FLORA of MELBOURNE

FLORA of MELBOURNE

A Guide to the Indigenous Plants of the Greater Melbourne Area

COMPILED BY THE FOLLOWING MEMBERS OF THE
AUSTRALIAN PLANTS SOCIETY MAROONDAH, INC.:

Marilyn Gray & John Knight (editors)
George Stolfo & John Armstrong (line drawings)

with the assistance of
Flora Anderson, Ros Savio and Bruce Schroder

HYLAND HOUSE

Titles published by
S.G.A.P. Maroondah Inc.

500 Australian Native Plants
Attracting Birds to Native Gardens
Guide to Darwinia and Homoranthus

This publication should be cited as follows:
Australian Plants Society Maroondah (2001) *Flora of Melbourne*, Hyland House, Melbourne

---

This third, enlarged edition published in 2001 by
Hyland House Publishing Pty Limited
PO Box 122
Flemington, Vic. 3031

First published 1991 by
Society for Growing Australian Plants Maroondah, Inc.

Second edition published 1993
by Hyland House Publishing

© Australian Plants Society Maroondah, Inc., 1991, 1993, 2001

Reprinted 2001

This book is copyright. Apart from any fair dealing for the purposes of private study, research, criticism or review, as permitted under the Copyright Acts, no part may be reproduced by any process without written permission. Enquiries should be addressed to the publisher.

National Library of Australia
Cataloguing in publication data

Flora of Melbourne: a guide to the indigenous plants of
the greater Melbourne area.

3rd enlarged ed.
Bibliography.
Includes index.
ISBN 1 86447 085 2.

1. Botany-Victoria-Melbourne. I. Australian Plants Society
Maroondah, Inc.

581.99451

Editors: Marilyn Gray, John Knight *et al.*
Illustrations, George Stolfo
Cover design by Rob Cowpe
Typeset by Solo Typesetting, South Australia
Printed by Brown Prior Anderson, Burwood, Victoria

Front cover, from left to right: *Trachymene anisocarpa*, *Isotoma fluviatilis*, *Acacia dealbata* leaves, *Patersonia occidentalis* flowers (white form), *Goodenia ovata*, and *Solanum aviculare* fruit

Table of Contents

Foreword

The *Flora of Melbourne* was more than seven years in its writing, illustration and compilation. The quality of its information, the writing of special sections, and the manner of dealing with individual species, clearly illustrate both the dedication and the expertise of the comparatively small group of people devoted to this labour of love.

Flora of Melbourne sets out to do a number of things: to show that we need to recognise just how fortunate we are in having such a rich flora at our back door, that we haven't been as considerate of it as we could and should have been, that the birds we all enjoy as residents or visitors in our gardens are very dependent on the bushland for food, nesting and living habitat, and that we can all do something towards reversing some of the vast damage done to this vital heritage by unchecked urban development, even within our own lifetimes.

It is not denied that we have done enormous damage to an environment that the Aborigines lived in harmony with for possibly 70,000 years or more but it is only in the last few decades that, apart from a few individuals, any number of people have made concerted efforts to bring about changes in attitudes.

We now see evidence of these changes in our national parks, our reserves, our local communities, and most importantly, in the halls of government.

But the process of awareness, training, education and implementation of conservation and revegetation policies are never ending.

Information is collected, collated and distributed through numerous publications and programs, and groups with special interest philosophies arise.

The Society for Growing Australian Plants (SGAP) is one such group. It had its beginnings in promoting the use of Australian plants in private and public gardens and over the years it has been exceedingly successful in achieving this aim. Later, broader conservation issues arose, and a different awareness evolved among certain groups of people; the ever-shrinking natural urban landscape was the focus of some of these concerns.

Many people, though, still say 'What can I do about it? I'm only one individual.' Herein lies one of the great strengths of *Flora of Melbourne*. It shows you just how involved you can become in regenerating a plot of badly treated bushland, or creating a broad habitat on your own land, including an all-important water area, and how to go about the practicalities of achieving this.

You will see how to readily identify the soil types in your area, and how best to use them for the purpose you have planned. The descriptions of nearly 1150 plants, together with over 900 line drawings, complemented by a number of colour plates will assist you in identifying any plant in your area, from the loftiest tree to the most delicate lily or ground orchid.

A section deals with the collection and storage, and the propagation of seed, and even how to recognise when it is ripe.

There is a strong and well-based philosophy expressed, that where possible . . . 'you should grow plants from seed collected locally'. While it may not always be an aim you are able to adhere to, the retention of genetic diversity is a desirable objective.

Another plant from a nursery may appear more attractive, but will it provide as adequate a habitat for the birds, animals and insects which have adapted to life in a local environment?

The commonsense, practical and easily located information in this publication will be invaluable to councils, schools, tertiary students, the horticulturalist with a special interest, or the lay person wishing to satisfy a curiosity about plants in his or her own local area, and finally to assist one's deeper involvement in the understanding of Melbourne's own floral diversity.

This is a book compiled by people who care about our native plants, who undoubtedly have extensive knowledge of and experience with them, and who wish to share this understanding and its attendant pleasures with you.

Bill Molyneux

Bill Molyneux is a horticultural botanist, author and nurseryman.

Acknowledgements

We gratefully acknowledge the support and assistance of a large number of people without whom this book would never have been completed. We have met enthusiasm and encouragement from all who have been approached no matter what the query or request.

This much-needed book on Melbourne's indigenous flora was initiated by John Knight. A sub-committee was subsequently formed under Marilyn Gray's leadership, with ongoing support from John. It is the encouragement of successive Committees of SGAP Maroondah Inc. and the members plus the financial support from the annual Melbourne Wildflower Show which has made this book possible.

While we are appreciative of all who have helped along the way there are three people who deserve special recognition. We have been very fortunate to have the continued assistance and guidance of Rodger and Gwen Elliot and David Albrecht. Rodger and Gwen, as members of SGAP Maroondah Inc. and authors of numerous books on Australian plants, have shared their knowledge and experiences freely with us as we have followed the long path culminating in the publication of the *Flora of Melbourne*. Access to their botanical library has also been invaluable. David Albrecht, botanist in charge of the Identification Service at the National Herbarium of Victoria, has shared with us his amazing knowledge of the indigenous plants of Melbourne. Among other things, he has assisted with information, checked our line drawings for accuracy and identified specimens.

The immense task of editing the Flora and the articles was undertaken by David Albrecht (Dicotyledons and Conifers), Berres Colville, Tim Entwisle (Ferns), David Jones (Orchids), Graeme Lorimer (other Monocotyledons) and Gretna Weste. We appreciate the time that each put into his or her section in our pursuit of accuracy. Grant Mattingley had the unenviable task of proof reading the whole manuscript.

We are indebted to Geoff Carr, Darcy Duggan, Rodger Elliot, Vivien Freshwater, Andrew Paget, Murray Ralph, Nick Romanowski, Roslyn Savio and the Soil Conservation Authority (now part of the Dept. of Conservation & Environment) for contributing supporting articles for the project, Adrian Rigg for preparing the soil map, and to Bill Molyneux who wrote the Foreword.

The staff at the Melbourne Herbarium has kept us up to date on botanical name changes as well as allowing us access to the pressed collections for research. The Flora Branch at the Department of Conservation and Environment has allowed us the use of its yet to be published report, has verified collections and distributions from its database, and has provided us with several plant lists of remnant reserves. Both groups kindly consented to read through and comment on our draft copy.

Photographs were generously provided by Flora Anderson, Ilma Dunn, Rodger Elliott, Marion and Bill King, John Knight, Alf Salkin, Bruce Schroder and Jim Willis.

The fine-line illustrations have been painstakingly drawn by George Stolfo, with some assistance from John Armstrong who also prepared the map of the Melbourne area and the text illustrations.

The task of typing the manuscript was carried out by Marilyn Gray with assistance from Brenda Martin and David Gray.

Members of Maroondah group have assisted in many ways: providing or collecting specimens to be drawn, contributing to the early research, working bees to collate information, local knowledge of plants. We sincerely thank all who have contributed in some way and apologise for any names unintentionally omitted: Bill Aitcheson, Dave Allen, Beth Armstrong, Julie and Andrew Banks, Joan Barrett, Eva Buchanan, Trix and Lewis Chambers, Kath Deery, Millicent Denton, Tommie and Bill Ellis, Chris Fletcher, Kahn Franke, Jean Galliott, Sue Guymer, Enid and Ian Haskins, Marge and Jim Landman, Neil Marriot, Brenda Martin, Lola and Charlie Mensch, Glad Moody, Helen and Tim Morrow, Libby Powell, Arnold Romijn, Rylice Sandell, Roger and Merilyn Serong, Alice Talbot, Marie and Alf Wallbridge, Pat and Jim Watson, Gretna Weste, Mary Whitehead, Nola Wilkinson, Margaret Williams, Joe Wilson. Lorraine Marshall spent many hours researching the orchids and contacting the relevant botanists for the most up to date information. She provided us with many specimens and escorted us to sites where rare orchids could be drawn in the field.

We are grateful to the many botanists and specialists who have provided valuable information from their own research and were always willing to answer our queries: Bob Bates, Peter Branwhite, David Cameron, Roger Carolin, Geoff Carr, Margaret Corrck, Pat Coupar, Phyl Dannat, Hansjoerg Eichler, Paul Gullen, Jeff Jeanes, David Jones, Graeme Lorimer, Annette Muir, Randall Robinson, Jim Ross, Neville Scarlett, Philip Short, Thelma and George (dec.) Spice, Neville Walshe, Jim Willis, Jeff Yugovic. Beth Gott allowed us to use her unpublished database on plant species used by the local Aborigines. David Cheal checked our plant communities for accuracy.

For their assistance in taking us on field trips, providing specimens to draw, contributing information and/or plant lists from all over the Melbourne area we would like to thank: Tracey Archer, Judy Barker, Paul Barnett, Robert Bender, Robyiyn Bennison, David Boekel, Jenny Caddaye, Stewart Campbell, Jenny Casamento, Tony Chapman, Ian Clarke, Graham Clutterbuck, Scott Coutts, Jean and David Edwards, Tony Faithfull, Michael Fendley, Ferntree Gully NP rangers, Vivien Freshwater, John Galea, Laurie Gilmore, the Harpers, Robyn Heath, Don Hill, Richard Hill, Margaret Keert, Joyce Kerfoot, Chris Kenyon, Richard Leppitt, Mike Love, Lisa Milley, Adam Muyt, James O'May, George Paras, David Parkes, Loris Peggie, Murray Ralph, Anne Read, Pam Richards, Nick Romanowski, Nicky Rose, Glyn Sago, Alf Salkin, Jan Shaw, Dale Tonkinson, Eric Ward, Neil Werrett, Mary White, Les Williams, Fiona Young, the Parks and Gardens staff of many municipal councils and shires.

Members of several groups assisted us in various ways. These include SGAP Keilor Plains, especially Carl Raynor, Ian Taylor and Barry White; SGAP Daisy Study Group; Australian Native Orchid Society (allowing our illustrator access to orchids on display at several shows) and especially Helen Richards; Bairnsdale and Latrobe Field Naturalists.

The staff of Research Publications have been extremely helpful, guiding us through the final stages of the book, offering advice and ideas and bending with us as we strove to collate the final copy ready for printing.

We gratefully acknowledge the financial support received through grants from Department of Conservation and Environment, Victoria, and Parkhills BDO, Chartered Accountants.

Finally our heartfelt thanks goes to our families who have supported us and borne the disruption of more than 7 years of research and meetings. They are Andy (dec.), Beth, David, Sue, Jill and Rene (who at last has her fridge free of specimens). Our children were all young when the project began and we thank them especially for their tolerance; Sarah, Erin (who have assisted with typing and collating) and Lauren; Darren, Keren and Liane; Michael and Naomi; Nicole and David; and Emma and Mandy (who have never known life without 'The Book').

Since the publication of *Flora of Melbourne* the editors have been inundated with information on the distribution of plants throughout our study area. As a result I have updated the localities listing to include as much new material as possible in the second edition. Thirty species have been added to the descriptions. Many of these have been only recently discovered within the Melbourne area.

We would be pleased to receive any additional information as it becomes available with a view to using it in future editions.

We would like to thank David Bainbridge, Bill Barker, Evan Clucas, Glen Jameson, Valentino Stajsic, Jason Stewart, Ian Taylor, Carina Watson as well as many of the previous contributors who have supplied new and updated information for this edition. The staff of the National Herbarium of Victoria have provided updated bulletins of the *Census of the Vascular Plants of Victoria* to ensure accuracy in botanical nomenclature.

The views expressed in Part 1 are not necessarily those of the Society for Growing Australian Plants Maroondah Inc.

Acknowledgements to the third edition

While it is never possible to claim that all vascular plants known from the greater Melbourne area have now been described, we hope that with this third edition we are coming closer to a picture of the range in species that occurred at the time of European settlement. The enormous work *Flora of Victoria*, edited by Neville Walsh and Tim Entwisle, has greatly contributed to an increased knowledge of our local flora. It is with deep appreciation that I thank the staff of the National Herbarium of Victoria for access to records and plant collections and to the draft copy of *Flora of Victoria* Vol. 4. Staff at the Arthur Rylah Institute have also very generously assisted this project, making available the latest version of the Victorian Flora Information System database.

After changes, additions and deletions to the previous editions of *Flora of Melbourne* the third edition includes 1200 species and 1254 taxa.

We are indebted to many people for providing updated lists, personal observations and new information which has been incorporated in this edition: Eva Buchanan, Geoff Carr, Gordon Carter, Ian Clarke, Michael Coleman, Catherine Coles, Pat Coupar, Fiona Cross, Rodger Elliot, Doug Frood, Peter Geoghan, Leony Graham, Joan Harper, Ruth Jackson, Glen Jameson, David Lockwood, Graeme Lorimer, Kathleen Loxton, Graham Patterson, Ron Pearson, Randall Robinson, Kevin Rule, Alf Salkin, Rob Scott, Jason Summers, Cameron Taylor, Jenny Tonkin, Dale Tonkinson, David Van Bockel, Eric Ward and Phillip Wierzbowski, Jeff Yugovic.

I am especially grateful to David Cameron for his fine-tuning of the plant list, John Knight, who once again edited and proof read all entries, and botanical editors Neville Walsh, who edited almost all of the new material, with assistance from Lynlee Smith (geraniums) and Jeff Jeanes (orchids).

Flora Anderson
John Armstrong
Marilyn Gray
John Knight
Roslyn Savio
Bruce Schroder
George Stolfo

Photographic Acknowledgements

Flora Anderson	30 38 55
Ilma Dunn	33 45 46
Rodger Elliot	11 21 23 25 27 32 39 40 44 50 51 54 59 63 69 70 74 and front cover plant photographs
Marilyn Gray	1 5 6 10 12 14 16–18 20
Bill King	48
Marion King	49 58
John Knight	4 9 15 26 28 29 31 34–37 41 42 47 52 53 56 57 60–62 64 65 67 68 71–73
Alf Salkin	22 66
Bruce Schroder	2 3 7 8 13 19
Jim Willis	24 43

Introduction

The publication of the *Flora of Melbourne* is the culmination of 7 years of dedication by a group committed to seeing indigenous plants appreciated as an important horticultural resource, and accepted as ecologically necessary in maintaining the survival of our local bushland environment for future generations.

It was written in response to many enquiries from a broad spectrum of the community: individuals, groups and organisations, each seeking information on local species suitable for home gardens, or the composition of the original plant communities of their area, to be used in revegetation projects. The encouragement and support of the community over this time has been the stimulus needed to keep going. Our reward will come from being involved, and encouraging others to participate, in saving what little remains of our precious remnant bushland.

Originally 'The Book', as it has become known to all involved, was planned as a horticultural guide, with details of 200 species of indigenous plants suitable for home gardens. Deciding on which species to include, and which to omit, was a much more demanding task than it might appear and was eventually abandoned in favour of a more detailed study of the known flora of Melbourne. Researching the original plant list showed just what a dearth of information existed on the plants of the Melbourne area.

Many hours of research were spent to develop a broad picture of which plants grew where. Numerous searches were made through the pressed collections at the Melbourne Herbarium. The State Library was also often visited to uncover its vast source of knowledge. Its store of older works helped us piece together an overview of Melbourne's original flora. References were made to numerous unpublished species check lists, many produced by botanists preparing management plans for specific areas. Field notes published in *Victorian Naturalist*, the journal of the Victorian Field Naturalist Club (some issues dating back over 50 years), were used to gain detailed species lists of many areas of Melbourne long since fallen victim to urban growth. Fruitful weekends were spent in the company of local experts, wandering through many of Melbourne's different habitats seeking out the many unfamiliar or little known species.

Over recent years the quest for knowledge on indigenous plants specific to local areas has exploded, as has the push for regeneration in remaining bushland areas and the revegetation of habitats in devastated areas. Work is being undertaken at a local level by concerned groups, with the publication of various booklets and pamphlets. While these works are of value to local people, they generally include only the more easily recognised plants and fall to give a picture of the overall situation in Melbourne.

With the completion of this book which contains detailed information of over 1100 species, both flowering and non-flowering, we have endeavoured to provide readers with an insight into the varied plant communities which once existed throughout the greater Melbourne area, and an idea of the original vegetation of each area. No attempt has been made to produce a genuine botanical 'flora', with its often difficult to follow identification keys. We believe that a book with simple, easily read text, and illustrations to aid identification, would far better suit the purpose of encouraging people from all walks of life to become involved in reversing the trend of the last 150 years, and hopefully rebuild the integrity and diversity of our quickly diminishing remnant bushland vegetation.

The Benefits of Growing Local Indigenous Plants

Conservation of natural bushland habitats is a world-wide issue. The greater Melbourne area prior to European settlement contained many unique habitats. Each included a great number of different species of flora and fauna, from the insects and tiny herbs to lofty trees, which were dependent on each other for survival.

The indigenous flora of an area is a group of plants which occur naturally having evolved over thousands of years to adapt perfectly to the conditions prevailing in their environment.

Fragmenting these habitats leads to a reduction of the natural life forms found at the site.

Changes to the environment, such as clearing of land for agriculture and urban development, affect directly the viability of ecosystems. Add to this an altered fire regime, increased water runoff, erosion and nutrient build up. Each of these factors favours the establishment of weed species over the local species, ultimately leading to the destruction of the original environment.

Replanting and encouragement of regeneration of remnant bushland areas, and roadside verges, with plants indigenous to that site is the first step in arresting the destruction and brings a number of benefits.

Once established, indigenous plants, being adapted to the local climate and soil conditions, win require less maintenance and watering than exotic species. Thus the long-term cost of replanting will be less than if exotics had been used for landscape improvement.

Where possible, plants for regeneration programs should be grown from a local source to protect genetic diversity.

The use of native grasses, herbs and sedges, which produce green growth during Summer, will lessen the potential fire hazard where planted along roadsides. An understorey of introduced, weedy grasses presents a much more flammable situation as they dry out over Summer.

Using indigenous plants preserves the unique local character of an area, presenting a unified visual landscape. As the replanted areas mature, populations of native birds, and even animals, will return, occupying previously lost habitats in a relatively short time. This has been seen along the Yarra River where platypus and koalas have returned to the area.

Naturally occurring regeneration will continue to maintain the habitat, so that the bushland will ultimately become self-supporting.

This book is written for the many individuals, environmental groups and school councils who are aware of the desperate need to preserve what little remains of the natural vegetation of the greater Melbourne area. Municipal councils and government departments are charged with the responsibility of restoring the integrity of areas under their control. The *Flora of Melbourne* will assist them in making the right decisions for the long-term, despite pressure to spread the environmental improvement dollar too thinly.

It is our hope that everyone will be encouraged to be involved in reclaiming areas devastated through misuse, so that future generations may also have the opportunity to appreciate the beauty of Melbourne's unique landscape.

If this book stimulates increased public awareness of the value of retaining and caring for our remnant indigenous plant habitats, and saves even one more bushland area from destruction, our time over the past 7 years will have been well spent.

Each of us is much richer for the experience.

John Knight

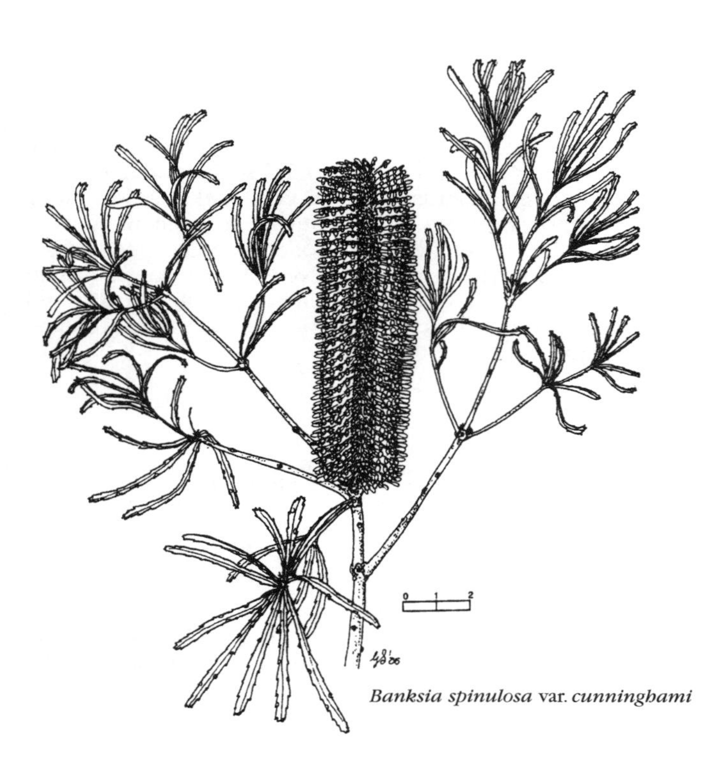

Banksia spinulosa var. *cunninghami*

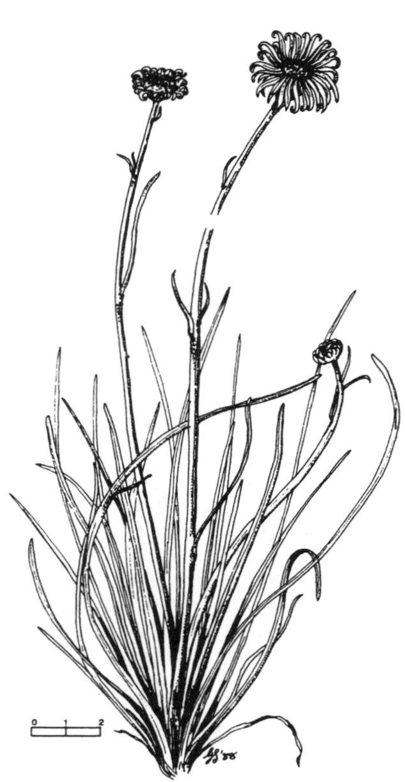

Brachyscome cardiocarpa

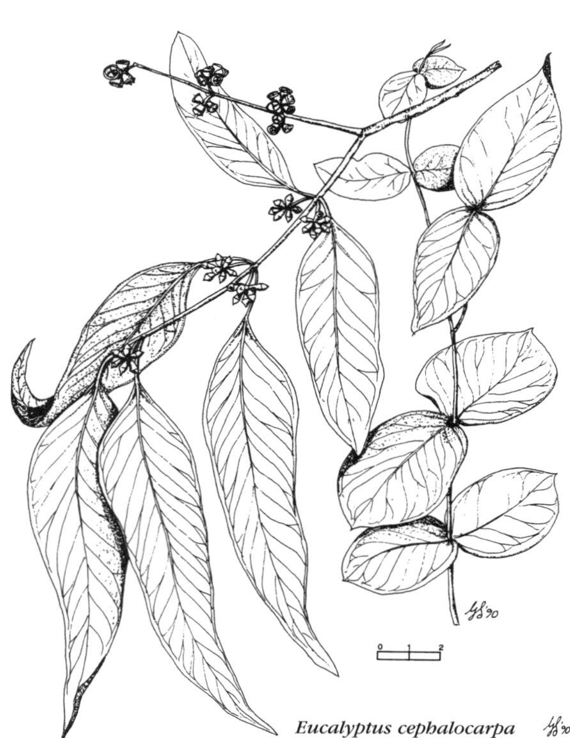

Eucalyptus cephalocarpa

SCALE: 0 1cm 2cm This scale representation on each plant equals 2 cm.

Part One

Chapter 1. Melbourne's Indigenous Plant Communities

Roslyn Savio*

Introduction

Plants do not grow in isolation. They grow in association with plants of the same species which interact with each other and their surrounding environment. A group of plants growing in a common environment, together with the ecological processes which determine these, is called a plant community and provides a habitat for animals, including birds, insects, spiders and reptiles. Each community can be distinguished by having more or less the same species of plants in similar proportions and the same physical vegetative structure made up of a number of intermingling layers. When these two characteristics are combined they form a description of how the plant community looks when viewed from above and in three dimensions or the side view.

A knowledge of plants in a community provides a guide as to the species of plants which may grow together naturally and the type of environment in which a particular plant can grow. The combined view is a picture of what the vegetation of Melbourne may have looked like prior to European settlement. Thus one could use this knowledge when aiming to reproduce a bird or animal habitat or simply a 'natural environment'.

It is recognised that when indigenous plants are used horticulturally or as part of a landscape design they are often not grown as part of a natural plant community. Other factors come into play such as usefulness for screening, colours of the flowers, the ability to grow quickly, shapes of the leaves, having a non-invasive root system, the ability to create shade, height and other design or horticultural requirements. It may not be possible (or even desirable) to recreate a plant community fully because of irrevocable changes to the environment that have occurred since European settlement. These changes include massive clearing, agriculture, polluted water, stormwater discharge, land fill, proximity to housing, weed invasion, the presence of exotic grasses, and also fertiliser application, incorporation of humus, Summer watering and artificial sub-surface drainage.

1. Influencing Factors on a Natural Community

Many factors may influence a plant community and are interdependent. Some of the most important of these are rainfall, temperature, wind, soil type and geology, topography, steepness of slopes, frequency of fire, grazing, altitude, aspect and the proximity of other plants and animals within the environment. In return the inhabitants themselves also influence these factors by altering soil, wind, sunlight and rainfall patterns, among others.

In the Melbourne area some of the major factors influencing the formation of the indigenous plant communities have been topography, geology, soil type and climate.

1.1 Topography

The topography of Melbourne divides into roughly four regions; the flat or undulating plains to the west and the north; the foothills of the east and north east, gradually rising to the foothills of the Dandenong Ranges and the Great Dividing Range; the coastal fringe around Port Phillip Bay, merging into the flat to undulating region to the east and south-east, and the numerous rivers and creeks flowing through the regions to create a variety of riparian and swamp environments. Topography also affects altitude, slope and aspect.

1.2 Soils

Soil types are the major influence on indigenous communities and follow a similar pattern to topography. The soil types are discussed in greater detail in Chapter 2, but are briefly described here as they form the basis for grouping the plants into communities.

The western plains are made up of heavy clays on younger basalt, which can extend east as far as the Plenty River and through to Richmond. In the hills of the east are the Silurian derived sedimentary clay soils of light grey loams over clay, often following rivers and creeks, with red loams on the east side of the Dandenongs. The south and south-east suburbs are a combination of deep sands free of lime around the Sandringham area, dark loams, clays and local sands. Collectively, these are known as Tertiary Sands.

1.3 Climate

The climate of Melbourne also varies from east to west, again affecting the formation of the plant communities. The east and northeastern hills generally have a higher rainfall than the western plains, the highest rainfall being on the Dandenong Ranges, averaging 625 mm in Spring, whereas the rainfall at Sydenham and Melton is 150 mm in Spring. The rainfall on the southern coastal fringe reflects that of the west, gradually increasing towards the east.

Temperatures are less varied with the mean maximum annual temperatures fairly uniform, the warmest mean temperatures around Melton and the coolest on Mt. Dandenong. Maritime influences are noticeable on mean minimum temperatures, the higher temperatures being around Port Phillip Bay and the near eastern and western suburbs. Cooler temperatures are found further inland, the coolest again being associated with increased altitude on Mt. Dandenong.

Wind patterns, evaporation, ground temperatures, seasonal distribution of rain are often factors influencing climate.

* Roslyn Savio is a landscape architect with working experience in the private development industry and in local and state government. Currently she has her own private practice in Croydon.

2. Definitions of Plant Communities

Plant community boundaries are rarely distinct lines but are more often broadly overlapping zones. Plant community descriptions relate to typical stands.

A plant community can be described in two ways. The first is a floristic description, when all the species growing at a variety of sites are identified as being inhabitants of the community. The plant community is characterised by particular species being consistently present and indicative of the local environment. It is defined by the presence of group(s) of species and the absence of other group(s). The floristic description can also include relative proportions of each species.

The second method is the structural approach, which disregards the environmental conditions and species present. This method recognises that the layers or strata within a plant community can also influence some of the environmental factors. If a slice is taken through a community, the vegetation is divided into a number of layers. The uppermost layers of vegetation form a canopy. When looked at from above, the amount of foliage cover per ground area of the uppermost layer, together with the height of the tallest layer, determines the type (and name) of the community. This is because the uppermost layer controls the solar energy used by the rest of the plant community. (Specht, R.L. 1970) This method distinguishes between the open forest or woodland with space between the treetops, and the rainforest where the canopy is closed and there is no space between the treetops.

In the Melbourne area plant communities can be divided into eighteen different structural types, listed in decreasing canopy height and density of the canopy foliage.

1. Tall Open-forest	Tree height: Foliage cover:	Greater than 30 m Density 30–70% (mid dense)
2. Open-forest	Tree height: Foliage cover:	10–30 m Density 30–70% (mid dense)
3. Low Closed-forest	Tree height: Foliage cover:	5–10 m Density greater than 70% (dense)
4. Low Open-forest	Tree height: Foliage cover:	5–10 m Density 30–70% (mid dense)
5. Woodland	Tree height: Foliage cover:	10–30 m Density 10–30% (sparse)
6. Open-woodland	Tree height: Foliage cover:	10–30 m Density less than 10% (very sparse)
7. Low woodland	Tree height: Foliage cover:	5–10 m Density 10–30% (sparse)
8. Low-open woodland	Tree height: Foliage cover:	5–10 m Density less than 10% (very sparse)
9. Closed-scrub	Shrub height: Foliage cover:	2–8 m Density 70–100% (dense)
10. Open-scrub	Shrub height: Foliage cover:	2–8 m Density 30–70% (mid-dense)
11. Closed-heath	Shrub height: Foliage cover:	0–2 m Density 70–100% (dense)
12. Open-heath	Shrub height: Foliage cover:	0–2m Density 30–70% (mid-dense)
13. Herbland	Herbs Foliage cover:	Density 30–70% (mid-dense)
14. Open-herbland	Herbs Foliage cover:	Density 10–30% (sparse)
15. Closed-tussock grasslands	Herbs Foliage cover:	Density 70–100% (dense)
16. Tussock grassland	Herbs Foliage cover:	Density 30–70% (mid-dense)
17. Grassland/Sedgeland	Herbs Foliage cover:	Density 30–70% (mid-dense)
18. Closed-grassland/ Sedgeland	Herbs Foliage cover:	Density 70–100% (dense)

3. Identification of Melbourne's Plant Communities

The names describing the plant communities of the Melbourne area are variable and somewhat imprecise, such as the traditional 'Dry Sclerophyll Forest'. For the sake of consistency, this book uses the names and descriptions of plant communities identified by David Cheal and others of the Department of Conservation and Environment's Flora Branch in their yet to be published report, *Vegetation Survey and Sites of Botanical Significance in the Melbourne Area*,[1] which David Cheal has generously made available, and the published *Floristic Vegetation Map of the Melbourne Area* (Cheal et al 1989). Where the boundaries of the Melbourne area of this book are not covered by this map then reference is made to another map, *Floristic Vegetation of the Upper Yarra Valley and the Dandenong Ranges*, (Parkes, D.M. 1980) and the plant communities given the names of the Flora Branch where applicable. It should be noted that the names are labels only and not a definition of the plant communities themselves.

Twenty-one communities of the Melbourne area are described in this chapter by specifying their structure, and the dominant and less frequent species for each of the different strata of the vegetation, from the upper storey or tree canopies down to the ground storey. It is important to note, however, that because the descriptions are based on site surveys of recent times, some species may be omitted because they were overlooked in the field due to seasonal differences or because they no longer exist, occur rarely or are unable to grow due to the pressure of settlement, lack of fire, grazing and weed invasion at a particular site. Many species may have also been overlooked as field surveys were not carried out at the site where they still remain. As a general rule, weed or introduced species of a particular plant community have been ignored in this description (although not in David Cheal's report), even though they may form a significant proportion of the plant community.

In order to co-ordinate the relationship between plant communities and regions of Melbourne, communities have been broadly grouped on Map 2 according to soil type and geographical area: A. Basalt Plains; B. Silurian-derived Sedimentary Hills; C. Tertiary Sands and D. Coastal areas. Within each plant community category, sub-communities have been listed according to their locality and are presented as a guide only. Readers will need to draw their own conclusion as to the particular plant community or sub-communities relevant to their chosen site. It should be remembered too that the boundaries of the areas are not distinct and that plant communities and sub-communities grade into each other.

A. Basalt Plains

The type of soil and the topography of the western regions of Melbourne area have greatly influenced the plant communities found there. Similar soils also extend north to Mernda and east to Richmond. They are mainly fertile, heavy clay soils over younger basalts of volcanic origin which are poorly draining. Volcanic activity has also influenced the topography by forming low-lying, undulating, expansive plains with occasional rocky outcrops of earlier sedimentary or other geological origin. As mentioned previously, the rainfall is much lower than elsewhere in the Melbourne area. These are sites of rare natural grasslands, adapted to high winds and shallow soils. Trees and shrubby plants find these conditions difficult and so are not a dominant feature of the Plains Grassland and Grassy Wetlands plant communities, although they can be common on the rocky escarpments and sedimentary hills. Watercourses and drainage lines flowing through the plains have formed riparian and escarpment plant communities such as Riparian Scrub, Chenopod Rocky Open scrub and Riparian Woodland.

1 Not all communities listed are included as they are outside the boundaries of the Melbourne area of this publication, or are not listed as a community on the map by Parkes.

As the rainfall increases towards the north and east and the topography becomes more hilly, soils are of sedimentary origins or have overlying gravel deposits. Trees become more dominant and the plant communities become Red Gum Woodlands and Box Woodlands.

1. **Plains Grasslands** (Median annual rainfall 550–700 mm)

Plains Grasslands were once quite spectacular, forming waving swards of native tussock grasses interspersed with small colourful flowering herbs. The dominant grass is *Themeda triandra* but other grasses can also be present in differing numbers and species, depending on their location. Some locations where different sub-communities can be found are listed as follows:

1.1 Scattered Areas West of Darebin Creek and East of Melton
This sub-community is a Closed-tussock Grassland where *Themeda triandra* is dominant. Occasionally, other grasses such as *Danthonia caespitosa, D. setacea* and *Stipa bigeniculata* are common but not many others. *Convolvulus erubescens* and *Oxalis perennans* are characteristic herb species.

1.2 Western Area, Sunshine and Taylors Lakes (minor occurrence)
Species of this sub-community are similar to those in 1.1, but with the addition of two other tussock grasses, *Danthonia duttoniana*, instead of *D. caespitosa*, and *Chloris truncata*, but not in large numbers. The sedge, *Schoenus apogon* and rush, *Juncus bufonius* are frequent associates. Herb species include not only the characteristic *Convolvulus erubescens* but also *Acaena echinata, Asperula conferta, Eryngium ovinum, Hypericum gramineum, Solenogyne dominii* and *Plantago gaudichaudii* interspersed amongst the tussocks.

1.3 Central West—Laverton, Somerton, north of Sunbury at Jacksons Creek, formerly at Taylors Lakes
Apart from *Themeda triandra*, the tussock grasses of 1.2 are rare to absent. Instead, the associated grasses of this Closed-tussock Grassland sub-community are frequently *Stipa gibbosa* and *Danthonia caespitosa* with *Agrostis avenacea*. The herbs and rushes are similar to those of 1.2 with the addition of *Calocephalus citreus, Leptorhynchos squamatus* and *Oxalis perennans* but not *Hypericum gramineum* or *Solenogyne dominii*.

1.4 Evans Street, Sunbury
The Closed-tussock Grassland here is dminated by *Themeda triandra* and *Danthonia caespitosa*. The soils supporting this sub-community are actually derived from shale and sandstone but the community is still influenced by nearby basalt soils. Some grasses not typical of Plains Grassland are present in large numbers such as *Danthonia eriantha, Dichelachne crinita* and *Pentapogon quadrifidus* but some of the herbs of 1.3 are also typical of this community. Some additional herb species more typical of Silurian soils can be found such as *Caesia calliantha, Drosera peltata* and *Oxalis radicosa* and the small shrubs *Bossiaea prostrata, Pimelea curviflora* and *Pimelea humilis*. It is possible that this community may be transitional to Red Gum Woodland and may once have had an open tree canopy.

2. **Grassy Wetlands** (Median annual rainfall 550–700 mm)

Throughout the plains, scattered amongst the grasslands, are small depressions in the heavy fertile soils called 'gilgais', often around one hectare in size. These tend to hold water in Winter but dry out and crack deeply in Summer. Thus these depressions have supported another plant community, called Grassy Wetlands, dominated by grasses, sedges and rushes forming Grassland/Sedgelands (Herblands) or Closed-grassland/Sedgeland. Other characteristic plants include many daisy species. These communities also occur less commonly around lake margins. Significant localities are described as follows:

2.1 Scattered areas west of the Maribyrnong River.
The characteristic tussock grasses of 1.2 are present but not frequent in Grassy Wetlands. More typical are *Eleocharis acuta, Juncus flavidus* and different grasses such as *Agrostis avenacea* and *Amphibromus neesii*. Some herbs also typical of Plains Grassland grow in this sub-community such as *Acaena echinata, Asperula conferta, Eryngium ovinum* and *Convolvulus erubescens* but others are notably different, such as *Brachyscome basaltica* var. *gracilis, Calotis* spp., *Eleocharis pusilla* and *Eryngium vesiculosum*.

2.2 Western area, margins of freshwater lakes (Lake Stanley at Ardeer)
The seasonally flooded margins of freshwater lakes and swampy drainage lines also support a Grassy Wetland plant community. The structure of these communities varies from small elevated islands in areas flooded longest to cover wider areas in less flooded situations. The most typical grasses are *Agrostis avenacea* and *Amphibromus neesii* and a sedge, *Eleocharis acuta* is also common. Herbs typical of wetland areas thrive, such as *Lobelia pratioides, Lythrum hyssopifolia* and *Myriophyllum* spp.

3. **Riparian Scrub** (Median annual rainfall 500–750 mm)

Where the basalt plains are cut by watercourses and drainage lines, different plant communities have developed. The heavy loamy soils here contain more organic matter, are waterlogged for much of the Winter and are still moist during Summer.

3.1 Western area, Jacksons Ck and Werribee R.
This sub-community has a woodland structure, the tree canopy being made up of *Eucalyptus camaldulensis* over an open understorey of two wattles, *Acacia melanoxylon* and *A. mearnsii*. The dominant characteristic of this community however, is a tall dense shrub layer beside the water, made up of *Callistemon sieberi, Hymenanthera dentata* and *Leptospermum lanigerum*. Beside the water are a number of emergent aquatics and other species tolerant of prolonged waterlogging. These include *Crassula helmsii, Persicaria decipiens, Isolepis cernua, I. inundata, I. nodosa, Juncus sarophorus* and *Triglochin procera*. *Phragmites australis* forms tall reed beds amongst the aquatics. Also characteristic of this sub-community are the dense swards of *Poa labillardieri*.

3.2 Northern and Western area, Merri Ck and tributaries
The Merri Creek sub-community has a structure more of an Open-woodland but with the same tree canopy and understorey. The characteristic dense shrub layer also contains similar plant species, but with *Bursaria spinosa* instead of *Callistemon sieberi*. Similar too are the reed beds of *Phragmites australis* which also support *Calystegia sepium*. The aquatic sedges and herbs of the stream margins include large numbers of *Bolboschoenus medianus, Schoenoplectus validus, Apium prostratum, Crassula helmsii, Epilobium hirtigerum, Hydrocotyle verticillata, Lobelia alata, Lythrum hyssopifolia, Persicaria decipiens* and *Selliera radicans*.

3.3 Northern area, Jacksons Ck at Bulla, Deep Ck at Sunbury, Warringal Parklands, Heidelberg
The tree canopy of this Open-woodland is the same as 3.1 and 3.2 but the understorey has a different species of wattle—*Acacia dealbata*. The shrub layer and reed beds are similar to those of 3.1, with slightly different grasses, sedges and rushes, consisting of *Agrostis avenacea, Carex appressa, Juncus pauciflorus, Microlaena stipoides* and *Poa labillardieri*. Herb species typical of this sub-community are *Alternanthera denticulata, Rubus parvifolius* and *Dichondra repens*. Emergent aquatics beside the watercourses include *Alisma plantago-aquatica, Eleocharis* spp. and *Triglochin* spp. Dense carpets of floating plants such as *Azolla* spp. and *Spirodela oligorrhiza* may also be found in the still parts of watercourses.

4. Riparian Woodland (Median annual rainfall 550–600 mm)

Riparian Woodland is a very restricted plant community of the western area, with only one isolated occurrence within the study area. It occurs beside watercourses which may be dry in Summer but achieve high levels of water in Winter, and where the soils are alluvial loams of moderate depth.

4.1 Western area, occasionally along the Werribee R.
The tree canopy is formed by *Eucalyptus baueriana*, together with the occasional *E. camaldulensis* and *E. viminalis*. Beneath the canopy is a dense shrubby understorey of *Callistemon sieberi*, *Leptospermum lanigerum* and *Melaleuca lanceolata* and the taller *Acacia mearnsii*. The herbs are unusual in that they are a mixture of species from rocky sites (eg *Einadia hastata*), woodlands (*Dichondra repens*, *Rumex brownii* and *Veronica plebeia*) as well as those more typical of riparian conditions (*Poa labillardieri* and *Urtica incisa*).

5. Chenopod Rocky Open Scrub (Median annual rainfall 600–650 mm)

Chenopod Rocky Open Scrub is also a plant community of very restricted distribution. While it is located in the west, it is not typical of basalt-derived soils, but of Ordivician and Silurian-derived sedimentary soils on steep topographically arid slopes. The soils have a thin upper layer and a poorly permeable lower layer with a high proportion of salts. It includes the so-called 'Melton Mallee' which is just outside the study area.

5.1 Isolated Occurrences at Janefield (Plenty River) and between Sunbury and Diggers Rest (Jacksons Creek)
The tree canopy of this Open-scrub (Woodland) community is dominated by stunted *E. leucoxylon* ssp. *connata* and *E. microcarpa*, which play host to *Amyema miquelii*. The understorey is tall and shrubby and made up of *Acacia acinacea*, *A. pycnantha*, *Cassinia longifolia* and the characteristic *Rhagodia parabolica*. Characteristic sub-shrubs are *Einadia hastata*, *E. nutans* and the succulent herb *Carpobrotus modestus*. Through these shrubs scrambles *Clematis microphylla*. Grasses are not so important but typical species are *Danthonia setacea*, *Poa* spp. and *Stipa* spp.
A variation of this community occurs on dry stony western-facing slopes of deeply incised rivers and streams. *Eucalyptus leucoxylon* ssp. *connata* is the more dominant eucalypt here and is more scattered.

6. Box Woodland (Median annual rainfall 600–700 mm)

Box Woodland plant communities can be found on the western side of Melbourne, usually on sedimentary-derived soils but sometimes on basalt outcrops. This has a bearing on the differences between plant species found within the sub-communities. Escarpment communities are also usually classified with Box Woodlands, as a dense shrubland.

6.1 Scattered areas from Melton South to Yan Yean
This sub-community is not dominated by a eucalypt, (although there is the occasional emergent *Eucalyptus leucoxylon* ssp. *connata* or *E. melliodora*), but by *Allocasuarina verticillata*, which occurs in dense stands, either as Open-forest, Low Open-forest or Woodland. It is characterised by exposed rocky outcrops of either basalt or sedimentary origin with thin skeletal soils. *Acacia* spp., typically *A. melanoxylon*, *A. pycnantha* and *A. implexa*, form either an open understorey or link up with the canopy. There are few other shrubs except for scattered *Bursaria spinosa*, *Exocarpos cupressiformis* and *Hymenanthera dentata*, through which scrambles *Clematis microphylla*. In the past there may have been more scattered shrubs such as *Acacia acinacea*, *A. paradoxa* and *Cassinia* spp. Grasses dominate the ground layer and include a number of *Danthonia* spp. such as *D. caespitosa*, *D. racemosa* and *D. setacea*, with *Dichondra repens* and *Microlaena stipoides* in shady areas.

6.2 North Western area across to Merri Ck
A Box Woodland sub-community dominated by the tall *Eucalyptus microcarpa*, is found on gently rolling sedimentary hills, forming an Open-forest, Woodland or Low Woodland, with the occasional *E. leucoxylon* ssp. *connata*. There is generally no understorey but the field layer is dominated by the *Danthonia* spp. mentioned in 6.1, together with other grasses and tufted plants including *Elymus scabrus*, *Stipa bigeniculata*, *Themeda triandra*, *Juncus subsecundus*, *Lomandra filiformis*, *Tricoryne elatior* and *Microlaena stipoides*. Broad-leaved herbs are uncommon but may include *Oxalis radicosa* in large numbers, and *Einadia nutans*.

6.3 Gellibrand Hill
Gellibrand Hill and other low rolling hills of the central north west are made up of poorly-structured, free draining soils of Devonian granodiorite origin. The sub-community formed here is a Woodland to Open-woodland of *Eucalyptus microcarpa*. Along the drainage lines and lower slopes is *E. camaldulensis*. The shrub layer would have been open with *Acacia acinacea* and *Bursaria spinosa* plus a ground storey similar to that described in 6.2.

7. Red Gum Woodland (Median annual rainfall 600–650 mm)

Red Gum Woodland has also developed on a range of soil types, including those of the basalt plains, with which it shares many plant species. The community was once widespread in the north and it is likely that it intermingled with Plains Grassland communities between Craigieburn and the Plenty River, sharing many species in common. As most existing Red Gum Woodland communities are heavily disturbed, their original composition is difficult to determine. Thus some sub-communities do not reflect the 'natural environment' so much as the management history. The basalt plains sub-community is described here.

7.1 Near Northern area, Bundoora and Campbellfield
This is a Red Gum Woodland of very old *Eucalyptus camaldulensis*, forming a very open and scattered canopy. There is usually no understorey but the ground storey is very dense. The structure is of tussock grasses such as *Agrostis aemula*, *Danthonia caespitosa*, *D. laevis*, *Poa sieberiana*, *Stipa bigeniculata* and *Themeda triandra* with other herbs, some tufted, between the tussocks. These include *Acaena agnipila*, *Senecio quadridentatus* and *Tricoryne elatior* in large numbers, with lesser numbers of *Carex inversa*, *Dichelachne crinita*, *D. micrantha*, *Dichondra repens*, *Haloragis heterophylla*, *Juncus subsecundus*, *Leptorhynchos tenuifolius*, *Lomandra filiformis*, *Lythrum hyssopifolia* and *Oxalis* spp.

B. Silurian-derived Sedimentary Hills

In the northeastern and eastern area of Melbourne, where the undulating plains give way to more hilly and mountainous topography, (often along the alignment of the Plenty River), Silurian-derived sedimentary soils are more frequently found.

These soils are generally light grey loams over clay which tend to be moist in Winter but dry out in the upper layer over Summer. Along the watercourses and drainage lines are even moister dark loams, clays and local sands. South of the Dandenong Ranges there are areas of gritty light grey loams over clay, with some red loams, while on the eastern face of the Dandenongs the soils become red loams.

As the soils change, so do the plant communities which they support. Open Woodlands on undulating hills give way to more densely forested steeper slopes. Species become much more diverse with trees and shrubs a greater feature of the structure of these communities, although grasses and herbs are still common. The main variables for the change in plant communities are soil fertility, depth of the upper layer of the soil, the amount of moisture available, rainfall and altitude.

Some plant communities are the same as for the Basalt Plains, notably Red Gum Woodland and Riparian Scrub, although the sub-communities themselves are different. Other typical plant communities of Silurian-derived soils range from Box Ironbark Woodland, the widespread Dry Sclerophyll Forest and associated Valley Sclerophyll Forest, and Swamp Scrub in the drier areas, through to Damp and Wet Sclerophyll Forests and Cool Temperate Rainforest communities of moister, higher altitudes.

1. Red Gum Woodland (Median annual rainfall 600–800 mm)

Bordering on the Basalt Plains and grading into sedimentary soils are large areas where Red Gum Woodland would have predominated, with a denser understorey.

1.1 Near Northeastern area, Bundoora, Yallambie, Kew, Burwood, Alamein

This sub-community is an Open-forest with dense stands of *Eucalyptus camaldulensis* and *E. melliodora*, found on low undulating hills. The understorey, if present, is made up of *Acacia implexa* and occasionally *A. mearnsii* or *A. melanoxylon*. As with Red Gum Woodland communities of the Basalt Plains, the ground layer is made up of tussock grasses, but with some changes in species. *Danthonia* spp. and *Themeda triandra* are still common, but *Poa morrisii* and *Microlaena stipoides* are also widespread. *Lomandra filiformis* is typical of the west but other species present include *Arthropodium strictum*, *Bossiaea prostrata*, *Dianella longifolia*, *Gonocarpus tetragynus*, *Opercularia ovata* and *Tricoryne elatior*.

1.2 Near Northeastern area, Lower Templestowe to Sth Morang

A sub-community of Woodland structure containing an open formation of *Eucalyptus camaldulensis* only, with an understorey of *Acacia mearnsii* and/or *A. melanoxylon*. Again there are no understorey shrubby species and grasses such as *Danthonia laevis*, *D. racemosa*, *Microlaena stipoides*, *Themeda triandra* and less commonly *Elymus scabrus* predominate the ground species with the lily *Tricoryne elatior*.

1.3 Eastern Suburbs and Bundoora

In these locations, *Eucalyptus camaldulensis* combines with *E. ovata* to form a Woodland on swamps and drainage lines. Small trees of *Acacia mearnsii* are moderately common as an understorey while *Themeda triandra* and *Danthonia geniculata* dominate the ground layer. The herbs growing between the tussocks are typical of waterlogged conditions and include *Drosera peltata* ssp. *peltata*, *Gonocarpus tetragynus*, *Luzula meridionalis*, *Schoenus apogon*, *Stylidium graminifolium* and *Wahlenbergia gracilenta*. Two orchids, typical of moist soils, are *Microtis unifolia* and *Thelymitra pauciflora*.

1.4 Near North to Northeastern area and Murrumbeena (restricted area)

This sub-community was once widespread on the low hills and plains around Melbourne, but, because of its management history of grazing, many species have disappeared. What is left is a Woodland of *Eucalyptus camaldulensis* associated with either *E. ovata* or *E. melliodora*. Again, shrubs are non-existent and the remaining ground storey is made up of *Danthonia* spp. (such as *D. laevis*, *D. setacea* and *D. racemosa*) and *Themeda triandra*, *Microlaena stipoides*, *Lythrum hyssopifolia* and *Oxalis* spp.

1.5 North Central area and Bundoora

Similar to 1.1, this Red Gum Woodland sub-community has the same structure and grows in similar soil but *Eucalyptus camaldulensis* is the only canopy tree. An additional understorey tree is *Acacia pycnantha*, while the ground storey contains the characteristic sub-shrub *Bossiaea prostrata* in addition to the grasses of 1.1. Other additional species include *Burchardia umbellata* and *Carex breviculmis*.

1.6 Near Northeastern area, Yarra River at Kew North along the Darebin Creek Valley to Bundoora

Another sub-community similar to 1.1 and 1.5 but containing *Eucalyptus ovata* as an occasional tree in association with *E. camaldulensis*. Additional tussock grasses are *Elymus scabrus*, *Stipa rudis* and *S. mollis*. Lilies are characteristic of this sub-community and *Caesia calliantha* and *Dianella revoluta* are included with those of 1.1. *Acaena agnipila* and *Convolvulus erubescens* are additional herbs.

1.7 Eastern areas (formerly), Bundoora

A sub-community of Red Gum Woodland was once widespread on drainage lines and swampy areas of the eastern suburbs, now remaining only at Bundoora, where *Eucalyptus ovata* is actually more dominant than *E. camaldulensis*, forming a Woodland structure. Except for the occasional *Acacia mearnsii* the understorey is absent, but there is a dense ground storey dominated by grasses, mainly *Themeda triandra*, but also *Danthonia geniculata*. The herbs and sedges in between the tussocks are typical of poorly drained areas and include *Drosera peltata* ssp. *peltata*, *Gonocarpus tetragynus*, *Luzula meridionalis*, *Schoenus apogon*, *Stylidium graminifolium* and the annual *Wahlenbergia gracilenta*. Two moisture-loving orchids, common in season are *Microtis unifolia* and *Thelymitra pauciflora*.

2. Riparian Scrub

A form of Riparian Scrub community is found on fertile heavy loams of recent alluvial soils. Now heavily weed invaded it generally forms Woodland to Open-woodland and Open-scrub with *Eucalyptus camaldulensis* as the dominant tree, where present.

2.1 Scattered areas near Streams, particularly beside the Yarra River

Beneath the tree canopy of *Eucalyptus camaldulensis* is a dense understorey of *Acacia dealbata*, *Callistemon sieberi*, *Coprosma quadrifida* and *Hymenanthera dentata*. The indigenous species of the ground storey include the rushes and sedges *Carex* spp., *Juncus* spp. and *Alternanthera denticulata*. Growing in the water is *Alisma plantago-aquatica*.

3. Box-Ironbark Woodland (Median annual rainfall 650–700 mm)

A plant community of very restricted distribution within the defined Melbourne region covered by this book, found only on the steep slopes of the Plenty River.

3.1 Yarrambat

The characteristic dominant tree species are *Eucalyptus leucoxylon* ssp. *connata* and *E. tricarpa*, often with *E. macrorhyncha*. These species occur elsewhere but not all together. It is an Open-forest formation with an open understorey of shrubs including *Acacia acinacea*, *A. pycnantha*, *Cassinia longifolia* and *Ozothamnus obcordatus* through which scrambles *Clematis microphylla*. Occasionally emergent from these shrubs is the taller *Exocarpos cupressiformis*. Beneath the shrubs are the tussock grasses *Danthonia geniculata*, *D. setacea*, *D. tenuior*, *Poa* spp. and *Stipa* spp. and small shrubs such as *Astroloma humifusum* and *Einadia hastata*. *Amyema miquelii* grows in the tree canopy.

4. Dry Sclerophyll Forest (Median annual rainfall 700–800 mm)

From Red Gum Woodland, plant communities grade into Dry Sclerophyll Forest. As the topography of Melbourne becomes more hilly towards the east, rainfall increases and the soils are of the type that are moist to near waterlogged in Winter and dry out in the upper layer in Summer. Dry Sclerophyll Forest is one of the most widespread communities of Silurian-derived sedimentary soils, containing a large number of varied sub-communities.

4.1 Eastern area from Doncaster North to Mernda

Dominating the tree canopy of this sub-community are *Eucalyptus goniocalyx*, *E. macrorhyncha* and *E. polyanthemos*, forming an Open-forest structure. *E. melliodora* is sometimes present which is indicative of deeper soils. The understorey is made up of 2 layers, with *Acacia mearnsii* and *Exocarpos cupressiformis* taller than the smaller shrubs *Acacia acinacea*, *A. genistifolia*, *Bursaria spinosa* and *Cassinia arcuata*. An even smaller shrub layer is not a common occurrence in this sub-community, but sometimes *Daviesia leptophylla* and *Dillwynia cinerascens* may be present. *Poa sieberiana* and *Themeda triandra* are widespread in the ground storey. Some herbs more characteristic of deeper soils are *Hypericum gramineum*, *Senecio quadridentatus* and *Wurmbea dioica*. Other components of the ground storey include the sedges and lilies *Arthropodium strictum*, *Burchardia umbellata*, *Dianella revoluta*, *Lepidosperma laterale* and *Lomandra filiformis*, the climber *Hardenbergia violacea* and other herbs and small shrubs such as *Astroloma humifusum*, *Drosera peltata* ssp. *peltata*, *Gonocarpus tetragynus*, *Pimelea humilis* and *Poranthera microphylla*.

4.2 East and Northeastern area, Doncaster to Yarrambat

Because of the more skeletal soils in this region, this Open-forest sub-community is more typical of Dry Sclerophyll Forest, supporting *Eucalyptus goniocalyx*, *E. macrorhyncha* and *E. polyanthemos* as the tree canopy. The understorey or shrub layer contains species of varying heights. A middle height layer of *Acacia genistifolia*, *Daviesia leptophylla* and *Dillwynia cinerascens* is interspersed with heathy species such as *Acrotriche serrulata*, *Correa reflexa*, *Hovea linearis* and *Leucopogon virgatus*. Also intermingled are taller shrubs such as *Bursaria spinosa*, *Cassinia longifolia* and *Exocarpos cupressiformis*. The ground storey is continuous beneath the shrub layer and dominated by tussock grasses. *Chionochloa pallida*, *Poa sieberiana* and *Themeda triandra* are characteristic species. Lilies and rushes similar to those in 4.1 are common, together with other herbs such as *Brunonia australis*, *Drosera peltata* and *Opercularia varia*.

4.3 Eastern area, East Burwood to Ringwood, Warrandyte and Hurstbridge

This is also an Open-forest sub-community of moister soils and grades into Damp Sclerophyll Forest. The typical trees of 4.1 are joined by *Eucalyptus obliqua* and *E. rubida*, but are not as common. The understorey is marginally different, although still in 2 layers. Beneath an open layer of taller shrubs and small trees such as *Acacia mearnsii* and *Exocarpos cupressiformis* and the occasional *Acacia melanoxylon* is an open shrub layer of mostly *Bursaria spinosa* and *Cassinia aculeata* with some *Kunzea ericoides*. The ground storey of tussock grasses is similar to that of 4.2 but also includes *Poa morrisii* and *Stipa rudis*. Some creeping grasses are also common, including *Microlaena stipoides* and *Deyeuxia quadriseta*. *Gahnia radula*, *Dianella revoluta* and *Lomandra filiformis* are found in the ground storey, together with typical moisture-loving herbs and ferns, *Acaena novae-zelandiae*, *Euchiton involucratus*, *Gonocarpus tetragynus*, *Poranthera microphylla* and *Adiantum aethiopicum* in localised areas.

4.4 Scattered Far Eastern areas, around Wattle Glen and Further Northeast

An Open-forest sub-community found on the crowns and slopes of hills is very similar to 4.2, having the same tree canopy, but with the lower storeys heathy in character. Additional species of the middle storey are *Cassinia aculeata*, *Gompholobium huegelii* and *Hardenbergia violacea* and heathy species such as *Epacris impressa* and *Pimelea linifolia*, but not *Correa reflexa*. An additional grass species to those of 4.2 is *Dichelachne micrantha*. Rushes, lilies and other herbs are also similar with the addition of *Microseris lanceolata* and the orchids *Thelymitra* spp. and *Microtis unifolia*, common in season.

4.5 Restricted areas, Mullum Creek, Donvale and the Pauline Toner Butterfly Reserve, Montmorency

On the deeper soils of the middle slopes of hills a different Open-forest sub-community is found. It contains the usual tree canopy species of 4.1, but associated eucalypt species are *Eucalyptus radiata* and *E. rubida*. Understorey shrubs are not as common as in other Dry Sclerophyll Forest sub-communities but do include species similar to those in 4.1 as well as *Correa reflexa* and *Platylobium obtusangulum*. The grasses of the ground storey consist mainly of tussocks of *Chionochloa pallida*, but also include *Danthonia* spp., *Deyeuxia quadriseta*, *Dichelachne sieberiana*, *Elymus scabrus*, *Microlaena stipoides*, *Poa sieberiana* and *Themeda triandra*.

Species uncharacteristic of Dry Sclerophyll Forests but typical of more fertile soils are *Dianella longifolia*, *Linum marginale* and *Senecio hispidulus*. *Clematis microphylla* and *Comesperma volubile* are unusually common. Heathy shrubs and other herbs include *Acrotriche serrulata*, *Astroloma humifusum*, *Burchardia umbellata*, *Dianella revoluta*, *Drosera peltata* spp. *auriculata*, *Gonocarpus tetragynus*, *Hardenbergia violacea*, *Hovea linearis*, *Hypericum gramineum*, *Lepidosperma laterale*, *Leptorhynchos tenuifolius*, *Lomandra filiformis*, *Opercularia varia*, *Senecio tenuiflorus*, *Stylidium graminifolium*, *Tricoryne elatior* and *Veronica calycina*.

At Lower Plenty near Plenty Gorge, a disturbed variation of this sub-community occurs with the same upper and lower storeys, except for *Acacia paradoxa* and *A. implexa* but missing some herb species such as *Burchardia umbellata*, *Comesperma volubile*, *Drosera peltata*, *Stylidium graminifolium* and many others.

4.6 Restricted area near Hurstbridge

This Open-forest sub-community represents a grading from Box Ironbark Woodland to Dry Sclerophyll Forest and includes *Eucalyptus tricarpa* in association with the typical trees of subcommunity 4.2. The understorey is dominated by *Acacia paradoxa*, *A. pycnantha* and *Cassinia longifolia* with the taller *Exocarpos cupressiformis* occasionally emerging. The most common grasses of the ground storey are *Chionochloa pallida* and *Poa sieberiana*, interspersed with a variety of heathy shrubs including *Acrotriche serrulata*, *Astroloma humifusum*, *Correa reflexa*, *Dillwynia phylicoides*, *Dianella revoluta*, *Gonocarpus tetragynus*, *Goodenia blackiana*, *Leucopogon virgatus* and *Stylidium graminifolium*.

5. Valley Sclerophyll Forest (Median annual rainfall 750–1000 mm)

Throughout the low rolling hills of the Dry Sclerophyll Forests are watercourses, gullies and drainage lines. Within these environments, often on alluvial soils, on sheltered slopes, and on slopes of north Mt. Dandenong, a related plant community known as Valley Sclerophyll Forest has developed. The species of these plant communities generally prefer moister conditions.

5.1 Far Eastern Area, from Doncaster East and Mullum Creek North to Hurstbridge

On sheltered slopes in these areas, the typical canopy is similar to those of Dry Sclerophyll Forest, forming an Open-forest of *Eucalyptus goniocalyx*, *E. obliqua*, *E. macrorhyncha* and *E. polyanthemos*. The understorey is generally two layered, with similar species but limited in diversity—a dense layer of *Acacia* spp., *Bursaria spinosa*, *Cassinia aculeata* and *C. arcuata* over a more open layer of heathy species—*Epacris impressa*, *Hardenbergia violacea*, *Hovea linearis*, *Platylobium obtusangulum* and *Pimelea humilis*. An occasional third layer is formed by the taller *Acacia melanoxylon*, *A. mearnsii* and *Exocarpos cupressiformis*. Tussock grasses are also similar and are as listed for sub-community 4.2, but *Microlaena stipoides* and the bracken *Pteridium esculentum* are included. The characteristic herb of the ground story is the common *Viola hederacea*, but the rest of the species are similar to those of many Dry Sclerophyll

Forest sub-communities: *Arthropodium strictum*, *Brunonia australis*, *Burchardia umbellata*, *Dianella revoluta*, *Lomandra filiformis*, *Euchiton involucratus*, *Gonocarpus tetragynus*, *Hypericum gramineum* and *Opercularia varia*.

5.2 Mullum Mullum Creek and Diamond Creek

The tree canopy of this Open-forest sub-community varies slightly from 5.1. *Eucalyptus goniocalyx*, *E. macrorhyncha* and *E. polyanthemos* are joined by *E. melliodora* and *E. radiata*. Again the understorey is two-layered, the tallest layer consisting of *Acacia melanoxylon* and *Exocarpos cupressiformis*. The second layer is an open combination of *Cassinia aculeata*, *C. arcuata* and *Coprosma quadrifida* mixed with smaller shrubs such as the characteristic *Spyridium parvifolium* and shrubs more typical of exposed sites: *Acrotriche serrulata*, *Correa reflexa*, *Daviesia leptophylla*, *Dillwynia cinerascens* and *Platylobium obtusangulum*. The ground storey is also similar to that of Dry Sclerophyll Forest and includes *Poa sieberiana* and *Themeda triandra* with *Dianella revoluta*, *Drosera peltata*, *D. whittakeri*, *Gonocarpus tetragynus*, *Lomandra filiformis*, *Senecio quadridentatus* and those typical of sheltered areas such as *Hydrocotyle hirta* and *Viola hederacea*. *Hardenbergia violacea*, *Comesperma volubile* and *Billardiera scandens* scramble through the shrubs.

5.3 Scattered in Eastern area from Mt. Waverley to Hurstbridge

The eucalypt species making up the tree canopy in this sub-community are the same as in 5.2 with *Eucalyptus blakelyi* also found in an area in Yarrambat. The tall understorey consists of *Exocarpos cupressiformis* with a number of wattles: *Acacia melanoxylon*, *A. mearnsii* and *A. dealbata*, and a second, dense layer of *Bursaria spinosa*, *Cassinia aculeata* and *Kunzea ericoides* with the occasional smaller shrub as for 5.2. The ground storey is slightly different, however, with *Microlaena stipoides* present amongst the *Poa* and *Danthonia* spp., *Themeda triandra*, *Arthropodium strictum* and *Lomandra filiformis*. Other moisture-loving herbs amongst the tussocks are *Acaena novae-zelandiae*, *Dichondra repens* and *Viola hederacea* with common herbs *Gonocarpus tetragynus* and *Hypericum gramineum*.

5.4 Scattered in the Northeastern area, such as Pound Bend near the Yarra River

On the small creeks and drainage lines between the low rolling hills in this area another Valley Sclerophyll Forest sub-community can be found dominated by *Eucalyptus ovata*. Also present are *E. melliodora*, *E. rubida*, plus the usual *E. polyanthemos* and *E. radiata*. The understorey is a very dense layer of shrubs such as *Acacia verticillata*, *Cassinia aculeata*, *Coprosma quadrifida*, *Ozothamnus ferrugineus* and *Pomaderris aspera*, with a taller layer of *Acacia melanoxylon* and *A. mearnsii*. The only low shrub is Goodenia ovata because of the shade caused by the taller shrubs. The ground storey has a diverse range of moisture-loving plants: *Acaena novae-zelandiae*, *Adiantum aethiopicum*, *Carex appressa*, *Dichondra repens*, *Gratiola peruviana*, *Gahnia radula*, *Juncus pallidus*, *Lomandra longifolia*, *Microlaena stipoides*, *Poa labillardieri*, *P. tenera* and *Prunella vulgaris*.

5.5 Scattered in the Far Eastern area, Glen Waverley, Mt. Waverley and Nunawading

A very open sub-community for sheltered slopes with a variable combination of species: *Eucalyptus obliqua* and *E. radiata* sometimes with *E. dives*, *E. goniocalyx* and *E. ovata*. The understorey is dense, commonly containing *Acacia mearnsii* with the occasional *Exocarpos cupressiformis*, a high proportion of *Bursaria spinosa*, together with *Kunzea ericoides* and *Leptospermum continentale*. Wattles other than *Acacia paradoxa* are rare. Many grasses are present in the ground storey: *Poa morrisii*, *Stipa rudis*, *Themeda triandra*, *Deyeuxia quadriseta* and *Microlaena stipoides*. Again the herbs are typical of Dry Sclerophyll Forest: *Dianella revoluta*, *Drosera peltata* ssp. *auriculata*, *Gonocarpus tetragynus*, *Hypericum gramineum*, *Lepidosperma laterale*, *Pimelea humilis* and *Poranthera microphylla*.

5.6 Widespread from the Far East to the Far Northeastern areas, Ringwood to Hurstbridge

This is also a sheltered slope Open-Forest sub-community with a tree canopy similar to that in 5.5 but more dense. The understorey is a combination of the tall *Acacia melanoxylon* with a dense layer beneath of tall shrubs such as *A. verticillata*, *Cassinia aculeata*, *Coprosma quadrifida* and *Ozothamnus ferrugineus*. Other shrubs typical of Damp Sclerophyll Forests are also scattered throughout the understorey: *Bedfordia arborescens*, *Olearia argophylla* and *Polyscias sambucifolius*. Smaller shrubs are not a feature but there is a dense ground storey of herbs typical of sheltered areas: *Acaena novae-zelandiae*, *Adiantum aethiopicum*, *Dichondra repens*, *Euchiton involucratus*, *Lagenifera stipitata*, *Oxalis exilis* and *Viola hederacea* and the grasses *Microlaena stipoides*, *Poa labillardiera* and *P. morrisii*. Dry Sclerophyll Forest herbs are also present including *Gonocarpus tetragynus*, *Hypericum gramineum*, *Lomandra filiformis* and *Pteridium esculentum* as well as the scramblers *Billardiera scandens* and *Clematis aristata*.

5.7 Scattered in Eastern area, Glen Waverley to St. Andrews

Instead of Silurian soils, this Open-forest sub-community is found on Quaternary alluvial soils beside permanent watercourses which are moist throughout the year. Hence it has a quite different tree canopy of *Eucalyptus viminalis* with *E. melliodora* on drier soils. The understorey is dense with a tall, fairly close tree layer of *Acacia dealbata*, *A. mearnsii* and *Pomaderris aspera* over a dense shrub layer of *Acacia verticillata*, *Bursaria spinosa*, *Kunzea ericoides*, *Ozothamnus ferrugineus* and *Prostanthera lasianthos*. Smaller shrubs are resticted to *Goodenia ovata*, possibly due to the shady conditions. *Lomandra longifolia*, *Microlaena stipoides*, *Prunella vulgaris* and *Pteridium esculentum* dominate the ground storey.

5.8 Upper Western Slopes, Dandenong Ranges, Ferntree Gully

On the exposed upper western slopes of Mt Dandenong and around Ferntree Gully, an Open-forest sub-community with the dominant tree components of *Eucalyptus goniocalyx* and *E. macrorhyncha* can be found. The understorey is fairly sparse, consisting of isolated specimens of *Exocarpos cupressiformis* and *Acacia stricta*. Of the extensive heathy ground storey *Poa* spp., *Gonocarpus tetragynus*, *Lomandra filiformis*, *Pimelea humilis* and *Viola hederacea* are the most common species, but others include *Deyeuxia quadriseta*, *Chionochloa pallida*, *Glycine clandestina*, *Oxalis perennans*, *Pteridium esculentum*, *Platylobium formosum*, *Stylidium graminifolium* and *Themeda triandra*.

5.9 Northern slopes of Mt. Dandenong, Montrose, Mt. Evelyn

On the northern slopes of the Dandenongs there is an Open-forest sub-community where the dominant tree species is *Eucalyptus obliqua* together with *E. radiata*. Less common are *E. goniocalyx* and *E. macrorhyncha*. The understorey of this sub-community most commonly consists of the tall *Exocarpos cupressiformis* and *Cassinia aculeata* but also some *Acacia mucronata*, *A. stricta*, *Leptospermum continentale*, *Lomatia ilicifolia* and *Ozothamnus ferrugineus* forming an upper layer. The lower layer is heathy with similar species to those of 7.2. *Acacia myrtifolia*, *Epacris impressa*, *Goodenia lanata* and *Pultenaea gunnii* are the most common, but *Acrotriche serrulata* and *Pimelea humilis* are also included. Other climbers are *Clematis aristata*, *Comesperma volubile* and *Glycine clandestina*. The ground storey is also species-rich with the major species being *Poa ensiformis*, *Tetrarrhena juncea*, *Gonocarpus tetragynus*, *Viola hederacea* and *Pteridium esculentum*. Other herbs include *Geranium potentilloides*, *Helichrysum scorpioides*, *Hypericum gramineum* and *Oxalis perennans*, the grasses *Deyeuxia quadriseta* and *Microlaena stipoides*, the fern *Adiantum aethiopicum* and an orchid *Dipodium roseum*.

5.10 Eastern area between Dandenong and Lysterfield

Another sub-community in the eastern area not found on Silurian soils but on soils derived from Devonian volcanic rocks that are nearly waterlogged in Winter and moist at depth in Summer. This is consequently a quite different Open-forest sub-community with a low, moderately dense tree canopy of *Eucalyptus melliodora* and *E. radiata*. The moderately dense understorey is made up of *Allocasuarina littoralis*, *Acacia mearnsii* and *A. implexa*. Lower shrubs are not common but may have included *Cassinia aculeata*. The ground storey is dominated by tussock grasses: *Danthonia geniculata*, *Poa morrisii*, *Stipa pubinodis* and *Themeda triandra* and the creeping *Microlaena stipoides*. Lilies and rushes are also common amongst the grasses: *Dianella* spp., *Lepidosperma laterale*, *Lomandra filiformis* and *L. longifolia* together with the spreading, shade tolerant *Dichondra repens*, *Euchiton involucratus*, *Hypericum gramineum*, *Poranthera microphylla* and *Veronica plebeia*.

6. Swamp Scrub (Median annual rainfall 650–900 mm)

Swamp scrub is widespread in the eastern area where soils are poorly drained along creeks and drainage lines in lowland areas.

6.1 Eastern area

The tree canopy can be absent, but when it is present its main component is *Eucalyptus viminalis* and/or the shorter *E. ovata*. This means the structure may vary from Open-forest to Woodland to Open-woodland to Closed-scrub. The most characteristic species of this plant community is the tall dense understorey of *Melaleuca ericifolia*, and also *Acacia verticillata*, *Coprosma quadrifida*, *Ozothamnus ferrugineus* and *Leptospermum continentale*. Smaller shrubs are not a feature of the ground storey, which is composed mainly of moisture-loving herbs, grasses and sedges such as *Acaena novae-zelandiae*, *Carex appressa*, *Hydrocotyle hirta*, *Lepidosperma laterale*, *Microlaena stipoides*, *Poa tenera*, *Prunella vulgaris* and *Senecio minimus*.

7. Sclerophyll Woodland (Median annual rainfall approx. 900–1100 mm)

Within the study group there is one sub-community of Sclerophyll Woodland south of the Dandenong Ranges which is effectively a hilly heathland. The surface layers of the soils are shallow and nutrient deficient over a clay layer which impedes drainage and leads to waterlogging in Winter.

7.1 Low Foothills, South of Belgrave

This sub-community occurs in the low foothills south of the Dandenongs. The major tree species is *Eucalyptus cephalocarpa* in association with some *E. obliqua*. *Amyema pendulum* grows through the tree canopy. There is no tall understorey of *Acacia* spp., but there is a heathy understorey in two layers of great diversity. The dominant shrub of the upper layer is *Leptospermum continentale*, but also present are *Allocasuarina paludosa*, *Banksia marginata*, *Cassinia aculeata*, *Hakea nodosa*, *H. ulicina* and *Leptospermum myrsinoides*, with *Billardiera scandens* scrambling through them. Of the lower layer, *Platylobium obtusangulum* and *Epacris impressa* are the most common. Other species which also contribute to the heathy character of this layer are *Acrotriche prostrata*, *Acacia myrtifolia*, *Gompholobium huegelii*, *Goodenia lanata*, *Hibbertia stricta* and *Pultenaea gunnii*. Also typical of heathlands are the species found in the ground storey dominated by *Gahnia radula* and *Gonocarpus tetragynus*. Less common are *Chionochloa pallida*, *Deyeuxia quadriseta*, *Empodisma minus*, *Lepidosperma laterale*, *Lindsaea linearis*, *Poa ensiformis*, *Stipa muelleri*, *Themeda triandra* and the lily, *Burchardia umbellata*.

8. Damp Sclerophyll Forest (Median annual rainfall 900–1200 mm)

There are two plant sub-communities of Damp Sclerophyll Forest found on the eastern face of the Dandenong Ranges, one of which has been disturbed by frequent fire, described in 8.1.

8.1 East side of Dandenong Ranges, between Olinda and Silvan

The dominant tree of this Open-forest sub-community is *Eucalyptus obliqua* with the occasional *E. radiata*. There are no understorey trees but there are a number of shrub species. Large shrubs include *Acacia verticillata* and *Ozothamnus ferrugineus*. Smaller shrubs include large numbers of *Spyridium parvifolium* with lesser amounts of *Goodenia lanata*, *G. ovata*, *Pultenaea scabra* and *Tetratheca ciliatum*. *Tetrarrhena juncea* and *Pteridium esculentum* dominate the ground storey along with other species such as *Gonocarpus tetragynus*, *Lepidosperma elatius*, *Poa ensiformis* and *Viola hederacea*.

8.2 East side of Dandenong Ranges, West side of Silvan Reservoir

This sub-community is more diverse but has the same tree canopy as 8.1. The upper shrub layer of the understorey is composed of *Acacia mucronata*, *Cassinia aculeata*, *Leptospermum continentale* and *Ozothamnus ferrugineus*. The lower layer is composed of *Acrotriche prostrata*, *Epacris impressa*, *Goodenia lanata* and *Pultenaea gunnii* intermingled with the ground storey species, made up of rushes, ferns, sedges, grasses and herbs, which include *Gonocarpus tetragynus*, *Pteridium esculentum* and *Tetrarrhena juncea* in large numbers with fewer *Billardiera scandens*, *Deyeuxia quadriseta*, *Gahnia radula*, *Lepidosperma laterale*, *Lindsaea linearis*, *Lomandra filiformis*, *Poa ensiformis* and *Xanthorrhoea minor* ssp. *lutea*.

9. Wet Sclerophyll Forest

Wet Sclerophyll Forest is Tall Open-forest found on sheltered south to east facing slopes of the Dandenong Ranges, generally on deep loamy soils, and is quite different in species to those previously listed.

9.1 South and East Facing Higher Altitude Slopes, between Mt. Dandenong and Belgrave

The dominant tree is *Eucalyptus regnans*. Beneath the tree canopy is a dense understorey tree layer of *Acacia dealbata*, with *Bedfordia arborescens*, *Hedycarya angustifolia*, *Olearia argophylla* and *Pomaderris aspera*. Smaller shrubs are not common except for *Sambucus gaudichaudiana* and dense stands of *Coprosma quadrifida*, deeply shading the lower layers and making ferns the most prevalent, particularly treeferns *Dicksonia antarctica* and *Cyathea australis*, and *Polystichum proliferum*. Also present in the ground storey are *Australina pusilla* ssp. *muelleri*, *Pteridium esculentum*, the rampant grass *Tetrarrhena juncea* with *Clematis aristata* scrambling through the ferns.

9.2 South and East Facing Lower Altitude Slopes, between Mt. Dandenong and Belgrave

In this sub-community the dominant tree species is *E. cypellocarpa* instead of *E. regnans*, with some *E. obliqua*. The understorey tree layer has fewer species than in 9.1, with only *Acacia dealbata*, *A. melanoxylon*, *Ozothamnus ferrugineus* and *Pomaderris aspera*, but the dense shrub layer of *Coprosma quadrifida* is still evident, combined with some *Acacia paradoxa* and *Goodenia ovata*. Ferns are not as obvious with only a few *Cyathea australis*, *Calochlaena dubia* and *Polystichum proliferum*. *Tetrarrhena juncea* is still rampant in the ground storey, with *Viola hederacea* also a common component. Other plant species include *Clematis aristata*, *Geranium potentilloides*, *Hydrocotyle hirta*, *Lepidosperma elatius*, *Oxalis perennans*, *Poa ensiformis*, *P. tenera*, *Pteridium esculentum* and *Rubus parvifolius*.

9.3 Streams, Drainage Lines, North of Mt. Dandenong, around Silvan
This sub-community[2] is similar to 9.2 with *Eucalyptus viminalis* added to the tree canopy, *Prostanthera lasianthos* to the shrub layer, the fern *Blechnum wattsii* and the herbs *Acaena novae-zelandiae*, *Dianella tasmanica*, *Galium propinquum* and *Stellaria flaccida* added to the ground storey.

9.4 South and East Facing Slopes, between Mt. Dandenong and Belgrave
Another sub-community that is quite widespread on the sheltered slopes of the ranges contains similar species to that of 9.2, but instead of *Eucalyptus obliqua* being common, the tree canopy is formed by an association of *E. cypellocarpa* and *E. regnans*. The understorey is made up of layers, the upper layer being *Acacia dealbata*, the lower layer consisting of *Cassinia aculeata*, *Olearia phlogopappa* and *Polyscias sambucifolius* in fairly dense numbers. Both species of tree fern are present with *Dicksonia antarctica* the more common of the two. *Dianella tasmanica* and *Polystichum proliferum* are widespread in the ground storey, with *Poa ensiformis* and *Viola hederacea* also common. Less widespread components of the ground storey are *Acaena novae-zelandiae*, *Clematis aristata*, *Geranium potentilloides*, *Hydrocotyle hirta*, *Pteridium esculentum*, *Senecio linearifolius*, *Stellaria flaccida* and *Tetrarrhena juncea*.

10. Cool Temperate Rainforest

The Cool Temperate Rainforest community is located in sheltered southerly or south-easterly creek gullies on high rainfall sedimentary slopes, at mid to low altitudes.

10.1 Sheltered Gullies, Eastern Slopes of the Dandenong Ranges
Forming a Low Closed-forest, the characteristic component of this plant community is *Atherosperma moschatum* and *Acacia melanoxylon* with a few emergent Eucalyptus regnans. The fairly dense understorey is made up of tall shrubs, particularly *Olearia argophylla*, but also *Bedfordia arborescens*, *Coprosma quadrifida*, *Hedycarya angustifolia* and *Pittosporum bicolor*. Below the shrubs is a layer of *Dicksonia antarctica* and *Cyathea australis* which are host to filmy ferns and other epiphytics such as *Asplenium bulbiferum* and *Microsorum diversifolium*. The ground storey, typically low in species diversity, includes *Australina pusilla* ssp. *muelleri* and *Polystichum proliferum*.

C. Tertiary Sands

The tertiary sands area of Melbourne contains plant communities growing on a variety of soil types derived from sandstone and wind-blown sand. These range from dark loams, clays and local sands and dark grey sands over clay, through to light grey loams over clay and deep sands free of lime. In broad geographical terms, the southeastern Tertiary sands region includes areas around Central Melbourne down through Brighton and Moorabbin to Frankston, and inland to Caulfield, Oakleigh, Springvale and Cranbourne. In turn, these soils support a range of diverse plant communities including the very species-rich Tea-tree heath on the deep sands, Grassy Low Open Forest and Wattle tea-tree scrub on sands and sandy clays, and the ubiquitous Red Gum Woodland. Swamp scrub also occurs along drainage lines between the dunes and is referred to in detail in 6.1.

The Tea-tree heaths, or 'heathlands' were quite spectacular in Spring and once covered 'hundreds of square miles'. They used to be quite extensive around Sandringham. Swamps were common around Carrum, originally spreading to Keysborough and covering about 185 hectares.

2 On the floristic vegetation map for the Upper Yarra Valley and Dandenong Ranges, this plant community is classified as a separate community of Riparian Wet Sclerophyll Forest.

1. Tea-tree Heath (Median annual rainfall 700–800 mm)

Tea-tree heaths occur on nutrient-deficient deep sands on undulating dunes and are now found mainly at Langwarrin, Cranbourne, Braeside, Frankston and inland from Frankston, with odd patches at Sandringham and Springvale.

1.1 Far Southern area, Frankston, Langwarrin and Braeside
The main sub-community is an Open-woodland to Low Open-woodland where the dominant tree species is *Eucalyptus pryoriana*, forming a low open canopy over a dense shrub layer which consists mainly of *Leptospermum myrsinoides* with *Acacia oxycedrus*, *Banksia marginata*, *Leptospermum continentale* and *Ricinocarpos pinifolius* from which *Exocarpos cupressiformis* emerges, forming a very open taller understorey. Typical of heathland, smaller flowering shrubs can be found in the ground storey: *Amperea xiphoclada*, *Aotus ericoides*, *Acianthus pusillus*, *Bossiaea cinerea*, *Correa reflexa*, *Dillwynia glaberrima*, *Epacris impressa*, *Hibbertia prostrata*, *Leucopogon virgatus* and *Monotoca scoparia* to name a few. Some rushes and sedges are also typical such as *Hypolaena fastigiata*, *Lepidosperma concavum* and *Lomandra filiformis* as well as the grass tree *Xanthorrhoea minor* ssp. *lutea* and *Pteridium esculentum*. In the shelter provided by the taller shrubs, some herbs thrive with *Centrolepis strigosa*, *Dichondra repens*, *Drosera whittakeri*, *Gonocarpus tetragynus*, *Lagenifera stipitata*, *Opercularia varia*, *Platysace heterophylla* and *Thysanotus patersonii* being fairly common. *Trachymene anisocarpa* is commonly seen after fires or other disturbance. Many orchids may be found in season, *Pterostylis nutans*, *P. longifolia* being the most common.

Because the soils are generally nutrient-deficient, grasses are not characteristic of heaths, although *Microlaena stipoides* is often present in the understorey. The Dodder Laurel, *Cassytha glabella* may be found scrambling amongst the shrubs and herbs.

1.2 Far Southern area, Frankston, inland Langwarrin and Cranbourne
This sub-community is generally lacking in a tree canopy and has a structure of Low Open-woodland, Closed-heath and Open-heath. It is dominated by a dense, tall shrub layer of mainly *Leptospermum myrsinoides*, but may also include *Allocasuarina paradoxa*, *Banksia marginata* and *Leptospermum continentale*. Beneath this layer are the smaller heathy shrubs: *Amperea xiphoclada*, *Aotus ericoides*, *Dillwynia glaberrima*, *D. sericea*, *Epacris impressa*, *Hibbertia acicularis*, *H. prostrata*, *Leucopogon virgatus*, *Monotoca scoparia* and *Ricinocarpos pinifolius*. The ground storey is similar to that of 1.1 but is not as species-rich. It does not include grasses but may have a number of orchids.

2. Wattle Tea-tree Scrub (Median annual rainfall 700–800 mm)

Wattle tea-tree scrub represents a diverse array of communities some of which may be natural and others that are largely the result of disturbance since settlement of what was formerly Grassy Low Open Forest or Swamp Heaths. The 'wattle' (*Acacia longifolia*) has been introduced and is in many areas now dominating. It occurs on shallow sands and sandy clays over moderately fertile, sticky, wet, dense grey clays which are waterlogged in Winter and remain moist at a moderate depth in Summer.

2.1 Far Southern area, Langwarrin
The original community is Open-forest dominated by *Eucalyptus cephalocarpa* or, where the soils are very heavy, *E. ovata*. There is a tall understorey of *Leptospermum continentale*, *Melaleuca ericifolia* and *Ozothamnus ferrugineus* with *Cassytha glabella* winding through them. Typical of poorly-drained soils are the ground storey of tall sedges such as *Lepidosperma longitudinale* and *Lepyrodia muelleri*. Between the sedges are moisture-loving herbs such as *Drosera peltata* ssp. *auriculata*, *Gonocarpus tetragynus*, *Hydrocotyle hirta*,

Isolepis marginata, *Lagenifera gracilis*, *L. stipitata* and *Opercularia varia*. Occasionally the small herb *Xanthosia dissecta* may be found. Differing from the Tea-tree heath nearby, grasses are common and include *Microlaena stipoides* and *Poa sieberiana*.

Other likely components of this community, but now found only where the sites are often slashed, are small herbs such as *Centrolepis aristata*, *C. strigosa*, *Drosera pygmaea*, *Gonocarpus micrantha*, *Goodenia humilis*, *Hypericum gramineum* and *Schoenus apogon*.

A variation of the main community is a greater occurrence of *Lepidosperma longitudinale* and *Leptospermum continentale* and fewer herbs. Other variations have a higher proportion of *Lepidosperma longitudinale* and *Schoenus brevifolius*, *Lepyrodia muelleri* and *Gahnia radula*.

2.2 Far Southern area, Cranbourne, Langwarrin, Frankston
In between the sand dunes where there are moist, poorly-drained depressions are sub-communities of Open-forest, Low Open-forest and Closed-scrub, with a canopy, where present, of *Eucalyptus cephalocarpa* and *E. ovata*. The understorey is a combination of *Leptospermum continentale*, *Melaleuca ericifolia*, *M. squarrosa* and *Ozothamnus ferrugineus*. The ground storey is dominated by *Gahnia sieberiana* with other sedges such as *Empodisma minus*, *Lepidosperma longitudinale*, *Schoenus apogon* and *S. brevifolius*. *Gonocarpus tetragynus*, *Pteridium esculentum* and *Xanthosia dissecta* grow among them.

2.3 Far Southern area, Langwarrin
Another sub-community of Wattle tea-tree scrub, now dominated by *Acacia longifolia*, is thought to be a heathland typical of waterlogged soils which no longer exists around Melbourne. This was Closed-scrub dominated by *Allocasuarina paludosa* and *Leptospermum continentale*, and had a field layer of species such as *Drosera peltata* ssp. *auriculata*, *Epacris impressa*, *Gahnia radula*, *Gonocarpus micranthus*, *G. tetragynus*, *Patersonia occidentalis*, *Schoenus tenuissimus*, *Thelionema caespitosum* and *Xanthosia dissecta*.

3. Grassy Low Open Forest (Median annual rainfall 800–900 mm)

In the flat to undulating areas inland from the coast to the south east where soils are mainly sands and sandy clays, the major vegetation type is Grassy Low Open-forest. The remnants are now mainly south and east of Seaford and Frankston, but could have extended northwest of these areas, through to Braeside, Caulfield and Melbourne.

The structure of the community is Low Open-forest and Open-forest as indicated by the name.

3.1 Widespread in Far Southern area, South of Seaford
This is a very species-rich sub-community and is the most typical. The characteristic dominant tree is *Eucalyptus radiata*, sometimes with *E. ovata* and occasionally *E. cephalocarpa* and *E. pryoriana*. The tall shrub or small tree understorey includes *Acacia mearnsii*, *A. paradoxa*, *Allocasuarina littoralis*, *Cassina aculeata*, *Exocarpos cupressiformis* and *Leptospermum continentale*. The lowest storey is made up of sedges and bracken (*Gahnia radula*, *Pteridium esculentum*), small shrubs: *Acrotriche serrulata*, *Astroloma humifusum*, *Bossiaea prostrata*, *Epacris impressa*, *Hibbertia riparia*, *Leucopogon virgatus* and *Pimelea humilis*, *Xanthorrhoea minor* ssp. *lutea*, and herbs, including orchids and lilies (*Arthropodium strictum*, *Burchardia umbellata*, *Chamaescilla corymbosa*, *Dianella revoluta*, *Gonocarpus tetragynus*, *Goodenia geniculata*, *Lagenifera gracilis*, *L. stipitata*, *Opercularia varia*, *Pterostylis longifolia*, *P. nutans*, *P. pedunculata*, *Thysanotus patersonii*, *Tricoryne elatior*). Grasses such as *Microlaena stipoides*, *Poa morrisii*, *P. sieberiana* and, to a lesser extent, *Deyeuxia quadriseta* can also be dominant features. Other plants such as *Billardiera scandens*, *Comesperma volubile*, *Dichondra repens*, *Drosera peltata* ssp. *auriculata*, *D. whittakeri*, *Hypericum gramineum*, *Lepidosperma laterale*, *Lomandra filiformis*, *Schoenus apogon* and *Viola hederacea* are less common. *Amyema pendulum* is present in the tree canopy.

3.2 Far Southern area, small area South of Cranbourne
Where there are relatively heavy soils, with sand overlying heavy clay which becomes waterlogged in Winter, a slightly different sub-community of Grassy Low Open Forest exists. Here the tree canopy generally contains only one species, *Eucalyptus radiata*, and rarely, *E. cephalocarpa*. Beneath the canopy is a tall shrubby understorey of *Acacia mearnsii*, *Leptospermum continentale* and occasionally *Melaleuca ericifolia*.

There are few typical heathland species and low shrubs in the ground storey, except for *Epacris impressa*, *Pteridium esculentum*, and grass species such as *Danthonia pilosa*, *D. semiannularis*, *Deyeuxia quadriseta*, *Microlaena stipoides*, *Poa sieberiana* and *Stipa rudis*. Other herbs and rushes present amongst the grasses include *Gonocarpus tetragynus*, *Lagenifera stipitata*, *Lomandra filiformis*, *Poranthera microphylla* and *Viola hederacea*. *Arthropodium strictum* and *Tricoryne elatior* are less common. *Amyema pendulum* is occasionally present in the tree canopy.

3.3 Far Southern area, South of Frankston
A sub-community similar to 3.1 but the dominant trees are *Eucalyptus pryoriana* and *E. viminalis*, rather than *E. radiata*. *Bursaria spinosa*, *Exocarpos cupressiformis* and *Ozothamnus ferrugineus* form a dense understorey. The ground storey species are few in number but include the shade-loving plants *Adiantum aethiopicum*, *Dichondra repens*, *Microlaena stipoides* and *Poa labillardieri*, and other species, including *Acaena novae-zelandiae*, *Billardiera scandens*, *Comesperma volubile*, *Drosera peltata* ssp. *auriculata*, *Dianella revoluta*, *Gahnia radula*, *Juncus pallidus*, *Lepidosperma laterale*, *Lomandra longifolia*, *Pteridium esculentum*, *Schoenus apogon* and *Themeda triandra*.

4. Red Gum Woodland

In some areas of the Tertiary Sands region, where there are not sands but sedimentary clay-loams, Red Gum Woodland communities dominated. These areas are flat, broad and swampy and remain waterlogged for much of the year.

4.1 Far Southern area, Northeast of Frankston
The dominant tree of this Woodland is *Eucalyptus camaldulensis* with an understorey of *Acacia paradoxa*, *Melaleuca ericifolia* and *Ozothamnus ferrugineus*. The ground storey layer consists of the herbs *Acaena novae-zelandiae*, *Senecio glomeratus*, *S. hispidulus*, the rushes and sedges *Eleocharis acuta*, *Juncus amabilis*, *J. pallidus* and *Lomandra longifolia*, grasses such as *Poa labillardieri* and *P. sieberiana* and *Clematis microphylla*.

4.2 Southeastern area, Braeside and Noble Park
Red Gum Woodland becomes Grassy Low Open Forest in these areas, grading into other more forested communities of sedimentary-derived soils to the east. Again the dominant tree is *Eucalyptus camaldulensis* with a very open understorey of mainly *Leptospermum continentale*, and some *Kunzea ericoides*. The ground storey species are dominated by Themeda triandra with other characteristic herbs, rushes and sedges, *Carex breviculmis*, *Dichondra repens*, *Drosera peltata* ssp. *peltata*, *Hypericum gramineum*, *Hypoxis hygrometrica*, *Juncus bufonius*, *J. holoschoenus*, *J. pallidus*, *Luzula meridionalis* and *Schoenus apogon*.

D. Coastal Areas

The coastal and near-coastal areas of Melbourne around Port Phillip Bay support a number of plant communities. East of the Maribyrnong River, the communities are Primary Dune Scrub and Coastal Banksia Woodland, while west of the Maribyrnong River the coast is host to Saltmarsh communities. The differences in soils and amount of rainfall account for the differences between east and west.

Coastal communities are amongst the most fragile, struggling for survival against continual pressure from wind, rain and tide. Destruction of even small areas of vegetation can cause rapid and severe erosion of unstable sand dunes.

1. Primary Dune Scrub (Median annual rainfall 600–800 mm)

There are two sub-communities of Primary Dune Scrub found along the coast.

1.1 Coastal Dunes Inland of Beaches, Eastern Shore of Port Phillip Bay

Because of the extreme influences of salt spray, wind exposure and early soil development from deep sands, the structure of the coastal dune plant community changes over short distances from Open-heath, Open-scrub, Open-woodland to Woodland.

On the seaward face, on the first line of defence, is a group of plants dominated by the grass, *Spinifex sericeus*, growing with *Atriplex cinerea*. As sites become more sheltered and the soils improve, shrubs are more frequent and become the second line of defence. The main shrub species is *Leptospermum laevigatum* but other species include *Acacia sophorae*, *Banksia integrifolia*, *Correa alba*, *Olearia axillaris* and *Ozothamnus turbinatus*. *Tetragonia implexicoma* scrambles through the shrubs forming dense mats. The ground storey comprises herbs such as *Actites megalocarpa*, *Apium annuum*, *Carpobrotus rossii* and *Isolepis nodosa*.

1.2 Low to High Exposed Cliffs, Eastern Shore of Port Phillip Bay

The cliffs are composed of sandy, more or less consolidated rock with the same influences as the coastal dunes, forming Closed-heath, Open-heath, Open-scrub and Woodland. Dense shrubs form the dominant vegetation, mainly *Acacia sophorae* and *Leptospermum laevigatum*. Other typical shrubs are *Leucopogon parviflorus* and *Rhagodia candolleana*, together with the distinctive *Alyxia buxifolia* and *Myoporum insulare*. Species which are also a feature in the dunes are *Tetragonia implexicoma*, *Dianella revoluta* var. *brevicaulis* and the grass *Distichlis distichophylla*.

2. Saltmarsh (Median rainfall 550–650 mm)

The Saltmarsh communities of the Melbourne area can be found on basalt-derived soils which are waterlogged for much of the year, particularly in Winter, with semi-saline to saline water. Like the Plains Grassland, the saltmarshes are treeless.

2.1 West of the Maribyrnong River

The saltmarsh community, or series of sub-communities, is quite distinctive, with a unique group of succulent or salt tolerant sedges and grasses. Its structure is of an Open-herbland, but the plant species tend to be distributed according to the depth and length of time they are inundated with saline water. The dominant species in the upper saltmarsh zones are the succulents *Sarcocornia quinqueflora* and *Suaeda australis* but the tallest plants are usually a number of salt tolerant sedge-type plants such as *Bolboschoenus caldwellii* and grasses such as *Puccinellia stricta*. *Triglochin striata* grows in depressions. Smaller growing species are *Distichlis distichophylla*, *Disphyma crassifolium* ssp. *clavellatum*, *Hemichroa pentandra* and *Samolus repens*. Closer to the beach is the shrub *Atriplex cinerea* in association with *Disphyma crassifolium* ssp. *clavellatum* and *Suaeda australis*.

The mangrove *Avicennia marina* forms an Open-scrub on intertidal mud-flats adjacent to saltmarshes, often near creek mouths. Other plant communities associated with saltmarshes are saline swamps of sedgelands composed of *Juncus krausii* and *Gahnia filum*, and on the seaward edge of the saltmarsh, a community influenced by the high tides: *Atriplex cinerea* and *Spinifex sericeus*.

3. Coastal Banksia Woodland (Median annual rainfall 800 mm)

Along the low-lying Kananook Creek is a unique community of Coastal Banksia Woodland. This is due to the environmental characteristics of this area, being flat, low, and having poorly draining, organic, slightly saline soils. Within this area are a number of sub-communities.

3.1 South of Patterson River (earlier extended north to Yarra River

The first sub-community is located on near-coastal sites south of the Patterson River where the soils are deep sand. The sites are less exposed than those of 1.1, therefore the community represents the third line of defence from salt-laden winds. This sub-community is a Woodland dominated by *Banksia integrifolia*. Beneath the tree canopy is a dense shrub layer of *Acacia sophorae*, *Leptospermum laevigatum*, *Leucopogon parviflorus*, *Myoporum insulare* and *Rhagodia candolleana*. The ground storey layer comprises rushes and herbs: *Carpobrotus rossii*, *Dichondra repens*, *Isolepis nodosa*, *Lepidosperma concavum*. Climbers and scrambling perennials through the shrubs, such as *Clematis microphylla*, *Muehlenbeckia adpressa* and *Tetragonia implexicoma*, are common.

3.2 Kananook Creek, between Patterson River and Frankston

The second sub-community is Closed-scrub and Woodland containing species typical of both Saltmarsh (*Atriplex hastata*, *Disphyma crassifolium* ssp. *clavellatum*, *Sarcocornia* spp. and *Suaeda australis*) and Swamp Scrub (*Melaleuca ericifolia* and *Phragmites australis*) because of the high water table. Species typical of free-draining coastal sites are also present: *Banksia integrifolia*, *Leptospermum laevigatum*, *Rhagodia candolleana* and *Tetragonia implexicoma*. Species more typical of this sub-community than elsewhere include *Leptinella reptans*, *Juncus krausii* and *Selliera radicans*.

Further Reading

Australian Surveying and Land Information Group, (1990) *Vegetation Atlas of Australian Resources* Vol 6, Third Series. Department of Administrative Services, Canberra.

Cheal, D.C., et al (Oct. 1989, unpublished) *Vegetation Survey and Sites of Botanical Significance in the Melbourne Area.* Flora Branch, Department of Conservation & Environment.

Cheal, D.C., Lau, J.A., et al, (1989) *Floristic Vegetation Map of the Melbourne Area.* Department of Conservation & Environment.

Cochrane, G.R., Fuhrer, B.A., Rotherham, E.R., Willis, J.H., (rev. 1973) *Flowers and Plants of Victoria.* A.M. & A.W. Reed, Sydney.

Costermans, Leon, (rev 1991) *Native Trees and Shrubs of South-Eastern Australia.* Rigby, Adelaide.

Director of Meteorology, (Sept. 1968) *Climatic Survey Region 10—Port Phillip Victoria.* Commonwealth of Aust., Bureau of Meteorology.

Gullan, P.K., et al (July 1979) *Sites of Botanical Significance in the Upper Yarra Region.* Environmental Studies Program, Ministry of Conservation, Victoria.

McDougall, K., (1987) *Sites of Botanical Significance in the Western Region of Melbourne.* Dept. of Geography, University of Melbourne, for Dept. Conservation, Forests & Lands.

Parkes, D.M., (1980) *Floristic Vegetation of the Upper Yarra Valley and Dandenong Ranges.* Map. Upper Yarra Valley and Dandenong Ranges Authority.

Specht, R.L. (1970) 'Vegetation' in Leeper, G.W. (ed.) *The Australian Environment.* CSIRO Aust. with M.U.P.

Willis, J.H., (1965) 'Native Plants of Brighton'. *Indigenotes.* (IFFA) Vol.4 No. 8, 1991 Melb.

Chapter 2. Soils of Melbourne

Soil Conservation Authority*

In using the soil map of Melbourne, it should be remembered that builders and developers often bulldoze the topsoil, and even the subsoil, during their activities. Clean filling may be removed or brought in. Also, in Melbourne, a truly staggering amount of soil is sold to the public and spread on their gardens as: 'mountain soil' from as far away as Toolangi, 'Cranbourne loam', 'sandy loam' or just 'topsoil'. Depending on its history, the soil in a given garden may therefore vary considerably from the natural undisturbed soil profiles. The map also employs broad groupings of soils within which there is some natural variation.

The area covered by this article is larger than that of the Melbourne study area of this book. As the map also covers all sections the text has been left intact.

1. Red Loams

In the rolling to hilly country between Silvan and Monbulk, the upper parts of the Dandenong Ranges and the hill crests at Chirnside Park, one finds red loam soils which are deep, friable, well-structured and mildly acidic. Other features include:

- excellent drainage
- low to moderate water holding capacity
- soil digging very easy whether dry, moist or wet; non-sticky
- soil structure allows extensive root development
- shrinking and swelling is minimal
- erodibility is low
- suits wide range of plants

Example 1: MOOROOLBARK (Melway Map 37.K5)
Tertiary basalt

Soil Profile:

0–20 cm	Dark brown friable loam, grading into
20–80 cm	dark reddish brown friable clay loam, over
80–120 cm	reddish brown or brown strongly weathered soft basalt.

2. Brown Loams over Clay

Very good soils have developed on the Older basalts of the lower Mornington Peninsula. Grey brown friable loam topsoils overlie well-structured yellow-red mottled clay subsoils. Other features include:

- good drainage
- good water holding capacity
- easily worked when moist, non-sticky, too soft when wet
- soil structure allows good root development

Example 2: BALDRY'S CROSSING (Melway Map 256.L10)
Tertiary (Older basalt)

Soil Profile:

0–30 cm	Grey brown friable loam, abruptly overlying
30–300 cm	yellow-red heavy textured clay, over
200+ cm	rock or decomposed basalt.

3. Dark Grey Sand over Clay

In the gently undulating to flat land between Kew and Mt Waverley, and in a large triangular area bounded by Toorak, Cheltenham and Dandenong, the topsoil is a black to dark grey sand, grading into light grey sand. This topsoil overlies a brown, red and grey mottled clay. These soils are also found in the Frankston-Mornington-Balnarring-Tyabb area but the topsoils are loamier, deeper and without stones. These soils are poor in plant nutrients. Other features include:

- clay subsoil prevents too rapid drainage
- suited to a large range of plants
- topsoil easily worked whether dry, moist or wet
- non-sticky
- in winter a perched watertable may occur above the clay affecting drainage

Example 3: KEW (Melway Map 45.J7)
Tertiary sands

Soil Profile:

0–30 cm	Black to dark grey sand; grading into
30–50 cm	light grey sand, with slight yellow-brown mottling and a concentration of buckshot (small iron stones) at depth; abruptly overlying
50–150+ cm	brown, red and grey, mottled compact clay; strongly weathered.

4. Light Grey Loams over Clay

In the north-eastern areas of Melbourne, which include: Kew to Croydon and from Bundoora to Rowville, the topsoil consists of a light grey loam with some stones or gravel. The topsoil overlies a compact yellow brown mottled clay with small and large angular stones often found at the junction. These soils are poor in plant nutrients and humus. Other features include:

- moderately well drained
- moderate to low in water holding capacity

* The Soil Conservation Authority is now part of the Deptartment of Conservation and Natural Resources.

- topsoil tends to set quite hard when dry and needs to be worked when moist as it is too soft when wet
- good for a wide range of plants
- scattered rock fragments in the subsoil can cause problems for digging

Example 4: BUNDOORA (Melway Map 10.A9)
Silurian sandstones and sandstones

Soil Profile:

0–15 cm	Light grey loam, with some stones and gravel, abruptly overlying
15–60+ cm	yellow brown mottled clay.

5. Gritty Light Grey Loam over Clay

Soils formed on granite rocks occur between Lysterfield and Hallam, Arthur's Seat, Mt Martha and in other areas. These soils consist of light grey gritty sandy loam, or loamy sand, over mottled yellow brown and grey clay. They are poor in nutrients and are also mildly acidic. Other features include:

- moderately well drained
- low water holding capacity in topsoil
- topsoil sets hard when dry and is moderately easy to dig when moist
- non-sticky
- waterlogging is common on lower slopes in Winter and Spring
- prone to water erosion

Example 5: MT MARTHA (Melway Map 150.G7)
Granite

Soil Profile:

0–30 cm	Light grey sandy loam; an abrupt transition to
30–100 cm	yellow brown sandy clay with a blocky structure;
100+ cm	decomposing granite.

6. Dark Loams, Clays, Local Sands

On the flood plain and swampy areas around Melbourne the soils consist of dark loams, clays and sands. These soils can be very good for a wide range of plants if they are adequately drained (watertable kept between 1 and 2 metres in depth). They are fair to poor in plant nutrients. Other features include:

- drainage variable
- if rusty mottling along old root channels in topsoil is present it indicates very poor drainage
- mildly acidic to neutral
- sand and clay contents will vary depending upon position on the floodplain (i.e. youngest terrace or an old levee)

Example 6: BANKSIA PARK, BULLEEN (Melway Map 32.D5)
Alluvial soil on Yarra floodplain

Soil Profile:

0–20 cm	Very dark grey brown silt loam to clay loam; grading into
20–60+ cm	grey brown silty clay loam to silty clay.

7. Deep Sands Free of Lime

Deep grey brown sands over yellow grey, frequently with a layer of dark brown hard cemented sand ('Coffee rock'), cover the sand-dune areas from Black Rock to Brighton, and along the coast of Port Phillip Bay as far as Rye. These soils are extremely poor in nutrients and strongly to mildly acidic. Other features include:

- rapid drainage
- very low water holding capacity
- very easily worked when wet, moist or dry
- non-sticky
- prone to wind erosion
- high water tables in some areas

Example 7: FRANKSTON (Melway Map 103.K8)
Sand

Soil Profile:

0–40 cm	Light grey sand, over
40–50 cm	coffee coloured sand, extending into
50+ cm	yellowish brown to brown sand.

8. Deep Sands with Lime

Between Cape Schanck and Sorrento, in rolling sand dune areas, the deep soils are grey to whitish sand that occasionally lie on a lime-cemented hard pan. The sandy topsoil contains a varying amount of lime and is lightly acid to alkaline, and the subsoils are alkaline. Other features include:

- excellent drainage
- very low water holding capacity
- very easily worked when wet, moist or dry
- non-sticky
- prone to wind erosion
- limited range of lime tolerant and salt wind tolerant plants

Example 8: SORRENTO (Melway Map 156.J9)
Aeolianite, calcareous and siliceous dune sand

Soil Profile:

0–90 cm	Uniform dark grey medium sand, over
90–200+ cm	yellow grey uniform sand. Over sand and calcarenite.

9. Heavy Clay on Younger Basalts

Over extensive areas to the north-west of Melbourne, stretching from Altona to Thomastown and from Richmond to Broadmeadows and beyond, one finds shallow dark and reddish brown heavy clays with a thin loamy topsoil. Basalt outcrops are common and basalt floaters occur extensively. Other features include:

- drainage very poor, waterlogged in wet weather
- soils very hard when dry and very sticky when wet, making them very difficult to cultivate
- slightly alkaline to slightly acidic
- clayey soil and low rainfall limits the range of plants
- clay dries very quickly in hot weather and can develop deep cracks. Large shrink-swell capacity. This can cause cracks in walls and pavements

Example 9: DAREBIN PARK, FAIRFIELD (Melway Map 31.D8)
Quaternary basalt

Soil Profile:

0–15 cm	Very dark grey brown clay, fissured and hard when dry but sticky and plastic when wet, grading into
15–70+ cm	dark grey brown to brown heavy clay, coarsely angular blocky structure.

Notes on Soil Descriptions Used

Acidity Acidity is measured on the pH scale. Soils are said to be neutral if they have a pH of 7, acidic if the pH is less than 7 and alkaline if they have a pH greater than 7.

Floaters Rocks and stones which occur irregularly within the soil profile are referred to as floaters.

Friable A friable soil is one which can be easily crumbled or broken up. A friable soil allows easy cultivation.

Hardpan The term hardpan refers to any layer compacted or cemented within or below a soil profile.

Humus That part of soil organic matter which has decomposed into a dark coloured soft material without a trace of the original plant tissue.

Mottled Spots or blotches of different colours or shades of colour interspaced with the dominant colour.

Organic Matter All the constituents of soil arising from living matter: includes remains of dead plants and microfauna, both fresh and decomposed.

Plant Nutrients The term 'poor' used with plant nutrients means that the nutrient levels are usually enough to permit growth of most Australian plants and many exotics. Indigenous plants are happy growing without additives such as fertiliser and soil improvers.

However, to grow a range of Australian plants soil conditions may be improved by the addition of appropriate amounts of:

—**organic material** will increase the humus content of the soil. This has an excellent effect on the soil structure in loams and clays while increasing water holding capacity and nutrient storage ability of all soils

—**fertilisers** or **animal manures** will increase the nutrient level of the soil

—**lime** or **dolomite** will neutralise acidity

—**sulphur** will neutralise or acidify an alkaline soil

—**gypsum** will improve and stabilise soil structure.

Soil Profile A vertical section of a soil through all its layers and extending into the bedrock. A profile can be seen when the soil is exposed in a road or railway cutting.

Structure Structure refers to the way soil particles group together. The particles in most soils consolidate into crumbs of various sizes. Some soils, such as beach sand, have particles which do not cling together and they have no structure. In contrast, some clay soils stick together in one solid mass and also lack structure. Soils which do not readily break into crumbs are poorly structured. Well-structured soils break up easily into crumbs with definite shapes and sizes. These crumbs, being irregular in size and shape, do not completely fill the space they occupy and result in a network of open spaces and passages which are filled by air, water or plant roots. In fact, an average soil may contain forty to sixty percent of these open spaces. The structure of the soil is very important to farmers and gardeners. A well-structured soil will easily take in water through the spaces between the lumps. Excess water will drain away through the spaces and be replaced with air. Most plants need both air and water near their roots to grow well. When surface soils lose their structure they are more easily eroded.

Texture Texture is the feel of the moist soil when worked between the fingers and is related to the relative proportions of particle size groups present (coarse and fine sand, silt, clay), as well as being influenced by organic matter and gravel. The texture has an important bearing on how much water the soil can hold, how easy it is to dig or plough, and its fertility.

Much of our agricultural production comes from soils with friable loam surface horizons. These soils contain moderate but variable amounts of all sizes of mineral particles together with organic matter.

Chapter 3. Regeneration of a House Block

Vivien Freshwater*

Why bother to retain bushland on a small block of land? Will it survive? Fortunately the move towards indigenous plants has fostered an awareness of just how important a small area of natural bush is in maintaining the local genetic diversity in plant species. Even small linear reserves are important in providing a corridor for bird and animal movement. Many species of insects have an association with a particular native plant species on which they lay their eggs, providing an immediate food source for their larvae.

Once you have acquired your bush block you should identify the indigenous and introduced plant species growing on it, as well as possible fauna habitats. The old dead tree could be an important habitat for possums, birds or bats.

Take a full year to complete your list of plant species, remembering that most orchids and lilies only appear in Spring and Summer. The identification of native grasses should be carried out in Summer, when most species are flowering. If you do not have sufficient knowledge for this task, either consult an expert, or collect plant specimens and take them to the Herbarium.

The aim of natural regeneration is to help the bush help itself. This means there should be minimal disturbance, and removal of weeds should only be carried out at the same rate as the indigenous plants are able to replace them. Experience shows the value of a long-term written plan before any revegetation work is undertaken. Natural bush regeneration takes time, so don't expect to complete the task of restoring your block in a couple of years.

It is preferable to use small hand tools when working in bushland. A kit consisting of a two-pronged daisy digger, secateurs and a pair of pliers will enable you to handle most weeds. Pliers are indispensable for removing small roots up to 10mm wide from moist soil without snapping them off. This is less destructive than digging. They are also useful when handling or moving blackberries.

Some weeds are more easily controlled than others, but if you plan your regeneration strategies to remove the introduced plants before they set seed, then you will save yourself a lot of time and effort. Probably the two introduced grasses most difficult to eliminate are Panic Veldt Grass (*Ehrharta erecta*) and Blown Grass (*Agrostis* species). The former is easily removed, but has many tiny seeds that seem to fall off the plant no matter how careful you are. The latter has a very matted root system. It is important to learn the growing and seeding habits of the weeds. With experience you learn to recognise the introduced grasses before they flower.

Each weed species has specific requirements for removal. Make a study of the various root systems, so that you will automatically know which technique and tool to use when removing them. For weeds with a more extensive root system, a garden fork is more appropriate and preferable to a mattock.

The timing for the removal of understorey trees such as Sweet Pittosporum (*Pittosporum undulatum*) can be critical. The removal of these trees will dramatically increase the light level, and in turn favour any weeds that are already established under them. It is therefore advisable to control these weeds before removing 'weedy' understorey trees. A small hot fire around the stump of *P. undulatum* will prevent regrowth and stimulate germination of soil-stored indigenous seeds.

Areas where there are few individual weeds can be restored fairly quickly. This will give you a lot of satisfaction, plus the incentive to tackle more heavily infested areas. The advantage of being 'on the spot' is that you can closely monitor the areas where you have carried out work, and constantly follow up in these areas.

The golden rule of bush regeneration is—**do not clear too large an area at one time.** Work out how much time you are prepared to spend doing follow-up and maintenance work and plan your weeding strategies accordingly. Weeds are fast colonisers of bare earth and if you overclear an area of one weed, for example Wandering Jew (*Tradescantia fluminensis*), you could find that other weed species will replace it, thus negating your work.

So start modestly. Remember that it is the quality of weed removal, rather than quantity, that will give you the best result.

You may need to reintroduce some indigenous plants to your bush block to give it the correct ecological balance. Study the surrounding bushland and make sure that you only use stock grown from local species, or better still, collect a small amount of local seed and grow your own plants. The latter at least ensures that you will not be introducing more weed species with foreign soil. Some plants such as Australian grasses can be reintroduced by direct seeding, but once again make sure that you use only local seed. It may be necessary to obtain a permit to collect seed from some areas. (See Permit Requirements in Chapter 7 Section 2).

Bush litter that lies thick on the ground forms part of the unique character of the Australian bushland but if you live in a fire-prone area it is prudent to keep the ground fuel level fairly low by removing small branches and excess bark. This needs to be carried out each Autumn and Spring, depending on the vegetation type. Some grasses such as Wire Grass (*Tetrarrhena juncea*) will need to be removed manually on a regular basis, unless you have native fauna to graze it. Other shrubs such as Hop Goodenia (*Goodenia ovata*) could be selectively thinned to encourage the germination of new

* Vivien Freshwater is a naturalist working in a voluntary capacity in bushland regeneration. She is one of the inaugural members of the Friends of Sherbrooke Forest.

plants and reduce the fire risk. Some Australian plant species such as *Senecio* spp. are early colonisers following clearing and have a 'weedy' appearance, but are in fact important food plants for the larvae of some moths. Many native sedges are food plants for butterfly larvae.

Our indigenous vegetation has a special charm and atmosphere all of its own. Its beauty is subtle, and can be fully appreciated by observing its finer details, such as grasses when in flower, or the delicate white flowers of plants such as the Bootlace Bush (*Pimelea axiflora*). It is all very precious—each small area that has survived the ravages of urbanisation.

Further Reading

Bradley, Joan (1988) *Bringing Back the Bush: The Bradley Method of Bush Regeneration*. Lansdowne Press, Sydney.

Buchanan, Robin A, (1990) *Bush Regeneration: Recovering Australian Landscapes*. TAFE, NSW.

Friends of Sherbrooke Forest, (revised ed 1989) *Weeds of Forests, Roadsides and Gardens*. Department of Conservation & Environment, Melbourne.

Regional Pest Plant Strategy Working Group (PITE Project), (Oct. 1991) *Environmental Weeds Kit (Identification & Control)*. A Free kit C/o PO Box 104, Lilydale 3140.

Senecio glomeratus

Chapter 4. Creating or Restoring a Wetlands Area

Nick Romanowski*

For most of the period of white settlement, wetlands throughout Australia have been drained without thought which seems ridiculous on this the driest and most drought-prone of continents. Wetlands are an important habitat for a large range of birds and other animals, and the home of many unusual waterplants quite different from the Australian plants most people are familiar with.

If you have the space for a wetland area, you will attract a surprising range of native fauna to your area, including animals which are primarily associated with water. Even a fairly small pond is worth having as it brings the distinctive feeling of water to a garden, and can add significantly to the range of Australian plants you can grow.

Many remnant bushland areas have some form of watercourse running through them. These are invariably degraded, generally choked with weeds, silted and/or eroded. Some have even been drained. Much care and sensitivity needs to be used to restore these to their original state.

This chapter is a brief guide to establishing wetlands, starting with an outline of the general requirements of waterplants. Further sections deal with the planning and preparation of new wetlands (including dealing with established weed problems) before they are filled with water, and with several potential problems.

Conditions for waterplants

Few waterplants will do well on pure clay, although some will colonise it and gradually change conditions until they are suitable for waterplants with other needs. Planting directly with clay-colonisers and allowing a natural succession of plants is not recommended because many introduced weeds grow better under these conditions than Australian plants.

It is worth preparing soil mixes to approximate soils found in long-established wetlands, and there are additional qualities which should be incorporated for best initial growth. Wetland soils are quite different from those you are used to growing land plants in; they are usually richer, and may contain large amounts of organic matter including decayed animal materials. Under water the structure of these soils may collapse, which means they will not allow gases in and may become anaerobic (lack oxygen). As a result, plant roots may not be able to absorb nutrients from the soil. Although many water plants will absorb most of their nutrient needs from water and the thin aerobic layer on the soil's surface, most will grow faster and better if planted in a rich mix which is open and shallow enough for oxygen to circulate through it. Mixes of this type will usually become quite like soils found naturally in wetlands over a period of time, and will have given waterplants a good boost in growth by this stage.

The main component of the mix should be the topsoil of the future wetland (up to 95% by volume). To this you may need to add: organic matter (up to 10% crumbled brown coal, peat, etc.); soil-openers to improve water and gas circulation (up to 10% vermiculite, peat, or coarse sand); and fertilizer (between 1% and 2% of manures or blood-and-bone), according to the nature of the original soil. Inorganic fertilizers leach differentially, ie some chemicals will leach more quickly than others, and may cause peculiar chemical effects. A skilled operator can do the mixing with a bulldozer, and spread it as a layer 5–10 cm deep wherever you intend to plant. Sterilisation of the soil is rarely needed; if there will be a reasonable depth of water over the soil layer, most weed seeds will drown without sprouting. To further reduce weed-seed germination, and also to restrict soil or nutrients leaching into the water, spread a 2–4 cm layer of coarse sand, washed river-gravel or similar material over the soil. The pond or wetland is now ready to be filled with water, but you may want to plant into the deeper sections before much water goes in.

In small ponds, the above method can be modified for planting in ordinary pots, but lay newspaper or hessian in the bottom of the pot first to prevent leakage of soil and fertiliser. In larger ponds or dams, you should include planting-shelves or shallows. These are shelves (of any width, depth or shape) on which the layers of soil and sand are spread. To reduce loss of soil over the edge, narrower shelves should slope slightly downwards, away from deeper water. Larger areas such as planting shallows don't have to be uniformly level, but should always slope gradually between different depths. Whether you use pots or plant directly on the bottom, remember that the actual planting depth is the distance from the surface to the top of the sand layer on the soil and should be chosen to suit the particular plants you are planning to grow.

Most waterplants will grow best in full sunlight, tolerating some shade for part of the day. Those which grow fully submerged need enough light for growth. In murky water they should be planted closer to the surface. Most waterplants prefer fairly soft water which should be reasonably close to neutral. Melbourne tapwater is quite satisfactory, but should be allowed to stand whenever possible to release chlorine; this is also important for good health of any fish you may keep. Hard or saline waters reduce the range of

* Nick Romanowski is a qualified zoologist with a special interest in all aspects of freshwater biology including aquaculture. He is manager and co-owner of 'Dragonfly Aquatics', a specialist waterplant nursery.

species which can be grown. Unlike most Australian land plants you are probably familiar with, many waterplants die away for part of the cooler months. Include some evergreen ones if they are required for permanent habitat for animals.

Planning for a wetland area

The first step in planning for a pond or wetland area is to decide how much water you can make available. (Work out the catchment of the area, and combine this with rainfall figures). If you are relying on rainfall alone to maintain the wetland, remember that a large proportion of rainfall is absorbed before any begins to run off the soil.

Australian wetlands are very varied; many dry out in warmer seasons, so a natural-looking wetland can be designed even where shortage of water is a regular Summer problem. Plants which tolerate drying out for part of the year are needed for such conditions, while others may require a minimum depth of water to grow in at all times.

The wetland does not necessarily have to be filled in just one year, but planting cannot be started until water levels are close to maximum. The larger the surface area relative to the volume of water, the greater will be the rate of evaporation; this can represent a loss of around one metre depth of water in some areas of Melbourne even in a normal Summer. If the plants you plan to grow will not tolerate large drops in water level, a reserve dam should be built at a higher point in the catchment for topping up. In the garden situation a tank may be used to collect and store water in readiness for Summer.

Preparing the area

Whether you are building a small pond for the garden or dealing with a natural wetland which has been drained, you will effectively be damming an area to retain water. All standard damming techniques must be used including topsoil removal, tying the wall into the substrate, sheepfoot rolling (about one in three dams made with just a bulldozer will not hold water properly), and provision of an overflow capable of handling maximum expected runoff for your area. When water demands are less than 100,000 litres per day, a permanent tapped siphon is a cheap and easy option which will not weaken the wall. (If a pipe is put through the dam wall, it must have water-impervious baffles attached, and be hand compacted into place before construction of the dam wall begins.)

Once the position and water-holding height of the future wall is known, a level may be used to mark out the boundary of the wetland or pond. Alternatively, this can be marked out beforehand and the wall built to hold water to this level. Whether you are starting from scratch or reclaiming a wetland, the surface will often have been contoured to improve drainage. To correct this, future islands, peninsulas, planting shelves and shallows should be marked out at this stage. Avoid building in too many such features and follow the present slope and variation of the future wetland as much as possible, both for natural appearance and economy in earthmoving.

With the completion of contouring and rolling, topsoil can be spread where it is needed. In most cases this is the planting shelves and shallows (with organic matter and fertiliser mixed in as described), and clay surfaces above water. Don't spread topsoil in deep water areas unless you have a specific reason for putting it there. Few waterplants grow at these depths, and the deeper areas will tend to silt up anyway. Don't speed up the process unnecessarily.

The finished wetland should be a complex of shallow areas sloping gradually to meet islands and peninsulas which have been prepared for conventional planting of Australian land plants. Finally, just add water!

Dealing with established weeds

An overgrown wetland or dam provides good habitat for some water animals such as dragonfly larvae and snails, but it is also in the last stages of turning into land, and many of the plants in it may be undesirable, introduced species. There are a number of ways to tackle cleaning out overgrown ponds or wetlands.

If you are only dealing with a small area, and are not in a hurry, it may be possible to do the work by hand and with a rake. The plants pull out of soft mud fairly easily, but you must be prepared to repeat the process regularly until new growth stops appearing. If the mud remaining is too deep it can usually be removed by a sludge pump, and is excellent used on gardens.

There are a number of types of mechanical excavator which will remove weed growth complete with mud in large-scale areas. Although this is a relatively expensive option, most of the work will be done in a single operation. Some pieces of weed will certainly remain, but these may be removed over a short period of time by hand. Alternatively, drain the entire wetland at the beginning of hot weather and allow it to dry, then remove all unwanted plants. This method is fairly quick and thorough, but also expensive, as you are effectively starting from scratch.

There are usually legal restrictions relating to the use of herbicides around and in water (for good reason—someone downstream of you will be the next person to get them!), and appropriate advice should be sought from local authorities before even considering their use. The only herbicide which is reasonably harmless to use over water is glyphosate, which is sold under a number of trade names (eg Roundup or Zero). This breaks down fairly quickly and does not appear to affect most water animals. However, many water plants are unaffected by it for at least part of their growth cycle, especially submerged ones. Other herbicides which will destroy waterplants will effectively kill most life in the water, and may still leave you with the problem of disposing of a mass of mud bound together with plant roots, if the mud is too deep for healthy underwater conditions.

Problems

Wetlands are usually located on watercourses which may flow dramatically at some times of the year and even dry out at others. In areas permanently or frequently submerged, erosion may become a problem. It is most easily prevented by establishing a carpet of living plants. Many larger Australian plants, such as trees, will grow in areas which are only flooded occasionally. These plants are described elsewhere in this book. However there are two types of erosion which must be contained with true waterplants.

Plants which will not break up under the full force of Winter flooding must be grown in permanently moving waters. It is useful to have some idea how deep the floodwaters may run, and for how long, as not all waterplants will tolerate prolonged deep submersion. In already eroded watercourses, the same methods may be used to protect exposed soil as on land eg mesh, rock rubble, even old tyres if these can be firmly pinned down. The outside curve of bends needs particular reinforcement. Any use of rock fill must avoid causing further undercutting while allowing new plantings to take hold.

The other form of erosion occurs where water levels vary considerably over a year. Plants for these conditions must tolerate being submerged for part of the year, and dry at others, or the result is a bare band of soil which is easily eroded by heavy rains or wind. Choice of plants in this case depends on how much the water level varies, and how long plants must survive the dry conditions. For example, in areas which are only covered in water for short periods of time, land plants which will tolerate short-term flooding are the most suitable. At another extreme, when water levels

MELBOURNE - SOIL TYPES

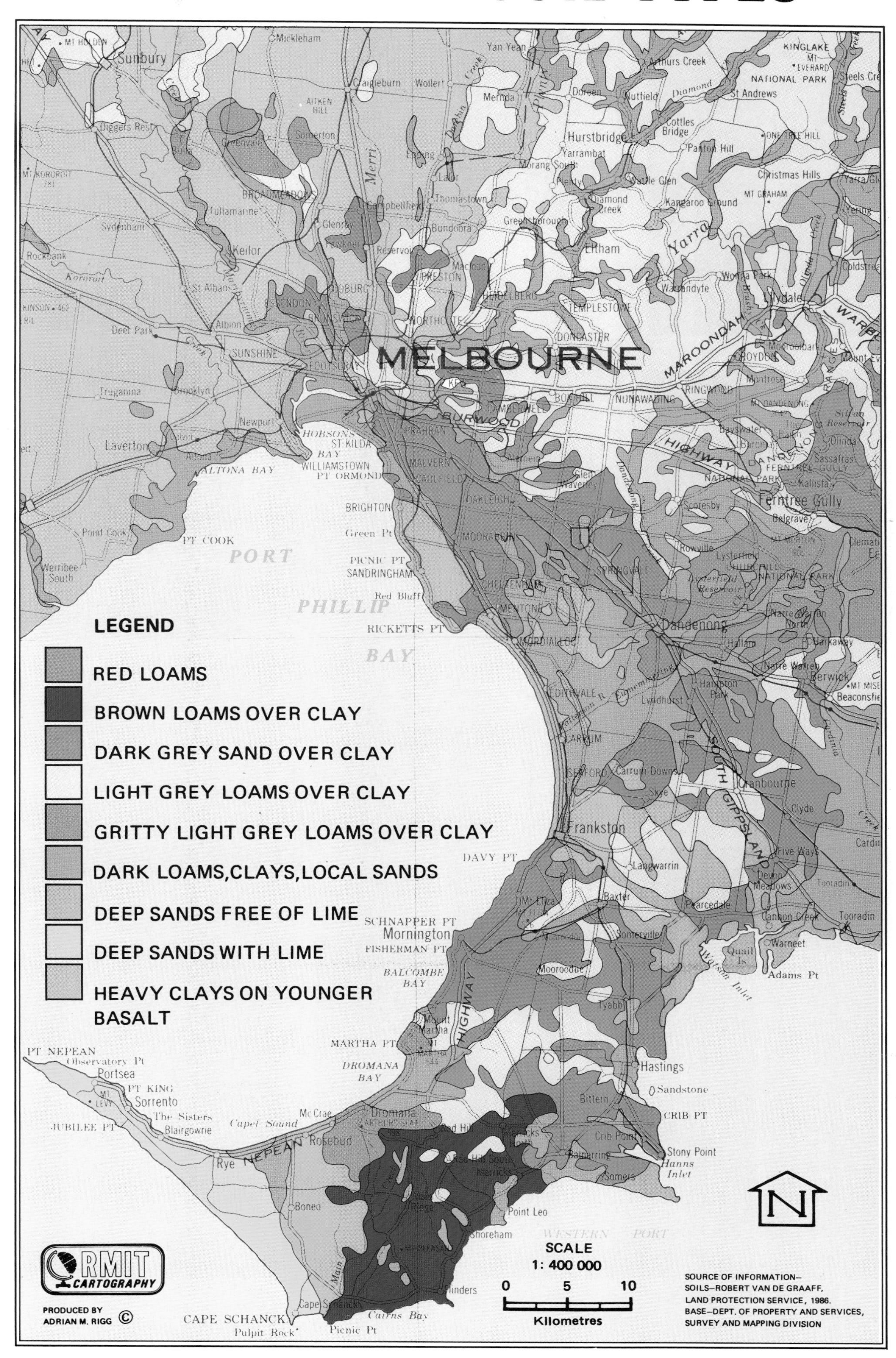

1

2

3

4

5

6

1. *Eucalyptus rubida* ssp. *rubida* Candlebark Gum
2. *Patersonia occidentalis* Long Purple-flag
3. *Podolepis jaceoides* Showy Podolepis
4. *Pomaderris lanigera* Woolly Pomaderris
5. *Stellaria flaccida* Forest Starwort
6. *Ajuga australis* Austral Bugle
7. *Stipa rudis* ssp. *rudis* Veined Spear-grass
8. *Pycnosorus globosus* Drumsticks
9. *Diuris punctata* Purple Diuris

7

8

9

may fall considerably over Summer, plants chosen must be able to survive dry conditions and also be able to grow in deep water.

Other problems in wetlands can be caused by too much plant growth; some plants can be very invasive, particularly *Eleocharis sphacelata*, *Phragmites australis* or either of the Australian *Typha* species. Although they make excellent and ornamental habitat for smaller water animals, waterfowl, and plants they are also fast spreading and can completely overgrow a dam or creek. The build up of silt and organic matter among their roots speeds up the ageing process of the water area, and the tall growth of *Typha* and *Phragmites* will completely screen the water from view with time. In large areas they may be kept contained by use of deep water channels, but you may need to remove seedlings once a year. In smaller ponds they are more manageable, and can be kept within bounds by planting them in a pot or other large container.

Some unwanted plants may appear around the water's edge. New plantings should be watched and seedlings removed by hand while small. Once plants are established it is usually more difficult for weeds to gain a toe-hold.

Like most Australian plants grown in their natural range, waterplants seem surprisingly trouble free. The most common problem affecting them is physical damage, and the most common culprits here are stock (particularly cattle) and yabbies. Stock of all kinds should be fenced out of wetland areas (they are a major cause of erosion and weed dispersal in any case), but yabbies require longer-term control. Some Australian fish such as cat-fish and golden perch will reduce their numbers to an acceptable level, but it may be several years before a yabby-filled dam can be planted.

One more aesthetic problem should be mentioned. Many people would like to grow native water-lilies but none of these will grow well (let alone flower) in most of Southern Australia. *Ottelia ovalifolia* with attractive, elongated floating leaves and large, showy, white flowers makes a good replacement. Other waterplants occurring naturally in the Melbourne area are described elsewhere in this book.

Water gardening adds new dimensions to an interest in Australian plants. A pond, dam or wetland draws a greater range of wildlife than land plants alone will attract, may take up surprisingly little space for the benefits it will bring, and requires as little maintenance as you would expect from any established indigenous planting.

Further Reading

Aston, H., (1973) *Aquatic Plants of Australia*. Melbourne University Press, Melbourne. (Many of the names used have now been revised.)

Nelson, K.D. (1985) *Design and Construction of Small Earth Dams*. Inkata Press, Melbourne.

Sainty, G.R & Jacobs, S.W.L, (1981) *Waterplants of New South Wales*. Water Resources Commission, NSW.

Seagrave, C. (1988) *Aquatic Weed Control*. Fishing News, Farnham, Surrey. (An English book, but many of the common weeds, or related species, occur here also.)

Triglochin striata

Chapter 5. Planning and Design of Bushland Restoration

Darcy Duggan*

Introduction

An important outcome of the growing community interest in environmental issues has been an awareness of the role that native bushland and wildlife species play in defining the character of different areas around Melbourne. Little wonder then that community groups are alarmed to see the decline and loss of native vegetation as Melbourne creeps further into the surrounding countryside.

However, opportunities do exist for all residents throughout Melbourne to play a vital role in the conservation of many rare and threatened native plant and wildlife species.

This can be achieved by:

1. Encouraging the re-establishment of these species in their own backyards; and
2. Participating in the protection, management and restoration of remnant bushland.

Given the generally small and isolated nature of most urban bushland remnants, these areas will require intensive and sensitive management.

The success of any project is dependent on a commitment to funding and effort. Most important of all is the need for a well planned and structured approach, based on sound ecological guidelines and principles.

Planning the Management of Natural Areas

The main objective of any bushland management program should be the creation of a 'manageable ecosystem', resulting in the rehabilitation of a native vegetation community and restoration of wildlife habitat.

This process of recreating the right conditions for regrowth of the desired plant community can be initiated by the removal of exotic and alien plants, and the encouragement of indigenous species to re-establish themselves.

It is vital therefore to recognise that each site will have individual and often diverse physical, chemical and biological characteristics (J. Rawlings 1990). The characteristics of a Eucalypt Woodland or Grassy Woodland community for example will differ markedly from that of a Coastal or Wet Forest community.

Understanding the history of the site and how it relates to its present condition is also critical in the planning and design of a project. There are a number of issues which must be considered such as:

- What is known about the original vegetation community structure and species diversity of a site?
- What seed or plant sources are available for revegetation works?
- What past disturbances and degree of alteration have occurred to bring about the current status of the site (eg, impact of grazing, altered fire regimes, clearing)?
- To what extent do changes in site conditions (eg filling) affect your ability to re-establish or restore a particular native vegetation community or ecosystem?

Researching historical references can often provide valuable information in reconstructing the original flora and fauna of an area, and in gaining a better understanding of the type and impact of disturbance processes. Useful sources of information include the Picture Collection (La Trobe Library), the Victorian Field Naturalists magazine, early journals including original surveyors' reports (former Dept of Lands—Victorian Archives annex—Laverton), local historical societies, and contacting older residents in an area.

Survey and study of other remnant vegetation areas nearby can be very valuable in gaining insight into the dynamics of a natural ecosystem. These sites are also extremely important for relocating species which may have been present, and in providing a source of material for re-introduction.

Stage 1: Site Assessment

Site assessment is a critical first stage of a project, and must involve consideration of the following:

- the history of the site and how it relates to its present condition;
- overall management objectives which will influence project planning and design.

Site Disturbance History

In determining the history of a site, it is necessary to work out the degree and type of disturbance that has occurred. Disturbance may be categorised as follows:

DEGREE—gap, patchy, marginal or all-pervasive.
FREQUENCY—one-off, periodic or continuous.
NATURAL—fire, landslips, storm damage and insect attack.
MAN-MADE—active and/or passive eg, fire, clearing, neglect.

Most bushland areas have been altered by one or more of these forms of disturbance, and will continue to fluctuate in response to environmental change. Some forms of disturbance are inevitable and part of the natural process of

* Darcy Duggan is a naturalist currently working in environmental planning. He is employed by the Yarra Bend Trust.

shaping the composition and structure of the wildlife and vegetation communities present.

Management must therefore focus on modifying the impact of disturbance initiated or magnified by human action. Major causes of site degradation include soil erosion, soil disturbance, nutrient input due to clearing and drainage discharge and rubbish dumping (hard rubbish and garden refuse).

Disturbance events causing site degradation are generally inter-related. For example, intense grazing and associated soil disturbance by rabbits will often result in soil erosion due to loss of vegetation cover. In some situations, selective grazing pressure of rabbits on vegetation may also favour the growth and spread of unpalatable weed species such as Serrated Tussock (*Nassella trichotoma*).

Setting Management Objectives

In setting management objectives for a given site, it is essential that the area is considered and managed on a whole catchment basis wherever possible.

Account must also be taken of the irreversible changes that have occurred at each site. It may not be desirable to revegetate a swamp site which has previously been drained. Many housing and industrial estates have been established over former swamps. Another constraint is proximity to housing. Tea-tree Heaths are very flammable and revegetation would need to be modified where this would be a danger. Soil conditions were greatly altered in some coastal areas where sand dunes were bulldozed onto low-lying areas.

Current site conditions and the nature and extent of various degradation processes that have occurred will influence short term objectives. These may include the following:

Retention and protection of existing remnant bushland areas to prevent further degradation and loss of species;

Restoration of moderately degraded sites;

Revegetation of totally degraded or modified areas.

In defining long term objectives for a project site, consideration should be given to the following:

- full restoration to reflect the original species diversity and community structure;
- rationalisation and extension of the boundaries of the site to provide a buffer between the core bushland and urban development. This approach will enhance the overall stability of a site;
- the protection and enhancement of sites of landscape, geological, historical or archeological interest;
- planning for appropriate community use of an area consistent with preserving and maintaining its values.

Major Factors to Consider in Site Analysis

The basic component of any site analysis is a flora and fauna survey. A good working knowledge and understanding of flora and fauna are therefore essential. It is impossible to identify problems such as weed invasion if you are unable to recognise the presence of weeds on site.

1. Flora survey and assessment

The initial flora survey should be carried out preferably during spring, when the majority of species including various annuals are evident. An ongoing survey throughout the year is also useful given the seasonal variations that occur within an area. This is especially the case for some sites where a large number of Winter annual and perennial species such as Angled onion (*Allium triquetrum*), Oxalis (*Oxalis pes-caprae*), Veldt grass (*Erharta longiflora*) and Quaking grass (*Briza maxima*) die back in the Summer. Additional surveys during this period allow a much greater appreciation of the extent of remnant vegetation present, without other weeds masking your view of the site.

When assessing existing vegetation, consideration must be given to the following:

- remnant indigenous species and vegetation community structure;
- native non-indigenous and ornamental/exotic species present, in particular invasive species and environmental weeds.

The relative significance of each plant species/community should be noted, for example:

- whether remnant indigenous species are of local, regional or state significance;
- historical value, landscape significance or wildlife habitat value;
- quality assessment of vegetation and extent of weed invasion. Identification of weed species present is essential in developing a management strategy for a given site (refer to Table 1 and further discussion).

2. Survey of existing fauna

This should include all resident and vagrant native and introduced animal and bird species. Assessment of the status or significance of each species should be made, as well as habitat needs and value of the site.

It is essential the habitat needs of wildlife are considered when developing a revegetation program. Recognition of the value of woody weeds (eg Boxthorn) in providing habitat to small bird species is important in ensuring the development of a staged program of removal of these species and replacement with suitable indigenous species. This factor is frequently overlooked in the desire to control and remove woody weeds in particular, and may result in the displacement or local extinction of remnant wildlife populations.

The presence of problem species such as rabbits must be identified and precautions taken to minimise damage. In developing a management program for these sites, priority must be given to establishing an integrated control and eradication program.

It is worth noting that the role of native fauna in ecosystem dynamics is only now beginning to be recognised. Recent observations and research suggest that the burrowing and feeding activities of small mammals such as the Bandicoot and Potoroo, may have played an important role in fire control through the reduction in ground litter along the edge of native grassland and woodland communities, in nutrient recycling and possibly in stimulating the regeneration of native herbaceous species reliant upon soil disturbance (J. Wombersley).

The extent of change in vegetation dynamics which has occurred as a result of the almost total elimination of small ground dwelling species is unknown.

In addition to a basic flora and fauna survey of a site, other factors that need to be considered during the very early phases of a project are:

1. Soil type and structure. May require a soil test to be carried out to determine pH, nutrient status etc. The nature of the soil influences both the dynamics and composition of a natural ecosystem and the extent to which ecological succession can occur. For example, the depth and physical, chemical and biological characteristics of topsoil will determine whether the status of a disturbed site is primary, secondary or intermediate in nature.

The biological status and 'health' of the soil is of particular importance. Only now are we beginning to realise the fundamental role that soil micro-organisms and associations between soil borne fungi and plant roots (mycorrhizas) play in nutrient cycling, water uptake and regeneration needs of native plants.

The original soils and topography may have altered resulting in the development of a completely different type of ecosystem from that previously present. This is certainly the case where these changes have been compounded by the introduction of various weed species.

2. Landscape significance and sensitivity of a site requiring the retention of strategic viewing areas or screening of intrusive features.

3. Local or Regional context of a site. Function of the site as a refuge for native plant and wildlife species, and existing or potential corridor connections with other natural areas eg road and stream reserves.

4. Planning constraints, ie area of land, existing underground or above ground services, ownership of land including legal status, covenants, planning controls and authorities or agencies responsible, boundaries (fencing), and planning controls affecting surrounding land use.

5. General topography of a site including its relationship to the surrounding landscape, levels, contours and specific features such as rocky escarpments.

6. Existing access into a site ie pedestrian, vehicular, parking facilities, general circulation through the area and preferred access routes which have least environmental impact.

Survey and Mapping

To facilitate the survey and mapping of an area, it is recommended that a series of colour aerial photos (preferably 1:1000) with associated contour and grid overlay transparencies be obtained. These are particularly useful in giving an overview of the area.

Grid overlays, comprising a series of 100 m x 100 m grids or sectors, are an extremely valuable tool for preparing base maps. By accurately locating and marking the coordinates of each grid sector on the ground, it is possible to use these reference points to map in the various features for each area. By transposing this information onto transparencies, it is then possible to build up a composite picture for each sector.

This detailed approach has proved very useful in that it provides a full and comprehensive understanding of the inherent features and problems for a given site, and allows the preparation of an appropriate management program. The other major advantage is that it also ensures accurate documentation and monitoring of the site and associated management works, which can then be readily interpreted and used by others working in the field.

Stage 2: Developing a Management Strategy and Action Plan

Quality Assessment

The combination of each of the various features of the site will determine its overall quality. Quality assessment is therefore extremely valuable in setting both management objectives, and in developing an appropriate works program.

A useful model for assessing and mapping site criteria with regard to the quality of remnant vegetation areas, has been developed by the National Trust (NSW) Bush Regeneration program. Quality ratings range from category 1—undisturbed sites of highest quality and ecological diversity, to category 4—severe disturbance and low diversity.

A simple colour code allows ready identification of different areas.

Red—areas where bushland has been completely replaced by exotic plant species; or
—bushland where only overstorey species remain and regeneration is absent due to infestation of the understorey by exotics or invading native alien species.*

Orange—areas where bushland is severely infested by exotics and/or invading native alien species; and
—where the regeneration of the dominant species of that plant community are being significantly suppressed.

Blue—areas of bushland with moderate infestation of exotics and/or invading native alien species.

Green—areas of bushland virtually free of exotic plants where the native plant communities display the structure, species composition and diversity typical of those communities in non-urban situations.

In determining an appropriate management strategy and actions for a given area, management requirements will differ markedly. The following comments can be made with regard to the general treatment of each category:

Red and Orange (Category 3 & 4) sites. Totally degraded or highly modified ecosystem.

This is by far the most common situation throughout Melbourne, and is characteristic of many areas such as urban waterways which have undergone extensive filling and gross modification over the years. Associated changes in soil properties and structure as well as massive weed invasion can pose serious problems and constraints, which will substantially affect the overall approach to revegetating these areas.

An intensive weed control program is generally required prior to revegetation of these sites. Depending on the extent of disturbance and nature of the site conditions, the best approach may be by simulating ecological succession through a staged program of re-introduction of native species.

Blue (Category 2) sites. Moderately fragmented or degraded ecosystem.

This situation is becoming more common, and is indicative of the general decline and degradation of the environment. The increased isolation and vulnerability of flora and fauna to disturbance or local extinction is strongly influenced by factors such as reduced fitness of remnant populations due to inbreeding or inability to regenerate as a result of competition and invasion by exotic species.

Weed control is again a critical first stage in treatment of these sites to prevent further degradation and loss of species, and to encourage natural regeneration wherever possible. Supplementary planting and re-introduction of species formerly associated with the vegetation community, as well as improvement of wildlife habitat (eg hollow logs), is also valuable in re-establishing ecological diversity and stability.

Green (Category 1) sites. Reasonably intact or high quality ecosystem—(an increasingly rare phenomenon these days).

Vegetation is comparatively intact structurally with low to moderate levels of weed invasion and disturbance. This situation offers the greatest potential in terms of full restoration of ecological diversity and stability.

In this situation, the most appropriate strategy must be protection of the site by minimising further disturbance and degradation, and encouraging natural regeneration. This can be achieved through sensitive weed control, requiring the use of selective control techniques such as hand weeding out from the edge of intact areas (modified Bradley method), and use of spot spraying and selective herbicides.

Table 1 Rating of Environmental Quality

quality of understorey vegetation				
primary physical disturbance	weed intrusion (impact of alien flora)	ecological balance	diversity of indigenous flora	rating
nil	nil to negligible	excellent	maximum attainable in vegetation type	1
(nil to) moderate	slight to moderate	reasonable	high to moderate	2
(nil to) severe	moderate to heavy	poor	significantly reduced	3
(nil to) severe	very heavy	drastically out of balance	low to absent	4

In the case of most remnant areas where all four site conditions may be present, the overall management approach must be broad based. High priority must be given to both

* For the purposes of the above coding system, 'invading native alien plant species' is defined as any non-indigenous native plant which is capable of naturalising in a native vegetation community.

the protection of rare or significant species, and rehabilitation of high quality remnant vegetation areas, to prevent further degradation and loss of species. Equal importance should also be given to the control of specific invasive weed species, to contain their spread and prevent invasion into adjoining high quality areas.

In addition to management of high quality conservation sites, it is also good 'politics' to give preference to a few high profile areas (eg roadside reserves, picnic areas) where possible. Being seen to be doing something in the eyes of the public is critical in raising community awareness and support for your work, and increases the likelihood of gaining ongoing or additional funding.

Adoption of this approach however will ultimately be a question of balance between existing labour and resources, and other management priorities which you have identified.

Other Planning and Design Issues

In addition to the assessment of the overall quality of a given site, there are a number of other factors which must also be considered when planning a project. These include issues such as:

1. Limitations relating to current information and availability of suitable revegetation materials

Lack of information regarding the original vegetation community structure and species diversity of a site, as well as a shortage of suitable seed/plant material for revegetation works, will be a major limitation to any project.

2. Current knowledge and level of expertise in revegetation techniques

Whilst considerable attention has been given to the development of successful strategies for the re-establishment of tree and shrub species in recent times, little attention has been given to ground flora.

There is an urgent need therefore for expanded field research and documentation in this area, particularly with regard to site and species interaction and dynamics. Wherever possible, a full complement of species must be included in any revegetation or restoration project.

In addition to encouraging natural regeneration, consideration should also be given to other techniques such as the use of tubestock, direct seeding (a potentially valuable method), transplanting material from threatened sites, and vegetative propagation, ie direct planting of cuttings and divisions of material on site.

3. Budget and resources

These issues are critical in influencing both the scale of the site works, and your ability to implement and maintain a project over the medium to long term. Lack of continuity and security of funding as well as over-commitment of resources is the most common cause of failure. Quality not quantity is the key to success in undertaking this work when faced with an uncertain funding future. A smaller project well done is more likely to gain support if it is seen to be successful.

Critical Aspects of Planning and Implementation

Given the dynamic nature of revegetation and bushland restoration projects, forward planning is critical in ensuring appropriate timing and implementation of each phase of the program. Initial site preparation, for example, may need to be undertaken up to 12–18 months in advance of planting the site. This is particularly the case when dealing with heavily weed infested areas. In this situation, it will always be an advantage to expend extra time and effort in treating invasive weeds eg Fennel (*Foeniculum vulgare*) and to carry out follow up treatment to eliminate regeneration from soil-stored seed, before you attempt to revegetate an area.

Timing of post-planting maintenance is also critical to prevent re-seeding of weeds, and re-colonisation of the site. There are some situations however, such as highly exposed sites, where allowing initial recolonisation of a site by weeds can benefit young native plants, by acting as a nurse crop in providing protection from wind. In these circumstances, maintenance should be deferred until the point of flowering and seed set of weeds.

The overall importance of site preparation and follow up maintenance and their reliance on a well planned and structured approach to the project, cannot be over-emphasised.

Timing is also essential for other aspects of a project such as seed collection, where for many species, seed is only available for a few days in the year.

Finally, there is the need to maintain accurate records and to systematically document all work that is carried out. This aspect of a project is frequently ignored, resulting in much valuable information regarding the success or failure of various strategies and revegetation techniques being lost. Maintaining photographic records of a site, especially before and after photos, is extremely valuable. Photographic slides are especially useful, both as an educational resource, and to use in gaining further funding and support for projects.

Summary

There are many clearly defined ecological principles which must be considered in developing an integrated management strategy. These include issues such as the importance of protecting existing remnant vegetation by minimising soil disturbance and damage to sites, retention and enhancement of wildlife habitat, use of local provenance genetic material in re-establishing plant species etc.

Treatment of causes of site disturbance and degradation is also critical. Weed invasion is without doubt a major environmental problem, and poses one of the greatest threats to the long term conservation of flora and fauna. This issue must therefore be given the highest priority in any project.

The extent of our ecological knowledge and understanding of native vegetation and wildlife management has expanded greatly over the last 10 years or so. We are still only scratching the surface however in many areas, and for this reason each of us has the opportunity of making an important contribution. Thorough documentation and monitoring of field research and trials undertaken, as well as exchange of information, aré an essential element to the success of this process.

Further Reading

Allen, M.F. (1988) *Reconstruction of Disturbed Arid Lands—An Ecological Approach*. Ed. E.B. Allen. American Association for the Advancement of Science (AAAS) 1988. Symposium 109.

Breckwoldt, R. (1983) *Wildlife in the Home Paddock*. Angus and Robertson, Sydney.

Buchanan, R.A. (1990) *Bush Regeneration: Recovering Australian Landscapes*. TAFE, NSW.

Carr, G.W. (1989) 'Perspectives on Environmental Weeds in Victoria'. *Weeds on Public Land—an Action Plan for Today*. Symposium presented by Weed Science Society of Victoria, Monash University, May 1988.

DePuit, E.J. & Redente, E.F., (1988) *Manipulation of Ecosystem Dynamics on Reconstructed Semi-arid Lands*. AAAS. Symposium 109.

Greening Australia Ltd, (1990) *Sowing the Seeds*. Direct Seeding and Natural Regeneration Conference Proceedings. 22–25 May, 1990.

McGee, P. (1986) *Mycorrhizal Associations of Plants in a Semi-arid Community*. Australian Journal of Botany 34, 585-593.

Rawlings, J. (1990) *Urban Bushland Management Handbook*. National Trust (NSW) unpublished Draft 3.

Stiller, D.M., Zimpfer, G.L., & Bishop, M. (1980) 'Application of Geomorphic Principles to Surface-mined Land Reclamation in Semi-arid west'. *Journal of Soil and Water Conservation*. 35: 274–277.

Wombersley, J. Director of Warrawong Wildlife Sanctuary, Adelaide Hills—South Australia. (personal communication)

Chapter 6. *Environmental Weed Invasions and their Conservation Implications*

Geoff Carr*

Introduction

The Victorian flora comprises over 3,200 indigenous species, about 30% of which occur in the Melbourne area. This is far from the only flora we have however: the exotic or introduced flora surrounds us at every turn and, more than any other factor, prejudices the survival of indigenous vegetation communities and plant species. In this chapter the size, origins, distribution and aspects of the biology and ecology of the exotic flora, as well as their significance as a threat to indigenous flora and fauna, are discussed. Particular attention will be focused on environmental weeds.

Some Definitions

Indigenous species are those plants which are native to, and evolved in, a particular area or country.

Exotic species are those species which have been introduced from overseas. They may or may not be naturalised.

Alien species refer to plants which occur naturally outside the Melbourne area.

Naturalised species have become established outside gardens, farms or plantations and their self-maintaining populations persist without direct reliance on humans.

Environmental weeds are plants which aggressively invade natural bushland and displace native flora and fauna. They may be exotic, alien or ecologically 'out-of-balance' indigenous species and adversely affect survival or regeneration of indigenous species. Several categories of environmental weeds are discussed below.

Noxious weeds are species which affect agricultural production.

Size of the Exotic Flora

Table 1 gives the statistics on the size of the indigenous, alien and exotic floras of Victoria. The information has been compiled from the *Census of the Vascular Plants of Victoria* (Ross 1990) and approximately 222 additional exotic species listed by others in the last 10 years. Unfortunately plant enthusiasts often neglect the weeds in favour of indigenous plants and naturalised exotic species may go unreported.

New species and new records are continually being added to the Victorian Census but the list of 'new' indigenous species is growing more slowly and should be more-or-less stable when the Australian flora is fully studied. Not so the exotic flora!

With about 1220 species (28% of the total flora), the exotic flora of Victoria is exceptionally large in proportion to the indigenous flora by both world and Australian standards.

The Melbourne region has a large indigenous flora but also an exceptionally large exotic flora. The Department of Conservation & Environment lists some 403 alien and exotic species (from quadrat data and species lists) but the real figure is much higher and few exotic species in Victoria do not occur in the Melbourne region. A tentative estimate of the number of alien and exotic species which occur in the Melbourne region is about 1000 species. This should be seen in the context of ongoing **extinction of indigenous species** and continual **addition of exotic species.**

It will be apparent to anyone who has witnessed the massive regional invasion of environmental weeds in indigenous vegetation, that these exotic species pose the greatest threat to indigenous species and the vegetation communities to which they belong.

Table 1 Numbers of taxa in the exotic and alien vascular flora of Victoria compared with the indigenous flora. Based on Ross (1990) and 222 additional naturalised exotic taxa (Carr).

Group	Naturalised flora			Indigenous flora		
	Families	Genera	Species and Infraspecific taxa	Families	Genera	Species and Infraspecific taxa
Ferns and Fern Allies	3	3	4	25	51	157
Gymnosperms (Conifers)	2	4	14	2	2	6
Monocotyledons	20	134	309	24	191	874
Dicotyledons	94	371	894	103	418	2107
Totals	119	512	1221 (28%)*	154	662	3144 (72%)*

*Percentage of total Victorian flora of approx. 4365 taxa.

* Geoff Carr, a botanical consultant, is a director of Ecological Horticulture P/L which is involved in vegetation surveys, studies for vegetation management, assessments, research and education. His special interests include research on Australian orchids and environmental weeds. He is a founder and past President of the Indigenous Flora & Fauna Association.

Origins of the Exotic Flora

The establishment of exotic plant species began on the day that Europeans set foot in Victoria. In March 1801, Lt. Jas. Grant in the 'Lady Nelson' called at Churchill Is. in Westernport Bay and planted food plants including peaches, apples, wheat, onions and potatoes. Documentation of the exotic flora in South Australia showed that only about 20 years after founding, 101 plant species had already become naturalised. This must have been closely comparable to the development of the exotic flora of the Melbourne region—both in the methods of introduction of exotic species and the composition of the exotic floras involved.

Plants have been either deliberately or accidentally introduced, and for some species, both probably apply.

Deliberate introduction of species for ornament or utility has been more significant than accidental introductions and it is estimated that between 65 and 70% of all naturalised exotic species in Victoria have been introduced this way, mostly for ornamental horticulture. This is illustrated by Guilfoyle's *Catalogue of Plants under Cultivation in the Melbourne Botanic Gardens* (1883). Of the several thousand species listed, at least 337 (27% of the current exotic flora) have become naturalised in Victoria. Indeed many hundreds of plant species are currently available in the nursery trade and they include some of the most destructively invasive of environmental weed species. Of the 570 species of serious or potentially serious Victorian environmental weeds (listed in the recent compilation by the author and co-workers), no less than 43% are commercially available.

The horticultural industries are by no means the only source of weed species—they are routinely used for soil stabilisation and in other environmental management practices. Of the numerous plant species advocated for soil stabilisation in Victoria by government agencies, 51 are seriously weedy.

The influx of exotic plant species into Victoria and Australia goes unchecked. Agricultural scientists, for example, continue to scour the world for potentially useful species (eg for fodder or for rehabilitation of saline land) which will ideally behave as weeds. In addition, current weed species (eg *Phalaris aquatica*, Canary Grass) are being genetically 'improved' to enhance their ability to flourish in a wider range of conditions. Plant quarantine laws are outdated by contrast with animal quarantine laws.

The **geographic origins** of the exotic flora reflect regions or countries with which historically we have had greatest political, economic and cultural ties. They come from climatically similar regions, especially those with a Mediterranean climate. The main regions or countries which have provided the exotic flora are (in decreasing order of importance): Europe and the British Isles, Mediterranean Basin, South Africa, Asia, South America, North America, Western Asia, Central America and Mexico, North Africa, China and New Zealand. Naturalised species originating in Australia (including Victoria) are discussed below.

Life Forms

A wide variety of life forms (or growth habits) is found in the exotic flora. They range from annuals (the most common life form) through perennial herbs to shrubs, vines and trees; some are purely aquatic and there is a larger range of succulents than in the indigenous flora. Life forms of the most serious environmental weed species in Victoria are given in the Appendix (Page 30).

Conservation Implications of Environmental Weed Invasions

Invasion by environmental weeds is a world-wide phenomenon and it is without doubt the most serious conservation threat to our indigenus flora and fauna. These invasions are part of the world-wide destruction and degradation of the flora (and by implication fauna) caused by human activity. Environmental weed invasions have been documented in many regions throughout the world.

Considering the conservation and economic implications, relatively little attention has so far been given to environmental weeds within Australia. For Victoria, several generalised or anecdotal accounts have been published. More recently an overview of an environmental weed invasion in the state gave rise to the preparation of a list of some 570 species regarded as environmental weeds in Victoria.

A local weed flora has been published by the Friends of Sherbrooke Forest and several pamphlets or booklets have appeared eg. those published by the City of Frankston and the Shire of Eltham. A further publication by the Regional Pest Plant Strategy Working Group treats cultivated 'garden-escape' environmental weeds in the Dandenong Ranges. All above-mentioned publications deal with weeds contained within and/or adjoining the Melbourne region.

The most detailed and comprehensive documentation of environmental weed invasion in Victoria has come from specific studies in connection with environmental effects statements, vegetation and species management investigations, and assessments of vegetation significance. Well over 100 such studies have been carried out in the Melbourne region.

Ecological studies on specific environmental weed species have also been carried out, sometimes in the Melbourne region.

What is the nature of the environmental problems posed by environmental weeds?

Indications are that the future of the flora and fauna of much of Victoria, and of Australia, is in jeopardy and faces annihilation at the community and species levels.

Almost all remnant bushlands are being invaded by weeds or will be invaded in the future. Without appropriate management we may expect gross changes in vegetation structure and composition. Communities will become impoverished and ultimately indigenous species will be unable to regenerate because of competition from weeds. With the destruction of the flora, the indigenous fauna, which is directly or indirectly dependent on indigenous vegetation, will also collapse. The extent and rate of this projected ecological collapse may be unprecedented in evolutionary time without appropriate management.

One of the most spectacular demonstrations of invasion, and a case which is regarded as a preview of the longer-term scenario is seen at the You Yangs, a low granite range southwest of Melbourne. Here indigenous vegetation has been substantially eliminated by invasions of *Chrysanthemoides monilifera* (Boneseed), *Myrsiphyllum asparagoides* (Bridal Creeper, Smilax Asparagus) and numerous exotic grasses, over a period of about 35 years.

The flora and fauna of the Melbourne region have already suffered severe degradation and destruction from a variety of causes related to settlement such as grazing and clearing but environmental weed invasions could now destroy most indigenous vegetation remnants. Already an alarming proportion of indigenous species in the Melbourne flora have become extinct, and many more are on the brink of extinction; the same applies regionally to vegetation communities.

Types of Environmental Weeds

It is convenient to recognise several different types of environmental weeds according to their origins, but it is also necessary to identify another kind of invasion—that of **genes** contributed to populations of indigenous species by hybridisation with alien and exotic species. A further problem of weediness concerns naturalised indigenous species. Both are discussed below.

Three groups of environmental weeds are recognisable according to geographical origins:

- species introduced deliberately or accidentally from overseas (exotic);
- Australian plant species from outside Melbourne (alien);
- Victorian species naturalised outside their natural geographic range, including 'garden escapees' and those which have been inadvertently dispersed.

Size of the Environmental Weed Flora

The recent list of environmental weeds in Victoria has about 570 entries. Most are species but a few hybrids and horticultural selections are included. This represents about 46% of the total exotic flora of Victoria. Almost all species on the list occur in the Melbourne region.

In any given reserve or larger area, the number of environmental weed species is invariably high, and many of these have the capacity to destroy indigenous vegetation over time. Statistics for representative areas in the greater Melbourne region are given in Table 2. The most serious environmental weed species in Victoria are listed in the Appendix.

Australian Plants as Environmental Weeds

About 120 species of Australian plants have been recorded as naturalised in Victoria outside their natural range, as 'escapees' from cultivation. They include species from all states and are amongst the most devastatingly invasive of all weeds (see Appendix). On present trends it is clear that many additional Australian plant species will become naturalised in Victoria.

The ease with which Australian plants naturalise is demonstrated in several locations where plantations of 'native' plants have been established in sites adjoining intact or partially intact indigenous vegetation. At Anglesea where two plantations contain about 50 Australian tree and shrub species, no less than 35 of these species have become naturalised and many are exceedingly serious threats (eg. *Melaleuca armillaris*, Bracelet Honey-Myrtle, and *M. diosmifolia*, Green Honey-myrtle).

A similar response is seen at Mt. Martha Park on the Mornington Peninsula where at least 102 species of Australian plants have been cultivated in regionally significant woodland. Of these species, 38% have become naturalised and now threaten the survival of the remnant vegetation. Examples include *Hakea suaveolens* (Sweet Hakea) and *Baeckea virgata* (Tall Baeckea).

Hybridisation between Indigenous, Alien and Exotic Species

Hybridisation between indigenous, alien and exotic species has been reported in many countries. In Victoria at least 12 such hybrids involving indigenous species have been recorded in six genera: *Acacia* (4 spp.), *Coprosma* (1), *Correa* (1), *Grevillea* (4), *Nicotiana* (1) and *Pittosporum* (1).

One very large hybrid population at West Barwon dam (Otway Ranges) involves *Acacia mucronata* x *A. longifolia* and numbers hundreds of individuals. How far or fast the genes of *A. longifolia* (naturally confined to East Gippsland and the Grampians in Victoria) will move through the extensive *A. mucronata* populations in the Otways, and the potential ecological consequences, is not known. *A. longifolia* was originally planted as garden specimens.

Of similar concern is the contamination of the gene pools of the regionally-rare *Grevillea rosmarinifolia* at Hurstbridge and Diamond Creek by alien *Grevillea* spp. Other species, involving *Grevillea baueri*, *G. juniperina* and other *G. rosmarinifolia* forms as well as hybrids, are cultivated in nearby gardens from which honey-eaters carry pollen to the local wild plants. The complex hybrid swarms resulting will cause the demise of the pure *G. rosmarinifolia* as hybrids are now

Table 2 Statistics on the weed flora of representative biological reserves or areas in the Melbourne region.

Reserve/area	Area (ha)	Broad vegetation communities present	Total no. of plant species recorded	Indig spp. (%)	Exotic spp. (%)	No. of environ weeds targeted for control or elimination	Refs
Gramatan Ave Heathland Sanctuary—City of Sandringham	0.27	Tea-tree Heath	107	50 (47%)	57 (53%)	57	Carr et al. 1991b
Hochkins Ridge Flora Reserve—Croydon Nth	18.6	Dry & Valley Sclerophyll Forest	378	227 (60%)	151 (40%)	67	Carr et al. 1991a
Moorooduc Quarry Reserve—Mt. Eliza	37	Wetland, Sclerophyll Woodland, Swamp Shrubland	314	182 (58%)	132 (42%)	88	Carr & McMahon 1988
Plenty Gorge Metropolitan Park—Mernda to Greensborough	1400	Dry & Valley Sclerophyll Forests, Wetlands Grassy Woodlands Grasslands	696	411 (59%)	285 (41%)	not applic	Carr et al. 1991c
Puffing Billy Corridor—Shire of Sherbrooke		Sclerophyll Forest Damp Sclerophyll Forest	176	95 (54%)	81 (46%)	57	McMahon et al. 1990
Shire of Eltham		Sclerophyll Forest	696	348 (50%)	348 (50%)	80	McMahon et al. 1989
Truganina Swamp/ Cherry Lake—Altona	350	Saltmarsh, Grassland	307	141 (46%)	166 (54%)	36	Carr et al. 1989

more abundant and more vigorous and out-compete their wild parents.

At Mt. Dandenong, hybridisation between a rare distinctive *Grevillea alpina* population and garden-grown *G. rosmarinifolia* is also reported. A comparable outcome to the *G. rosmarinifolia* Hurstbridge hybridisation is predictable.

Hybrids of this kind will become increasingly common, as will hybrids between local and non-local provenances of the same species where the latter are cultivated near natural populations. This has been termed 'genetic pollution' and the introduction of foreign genes may have harmful ecological consequences. The most obvious potential for 'genetic pollution' is seen in *Eucalyptus camaldulensis* around Melbourne. Numerous wild populations of this species probably now contain 'foreign' genes because of extensive planting of Northern Victorian Red Gums, for example on the freeway around Yarra Bend Park and Latrobe University campus. Seed from these populations can no longer be used for revegetation purposes, and this is yet another convincing argument for planting **local provenances** of indigenous species wherever the latter are required.

Ecologically 'out-of-balance' Indigenous Species

In recent decades population explosions of several Victorian indigenous species have occurred, either in vegetation communities in which the species normally occurs, or in adjoining vegetation communities. Such species may be as destructively invasive as any truly exotic environmental weed species. The most serious of these species in Victoria are *Acacia sophorae* (Coast Wattle), *Kunzea ambigua* (White Kunzea), *K. ericoides* (Burgan) and *Leptospermum laevigatum* (Coast Tea-tree).

In the Melbourne region *A. sophorae* is highly invasive in coastal and near-coastal heath, woodland and forest, as is *L. laevigatum*. *K. ericoides* has recently been reported as a serious vegetation management problem in several areas.

The reasons for the upsurge in these indigenous species are poorly understood but may involve altered fire regimes (*Leptospermum laevigatum* and *Acacia sophorae*), increased grazing pressure by kangaroos, wallabies and stock (*Kunzea ericoides*), and increased seed dispersal by vehicles and exotic animals (*A. sophorae*). A further species, *Tetrarrhena juncea* (Forest Wire-grass), is considered a problem in Sherbrooke Forest as a result of reduced grazing by wombats. It inhibits regeneration of other species and reduces availability of lyrebird feeding sites.

In future, indigenous species will increasingly require active management to prevent ecological imbalance, especially in remnant vegetation.

Dispersal

Dispersal of weed seeds or plant parts is a key attribute determining the success of weed species. Some produce no seed, instead reproducing exclusively from bulbs, corms, fragmented stems, stolons or leaves, for example *Salix fragilis* (Crack Willow), *Oxalis pes-caprae* (Soursob) and *Vinca major* (Blue Periwinkle). The latter has dispersed along vast tracts of riverine environments in East Gippsland indicating that seed production is not a prerequisite for success.

Many different seed dispersal mechanisms are evident in the alien and exotic flora. This has important implications from a vegetation management perspective because some control may be effected to reduce dispersal of environmental weeds.

A very large proportion of species is dispersed by seed adhering to animals' fur, people's clothing, in mud on feet, and the like. This may be good reason for limiting access of people in certain areas, and is of critical importance in stock-grazing of indigenous vegetation.

Fleshy seeds and fruit (some 8% of the Victorian non-indigenous flora), as well as a range of other weeds including grasses and clovers (*Trifolium* spp.), are eaten by a large range of birds and mammals, such as gulls, silvereyes, currawongs, emus, blackbirds, starlings, cattle, horses, sheep and foxes, and even lizards, and dispersed over a wide area. Some of the most devastating weeds originate in gardens and are dispersed by birds, especially the exotic blackbird. Examples of species with fleshy fruits or seeds dispersed in this way are given in the Appendix.

There is a continual weed seed rain into indigenous vegetation from surrounding areas. In the case of wind dispersed species (notably of the family *Asteraceae*) seeds may come from a great distance.

The dumping of garden rubbish is one of the most significant of all means by which exotic plants find their way into indigenous vegetation and corms, bulbs, tubers, stem leaves and whole plants may become established in this way. Education to prevent this common practice is urgently needed.

A final but exceedingly important seed dispersal mechanism is via the motor vehicle. One Canberra scientist recovered and germinated seed of no less than 116 plant species from sludge in a car wash, including very serious environmental weeds!

The most significant management lessons from seed dispersal stories are the following:

- given the extremely effective dispersal of weeds, sometimes over long distances, there is no safe place where weeds may be tolerated as posing no threat to indigenous vegetation. When cultivation of serious environmental weeds is finally banned the ban should be universal and not restricted to certain places;
- it is pointless to control or eliminate weed populations in bushland if there is a constant rain of seed of garden-grown weed species from adjoining properties.
- restriction of access in certain areas of reserves (people, horses and/or vehicles) is often advisable to limit spread of weeds.
- stock grazing on public land and in indigenous vegetation in general is disastrous.
- drainage water from roads and tracks should be very carefully controlled because of its role in seed dispersal as well as creating physical environments conducive to weed invasions.

The Conservation Implications

Vegetation Management

Vegetation requires management. Gone are the days when nature 'looked after itself', when an area culd be simply fenced and left to its own devices.

The need for active vegetation management—not only that in reserves but **all** indigenous vegetation remnants—is very poorly appreciated. In the Melbourne region, as elsewhere, adequate vegetation management is a lamentably rare phenomenon, either on public or private land. If we neglect management of private land then we may consign its vegetation and fauna to the scrap heap of history. Degradation is frequently irreversible.

An array of harmful vegetation management procedures is routinely practised by public and private management agencies and individuals. Such practices include inappropriate fire regimes, vegetation clearance, mowing, altered water cycles, nutrient enrichment of soils and water, stock grazing, non-renewable resource exploitation, soil compaction and disturbance, and planting of environmental weeds.

The discipline of indigenous vegetation management is still in its infancy and little published information is available. Unfortunately there is often a lack of appreciation, even amongst practitioners, that for vegetation management 'near enough' is not good enough. A full inventory of indigenous and exotic plant species is required as well as information on the structure and composition of vegetation (ie quadrat data) and the physical environment. Management plans can be formulated on the basis of this information. Indigenous animals should not be overlooked since management for vegetation objectives may be antagonistic to faunal values.

Vegetation management plans have been prepared for many reserves (see Further Reading) but the necessary amount of management is seldom possible because of inadequate financial resources and/or available expertise. Too often the perception prevails that 'it will happen in good time'. For most regional vegetation it is now the eleventh hour; a lost opportunity or failure of timing may mean consigning vegetation and fauna to annihilation.

An excellent case in point is the phoenix-like recovery of (now) exceedingly rare heath vegetation, ostensibly eliminated by invading *Leptospermum laevigatum* (Coast Tea-tree) at Sandringham. An astonishing recovery from soil-stored seed occurred after fire destroyed the tea-tree. If this site had not been weeded in the first six months after fire, it would have been irredeemably lost. A second opportunity would **never** arise. Furthermore, ongoing maintenance of the site is mandatory.

The Future?

The conservation scenario sketched in this chapter is disturbing but we cannot believe that it is an inevitable consequence of settlement or we will consign the results of millions of years of evolutionary history to oblivion. A great deal can be done to maintain the integrity of the flora and fauna both for its own sake (always the primary imperative) and for the benefit of future generations. To achieve this something approximating a revolution needs to occur—a major change in awareness, communication and action which needs to be Australia-wide.

The initiatives listed below are essential to tackle environmental weed invasions on the broadest front.

- overhaul of all plant importation and quarantine laws;
- horticultural, agricultural and land management practices using exotic species must be revised. It should be illegal to cultivate or trade in environmental weeds;
- the vast array of deleterious land management practices must be curtailed or revised;
- research and documentation of environmental weed invasions is required;
- education at all levels;
- action on weed monitoring and control must take place, **prevention** rather than cure being the watchword.

Appendix: Very Seriously Invasive Environmental Weed Species in Victoria

Life Form

A	— Annual	Ea	— Emergent aquatic herb	Ls	— Large shrub
P	— Perennial	Pb	— bulbous perennial	Pc	— Cormous perennial
Pt	— Tuberous perennial	Rc	— Root climber	S	— Small to medium shrub
T	— Tree	V	— Vine	X	— Succulent perennial herb, subshrub or shrub

Origin

Af	— Africa	Am	— America	Arg	— Argentina	As	— Asia
C	— Central	Cal	— California	Ch	— China	E	— East
Eur	— Europe	E/as	— Eurasia	Hem	— Hemisphere	Is	— Islands
Jap	— Japan	Med	— Mediterranean	N	— North	NSW	— New South Wales
NZ	— New Zealand	Qld	— Queensland	S	— South	Tas	— Tasmania
Tem	— Temperate	Vic	— Victoria	W	— West	WA	— Western Australia

Latin name	Common name	Family	Life form	Origin
Acacia baileyana	Cootamundra Wattle	Mimosaceae	T	NSW
Acacia decurrens	Early Black Wattle	Mimosaceae	T	NSW
Acacia elata	Cedar Wattle	Mimosaceae	T	NSW
Acacia longifolia	Sallow Wattle	Mimosaceae	Ls/T	Vic, NSW, Qld
Acacia saligna	Golden Wreath Wattle	Mimosaceae	Ls/T	WA
Acacia sophorae	Coast Wattle	Mimosaceae	Ls	Vic, NSW, Qld, Tas
Acer pseudoplatanus	Sycamore Maple	Aceraceae	T	Eur
Agrostis capillaris	Brown-top Bent	Poaceae	P	N Hem
Agrostis stolonifera	Creeping Bent	Poaceae	P	N Hem
Allium triquetrum	Angled Onion	Liliaceae	Pb	W Med
Alstroemeria aurea	Alstroemeria	Liliaceae	Pt	Chile, Arg
Ammophila arenaria	Marram Grass	Poaceae	P	Eur
Anthoxanthum odoratum	Sweet Vernal-grass	Poaceae	P	Eur
Artemisia verlotiorum	Chinese Wormwood	Asteraceae	P	Eur, As
Avena fatua	Wild Oat	Poaceae	A	Med
Brassica tournefortii	Mediterranean Turnip	Brassicaceae	A	As
Briza maxima	Large Quaking-grass	Poaceae	A	Med
Bromus catharticus	Prairie Grass	Poaceae	A	S Am
Bromus diandrus	Great Brome	Poaceae	A	Med
Carpobrotus edulis	Hottentot Fig	Aizoaceae	X	S Af
Carrichtera annua	Wards Weed	Brassicaceae	A	Med
Chrysanthemoides monilifera ssp. *m.*	Boneseed	Asteraceae	Ls	S Af
Coprosma repens	New Zealand Mirror-bush	Rubiaceae	Ls	NZ
Coprosma robusta	Karamu	Rubiaceae	Ls/T	NZ
Cortaderia jubata	Pink Pampas Grass	Poaceae	P	S Am
Cortaderia selloana	Pampas Grass	Poaceae	P	S Am
Cotoneaster divaricata	Cotoneaster	Rosaceae	Ls	As

Latin name	Common name	Family	Life form	Origin
Cotoneaster glaucophyllus	Cotoneaster	Rosaceae	Ls	Ch
Cotoneaster pannosus	Cotoneaster	Rosaceae	Ls	E As
Crataegus monogyna	Hawthorn	Rosaceae	Ls/T	Eur
Critesion marinum	Sea Barley-grass	Poaceae	A	Med
Crocosmia x *crocosmiiflora*	Montbretia	Iridaceae	Pc	S Af
Cynara cardunculus	Artichoke Thistle	Asteraceae	P	Med
Cytisus multiflorus	White Spanish Broom	Fabaceae	Ls	Spain, Portugal
Cytisus palmensis	Tree Lucerne	Fabaceae	Ls/T	Canary Is
Cytisus scoparius	English Broom	Fabaceae	S	Eur
Delairea odorata	Cape Ivy	Asteraceae	V	S Af
Dipogon lignosus	Dipogon	Fabaceae	V	S Af
Ehrharta calycina	Perennial Veldt Grass	Poaceae	P	S Af
Ehrharta erecta	Panic Veldt Grass	Poaceae	P	S Af
Ehrharta longiflora	Annual Veldt Grass	Poaceae	A	S Af
Eragrostis curvula	African Love-grass	Poaceae	P	S Af
Erica arborea	Tree Heath	Ericaceae	Ls	Med, SW Eur
Erica baccans	Berry-flower Heath	Ericaceae	S	S Af
Erica lusitanica	Spanish Heath	Ericaceae	S	SW Eur
Foeniculum vulgare	Fennel	Apiaceae	P	Eur, W As
Fraxinus rotundifolia ssp. *rotundifolia*	Desert Ash	Oleaceae	T	Med, SW As
Freesia leichtlinii	Freesia	Iridaceae	Pc	S Af
Galium aparine	Cleavers	Rubiaceae	A	Eur
Genista linifolia	Flax-leaf Broom	Fabaceae	S	Med
Genista monspessulana	Montpellier Broom	Fabaceae	S	Med
Gladiolus undulatus	Gladiolus	Iridaceae	Pc	S Af
Hakea salicifolia	Willow-leaf Hakea	Proteaceae	Ls	NSW, Qld
Hakea suaveolens	Sweet Hakea	Proteaceae	Ls	WA
Hedera helix	Ivy	Araliaceae	Rc	Eur
Holcus lanatus	Yorkshire Fog	Poaceae	P	Eur, As
Homeria flaccida	One-leaf Cape Tulip	Iridaceae	Pc	S Af
Homeria miniata	Two-leaf Cape Tulip	Iridaceae	Pc	S Af
Hypericum androsaemum	Tutsan	Clusiaceae	S	Eur, N Af, W As
Hypericum calycinum	Large-fl. St Johns Wort	Clusiaceae	S	SE Eur, W As
Hypericum perforatum	St Johns Wort	Clusiaceae	P	Eur, W As
Ilex aquifolium	Holly	Aquifoliaceae	T	Eur
Juncus acutus	Sharp Rush	Juncaceae	P	Med,Eur,SAm,N Am,S Af
Juncus effusus	Soft Rush	Juncaceae	P	temp N Hem
Lagurus ovatus	Hares-tail	Poaceae	A	Med
Leersia oryzoides	Cut-grass	Poaceae	Ea(P)	Eur, temp As, N Am
Leptospermum laevigatum	Coast Tea-tree	Myrtaceae	Ls/T	Vic, NSW, Tas
Leycesteria formosa	Himalayan Honeysuckle	Caprifoliaceae	Ls	Himalaya
Lonicera japonica	Japanese Honeysuckle	Caprifoliaceae	V	E As
Lotus corniculatus	Birds-foot Trefoil	Fabaceae	A	Eur
Lotus uliginosus	Greater Birds-foot Tref.	Fabaceae	P	Eur
Lycium ferocissimum	African Box-thorn	Solanaceae	Ls	S Af
Marrubium vulgare	Horehound	Lamiaceae	P	Eur
Melaleuca armillaris	Giant Honey-Myrtle	Myrtaceae	Ls/T	Vic, NSW, Qld Tas
Mesembryanthemum cystallinum	Ice Plant	Aizoaceae	A	S Af
Myrsiphyllum asparagoides	Bridal Creeper	Liliaceae	Pt	S Af
Myrsiphyllum scandens	Myrsiphyllum	Liliaceae	Pt	S Af
Nassella neesiana	Chilean Spear-grass	Poaceae	P	S Am
Nassella trichotoma	Serrated Tussock	Poaceae	P	S Am
Oenothera glazioviana	Evening Primrose	Onagraceae	P	garden origin
Oxalis pes-caprae	Soursob	Oxalidaceae	Pb	S Af
Paraserianthes lophantha	Cape Wattle	Mimosaceae	Ls/T	WA
Paspalum dilatatum	Paspalum	Poaceae	P	S Am
Paspalum distichum	Water Couch	Poaceae	Ea(P)	cosmopolitan
Passiflora mollissima	Banana Passionfruit	Passifloraceae	V	S Am
Pennisetum alopecuroides	Swamp Foxtail-grass	Poaceae	P	As, Pacific
Pennisetum clandestinum	Kikuyu	Poaceae	P	E Af
Pennisetum macrourum	African Feather-grass	Poaceae	P	S Af
Phalaris aquatica	Toowoomba Canary-grass	Poaceae	P	Med
Phalaris arundinacea	Reed Canary-grass	Poaceae	Ea(P)	N Hem, S Af
Phleum pratense	Timothy Grass	Poaceae	P	Eur
Pinus pinaster	Cluster Pine	Pinaceae	T	Med
Pinus radiata	Monterey Pine	Pinaceae	T	Cal
Pittosporum undulatum	Sweet Pittosporum	Pittosporaceae	T	E Vic, NSW, Qld
Polygala myrtifolia	Myrtle-leaf Milkwort	Polygalaceae	S	S Af
Prunus cerasifera	Cherry-plum	Rosaceae	T	E/as
Prunus laurocerasus	Cherry Laurel	Rosaceae	T	E Eur, W As
Psoralea pinnata	Blue Psoralea	Fabaceae	Ls	S Af
Pyracantha angustifolia	Orange Firethorn	Rosaceae	Ls	Ch
Pyracantha crenulata	Nepal Firethorn	Rosaceae	Ls	Himalaya
Rhamnus alaternus	Italian Buckthorn	Rhamnaceae	Ls	Eur
Romulea rosea	Common Onion-grass	Iridaceae	Pc	S Af

Latin name	Common name	Family	Life form	Origin
Rosa rubiginosa	Sweet Briar	Rosaceae	Ls	Eur
Rubus cissburiensis	Blackberry	Rosaceae	Ls	Eur
Rubus discolor	Blackberry	Rosaceae	Ls	Eur
Rubus polyanthemus	Blackberry	Rosaceae	Ls	Eur
Rubus rosaceus	Blackberry	Rosaceae	Ls	Eur
Rubus ulmifolius	Blackberry	Rosaceae	Ls	Eur
Rubus vestitus	Blackberry	Rosaceae	Ls	Eur
Rumex sagittátus	Climbing Dock	Polygonaceae	V	S Af
Salix cinerea	Grey Sallow	Salicaceae	Ls/T	Eur, W As, N Af
Salix x *rubens*	Crack Willow	Salicaceae	T	Eur
Salpichroa origanifolia	Pampas Lily-of-the-Valley	Solanaceae	Pt	S Am
Senecio angulatus	Climbing Groundsel	Asteraceae	V	S Af
Solanum pseudocapsicum	Madeira Winter Cherry	Solanaceae	S	S Am
Sollya heterophylla	Bluebell Creeper	Pittosporaceae	V	WA
Sparaxis bulbifera	Harlequin-flower	Iridaceae	Pc	S Af
Spartina maritima	Cord-grass	Poaceae	Ea(P)	W Eur
Spartina townsendii	Townsends Cord-grass	Poaceae	Ea(P)	Eur (hybrid)
Thinopyrum junceum	Sea Wheat-grass	Poaceae	P	W & N Eur
Tradescantia albiflora	Wandering Jew	Commelinaceae	P	S Am
Trifolium arvense	Hares-foot Clover	Fabaceae	A	Eur, W As
Trifolium repens	White Clover	Fabaceae	P	Eur, As
Typha latifolia	Great Reedmace	Typhaceae	Ea(P)	temp N Hem, N&C Af, S Am
Ulex europaeus	Gorse	Fabaceae	Ls	W Eur
Vinca major	Blue Periwinkle	Apocynaceae	P	Med
Vulpia bromoides	Squirrel-tail Fescue	Poaceae	A	Eur, W As, Af
Watsonia meriana var. *bulbillifera*	Bulbil Watsonia	Iridaceae	Pc	S Af
Zantedeschia aethiopica	White Arum Lily	Araceae	Pt	S Af

Further Reading

Arnold, A.H. (1987) 'Exotic Plant Invasions in Coastal Ecosystems', in proceedings *National Workshop on Coastal Management, Queenscliffe and Gosford*, Institute of Parks and Recreation, Canberra.

Audas, J.W. (1937) *The Flora of Mitcham*, Mitcham Naturalists Club, Mitcham.

Australian Institute of Agricultural Science (1976) *The Threat of Weeds to Bushland: A Victorian study*, Inkata Press, Melbourne.

Buchanan, R.A. (1989) *Bush Regeneration: Recovering Australian Landscapes*. TAFE, NSW.

Burrell, J.P. (1981) 'Invasion of coastal heaths of Victoria by *Leptospermum laevigatum* (J. Gaertn.) F. Muell.', *Australian Journal of Botany*, vol. 29.

Calder, M. (1988) 'Why bother to control alien plants in national parks and other parks?' in *Weeds on public land—an action plan for today*, (ed. R.G. Richardson), Proceedings of the Weed Science Society of Victoria and the School of Environmental Science, Monash University, Melbourne.

Carr, G.W. (1993) 'The naturalised flora of Victoria and conservation consequences of weed invasion', *Flora of Victoria* Vol 1. National Herbarium of Victoria, Melbourne.

Carr, G.W. & McMahon, A.R.G. (1988) *Vegetation and management of Quarry Reserve, Mt. Eliza, Victoria*, Report for City of Frankston, Ecological Horticulture P/L, Clifton Hill, Victoria.

Carr, G.W., McMahon, A.R.G. & Race, G.J. (1991) *The vegetation and management of Gramatan Avenue Heathland Sanctuary, City of Sandringham, Victoria*, Report for City of Sandringham, Eco. Hort. P/L, Clifton Hill, Victoria.

Carr, G.W. et al (1991) *The vegetation and management of Hochkins Ridge Flora Reserve, North Croydon, Victoria*, Report for the Hochkins Ridge Flora Reserve Committee of Management. Eco. Hort. P/L, Clifton Hill, Victoria.

Carr, G.W. et al (1989) *The vegetation, botanical significance and management of Cherry Lake, Lower Kororoit Creek and Truganina Swamp, Altona, Victoria*, Report for MMBW, Melbourne. Eco. Hort. P/L, Clifton Hill, Victoria.

Carr, G.W., Reid, J. & Albrecht, D. (1987) *The vegetation, fauna and management of Antonio Park, City of Nunawading, Victoria*, Report for the City of Nunawading, Eco. Hort. P/L, Clifton Hill, Victoria.

Carr, G.W., Todd, J.A. & Race, G.J. (1991) *Vegetation of Plenty Gorge Metropolitan Park, Greensborough—Mernda, Victoria, and its management. Part A. Significance and management issues*, Report for the MMBW, Eco. Hort. P/L, Clifton Hill, Victoria.

Carr, G.W., Yugovic, J.V. & Robinson, K. (1992) *Environmental Weeds in Victoria: an Overview*, Dept. Conservation & Environment & Eco. Hort. P/L, Melbourne.

Cheal, D.C. (1988) *Botanical Assessment of grasslands, Merri Creek-Somerton-Cooper Street*, Resource Assessment Report 88-1. Dept Conservation, Forests & Lands, Melbourne.

Cheal, D.C. et al (in prep) *Vegetation survey and sites of botanical significance in the Melbourne area*, Dept Conservation & Environment, Victoria.

City of Frankston, Shires of Hastings & Mornington (undated) *Mornington Peninsula Pest Plants*, Pamphlet, City of Frankston, Shires of Hastings & Mornington, Victoria.

Elliot, R. (1986) 'Check bushland invaders now', *Your Garden*, vol. 39(1) Melbourne.

Friends of Sherbrooke Forest and Department of Conservation, Forests & Lands (1989) *Weeds of Forests, Roadsides and Gardens*, Second edn, Department of Conservation, Forests & Lands, Victoria.

Frood, D. & Calder, M. (1987) *Nature Conservation in Victoria*, Vols 1 & 2, Victorian National Parks Association, Melbourne.

Garnett, S.T. (3 Aug 1987) 'Exotic peril to Australia's balance', *The Age*, Melbourne.

Gleadow, R.M. & Ashton, D.H. (1981) 'Invasion by *Pittosporum undulatum* of the forests of central Victoria. I. Invasion patterns and plant morphology', *Australian Journal of Botany*. vol. 29.

Gullan, P.K. (1988) 'Weeds in Victoria, where are we?', in *Weeds on public land—an action plan for today*, ed. R.G. Richardson: Proceedings of symposium presented by the Weed Science Society of Victoria and the School of Environmental Science, Monash University, Melbourne.

Holzner, W., Werger, M.G.A. & Ikasima, J. eds. (1983) *Man's impact on vegetation*, Dr W. Junk Publishers, The Hague.

Humphries, S.E., Groves, R.H. and Mitchell, D.S. (in press). *Plant invasions of Australian ecosystems: a status review and management directions*. Report to Australian National Parks and Wildlife Service. Endangered Species Program, project no 58.

Judd, T. (1990) *Invasion of native plant communities by Kunzea ambigua, Kunzea ericoides and Leptospermum laevigatum*, Ph.D. thesis, Department of Botany, University of Melbourne, Victoria.

Kloot, P.M. (1983) 'Early records of alien plants naturalised in South Australia', *Journal of the Adelaide Botanic Gardens*, vol. 6, Adelaide Botanic Gardens, S.A.

Lunt, I.D. (1988) *Derrimut Grassland Vegetation Report. Part I. The Vegetation and its Management*, Report to the Department of Conservation, Forests & Lands, Victoria.

McIntyre, S. (1990) 'Invasion of a Nation: Our Role in the Management of Exotic Plants in Australia', *Australian Biologist* Vol 3.

McMahon, A.R.G. et al (1989) *An assessment of the environmental weed problem within the Shire of Eltham and formulation of a management strategy*, Report prepared for the Shire of Eltham, Victoria.

McMahon, A.R.G. et al (1989) *An assessment of the environmental weed problem within the Shire of Eltham and formulation of a management strategy*, Report prepared for the Shire of Eltham, Victoria.

McMahon, A.R.G. et al (1989) *A review of the sites of significance in the Upper Yarra and Dandenong Ranges region*. Prepared for the Upper Yarra and Dandenong Ranges Authority. Eco. Hort. P/L, Clifton Hill, Victoria.

McMahon, A.R.G., Robinson, R.W. & Bedggood, S.E. (1990) *Preliminary assessment of the biological impacts of the proposed Puffing Billy railway extension*, Shire of Sherbrooke. Eco. Hort. P/L, Clifton Hill, Victoria.

Montrose Environmental Group (inc). *Garden Escapees: A Blot on the Montrose Landscape*, Montrose Environmental Group (inc)., Victoria.

Parsons, W.T. (1973) *Noxious weeds of Victoria*, Inkata Press, Melbourne.

Regional Pest Plants Strategy Working Group (1991) *Environmental Weed Kit*, (Identification and Control) Free kit produced by RPPSWG, Melbourne.

Robin, J.M. & Carr, G.W. (1983) 'Weed Invasions and Horticulture—an Ecological Rethink', *Australian Horticulture*, vol. 81.

Ross, J.H. (1990) *A Census of the Vascular plants of Victoria*, 3rd edition, National Herbarium of Victoria, Department of Conservation, Forests & Lands, Victoria.

Short, P.S. (1987) 'Recording and distribution of weeds in Victoria', *Victorian Naturalist*, vol. 104, Victoria.

Willis, J.H. (1965) 'Native Plants of Brighton', *Brighton Historical Society Newsletter* No. 9 (Reprinted in 'Indigenotes' Vol 4 (8) 1991). Victoria.

Leptospermum laevigatum

Chapter 7. Seed Collection

Section 1 Guidelines

Darcy Duggan

The availability of seed of local Australian species is critical for both nursery propagation and direct seeding to enable revegetation and conservation of natural areas.

Seed collecting is an interesting and rewarding way to discover and explore the local flora and fauna of an area. The techniques involved in collecting seed are easily learnt and can be carried out by almost anyone, and it provides an opportunity for an interested member of the community to play a small but vitally important part in the conservation and protection of our natural heritage.

It is essential however, that all people undertaking seed collection have a good understanding of the basic principles associated with this task, and follow a few simple guidelines.

These can be outlined as follows:

Ethics of Seed Collecting

1. Respect

Most urban remnant vegetation sites are now small and isolated with often fragmented and declining populations of local native species. These sites are now extremely vulnerable to disturbances such as trampling of ground flora and excessive damage to foliage. It is absolutely fundamental therefore, that seed collectors treat all remnant natural areas with care and respect.

When working in an area:

- move carefully and watch where you walk to avoid damage to native ground flora;
- when collecting seed from shrub and overstorey species, minimise damage to vegetation by avoiding excessive pruning or breaking foliage;
- if working with a group, spread out over the site. Small groups are preferable compared with large groups of enthusiastic, well intentioned people who can inadvertently cause a lot of damage;
- carefully select sites to suit the skills level of groups. Sensitive areas should be avoided when working with inexperienced groups such as school children;
- exercise caution when disclosing the location of rare or endangered species to minimise the loss of these sites through 'poaching'. Ensure collection of seed or propagation material of these species is undertaken by experienced and trusted collectors.

2. Integrity

Maintaining the genetic diversity and integrity of a given species is critical to its long term protection and conservation.

The local flora of an area may comprise one or more plant communities. A plant community is made up of populations of numerous different plant species, which over a long period have evolved and adapted to suit the soils and climatic conditions of a given area. This has led to the development of local forms or varieties of particular plant species, with different genetic make-up.

The term 'provenance' is used to identify the location from where the seed or cutting material was collected. To conserve the character and genetic make-up of a local population therefore, it is necessary to collect and propagate seed from that local provenance, and make sure that propagated plants are planted back into the same area.

Seed collecting however is a subjective exercise.

There is often a tendency to either consciously or subconsciously search for superior healthy plants with a heavy seed load. This temptation must be avoided, as it is critically important to take a broad sample of the local gene pool of a species, to maintain the genetic diversity within a given population of plants. This can best be achieved by collecting seed from all individuals irrespective of seed load. It is far better to collect a small amount of seed from a large number of plants than vice versa.

In general no more than 20% of the seed present from any given plant should be collected.

There are often problems in collecting seed from rare or isolated individuals. For example the seed may have a low viability due to self pollination and/or incrossing between related individuals; and represents only a small or distorted component of the original gene pool.

3. Documentation

Thorough documentation is essential to ensure the integrity of seed and propagating material which has been collected.

The process of documentation is straightforward and is outlined as follows:

- locate the remnant vegetation site;
- identify species present;
- collect a plant pressing showing fruits, flowers and leaves to confirm identification. It is useful to establish a small herbarium of plants collected from a given site for research and as an educational aid.

If there is any doubt as to the identity of a plant in the field, it is essential that it be properly identified before seed is collected from it. In this way, many hours of valuable time and energy can be saved by not collecting seed from what might turn out to be either a weed or non-indigenous species.

Much of Chapter 7 is reproduced with permission from Vol 3, No. 11 (1990) of Indigenotes, the newsletter of the Indigenous Flora and Fauna Association.

4. Keep notes for each site

Record things such as flowering and maturation times of species present, general status of the vegetation community, environmental pressures affecting the site, eg weed invasion, rabbit grazing, disturbance etc.

These site records are valuable in developing a management strategy for the area. It is useful to record the changes in a site over a period of time, hence it is important to revisit the site regularly, but especially during Spring and Summer to monitor the rate of development and maturation of seed and the variations from year to year.

5. Labelling

Each collection of seeds should be immediately labelled with the name of the species, date, name of collector, location (eg Melway map reference), soil type, aspect, and any other relevant observations (eg wildlife habitat).

Factors to Consider when Collecting Seed

There are a number of interrelated characteristics of a plant species and its seed, which influence both the techniques used to collect it, as well as the success or cost efficiency of the exercise in meeting your particular needs. For example you may require only a small amount of seed for propagation, or require bulk amounts for direct sowing and revegetation trials.

1. The number of plants in an area (more or less than 100 per ha). The greater the number of plants from which seed is collected, the greater the genetic diversity of the gene pool of a given collection.

2. Height of seed pods from the ground (more or less than 2 m). Pod or seed capsule location is an important factor when considering the ease of collection and the tools required to collect the seed e.g. hand saw, step ladder, cherry picker, long handled pruners, climbing gear.

It is often claimed that seed from the middle and upper reaches of a tree or shrub is generally of a better quality and viability than that collected lower down.

3. The number of seed pods per plant is both genetically and environmentally controlled. Some species (e.g. *Acacia*) exhibit distinct cycles in seed production (i.e. every 4 to 7 years a high seed yield is produced whilst in other years little or no seed matures). It is important therefore to have seed in storage to offset the lack of seed in a poor year. Environmental factors such as soil moisture and nutrient levels, temperature and rainfall will affect the health and growth of a plant and the amount of seed produced in a given year. Seed production is also clearly influenced by other factors such as strong winds which dislodge flowers and or pods, heavy frosts or attack by insect predators.

4. Number of seeds per pod This affects the amount of effort required to collect a required quantity of seed.

5. Pod size Determines the ease of collection and handling of a given species.

6. Seed Retention The time between flowering, seed maturation and seed shed of different species is highly variable, and may be as short as several weeks. For some plants such as *Eucalyptus*, which produce woody capsules, it may be up to one year or more after flowering before seed is mature and ready to collect (see Section 5).

A number of groups of plants retain the seed for several years within woody capsules until fire or some other environmental factor triggers seed dispersal. Genera such as *Callistemon*, *Leptospermum*, *Banksia*, *Hakea* and *Melaleuca* fall into this category. The advantage of this characteristic is that seed is generally available for collection at any time of the year.

In most other species however, seed is not retained, but dispersed fairly quickly after maturation. For most 'pea' species, e.g. *Kennedia*, *Bossiaea*, *Eutaxia*, *Pultenaea*, *Hardenbergia*, the seed is dispersed within four to five weeks after flowering, and is often forcibly ejected from the seed pods. In some species the seed may be dispersed up to 2 metres from the parent plant.

The *Acacia* group displays a fair degree of variation in the rate of seed retention which can be related to certain physical characteristics of the seed. *A. melanoxylon* and *A. implexa* both have a well developed aril (an appendage which attaches the seed to the inside of the pod), allowing seed to be retained on the plant for 4 to 6 weeks after the pods split open. *A. pycnantha* on the other hand has a greatly reduced aril resulting in seed being shed as soon as the pods split open.

Monitoring of an area from which seed is to be collected, and the timing of collection, is critical in maximising the yield of seed from many species.

7. Distance travelled to collect seed (travelling time more or less than 50% of time spent). This factor affects both the cost and efficiency of seed collecting, especially if collecting large quantities of seed, or a variety of different species from a site.

8. Differential Ripening. In some plant species such as native grasses, seed on the same plant ripens at different times. The timing of collection is less critical, as seed can be collected over a period of time.

9. Difficulty in collecting seed. Various native plants are 'armed' with spines or prickly foliage, making seed collection a somewhat painful and unpleasant experience. Thick protective clothing and leather gloves may therefore be required.

Some plants such as *Hakeas*, have thick woody capsules which are difficult to remove and may have to be cut off the plant.

10. Recognising when seed is mature and ready to collect is generally a combination of observation and common sense. The most obvious telltale sign is a change in colour and appearance of seed or seed pods from green to brown or black. Colour change is usually associated with a drying out and hardening of seed pods.

If unsure, a test sample of seed should be taken and examined. For example in *Stipa* (a native grass) if the seed is dark in colour, has a hard seed coat (requires fair pressure to split seed if squeezed between fingernails) and the seed is easily removed from the flower head, then it is mature and ready to collect.

In *Eucalyptus*, there is usually a discernible colour change in the capsules from green to red/brown. When a sample of capsules is placed in a paper bag and seed is shed within 3 to 4 days after collection (and the seed is dark in colour as opposed to pale) then it is ready to collect. You may also notice the valves in the opening of each capsule start to split open, indicating it is ready for collection (see Section 4).

Methods of Collection

A number of different methods and a range of equipment and materials are required. The method chosen is dictated by the type of plant being collected.

Basic equipment and materials include:

- notebook and pen
- lots of large paper bags or envelopes
- plastic ground sheets
- a few plastic garbage bags
- old nylon stockings

Three broad categories of plants are annuals and herbaceous species, shrubs, and tall trees. Suggested collection methods for each category are as follows:

1. Annuals and Herbaceous species

This category includes native grasses, lilies and wildflower species. Collection is by hand, is intensive, time consuming and often tedious.

Grasses. Collect by running fingers in an upward motion along the flower head. If seed is mature, it should pull out with gentle pressure. It is important to keep awns intact as these aid germination. Place in a paper bag.

Another effective method is to grasp a handful of flower stalks and cut using secateurs or scissors. This is a particularly useful method for species such as *Poa* and *Danthonia* which have small seeds, and a distinctive tussock habit. Seed heads can then be threshed to remove seed.

***Dianella* (Flax Lilies).** Seed is contained within fleshy fruits which change colour from green to purple. Fruits drop to the ground when mature or can be gently picked off by hand. It is recommended the fruits be placed in a plastic bag as they tend to make paper bags go soggy.

***Arthropodium* (Chocolate Lilies) and Bulbine Lilies.** Seed of these species is contained in small round capsules along the stem which visibly dry out and split open. Seed disperses quickly. It is best to collect the whole stem and place it upside down in a large paper bag to allow seed to shed in the bag.

***Brunonia* (Blue Pincushions).** These have tight clustered flower heads. The seed is ready to be collected when heads can be gently picked off.

Asteraceae e.g. *Bracteantha*, *Helichrysum*, *Rhodanthe*, *Vittadinia*, *Senecio*: The seed of this group is small and attached to a pappus; it is generally ready to collect when the flowers start to dry and develop a fluffy appearance. Light pressure with fingers should easily dislodge seed. Remove the flower head and place in a paper bag.

It is also possible to use a small portable vacuum cleaner to collect fine herbaceous seed of this type.

Ground cover and prostrate species, e.g. *Eutaxia microphylla*, *Convolvulus erubescens*: collection of seed from these species can be very tedious and fiddly, hand picking individual pods. A more effective method is to gently lift the foliage and carefully slide a sheet of corrugated cardboard under the plant. Tap mature pods or seed onto the cardboard. Carefully remove the cardboard with the seed in place.

Bossiaea prostrata (Creeping Bossiaea). Pods split open and forcibly eject seed. Maturation of pods therefore needs to be carefully monitored. These will first start to swell and then dry out and darken in colour. To check if they are ready, lightly squeeze pods with fingers and the pods should split open easily. Seed is light brown or tan in colour when mature. It is easier to collect the pods whole and remove the seed later.

2. Woody shrubs and small trees

Different methods can be employed—depending on the dispersal strategy of the species and the time lag involved. A ground sheet may be placed at the base of the plant, and seed pods can be hand picked, or seed knocked onto the ground sheet. This method can be very efficient and time saving, and is suitable for a range of species—especially *Acacia* spp., and fleshy fruited species e.g. *Hymenanthera*, *Coprosma* and *Myoporum*.

Alternatively seed may be hand picked and placed directly into a foam box or paper bag.

By far one of the most difficult groups to collect from are the 'peas' e.g. *Dillwynia*, *Pultenaea*, *Daviesia*. The seed of these species is generally ejected over a very short period (1–2 days). It is critical therefore, that these species are actively monitored to ensure correct timing of collection. Key indicators to look for are swelling of pods and colour change from green to brown.

Two methods have proven successful in collecting seed of these species:

Selective and careful pruning of shrubs with seed pods attached, which are then placed into large paper bags. As the material dries out, the pods open releasing seed.

This method is far more successful compared with hand stripping of pods from the plant. The attachment of pods to the branches would appear to be essential to the pods' splitting open.

When it is not possible to regularly monitor a site, branches with pods attached may be **enclosed in old nylon stockings** which are then tied firmly in place. Seed will be shed into the stockings, which must then be carefully removed from the plants.

3. Tall tree species

These can present problems because of the height of the trees and difficulty of access. It may be possible to collect seed from the lower branches using secateurs. For higher branches a tree lopper, commando saw, climbing gear or even a cherry picker may be required.

Wherever possible, attempt to coordinate seed collection with annual pruning work undertaken by the local council or SEC.

Royalties

In Victoria, under the Forests Act, royalties are payable on commercial quantities of seed collected from all public land managed by the Department of Conservation and Environment. Enquiries should be made to the relevant regional office of the Department.

Section 2 Permit Requirements (Vic)

Department of Conservation and Natural Resources

At present, permits under the Flora and Fauna Guarantee Act are required for collecting seed or other propagating material from protected flora on public land.

A written permit is required from the local Regional Office of the Department of Conservation and Environment, or if the collection relates to a number of regions, to the Flora Branch of the Department. The application form should be accompanied by a covering letter explaining the purpose of the seed collecting.

It is advisable to obtain verbal permission from the Department's Regional Flora and Fauna Guarantee Officer before any particular collection takes place, to regulate over-collection.

Conditions are attached to permits which are granted. These include that vegetation disturbance is minimized, that sufficient seed is left to ensure natural regeneration, and that vehicles should be confined to existing tracks.

In National and State Parks seed collection requires a research permit under the National Parks Act. Applications should be made to the National Parks and Public Land Division of the Department of Conservation and Environment phone (03) 412 4011.

On private land permission should be sought from the owner, and this is considered sufficient, except in the case of declared critical habitat (none is yet declared however).

The collection of tree ferns and grass trees requires special permission from the Department.

Protected Flora and Communities Found within the Melbourne Region

Approximately 680 species of flora have been declared protected in Victoria under the Flora and Fauna Guarantee Act 1988. Five plant communities are also protected within Victoria. Those species and the one community found within the Melbourne region are listed below. For further information on all protected species contact the Flora & Fauna Guarantee Section of Department of Conservation & Environment, 250 Victoria Pde, East Melbourne 3002 (03) 412 4011.

Communities

Western (Basalt) Plains Grassland Community. Every plant of that community is protected wherever it occurs within the Basalt community. The basalt community in Melbourne is shown on Map 2. It is also discussed in detail in Chapter 1.

Species and/or Genera

Acacia spp. All except *A. dealbata*, *A. implexa*, *A. melanoxylon*, *A. paradoxa*.
Agrostis adamsonii
Allocasuarina luehmannii
Boronia parviflora
Bracteantha spp.
Brunonia australis
Calytrix tetragona
Chrysocephalum spp.
Comesperma polygaloides
Correa spp.
Epacridaceae—all species
Euphrasia scabra
Gompholobium huegelii
Grevillea spp.
Hardenbergia violacea
Helichrysum spp.
Lepidium pseudohyssopifolium
L. pseudotasmanicum
Leucochrysum albicans
Orchidaceae—all species
Ozothamnus spp.
Prostanthera spp.
Psoralea parva
Psoralea tenax
Pteridophyta—Clubmosses, ferns and fern allies except *Pteridium esculentum*
Rhodanthe spp.
Rutidosis leptorrhynchoides
Senecio macrocarpus
Stylidium spp.
Thesium australe
Thysanotus spp.
Xanthorrhoea spp.

Section 3 *The Separation, Cleaning and Storage of Seeds*

Andrew N. Paget*

These notes explain first how to separate the seeds from the various types of ripe fruits that you have collected, and then how to clean the seeds. Once separated and cleaned they should be stored as described or sown immediately. The information refers mainly to the handling of seed on a large scale but is also applicable to smaller quantities.

Some of the section on separation and cleaning, and the directions for storage, have been supplied by Darcy Duggan.

Separation

When collected, seed pods and capsules need to be dried out to fully release the seed. The method used depends on the type of seed and the ease with which it is released.

Two options are to spread pods out onto sheets on the floor, turning the pods regularly to prevent sweating and ensure even drying, or to suspend seed from the ceiling in sheets. (Duggan)

Drying cabinet

For most fruits a drying cabinet is required to dry the fruits until seeds are released. This cabinet is best fairly well sealed and heated with a small fan heater to move the air around. The fruits can be put into brown paper bags or wooden boxes and placed on racks in this cabinet for several days until they open. Vigorous shaking when the fruits have opened will help to remove all the seed. Small quantities of seed can be separated by placing capsules into a brown paper bag and situating it in a warm position.

Burning

For Banksias, a drying cabinet is not hot enough, and the cones must be burnt for the follicles to open and release their seeds. Either burning with a blow-torch, or on a small bonfire is effective; or you can place them in a paper bag in a warm oven.

Bashing

Some fruits, like Blackwoods (*Acacia melanoxylon*), are reluctant to let go of their seeds. We put such fruit into a

* Andrew Paget is a botanist who has developed an interest in indigenous flora. He is a partner in 'Bushland Flora', a wholesale and retail nursery devoted to collecting and growing indigenous species.

rubbish bin and beat them with a large broom handle to separate them. It is advisable to use a dust mask when doing this to avoid the dust created.

Cleaning

Seed cleaning is an essential process. Removal of trash is important, as this often harbours insects which may attack seed and reduce viability. For small quantities of seed you may need to use a combination of graded sieves and/or winnowing in a light breeze to remove chaff. (Duggan)

Mush, dry and scrunch

For fleshy fruits we find that the best method to obtain clean seed is to put the fruits into a bowl and add some water. Mush all the fruits up, trying to squeeze the flesh off the seeds. Drain off as much liquid as possible and spread out the pulp onto absorbent paper. Put this into the drying cabinet or a warm oven. This is the important stage because if the pulp does not dry quickly enough or well enough it will go mouldy. Once dried the pulp can be scrunched up and all the clean seeds should separate easily. This method is suitable for *Actrotriche* spp., *Astroloma humifusum*, *Billardiera scandens*, *Coprosma* spp., *Dianella* spp., *Persoonia juniperina*, *Polyscias sambucifolius*, *Rubus parvifolius* and *Solanum* spp.

Sieving

Sieves of various mesh sizes are essential in cleaning most seeds. In ideal situations it will be possible to select two sieves for each seed being cleaned. One will be larger than the seed, to allow the seeds to fall through but catch larger trash. The second sieve will be just smaller than the seed to catch the seeds but discard smaller trash.

It is difficult and expensive to obtain a good range of sieves. A set of 2 sieves which are useful for most seeds is available from 'Gemrocks' at Nunawading. A wide range is available through 'Greer Wire Industries', Thomastown or 'Hannafords' (manufacturers of 'Seedmaster' seed cleaning machines) of 64 East Avenue, Beverley. South Australia, 5009.

Rubbing

Rubbing grass heads between 2 rubber mats is a method we have found useful for separating *Danthonia* seeds. These seeds will not germinate while still enclosed in the heads, but rubbing them separates them easily. Again masks are recommended to avoid inhaling the dust created.

Storage

Low temperature and humidity conditions are important to maintain viability of seed. Satisfactory short term storage may be achieved by placing seed in paper envelopes and storing in a cool dark cupboard fumigated with moth balls (Napthalene). For longer term storage, place seed in screw top glass jars.

Clear labels with relevant data, including name of species, site and date of collection, are essential.

Section 4 *Recognising Ripe Indigenous Fruit and Seeds*

Andrew N. Paget

The following notes are intended as a guide to judging when fruit or seeds are ripe. They relate to the Knox area of Melbourne, but may be useful in other areas also.

Colour changes

The fruit or seeds of most species change colour distinctly when they ripen:

Acacia spp.—most turn from creamy green to shiny black. Some (like *A. ulicifolia*) do not attain a high gloss finish.

Acaena spp.—turn from green to light grey-brown.

Acrotriche spp.—have a creamy bloom on the green succulent fruit.

Alisma plantago-aquatica—turns pale red-brown from green.

Amperea xiphoclada—the seeds inside the green fruit turn from cream to black and shiny.

Amyema spp.—turn slightly yellower when ripe, are plump, and break off easily.

Arthropodium spp.—seeds turn black.

Astroloma humifusum—fruit becomes glaucous when ripe, and seeds turn red-brown.

Billardiera longiflora—fruit turns purple from green, and seeds turn dark maroon.

Billardiera scandens—fruits turn translucent khaki, and seeds turn red-brown.

Bulbine bulbosa—seeds turn from creamy to grey-brown.

Burchardia umbellata—seeds turn from cream to red-brown.

Bursaria spinosa—fruits turn from green to red-brown, and the seeds also become red-brown.

Caesia parviflora—seeds turn black when ripe, inside green capsules.

Cassytha glabella and *C. pubescens*—seeds turn red-brown within green fruits.

Cassytha melantha—seeds turn almost black.

Centipeda minima—seeds turn from green to creamy yellow-green.

Coprosma quadrifida—fruit turns from green to red.

Cymbonotus preissianus—seeds turn from cream to black.

Cynoglossum spp.—seeds change from green to a grey-brown colour.

Danthonia spp.—most have seed heads which turn from green to fawn-cream when ripe.

Dianella spp.—fruit turns purple when ripe and seeds are shiny and black.

Diplarrena moraea—mature seeds are red-brown.

Drosera spp.—seeds are black.

Einadia nutans—ripe fruits are red, and the mature seeds are almost black.

Exocarpos cupressiformis—fruit turns red, seeds turn dark brown.

Exocarpos strictus—fruit turns pale silvery-pink, seeds turn dark brown.

Gahnia sieberiana—mature seeds turn red-orange.

Glycine clandestina—ripe pods turn almost black, and mature seeds inside are red-brown.

Goodia lotifolia—mature seeds are almost black.

Gynatrix pulchella—the fruits turn grey, and the ripe seeds inside are red-brown.
Hedycarya angustifolia—ripe fruit is orange.
Hibbertia stricta—ripe seeds are mottled red-brown.
Hovea linearis—seeds change from cream to dark grey, and the pods turn from green to grey-brown.
Hypericum gramineum—capsules turn from green to red-brown, and mature seeds are also red-brown.
Indigofera australis—seeds are red-brown.
Lagenifera spp.—seeds turn from green to grey-brown.
Leptorhynchos tenuifolius—seeds are almost black.
Linum marginale—seeds are shiny red-brown at maturity.
Lomandra spp.—creamy seeds are shiny red-brown.
Luzula meridionalis vars.—seeds almost black when mature.
Pandorea pandorana—fruit changes from green to yellowish then progressively becomes mottled with brown. At maturity the seeds are papery red-brown.
Patersonia occidentalis—mature seeds change from creamy to shiny red-brown.
Pelargonium inodorum—seeds are dark grey on maturity.
Persoonia juniperina—green fruit becomes yellow, and mature seeds are red-brown.
Pimelea spp.—most seeds are black, inside leathery fruit.
Pittosporum bicolor—mature fruit opens to reveal dark red sticky seeds.
Polyscias sambucifolius—clusters of ripe fruit are translucent grey-lilac.
Prostanthera lasianthos—green seeds change to grey.
Pultenaea spp.—green pods turn red-brown, and seeds within change from green to almost black.
Ranunculus spp.—green seeds turn yellowish, and fall if brushed.
Ricinocarpos pinifolius—green burr-like fruits turn red-brown and split open when ripe.
Rumex brownii—green fruit turns red-brown when ripe.
Sambucus gaudichaudiana—ripe fruit changes from green to a translucent creamy colour.
Solanum aviculare—green fruit turns dark orange-red, and seeds are red-brown.
Solanum laciniatum—green fruit turns yellow-orange and seeds are red-brown.
Sphaerolobium vimineum—green pods change through purple tinges to grey-brown.
Stylidium graminifolium—green capsules turn fawn-grey, and seeds change from cream to red-orange on ripening.
Thelymitra spp.—Most capsules turn grey-brown, and seeds from creamy to brown.
Themeda triandra—fruit (awn and florets) turns dark red-brown and shiny, from green-cream.
Thysanotus spp.—seeds turn from creamy-green to black.
Tricoryne elatior—seeds within green fruit turn black.
Viminaria juncea—pods enclosing ripe seeds turn grey-brown.
Viola hederacea—seeds turn dark maroon from creamy.
Wahlenbergia spp.—ripe seeds are red-brown, and capsules turn from green through yellow-green to grey-brown.
Wurmbea dioica—cream seeds mature to red-brown.
Xanthorrhoea minor—ripe seeds are black in colour.

Other Changes

Other observable changes which will indicate the fruit or seeds are ripe are:

Valves formed:

Allocasuarina spp., *Eucalyptus* spp., *Kunzea ericoides*, *Leptospermum* spp., and *Melaleuca* spp.

Ease of removal:

Most fruit and seeds are easier to remove when they are ripe than when immature. This is an easy way of determining ripeness of: *Acaena* spp., *Amyema* spp., *Billardiera* spp., *Brachyscome* spp., *Carex* spp., *Centipeda minima*, *Clematis* spp., *Cynoglossum* spp., *Lagenifera* spp., *Leptorhynchos* spp., *Persoonia* spp., *Ranunculus* spp., *Triglochin* spp., and most native grasses.

Fruit opening

This is the easiest way of telling that the seeds of the following species are ripe: *Acacia* spp., *Arthropodium* spp., *Bulbine bulbosa*, *Burchardia umbellata*, *Bursaria spinosa*, *Chamaescilla corymbosa*, *Comesperma* spp., *Cymbonotus preissianus*, *Derwentia derwentiana*, *Diplarrena moraea*, *Hypericum gramineum*, *Juncus* spp., *Kunzea ericoides*, *Linum marginale*, *Lomandra* spp., *Lomatia* spp., *Pandorea pandorana*, *Patersonia* spp., *Pittosporum* spp., *Villarsia* spp., *Wahlenbergia* spp., *Wurmbea dioica*, and *Xanthorrhoea minor*.

Timing

It is essential to keep good records of when you collect seeds as the timing varies little from year to year. Once you have collected them one year, you can go back within a couple of weeks the following year and expect to find them ripe. To this end, Operation Revegetation has compiled a seed collecting calendar with the time of the year (in half-months) the seed of each species ripens in the Knox area.

Section 5 *Seed Collection Times for a Range of species in Melbourne*

Murray Ralph*

This list has been put together from the Victorian Indigenous Nurseries Co-operative's seed collection records compiled over the last few years.

Times given are the most likely periods for seeds of a particular species to be collected. However depending on the season, local microclimate and aspect, and the area of Melbourne in which you are collecting, seed may ripen up to a few weeks earlier or later. Careful observation over time is the key to success.

The length of time for which mature seed is held on the plant varies from species to species. Some species can hold seed for up to several years, while other species release them immediately after ripening. Seed on many species ripens progressively with both mature and immature seed present on the same plant, so several visits may be required to collect quantities needed. Quantities of seed produced varies greatly from year to year with some species producing large crops of seed on a cyclical basis.

* Murray Ralph spent 12 months working with the CSIRO for the National Seed Collection Project. He became interested in the importance of propagating indigenous plants and was manager of 'Victorian Indigenous Nursery Co-operative' in East Brunswick for 4½ years. He now collects seed on contract.

Duration of time seed remains on the plant after maturity is indicated by the following:

*	one to two days	***	up to several months
**	one to two weeks	****	up to several years

Tree and Shrub Species

Acacia spp.—seeds of most *Acacia* spp. in the Melbourne region mature around late December to early January and generally drop soon after maturity so close attention is warranted.

A. acinacea	Late December	****
A. dealbata	Late December	*
A. genistifolia	Late Dec–early Jan	*
A. implexa	January	*
A. mearnsii	Late December	*
A. melanoxylon	January	**
A. mucronata	Mid Dec–Jan	*
A. myrtifolia	Mid–late Dec	*
A. paradoxa	Late Dec	*
A. pycnantha	Mid Dec–early Jan	*
A. retinodes	Late Jan–early Feb	*
A. verniciflua	Mid Dec–early Jan	*
A. verticillata	Mid December	*

Allocasuarina spp.—Seed cones tend to be persistent and can be collected all year round. Late Summer to Autumn tends to be the best time as the current year's crop matures at this time.

Allocasuarina luehmannii seed not persistent—late Summer.

Alyxia buxifolia	Late December	**
Atriplex cinerea	Early January	**
Banksia integrifolia	March	***
Banksia marginata	Late Dec–March	***
Bursaria spinosa	March–April	**
Callistemon sieberi	All year round	****
Callitris glaucophylla	March	***
Cassinia spp.	Late Jan–mid Feb	**
Coprosma quadrifida	Late Dec–Jan	**
Daviesia spp.	December	*
Dillwynia cinerascens	Mid Dec	*
Dodonaea viscosa ssp. *spatulata*	Mid–late Dec.	**

Eucalyptus spp.—vary throughout the year from species to species, with some having persistent seed.

E. camaldulensis	March–Nov	***
E. cephalocarpa	April–August	***
E. cypellocarpa	Jan–June	***
E. dives	All year	****
E. goniocalyx	All year	****
E. leucoxylon ssp. *connata*	Oct–June	***
E. macrorhyncha	All year	****
E. melliodora	Dec–Sept	***
E. microcarpa	Nov–August	***
E. obliqua	All year	****
E. ovata	All year	****
E. polyanthemos ssp. *vestita*	Dec–June	***
E. radiata	All year	****
E. rubida	Feb–May	***
E. viminalis	July–April	***
E. yarraensis	Variable	***
Eutaxia microphylla	Early–Mid Dec	*
Goodia lotifolia	December	*
Grevillea spp.	December	*
Gynatrix pulchella	Late December	**
Hakea spp.	All year	****
Hymenanthera dentata	January	**
Indigofera australis	Late Dec–early Jan	*
Kunzea ericoides	March	***
Lavatera plebeia	December	*
Leptospermum spp.	All year	****
Leucophyta brownii	March	**
Melaleuca spp.	All year	****
Olearia lirata	December	**
Olearia ramulosa	December	**
Ozothamnus ferrugineus	January	**
Ozothamnus obcordatus	Dec–Jan	**
Platylobium spp.	December	*
Pomaderris spp.	Late Dec–early Jan	**
Prostanthera lasianthos	January	*
Pultenaea daphnoides	December	*
Rhagodia candolleana	February	**
Rhagodia parabolica	Mid–late Jan	**
Senna artemisioides ssp. *filifolia*	Late Jan–early Feb	*
Solanum spp.	Jan–Feb	**
Viminaria juncea	Jan–Feb	*

Tussock Habit—Native Grasses

Agrostis spp.	Late Dec–Jan	*
Carex spp.	Dec–Jan	**
Chloris truncata	Dec–Feb	**
Danthonia spp.	Late Nov–mid Dec	**
Dianella longifolia	Late December	**
Dianella revoluta	Mid–late December	**
Dianella tasmanica	January	**
Dicanthium sericeum	February	**
Elymus scabrus	December	*
Juncus spp.	Dec–Jan	**
Lomandra longifolia	Late Dec–Jan	*
Microlaena stipoides	December	*
Poa spp.	Mid–late December	**
Stipa spp.	Late Nov–Dec	**
Themeda triandra	Late Dec–early Jan	*

Groundcovers—Climbers

Atriplex semibaccata	Jan–Feb	**
Bossiaea prostrata	Mid December	*
Carpobrotus spp.	Dec–Jan	**
Clematis aristata	Dec–Jan	**
Clematis microphylla	December	*
Einadia nutans	December	*
Enchylaena tomentosa	February	**
Hardenbergia violacea	December	*
Kennedia prostrata	December	*

Herbs

Acaena spp.	Dec–Jan	*
Brachyscome spp.	Dec–Feb	*
Bracteantha viscosa	Mid December	*
Brunonia australis	Late Dec–mid Jan	**
Calocephalus spp.	Feb–early March	**
Calotis spp.	Dec–Jan	**
Chrysocephalum apiculatum	Late Dec–early Jan	**
Chrysocephalum semipapposum	Jan	**
Convolulus erubescens	February	*
Craspedia variabilis	January	**
Eryngium ovinum	February	**
Goodenia pinnatifida	Dec–Feb	*
Helichrysum rutidolepis	Dec–Jan	**
Helichrysum scorpioides	Dec–Jan	**
Leptorhynchos squamatus	December	*
Nicotiana spp.	December	*
Pimelea spp.	Late Nov–Feb	*
Podolepis jaceoides	Mid Dec–mid Jan	**
Ptilotus spp.	January	**
Pycnosorus spp.	January	**
Rutidosis leptorrhynchoides	Dec–Jan	*
Rumex spp.	December	*
Senecio spp.	Late Nov–Jan	*
Velleia paradoxa	Mid Dec–early Jan	*
Vittadinia spp.	Nov–early Jan	*
Wahlenbergia communis	Jan	**
Wahlenbergia stricta	Late Dec–Jan	**

Bulbs and Tuberous Species

Arthropodium spp.	Dec–Jan	**
Arthropodium minus	Mid–Late Dec	**
Bulbine bulbosa	Late Nov–early Dec	*
Burchardia umbellata	Dec–early Jan	*
Caesia spp.	Late Dec–early Jan	**
Stylidium graminifolium	Mid–late Dec	*
Tricoryne elatior	Jan–Feb	*

Chapter 8. Propagation of Indigenous Plants of Melbourne

Rodger Elliot*

With the increasing interest in the value and importance of conserving and growing Melbourne's local plants there is also a coinciding interest in the propagation of these species.

A number of nurseries in the Melbourne region now specialise in propagating indigenous flora and they make many species available which were previously difficult to obtain. However there is a great feeling of achievement when propagating your own plants successfully. There is also the added pleasure of being able to give away any of your excess plants to friends, neighbours or local schools.

Some people may be reluctant to propagate their local plants because they believe it may be too difficult to achieve success. There is however very little difference in propagating our local plants as compared to plants from anywhere else. Generally the propagation principles are the same, with any differences in technique being only slight and of minor concern. The base line with plants, wherever they originate from, is that some are easy to propagate and others difficult and very frustrating, which hopefully adds up to interesting times if you are involved in propagation.

The information on propagation supplied here is purely an introductory exercise and there may be times when the reader will hunger for more detail. There are many excellent publications which can provide information at a greater depth. See Further Reading at the end of this chapter.

Equipment for Propagation

Before undertaking sowing of seed, preparation of cuttings or other propagation methods, thought must be given as to the type of equipment required for success. This equipment can vary from being very simple to highly sophisticated, but most species can be propagated with the simplest of equipment, provided certain conditions are maintained, and these are discussed in more detail below.

Containers

Any containers used must be able to hold the propagation medium and at the same time provide excellent drainage. Suitable new or used containers can be from a wide range of materials. Used containers should be thoroughly washed and sterilised prior to use. Many containers are made specifically for plant cultivation, but there are also other items that can be used such as plastic margarine or ice cream containers, if efficient drainage holes are provided.

Propagating Structures

The next requirement is for some form of structure in which to carry out the propagation. Germination of seed can be done in the open if desired, but problems can be experienced in the form of animals, children, or heavy rain or hail and your efforts, as well as perhaps valuable seed, may be wasted.

For seedlings, one of the simplest structures is a box covered with plastic sheeting, into which seed trays or pots are placed. This can also be used for cuttings. A simple structure is also provided by polystyrene boxes which are commonly used for packaging fruit. Two wire hoops placed at each end and covered by a sheet of plastic make the unit complete.

Possibly the simplest method for propagating cuttings is to place a plastic bag or upturned bottle over a pot of cuttings. It is important however that these items, and also the fruit-box structure, should not be exposed to direct sunshine as young seedlings or cuttings may be scorched.

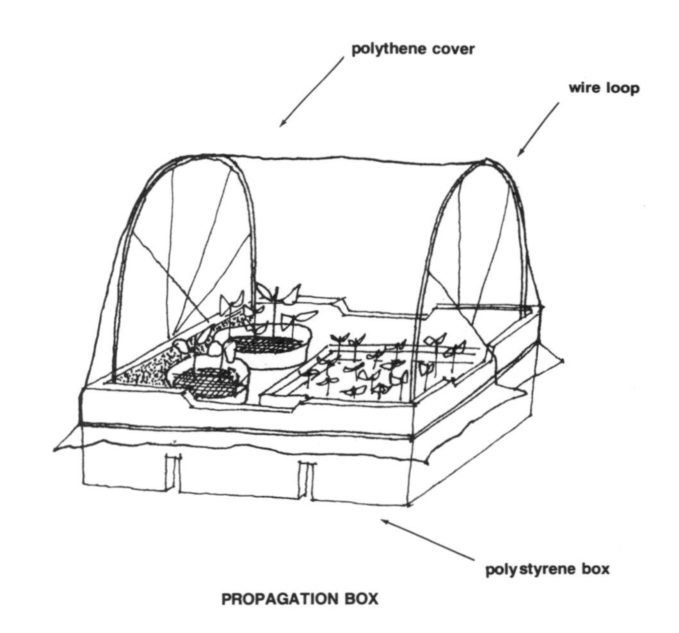

PROPAGATION BOX

A common propagating structure is the cold frame, and it is suitable for most propagation requirements. Cold frames can be easily constructed in wood or brick with a hinged upper frame covered by glass or plastic sheeting.

From cold frames the next stage is to plastic or glass houses. These should be sited in sunny areas. They will need shading during late spring to early summer. This can be done by painting with white glasshouse paint, or by covering with shadecloth. Undoubtedly these larger structures do

* Rodger Elliot is a professional horticulturist operating a wholesale nursery for Australian plants. He regularly writes articles for magazines and journals and is the author of many books on native plants and co-author of the *Encyclopaedia of Australian Plants*.

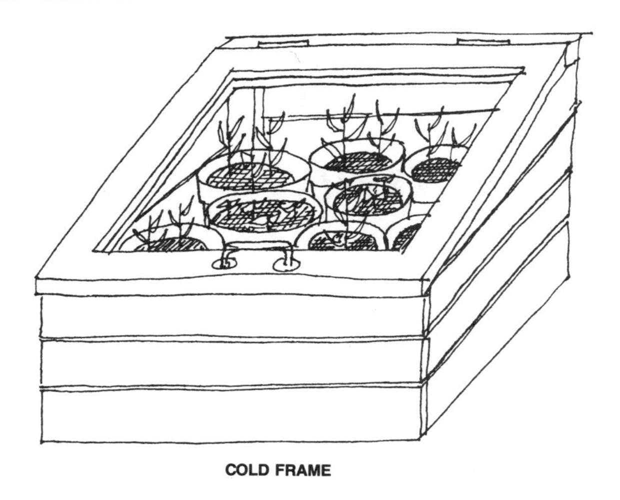

COLD FRAME

have advantages over smaller ones. You can work undercover on inclement days, and they generally will hold a greater number of seedling trays and pots, thus allowing for the production of more plants.

In propagation from cuttings often there are specific conditions required for success. Different methods and equipment can be employed to achieve those desired.

Warmth is an important aspect. If a cold frame or glasshouse is positioned well the warmth available from the sun can be all that is necessary for successful propagation. Electrically heated propagating units, as well as heating mats, are now readily available if you wish to build them into a new structure, or incorporate them into an existing one.

It is worth repeating here that in most cases you do not need sophisticated equipment to propagate plants. Plants have been propagated for thousands of years now, and in some cases equal success was achieved with early methods in comparison with today's modern technology, (eg. the propagation of grapes in the 16th century). It is therefore suggested that if you are just starting in propagation, begin with simple equipment. Then later on you can change or upgrade to different units or incorporate heating etc., if you feel the need to do so.

Propagation Hygiene and Materials

Hygiene

This is one of the most important aspects of propagation. It can mean the difference between success or failure. It is wise to make sure all containers have been treated in some way to eliminate all diseases or pests, especially if the containers have been used before. This can be achieved by soaking the containers in a germicide (as directed on the label), or bleach at the ratio of 1 part bleach to 19 parts water. They should then be thoroughly aired so there are no fumes left that may damage plant material. All tools, especially secateurs, should be regularly cleaned using a similar solution.

Regular treatment of propagation structures is beneficial, as there may often be a build-up of fungi and moulds. Initially they may not have much effect on cuttings and young plants, but in some cases there is a breaking point when there is an extremely quick expansion of a disease which can attack cuttings or seedlings within the structure, if not noticed and treated immediately. It is recommended that every 9–12 months structures be thoroughly washed with a germicide, then left for a day or so to enable complete airing before again filling them with propagation material.

It is also ideal that all media used for propagation, especially if it contains sand or soil, be treated to eliminate any diseases. A simple method which helps but does not entirely eliminate diseases, is to pour boiling water over the propagating mix. This has the disadvantage of making the mix very wet, and it therefore must be dried a little before use. For small quantities, moist media can be placed in a sealed plastic bag and located in a sunny site. It should be left there for 3–5 sunny days, with the bag being turned over each day.

Another method suitable for small quantities is to place the propagation mix in an oven at 95°C for 30 minutes. It is best if the mixture has been kept moist for 3 days prior to this treatment. Selected chemicals can be used but this is a somewhat more complex treatment, and the propagation mixture must be allowed to stand for some time before use, for if any trace of the chemical remains it could prove toxic to the cuttings or seedlings. Small steam sterilising units suitable for home propagators are also available.

Propagation materials

There are many different views on which are the best materials for use in propagation. Today a wide range of materials are used with success. With propagation it is necessary to find the mixture that best suits your needs and your own situation. If you have success with a mixture there is certainly no need to change it because it differs from that used by anyone else.

Some components that are frequently used in propagation mixes are sand, peat moss, perlite, vermiculite, pinebark, sawdust and topsoil. These materials need to be mixed in different proportions, depending on the aspect of propagation for which they are to be used and the conditions under which propagation is to take place.

Seed Raising Media

For raising seedlings there is quite a wide range of mixtures that can be used. The main pre-requisites for a sowing mixture are that it must be very well drained and at the same time it must be well aerated, i.e. it must not pack too tightly and become waterlogged. Propagation sand or coarse river sand with peat moss, pine peat and good quality topsoil can be used in varying quantities to achieve suitable germination results.

Perlite is also used and the following formula has proved successful—1 part peatmoss, 1 part perlite plus 1 part good quality sterilised loam.

Cutting Media

For cuttings the most commonly used materials are sharp, coarse river sand and peatmoss. A widely accepted mixture is 3 parts of sand to 1 part of peatmoss. This is suitable for the majority of Australian plants. If for some reason you do not have success with this mixture, then try some variations such as a 50/50 mix. Even 100% coarse sand is worth a try, and some native plant propagators find this quite adequate. Another suitable mixture is 50% peatmoss and 50% perlite. Some growers use 1 part of peatmoss to 2 parts of perlite. Both of these ingredients are sterile, so there is no need for sterilising treatment before use.

Propagation from Seed

For information on the collection of seed, separation, cleaning and storage, see Chapter 7 on Seed Collection.

Seed of some species can be sown immediately after it has been separated from the capsules, follicles or other fruits, eg. *Callistemon*, *Eucalyptus*, *Melaleuca* and *Stylidium*. However there are some species which need pre-sowing treatment that may help to promote seed germination. There is a range of pre-sowing treatments which can be used.

1. Treatment of seed with hard outer coatings.
Seeds of this type can remain viable in the wild for many years. Pre-sowing treatment is desirable to allow water to penetrate to the embryo and hasten germination. The main group of plants which respond to this treatment are the legumes, eg. *Acacia* species and all the pea plants. Some of

the hard-seeded lilies also respond well. Various methods can be employed.

(a) Pour freshly boiled water onto the seed in a container and allow them to soak for 1–24 hours. Fertile seeds will swell. This is the simplest and most commonly used method. Do not boil the seeds in water as this usually damages the embryo.

freshly boiled water poured onto seeds

(b) Scarify the seeds by rubbing them between sandpaper or wet-and-dry paper.

(c) Nick the seed coat with a sharp implement (nail-clippers are ideal). This method is best used for large seeds, otherwise damage to the embryo can occur.

2. Stratification.
Seeds are subjected to periods of low temperatures, 0°C to −4°C for varying periods, eg. 3–10 weeks. This must be done in advance, to allow for the proposed sowing date. Some genera which are known to respond well to this treatment include *Billardiera*, *Eucalyptus* and *Wahlenbergia*.

3. Dormancy-breaking.
Many species will not germinate from freshly collected seed because of a dormancy period before maturity. Much better results are attained if the seed is sown 8–12 months after collection. Many of the native grasses are in this group, eg. *Themeda triandra*, Kangaroo grass. Seed needs to be stored in airtight containers at between 3°C and 15°C. It is thought that seed of *Billardiera*, *Patersonia*, some *Acacia* and *Kennedia* species also have dormancy periods.

4. Leaching.
Some species contain inhibitors and on occasions these can be leached from the seeds. The simplest method is to soak the seed in containers of cold water for extended periods. Another is to put the seeds in a permeable container (nylon stockings or pantyhose are useful) and place it in flowing water. Some success has been achieved by immersing such a container in a toilet cistern. *Billardiera* may respond well to this treatment.

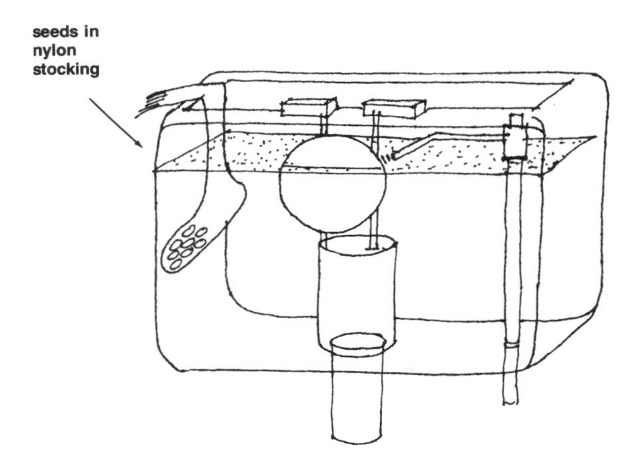
seeds in nylon stocking

5. Fermentation.
Some fleshy fruits can be placed in a plastic bag and stored in a warm humid site, allowing the fruits to ferment. *Astroloma*, *Billardiera* and *Dianella* may respond favourably to this treatment.

There is still a need for much experimentation with pre-sowing treatments, and the results need to be recorded and published as they would have value for future work.

Sowing of Seed

Containers for seed propagation should be from 4–8 cm deep. The propagation medium is filled to within about 1cm of the top. It should only be gently firmed. Compacting the medium too firmly can inhibit root growth of seedlings.

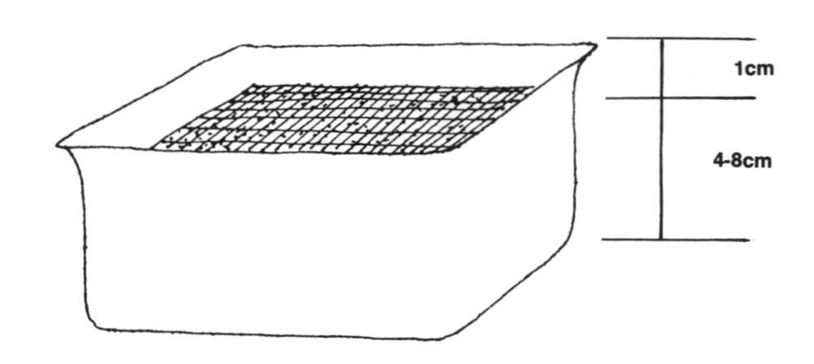

Perhaps the main rule with sowing is not to spread seed too thickly over the propagating medium. This may initially provide a lot of plants, but in most cases the end result is poor quality seedlings because of the intense competition. Many of the seedlings may die due to disease, which can spread readily among overcrowded seedlings.

Very fine seed can be difficult to spread lightly and evenly. By placing the seed and dry fine sand in a salt or pepper shaker and then dispersing the mixture over the propagation medium there is less likelihood of seedling overcrowding.

A general practice that works well is to cover the seed with propagating mixture to a depth equal to the size of the seeds. Therefore with fine seed it is only necessary for it to be barely covered. If the bog or capillary methods (see below) are used the seed does not always need to be covered.

When sowing seed, always make sure that the containers are properly labelled with the plant name and date of sowing.

The first watering must be sufficient to thoroughly soak the medium, but without dispersing the seed. A fine spray nozzle on the hose or watering can is therefore recommended. Alternatively the container should be placed in another container of water and allowed to soak. See Alternative Watering Methods, below. A fungicide can be added to the water if desired, as this can help to combat disease.

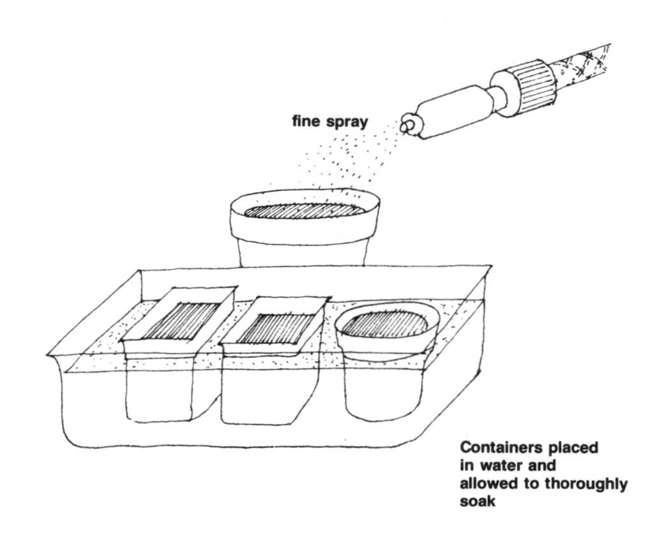

Containers placed in water and allowed to thoroughly soak

Seedling containers should be placed in a well ventilated area and generally kept moist but not wet. Germination time varies considerably from species to species. Acacias and pea plants (after treatment) are often quickest to germinate, while others such as *Epacris* spp. can take much longer. If you have any precious seeds that have not germinated, don't throw them out too soon. If the seeds don't germinate within a season put the containers aside under a tree or in a similar situation. You may be surprised to find them full of seedlings at a later date.

Some species will often not germinate until there is a continuous spell of cool weather, with plenty of rain, eg. *Billardiera* species. Seed sown in early spring may not germinate until after autumn rains.

Alternative Watering Methods

Bog Method.
With many species of the Myrtle family, eg. *Callistemon*, *Kunzea*, *Leptospermum* and *Melaleuca* this method is very successful, and it is worth trying, especially with those which occur naturally in waterlogged soils or are subject to inundation for short periods. This includes aquatic species such as *Myriophyllum*.

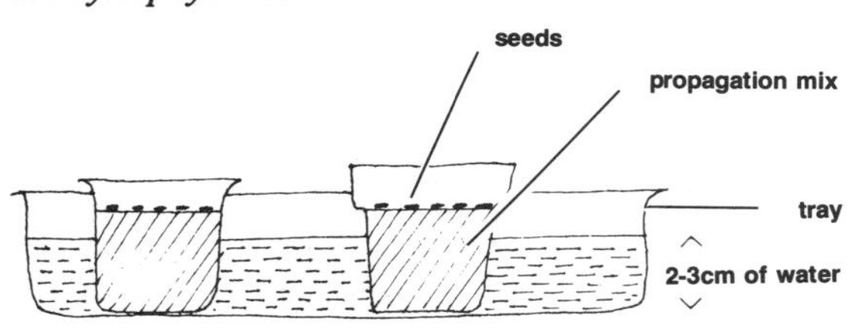

It is a simple and time-saving method. The seed should be sown in the normal manner, but it is not always necessary for it to be covered with propagating mix. The seedling container is then placed in another container that has a water level of about 2–3 cm deep. The seed is then kept continually moist by capillary action and therefore there is no need for overhead watering which can disperse fine seed and possibly damage or kill very young seedlings. It is an excellent method for keeping the seedling mix moist if you are likely to be away for a few days.

As the seed germinates and the seedlings develop they should be watched carefully. When the seedlings are about 0.5–1 cm tall the container should be removed from the water so that the seedlings do not suffer from waterlogging which can kill some of the young roots and eventually the plants.

Capillary method.
This is an adaptation of the Bog Method. It differs in having sand in a container with a bottle feed to keep the moisture at a constant level. The container with seeds is partially buried in the moist sand. It is ideal for people who may be away for periods of longer than 2–3 days.

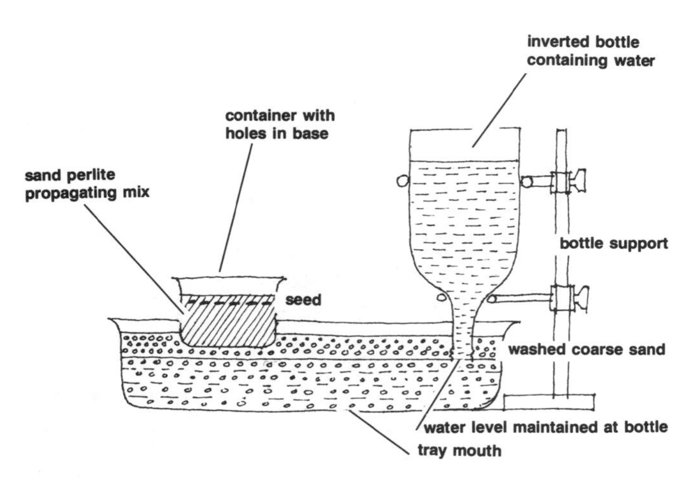

Post-germination Treatment

As seeds germinate it is best in most cases to pot them on into individual containers, as soon as they can be handled easily. This is likely to prevent poor development of roots if seedlings are retained in smaller containers, with stronger and more healthy roots being the end product. Forestry tubes or similar sized pots, into which the seedlings can be transplanted, are ideal.

If you find the roots of the seedlings are very long, do not be afraid to prune them. Many people still believe that the roots of Australian plants should not be cut or otherwise interfered with, however experience and research have found this not to be the case when handling young seedlings. They respond well to this procedure. It prevents the roots being squeezed into a small area where they can become bent or disfigured, which can often mean that they do not develop properly and are unable when planted out to support the trunk and foliage.

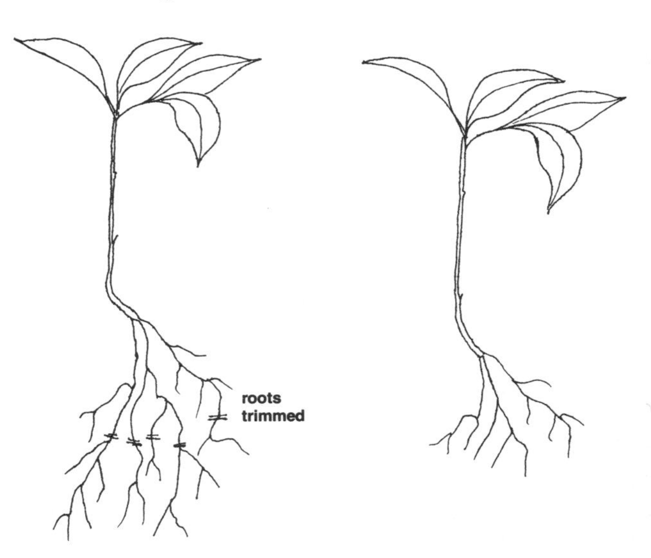

After transplanting seedlings into individual pots they should be well watered and placed in a protected shady spot for 4–7 days, to allow them to recuperate from their previous treatment. The addition of one of the commercially available plant starters and root stimulants, at the watering stage, can be beneficial.

Propagation from Cuttings

Plants are grown from cuttings for a number of reasons including the following.

(a) There is often difficulty in obtaining seed of many species.
(b) The same forms or varieties can be perpetuated, which is not always the case in seedling grown plants.
(c) Some plants are much easier to grow from cuttings than from seed, eg. species of *Correa*, *Epacris* and *Goodenia*.

Some people are often reluctant to try growing plants from cuttings, with the idea that it is too difficult. There are many of the indigenous plants of Melbourne that are extremely easy to propagate by this method, including *Brachyscome multifida*, *Goodenia lanata*, *Mentha australis* and *Myoporum parvifolium*.

To achieve success with cuttings there are some important guidelines which should be followed, however experience is usually the best teacher, so if at first you don't succeed, have a chat with someone about what might have gone wrong, then try again.

Collection of Cutting Material

One of the most important steps to success is to start with healthy material in good condition. The question is often asked as to when is the best time to take cuttings of Australian plants, and the answer is the nebulous 'when the material is in the optimum state for propagation'. This is usually after flowering has finished and there is new foliage growth which has begun to 'harden off' beyond the soft and floppy stage.

Cuttings can therefore be taken at varying times, depending on the plant species. Best results are usually gained between October and March, when there is warm weather and therefore more favourable propagating conditions. Artificial heating of propagation units can extend the propagation season. See below for further information on this aspect.

There are some special points worth noting while collecting material.

(1) Cutting material is best collected in the cooler times of the day, such as early morning, before the sun has been on the foliage, or in early evening, when the foliage is again cool. On collection the foliage can be cooled further by spraying with water.

(2) Cuttings are best collected from young plants, as research has shown that this type of material is usually capable of producing roots much more quickly than that from older plants.

(3) Always use disease-free material. Collect cuttings from branches that do not touch the ground, and if possible choose those that do not have black spots or markings or have not been splashed with earth and water during heavy rains. This will mean there is less likelihood of any earth-borne fungi being on the plant material.

(4) Collect material that is not too soft or too rigid, unless nothing else is available. Cuttings should have a springiness, and a useful guide is to bend the tips back until they touch the stem, then let go. If they return fairly quickly to the original position then it is likely to be good material for cuttings.

(5) At all times cutting material should be kept slightly moist, to retain it in good condition.

(6) If cuttings need to be transported for half an hour to over a period of some days, small quantities can be wrapped in newspaper and placed in an insulated cooler. Alternatively large quantities can be placed in a moistened woven polypropylene bag (often recycled fertilizers or stock food bags), which usually prevents the cuttings from sweating, as is prone to happen in clear polythene bags. Plastic garbage bags are not recommended, as they can release ethylene gas, which is detrimental to retaining cuttings in good condition.

Preparation of Cuttings

There are a number of different methods in preparing cuttings for propagation. Stem cuttings are by far the most commonly used. Single node cuttings or single bud cuttings can also be successful but are beyond the scope of this chapter. See Further Reading for specialised publications which cover these subjects in detail.

Preparation of Stem Cuttings

Most cuttings should be around 7–15 cm long, although there is no strict rule. Some plants, eg. *Astroloma humifusum* may not produce much material that is suitable for cuttings of this size. Therefore smaller cuttings must be used. If tip growth is too soft it will be likely to wilt and therefore should be removed by cutting or pinching just above a node. In some species the removal of the growing shoot may spoil the future shape of the plant, in which case it is best to use material with firm tip growth.

The lower cut should be just below a node, as this is the point from which roots will usually be produced. There are exceptions to most rules, and with species such as *Hardenbergia violacea* and *Pandorea pandorana* the lower cut can be done at the internode—the region of stem between the leaf nodes. Roots will develop from that cut area. It is worth experimenting with other species in the same manner.

The next step is to remove the leaves from the lower half of the cutting. In many cases they can be taken off with a quick downwards movement of the fingers, eg. *Brachyscome multifida*, *Epacris impressa* and *Myoporum parvifolium*, but once again experience will show which plants cannot be treated in this way. Some will be very prone to ripping of the outer layer of the cutting, which may cause the cutting to die. If ripping occurs, try pulling off the leaves with an upwards motion, or removal of the leaves by secateurs may be necessary.

In some plants such as those with broad-leaves, slight wounding of the base of the cutting will help to promote root growth. This can usually be done by allowing the lowest leaves to be pulled downwards, or the wound can be made with a sharp blade.

With large-leaved species it is usually desirable for the leaves to be removed with secateurs. It is the practice of some propagators to reduce the size of the remaining leaves on the cuttings. This reduces the need for the cutting to provide moisture to sustain large amounts of foliage, however in some cases cutting can also cause dieback to occur, which may spread rapidly to other parts of the cutting. **It is most important to use clean secateurs for this process, as it is in all aspects of propagation.**

If large leaves are allowed to remain on cuttings, they can prevent water from reaching the propagating medium, and extra care should be taken to prevent it from drying out.

The next step is to place the cuttings in the selected propagation medium.

The application of a hormone root stimulant can be beneficial in producing more roots of better quality, but it is not imperative that it should be used. Hormone powders or liquids for plant propagation are readily available from nurseries and garden stores.

Management of Cuttings

From this stage there are very specific aspects which, if handled in the right manner, should produce good results. There are four major requirements for cuttings to be maintained in a living state to eventually produce roots. They are: (i) Air, (ii) Light, (iii) Water and (iv) Heat.

If these can be maintained in the right balance all the time the results will usually be excellent. There are however so many variations that can alter the environment very quickly, thus reducing the success rate for which we may hope.

1. Air.

A well-aerated propagation medium is important, as it allows for the provision of oxygen around the base of the cuttings, enabling callus and root production. Air movement within the propagation structure will also impede any fungal build-up on the cuttings.

2. Light.

Light enables the cuttings to carry out normal leaf function, eg. photosynthesis. Excessive light often leads to an increase in temperature and therefore drying out of the atmosphere and leaf surface, which is not beneficial. Lack of adequate light may lead to low temperatures and an excessive build up of moisture which can be detrimental for plant growth.

3. Water.

Water is of utmost importance, as there must be a humid atmosphere to reduce moisture loss from the cuttings and the propagation medium. The medium should be kept moist, but not wet, as waterlogging will reduce the access of air to the base of the cuttings. A humid atmosphere will reduce the leaf temperature, which ideally should be below that of the root area. Regular spraying of the leaf surfaces is usually beneficial in maintaining the conditions mentioned above. This action can be maintained by installing an automatic misting system, but this is not necessary for success.

4. Temperature.

Temperature plays an important role in the production of roots. The optimum temperature for most cuttings is in the range of 20–27°C during the daytime, and about 15°C at night. Best results are usually obtained if the top of the cutting is 5–10°C below the temperature at the base. This means that root production is not impeded by effort put into leaf-bud growth. The use of bottom heat equipment can help greatly in maintaining a suitable temperature. There should be careful control of ventilation in the propagation area, and there is usually the need for some form of shading to restrict temperatures from rising excessively during the summer months.

If you can provide suitable conditions, having regard to the above four requirements, you will be well on the way to success, especially if you have collected good quality cutting material. For further information on these subjects it is worth considering publications which are devoted entirely to propagation, see Further Reading.

Propagation by Division

There are a number of Melbourne's indigenous plants that may be propagated by division. They are mainly monocotyledons that are clumping, tufting, have creeping rhizomes or have the capacity to form roots and self-layer at nodes on the creeping stems.

Plants in these categories include the following.

(a) Lilies and irises—such as *Dianella*, *Diplarrena*, *Libertia*, *Patersonia* and *Thelionema*.
(b) Grasses such as *Agrostis*, *Danthonia*, *Poa*, *Stipa* and *Themeda*.
(c) Rushes and sedges, such as *Carex*, *Isolepis*, *Juncus*, *Schoenus* and *Xyris*.

Although the majority of ferns are propagated from spore, a number of ferns and their allies can be grown from divisions, including some species in the genera of *Calochlaena*, *Doodia*, *Gleichenia*, *Pteris*, *Rumohra*, *Selaginella* and *Sticheris*.

There are quite a number of dicotyledons which are herbaceous perennials, and these are readily propagated by division. The following genera include species which respond well to this form of propagation: *Calotis*, *Goodenia*, *Helichrysum*, *Hydrocotyle*, *Myriophyllum*, *Pratia*, *Samolus*, *Selliera*, *Viola* and *Wahlenbergia*.

Division is a very simple method that does not need great expertise or many special tools. There are however some points which can have a significant effect on the success of plant divisions.

(1) Prevent any unnecessary damage to plant tissue.
(2) Each division must have ample healthy young roots to be able to provide food for the foliage. There should be a balance between the root system and the upper growth.
(3) Divisions must retain buds and growing points.
(4) Hygiene is very important.

As, in most cases, plants being divided have been growing in soil, either in a garden or a container, there could be diseases present that would spread readily in this propagation method. A recommended procedure is to thoroughly drench the soil area in and around the plant, 10–14 days before division, using a fungal drench and root stimulant.

The best time to divide plants is when new roots are beginning to be formed. This is usually after a growth flush. In Melbourne and its environs the period between the end of June and the middle of September has been found to be suitable. If division is done in late autumn there can be difficulty in establishing the divisions, unless they can be placed in a warm sheltered propagating structure, such as a cold frame, a glasshouse or polyhouse.

While dividing plants, always keep foliage and roots moist. Division should be carried out in a location sheltered from sun and winds which will dry the divisions.

After the plant has been removed from the ground or a container, loosen soil around the roots. If difficulty is experienced, place the plant and soil in water, agitating it as you remove the soil with the fingers. The use of water from a hose can also help to dislodge soil which is firmly attached. This also eliminates excessive damage to the root system. Some clumps can be separated with the hands, others may need to be cut with a clean sharp knife or secateurs.

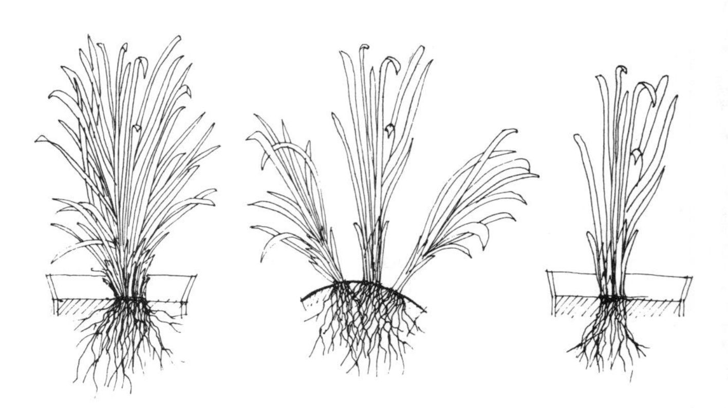

For best results it is recommended that there be 3–5 growth points per division. Very small divisions initially produce more plants, but the success rate is often greatly reduced.

Any dead growth, on foliage or roots, should be removed. After balancing the amount of foliage as compared with the root system, the division is then ready for potting into containers.

Propagation of Ferns

Ferns are usually propagated from spore, but some may be done by division, see above.

Propagation from spore is a somewhat specialised process, and is dealt with here in simple terms. If further information is desired, it can be gained from specialist fern publications and societies.

Ferns differ from the majority of other plants in producing spore rather than seeds. If propagation conditions are right these will develop on the propagation medium surface as small heart-shaped prothalli, with separate male and female organs. Sperm travels from the male to the female section to achieve fertilisation and the development of a sporeling begins.

Collection of Spore

Spore develops on the underside of typical fern fronds or there may be special fertile fronds which are often narrower than the typical fronds.

It is best to collect mature fronds and place them in folded paper, a paper bag or envelope and store the package in a warm dry place. Never use plastic bags, as moulds can develop and ruin the spore.

The very fine, dust-like spore is shed after a few days and should be sown as soon as possible.

Sowing of Spore

A precis of the steps for the sowing of spore.

(1) Fill the lower third of a sterile pot with coarse propagating sand.

(2) Add sowing medium, firmly packed to within about 3 cm of container rim. A mixture of thoroughly wetted peat moss and finely chopped tree fern fibre is a recommended medium for raising the spore.

(3) Pour boiling water quickly into the pot until all the medium is covered, or place the pot in a pre-heated oven 93–95°C, for 30–45 minutes.

(4) When pot and mixture have drained and cooled to be barely warm, spread the spore thinly over the surface using a spoon or a knife.

(5) Moisten the spore layer with an atomiser water spray.

(6) Cover the pot with a sheet of glass or polythene.

(7) Place the pot into another container. Add clean water to about one third of the pot's depth, (similar to the bog method of seed germination. Maintain the water level until true fronds appear.

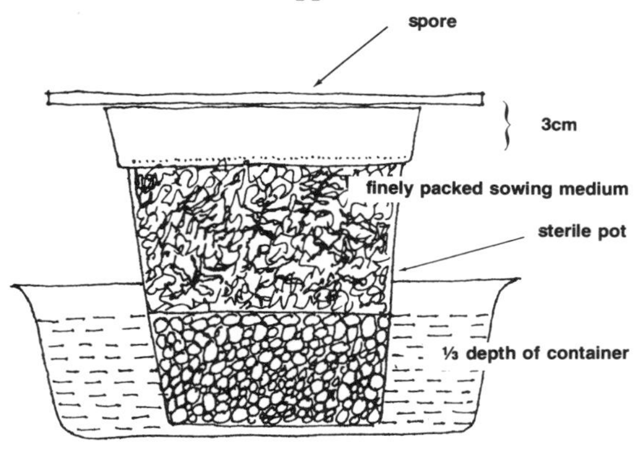

(8) Envelop the pot with a sheet of newspaper for 2–3 weeks.

(9) Leave the pot and container in a sheltered location.

(10) When sporelings develop, harden them off by removing glass or polythene.

(11) Prick out sporelings as small clusters. When further developed they can be separated into individual plants and re-potted.

(12) Ensure that young plants are given protection from sun and winds until they become established.

Propagation of Orchids

Removal of orchids from the wild is illegal, (unless permission is granted by appropriate Government authorities), and not in the interests of conservation of our native bushland, unless some special development within an area means the plants would be destroyed anyway.

The propagation of orchids is a specialised operation. Many orchids have a symbiotic relationship with bacteria, and unless such a relationship can be maintained the orchids will die.

Orchid propagation is not covered in this chapter, but there is an excellent book on their propagation and cultivation, published by the Australasian Native Orchid Society, recommended for those with an interest in this topic. See Further Reading below. The Society also offers excellent service for members, and details of membership will be found in Appendix 3.

Further Reading

Elliot, G. M. (1981) *Fun with Australian Plants.* Hyland House, Melbourne.

Elliot, G. M. (1985) *The Gardener's Guide to Australian Plants.* Hyland House, Melbourne.

Elliot, W.R. and Jones, D.L. (1980) *Encyclopaedia of Australian Plants Suitable for Cultivation, Vols 1–5.* Lothian, Melbourne.

Gardiner, A. (1988) *Modern Plant Propagation.* Lothian, Melbourne.

Handreck, K. & Black, N. (1984) *Growing Media for Ornamental Plants & Turf.* NSW University Press, Kensington NSW.

Hartman, H.T. & Kester, D.E. (1975) *Plant Propagation Principles and Practices.* Prentice Hall, U.S.A.

Jones, D. L. (1987) *Encyclopaedia of Ferns.* Lothian, Melbourne.

Jones, D. L. (1988) *Native Orchids of Australia.* Reed Books, Sydney.

Langkamp, P.J. (Ed.) (1987) *Germination of Australian Native Plant Seed.* Inkata Press, Melbourne.

Macdonald, B. (1986) *Practical Woody Plant Propagation for Nursery Growers.* Timber Press, Oregon U.S.A.

McMillan Browse, P.D.A. (1979) *Hardy, Woody Plants from Seed.* Grower Books, London, U.K.

Plumridge, J. (1977) *How to Propagate Plants.* Lothian, Melbourne.

Richards, H., Wootton, R. & Datodi, R. (1984) *Cultivation of Australian Native Orchids.* Australian Native Orchid Society (Vic. Group) Melbourne.

Wrigley, J. & Fagg, M. (1988) *Australian Native Plants* 3rd Ed. Collins, Sydney.

Part Two

Plant Descriptions

Prostanthera lasianthos var. *lasianthos*

SCALE: 0 1cm 2cm The scale representation on each plant equals 2cm.

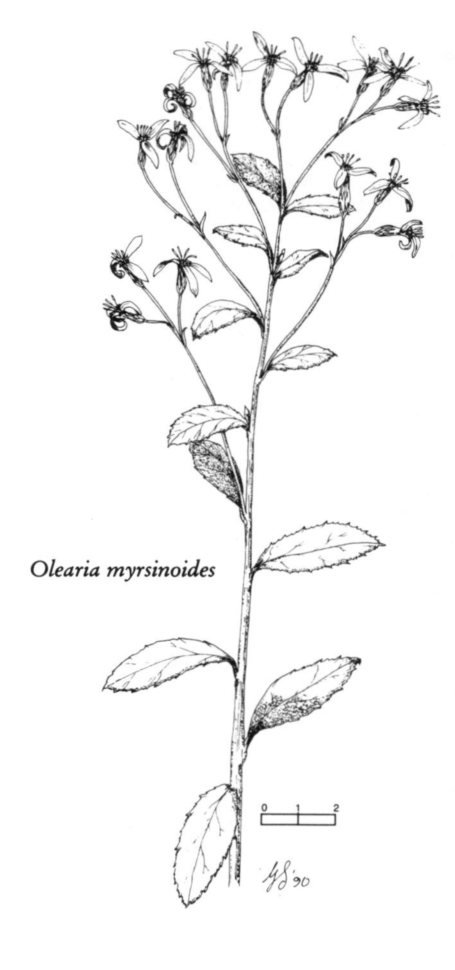

Olearia myrsinoides

Explanation of the Plant Descriptions

Botanical Nomenclature follows '*A Census of the Vascular Plants of Victoria*', 4th Edition, J.H. Ross (January 1993).

The *Flora of Melbourne* has been listed **alphabetically** in groups according to easily recognisable flowering and non-flowering characteristics.

A total of 1152 plants indigenous to Melbourne have been described. This represents a little over ⅓ of the Victorian indigenous flora. It is estimated that about 70 species are now extinct within Melbourne, with many more known from very few plants.

No attempt has been made to describe introduced (Australian or exotic) species although botanists are still undecided about the origins of a few species included here.

Synonyms have been used to explain recent name changes. Botanical revision is an on-going process and many new names are found within the text. Names that have been incorrectly applied to species are also listed under the term 'synonym'.

Where several species of a genus occur in the Melbourne area, a general introduction to that genus has often been used. Features common to all the indigenous Melbourne species are discussed as well as specific generic characteristics and pertinent horticultural notes.

Botanical terms have been kept to a minimum throughout the text. An illustrated **glossary** explains all terms used.

The description of each plant refers as much as possible to local forms. Plants frequently vary in habit and foliage throughout their range. In some cases more than one form may exist within the Melbourne area. These are detailed where known.

While plants may grow in a large variety of **habitats** throughout Australia, we have chosen to list only the typical sites where one would expect to find a given species in Melbourne. These habitats are explained in Chapter 1.

The Australia-wide and world-wide **distribution** has been included to show the broader perspective of the indigenous plants of Melbourne.

The **size** usually refers to the ultimate height of the tallest part of the plant. Some plants have rosettes or tufts of leaves which are considerably shorter than the flowering stems. The foliage description will indicate the size of these plants when not in flower. Size is always given as height x width.

The size of any plant should only be used as a general guide. Cultivated plants are often larger or denser than those growing in remnant bushland. Other factors affecting ultimate size are amount of available moisture, soil type and habitat. A tree may be quite stunted on the coast where it grows on sandy, well drained soil and contends with salt-laden winds whereas the mountain form would usually be tall and straight.

Many features are common to a great many of the plants. **Foliage** may vary considerably in colour, texture and surface covering. The most common leaf colour is green and this may be assumed unless mentioned otherwise. Reference may be made to the lower surface of the leaf which is paler or brownish in appearance in some species. Leaves are also smooth and glabrous (hairless), and arranged in an alternate pattern unless otherwise stated. Leaf size is length x width.

Flowering times should be used as a guide only and, where possible, relate to Melbourne conditions. Flowering is often variable, and months stated indicate the period during which it is most likely to occur. Some plants also have sporadic flowering at other times of the year. Climatic conditions may influence the timing and duration of flowering. Other influencing factors are altitude and proximity to the sea. Cultivation may also affect length or time of flowering.

The **drainage requirements** of a plant refer to the amount of moisture retained in the soil over a period of time. 'Soil' is a combination of solid particles and open spaces. The solid particles, both organic and inorganic, comprise, in most soils, less than half the total volume of soil. The balance, even in poorly drained soils, is open space, known as 'pore space'. Pore space is the most important factor in determining the drainage qualities and structure of soil. It is filled with water, air and plant roots; the proportion of air:water varies with rainfall.

In well drained soils excess water does not accumulate, but moves readily through the pore spaces, allowing oxygen to become available to the plant roots quickly. Moist, well drained soils never dry out, but after wet periods excess water remains in the soil for only short periods. Moist or swampy soils are often poorly drained remaining wet for most of the year, and may retain free water for some months. Wet, boggy or waterlogged soils are highly water-retentive and remain wet all year, except that in times of drought, they may dry to varying degrees. Soils subject to periodic inundation are generally poorly drained, and free water is held above ground for varying times, particularly during Winter. However these soils may become quite dry during Summer. The section on requirements deals as much with horticultural needs as the conditions in which a plant occurs naturally. Many species will adapt to different conditions while others will succeed only in specific situations.

Propagation methods for each plant are mentioned in the text. Chapter 8 deals with the procedures to be used for each method.

The reader may assume that unless otherwise mentioned all plants are **frost hardy**. Plants which grow in the understorey rarely come into contact with frosts in their natural environment.

Most Australian plants benefit from pruning after flowering. This will produce more vigorous growth or a more desirable shape for a garden specimen.

The **fine-line drawings** of over 950 plants are an added identification guide. We have attempted to illustrate a species from every genus. The scale representation on each illustration is 2 cm. Live specimens have been used for most of the illustrations. Where this was not possible pressed herbarium specimens were referred to. A composite of photographs was used for a few of the rarer orchids.

The **reserves and localities** used represent the range of

habitats found within the Melbourne region, as well as examples from a broad spectrum of suburbs, enabling readers to obtain an idea of the original vegetation of their area. The key on the bookmark may be used as a quick reference, while a more detailed listing may be found in Appendix 2. All reserves and localities are shown on the Map inside the front and back covers. Suburb names have been used when locations have been obtained from herbarium specimens or personal knowledge, and do not coincide with the numbering system. At times a reserve/locality number has been used when a plant is known to come from that general area, even though it may no longer be at that specific site. Species that are known to be extinct within a particular area or reserve are marked #, eg 67#.

In order to protect species which are becoming rare or are endangered, specific locations are not given. This is the case with all orchids, where indiscriminate collection or picking has contributed to the decline in orchid populations.

We have attempted to verify the placement of species on the lists given to us. In some cases, especially with older lists, plants may have been misidentified. In other cases subsequent revision of species has made it difficult to be sure which species or subspecies was originally referred to. The authors would be pleased to receive any information regarding plants inadvertently omitted from or added to this list. Space did not permit the inclusion of every list available for the Melbourne area.

Indigenous plants should never be removed from remnant bushland sites. Seed and cuttings should only be taken with permission of the land owner and, where public land is involved, a permit may be necessary. (See Chapter 7)

Abbreviations

F — Full sun in an open position
P — Partial sun (full sun for only part of the day), filtered sun or dappled shade (with overhead canopy)
N — Full shade

ssp. — subspecies
var. — variety
spp. — more than one species
? — unconfirmed listing
Rges — Ranges
R — River
Pt — Point

Vic — Victoria
NSW — New South Wales
SA — South Australia
NT — Northern Territory
Qld — Queensland
Tas — Tasmania
WA — West Australia

NZ — New Zealand
PNG — Papua/New Guinea
Af — Africa
N Am — North America
S Am — South America
W Ind — West Indies
N Cal — New Caledonia
Mal — Malaysia
Poly — Polynesia
Indon — Indonesia
Eur — Europe

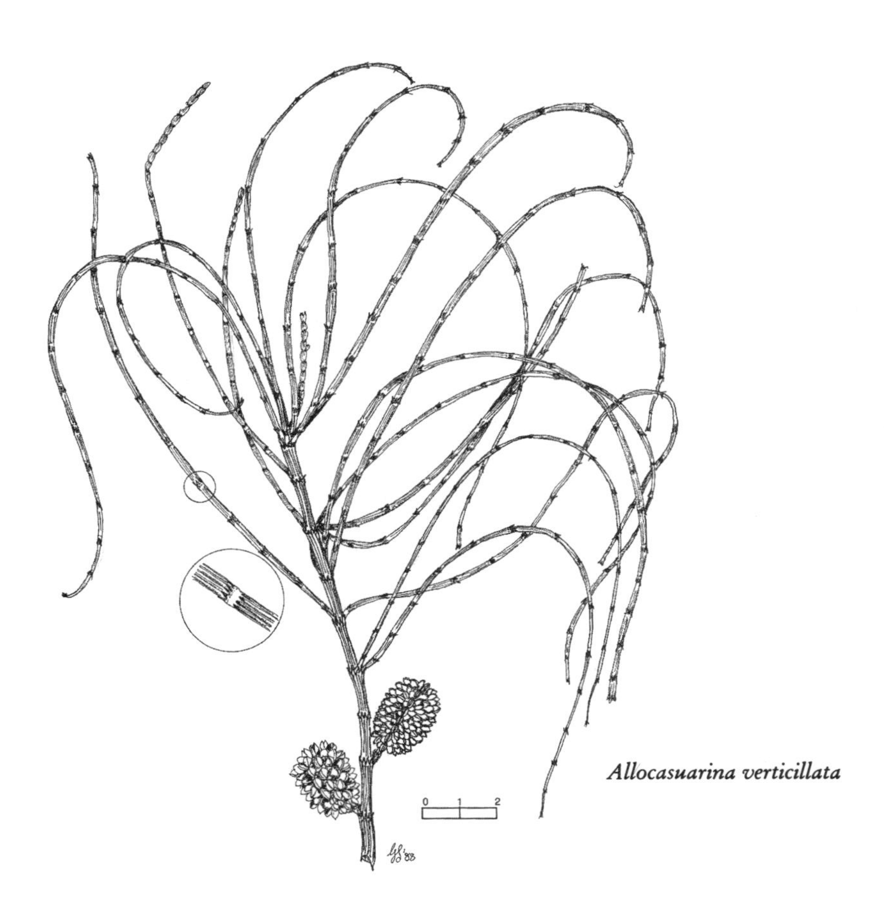

Allocasuarina verticillata

Flowering Plants Dicotyledons

Acacia Mimosaceae

The wattles are a very large genus represented by 23 species within the Melbourne area. They range in height from tall forest trees to prostrate shrubs, occurring in a wide range of habitats. Many are found as understorey shrubs in open forest. Their form and foliage are equally diverse. The true leaves of acacias are divided and fern-like and are most conspicuous when plants are seedlings. Some species retain these divided leaves while others form leaf-like structures called phyllodes. The yellow flowers are tightly clustered into globular flowerheads (or balls) or cylindrically-shaped spikes (or rods). The pods that form after fertilisation contain hard seeds which are an important food source for many birds. Pruning after flowering improves the shape of the shrubs and can extend the life of the plant. The seeds, gum, wood and bark of many species were used extensively by the local Aborigines as sources of food, fibre, medicine, implements and containers. Propagation is generally by seed, treated by immersing in boiling water, then soaking for 24 hours. (See Propagation) Some species can also be propagated by cuttings.

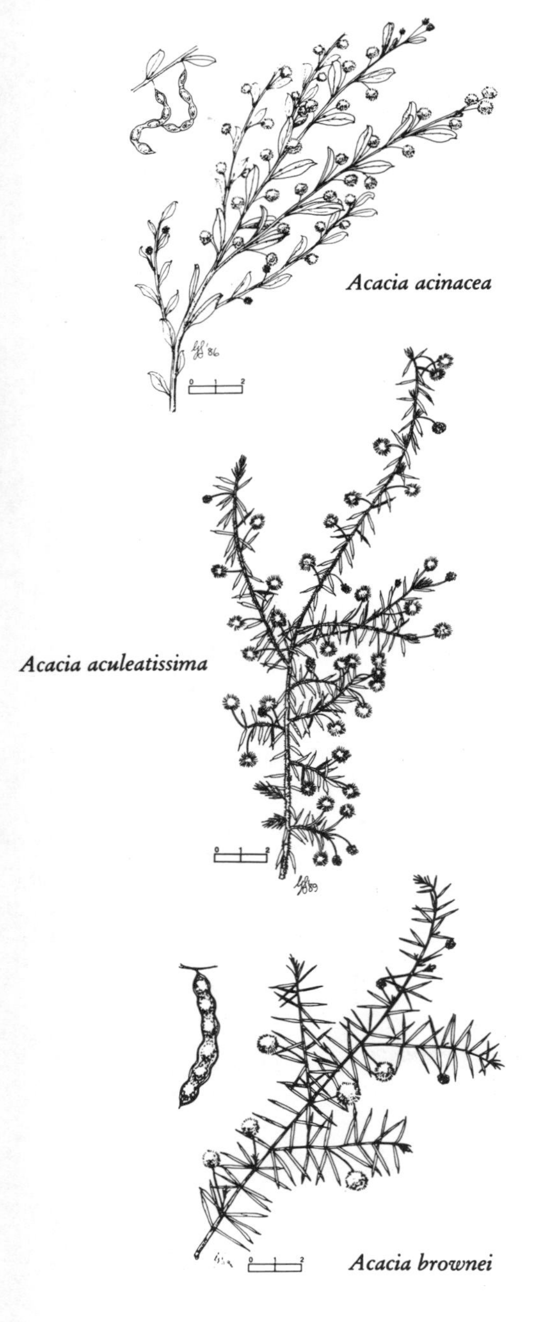

Acacia acinacea

Acacia aculeatissima

Acacia brownei

Acacia acinacea — Gold Dust Wattle

Size: 0.5–2.5 m x 2–4 m **F P**
Habitat: Dry sclerophyll forest, chenopod rocky open scrub, box ironbark, red gum and box woodland
Form: Open spreading shrub, denser in cultivation
Foliage: Small rounded or oblong phyllodes to 10 mm long, sometimes larger
Flowers: In profuse bright yellow balls along arching branches; August to November
Requirements: Adaptable to well drained soils
Comments: A good low screening plant which will often self seed in the garden. Annual pruning is beneficial.
Localities: Melton, 14, 16, 22, 24–26, 29, 31–39, 41, 42, 56, 58
Distribution: Vic, NSW, SA

Acacia aculeatissima — Thin-leaf Wattle, Snake Wattle

Size: 0.2–0.6 m x 1–2 m **P**
Habitat: Dry sclerophyll forest
Form: Light open sprawling shrub
Foliage: Fine prickly phyllodes 10-15 mm long
Flowers: In yellow balls along wiry branches; June to December
Requirements: Well drained clay soils. Withstands extended periods of dryness once established.
Comments: Excellent for rockeries or banks. Withstands light pruning. A natural hybrid between *A. aculeatissima* and *A. verticillata* occurs in Warrandyte. It has grey phyllodes, is more upright in form than *A. aculeatissima*, and the flowerheads are intermediate between the two parents.
Localities: 34, 34A, 40-42, 44, 46–49, 50A, 51, 62–64
Distribution: Vic, NSW

Acacia brownei — Heath Wattle, Golden Prickly Wattle

Size: 0.5–1 m x1–2 m **P**
Habitat: Tea-tree heath, gravelly hillsides of dry sclerophyll forests
Form: Small spreading shrub
Foliage: Stiff narrow prickly phyllodes to 25 mm long
Flowers: In profuse golden yellow balls along arching stems; June to November
Requirements: Light soils tolerating dryness once established
Comments: An excellent garden plant, it differs from *A. ulicifolia* in that its phyllodes are longer and not markedly broader at base and the flowers are deeper yellow. Not common in Melbourne.
Localities: Warrandyte, Springvale, 50A, 51, 53, 59, 71, 74, 75
Distribution: Vic, Qld, NSW
Synonym: *A. ulicifolia var. brownei*

10

11

12

14

13

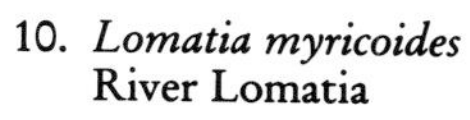

10. *Lomatia myricoides* River Lomatia
11. *Indigofera australis* Austral Indigo
12. Saltmarsh vegetation
13. *Pimelea linifolia* ssp. *linifolia* Slender Rice-flower
14. *Muehlenbeckia florulenta* Tangled Lignum
15. *Lobelia gibbosa* Tall Lobelia
16. *Gahnia filum* Chaffy Saw-sedge
17. *Hardenbergia violacea* Purple Coral Pea
18. *Pittosporum bicolor* Banyalla
19. *Swainsona lessertiifolia* Coast Swainson-pea
20. *Acacia verticillata* Prickly Moses

16

17

15

18

19

20

21

22

23

24

25

26

27

21. *Kennedia prostrata*
Running Postman
22. *Eryngium ovinum*
Blue Devil
23. *Dichanthium sericeum*
Silky Blue-grass
24. *Diuris fragrantissima*
Fragrant Doubletail
25. *Eucalytpus camaldulensis*
River Red Gum
26. *Acacia pycnantha*
Golden Wattle
27. *Stypandra glauca*
Nodding Blue Lily
28. *Ottelia ovalifolia*
Swamp Lily
29. *Leucochrysum albicans*
Hoary Sunray

28

29

Acacia dealbata

Silver Wattle

Size: 6–30 m x 5–10 m **F P**
Habitat: Wet, damp and valley sclerophyll forests, riparian scrub, red gum woodland, grassy low open forest
Form: Fast-growing open tree
Foliage: Bluish-green bipinnate leaves to 130 mm long
Flowers: Flowers in profuse lemon balls arranged in terminal racemes; July to October
Requirements: Easily grown, prefers deep moist soil
Comments: A useful tree for erosion control. An important aboriginal plant, the seeds and gum were eaten and axe handles were made from the wood. The gum was also used as an adhesive or mixed with burnt wattle bark to produce an ointment. Host to the Imperial Blue Butterfly caterpillar when less than 3 m high. Used for perfume manufacture in France where it is called Mimosa.
Localities: 1, 16, 19, 23–29, 32–36, 38, 39, 41, 42, 44, 46–53, 55–59, 61, 62, 64, 71, 75, 76
Distribution: Vic, NSW, Tas

Acacia dealbata

Acacia genistifolia

Acacia gunnii

Acacia genistifolia

Spreading Wattle

Size: 1–3 m x 1–3 m **F P**
Habitat: Dry and valley sclerophyll forests
Form: Fast-growing, open spreading shrub
Foliage: Narrow prickly phyllodes to 30 mm long
Flowers: In perfumed lemon to cream balls. Long flowering; August to October and January to May
Requirements: Reliable shrub tolerating wet or dry soil
Comments: Because of its prickly foliage, this plant is a good refuge for small birds. Often self seeds in the garden.
Localities: Sth Morang, Murrumbeena#, 33, 34A–38, 41, 42, 49, 51, 53, 58, 59, 62, 63, 67#, 74
Distribution: Vic, NSW, Tas
Synonym: *A. diffusa*

Acacia gunnii

Ploughshare Wattle

Size: 0.3–1 m x 1–2 m **F P**
Habitat: Exposed positions in box ironbark woodland, dry sclerophyll forest
Form: Prickly, low open spreading shrub
Foliage: Triangular phyllodes to 15 mm long, tapering to a pungent point
Flowers: In pale yellow balls; June to October
Requirements: Well drained soils tolerating dryness once established
Comments: A useful ground cover for erosion control. Not common in the Melbourne area.
Propagation: Seed, cuttings
Localities: Diamond Ck
Distribution: Vic, Qld, NSW, Tas, SA

Acacia implexa

Lightwood, Hickory Wattle

Size: 5–15 m x 4–7 m **F P**
Habitat: Common in dry or valley sclerophyll forests, red gum, box and riparian woodlands
Form: Fast-growing, upright small tree
Foliage: Sickle-shaped phyllodes to 20 cm x 20 mm
Flowers: In perfumed cream balls arranged in racemes; December to March
Requirements: Adaptable plant tolerating both wet and dry, well drained clay soil
Comments: An attractive, long-lived screen or shade tree, useful for erosion control. Its phyllodes are used for dyeing and the bark for tanning. The fibres produced twine.
Propagation: Seeds, cuttings
Localities: 8, 14, 16, 18, 21, 23–26, 28, 29, 31–39, 42, 44, 47–49, 50A, 51, 53, 58, 60-65, 67, 68, 69A, 71,
Distribution: Vic, Qld, NSW

Acacia implexa

Acacia lanigera

Woolly, or Hairy Wattle

Size: 0.3–2 m x 1–3 m **F P**
Habitat: Dry sclerophyll forest, box ironbark woodland
Form: Small, rigid open shrub
Foliage: Sharp slightly curved grey-green phyllodes to 70 mm long. New growth is covered with whitish hairs.
Flowers: In bright yellow balls; May to October
Requirements: Well drained rocky and clay soils. Tolerates short periods of wetness.
Comments: Useful for planting under established trees and soil binding. Showy in flower.
Propagation: Seed, cuttings
Localities: Research, ?42
Distribution: Vic, NSW

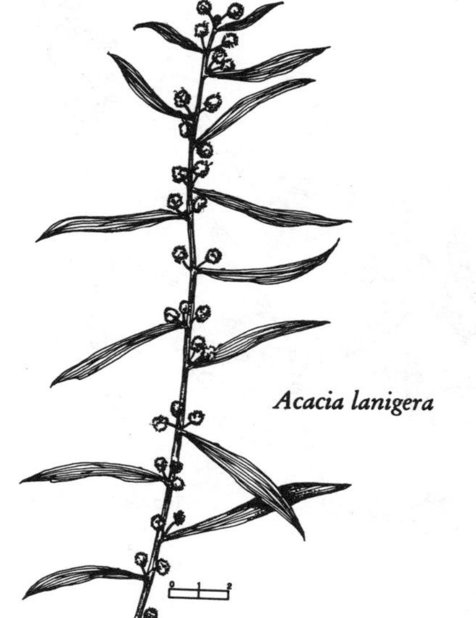

Acacia lanigera

SCALE: 0 1cm 2cm The scale representation on each plant equals 2cm.

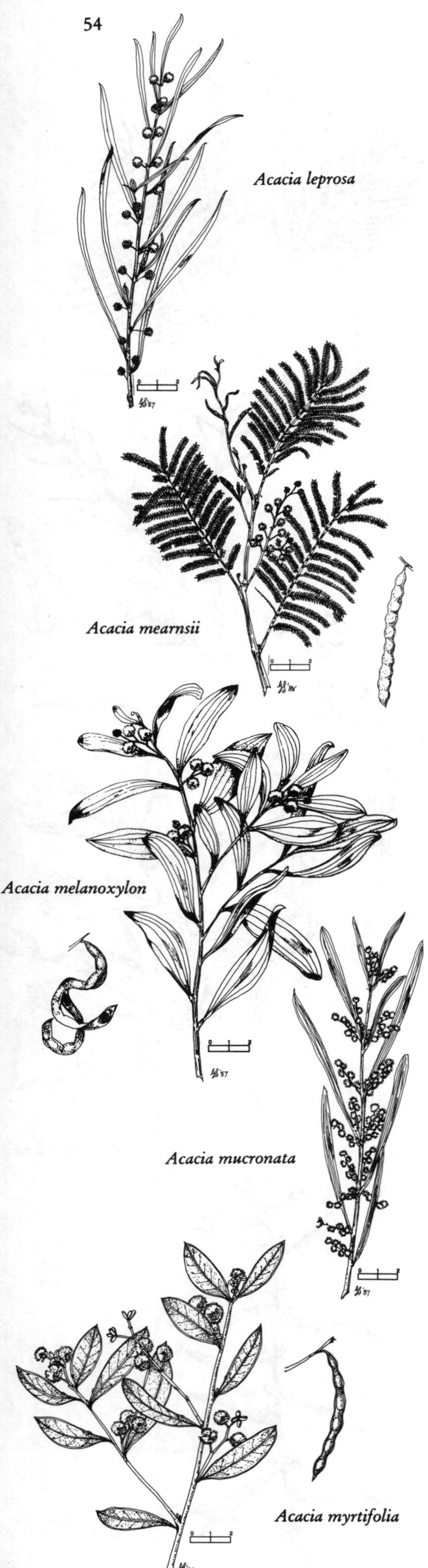

Acacia leprosa

Cinnamon Wattle

Size: 3–12 m x 2–6 m **P N**
Habitat: Damp and valley sclerophyll forests
Form: Fast-growing medium shrub or small tree of dense weeping habit
Foliage: Bright green fragrant and sticky phyllodes, variable in size from 30–150 mm long and up to 25 mm wide
Flowers: In abundant scented lemon to yellow balls; August to December
Requirements: Moist, well drained soils
Comments: This reliable wattle makes an excellent tall screening plant. Weeping forms are attractive planted near water. Foliage has a cinnamon fragrance on humid days or when crushed. *A. leprosa x paradoxa* occurs in dry sclerophyll forest in the Croydon/Warrandyte and Lysterfield areas.
Localities: 40, 42, 43, 47, 50A, 51, 53, 55–58, 60, 61
Distribution: Vic, NSW

Acacia mearnsii

Black Wattle

Size: 8–25 m x 6–10 m **F P N**
Habitat: Widespread in dry and valley sclerophyll forests, grassy low open forest, red gum and riparian woodland, plains grassland, escarpment above riparian scrub
Form: Very fast growing open spreading tree
Foliage: Bipinnate dark green leaves to 20 cm long
Flowers: Strongly scented pale yellow balls in dense racemes; September to December
Requirements: Prefers well drained soils
Comments: This attractive tree can be short-lived and is often subject to borer attack. Its bark, seed pods, leaves and flowers can be used for dyeing. The wood was used for aboriginal weapons and bark provided twine and medicine. The gum was a source of food, drink and adhesive. Seed germinates readily after fire.
Localities: Tarneit, Melton, St Albans, 1, 8, 14, 16, 18, 21–23, 25, 26, 28–31, 33–51, 53, 50–76
Distribution: Vic, NSW, Tas, SA

Acacia melanoxylon

Blackwood

Size: 5–30 m x 4–15 m **F P**
Habitat: Widespread in cool temperate rainforest to dry sclerophyll forests, grassy low open forest, red gum woodland, riparian scrub, plains grassland
Form: Fast-growing upright tree with a heavy canopy
Foliage: Phyllodes are dull green and variable, to 15 cm x 10–30 mm
Flowers: In cream balls, arranged in short racemes; July to October
Requirements: Prefers deep moist soil but adaptable, tolerating dryness once established
Comments: A long-lived tree providing good screening and shade. It tends to sucker if its roots are damaged. Grows as a more stunted tree on the escarpments of the basalt plains. Excellent timber for furniture-making. Its fibre was used to make fishing lines by the Aborigines. Also provided weapons and medicine.
Localities: Sunshine, St Albans, 1, 8, 14, 16, 19, 21, 23, 25, 26, 28, 29, 32–36, 38–51, 53–69A, 71, 74–76
Distribution: Vic, Qld, NSW, Tas, SA

Acacia mucronata

Variable Sallow Wattle, Narrow-Leaf Wattle

Size: 2–6 m x 2–5 m **F P**
Habitat: Damp and valley sclerophyll forests
Form: Spreading or erect shrub of variable habit
Foliage: Light green linear phyllodes from 3–20 cm long
Flowers: In cream to yellow spikes; August to October
Requirements: Moist well drained soils. Drought resistant once established
Comments: A good screen plant but requires pruning. Suckers, especially after fires.
Localities: 42, 47, 49, 50A, 51, 53, 55, 56, 58, 61
Distribution: Vic, NSW, Tas

Acacia myrtifolia

Myrtle Wattle

Size: 1–3 m x 1–2 m **F P N**
Habitat: Sclerophyll woodland, damp and valley sclerophyll forests
Form: Fast-growing rounded or erect shrub
Foliage: Broad phyllodes often with yellow margins, to 60 mm long. New growth is bronze.
Flowers: Profuse, in cream to yellow balls, arranged in racemes; July to October
Requirements: Most soils
Comments: An ornamental bush, with reddish stems, it provides a low screen. A heavy prune can be beneficial. This wattle is quite variable throughout its range.
Localities: 34A, 35, 42, 43, 46–51, 53–56, 58–65
Distribution: All states

Acacia oxycedrus

Spike Wattle

Size: 1–10 m x 2–5 m **F P**
Habitat: Tea-tree heath, dry sclerophyll forest
Form: Stiffly spreading shrub to small tree
Foliage: Rigid dark green phyllodes to 40 mm long, tapering to a sharp point
Flowers: In showy bright yellow spikes; June to November
Requirements: Adaptable, withstanding wet periods
Comments: A useful windbreak, its prickly foliage provides a good bird refuge or protective barrier. The local form is unlikely to grow taller than 3 m. *A. oxycedrus* x *sophorae* occurs in Oakleigh, Parkdale and Frankston.
Propagation: Seed, cuttings
Localities: 45#, 49, 50A#, 63, 67–71, 73–75
Distribution: Vic, NSW, SA

Acacia paradoxa

Hedge Wattle, Kangaroo Thorn

Size: 2–4 m x 2–5 m **F P**
Habitat: Widespread in dry sclerophyll forest, grassy low open forest, red gum woodland, plains grassland
Form: Fast-growing dense and spreading shrub covered with thorns
Foliage: Dark green oblong to narrow phyllodes with wavy edges, to 30 mm long
Flowers: Abundant in large golden yellow balls; August to November
Requirements: Will adapt to any situation
Comments: A very ornamental wattle, it has been declared a noxious weed in rural areas. Its thorny habit makes it a refuge for birds.
Propagation: Seed, cuttings
Localities: 12, 13, 16, 21, 23–26, 29, 30, 32, 33, 34A–39, 42, 44–49, 50A, 51, 53–55, 60–71, 73–76
Distribution: All states
Synonym: *A. armata*

Acacia pycnantha

Golden Wattle

Size: 3–10 m x 2–5 m **F P**
Habitat: Widespread in dry, damp and valley sclerophyll forests, plains grassland, red gum woodland
Form: Erect or spreading small tree with glaucous bark while young
Foliage: Bright green, broad curved phyllodes to 20 cm x 10–50 mm wide
Flowers: Profuse, in perfumed golden balls arranged in long racemes; July to October
Requirements: Well drained soil
Comments: Australia's floral emblem, this tree is fast-growing and drought resistant. Pruning whilst young encourages denser growth. It is a screening and windbreak tree and is useful for erosion control. An important aboriginal plant for food, containers, medicine and glue.
Propagation: Seed or cuttings
Localities: Montrose, 1, 4, 14, 16, 21–26, 28–30, 32–44, 47, 48, 50-53, 56, 58, 61–65, 72, 74
Distribution: Vic, NSW, SA

Acacia retinodes

Wirilda, Swamp Wattle

Size: 4–8 m x 3–5 m **F P**
Habitat: Riparian scrub, coastal banksia and riparian woodlands
Form: Spreading tall shrub or small tree
Foliage: Long narrow bluish-green phyllodes to 20 cm long
Flowers: In lemon-yellow perfumed balls, arranged in racemes; intermittent all year, peaking November to January
Requirements: Adaptable to all soils and conditions including salt and moderate lime
Comments: This quick growing ornamental wattle can be induced to sucker by severing its roots. It can self-seed and needs to be watched near bush areas.
Localities: 8, 16, 18, 19, 26, 29, 33, 50A, 61, 67
Distribution: Vic, Tas, SA

Acacia sophorae

Coastal Wattle

Size: Variable 1–8 m x 4–8 m **F**
Habitat: Dominant in primary dune scrub, coastal banksia woodland, invasive in grassy low open forest
Form: Dense mounded shrub to small tree
Foliage: Broad elliptical phyllodes to 15 cm long
Flowers: In sulphur-yellow spikes; July to October
Requirements: Well drained moist to dry soils
Comments: Taller forms make excellent screens and windbreaks. A useful soil-binding and erosion control plant, especially for front line dune stabilisation as it tolerates salt-laden winds. The green seeds were cooked in their pods and eaten by the Aborigines.
Localities: 32, 64, 67–69A, 71, 72, 74, 75
Distribution: Vic, Qld, NSW, Tas, SA

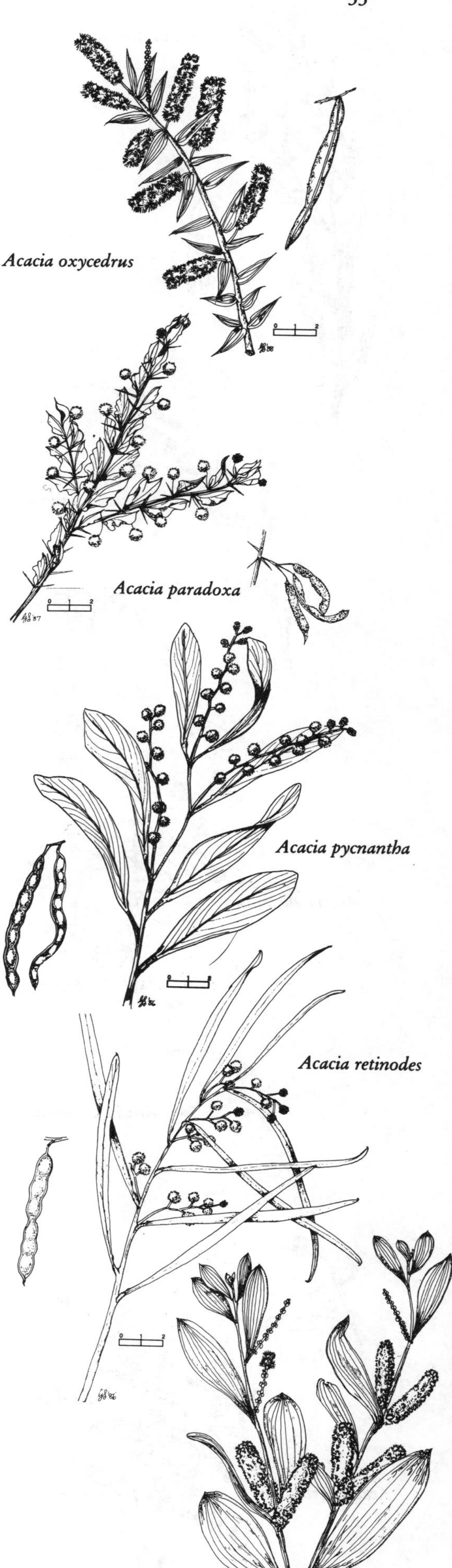

Acacia oxycedrus

Acacia paradoxa

Acacia pycnantha

Acacia retinodes

Acacia sophorae

SCALE: 0 1cm 2cm

The scale representation on each plant equals 2cm.

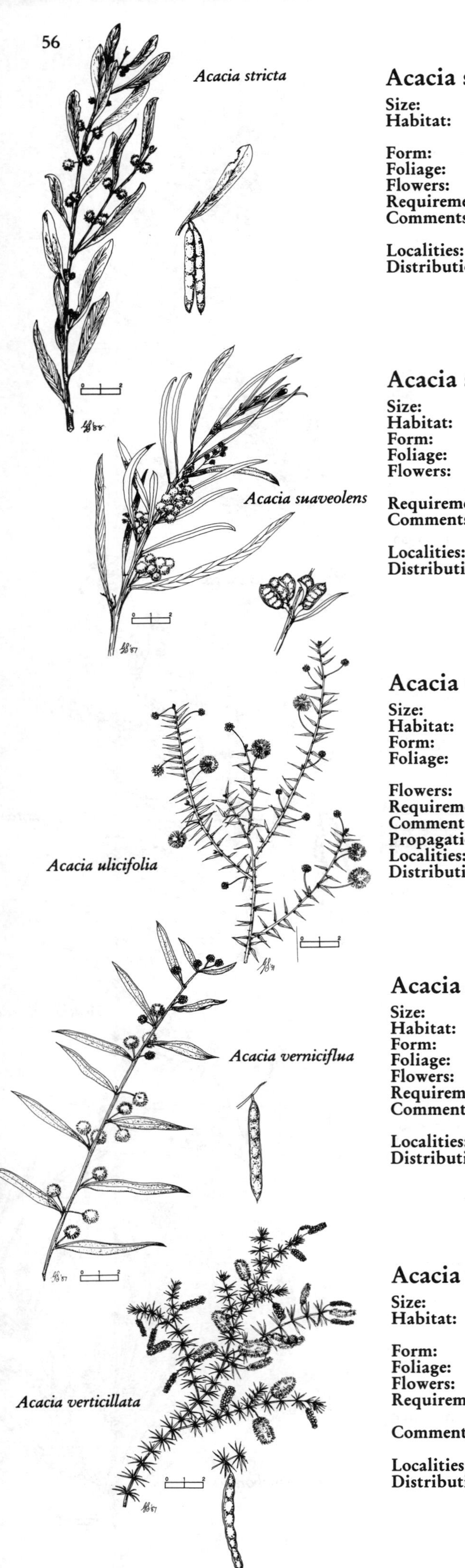

Acacia stricta

Hop Wattle, Straight Wattle

Size: 2–5 m x 2–4 m **F P N**
Habitat: Valley sclerophyll forest, coastal banksia woodland, grassy low open forest, tea-tree heath
Form: Open upright shrub
Foliage: Erect narrow elliptical dull grey-green phyllodes to 15 cm long
Flowers: In pale yellow balls; May to October
Requirements: Reliable in most soils
Comments: A quick growing low windbreak ideal for planting under existing trees. It is drought hardy and tolerates coastal exposure.
Localities: 34A, 42, 44, 46, 47, 49–56, 58, 59, 61, 66, 67#, 70, 74
Distribution: Vic, Qld, NSW, Tas, SA

Acacia suaveolens

Sweet Wattle

Size: 1–3 m x 2–5 m **F P**
Habitat: Tea-tree heath, wattle tea-tree scrub
Form: Open spreading shrub
Foliage: Bluish-green narrow phyllodes to 15 cm long
Flowers: In perfumed cream balls arranged in racemes; April to October, followed by pale bluish seed pods
Requirements: Well drained dry soils
Comments: A fast-growing wattle, it is a very ornamental low screen or windbreak, especially for coastal areas. Responds well to pruning after flowering.
Localities: 66–69, 74, 75
Distribution: Vic, Qld, NSW, Tas, SA

Acacia ulicifolia

Juniper Wattle

Size: 1–2 m x 1–2 m **P**
Habitat: Valley sclerophyll forest, tea-tree heath, grassy low open forest
Form: Open rounded shrub
Foliage: Very narrow dark green prickly phyllodes to 10 mm long, broader at the base
Flowers: Singly, in cream to pale yellow balls; March to September
Requirements: Prefers moist well drained soils
Comments: Used as a low screen it provides a prickly barrier and bird refuge.
Propagation: Seeds, cuttings
Localities: 34A, 41, 42, 50A–53, 67, 69#, 74, 75
Distribution: Vic, Qld, NSW, Tas

Acacia verniciflua

Varnish Wattle

Size: 3–5 m x 3–5 m **F P**
Habitat: Damp and valley sclerophyll forests, grassy low open forest
Form: Slightly weeping open tall shrub or small tree
Foliage: Light shiny green curved phyllodes to 15 cm long
Flowers: Profuse, in pale to bright yellow balls; July to January
Requirements: Tolerates both wet and dry conditions
Comments: A quick growing light screening plant with sticky new growth. Seeds and pods provided food for the Aborigines.
Localities: Eltham, 33, 44, 47, 51, 52, 55, 59, 74, 76
Distribution: Vic, Qld, NSW, Tas, SA

Acacia verticillata

Prickly Moses

Size: 2–6 m x 3–5 m **P**
Habitat: Widespread in wet, damp and valley sclerophyll forests, wattle tea-tree and riparian scrub
Form: Variable open shrub
Foliage: Fine prickly phyllodes to 20 mm long
Flowers: In light yellow spikes; June to December
Requirements: Tolerates most garden conditions, including alkaline soils. Withstands periods of waterlogging.
Comments: Pruning whilst young encourages a bushy habit. It is a useful bird refuge. Fishing line was made from the fibre.
Localities: 16, 26, 29, 30#, 33–36, 40–44, 46–51, 53–64, 67#, 70, 74–76
Distribution: Vic, NSW, Tas, SA

Acaena **Rosaceae**

Acaena agnipila

Hairy Sheep's Burr

Size: 20–50 cm x 30 cm **F P N**
Habitat: Plains grassland, grassy wetland, red gum woodland, dry sclerophyll forest
Form: Rosette or tufted perennial herb
Foliage: Narrowly-obovate to oblanceolate pinnate leaves to 15 cm long, including stalk, with more than 4 pairs of leaflets. Moderately hairy upper surface, densely hairy below.
Flowers: Flowers are in a spike with dark purple stamens; October to November. Spines of the burr are of equal length, with slender barbs on the end.
Requirements: Well drained soils
Comments: *A. echinata* and *A. ovina* are very similar to *A. agnipila* and the 3 species may be difficult to tell apart, especially if flowerheads or burrs are not present. All 3 lack stolons and are propagated by seed.
Localities: St Albans, 6, 21, 25, 26, 28, 35, 36, 39, 50A, 51, 55, 56, 74, 76
Distribution: Vic, Qld, NSW, Tas, SA

Acaena agnipila

Acaena anserinifolia = A. novae-zelandiae

Acaena echinata

Sheep's Burr

Size: 25–40 cm high **F P**
Habitat: Grassy wetland, plains grassland, red gum woodland, valley sclerophyll forest
Form: Perennial herb with erect stems
Foliage: Narrowly obovate to oblanceolate, pinnate leaves 60–150 mm long, with 9–15 ovate to oblong toothed leaflets. Hairs on undersurface are confined to the major veins.
Flowers: Tiny flowers with dark purplish stamens form a cylindrical spike 50–150 mm long; August to November. Spines of the burr are unequal in length.
Requirements: Moist soil
Localities: Eltham, Research, 2, 4–7, 10, 12, 16–18, 20, 21, 23, 24, 26, 28, 31, 32, 36, 41, 42, 44, 59, 60, 62–65, 69A, 74
Distribution: All states except NT

Acaena echinata

Acaena novae-zelandiae

Bidgee Widgee

Size: Prostrate x 1–4 m **F P N**
Habitat: Widespread in wet, damp and valley sclerophyll forests, swamp and riparian scrub, plains grassland, riparian and red gum woodland
Form: Rambling stoloniferous mat plant
Foliage: Oblong pinnate leaves to 40 mm. 11 oblong leaflets with toothed margins, increasing in size along the stalk to 10 mm long.
Flowers: Globular greenish-white flowerheads on stalks to about 20 cm long; October to January. Fruits form reddish globular heads to 25 mm covered with spines.
Requirements: Adaptable, tolerating wet or dry conditions
Comments: A useful soil-binding plant and ground cover. The burrs can be a problem on clothing. Early settlers used the leaves as a tea substitute.
Propagation: Seeds, cuttings, division
Localities: 5, 6–8, 10, 16, 21, 26–36, 38, 40–44, 46–65, 67, 69A–76
Distribution: Vic, Qld, NSW, Tas, SA
Synonym: *A. anserinifolia*

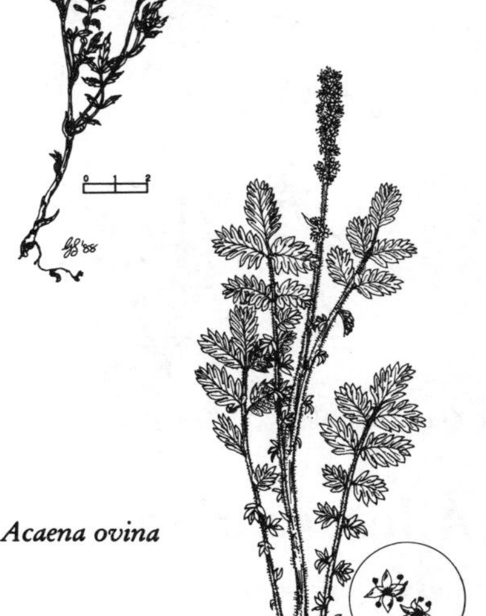

Acaena novae-zelandiae

Acaena ovina

Australian Sheep's Burr

Size: 10–50 cm high **F P**
Habitat: Damp and dry sclerophyll forests, red gum and riparian woodland, plains grassland, grassy low open forest
Foliage: Tuft or rosette. Leaves to 120 mm long have 5 or more pairs of leaflets. May be glabrous or sparsely hairy above, more densely hairy below.
Flowers: Flowers are in a spike; September to November. Green burrs have 15–50 short spines with 3–6 much longer.
Localities: 4, 8, 15, 16, 26, 28, 29, 31, 32, 34A–36, 42, 44, 45, 47–49, 54, 56, 58, 63–67, 71, 74
Distribution: Vic, Qld, NSW, Tas, SA

Acaena ovina

SCALE: 

The scale representation on each plant equals 2cm.

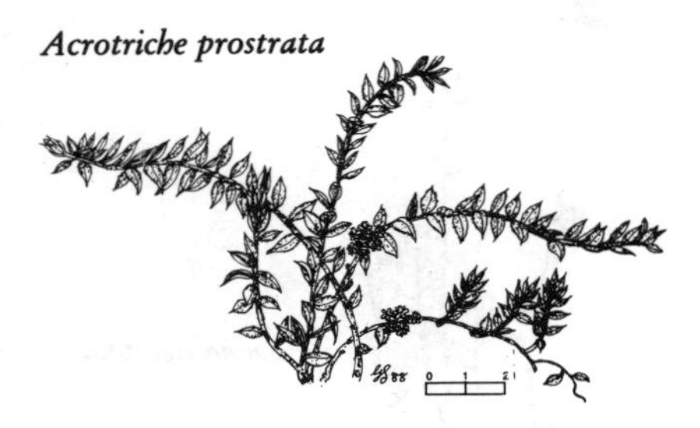
Acrotriche prostrata

Acrotriche — Epacridaceae

Acrotriche prostrata — Trailing Ground-Berry

Size: Prostrate x 1–2 m — P N
Habitat: Damp and valley sclerophyll forests, sclerophyll woodland, grassy low open forest
Form: Open trailing plant
Foliage: Small dark green triangular leaves to 20 mm long
Flowers: Greenish translucent, tubular flowers which produce copious amounts of nectar, clustered on old wood; May to September.
Requirements: Moist friable soil
Comments: Edible fruits are globular, succulent drupes. It is ideal for growing with ferns.
Propagation: Cuttings
Localities: 55, 56, 58–62, 64, 65, 74–76
Distribution: Endemic to Vic

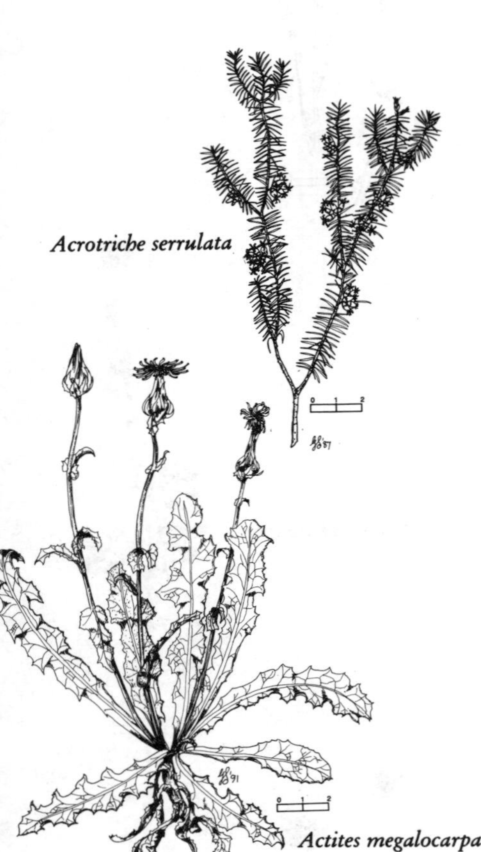
Acrotriche serrulata

Actites megalocarpa

Acrotriche serrulata — Honey Pots

Size: 10-30 cm x 0.5–1 m — P
Habitat: Sclerophyll woodland, grassy low open forest, dry and valley sclerophyll forests
Form: Slow-growing, dense ground-covering shrub
Foliage: Hairy leaves to 10 mm long, tapering to a point
Flowers: Greenish translucent, tubular flowers clustered on old wood; May to October
Requirements: Most well drained soils tolerating dry periods
Comments: Flowers have a strong honey fragrance, and are rich in nectar. Used for food and drink by the Aborigines.
Propagation: Cuttings
Localities: Research, 29, 34–37, 40–44, 47–56, 58–65, 67–70, 74–76
Distribution: Vic, NSW, Tas, SA

Actites — Asteraceae

Actites megalocarpa — Dune Thistle

Size: 0.1–0.6 m high — F
Habitat: Primary dune scrub and coastal cliffs
Form: Erect fleshy rhizomatous perennial herb usually forming an open clump
Foliage: Variable, thick glossy oblong leaves from 1.5–17 cm x 5–45 mm, stiff and stem-clasping with prickly teeth
Flowers: Yellow daisy flowerheads; September to June
Requirements: Well drained sandy soil
Comments: Tolerates exposure to salt spray but more stunted, reaching full height in a sheltered position. Probably extinct within the Melbourne area.
Propagation: Seed, division
Localities: Collected on Brighton Beach, 1887; 69A, 74
Distribution: All states

Ajuga australis

Ajuga — Lamiaceae

Ajuga australis — Austral Bugle

Size: 20–30 cm x 30–50 cm — F P
Habitat: Valley and dry sclerophyll forests, red gum woodland
Form: Erect or spreading perennial herb
Foliage: A basal rosette of velvety, grey-green toothed leaves to 120 mm long, leaves decreasing in size up the stem.
Flowers: Erect spikes of purple tubular flowers, sometimes blue or pink; September to February.
Requirements: Well drained soils, tolerates extended dry periods once established
Comments: A useful plant for erosion control in sandy soils. It will grow in sheltered coastal areas. Suckers vigorously in open soils. A decoction for sores was made from the leaves by the Aborigines.
Propagation: Seed, cuttings or division
Localities: 29, 34A, 35, 38, 39, 41, 42, 67#
Distribution: Vic, Qld, NSW, Tas, SA

Allocasuarina — Casuarinaceae

Allocasuarinas are medium shrubs to tall trees. They are found in coastal areas with some growing inland. Most species are dioecious. Male plants have flower spikes from yellow to brown at the ends of branchlets, while female plants bear globular reddish flowers along the trunk and branches, followed by seed cones. Foliage is reduced to whorls of leaf teeth along the branchlets at the nodes. Allocasuarinas respond well to pruning if necessary. They are all ornamental and make excellent screening or windbreak plants. The timber provides excellent firewood. The local Aborigines ate the shoots and young cones and made implements and weapons from the wood. Propagation is by seed.
Synonym: All species in the Melbourne region were formerly placed in the genus *Casuarina*.

Allocasuarina littoralis

Black Sheoke

Size:	4–8 m x 2–5 m **F P**
Habitat:	Widespread in grassy low open forest, dry and valley sclerophyll forests, red gum woodland
Form:	Upright small tree with fine branchlets
Flowers:	Female flowers reddish to crimson. Male flower spikes dark brown; March to June
Requirements:	Well drained soils
Comments:	The bark on old trees is dark and deeply furrowed and is ideal for growing epiphytic orchids.
Localities:	Research, 29–35, 42, 44, 47, 49, 50A, 51, 53, 54, 56, 60-67#, 69A, 71, 74–76
Distribution:	Vic, Qld, NSW, Tas
Synonym:	*Casuarina littoralis*

Allocasuarina luehmannii

Bull Oak, Buloke

Size:	5–15 m x 5–10 m **F**
Habitat:	Box woodland
Form:	Fast-growing upright tree with fine dull green branchlets
Flowers:	Yellow spikes to 25 mm long on male trees; October to November.
Requirements:	Prefers heavy soil. Tolerates periods of dryness and inundation.
Comments:	Roots may produce suckers. The cones are distinctive being squat with only 2 or 3 rows of valves. Occurring in few sites within the Melbourne area, it has become depleted in Victoria.
Localities:	Melton, 9, 16, 26, 32–34
Distribution:	Vic, Qld, NSW, SA
Synonym:	*Casuarina luehmannii*

Allocasuarina paludosa

Swamp Sheoke

Size:	0.5–2 m x 1–2 m **F**
Habitat:	Tea-tree heath, sclerophyll woodland, grassy low open forest
Form:	Slow-growing open or dense shrub, branchlets grey-green, sometimes hairy in furrows
Flowers:	Brown male flowers; March to October
Requirements:	Moist well drained clay or sandy soils
Comments:	Unlike most *Allocasuarina* spp., it may have both male and female flowers on the same plant. A groove down the centre of each ridge along the branchlets is a distinguishing feature.
Localities:	45#, 59, 63–65, 70, 71, 74–76
Distribution:	Vic, NSW, Tas, SA
Synonym:	*Casuarina paludosa*

Allocasuarina paradoxa

Dwarf Sheoke

Size:	0.5–2 m x 1–2 m **F P**
Habitat:	Tea-tree heath
Form:	Upright open to dense shrub
Flowers:	Reddish-brown male flowers; September to November
Requirements:	Well drained sandy soil
Comments:	Commonly found with *A. paludosa* with which it may be easily confused but *A. paradoxa* prefers better drainage. It is hairless and ridges are smooth.
Localities:	67–70, 73–75
Distribution:	Endemic to Vic
Synonym:	Plants from the Melbourne region were commonly referred to as *A. pusilla*, which occurs in western Victoria.

Allocasuarina verticillata

Coast or Drooping Sheoke

Size:	4–11 m x 3–6 m **F**
Habitat:	Widespread in primary dune scrub, box, red gum and box ironbark woodlands, chenopod rocky open scrub
Form:	Small erect tree with a dense rounded crown and drooping greyish-green branchlets
Flowers:	Yellow to brown male flowers; March to December
Requirements:	Well drained soils
Comments:	The golden effect provided by the dense flowers is an attractive feature of this tree. The dark furrowed bark is useful for growing epiphytic orchids.
Localities:	Melton Sth, 14, 16, 18, 23, 25, 26, 29, 32–34A, 36, ?42, 44, 67, 69A, 71, 74, 76
Distribution:	Vic, NSW, Tas, SA
Synonym:	*A. stricta, Casuarina stricta*

Illustrated p. 51

Allocasuarina littoralis

Allocasuarina luehmannii

Allocasuarina paludosa

Allocasuarina paradoxa

The scale representation on each plant equals 2cm.

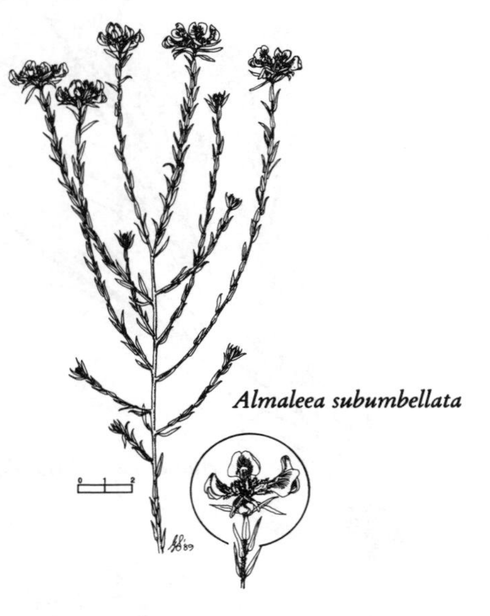

Almaleea subumbellata

Almaleea

Fabaceae

Almaleea subumbellata

Wiry Bush-pea

P

Size: 0.3–0.6 m high
Habitat: Swamp scrub
Form: Slender, erect, or trailing shrub
Foliage: Concave, lanceolate leaves to 12 mm long with minute free stipules. Leaves are usually pressed up along the stems.
Flowers: Terminal clusters of yellow and red flowers; October to December. Hairy oblong bracteoles.
Requirements: Moist to wet soils
Comments: An attractive low shrub with yellowish branchlets. When found in sedge swampland the plant may reach 1.5 m tall, its slender stem being supported by surrounding scrub.
Localities: 47, 54, 59
Distribution: Vic, Tas
Synonym: *Pultenaea subumbellata*

Alternanthera denticulata

Alternanthera

Amaranthaceae

Alternanthera denticulata

Lesser Joy Weed

F P

Size: 15–30 cm x 0.5 m
Habitat: Damp depressions in red gum, riparian and box woodlands, grassy wetlands, dry sclerophyll forest
Form: Low straggling perennial herb
Foliage: Narrow leaves from 20-100 mm long
Flowers: Short spikes of silvery-white paper flowers most of the year
Requirements: Moist well drained soils
Comments: This plant may be useful beside ponds. Prune after flowering to encourage a bushy habit. A small compact form to 15 cm wide is found on drier grasslands and box woodland of the basalt plains, rather than the usual riparian habitat. It is in the Melton area, amongst *Allocasuarina luehmannii* and has rounded leaves, white flowerheads which are twice the size of the normal form, and very short internodes.
Propagation: Seed, cuttings
Localities: Derrimut, Deer Park, Melton, 6, 8, 9, 11, 16–18, 25–30, 34A–36, 41, 42, 60, 62, 64, 67, 71, 74
Distribution: Vic, Qld, NSW, Tas, SA

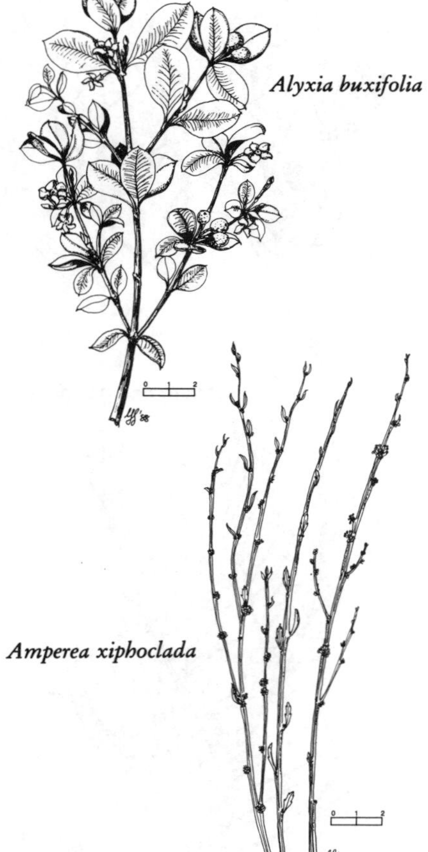

Alyxia buxifolia

Amperea xiphoclada

Alyxia

Apocynaceae

Alyxia buxifolia

Sea Box

F

Size: 1–2 m x 1–3 m
Habitat: Exposed coastal cliffs and primary dune scrub, grassy low open forest
Form: Slow-growing dense spreading shrub
Foliage: Leathery, dark green, glossy oval leaves to 30 mm long; paired or in 3s
Flowers: Sessile cluster of scented white flowers with 5 petals twisted sideways; October to February
Requirements: Well drained soils
Comments: A useful coastal plant tolerant of salt spray, its fruits are very attractive bright red drupes. It could make a decorative container plant.
Propagation: Seed, cuttings—slow to strike
Localities: Seaford, 67, 69A, 74
Distribution: Vic, NSW, Tas, SA, WA

Amperea

Euphorbiaceae

Amperea xiphoclada

Broom Spurge

F P

Size: 0.3–0.8 m x 0.4–0.5 m
Habitat: Tea-tree heath, dry sclerophyll forest
Form: Wiry shrub with rigid stems arising from a woody rootstock
Foliage: Smooth dark green narrow leaves to 20 mm long; scale-like leaves on flowering stems
Flowers: Clusters of insignificant brown and cream flowers; September to February
Requirements: Moist well drained soils
Comments: Useful in landscaping for creating a natural bush appearance.
Propagation: Seed, cuttings
Localities: 49, 55, 56, 63, 67, 69–71, 73–76
Distribution: Vic, Qld, NSW, Tas, SA

Amyema

Loranthaceae

Although parasitic, mistletoes are not a problem in forested areas because of the number of host trees available. On cleared land few trees remain. This may cause heavier infestation on each tree which may result in the tree's death. The mistletoe bird eats the berries and deposits the seeds on branches of the host trees. To propagate, the sticky seed needs to be collected and placed on the bark of a suitable host.

Amyema linophyllum ssp. orientale

Slender-leaf Mistletoe

P

Habitat: Box woodland on *Allocasuarina luehmannii*
Form: Pendulous clump, young stems and leaves densely covered with white hairs
Foliage: Pairs or clusters of blue-green needle-like leaves to 120 mm long, with blunt tips
Flowers: 3 groups of 3 red flowers, whitish on the outside, on a common woolly stalk. The outer 2 flowers are stalked, the central flower sessile; October to February. The bud is 15–25 mm long, the globular berry is 5 mm.
Comments: On few sites in Melbourne, as it is dependent on *Allocasuarina luehmannii*. Also becoming rare within Victoria.
Localities: Melton, Werribee#, 9
Distribution: Vic, Qld, NSW, SA

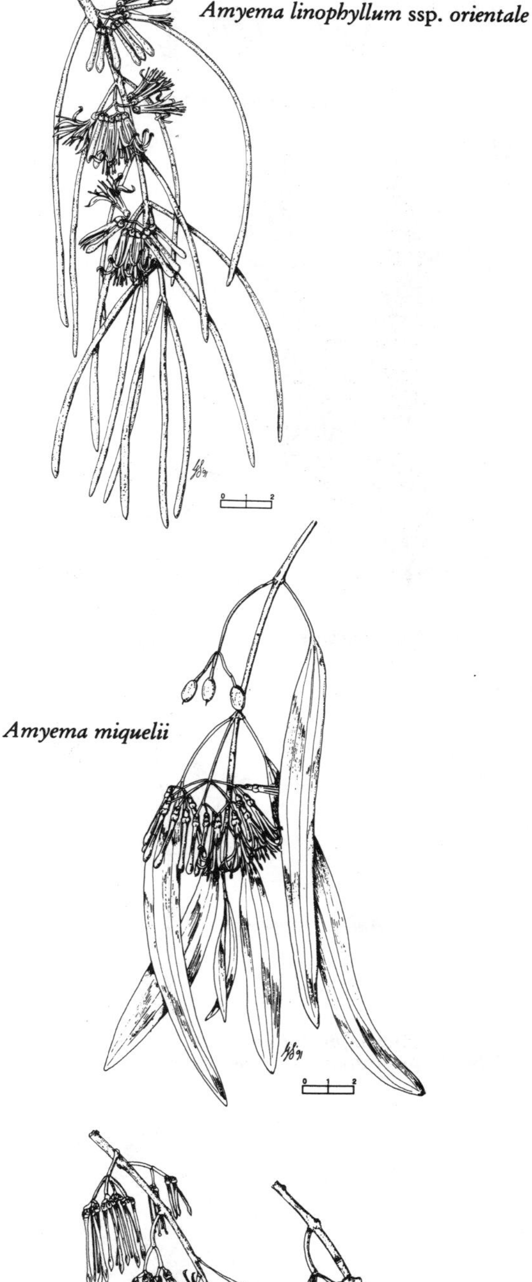

Amyema linophyllum ssp. *orientale*

Amyema miquelii

Amyema miquelii

Box Mistletoe

P

Size: Drooping, to 3 m long
Habitat: Box and red gum woodlands
Form: Open pendulous clumps on host tree
Foliage: Curved, bronze-green linear leaves to 20 cm long
Flowers: Drooping clusters of 4–5 groups of 3 attractive, stalked orange-red flowers, each group on a common stalk. Flowering occurs sporadically throughout the year. The bud is 15–30 mm long. Fruit is a cylindrical to pear-shaped berry to 12 mm.
Comments: This parasitic plant may eventually kill the host branch. Its common host plant is *Eucalyptus* spp., but it is also found on *Acacia* spp.
Localities: Research, 25, 36, 42
Distribution: All states

Amyema pendulum

Drooping Mistletoe

P

Habitat: Sclerophyll woodland, wet, damp and valley sclerophyll forest, grassy low open forest
Form: Very similar but larger than *A. miquelii* with lanceolate leaves to 20 cm long.
Flowers: The main distinguishing feature is the flower cluster which has 3–4 groups of 3 or 4 flowers. While the 2 outer flowers are stalked the central flower is sessile. The bud is 30–35 mm long and the berry elliptical to 10 mm long. Flowering mainly Summer.
Localities: Sth Morang, 26, 29#, 33–36, 39, 42, 44, 47–51, 53–58, 60–62, 64, 65, 67#, 71–76
Distribution: Vic, NSW, SA

Amyema preissii

Wire Leaf Mistletoe

P

Habitat: Coastal and basalt plains
Foliage: Similar to *A. linophyllum* but has glabrous bright green foliage. Needle-like leaves to 100 mm long are paired, alternate or clustered.
Flowers: Red flowers in 2 (rarely 3) groups of 3, central flower sessile; November to April. Globular berry to 10 mm wide.
Comments: Host plants are *Acacia* spp., especially *A. mearnsii* and *Allocasuarina* spp.
Localities: Probably occurred along the Eastern coast-line of Port Phillip Bay.
Distribution: All mainland states

Illustrated p. 79

Amyema quandang var. quandang

Grey Mistletoe

P

Habitat: Valley sclerophyll forest
Form: Grey, shortly hairy plant
Foliage: Lanceolate to elliptical leaves to 100 mm long, often curved, in pairs or scattered
Flowers: Dark red flowers are held upright in 2 groups of 3; most of the year. Fruit is a pear-shaped berry to 10 mm long.
Comments: Always found on *Acacia* spp., especially *A. dealbata* locally.
Localities: Olinda Ck, Lilydale, 35, 42, 44, 61
Distribution: All mainland states

Illustrated p. 79

The scale representation on each plant equals 2cm.

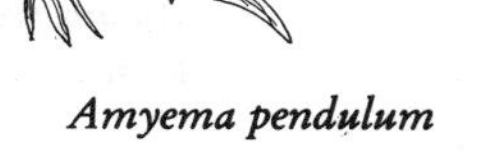

Amyema pendulum

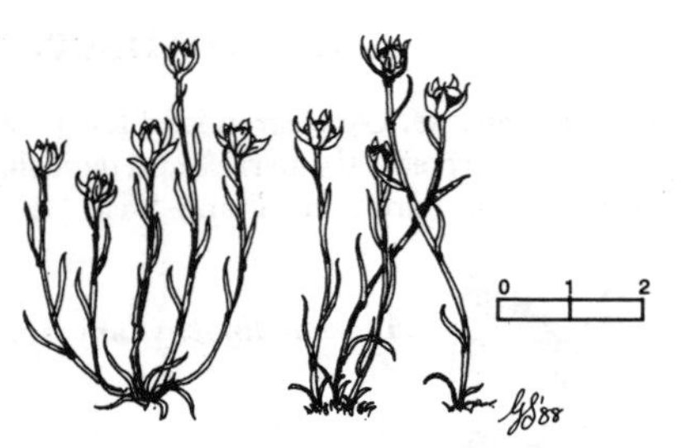

Angianthus preissianus

Angianthus — Asteraceae

Angianthus preissianus — Common Cup Flower, Salt Angianthus

F

Size: 10–30 cm x 15 cm
Habitat: Saltmarshes, primary dune scrub
Form: Annual matting herb
Foliage: Hairy, narrow silvery-grey leaves to 10 mm long
Flowers: In whitish subglobular terminal flowerheads; October to December
Requirements: Prefers moist sandy soils
Comments: Unknown in cultivation and locally rare, it would be worth trying.
Propagation: Seed
Localities: Williamstown, 67#
Distribution: Vic, SA, WA

Aotus ericoides

Aotus — Fabaceae

Aotus ericoides — Common Aotus

F P

Size: 0.5–1.5 m x 0.5–1.5 m
Habitat: Tea-tree heath
Form: Fast-growing bushy upright shrub
Foliage: Slender hairy light green leaves to 20 mm long
Flowers: Clusters of small yellow and red pea flowers; August to December
Requirements: Adaptable to well drained soils, tolerating both wet or dry periods
Comments: A very showy plant when in bloom, it requires pruning after flowering.
Propagation: Scarified seed, cuttings
Localities: St. Kilda#, 45#, 63, 67–69, 70, 71, 73–75
Distribution: All states

Apium annuum

Apium prostratum ssp. *prostratum* var. *prostratum*

Apium — Apiaceae

Apium annuum

F

Size: to 15 cm high
Habitat: Wet depressions in plains grassland, grassy low open forest, primary dune scrub
Form: Erect annual or biennial herb
Foliage: Broadly ovate leaves divided into 3–5 elliptic to obovate segments, 2 or 3 times longer than wide, which may be entire, lobed or further divided
Flowers: Sessile umbels of 4–10 tiny white flowers; September to November
Requirements: Moist sandy soil
Comments: The globular fruit have narrow ribs.
Propagation: Seed
Localities: Laverton, Altona, Seaford, 2, 3, 74
Distribution: Vic, SA, WA

Apium prostratum ssp. prostratum var. prostratum — Sea Celery

F

Size: 10–30 cm x 1–2 m
Habitat: Widespread in fresh or brackish swamps of coastal banksia woodland and riparian scrub
Form: Trailing perennial
Foliage: Smooth, divided or entire celery-like leaves with narrow to lanceolate segments. Leaves are 7–12 times longer than their width.
Flowers: Inconspicuous cream to green flowers in umbels; December to April
Requirements: Moist well drained sandy soils
Comments: Globular fruits have corky ribs. Occurs further inland than var. *filiforme*. Suitable for a rockery. It may be used as a celery substitute.
Propagation: Seed, division
Localities: Mordialloc, Carrum, 2, 16, 25, 26, 28, 35, 67, 69A, 74
Distribution: All states; NZ

Apium prostratum ssp. *prostratum* var. *filiforme*

Apium prostratum ssp. prostratum var. filiforme

F

Habitat: Coastal river mouths and exposed foreshores, primary dune scrub
Comments: Leaves are always divided, often several times, and they are only 2–3 times longer than wide. Segments vary in shape from elliptic to cuneate. Stems are also finer than var. *prostratum*.
Localities: Ricketts Point
Distribution: All states except NT; NZ

Asperula — Rubiaceae

Asperula conferta

Common Woodruff

Size: to 20 cm x 0.5–1 m — P
Habitat: Widespread on primary dune scrub, grassy wetlands, red gum woodland, plains grassland, valley sclerophyll forest
Form: Low spreading perennial herb with squarish glabrous stems, becoming round with age
Foliage: Bright green linear pointed leaves to 10 mm long, in whorls of 6, margins and midrib on underside roughly hairy
Flowers: Dioecious, white terminal flowers, females in groups of 3 and shorter than males; September to December
Requirements: Well drained soils
Comments: A useful low groundcover for a moist, shady spot.
Propagation: Cuttings
Localities: Eltham, 6, 12, 13, 15–18, 25, 26, 28, 29, 31, 32, 34A, 35, 41, 42, 45, 49, 54–56, 58–67#, 74
Distribution: Vic, Qld, NSW, SA

Asperula euryphylla

Broad-Leaf Woodruff

Size: Weak branches to 15 cm high — P
Habitat: Damp and wet sclerophyll forests
Form: Wiry perennial herb, rectangular stems covered in fine hairs, scrambling amongst other plants
Foliage: Whorls of 6 downy or glabrous, obovate to oblanceolate leaves to 12 mm long
Flowers: Dioecious, 1–3 white flowers in terminal clusters; November to December
Requirements: Moist well drained soils
Localities: 55–57, 61
Distribution: Vic, SA

Asperula scoparia

Prickly Woodruff

Size: 10 cm x 0.5–1 m — P N
Habitat: Damp and dry sclerophyll forests, plains grassland, grassy wetlands
Form: Moss-like perennial herb with rough hairy stems
Foliage: Whorls of 6 stiff, prickly narrow leaves
Flowers: Dioecious, small clusters of tiny white flowers; September to February
Requirements: Moist well drained soils
Comments: Ideal used under other plants or around rocks.
Localities: 2, 4–7, 10, 12, 16–18, 20, 26, 28, 34A, 36, 37, 39, ?42, 43, 49, 55, 56, 58, 71
Distribution: Vic, Qld, NSW, Tas, SA

Asterolasia — Rutaceae

Asterolasia asteriscophora

Lemon Star Bush

Size: 1.5 m x 1 m — P
Habitat: Damp and valley sclerophyll forests
Form: Slender upright shrub
Foliage: Dull green soft hairy leaves to 25 mm long, locally smaller to 10 mm long
Flowers: Lemon-yellow star-like flowers, solitary or in clusters; September to November
Requirements: Moist well drained soils
Comments: A reliable garden plant needing annual pruning. Lasts well as a cut flower. The local form often has white flowers.
Propagation: Cuttings
Localities: Belgrave, Upper Ferntree Gully
Distribution: Vic, NSW

Astroloma — Epacridaceae

Astroloma humifusum

Cranberry Heath

Size: 10-50 cm x 1–1.5 m — F P
Habitat: Red gum woodland, dry sclerophyll forest, tea-tree heath, grassy low open forest
Form: Dense spreading mat-like plant
Foliage: Blue-green, stiff, prickly narrow leaves to 10 mm long
Flowers: Bright red tubular flowers along branches most of the year, especially May to September
Requirements: Well drained soils tolerating dry periods once established
Comments: The pale green globular fruit are edible. An excellent plant for rockeries, embankments, under shrubs or in hanging baskets. The flowers are generally hidden by the foliage. Responds well to pruning.
Propagation: Cuttings—difficult. Use very young firm growth.
Localities: 26, 34A–42, 44, 45#, 47–49, 50A, 51, 58, 62–69A, 74–76
Distribution: Vic, NSW, Tas, SA, WA

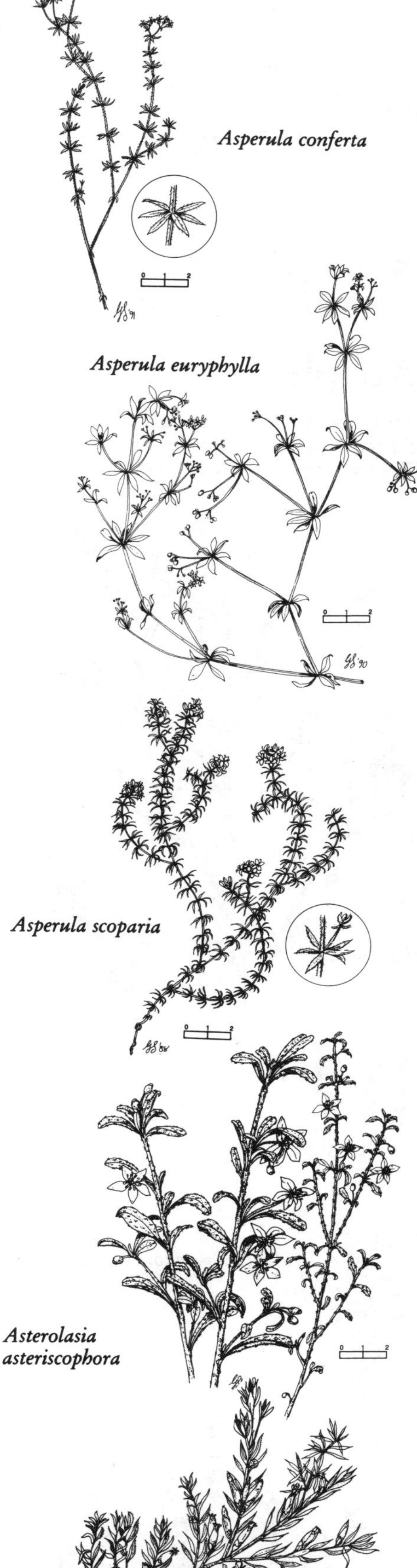

Asperula conferta

Asperula euryphylla

Asperula scoparia

Asterolasia asteriscophora

Astroloma humifusum

SCALE: 0 1cm 2cm — The scale representation on each plant equals 2cm.

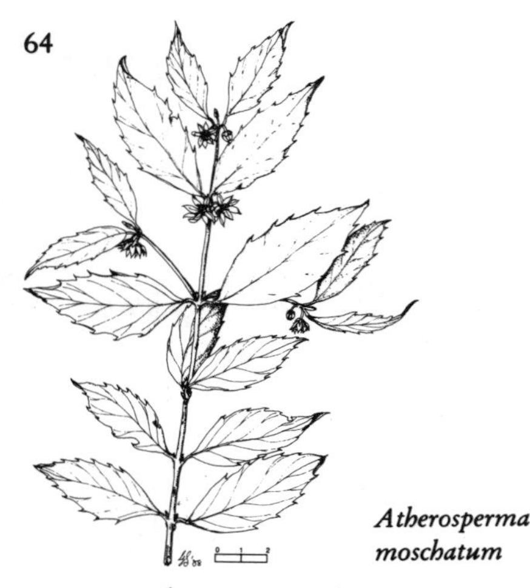

Atherosperma moschatum

Atherosperma — Monimiaceae

Atherosperma moschatum

Southern or Black Sassafras

P N

Size: 10–25 m x 2–5 m
Habitat: Cool temperate rainforest, wet sclerophyll forest
Form: Dense narrow conical tree
Foliage: Shiny green lanceolate leaves, whitish below, 40–90 mm x 15–40 mm
Flowers: Pendent velvety cream perfumed flowers; March to July
Requirements: Cool moist well drained soils
Comments: A slow-growing tree with nutmeg-scented bark and musky leaves.
Propagation: Seed, cuttings—can be very slow to strike
Localities: 57, 58
Distribution: Vic, Qld, NSW, Tas

Atriplex — Chenopodiaceae

Atriplex species are commonly known as saltbushes as they can grow in saline soil. Flowers are unisexual: the males are globular forming clusters or spikes; the females form clusters in lower axils. *Atriplex* are fire-resistant, drought tolerant and excellent for soil erosion control. The seeds were ground and cooked by the Aborigines.

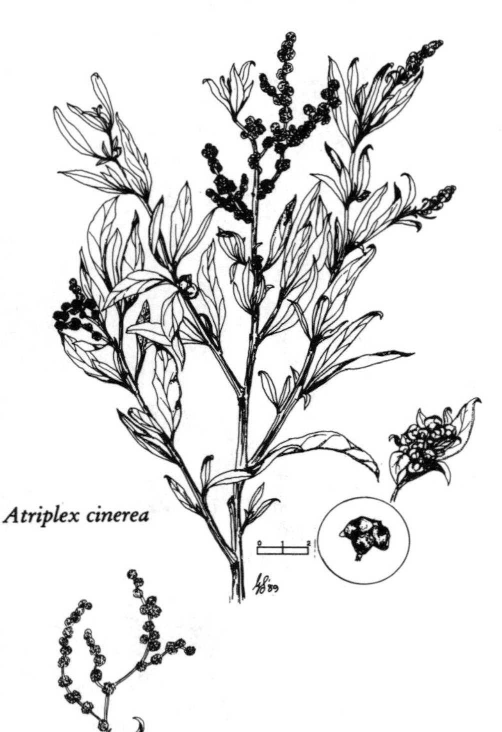

Atriplex cinerea

Atriplex billardieri

Glistening Saltbush

F

Size: 15–40 cm x 0.5–1 m
Habitat: Coastal cliffs and foreshores near high tide line, primary dune scrub
Form: Small succulent perennial herb
Foliage: Glistening, oblong yellow-green leaves to 10 mm long
Flowers: Small greenish flowers, male flowers in small clusters in the upper axils, females 1–2 in lower axils on the same plant
Requirements: Well drained sandy soil
Comments: An endangered species in Melbourne.
Localities: St. Kilda#, 67
Distribution: Vic, Tas
Synonym: *Theleophyton billardieri*

Atriplex cinerea

Coast or Grey Saltbush

F P

Size: 1–2 m x 2–3 m
Habitat: Exposed primary dune scrub, sandy shorelines above high tide level
Form: Fast-growing dense spreading shrub with brittle branches
Foliage: Silver-grey lanceolate to oblong leaves to 80 mm long
Flowers: Male and female flowers usually occur on separate plants (dioecious). Male flowers are reddish-purple in dense globular clusters; female flowers are cream in axillary clusters; September to March
Requirements: Well drained soils
Comments: This saltbush has fleshy, triangular fruit. Its leaves can be eaten after cooking. A good low screen for coastal gardens.
Propagation: Seed, cutting
Localities: 2, 3, 67, 69A, 74
Distribution: All states

Atriplex paludosa ssp. *paludosa*

Atriplex paludosa ssp. paludosa

Marsh Saltbush

F

Size: 1 m x 1–2 m
Habitat: Saltmarshes and tidal flats
Form: Open silvery-grey shrub
Foliage: Scaly ovate to oblong leaves to 25 mm long
Flowers: Dioecious, the male flowers are in slender spikes, the females in axillary clusters; most of the year
Requirements: Boggy saline soils
Comments: Useful in saline areas.
Localities: 2, 3
Distribution: Vic, NSW, Tas, SA, WA

Atriplex semibaccata

Berry or Creeping Saltbush

F P

Size: 10–30 cm x 1–3 m
Habitat: Primary dune scrub, riparian scrub, red gum woodland, coloniser of disturbed ground
Form: Spreading perennial shrub
Foliage: Oblong toothed leaves to 30 mm long, grey-green above, mealy below
Flowers: Male flowers in small dense clusters in upper axils, female flowers scattered in lower axils, singly or in small clusters, on the same plant; most of the year, peaking November to February. Followed by red succulent fruit.
Requirements: Well drained soils. Salt tolerant
Comments: A useful groundcover to control soil erosion.
Localities: Maribyrnong, Derrimut, Melton, 2–4, 6, 16, 18, 21–29, 32, 35, 71
Distribution: All mainland states

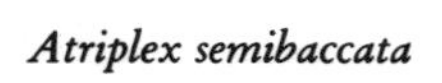

Atriplex semibaccata

Atriplex suberecta

Sprawling or Lagoon Saltbush

Size: 0.3–0.6 m x 1–2 m **F**
Habitat: Saltmarshes and disturbed areas
Form: Sprawling annual herb with ascending stems
Foliage: Wedge-shaped leaves to 70 mm long are green above and mealy white below
Flowers: Male flowers clustered near the ends of branches, females in dense axillary clusters; all year
Requirements: Tolerates boggy saline soils
Comments: Often found alongside railway lines. May be introduced in these situations.
Localities: Melbourne, Footscray, Sunshine, Rockbank, Melton, 2–4, 10
Distribution: Vic, Qld, NSW, SA, WA
Synonym: Separated from *A. muelleri* which occurs in Northern Australia

Australina pusilla ssp. *muelleri*

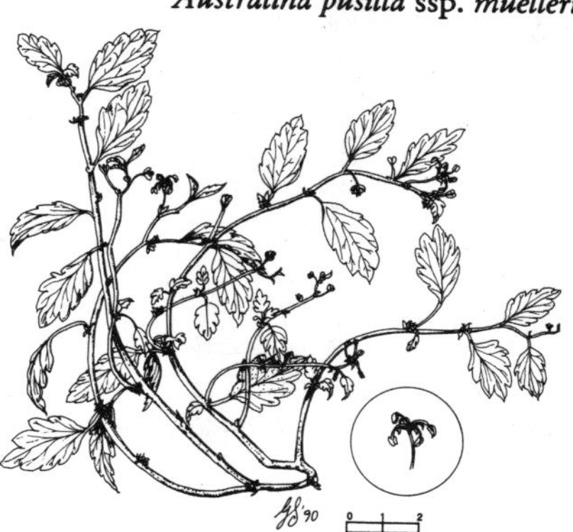

Australina — Urticaceae

Australina pusilla ssp. muelleri

Smooth or Shade Nettle

Size: 20–40 cm x 0.5–1 m **N**
Habitat: Cool temperate rainforest, damp and wet sclerophyll forests
Form: Loosely-branched perennial herb
Foliage: Dark green ovate to lanceolate leaves to 50 mm long
Flowers: Insignificant hairy male and female flowers without petals on semi-succulent stems; November to February
Requirements: Moist well drained soils
Comments: A non-stinging herb ideal for growing with ferns.
Propagation: Seed, cutting, root division
Localities: 57, 58, 60
Distribution: Vic, Qld, NSW, Tas
Synonym: *A. muelleri* is now included in *A. pusilla*

Avicennia — Verbenacaea

Avicennia marina

White or Grey Mangrove

Size: 3–8 m x 2–5 m **F**
Habitat: Coastal shallows and estuaries, saltmarshes
Form: Slow-growing dense shrub or small tree
Foliage: Shiny dark green ovate-lanceolate leaves to 60 mm long
Flowers: Sweetly scented yellow to cream flowers; January to March
Requirements: Restricted to sites inundated at high tide
Comments: An excellent plant for stabilising mud flats, there are now only a few remnant stands left around Port Philip Bay. The Aborigines roasted and ate the fruit. The durable timber is used for marine construction.
Propagation: Seed—germinates on the tree before dropping. Seedlings can be transplanted but pots need flushing with brackish water.
Localities: Williamstown, 3#
Distribution: All mainland states

Avicennia marina

Ballantinia — Brassicaceae

Ballantinia antipoda

Southern Shepherds Purse

Size: 2–10 cm high **F P**
Habitat: Basaltic and granitic sites in moss mats in seepage areas
Form: Tiny, much branched hairy annual herb
Foliage: Leaves pinnate, lanceolate to ovate in outline
Flowers: Masses of tiny white flowers with shortly-clawed petals; Spring
Requirements: Well drained moist soil
Comments: This little herb would make an interesting container plant. Extinct in Melbourne mainly due to grazing and rabbits, it is now known from 1 Victorian site.
Propagation: Seed
Localities: An early collection in Werribee
Distribution: Vic, Tas
Synonym: *Cuphonotus antipodus, Capsela antipodus, Hutchinsia australis*

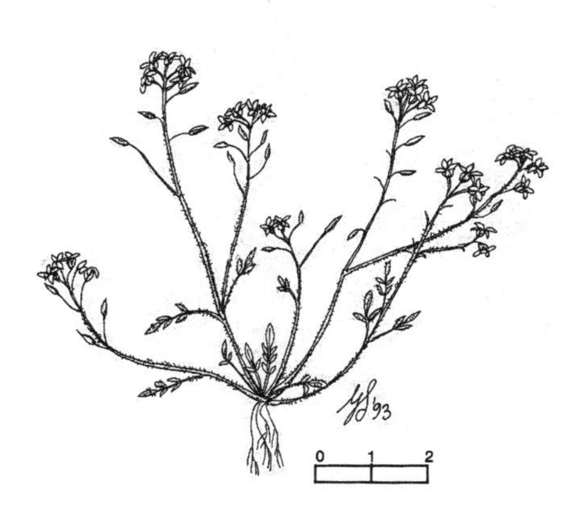

Ballantinia antipoda

SCALE: 0 1cm 2cm — The scale representation on each plant equals 2cm.

Banksia — Proteaceae

Banksia integrifolia var. integrifolia — Coast Banksia

F

Size: 10–20 m x 5–10 m
Habitat: Coastal banksia woodland, primary dune scrub
Form: Open erect or spreading tree
Foliage: Dark green leaves with silvery underside, linear to obovate to 15 cm long
Flowers: Pale yellow flowers borne on terminal spikes or brushes, 50–150 mm long. Flowering may occur at any time of the year, but mainly February to September
Requirements: Well drained soils responding to Summer watering
Comments: A sturdy ornamental windbreak with rough bark which can become gnarled and fissured with age. The seed is shed from woody cones when mature. It is useful for beach erosion control. The nectar from banksia cones was used to make drinks by the Aborigines. Paint brushes came from the stamens.
Propagation: Seed
Localities: 67, 69A, 74, 75
Distribution: Vic, Qld, NSW, Tas

Banksia integrifolia var. *integrifolia*

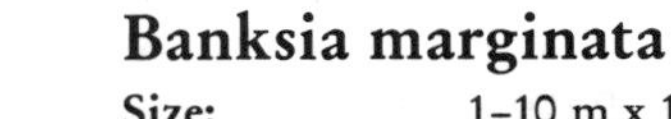

Banksia marginata — Silver Banksia

F P

Size: 1–10 m x 1–5 m
Habitat: Widespread from coast to ranges in tea-tree heath, grassy low open forest, riparian scrub, sclerophyll woodland, valley sclerophyll forest
Form: Variable dense to open shrub or small tree, depending on its habitat
Foliage: Stiff linear to obovate leaves to 100 mm long, silver below, toothed or entire, with a truncate tip.
Flowers: Pale to bright yellow flower spikes 40–100 mm; September to April
Requirements: Prefers good drainage tolerating soils which can be wet in Winter and dry in Summer
Comments: Bushy forms make excellent screening plants. Attractive woolly brown new growth can be encouraged by pruning. Seed is shed when mature. Cut flowers keep well. The forms presently found in the Melbourne area are unlikely to exceed 5 m. A tree form once occurred on the basalt plains in the Shire of Bulla and was referred to in early surveying reports. It now remains to the north west of the study area.
Propagation: Seed; specific forms must be grown from cuttings.
Localities: Olinda, Wonga Park, Mt. Cottrell, 1, 16, 26, 29, 43, 49, 50, 51, 54–56, 58, 59, 61–63, 67, 69–71, 73–76
Distribution: Vic, NSW, Tas, SA

Banksia marginata

Banksia spinulosa var. cunninghamii — Hairpin Banksia

F P

Size: 2–4 m x 2–5 m
Habitat: Valley sclerophyll forest, sclerophyll woodland
Form: Dense erect or spreading shrub
Foliage: Narrow dark green toothed leaves to 100 mm long
Flowers: Golden yellow spikes to 20 cm long with black hooked styles; February to July. Seed is retained in the cone.
Requirements: Prefers moist well drained soils but will tolerate dryness once established
Comments: An excellent shrub for growing under established trees. Light pruning encourages bushiness and makes an attractive screen. This variety does not produce a lignotuber and is not appropriate for areas with alkaline soils.
Propagation: Seed, Cuttings
Localities: 47, 51, 55
Distribution: Vic, Qld, NSW

Illustrated title page

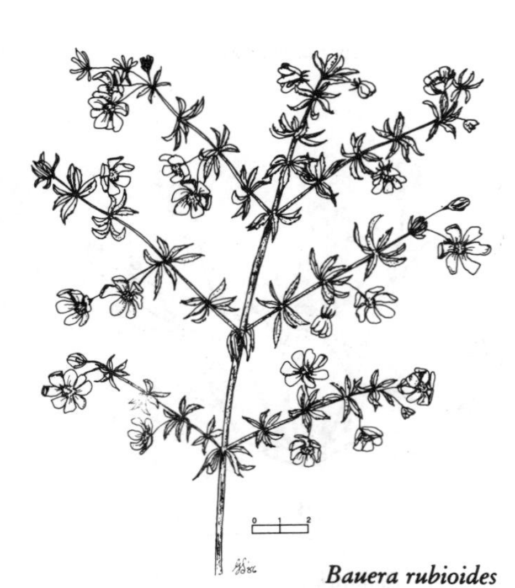

Bauera rubioides

Bauera — Baueraceae

Bauera rubioides — Wiry Bauera, River or Dog Rose

P N

Size: 1–2 m x 1–2 m
Habitat: Wet and sclerophyll forest
Form: Fast-growing dense scrambling shrub
Foliage: Pairs of leaves divided into 3 narrow sessile leaflets to 12 mm long, giving the appearance of whorls of 6 leaves
Flowers: Showy display of pink, sometimes white, open flowers most of the year
Requirements: Well drained moist soils, tolerating short periods of waterlogging
Comments: A hardy garden plant requiring regular light pruning.
Propagation: Cuttings, seeds
Localities: Montrose, 55–57
Distribution: Vic, Qld, NSW, Tas, SA

Bedfordia **Asteraceae**

Bedfordia arborescens

Blanket Leaf

Size: 3–7 m x 2–4 m **P N**
Habitat: Cool temperate rainforest, wet and valley sclerophyll forests
Form: Tall shrub or small spreading open tree
Foliage: Soft lanceolate leaves, dark green above, woolly white below, 15–25 cm long
Flowers: Small yellow daisy flowerheads in loose woolly clusters; October to January
Requirements: Deep well drained moist soils
Comments: A cool root system is necessary for this undershrub. This may be attained through mulching. Its rough bark may be suitable for epiphytic orchids or ferns.
Propagation: Seed
Localities: 42, 55–57
Distribution: Vic, NSW

Beyeria **Euphorbiaceae**

Beyeria viscosa

Pinkwood

Size: 3–6 m x 2–4 m **P**
Habitat: Damp sclerophyll forest, along gullies
Form: Medium to tall sticky shrub
Foliage: Shiny dark green oblong leaves to 100 mm long with dense white hairs below and edges recurved
Flowers: Pale yellow to cream flowers; July to January. Dioecious, female flowers are solitary, male flowers in clusters of 1–3. Fruit is a rounded capsule to 8 mm long.
Requirements: Well drained light to medium soil
Comments: Typically a plant of East Gippsland, it is known in Melbourne from a single stand on Mt. Dandenong. An excellent screening plant which responds well to pruning.
Propagation: Seed, cuttings
Localities: 55
Distribution: Vic, NSW, Tas, SA, WA

Billardiera **Pittosporaceae**

Billardiera longiflora

Purple Apple Berry

Size: Slender climber **P**
Habitat: Cool temperate rainforest, wet and valley sclerophyll forests, grassy low open forest
Form: Slender quick-growing light climber
Foliage: Shiny narrow dark green to purplish leaves to 50 mm long
Flowers: Pendent tubular flowers to 30 mm, bright greenish-yellow tinged with purple; August to January
Requirements: Moist well drained soils
Comments: Grows well under established eucalypts provided it has extra summer moisture. An attractive feature is the glossy purple berries which follow the flowers. It tolerates full sun in cool areas.
Propagation: Seed, cuttings
Localities: Kalorama, ?42, 57, 74, 76
Distribution: Vic, NSW, Tas

Billardiera scandens var. scandens

Common Apple Berry, Apple Dumpling

Size: Adaptable light climber **F P N**
Habitat: Widespread in damp, dry and valley sclerophyll forests, sclerophyll woodland, grassy low open forest
Form: Soft climber, bushier if grown in an open aspect
Foliage: Dark green linear-lanceolate leaves to 50 mm long, with wavy margins. New growth is soft, light green and hairy.
Flowers: Greenish-yellow tubular flowers throughout the year, with the main flowering period from June to January.
Requirements: Well drained dry to moist soils
Comments: The light green berries are edible. Grows under established trees.
Propagation: Seed, cuttings
Localities: 30#, 34–38, 40–64, 67, 69–71, 74–76
Distribution: Vic, Qld, NSW, Tas, SA

Billardiera scandens var. brachyantha

Habitat: Dry sclerophyll forest
Comments: A more shrubby, hairier variety with 2–3 flowers grouped together. Flower stalks and petals are shorter.
Localities: Eltham, 42
Distribution: Endemic to Vic

SCALE: 0 1cm 2cm — The scale representation on each plant equals 2cm.

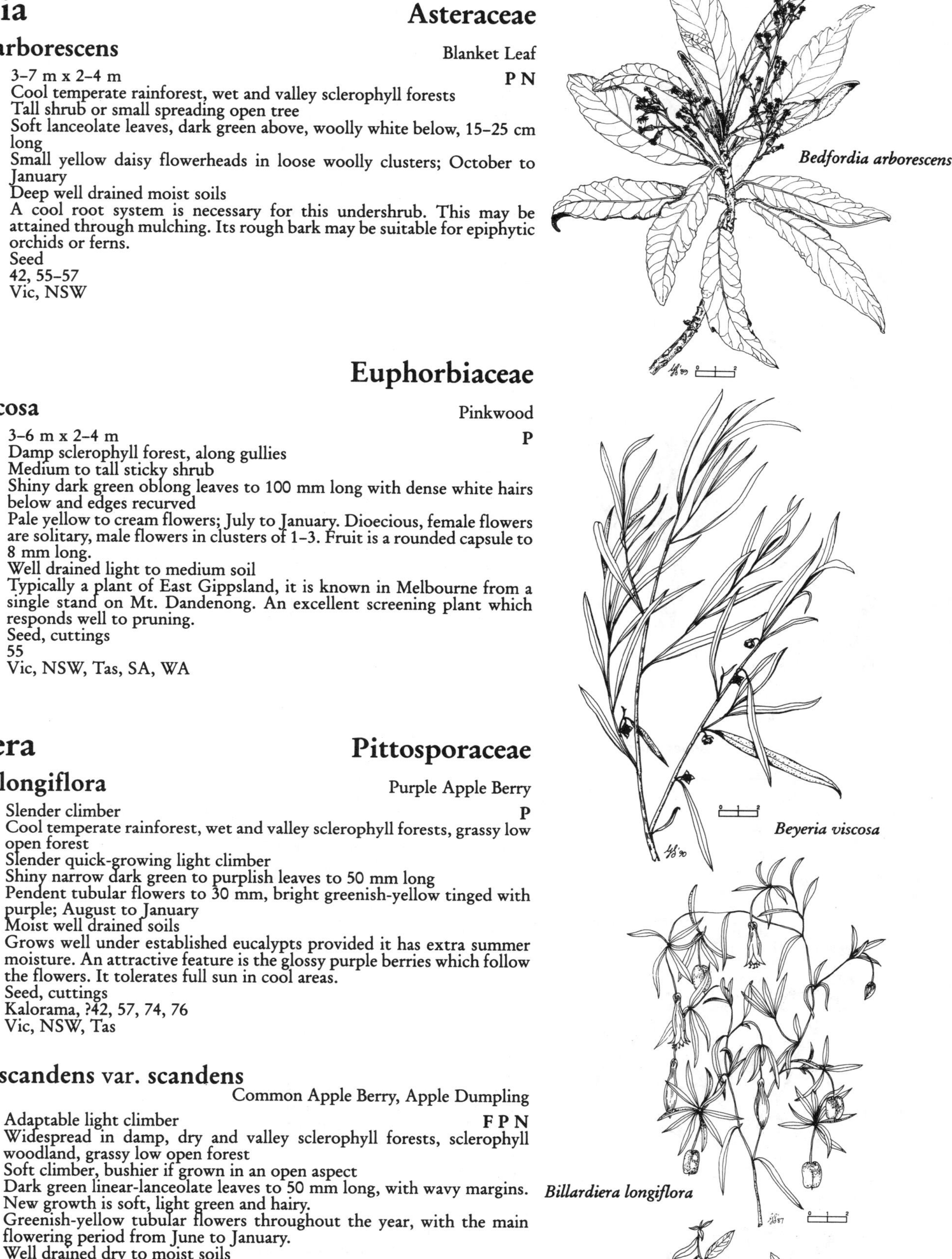

Bedfordia arborescens

Beyeria viscosa

Billardiera longiflora

Billardiera scandens var. *scandens*

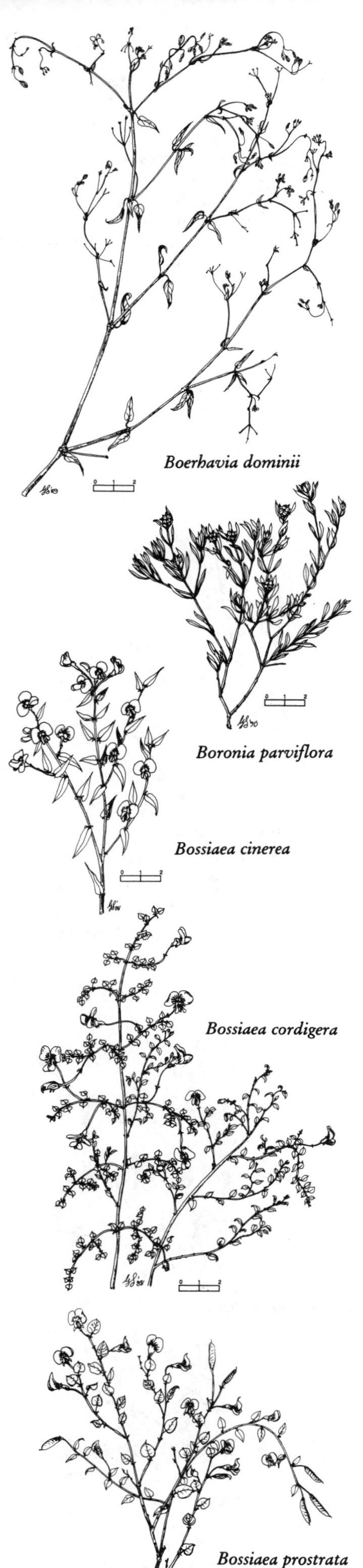
Boerhavia dominii

Boronia parviflora

Bossiaea cinerea

Bossiaea cordigera

Bossiaea prostrata

Boerhavia — Nyctaginaceae

Boerhavia dominii — Tah Vine

Size: Prostrate x 1–2 m — **F P**
Habitat: Saltmarsh
Form: Trailing or climbing perennial
Foliage: Dark green to 25 mm long, broad basal leaves with narrower upper leaves, wavy margins
Flowers: Dull pink flowers, either solitary or in umbels of 2–4; August to December
Requirements: Dry situations
Comments: A useful ground cover for dry areas but could become a weed in ideal conditions. The tap root was baked and eaten by the Aborigines.
Propagation: Seed, cuttings
Localities: Altona
Distribution: All mainland states
Synonym: *B. diffusa*

Boronia — Rutaceae

Boronia parviflora — Swamp Boronia

Size: 0.3–0.5 m x 0.3–0.5 m — **P**
Habitat: Swamp margins of tea-tree heath
Form: Diffuse or trailing dwarf shrub
Foliage: Elliptical reddish leaves to 20 mm long
Flowers: White or pink flowers in clusters at the end of branchlets; August to December
Requirements: Moist peaty soil
Comments: Summer moisture is required. A light mulch will keep the roots cool.
Propagation: Cuttings
Localities: 66#, 67#, 74, 75
Distribution: Vic, Qld, NSW, Tas, SA

Bossiaea — Fabaceae

Bossiaea cinerea — Showy Bossiaea

Size: 1–2 m x 1–2 m — **F P**
Habitat: Tea-tree heath, coastal banksia woodland
Form: Dense low, rounded or spreading shrub
Foliage: Alternate dull green, stalkless triangular leaves to 20 mm long, with bronze new growth
Flowers: Profuse yellow and red pea flowers occurring singly along stems; August to December
Requirements: Adapts to most well drained soils
Comments: An ornamental shrub which may be pruned hard. It prefers dappled shade and tolerates some coastal exposure and light frosts.
Propagation: Scarified seed, cuttings
Localities: Port Melbourne#, 42, 63, 65#–71, 73–76
Distribution: Vic, NSW, Tas, SA

Bossiaea cordigera — Wiry Bossiaea

Size: Prostrate—20 cm x 1–2 m — **P**
Habitat: Sclerophyll woodland
Form: Ornamental spreading shrub
Foliage: Pairs of small dark green heart-shaped leaves to 5 mm long
Flowers: Single yellow and red pea flowers; November to February
Requirements: Well drained moist soil
Comments: A wiry shrub which scrambles over other plants.
Localities: 59
Distribution: Vic, Tas

Bossiaea prostrata — Creeping Bossiaea

Size: Prostrate x 0.5–1.5 m — **F P N**
Habitat: Dry and valley sclerophyll forests, grassy low open forest, red gum and sclerophyll woodlands, plains grassland
Form: Spreading or matting ground cover
Foliage: Oval to oblong grey-green leaves to 10 mm long
Flowers: Yellow and brown pea flowers; October to November
Requirements: Easy to grow in all well drained soils
Comments: This attractively foliaged plant grows well under other plants. Common throughout most of Melbourne, it remains in isolated areas on the basalt plains.
Localities: Tottenham, 7, 12, 13, 16, 25, 26, 28–36, 38, 39, 41, 42, 44–51, 53–56, 58–67, 69–71, 74–76
Distribution: Vic, Qld, NSW, Tas, SA

Brachyloma **Epacridaceae**

Brachyloma ciliatum

Fringed Brachyloma or Daphne Heath

Size: 0.5 m x 0.5–1 m **P**
Habitat: Tea-tree heath
Form: Slow-growing open shrub
Foliage: Small dull green oval to oblong pointed leaves to 10 mm long, margins hairy
Flowers: Small white to cream tubular flowers, hairy inside; September to December
Requirements: Prefers sandy well drained soil
Comments: Useful as an undershrub, this plant tolerates light frosts and needs cool roots. Regenerates well after a fire. The fruit was eaten raw by the Aborigines.
Propagation: Cuttings
Localities: Baxter, 67#, 74, 75
Distribution: Vic, Tas, SA

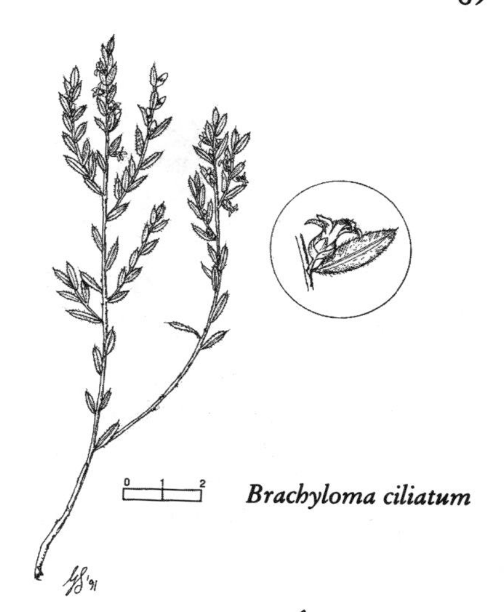

Brachyloma ciliatum

Brachyscome **Asteraceae**

A member of the daisy family, these plants are widespread, occurring in many habitats throughout Melbourne. Most require moist conditions or Summer watering. Seventeen species occur in the Melbourne area; several of these are already extinct while most are rare or endangered. They are perennial herbs with the typical daisy flowerhead which consists of many disc florets surrounded by petal-like ray florets. They adapt well to cultivation and are excellent for the small garden, rockeries or container growing. A heavy prune after flowering is beneficial. Propagation is by seed, cutting or division with many striking readily from cuttings.

Brachyscome aculeata

Hill Daisy

Size: 0.2–0.6 m high **F P**
Habitat: Riparian scrub
Form: Basal rosette
Foliage: Linear to wedge-shaped leaves to 100 mm long
Flowers: Branched flowering stems with numerous erect white flowerheads, 20 mm across; intermittent from late Spring to late Autumn
Requirements: Ample moisture
Comments: A very restricted range in Melbourne.
Localities: Lilydale#, 29
Distribution: Vic, Qld, NSW, Tas, SA

Brachyscome basaltica var. gracilis

Basalt Daisy

Size: 0.3–0.6 m high **F**
Habitat: Grassy wetlands, plains grassland
Form: Small perennial herb
Foliage: Narrow-linear leaves to 90 mm long, scattered along the stems
Flowers: Numerous white flowerheads to 18 mm across, held erect; September to November
Requirements: Moist soils
Comments: A good bog plant from the basalt plains but now locally rare.
Localities: Werribee, Sydenham, Bundoora, Derrimut, 7, 11, 16, 17#, 26
Distribution: Vic, NSW, SA

Brachyscome cardiocarpa

Swamp Daisy

Size: 10–30 cm x 20 cm **F P**
Habitat: Swamp scrub, grassy wetland, depressions in tea-tree heath
Form: Fast-growing tufted perennial herb
Foliage: Rosette of grass-like dark green or purplish leaves to 20 cm long
Flowers: Single white or blue flowerheads 40 mm across, on long erect stems; June to December.
Requirements: Moisture is essential
Localities: Black Rock, Scoresby, Bayswater, Kilsyth, Springvale, Montrose, 29#, 49, 58, 63, 65#, 67#, 74
Distribution: Vic, NSW, Tas, SA *Illustrated p. 1*

Brachyscome ciliaris

Variable Daisy

Size: 7–11 cm high **F**
Habitat: Plains grassland
Form: Spreading annual or perennial herb
Foliage: Pinnate leaves to 60 mm long, leaflets narrow, covered in white woolly hairs
Flowers: Profuse white or blue flowerheads on wiry, down-covered stems; most of the year, peaking August to December
Requirements: Well drained soil
Comments: An excellent container plant.
Localities: Collected in Werribee in 1899; 74
Distribution: All states

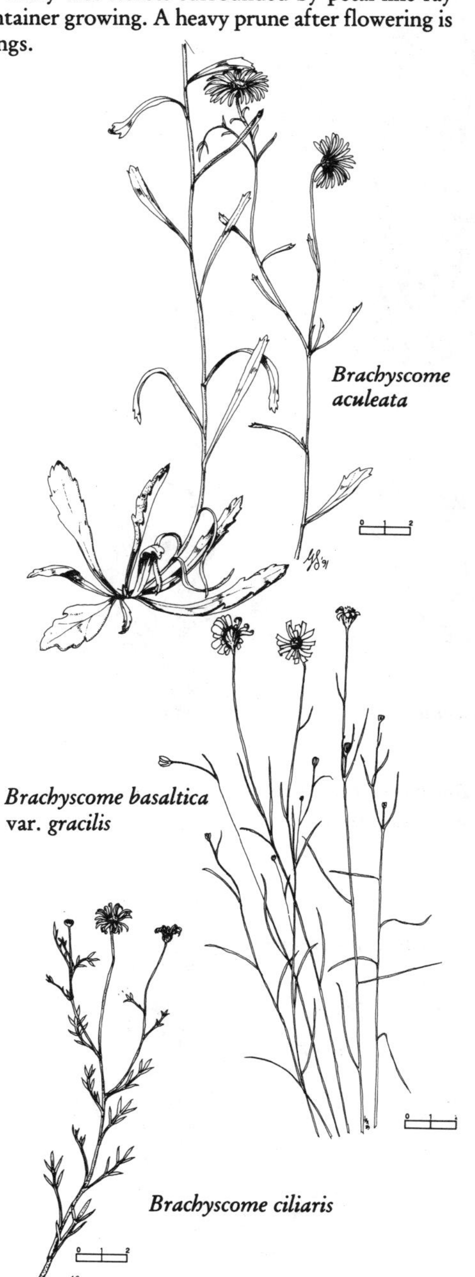

Brachyscome aculeata

Brachyscome basaltica var. *gracilis*

Brachyscome ciliaris

SCALE: 0 1cm 2cm The scale representation on each plant equals 2cm.

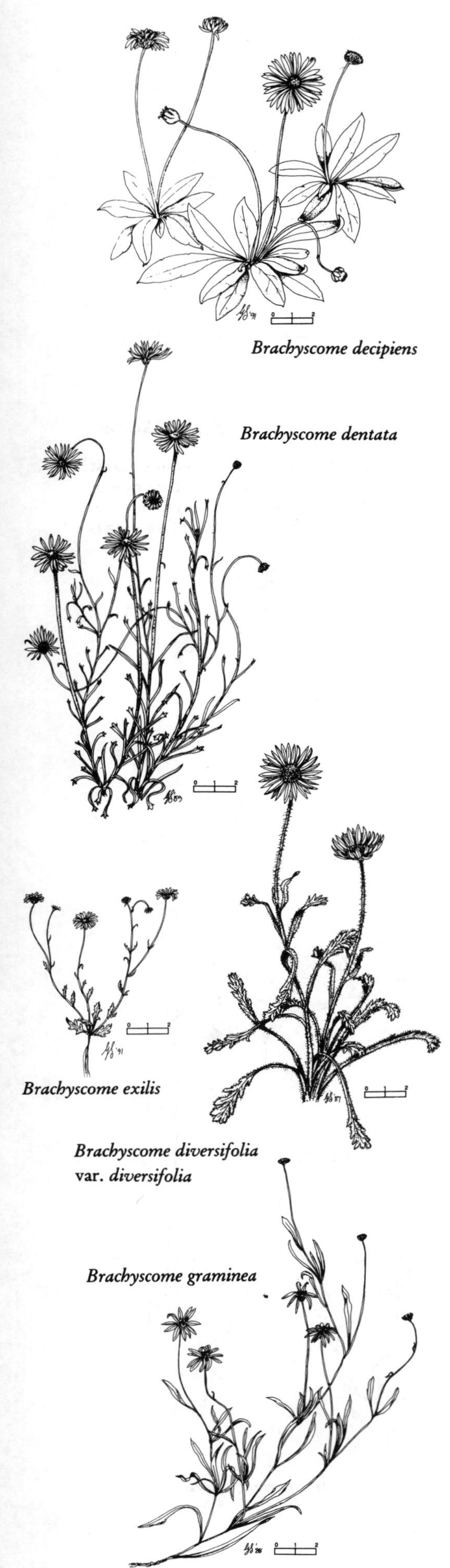

Brachyscome decipiens

Brachyscome dentata

Brachyscome exilis

Brachyscome diversifolia var. *diversifolia*

Brachyscome graminea

Brachyscome decipiens
Field Daisy

Size: 3–20 cm high **F P**
Habitat: Plains grasslands, red gum woodland, dry and valley sclerophyll forests
Form: Perennial herb in a basal rosette
Foliage: Flat tuft of broad leaves to 16 cm long,
Flowers: White or blue flowerheads 40 mm across on erect stalks; August to March
Requirements: Moist to wet soils
Comments: An excellent container or rockery plant. Locally rare.
Localities: Coldstream, Eltham–Warrandyte, 25, 26, 29#, 34A, 45, 49, 50A, 63, 64, 67#
Distribution: Vic, NSW, Tas, SA

Brachyscome dentata
Golden or Lobe-seed Daisy

Size: 15–30 cm x 0.3–0.6 m **F**
Habitat: Grassy wetlands, riparian scrub, box woodland, plains grassland
Form: Spreading to erect perennial herb
Foliage: Narrow leaves to 30 mm long
Flowers: White flowerheads; October to December
Requirements: Well drained soils and protection from slugs and snails
Localities: Sunbury, Tottenham, St Albans, Keilor, Williamstown, Melton Sth, Laverton Nth, 2, 4, 7, 10–12, 16, 17#, 25, 26
Distribution: Vic, Qld, NSW, SA
Synonym: *B. heterodonta*

Brachyscome diversifolia var. diversifolia
Tall or Large-headed Daisy

Size: 20–50 cm high **F P**
Habitat: Primary dune scrub, coastal banksia woodland, dry sclerophyll forest
Form: Robust tufted herb
Foliage: Soft, hairy, lobed bright green leaves to 100 mm long
Flowers: Single white flowerheads, 20–40 mm across on erect hairy stalks; intermittent, peaking from October to February.
Requirements: Well drained soils
Comments: Suitable for cut flowers. Endangered in Melbourne, it has disappeared from most of its range.
Localities: Warrandyte, 67#
Distribution: Vic, Qld, NSW, Tas, SA

Brachyscome exilis
Slender Daisy

Size: 5–15 cm high **F P**
Habitat: Saline areas and near brackish wetlands
Form: Small herb
Foliage: Few broad hairy leaves to 10 mm long
Flowers: Terminal bunches of white flowerheads; August to November
Requirements: Adaptable to dry or wet conditions
Comments: A rare Victorian plant it is now believed to be extinct within the Melbourne area.
Localities: Collected from the Eltham and St. Albans areas.
Distribution: Vic, NSW, SA, WA

Brachyscome graminea
Grass Daisy

Size: 0.3–0.7 m high **F P**
Habitat: Margins of brackish swamps in riparian scrub, tea-tree heath, grassy wetlands
Form: Sprawling perennial herb
Foliage: Bright green grass-like leaves to 50 mm long
Flowers: Numerous single-stemmed white, pink, lilac or deep blue flowerheads to 20 mm wide; September to March
Requirements: Moist soils
Comments: A good container plant but must not dry out.
Localities: Port Phillip Bay, 29, 30#, 34A, 67#
Distribution: Vic, Qld, NSW, Tas, SA

Brachyscome leptocarpa
Downy or Small Hairy Daisy

Size: 2–25 cm high **F**
Habitat: Plains grasslands
Form: Slender annual herb
Foliage: Hairy leaves to 30 mm long, basal leaves are narrow while stem leaves are entire or toothed
Flowers: Few white to mauve flowerheads; September to November
Requirements: Dry well drained soils
Localities: An early collection from Werribee
Distribution: Vic, NSW, SA

Illustrated p. 79

Brachyscome multifida var. multifida

Cut Leaf Daisy

F P

Size: 10–40 cm x 0.2–1 m
Habitat: Box woodland, dry sclerophyll forest, sheltered rocky areas
Form: Fast growing, low spreading perennial
Foliage: Soft dark green pinnate leaves to 70 mm long
Flowers: Profuse variable lilac-blue, mauve, pink or white flowerheads, held erect. Flowers most of the year peaking in Spring and Summer.
Requirements: Moist clay soils, tolerating dryness once established
Comments: A very popular and ornamental plant. Spreads by underground suckers and roots at nodes making it a useful soil binder.
Propagation: Stem cutting, which strikes readily.
Localities: Bundoora, 36, 55, 63
Distribution: Vic, Qld, NSW

Brachyscome multifida var. *multifida*

Brachyscome parvula var. parvula

Coast Daisy

F

Size: 10–40 cm high
Habitat: Marshes of primary dune scrub
Form: Tufted perennial herb
Foliage: Blunt linear to spathulate leaves to 70 mm long
Flowers: Single white flowerheads to 10 mm; November to January
Requirements: Wet soils
Comments: Useful as a bog plant. Locally rare.
Localities: Mordialloc, 67
Distribution: Vic, Tas, SA

Brachyscome parvula var. *parvula*

Brachyscome perpusilla

Rayless Daisy

F

Size: to 10 cm high
Habitat: Grassy wetlands
Form: Tiny annual tufted herb
Foliage: Pinnate leaves 4–30 mm long
Flowers: Yellow flowerheads with minute ray florets on branched stalks; July to October
Requirements: Moist well drained soils
Localities: Werribee
Distribution: Vic, NSW, SA, WA

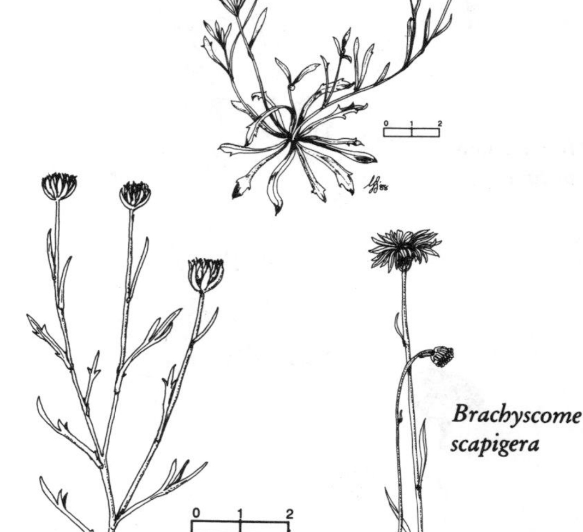

Brachyscome perpusilla

Brachyscome scapigera

Brachyscome scapigera

Tufted Daisy

F P

Size: 15–40 cm high
Habitat: Dry sclerophyll forest
Form: Densely clumping perennial herb
Foliage: Entire linear-lanceolate leaves to 19 cm long
Flowers: Few white to lilac flowerheads to 20 mm wide on unbranched stalks; September to January
Requirements: Moist soils, becoming dormant when dry
Comments Useful for rockeries and containers. May be extinct locally.
Localities: Collected from Research, Eltham.
Distribution: Vic, Qld, NSW

Brachyscome spathulata

Coarse Daisy

F P

Habitat: Riparian scrub
Comments: One of the *B. aculeata* group with which it is often combined, it is distinguished by the bright blue flowerheads and pointed bracts. The unbranched flowering stalks rise from a rosette of oblanceolate to broad-spathulate toothed leaves.
Localities: An early collection from along the Merri Creek, 1896
Distribution: Vic, NSW, Tas
Synonym: *B. scapiformis*

Illustrated p. 79

Brachyscome trachycarpa

Smooth Daisy

F

Size: 10–40 cm high
Habitat: Sandy woodlands and rocky areas
Form: Small erect herb
Foliage: Narrow entire or lobed leaves to 35 mm long
Flowers: White to lilac flowerheads; most of the year
Comments: Appears to be locally extinct.
Localities: Collected at Werribee
Distribution: All mainland states

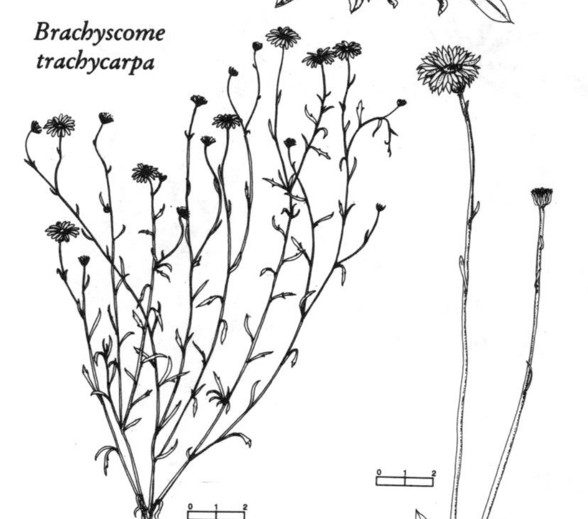

Brachyscome trachycarpa

Brachyscome uliginosa

Brachyscome uliginosa

Small Swamp Daisy

F

Size: to 30 cm high
Habitat: Valley sclerophyll forest
Form: Creeping tufted herb
Foliage: Narrow pale green foliage to 60 mm long
Flowers: Single white or mauve flowerheads on long stems; September to January
Requirements: Moist soils
Comments: Similar to *B. scapigera*. A good container plant. Locally rare.
Localities: Eltham
Distribution: Vic, SA

SCALE: 0 1cm 2cm — The scale representation on each plant equals 2cm.

Bracteantha

Asteraceae

Bracteantha are referred to as everlasting daisies. Their flowers are long-lasting and often very showy. Petal-like bracts surround many tiny flowers, giving a daisy-like appearance. Useful as cut flowers, they also dry well. *Bracteantha* are very adaptable and make excellent garden or container subjects. It is preferable to prune them back in late Winter to encourage new growth. Propagation is by seed or cuttings.
Synonym: Previously included in the genus *Helichrysum*

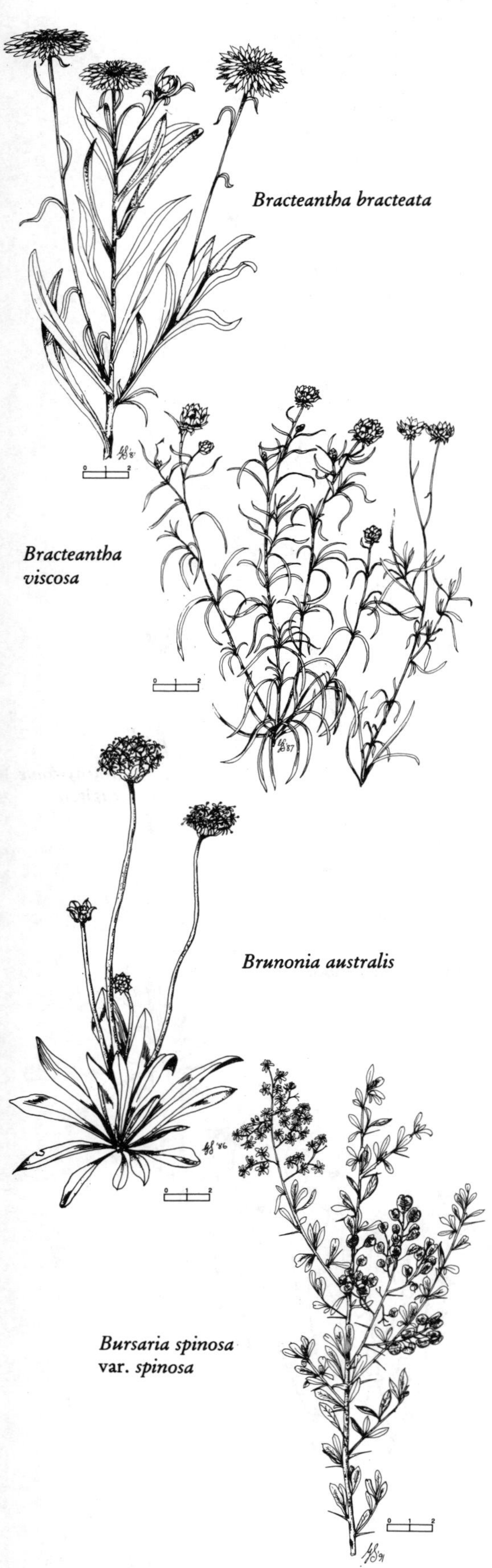

Bracteantha bracteata

Bracteantha viscosa

Brunonia australis

Bursaria spinosa var. *spinosa*

Bracteantha bracteata

Golden Everlasting, Straw Flower, Paper Daisy

Size: 0.3–1.2 m x 0.6 m — F
Habitat: Tea-tree heath, dry sclerophyll forest
Form: Fast growing erect annual or perennial herb
Foliage: Soft, stalkless, fresh green oblong leaves 15–120 mm long; upper leaves are narrower
Flowers: Flowerheads are surrounded by numerous shiny, bright yellow bracts, providing a very showy display; late Spring to Autumn
Requirements: Dry well drained soil
Comments: A spectacular daisy which is ideal for rockeries and containers. It is very variable in form and colour throughout its range. The forms generally available in nurseries are perennials from outside the Melbourne area. Hard pruning increases vigour. Locally rare.
Localities: Warrandyte, 30, 32, 34A, 67, 74, 75
Distribution: All states
Synonym: *Helichrysum bracteatum*

Bracteantha viscosa

Sticky Everlasting

Size: 0.5–0.8 m x 0.3–1 m — F P
Habitat: Dry sclerophyll forest, red gum and box woodlands, often on shallow stony soils
Form: Much-branched sticky biennial or perennial herb, dense or straggly
Foliage: Linear dark green leaves to 90 mm long, margins recurved
Flowers: Showy bright yellow flowerheads to 40 mm at the ends of branches; August to April
Requirements: Well drained soils
Comments: Pruning is necessary to encourage bushiness and to extend the life of this very attractive daisy. Responds to extra Summer moisture.
Localities: Diamond Creek, Warrandyte, Montrose, Sth of Melton, 32, 36, 67#
Distribution: Vic, Qld, NSW
Synonym: *Helichrysum viscosum*

Brunonia

Brunoniaceae

Brunonia australis

Blue Pincushion

Size: 10–50 cm x 10–15 cm — F P
Habitat: Tea-tree heath, dry and valley sclerophyll forests, red gum woodland, plains grassland
Form: Perennial herb
Foliage: Rosette of spoon-shaped light green hairy leaves to 100 mm long
Flowers: Dense blue pincushion-like flowerheads on stems to 50 cm high; October to January
Requirements: Moist well drained soil, tolerant of extended dry periods
Comments: Often short-lived in cultivation, it makes an excellent container plant. Treat as an annual and collect seeds to replant. Informal drifts provide a natural look.
Propagation: Seed sown fresh, division—in July to August.
Localities: 12, 26, 29#, 34A–39, 41–44, 46–53, 55, 56, 58, 59, 62, 63, 67#, 68, 74–76
Distribution: All states

Bursaria

Pittosporaceae

Bursaria spinosa var. spinosa

Sweet Bursaria, Blackthorn

Size: 2–6 m x 2–3 m — F P
Habitat: Widespread in grassy low open forest, riparian scrub, dry and valley sclerophyll forests, red gum and riparian woodlands
Form: Slender to rounded shrub or small tree with spines along the branches
Foliage: Shiny narrow dark green leaves, variable to 25 mm long and 10 mm wide
Flowers: Masses of fragrant, creamy-white bunches of flowers at the end of branches; December to March
Requirements: Well drained soils
Comments: Clusters of bronze seed capsules follow flowering on this easily grown plant. It is the food plant of the Eltham Copper Butterfly.
Propagation: Seed, cuttings
Localities: 1, 14, 16, 18, 22, 25, 26, 28, 30–56, 58–69, 74, 76
Distribution: All states except NT

Bursaria spinosa var. macrophylla

Habitat: Plains grassland, riparian scrub
Comments: Leaves are longer (more than 25 mm) and wider (more than 10 mm) than *B. spinosa* var. *spinosa* and the branches are spineless.
Localities: Seaford, Kororoit Ck, 4, 26, 28–30, 34A, 44, 69A, 74
Distribution: Vic, Qld, NSW, Tas, SA

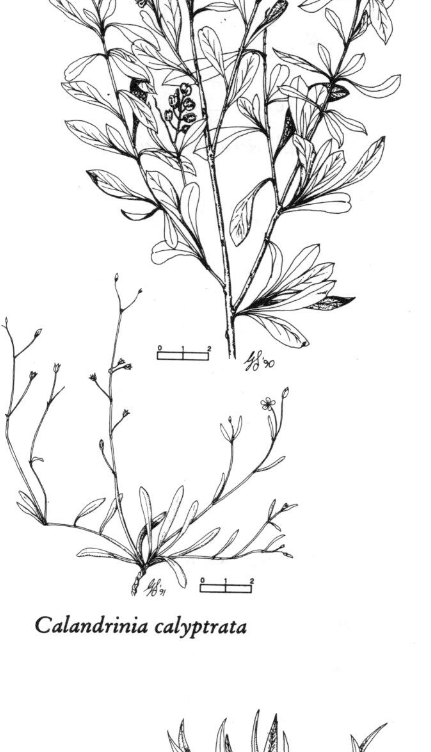

Bursaria spinosa var. *macrophylla*

Calandrinia calyptrata

Calandrinia — Portulacaceae

Calandrinia calyptrata — Pink Purslane, Small Leaf Parakeelya

Size: Prostrate—10 cm x 10–30 cm **F**
Habitat: Primary dune scrub, coastal banksia, box and red gum woodlands, chenopod rocky open scrub
Form: Rosetted annual growing from Winter to Spring
Foliage: Succulent leaves to 35 mm long, tapered at each end, often reddish
Flowers: Terminal sprays of small pink flowers held high above the foliage on slender leafless stems; August to October
Requirements: Prefers well drained, dry soils in warm to hot areas
Comments: Seeds of calandrinias were ground by the Aborigines to make bread. Disappeared from much of its range.
Propagation: Seed, cuttings
Localities: Brighton 1887; 14, 16, 26, 30#, 35, 42, 67#
Distribution: All states except Qld

Calandrinia eremaea — Small Purslane

F

Comments: Similar to *C. calyptrata*, but leaves are longer, to 40 mm, thicker, more cylindrical and stem-clasping at the base. Flowers are pink or white. May be locally extinct.
Localities: near Werribee R 1890
Distribution: Vic, NSW, SA, NT

Callistemon — Myrtaceae

Callistemon sieberi — River Bottlebrush

Size: 3–10 m x 2–6 m **F P**
Habitat: Widespread in riparian scrub and woodland
Form: Open to dense weeping shrub
Foliage: Stiff narrow green leaves to 100 mm long; silky, silver new growth
Flowers: Scattered cream or pink bottlebrushes to 80 mm long; November to May
Requirements: Very adaptable, prefers very wet to moist conditions in heavy clay soil but tolerates dryness once established
Comments: An attractive screening shrub which benefits from pruning to encourage more prolific flowering.
Propagation: Seeds using bog method, cuttings
Localities: Keilor, 8, 14, 16, 19, 23, 26–36, 42, 47
Distribution: Vic, NSW, Tas, SA
Synonym: *C. paludosus*

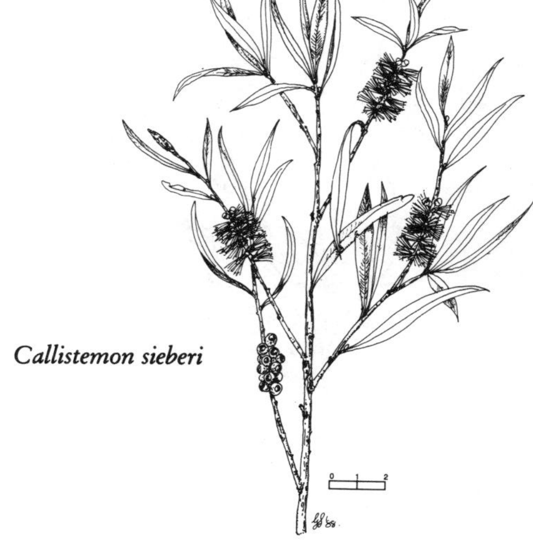

Callistemon sieberi

Callitriche — Callitrichaceae

Callitriche brachycarpa — Water Starwort

P

Habitat: Moist areas of dry sclerophyll forest, riparian scrub
Form: Very small prostrate herb
Foliage: Entire oblanceolate to ovate leaves to 7 mm long
Flowers: Pale brown fruit with an inconspicuous wing
Requirements: Moist soils
Comments: A rare plant, with a restricted range in Melbourne. Also found north of Hurstbridge and in the Otways/Apollo Bay area.
Localities: Hurstbridge, 29
Distribution: Vic, Tas

Callitriche cyclocarpa — Water Starwort

Habitat: Floodwaters
Form: Tangled aquatic herb rooting from the nodes
Foliage: Leaves oblanceolate to 4 mm long, lower leaves occasionally more linear
Comments: Similar to *C. umbonata*. Distinguished by the black fruit which lacks a basal projection and is scarcely winged. An endangered plant, probably extinct in Melbourne.
Localities: Early collections were made in Springvale and an undefined central Melbourne site.
Distribution: Endemic to Vic

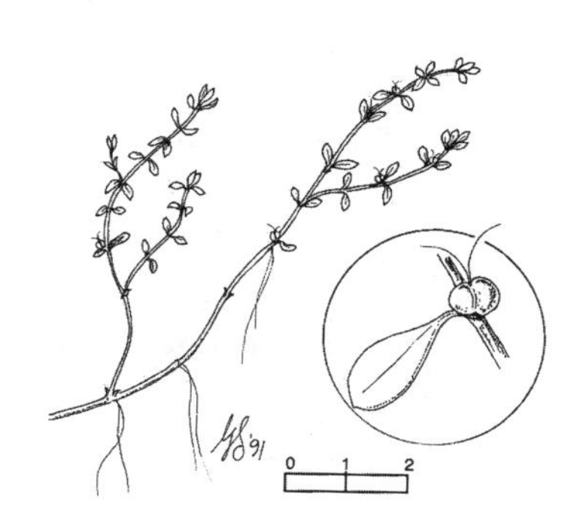

Callitriche brachycarpa

SCALE: 0 1cm 2cm — The scale representation on each plant equals 2cm.

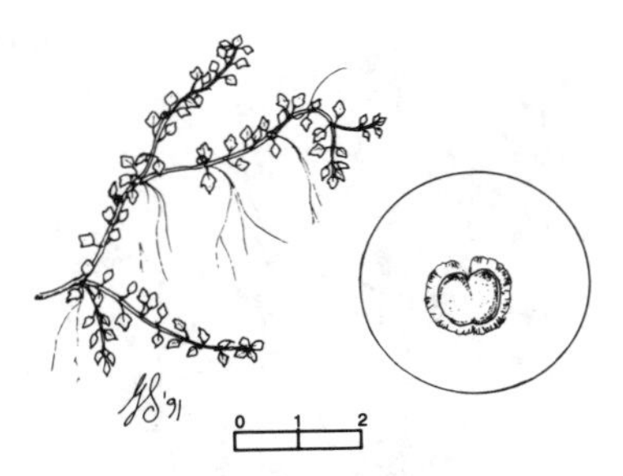

Callitriche muelleri

Callitriche muelleri

Round Water Starwort

P N

Size:	Prostrate x 10–20 cm
Habitat:	Boggy sites and wet areas, also aquatic
Form:	Creeping herb
Foliage:	Very small dark green rhomboidal leaves, 2–7 mm long, with a single tooth on each side
Flowers:	Insignificant, pairs of male and female flowers in each leaf axil; October to February. Tiny fruit has a conspicuous wing.
Requirements:	Damp to wet conditions
Comments:	It would make an attractive mat plant for bog gardens and pond margins.
Propagation:	Division
Localities:	Lilydale, 35, 49#, 60
Distribution:	Vic, Qld, NSW; NZ

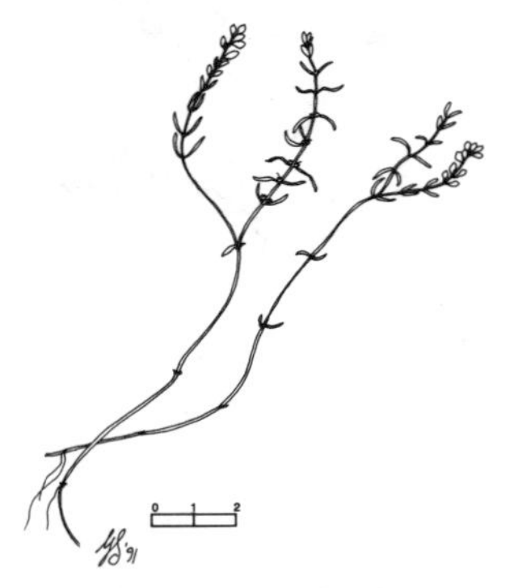

Callitriche umbonata

Callitriche palustris

Water Starwort

P

Habitat:	Riparian scrub, valley sclerophyll forest
Form:	Floating or creeping stems
Foliage:	Pairs of linear-lanceolate leaves to 3 mm long
Comments:	Flowers have conspicuous bracts. Fruit is stalkless. Suitable for aquariums.
Localities:	Keilor, Warrandyte North, 16, 19, 26, 32
Distribution:	Vic, NSW; PNG, New Caledonia

Callitriche umbonata

Water Starwort

P

Habitat:	Grassy wetland
Form:	Aquatic or terrestrial herb
Foliage:	Lower leaves of aquatic plants linear to 10 mm, upper rosette of leaves are obovate to 8 mm long on a broad stalk; terrestrial plants lack linear leaves.
Flowers:	Single white axillary flowers; August to December. Tiny dark brown fruit has a narrow pale brown wing projecting at the base.
Localities:	Early collections from Darebin Creek in 1852 and unnamed inner Melbourne sites.
Distribution:	Vic, NSW, Tas, SA

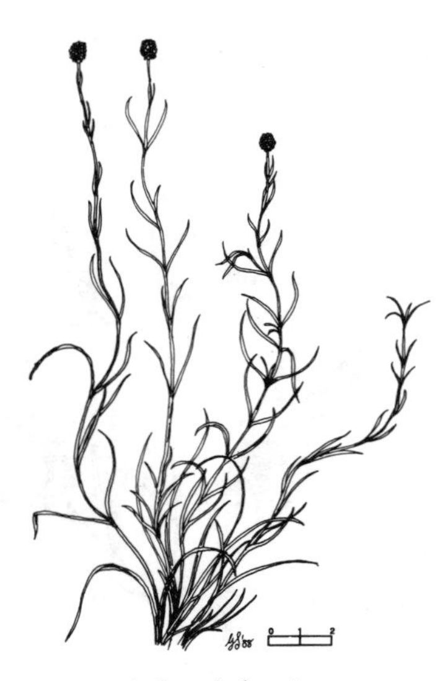

Calocephalus citreus

Calocephalus — Asteraceae

Calocephalus brownii = Leucophyta brownii

Calocephalus citreus

Lemon Beauty Heads

F P

Size:	0.2–0.5 m x 0.3–1 m
Habitat:	Plains grassland, red gum woodland
Form:	Tufted perennial herb
Foliage:	Silvery-grey pointed leaves to 100 mm long
Flowers:	Bright yellow oblong flower heads held erect; October to February
Requirements:	Well drained soils, tolerating dry periods once established
Comments:	An attractive plant, suitable for mass planting in the garden or as a container plant. Flowers dry well.
Propagation:	Cuttings, division
Localities:	2, 4, 5, 7, 10, 12, 13, 15–18, 20, 25, 26
Distribution:	Vic, Qld, NSW, Tas, SA

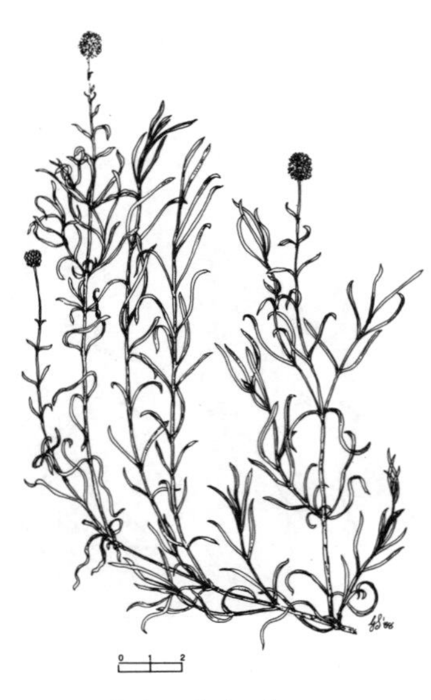

Calocephalus lacteus

Calocephalus lacteus

Milky Beauty Heads

F P

Size:	15–30 cm x 10–30 cm
Habitat:	Plains grassland, red gum woodland, dry sclerophyll forest
Form:	Small sprawling shrub
Foliage:	Soft, grey, blunt leaves to 25 mm long
Flowers:	White globular to oblong button flowerheads; September to February.
Requirements:	Well drained soils tolerating dryness once established
Comments:	Locally rare
Propagation:	Seed, cuttings
Localities:	St. Kilda#, Sunbury, 2, 4, 5, 24–26, 28, 35, 36, 67#
Distribution:	Vic, NSW, Tas, SA

Calotis

Asteraceae

Low perennial shrubs with daisy flowerheads, followed by round burr-like fruiting heads. Propagate by seed or cuttings.

Calotis anthemoides

Common Burr Daisy

Size: 10–20 cm x 20–30 cm **F P**
Habitat: Grassy wetlands, plains grassland
Form: Erect glabrous perennial herb
Foliage: Tuft of finely divided basal leaves to 115 mm long
Flowers: Showy white or lilac flowerheads to 15 mm wide in Spring.
Comments: Locally rare plant of moist to wet areas
Localities: Laverton Nth, Altona, 2
Distribution: Vic, NSW

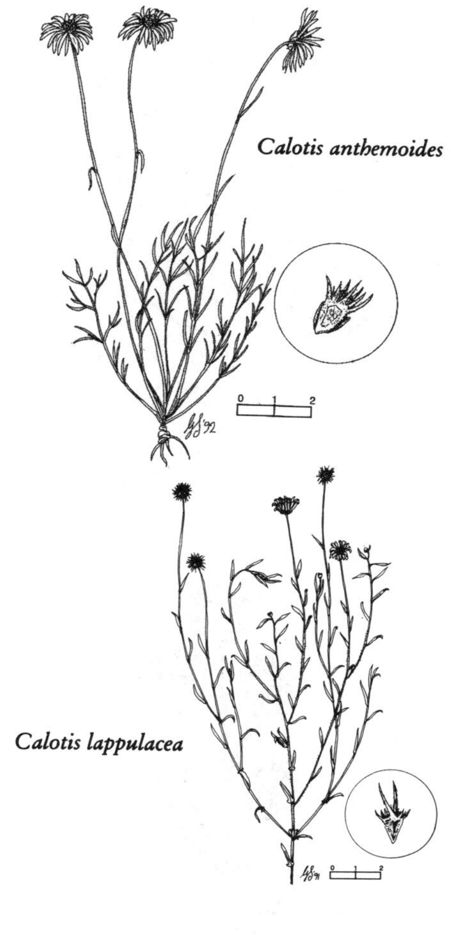

Calotis anthemoides

Calotis cymbacantha

Showy Burr Daisy

Size: 10–30 cm high **F**
Habitat: Plains grassland
Form: Erect, branched annual herb, covered in downy hairs
Foliage: Oblong to broad-linear leaves with 3–7 lobes; stalked basal leaves to 90 mm long, sessile stem leaves to 80 mm long
Flowers: Yellow flowerheads to 20 mm wide in loose leafy cymes; February to March, July to October
Requirements: Well drained soil
Comments: Although widespread, this plant is very rare; in Victoria it is usually found only in the drier North West region.
Localities: St. Albans
Distribution: Vic, Qld, NSW, SA, WA, NT

Illustrated p. 79

Calotis lappulacea

Yellow Burr Daisy

Size: 0.3–0.5 m x 0.3–1 m **F P**
Habitat: Box woodland and cleared land
Foliage: Hairy; wedge-shaped lower leaves to 60 mm long; sessile stem leaves, lobed to toothed or narrow and entire, to 25 mm long
Flowers: Yellow daisy flowerheads to 10 mm wide most of the year
Requirements: Dry, well drained soils
Comments: A very showy plant, ideal for rockeries. The prickly burrs limit its placement to areas away from paths.
Localities: Toolern Vale
Distribution: Vic, Qld, NSW, SA, WA

Calotis lappulacea

Calotis scabiosifolia var. scabiosifolia

Rough Burr Daisy

Size: 0.3–0.5 m x 0.5–1 m **F P**
Habitat: Plains grassland, red gum woodland
Form: Hairy perennial herb spreading by stolons to form tufts
Foliage: Basal leaves are lanceolate and toothed or lobed to 20 cm long; stem leaves are narrow, toothed or entire and sessile
Flowers: Showy white or lilac flowerheads to 25 mm across, singly on long stalks; August to November.
Comments: Suited to container growing and is drought resistant. Now locally rare.
Localities: Tottenham, Sydenham, Laverton Nth, 17#, 18
Distribution: Vic, Qld, NSW, SA

Calotis scabiosifolia var. *scabiosifolia*

Calotis scabiosifolia var. integrifolia

P

Comments: Montane form. Leaves are linear and usually without teeth.
Localities: 55
Distribution: Vic, NSW

Calotis scapigera

Tufted Burr Daisy

Size: 0.1–0.5 m x 0.5–1 m **F P**
Habitat: Grassy wetland, swamps and depressions in red gum woodland
Foliage: Tufts of narrow leaves to 100 mm long
Flowers: White or lilac flowerheads; October to May
Requirements: Moist, heavy well drained soil
Comments: An excellent ground cover. Its suckering habit assists in controlling soil erosion.
Propagation: Root cuttings from runners strike readily.
Localities: Sydenham, 7, 12, 16–18, 26
Distribution: Vic, Qld, NSW, SA

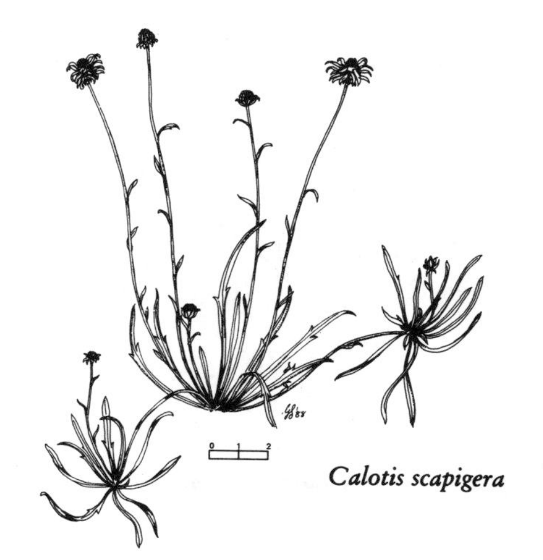

Calotis scapigera

SCALE: 0 1cm 2cm

The scale representation on each plant equals 2cm.

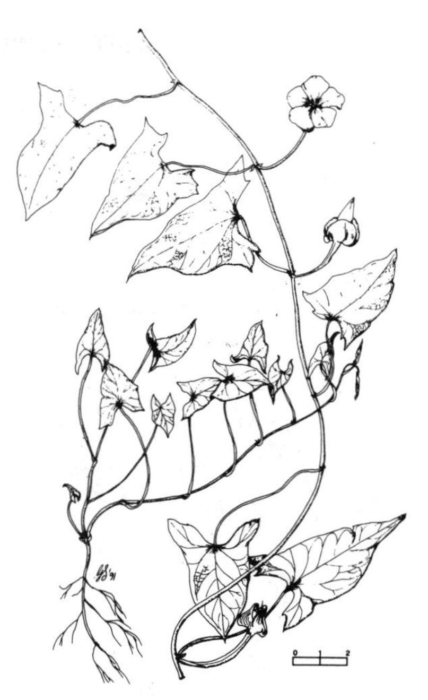

Calystegia marginata

Calystegia — Convolvulaceae

Calystegia marginata — Forest Bindweed

Size: Twining stems to 1–2 m — **P N**
Habitat: Damp and valley sclerophyll forests
Form: Slender climber
Foliage: Shiny arrow-shaped leaves to 60 mm long
Flowers: Solitary white to pale pink funnel-shaped flowers 20–30 mm long and 20 mm across on long stalks; October to January
Requirements: Moist to wet areas
Comments: Masses of short-lived flowers are produced. Regular pruning is beneficial. Water must be available during dry periods to keep this plant growing attractively. Locally rare.
Propagation: Cuttings, seeds (Refer to treatment of hard coated seeds.)
Localities: 42, 55–58
Distribution: Vic, Qld, NSW

Calystegia sepium — Large Bindweed

Size: Twining stems to 1–4 m long — **P**
Habitat: Riparian scrub, grassy wetland, valley sclerophyll forest
Comments: An attractive climber similar to *C. marginata* except that it has larger flowers and foliage. It may regenerate prolifically after fire but is never rampant. The roots were an important food source for the Aborigines.
Localities: Kororoit Ck, 4, 7, 16, 19, 26–29, 35, 42, 62, 63, 74
Distribution: All states except NT — *Illustrated p. 79*

Calytrix tetragona

Calytrix — Myrtaceae

Calytrix tetragona — Fringe Myrtle

Size: 1–2 m x 1–2 m — **F P**
Habitat: Riparian scrub amongst rocks
Form: Open erect or spreading shrub
Foliage: Fine, green, crowded aromatic leaves to 6 mm long
Flowers: Dense terminal heads of white flowers; August to November
Requirements: Well drained soils, tolerating extended dry periods and occasional inundation
Comments: Very attractive in flower. It makes an excellent container plant. Pruning promotes bushiness. An attractive feature of *Calytrix* is the deep red calyx which persists after flowering.
Propagation: Seed, cuttings
Localities: Diggers Rest#, Sunbury, 16, 26
Distribution: All states except NT

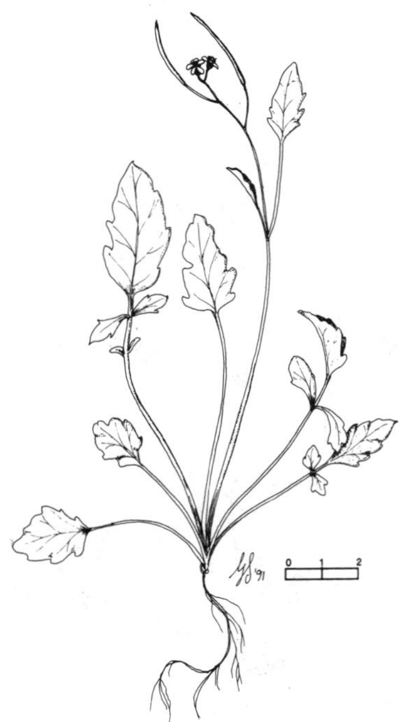

Cardamine gunnii

Cardamine — Brassicaceae

Cardamine dictyosperma = Rorippa dictyosperma

Cardamine gunnii — Common Bitter Cress

Size: 10–30 cm high — **P**
Habitat: Swamps of tea-tree heath, cool temperate rainforest
Form: Soft, tufted perennial herb
Foliage: Pinnate basal leaves on long stalks, segments spathulate, sometimes only the terminal leaflet developing
Flowers: Tiny white flowers held above the foliage on slender stalks; Spring to early Summer. Fruit a narrow cylindrical pod to 30 mm long on elongated stalks.
Requirements: Moist to wet soils
Comments: The leaves and stems of *Cardamine* species were an important food source for the Aborigines.
Localities: 57, 58, 67#
Distribution: Vic, NSW, Tas, SA
Synonym: Previously included with *C. debilis*

Cardamine laciniata = Rorippa laciniata

Cardamine paucijuga

Bitter Cress

Size: to 0.4 m high **P**
Habitat: Riparian and swamp scrub
Form: Erect annual herb
Foliage: Rosette of pinnate leaves, 1–4 pairs of linear to ovate leaf segments.
Flowers: Tiny white, occasionally pink, flowers in terminal clusters held above the foliage on a long flowering stem; June to November. Fruit to 30 mm long.
Requirements: Rich soil in moist or dry conditions
Comments: Similar to *C. gunnii*. Locally very rare.
Localities: An early collection along the Merri Creek may have been this species; 61
Distribution: All states except NT

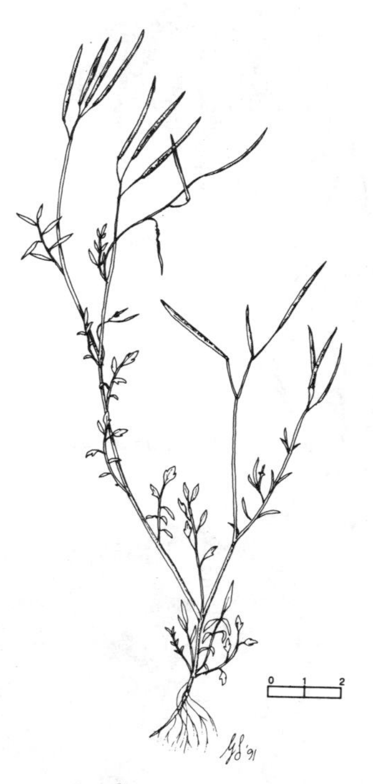

Cardamine paucijuga

Cardamine tenuifolia

Slender Bitter Cress

Size: stems to 1 m long **P**
Habitat: Swamp margins, plains grassland, valley sclerophyll forest
Form: Slender stoloniferous perennial herb with leaves scattered along the weak stems
Foliage: Pinnate leaves have 1–5 pairs of narrow segments
Flowers: Clusters of small pink or white flowers to 10 mm across; October to March. Fruit to 40 mm long.
Requirements: Moist to wet soils subject to inundation
Comments: On the basalt plains plants are protected by large boulders. Their leaves were much larger (to 70 mm long) than the finer leaves of plants east of Melbourne.
Localities: 18, 34A, 47
Distribution: All states except Qld

Carpobrotus

Aizoaceae

Carpobrotus modestus

Inland Noonflower or Pigface

Size: Prostrate x 1–3 m **F**
Habitat: Chenopod rocky open scrub
Form: Spreading succulent perennial
Foliage: Linear 3-sided leaves to 70 mm long
Flowers: Profuse sessile light purple flowers to 20 mm, shading to white at the base; August to January
Requirements: Well drained soils
Comments: The flowers only open on sunny days.It is salt and drought tolerant and is useful as a soil binder. The Aborigines ate the fruit and leaves raw. The leaves were sometimes cooked.
Propagation: Seed, cuttings, division of layered stems
Localities: 1, 29#, 32, 34A–36
Distribution: Vic, SA, WA

Carpobrotus rossii

Ross' Noonflower, Karkalla

Size: Prostrate x 2–3 m **F P**
Habitat: Coastal banksia woodland, primary dune scrub
Comments: Similar to *C. modestus* but with longer leaves, to 100 mm and larger flowers to 50 mm across. The globular purplish-red fruit were eaten fresh or dried by the Aborigines. They also ate the salty leaves with meat. Grows in sandy soil.
Localities: Seaford, 16, 26, 67–69, 74
Distribution: Vic, Tas, SA, WA

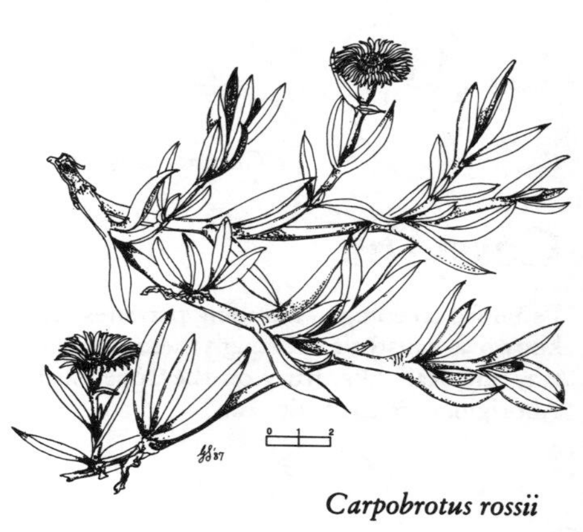

Carpobrotus rossii

Cassia nemophila var. nemophila = Senna artemisiodes ssp. filifolia

Cassinia

Asteraceae

Erect shrubs found in open forest. Fast growing, they provide quick screens while other plants grow. All need pruning to maintain shape and prevent woodiness. Flowers last for a long time and can be dried. The foliage may cause skin irritations. Propagate easily from seed or cuttings.

Cassinia aculeata

Common Cassinia, Dogwood

Size: 2–4 m x 1–2 m **P**
Habitat: Widespread in wet to dry sclerophyll forests, grassy low open forest, sclerophyll woodland, from coast to foothills
Form: Upright open shrub
Foliage: Dark green linear leaves to 40 mm long
Flowers: Crowded, domed heads of small whitish flowers; November to March, buds often pink
Requirements: Heavy, moist, well drained soils
Localities: 29, 33–44, 46–64, 67, 68, 70–76
Distribution: Vic, NSW, Tas, SA

Illustrated p. 79

SCALE: 0 1cm 2cm The scale representation on each plant equals 2cm.

Cassinia arcuata

Cassinia longifolia

Cassinia arcuata

Drooping Cassinia, Chinese Scrub

Size: 1–3 m x 1–2 m **F P**
Habitat: Box and box ironbark woodland, dry and valley sclerophyll forests, especially on disturbed ground, grassy low open forest
Form: Open rounded shrub
Foliage: Drooping linear leaves to 10 mm long, with spicy aroma
Flowers: Long, pendulous plumes of shiny pale brown flowerheads; November to February
Requirements: Well drained soils
Comments: This graceful plant is very easy to grow.
Localities: Sunbury, 16, 18, 21, 25, 26, 32, 33, 35–42, 44, 46–51, 55, 56, 58, 60–64, 68, 70–72, 74–76
Distribution: Vic, NSW, SA, WA

Cassinia longifolia

Shiny Cassinia, Cauliflower Bush

Size: 2–4 m x 2–3 m **P N**
Habitat: Valley and dry sclerophyll forests, grassy low open forest, box and red gum woodland
Form: Medium to large shrub
Foliage: Lanceolate leaves to 80 mm long. Leaves are hairy below and sticky when young.
Flowers: Dense terminal clusters of small white flowers, to 15 cm across; November to March
Requirements: Moist, well drained soil
Comments: An adaptable shrub to most conditions.
Localities: Sth Morang, Sth of Melton, 14, 16, 25, 26, 29, 32, 34–36, 38, 39, 41, 42, 44, 47, 48, 50–53, 55–60, 63, 71, 74, 76
Distribution: Vic, Qld, NSW, Tas

Cassinia trinerva

Three-Veined Cassinia

Size: 2–3.5 m x 1.5–3 m **P N**
Habitat: Damp and wet sclerophyll forests
Form: Dense rounded shrub
Foliage: Narrow, 3-veined, dark green leaves to 80 mm long, pale underneath.
Flowers: Broad flat clusters of whitish flowers; November to March
Requirements: Moist, well drained heavy soil
Localities: Wantirna, 57, 58
Distribution: Vic, NSW, Tas

Illustrated p. 79

Cassytha **Lauraceae**

Perennial creeping or climbing parasites, cassythas become rootless at maturity attaching to their hosts by a wedge inside attachment cups known as haustoria. Through these attachments they are able to gain some of their nutritional requirements from the host plant. Leaves are tiny and scale-like, hairy on the upper surface. Forming a tangled mass, large cassythas may kill their host. Propagation is by seed. The Aborigines ate the fruit raw.

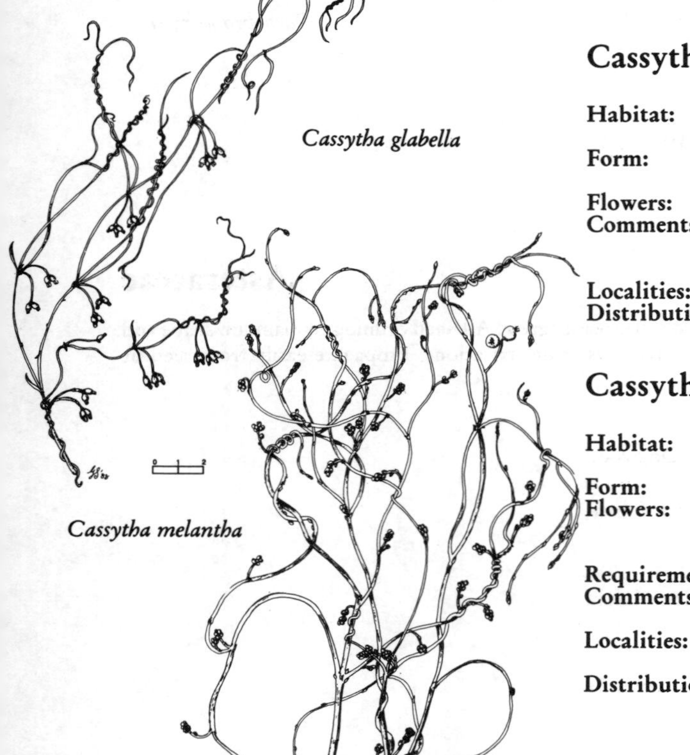

Cassytha glabella

Cassytha melantha

Cassytha glabella

Slender or Tangled Dodder Laurel

F P

Habitat: Tea-tree heath, wattle tea-tree scrub, damp and valley sclerophyll forests
Form: Light parasitic creeper with fine, glabrous stems less than 1 mm thick, twining over grasses and small shrubs
Flowers: Clusters of tiny white flowers are followed by orange or red fruit
Comments: A most attractive species which is readily controlled by pulling the threadlike stems away from the host plant. The Aborigines infused the fruit to treat fever.
Localities: 36, 41–43, 49, 50A, 58–61, 63, 64, 67–76
Distribution: All states except NT

Cassytha melantha

Coarse or Large Dodder Laurel

F P

Habitat: Damp, dry and valley sclerophyll forests, coastal banksia and box woodlands
Form: Rapidly growing parasitic creeper
Flowers: Minute white flowers in spikes; June to October. The outside of the flowers are covered in dense black hairs. Globular green to black fruit follow the flowers.
Requirements: Prefers light well drained soil
Comments: Growing well above the ground, this most robust species can strangle or break its host plant, often eucalypts.
Localities: 14, 16, 26, 27, 32, 34A–36, 40–42, 44, 47–49, 50A, 51, 54–56, 60, 62, 67, 69A, 74–76
Distribution: Vic, NSW, Tas, SA, WA

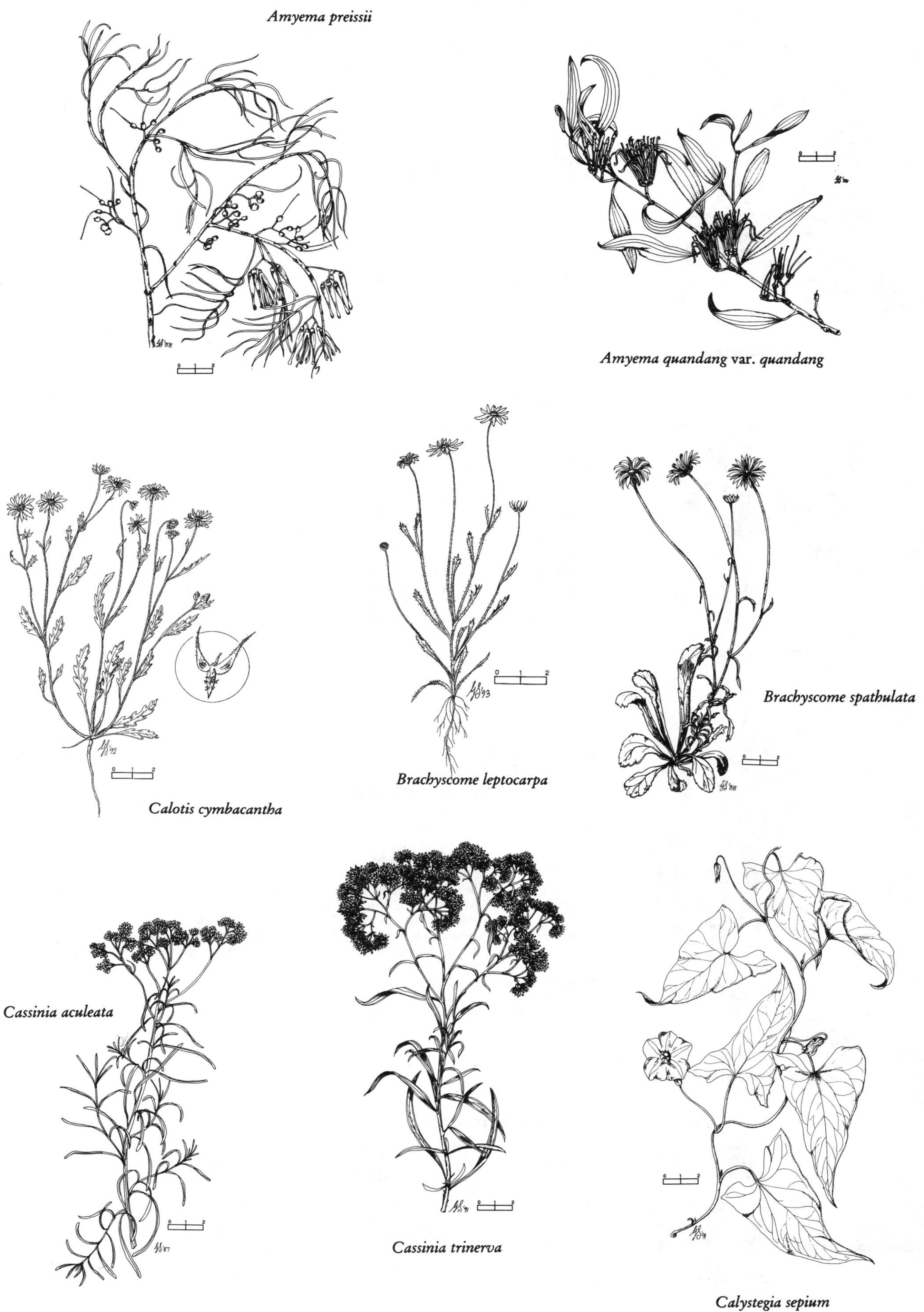

SCALE: 0 1cm 2cm The scale representation on each plant equals 2cm.

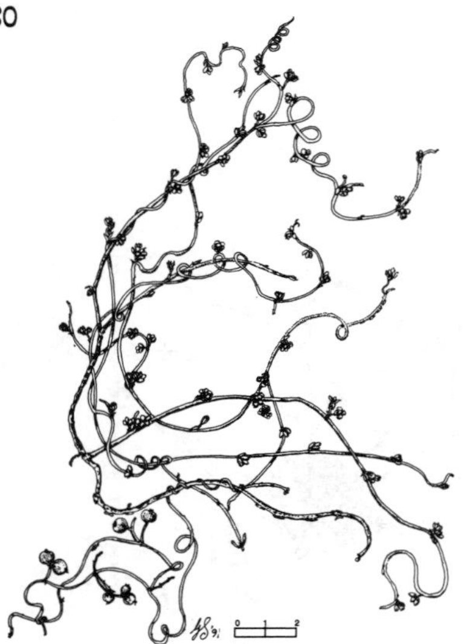
Cassytha pubescens

Cassytha pubescens
Downy Dodder Laurel

F P

Habitat: Widespread in tea-tree heath, dry, damp and valley sclerophyll forests, red gum woodland
Form: Light, parasitic creeper, somewhat more robust than *C. glabella* with stems to about 2 mm thick. The stems, buds and fruit are usually hairy.
Flowers: Flowering occurs from December to April, with many tiny white flowers tightly clustered in a spike from 25–100 mm long, followed by greenish-white fruit.
Localities: St. Kilda#, 40–42, 44, 47, 48, 50–56, 58, 60, 62, 63, 65#–70, 73–76
Distribution: Vic, Qld, NSW, SA, Tas; NZ
Synonym: *C. phaeolasia*

Casuarina spp. = Allocasuarina spp.

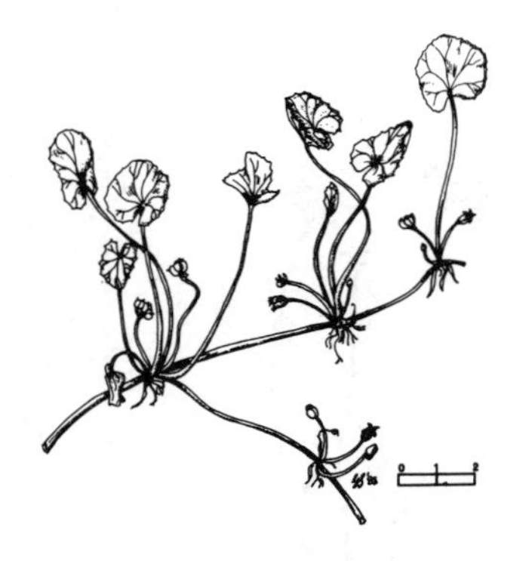
Centella cordifolia

Centella — Apiaceae

Centella cordifolia
Swamp Pennywort

Size: Prostrate x 1–2 m — F P
Habitat: Widespread in swamp and riparian scrub, damp, valley and dry sclerophyll forests, grassy low open forest
Form: Fast-growing creeping perennial herb
Foliage: Light green heart-or kidney-shaped leaves to 40 mm long
Flowers: Umbels of tiny white to pink flowers on long stalks; August to January
Requirements: Moist to wet soils
Comments: Grows well around pools and in boggy areas but may become invasive.
Propagation: Cuttings, division of stems
Localities: Montrose, 28, 29, 34A–36, 40–42, 44, 46–48, 50, 51, 53, 54, 56, 59, 60, 62–64, 70, 74–76
Distribution: All states except NT

Centipeda — Asteraceae

Centipeda cunninghamii
Common Sneezeweed

Size: 0.1–0.5 m x 30 cm — F P
Habitat: Grassy wetland, grassy low open forest, riparian scrub
Form: Fast-growing perennial herb
Foliage: Sessile coarsely-toothed oblanceolate leaves to 30 mm long, may be hairy or glabrous
Flowers: Sessile, globular greenish-yellow flowerheads; November to March
Requirements: Moist soils, tolerating inundation. Ideally suited to growing in hot inland areas, provided moisture is available.
Comments: Pruning is necessary to promote compact growth. The Aborigines and early settlers used this plant to treat many disorders including colds and infected eyes. Becoming rarer in Melbourne.
Propagation: Seed or cuttings
Localities: Eltham, 5, 6, 18, 30#, 34A, 35, 40, 42, 51, 60, 67#
Distribution: All mainland states

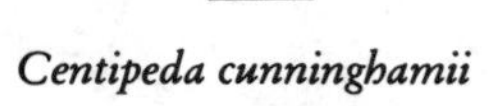
Centipeda cunninghamii

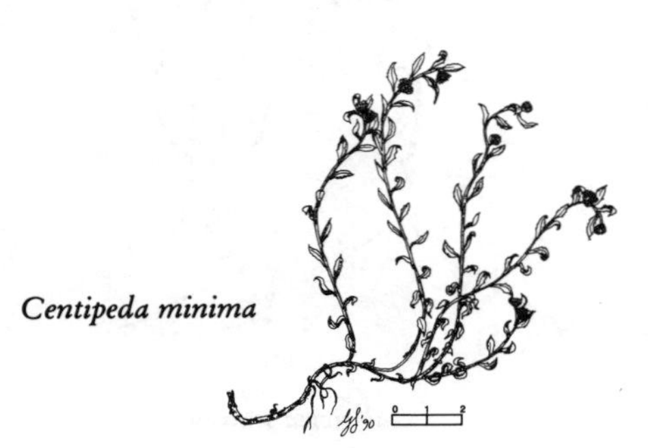
Centipeda minima

Centipeda minima
Spreading Sneezeweed

Size: Prostrate—20 cm x 10–30 cm — P
Habitat: Widespread in swamp scrub, red gum woodland, valley sclerophyll forest, in flood-prone areas
Form: Spreading annual herb
Foliage: Similar to *C. cunninghamii*, but shortly stalked and more ovate, to 15 mm long, with a few teeth near the apex
Flowers: Flowerheads are smaller than *C. cunninghamii*
Requirements: Moist soils which may dry out in Summer
Comments: The Aborigines crushed the herb to treat colds. Becoming locally rare.
Localities: 12, 26, 34–36, 54, 61–63, 74, 75
Distribution: All states

Ceratophyllum Ceratophyllaceae

Ceratophyllum demersum Common Hornwort

Size: stems 0.3–0.6 m long
Habitat: Aquatic, submerged in 0.3–1 m water
Form: Rootless perennial herb
Foliage: Dark green dissected leaves to 40 mm long, segments linear and forked, spine-tipped teeth along margins; crowded in whorls of 7–12
Flowers: Inconspicuous greenish axillary flowers, male and female singly at different nodes; Summer
Requirements: Fresh or brackish stagnant to slow-moving water
Comments: Known from one area in the Melbourne area it may have once been more common. Useful in a pond providing fish habitat, but needs periodic thinning to prevent small ponds being overgrown.
Propagation: Stem cuttings in water
Localities: Werribee River
Distribution: Vic, Qld, NSW, SA, NT

Chamaesyce drummondii = Euphorbia drummondii

Chenopodium Chenopodiaceae

Annual or perennial herbs or shrubs with small unisexual or bisexual flowers clustered in the leaf axils or in terminal panicles. Terminal clusters are often male or bisexual flowers while female flowers occur in lateral clusters. They grow in drier areas and are salt tolerant. Some are fire retardant due to the high salt content of their foliage while others provide animal fodder. The leaves and seeds of some species were eaten by the Aborigines. Propagation is by seed or cutting.

Chenopodium desertorum ssp. microphyllum Small-leaf Goosefoot

Size: 0.4 m x 0.8 m **F**
Habitat: Chenopod rocky open scrub
Form: Mealy-white, much branched perennial herb
Foliage: Pale greenish blunt, broadly lanceolate leaves to 10 mm long
Flowers: Small loose clusters of sessile, mealy flowers in Winter and Spring; male and bisexual flowers terminal, female flowers lateral
Requirements: Moist soils
Comments: Locally rare.
Localities: Melton, Mt Cottrell, 16
Distribution: Vic, NSW, SA, WA
Synonym: *C. pseudomicrophyllum*

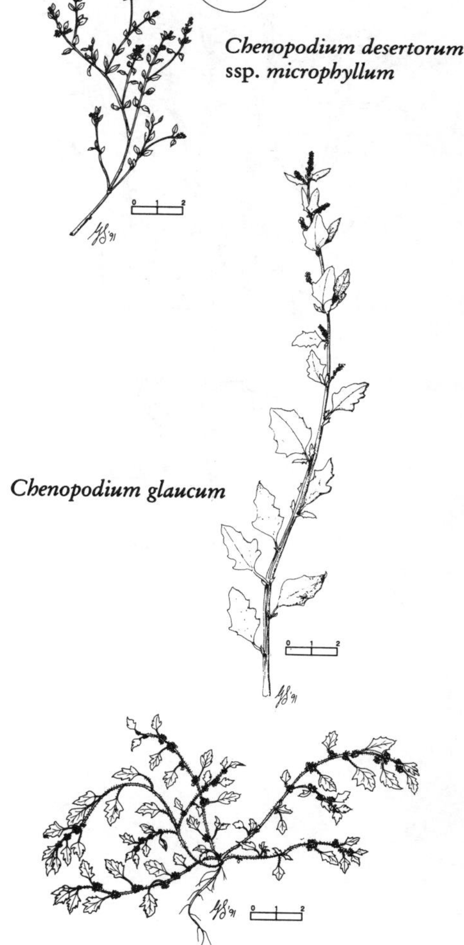

Chenopodium desertorum ssp. *microphyllum*

Chenopodium glaucum

Chenopodium glaucum Glaucous Goosefoot

Size: Prostrate–0.5 m x 1 m **F P**
Habitat: Primary dune scrub, saltmarshes, plains grassland
Form: Prostrate to erect branched annual herb
Foliage: Somewhat succulent, broadly lanceolate bright green leaves, densely mealy below, to 25 mm long
Flowers: Panicles of small dense clusters of mauve or green flowers in a cyme; December to June. Terminal clusters bisexual, lateral clusters female or bisexual.
Requirements: Moist saline soil
Comments: A second form is found near Rockbank in saline soils. Named *C. ambiguum* in the past, it is presently included in *C. glaucum.* It is prostrate and has small brownish leaves. There are only 2 known sites where this form still grows in Melbourne.
Localities: 3–5, 11, 22, 67#, 71
Distribution: Vic, NSW, Tas, SA, WA

Chenopodium pumilio Small Crumbweed, Rough-leaved Goosefoot

Size: Prostrate–25 cm high **F**
Habitat: Riparian scrub, grassy wetland
Form: Hairy aromatic annual herb
Foliage: Pale green oak-like leaves to 20 mm long
Flowers: Minute white flowers in compact clusters; March to July
Requirements: Grows in sandy soils
Localities: Early collections in Altona, St Kilda; Mt Cottrell, 9, 11, 16, 23, 26, 35
Distribution: All states

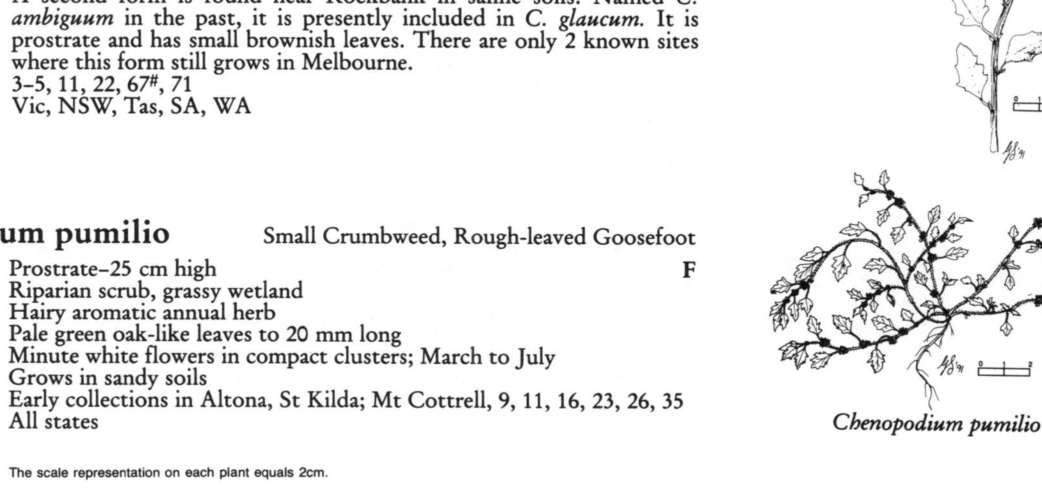

Chenopodium pumilio

SCALE: 0 1cm 2cm The scale representation on each plant equals 2cm.

Chrysocephalum apiculatum

Chrysocephalum — Asteraceae

Chrysocephalum apiculatum — Common Everlasting, Yellow Buttons

Size: Prostrate-30 cm x 1–2 m — **F**
Habitat: Widespread in plains grassland, red gum and box woodland, dry sclerophyll forest, tea-tree heath
Form: Variable, dense, spreading perennial herb
Foliage: Silver-grey obovate leaves to 60 mm long, densely hairy
Flowers: Terminal clusters of rounded, bright yellow flowerheads most of the year, peaking September to December
Requirements: Well drained soils
Comments: An excellent rockery plant with contrasting foliage. It should be pruned regularly to encourage new growth. The Keilor Plains form is smaller, more straggly in habit, with a finer leaf.
Propagation: Seed, cuttings
Localities: Warrandyte, 1, 4, 5, 7, 10, 12, 13, 15–18, 26, 29, 30, 35, 37, 50A, 55, 58, 67, 69, 69A, 74, 76
Distribution: All states
Synonym: *Helichrysum apiculatum*

Chrysocephalum semipapposum

Chrysocephalum semipapposum — Clustered Everlasting

Size: 0.3–1 m x 1–3 m — **F P**
Habitat: Box and red gum woodlands, damp to dry sclerophyll forests, plains grassland
Form: Variable, dense perennial herb, erect stems produced from a creeping rhizome. Individual stems live for 2 years, some forms developing secondary stems in their second year.
Foliage: Sticky grey-green narrow leaves 20–50 mm long
Flowers: Dense terminal clusters of small yellow flowerheads; October to May
Requirements: Variable, from moist to dry soils
Comments: Requires hard pruning of old growth. Three distinct forms occur within Melbourne.
Form 1: Large, robust grey-leafed form to 1 m high from damp sclerophyll forests and moist sites. May form very large patches to 3 m across. Stems are well spaced along the rhizome. Leaves to 50 mm long and 5 mm wide are broader at the tip. Flowers are orange yellow.
Localities: Baxter, 32, 34–39, 44, 49, 50A, 51, 55, 56, 58, 62, 63, 65–67
Form 2: Tight tussock forming clumps to 0.5 m high, from drier areas. Foliage is similar, to 30 mm long and silvery to green depending on the amount of sun received. Flowers are golden-yellow.
Localities: Eltham, 41, 42
Form 3: Drought tolerant, very tightly clumping sub-shrub to 0.4 m high. Stems are very straight in the first year, then arching with secondary stems to 100 mm high, rising erect from them. Leaves very narrow to 30 mm long, tightly revolute and falcate. Pale yellow flowers in smaller clusters on both primary and secondary stems. An excellent plant for cultivation which flowers later and responds well to Summer watering.
Localities: Hurstbridge, Sydenham, Melton Sth, 13–16, 25, 26, 32
Propagation: Seed, cuttings
Distribution: All states
Synonym: *Helichrysum semipapposum*

Ciclospermum — Apiaceae

Ciclospermum leptophyllum — Slender Celery

Size: 0.3–0.7 m high — **P N**
Habitat: Riparian scrub
Form: Slender open annual herb
Foliage: Divided leaves to 40 mm, with very narrow leaf segments
Flowers: Umbels of tiny whitish flowers at or near the ends of branches; December to February. Fruit deeply ribbed.
Requirements: Moist soils
Comments: Can become invasive especially in disturbed areas. A cosmopolitan weed, it is considered to be introduced to Australia by some authorities.
Propagation: Seed
Localities: Early collection from Darebin Creek
Distribution: All mainland states; America
Synonym: *Apium leptophyllum*

Clematis

Ranunculaceae

Clematis aristata

Austral Clematis, Goat's or Old Man's Beard, **F P N**

Habitat: Widespread in wet, damp and valley sclerophyll forests, grassy low open forest
Form: Vigorous climber
Foliage: Trifoliate shiny green leaves, leaflets ovate to 80 mm long. Juvenile leaves have silvery top markings, purplish below
Flowers: Masses of creamy white starry flowers to 60 mm across; August to March
Requirements: Easily grown in well drained soils
Comments: This very showy climber is dioecious. Attractive feathery seed heads persist on the female plant for some time. Will grow well under established eucalypts if watered during Summer.
Propagation: Fresh seed, stem cuttings
Localities: 33–34A, 40–44, 46, 47, 49, 50A, 51–53, 55–60, 62–64, 70, 74, 76
Distribution: Vic, Qld, NSW, Tas

Clematis aristata

Clematis microphylla var. microphylla

Small-leafed Clematis **F P**

Habitat: Dry sclerophyll forest, box, riparian and coastal banksia woodlands, primary dune scrub, plains grassland, grassy low open forest
Form: Variable medium-sized climber
Foliage: Oblong, dull green leaves to 30 mm long, divided 2–3 times
Flowers: Dioecious; masses of cream starry flowers; July to November. Feathery fruit persists on the female plant for some time.
Requirements: Well drained soils
Comments: Leaves can relieve skin irritations but may cause blisters unless used in moderation. The Aborigines cooked and kneaded the tap root to make dough.
Propagation: Seed, stem cuttings
Localities: 1, 14, 16, 18, 24–26, 28–30, 32–39, 41, 42, 44, 47, 48, 50A, 52, 53, 60–64, 67, 69A, 71, 74, 76
Distribution: All states except NT

Illustrated p. 106

Comesperma

Polygalaceae

Comesperma are small shrubs or twiners with attractive pea-like flowers. They prefer well drained soils with some shelter. Propagation is by seed or cuttings.

Comesperma calymega

Blue Spike Milkwort **F P**

Size: 0.3–0.5 m x 0.3–1 m
Habitat: Tea-tree heath
Form: Dwarf erect shrub
Foliage: Thick elliptic to lanceolate leaves to 20 mm long
Flowers: Dense terminal racemes of small blue flowers; October to January
Requirements: Well drained soil
Localities: Olinda, 67, 68, 71, 73–75
Distribution: Vic, Tas, SA, WA

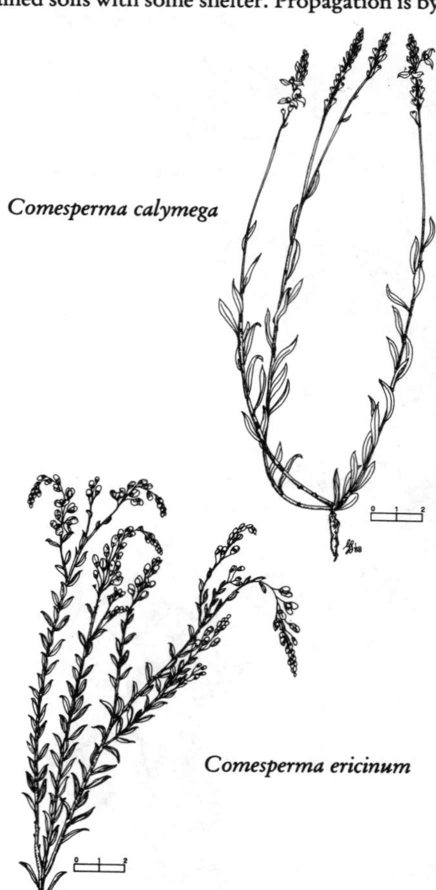

Comesperma calymega

Comesperma ericinum

Comesperma ericinum

Heath Milkwort **P**

Size: 0.5–1.5 m x 1–2 m
Habitat: Tea-tree heath, valley sclerophyll forest
Form: Slender erect shrub
Foliage: Numerous narrow to oblong dark green leaves to 15 mm long
Flowers: Profuse terminal racemes of small pink flowers; October to February
Requirements: Adaptable, tolerating wet periods
Comments: This attractive shrub benefits from pruning after flowering. Suitable for growing in containers. Locally rare.
Localities: Montrose, 49, 50–51, 53, 54, 56, 67#
Distribution: Vic, Qld, NSW, Tas

Comesperma polygaloides

Small Milkwort **F**

Size: 0.3–0.6 m x 0.3 m
Habitat: Plains grasslands, red gum woodland, in sandy, clay and granite areas
Form: Small slender shrub
Foliage: Narrow bluish-green leaves
Flowers: Profuse terminal racemes of purple or mauve flowers
Requirements: Well drained soils
Comments: Suitable for growing in containers. A vulnerable plant in Victoria, there are few sites where it remains in Melbourne. It occurred until recently at Taylors Lakes when this area was cleared for housing.
Localities: St Albans#, Footscray#, Port Melbourne#, Sunbury, 5, 7, 17#, 18, 26, 35
Distribution: Vic, SA, WA

SCALE: 0 1cm 2cm The scale representation on each plant equals 2cm.

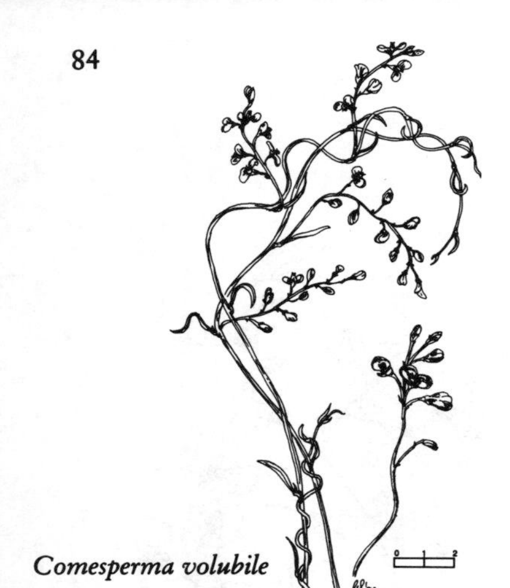
Comesperma volubile

Comesperma volubile

Love Creeper

P

Habitat:	Widespread in grassy low open forest, dry and valley sclerophyll forests, tea-tree heath
Form:	Open slender twiner
Foliage:	Almost leafless, with a few narrow leaves to 10 mm long
Flowers:	Loose racemes of blue flowers; August to December
Requirements:	Well drained soil with roots protected from drying out
Comments:	This beautiful creeper is difficult to establish, possibly requiring a symbiotic relationship with an undetermined organism for successful growth.
Propagation:	Seed, cuttings—difficult, needing leaves on stem
Localities:	Research, 34, 34A, 36, 37, 41–44, 46–53, 55–64, 67, 68, 70, 71, 73–76
Distribution:	All states except NT

Convolvulus — Convolvulaceae

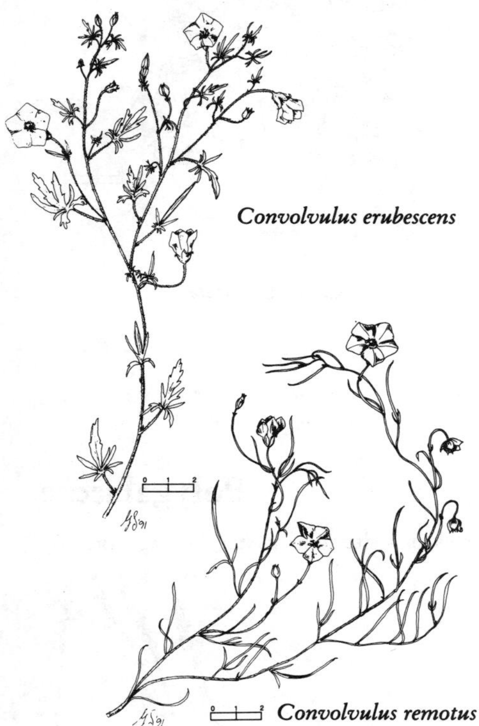
Convolvulus erubescens

Convolvulus remotus

Convolvulus erubescens

Australian, Blushing or Pink Bindweed

F

Size:	10–30 cm x 0.5 m
Habitat:	Tea-tree heath, red gum woodland, plains grassland, dry and damp sclerophyll forests
Form:	Fast-growing trailing or climbing perennial
Foliage:	Hairy grey-green leaves 15–60 mm long, with several lobes at the base, central lobe often much longer
Flowers:	Very showy rosy pink funnel-shaped flowers, on stalks 15–35 mm long; August to February
Requirements:	Well drained hot dry areas
Comments:	Ideal for tubs and hanging baskets or as a ground cover. The Aborigines used a boiled extract to treat diarrhoea and stomach ache. The woody taproot was cooked in baskets, then kneaded into dough.
Propagation:	Cuttings; woody seed coat needs to be sliced to expose seed before germination.
Localities:	1, 2, 4–9, 12, 13, 15–18, 20, 21, 24–26, 28–32, 34–36, 39, 42, 45#, 67#, 71, 74, 76
Distribution:	All states

Convolvulus remotus

F

Size:	Prostrate x 0.3–0.6 m
Habitat:	Red gum woodland, plains grassland
Form:	Small trailing plant
Foliage:	Entire, bright green leaves 15–70 mm long, sometimes with 2 long linear lobes at the base. Hairs are pressed against the leaf surface rather than erect as in *C. erubescens*.
Flowers:	Pink flowers, singly or in pairs; September to December
Comments:	Good ground cover for hot areas. Locally rare, found only on the basalt plains.
Localities:	Bundoora, Laverton Nth, 2, 21, 28
Distribution:	All mainland states

Coprosma — Rubiaceae

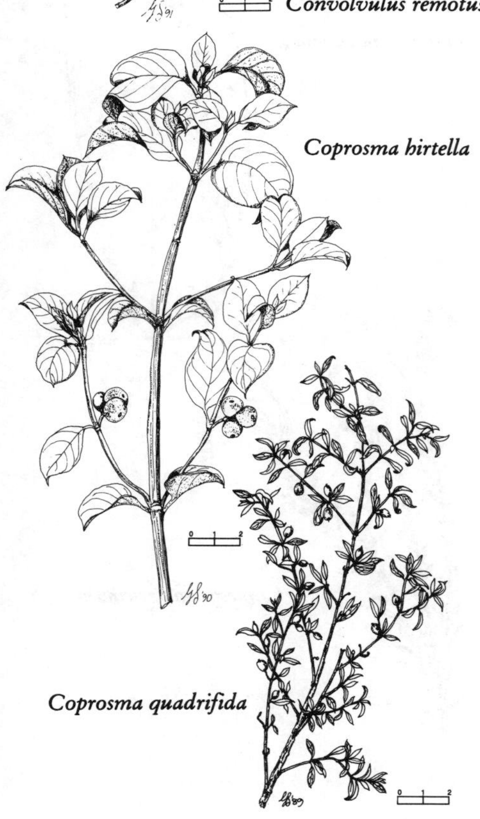
Coprosma hirtella

Coprosma quadrifida

Coprosma hirtella

Rough Coprosma

P

Size:	1–2 m x 0.5–1.5 m
Habitat:	Wet, damp and valley sclerophyll forests
Form:	Slender understorey shrub
Foliage:	Rough dull green broad elliptical leaves, pointed at ends, to 70 mm long
Flowers:	Insignificant greenish clusters of unisexual flowers; August to October; followed by attractive reddish-orange drupes to 10 mm long
Requirements:	Moist, well drained sheltered position
Comments:	Easily grown. The drupes are edible but leave an unpleasant taste.
Propagation:	Fresh seed, cuttings
Localities:	55–58
Distribution:	Vic, NSW, Tas

Coprosma quadrifida

Prickly Currant Bush

P N

Size:	2–4 m x 1–1.5 m
Habitat:	Cool temperate rainforest, wet and damp sclerophyll forests, sclerophyll woodland, swamp scrub
Form:	Open, upright, spiny shrub
Foliage:	Dull lanceolate to elliptic leaves to 15 mm long
Flowers:	Inconspicuous single greenish flowers; September to November; followed by small edible red drupes; January to March.
Requirements:	Moist well drained soil
Comments:	A useful plant to grow with ferns. A form growing at the head of the Werribee River has larger leaves to 50 mm long.
Propagation:	Seed, cuttings
Localities:	Sth Morang, 1, 26, 29–36, 41, 42, 44, 47, 50, 51, 53, 55–59, 62–64, 70
Distribution:	Vic, NSW, Tas

30

31

32

33

34

35

36

37

38

30. *Banksia marginata*
Silver Banksia
31. *Thelionema caespitosum*
Blue Grass-lily
32. *Acacia myrtifolia*
Myrtle Wattle
33. *Lomandra filiformis*
ssp. *coriacea*
34. *Wurmbea dioicia*
Early Nancy
35. *Comesperma ericinum*
Heath Milkwort
36. *Ricinocarpos pinifolius* with
Dampiera stricta
Wedding Bush & Blue Dampiera
37. *Calochilus robertsonii*
Common or Purple Beard-orchid
38. *Dillwynia sericea*
Showy Parrot-pea

39 40 41 42 43 44 45 46 47 48

39. *Grevillea alpina* Alpine Grevillea
40. *Acacia dealbata* Silver Wattle
41. *Olearia lirata* Snowy Daisy Bush
42. *Chiloglottis valida* Common Bird-orchid
43. *Notelaea ligustrina* Native Mock Olive
44. *Eucalyptus regnans* with *Bedfordia arborescens* Mountain Ash, Blanket Leaf
45. *Prostanthera lasianthos* Victorian Christmas Bush
46. *Lomandra filiformis* ssp. *filiformis* Wattle Mat-rush
47. *Doodia media* Common Rasp Fern
48. *Banksia spinulosa* Hairpin Banksia

Correa

Rutaceae

Correas are widespread in varied habitats from exposed coastal to mountain areas. Nectar-producing flowers occur over a long period, attracting honeyeaters. The flowers are bell-shaped except for *C. alba* which has an open star-like flower. The leaves when crushed produce a distinctive aroma. Pruning after flowering is beneficial to maintain shape. All require a well drained position. They make attractive tub specimens. Correas are usually propagated easily from cuttings whilst seeds are very difficult to germinate.

Correa alba

White Correa

Size: 0.5–2 m x 1–3 m **F P**
Habitat: Primary dune scrub
Form: Dense spreading shrub, dwarfed by wind and salt spray
Foliage: Thick, round to oval grey-green leaves, pale and hairy below, to 40 mm long
Flowers: Waxy white starry flowers most of the year
Requirements: Well drained soils, tolerating moisture or extended dry periods once established
Comments: A useful plant for soil binding or as a low screen. The leaves were used by early settlers to make a tea substitute.
Localities: Seaford, 67, 74
Distribution: Vic, NSW, Tas, SA

Correa glabra

Rock or Smooth Correa

Size: 1–3 m x 1–3 m **F P N**
Habitat: Widespread in riparian scrub, on low rocky outcrops, and escarpments
Form: Variable dense upright to spreading shrub
Foliage: Dark green oblong leaves, usually with wavy edges, to 40 mm long
Flowers: Solitary pale green bells most of the year, peaking May to August
Requirements: Well drained soils
Comments: An attractive, easily grown shrub, ideal as a low screen. Tolerant of lime.
Localities: Essendon, Sunshine, Kororoit Ck, 14, 16, 26, 28, 29, 32, 33, 34A–36, 41, 42, 47, 50A, 51
Distribution: Vic, Qld, NSW, SA

Correa reflexa

Native Fuchsia, Common Correa

Size: 0.3–2 m x 1–2 m **F P N**
Habitat: Dry, damp and valley sclerophyll forests, sclerophyll woodland, tea-tree scrub, grassy low open forest
Form: Very variable—open upright to spreading shrub
Foliage: Dull green, hairy, broadly ovate leaves to 50 mm long
Flowers: Solitary, large, usually light green bells; March to September. A form with red flowers and yellow tips is known from Donvale, Croydon, Boronia, Dingley and Frankston.
Requirements: Well drained soils
Comments: A prostrate form has been reported from Seaford. Other Victorian forms may be prostrate or medium-sized shrubs, with flowers of cream or red with yellow-green tips. An excellent plant for dry shady positions, establishing well under existing trees. Forms collected from wetter mountain areas require some moisture.
Localities: St. Kilda#, Eltham, 30#, 33, 34A–37, 40–44, 46–53, 55, 56, 58, 59, 61–65#, 67–71, 73–76
Distribution: All states except NT *Also illustrated p. ix*

Correa reflexa x glabra

Size: 1.5 m x 1.5 m **F P**
Comments: A natural hybrid occurring in the Warrandyte/Croydon North area. Similar in appearance to *C. glabra* but with bright green wrinkly leaves, hairy below, to 25 mm long. Grows in dry, clay soil.
Localities: 41, 42, 51, 53

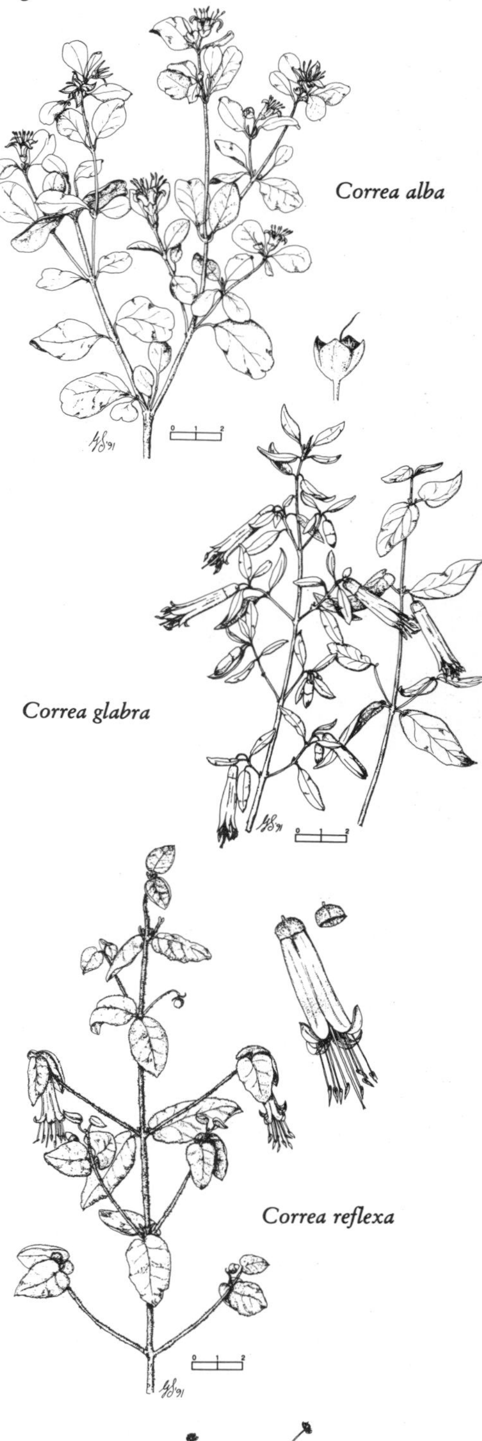

Correa alba

Correa glabra

Correa reflexa

Cotula

Asteraceae

Cotula australis

Common Cotula

Size: Prostrate–20 cm x 1 m **P N**
Habitat: Widespread in coastal banksia, red gum and sclerophyll woodland, riparian scrub, dry sclerophyll forest, near water
Form: Spreading annual or perennial herb
Foliage: Hairy pinnate leaves to 20 mm long
Flowers: Slender, long-stalked, solitary white and yellow-green flower heads; September to February
Requirements: Moist soils
Comments: A useful ground cover for difficult shady areas but may become invasive.
Propagation: Seed, cuttings, division
Localities: 16, 23, 25, 26, 29, 30, 32, 34A-36, 38, 41, 42, 44, 49, 51, 58, 63, 64, 67–71, 74
Distribution: All states

Cotula australis

SCALE: 0 1cm 2cm The scale representation on each plant equals 2cm.

Cotula reptans = Leptinella reptans

Cotula vulgaris var. australasica — Slender Cotula

Size: to 20 cm high — **F P**
Habitat: Saltmarshes, moist tea-tree heath
Form: Slender annual herb
Foliage: Thread-like leaves to 40 mm long forming a tangled mass
Flowers: Pale yellow button flowers; August to November
Requirements: Moist soil, tolerating saline conditions
Localities: Seaholme 1942, 67#
Distribution: Vic, Tas, SA, WA

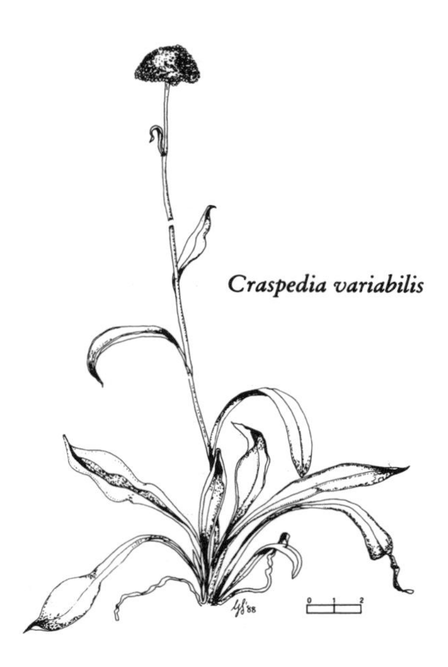

Craspedia variabilis

Craspedia — Asteraceae

Craspedia chrysantha = Pycnosorus chrysanthes

Craspedia globosa = Pycnosorus globosus

Craspedia variabilis — Common Billy Buttons

Size: 30 cm x 0.5–1 m — **F P**
Habitat: Widespread in grassy wetlands, plains grasslands, riparian scrub, tea-tree heath, grassy low open forest, dry and valley sclerophyll forest, sclerophyll woodland
Form: Variable tufted perennial herb
Foliage: Basal rosette of broad hairy leaves to 20 cm long
Flowers: Yellow globular heads to 20 mm held erect singly on long stalks from 15–50 cm high; September to November
Requirements: Moist to boggy soils
Comments: Spectacular in flower it may be grown in containers or rockeries or used in massed plantings. An excellent dried flower. A taller form grows in swampy areas to the north of the study area.
Propagation: Seed, division
Localities: St Albans, Sunbury, Eltham, Baxter, 2, 7, 15, 16, 26, 29#, 33–37, 42, 44, 46, 47, 49–51, 55, 58, 59, 63, 67#, 70
Distribution: All states
Synonym: *Craspedia glauca*

Crassula — Crassulaceae

Crassula colorata var. acuminata — Dense Crassula

Size: 1–15 cm high — **F**
Habitat: Plains grassland, chenopod rocky open scrub, grassy low open forests
Form: Erect, succulent annual herb
Foliage: Crowded, obovate leaves to 4 mm long, becoming red with age
Flowers: Dense clusters of tiny, sessile, pink 5-petalled flowers; August to October
Requirements: Moist soils
Comments: Would be attractive as a rockery plant. Distinguished from *C. sieberiana* ssp. *tetramera*, with which it often occurs, by a cluster of brown nodules near the base of each fruit. Locally rare.
Localities: 2, 74
Distribution: Vic, NSW, SA, WA; NZ
Synonym: *C. colorata* var. *tuberculata*

Crassula decumbens var. *decumbens*

Crassula decumbens var. decumbens — Rufous or Spreading Stonecrop

Size: Prostrate–8 cm high — **P**
Habitat: Primary dune scrub, red gum woodland, tea-tree heath, valley sclerophyll forest
Form: Widespread, small reddish erect or prostrate annual herb with repeatedly branched stems
Foliage: Succulent, linear-lanceolate leaves to 8 mm long
Flowers: Stalked, tiny white or red-tinged flowers in clusters.
Requirements: Moist, boggy areas
Localities: 2, 4, 23, 25, 26, 31, 32, 35, 42, 43A, 44, 49, 51, 67#–71, 74
Distribution: Vic, NSW, Tas, SA, WA; S Am, S Af
Synonym: *C. macrantha*

Crassula helmsii

Swamp Stonecrop

Size:	10–30 cm high **F**
Habitat:	Widespread in riparian scrub and woodland, valley sclerophyll forest, grassy low open forest
Form:	Fast growing aquatic or creeping perennial herb
Foliage:	Pairs of succulent, narrow green or reddish oblong leaves to 15 mm long
Flowers:	Insignificant, stalked, solitary, white 4-petalled flowers along ends of branches; November to April
Requirements:	Aquatic or bog conditions
Comments:	A rapid grower which may become invasive. Submerged forms have longer branches that float on the surface, and broader leaves. Plants growing in moist soils form small clumps with densely clustered leaves. Makes an excellent aquarium plant.
Propagation:	Seed, stem cuttings, division
Localities:	Diamond Ck, 4, 8, 14, 16, 26, 28, 34A, 35, 36, 42, 44, 60, 62, 63, 71, 74–76
Distribution:	All states except NT; NZ

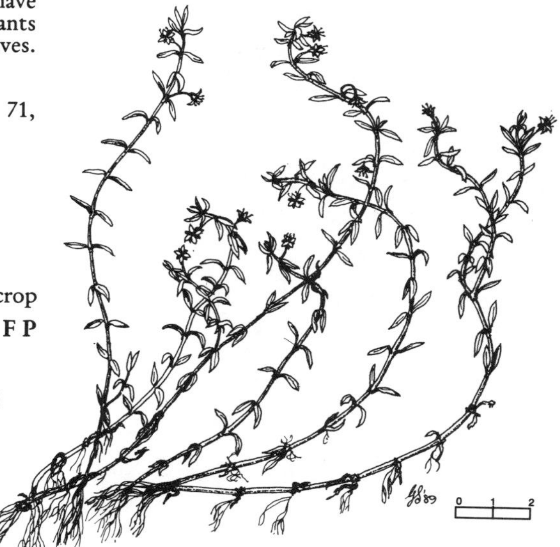

Crassula helmsii

Crassula pedicellosa

Stalked Stonecrop

Size:	to 10 cm high **F P**
Habitat:	Tea-tree heath, grassy wetlands
Form:	Tufted erect annual herb
Foliage:	Green to purplish-red oblanceolate to elliptic leaves to 12 mm long
Flowers:	Tiny cream flowers in terminal clusters; August to October
Requirements:	Moist sandy soils
Localities:	5, 74
Distribution:	Vic, Tas, SA, WA

Crassula peduncularis

Purple Stonecrop

Size:	to 5 cm high **P N**
Habitat:	Sheltered marshy sites in box woodland and coastal banksia woodland
Form:	Tiny upright annual herb with much-branched red stems
Foliage:	Succulent, oval purplish leaves to 5 mm long
Flowers:	Long-stalked, single red-tinged flowers in Summer
Comments:	Very restricted range in moist soils
Localities:	24, 67#
Distribution:	Vic, NSW, Tas, SA, WA; NZ, S Am
Synonym:	*C. purpurata*

Crassula sieberiana ssp. sieberiana

Austral Stonecrop

Size:	1–10 cm high **F P**
Habitat:	Wet crevices in red gum and box woodland, grassy wetland, plains grassland, riparian and chenopod rocky open scrub, tea-tree heath
Form:	Succulent perennial herb forming dense colonies. Roots frequently grow from shoots. Fleshy, decumbent branches have segmented, swollen nodes, especially below the leaves, with basal internodes from 3–5 mm long.
Foliage:	Tiny linear-lanceolate leaves to 8 mm long are green to greyish-brown
Flowers:	Minute 4-petalled cream, pink or red cup-shaped flowers in dense, spike-like clusters; October to June
Requirements:	Moist to wet soils
Comments:	Grow as a rockery plant.
Localities:	Research, Belgrave Heights, 4, 6, 12, 14, 16–18, 21, 23–26, 29, 32, 34A–36, 42, 49, 50A, 51, 55, 57–59, 67, 68, 69A, 75
Distribution:	Vic, Qld, NSW, Tas, SA; NZ

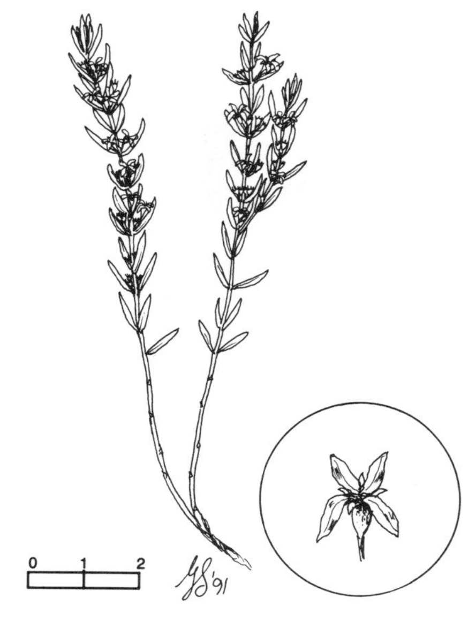

Crassula sieberiana ssp. *sieberiana*

Crassula sieberiana ssp. tetramera

Size:	to 15 cm high **P**
Habitat:	Tea-tree heath, valley sclerophyll forest
Form:	Erect annual with normal basal root system. Wiry-woody branches are not segmented and basal internodes are longer to 12 mm.
Flowers:	Axillary in leaf-like bracts; August to November. The calyx is twice as long as the petals in the coastal form.
Comments:	Often occuring with *C. colorata* var. *acuminata* which is distinguished by its 5 petals.
Localities:	Melton, Werribee, Diamond Ck, Research, 32, 36, 69–72, 74
Distribution:	All states

SCALE: 0 1cm 2cm The scale representation on each plant equals 2cm.

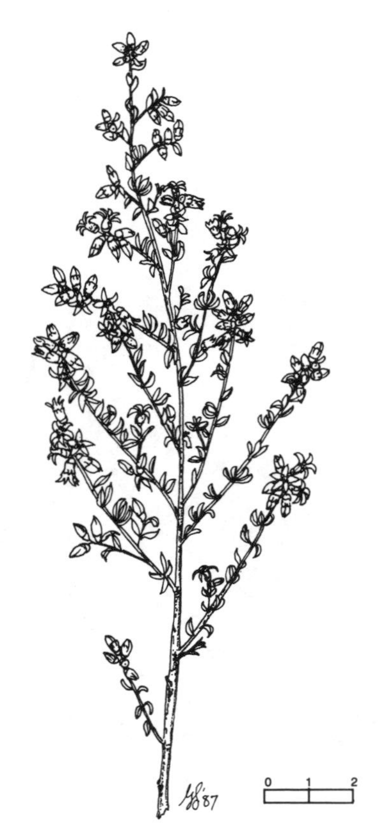

Cryptandra amara

Cryptandra — Rhamnaceae

Cryptandra amara var. amara — Bitter Cryptandra

F P

Size: 0.3–0.6 m x 0.5 m
Habitat: Box woodland
Form: Slow growing, wiry spreading shrub
Foliage: Green, narrow to obovate leaves to 6 mm long, rarely slightly hairy, on stiff, spiny branchlets
Flowers: Clusters of small white or reddish flowers; April to October
Requirements: Well drained soils, tolerating dryness once established
Comments: A very showy plant, especially suited to container growing or massed planting in a rockery. Requires light pruning after flowering to maintain a compact shape.
Propagation: Cuttings—can be slow to strike
Localities: Diggers Rest, Bulla
Distribution: Vic, Qld, NSW, Tas, SA

Cuscuta — Cuscutaceae

Cuscuta tasmanica — Golden Dodder

F

Habitat: Saltmarshes
Form: Leafless, rootless parasite which twines around low herbs, absorbing their nourishment through specialised attachments. Often parasitises *Wilsonia* spp. and *Chenopodium* spp. Slender stems are pale yellow.
Flowers: Creamy flowers are in small, dense, stalked clusters; December to May.
Comments: It has little ornamental value and plants may become a weed in gardens. May be extinct within Melbourne.
Localities: Collected in St. Kilda in 1905, Altona#; 4
Distribution: Vic, NSW, Tas, SA, WA

Cymbonotus — Asteraceae

Cymbonotus lawsonianus — Bear's Ear

F

Size: Prostrate x 10–30 cm
Habitat: Red gum woodland, plains grassland, dry or valley sclerophyll forest
Form: Perennial herb forming a flat rosette
Foliage: Ovate to lanceolate toothed leaves to 100 mm long, white and hairy underneath
Flowers: Single yellow daisy flowers on short woolly stalks; September to November
Requirements: Moist, rich well drained soils
Comments: Suitable for rockeries but may become a weed in cultivated or disturbed soil. Fruit are deeply curved and smooth on the convex side. Used by the early settlers in an ointment to heal wounds. Very rare.
Propagation: Seed, division
Localities: Sydenham#, St. Albans#, Greensborough, 20#, 21#, 30#, 42, 58#
Distribution: All states except NT

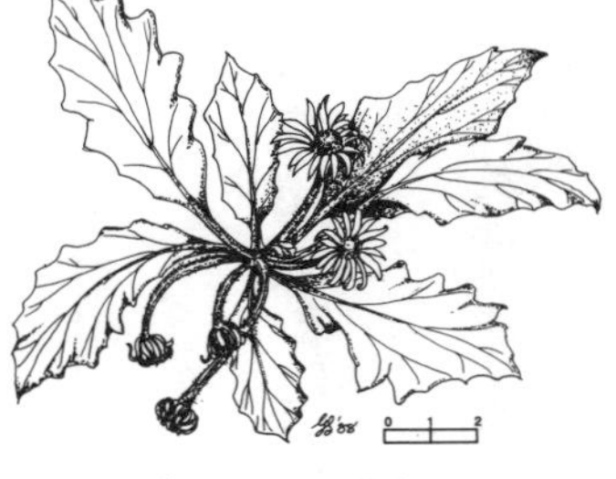
Cymbonotus preissianus

Cymbonotus preissianus — Australe Bear's Ear

P N

Habitat: Dry and damp sclerophyll forest, red gum woodland, grassy low open forest
Comments: Differs from *C. lawsonianus* in preferring sheltered situations. Leaves are velvety and strap-like. Fruits are only slightly curved, and rough on the convex side.
Localities: 29#, 34A–39, 41, 42, 55, 58, 67#, 74, 76
Distribution: Vic, NSW, Tas, SA, WA

Cynoglossum australe

Cynoglossum — Boraginaceae

Cynoglossum australe — Austral Hound's Tongue

F P

Size: 0.3–1 m x 0.5–2 m
Habitat: Plains grassland, amongst rocks
Flowers: Similar to *C. suaveolens* but with small, slightly fragrant light blue flowers; October to February. Forked flowering stems are leafless and many-flowered.
Requirements: Dry, well drained soil
Comments: Locally endangered, it may already be extinct in the Melbourne region.
Localities: Early collections from Darebin Creek, Melbourne
Distribution: All states except Qld

Cynoglossum latifolium

Forest Hound's Tongue

P

Size: 0.5–1.5 m x 0.5–2 m
Habitat: Damp and wet sclerophyll forests and gullies
Form: Weak-stemmed prickly perennial
Foliage: Oval, hairy 5-veined leaves to 80 mm long
Flowers: Small bluish flowers on longer stalks (>15 mm) than *C. suaveolens* and *C. australe*, singly in axils or in few-flowered loose racemes; sporadically. Stalks do not recurve in fruit.
Requirements: Moist soil in sheltered areas
Localities: 56–58
Distribution: Vic, Qld, NSW, Tas

Cynoglossum suaveolens

Sweet Hound's Tongue

F P

Size: 0.1–1 m x 0.5–1.5 m
Habitat: Plains grassland, coastal banksia woodland, damp and dry sclerophyll forest
Form: Erect to spreading perennial herb
Foliage: Basal rosette with wavy lanceolate to oblong leaves to 120 mm long, becoming smaller and sessile on stems. Leaf surface is covered in stiff hairs.
Flowers: Highly fragrant, stalked, small white flowers with yellow centres, on terminal leafy flowering stems; most of the year. Flower stalk curves downwards in fruit.
Requirements: Well drained heavy soil
Comments: This most desirable plant is useful for containers or on embankments where it acts as a soil binder. It responds well to light pruning.
Propagation: Seed, cuttings, division
Localities: Kororoit Ck, Rockbank, 18, 25, 26, 28, 30#, 35, 42, 44, 47, 49, 50A, 55, 56, 59, 67#, 69A, 74
Distribution: Vic, Qld, NSW, Tas, SA

Cynoglossum latifolium

Cynoglossum suaveolens

Dampiera

Goodeniaceae

Dampiera stricta

Blue Dampiera

F P

Size: 0.3–0.8 m x 0.3–2 m
Habitat: Dry sclerophyll forest, tea-tree heath
Form: Suckering perennial herb
Foliage: Thick, elliptical leaves, sometimes hairy, to 50 mm long
Flowers: Single or clustered bright blue to mauve-blue flowers with yellow centres; May to June
Requirements: Moist soils with reasonable drainage
Comments: Excellent garden or container plant providing a natural look. Hard pruning is beneficial. Locally rare.
Propagation: Suckers, cuttings can be slow
Localities: Eltham, ?42, 44
Distribution: Vic, Qld, NSW, Tas

Daucus

Apiaceae

Daucus glochidiatus

Austral Carrot

F P

Size: 0.75 m high
Habitat: Plains grassland, dry and valley sclerophyll forest, coastal banksia woodland
Form: Slender carrot-like annual with erect stems branching at the base and covered in stiff hairs
Foliage: Pinnate leaves, ovate segments have narrow lobes
Flowers: Terminal umbels of tiny white or pink flowers; August to November. Fruit spiny.
Requirements: Dry soils
Comments: May become a weed under ideal conditions.
Propagation: Seed
Localities: Diamond Ck, Laverton Nth, 12, 26, 29#, 34A, 36, 38, 41, 42, 44, 53, 55, 62, 63, 67#, 75
Distribution: All states

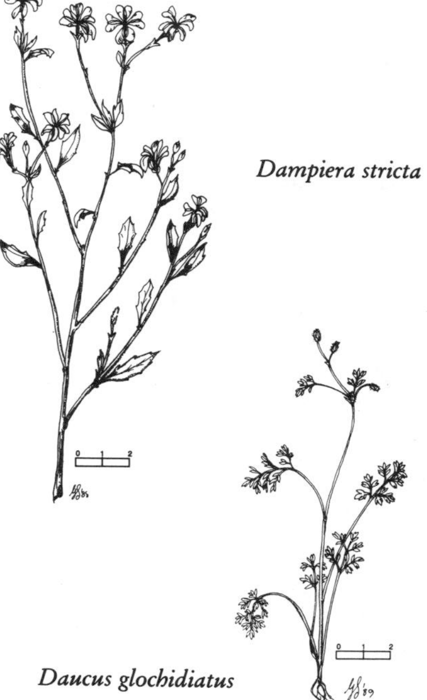

Dampiera stricta

Daucus glochidiatus

SCALE: 0 1cm 2cm The scale representation on each plant equals 2cm.

Daviesia **Fabaceae**

These 3 species are frequently found as understorey shrubs in open forests where they will tolerate a wide range of well drained soils. Masses of pea-shaped flowers, commonly yellow and brown, make them very showy in Spring. They are followed by triangular seed pods which are a distinguishing feature. Plants will benefit from an annual pruning after flowering. Propagation is by scarified seed or cuttings.

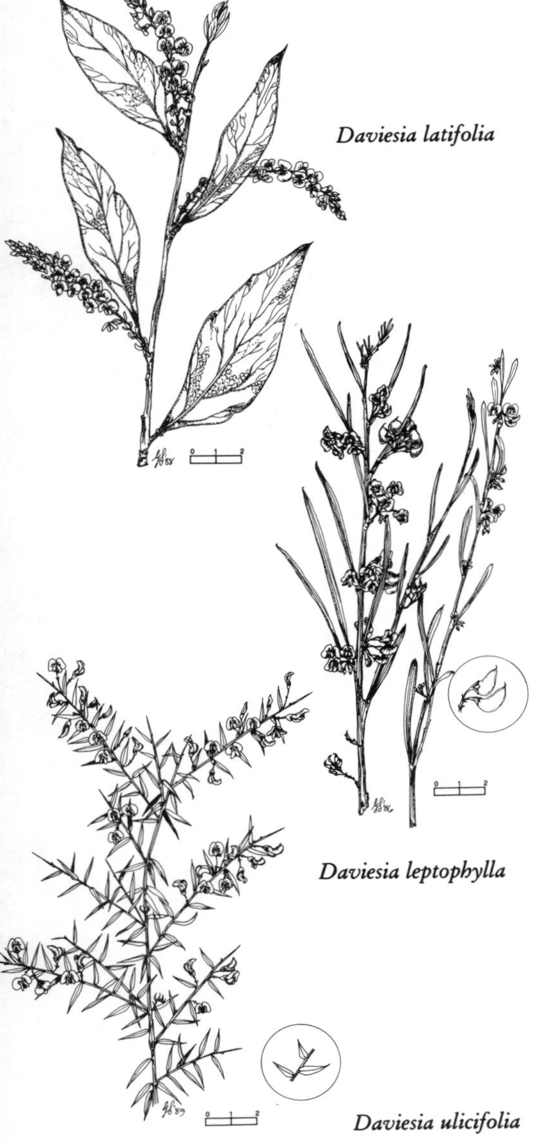

Daviesia latifolia

Daviesia leptophylla

Daviesia ulicifolia

Daviesia latifolia

Hop Bitter-pea

Size: 1–3 m x 1–2 m **F P**
Habitat: Dry, damp and valley sclerophyll forests, grassy low open forest, disturbed areas
Form: Open spreading shrub
Foliage: Dull green ovate-elliptic leaves with wavy edges to 100 mm long and a strong network of veins
Flowers: Dense racemes of fragrant yellow and brown flowers; September to December
Requirements: Adaptable to most soils
Comments: Useful in massed plantings for screening or hedges. Leaves have medicinal properties and were substituted for hops.
Localities: Epping, Springvale#, 34A, 42–44, 47–49, 50A, 51, 54, 56, 58, 61–64, 67#, 74, 76
Distribution: Vic, Qld, NSW, Tas

Daviesia leptophylla

Narrow Leaf, or Slender Bitter-pea

Size: 1–2 m x 1–2 m **F P**
Habitat: Widespread in valley and dry sclerophyll forests, sclerophyll and coastal banksia woodland
Form: Open erect shrub
Foliage: Stiff dull green linear leaves to 100 mm long
Flowers: Many short racemes of yellow and red flowers; September to January
Localities: Hawthorn#, Hampton#, Clayton#; Epping, Research, 34, 34A, 36, 37, 41, 42, 44, 46–51, 53–56, 58, 62–64, 67#, 74, 75
Distribution: Vic, NSW, SA
Synonym: *D. virgata*

Daviesia leptophylla x latifolia

Comments: A natural hybrid with characteristics mid-way between each parent. Frequently confused with *D. mimosoides* which does not occur within the Melbourne area.
Localities: Knox, 35, 38, 39, 42, 43, 47, 48, 50A, 74

Daviesia ulicifolia

Gorse Bitter-Pea

Size: 1.5 m x 1–2 m **P**
Habitat: Dry sclerophyll forest, tea-tree heath, riparian scrub
Form: Stiff, tangled, prickly shrub
Foliage: Dark green prickly, narrow-lanceolate leaves to 25 mm long, midrib prominent
Flowers: 1–3 flowers in leaf axils; July to November
Localities: 29, 49, 55, 67, 68
Distribution: Vic, Qld, NSW, SA, WA

Derwentia **Scrophulariaceae**

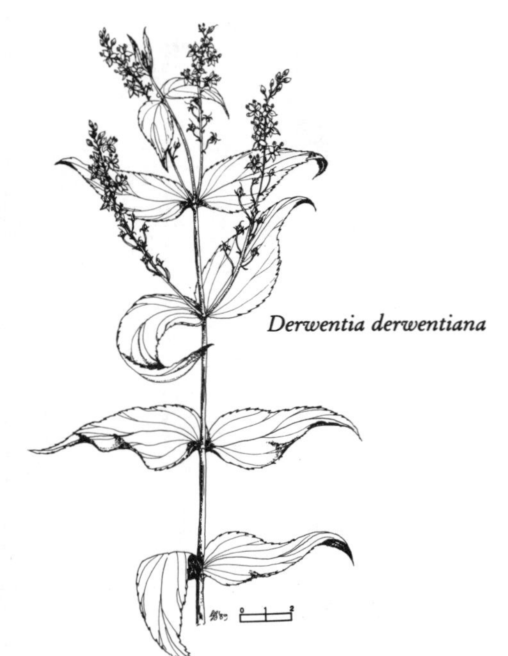

Derwentia derwentiana

Derwentia derwentiana

Derwent Speedwell

Size: 0.6–1 m x 1 m **P N**
Habitat: Valley, damp and wet sclerophyll forests, riparian scrub
Form: Upright to straggly open perennial
Foliage: Dark green lanceolate leaves with toothed edges, to 100 mm long
Flowers: Terminal sprays of white or pale blue 4-petalled flowers; November to January
Requirements: Moist well drained soil
Comments: Fast growing perennial which may die back in Summer. Hard pruning encourages more vigorous growth.
Propagation: Cuttings, division
Localities: 29, 42, 44, 50A, 55–58, 60
Distribution: Vic, Qld, NSW, Tas, SA
Synonym: *Veronica derwentiana, Parahebe derwentiana*

Desmodium — Fabaceae

Desmodium gunnii

Slender Tick-trefoil

Size: 0.2–0.5 m x 1–2 m — P
Habitat: Damp and valley sclerophyll forests, grassy wetlands
Form: Light scrambling undershrub, occasionally rooting at the nodes
Foliage: Trifoliate with smooth round dark green leaflets to 25 mm long
Flowers: Pink pea flowers in loose racemes to 120 mm occur most of the year. Fruit is a pod to 24 mm with 3–6 tooth-like segments, covered in small bristles.
Requirements: Moist soils
Comments: An evergreen undershrub which may form large mats in moist conditions. Needs to be grown among other plants.
Propagation: Scarified seed, cuttings
Localities: 6, 36, 42, 55–58, 60
Distribution: Vic, Qld, NSW, Tas
Synonym: *D. varians* var. *gunnii*

Desmodium varians

Slender Tick-trefoil

Size: 0.2–0.5 m x 0.2–0.5 m — F P
Habitat: Dry sclerophyll forest, plains grassland, crevices in escarpments
Form: Slender scrambling undershrub which dies back to its rootstock in Summer
Foliage: Yellow-green trifoliate leaves, leaflets linear with sunken veins
Flowers: Yellow-orange pea flowers in loose racemes; Winter to Spring
Requirements: Well drained soils, tolerating dry periods once established
Comments: Juvenile leaflets may be rounded and the plant may be easily mistaken for *D. gunnii* at this stage. When regrowth takes place a terminal flower spike develops at the end of the new shoot first before lateral shoots develop.
Localities: Essendon, Kororoit Ck, 17#, 34A, 41, 42, 59
Distribution: Vic, Qld, NSW, SA

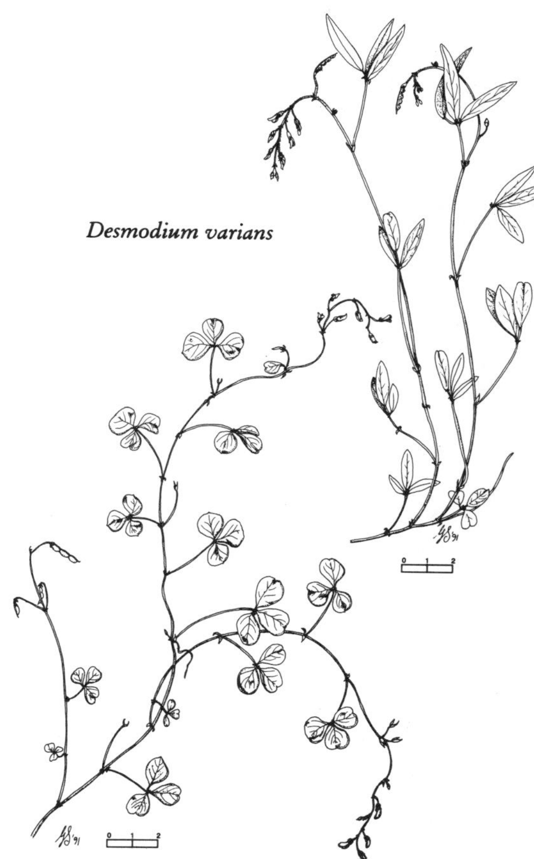

Desmodium varians

Desmodium gunnii

Dichondra — Convolvulaceae

Dichondra repens

Kidney Weed

Size: Prostrate creeping herb — P N
Habitat: Widespread in plains grassland, red gum and coastal banksia woodland, riparian scrub and woodland, dry and valley sclerophyll forests and grassy low open forest
Form: Dense spreading herb rooting at nodes to form mats
Foliage: Hairy kidney-shaped leaves to 40 mm long
Flowers: Tiny greenish flowers; September to December
Requirements: Well drained soils
Comments: Alternative to grass where foot traffic is light. It grows more vigorously under cultivation.
Propagation: Seed, division of suckers. Seed available from most commercial outlets is not the local form but is in fact the American species *D. micrantha*.
Localities: 2, 4–6, 8, 9, 12, 14, 16–18, 21, 23–32, 34A–48, 50A–52, 54–71, 74–76
Distribution: All states

Dichondra repens

Dillwynia — Fabaceae

The dillwynias are most attractive small shrubs occurring in dry sclerophyll forests or in heathlands. They are tolerant of a wide range of well drained soils. A display of showy yellow or yellow and red pea flowers occurs during Spring. They may be distinguished from the other genera with pea flowers by the groove in the upper surface of the leaf. Pruning after flowering is beneficial. Propagation is by scarified seed or cuttings.

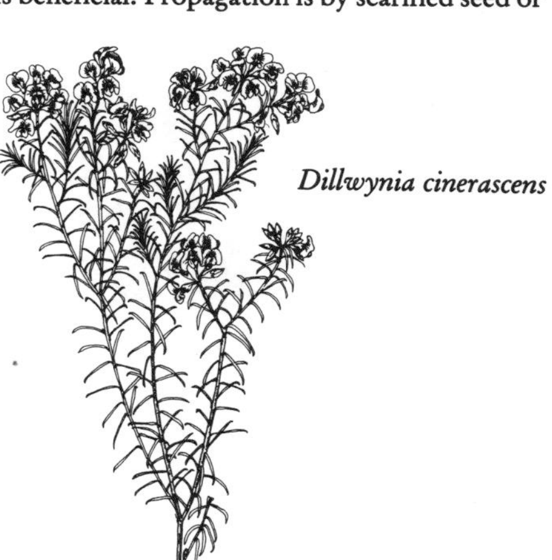

Dillwynia cinerascens

Dillwynia cinerascens

Grey Parrot Pea

Size: 0.6–1.5 m x 0.5–1.5 m — P
Habitat: Tea-tree heath, dry and valley sclerophyll forests, plains grassland
Form: Open, erect or spreading understorey shrub
Foliage: Terete greyish-green leaves to 20 mm long
Flowers: Terminal clusters of yellow and orange pea flowers; July to November
Requirements: Dry soils
Comments: An adaptable shrub for a shady situation.
Localities: Sydenham, Oaklands, Tottenham, Laverton Nth, Sunshine, 12, 15, 16, 26, 33–36, 38–44, 46–56, 58, 62–64, 67–69, 71, 73–76
Distribution: Vic, Tas, SA, WA

SCALE: 0 1cm 2cm — The scale representation on each plant equals 2cm.

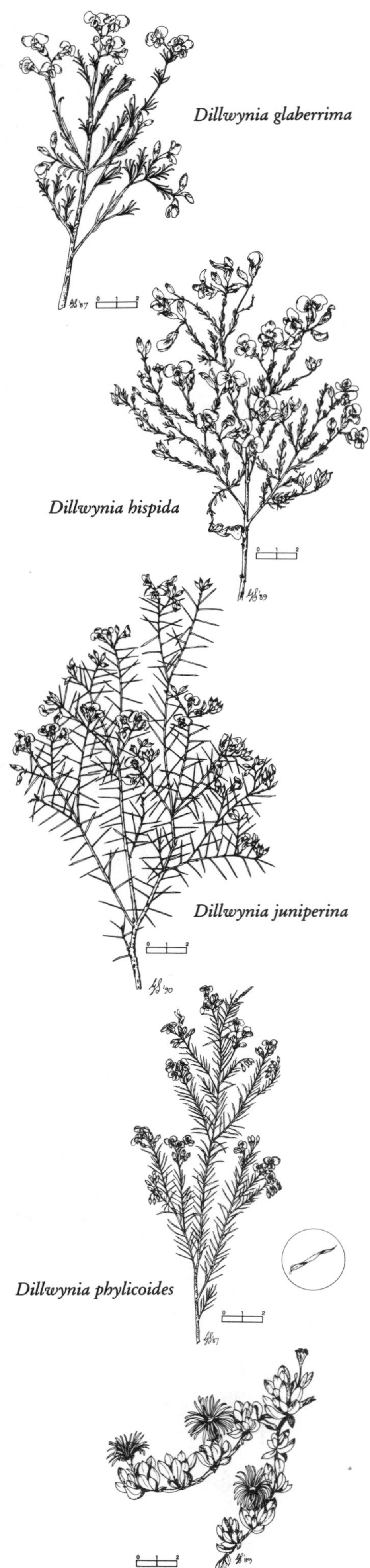
Dillwynia glaberrima

Dillwynia hispida

Dillwynia juniperina

Dillwynia phylicoides

Disphyma crassifolium ssp. clavellatum

Dillwynia glaberrima
Heath or Smooth Parrot Pea

Size: 1–2 m x 1–2 m — F P
Habitat: Valley sclerophyll forest, tea-tree heath, grassy low open forest
Form: Wiry, open shrub
Foliage: Glabrous terete green leaves to 25 mm long
Flowers: Terminal racemes of bright yellow and red flowers; August to December.
Comments: Useful for planting under established trees.
Localities: 37, 42, 44, 47, 49, ?50A, 59, 60, 61, 67–71, 73–76
Distribution: Vic, Qld, NSW, Tas, SA

Dillwynia hispida
Red Parrot Pea

Size: 0.2–0.6 m x 0.3–1 m — P
Habitat: Tea-tree heath
Form: Slender erect shrub
Foliage: Crowded terete leaves to 10 mm long with stiff spreading hairs
Flowers: Well displayed large red to orange flowers in terminal heads; September to November
Requirements: Prefers sandy, moist, well drained situations
Comments: Very showy plant in containers and hanging baskets but difficult to maintain in the garden.
Localities: The only occurrence of this plant within the Melbourne area is at Sandringham. This may be an incorrect collection.
Distribution: Vic, NSW, SA

Dillwynia juniperina
Prickly Parrot Pea or Juniper Pea Bush

Size: 1–1.5 m x 1–1.5 m — P
Habitat: Red gum woodland
Form: Prickly shrub
Foliage: Linear leaves to 15 mm long, providing excellent bird refuge
Flowers: Yellow and red flowers clustered near the ends of branches; September to November
Requirements: Very adaptable in well drained dry situations
Comments: Known from very few sites in Melbourne.
Localities: 29, 35
Distribution: Vic, Qld, NSW

Dillwynia phylicoides
Small-leaf Parrot Pea

Size: 0.5–1.5 m x 1–2 m — P
Habitat: Dry sclerophyll forest
Form: Spreading to erect shrub
Foliage: Narrow twisted leaves to 10 mm long
Flowers: Profuse terminal clusters of yellow and red flowers; September to December
Requirements: Well drained soil
Comments: A very hardy and ornamental species that deserves to be more widely grown. Responds very well to hard pruning.
Localities: Hurstbridge, 36, 41, 47#
Distribution: Vic, Qld, NSW
Synonym: *D. retorta* var. *phylicoides*

Dillwynia sericea
Showy Parrot Pea

Size: 0.6–1.5 m x 0.5–1.5 m — F P
Habitat: Dry sclerophyll forest, sclerophyll woodland, tea-tree heath
Form: Small erect shrub
Foliage: Narrow hairy leaves to 20 mm long
Flowers: Cylindrical leafy spikes of yellow and red, apricot, or orange flowers; August to December
Requirements: Very adaptable, tolerating extended dry periods once established
Comments: Useful as a low screen or container plant but requires regular pruning after flowering.
Localities: 16, 20#, 26, 36, 42, 44, 46, 47, 49#, 50A, 67#, 71, 73–76
Distribution: Vic, Qld, NSW, Tas, SA

Illustrated p. 106

Disphyma — Aizoaceae

Disphyma crassifolium ssp. clavellatum
Rounded Moon-flower

Size: Prostrate x 1–2 m — F
Habitat: Coastal banksia woodland, saltmarshes
Form: Spreading perennial herb
Foliage: Succulent, cylindrical leaves to 50 mm long
Flowers: Daisy-like pink or magenta flowers with white centre, to 50 mm wide; October to February
Requirements: Very reliable in most soils. Tolerates saline conditions.
Comments: Useful for soil erosion on embankments. The attractive foliage varies from green through to purple and was eaten raw by the Aborigines.
Propagation: Stem or leaf cuttings, or seed
Localities: Footscray, 1–4, 32, 67, 69A, 72, 74
Distribution: Vic, Qld, NSW, Tas, SA
Synonym: *D. clavellatum*, *D. australe*

Dodonaea

Sapindaceae

Dodonaea viscosa ssp. spatulata

Wedge-Leaf Hop Bush

Size: 1–3 m x 1–3 m **F P**
Habitat: Dry sclerophyll forest, riparian scrub, box woodland, grassy low open forest
Form: Open to dense spreading shrub
Foliage: Obovate to spathulate leaves to 75 mm long
Flowers: Inconspicuous unisexual flowers in clusters; August to November; followed by showy red or blackish-brown capsules with 3–4 papery wings
Requirements: Well drained soils
Comments: A very hardy shrub tolerating extended dry periods once established and moderate coastal exposure. Pruning is beneficial. Plants in the Melbourne area have been incorrectly referred to as *D. cuneata*. The typical form *D. viscosa* ssp. *viscosa* does not occur in the study area.
Propagation: Seed, cuttings—especially to perpetuate forms with attractively coloured capsules
Localities: Keilor, Greensborough, Research, 1, 9, 14, 16, 18, 22, 23, 26, 29, 31, 32, 35, 36, 74, 76
Distribution: All states except NT
Synonym: *D. viscosa* ssp. *cuneata*

Also illustrated p. 106

Dodonaea viscosa ssp. *spatulata*

Drosera

Droseraceae

Droseras are small carnivorous perennial herbs. Known as Sundews, they trap insects on special sticky hairs on their leaves. All droseras require damp soil for at least part of the year. The main growing season is from Autumn to Spring, usually with a dormant period during Summer when plants die back to their roots. Most make excellent container plants, preferring a damp peaty soil and plenty of light. Propagation is by seed sown in Spring, or by leaf cutting.

Drosera binata

Forked Sundew

Size: 0.2–0.8 m high **F P**
Habitat: Tea-tree heath, valley sclerophyll forest
Form: Erect perennial herb
Foliage: Narrow pale green to reddish forked leaves from 5–60 cm long
Flowers: Flowering stem is up to 80 cm long, with many white flowers, each 25 mm across. The main flowering is from September to April.
Requirements: Needs continuously damp peaty soil
Comments: Excellent pot or basket plant. Use peat and sand, or sphagnum moss, in a shallow container.
Propagation: Easy from seed, leaf or stem cutting
Localities: Moorabbin#, 42, 67#, 74, 75
Distribution: All states

Drosera glanduligera

Scarlet Sundew

Size: Basal rosette to 3 cm high **F P**
Habitat: Swamps and moist banks of red gum woodland and tea-tree heath
Form: Tiny rosette
Foliage: Elliptical leaves to 15 mm long
Flowers: Terminal clusters of orange flowers fading to pink; August to October
Requirements: Moist acidic, peaty soil
Comments: Usually grows in dense colonies.
Localities: 12, 26, 35, 45, 67#, 74, 75
Distribution: Vic, NSW, Tas, SA, WA

Drosera macrantha

Bridal Rainbow or Climbing Sundew

Size: 0.4–0.8 m high **F P**
Habitat: Damp and valley sclerophyll forest, tea-tree heath, swamp scrub, grassy low open forest, sclerophyll woodland
Form: Weakly climbing perennial herb with a tuberous rootstock
Foliage: Rounded, cupped, yellowish-green leaves to 90 mm long
Flowers: Terminal clusters of white or pink sweetly perfumed flowers; June to October
Requirements: Sandy loam or clay soils which are moist during the growing period but dry out in Summer
Propagation: Seed
Localities: 29, 30, 32, 34A, 41, 42, 49, 53, 58, 67, 69, 70, 71, 73–76
Distribution: Vic, Tas, SA, WA
Synonym: *D. macrantha* ssp. *planchonii*, *D. planchonii*

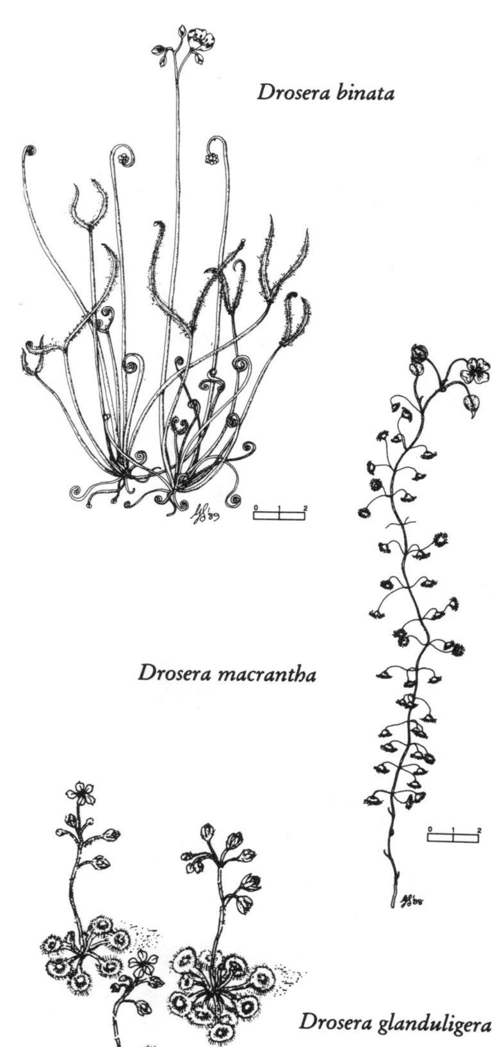

Drosera binata

Drosera macrantha

Drosera glanduligera

SCALE: 0 1cm 2cm — The scale representation on each plant equals 2cm.

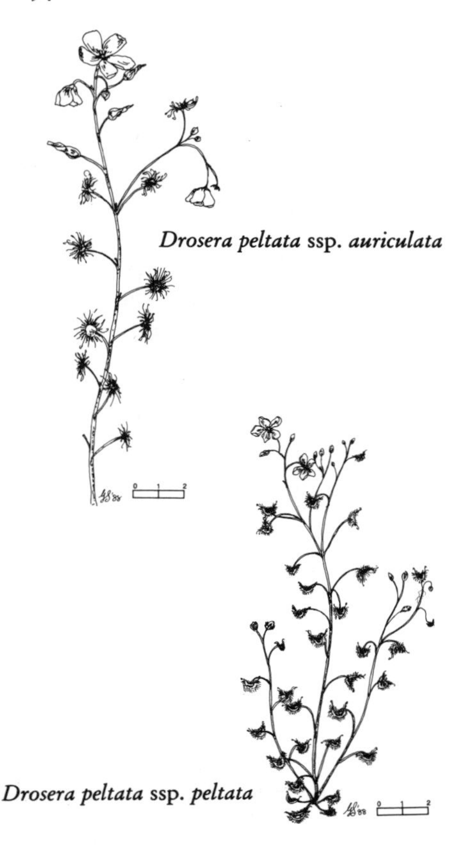

Drosera peltata ssp. *auriculata*

Drosera peltata ssp. *peltata*

Drosera peltata ssp. auriculata

Tall Sundew

Size: 0.1–0.8 m high **F P**
Habitat: Widespread in wattle tea-tree scrub, tea-tree heath, grassy low open forest, dry and valley sclerophyll forest
Form: Upright perennial herb with a tuberous root
Foliage: Sparsely foliaged with few dark green spathulate leaves to 12 mm long
Flowers: Loose terminal cluster of white to pale pink flowers; August to December
Requirements: Adaptable to most soils which are damp during growth periods and dry out in Summer
Comments: The size of the seeds is the most reliable distinguishing feature between the 2 subspecies of *D. peltata*. They are linear, to about 1 mm long in ssp. *auriculata*.
Propagation: Seed
Localities: 29#, 32–36, 38, 41–51, 53–56, 58–64, 67–71, 73–76
Distribution: Vic, Qld, NSW, Tas, SA
Synonym: *D. auriculata*

Drosera peltata ssp. peltata

Pale Sundew

Size: 0.1–0.5 m high **F P**
Habitat: Plains grassland, red gum woodland, dry and valley sclerophyll forests, tea-tree heath
Comments: This subspecies differs from *D. peltata* ssp. *auriculata* in that it usually has a basal rosette of pale green leaves and usually has hairy rather than smooth buds. Seeds are ovoid and less than 0.6 mm long.
Localities: 7, 12, 13, 16, 25, 26, 29–31, 34A–36, 42, 44, 47, 49–52, 56, 58, 69A–71, 74–76
Distribution: All states except NT

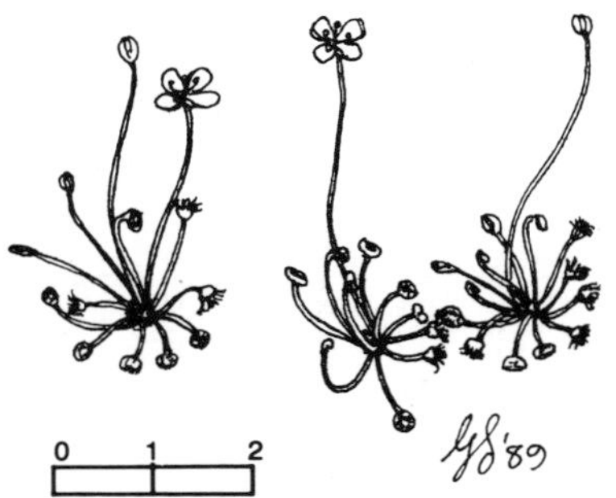

Drosera pygmaea

Drosera pygmaea

Pygmy, or Tiny Sundew

Size: 2 cm high **F**
Habitat: Grassy low open forest, swamp scrub
Form: Tiny basal rosette
Foliage: Bronze round leaves to 2 mm diameter on a fine stalk to 8 mm long
Flowers: Single white flower 4 mm wide on an erect stalk to 20 mm; June to January
Requirements: Moist, sandy soil
Propagation: May be propagated from vegative propagules (minute bud-like, lens-shaped structures) which form in the centre of the rosette.
Localities: Heathmont, The Basin, Rowville, Baxter, 54, 61, 67#, 69A, 73–76
Distribution: All states

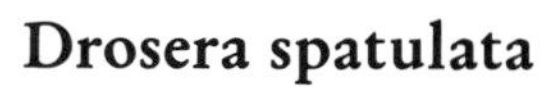

Drosera spathulata

Drosera spatulata

Spoon-leaf or Rosy Sundew

Size: 5–20 cm x 2 cm **P**
Habitat: Tea-tree heath and swamp scrub
Form: Tuberous basal rosette
Foliage: Crowded spathulate reddish leaves to 10 mm long
Flowers: Small white, pink or red flowers on an erect stem to 200 mm high, throughout the year
Comments: An attractive container plant. Endangered locally.
Localities: Cheltenham#, 67#, 74, 75
Distribution: Vic, Qld, NSW, Tas

Drosera whittakeri

Drosera whittakeri

Scented Sundew

Size: 2–4 cm x 2–4 cm **F P**
Habitat: Widespread in tea-tree heath, grassy low open forest, red gum woodland, plains grassland, dry and valley sclerophyll forest
Form: Tuberous, round flat basal rosette
Foliage: Green, bronze or red spathulate leaves to 25 mm long
Flowers: Single large, perfumed white flower to 30 mm on a thick, erect stalk to 40 mm; July to October
Requirements: Prefers acidic peaty soil which is moist during the growing season
Comments: May form large colonies in moist areas. An excellent container plant.
Localities: 12, 16, 25, 26, 29#, 30#, 34A–36, 38, 39, 41–44, 46–51, 53–56, 58–64, 67#, 70, 71, 73–76
Distribution: Vic, SA

Eclipta

Asteraceae

Eclipta platyglossa

Yellow Twin-heads

Size: 15–25 cm high **F P**
Habitat: Grassy wetlands
Form: Hairy annual or biennial herb
Foliage: Pairs of lanceolate leaves to 50 mm long
Flowers: Tiny yellow daisy flowers with bi-lobed rays; late Spring and Summer
Requirements: Tolerates heavy, wet soil
Comments: Suitable for a bog garden. Very rare in the Melbourne area and in danger of extinction.
Propagation: Seed, cuttings
Localities: Werribee#, Derrimut on private property
Distribution: All states except Tas

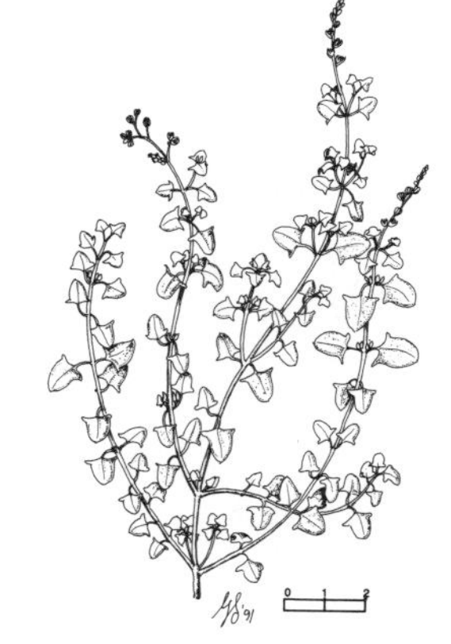

Einadia hastata

Einadia

Chenopodiaceae

Einadia hastata

Saloop, Berry Saltbush

Size: 10–20 cm x 20–50 cm **F P**
Habitat: Riparian and chenopod rocky open scrub, riparian, box and red gum woodland, primary dune scrub, tea-tree heath
Form: Many-branched rigid procumbent undershrub
Foliage: Green hastate leaves to 20 mm long
Flowers: Clusters of insignificant cream flowers followed by small succulent red berries
Requirements: Well drained soils, tolerating dryness
Comments: Regular light pruning promotes dense bushy growth. Saltbushes are useful in revegetating salt affected areas.
Propagation: Cuttings
Localities: West Melton, 9, 14, 16, 26, 29, 32, 34A–36, 67#, 69
Distribution: Vic, Qld, NSW
Synonym: *Rhagodia hastata*

Einadia nutans ssp. nutans

Nodding or Climbing Saltbush

Size: 30 cm x 1.2 m **F P**
Habitat: Dry sclerophyll forest, plains grassland, riparian and chenopod rocky open scrub, riparian, red gum and box woodland, primary dune scrub
Form: Sprawling or scrambling shrub
Foliage: Broadly lanceolate grey-green leaves to 30 mm long
Flowers: Insignificant clusters of greenish flowers followed by succulent red berries in Summer and Autumn
Requirements: Tolerates dry soils
Comments: A useful groundcover for dry banks and rockeries, drought resistant once established. It is also a valuable fire retardant.
Propagation: Cuttings
Localities: 2, 4, 8, 9, 12, 14–16, 18, 21–26, 28–36, 38, 39, 42, 49, 65#, 67#, 69A, 71
Distribution: All states except WA
Synonym: *Rhagodia nutans*

Einadia nutans ssp. *nutans*

Einadia trigonos ssp. trigonos

Lax or Fishweed Goosefoot

Size: Prostrate or procumbent **P**
Habitat: Red gum woodland
Form: Low straggling herbaceous perennial
Foliage: Greyish-green arrow-shaped leaves to 15 mm long
Flowers: Insignificant flowers followed by dry black berries
Requirements: Moist well drained soil
Comments: A rare plant for Melbourne, known from few sites.
Propagation: Cuttings
Localities: 32
Distribution: Vic, NSW, Qld
Synonym: *Chenopodium trigonon*

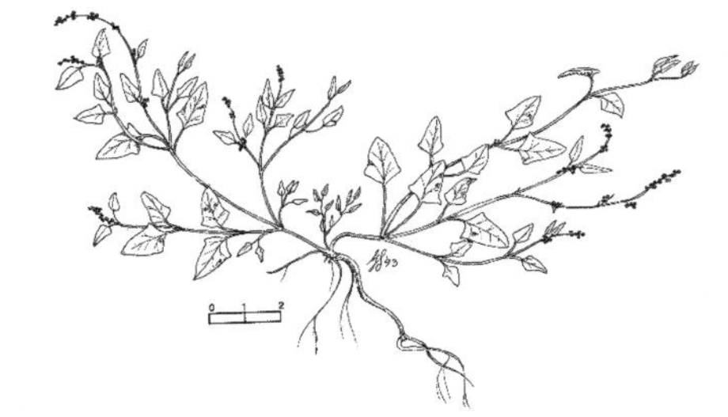

Einadia trigonos ssp. *trigonos*

Elatine

Elatinaceae

Elatine gratioloides

Waterwort

Size: Prostrate x 0.3–2 m **F**
Habitat: Aquatic, in still water or muddy sites, of red gum and box woodland, grassy wetland and plains grassland
Form: Fast growing annual herb
Foliage: Bright green ovate to elliptic leaves 2–20 mm x 1–4 mm
Flowers: Solitary pinkish-green flowers in leaf axils most of the year
Requirements: Shallow water or boggy site subject to inundation
Comments: Makes a good aquarium or bog garden plant, regenerating readily in boggy conditions. Locally rare.
Propagation: Cuttings, seed sown in mud
Localities: Deer Park, Rockbank, 2, 6, 7, 17#, 18, 24, 26
Distribution: All states

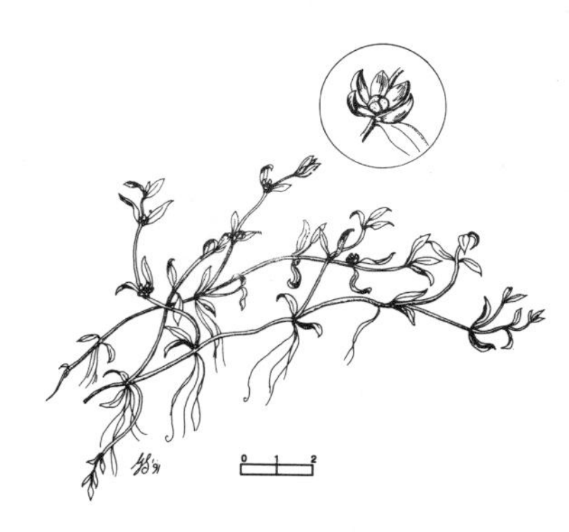

Elatine gratioloides

SCALE: 0 1cm 2cm The scale representation on each plant equals 2cm.

Enchylaena tomentosa

Enchylaena — Chenopodiaceae

Enchylaena tomentosa — Barrier or Ruby Saltbush

Size:	Prostrate–1 m x 0.5–1 m **F P**
Habitat:	Riparian and chenopod rocky open scrub, red gum and box woodland, plains grassland, primary dune scrub
Form:	Low spreading or upright woody shrub
Foliage:	Bluish-green to dark green succulent leaves, narrowly cylindrical to 10 mm long or linear with margins recurved, to 20 mm long
Flowers:	Insignificant greenish flowers in Spring and early Summer, followed by succulent green berries which change to yellow or red.
Requirements:	Very adaptable tolerating poor soils, dryness and some salinity
Comments:	An attractive plant, useful as an undershrub in dryland plantings, and suitable for containers. Pruning is beneficial. There are two forms within the Melbourne area, an upright form with smaller and paler terete leaves and red berries favouring drier areas and a prostrate form with darker linear leaves and yellower berries, preferring alluvial soils. The Aborigines ate the sweet berries and used the leaves as a green vegetable.
Propagation:	Cuttings, seed
Localities:	Avondale Heights, 1, 2, 4, 12, 14–16, 21–26, 28, 29, 32, 34A, 67#, 74
Distribution:	All mainland states

Epacris — Epacridaceae

The 3 *Epacris* species of Melbourne commonly occur in heathlands and as understorey shrubs. They are upright plants with tubular flowers borne on the upper branches from late Autumn to Spring. All make good tub specimens, especially if massed. Often spindly, they respond to hard pruning after flowering. Root protection is necessary if grown in full sun. Propagation is by seed or cuttings which strike well provided young growth is used.

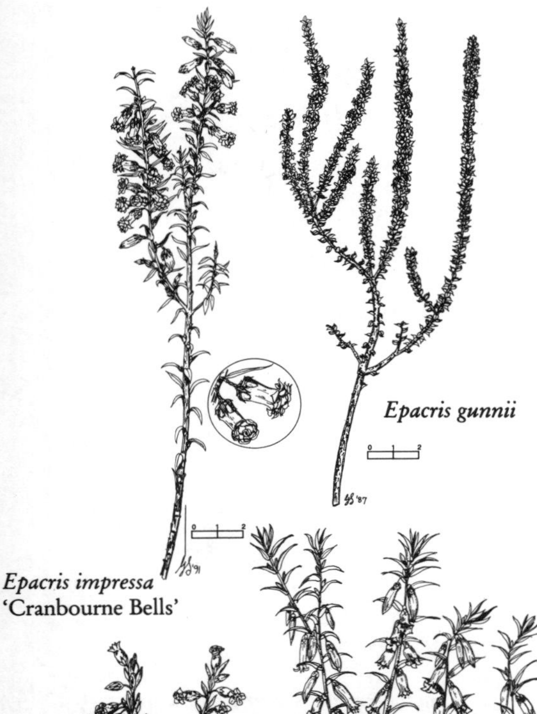
Epacris gunnii

Epacris impressa 'Cranbourne Bells'

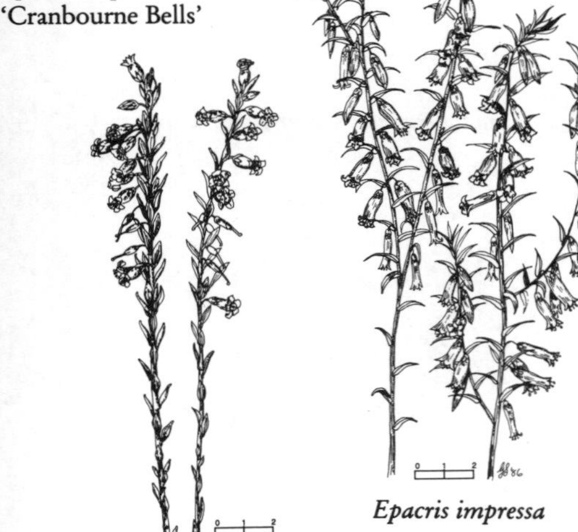
Epacris impressa

Epacris obtusifolia

Epacris gunnii

Size:	0.5–1 m x 0.5–1 m **P**
Habitat:	Swamp scrub, valley sclerophyll forest
Form:	Straggly, upright shrub
Foliage:	Crowded, prickly, heart-shaped leaves to 6 mm long
Flowers:	Very small white flowers sometimes tinged with pink; April to October
Requirements:	Moist well drained soils which should not dry out in Summer
Comments:	A most attractive rockery plant, also suitable for containers. It is frost and snow tolerant. Locally rare through clearing.
Localities:	Montrose, Heathmont, Knox#
Distribution:	Vic, Tas
Synonym:	*E. microphylla* var. *gunnii*

Epacris impressa — Common Heath
Victoria's floral emblem

Size:	0.5–1.5 m x 0.2–0.6 m **P**
Habitat:	Widespread in tea-tree heath, wattle tea-tree scrub, low grassy open forest, sclerophyll woodland, dry, damp and valley sclerophyll forests
Form:	Open, wiry shrub
Foliage:	Prickly, tapering leaves to 15 mm long
Flowers:	Masses of white, pink or red flowers; March to November
Requirements:	Moist, well drained soil, tolerating limited dry or wet periods once established
Comments:	An attractive rockery plant, particularly when planted in groups. Makes an excellent cut flower. A form from Cranbourne, with double white flowers, is sold as 'Cranbourne Bells'. Its only known habitat has now been destroyed.
Localities:	St. Kilda#, Eltham, 29, 33–35, 40–44, 46–56, 58–64, 67–71, 73–76
Distribution:	Vic, NSW, Tas, SA

Epacris obtusifolia — Blunt-leaf Heath

Size:	1–2 m x 0.6–1.5 m **P**
Habitat:	Moist tea-tree heath
Form:	Narrow erect shrub
Foliage:	Erect, blunt-tipped oblong-elliptical leaves from 5–12 mm long
Flowers:	Masses of small white to cream perfumed flowers; June to December
Requirements:	Moist sandy or peaty soil
Comments:	Locally rare.
Localities:	66#, 67#, 73–75
Distribution:	Vic, Qld, NSW, Tas, SA

Epilobium

Onagraceae

Epilobium billardierianum ssp. billardierianum

Smooth Willow Herb

Size: 0.1–1 m, variable depending on moisture **F P**
Habitat: Widespread in red gum woodland, riparian and swamp scrub, valley and dry sclerophyll forest, wattle tea-tree scrub
Form: Erect hairy perennial herb with sprawling base and leafy stems
Foliage: Pairs of blunt, bluish-green ovate stem-clasping leaves to 35 mm x 6–18 mm, densely toothed with up to 40 teeth per side. Lower leaves often red.
Flowers: Single lilac, pink or white flowers to 15 mm long, along upper stems; December to March. Densely covered in tiny flattened hairs. Stalk lengthens to 20 mm in fruit. Capsule to 70 mm long.
Requirements: Will grow almost anywhere
Comments: The seed capsules of *Epilobium* spp. open to reveal small seeds densely covered in white hairs. May become invasive under ideal conditions.
Propagation: Seed
Localities: 2, 4–6, 11, 12, 18, 21, 26, 29#, 34A–36, 39, 41, 42, 44, 51, 52, 54, 55, 62, 63, 67, 72, 74, 75
Distribution: Vic, NSW, Tas, SA, WA; NZ

Epilobium billardierianum ssp. *billardierianum*

Epilobium billardierianum ssp. *cinereum*

Epilobium billardierianum ssp. cinereum

Size: to 0.3 m high
Habitat: Damp and valley sclerophyll forests, swamp scrub
Comments: Leaves are narrower, to 2–7 mm, than ssp. *billardierianum*, with 0–6 coarser teeth per side. Flowers have erect as well as flattened hairs. Grows well in wet conditions.
Localities: 16, 53, 56, 57, 58, 60, 62, 63, 70, 74, 76
Distribution: All states; NZ
Synonym: *E. cinereum*

Epilobium billardierianum ssp. intermedium

Comments: Differs from the above ssp. in that lanceolate leaves have 6–20 small irregular teeth per side and margins are often wavy. Stems are often branched and have glandular and erect hairs towards the end, near the inflorescence.
Localities: Montrose
Distribution: Vic, NSW, Tas, SA, WA

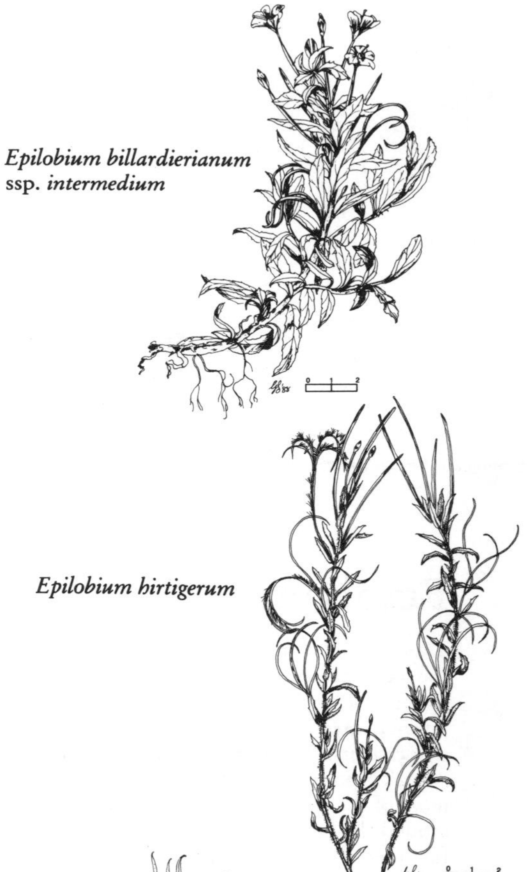

Epilobium billardierianum ssp. *intermedium*

Epilobium hirtigerum

Epilobium hirtigerum

Narrow Leaf or Hoary Willow Herb

Size: 0.2–1.4 m high **F P**
Habitat: Widespread in plains grassland, red gum and sclerophyll woodland, riparian scrub, valley sclerophyll forest, grassy low open forest
Form: Variable, erect perennial herb with spreading hairs
Foliage: Narrow, pointed sessile leaves to 60 mm long, usually alternate, with widely-spaced teeth. New growth is covered in white hairs.
Flowers: Single small pink or white flowers to 7 mm long; November to March. Covered in spreading hairs. Capsule to 60 mm long on stalk lengthened to 15 mm.
Requirements: Moist soils
Propagation: Seeds
Localities: 4, 12, 16–18, 26, 28, 34A–36, 41, 42, 53, 54, 64, 69A, 70, 74, 76
Distribution: All states except NT; NZ, Java, S Am

Eremophila

Myoporaceae

Eremophila deserti

Turkey Bush

Size: 1–4 m x 2 m **F**
Habitat: Box woodland
Form: Erect much-branched shrub
Foliage: Thick narrowly oblanceolate leaves to 50 mm long, with hooked tip
Flowers: Drooping cream bell-shaped flowers in groups of 1–4; May to October
Requirements: Well drained stony or sandy soils
Comments: The yellow drupes following flowering are eaten by emus and turkeys but are poisonous to stock. It is now very rare in the Melbourne area reproducing successfully in two sites.
Propagation: Cuttings
Localities: Spasmodic on the basalt plains, remaining in Keilor, Essendon and Melton, 16, 22, 26
Distribution: Vic, Qld, NSW, SA, WA
Synonym: *Myoporum deserti*

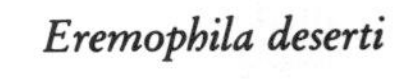

Eremophila deserti

SCALE: 0 1cm 2cm The scale representation on each plant equals 2cm.

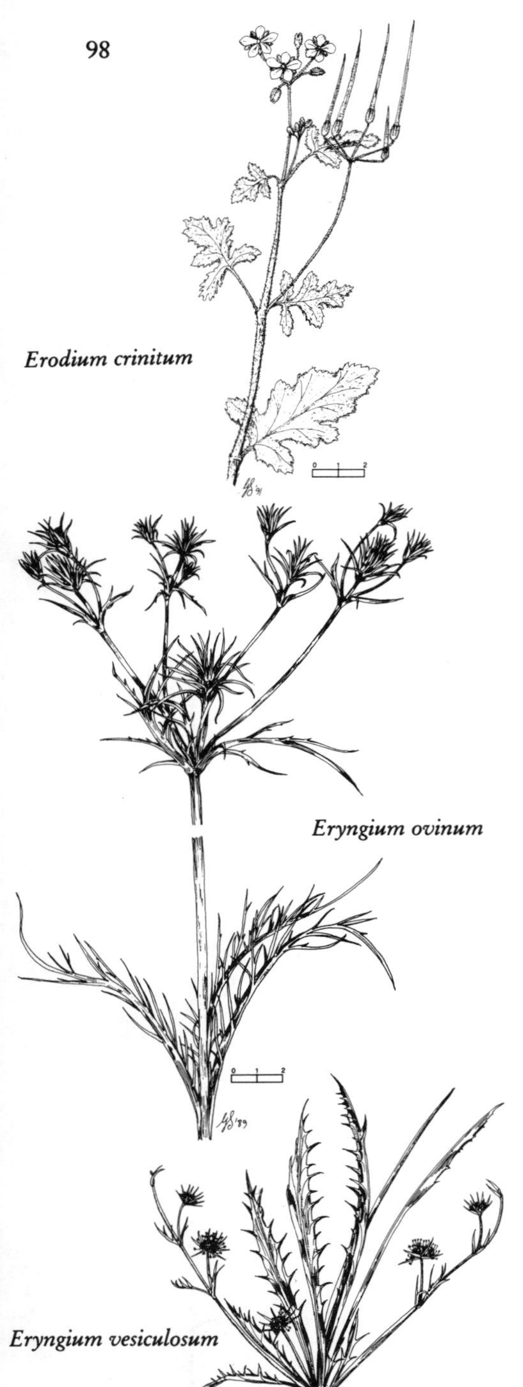
Erodium crinitum

Eryngium ovinum

Eryngium vesiculosum

Erodium — Geraniaceae

Erodium crinitum

Blue Heron's Bill, Native Crowfoot

Size: 0.1–0.8 m x 0.3–1 m — F P
Habitat: Coastal banksia woodland, tea-tree heath, plains grassland
Form: Fast growing, open, spreading annual or biennial herb
Foliage: Deeply divided dark green leaves from 15–40 mm long
Flowers: Clusters of 2 to 6 blue flowers with yellow or white veins near the base; July to October
Requirements: Tolerates extended dry periods in sandy soil
Comments: It is a useful container plant, with interesting fruit. The roots are edible. Locally rare.
Propagation: Seed or cuttings
Localities: 2, 12, 16, 21, 26, 34A, 49, 67#, 71
Distribution: All states

Eryngium — Apiaceae

Eryngium ovinum

Blue Devil, Eryngo

Size: 0.1–0.6 m x 0.3–0.5 m — F
Habitat: Plains grassland, red gum woodland
Form: Fast growing, stiffly erect perennial herb with ribbed stems
Foliage: Prickly; basal leaves finely divided from 10–25 cm long, stem leaves smaller.
Flowers: Globular to ovoid flowerheads to 25 mm long with rigid sharply-pointed metallic blue to purplish bracts; August to February
Requirements: Moist well drained soils
Comments: A very decorative but extremely prickly plant for a container or rockery.
Propagation: Seed
Localities: Melton, Tottenham, St Albans, Hampton#, 2, 4, 5, 7, 10, 12, 13, 15–18, 20, 24–26, 28, 29, 35, 67#
Distribution: All states; S Am
Synonym: *E. rostratum*

Eryngium vesiculosum

Prickfoot

Size: 10–20 cm x 0.3–0.6 m — F P
Habitat: Swamp scrub, grassy wetlands, valley sclerophyll forest
Form: Tufted perennial herb
Foliage: Bright green oblanceolate leaves with sharply toothed edges, from 5–20 cm long; stem leaves shorter and lobed
Flowers: Small globular pale blue flower heads; October to February
Requirements: Moist soil, withstands wet conditions
Comments: It is an interesting plant for a bog garden or container, the base of which should be immersed in water.
Propagation: Root cuttings, seeds
Localities: Bundoora, Moorabbin, Carrum, 2, 4, 6, 7, 17#, 18, 28, 29, 35, 41, 42, 44, 51, 54, 67#, 71
Distribution: All states except NT; NZ

Eucalyptus — Myrtaceae

Twenty-eight *Eucalyptus* species occur within the Melbourne area. They are found in most habitats covering a wide variety of soil types. All the local species have white to cream flowers. Their bark, foliage, flower size and number, and bud and capsule shape provide identifying features. The paired leaf arrangement typical of eucalypt seedlings contrasts with the alternate arrangement of adult leaves. Seedling and juvenile leaves may differ from adult leaves in a number of other features, including, size, shape, colour, and presence or absence of surface wax or hairs. Propagation is by seed collected from mature capsules.

Bark type is also a useful aid to identifying most of the indigenous eucalypts. The most common type belongs to the 'Gums'. The bark on most of the trunk and on the branches is smooth and is shed annually leaving a cream or grey trunk. Some gums retain old, darker bark around the base, sometimes extending up the tree. 'Stringybarks' are usually tall and straight and are easily identified by the thick, widely furrowed dead bark which is retained on the trunk and branches, weathering to grey or grey-brown. The long fibres can be pulled off in strands. The adult leaves of most stringybarks are asymmetrical and their intermediate leaves are noted for their larger size and variety of shapes. The outer bark of the 'Boxes' is persistent on the trunk, short-fibred, thin and flaky or scaly. The wood is close-grained providing excellent fuel. Flowers are in clusters forming a panicle. The term 'Peppermint' alludes to the strong peppermint smell of the leaves of 2 of the Melbourne species when crushed. The bark is grey and persistent, the fibres closely interlaced. There is only one 'Ironbark' in Melbourne. Its bark is hard, thick and deeply furrowed.

The Aborigines used eucalypts extensively for many products. Food was obtained from the seed, nectar and manna of many species. Many medicinal concoctions were derived from the leaves and gum. Bark provided containers, canoes and fibre for string. Many implements were made from the wood.

Although most local eucalypts may obtain their maximum size under ideal conditions it is most unlikely that these dimensions would be reached in cultivation.

Eucalyptus albens

White Box

Size: 8–25 m x 10–15 m **F P**
Habitat: Box woodland
Form: Medium to tall upright tree with dense spreading canopy
Foliage: Juvenile—glaucous ovate to rounded leaves 50–150 mm x 50–115 mm
Adult—Grey to bluish-green broadly lanceolate leaves to 15 cm x 30 mm, densely veined
Flowers: Terminal clusters of 3–7 sessile, long (to 18 mm), tapered glaucous buds, often ridged. Very showy creamy flowers; February to June. Glaucous barrel-shaped fruits have sunken valves.
Requirements: Well drained drier soils
Comments: An attractive fast growing tree with whitish-grey bark and hard, durable timber. Useful as a shade and windbreak tree, providing excellent honey.
Localities: The only occurrence within the Melbourne area is in Melton South.
Distribution: Vic, Qld, NSW, SA

Eucalyptus albens

Eucalyptus aromaphloia = Eucalyptus ignorabilis

Eucalyptus baueriana

Blue Box, Round-leaf Box

Size: 12–30 m x 8–15 m **F**
Habitat: Riparian and box woodland
Form: Medium tree with dense crown
Foliage: Juvenile—thin, round pale to grey-green leaves 60–70 mm x 50–120 mm
Adult—thin, pale green ovate to broad-lanceolate leaves to 90 mm x 60 mm
Flowers: Clusters of 7 club-to diamond-shaped buds followed by profuse terminal bunches of white flowers October to January. Fruit are funnel-shaped.
Requirements: Well drained moist loams
Comments: An excellent tree for larger gardens, providing shade.
Localities: Mt Cottrell, 8
Distribution: Vic, NSW

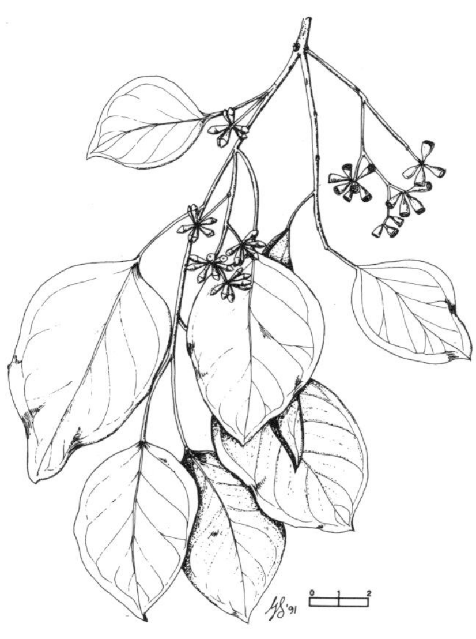

Eucalyptus baueriana

Eucalyptus baxteri

Brown Stringybark

Size: 3–40 m x 4–20 m **F P**
Habitat: Damp and valley sclerophyll forests of foothills
Form: Variable, medium-sized tree with a rounded crown locally, smaller in exposed areas
Foliage: Juvenile—opposite and ovate at first, paler green and hairy below, 30–70 mm x 20–50 mm, with wavy edges
Intermediate—larger to 130 mm x 80 mm
Adult—thick, glossy green broad-lanceolate leaves, 15 cm x 30 mm
Flowers: Clusters of 7–15 club-shaped and warty buds on a thick stalk. Profuse white flowers December to April. Large, round fruit with the rim near the top.
Requirements: Well drained soils
Comments: A good shelter and shade tree. Timber is used for buildings, poles and fuel. The size of this tree is determined by the quality of the soil on which it is grown.
Localities: Montrose, 34A, 42, 43, 47, 51, 54, 55, 56, 61
Distribution: Vic, NSW, SA *Illustrated p. 106*

Eucalyptus behriana

Bull Mallee

Comments: After further research for the second edition it is improbable that *E. behriana* occurred within the Melbourne area. Its closest distribution is in the Bacchus Marsh/Long Forest area.

Eucalyptus blakelyi

Blakely's Red Gum

Size: 15–24 m x 10–15 m **F P**
Habitat: Box-ironbark woodland
Form: Medium-sized tree with a short trunk and a large dense crown
Foliage: Juvenile—alternate, thick, ovate to nearly round grey-green leaves to 140 mm long x 100 mm
Adult—dull green, lanceolate, falcate leaves to 16 cm x 20 mm
Flowers: Clusters of 5–10 yellowish-green buds, caps elongated and conical. White flowers; August to January. Small ovoid fruit with a small rim and 3–4 strongly projecting valves.
Requirements: Heavy, moist soils
Comments: The grey bark sheds in large sheets or flakes to leave a smooth surface with light patches. Found in a very localised area within Melbourne. Its durable red timber is useful for fence posts and firewood. It is also a valuable honey tree. Growing from a lignotuber it responds well to coppicing or hard pruning. Relatively slow growing, *E. blakelyi* makes a good shade and windbreak tree suited to large suburban gardens.
Localities: Yarrambat, Diamond Ck, 36
Distribution: Vic, Qld, NSW

Eucalyptus blakelyi

SCALE: 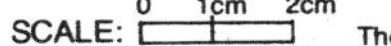

The scale representation on each plant equals 2cm.

Eucalyptus camaldulensis

Eucalyptus camaldulensis

River Red Gum

Size: 12–50 m x 15–35 m **F**
Habitat: Plains grassland, riparian scrub and woodland, red gum woodland
Form: Large open spreading tree
Foliage: Juvenile—bluish-green broad-lanceolate leaves to 26 cm x 80 mm
Adult—dull narrow-lanceolate leaves to 25 cm x 20 mm. Forms from the Melbourne area generally have smaller foliage than those from inland areas.
Flowers: Long-stalked buds in clusters of 7–11, with caps contracting abruptly to a point. Profuse white flowers; November to March. Fruit is small with 4 strongly projecting valves.
Requirements: Damp alluvial soils, deep subsoils. Tolerates very dry periods and inundation once established.
Comments: A widespread eucalypt which has almost disappeared from the grassy woodlands of eastern Port Phillip Bay. Excellent for planting in parklands and broadacres but too large for the small suburban garden. It is very valuable as a honey tree and for its durable timber. Its bark is greyish with brown or reddish patches peeling or flaking during late Summer/Autumn. Selected forms are being planted to combat salinity in inland soils. An important species to the Aborigines, many trees are renowned as corroboree or canoe trees. Food, containers and clubs were other by-products while the gum treated burns and diarrhoea.
Localities: Melton, Wonga Park, Caulfield, Dandenong, Brighton, 4, 6, 8, 14, 16, 18, 19, 21, 23–36, 44, 45, 60, 61, 63, 65–69A, 71, 72, 74
Distribution: All mainland states

Eucalyptus camphora

Eucalyptus camphora

Mountain Swamp Gum

Size: 8–20 m x 5–12 m **F P**
Habitat: Valley sclerophyll forest
Form: Slow growing medium tree with short crooked trunk and rounded crown
Foliage: Juvenile—thick, dull to glossy green ovate to nearly round leaves to 80 mm x 40 mm, often notched at the apex; larger in intermediate stage
Adult—thick, dark green elliptic to ovate leaves to 130 mm x 60 mm, densely veined.
Flowers: Clusters of 3–7 shiny diamond-shaped buds followed by white flowers; March to April. Funnel-shaped fruit are flat-topped with 3–4 small erectly projecting valves.
Requirements: Heavy wet soils, tolerating heavy frosts
Comments: Similar to *E. ovata* but has broader leaves and smaller fruit with exserted valves. Rough scaly bark persists at the base of the tree, peeling in long strips from most of the trunk and the branches. Useful as a shade tree in wet areas, and to control poor drainage. Locally rare.
Localities: Diamond Ck, Wonga Park
Distribution: Vic, Qld, NSW

Eucalyptus cephalocarpa

Silver Leafed Stringbark, Mealy Stringybark

Size: 8–20 m x 5–15 m **F P**
Habitat: Damp and valley sclerophyll forests, sclerophyll woodland, grassy low open forest, wattle tea-tree scrub
Form: Medium-sized straight or crooked tree with dense canopy
Foliage: Juvenile—sessile, round to ovate silver leaves to 110 mm x 60 mm
Adult—grey-green lanceolate leaves 20 cm x 25 mm
Flowers: Silvery clusters of 7–11 stalkless, diamond-shaped buds. Profuse white to cream flowers March to August. Fruit is often flat topped and silvery.
Requirements: Most soils, withstanding periods of inundation.
Comments: The new foliage is an attractive feature while its juvenile foliage is used for wool dyeing and decoration. A valuable honey tree.
Localities: Montrose, 34, 42–51, 54, 56–64, 67#, 70, 73–76
Distribution: Endemic to Vic
Synonym: *E. cinerea* ssp. *cephalocarpa* *Illustrated p. 106*

Eucalyptus cypellocarpa

Eucalyptus cypellocarpa

Mountain Grey Gum

Size: 10–65 m x 12–30 m **F P**
Habitat: Wet and damp sclerophyll forests of foothills
Form: Upright tree with dense canopy, but growth is stunted in drier soils
Foliage: Juvenile—broad, stalkless, 17 cm x 70 mm
Intermediate—very long to 35 cm
Adult—falcate or lanceolate to 20 cm x 25 mm
Flowers: Thick stalked elongated buds in clusters of 7. White flowers usually from December to July. Goblet-shaped fruit have enclosed valves.
Requirements: Prefers deep moist soil however it is adaptable to most conditions
Comments: This tree provides timber for the building industry, produces abundant honey and has potential for parkland and broadacre planting. The greyish bark sheds in strips in late Summer/Autumn to reveal yellow or whitish patches while that at the base may be rough and flaky. This species has been confused with *E. goniocalyx*.
Localities: Kalorama, 55, 56
Distribution: Vic, NSW

Eucalyptus dives

Broad-leafed or Blue Peppermint

Size: 8–25 m x 6–15 m **F P**
Habitat: Valley sclerophyll forest, sclerophyll woodland, usually on poor soils
Form: Moderately dense low branching, spreading tree with large canopy
Foliage: Juvenile—broad, thick-textured blue to grey-green stem-clasping leaves, to 15 cm x 70 mm
Adult—aromatic, firm dull green broad-lanceolate leaves to 15 cm x 30 mm
Flowers: Profuse clusters of 7–15 club-shaped buds followed by white flowers September to December. Pear-shaped fruit have flat rims.
Requirements: Adaptable to all but wet soils, tolerating dry and stony conditions
Comments: Trees provide shade and windbreaks. If coppiced, new growth is useful as cut foliage.
Localities: 33, 44, 45, 47, 56, 60, 73
Distribution: Vic, NSW

Eucalyptus dives

Eucalyptus globoidea

White Stringybark

Size: 10–30 m x 8–20 m **F P**
Habitat: Valley sclerophyll forest
Form: Upright tree with compact canopy
Foliage: Juvenile—ovate, hairy leaves, paler below, 30–60 mm x 20–40 mm, edges wavy
Adult—glossy and lanceolate, 60–100 mm x 25 mm, generally smaller than other stringybarks
Flowers: Pointed buds in groups of 7–15 on flattened stalks. White to cream flowers at various times followed by hemispherical fruit.
Requirements: Will adapt to a wide range of moist soils
Comments: A useful shade tree for parks, it has a high yield of pollen for honey production. The trunks provide straight timber for poles. Restricted within the Melbourne area.
Localities: Dandenong Ck valley, 47, 49–51
Distribution: Vic, NSW

Eucalyptus globoidea

Eucalyptus goniocalyx

Long-leaved Box, Bundy

Size: 8–20 m x 6–15 m **F P**
Habitat: Dry, valley and damp sclerophyll forests
Form: Fast growing tree with a crooked trunk and large rounded crown
Foliage: Juvenile—bluish to light green and sessile, round to broad leaves to 110 mm x 100 mm
Adult—long, tapering shiny leaves to 24 cm x 30 mm
Flowers: Broad flat stalk has up to 7 cylindrical buds. Cap conical. White to cream flowers; March to August. Fruit cup-shaped.
Requirements: Tolerates dry and poor soils
Comments: This species is not considered a true box as its bark is thick and subfibrous and it has flowers in axillary clusters rather than in terminal panicles.
Localities: 33–44, 46–49, 50A–56, 58–63
Distribution: Vic, NSW, SA

Illustrated p. 106

Eucalyptus ignorabilis

Scent Bark

Size: 12–20 m x 7–15 m **F**
Habitat: Damp sclerophyll forest
Form: Spreading tree with open to dense canopy on open sites, taller on better soils
Foliage: Juvenile—grey-green, stalked, at first lanceolate, quickly becoming stalked, narrow-elliptical or broad-lanceolate, to 50 mm x 8 mm
Adult—long, narrow green to blue green pendulous leaves, 140 mm x 25 mm
Flowers: Egg-shaped buds in 7s. White to cream flowers from January to April are followed by small top-shaped fruit.
Requirements: Moist loams, tolerating wet periods but not inundation
Comments: A large shade tree with pinkish brown wood. The young bark is aromatic when crushed. This species is confused and currently subject to revision. The Melbourne form is now known as *E.* aff. *aromaphloia* and may become a new species.
Localities: Diamond Ck, Wantirna, 44, 50A, 59
Distribution: Vic, NSW
Synonym: Recently segregated from *E. aromaphloia*

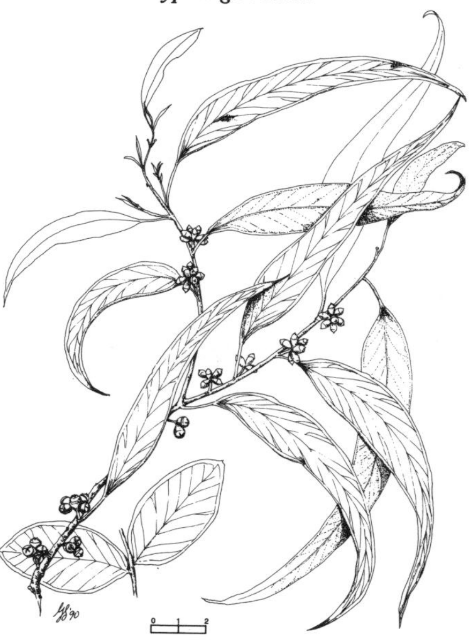

Eucalyptus ignorabilis

SCALE: 0 1cm 2cm — The scale representation on each plant equals 2cm.

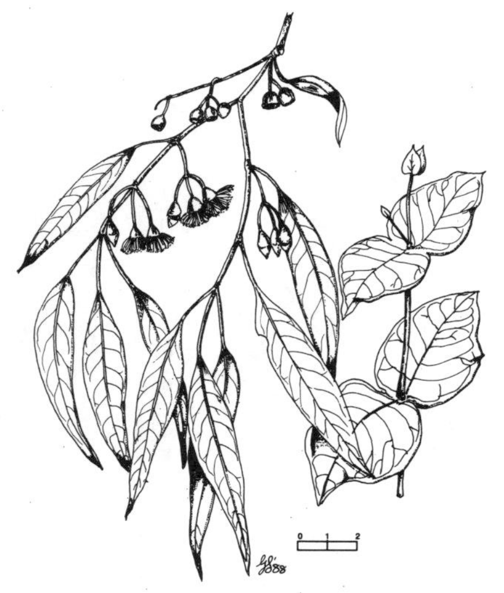

Eucalyptus leucoxylon ssp. *connata*

Eucalyptus leucoxylon ssp. connata

Yellow Gum, White Ironbark, S.A. Blue Gum

Size: 10–20 m x 6–20 m **F P**
Habitat: Box ironbark, red gum and box woodlands, chenopod rocky open scrub, dry sclerophyll forest
Form: Upright tree with spreading crown
Foliage: Juvenile—sessile heart-shaped green or blue-green leaves to 90 mm x 60 mm, becoming connate (or joined at the base)
Adult—stalked olive-green to green, narrow to lanceolate leaves to 14 cm x 25 mm
Flowers: Conical buds in 3s on long thin stalks followed by profuse cream to white flowers; May to September. Fruit are hemispherical, or sometimes slightly subcylindrical with sunken valves.
Requirements: Prefers heavy soil but is very adaptable, tolerating drought once established. Grows on sandstone in the basalt plains area.
Comments: Bark is rough at the base, cream or light-grey above, shedding to leave yellowish patches. It is an excellent tree for larger gardens, providing shade and shelter. *E. leucoxylon* is an excellent honey-producing tree and also a valuable source of timber and fuel. The Aborigines made clubs and shields from its wood. Early settlers used oil distilled from its leaves for a variety of purposes including remedy for coughs and colds, insecticide and disinfectant. The form commonly available through the nurseries, erroneously known as *E. leucoxylon* "Rosea", is not the local Melbourne form.
Localities: 1, 14, 16, 26, 29, 31, 32, 34A–36, 49
Distribution: Endemic to Vic
Synonym: Segregated from *E. leucoxylon* ssp. *leucoxylon*

Eucalyptus macrorhyncha

Eucalyptus macrorhyncha

Red Stringybark

Size: 10–35 m x 10–20 m **F P**
Habitat: Dry and valley sclerophyll forests
Form: Medium to tall upright tree with rounded canopy
Foliage: Juvenile—ovate, shortly stalked hairy leaves with wavy margins, 30–50 mm x 20–30 mm
Adult—glossy, lanceolate leaves 60–150 mm x 30–50 mm
Flowers: Diamond-shaped buds with long caps in clusters of 7–11, on a flattened stalk. Profuse white to cream flowers January to April. Globular fruit has valves projecting.
Requirements: Prefers well drained clay loam soil. It does not tolerate wet soils.
Comments: The red-brown bark is deeply fissured. Its flowers exude a sweet honey aroma, and produce excellent honey. The roots are sensitive to compaction of soil.
Localities: 29, 33–53, 55, 56, 58, 60, 62–66
Distribution: Vic, NSW, SA

Eucalyptus melliodora

Yellow Box

Size: 10–30 m x 8–25 m **F P**
Habitat: Dry and valley sclerophyll forests, red gum and box woodlands
Form: Variable open to dense tree
Foliage: Juvenile—grey-green oval leaves to 110 mm x 50 mm
Adult—narrow leaves ranging from light green to greyish or blue, 60–140 mm x 12–25 mm
Flowers: Club-shaped buds in clusters of 3–7, followed by profuse, perfumed white to cream flowers; September to March. Fruit are hemispherical to sub-globular.
Requirements: Well drained loams and alluvial soils
Comments: This attractive tree is highly regarded for timber and honey. The bark is rough and brownish with yellow tinges at the base, smooth and cream on upper branches. Whilst too large for suburban gardens, it is an excellent tree for broadscape planting.
Localities: Mt. Cottrell, Brighton, Mooroolbark, 9, 16, 23, 25, 26, 29–32, 34–39, 41, 42, 44–49, 50A, 51, 53, 56, 58, 60–64, 67#, 69A
Distribution: Vic, Qld, NSW *Illustrated p. 106*

Eucalyptus microcarpa

Eucalyptus microcarpa

Grey or Inland Grey Box, Narrow Leaf Box

Size: 10–25 m x 10–15 m **F**
Habitat: Box woodland, chenopod rocky open scrub
Form: Small to medium spreading tree, with ascending branches
Foliage: Juvenile—ovate to broad dull green leaves 30–120 mm x 20–50 mm
Adult—dull green narrow leaves to 15 cm x 25 mm
Flowers: 4–8 diamond-shaped buds with hooked ends on thin stalks. White flowers February to August. Fruit varies from cup to barrel-shaped.
Requirements: Heavy soils, tolerating wet winters and dry summers
Comments: This shade or windbreak tree is valued for its timber and honey. The scaly grey bark becomes smooth on small branches.
Localities: Mt Cottrell-Melton, Toolern Vale, 9, 14, 16, 24–26, 29
Distribution: Vic, Qld, NSW, SA

Eucalyptus nortonii
Large-leaved Box

Size: 10–15 m x 5–8 m **F P**
Habitat: Red gum woodland
Form: Rounded, sparsely crowned small to medium tree, with a crooked trunk
Foliage: Juvenile—stalkless, rounded bluish-grey leaves 40–90 mm x 30–80 mm, with toothed edges
Adult—stalked, grey to light green lanceolate leaves to 25 cm x 35 mm
Flowers: Broad, flat, mealy stalk has up to 7 mealy cylindrical buds. White flowers in axillary clusters; August to October. Smooth or ribbed barrel-shaped fruit is mealy.
Requirements: Well drained soil
Comments: Very similar to *E. goniocalyx* but has larger, glaucous buds and fruit. An ornamental tree for home gardens and street planting. It has a disjunct distribution in Victoria with one stand occurring in Gresswell Forest.
Localities: 35
Distribution: Vic, NSW

Eucalyptus obliqua

Eucalyptus obliqua
Messmate

Size: 4–70 m x 6–35 m **F P**
Habitat: Widespread in wet, damp, valley and dry sclerophyll forests, sclerophyll woodland, grassy low open forest
Form: Tall upright tree with a dense canopy
Foliage: Juvenile—glossy, pendent, broadly ovate leaves, 60–80 mm x 30–40 mm
Intermediate—20 cm x 14 cm
Adult—shiny oblique leaves, 90–150 mm x 30 mm
Flowers: Club-shaped buds without scars, in clusters of 7–15 followed by profuse white to cream flowers December to March. Wine-glass shaped fruit have sunken valves.
Requirements: Moist well drained soils, tolerating short dry periods
Comments: Important for its honey and hardwood. It is an excellent shelter and shade tree for larger areas. The bark provided string for bags and nets, and tinder for fire-making. A tall tree locally, it becomes a stunted shrub in exposed coastal areas outside the Melbourne region.
Localities: 34, 37, 42–44, 46–49, 50–63, 74, 76
Distribution: Vic, Qld, NSW, Tas, SA

Eucalyptus ovata

Eucalyptus ovata
Swamp Gum

Size: 8–30 m x 8–20 m **F P**
Habitat: Widespread in damp and valley sclerophyll forests, riparian and red gum woodland, grassy low open forests, swamp and riparian scrub
Form: Fast growing upright tree with open to moderately dense canopy
Foliage: Juvenile—dull green elliptic leaves 30–100 mm x 30–70 mm, becoming intermediate after only a few pairs
Intermediate—larger, 110–150 mm x 50–80 mm
Adult—shiny broad-lanceolate to ovate leaves to 15 cm x 30–50 mm with wavy edges and uneven bases
Local coastal forms seem to have smaller leaves than forms further inland.
Flowers: Usually 7 diamond-shaped buds in a cluster followed by white to cream flowers. Flowering time can vary, usually March to June. Fruit is funnel-shaped and flat topped.
Requirements: Moist soils, tolerating inundation during Winter and Summer dryness
Comments: Rough bark persists for some way up the trunk. Long strips are shed in Summer and Autumn from the upper trunk and branches to reveal greyish new bark. It is a useful shade tree for swampy areas and creek banks. The leaves are eaten by koalas.
Localities: 26, 29, 32, 33, 34A, 35, 37, 38, 40–45, 47, 49–51, 53–56, 58–67, 70–76
Distribution: Vic, NSW, Tas, SA

Eucalyptus ovata x camaldulensis = Eucalyptus studleyensis

Comments: A naturally occurring hybrid found in Studley Park/Yarra Bend and along the Yarra Valley. It has rough bark and grows to 12 m high.

Eucalyptus pauciflora ssp. *pauciflora*

Eucalyptus pauciflora ssp. pauciflora
Snow Gum, White Sallee

Size: 8–12 m x 6–10 m **F P**
Habitat: Dry sclerophyll forest, red gum woodland
Form: Rounded low-branching tree locally, low stunted tree in alpine areas
Foliage: Juvenile—weeping blue-green ovate leaves to 18 cm x 75 mm
Adult—thick, shiny bright green leaves broadly lanceolate to 19 cm x 20–70 mm
Flowers: Clusters of 7–15 club-shaped buds without distinct scars, on thick stalks. White to cream flowers October to January. Fruit are cup-shaped.
Requirements: Well drained conditions
Comments: The beautiful white to cream trunk makes this tree well worth growing. It provides honey, fuel and assists with soil erosion control. Although trees may grow larger than 12 m, they are unlikely to do so under Melbourne conditions. It is tolerant of extreme exposure to cold.
Localities: Lilydale, Mooroolbark, 67#, 69A–71, 73–75
Distribution: Vic, NSW, Tas

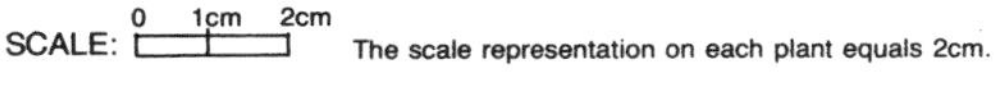

The scale representation on each plant equals 2cm.

Eucalyptus polyanthemos ssp. *vestita*

Eucalyptus polyanthemos ssp. vestita

Red Box

Size: 7–25 m x 5–15 m **F P**
Habitat: Dry and valley sclerophyll forests
Form: Slow growing, small to medium tree sometimes with a crooked trunk, with compact to spreading crown
Foliage: Juvenile—rounded grey-green leaves, 65 mm x 30–80 mm
Adult—ovate to broad-lanceolate bluish-green leaves, 50–90 mm x 15–30 mm
Flowers: Terminal bluish club-shaped buds in groups of 3–7. White or cream flowers; September to January. Fruit barrel-shaped.
Requirements: Requires good drainage and will tolerate poor stony soils
Comments: An ornamental tree with attractive blue-grey foliage which is used for floral decoration. The red wood is hard and durable and makes excellent fuel. A profusely flowering tree which produces copious quantities of excellent honey.
Localities: Sth Morang, Research, 29, 33–36, 40–42, 44, 47–49, 50A, 51
Distribution: Vic, NSW

Eucalyptus pryoriana

Eucalyptus pryoriana

Gippsland Manna Gum

Size: 8–16 m x 5–12 m **F**
Habitat: Tea-tree heath, wattle tea-tree scrub
Form: Well-branched, spreading medium tree with a dense crown
Foliage: Juvenile—dark green, paler below, stalkless lanceolate leaves 80–150 mm x 25 mm
Adult—narrower dark green stalked leaves to 180 mm x 20 mm
Flowers: Stalkless pointed buds in 3s. White flowers March to May. Cup-shaped fruit have projecting valves.
Requirements: Well drained sandy soil
Comments: Thick fibrous bark persists on the trunk and larger branches, shedding on smaller branches. An ideal tree for larger coastal gardens, it is also a good windbreak and shelter tree providing honey and fuel. This tree is an important koala fodder tree.
Localities: 67–71, 74–76
Distribution: Endemic to Vic
Synonym: *E. viminalis* var. *racemosa*

Eucalyptus radiata

Narrow-leaved Peppermint

Size: 10–30 m x 6–20 m **F P**
Habitat: Widespread in damp and valley sclerophyll forests, sclerophyll woodland, grassy low open forests
Form: Attractive low branching tree with dense canopy
Foliage: Juvenile—lanceolate or occasionally broad-lanceolate, thin-textured and stem-clasping, becoming elongated, to 15 cm x 35 mm
Adult—aromatic, thin-textured, narrow, to 15 cm x 20 mm
Flowers: Numerous small club-shaped buds without distinct scars in clusters. Profuse white flowers; October to January. Small cup-shaped fruit.
Requirements: Well drained soils
Comments: This graceful upright tree provides shade and shelter. Its leaves are distilled for oil. Some forms have an attractive weeping habit.
Localities: 26, 33–34A, 40–51, 53–56, 58–63, 67#, 71, 73–76
Distribution: Vic, NSW *Illustrated p. 106*

Eucalyptus regnans

Eucalyptus regnans

Mountain Ash

Size: 25–95 m x 15–30 m **F**
Habitat: Cool temperate rainforest, wet sclerophyll forest
Form: Fast growing upright tree with a small open canopy
Foliage: Juvenile—broad with wavy edges, 17 cm x 80 mm
Adult—lanceolate to 140 mm x 10–70 mm
Flowers: Club-shaped buds in paired clusters of 7–15. Profuse white to cream flowers; December to May. Fruit are shaped like a top.
Requirements: Deep rich loams which are moist and well drained
Comments: A rough finely fibrous bark is persistent to 15 m. It is smooth and greyish above with long ribbons of shedding bark often hanging from the tree. The tallest flowering plant in the world, *E. regnans* produces excellent hardwood timber and is also used in paper manufacturing. Unlike most eucalypts, individuals are killed by intense fire and regeneration is usually exclusively from seed.
Propagation: Seed, may germinate better if moistened and placed in the refrigerator for 3–4 weeks.
Localities: 55, 57
Distribution: Vic, Tas

Eucalyptus rubida ssp. rubida

Candlebark Gum

Size: 10–25 m x 10–20 m **F P**
Habitat: Dry and valley sclerophyll forests
Form: Upright tree with dense spreading to rounded crown
Foliage: Juvenile—sessile, silvery rounded leaves 45 mm x 30–55 mm
Adult—long narrow dark green leaves 7.5–24 cm x 10–25 mm
Flowers: Sessile buds with domed caps, in 3s. White flowers November to February. Domed fruit have projecting valves.
Requirements: Well drained drier soils
Comments: A decorative shade tree with a smooth white trunk which develops red or pink patches before the bark is shed in strips. It withstands very cold conditions and is a good honey producer. An important koala food tree.
Localities: Mooroolbark, Montrose, 33–34A, 36, 38–42, 44, 51, 53, 56, 58, 62, 63
Distribution: Vic, Qld, NSW, Tas, SA

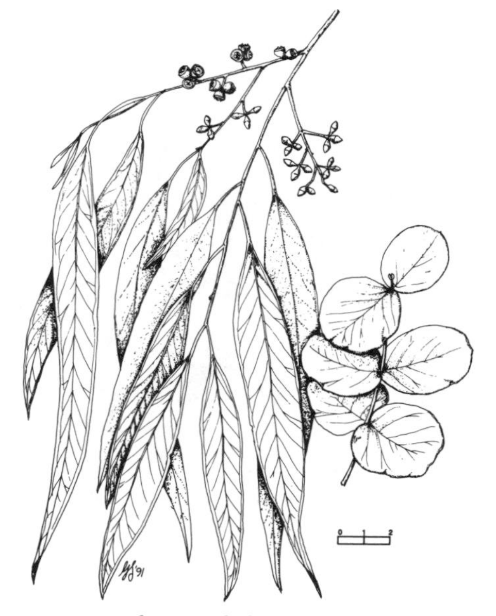

Eucalyptus rubida ssp. *rubida*

Eucalyptus sideroxylon ssp. tricarpa = Eucalyptus tricarpa

Eucalyptus tricarpa

Red Ironbark, Mugga

Size: 10–30 m x 10–20 m **F P**
Habitat: Box ironbark woodland, dry sclerophyll forest
Form: Upright to spreading tree with an open crown
Foliage: Juvenile—bluish, oblong leaves, 40–150 mm x 20 mm
Adult—narrow grey-green leaves to 140 mm x 18 mm
Flowers: Large diamond-shaped buds in 3s on long stalks. Profuse cream or pink flowers; May to December. Large barrel-shaped fruit.
Requirements: Well drained soils, tolerating extended dry periods
Comments: The rough, black bark and bluish foliage make this ornamental tree very popular. The flowers of the local form are usually cream. It is valued for its honey and durable timber. Essential oils are extracted from the foliage. The wood was used to make shields.
Localities: 35, 36, 42
Distribution: Vic, Qld, NSW
Synonym: *E. sideroxylon* ssp. *tricarpa*

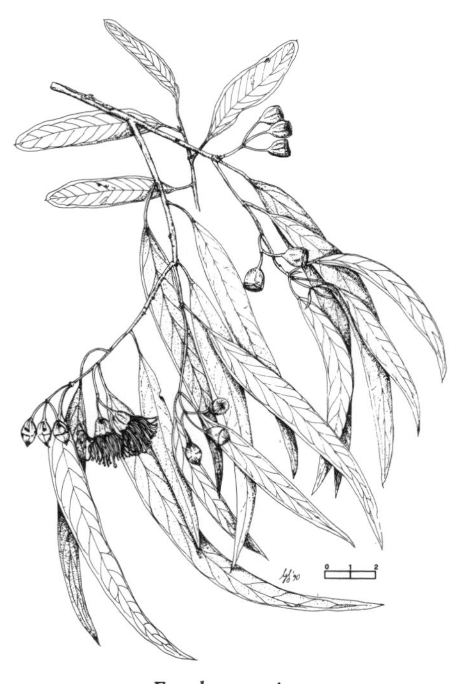

Eucalyptus tricarpa

Eucalyptus viminalis

Ribbon or Manna Gum

Size: 10–50 m x 8–15 m **F**
Habitat: Widespread along watercourses of wet and valley sclerophyll forests, sclerophyll and riparian woodland, grassy low open forest
Form: Fast growing tall upright tree with open crown
Foliage: Juvenile—dark green lanceolate to broad-lanceolate leaves 35–65 mm x 10–30 mm
Adult—narrow, often sickle-shaped to 20 cm long
Flowers: Egg-shaped buds in clusters of 3 on a flattened stalk. White flowers January to May. Round fruit with 3 or 4 projecting valves.
Requirements: Very adaptable, with tallest specimens found in moist deep loam soils in mountain areas
Comments: Bark is shed in ribbons during Summer leaving the upper trunk and branches white. Rough bark often persists at the base. This ornamental tree is best suited to large gardens and parklands. It is used for timber, pulp, honey production and is an important koala food tree. An important source of manna to the Aborigines, it was also used to obtain medicines and make implements.
Localities: Malvern#, 16, 23, 25, 26, 29, 32–36, 38, 42, 44, 45#, 47–49, 50A, 53, 55–58, 60–67, 73–76
Distribution: Vic, Qld, NSW, Tas, SA *Illustrated p. 106*

Eucalyptus yarraensis

Yarra Gum

Size: 10–20 m x 5–10 m **F P**
Habitat: River flats and flood plains of valley sclerophyll forest
Form: Small to medium tree with a short trunk and dense spreading crown
Foliage: Juvenile—dull green oval leaves 50–80 mm x 30–50 mm, not always opposite
Adult—elliptic or broad-lanceolate leaves 60–100 mm x 30–50 mm, with wavy edges
Flowers: Small diamond-shaped buds in clusters of 7. White flowers in January are followed by small hemispherical fruit.
Requirements: Tolerates heavy soil and limited inundation
Comments: Rough black fibrous bark persists on the trunk and sometimes on large branches. It makes a good shade and windbreak tree.
Localities: Yarra Valley between Lilydale and Healesville, Yarrambat; 47, 62, 63
Distribution: Endemic to Vic

Eucalyptus yarraensis

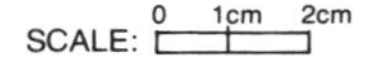

The scale representation on each plant equals 2cm.

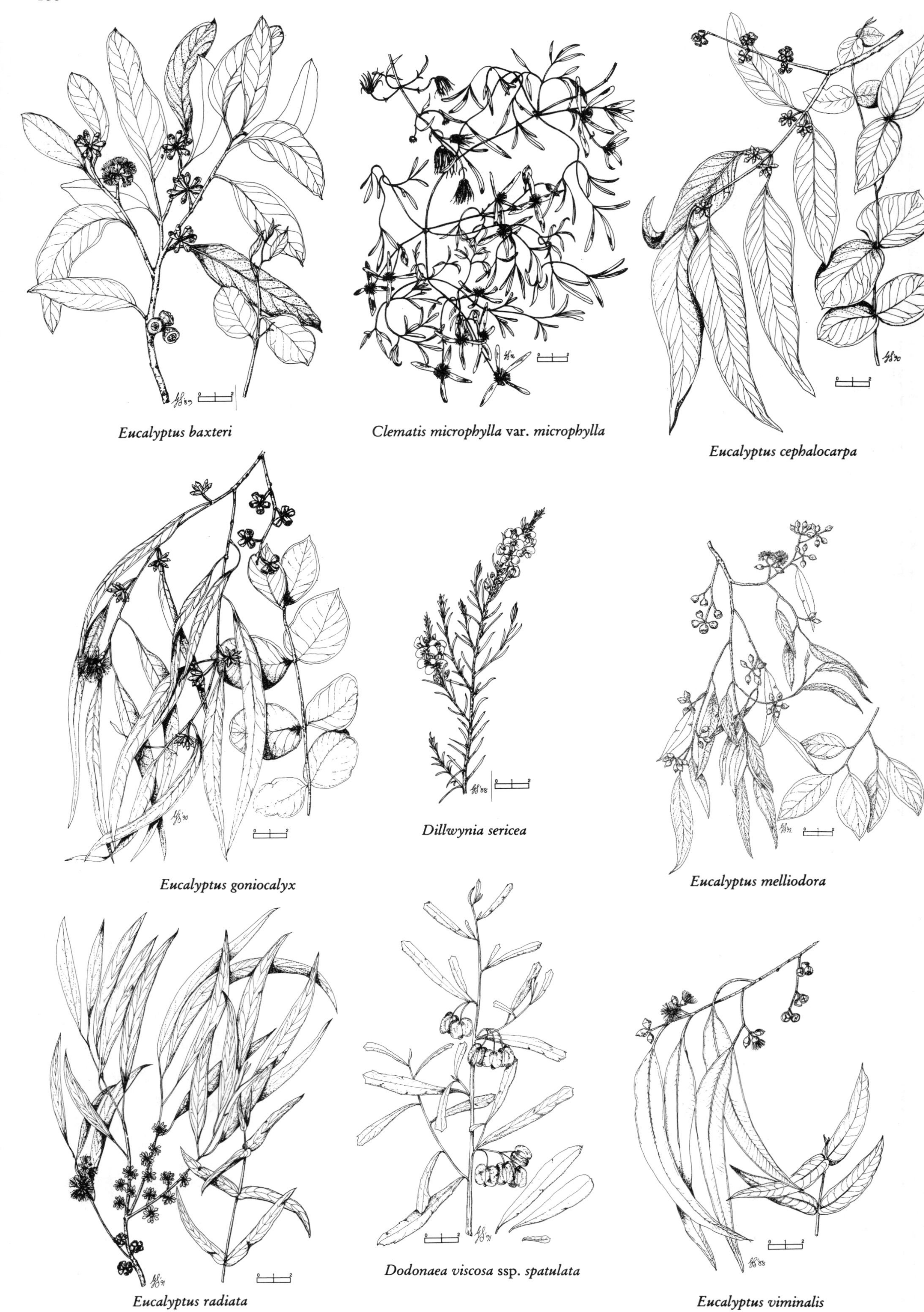

Eucalyptus baxteri

Clematis microphylla var. *microphylla*

Eucalyptus cephalocarpa

Eucalyptus goniocalyx

Dillwynia sericea

Eucalyptus melliodora

Eucalyptus radiata

Dodonaea viscosa ssp. *spatulata*

Eucalyptus viminalis

Euchiton

Asteraceae

Euchiton gymnocephalus

Creeping Cudweed

Size: to 30 cm high
Habitat: Riparian scrub, valley sclerophyll forest, wattle tea-tree scrub
Form: Stoloniferous perennial herb
Comments: Differs from *E. involucratus* in that leaves are shorter, usually less than 40 mm long, floral leaves are also shorter. Basal rosette is persistent when flowering.
Localities: 26, 28, 29, 35, 39, 41, 42, 47, 49, 51, 52, 56, 58, 60, 62, 63, 67, 69A, 70, 74–76
Distribution: ?All states
Synonym: *Gnaphalium gymnocephalum, G. japonicum, G. collinum*. Separated from *Euchiton involucratus.*

Euchiton gymnocephalus

Euchiton involucratus

Common or Star Cudweed

Size: 10–50 cm high **F P**
Habitat: Widespread in dry and valley sclerophyll forests, box and coastal banksia woodland, riparian scrub
Form: Erect, unbranched woolly annual or perennial herb, tufted to shortly rhizomatous
Foliage: Leaves usually glabrous above, cottony-white underneath, to 20 cm long but usually smaller; basal rosette withering before flowering; narrowly elliptic, oblanceolate or linear stem leaves have a distinct mid-vein and may be almost stem-clasping
Flowers: Globular terminal clusters of brownish flowerheads to 2 mm wide, lacking ray florets, most of the year, surrounded by green leaf-like bracts much larger than the flowerheads. Flowerhead has more than one bisexual floret.
Requirements: Moist, well drained soils
Propagation: Seed, cuttings, division
Localities: Eltham, 6, 16–18, 28, 34A, 36, 40–42, 44, 47, 50–56, 58, 60, 62–65, 67, 69A, 74, 76
Distribution: All states
Synonym: *Gnaphalium involucratum*

Euchiton sphaericus

Common Cudweed

Size: 0.3–0.6 m high
Habitat: Box woodland, plains grassland, valley sclerophyll forest
Form: Tufted annual herb, lacking a rosette
Foliage: Leaves similar to *E. involucratus*, to 80 mm long.
Flowers: Flowerheads less than 2 mm wide in dense terminal clusters to 25 mm across. Single bisexual floret per flowerhead. July to December
Localities: 9, 14, 25, 26, 41, 42, 56, 62
Distribution: All states; NZ
Synonym: *Gnaphalium sphaericum*. Separated from *Euchiton involucratus.*

Euchiton sphaericus *Euchiton involucratus*

Euphorbia

Euphorbiaceae

Euphorbia drummondii

Flat Spurge, Caustic Weed

Size: Prostrate x 20–30 cm **F**
Habitat: Box woodland, plains grassland, saltmarshes
Form: Annual or short-lived perennial matting plant
Foliage: Pairs of ovate to oblong blue-green leaves with reddish margins to 8 mm long
Flowers: Minute green flowers with reddish glands, singly or in small clusters; July to September, March to May
Requirements: Dry soils
Comments: Watering may encourage a longer life span. The stems contain a milky sap which was used by the Aborigines to treat snake bite, dysentery, genital diseases and wounds.
Propagation: Seed
Localities: 4, 9, 12, 14–16, 25, 26, 34A
Distribution: All mainland states
Synonym: *Chamaesyce drummondii*

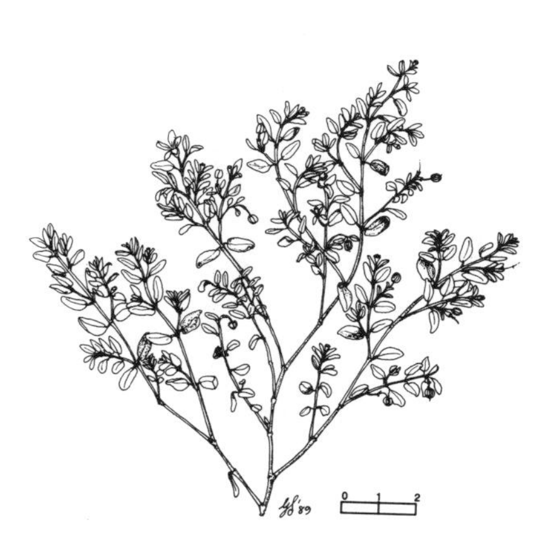

Euphorbia drummondii

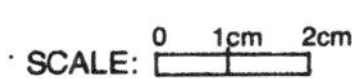

The scale representation on each plant equals 2cm.

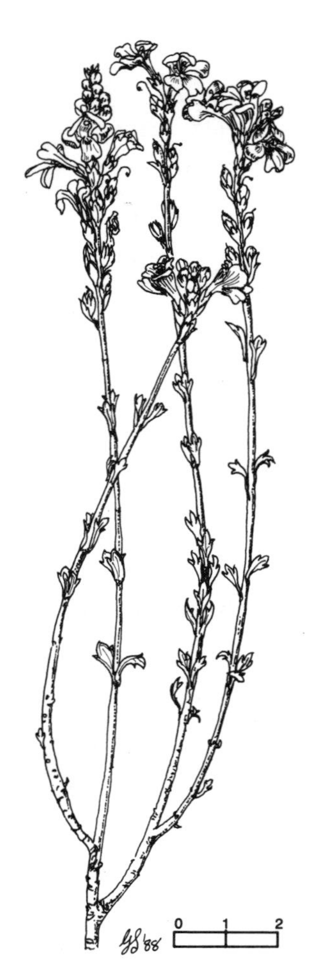

Euphrasia collina ssp. *collina*

Euphrasia — Scrophulariaceae

Euphrasia collina ssp. collina — Purple Eyebright

Size: 0.2–0.8 m x 0.2–0.5 m — F P
Habitat: Was widespread in tea-tree heath, sclerophyll woodland
Form: Small, upright perennial herb
Foliage: Pointed, oval to oblong toothed leaves to 15 mm long x 5 mm
Flowers: Upper branches densely covered with white to pink and mauve hooded flowers; August to February. Flowering growth dies back each year.
Requirements: Well drained moist soils.
Comments: This very attractive small herb has disappeared from most Melbourne localities. It is semi-parasitic and has the ability to photosynthesise as well as obtain nutrients by attaching to the roots of host plants. It has proven difficult to propagate and grow. There are many subspecies and affiliated species.
Propagation: Seeds. Difficult
Localities: Dandenong, 49, 58, 59, 67, 74
Distribution: Vic, NSW, Tas, SA

Euphrasia collina ssp. muelleri

Size: 0.4 m high
Habitat: Heathlands, once widespread
Comments: This subspecies is now very rare in Victoria. It has lilac to purple flowers; July to November.
Localities: Frankston#, Mentone#, Sandringham#
Distribution: Vic, NSW, SA

Euphrasia collina ssp. paludosa

Size: 0.5 m high
Habitat: Swamp scrub, valley sclerophyll forest
Comments: Flowers are white or white with blue through to pink markings in the throat. Masses of flowers are produced from September to February.
Localities: Outer Eastern suburbs and Dandenong Ranges, to Dandenong
Distribution: Vic, Qld, NSW, SA

Euphrasia collina ssp. trichocalycina

Size: 0.6 m x 0.3–0.5 m
Habitat: Dry sclerophyll forest
Comments: Prefers an open situation. Leaves narrow-ovate to oblong. Racemes of 20–50 flowers, white or white with lavendar markings; August to November. Now extinct within Melbourne and rare in Victoria.
Localities: Collected in Ringwood 1924
Distribution: Vic, SA

Euphrasia scabra — Yellow Eyebright

Size: 0.1–0.5 m x 0.1–0.5 m — F P
Habitat: Moist grassy sites on primary dune scrub, saltmarshes
Form: Semi-parasitic, erect hairy annual herb
Foliage: Pairs of ovate to elliptic, toothed or lobed leaves to 15 mm long, with 1–5 pairs of teeth
Flowers: Dense terminal spikes of yellow flowers, (often mauve in alpine areas); October to April
Requirements: Moist well drained soils
Comments: Once widespread in southern Australia, it is now endangered throughout its range. It is extinct in Melbourne and survives in a few ungrazed sites in the Victorian alps. Would make an attractive container plant if problems of cultivation could be overcome.
Propagation: Seeds. Difficult.
Localities: Collected in Port Melbourne in 1850.
Distribution: Vic, NSW, Tas, SA, WA

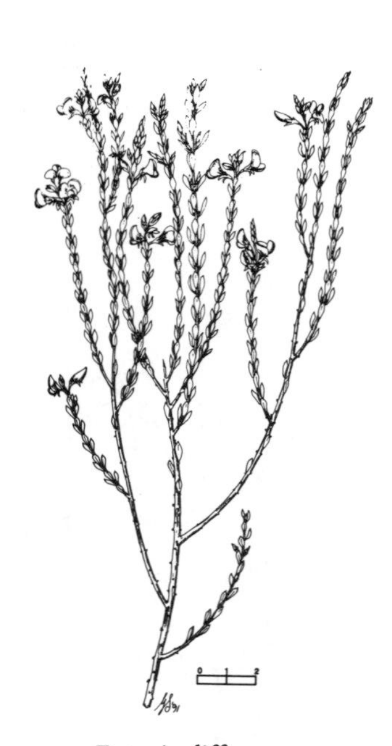

Eutaxia diffusa

Eutaxia — Fabaceae

Eutaxia diffusa

Size: 0.5–1.2 m x 0.8–1.2 m — F
Habitat: Coastal cliffs, box woodland
Comments: Differs from *E. microphylla* in that it is upright in form with soft branches and lanceolate leaves. Flowers are paler yellow often without any red. This species also occurs around Long Forest and Exford just outside the study area.
Localities: Melton area, 16, 22, 74
Distribution: Vic, NSW, SA
Synonym: *E. microphylla* var. *diffusa*

Eutaxia microphylla var. microphylla

Small-leaved Eutaxia

Size: Prostrate or procumbent x 0.5–1.5 m **F P N**
Habitat: Plains grassland, red gum woodland
Form: Variable low growing shrub
Foliage: Crowded, narrow, greyish-green leaves to 7 mm long. Branchlets on older growth become spiny.
Flowers: Profuse yellow and red pea flowers; August to October
Requirements: Adapts to most soils and, once established, tolerates waterlogging and extended dry periods.
Comments: This attractive ground cover makes an excellent container plant. It can be used on pool edges or rockeries, and may be used to control soil erosion in small areas. Responds well to pruning.
Propagation: Scarified seed, cuttings
Localities: 4, 5, 7, 12, 16, 26, 29, 35
Distribution: All states except NT

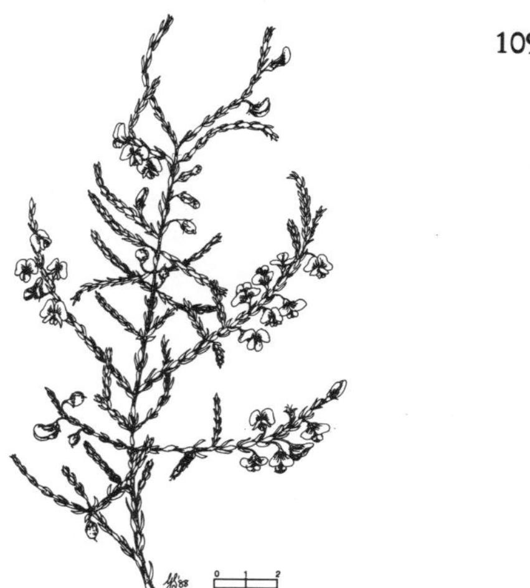

Eutaxia microphylla var. *microphylla*

Exocarpos

Santalaceae

Exocarpos cupressiformis

Wild Cherry, Cherry Ballart

Size: 3–8 m x 3–5 m **F P**
Habitat: Widespread in grassy low open forest, dry, damp and valley sclerophyll forests, red gum and box woodland, tea-tree heath
Form: Dense, rounded shrub to small tree
Foliage: Leaves reduced to tiny scales on pendulous yellow-green to dark green branchlets
Flowers: Insignificant spikes of cream flowers are followed by globular green nuts on fleshy orange to red, edible stalks.
Requirements: Well drained soils, tolerating poor and dry conditions
Comments: Whilst a very attractive tree it needs a symbiotic relationship with another plant to grow. Plants respond well to pruning. They are brittle in the wind but coppice readily. The timber is excellent for turning and furniture. It was used by the local Yarra tribe to make spear throwers.
Propagation: Difficult. Minimal success with stem cuttings but root cuttings may be more successful. Suckering can be attained by damaging roots. Seed was successfully germinated after fruit was fed to hens and then sown with seeds of *Themeda triandra*. (IFFA Vol 4, No. 2 1991)
Localities: Melton Sth, 14, 26, 29, 30–33, 34A–69A, 71–76
Distribution: Vic, Qld, NSW, Tas, SA

Exocarpos strictus

Pale Fruit Ballart or Dwarf Cherry

Size: 1–2.5 m x 1–3 m **F P**
Habitat: Damp, valley and dry sclerophyll forest, red gum woodland, grassy low open forest
Form: Upright to spreading broom-like shrub
Foliage: Light to dark green flattened branchlets, becoming pendulous. Leaves are tiny scales.
Flowers: Minute clusters of flowers, August to November are followed by green to purplish-black fruit on a succulent white to mauve stalk.
Requirements: Well drained soils
Comments: Forms dense thickets in its natural habitat.
Propagation: As *E. cupressiformis*
Localities: 26, 32, 33, 42, 43, 54, 55, 58, 60, 67#, 74, 76
Distribution: Vic, NSW, Tas, SA

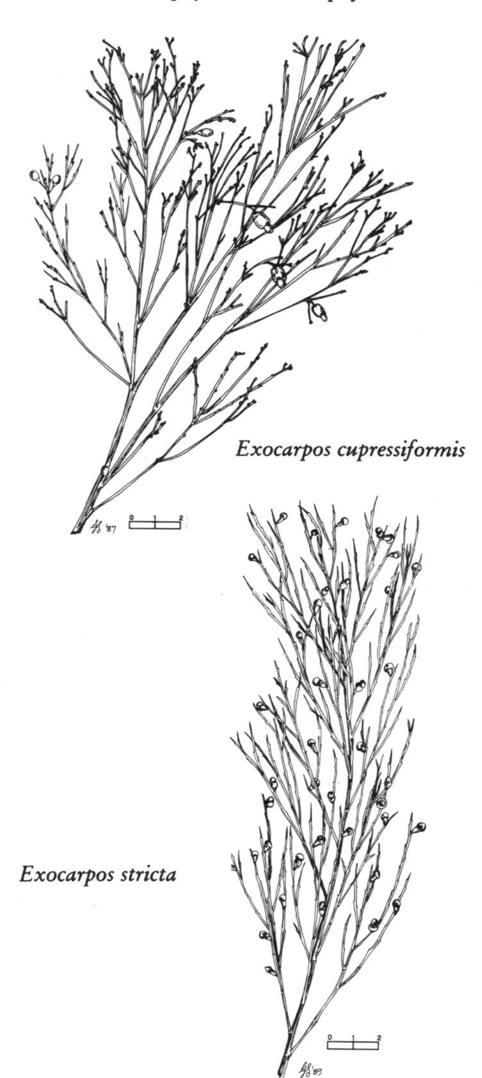

Exocarpos cupressiformis

Exocarpos stricta

Frankenia

Frankeniaceae

Frankenia pauciflora var. pauciflora

Southern or Common Sea Heath

Size: Prostrate-30 cm x 0.3–1 m **F P**
Habitat: Coastal saltmarshes, primary dune scrub
Form: Spreading mat-like shrub
Foliage: Narrow to oblong green to grey-green leaves to 7 mm long, hairy underneath
Flowers: Masses of small pink flowers in terminal clusters, occurring most of the year, peaking August to February
Requirements: Well drained soils, tolerating extended dry periods once established
Comments: An attractive plant for rockeries and containers, responding well to pruning to maintain denseness. It is useful for binding soil especially in saline areas. The Victorian form has been referred to as var. *gunnii*.
Propagation: Seed, cuttings, division of suckers
Localities: 2–4, 67, 74
Distribution: All states except Qld
Synonym: *F. pauciflora* var *gunnii*

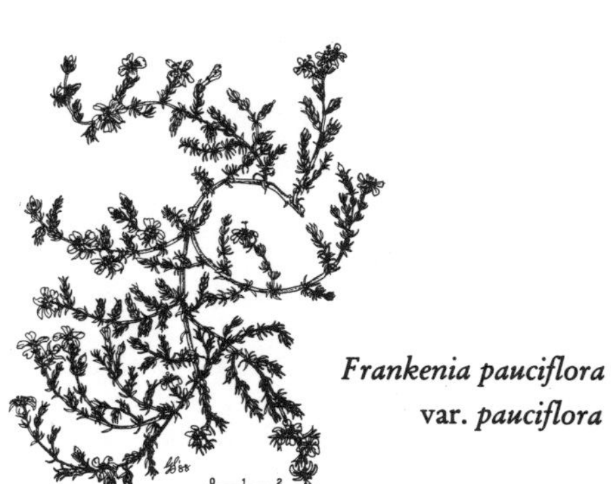

Frankenia pauciflora var. *pauciflora*

The scale representation on each plant equals 2cm.

Galium

Rubiaceae

Spreading annual, biennial or perennial herbs found in a wide range of habitats, although generally in sheltered positions. Stems are usually quadrangular and leaves often have bristle-like hairs. Flowers are in axillary or terminal branched clusters and have a very short floral tube. Useful as ground covers in shady moist areas or for cascading over containers. Propagation is by seed, cuttings or division of creeping rhizomes. *Galium* spp. are very similar to *Asperula* spp., the latter distinguished by the dioecious nature of the plants, the longer floral tube and the fleshy fruit.

Galium australe

Galium binifolium

Galium ciliare

Galium australe

Bedstraw, Tangled Bedstraw

P

Habitat: Grassy low open forest, riparian scrub, valley sclerophyll forest, occasionally epiphytic on tree ferns
Form: Often hairy perennial with tangled, weak stems
Foliage: Whorls of 4 dark green to brown, elliptical leaves to 12 mm long, often unequal in length
Flowers: Axillary clusters of 1–7 white flowers; December to February. Fruit covered in brown hooked hairs.
Localities: Baxter, 29#, 42, 49
Distribution: Vic, NSW, Tas, SA, WA

Galium binifolium

Reflexed Bedstraw

P

Habitat: Damp sclerophyll forest
Form: Straggling annual or biennial herb
Foliage: Narrow elliptical leaves to 12 mm long, usually unequal in length (2 long and 2 short), especially on the lower parts of stems, often bent downwards
Flowers: Cream to yellowish flowers sometimes have reddish or purple tinges; September to November. 1 or 2 axillary clusters of up to 8 flowers in leaf axils.
Localities: 56
Distribution: Vic, NSW, SA

Galium ciliare

Bedstraw

Size: 10–40 cm x 0.3–1 m **P**
Habitat: Woodland, also usually on grasslands of basaltic plains
Form: Erect usually unbranched stems are glabrous or have spreading hairs
Foliage: Glossy, yellowish, ovate to round leaves to 10 mm long with recurved margins, in whorls of 4–5
Flowers: Yellow to cream axillary or terminal clusters on long stalks to 15 mm long; September to December
Requirements: Well drained soil
Comments: Similar to *G. propinquum* which has non-glossy leaf blades tapering to the stalk, and short or absent flower stalks.
Localities: Known from an early collection from the Dandenong area.
Distribution: Vic, Qld, NSW, Tas

Galium compactum

Bedstraw

Size: Prostrate–30 cm x 0.2–0.6 m **F**
Habitat: Dry sclerophyll forest
Form: Compact perennial with short hairy stems
Foliage: Tiny, light green pointed ovate leaves to 6 mm, in whorls of 4–5. Scattered bristles on leaves, mainly on recurved margins.
Flowers: 1 or 2 axillary yellowish-green flowers tinged with purple on stalks shorter than the leaves; September to December
Requirements: Very well drained soils, tolerating limited periods of dryness and coastal exposure
Comments: A useful compact plant for rockeries or a container. An endangered plant in Victoria, it is now extinct in Melbourne.
Localities: Research#
Distribution: Vic, SA

Galium gaudichaudii

Rough Bedstraw

Size: Prostrate–30 cm x 0.5–2 m **P**
Habitat: Wet sclerophyll rainforest, riparian scrub, damp and valley sclerophyll forests, grassy low open forest
Form: Spreading perennial herb with strong tap root
Foliage: Narrow leaves to 12 mm long, in whorls of 4–5, margins recurved
Flowers: Very small almost sessile cream flowers in terminal and axillary clusters; September to December. Buds are purplish.
Requirements: Moist, well drained soils
Comments: The most common Victorian species. It may become invasive in ideal conditions.
Propagation: Seed, cuttings
Localities: 16, 26, 29, 32, 34A, 36, 41, 42, 53, 55, 57, 58, 64, 74, 76
Distribution: Vic, Qld, NSW, Tas, SA

Galium migrans

P

Habitat: Rock crevices in escarpment vegetation, riparian woodland and scrub, valley sclerophyll forest
Form: Straggling hairy perennial preferring moist situations
Foliage: Bright, light green elliptical to almost linear leaves to 10 mm long, upper leaves becoming narrower, in whorls of 4.
Flowers: Clusters of 5–15 yellowish to white flowers on long, branched thread-like stalks; September to November
Comments: Differs from *G. binifolium* principally in having leaves of equal length.
Localities: Kororoit Ck, Melton Sth, 8, 18, 28, 36, 56
Distribution: Vic, Qld, NSW, SA, WA

Galium propinquum

Maori Bedstraw

Size: Prostrate–20 cm x 0.5–1 m — P N
Habitat: Coastal banksia, box and riparian woodlands, valley sclerophyll forest, grassy low open forest
Form: Vigorous tangled perennial herb
Foliage: Dull to yellowish green oval leaves to 15 mm long, in whorls of 4–5
Flowers: Few tiny white to cream or yellow flowers in clusters; September to December
Requirements: Moist well drained soils
Comments: Grows well in densely shaded areas, spreading by rhizomes. *G. gaudichaudii* is distinguished from *G. propinquum* by its narrower leaves and more compact habit.
Propagation: Seed, cuttings, division
Localities: 8, 14, 34A, 36, 42, 44, 58, 60, 67#, 74, 76
Distribution: Vic, Qld, NSW, SA; NZ

Geranium — Geraniaceae

Geranium potentilloides

Crane's Bill

Size: Prostrate x 0.5 m-1.5 m — P N
Habitat: Widespread in damp and valley sclerophyll forests
Form: Creeping perennial herb
Foliage: Hairy, almost round leaves with 5–7 lobes, often purplish below. Stem leaves, 70 mm x 50 mm, on stalks to 40 mm long. The larger basal leaves are usually deciduous.
Flowers: Solitary open pink to almost white flowers, 10–15 mm wide; September to March. Fruit is beaked to 10 mm long.
Requirements: Moist shaded conditions
Comments: Although not ornamental it is useful for stabilising soils in shaded situations. The thick tap root of some *Geranium* species was cooked for food by the Aborigines.
Propagation: Seed, cuttings, division of layered stems
Localities: 34A, 35, 42, 44, 50A, 51, 53, 55–60, 64, 74
Distribution: Vic, NSW, Tas, SA; NZ, Antarctic Islands

Geranium retrorsum

Grassland Crane's Bill

Size: Prostrate–30 cm x 0.6–1 m — P
Habitat: Red gum, box and riparian woodland, plains grassland
Form: Creeping perennial herb
Foliage: Hairy, ovate to kidney-shaped stem leaves to 90 mm x 30 mm with 3–7 deeply dissected narrow lobes, held on stalks to 70 mm long. Basal leaves somewhat larger and more deeply dissected.
Flowers: Paired pink flowers with long hairs on sepal margins and hairs on stalks pressed backwards; July to January. Fruit beaked to 15 mm long.
Requirements: Most soils, preferring shade
Comments: Does not self layer.
Localities: 2, 5, 8, 10, 12, 15–18, 26, 28, 35, 44, 47, 48, 53, 60, 71, 74
Distribution: Vic, NSW, Tas, SA, WA; NZ

Geranium solanderi

Austral Crane's Bill

Size: Prostrate–0.5 m x 0.6–1.5 m — P
Habitat: Widespread in red gum woodland, riparian scrub, dry and valley sclerophyll forests, grassy low open forest
Form: Hairy, creeping perennial herb
Foliage: Stem leaves 5–7 lobed, kidney-shaped to almost round to 100 mm x 40 mm, paler green below, on long hairy stalks. Basal leaves larger and more deeply dissected. Leaves age orange to red.
Flowers: Paired pink flowers on stalks with reflexed or spreading hairs; October to February. Fruit beaked to 12 mm long.
Requirements: Well drained soils but tolerates moisture
Comments: Similar to the other species. Cultivated plants form a dense cover in permanently damp areas. The Aborigines roasted the taproot.
Localities: 1, 10, 13, 18, 25, 26, 29, 31, 32, 34A–36, 39, 41, 42, 44, 46–48, 50A, 51, 53, 55–58, 60, 62, 63, 71, 74–76
Distribution: All states except NT; NZ

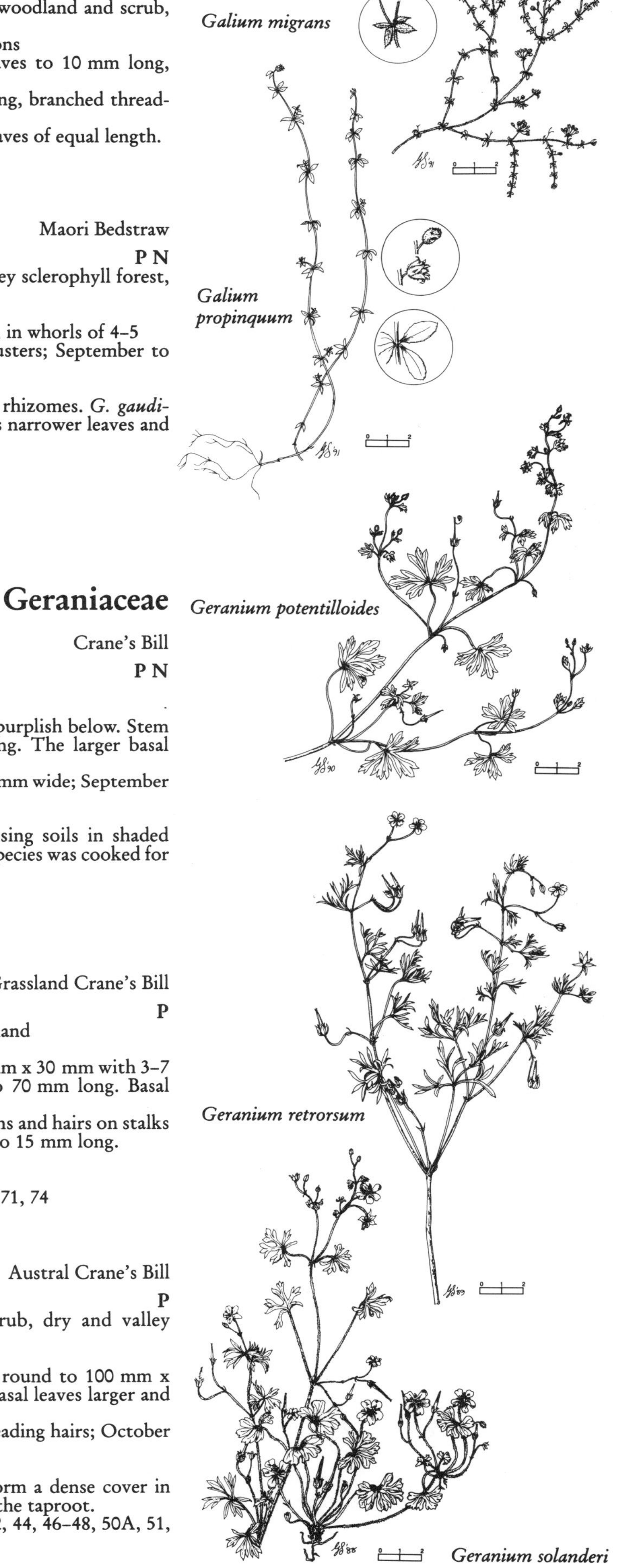

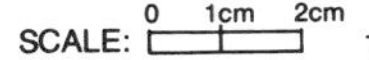
SCALE: 0 1cm 2cm — The scale representation on each plant equals 2cm.

Glycine clandestina

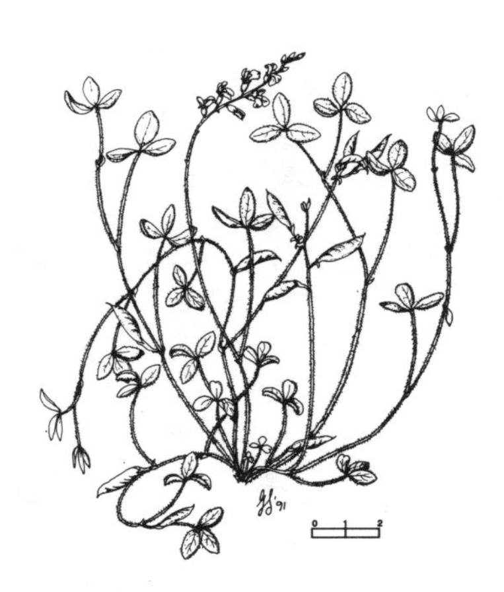

Glycine latrobeana

Glycine tabacina

Glossostigma — Scrophulariaceae

Glossostigma elatinoides — Small Mudmat

Size: Prostrate x 0.3–1 m — F
Habitat: In and beside freshwater swamps and shallow pools, in box woodland
Form: Semi-aquatic creeping perennial herb rooting at leaf nodes to form a mat
Foliage: Pairs of erect, stalked oblanceolate leaves to 15 mm long, along prostrate stems
Flowers: Tiny, single pale blue or mauve 5-petalled flowers on erect stalks shorter than the leaves; December to April
Requirements: Mud or shallow water to 0.1 m, on clay
Comments: Useful in stabilising the edges of clay-based pools where it will form green mats beneath the water. Locally rare.
Propagation: Fresh seed, cuttings, division
Localities: Melton South, 42
Distribution: Vic, NSW, Tas, SA; NZ

Glycine — Fabaceae

Glycine clandestina — Twining Glycine

Size: Twining 0.3–2 m tall — P N
Habitat: Widespread in tea-tree heath, red gum woodland, dry and valley sclerophyll forests
Form: Slender open twiner
Foliage: Hairy, trifoliate leaves, leaflets narrow-ovate to 40 mm long, on stalks of equal length. The stalk of the terminal leaflet lacks small stipule-like structures, called stipels.
Flowers: Racemes of small bluish-mauve pea flowers; October to January
Requirements: Moist well drained soils tolerating dry periods once established
Comments: A dainty twiner for climbing through other plants, usually not noticed until it flowers.
Propagation: Scarified seed, cuttings
Localities: 29#, 34A–38, 41–44, 47, 49, 50A–53, 55–61, 63–67#, 71, 74, 76
Distribution: All states except NT

Glycine latrobeana — Clover or Purple Glycine

F P

Habitat: Plains grassland, box woodland and dry sclerophyll forests
Form: A trailing rather than climbing plant with short stems
Foliage: Obovate leaves, 20 mm x 12 mm, broader than *G. clandestina*
Flowers: Racemes of 3–8 deep purple pea-like flowers; September to December
Requirements: Moist well drained soils
Comments: An endangered plant Australia-wide, it is also at risk in Melbourne.
Localities: Werribee#, Diggers Rest#, Melton South, Research-Eltham, 34A, 55, 58
Distribution: Vic, NSW, Tas, SA

Glycine microphylla

P N

Habitat: Damp sclerophyll forest
Form: Stoloniferous twiner, rooting at the nodes of above ground stems
Foliage: Trifoliate leaves, leaflets lanceolate to 15–50 mm long, terminal leaflet often larger, on stalks of equal length. Pair of stipels on the stalk of the terminal leaflet. Leaflets of first leaves broader.
Flowers: Racemes of small violet flowers with a white spot; October to April
Requirements: Tolerates poorly drained soils in Winter
Comments: Similar to *G. clandestina* but smaller, the main distinguishing feature being the presence of the stipels.
Localities: 42, 58
Distribution: Vic, Qld, NSW, Tas, SA; Norfolk Is
Synonym: Previously included with *G. clandestina*

Glycine tabacina — Vanilla or Variable Glycine

Size: Stems 0.2–2 m long — F P
Habitat: Dry sclerophyll forest, plains grassland, riparian scrub, red gum woodland
Form: Creeping or trailing perennial
Foliage: Trifoliate leaves, side leaflets elliptic to ovate to 15 mm long, terminal leaflet larger and narrower to 50 mm long. The stalk of the terminal leaflet is markedly longer than the stalks of the 2 lateral leaflets.
Flowers: Racemes of 4–12 blue to purple pea flowers; December to May
Requirements: Well drained soils, tolerating dryness once established
Comments: This species is not tolerant of heavy frost. The Aborigines chewed the tap root which is liquorice flavored.
Propagation: Seed, cuttings
Localities: Kororoit Ck, Melton Sth, 6, 7, 12, 16–18, 21, 23, 25, 26, 28, 29, 31#, 35, 38, 39
Distribution: Vic, Qld, NSW, SA, WA

Glycyrrhiza **Fabaceae**

Glycyrrhiza acanthocarpa
Native or Southern Liquorice

F P

Size: 0.6–1.5 m x 0.5–1 m
Habitat: Sedimentary rises
Form: Erect sticky shrub
Foliage: Aromatic pinnate leaves to 60 mm, 9–13 oblong-lanceolate leaflets to 20 mm
Flowers: Long axillary racemes, to 80 mm, of lilac pea flowers, along the upper part of the stalk; September to February. Fruit a rusty-brown burr-like pod.
Requirements: Moist soils
Comments: Responds well to hard pruning. Plants die back over Summer. Little known, it may be extinct within the Melbourne area.
Propagation: Scarified seed, cuttings
Localities: An early collection from Mentone. Possibly once occurred on sedimentary rises on the basalt plains.
Distribution: Vic, Qld, NSW, SA, WA

Gnaphalium **Asteraceae**

Gnaphalium collinum, G. gymnocephalum, G. japonicum = Euchiton gymnocephalus

Gnaphalium indutum
Tiny Cudweed

F

Size: 10–50 mm x 150 mm
Habitat: Grassy wetlands, red gum woodland, coastal banksia woodland and tea-tree heath
Form: Tiny wiry herb
Foliage: Narrow woolly grey leaves to 10 mm long
Flowers: Deeply clustered terminal creamy-brown flowerheads surrounded by larger bracts. Flowering occurs mainly in the warmer months.
Requirements: Open well drained situation
Comments: While rarely cultivated it has potential as a small rockery plant.
Propagation: Seed, cuttings
Localities: Seaford, 5, 7, 35, 42, 67#, 68, 70, 74
Distribution: All states except NT

Gnaphalium indutum

Gnaphalium involucratum = Euchiton involucratus

Gnaphalium luteo-album = Pseudognaphalium luteo-album

Gnaphalium sphaericum = Euchiton sphaericus

Gompholobium huegelii

Gompholobium **Fabaceae**

Gompholobium huegelii
Common Wedge-pea, Karalla

P

Size: 0.3–1 m x 0.3–1 m
Habitat: Tea-tree heath, sclerophyll woodland, dry sclerophyll forest
Form: Open spreading shrub
Foliage: Trifoliate leaves with narrow, pointed bluish-green leaflets to 25 mm long
Flowers: Large, bright yellow pea flowers; September to February. Buds and backs of petals are dark olive green.
Requirements: Well drained soils
Comments: A very attractive plant when in flower, displayed to best advantage when grouped with other plants. Tip pruning encourages bushiness. An excellent container plant.
Propagation: Scarified seed, cuttings
Localities: Hurstbridge, Warrandyte, 50–51, 53, 56, 59, 60, 67–71
Distribution: Vic, Qld, NSW, Tas

SCALE: 0 1cm 2cm The scale representation on each plant equals 2cm.

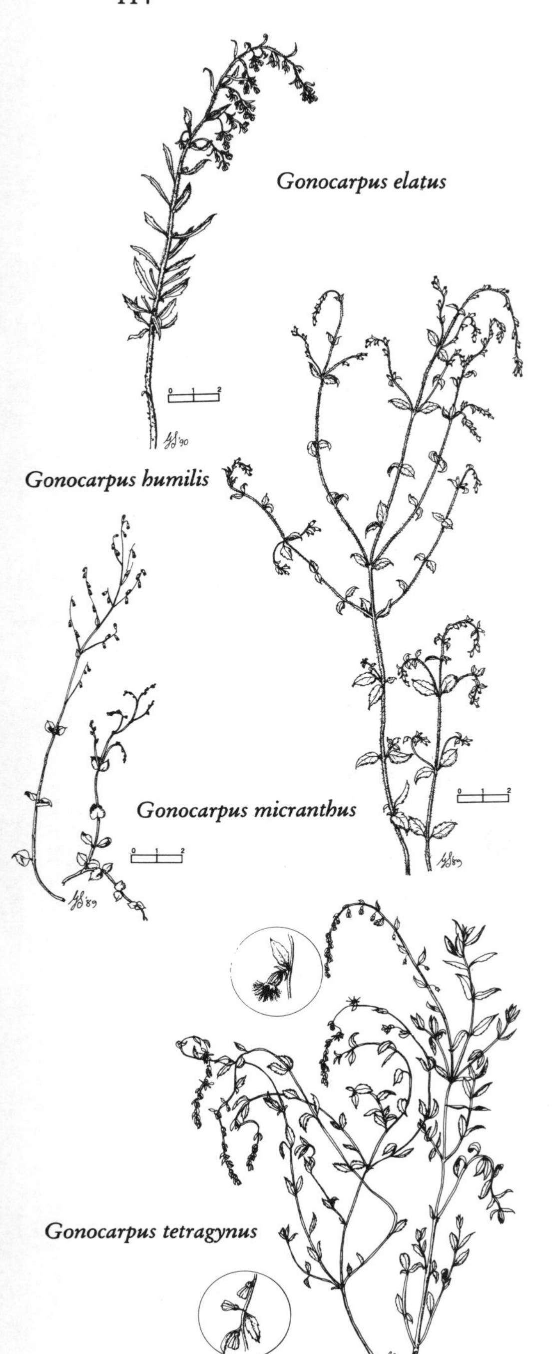

Gonocarpus — Haloragaceae

Gonocarpus elatus

Tall Gonocarpus, Raspwort

Size: 0.2–0.6 m x 0.3–1 m — F P
Habitat: Exposed rocky hillsides in box woodlands
Form: Dense perennial herb with hairy stems and leaves
Foliage: Variable green to reddish leaves, narrow to ovate, entire or toothed, 10–60 mm long
Flowers: Spikes of very small reddish-brown with yellow-green flowers; October to January. Small round to oval fruit after flowering.
Requirements: Well drained soils
Comments: The common name refers to the stems of raspworts, which are rough to the touch and 4-ribbed. Locally rare.
Propagation: Cuttings
Localities: Jacksons Ck Keilor, 26
Distribution: Vic, Qld, NSW, SA
Synonym: *Haloragis elata*

Gonocarpus humilis

Raspwort

Size: to 0.7 m high — P
Habitat: Grassy low open forest, damp and valley sclerophyll forests
Form: Semi-prostrate to bushy shrub with minute spreading stem hairs
Foliage: Widely spaced decussate pairs of broad, toothed leaves to 10 mm long
Flowers: Terminal spikes of tiny greenish-yellow flowers; November to February
Requirements: Moist soils
Comments: Grows amongst thick undergrowth. Difficult to distinguish from *G. teucrioides* (which does not occur within the Melbourne area) but tends to have less stiffly erect stems and alternate flowers.
Localities: The Basin, Kalorama 41, 44, 54–56, 60, 69, 74, 75
Distribution: Vic, Qld, NSW, Tas, SA

Gonocarpus micranthus

Creeping Raspwort

Size: Prostrate x 0.5 m — P
Habitat: Damp, peaty ground in wattle tea-tree scrub, tea-tree heath and swamp scrub, from coast to foothills
Form: Matting plant
Foliage: Decussate pairs of small, roundish, bright green leaves to 10 mm long
Flowers: Minute red flowers near ends of stems; December to February. Very small grey to reddish fruit.
Requirements: Boggy soils, tolerating dry periods
Localities: The Basin, Montrose, 47, 48, 51, 54, 56, 62–64, 67–71, 73–76
Distribution: Vic, Qld, NSW, Tas, SA; NZ
Synonym: *Haloragis micrantha*

Gonocarpus tetragynus

Common or Poverty Raspwort

Size: 10–30 cm x 20–40 cm — F P
Habitat: Valley and dry sclerophyll forests on slopes, sclerophyll and red gum woodlands, grassy low open forest, tea-tree heaths and scrubs, and plains grassland
Form: Low bushy herb covered in short white appressed stem hairs
Foliage: Small lanceolate to elliptic serrated leaves to 12 mm long, pairs decussate
Flowers: Loose spikes of tiny pinkish-red flowers; December to February
Requirements: Moist to dry, well drained soils
Localities: 6, 12, 13, 16, 24–26, 28, 31, 32, 35, 36, 38–71, 73–76
Distribution: Vic, Qld, NSW, Tas, SA
Synonym: *Haloragis tetragyna*

Goodenia — Goodeniaceae

Nine species of *Goodenia* are found in the Melbourne area. With the exception of *G. ovata*, all are perennial herbs, forming tufts or rosettes. Most grow in moist well drained habitats, tolerating periods of inundation, and are excellent used as ground covers in the garden. Easily cultivated, goodenias are mostly insignificant until in flower when they are covered with bright yellow flowers, often on long stalks, usually for lengthy periods. Propagation is usually by stem cuttings or division of stolons (where applicable) although leaf cuttings are worth trying for some species.

Goodenia blackiana

Size: Prostrate–10 cm x 10–20 cm — F P
Habitat: Dry and valley sclerophyll forest
Form: Stoloniferous tufted woolly perennial herb
Foliage: Erect obovate to narrow-oblanceolate leaves to 60 mm long with a few scattered teeth, glabrous above, densely woolly below
Flowers: Single terminal yellow flowers on long erect stalks to 100 mm; September to February. Bracteoles linear to 12 mm long.
Requirements: Well drained soils
Comments: Similar to *G. geniculata* which has longer leaves with a persistent covering of stiffer hairs on both sides, and shorter bracteoles. An excellent rockery or container plant due to its long flowering time.
Localities: Hurstbridge, 36, 50A
Distribution: Vic, SA

Goodenia elongata

Lanky Goodenia

Size: 20–50 cm x 0.5–1.5 m — **P**
Habitat: Valley sclerophyll forest, swamp scrub, swampy heathland
Form: Creeping perennial herb
Foliage: Lanceolate to ovate slightly hairy leaves from 10–50 mm long, sometimes with scattered teeth. Smaller stem leaves.
Flowers: Large solitary yellow flowers to 25 mm on long slender stalks; October to January
Requirements: Damp soil, tolerating waterlogging
Comments: This plant may form large colonies in shaded, moist conditions. Pruning after flowering is beneficial.
Propagation: Cuttings—firm new growth
Localities: 36, 42, 47, 51, 54, 55, 67#, 74, 75
Distribution: Vic, NSW, Tas, SA

Goodenia elongata

Goodenia geniculata

Goodenia geniculata

Bent Goodenia

Size: 5–10 cm x 10–50 cm — **F P**
Habitat: Grassy low open forest, tea-tree heath
Form: Perennial matting herb
Foliage: Rosettes of glossy oblanceolate leaves to 100 mm long, covered in stiff hairs. Young foliage is lobed.
Flowers: Large, solitary pale to bright yellow flowers on stalks longer than the foliage; August to February. Stalk bends after flowering.
Requirements: Adaptable, tolerating wet or dry periods
Comments: An excellent rockery or container plant due to its long flowering time. Spreads by suckering.
Propagation: Cuttings, division
Localities: Eltham, 29, 35, 36, 49, 67–71, 74–76
Distribution: Vic, NSW, Tas, SA

Goodenia gracilis

Slender Goodenia

Size: 20–50 cm x 10–30 cm — **F**
Habitat: Grassy wetlands
Form: Very attractive erect perennial herb
Foliage: Narrow leaves from 25–150 mm long on long stalks
Flowers: Loose clusters of single, small yellow flowers on tall branched stalks; September to February
Requirements: Tolerates periodic inundation
Comments: Locally rare.
Propagation: Seed
Localities: Deer Park, Laverton-Werribee, 16–18, 35
Distribution: Vic, Qld, NSW, NT

Goodenia heteromera

Spreading Goodenia

Size: Prostrate–20 cm x 0.5–2.5 m — **F P**
Habitat: Grassy wetlands
Form: Vigorous perennial stoloniferous herb, forming dense mats
Foliage: Lanceolate leaves to 80 mm long
Flowers: Single yellow flowers are held on long stalks which arise from a cluster of smaller stem leaves.
Requirements: Moist to wet heavy soil
Comments: Useful for soil erosion in small areas.
Localities: Laverton, Werribee
Distribution: Vic, Qld, NSW, SA

Goodenia gracilis

Goodenia humilis

Goodenia humilis

Swamp Goodenia

Size: 5–10 cm x 0.5–1.5 m — **F**
Habitat: Valley sclerophyll forest, wattle tea-tree scrub and swamp scrub
Foliage: Narrow lanceolate leaves to 100 mm long
Flowers: Profuse terminal clusters of yellow flowers; November to March
Requirements: Moist to wet soil
Comments: A very adaptable suckering, matting plant. Ideal planted around clay-based pools.
Localities: Montrose, 34A, 35, 50A, 54, 60–65, 67#, 69, 69A, 71, 72, 74–76
Distribution: Vic, NSW, Tas, SA

Goodenia lanata

Woolly or Trailing Goodenia

Size: Prostrate x 0.5–1.5 m — **F P**
Habitat: Damp and valley sclerophyll forests, sclerophyll woodland
Form: Hairy trailing herb, rooting at the nodes
Foliage: Dark green, coarsely-toothed obovate leaves to 80 mm long, paler below. Stem leaves are small and fleshy.
Flowers: Attractive solitary yellow flowers on long stalks; October to December.
Requirements: Tolerates extended dry periods once established.
Comments: Good in a container amongst other plants. Hard pruning will rejuvenate leggy plants.
Localities: 37, 41–44, 49–52, 54–56, 58, 59
Distribution: Vic, Tas

Illustrated p. 172

SCALE: 0 1cm 2cm — The scale representation on each plant equals 2cm.

Goodenia ovata

Goodenia ovata
Hop Goodenia

Size: 1–2.5 m x 1–3 m **F P N**
Habitat: Widespread from wet sclerophyll forest to grassy low open forest, box and red gum woodlands, also coastal cliffs
Form: Small to medium open shrub
Foliage: Light green ovate, toothed leaves to 100 mm long
Flowers: Sprays of 3–6 yellow flowers; August to February
Requirements: Damp soils, tolerating waterlogging
Comments: An understorey plant that can become straggly unless pruned. Useful as a cut flower. It is an early coloniser after fire or clearing.
Localities: 1, 14, 16, 22, 23, 26, 29–36, 40, 42–44, 46–51, 53–64, 67, 69A–71, 74, 76
Distribution: All states except WA

Goodenia pinnatifida
Cut-leaf Goodenia, Mother Ducks, Scrambled Eggs

Size: 0.2–0.5 m x 0.2–0.6 m **F**
Habitat: Red gum woodland, plains grassland, grassy wetlands
Form: Tufted annual or perennial herb
Foliage: Deeply and narrowly lobed oblong leaves to 80 mm long
Flowers: Profuse clusters of large, bright yellow flowers to 50 mm; October to November and March to May.
Requirements: Tolerates dryness, but Summer watering will increase flowering time
Comments: An excellent garden or container plant for warm areas. May completely die back during dry Summers, regenerating naturally from underground rhizomes following rain. Locally rare.
Propagation: Seed, cuttings, stolons
Localities: Tottenham, St. Albans, Nth Melbourne, Sunbury, Werribee, 2, 10, 16, 26, 28, 35, 67#
Distribution: Vic, Qld, NSW, SA, WA *Illustrated p. 172*

Goodia lotifolia

Goodia — Fabaceae

Goodia lotifolia
Golden Tip, Clover Tree

Size: 1–5 m x 1–5 m **F P**
Habitat: Damp to dry sclerophyll forests, sclerophyll woodland (on sandstone)
Form: Fast growing open shrub
Foliage: Trifoliate leaves with ovate bluish-green leaflets to 25 mm long, paler below
Flowers: Profuse racemes of fragrant yellow pea flowers with reddish markings; September to December
Requirements: Well drained soils, intolerant of alkaline soil
Comments: Very showy in flower. Pruning after flowering is necessary to maintain bushy growth. Heavy pruning may induce suckering.
Propagation: Scarified seed, stem or root cuttings
Localities: Sunbury, 16, 26, 42, 47, 49, 55–59
Distribution: All states except NT

Gratiola peruviana

Gratiola — Scrophulariaceae

Gratiola peruviana
Austral Brooklime

Size: 30 cm x 0.5–1.5 m **P N**
Habitat: Edges of swamps and creeks in riparian scrub, grassy low open forest, valley sclerophyll forests
Form: Sprawling or erect perennial herb
Foliage: Pairs of pale green, glabrous ovate stem-clasping leaves to 45 mm long x 5–27 mm with lightly-toothed margins. Sometimes leaves have sparse non-gland tipped hairs.
Flowers: Solitary pale pink, rarely purple or white, tubular flowers to 12 mm, either stalkless or shortly stalked, in leaf axils; October to May
Requirements: Easily grown in most conditions, it prefers a moist position but tolerates waterlogging and drying out once established
Comments: A suckering plant, it is excellent for planting beside ponds or in terrariums. The leaves have a powerful laxative effect, and were also used to treat dizziness and loss of appetite.
Propagation: Cuttings, division
Localities: 16, 26, 30, 34A, 35, 42, 44, 45, 47, 49, 56–58, 60, 67#, 71, 74, 75
Distribution: Vic, NSW, Tas, SA, WA; NZ, Sth Am
Synonym: *G. latifolia*

Gratiola pubescens

Gratiola pubescens
Brooklime

Size: Prostrate–20 cm x 0.6–1.5 m **P**
Habitat: Swamp scrub
Flowers: Pale pink flowers with a yellow throat, stalks to 25 mm; October to January
Requirements: Damp areas which dry out in Summer
Comments: Similar to *G. peruviana* but with densely glandular, pubescent hairs. Leaves are shorter, to 26 mm, and narrower. Locally rare due to drainage of habitat.
Localities: Kilsyth, Montrose, Mooroolbark, 74, 75
Distribution: Vic, NSW, Tas, SA, WA

49 50 51 52 53 54 55 56 57 58

49. *Epacris impressa* Common Heath
50. *Goodenia ovata* Hop Bush
51. *Amyema pendulum* Drooping Mistletoe
52. *Drosera peltata* ssp. *auriculata* Tall Sundew
53. *Patersonia fragilis* Short Purple-flag
54. *Bursaria spinosa* Sweet Bursaria
55. *Isopogon ceratophyllus* Horny Cone-bush
56. *Lythrum salicaria* Purple Loose-strife
57. *Lomandra longifolia* Spiny-headed Mat-rush
58. *Xanthorrhoea minor* ssp. *lutea* Small Grass Tree

59

60

61

62

64

59. *Themeda triandra* Kangaroo Grass
60. *Kunzea ericoides* Burgan
61. *Platylobium formosum* Handsome Flat-pea
62. *Correa reflexa* Native Fuchsia
63. *Eucalyptus polyanthemos* ssp. *vestita* Red Box
64. *Caladenia dilatata* Green Comb Spider Orchid
65. *Stackhousia monogyna* Candles
66. *Tetratheca ciliata* Pink Bells
67. *Hibbertia stricta* Erect Guinea-flower
68. *Spyridium parvifolium* Dusty Miller

63

67

65

66

68

Grevillea

Proteaceae

Grevillea alpina

Alpine or Mountain Grevillea, Cat's Claw

Size: Variable, 1–2.5 m x1–2 m — P
Habitat: Dry sclerophyll forest in foothills
Form: Dense upright shrub (Mt. Dandenong form described)
Foliage: Hairy oval leaves to 12 mm long, paler below
Flowers: Clusters of hairy, bright red and yellow flowers in terminal clusters; August to December
Requirements: Well drained soils
Comments: Flowering for a long time, this showy plant does best as an understorey shrub. Frequent pruning when young encourages bushiness in most forms. *G. alpina* is very variable over its range in habit and flower colour, with shades from white and green through yellow and gold to pinks and reds. All make attractive tub specimens. The local form makes a reliable garden plant.
Propagation: Cuttings
Localities: 55, 56
Distribution: Vic, NSW, Tas

Grevillea alpina

Grevillea infecunda

Anglesea Grevillea

Size: 0.3–0.6 m x 1.5–2.5 m — F P
Habitat: Tea-tree heath
Form: Low spreading shrub, hairy young growth and branchlets
Foliage: Oblong, holly-like, flat to concave leaves to 60 mm long, teeth sharply pointed. Leaves paler and silky below
Flowers: Terminal red and green toothbrush-like flowers to 40 mm long; September to January
Requirements: Well drained sandy soil tolerating dryness once established
Comments: This unusual species never sets seed but forms colonies by suckering. Responds well to pruning and fire. Now only found in the Anglesea area it was recorded in 1950s occurring in scrub near Brighton. It is also possible that another grevillea collected near Oakleigh (1911) may have been this species.
Propagation: Stem and root cuttings
Localities: Brighton-Sandringham area#
Distribution: Endemic to Vic
Synonym: Segregated from *G. aquifolium*

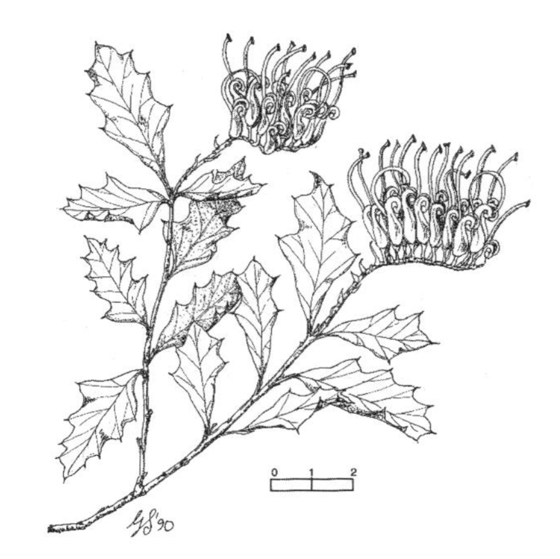

Grevillea infecunda

Grevillea rosmarinifolia

Rosemary Grevillea

Size: Variable, 1–3 m x 2–3 m — F P
Habitat: Dry sclerophyll forest, plains grassland
Form: Dense rounded shrub
Foliage: Stiff, prickly needle-like or linear flat leaves to 40 mm long
Flowers: Racemes of red and cream, or greenish, spidery flowers drooping from the ends of branches most of the year, peaking Winter and Spring
Requirements: Well drained soils
Comments: The dense prickly foliage provides an excellent bird habitat and pruning will encourage more compact growth. Some people suffer allergic reactions to the prickly leaves. The local forms of *G. rosmarinifolia* have a very limited distribution within the Melbourne area.

The form from the basalt plains, which is sold as 'Lara Dwarf', is a small, slow-growing compact form with grey leaves and cream and pink flowers. The sole surviving plant in its natural habitat occurs just outside the Melbourne area.

The Hurstbridge/Eltham form is low growing, up to 1 m x 1 m. It has prickly bluish-green linear leaves to 15 mm long and cream flowers with pink tonings.

The Plenty Gorge form is more upright to 1.5 m x 1 m. Leaves are darker green, longer to 25 mm and broader to 3–4 mm and the flowers have stronger pink tonings.

A naturally occurring hybrid between *G. rosmarinifolia* and *G. lanigera* is found in Wattle Glen.

Propagation: Cuttings
Localities: Werribee#, Hurstbridge, Diamond Ck, Craigieburn, 26, 29#, 34, 34A, 36, 42
Distribution: Vic, NSW
Synonym: The forms to the north-east of Melbourne have previously been referred to as *G. glabella*.

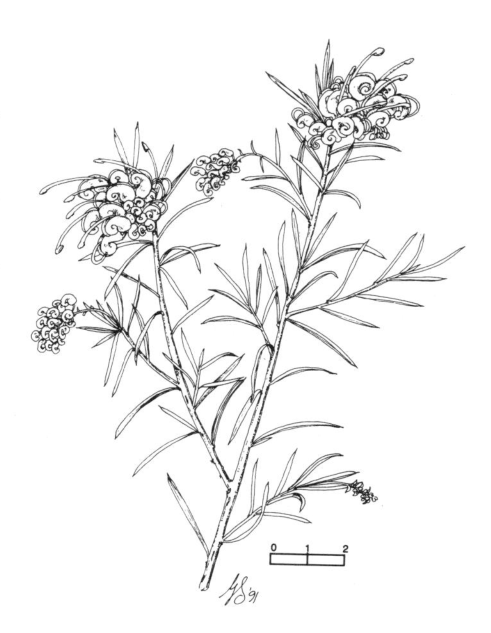

Grevillea rosmarinifolia

SCALE: 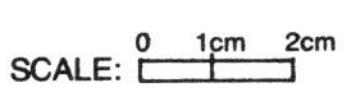

The scale representation on each plant equals 2cm.

Gynatrix pulchella

Gynatrix — Malvaceae

Gynatrix pulchella — Hemp Bush

Size: 2–4 m x 1.5–3 m — P
Habitat: Damp and valley sclerophyll forests, riparian scrub, red gum woodland, often on rocky sites
Form: Open woody shrub
Foliage: Hairy heart-shaped leaves to 100 mm long with rounded teeth along the edges, pale green below
Flowers: Panicles of fragrant, small greenish-white flowers; August to October. Male and female flowers on different plants, with shorter petals on the female flowers.
Requirements: Well drained moist soil
Comments: Often profuse in flowering. Can become straggly, but regular pruning will overcome this. The Aborigines made string from the bark.
Propagation: Seed, cuttings
Localities: Diamond Ck, 23, 26–30, 32, 33, 34A–36, 41, 42, 51, 56, 62–66
Distribution: Vic, NSW, Tas

Hakea — Proteaceae

Four hakeas occur in the Melbourne region, growing in open forest and heathland. All have pungent-tipped foliage and clusters of flowers in the leaf axils. Their seeds are protected by large woody fruit which open after fire or damage. A favourite among birds, they provide food and protection from predators. Propagation is by seed.

Hakea nodosa

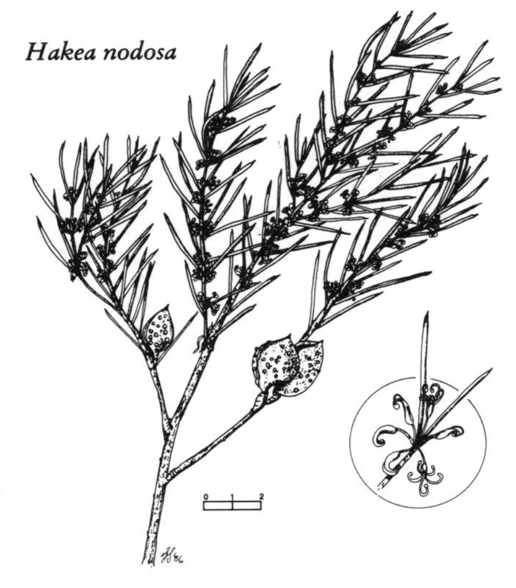

Hakea nodosa — Yellow Hakea

Size: 1–3 m x 1–2 m — F P N
Habitat: Swamp scrub, sclerophyll woodland, valley sclerophyll forest, from coast to foothills
Form: Erect, dense to open shrub
Foliage: Blue-green needles to 40 mm long, not as sharp as the other species
Flowers: Masses of small fragrant yellow flowers; April to August. Oval warty fruit to 30 mm long.
Requirements: Tolerates poor drainage but grows well in dry or moist conditions
Comments: Attractive in flower this quick growing shrub provides a good low screen. Plants may be invigorated by hard pruning.
Localities: 29, 47, 49–51, 54–56, 59–61, 63, 64, 67#, 70, 74, 75,
Distribution: Vic, Tas, SA

Hakea sericea — Silky Hakea, Bushy Needlewood

Size: 2–5 m x 1–3 m — F P
Habitat: Sclerophyll woodland, box and red gum woodland, valley sclerophyll forest
Form: Fast-growing erect open to dense shrub
Foliage: Stiff prickly needles to 60 mm long
Flowers: Masses of fragrant, hairy, white, or occasionally pink, flowers; May to September. Prominent rough fruit to 40 mm long have a double-pointed beak.
Requirements: Adaptable to any conditions
Comments: The prickly foliage provides a safe habitat for birds. Pruning is beneficial. Due to the indiscriminate planting of this species, and possible garden escapes, it is uncertain what the true range of this species is in Melbourne. This species is presently undergoing revision. It appears that it is different to the typical *H. sericea* which occurs in south-east NSW.
Propagation: Seed, cuttings
Localities: Montrose, 18, 29, 33–34A, 42, 47–49, 54, 56, 58, 62–64, 74, 75
Distribution: Vic, NSW, Tas *Illustrated p. 172*

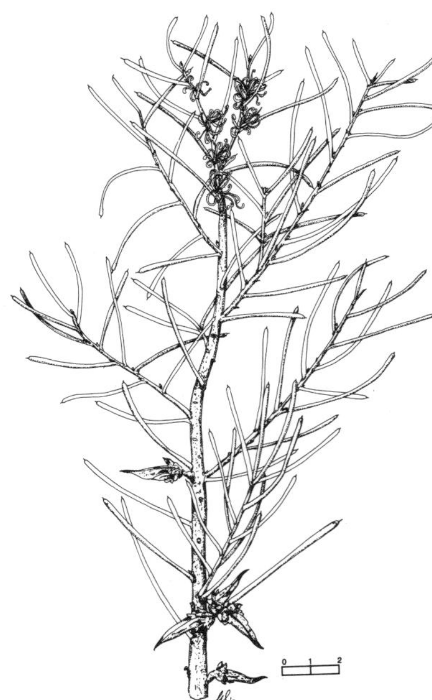

Hakea teretifolia ssp. *hirsuta*

Hakea teretifolia ssp. hirsuta — Dagger Hakea

Size: 2–3 m x 1–3 m — F
Habitat: Sclerophyll woodland
Form: Dense, upright to spreading shrub
Foliage: Stiff, sharp needle-like leaves to 50 mm long, new growth hairy and white
Flowers: Masses of very hairy white flowers; November to February. Fruit are narrow and dagger-shaped to 30 mm long with a sharp point.
Requirements: Whilst occurring naturally on moist sandy soil, it is adaptable to any well drained situation
Comments: Seed germinates readily after fires, forming dense stands.
Localities: Narre Warren East 1907; 49, 50A, 61, 74. Occurred in swamps near the Dandenong Rges in 1853.
Distribution: Vic, Qld, NSW, Tas

Hakea ulicina

Furze Hakea

Size:	1–3 m x 1–2 m **F P**
Habitat:	Tea-tree heath, sclerophyll woodland, dry and valley sclerophyll forest
Form:	Rigid upright shrub
Foliage:	Narrow, pointed leaves to 20 cm long
Flowers:	Small clusters of white to cream flowers; July to November. Clusters of smooth short-beaked fruit to 20 mm long.
Requirements:	Well drained dry to moist soils
Comments:	Stands of this narrow erect hakea form an interesting landscape feature.
Localities:	Montrose, 34, 49–51, 54, 56, 58–61, 63, 64, 67#, 70, 73–75
Distribution:	Vic, NSW, Tas

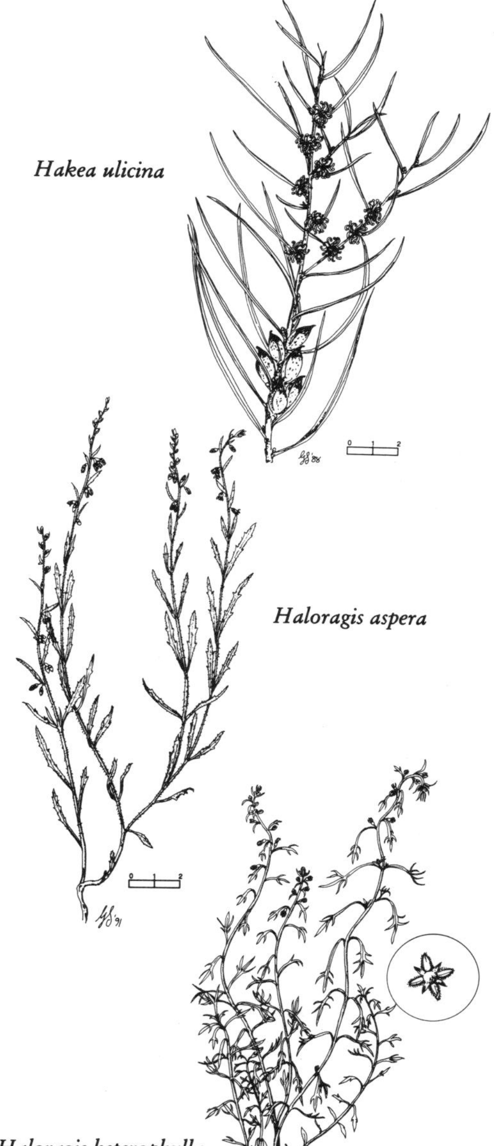

Hakea ulicina

Haloragis aspera

Haloragis heterophylla

Haloragis — Haloragaceae

Haloragis aspera

Rough Raspwort

Size:	10–25 cm high **F P**
Habitat:	Plains grassland, box woodland
Form:	Erect perennial herb
Foliage:	Sessile grey-green lanceolate leaves to 50 mm long, hairy and usually toothed
Flowers:	Small clusters of red to green flowers in spikes at the end of stems; Spring to Autumn. Anthers are yellow.
Requirements:	Moist heavy clay soils
Comments:	Stems are rough and hairy, the hairs ending in a hook. The stems grow from underground stolons.
Propagation:	Seed, division
Localities:	5, 7, 12, 17#, 18, 26, 28, 63
Distribution:	All states

Haloragis heterophylla

Variable Raspwort

Size:	0.1–0.5 m high **F P**
Habitat:	Widespread in riparian scrub and plains grassland
Comments:	Perennial herb similar to *H. aspera* but more slender, with leaves that have fewer more deeply incised teeth. Flowers have red anthers and occur during Spring and Summer. Fruit are smaller.
Localities:	Warrandyte, 5, 12, 18, 25, 26, 28, 35, 38, 44, 62, 71, 74
Distribution:	Vic, Qld, NSW, Tas, SA

Halosarcia — Chenopodiaceae

Halosarcia halocnemoides ssp. halocnemoides

Shrubby Samphire or Glasswort

Size:	5–15 cm high **F**
Habitat:	Saltmarshes
Form:	Erect branched sub-shrub. Stems are succulent and composed of glossy segments which are usually red or yellow.
Foliage:	Reduced to rim on segments
Flowers:	In short terminal spikes 5–20 mm long; November to April
Requirements:	Withstands extreme salinity and poor drainage
Propagation:	Seed
Localities:	Footscray, 2–4
Distribution:	Vic, SA, WA
Synonym:	*Arthrocnemum halocnemoides*

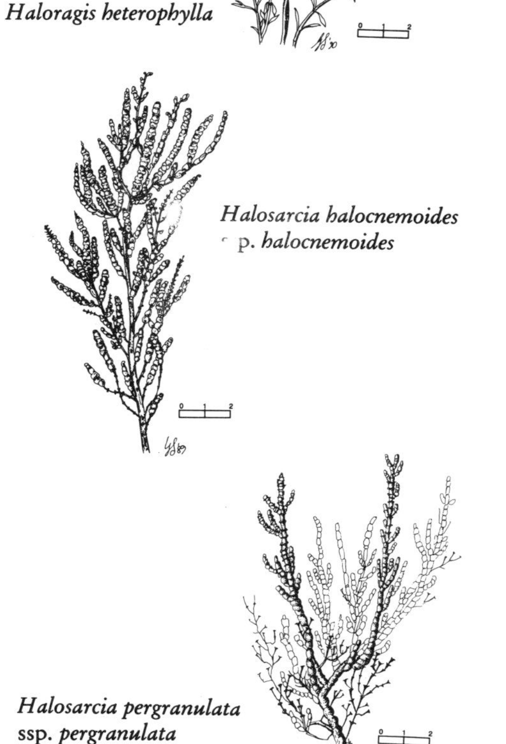

Halosarcia halocnemoides ssp. *halocnemoides*

Halosarcia pergranulata ssp. *pergranulata*

Halosarcia pergranulata ssp. pergranulata

Size:	0.2–0.6 m high **F**
Habitat:	Saltmarshes
Comments:	Similar to *H. halocnemoides*, but in the Melbourne region it is a larger, erect or ascending (rarely decumbent) shrub. It has conspicuous fertile spikes 10–50 mm long. The seed is ribbed and more granular.
Localities:	2–4
Distribution:	All mainland states
Synonym:	*Arthrocnemum halocnemoides* var. *pergranulata*

The scale representation on each plant equals 2cm.

Hardenbergia violacea

Hardenbergia — Fabaceae

Hardenbergia violacea

Purple Coral Pea, False Sarsparilla

F P

Habitat: Red gum woodland, dry and valley sclerophyll forests
Form: Fast growing dense creeper or wiry scrambler
Foliage: Leathery dark green ovate to lanceolate leaves to 100 mm long
Flowers: Sprays of mauve to purple, or sometimes pink or white, pea flowers massed along branches; July to November
Requirements: Well drained soils
Comments: A very showy scrambling climber with many forms and cultivars. The local form has dark purple flowers with a prominent green centre. It is useful for covering embankments or providing a light screen. The flowers are a source of dye. The cultivar "Happy Wanderer" is the most commonly available form of *H. violacea*. Bushy forms of *H. violacea* are also sold.
Propagation: Scarified seed
Localities: 1, 16, 21, 25, 26, 29, 30, 32–44, 46–56, 58–64, 67#, 74, 76
Distribution: All states

Hedycarya — Monimiaceae

Hedycarya angustifolia

Austral or Native Mulberry

N

Size: 3–7 m x 4 m
Habitat: Fern gullies of cool temperate rainforest, wet and damp sclerophyll forests
Form: Slender, large shrub or small tree
Foliage: Toothed, glossy dark green oval leaves to 120 mm long, pale green below, conspicuously veined
Flowers: Inconspicuous pale green male and female flowers during Spring
Requirements: Rich, moist well drained soil
Comments: The yellow fruit resembles a mulberry but is inedible. The Aborigines used the stems and wood for spear ends and firemaking.
Propagation: Cuttings
Localities: 49#, 55–58
Distribution: Vic, Qld, NSW

Hedycarya angustifolia

Helichrysum — Asteraceae

Helichrysums are referred to as everlasting daisies. Their flowers are long-lasting and often very showy. They are very adaptable and brighten up a rockery or bush garden. It is preferable to prune them back in late Winter to encourage new growth. Propagation is by seed or cuttings. Due to a recent botanical revision, *Helichrysum* species have been separated into 4 genera.

Helichrysum apiculatum = Chrysocephalum apiculatum

Helichrysum bracteatum = Bracteantha bracteata

Helichrysum dendroideum = Ozothamnus ferrugineus

Helichrysum leucopsideum

Satin Everlasting

F P

Size: 0.1–0.5 m x 0.6 m
Habitat: Coastal banksia and sclerophyll woodlands
Form: Erect hairy perennial herb
Foliage: Narrow leaves to 50 mm long, white and woolly below
Flowers: Single white paper daisy flowers with yellow centres on long stalks; October to March
Requirements: Adaptable but prefers well drained soil
Localities: Port Phillip Bay area, Belgrave, 55, 56
Distribution: All states except Qld

Helichrysum obcordatum = Ozothamnus obcordatus

Helichrysum leucopsideum

Helichrysum paralium = Ozothamnus turbinatus

Helichrysum rosmarinifolium = Ozothamnus rosmarinifolius

Helichrysum rutidolepis
Pale Everlasting

Size: 0.2–0.5 m x 0.5–1.5 m **F P**
Habitat: Wet sites in red gum woodland, plains grassland, grassy wetland, dry sclerophyll forest
Form: Erect, hairy rhizomatous perennial herb with stems branching from above the base
Foliage: Stem-clasping and grey-green, lower leaves broadly oblanceolate, upper leaves narrower
Flowers: Single yellow button flowerheads 15–20 mm wide; Spring
Requirements: Moist well drained soil
Comments: An interesting rockery plant spreading by stolons. Locally rare. The species *H.* sp. aff. *rutidolepis* is now included as part of this species.
Localities: Diamond Ck, 2, 7, 16, 17#, 26, 61
Distribution: Vic, Qld, NSW, SA

Helichrysum rutidolepis

Helichrysum scorpioides
Curling or Button Everlasting

Size: 30 cm x 20–30 cm **F P**
Habitat: Widespread in tea-tree heath, sclerophyll woodland, dry sclerophyll forest
Form: Woolly perennial herb spreading by underground stems to form a dense mat. Branched from the base.
Foliage: Basal clump of broad velvety leaves to 70 mm long. Stem leaves become smaller. Similar to *H. rutidolepis* but upper surface of leaves has coarse glandular hairs.
Flowers: Single flat yellow flowerheads 20–30 mm wide, larger than *H. rutidolepis*, surrounded by brown papery bracts, held on long stems; September to December
Requirements: Well drained soils
Comments: An attractive rockery plant which dies back after flowering. Flowers dry well.
Localities: 16, 26, 30, 33, 34A, 36, 41–56, 58, 59, 61–64, 67–69, 71, 74–76
Distribution: Vic, Qld, NSW, Tas, SA

Helichrysum scorpioides

Helichrysum semipapposum = Chrysocephalum semipapposum

Helichrysum viscosum = Bracteantha viscosa

Helipterum albicans ssp. albicans var. albicans = Leucochrysum albicans ssp. albicans var. albicans

Helipterum anthemoides = Rhodanthe anthemoides

Helipterum australe = Triptilodiscus pygmaeus

Helipterum corymbiflorum = Rhodanthe corymbiflorum

Hemichroa
Chenopodiaceae

Hemichroa pentandra
Trailing Jointweed

Size: Prostrate x 30 cm **F**
Habitat: Saltmarshes and shorelines
Form: Spreading perennial herb
Foliage: Succulent, narrowly-ovate leaves to 12 mm long
Flowers: Single, tiny white flowers along the stems enclosed in papery bracts; November
Requirements: Wet salty soil
Propagation: Cuttings
Localities: 2–4, 67, 74
Distribution: Vic, NSW, Tas, SA, WA

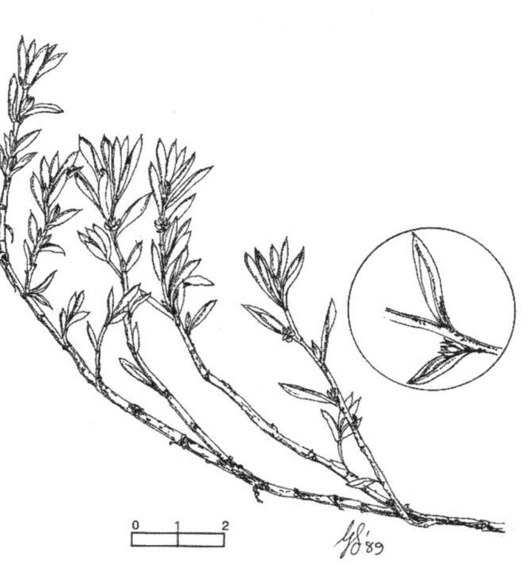

Hemichroa pentandra

SCALE: 0 1cm 2cm The scale representation on each plant equals 2cm.

Hibbertia

Dilleniaceae

The guinea flowers are small shrubs with masses of showy yellow flowers. All make excellent garden or container plants. Pruning after flowering encourages compact growth. Propagate from cuttings.

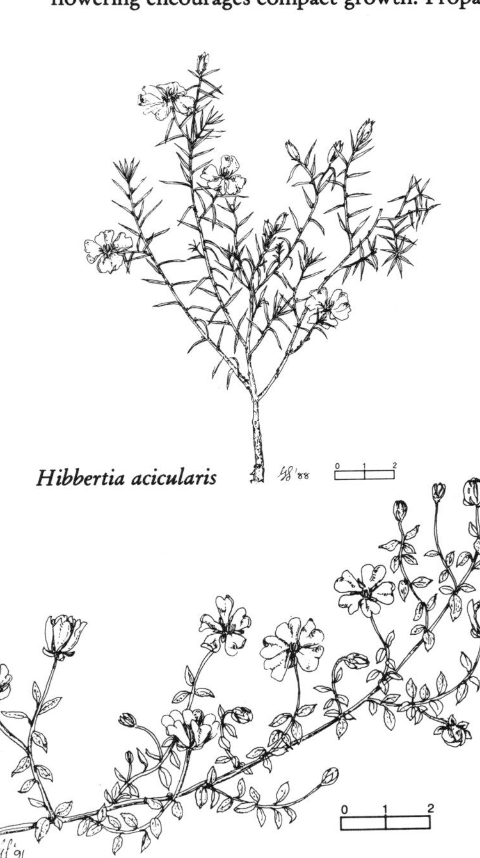

Hibbertia acicularis

Hibbertia empetrifolia

Hibbertia acicularis

Prickly Guinea-flower

Size: Prostrate-30 cm x 0.3–0.6 m **F P**
Habitat: Tea-tree heath, sclerophyll woodland
Form: Erect or sprawling small shrub
Foliage: Narrow pointed leaves to 12 mm, yellow below
Flowers: Masses of bright yellow flowers; September to February
Requirements: Well drained soils
Comments: On coastal sands it is a compact, rounded shrub, but varies according to competition from other plants. New growth is bright red and tip pruning accentuates this feature.
Localities: 67, 69, 70, 73–75
Distribution: Vic, Qld, NSW, Tas

Hibbertia empetrifolia

Trailing Guinea-flower

Size: 0.6–1 m x 2 m **F P**
Habitat: Valley sclerophyll forest
Form: Wiry trailing shrub covered in tiny bristly hairs
Foliage: Rough dark green elliptical leaves to 10 mm long, margins slightly recurved
Flowers: Masses of bright yellow flowers to 10 mm; August to October
Requirements: Well drained soils
Comments: Excellent scrambling shrub for embankments and under established trees and shrubs, providing a massed display. Grows more vigorously in moist soils, and may smother smaller plants. It may be encouraged to climb fences or pruned to form a low hedge.
Localities: 51, 53
Distribution: Vic, Qld, NSW, Tas
Synonym: *H. astrotricha, H. billardieri*

Hibbertia obtusifolia

Hibbertia obtusifolia

Showy or Grey Guinea-flower

Size: 0.3–0.6 m x 1 m **P**
Habitat: Dry sclerophyll forest, box ironbark woodland
Form: Open rounded to spreading shrub
Foliage: Hairy broad to rounded grey-green leaves to 20 mm long
Flowers: Masses of large golden yellow flowers; August to February
Requirements: Well drained soil, tolerating dry shade once established
Comments: Very showy rockery or container plant with some flowers appearing throughout the year. The prostrate form commonly available from nurseries is not local to the Melbourne area.
Localities: 42, 44, 47, 49, 50A, 51,
Distribution: Vic, Qld, NSW, Tas

Hibbertia procumbens

Spreading Guinea-flower

Comments: After further research this species was found to be incorrectly included in the first edition.

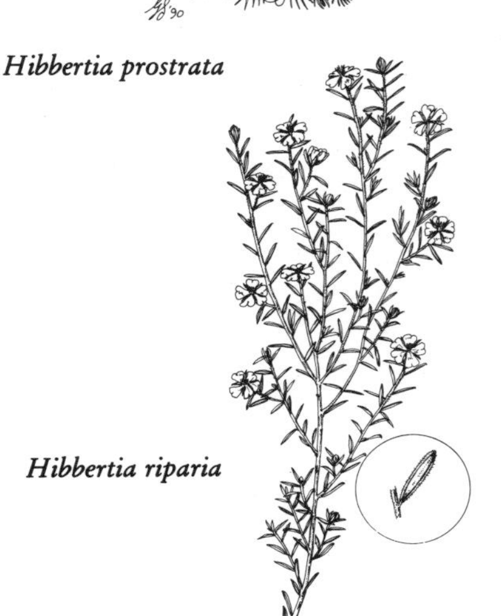

Hibbertia prostrata

Hibbertia prostrata

Stalked or Bundled Guinea-flower

Size: 0.3–0.6 m x 0.3 m **F P**
Habitat: Tea-tree heaths
Form: Low erect sub-shrub
Foliage: Soft, hairy needle-like leaves to 25 mm long in dense clusters along the stems
Flowers: Clusters of yellow flowers for a long period, peaking September to November
Requirements: Moist well drained sandy soil
Comments: The plant is at first upright, the stems bending to the ground as they become too tall to support their own weight. Difficult in clay soils.
Localities: Port Melbourne[#], 61, 67–71, 73–76
Distribution: Vic, Qld, NSW, Tas, SA
Synonym: *H. fasciculata*

Hibbertia riparia

Hibbertia riparia

Erect Guinea-flower

Size: 0.3–1 m x 0.6 m **F P**
Habitat: Sclerophyll woodland, grassy low open forest, valley sclerophyll forest, tea-tree heath
Form: Open erect shrub
Foliage: Narrow, sometimes stiff leaves to 10 mm long, variable in hairiness
Flowers: Sessile yellow flowers during Spring and Summer
Requirements: Moist well drained soil, responding to Summer watering.
Localities: 47, 48, 64, 69, 70, 74, 76
Distribution: All states except NT
Synonym: Previously referred to as *H. stricta*

Hibbertia sericea var. sericea

Hibbertia sericea var. sericea — Silky Guinea-flower

Size: 0.3–1 m x 0.6 m — **F P**
Habitat: Tea-tree heath
Form: Small erect shrub covered in silky hairs
Foliage: Dark green oblong leaves to 25 mm long
Flowers: Profuse terminal clusters of yellow flowers; October to December
Requirements: Well drained soil
Comments: Cut back after flowering.
Localities: 33, 34A, 67–71, 73–75
Distribution: Vic, Qld, NSW, Tas, SA

Hibbertia stricta var. stricta — Erect Guinea-flower

Size: 0.4–1 m x 0.3–1 m — **F P N**
Habitat: Widespread in sclerophyll woodland, valley sclerophyll forest, tea-tree heath
Form: Showy rounded to erect shrub
Foliage: Narrow dull grey-green leaves to 12 mm long
Flowers: Light yellow distinctly stalked flowers may occur at any time, peaking August to November
Requirements: Well drained moist soils
Comments: Drought tolerant once established. Similar to *H. riparia* which has either sessile or sub-sessile flowers.
Localities: Newport#, 33, 34A, 35, 44, 46, 47, 49–51, 58–63, 65–68, 74, 75
Distribution: All states
Synonym: Previously referred to as *H. australis*

Hibbertia stricta var. *stricta*

Hibbertia virgata var. virgata — Twiggy Guinea-flower

Size: 0.3–0.6 m x 0.6–1 m — **F P**
Habitat: Tea-tree heath
Form: Open, twiggy shrub
Foliage: Narrow channelled leaves to 20 mm long, grouped along the stems
Flowers: Very showy, bright yellow flowers to 25 mm wide, produced over a long period from Winter to Spring
Localities: Baxter, 74
Distribution: Vic, Qld, NSW, Tas, SA

Hovea — Fabaceae

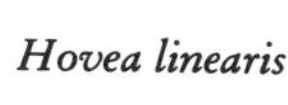

Hovea linearis

Hovea linearis — Common Hovea, Blue Bonnet, Bird's Eye

Size: 0.3–0.6 m x 0.3 m — **P N**
Habitat: Dry and valley sclerophyll forest, tea-tree heath
Form: Open trailing sub-shrub
Foliage: Variable olive-green leaves, lower leaves oval, becoming narrower and longer up the stem to 65 mm long
Flowers: Small mauve (or rarely white) pea flowers along the stems August to October. Rounded green seed pods turn black when ripe.
Requirements: Dry well drained soil
Comments: A dainty little plant to grow amongst other plants and under eucalypts.
Propagation: Scarified seed, cuttings
Localities: 34, 34A, 36, 37, 39–44, 46–56, 58, 59, 62–64, 67#, 70
Distribution: Vic, Qld, NSW, Tas, SA
Synonym: *H. heterophylla*

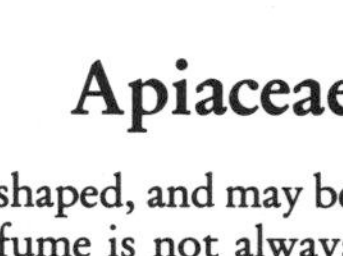

Hydrocotyle — Apiaceae

Hydrocotyles are either prostrate stoloniferous perennial herbs or small erect annuals. Their leaves are circular to kidney-shaped, and may be entire or lobed, usually with toothed margins. The inconspicuous flowers are grouped together in umbels. Their perfume is not always pleasant. They are useful ground covers when grown in shady, moist areas. Propagation is by seed, division of rooted nodes or cuttings.

Hydrocotyle callicarpa — Small or Tiny Pennywort

Size: 2.5–8 cm high — **F P N**
Habitat: Valley sclerophyll forest, primary dune scrub, grassy low open forest
Form: Erect annual herb
Foliage: Kidney-shaped stalkless leaves to 10 mm across, deeply divided into 3–5 lobed segments
Flowers: 6–16 minute light green flowers, in umbels on long stalks; August to November
Requirements: Moist well drained soil
Localities: 35, 36, 41, 42, 44, 47, 48, 53, 55, 67#, 74–76
Distribution: Vic, NSW, Tas, SA, WA

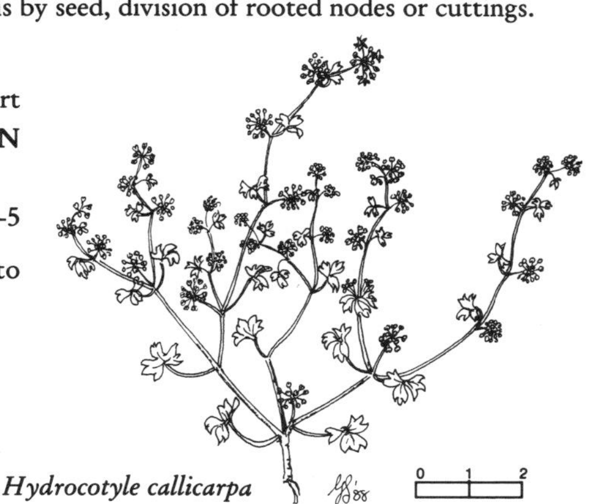

Hydrocotyle callicarpa

SCALE: 0 1cm 2cm — The scale representation on each plant equals 2cm.

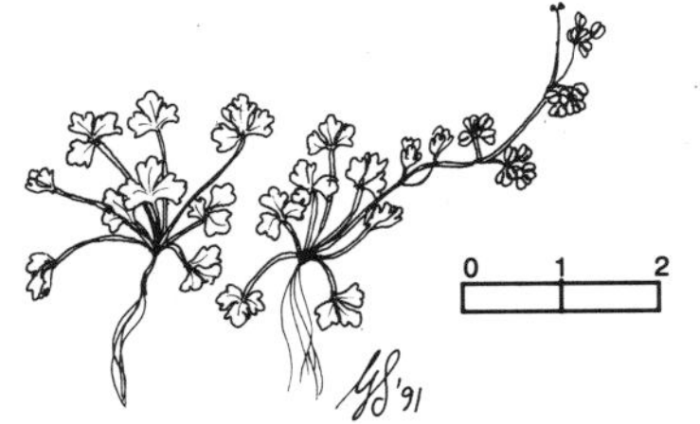

Hydrocotyle capillaris

Hydrocotyle capillaris

Thread Pennywort

F P

Size: 12 mm x 25 mm
Habitat: Valley sclerophyll forest, grasslands, saltmarshes
Form: Wiry, erect annual
Foliage: 3–5 lobed leaves to 8 mm long
Flowers: Nearly stalkless umbels of tiny white flowers
Comments: Locally rare.
Localities: Werribee 1911, Research, 3, 41, 42
Distribution: Vic, NSW, Tas, SA, WA

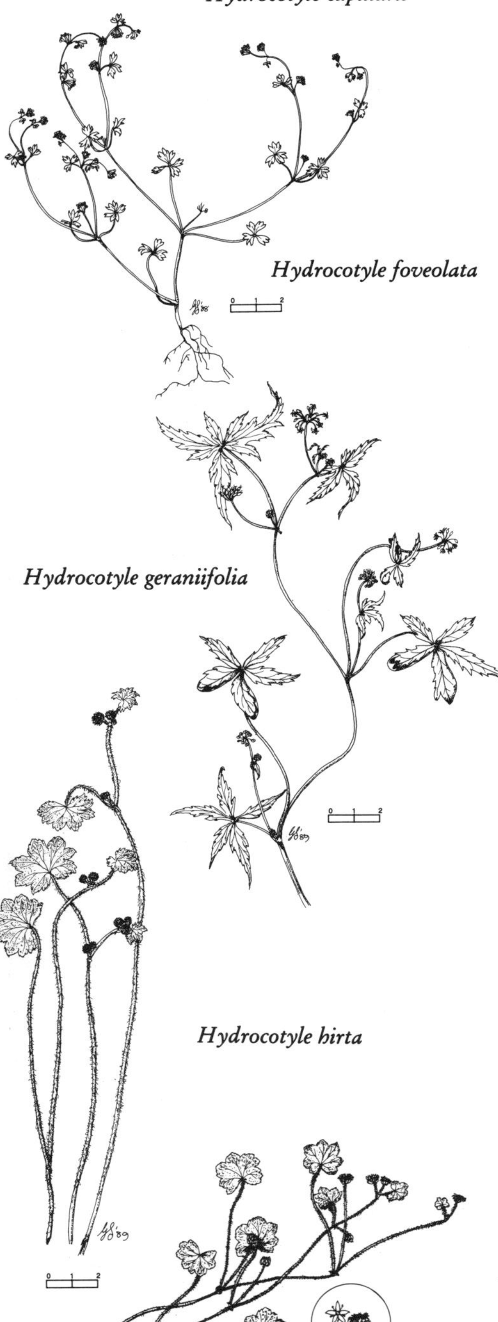

Hydrocotyle foveolata

Hydrocotyle geraniifolia

Hydrocotyle hirta

Hydrocotyle foveolata

Yellow Pennywort

P

Size: to 10 cm high
Habitat: Valley sclerophyll forest, tea-tree heath
Form: Tiny erect annual
Foliage: Yellowish, 3-lobed leaves with scattered long hairs, each lobe having 3 blunt teeth
Flowers: Stalkless clusters of 3–6 tiny flowers; September to November.
Localities: Warrandyte, 36, 41, 44, 50A, 51, 54, 55, 74, 75
Distribution: Vic, Tas, SA

Hydrocotyle geraniifolia

Forest Pennywort

P N

Habitat: Fern gullies of wet and valley sclerophyll forest
Form: Trailing perennial herb
Foliage: Dark green leaves are deeply divided into 3–5 toothed, lanceolate segments
Flowers: Umbels of stalked small white flowers; Summer
Requirements: Moist soil
Localities: 55–58
Distribution: Vic, NSW

Hydrocotyle hirta

Hairy Pennywort

P

Habitat: Damp, wet and valley sclerophyll forests, swamp and wattle tea-tree scrub
Form: Carpeting perennial herb
Foliage: Hairy stems and round or kidney-shaped leaves to 25 mm long on long stalks
Flowers: Tiny stalkless pale yellow flowers in a tight cluster; Summer
Comments: Spreads by above ground creeping stems.
Localities: 34A, 42, 44, 47, 54–58, 60, 71, 74–76
Distribution: All states

Hydrocotyle hirta

Hydrocotyle laxiflora

Stinking Pennywort

P N

Size: 10–20 cm x 1–2 m
Habitat: Riparian woodland, dry and valley sclerophyll forests
Form: Creeping perennial herb
Foliage: Hairy, round or kidney-shaped leaves to 40 mm long with 5–11 scalloped lobes
Flowers: Globular umbels of tiny greenish-yellow flowers to 20 mm across; mainly October to December, emitting a strong offensive odour. Male flowers are on long stalks whilst female flowers occur on shorter stalks.
Requirements: Moist soils on poor sites
Comments: Spreads by underground rhizomes. A useful groundcover in shady bush areas.
Localities: 26, 29#, 35, 39, 41, 42, 44, 47–49, 50A, 58–60, 62–67, 69#, 71, 72, 74, 76
Distribution: Vic, Qld, NSW, Tas, SA

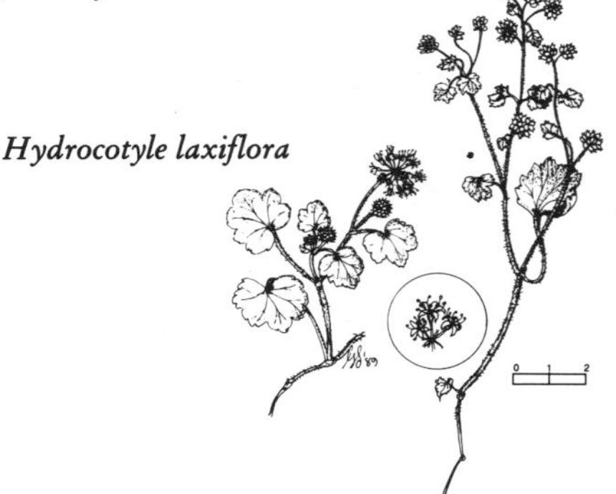

Hydrocotyle laxiflora

Hydrocotyle medicaginoides

Trefoil Pennywort

P

Size: to 15 cm high
Habitat: Wattle tea-tree scrub
Form: Slender annual herb
Foliage: Fan-shaped leaves to 15 mm long have 3 deeply cut lobes
Flowers: Globular umbel of almost sessile greenish-white flowers tinged with purple; September to November
Requirements: Moist soil, tolerating some saltiness
Comments: Locally rare.
Localities: 74
Distribution: Vic, SA, WA

Hydrocotyle muscosa

Mossy Pennywort

Size: to 20 cm high — P
Habitat: Freshwater swamps and along watercourses in grassy low open forest
Form: Dense matting perennial herb with thread-like stems, spreading by underground stolons
Foliage: Round shiny leaves to 15 mm across, deeply divided into 5 wedge-shaped leaflets, each entire or 3-toothed at the end; long hairs below.
Flowers: Small long-stalked umbels of 3–4 sessile deep purplish-red flowers; September to March
Requirements: Moist to wet soils
Localities: 60
Distribution: Vic, Tas, SA

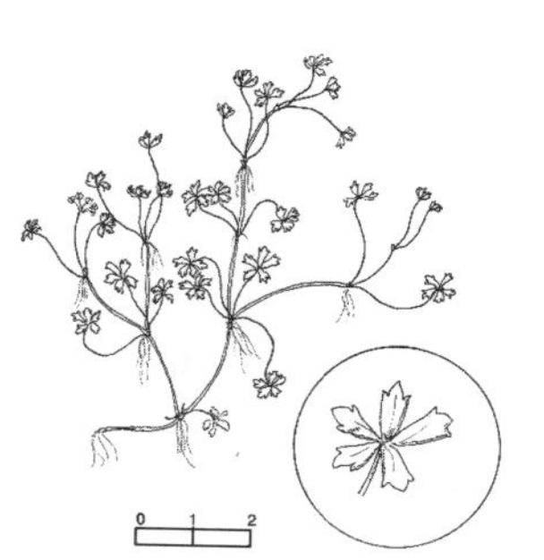

Hydrocotyle muscosa

Hydocotyle sibthorpioides

Shining Pennywort

Size: Prostrate x 0.6–2 m — P
Habitat: Valley sclerophyll forest, grassy wetlands
Form: Trailing perennial matting herb
Foliage: Hairy, shiny light green circular leaves
Flowers: Tiny stalkless green flowers in terminal, globular umbels
Requirements: Moist soils, tolerating some sun
Comments: Often found in poorly drained lawns.
Localities: Laverton Nth, Rockbank, 17, 35, 41, 42, 69A
Distribution: Vic, NSW, Tas; PNG

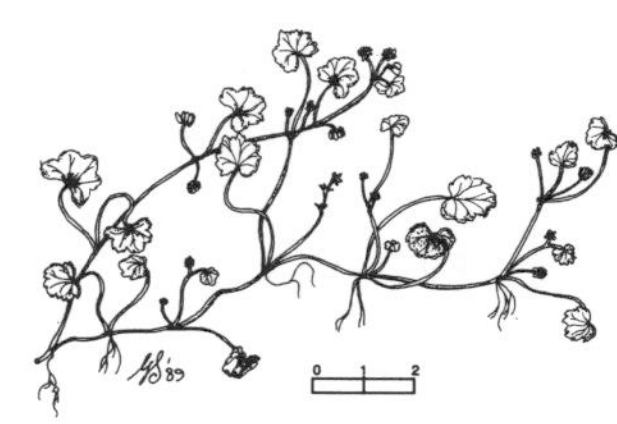

Hydrocotyle sibthorpioides

Hydrocotyle tripartita

Slender Pennywort

P

Habitat: Grassy low open forest, box woodland
Form: Hairy, slender trailing perennial herb
Foliage: Leaves deeply divided into 3 toothed segments
Flowers: Minute, almost stalkless, purplish-red flowers in umbels all year, peaking November to March
Requirements: Moist soils
Localities: St. Kilda#, 17#, 18, 34A, 44, 60, 67#
Distribution: Vic, Qld, NSW, Tas, SA

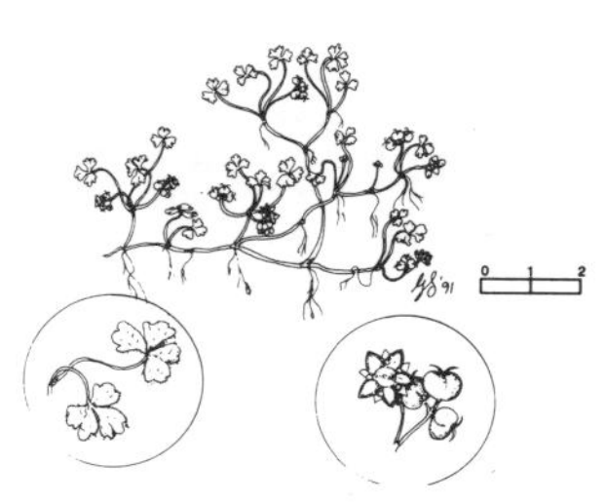

Hydrocotyle tripartita

Hydrocotyle verticillata

Common or Shield Pennywort

P

Habitat: Freshwater swamps in riparian and wattle tea-tree scrub, valley sclerophyll forest
Form: Creeping perennial herb
Foliage: Circular light green leaves to 60 mm across, leaf attached to the stalk on its undersurface (peltate)
Flowers: Flower stalks rise from creeping roots, having whorls of small umbels of white flowers; November to April
Requirements: Wet soil
Localities: 28, 35, 36, 67#
Distribution: Vic, Qld, NSW, SA

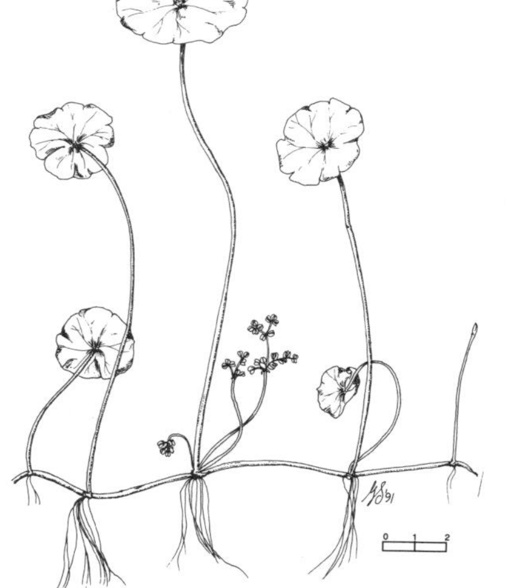

Hydrocotyle verticillata

Hymenanthera — Violaceae

Hymenanthera dentata

Tree Violet

Size: 2–4 m x 1–2.5 m — F P
Habitat: Riparian scrub, box woodland
Form: Rigid, often spiny, spreading shrub
Foliage: Dark green oblong, toothed leaves to 50 mm long, paler green below
Flowers: Masses of fragrant tiny cream bell flowers hanging along branches; September to November, followed by pale green to purple berries
Requirements: Well drained soils responding to extra watering
Comments: A variable shrub being lush in lightly shaded gullies but becoming stunted and spiny in exposed rocky areas.
Propagation: Seeds, cuttings
Localities: Werribee R., Seaford, 8, 14–16, 18, 23–30, 32–36, 39, 42, 44, 47, 61–64
Distribution: Vic, NSW, Tas, SA
Synonym: The variety *angustifolia* has now been combined with this species.

Hymenanthera dentata

Hymenanthera sp. aff. dentata

Size: to 1.5 m high — F
Habitat: Plains grassland, escarpments
Form: Intricately branched shrub, branches spine-tipped
Comments: Differs from *H. dentata* in that leaves are smaller and dark green and bluer fruit is often spotted. Flowers slightly later in the Melbourne area. Prefers drier sites. A threatened species which occurs on private property and is therefore not protected. Confused with the weed Boxthorn by landowners.
Localities: Deer Park, Rockbank, St Albans, Melton, Mt Cottrell
Synonym: Incorrectly referred to as *H.* sp. aff. *crassifolia*.

SCALE: 0 1cm 2cm — The scale representation on each plant equals 2cm.

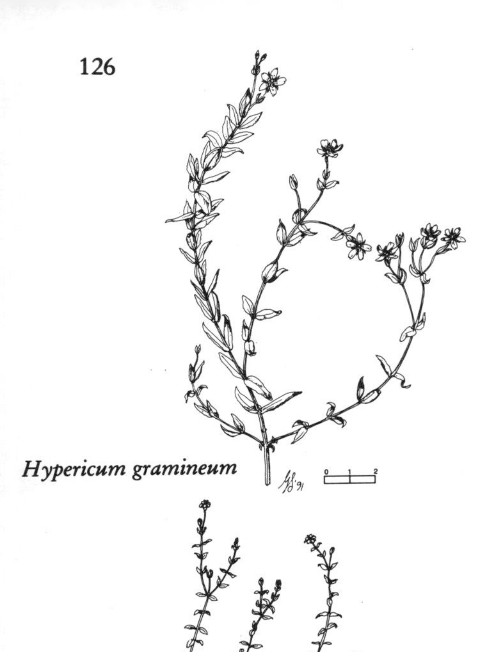

Hypericum gramineum

Hypericum japonicum

Hypericum — Hypericaceae

Hypericum gramineum

Small St. John's Wort

Size: to 25 cm x 5–20 cm — F P
Habitat: Widespread in sclerophyll and red gum woodlands, grassy low open forest, wattle tea-tree scrub, plains grassland, dry and valley sclerophyll forests
Form: Erect perennial herb, stems often ridged
Foliage: Stem-clasping blue-green oblong leaves to 20 mm long, wavy on edges
Flowers: Cup-shaped orange-yellow flowers to 10 mm across in loose clusters above the leaves; October to January
Requirements: Most soils tolerating moisture and Summer dryness
Propagation: Seed
Localities: 5–7, 10–12, 16–18, 24, 26, 28, 32, 34A–36, 38–44, 46–68, 69A–71, 74–76
Distribution: All states

Hypericum japonicum

Matted St. John's Wort

Size: to 10 cm x 15 cm — P
Habitat: Damp sclerophyll forest, swamp and wattle tea-tree scrub
Form: Weak, trailing or matted herb, smaller than *H. gramineum*
Foliage: Oval to oblong, green leaves are not stem clasping
Foliage: Solitary or few yellow flowers, to 8 mm wide; Spring and Summer
Requirements: Moist soils, tolerating Summer dryness
Localities: Montrose, 29#, 40, 42, 54, 56, 57, 67, 71, 74
Distribution: All states except NT

Indigofera — Fabaceae

Indigofera australis

Austral Indigo

Size: 1–2 m x 1–2 m — F P N
Habitat: Widespread in riparian scrub, valley and damp sclerophyll forests, grassy low open forest
Form: Open, spreading to erect shrub
Foliage: Pinnate blue-green leaves with elliptical leaflets 10–30 mm long
Flowers: Sprays of mauve, occasionally pink or white, pea flowers; September to December
Requirements: Adaptable to any well drained soil. Lime tolerant
Comments: Very attractive in flower, it is a useful shrub for understorey planting. Pruning is important to maintain bushiness and vigour. The crushed roots were used by the Aborigines to poison fish. They also obtained blue dye from the flowers.
Propagation: Scarified seed
Localities: Research, St Albans, 1, 10, 16, 26, 27, 29, 30, 32–35, 37, 41, 42, 44, 47–49, 50A, 51, 53, 55–67#, 74, 76
Distribution: All states

Indigofera australis

Isoetopsis — Asteracea

Isoetopsis graminifolia

Grass cushions

Size: 20–50 mm high — F
Habitat: Plains grasslands, red gum woodland
Form: Tufted, stemless annual herb
Foliage: Grass-like leaves to 50 mm long
Flowers: In greenish-white, papery flowerheads at the base of the leaves; August to November
Requirements: Dry soils
Comments: Once more widespread in Melbourne it is now known from very few sites.
Propagation: Seed
Localities: Sydenham, Rockbank, St Albans, Sunbury, Bundoora, 26, 42, 49
Distribution: All states

Isopogon ceratophyllus

Isopogon — Proteaceae

Isopogon ceratophyllus

Horny Cone-bush

Size: 0.2–0.6 m x 0.5–1.2 m — F P
Habitat: Tea-tree heath
Form: Stiff, rounded dwarf shrub
Foliage: Rigid, very prickly, finely divided light green leaves to 80 mm long, segments narrow to triangular
Flowers: Terminal golden-yellow flowerheads to 30 mm wide amongst the leaves; September to November. Fruiting cones to 20 mm wide.
Requirements: Moist well drained sandy soil, tolerating dryness once established
Comments: A slow growing plant, difficult to maintain for long periods unless in ideal conditions. Must be moist for extended periods. Locally rare.
Propagation: Seed, cuttings—using firm young growth
Localities: Baxter, 67–69, 73–75
Distribution: Vic, NSW, Tas, SA

Isotoma **Campanulaceae**

Isotoma fluviatilis ssp. australis — Swamp Isotome

Size: Prostrate x 1 m **F P**
Habitat: Plains grassland, riparian and wattle tea-tree scrub in bogs and swamps
Form: Dense matting plant
Foliage: Crowded, narrow slightly toothed leaves to 10 mm long
Flowers: Small blue starry flowers; October to November
Requirements: Moist to wet conditions
Comments: An excellent self-layering ground cover for damp areas and poolside plantings. Plant 30 cm apart to establish a quick cover. Restricted to very few sites.
Propagation: Seeds, cuttings, division
Localities: Knox, 17#, 26, 29#, 35, 42, 49, 67#, 75
Distribution: Vic, Qld, NSW, Tas, SA; NZ

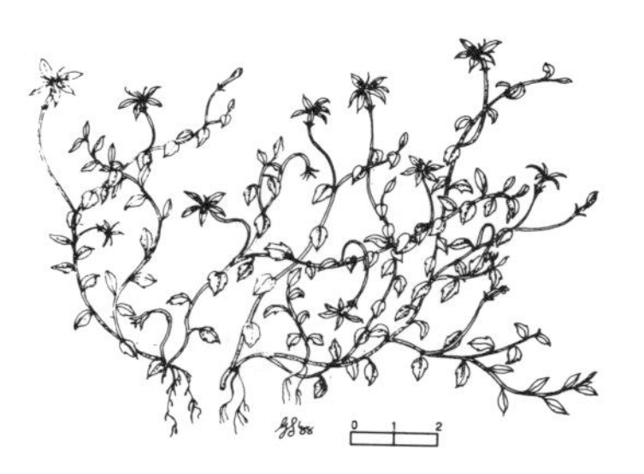

Isotoma fluviatilis ssp. *australis*

Ixiolaena **Asteraceae**

Ixiolaena leptolepis — Stalked Plover Daisy

Size: 10–40 cm x 10–40 cm **F**
Habitat: Plains grasslands
Form: Upright perennial herb
Foliage: Rough linear to lanceolate leaves to 15 mm long, pointed at the end
Flowers: Long stalked, rounded flowerheads of many yellow tubular florets; August to November
Requirements: Well drained heavy soils, tolerating lime and short periods of wetness
Comments: Stems and branches are covered with loose cottony hairs. Locally rare. This species is presently undergoing revision.
Propagation: Seed, cuttings
Localities: Sydenham
Distribution: All mainland states

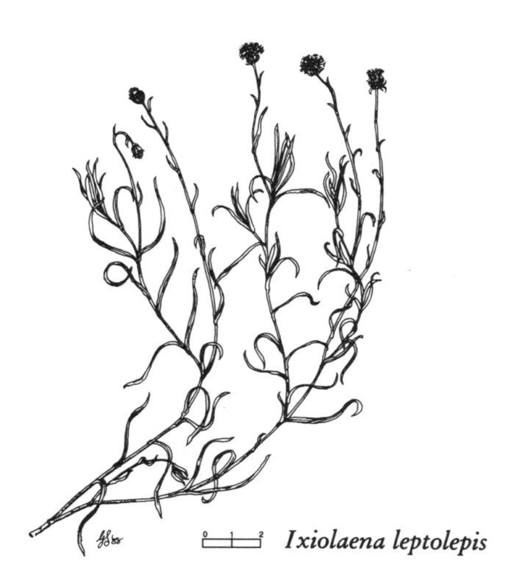

Ixiolaena leptolepis

Ixiolaena sp. — Woolly Buttons

Size: to 0.5 m high **F**
Habitat: Grasslands and floodplains of the basalt plains
Form: Perennial shrublet
Foliage: Soft, narrow-linear grey leaves. The leaves and branches are covered in white cottony hairs.
Flowers: Single yellow flowerheads are held erect on long stalks; September to January.
Requirements: Well drained heavy soil, tolerating dry periods but responds to Summer watering in the garden
Comments: An endangered plant in Melbourne. This species is undergoing review and may be found to be conspecific with *Ixiolaena leptolepis*.
Localities: St Albans 1938, Sydenham 1950; Laverton, Deer Park
Distribution: Vic, NSW, Tas
Synonym: *Leptorhynchos panaetioides*

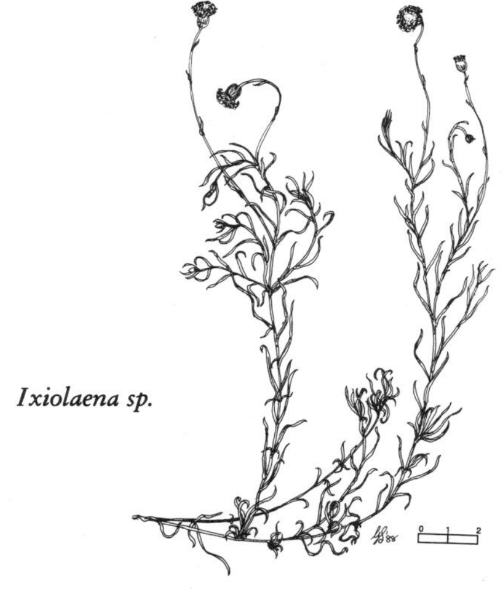

Ixiolaena sp.

Kennedia **Fabaceae**

Kennedia prostrata — Running Postman, Scarlet Runner

Size: Prostrate x 1–2.5 m **F P**
Habitat: Widespread in plains grassland, red gum woodland, riparian scrub, dry and valley sclerophyll forests, tea-tree heath, grassy low open forest
Form: Open trailing or densely matting perennial
Foliage: Crinkly and hairy grey-green trifoliate leaves, leaflets 6–18 mm long
Flowers: Single scarlet pea flowers scattered along stems; April to December
Requirements: Well drained soils
Comments: Drought tolerant once established. Recolonises in disturbed areas and after fire. Grows well in a hanging basket. The Aborigines sucked the nectar and also used the stems as twine.
Propagation: Scarified seed, cuttings
Localities: Altona, 1, 10, 12, 15, 16, 21, 26, 29, 30, 32–39, 41, 42, 44, 46–49, 50A, 51, 53, 55, 56, 58, 61–63, 65#–69A, 71, 72, 74–76
Distribution: All states except NT

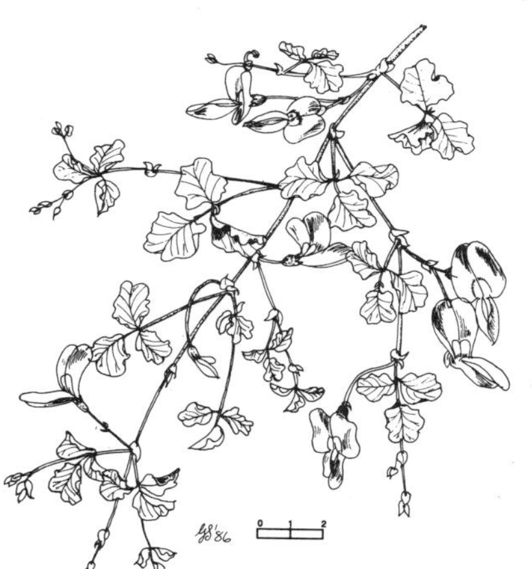

Kennedia prostrata

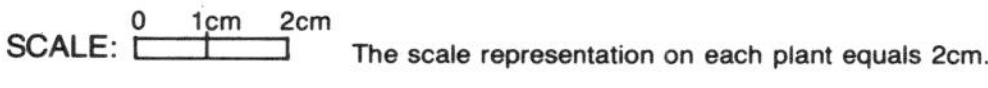

The scale representation on each plant equals 2cm.

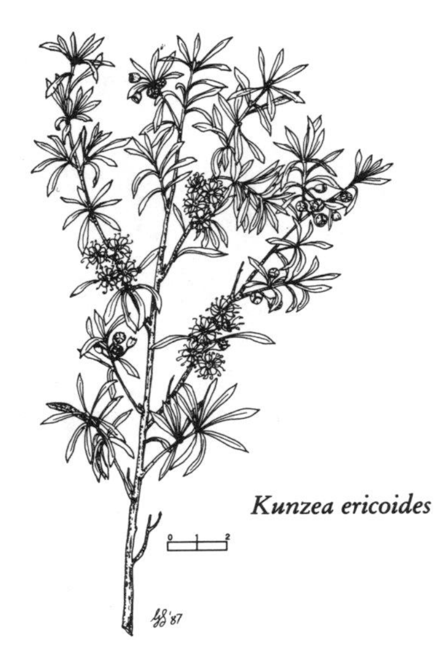
Kunzea ericoides

Kunzea — Myrtaceae

Kunzea ericoides

Burgan
F P

Size:	2–5 m x 2–4 m
Habitat:	Dry and valley sclerophyll forests
Form:	Dense to open weeping shrub
Foliage:	Variable, generally narrow dark green leaves from 8–25 mm long
Flowers:	Masses of long-stalked white flowers along the stems; November to February
Requirements:	Adaptable, tolerating wet and dry periods
Comments:	A very attractive, fast-growing shrub, particularly the weeping form. Suitable for screening. It tolerates hard pruning. Seeds are shed annually and it may revegetate a cleared area quickly. The wood was important to the Aborigines for making fighting implements.
Propagation:	Seed, cuttings
Localities:	30, 31, 33–35, 39–42, 44, 47–49, 50A–56, 59, 61–63, 67#, 71, 74
Distribution:	Vic, Qld, NSW
Synonym:	*Leptospermum phylicoides*

Lagenifera — Asteraceae

Lagenifera is closely related to Brachyscome, differing in the fruit, which is bottle-shaped instead of blunt.

Lagenifera gracilis

Lagenifera gracilis

Slender Bottle Daisy
F P

Size:	to 25 cm x 8 cm
Habitat:	Widespread in grassy low open forest, wattle tea-tree scrub, dry and valley sclerophyll forests
Form:	Perennial herb with fleshy roots
Foliage:	Basal rosette of dark green obovate to spathulate leaves, lighter below, to 55 mm long, with 2–4 pairs of teeth and wavy margins
Flowers:	Small mauve or white flowerheads on smooth, often blackish, wiry stalks 8–25 cm high; October to February
Requirements:	Damp well drained soils
Comments:	This tiny daisy is suitable for containers and can be established under trees, provided moisture is available.
Propagation:	Seed
Localities:	34A, 40–42, 44, 47, 48, 50, 51, 53–56, 59, 63, 64, 74–76
Distribution:	All states

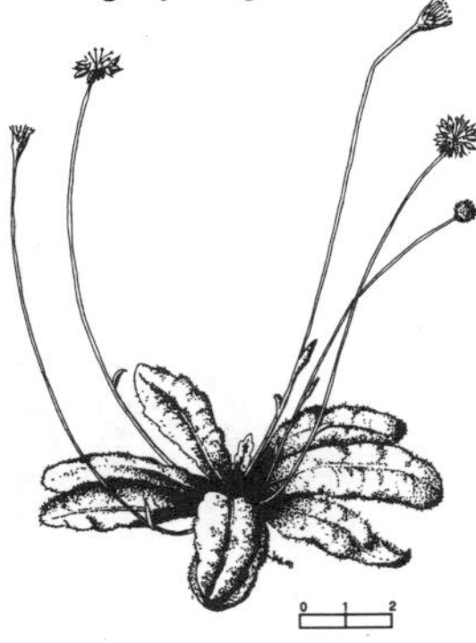
Lagenifera huegelii

Lagenifera huegelii

Coarse Bottle Daisy
F P

Size:	7–35 cm high
Habitat:	Dry sclerophyll forest, box woodland
Form:	Small, hairy perennial herb with fleshy roots
Foliage:	Deeply lobed oblanceolate basal leaves to 140 mm long, with 4–10 pairs of blunt teeth on wavy margins. Hairy flower stalks, 10–350 mm high, bear a few small, sessile, mostly entire, leaves, to 8 mm long.
Flowers:	White, pink or blue flowerheads; September to November and March to June
Requirements:	Moist well drained clay soil
Comments:	Locally rare.
Localities:	Eltham, Research, Sth of Melton
Distribution:	Vic, Tas, SA, WA

Lagenifera stipitata

Lagenifera stipitata

Common Lagenifera, Blue Bottle Daisy
F P

Size:	5–25 cm high
Habitat:	Wet, damp and valley sclerophyll forests, grassy open forest, tea-tree heath, wattle tea-tree scrub
Form:	Small stoloniferous perennial herb with a slender, hairy flower stalk to 25 cm high, and fibrous roots
Foliage:	May have a basal rosette; leaves similar to *L. gracilis* but hairy
Flowers:	Mauve flowerheads to 12 mm wide; Spring and Autumn
Requirements:	Adaptable to moist well drained soils
Propagation:	Seed, division
Localities:	34A–36, 38, 41–44, 47, 48, 50–53, 55–58, 60, 61, 63, 67#, 69A–71, 74–76
Distribution:	All states

Lasiopetalum — Sterculiaceae

Lasiopetalum baueri — Slender Velvet Bush

Size:	1–1.5 m x 1 m	**F**
Habitat:	Coastal cliffs and primary dune scrub	
Form:	Dense, erect, small shrub with a velvety covering of star-like hairs	
Foliage:	Narrow grey-green leaves, with recurved margins, to 45 mm long, hoary or rust-coloured below	
Flowers:	Small drooping clusters of hairy greyish-pink to white flowers. The petal-like organs are actually calyx lobes. October to February.	
Requirements:	Dry, well drained soil	
Comments:	An attractive plant which is now locally very rare. One plant remains in the Sandringham area.	
Propagation:	Cuttings	
Localities:	67	
Distribution:	Vic, NSW, Tas, SA	

Lasiopetalum baueri

Lavatera — Malvaceae

Lavatera plebeia var. plebeia — Australian Hollyhock

Size:	0.5–2.5 m high	**F**
Habitat:	Coastal limestone in saltmarshes or basalt plains in riparian scrub	
Form:	Erect annual or perennial herb with downy star-shaped hairs	
Foliage:	Dark green, broadly ovate, 5–7 lobed leaves, 20–120 mm across, on long stalks	
Flowers:	Clusters of large, attractive, prominently-veined flowers, pink, white or lilac with lemon centres, petals notched; July to December	
Requirements:	Adaptable to most conditions	
Comments:	A short lived plant, it may shoot again from its woody base if pruned back hard. It is a useful background plant for a sunny rockery. The Aborigines baked the stems before chewing them. A locally rare plant of Port Phillip Bay.	
Propagation:	Seed	
Localities:	Port Melbourne 1850, Altona, 16, 18, 26, 32	
Distribution:	All states	

Lavatera plebeia var. *plebeia*

Lavatera plebeia var. tomentosa

		F
Habitat:	Coastal primary dune scrub	
Comments:	A stouter shrub covered in dense velvety hairs. White flowers most of the year. Remains in one location in the Melbourne area.	
Localities:	Altona	
Distribution:	Vic, Tas, SA, WA	

Lawrencia — Malvaceae

Lawrencia spicata — Salt Lawrencia

Size:	0.3–1.8 m high	**F**
Habitat:	Saltmarshes, peat swamps of tea-tree heath	
Form:	Erect perennial rising from a basal rosette	
Foliage:	Elliptic to narrowly ovate, toothed, long-stalked basal leaves, to 115 mm x 60 mm; stem leaves smaller, becoming sessile and entire	
Flowers:	Dense cylindrical, terminal spikes of pale yellow to white flowers; October to February.	
Requirements:	Moist salty soil	
Comments:	Flowers emit a strong odour. Locally rare and endangered within the Melbourne area.	
Propagation:	Seed	
Localities:	2, 3, 7, 67#	
Distribution:	Vic, Tas, SA, WA	

Lawrencia spicata

Lepidium — Brassicaceae

Lepidium aschersonii — Swamp or Spiny Pepper Cress

Size:	30 cm high	**F**
Habitat:	Saltmarshes	
Form:	Branched shrubby perennial herb covered in short hairs. Branchlets end in a spine.	
Foliage:	Basal leaves bipinnate to 120 mm long; sessile upper leaves becoming smaller and lanceolate	
Flowers:	Short racemes of tiny greenish-white flowers; November to December	
Requirements:	Moist soils, salt tolerant	
Comments:	This is an endangered species Australia-wide which is now extinct in Melbourne. The leaves of *Lepidium* species were steamed by the Aborigines prior to eating.	
Propagation:	Seed	
Localities:	Was collected at Williamstown	
Distribution:	Vic, NSW, WA	

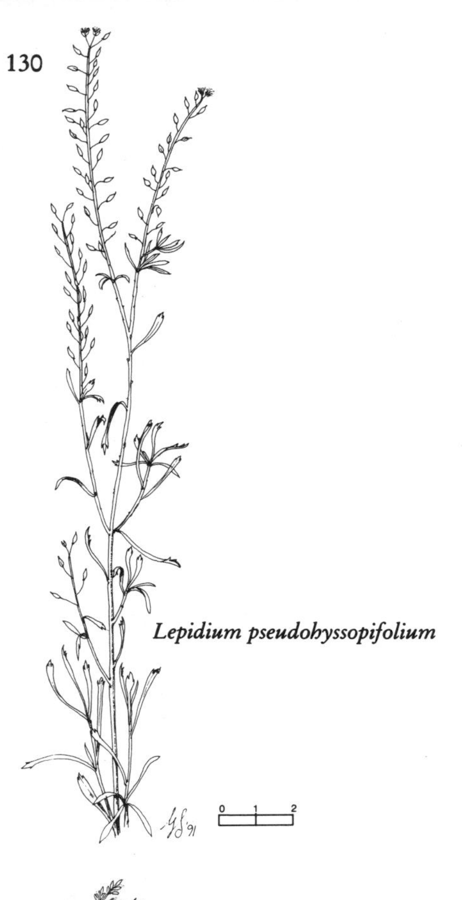

Lepidium pseudohyssopifolium

Lepidium pseudohyssopifolium

Pepper Cress

F P

Size: 0.4 m high
Habitat: Plains grassland, riparian scrub, box woodland
Form: Erect, annual or perennial herb with glabrous stems
Foliage: Leaves are variable in size and shape from narrow and entire to 20 mm long, to broadly lanceolate and pinnate or toothed, to 90 mm long.
Flowers: Long spikes of tiny white flowers on glabrous stalks; June to September.
Requirements: Tolerates dry periods but responds well to summer watering
Comments: Rare throughout its range, it is endangered in Melbourne.
Localities: Early collections from Port Melbourne and Werribee; Sunbury, Essendon, Werribee, 16, 26, 31#, 32, 35, 36, 67#
Distribution: Vic, Qld, NSW, SA, WA
Synonym: Was previously confused with *L. hyssopifolium*

Lepidium pseudotasmanicum

Peppercress

P

Size: 20–30 cm high
Habitat: Riparian scrub
Form: Erect, branching annual or biennial herb
Comments: The major feature distinguishing this species from *L. pseudohyssopifolium* is the hairy flower stalk which is shorter or equal to the length of the fruit. Also endangered in the Melbourne area.
Localities: Yarra R., 44, 49
Distribution: Vic, Qld, NSW, Tas, WA

Leptinella — Asteraceae

Leptinella reptans

Creeping Cotula

F P

Size: Prostrate x 1 m
Habitat: Bogs in riparian scrub, coastal banksia woodland
Form: Self-layering perennial herb
Foliage: Pinnate leaves to 100 mm long
Flowers: Yellowish button flowers throughout the year
Requirements: Tolerates permanently wet soil
Propagation: Cuttings, division
Comments: Previously included with *L. reptans*, *L. longipes* possibly also occurred within the Melbourne area. It may be distinguished by its almost glabrous, semisucculent leaves. Segments are larger with blunt ends.
Localities: 28, 30, 42, 67#, 74
Distribution: Vic, Qld, NSW, Tas
Synonym: *Cotula reptans*

Leptinella reptans

Leptorhynchos — Asteraceae

Perennial herbs or sub-shrubs. The long flowering time of *Leptorhynchos* spp. makes them useful container or rockery specimens. The yellow flowerheads are held singly above the foliage on long stems and may be used, cut or dried, for decoration. Propagation is by seed or cutting.

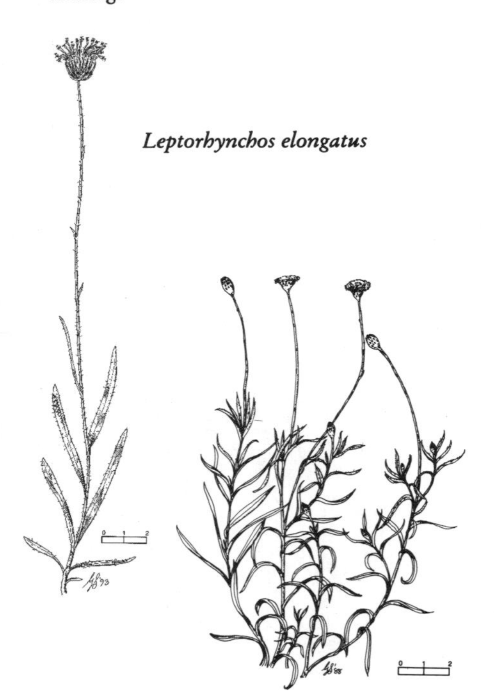

Leptorhynchos elongatus

Leptorhynchos squamatus

Leptorhynchos elongatus

Lanky Buttons

F

Size: 0.2–0.5 m x 0.2–0.6 m
Habitat: Dry sclerophyll forest
Form: Annual or perennial herb
Foliage: Linear-lanceolate leaves to 75 mm long
Flowers: White to pale yellow flowerheads; October to December.
Requirements: Well drained soil
Comments: A rare plant throughout Victoria, it is now extinct in Melbourne.
Localities: Early collection near Melbourne; 42#
Distribution: All states except WA

Leptorhynchos panaetioides = Ixiolaena sp.

Leptorhynchos squamatus

Scaly Buttons

F P

Size: 15–30 cm x 0.4 m
Habitat: Plains grassland, red gum woodland, valley sclerophyll forest
Form: Low spreading herb
Foliage: Linear-lanceolate, deep green leaves to 20 mm long, woolly white below, often concentrated on one side of the stem
Flowers: Small yellow flowerheads held above the foliage on long scaly stalks; September to January
Requirements: Well drained moist soils
Comments: Summer watering is beneficial. The local form has flowering stems to only 15 cm high.
Propagation: Seed, cutting, division
Localities: 2, 4, 5, 7, 10, 12, 13, 16–18, 25, 26, 28, 29, 34A, 35, 38, 39, 41, 42, 45, 49, 50A, 61, 67#
Distribution: Vic, Qld, NSW, Tas, SA

Leptorhynchos tenuifolius

Wiry Buttons

Size: 10–30 cm x 30 cm **F P**
Habitat: Plains grassland, red gum woodland, dry and valley sclerophyll forests, tea-tree heath, grassy low open forest
Form: Wiry, branched perennial
Foliage: Very narrow dark green leaves, woolly white below. Margins are rolled under.
Flowers: Single yellow flowerheads, to 10 mm wide, held erect; September to January
Requirements: Prefers well drained situations but accepts some moisture.
Localities: Kilsyth, 16, 26, 28, 35, 40–42, 44, 46–51, 54, 58–60, 62–67, 69, 69A, 71, 74–76
Distribution: Vic, SA

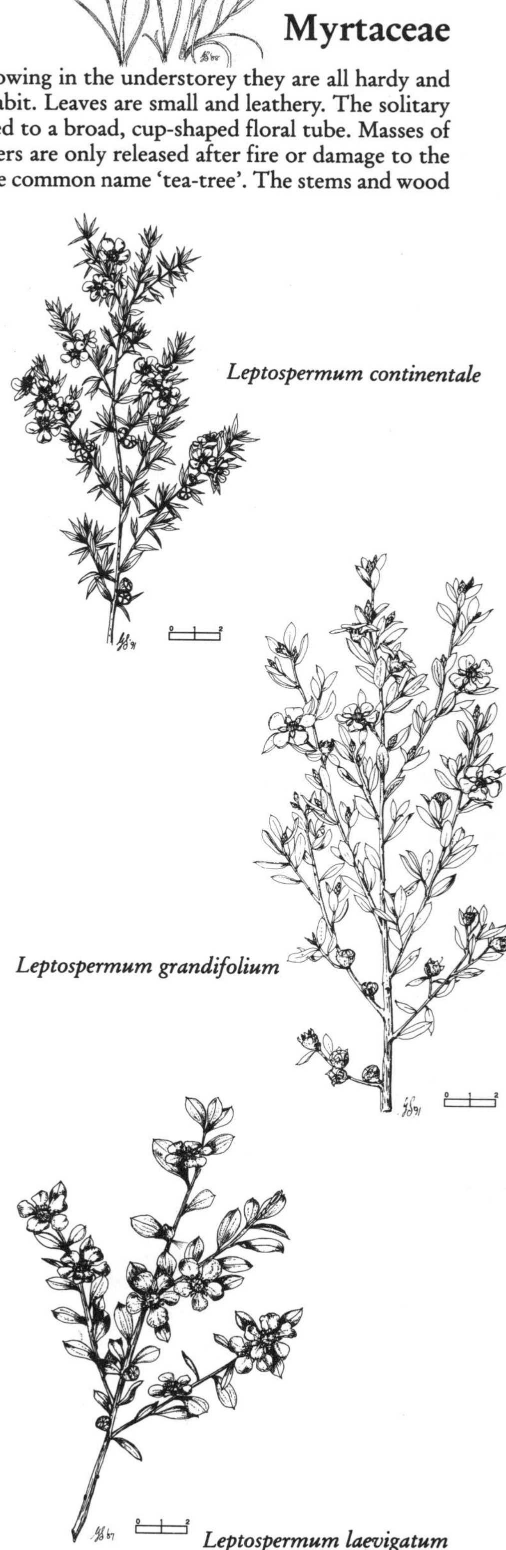

Leptorhynchos tenuifolius

Leptospermum

Myrtaceae

The 6 species of *Leptospermum* local to Melbourne are shrubs or small trees. Generally growing in the understorey they are all hardy and make attractive garden specimens, most providing a good screen through their compact habit. Leaves are small and leathery. The solitary white or pink flowers cover the plant for several months. The often large petals are attached to a broad, cup-shaped floral tube. Masses of seed are stored in woody capsules. Some species drop their capsules after a year while others are only released after fire or damage to the plant. The leaves of some species were used by the early settlers as a tea substitute, hence the common name 'tea-tree'. The stems and wood were used by the Aborigines to make pegs and spears. Propagation is by seed or cuttings.

Leptospermum continentale

Prickly Tea-tree

Size: 1–4 m x 1–2 m **F P**
Habitat: Widespread in damp and valley sclerophyll forests, sclerophyll woodland, swamp and wattle tea-tree scrub, grassy low open forest, tea-tree heath
Form: Rigidly upright, dense or straggling shrub or small tree
Foliage: Leaves rigid, prickly and concave, variable, narrow-lanceolate to lanceolate to 12 mm x 3 mm; hairy, especially on young shoots
Flowers: Masses of white flowers to 10 mm wide; October to March
Requirements: Adaptable, tolerating moisture
Comments: Two forms of this species exist in Melbourne. The form occurring in open forests is tall and broad with scattered leaves that are sparsely hairy below in the centre only. The heathland form is smaller, low-branching and denser with shorter and narrower leaves that are more clustered and hairier below. The heathland form also has smaller flowers and flowers earlier. The two forms co-exist in the Montrose and Langwarrin areas. *L. continentale* is often confused with *L. scoparium* which does not occur in the Melbourne area.
Localities: Toolern Vale, 33–35, 40, 42–51, 53–68, 69A, 71, 73–76
Distribution: Vic, NSW, SA
Synonym: A newly named species, it was known as *L. juniperinum*, a species which only occurs in NSW.

Leptospermum continentale

Leptospermum grandifolium

Mountain Tea-tree

Size: 1.5–6 m high **F P**
Habitat: Damp sclerophyll forest
Form: Dense shrub to small rounded tree
Foliage: Large oblong glossy leaves to 30 mm long, paler and silky below, ending in a sharp point. New growth is silver and hairy.
Flowers: Large white flowers to 18 mm wide, borne at the ends of side branches; October to January. Woolly calyx tube persists as woolly base to large woody fruit
Requirements: Adaptable, preferring moist to wet soil
Localities: The Patch, Wattle Glen, 29, 47, 56
Distribution: Vic, NSW

Leptospermum grandifolium

Leptospermum juniperinum—see L. continentale

Leptospermum laevigatum

Coast Tea-tree

Size: 2–8 m x 2–4 m **F P**
Habitat: Primary dune scrub, tea-tree heath, coastal banksia woodland, grassy low open forest
Form: Tall shrub or small tree
Foliage: Thick, flat, dull green obovate leaves to 30 mm long
Flowers: Stalkless white flowers in pairs to 20 mm wide; August to October
Requirements: Well drained soil tolerating dryness once established
Comments: Attractive in flower this adaptable shrub makes a useful screen plant if pruned. Its twisted, gnarled trunk and flaking bark adds interest. It is suitable for front-line coastal planting. Great care needs to be taken when introduced outside its normal habitat as it may become an environmental weed. It has already spread further inland since European settlement. A naturally occurring hybrid with *L. myrsinoides* is found in the Mordialloc and Frankston areas.
Localities: 65–70, 74, 75
Distribution: Vic, NSW, Tas

Also illustrated p. 33

Leptospermum laevigatum

SCALE: 0 1cm 2cm The scale representation on each plant equals 2cm.

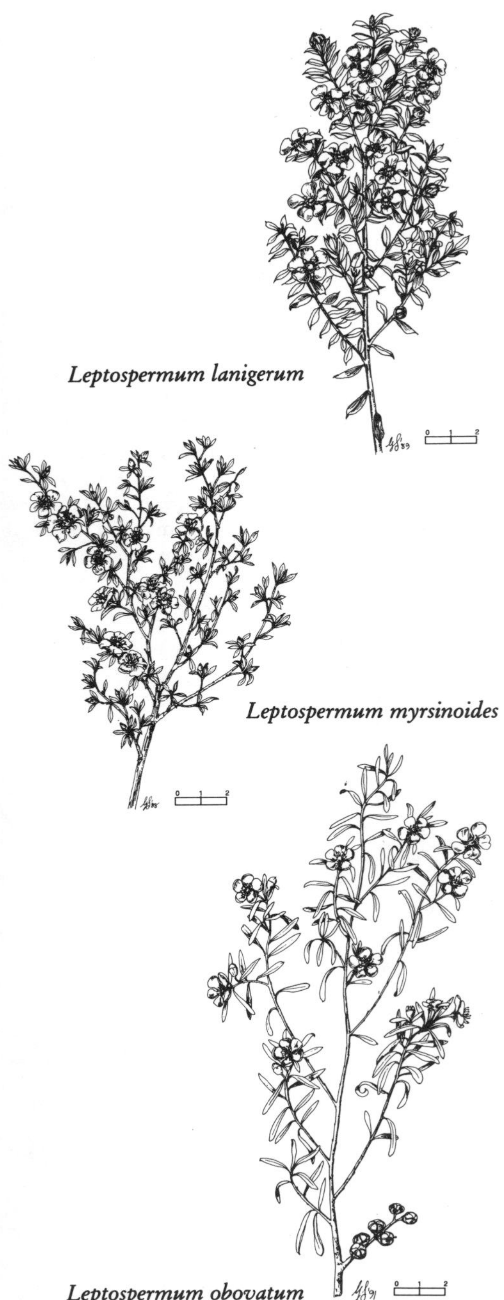

Leptospermum lanigerum

Leptospermum myrsinoides

Leptospermum obovatum

Leptospermum lanigerum

Woolly Tea-tree

Size: 2–6 m x 1–3 m — F P
Habitat: Riparian scrub and woodland, valley sclerophyll forest, tea-tree heath
Form: Dense shrub to erect small tree
Foliage: Variable oblong to narrowly oblanceolate greyish leaves 5–15 mm long, ending in a point. Young growth is silver and hairy on both sides, the upper surface becoming glabrous with age.
Flowers: Masses of white flowers to 15 mm wide; September to January. Densely hairy floral tube and capsule.
Requirements: Moist soils
Comments: An ornamental shrub, the grey-leafed forms provide an attractive foliage contrast. Regular pruning encourages a dense shrub. The wood was an important resource for the Aborigines, providing kangaroo spears and double-barbed spears.
Localities: Sunshine, 1, 8, 14, 16, 26, 28–30#, 33–36, 42, 47, 49, 54–57, 59, 66#–68, 74
Distribution: Vic, NSW, Tas, SA

Leptospermum myrsinoides

Heath or Silky Tea-tree

Size: 0.5–2.5 m x 1 m — F P
Habitat: Sclerophyll woodland, valley sclerophyll forest, tea-tree heath
Form: Compact or wiry shrub
Foliage: Dull green oblanceolate to obovate leaves to 10 mm long, concave above
Flowers: White or pink flowers to 15 mm wide, singly or paired, on pinkish stems; September to November. Only the base of the calyx has silky hairs.
Requirements: Adaptable, tolerating poor drainage
Comments: An attractive shrub for understorey planting.
Localities: Canterbury#, 37, 49, 50A, 59, 65–71, 73–75
Distribution: Vic, NSW, SA

Leptospermum obovatum

River or Blunt-leaf Tea-tree

Size: 2–4 m x 1.5–2 m — P
Habitat: Riparian scrub
Form: Dense erect shrub
Foliage: Thick, aromatic narrow to broad leaves with blunt tip, variable from 5–20 mm long
Flowers: Creamy white flowers to 12 mm wide, singly or in pairs; November to January
Requirements: Moist soils
Comments: Not common in the Melbourne area.
Localities: Yarra R, 31, 32, 34A, 35
Distribution: Vic, NSW

Leptostigma — Rubiaceae

Leptostigma reptans

Dwarf Nertera

Size: Prostrate x 20 cm — P N
Habitat: Valley sclerophyll forest
Form: Hairy, small spreading herb, rooting at the nodes
Foliage: Pointed, ovate leaves to 10 mm long
Flowers: Tiny tubular cream flowers to 12 mm long covered in long hairs, between terminal pairs of leaves; November to January. Attractive orange-red drupes follow flowering.
Requirements: Moist to wet soil
Comments: Suitable for a terrarium or beside ponds. It has regional significance in Melbourne as it is now known from very few locations locally.
Propagation: Division
Localities: 44
Distribution: Vic, NSW
Synonym: *Nertera reptans*

Leucochrysum albicans ssp. *albicans* var. *albicans*

Leucochrysum — Asteraceae

Leucochrysum albicans ssp. albicans var. albicans

Hoary Sunray

Size: 10–30 cm x 30 cm — F P
Habitat: Amongst rocks in dry sclerophyll forest
Form: Dense clumping perennial herb
Foliage: Long, narrow, hairy grey leaves to 100 mm long
Flowers: Yellow flowerheads, surrounded by showy white or yellow papery bracts, held on stems above the leaves; November to March
Requirements: Well drained soils
Comments: A very attractive rockery or container plant, it is useful as a cut or dried flower. Prune hard after flowering to promote bushiness.
Propagation: Fresh seed, cuttings
Localities: Eltham, Diamond Ck, 34A, 42
Distribution: Vic, Qld, NSW, Tas, SA
Synonym: *Helipterum albicans* ssp. *albicans* var. *albicans*

Leucophyta

Asteraceae

Leucophyta brownii

Cushion Bush

Size:	0.2–1 m x 0.5–2 m **F P**
Habitat:	Coastal headlands, primary dune scrub
Form:	Densely tangled rounded shrub
Foliage:	Grey hairy scale-like leaves
Flowers:	Pale yellow globular heads borne terminally; September to December
Requirements:	Well drained dry conditions, tolerates alkaline soil
Comments:	An attractive low shrub which withstands wind and salt spray and responds well to pruning. The grey foliage is able to reflect available light at night time making this an ideal plant for defining pathways in dimly lit areas.
Propagation:	Seed, cuttings—without mist
Localities:	Werribee#, St. Kilda, Williamstown, Mordialloc, Seaford, 67, 69A, 74
Distribution:	Vic, NSW, Tas, SA, WA
Synonym:	*Calocephalus brownii*

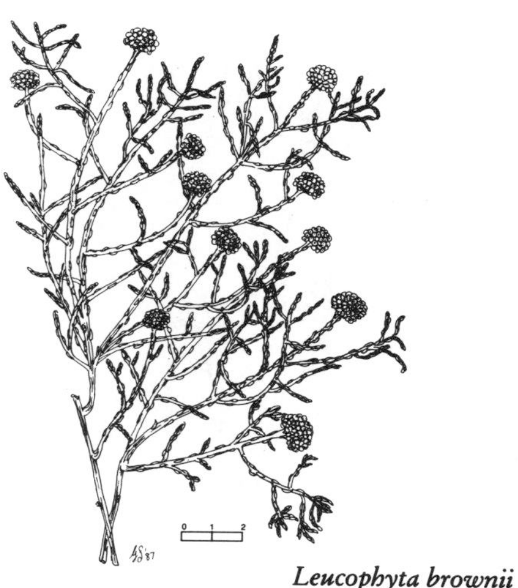

Leucophyta brownii

Leucopogon

Epacridaceae

Understorey shrubs of heathlands, Leucopogons are called 'Beard heaths' due to the dense beard of hairs on the corolla lobes. Flowers are followed by small, succulent drupes, which were eaten by the Aborigines. They require well drained soil and a cool rootrun. Propagation is by cuttings. Care needs to be taken with their fragile roots.

Leucopogon australis

Spike Beard Heath

Size:	1–1.5 m x 0.5–0.75 m **P**
Habitat:	Tea-tree heath
Form:	Upright shrub
Foliage:	Narrow dull green leaves to 50 mm long with parallel veins
Flowers:	Strongly perfumed tiny white flowers, densely bearded, in rigid terminal and axillary spikes shorter than leaves; September to November. Yellow or white drupes
Requirements:	Well drained damp sandy soil
Comments:	The branches are pale and acutely angled in section.
Localities:	67#, 75
Distribution:	Vic, Tas, SA, WA

Leucopogon ericoides

Pink Beard Heath

Size:	0.5–1.5 m x 0.7 m **P**
Habitat:	Tea-tree heath, dry sclerophyll forest
Form:	Upright wiry shrub
Foliage:	Prickly, narrow, dark green leaves to 10 mm long, margins curved under
Flowers:	Small clusters of white to pink bearded flowers in leaf axils follow pink buds; July to November. Drupes dryish.
Requirements:	Well drained soil, tolerating dry periods once established
Comments:	An attractive long-flowered plant, best when intermingled with other small shrubs.
Localities:	Eltham, 42, 44, 47, 63, 73–75
Distribution:	Vic, Qld, NSW, Tas, SA

Leucopogon parviflorus

Coast Beard Heath

Size:	1–4 m x 2–3 m **F P**
Habitat:	Coastal banksia woodland, primary dune scrub
Form:	Variable; much branched stunted shrub when exposed, small tree in scrub
Foliage:	Stiff elliptic to obovate leaves, paler below, to 30 mm long; new growth bright green
Flowers:	Masses of densely bearded white flowers tinged with maroon, in axillary spikes usually longer than the leaves; July to November. Edible round, white drupes
Requirements:	Well drained soils
Comments:	Bark is most attractive on old gnarled plants. It differs from *L. australis* in that leaves are broader and shorter, and the flowers lack perfume.
Localities:	Mordialloc, 67, 74, 75
Distribution:	All states except NT

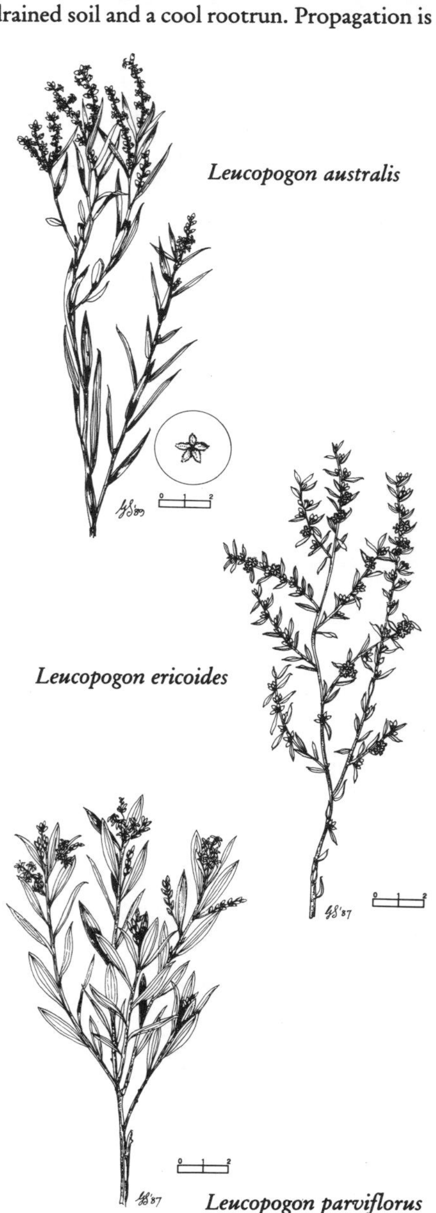

Leucopogon australis

Leucopogon ericoides

Leucopogon parviflorus

SCALE: 0 1cm 2cm The scale representation on each plant equals 2cm.

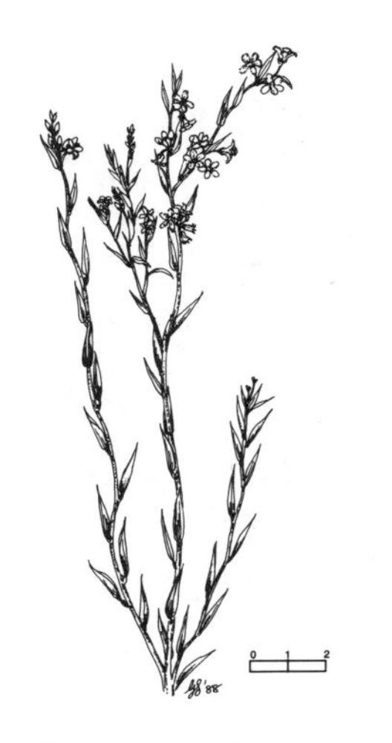
Leucopogon virgatus var. *virgatus*

Leucopogon virgatus var. **virgatus** — Common Beard Heath

Size: 0.3–1 m x 0.2–0.6 — F P
Habitat: Tea-tree heath, dry sclerophyll forest, grassy low open forest
Form: Upright wiry shrub
Foliage: Pointed concave, lanceolate leaves to 20 mm long, with 3 conspicuous parallel ribs on the underside. Some leaves are stem-clasping, others are spreading.
Flowers: Dense axillary spikes of fragrant, white bearded flowers at the ends of branches; July to December
Requirements: Well drained soils, tolerating some dryness once established; lime tolerant
Comments: An excellent garden plant, ideal for filling small gaps between other shrubs. Old plants may be rejuvenated by hard pruning.
Localities: Port Melbourne#, Clayton, 33, 34A, 41, 42, 44, 46–51, 53, 58, 65#, 67–70, 73, 76
Distribution: Vic, Qld, NSW, Tas, SA

Levenhookia — Stylidiaceae

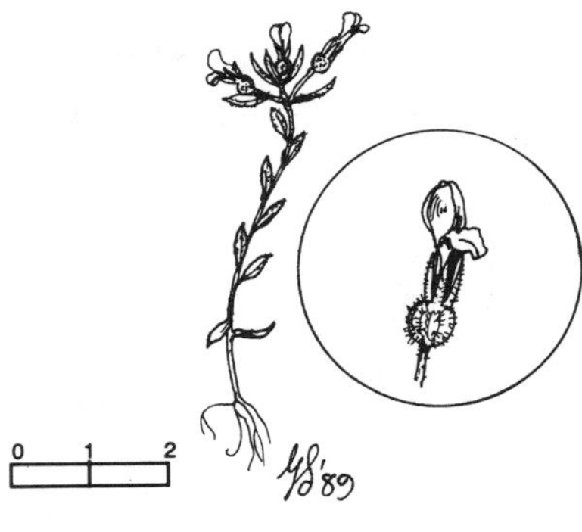
Levenhookia dubia

Levenhookia dubia — Hairy Stylewort

Size: 15–55 mm high — P
Habitat: Grassy wetlands, valley sclerophyll forest, tea-tree heath
Form: Inconspicuous, erect glandular-hairy herb with reddish stems
Foliage: Small obovate leaves to 6 mm long, lower leaves reddish and smaller than the upper green ones
Flowers: Small terminal clusters of tiny whitish flowers with a pale pink lip; September to October
Requirements: Damp well drained soils
Comments: A short lived plant, which is usually abundant in times of good rainfall, but disappears during drier periods.
Propagation: Seed
Localities: Laverton Nth, Eltham, 29#, 34A, 42, 49, 58, 67#
Distribution: Vic, NSW, Tas, SA, WA

Levenhookia sonderi — Slender Stylewort

Size: 2–6 mm high — F P
Habitat: Wet depressions in valley sclerophyll forest, grassy wetlands, tea-tree heath
Form: Tiny short-lived herb with green stems
Foliage: Round, green glandular leaves to 5 mm long
Flowers: Small terminal clusters of white or pinkish flowers have a purple lip
Requirements: Wet winter soils.
Localities: was in Eltham, Research; Belgrave, 7, 41, 42, 67#
Distribution: Endemic to Vic

Lilaeopsis — Apiaceae

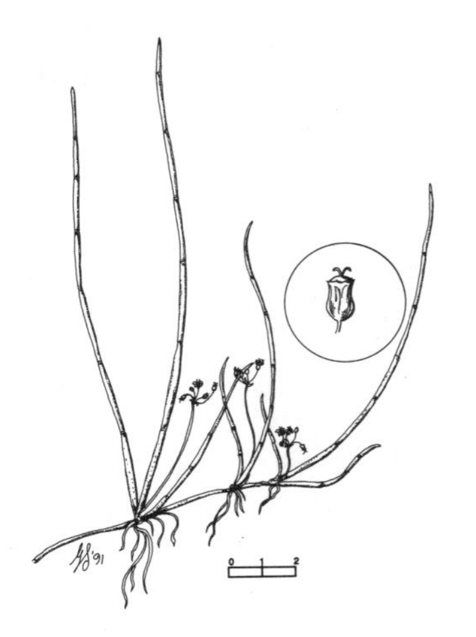
Lilaeopsis polyantha

Lilaeopsis polyantha — Creeping Crantzia

Size: 2–25 cm high — F P
Habitat: Aquatic, in shallow water of saltmarshes, primary dune scrub
Form: Tangled perennial creeping herb
Foliage: Tufts of narrow, terete, yellow-green leaves to 25 cm long, standing erect. The leaves are hollow and partitioned.
Flowers: Tiny purplish flowers, 2–6 per umbel, on upright stalks to 30 mm long; October to May
Requirements: Usually fresh but tolerates brackish water
Comments: Tufts of leaves and flowers occur at nodes on the creeping rhizomes. Known at very few locations in Melbourne.
Propagation: Seed, division
Localities: Seaford, 2, 4, 74
Distribution: Vic, NSW, SA
Synonym: *L. australica*

Limonium — Plumbaginaceae

Limonium australe — Yellow or Native Sea Lavender

Size: 0.3–0.5 m x 0.2–0.5 m — F
Habitat: Coastal mudflats and saltmarshes
Form: Rosetted perennial herb
Foliage: Leathery, glossy green obovate-oblong leaves to 90 mm long
Flowers: Broad panicle of flowers on angular flowering stalks 10–40 cm high. Pale pink or white papery calyx is more conspicuous than the yellow flowers.
Requirements: Moist or wet soil, tolerating salt
Comments: An attractive plant for a rockery or container.
Propagation: Seed
Localities: Early collections around Port Phillip Bay
Distribution: Vic, Qld, NSW

Limosella — Scrophulariaceae

Limosella australis — Australian Mudwort

Size: Prostrate — F
Habitat: Swamp scrub
Form: Perennial, stoloniferious semi-aquatic herb forming mats
Foliage: Basal tufts of narrow, oblong to spathulate leaves 10–40 mm long
Flowers: Single, small shortly-tubular, white or pale pink 5-lobed flowers on stalks shorter than the leaves; September to November
Requirements: Mud or shallow water
Comments: A useful matting plant for bogs or ponds.
Propagation: Division
Localities: Springvale
Distribution: All states except NT; NZ, Af

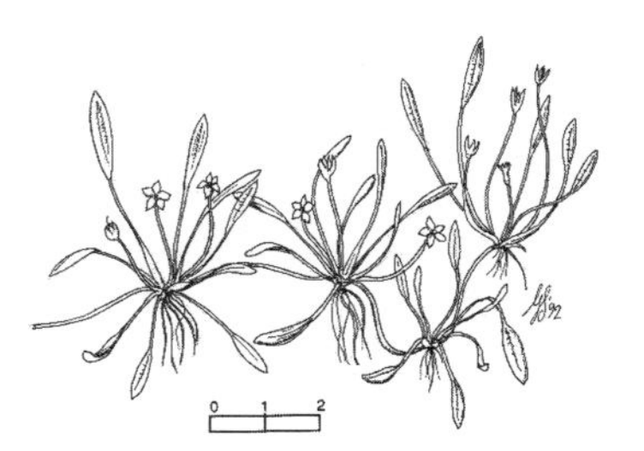

Limosella australis

Linum — Linaceae

Linum marginale — Native or Wild Flax

Size: 0.3–0.8 m x 0.3 m — F P
Habitat: Widespread in grassy wetland, red gum woodland, dry sclerophyll forest, tea-tree heath
Form: Slender erect perennial
Foliage: Ascending, narrow, sessile, bluish leaves to 20 mm long
Flowers: Terminal clusters of open, clear blue flowers with darker veins; most of the year, peaking September to May. The fruit is a round papery capsule.
Requirements: Moist well drained soils
Comments: The plant produces a thick tuberous rootstock, and may be cut back hard each year in late Autumn to encourage vigorous new growth. Fibre from the flax was used by Aborigines to make cord and fish nets. The seeds were used as food.
Propagation: Seed
Localities: St Albans, 2, 4, 16–18, 26, 28–30, 32, 34A, 35, 38, 40–42, 44, 47–49, 50A, 51, 55–57, 67#, 74
Distribution: All states except NT; NZ

Linum marginale

Lissanthe — Epacridaceae

Lissanthe strigosa — Peach Heath

Size: 0.2–1 m x 0.5 m — P
Habitat: Dry sclerophyll forest
Form: Rigid open shrub
Foliage: Stiff, narrow, green prickly leaves to 15 mm long with recurved margins. The underside is paler with conspicuous veins.
Flowers: Clusters of small pink or white urn-shaped flowers; August to November. Round, whitish, fleshy drupes follow flowering.
Requirements: Well drained soils
Comments: The drupes are edible.
Propagation: Cuttings—slow to strike
Localities: Research, 32, 36, 42
Distribution: Vic, Qld, NSW, Tas, SA

Lissanthe strigosa

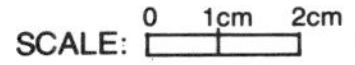

The scale representation on each plant equals 2cm.

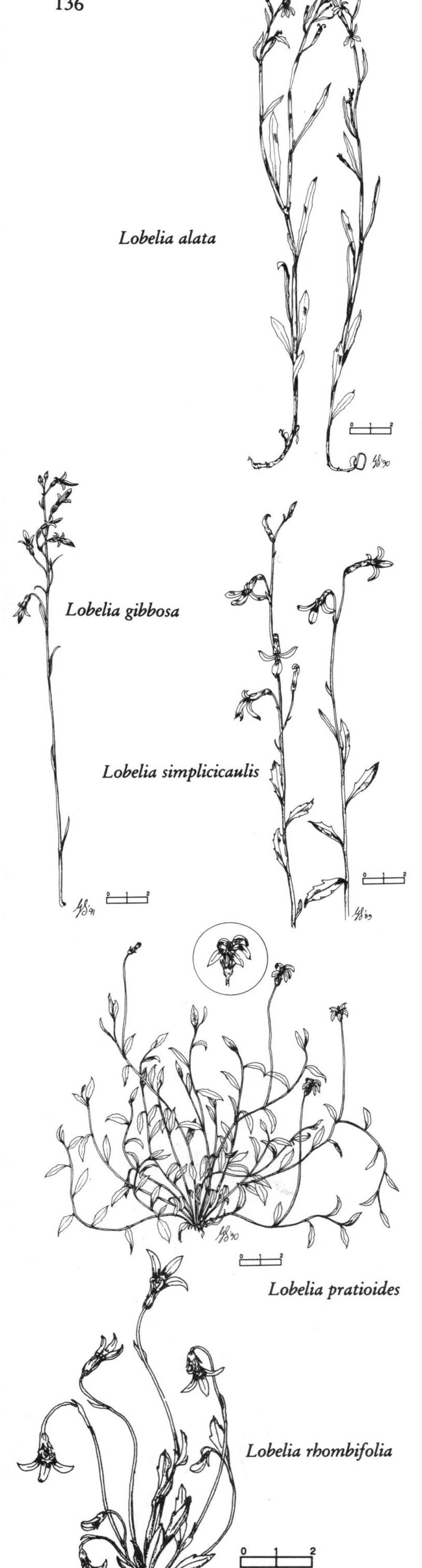

Lobelia — Campanulaceae

Lobelia alata

Angled Lobelia

Size:	Prostrate-30 cm high	F P
Habitat:	Damp and valley sclerophyll forests, sclerophyll woodland, riparian scrub, tea-tree heath	
Form:	Erect perennial herb spreading by layering	
Foliage:	Soft, narrow toothed leaves, the lower ones broader and longer, to 50 mm long	
Flowers:	Small pale blue fan-shaped flowers, singly in upper leaf axils; most of the year	
Requirements:	Moist soils	
Comments:	Suitable for a bog garden, this lobelia is easily recognised by its angular or narrowly winged stems.	
Propagation:	Division	
Localities:	Sunshine, Melton Sth, 14, 16, 26, 28, 35, 36, 42, 44, 46, 47, 51, 53–56, 59, 62–64, 67, 69A–71, 74–76	
Distribution:	All states except NT; NZ, S Af, S Am	

Lobelia gibbosa

Tall Lobelia

Size:	10–50 cm x 10 cm	P
Habitat:	Tea-tree heath	
Form:	Slender erect annual herb	
Foliage:	Scattered, narrow sessile leaves to 30 mm long, usually withering during flowering	
Flowers:	One-sided spike of deep blue tubular flowers, split to the base, white markings sometimes on the lower lobes; November to March. Seeds are tiny.	
Requirements:	Moist well drained soil	
Comments:	This herb is eye-catching in a small rockery.	
Propagation:	Seed	
Localities:	53, 55, 67#, 74	
Distribution:	All states except NT	

Lobelia pratioides

Poison Lobelia

Size:	Prostrate, spreading herb	P
Habitat:	Grassy wetlands, plains grassland, valley sclerophyll forest	
Form:	Loosely matting dioecious herb	
Foliage:	Dull green oblanceolate to cuneate leaves 10–50 mm long	
Flowers:	Single blue and white flowers are on hairy stalks longer than the leaves; November to January.	
Requirements:	Wet soils	
Comments:	An attractive plant for growing in a shaded garden, however the foliage is poisonous to stock.	
Localities:	4, 5, 7, 17#, 18, 24, 26, 67#, 69A, 75	
Distribution:	Vic, NSW, Tas, SA	

Lobelia rhombifolia

Branched or Tufted Lobelia

Size:	10–40 cm high	P
Habitat:	Swampy tracts in damp sclerophyll forest	
Form:	Much branched, erect or spreading annual herb	
Foliage:	Lobed oblong leaves to 25 mm long, upper leaves smaller and narrower	
Flowers:	Single dark blue to light purple flowers with a white and yellow throat, terminal on long stalks; September to November.	
Localities:	Northern slopes of Mt Dandenong, 49, 56, 58, 59	
Distribution:	Vic, Tas, SA, WA	

Lobelia simplicicaulis

Size:	to 0.8 m high	F P
Habitat:	Dry and valley sclerophyll forests. tea-tree heath	
Comments:	Similar to *L. gibbosa*. Stems are branched. Lower leaves are larger and lanceolate, to 40 mm long, and stem-clasping with toothed margins, becoming smaller and linear further up the stem. The lower leaves on coastal forms are narrow-lanceolate to 20 mm long. Seeds are much larger.	
Localities:	Cheltenham 1901; Kalorama, Olinda, 42, 49, 55–59	
Distribution:	Vic, Qld, NSW, Tas, SA	
Synonym:	*L. gibbosa* var. *simplicicaulis*	

Lomatia

Proteaceae

Lomatia fraseri

Forest or Tree Lomatia

Size: 2–7 m x 1–4 m **P N**
Habitat: Wet and damp sclerophyll forests
Form: Rounded shrub to small tree
Foliage: Stiff, leathery, narrowly elliptical leaves to 15 cm long, usually sharply and distantly toothed, silver-velvety hairs below
Flowers: Loose terminal or axillary racemes of creamy spider flowers, hairy on the outside; December to February
Requirements: Deep, moist well drained soil, tolerating some wetness
Comments: A very attractive small tree or shrub for a sheltered moist position. The interestingly-shaped seed follicles are also a feature. Plants are usually slow growing.
Propagation: Seed, cuttings
Localities: Mt Dandenong, 57, 58
Distribution: Vic, NSW

Illustrated p. 172

Lomatia ilicifolia

Lomatia ilicifolia

Holly Leaf Lomatia

Size: 0.5–2 m x 1 m **F P**
Habitat: Damp and dry sclerophyll forests, sclerophyll woodland, grassy low open forest
Form: Stiff erect shrub
Foliage: Dull green, leathery, crinkly, ovate to broad-lanceolate holly-like leaves to 15 cm long, prominent veins
Flowers: Racemes of glabrous cream flowers held above the foliage; December to February
Requirements: Well drained soil
Comments: A slow growing shrub regenerating vigorously from a lignotuber and flowering well after fire. It has attractive foliage and fruit. The new growth is very colourful with shades of bronze and red.
Propagation: Seed, cuttings
Localities: 42, 50A, 54–56, 58, 59
Distribution: Vic, Qld, NSW

Lomatia myricoides

River or Long-leaf Lomatia

Size: 2–5 m x 1–3 m **P N**
Habitat: Riparian scrub
Form: Open rounded shrub or small tree
Foliage: Dull green, narrow-lanceolate leaves to 20 cm long, veins not prominent. Margins with few distant teeth or rarely almost entire.
Flowers: Short axillary racemes of glabrous, perfumed, cream flowers; December to February
Requirements: Moist well drained soil. Tolerates short periods of wetness.
Comments: Attractive slow-growing small tree which flowers well in the garden with Summer watering.
Propagation: Seed, cuttings
Localities: Wonga Park, 34A, 42
Distribution: Vic, NSW

Illustrated p. 172

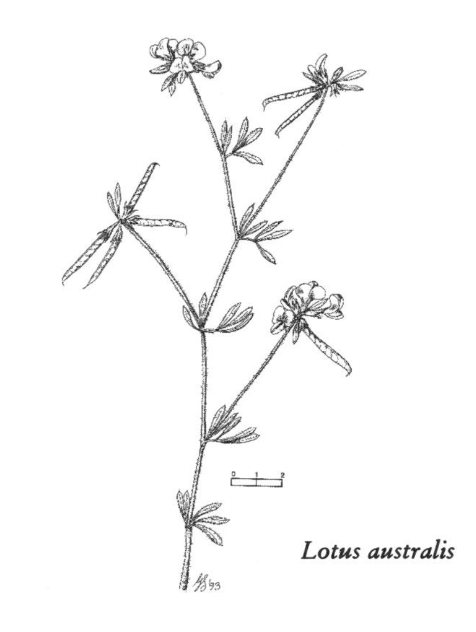

Lotus australis

Lotus

Fabaceae

Lotus australis

Austral Trefoil

Size: 0.3–0.6 m x 0.6 m **F**
Habitat: Plains grassland
Form: Open rounded perennial herb
Foliage: Soft light green trifoliate leaves, leaflets narrow to 40 mm long
Flowers: Pale pink or white pea flowers in terminal umbels, held erect on long stalks; October to March
Requirements: Moist well drained soils withstanding dry periods once established
Comments: An attractive rockery plant resistant to salt spray.
Propagation: Scarified seed
Localities: Early collections in Braybrook 1897, Sydenham 1907; 29
Distribution: All states

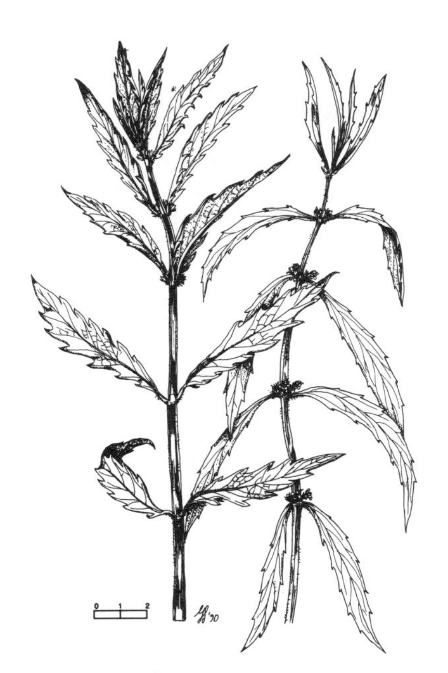

Lycopus australis

Lycopus

Lamiaceae

Lycopus australis

Australian Gypsywort

Size: to 1 m high **P N**
Habitat: Riparian scrub, valley sclerophyll forest, coastal banksia woodland
Form: Leafy, erect, slightly branched herb
Foliage: Pairs of aromatic, lanceolate leaves with jagged edges to 100 mm long
Flowers: Dense clusters of tiny, 4-lobed white flowers in leaf axils; December to April
Requirements: Moist to wet soil
Comments: The branches are quadrangular in cross section. An interesting foliage plant for a damp area. Not found in many locations in Melbourne.
Propagation: Cuttings
Localities: Diamond Ck, Yarra R, Seaford, 30, 35, 36, 42, 62, 63, 74
Distribution: Vic, Qld, NSW, Tas, SA

SCALE: 0 1cm 2cm — The scale representation on each plant equals 2cm.

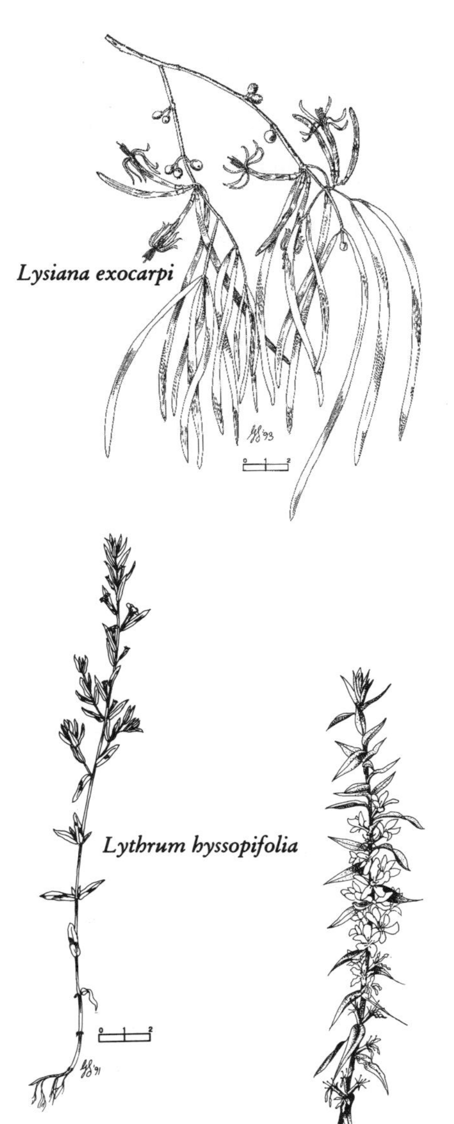
Lysiana exocarpi

Lythrum hyssopifolia

Lythrum salicaria

Lysiana — Loranthaceae

Lysiana exocarpi — Harlequin Mistletoe

Habitat: Box woodland
Form: Drooping stem parasite
Foliage: Narrow, curved bluish-green leaves to 150 mm long
Flowers: Groups of 2 or 3 curved, tubular bright red flowers to 50 mm long, greenish towards the end; January to August. Fruit is a green drupe ripening to red or purple.
Comments: A parasitic plant, infesting many host species in dry areas. The fruit was eaten by the Aborigines. Locally rare.
Propagation: Mistletoe birds eat the berries and deposit seeds on the branches of host trees.
Localities: Diggers Rest 1904; 9, 26
Distribution: Vic, NSW, SA

Lythrum — Lythraceae

Lythrum hyssopifolia — Small or Lesser Loosestrife

Size: Prostrate-30 cm x 20–30 cm — F P
Habitat: Swamp and riparian scrub, grassy wetlands, red gum woodland, valley sclerophyll forest, grassy low open forest
Form: Trailing or erect annual herb
Foliage: Oblong to oblanceolate, sessile leaves to 25 mm long
Flowers: Single, tiny pink tubular flowers with spreading petals in leaf axils along the stem; November to April
Requirements: Moist soils, tolerating dry summers
Comments: Stems are ribbed or angular.
Propagation: Seed, cuttings
Localities: 4–7, 9, 12, 16–18, 24–26, 28, 29, 31, 34A–36, 40–42, 44, 46, 47, 49–51, 53–61, 63, 65–69A, 71, 74–76
Distribution: All states except NT

Lythrum salicaria — Purple Loosestrife

Size: 1–2 m x 1 m — F
Habitat: Semi-aquatic in riparian scrub, valley sclerophyll forest
Form: Erect, hairy perennial, dying back after Summer
Foliage: Sessile, lanceolate leaves to 75 mm long, in pairs
Flowers: Clusters of tubular, purple to magenta flowers with spreading petals, crowded in terminal spikes; November to March
Requirements: Moist soils or shallow water
Comments: A very showy plant for bog gardens or beside pools, the stems should be cut back to the rootstock after flowering. Locally rare now but was collected from the banks of the Yarra River in 1856.
Propagation: Cuttings, division, will self-seed
Localities: Werribee, Warrandyte Nth, 16, 26, 30, 33, 35
Distribution: Vic, Qld, NSW, Tas, SA

Maireana — Chenopodiaceae

Woody perennials or small shrubs commonly called Bluebush. All local *Maireana* spp. have hairy to quite woolly branches. Leaves are sometimes succulent. In each of these species the minute greenish flowers are bisexual and sessile. The main identifying characteristic is the shape of the fruiting body. While all have horizontal wings, the upper and lower portions are unique to each species. *Maireana* spp. are found in open flat, often saline, areas. Propagation is by seeds or cuttings, without the use of mist.

Maireana brevifolia — Small-leaf or Short-leaf Bluebush, Cottonbush

Size: 1 m x 0.6–1 m — F
Habitat: Riparian scrub, box woodland
Form: Erect, sometimes dense shrub
Foliage: Succulent, obovoid glabrous leaves to 5 mm long, narrowing to a short stalk. Each leaf axil contains a tuft of wool.
Flowers: Solitary flowers followed by light brown fruit with 5 fan-shaped wings of equal size, inner lobes fleshy; December to July
Requirements: Dry well drained soils, tolerating salt
Comments: One small colony has recently been discovered within the Melbourne area.
Localities: Keilor
Distribution: All mainland states
Synonym: *Kochia brevifolia*

Maireana decalvans

Black Cottonbush

Size: 0.3–0.5 m x 0.5–1 m **F P**
Habitat: Seasonally waterlogged sites in box woodland, plains grassland
Form: Erect or spreading bushy perennial shrub with woolly leaf axils
Foliage: Succulent, terete, hairless blue-green leaves to 8 mm long
Flowers: Single flowers are followed by pale green fruit. The fruit has a hemispherical base and a single wing which is flat with a radial slit; November to May
Requirements: Prefers heavy soils, tolerating drying out in Summer.
Localities: Laverton Nth, Deer Park, Mt Cottrell, Melton Sth, Sydenham, 16, 26
Distribution: Vic, Qld, NSW, SA
Synonym: *Kochia villosa* var. *tenuifolia*

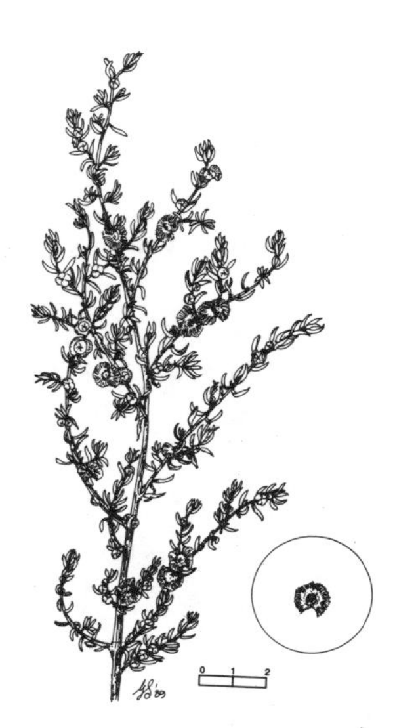
Maireana decalvans

Maireana enchylaenoides

Wingless Fissure-weed or Bluebush

Size: 10–20 cm x 0.3–0.6 m **F**
Habitat: Box woodland
Form: Slender, weak, sparsely branched perennial herb
Foliage: Dull, narrow, oblong, hairy leaves to 10 mm long
Flowers: Single flowers are followed by fruit with 5 small, crescent-shaped, overlapping wings which are inflated on their edges; September to March. Fruit turns black when dry.
Requirements: Loam soil
Localities: 9, 16, 21, 22, 26, 32
Distribution: Vic, Qld, NSW, SA, WA
Synonym: *Kochia crassiloba*

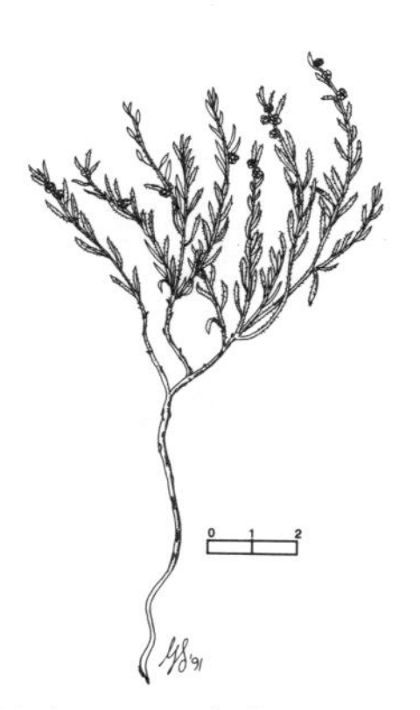
Maireana enchylaenoides

Maireana pentagona

Slender Fissure-weed

Size: 10–30 cm x 30–50 cm **F P**
Habitat: Plains grassland
Form: Small woolly, prostrate to ascending perennial herb
Foliage: Narrow leaves to 12 mm long
Flowers: Single flowers crowded towards the end of stems. Tiny pentagonal fruit are covered in dense hairs; August to September.
Requirements: Heavy soil
Localities: 26
Distribution: Vic, NSW, SA, WA
Synonym: *Kochia pentagona*

Mazus

Scrophulariaceae

Mazus pumilio

Swamp Mazus

Size: 3 cm x 0.5–1 m **F P N**
Habitat: Swamp margins of valley sclerophyll forest, tea-tree heath
Form: Suckering mat plant
Foliage: Glossy obovate-spathulate leaves, 8–65 mm long, with toothed, wavy margins
Flowers: Solitary, white or mauve flowers with 2 white humps on lower lip, on stalks to 25 mm long; October to March. Several flowers on branched stalks in sheltered areas.
Requirements: Moist to wet soil
Comments: Suckering from stolons to form a carpet, it is useful in boggy areas and on pond edges.
Propagation: Division
Localities: Montrose, 34A, 51, 53, 67#
Distribution: Vic, Qld, NSW, Tas, SA; NZ

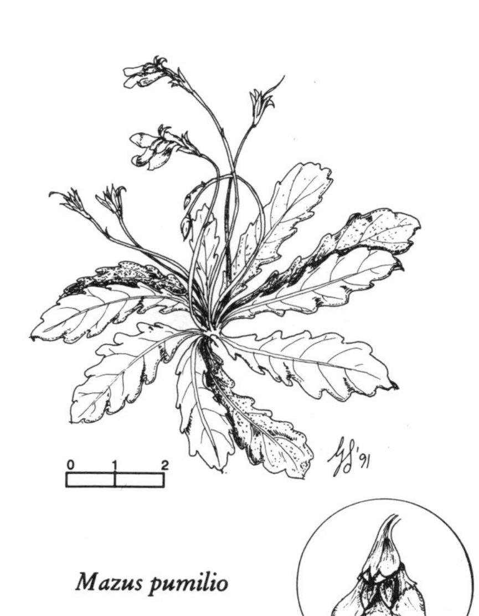
Mazus pumilio

The scale representation on each plant equals 2cm.

Melaleuca

Myrtaceae

Fast-growing medium to large shrubs or small trees. Only two of the locally occurring species have the characteristic paper bark. The papery bark of these species was used by the Aborigines to wrap up their babies, and for blankets, bandaging and roofing. Cream to yellow bottlebrush flowers are followed by a cluster of woody seed capsules which open after fire or damage to the plant. Melaleucas may form dense copses and tolerate a wide range of conditions. Propagation is by seed, using the bog method, or cuttings.

Melaleuca ericifolia

Melaleuca ericifolia

Swamp Paperbark

Size: 2–9 m x 3 m **F P**
Habitat: Red gum woodland, valley sclerophyll forest, swamp and wattle tea-tree scrub, coastal banksia woodland
Form: Erect, open to bushy shrub or small tree
Foliage: Narrow dark green leaves to 15 mm long, with blunt tips
Flowers: Masses of terminal short cream brushes to 20 mm long, more than 10 mm wide; October to November
Requirements: Moist or wet fertile soils, tolerating dry conditions once established
Comments: A very adaptable plant, useful in wet garden areas, it may sucker to form a dense copse. Responds well to pruning. With age, trunks take on interesting forms. The pale papery bark is used in bark paintings. Aborigines made clubs from young stems with a root attached. The nectar produced a sweet drink and the oil from the crushed leaves treated colds.
Localities: Melbourne#, Albert Park#, 1, 23, 29–35, 42, 44, 46, 47, 49–51, 54–56, 58, 60, 61–67#, 69–76
Distribution: Vic, Qld, NSW, Tas

Melaleuca lanceolata

Melaleuca lanceolata

Moonah

Size: 1–8 m x 3–6 m **F**
Habitat: Primary dune scrub, riparian scrub and woodland
Form: Dense large shrub or small tree, stunted in exposed coastal areas
Foliage: Thick, dull green, linear leaves to 12 mm long, often curved down
Flowers: Cream to white terminal spikes to 50 mm long; October to March
Requirements: Well drained soils, tolerating limestone and periods of inundation
Comments: An adaptable species, useful as a front line coastal plant. Locally, it commonly grows in coastal areas, but may also be found scattered in riverine sites, on basalt.
Localities: Werribee R, Richmond, Seaford, 69, 74
Distribution: Vic, Qld, NSW, SA, WA

Melaleuca parvistaminea

Size: 2–4 m x 3–5 m **F P**
Habitat: Riparian and swamp scrub, coloniser of disturbed areas
Form: Medium shrub very similar to *M. ericifolia*
Comments: Main differences include the rough bark and its non-suckering habit, although it may still form thickets. The canopy is broader and leaves smaller, to 11 mm long, with visible oil glands. The cream brushes are longer and less than 10 mm wide. Prefers infertile shallow soils in moist areas. Both species are occasionally seen growing together.
Localities: Werribee R, Yarra R above Kew
Distribution: Vic, NSW
Synonym: Was included with *M. ericifolia*, also referred to as *M.* sp. aff. *ericifolia*.

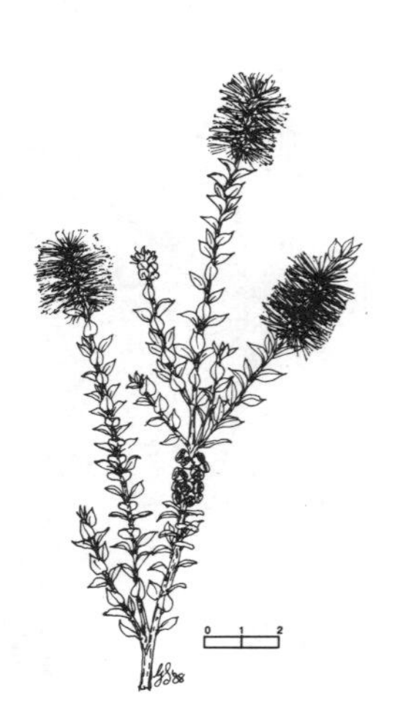

Melaleuca squarrosa

Melaleuca squarrosa

Scented Paperbark

Size: 2–5 m x 1–2 m **F P**
Habitat: Damp and valley sclerophyll forests, swamp and wattle tea-tree scrub
Form: Erect, open to compact large shrub or rarely, a small tree to 10 m high
Foliage: Stiff dark green ovate to triangular leaves to 18 mm long, crowded in pairs and distinctly decussate
Flowers: Profuse terminal spikes of scented cream to yellow flowers; September to February
Requirements: Moist to wet soils
Comments: An attractive shrub responding well to pruning, it also grows well near the coast and is salt tolerant.
Localities: Montrose, 33, 34A, 49, 50A, 56, 58, 59, 67, 70, 71, 73–76
Distribution: Vic, NSW, Tas, SA

Mentha — Lamiaceae

Small aromatic perennial herbs widespread in damp places, spreading by suckering. The mint leaves of some species have been used in drinks or as insect repellants. The Aborigines used them for medicinal purposes. All species are relatively uncommon in Melbourne. Propagation is by division or cuttings.

Mentha australis

River Mint

Size: 0.2–0.8 m x 0.3–1 m — **F P N**
Habitat: Riparian scrub, valley sclerophyll forest
Form: Slender, sprawling or erect herb with square stems
Foliage: Pairs of lanceolate leaves to 50 mm long
Flowers: Clusters of small tubular white to pale mauve flowers towards the end of upright stems in whorls of 7–10 flowers; September to March. Calyx covered in grey hairs.
Requirements: Moist to wet soils
Comments: A useful plant by ponds and near pathways where the foliage, when brushed, imparts a delightful mint fragrance. The Aborigines used the leaves to flavor food and as a decoction for coughs and colds. Locally rare.
Localities: Yarra R., Sunbury, 16, 26, 27, 29#–31, 33, 34A–36, 42, 57, 58
Distribution: All states

Mentha diemenica var. diemenica

Slender or Wild Mint

Size: 10–30 cm x 0.5 m — **F P N**
Habitat: Grassy wetlands, red gum woodland
Form: Slender herb similar to *M. australis*
Foliage: Ovate to oblong leaves to 20 mm long, covered in downy hairs
Flowers: Whorls of 2–8 bright pink to violet flowers
Requirements: Moist soil, tolerating periodic inundation
Localities: Laverton Nth, Bulla, 1, 17#, 18, 35
Distribution: All states except NT

Mentha laxiflora

Forest Mint

Size: 15–40 cm x 1 m — **P N**
Habitat: Wet, damp and valley sclerophyll forests
Form: Open spreading herb with erect stems
Foliage: Bluntly-toothed lanceolate leaves to 50 mm
Flowers: Dense clusters of mauve, or rarely white, short-stalked flowers; September to March
Localities: 55, 57, 58
Distribution: Vic, NSW

Mentha satureioides

Creeping Mint, Native Pennyroyal

Size: 15 cm high — **P N**
Habitat: Grassy wetland, red gum woodland
Form: Hairy stems with entire, oblong to oblong-lanceolate leaves to 30 mm long
Flowers: White flowers in whorls of 4–8; December to March.
Comments: Forms mats in sheltered areas.
Localities: 6, 25, 26
Distribution: Vic, Qld, NSW, SA, WA

Microseris — Asteraceae

Microseris lanceolata

Yam Daisy, Native Dandelion

Size: Prostrate-40 cm x 15–25 cm — **P**
Habitat: Plains grassland, red gum woodland, dry sclerophyll forest
Form: Tufted perennial herb, regenerating annually from a fleshy tuberous root
Foliage: Shiny, long narrow toothed leaves to 20 cm long
Flowers: Single bright yellow daisy flowerhead on a stalk 20–50 cm high; July to November. Fluffy white seed heads follow. The pappus on the narrowly-coned seed is scaly.
Requirements: Well drained soils
Comments: The flowerhead is distinguished from the dandelion as the bud droops before opening. The tuberous rootstock was a staple part of the aboriginal diet. This form was once also prevalent on the basalt plains. A second form, found in inundated areas of the basalt plains, is distinguished by the slightly waisted seed (or achene) which has a very fine, capillary-like pappus and a branched or forked taproot. Once common in moist hollows of Altona Meadows, it is still found in Laverton, although very rare.
Propagation: Seed
Localities: Eltham, 1, 7, 33–35, 37, 41, 42, 44, 45, 47–49, 50A–52, 61, 63#, 67#, 74, 76
Distribution: All states except NT
Synonym: *M. scapigera*

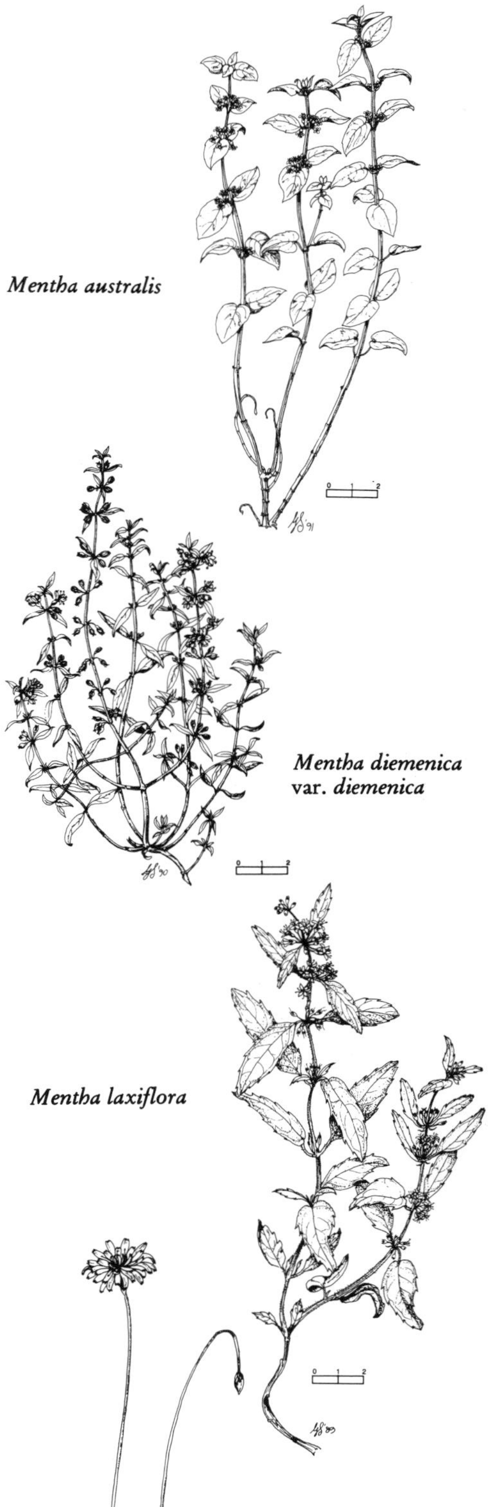

Mentha australis

Mentha diemenica var. *diemenica*

Mentha laxiflora

Microseris lanceolata

SCALE: 0 1cm 2cm — The scale representation on each plant equals 2cm.

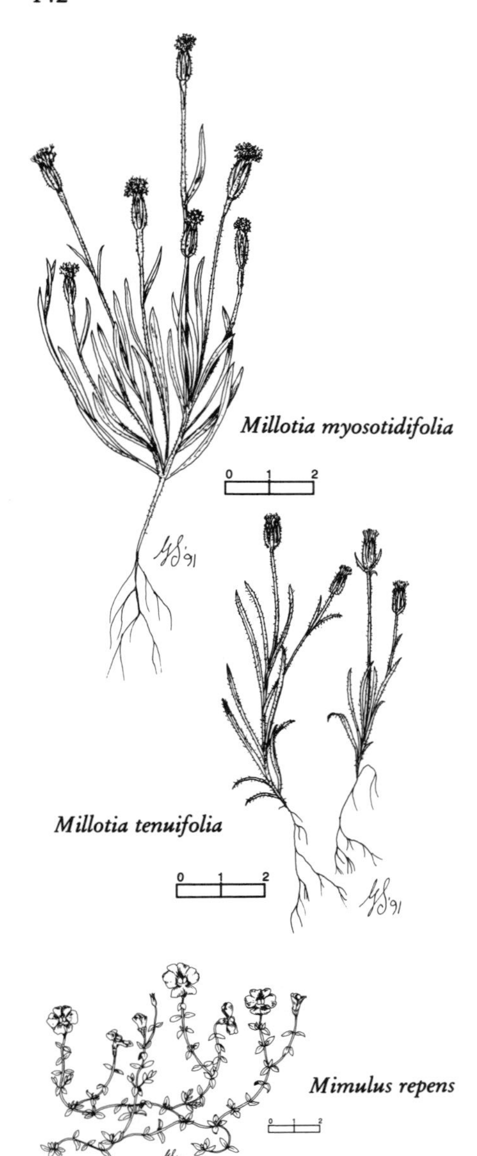

Millotia myosotidifolia

Millotia tenuifolia

Mimulus repens

Millotia — Asteraceae

Millotia myosotidifolia — Broad-leaf Millotia

Size: 10–20 cm x 15–25 cm — F P
Habitat: Red gum woodland
Form: Erect annual herb covered in white woolly hairs
Foliage: Soft, stem-clasping, narrow-linear to oblanceolate leaves to 50 mm long, at the lower end of the flower stalks
Flowers: Terminal creamy-white flowerheads, without ray florets, singly on long erect stalks; July to September. Bracts oblong, sparsely woolly with broad green midribs. Tiny flowers have 5 pointed petals and prominent anthers.
Requirements: Well drained soils
Comments: Probably extinct within the Melbourne area.
Localities: Collected in Epping 1902
Distribution: Vic, NSW, Tas, SA, WA

Millotia tenuifolia — Soft Millotia

Size: 25–140 mm x 10–30 cm — F
Habitat: Coastal cliff faces
Form: Aromatic annual herb with white-woolly and straight pale golden hairs
Foliage: Soft, grey, thread-like leaves to 25 mm long
Flowers: Single cream oblong flowerheads surrounded by narrow pointed green bracts, held above the leaves; August to November. Anthers are enclosed by 3–4 rounded petals.
Requirements: Well drained soil
Propagation: Seed
Localities: 67#
Distribution: Vic, NSW, Tas, SA, WA

Mimulus — Scrophulariaceae

Mimulus repens — Creeping Monkey-flower

Size: Prostrate x 0.5–1 m — F P
Habitat: Saltmarshes, grassy wetlands, riparian scrub
Form: Spreading perennial herb
Foliage: Pairs of succulent, stalkless, oval leaves to 6 mm long, crowded along stems
Flowers: Single mauve flowers with downy yellow centre on very short stalks; Spring and Autumn
Requirements: Moist soils tolerating salt and periods of inundation
Comments: Useful for planting by a water feature, it spreads by rooting at the nodes wherever it is in contact with soil.
Propagation: Division
Localities: Laverton, 4, 11, 16, 26, 67#, 72, 74
Distribution: All states; NZ

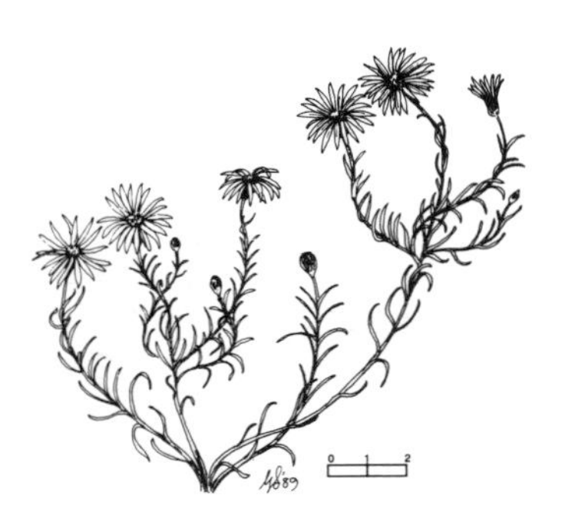

Minuria leptophylla

Minuria — Asteraceae

Minuria leptophylla — Minnie Daisy

Size: 10–30 cm x 20–50 cm — F
Habitat: Plains grassland
Form: Perennial herb forming a compact rounded mound
Foliage: Soft narrow bright green leaves 5–25 mm long
Flowers: White or mauve daisy-like flowerheads with yellow centres, on short stalks above the leaves; most of the year
Requirements: Very well drained soil tolerating dry periods once established
Comments: A very showy plant, useful for rockeries or border planting in dry areas. The local form is quite small to 15 cm high with short leaves to 10 mm long. Restricted to a few sites within the Melbourne area.
Propagation: Seed, cuttings
Localities: St Albans, Sydenham, Nth Sunshine, 7, 16–18, 26
Distribution: All mainland states

Mitrasacme distylis

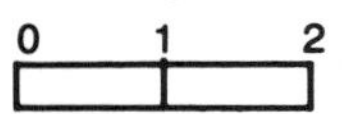

Mitrasacme — Loganiaceae

Mitrasacme distylis — Tiny Mitrewort

Size: to 25 mm high
Habitat: Coastal
Form: Slender erect annual herb
Foliage: Leaves differ from *M. paradoxa* in that they are narrow, 4 mm long, and not joined at the base
Flowers: Single tiny terminal flowers; October to November.
Localities: Collected around Port Phillip area in 1880s
Distribution: Vic, Tas, SA

Mitrasacme paradoxa

Wiry Mitrewort

Size: 25–150 mm high **P**
Habitat: Primary dune scrub, dry sclerophyll forest
Form: Inconspicuous erect annual herb with thread-like stems, and leaves mostly in a basal rosette
Foliage: Pairs of tiny, narrowly-oblong to ovate stem leaves (or bracts) to 8 mm long, hairy on top and joined at the base
Flowers: Umbels of 2–5 tiny white flowers on fine stems; September to December
Requirements: Well drained soils
Comments: An easily overlooked plant which is becoming rarer in Melbourne.
Propagation: Cuttings
Localities: Early collections—Mentone, Werribee; 41, 67#
Distribution: Vic, NSW, Tas, SA, WA

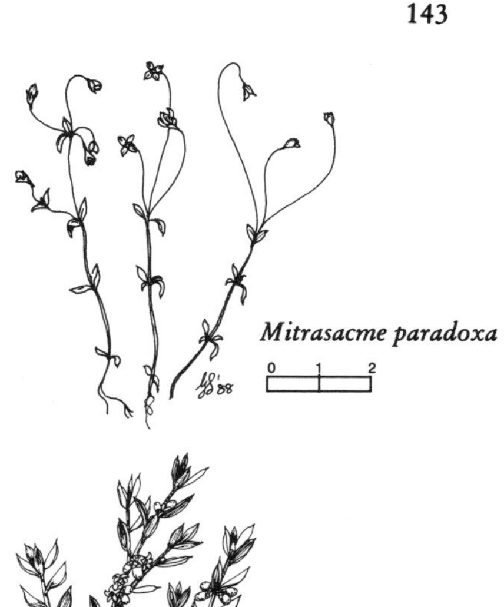

Mitrasacme paradoxa

Monotoca — Epacridaceae

Monotoca scoparia

Prickly Broom-heath

Size: 1–2.5 m x 1–2 m **F P**
Habitat: Tea-tree heath on poor, sandy or shallow soils, dry sclerophyll forest
Form: Rigid, erect shrub
Foliage: Stiff, prickly, dark green leaves with margins curved under, whitish below, to 14 mm long
Flowers: Tiny cream broadly tubular flowers in small clusters; March to June; followed by small edible pale creamy-yellow drupes
Requirements: Moist, well drained soils
Propagation: Cuttings are difficult
Localities: 34, 51, 59, 67–71, 73–75
Distribution: Vic, Qld, NSW, Tas, SA

Monotoca scoparia

Montia — Portulacaceae

Montia australasica = Neopaxia australasica

Montia fontana

Water-blinks

Size: to 20 cm high **P**
Habitat: Swampy grassland
Form: Tiny tufted annual herb. Similar to *Neopaxia australasica* but does not spread by rhizomes.
Foliage: Smaller paired leaves varying from narrow to spathulate, to 20 mm long
Flowers: Inconspicuous pinkish flowers; September to November.
Localities: Croydon, 1940#
Distribution: Vic, NSW, SA; NZ

Muehlenbeckia adpressa

Muehlenbeckia — Polygonaceae

Muehlenbeckia adpressa

Climbing Lignum

Size: Climber **F**
Habitat: Coastal banksia woodland, primary dune scrub
Form: Wiry trailing or climbing perennial
Foliage: Heart-shaped to ovate bright green leaves with wavy margins, variable 8–80 mm x 6–35 mm
Flowers: Axillary spikes of small greenish-yellow flowers; September to December; followed by dark reddish fruit
Requirements: Well drained sandy soils
Comments: A useful moderately vigorous climber for fences and retaining walls, tolerating salt exposure and dryness. The Aborigines ground the fruit of *Muehlenbeckia* spp. into flour.
Propagation: Cuttings
Localities: 67–69, 74
Distribution: Vic, NSW, Tas, SA, WA

Muehlenbeckia florulenta

Tangled Lignum

Size: 1–2.5 m x 1–2 m **F**
Habitat: Saltmarshes, grassy wetlands, riparian scrub
Form: Rigid, densely tangled, almost leafless, shrub
Foliage: Small narrow leaves found briefly on new growth. Branchlets are grey-green with parallel ridges.
Flowers: Spikes of small creamy-yellow flowers most of the year. Fruit is dry.
Requirements: Moist soil tolerating occasional inundation
Comments: An interesting plant which may form dense, impenetrable stands in ideal conditions. It is found on the edges of swamps on the basalt plains around Melbourne.
Propagation: Cuttings
Localities: Keilor, Laverton Nth, Sunshine, Sydenham, Melton, 4, 6, 11, 16, 26
Distribution: All mainland states
Synonym: *M. cunninghamii*

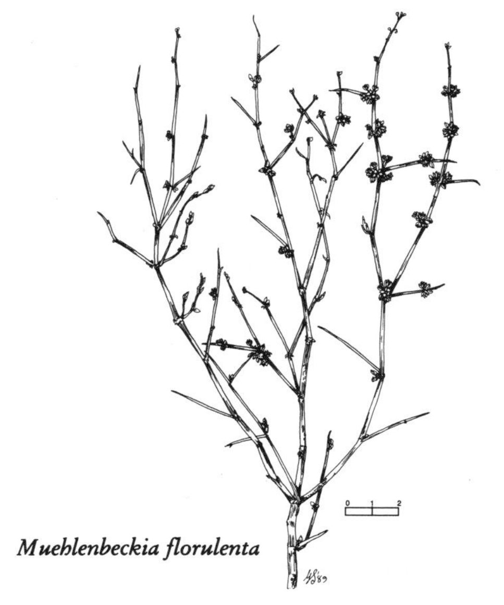

Muehlenbeckia florulenta

SCALE: 0 1cm 2cm The scale representation on each plant equals 2cm.

Muellerina eucalyptoides

Muellerina — Loranthaceae

Muellerina eucalyptoides — Creeping Mistletoe

F P

Habitat: Red gum and box woodlands, valley, damp and wet sclerophyll forests, grassy low open forest
Form: Erect dense parasitic climber becoming pendulous under its own weight
Foliage: Thick, blunt pale green leaves to 75 mm long
Flowers: Very attractive large red and greenish flowers in loose clusters in Spring and Summer; followed by green sticky pear-shaped fruit.
Comments: Parasitic on a variety of hosts, but usually eucalypts, its long roots creep along the branches. Healthy host plants are usually able to cope with minor infestations. Some plants may eventually weaken to the stage where branches die and break off. Removing and burning infested branches is recommended if infestation becomes too dense. Mistletoes are the host plants of the Imperial White Butterfly.
Propagation: Mistletoe bird deposits seed on branches of host tree.
Localities: 18, 19, 21, 23, 25, 26, 28, 31, 32, 34A, 42, 44, 50, 51, 57, 58, 60, 63, 67, 69A, 71, 74–76
Distribution: Vic, Qld, NSW, SA

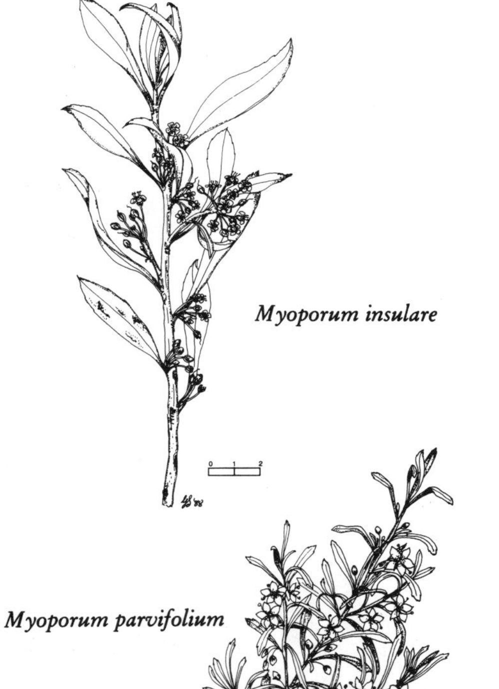

Myoporum insulare

Myoporum parvifolium

Myoporum viscosum

Myoporum — Myoporaceae

Myoporum deserti = Eremophila deserti

Myoporum insulare — Boobialla

F

Size: 1–6 m x 3 m
Habitat: Coastal banksia woodland, primary dune scrub
Form: Dense, rounded large shrub or small tree
Foliage: Thick, smooth lanceolate leaves, succulent beside the sea, to 100 mm long, small teeth towards the tip
Flowers: Clusters of fragrant white flowers with purple spots; October to November. Fruit is an edible, round purplish-green drupe.
Requirements: Well drained sandy soil tolerating dryness once established
Comments: Salt tolerant, it makes an excellent front line coastal plant. Useful for screening or a windbreak. Bark on old plants develop attractive tessellation. *Myoporum* spp. are useful fire retardant plants.
Propagation: Cuttings
Localities: Sunbury, Keilor, Seaford, 16, 26, 30#, 33, 67, 69A, 72, 74
Distribution: Vic, NSW, Tas, SA, WA

Myoporum parvifolium — Creeping Boobialla

F P N

Size: Prostrate x 2–4 m
Habitat: Saltmarshes, grassy wetlands
Form: Dense matting groundcover
Foliage: Thick, narrow to oblong leaves to 40 mm long, but usually smaller
Flowers: Masses of small, star-like white or pink flowers with purple spots; November to February. Edible green to purplish drupes
Requirements: Well drained soil, tolerating dryness once established
Comments: A very adaptable ground cover, it is excellent in rockeries. Its layering habit is useful for soil and sand binding. Other colour and leaf forms are available at nurseries. Possibly extinct within the Melbourne area.
Propagation: Cuttings, division at nodes
Localities: Early collections: Newport, Altona, Werribee, Moorabbin, 67#
Distribution: Vic, NSW, Tas, SA, WA

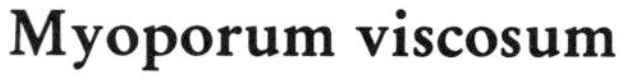

Myoporum viscosum — Sticky Boobialla

F

Size: 0.5–2 m x 1.5–2 m
Habitat: Rocky outcrops of riparian and chenopod rocky open scrub, coastal cliffs
Form: Dense shrub
Foliage: Thin, dark green, finely toothed ovate leaves to 50 mm long, paler below. Young growth is sticky.
Flowers: Clusters of white flowers with purple spots and hairy centres; September to December. Edible round yellow drupes
Requirements: Well drained dry soils
Comments: A useful shrub for coastal or dry areas, tolerating exposed salty conditions and extended droughts once established.
Propagation: Cuttings
Localities: 16, 26, 29, 30, 32, 33, 34A–36, 67
Distribution: Vic, SA, WA

Myosotis

Boraginaceae

Myosotis australis

Austral Forget-me-not

F

Size: 10–30 cm high
Habitat: Dry sclerophyll forest, grassy low open forest
Form: Slender hairy, annual herb with 1 to several erect stems from a basal rosette
Foliage: Lower leaves narrowly obovate to 40 mm long, upper leaves becoming smaller and stem clasping
Flowers: Terminal racemes of tiny white or pale blue flowers; August to November. Calyx hairy. Bracts have upward hooked hairs.
Requirements: Well drained soil
Comments: Fast disappearing within the Melbourne area.
Propagation: Seed
Localities: 30#, 34A, 42, 63, 67#, 74, 76
Distribution: Vic, NSW, Tas, SA, WA; NZ, PNG

Myosotis australis

Myosotis exarrhena

Sweet Forget-me-not

Habitat: Rocky sites
Comments: A perennial herb with larger flowers than *M. australis*. The fragrant white flowers have lobes as long as the tube, stamens are exserted, and calyx is glabrous. Recorded last century in the Melbourne area it may well be extinct now.
Localities: Frankston 1899, 29#
Distribution: Vic, NSW, Tas
Synonym: *M. suaveolens*

Myriocephalus

Asteraceae

Myriocephalus rhizocephalus

Woolly Heads

P

Size: 2–7 cm x 5–20 cm
Habitat: Temporarily moist depressions in red gum woodland, grassy wetlands
Form: Annual stemless herb forming a clump
Foliage: Grass-like yellowish-green leaves held vertically to 70 mm long
Flowers: Woolly, daisy-like flattened flowerheads, whitish bracts with yellow centres, intermixed with the leaves; September to November. Flowerheads are compound and composed of a number of partial flowerheads, each containing only one flower.
Requirements: Moist well drained soils
Comments: Short lived annual, shriveling quickly as soil dries out.
Propagation: Seed
Localities: Laverton Nth, St Albans, Werribee
Distribution: Vic, Qld, NSW, SA, WA

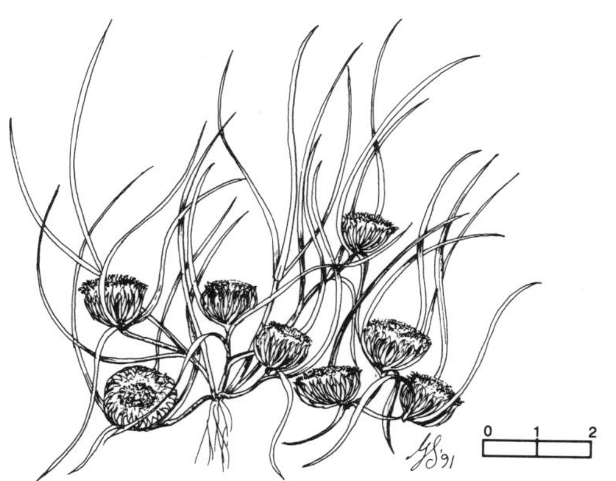

Myriocephalus rhizocephalus

Myriophyllum

Haloragaceae

Annual or perennial herbs, most of the local myriophyllums, or water milfoils, are aquatic for part of the year. Others live in marshes. The plants alter their appearance as water dries up. The submerged leaves are very similar in those species with pinnate foliage. Emergent leaves are entire, toothed or lobed. Single sessile flowers occur in the upper axils of the emergent leaves, male flowers above female along the stem. Petals are absent on female flowers. The aquatic species are useful for aquariums. They may be used in and around large pools but some may become invasive. Propagation is by cuttings placed in water or a wet medium, or by division of layered stems.

Myriophyllum amphibium

Broad Water-milfoil

P

Habitat: Semiaquatic in swamps and waterholes of wattle tea-tree scrub, red gum woodland and dry sclerophyll forest
Form: Mat-forming perennial herb with layering, prostrate stems
Foliage: Paired, obovate to oblanceolate leaves to 10 mm long
Submerged leaves entire or sometimes with 1 or 2 lobes
Flowers: Red flowers; November to February. Purplish black fruit.
Requirements: Moist soil
Comments: May be tolerant to low salinity and high levels of heavy metal pollution. Locally rare.
Localities: 35, 42, 75
Distribution: Vic, Tas, SA

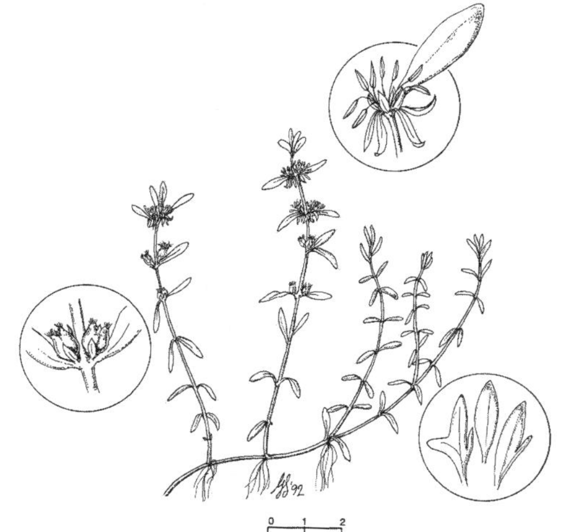

Myriophyllum amphibium

SCALE: 0 1cm 2cm The scale representation on each plant equals 2cm.

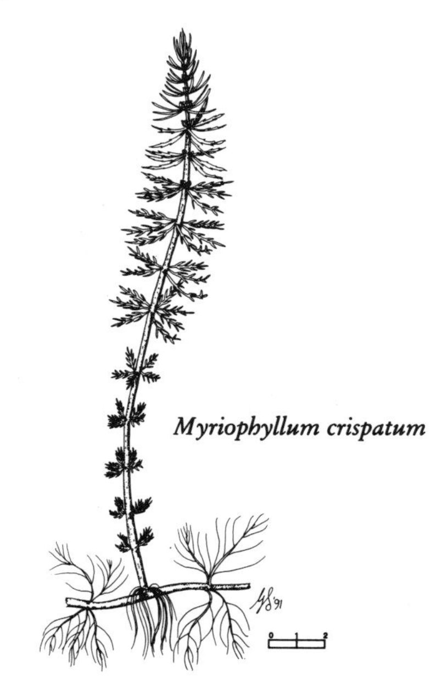

Myriophyllum crispatum

Myriophyllum caput-medusae

Coarse Water-milfoil

Size: Stems 0.3–2 m long **F P**
Habitat: Aquatic, in riparian scrub
Form: Perennial herb, sparsely branched below the water line, profusely above
Foliage: Submerged—whorls of 3–5 pinnate leaves to 20 mm long
Emergent—glaucous, often with purplish tip, in whorls of 3–5, becoming alternate. Leaves lobed, becoming entire, ovate to oblong, to 8 mm long.
Flowers: Yellow to reddish male flowers above green female flowers, in simple or branched spikes arising from the upper submerged leaves. Olive-brown cylindrical fruit with dense, fine spines; November to February.
Comments: Plants grow in water up to 2 m deep.
Localities: Kew, possibly Merri Ck
Distribution: Vic, NSW, SA
Synonym: Previously included under *M. elatinoides*

Myriophyllum crispatum

Size: 0.25–0.6 m high **F P**
Habitat: Widespread in swamps, still or slow flowing water. Will grow in water to 1 m deep.
Form: Erect perennial herb on short rhizomes
Foliage: Whorls of 5–8 leaves
Submerged—ovate in outline, pinnate to 30 mm long, segments thread-like
Intermediate—narrow to broadly lanceolate in outline, pinnate, lowest very short, upper to 17 mm long, toothed
Uppermost—terete, entire, 5–18 mm long
Flowers: Cream to reddish-brown flowers; October to April. Cubic fruit yellow brown to deep red.
Requirements: Moist to wet soil
Comments: This robust species can be recognised by the dense wavy hairs on the stems and on some leaves where the plant is not submerged. The emergent stem is spindle-shaped.
Localities: Basalt plains, 34A, 42
Distribution: All states except NT
Synonym: Previously included under *M. propinquum*

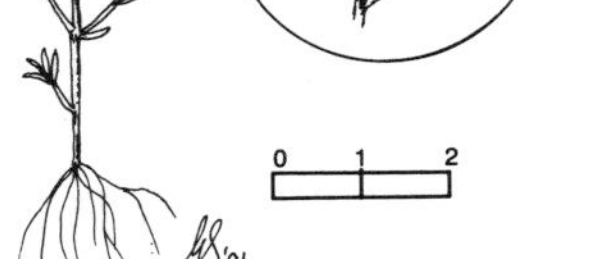

Myriophyllum integrifolium

Myriophyllum integrifolium

Tiny Water-milfoil

Size: 20–40 mm high **P**
Habitat: Valley sclerophyll forest, grassy low open forest
Form: Tiny, erect or trailing annual herb
Foliage: All leaves entire, or the lowermost rarely trifid, 1.2–3.5 mm long, upper ones shorter
Flowers: Red flowers are single and fruit is rounded
Localities: 42, 62, 66, 67, 75
Distribution: Vic, Tas, SA

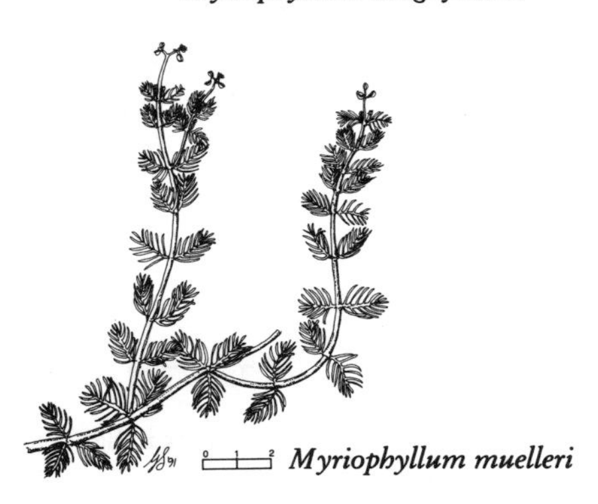

Myriophyllum muelleri

Myriophyllum muelleri

Size: to 0.6 m high **F P**
Habitat: Aquatic in grassy wetlands, growing in up to 60 cm of water
Form: Slender annual herb, rooting at the base
Foliage: Sessile pinnate leaves to 11 mm long, spreading at right angles from the stem. The leaves become thicker and smaller and the plant sterile if the water dries up.
Flowers: Single hooded red male flower at the end of flowering stem, single creamy yellow female flower in each axil immediately below. Cylindrical silvery-grey fruit.
Localities: Laverton, Werribee, 11
Distribution: Vic, Tas, SA, WA

Myriophyllum salsugineum

Myriophyllum salsugineum

Size: Stems 0.3–2 m long **F P**
Habitat: Aquatic, in slow-moving watercourses, tolerating brackish and calcareous water
Foliage: Similar to *M. caput-medusae* but all leaves are in whorls of 4–5.
Submerged pinnate leaves to 25 mm long
Emergent leaves—4–8 whorls, green to purplish, entire and ovate to 8 mm long, in single unbranched stem.
Flowers: Simple unbranched spike of green male flowers with a reddish tinge and petalless dark red and green female flowers in the axils of emergent leaves; September to February peaking in Summer. Cubic or roundish fruit is smooth.
Comments: Normally in water up to 2 m deep, it has been found in very deep water to 6 m.
Localities: Highett, Mt Eliza 1885
Distribution: Vic, NSW, Tas, SA, WA
Synonym: Previously included under *M. elatinoides*

Myriophyllum simulans

Size: to 0.4 m high **F P**
Habitat: Aquatic, growing in water to 0.5 m deep, or in mud and seepage areas of wattle tea-tree scrub
Form: Perennial herb with erect, weak, often reddish stems, rooting at nodes
Foliage: Submerged leaves—whorls of 4–5, close together and pinnate, to 25 mm long, segments thread-like
Emergent—irregular whorls of 3–4 entire, narrow leaves to 15 mm long, fleshy and toothed
Flowers: Reddish male and female flowers often on different shoots; September to December. Fruit cubic, reddish purple.
Comments: Very variable species in both habitat and appearance, needing some drying out for good setting of fruit. Emergent leaves grow on previously submerged stems.
Localities: Basalt plains, 75
Distribution: Vic, Qld, NSW, Tas, SA
Synonym: Previously included under *M. propinquum*

Myriophyllum simulans

Myriophyllum variifolium

Size: stems 0.3–0.5 m long **F P**
Habitat: Aquatic, in valley sclerophyll forest, tea-tree heath
Form: Aquatic perennial herb, erect in deep water to 2 m, prostrate and rooting at nodes in shallow water.
Comments: Very similar to *M. simulans*. All emergent leaves are whorled. Male flowers are yellow to red, female are white; fruit—cylindrical and yellow-brown.
Localities: Basalt plains, Montrose, 60, 61, ?67#
Distribution: Vic, Qld, NSW, Tas, SA
Synonym: Previously included under *M. propinquum*

Myriophyllum verrucosum

Red Water-milfoil

Size: Stems from 0.1–1.5 m **F P**
Habitat: Aquatic, in water usually less than 2 m deep, but will grow in water up to 4 m deep. Also permanently wet or muddy swamps in grassy wetlands
Form: Sparsely branched perennial rooting at lower nodes, only tips emergent
Foliage: Whorls of 3–4 leaves
Submerged—bright to dark green pinnate leaves to 12 mm long, rounded tips
Intermediate—in 1–2 whorls
Emergent—mid green, bluish or reddish-purple leaves, dissected and lanceolate to ovate to 9 mm long
Flowers: Flowers may be produced throughout the year, but mostly during the warmer months. Male flowers are yellow or occasionally pink. Female flowers have deciduous petals. Cubic fruit is straw, red or grey colored.
Comments: The most widespread *Myriophyllum*, it can be found in deep fast flowing water as well as shallow brackish or calcareous situations. Swamp-grown plants flower and fruit prolifically as water levels begin to fall during Summer.
Localities: Altona, Braybrook#, Melbourne#, Caulfield#, 16, 35
Distribution: All mainland states

Myriophyllum verrucosum

Neopaxia — Portulacaceae

Neopaxia australasica

White Purslane

Size: Prostrate creeper **F P**
Habitat: Swamps and bogs of tea-tree heath, swamp scrub, grassy wetlands, sometimes aquatic in running water
Form: Spreading perennial herb, rooting at nodes
Foliage: Erect, narrow succulent leaves 30–100 mm x 1–4 mm, emergent in water
Flowers: Long-stalked, small white flowers in terminal groups of 1–4; November to March
Requirements: Moist to wet soils
Comments: A pretty little creeper for pond edges and bog gardens which may become invasive in ideal conditions. The alpine form has thicker foliage and is more floriferous.
Propagation: Division
Localities: Laverton Nth, Seaford, 33, 34A, 35, 42, 61, 67#, 69A, 71, 74, 75
Distribution: Vic, NSW, Tas, SA, WA; NZ
Synonym: *Claytonia australasica, Montia australasica*

Neopaxia australasica

Nertera reptans = Leptostigma reptans

SCALE: 0 1cm 2cm The scale representation on each plant equals 2cm.

Nicotiana — Solanaceae

Nicotiana suaveolens

Nicotiana maritima

Coast Tobacco

Size: to 0.7 m high
Habitat: Along watercourses in red gum woodland
Form: Upright annual herb with white- or grey-woolly hairs at the base of the stems
Foliage: Basal rosette of woolly ovate or elliptic leaves 2–22 cm long with wavy margins, stalks winged
Flowers: Branched flowering stem with terminal clusters of cream tubular flowers to 25 mm long most of the year, peaking in Spring. Calyx hairy.
Requirements: Sandy soil
Comments: Similar to *N. suaveolens*. Now extinct in Victoria the last collection for Melbourne was in 1883.
Localities: Port Phillip area, 30#
Distribution: Vic, SA

Nicotiana suaveolens

Scented or Austral Tobacco

Size: 0.3–1.5 m F
Habitat: Rocky gullies of riparian scrub, box woodland
Form: Fast growing upright annual herb
Foliage: Basal rosette of fleshy, oblanceolate, dull green leaves 10–35 cm; few stem leaves are smaller and narrower.
Flowers: Terminal white to cream tubular flowers to 45 mm long in loose clusters; April to September
Requirements: Well drained dry sandy soil
Comments: Flowers are very fragrant at night. The crushed leaves were chewed as a substitute for tobacco. Locally rare.
Propagation: Seed, cuttings
Localities: Sunbury, Keilor, Essendon, Maribyrnong, Kew, 16, 26, 29
Distribution: Vic, Qld, NSW, SA

Notelaea — Oleaceae

Notelaea ligustrina

Notelaea ligustrina

Native or Privet Mock Olive

Size: 2–8 m x 3 m P N
Habitat: Cool temperate rainforest, wet sclerophyll forest
Form: Dense upright tall shrub or small tree
Foliage: Pairs of dull green, lanceolate leaves 40–90 mm long, paler below
Flowers: Racemes of insignificant creamy-yellow flowers; September. Oval, fleshy drupes to 10 mm long, white, pink, purple or black.
Requirements: Well drained, moist loamy soils
Comments: A useful screen plant for shady areas. Known from one location in the Melbourne area.
Propagation: Seed, cuttings
Localities: 57
Distribution: Vic, NSW, Tas

Olearia — Asteraceae

Widespread through many habitats, 13 species occur in the Melbourne area. A member of the daisy family, they have flowerheads consisting of multiple tubular florets surrounded by ray florets. They are woody shrubs, varying from small shrublets to small trees, all requiring pruning to encourage bushiness. Usually flowering profusely for several months, they are an attractive addition to the garden. Propagation is by seed or cutting.

Olearia argophylla

Olearia argophylla

Musk Daisy-bush

Size: 3–8 m x 3–5 m P N
Habitat: Moist gullies of cool temperate rainforest, wet, damp and valley sclerophyll forests
Form: Fast growing tall shrub or small tree
Foliage: Large, shiny, dark green, slightly-toothed elliptical leaves to 15 cm long, silvery below, with musky aroma
Flowers: Large terminal clusters of small white flowers with 3–5 ray florets; October to December
Requirements: Moist, rich, well drained soils
Comments: The largest *Olearia* sp., it is a very attractive tree for a shady area.
Localities: 42, 55–58, 60
Distribution: Vic, NSW, Tas

Olearia asterotricha

Rough Daisy-bush

Size: 1–2 m x 1 m **P**
Habitat: Grassy low open forest, valley sclerophyll forest
Form: Erect shrub
Foliage: Variable; rough and hairy, dull green linear leaves to 30 mm long, pale below, margins rolled under and/or lobed
Flowers: Single blue to mauve flowerheads with 12–24 ray florets, on long stalks; November to January
Requirements: Moist soils
Comments: Branchlets and foliage are covered with star-shaped hairs. A form with larger leaves also occurs in Mallacoota. It has leaves to 60 mm long with lobed margins which are hardly or not rolled under.
Localities: Sth Belgrave, Dandenong, Upper Beaconsfield
Distribution: Vic, NSW

Olearia asterotricha

Olearia axillaris

Coast Daisy-bush

Size: 1–2 m x 1–2 m **F**
Habitat: Primary dune scrub, coastal cliffs
Form: Erect, dense shrub
Foliage: Hoary narrow leaves to 25 mm long, becoming glabrous and dark green above and woolly-white below, margins rolled under
Flowers: Small, stalkless yellow flowerheads along upper branches, ray florets minute; February to April
Requirements: Well drained dry sandy soil
Comments: An interesting foliage plant with aromatic leaves, resistant to salt spray.
Localities: Seaford, 67, 74
Distribution: Vic, NSW, Tas, SA, WA

Olearia axillaris

Olearia ciliata

Fringed Daisy-bush

Size: 20–40 cm x 40–60 cm **F P**
Habitat: Tea-tree heath
Form: Small dense shrub
Foliage: Narrow, pointed, bright green leaves with margins rolled under, to 25 mm long, crowded along stems
Flowers: Single bright blue to purple flowerheads to 30 mm across, with yellow centres, held above foliage on reddish stems 5–25 cm long
Requirements: Well drained light soils tolerating lime
Comments: An attractive little shrub, useful for growing amongst other plants in a rockery. An endangered Melbourne species which may already be extinct.
Localities: 67#
Distribution: Vic, NSW, Tas, SA, WA

Olearia ciliata

Olearia decurrens

Clammy Daisy-bush

Size: 1–2 m x 1 m **F P**
Habitat: Box and red gum woodlands
Form: Erect open shrub
Foliage: Sticky, narrow-oblanceolate, bright green leaves 10–50 mm long, flat, usually with a few teeth or lobes
Flowers: Loose terminal panicles of white flowerheads with yellow centres; December to March. Ray florets 3–5.
Requirements: Well drained soils
Comments: A sticky shrub with aromatic leaves.
Localities: Diggers Rest 1901, Holden, Bulla
Distribution: Vic, NSW, SA

Olearia erubescens

Moth Daisy-bush

Size: 0.3–0.5 m x 0.5 m **F P**
Habitat: Dry and damp sclerophyll forests
Form: Small spindly shrub
Foliage: Dark green oblong to lanceolate toothed leaves to 40 mm long, paler below with white or rusty hairs. Young growth reddish.
Flowers: Small loose panicles of white to pink flowerheads with yellow centres, on long stalks to 50 mm; September to November. Ray florets 4–8.
Requirements: Well drained soils tolerating dryness once established
Comments: A straggly shrub by nature, it looks good planted amongst other shrubs. This species is often confused with O. *myrsinoides* which has shorter, broader and blunter leaves and less than 4 ray florets per flowerhead.
A form resembling O. *speciosa* but believed to be a hybrid with O. *argophylla* is found in isolated patches on Mt. Dandenong and in Mt. Evelyn. It has larger, ovate, lighter green leaves and generally lacks the reddish new growth. There are also more flowers in the panicle than O. *erubescens*. Further research is required to clarify its relationship to O. *speciosa*.
Localities: Eltham, 49, 55, 56
Distribution: Vic, NSW, Tas, SA

Olearia erubescens

The scale representation on each plant equals 2cm.

Olearia glandulosa

Olearia glutinosa

Olearia lirata

Olearia phlogopappa var. phlogopappa

Olearia glandulosa

Swamp Daisy-bush

F P

Size: 1–2 m x 1 m
Habitat: Swamp scrub
Form: Open, erect shrub
Foliage: Fine, sessile dark green leaves to 60 mm long, sticky to touch. The tightly rolled margins have several glandular swellings along their length.
Flowers: Dense terminal panicles of white or bluish flowerheads with yellow centres; November to April. Ray florets 12–15.
Requirements: Moist soils, tolerating some waterlogging in Winter
Comments: An attractive plant for a damp place in the garden. Locally rare.
Localities: Kilsyth
Distribution: Vic, NSW, Tas, SA

Olearia glutinosa

Sticky Daisy-bush

F

Size: 2 m x 1.5 m
Habitat: Primary dune scrub
Form: Dense rounded shrub
Foliage: Sticky, narrow, greyish leaves to 30 mm long, pointed at the end
Flowers: Terminal clusters of blue or white flowerheads with 6–8 ray florets; December to February
Requirements: Well drained sandy soil
Comments: A useful plant for coastal gardens, resistant to salt spray.
Localities: Seaford, 5, 67, 74
Distribution: Vic, NSW, Tas

Olearia lirata

Snowy Daisy-bush

P N

Size: 2–5 m x 2–3 m
Habitat: Moist gullies in damp and valley sclerophyll forests, grassy low open forest
Form: Soft open shrub
Foliage: Dark green lanceolate leaves to 16 cm long, whitish below
Flowers: Masses of small white flowerheads with about 15 ray florets, in large, loose panicles at or near the ends of branches; September to December.
Requirements: Moist well drained soil
Comments: An excellent shrub brightening a sheltered position in Spring.
Localities: 34, 34A, 42–44, 47, 49, 50A–59, 61–64, 74–76
Distribution: Vic, NSW, Tas

Olearia myrsinoides

Silky Daisy-bush

F P

Size: 0.3–1.5 m x 1 m
Habitat: Dry and valley sclerophyll forests
Form: Small open spreading shrub
Foliage: Shiny dark green obovate leaves to 20 mm long, silvery-greyish below, with serrated margins
Flowers: Tight clusters of flowerheads with yellow centres, and 3 white ray florets; October to February
Requirements: Well drained soils
Comments: Similar to O. *erubescens* which has longer, narrower, more pointed leaves, reddish new growth and more than 4 ray florets.
Localities: Sth Morang, Park Orchards, Wantirna, Warrandyte, Montrose, 40, 43, 47, 49–53, 56, 58
Distribution: Vic, NSW, Tas *Illustrated p. 49*

Olearia phlogopappa var. phlogopappa

Dusty Daisy-bush

F P

Size: 1–3 m x 1–2 m
Habitat: Valley sclerophyll forest
Form: Fast growing open to dense shrub
Foliage: Grey-green oblong leaves to 80 mm long, white below, with wavy, toothed margins
Flowers: Masses of long-stalked white, pink, blue or mauve flowerheads with yellow centres, in axillary clusters, in the upper branches; August to January. Ray florets 8–15.
Requirements: Well drained soils
Comments: One of the most attractive *Olearia* species. White is the most common colour form locally but others may be grown from selected clones.
Localities: 34, 47, 50, 50A, 55
Distribution: Vic, NSW, Tas

Olearia ramulosa var. ramulosa — Twiggy Daisy-bush

Size: 0.5–2.5 m x 1 m — F P
Habitat: Widespread in red gum woodland, damp sclerophyll forest, grassy low open forest, tea-tree heath, primary dune scrub
Form: Open spindly, often sprawling, shrub
Foliage: Narrow crowded leaves to 8 mm long, white below, sometimes sticky, with margins rolled under
Flowers: Masses of small, white or mauve flowerheads along branches; September to May. Ray florets 3–15.
Requirements: Well drained soils
Comments: Attractive garden plant especially the mauve, suckering form. Grows well in an understorey situation. Pruning as the flowers begin to fade usually encourages a further flush of flowers.
Localities: 30–32, 34A, 35, 42, 44, 58, 60, 66–71, 73–76
Distribution: All states except NT

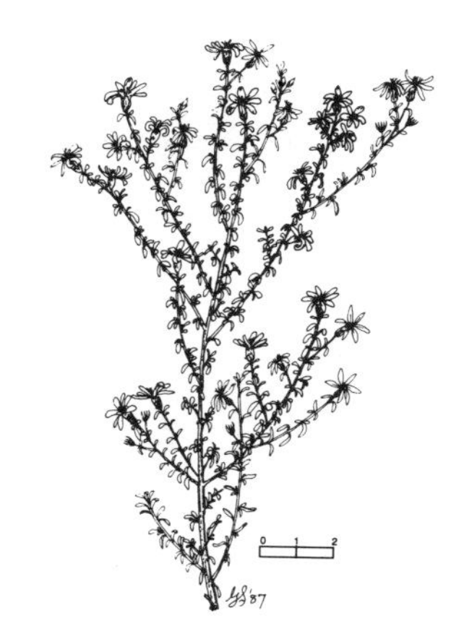

Olearia ramulosa var. *ramulosa*

Olearia rugosa — Wrinkled Daisy-bush

Size: 1–2 m x 1 m — P
Habitat: Damp sclerophyll forest
Form: Upright shrub
Foliage: Rough, deeply wrinkled, broadly-ovate leaves to 70 mm long, brown hairs below, toothed or entire on the same plant. Network of veins prominent.
Flowers: Small panicles of white flowerheads held erect on stiff stalks; October to November
Requirements: Moist well drained soil
Comments: An attractive foliage plant for a sheltered position.
Localities: Mt. Dandenong 1901, Belgrave 1932; Olinda
Distribution: Endemic to Vic

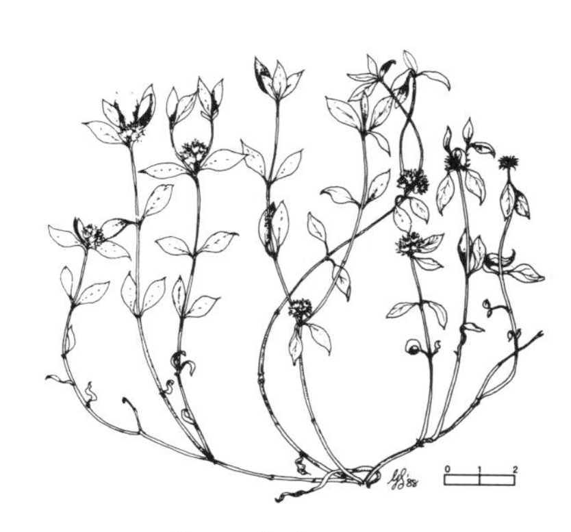

Opercularia ovata

Opercularia — Rubiaceae

Opercularia ovata — Broad Stinkweed

Size: to 15 cm x 5–30 cm — F P
Habitat: Red gum woodland, dry and valley sclerophyll forests, grassy low open forest
Form: Smaller than O. *varia* with a similar densely sprawling habit. Branching occurs from several points off an underground rhizome.
Foliage: Leaves are lighter green and ovate, on lax, somewhat angular stems. A narrow-leaf form occurs in Watsonia.
Flowers: Spherical cluster contains 10–18 flowers.
Localities: 34A, 35, 38, 39, 41, 42, 47–49, 50A-52, 54, 55, 59, 62–69, 74, 76
Distribution: Vic, Tas, SA

Opercularia varia — Variable Stinkweed

Size: 5–25 cm x 5–30 cm — P N
Habitat: Dry and valley sclerophyll forests, grassy low open forest, tea-tree heath, wattle tea-tree scrub
Form: Sprawling or upright perennial herb forming a clump
Foliage: Scattered pairs of sessile, narrow to lanceolate leaves to 12 mm long, with margins rolled under
Flowers: Inconspicuous green or purple flowers in tight hemispherical clusters of 2–7; Spring. Spiky green fruit are larger than flowers.
Requirements: Moist, well drained soils
Comments: Branching occurs from a single short basal stem. The leaves exude an unpleasant aroma when crushed.
Propagation: Seeds, cuttings
Localities: Research, 34A, 36, 40–42, 44–48, 50–51, 53–56, 58–60, 62, 67#, 69A–71, 74–76
Distribution: Vic, Qld, NSW, Tas, SA

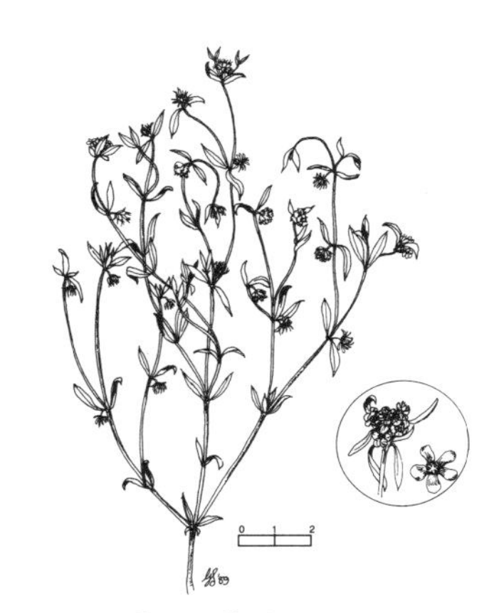

Opercularia varia

Oreomyrrhis — Apiaceae

Oreomyrrhis eriopoda — Hairy Carroway

Size: 15–40 cm high — F P
Habitat: Dry sclerophyll forest, box woodland
Form: Rosetted perennial herb
Foliage: Basal tuft of hairy, bipinnate, grey-green leaves to 20 cm long
Flowers: Terminal umbels of 12–35 tiny white flowers with purple anthers on erect stems to 40 cm long; September to November. Large brown or purplish fruit, like carroway seeds, develop on long stalks.
Requirements: Well drained soils
Comments: Locally rare
Propagation: Seed
Localities: 26, ?42, 55
Distribution: Vic, NSW, Tas, SA

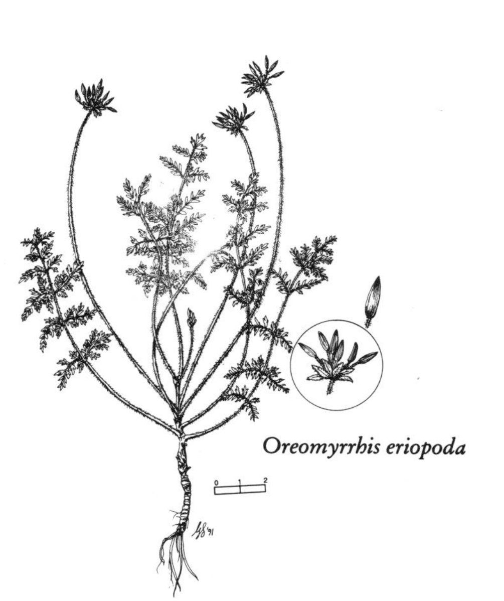

Oreomyrrhis eriopoda

SCALE: 0 1cm 2cm — The scale representation on each plant equals 2cm.

Oxalis **Oxalidaceae**

Oxalis is a widespread genus found throughout Australia and overseas which may become invasive in the garden. The local spp. are usually hairy with trifoliate clover-like leaves and small yellow flowers which are followed by cylindrical fruit. Propagation is by seed.

Oxalis perennans

Oxalis exilis

F P

Habitat: Damp and valley sclerophyll forests, box woodland, riparian scrub, grassy low open forest
Comments: Similar to *O. perennans* but smaller. Flowers are usually solitary, and fruit capsules shorter, to 9 mm long, and broader. Prefers rich peaty soils beside creeks. Some authors consider *O. perennans* and *O. exilis* to be conspecific.
Localities: Sth of Melton, 17#, 18, 21, 28, 34A, 36, 42, 44, 47, 48, 53–56, 69A, 71, 74, 76
Distribution: Vic, Qld, NSW, SA

Oxalis perennans

Size: 30 cm high **F P**
Habitat: Widespread in grassy wetlands, plains grassland, red gum woodland, valley sclerophyll forest
Form: Erect or creeping herb
Foliage: Wedge-shaped leaflets; individual leaves to 15 mm long on stalks 10–40 mm long
Flowers: 2–3 yellow flowers on stalks as tall or taller than leaves; throughout the year. Slender hairy fruit capsules from 4–30 mm long, held erect.
Requirements: Heavy soil
Comments: Stem hairs on this species point upwards. The stout tap root is edible.
Localities: 2, 4, 6, 8, 9, 14–18, 21, 23, 26, 28, 31, 32, 34A–36, 42, 46–49, 50A, 54–57, 61, 65–68, 69A, 74
Distribution: All mainland states; NZ
Synonym: Has been confused in the past with the introduced species *O. corniculata* and may occur in other areas.

Oxalis radicosa

F P

Habitat: Box woodland
Comments: Also similar to *O. perennans* but found on sandy soil. Dense stem hairs are widely spreading or bent backwards. Leaflets have rounded lobes. Fruit capsules are 10–20 mm long. Flowering March to November.
Localities: 9, 11, 12, 17#, 18, 26, 28, 71
Distribution: Vic, Qld, NSW, SA; Af, S Asia, Pacific

Ozothamnus **Asteraceae**

Ozothamnus spp. belong to the group of daisies known as everlastings. They are all shrubby in habit. The flowerheads are in broad flat terminal clusters and are long-lasting. They are useful as fillers in dried flower arrangements. *Ozothamnus* spp. are very adaptable and make excellent garden subjects. It is preferable to prune them back in late winter to encourage bushiness. Propagation is by seed or cuttings.
Synonym: *Helichrysum*

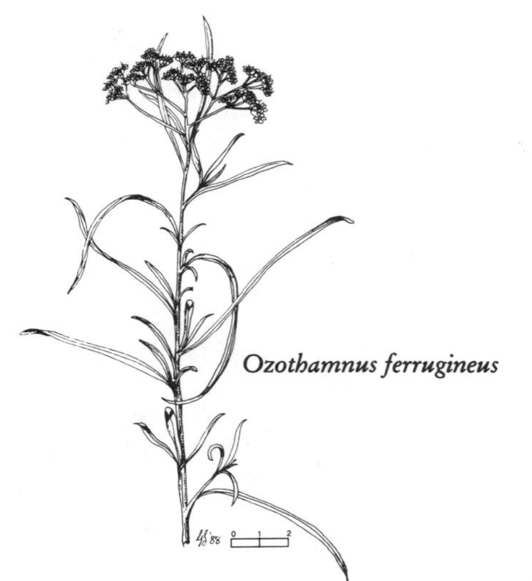

Ozothamnus ferrugineus

Ozothamnus ferrugineus

Tree Everlasting

Size: 2–6 m x 1–3 m **F P**
Habitat: Wet, damp and valley sclerophyll forests, red gum woodland, swamp and wattle-tree scrub, grassy low open forest
Form: Open rounded shrub or small tree
Foliage: Narrow dark green leaves to 70 mm long, whitish below
Flowers: Broad clusters of white flowerheads at the ends of branches; November to February
Requirements: Moist well drained soil
Comments: The yellow-green bracts which surround the flowers before they open is a useful feature to distinguish *O. ferrugineus* from *Cassinia* spp. It is very widespread and common in moist areas. A hybrid occurs between *O. ferrugineus* and *O. rosmarinifolius* in the foothills of the Dandenongs.
Localities: Seaford, 29#, 30, 33–37, 41, 42, 44, 47–60, 62–67#, 69A–71, 74–76
Distribution: Vic, NSW, Tas, SA
Synonym: *Helichrysum dendroideum*

Ozothamnus obcordatus
Grey Everlasting

Size: 1–2 m x 1 m **F P**
Habitat: Dry sclerophyll forest, box and box ironbark woodland, on shallow stony soil
Form: Slender erect shrub
Foliage: Broadly elliptic, obovate or wedge-shaped, shiny dark green leaves to 15 mm long, white below
Flowers: Numerous dense clusters of tubular yellow flowers; October to January
Requirements: Well drained dryish conditions
Comments: A showy shrub for a difficult spot.
Localities: Sth of Melton, 26, 34A–36, 42, 51
Distribution: Vic, Qld, NSW, Tas
Synonym: *Helichrysum obcordatum*

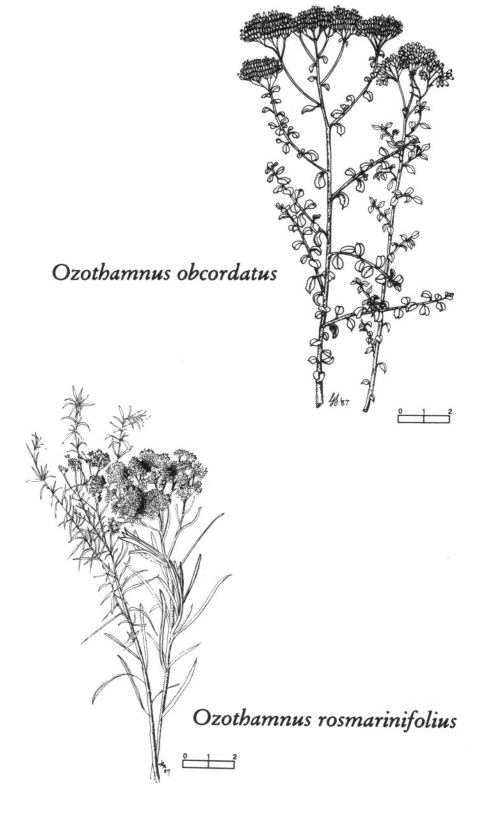

Ozothamnus obcordatus

Ozothamnus rosmarinifolius
Rosemary Everlasting

Size: 1.5–3 m x 1–2 m **F P**
Habitat: Swamp scrub
Form: Upright shrub
Foliage: Rough, narrow dark green leaves to 40 mm long, white below, with margins rolled under, leaves held erect
Flowers: Clusters of whitish flowers with yellow or crimson bracts; December to March
Requirements: Well drained, moist soil
Localities: Dingley#; Montrose, 54, 60, 67#, 74
Distribution: Vic, Tas
Synonym: *Helichrysum rosmarinifolium*

Ozothamnus rosmarinifolius

Ozothamnus turbinatus
Coast Everlasting

Size: 1–3 m x 1.5 m **F**
Habitat: Exposed sites on cliffs and primary dune scrub
Form: Dense upright to rounded hairy shrub
Foliage: Stiff, narrow grey-green leaves to 25 mm long, woolly white below, tinged yellow at the base, margins rolled under
Flowers: Dense clusters of cream tubular flowers surrounded by hairy yellow bracts; February to May
Requirements: Sandy, well drained soil
Comments: Easily grown, it benefits from hard pruning.
Localities: Seaford, 67#, 74
Distribution: Vic, Qld, NSW, Tas, SA
Synonym: *Helichrysum paralium*

Ozothamnus turbinatus

Pandorea — Bignoniaceae

Pandorea pandorana
Wonga Vine

F P
Habitat: Wet, damp, valley and dry sclerophyll forests, grassy low open forest
Form: Dense vigorous climber
Foliage: Glossy dark green pinnate leaves, 5–11 lanceolate leaflets to 50 mm long with the longest leaflet at the end
Flowers: Bunches of tubular creamy-white flowers with maroon markings in the throat and at the tips of the corolla lobes; September to January
Requirements: Moist well drained soil
Comments: Very showy in flower, this strong climber grows well amongst established trees or over a pergola. It prefers a shaded position. Many horticultural varieties are grown but most are not the local form.
Propagation: Seed, cuttings
Localities: 42, 43, 50A–53, 55–58, 61, 74–76
Distribution: Vic, Qld, NSW, Tas

Pandorea pandorana

Parahebe derwentiana = Derwentia derwentiana

Parietaria — Urticaceae

Parietaria debilis
Shade or Forest Pellitory, Smooth Nettle

Size: 20–30 cm high **F P N**
Habitat: Riparian scrub, valley sclerophyll forest, coastal banksia woodland
Form: Straggling annual herb
Foliage: Thin, flat, ovate light green leaves to 30 mm long, young growth hairy
Flowers: Masses of small hairy greenish flowers in clusters of 3, hanging from leaf axils; August to December
Requirements: Adaptable to most conditions. Tolerates limestone
Comments: Closely related to *Urtica incisa*, the stinging nettle, but the hairs do not sting when touched. Locally rare.
Propagation: Seed, cuttings
Localities: 28, 49, 58, 67
Distribution: All states

SCALE: 0 1cm 2cm — The scale representation on each plant equals 2cm.

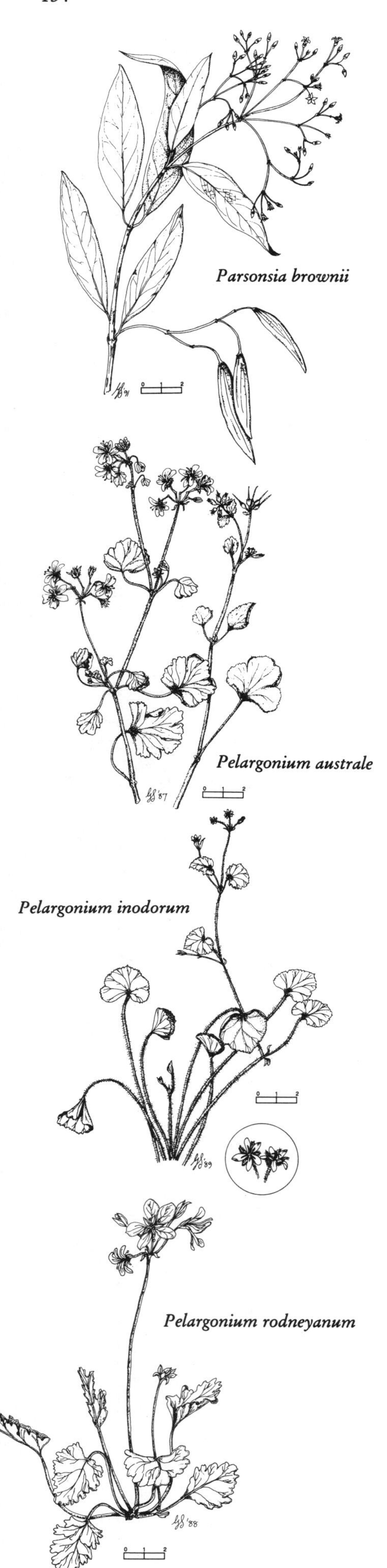

Parsonsia — Apocynaceae

Parsonsia brownii

Twining Silkpod

P N

Habitat: Wet sclerophyll forest, cool temperate rainforest
Form: Vigorous climber
Foliage: Dark green; long, narrow juvenile leaves to 100 mm x 5 mm; lanceolate adult leaves yellowish below, to 120 mm x 40 mm
Flowers: Loose clusters of small, hairy, yellow-brown flowers; September to January. Cylindrical seed pods to 80 mm long hang vertically, producing seeds with silky hairs from August to October.
Requirements: Moist well drained soil
Comments: A good climber for a shady area but may overgrow small plants. Pruning will produce a more bushy plant.
Propagation: Fresh seed, cuttings
Localities: Rowville, 56, 57
Distribution: Vic, NSW, Tas

Pelargonium — Geraniaceae

Pelargonium australe

Austral Stork's-bill

F P

Size: 0.3–0.6 m x 0.3–1 m
Habitat: Widespread on rocky outcrops in riparian scrub, damp and valley sclerophyll forests, coastal banksia woodland, primary dune scrub
Form: Soft, hairy, perennial herb forming a clump
Foliage: Pairs of aromatic, rounded, lobed leaves from 20–90 mm long, on stalks to 130 mm; velvety below
Flowers: Clusters of up to 12 pink or white 5-petalled flowers with crimson to purple veins, on long stalks; October to February. Calyx is covered in long spreading hairs.
Requirements: Well drained soils, tolerating dryness once established
Comments: An interesting rockery plant which is useful as a soil or sand binder. May die back to its rootstock during Summer, resprouting following Autumn rains.
Propagation: Seed, cuttings
Localities: Altona, St Albans, 2, 10, 16, 26, 27, 29, 30, 32, 33, 34A, 36, 42, 46, 49, 55, 58, 59, 61, 67, 72, 74–76
Distribution: All states except NT

Pelargonium inodorum

Kopata

F P

Size: 5–35 cm x 0.3–0.7 m
Habitat: Dry, valley and damp sclerophyll forests, grassy low open forest
Form: Sprawling annual or short-lived perennial herb
Foliage: Light green, ovate-cordate leaves to 80 mm long, with rounded lobes, on stalks to 50 mm long
Flowers: Clusters of tiny, deep pink flowers with darker veins; October to March
Requirements: Well drained soils
Propagation: Seed, cuttings
Localities: 34A, 42, 44, 54–59, 74, 75
Distribution: All states except NT; NZ

Pelargonium rodneyanum

Magenta Stork's-bill

F P

Size: 10–30 cm x 30–50 cm
Habitat: Rocky outcrops on plains grassland
Form: Perennial herb with a loose rosette of leaves growing from a tuberous root
Foliage: Dark green ovate leaves to 40 mm long with bluntly toothed edges, on long stalks to 100 mm long
Flowers: Small clusters of magenta flowers with darker veins, on long flowering stems; November to February
Requirements: Well drained soils
Comments: A very showy plant, excellent for a rockery or container, but needs root protection.
Propagation: Seed, cuttings
Localities: Melton, Rockbank, Sunbury, 16, 26, 30, 33
Distribution: Vic, NSW, SA, WA

Persicaria

Polygonaceae

Annual or perennial herbs. *Persicaria* spp. grow in either permanently or seasonally wet sites. They are usually erect or have decumbent stems which may root at the nodes. Spikes of many small flowers occur at or near the end of branches. Propagation is by seed or division. The seeds provide an important food source for water birds.

Synonym: Previously included with *Polygonum*

Persicaria decipiens (2 variants)

Persicaria decipiens

Slender Knotweed

Size: Prostrate-0.6 m x 1 m **F P N**
Habitat: Widespread in riparian scrub and woodland, red gum woodland, valley and damp sclerophyll forests
Form: Aquatic to semi-aquatic; glabrous, erect to spreading annual herb
Foliage: Almost sessile, lanceolate leaves to 15 cm long, often with a dark blotch. Sheathing stipules are fringed with bristles.
Flowers: Small pink flowers in slender spikes to 50 mm long, flowering stalk sometimes branched; most of the year
Localities: 4, 8, 14, 21, 26–28, 30–33, 34A–36, 42, 44, 49, 53, 56–58, 60, 62, 67, 68, 74
Distribution: All states
Synonym: *Polygonum minus*, *Polygonum decipiens*

Persicaria hydropiper

Waterpepper

Size: 0.6–1 m high **F P**
Habitat: Shallow water, swamps and depressions in riparian scrub, box woodland, valley sclerophyll forest
Form: Upright glabrous annual herb
Foliage: Lanceolate leaves from 30-90 mm long, with a hot peppery taste, sheathing stipules have bristled margins
Flowers: Small green or white flowers scattered along pendulous spikes to 15 cm long; December to February
Requirements: Wet soil or shallow water at edge of ponds
Comments: The Aborigines roasted and peeled the stem for food and used the leaves to poison fish.
Localities: 14, 16, 21, 26–28, 33, 34A–36, 42, 57
Distribution: Vic, NSW, Qld; NZ
Synonym: *Polygonum hydropiper*

Persicaria lapathifolia

Pale Knotweed

F P

Habitat: Valley sclerophyll forest
Form: Branching, erect annual herb
Foliage: Large leaves, to 20 cm long, often have a central brown blotch and ribbed stipules without bristles
Flowers: Dense, thick spikes to 70 mm long, of dull pink flowers, in terminal panicles throughout the year
Comments: Similar to *P. hydropiper* but somewhat taller, it may form prolific stands in ideal conditions.
Localities: 34A–36, 42, 44, 59, 62, 63, 71
Distribution: All states except WA; NZ
Synonym: *Polygonum lapathifolium*

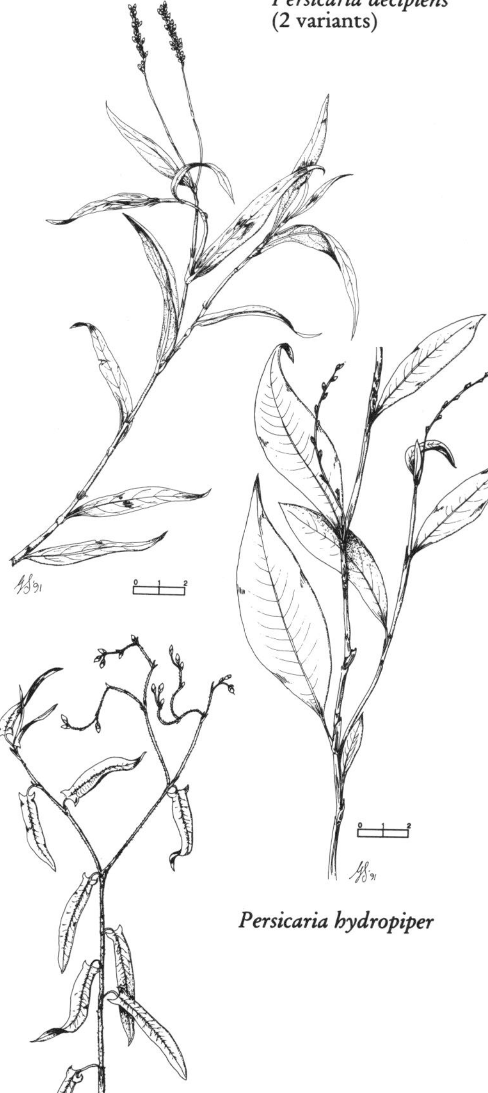

Persicaria hydropiper

Persicaria praetermissa

Persicaria praetermissa

Spotted Knotweed

P

Habitat: Valley sclerophyll forest
Form: Straggling perennial herb
Foliage: Lanceolate leaves are lobed at the base and hairy along their midribs
Flowers: Pink flowers are in short spikes in leaf axils; December to April
Comments: Confused with *P. strigosa* which does not occur in Melbourne.
Localities: Knox, 30, 33, 34A–36, 42, 51
Distribution: Vic, Qld, NSW, Tas
Synonym: Segregated from *Polygonum strigosum*

Persicaria prostrata

Creeping Knotweed

F P

Habitat: Grassy wetlands, plains grassland, valley sclerophyll forest
Form: Prostrate or decumbent perennial herb with some stems ascending, forming mats 1 m or more across
Foliage: Lanceolate leaves to 55 mm long are usually glabrous, but stems and leaf stalks are hairy. Hairy brownish sheathing stipule.
Flowers: Dense oval spikes to 20 mm long, of greenish flowers, in leaf axils; October to July
Localities: 9–11, 17#, 18, 26, 30, 33, 34A, 35, 42
Distribution: All states
Synonym: *Polygonum prostratum*

SCALE: 0 1cm 2cm The scale representation on each plant equals 2cm.

Persicaria subsessilis

Persoonia juniperina

Persicaria subsessilis

Hairy Knotweed

F P

Habitat: Riparian scrub
Form: Coarsely hairy, erect, annual or perennial herb
Foliage: Lanceolate leaves to 100 mm long
Flowers: Slender spikes, to 50 mm long, of white or pink flowers, in terminal panicles
Localities: 19, 32, 42
Distribution: Vic, Qld, NSW, Tas
Synonym: *Polygonum subsessile*

Persoonia — Proteaceae

Persoonia juniperina

Prickly Geebung

Size: 0.3–2 m x 0.6–0.8 m — **F P**
Habitat: Heathy understorey of dry and valley sclerophyll forests, grassy low open forest, tea-tree heath
Form: Erect or rounded small shrub
Foliage: Fine, prickly, light green leaves to 25 mm long, crowded towards the tips of branches
Flowers: Single yellow tubular flowers in leaf axils; December to March
Requirements: Well drained soils
Comments: An attractive shrub which may reach 2 m high in protected coastal heaths but is usually smaller in drier areas. The fleshy green drupes that follow flowering are edible.
Propagation: Cuttings, which are slow to form roots
Localities: Clayton#, 29, 49–51, 53–56, 59, 67#, 69, 73–75
Distribution: Vic, NSW, Tas, SA

Pimelea — Thymelaeaceae

Pimeleas are attractive small shrubs. Most species display striking terminal heads of flowers, often surrounded by large bracts. Leaves are almost always in pairs. Pimeleas grow in sheltered, well drained positions in the garden, some tolerating full sun. They are an important source of nectar for butterflies. Propagate from cuttings.

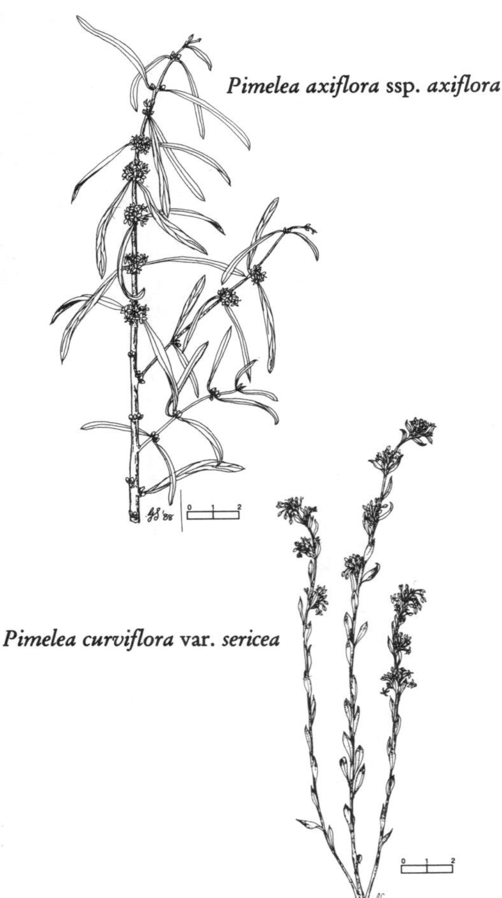

Pimelea axiflora ssp. *axiflora*

Pimelea curviflora var. *sericea*

Pimelea axiflora ssp. axiflora

Bootlace Bush, Tough Rice-flower

Size: 1–3 m x 1–2 m — **P N**
Habitat: Wet, damp and valley sclerophyll forests
Form: Open, erect or arching shrub
Foliage: Narrow dark green leaves, 10–80 mm long, paler below
Flowers: Dioecious; sessile clusters of small creamy-white flowers in each leaf axil, surrounded by 2–4 small, brown or green papery bracts; September to November.
Requirements: Moist well drained soil
Comments: The tough bark was stripped off by the Aborigines to make nets and headbands. The early settlers used it for bootlaces.
Localities: Kalorama, 49, 55–58
Distribution: Vic, NSW, Tas

Pimelea curviflora var. sericea

Curved Rice-flower

Size: 15–30 cm x 0.2–0.6 m — **F P**
Habitat: Widespread in plains grassland, red gum woodland, damp, valley and dry sclerophyll forests
Form: Erect hairy sub-shrub
Foliage: Dull green, elliptical leaves to 20 mm long, margins incurved, arranged alternately on stems
Flowers: Small terminal heads or axillary clusters of yellow-green flowers, sometimes dark red on tips, with 0–2 bracts; October to January
Requirements: Well drained soil
Comments: A variable species with many varieties, the local variety is low and spreading with upright branches.
Localities: Brighton#, Hawthorn#; Doncaster, Elsternwick, Montrose, 2, 7, 10, 12, 13, 15, 16, 21, 25, 26, 28, 29, 32, 34A, 35, 38–42, 44, 49, 51, 56, 58, 65–67#, 69A
Distribution: Vic, Qld, NSW, Tas, SA

Pimelea flava ssp. flava

Yellow Rice-flower

Size: 0.5–2 m x 0.5 m **P N**
Habitat: Damp and valley sclerophyll forests
Form: Erect, few-stemmed, slender shrub, young stems hairy
Foliage: Broad yellow-green leaves to 20 mm long, crowded along stems
Flowers: Masses of yellow flowers in terminal heads, surrounded by 2–4 ovate bracts, often larger than the leaves; August to December
Requirements: Moist well drained soils
Comments: Usually dioecious, but may be monoecious.
Localities: Kalorama, Montrose, 49, 50A, 51, 56, 59
Distribution: Vic, Tas, SA

Pimelea glauca

Smooth Rice-flower

Size: 0.3–0.6 m x 0.6 m **F P**
Habitat: Plains grassland, primary dune scrub
Form: Erect, many-branched glabrous shrub
Foliage: Narrowly-ovate, pointed, bluish-green leaves to 20 mm long
Flowers: Hairy; terminal, erect hemispherical heads, to 30 mm wide, of creamy-white flowers; July to February. 4 ovate bracts with pointed tips. The outer pair are glabrous but the inner pair have hairy margins.
Requirements: Well drained soils
Comments: The massed floral display makes this an excellent garden plant.
Localities: Laverton, Tottenham, 2, 4, 5, 10, 12, 15, 16, 18, 26, 29, 33, 34A, 41, 67#
Distribution: Vic, Qld, NSW, Tas, SA

Pimelea humilis

Common or Small Rice-flower

Size: 10–50 cm x 0.3–1 m **F P**
Habitat: Widespread in red gum woodland, valley and dry sclerophyll forests, grassy low open forest, tea-tree heath
Form: Erect or straggling perennial sub-shrub, usually with unbranched stems and a suckering habit. Young stems are densely hairy.
Foliage: Elliptic leaves are green to grey-green to 15 mm long
Flowers: Bracts (4–6) surrounding the dense creamy-white flowerheads are larger than the leaves; September to January
Requirements: Moist, well drained soils
Comments: Generally smaller than *P. glauca* from which it is distinguished by the hairy stems and the glabrous inner floral bracts. It tolerates dryness once established but with extra Summer moisture this attractive small shrub is more vigorous and the flowers tend to last longer.
Localities: 12, 16, 25, 26, 28, 29, 32–36, 38–45, 47–56, 58, 59, 62–67, 69A, 71, 73–76
Distribution: Vic, NSW, Tas, SA

Pimelea ligustrina ssp. ligustrina

Tall Rice-flower

Size: 0.5–2.5 m x 1–1.5 m **P N**
Habitat: Wet and damp sclerophyll forests
Form: Slender or bushy upright shrub
Foliage: Broad, thin-textured, shiny leaves, paler below, 10–75 mm long
Flowers: Masses of white flowers in large terminal clusters held on long, curving stalks. The yellow-tipped anthers are prominent; October to December. The 4 green bracts are broadly ovate, with pointed tips, sometimes silky hairs on the inside and margins.
Requirements: Moist well drained soil
Comments: A showy shrub for a moist, sheltered position.
Localities: Olinda, Mt Dandenong, 57, 58
Distribution: Vic, Qld, NSW, Tas, SA

Pimelea linifolia ssp. linifolia

Slender Rice-flower

Size: Prostrate-1.2 m x 1 m **F P**
Habitat: Riparian scrub, valley sclerophyll forest
Form: Variable, prostrate, erect or clump-forming, depending on habitat
Foliage: Narrow-elliptical dark green leaves to 30 mm long, margins curved inwards
Flowers: Terminal clusters of hairy white or pink flowers on long stalks. Flower-heads may be erect or nodding; July to January. The 4 broad bracts may be green or reddish.
Requirements: Well drained soils
Comments: Pruning will encourage branching. The local form is smaller, to 0.5 m high and leaves are shorter, to 15 mm long.
Localities: St. Albans, Hurstbridge, 16, 26, 29, 41, 42, 53, 56
Distribution: Vic, Qld, NSW, Tas, SA

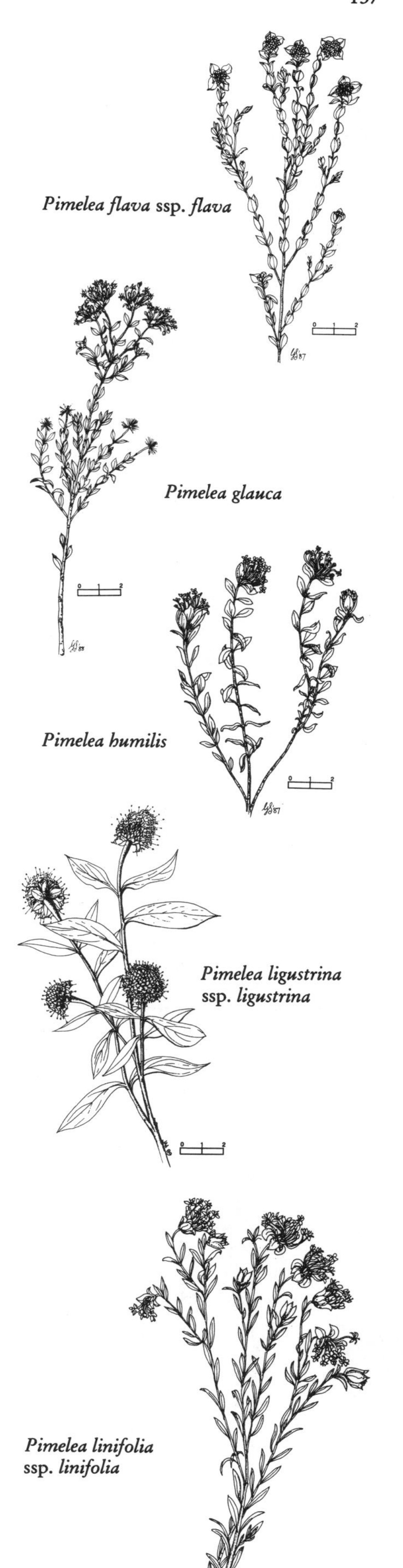

Pimelea flava ssp. *flava*

Pimelea glauca

Pimelea humilis

Pimelea ligustrina ssp. *ligustrina*

Pimelea linifolia ssp. *linifolia*

SCALE: 0 1cm 2cm The scale representation on each plant equals 2cm.

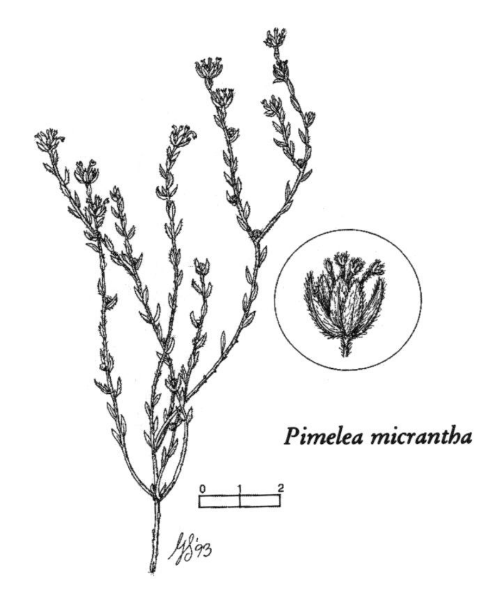

Pimelea micrantha

Pimelea micrantha

Silky Rice-flower

F P

Size: 10–40 cm high
Habitat: Riparian scrub on escarpments
Form: Erect sub-shrub, young stems covered in dense white hairs
Foliage: Hairy, pale grey-green narrowly elliptic to elliptic leaves to 10 mm long, alternate or opposite
Flowers: Compact terminal heads or axillary clusters of 3–8 tiny hairy flowers; bracts either absent or similar to the leaves; August to December
Requirements: Well drained soil
Comments: A species of north western Victoria which was recently discovered within the Melbourne area.
Localities: Taylors Lakes, Keilor Nth
Distribution: Vic, NSW, SA, WA
Synonym: *P. curviflora* var. *micrantha*

Pimelea octophylla ssp. octophylla

Woolly Rice-flower

F P

Size: 0.4–1 m x 0.5 m
Habitat: Tea-tree heath, sclerophyll woodland
Form: Slender, erect, open hairy shrub
Foliage: Green to dark bluish-green elliptical leaves to 20 mm long, covered in long, fine white hairs when young
Flowers: Masses of perfumed, woolly, creamy-yellow flowers in nodding heads; October to December. 6–12 (usually 8) densely hairy pale green bracts, no wider than the leaves.
Requirements: Well drained sandy soils
Comments: Leaves are alternate on this distinctive species.
Localities: Black Rock, Baxter, 59, 67, 68, 74, 76
Distribution: Vic, SA

Pimelea octophylla ssp. *octophylla*

Pimelea pauciflora

Poison Rice-flower

F P

Size: 1–3 m x 0.5–2 m
Habitat: Damp sclerophyll forest
Form: Slender, erect, many-branched shrub
Foliage: Dull green, narrow-elliptical leaves to 20 mm long
Flowers: Dioecious; few greenish-yellow flowers in clusters on short side branches, surrounded by 2–4 bracts which are longer than the flowerhead; October to December. Succulent red drupes follow flowering.
Requirements: Moist, well drained soils
Comments: A completely hairless, dioecious species which often forms dense thickets along mountain streams and moist, open areas. The tough bark was peeled and used to make nets by the Aborigines.
Localities: Lilydale, 50A
Distribution: Vic, NSW, Tas

Pimelea phylicoides

Heath Rice-flower

F

Size: 30–50 cm x 30 cm
Habitat: Tea-tree heath
Form: Erect, much branched shrub
Foliage: Green to blue-green elliptic leaves to 10 mm long, almost sessile, slightly toothed and hairy
Flowers: Small erect terminal flowerheads of hairy greenish-yellow, cream or white flowers; August to January. 3–6 hairy bracts broader than the leaves.
Requirements: Well drained sandy soil
Comments: Young stems are densely hairy.
Localities: Black Rock, 67#–69
Distribution: Vic, Tas, SA

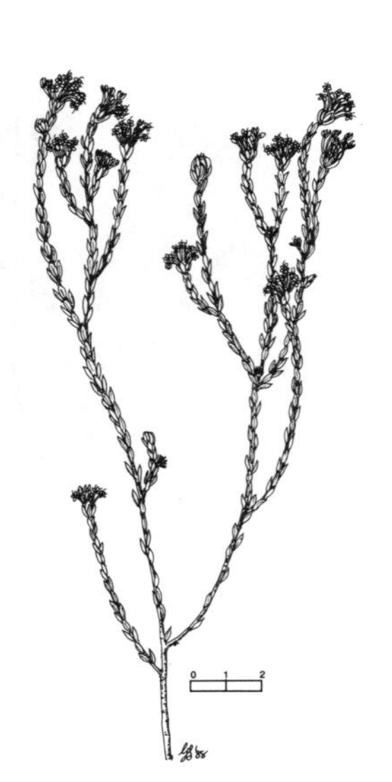

Pimelea phylicoides

Pimelea spinescens ssp. spinescens

Rice-flower

F

Size: 5–30 cm high
Habitat: Grasslands of basalt plains
Form: Low stunted shrub usually with leafless, spiny branchlets to 28 mm long
Foliage: Narrowly elliptic leaves to 10 mm long
Flowers: Insignificant terminal clusters of 6–12 tiny pale yellow glabrous flowers; April to October, inside 4 glabrous bracts to 7 mm long. Dioecious.
Requirements: Well drained soil
Comments: The only *Pimelea* sp. to have spines. It is smaller than *P. serpyllifolia* which grows behind sand dunes around the coast, south of the study area.
Localities: St Albans, Essendon, Sunshine, Deer Park, Rockbank, Altona, 4, 7, 10, 17#, 18, 20, 26
Distribution: Endemic to Vic
Synonym: Recently separated from *P. serpyllifolia*

Pittosporum

Pittosporaceae

Pittosporum bicolor

Banyalla

P N

Size: 3–10 m x 3–4 m
Habitat: Sheltered gullies of wet and damp sclerophyll forests
Form: Upright bushy shrub or small tree
Foliage: Glabrous dark green lanceolate leaves to 80 mm long, paler and hairy below. New growth is much lighter than the old leaves.
Flowers: Single, yellow, bell-shaped flower with maroon tones on the back, in leaf axils; September to November; followed by small grey fruit and sticky red seeds.
Requirements: Moist, humus-rich, well drained soils
Comments: An interesting shrub for a shaded position although it lacks the perfume of other species. Seeds often germinate on tree fern trunks. It does not become naturalised and cause an environmental problem like *P. undulatum* from East Gippsland.
Propagation: Seed, cuttings
Localities: 55, 57, 58
Distribution: Vic, NSW, Tas

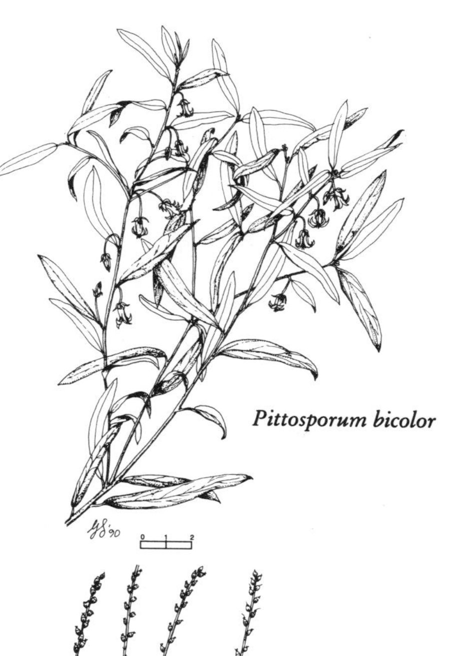

Pittosporum bicolor

Plantago

Plantaginaceae

Plantago debilis

Slender or Shade Plantain

P

Habitat: Damp and valley sclerophyll forests, grassy low open forest
Form: Rosetted perennial herb
Foliage: Oblanceolate leaves, to 15 cm x 30 mm are entire, broader and downy
Flowers: Smaller, usually glabrous, pale green flowers are widely spaced on the slender flower stalks.
Comments: Similar to *P. varia.* There is presently a lot of confusion within the genus *Plantago* and future revision will clarify this.
Localities: 34A, 36, 37, 42, ?56–58, 74
Distribution: All states

Plantago gaudichaudii

Narrow-leaf Plantain

F

Habitat: Plains grassland, red gum woodland
Foliage: Similar to *P. varia* but has narrower, linear leaves to 30 cm x 7 mm with fine brown hairs at the base. Usually glabrous.
Flowers: Compact flowering spikes to 100 mm long; August to October
Comments: A second form from the basalt plains has erect incurved leaves to 25 cm long, with the top half distantly toothed. Central vein is dominant.
Localities: 2, 7, 10, 12, 13, 17#, 18, 20, 26, 58
Distribution: Vic, Qld, NSW, Tas, SA

Plantago hispida

Plantain

F

Habitat: Box woodland
Foliage: Erect, shortly-stalked, blunt oblanceolate leaves to 145 mm long, entire or with widely-spaced lobes. Densely hairy, with a tuft of short, white or slightly tawny hairs at the base. Leaves dry to greyish-green.
Flowers: Compact flowering spikes to 80 mm long; August to November
Localities: Sunbury
Distribution: All states except NT

Plantago varia

Variable Plantain

F P

Size: 8–30 cm high
Habitat: Widespread in red gum woodland, dry, damp and valley sclerophyll forests, grassy low open forest
Form: Rosetted perennial herb
Foliage: Soft, linear-elliptic to oblanceolate hairy leaves to 20 cm x 5–20 mm, with 3 veins and sometimes toothed margins, ascending or erect. Dense tuft of brown hairs at the leaf base.
Flowers: Dense spikes (15–140 mm long) of tiny brownish flowers with hairy bracts, on leafless, upright flower stalks; most of the year
Requirements: Well drained soils
Comments: All local species are similar. Shape of the leaves help to distinguish this species as does the darker colour of the dried leaves.
Propagation: Seed
Localities: 7, 12, 13, 16, 18, 25, 26, 28, 29, 31, 32, 34A–36, 38, 39, 41–45, 47–49, 50A–53, 55, 56, 58, 62, 63, 67#, 71, 74, 76
Distribution: All states; NZ

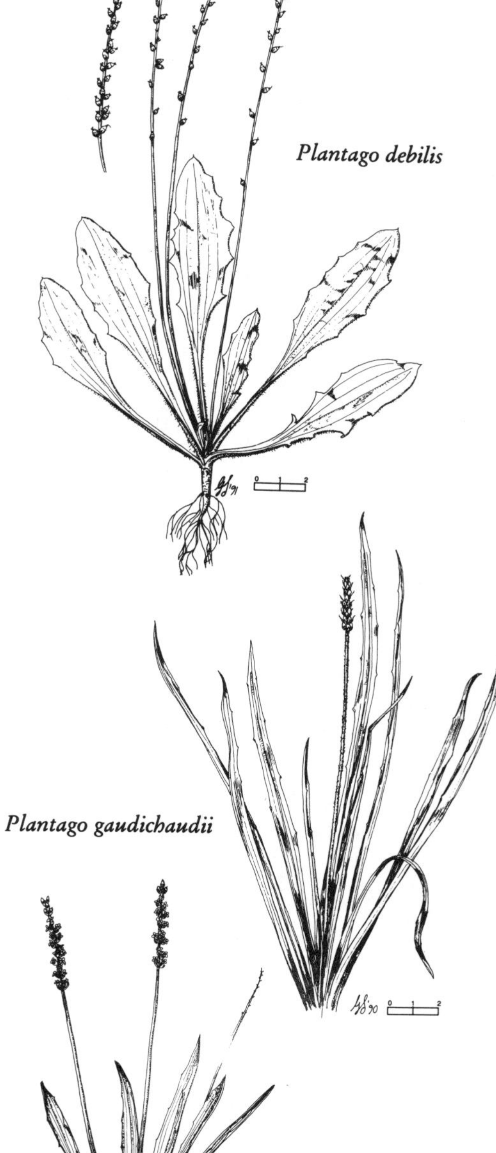

Plantago debilis

Plantago gaudichaudii

Plantago varia

SCALE: 0 1cm 2cm — The scale representation on each plant equals 2cm.

Platylobium **Fabaceae**

Platylobium formosum

Platylobium formosum

Handsome Flat-pea

F P

Size:	0.3–1.5 m x 1–1.5 m
Habitat:	Damp and valley sclerophyll forests, tea-tree heath
Form:	Wiry, upright or scrambling shrub
Foliage:	Pairs of sessile, dark green, leathery, heart-shaped leaves to 60 mm long, with raised network of veins
Flowers:	Large yellow and red pea flowers on long hairy stalks, 2–3 in leaf axils; September to December. Stalked pods to 40 mm are broad, flat and hairy with a satiny interior.
Requirements:	Moist well drained soils
Comments:	A useful plant for a shady area where it will scramble through other plants. The bright flowers only open on a sunny day.
Propagation:	Scarified seed, cuttings
Localities:	34A, 42–45, 47, 49–51, 55, 56, 58–61, 71, 74, 76
Distribution:	Vic, Qld, NSW, Tas

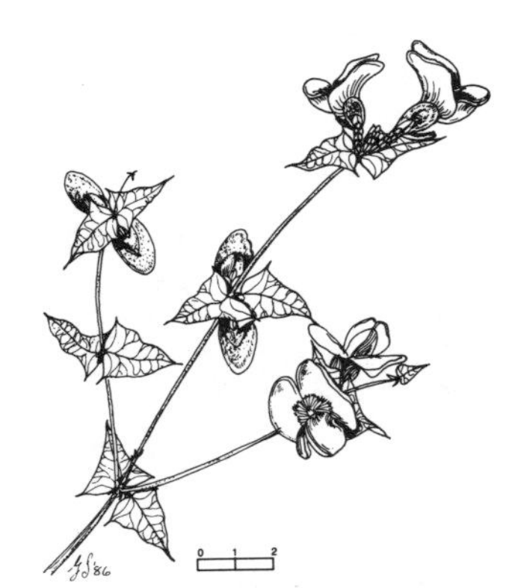
Platylobium obtusangulum

Platylobium obtusangulum

Common Flat-pea

F P

Size:	0.6–1 m x 1 m
Habitat:	Dry and valley sclerophyll forests, sclerophyll and red gum woodlands, tea-tree heath, grassy low open forest
Form:	Similar but less vigorous than *P. formosum*
Foliage:	Leaves are triangular or arrow-shaped to 30 mm long with 1–3 sharp points
Flowers:	Flowers (1–3 in axils) are on short stalks hidden by bracts. Pods are also shorter.
Requirements:	Prefers drier well drained soils.
Localities:	Highett, 32–35, 37–56, 58, 59, 62–71, 73–76
Distribution:	Vic, Tas, SA

Platysace **Apiaceae**

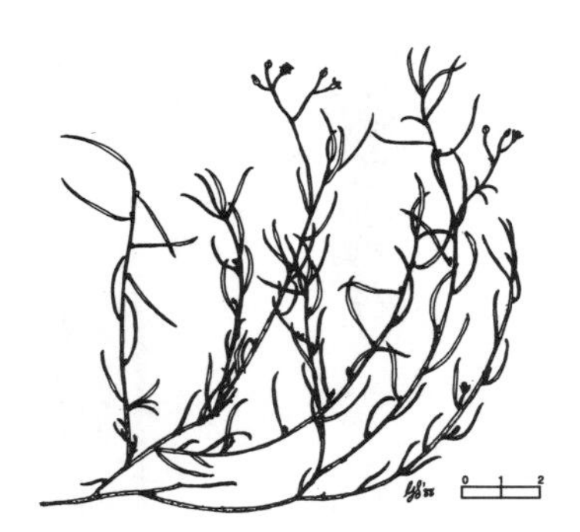
Platysace heterophylla

Platysace heterophylla

Slender Platysace

P

Size:	20–35 cm x 10 cm
Habitat:	Tea-tree heath, grassy low open forest
Form:	Trailing or tufting perennial herb
Foliage:	Very narrow leaves to 25 mm long, sometimes dark red. Lower leaves may be divided into three.
Flowers:	Small compound umbels of tiny, white, starry flowers on very slender stalks; October to January
Requirements:	Well drained soils, tolerating extra moisture in Winter
Propagation:	Seed, cuttings
Localities:	60, 67, 69, 70, 73–76
Distribution:	Vic, SA

Platysace lanceolata

Platysace lanceolata

Shrubby Platysace

P

Size:	0.6–1.5 m x 0.5–1 m
Habitat:	Dry sclerophyll forest
Form:	Open to dense rounded shrub
Foliage:	Very variable, lanceolate to nearly round, dark green leaves to 40 mm long. The local form has smaller, ovate to almost round leaves to 10 mm long.
Flowers:	Brown or pinkish flowerbuds open to tiny white flowers in rounded compound umbels to 30 mm wide; December to February
Requirements:	Well drained soils
Comments:	An attractive small shrub for a lightly shaded position, tolerating periods of dryness once established. Locally rare.
Propagation:	Seed, cuttings
Localities:	Warrandyte Nth
Distribution:	Vic, Qld, NSW

Podolepis

Asteraceae

Podolepis jaceoides

Showy Podolepis

Size:	0.3–0.6 m x 0.3 m **F P**
Habitat:	Plains grassland, grassy wetland, red gum woodland, valley sclerophyll forest, tea-tree heath
Form:	Erect tufted perennial herb
Foliage:	Dark green lanceolate leaves to 100 mm in a basal rosette; stem leaves smaller and linear
Flowers:	Showy, bright yellow daisy flowerheads to 50 mm wide, borne singly on long stems. Outer ligulate florets deeply 3–5-lobed; October to December
Requirements:	Well drained soils
Comments:	A spectacular plant in flower which grows better and flowers longer with extra Summer watering. The Aborigines baked the roots before eating. Two forms are found within the Melbourne area, both occurring together on the basalt plains. One form has few spathulate leaves and flower stalks which have 1 (or rarely) 3 flowers. The form more common in the foothills grows in clumps to 30 cm wide. It has narrow-linear leaves and branched flower stalks, each producing up to 12 flowers. The flowers are slightly smaller and more orange-yellow. Both are becoming rarer within the Melbourne area.
Propagation:	Seed
Localities:	Sunbury, Laverton, Werribee, Tottenham, Deer Park, Bundoora, Cheltenham#, 26, 42, 44, 47, 61, 67#
Distribution:	Vic, Qld, NSW, Tas, SA

Podolepis jaceoides

Podotheca

Asteraceae

Podotheca angustifolia

Sticky Long-heads

Size:	0.2–30 cm high **F**
Habitat:	Coastal banksia woodland
Form:	Erect annual herb, branching from the base
Foliage:	Sticky and hairy, narrow to oblanceolate, curved, dull green leaves 10–80 mm long
Flowers:	Terminal, narrow, woolly yellow flowerheads, to 40 mm long, on thick stalks above the foliage. Ray florets very small; September to October
Requirements:	Dryish, well drained soils
Comments:	A very sticky daisy which tolerates limestone. Presumed extinct within the Melbourne area.
Propagation:	Seed
Localities:	Cheltenham 1909, 67# 1909
Distribution:	Vic, NSW, Tas, SA, WA
Synonym:	*Podosperma angustifolium*

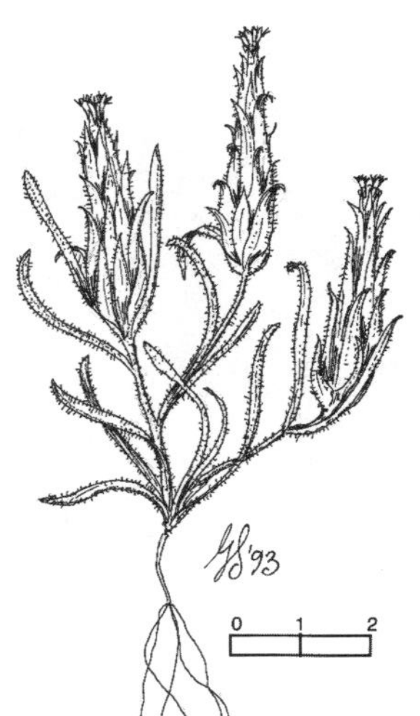

Podotheca angustifolia

Polygonum

Polygonaceae

Polygonum hydropiper = Persicaria hydropiper

Polygonum lapathifolium = Persicaria lapathifolia

Polygonum minus = Persicaria decipiens

Polygonum plebium

Small Knotweed

Size:	Prostrate x 30 cm **F P**
Habitat:	Low-lying areas of basalt plains
Form:	Compact, much-branched annual herb
Foliage:	Narrow oblong leaves to 15 mm long, with a silvery sheath at the base
Flowers:	Tight clusters of 2–5 small, white or pink flowers in leaf axils; mostly Summer
Requirements:	Damp, muddy soils
Propagation:	Seed
Localities:	Probably occurred within the south west section of the study area. Known to occur at Lara.
Distribution:	Vic, Qld, NSW, SA, NT

Polygonum plebeium

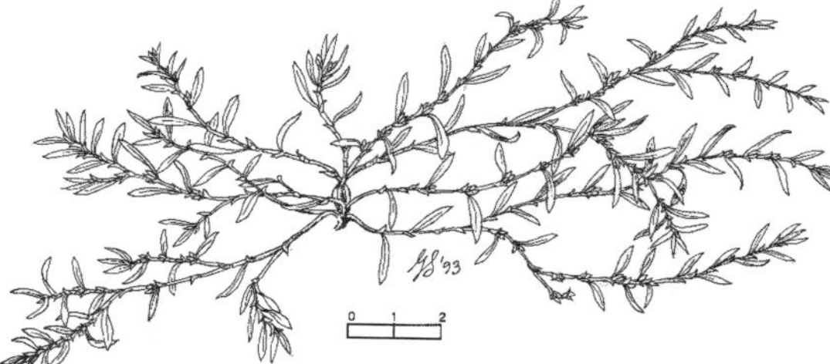

Polygonum prostratum = Persicaria prostrata

Polygonum subsessile = Persicaria subsessilis

Polypompholyx tenella = Utricularia tenella

SCALE: 0 1cm 2cm The scale representation on each plant equals 2cm.

Polyscias sambucifolius

Polyscias — Araliaceae

Polyscias sambucifolius
Elderberry Panax — P N

Size: 1–6 m x 1–3 m
Habitat: Damp, wet and valley sclerophyll forests
Form: Very variable, slender shrub or small tree
Foliage: Variable pinnate leaves; local form—leaflets narrow to lanceolate, dark green, paler below, to 110 mm long
Flowers: Clusters of small yellow-green flowers; November to January. Succulent blue berries in Summer.
Requirements: Moist well drained soil
Comments: An interesting foliage plant suitable for indoor usage.
Propagation: Cuttings, root suckers
Localities: Kalorama, 42–44, 50A, 55–58
Distribution: Vic, NSW

Pomaderris — Rhamnaceae

An attractive genus, ranging from low shrubs to small trees, often found in moist forests or near streams. Leaves are typified by the raised veins and the grey or rusty-brown star-shaped hairs on the underside. Well displayed clusters of flowers last only for a short time. Propagation is by seed or cuttings.

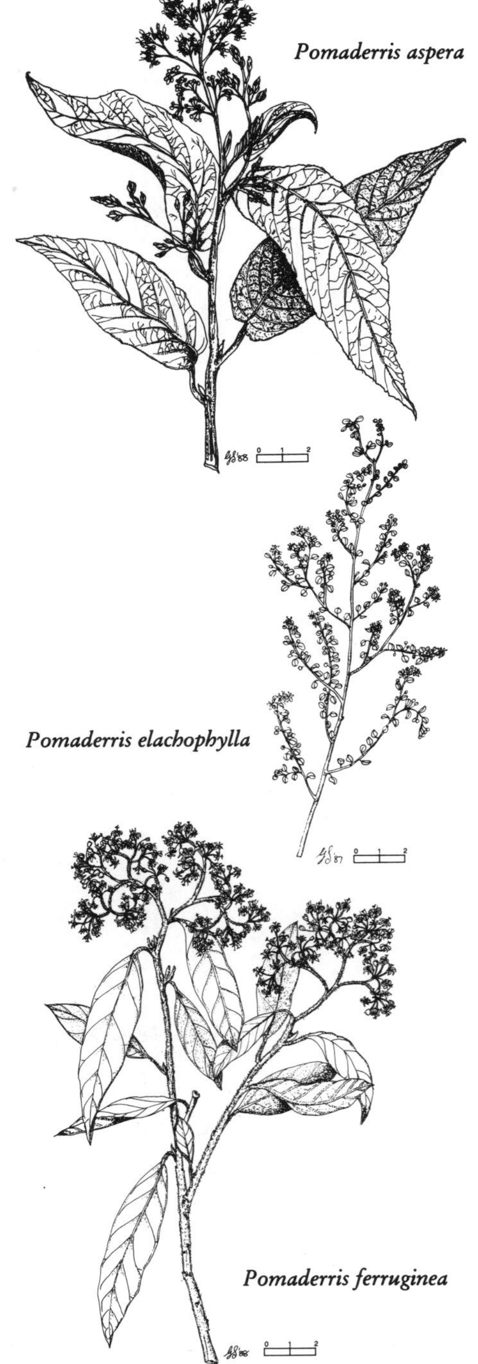

Pomaderris aspera

Pomaderris elachophylla

Pomaderris ferruginea

Pomaderris aspera
Hazel Pomaderris — P N

Size: 3–12 m x 2–4 m
Habitat: Wet, damp and valley sclerophyll forests, riparian scrub
Form: Slender leafy shrub or small tree
Foliage: Large, soft lanceolate leaves to 140 mm long, with deep veins; dark green above, paler below with pinkish-brown hairs and brown veins
Flowers: Masses of yellow-green flowers in terminal sprays; October to December. Petals absent.
Requirements: Moist, well drained, humus-rich soil
Comments: A middle storey shrub or tree with interesting markings on the bark as the plant ages. Pegs were made from the wood by the Aborigines to stretch skins.
Localities: 16, 26, 29, 32–34, 36, 42, 44, 49, 50A, 51, 55–59, 62, 63
Distribution: Vic, NSW, Tas

Pomaderris elachophylla
Small-leaf or Lacy Pomaderris — P

Size: 1–3 m x 0.5–2 m
Habitat: Valley sclerophyll forest
Form: Erect wiry open shrub
Foliage: Tiny, elliptic dark green leaves to 6 mm long, paler below with scattered brown hairs
Flowers: Small axillary clusters of tiny creamy flowers; October to November; petals absent
Requirements: Moist well drained soils
Comments: Easily identified by its tiny leaves. It is rare within the Melbourne area.
Localities: Hurstbridge
Distribution: Vic, NSW, Tas

Pomaderris elliptica
Smooth Pomaderris — P

Size: 1–4 m x 1–3 m
Habitat: Valley sclerophyll forest
Form: Tall erect or rounded shrub
Foliage: Smooth, thin, elliptic leaves to 100 mm long, pale grey below with minute hairs and raised brown veins
Flowers: Large rounded clusters of yellow flowers held above the foliage; September to October
Requirements: Moist well drained soils
Comments: One of the most attractive *Pomaderris* spp., easily grown in light shaded gardens. Rare within the Melbourne area.
Localities: Lilydale
Distribution: Vic, Qld, NSW, Tas
Synonym: *P. multiflora*

Pomaderris ferruginea
Rusty Pomaderris — F P

Size: 1–4 m x 1–1.5 m
Habitat: Valley sclerophyll forest
Form: Open softly hairy shrub
Foliage: Dull green, broad-lanceolate leaves to 100 mm long, glabrous above, pale brown and softly hairy below
Flowers: Large terminal sprays of hairy, whitish or yellow flowers; September to October
Requirements: Moist, well drained soils
Comments: Beautiful flowering shrub which tolerates short dry periods once established. Young growth is a most attractive rusty red.
Localities: Along the Yarra R, Lilydale Nth, 42
Distribution: Vic, Qld, NSW

Pomaderris lanigera

Woolly Pomaderris

Size: 1–3 m x 1–2 m **F P**
Habitat: Dry and valley sclerophyll forests
Form: Erect hairy shrub, hairs often rusty
Foliage: Large, lanceolate leaves to 120 mm long, pale green below with dense brown hairs on veins; hairy on both sides of leaf
Flowers: Large rounded terminal clusters of yellow flowers; September to October
Requirements: Moist well drained soil
Comments: A most attractive low screening plant.
Localities: Mooroolbark, Wantirna, 54, 55
Distribution: Vic, Qld, NSW

Pomaderris lanigera

Pomaderris paniculosa ssp. paralia

Size: 1–1.5 m x 1–1.5 m **F P**
Habitat: Coastal banksia woodland
Form: Open rounded shrub
Foliage: Ovate to elliptic leaves to 50 mm long, glabrous, shiny green above, pale and densely hairy below
Flowers: Many small cream flowers in terminal and axillary panicles; September to October
Requirements: Well drained sandy soil
Comments: An attractive coastal shrub with reddish new growth.
Localities: Seaford, ?Brighton, 74
Distribution: Vic, Tas, SA, WA
Synonym: Separated from *P. oraria*

Pomaderris paniculosa ssp. *paralia*

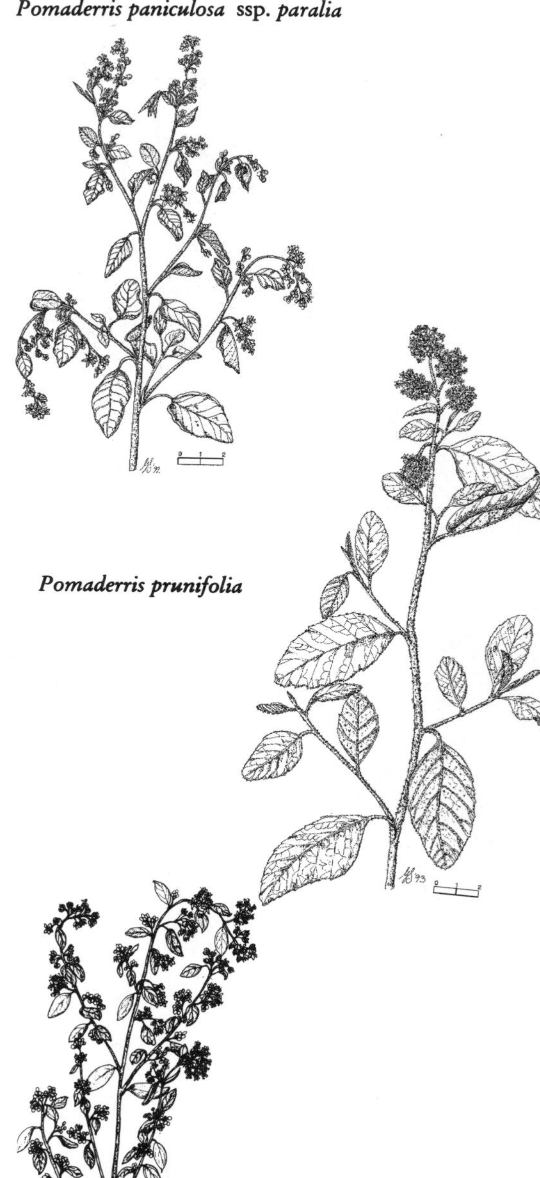

Pomaderris prunifolia

Pomaderris racemosa

Pomaderris prunifolia

Plum-leaf Pomaderris

Size: 1–4 m x 1–4 m **F P N**
Habitat: Valley sclerophyll forest
Form: Open rounded shrub
Foliage: Rough, dark green, elliptic to lanceolate leaves to 50 mm long, paler below
Flowers: Small, rounded clusters of pale yellow flowers; October to November. Petals absent.
Requirements: Moist well drained soils
Comments: More tolerant than most to drying out in Summer if it is in a shaded position.
Localities: 33, 34A, 36, 41, 42, 50A
Distribution: Vic, Qld, NSW

Pomaderris racemosa

Slender or Cluster Pomaderris

Size: 2–5 m x 1–2 m **F P N**
Habitat: Riparian scrub
Form: Slender shrub or, rarely, small lightly-branched tree
Foliage: Thin, dark green ovate leaves to 25 mm long, with margins turned down, pale green below.
Flowers: Small clusters of yellow flowers in leaf axils; October to November. Petals absent.
Requirements: Well drained soils
Comments: Ideal for planting in areas where space is limited, as growth is mostly erect.
Localities: 32, 34A, 36, 42, 50A, 62, 63
Distribution: Vic, Tas

Pomaderris vacciniifolia

Round-leaf Pomaderris

Size: 2–3.5 m x 3 m **F P**
Habitat: Valley sclerophyll forest
Form: Large straggling, spreading shrub
Foliage: Smooth, dark green, elliptic leaves to 20 mm long, with inconspicuous veins, pale grey below
Flowers: Small sprays of creamy flowers in leaf axils; October to November
Requirements: Well drained soils
Comments: A rare plant with a restricted range in Melbourne.
Localities: 42
Distribution: Endemic to Vic

Illustrated p. 172

SCALE: 0 1cm 2cm

The scale representation on each plant equals 2cm.

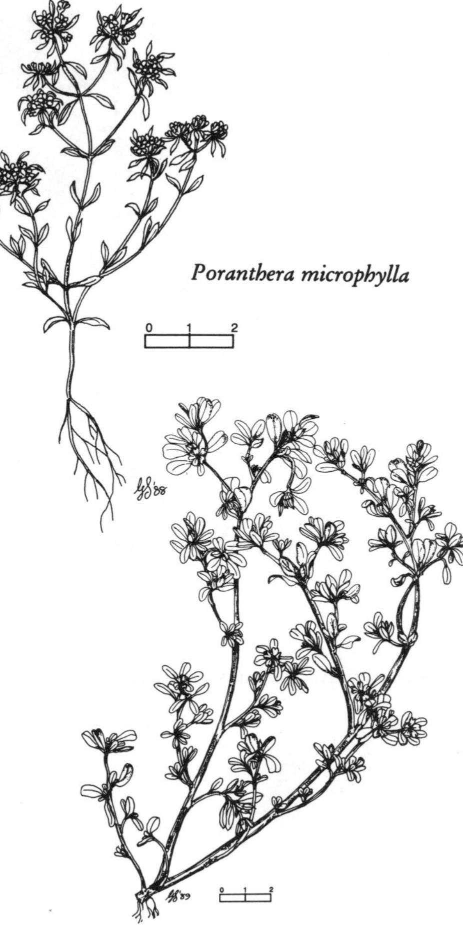
Poranthera microphylla

Portulaca oleracea

Poranthera — Euphorbiaceae

Poranthera microphylla — Small Poranthera

Size: 3–10 cm x 10 cm — F P
Habitat: Red gum and box woodland, dry and valley sclerophyll forests, grassy low open forest
Form: Trailing to erect annual herb
Foliage: Greyish, oval to spathulate leaves to 10 mm long
Flowers: Tiny white flowers in short, leafy heads at the end of branchlets; August to December
Requirements: Well drained soils
Comments: A relatively inconspicuous plant amongst grasses in the understorey. In moist areas, or in cultivation it becomes more vigorous and may spread 30 cm or more. It self-sows readily in the garden and can add a natural look to a low maintenance area.
Propagation: Seed
Localities: Sth of Melton, 34A–36, 38, 40–67#, 69A–71, 74–76
Distribution: All states; NZ

Portulaca — Portulacaceae

Portulaca oleracea — Common Purslane

Size: Prostrate x 0.4–0.7 m — F
Habitat: Wide-ranging, red gum woodland, damp sclerophyll forest, tea-tree heath, primary dune scrub, also disturbed areas
Form: Trailing or matting annual herb with red stems
Foliage: Succulent, oblong to wedge-shaped leaves to 25 mm long
Flowers: Sessile yellow flowers, single or clustered in leaf axils; August to March
Requirements: Adaptable in well drained soil
Comments: Salt tolerant. It may become a garden weed. Both the Aborigines and early settlers used to eat the leaves, raw or cooked, as a vegetable. The seeds were ground to make bread and cakes.
Propagation: Seed, cuttings
Localities: 25, 26, 35, 42, 58, 67, 71
Distribution: All states

Pratia — Campanulaceae

Carpeting perennial herbs, pratias provide a colorful groundcover in damp to wet soils. The flowers are similar to those of *Isotoma fluviatalis* but the tubular flower is split to the base in pratias. They are useful for binding soil and can be used as a grass alternative in low traffic areas. They may become invasive under ideal conditions but are easily controlled. Propagation is by division.

Pratia concolor — Poison Pratia

Size: Prostrate–30 cm x spreading — P N
Habitat: Poorly drained areas in plains grassland, grassy wetland
Form: Perennial herb, with trailing stems radiating from the centre
Foliage: Sessile, ovate-lanceolate to lanceolate grey-green leaves to 30 mm long, with finely toothed margins. Leaves are always on one plane.
Flowers: Small white to pale pink starry flowers; December to February; followed by succulent green fruit
Requirements: Moist to wet heavy soils
Comments: *P. concolor* has the largest leaves of the local pratias. The milky sap contains alkaloids which are suspected of stock poisoning.
Propagation: Cuttings, division
Localities: 17#, 18
Distribution: Vic, Qld, NSW, SA

Pratia irrigua

Pratia irrigua — Fleshy or Salt Pratia

Size: Prostrate or slightly ascending — F P
Habitat: Saltmarshes, riparian scrub
Form: Weak or trailing herb
Foliage: Shiny, entire or inconspicuously-toothed leaves to 25 mm long, variable, often narrowly elliptic in shape. Usually (but not always) succulent.
Flowers: Minute white or bluish flowers on stalks shorter or longer than the leaves
Comments: Locally rare.
Localities: Rockbank, Port Melbourne, 2, 4, 7, 29, 30#, 35
Distribution: All states except Qld
Synonym: *Pratia platycalyx*

Pratia pedunculata

Matted Pratia

Size:	Prostrate x 2–3 m **F P**
Habitat:	Swamp edges in plains grassland, grassy wetland, red gum woodland, valley sclerophyll forest, tea-tree heath
Form:	Dense matting plant
Foliage:	Tiny, toothed, oval green leaves to 8 mm long
Flowers:	Masses of starry, blue or white flowers singly in leaf axils; November to February
Requirements:	Moist soils, tolerating extended wetness
Comments:	A most attractive suckering plant flowering well in full sun provided it has some protection or is kept moist.
Localities:	17#, 18, 35, 42, 71, 74
Distribution:	Vic, Qld, NSW, Tas, SA

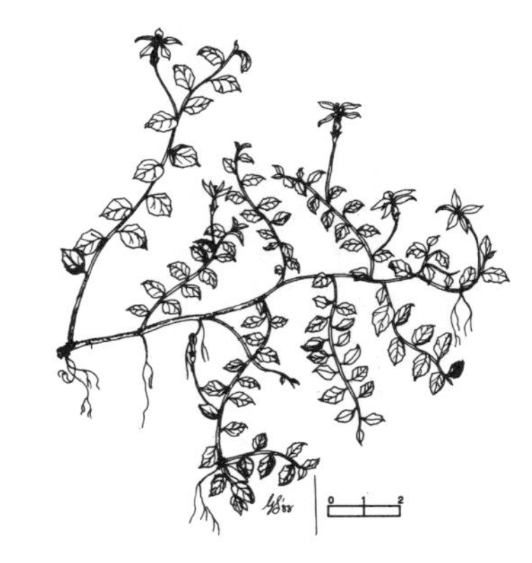

Pratia pedunculata

Pratia platycalyx = P. irrigua

Prostanthera — Lamiaceae

Prostanthera lasianthos var. lasianthos

Victorian Christmas Bush

Size:	2–8 m x 2–5 m **F P N**
Habitat:	Wet, damp and valley sclerophyll forests
Form:	Compact tall shrub or upright small tree
Foliage:	Pairs of dark green, toothed, lanceolate leaves to 100 mm long; minty aroma when crushed
Flowers:	Long, loose, terminal leafless racemes of hairy, white flowers, spotted with orange and purple; November to January
Requirements:	Moist, well drained loamy soils
Comments:	A spectacular tree in flower, it is useful as a screen plant but needs protection from strong winds. It is very variable in form according to its origins. Mulching is beneficial and plants respond to Summer watering. A pink flowering form from Kallista is available.
Propagation:	Fresh seed, cuttings
Localities:	33–34A, 42, 44, 47, 49, 50–51, 55–59, 61–63
Distribution:	Vic, Qld, NSW, Tas

Illustrated p. 49

Prostanthera melissifolia

Balm Mint Bush

Size:	1–3 m x 2–3 m **P N**
Habitat:	Wet sclerophyll forest
Form:	Fast-growing, dense rounded shrub
Foliage:	Pairs of dark green, coarsely-toothed ovate leaves to 40 mm long, paler below. Strong mint aroma. Branchlets square.
Flowers:	Loose terminal sprays of mauve to pink flowers cover the shrub; October to December
Requirements:	Moist, well drained soils
Comments:	An excellent shrub for a moist, sheltered position, preferably placed near a pathway as contact releases the minty fragrance. Pruning after flowering maintains bushiness and vigour.
Propagation:	Cuttings
Localities:	57
Distribution:	Vic, NSW

Prostanthera melissifolia

Prunella — Lamiaceae

Prunella vulgaris

Self-heal

Size:	7–150 mm x 10 cm **F P N**
Habitat:	Widespread in riparian and swamp scrub, red gum woodland, valley, damp and wet sclerophyll forests, tea-tree heath
Form:	Fast growing, spreading perennial herb
Foliage:	Pairs of lightly hairy, dark green ovate leaves to 60 mm long; stems reddish and quadrangular
Flowers:	Terminal heads of sessile, dark purple, rarely pink, flowers, held erect; mainly November to February
Requirements:	Moist soils
Comments:	A spreading groundcover for damp areas. In ideal conditions this plant may become invasive.
Propagation:	Cuttings
Localities:	28, 30, 33–36, 38, 40–44, 46–51, 53–67#, 71, 74, 76
Distribution:	All except NT; NZ

Prunella vulgaris

SCALE: 0 1cm 2cm — The scale representation on each plant equals 2cm.

Pseudognaphalium luteo-album

Pseudognaphalium — Asteraceae

Pseudognaphalium luteoalbum — Jersey Cudweed

Size: 20–50 cm high **F P N**
Habitat: Widespread in saltmarshes, plains grassland, valley and damp sclerophyll forest, swamp scrub, grassy low open forest
Form: Slender, erect, white-woolly annual or biennial herb
Foliage: Densely woolly, grey leaves; lower leaves obovate to 50 mm long, stem leaves smaller, sessile and more linear
Flowers: Terminal clusters of creamy-yellow flowerheads, without ray florets; September to March
Requirements: Adaptable, tolerating dryness once established
Comments: An easily grown plant which is often found in disturbed soil. May become invasive. The Aborigines made a drink from the leaf to treat general sickness.
Propagation: Seed
Localities: Sth of Melton, 4, 5, 16, 29#, 34A, 35, 39, 42, 44, 48, 49, 54, 55, 57–60, 67, 68, 69A, 74, 75
Distribution: All states; NZ
Synonym: *Gnaphalium luteoalbum*

Psoralea — Fabaceae

Psoralea adscendens — Dusky Scurf-pea, Mountain Psoralea

Size: Prostrate–0.6 m x 0.5–1 m **P**
Habitat: Plains grasslands
Form: Spreading perennial herb
Foliage: Dark green trifoliate leaves on long stalks to 150 mm long, leaflets lanceolate to 50 mm long
Flowers: Erect spike of purple, rarely pink or white, pea flowers on long stalks to 250 mm long; November to January. Calyx is covered in shaggy black hair.
Requirements: Moist well drained soils
Comments: Responds well to Summer watering. Attractive in a rockery or draping over logs. An endangered Melbourne species.
Propagation: Scarified seed
Localities: Was collected in St. Albans, Altona, Sth Morang
Distribution: Vic, NSW, Tas, SA

Psoralea parva — Small Scurf-pea

Size: Prostrate or scrambling **F**
Habitat: Plains grasslands
Form: Small trailing perennial herb
Foliage: Leaves on shorter stalks than other species with 3–5 narrow or oblanceolate leaflets to 25 mm long
Flowers: Dense clusters of tiny, sessile, lilac to white pea flowers; October to December. Calyx is covered in dense white hairs.
Comments: An endangered plant nationally, it is locally very rare.
Localities: Werribee, 17#
Distribution: Vic, NSW, SA

Psoralea tenax

Psoralea tenax — Tough Scurf-pea, Emu-foot

Size: 0.5 m high **F P**
Habitat: Plains grasslands
Form: Slender, trailing or erect perennial herb with angular ridges along stems
Foliage: Long-stalked dark green leaves have 5–7 sessile, narrow leaflets to 30 mm long, (rarely to 70 mm long) covered in small black dots
Flowers: Spikes, to 100 mm long, of tiny bluish pea flowers in leaf axils on long slender stalks to 20 cm long; August to March. Calyx hairs paler and shorter than *P. adscendens*.
Requirements: Moist soils
Comments: Appreciates Summer watering. Extinct throughout most of its Melbourne range and now rare on the Keilor basalt plains.
Propagation: Scarified seed
Localities: Was north east of Melbourne; St. Albans#, Sydenham, Sunshine, Werribee, 17#, 20#
Distribution: Vic, Qld, NSW

Ptilotus

Amaranthaceae

Ptilotus macrocephalus

Tall Mulla Mulla, Featherheads

Size: 0.6–1 m x 0.6 m **F**
Habitat: Plains grassland, red gum and box woodlands
Form: Erect, sparsely hairy perennial herb with a long, fleshy tap root
Foliage: Narrow, linear to elliptic leaves 50–100 mm long, margins wavy
Flowers: Single, terminal, fluffy, greenish-yellow flowerheads to 120 mm x 60 mm, on stems to 0.6 m high; October to November
Requirements: Well drained light or heavy soils
Comments: A very showy plant now found in only a few isolated places locally. Useful as a cut flower.
Propagation: Seed
Localities: Werribee, Sunbury, Bundoora, Sydenham, Diggers Rest, Laverton Nth, Deer Park, Rockbank, 26
Distribution: All mainland states

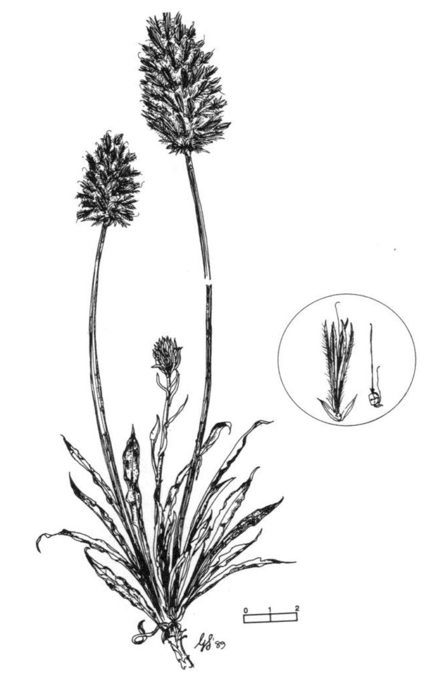

Ptilotus macrocephalus

Ptilotus spathulatus

Pussy Tails

Size: Prostrate x 10–40 cm **F**
Habitat: Plains grassland, primary dune scrub, box woodland
Form: Tufted perennial herb with a thick woody root
Foliage: Broad, spathulate leaves on prostrate stems, basal leaves to 60 mm long, stem leaves smaller; dark green above, paler below
Flowers: Single, terminal fluffy, pale green to brown erect flowerheads to 60 mm long, at the end of prostrate branches; October to November and March to June
Requirements: Well drained soils
Comments: A tiny, attractive plant restricted locally to a few remnant sites. The taproot was eaten by the Aborigines.
Propagation: Seed
Localities: Williamstown, St. Albans, Sunbury, Keilor, Bundoora, 1, 17#, 26, 29, 34A
Distribution: Vic, NSW, Tas, SA, WA *Illustrated p. 172*

Pultenaea

Fabaceae

A large family of shrubby understorey plants, the Pultenaeas are represented by 13 species locally. All are very showy, with bright orange-yellow and red 'egg and bacon' pea flowers during Spring. They make an attractive feature in the garden growing happily in rockeries or under trees. Planting in drifts gives the best effect. Good drainage, mulching and pruning after flowering are beneficial. *Pultenaea* spp. are distinguished from similar pea genera by the conspicuous stipules, (a pair of small leaf-like appendages) which are united behind the leaf stalk, and have rough margins. They also have a pair of bracteoles (small bracts) at the base of, or on, the flower calyx. Propagation is by scarified seed or cuttings.

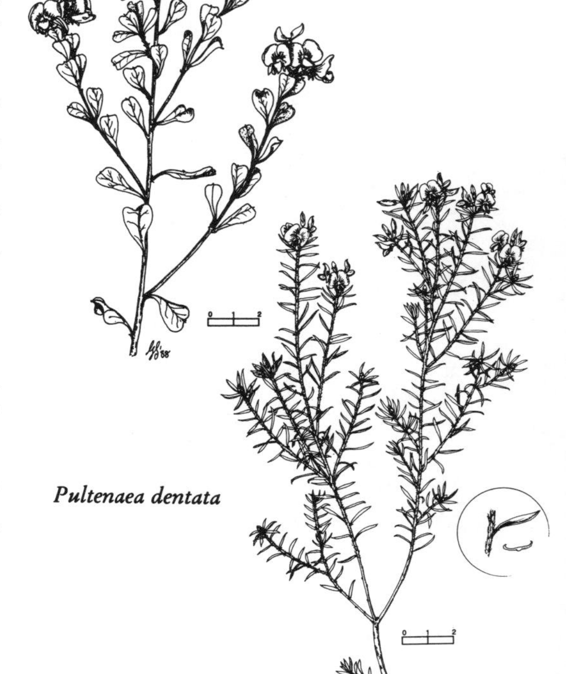

Pultenaea daphnoides

Pultenaea dentata

Pultenaea daphnoides

Large-leaf Bush-pea

Size: 1–3 m x 0.5–2 m **F P N**
Habitat: Dry sclerophyll forest, grassy low open forest
Form: Erect, branching shrub
Foliage: Large, flat, wedge-shaped olive green leaves to 30 mm long, paler below, with midvein produced into a slender stiff point. Stipules small.
Flowers: Large yellow and brown flowers in dense, terminal heads; August to November. Narrow, hairy bracteoles attached to middle of silky calyx tube.
Requirements: Well drained soils tolerating dryness once established, but appreciates extra moisture in full sun
Comments: An attractive soft shrub which, like many other species, is more stunted in coastal areas.
Localities: Sth Morang, 34–36, 49, 55, 56, 76
Distribution: Vic, NSW, Tas, SA

Pultenaea dentata

Clustered Bush-pea

Size: 0.3–1 m x 0.5 m **P**
Habitat: Valley sclerophyll forest, grassy low open forest
Form: Hairy, wiry shrub
Foliage: Scattered, stiff, linear-elliptic leaves to 10 mm, margins curved inwards; stipules 1–2 mm long
Flowers: Compact sessile clusters of yellow and red flowers; September to December. Bracteoles 3-lobed.
Requirements: Moist well drained soils
Comments: Locally rare.
Localities: Clayton#, 42, 66#, 67#, 74
Distribution: Vic, NSW, Tas, SA

SCALE: 0 1cm 2cm The scale representation on each plant equals 2cm.

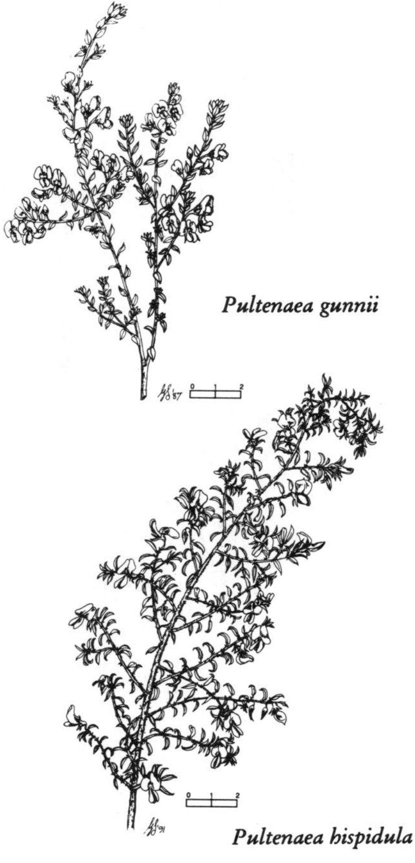

Pultenaea gunnii

Pultenaea hispidula

Pultenaea gunnii

Golden Bush-pea

Size: 0.5–1.5 m x 0.5 m — F P
Habitat: Damp, valley and dry sclerophyll forests, sclerophyll woodland
Form: Wiry erect or straggling shrub
Foliage: Tiny ovate, dark green leaves to 6 mm long, margins recurved, concave below. Tight rosettes of leaves often at ends of branchlets. Stipules tiny and dark brown.
Flowers: Terminal clusters of bright yellow-orange and dark red flowers; September to October. Small lanceolate bracteoles attached in the centre of the calyx tube.
Requirements: Well drained soils
Comments: Spectacular in flower, it grows well under established trees, with other shrubs. *P. gunnii* x *P. scabra* occurs in Heathmont, Montrose and Clayton.
Localities: 34, 34A, 36, 41–44, 47, 49–56, 58–61, 63, 64, 67#, 73, 74
Distribution: Vic, Tas

Pultenaea hispidula

Rusty Bush-pea

Size: 1–1.5 m x 1 m — F P
Habitat: Damp sclerophyll forest
Form: Hairy, much-branched shrub with arching branchlets
Foliage: Crowded, concave, oblong leaves to 9 mm long, hairy particularly on lower surface. Stipules reddish-brown, 2–3 mm long.
Flowers: Single yellow flowers in leaf axils, or terminal on short branchlets; September to December. Variable brown bracteoles are somewhat leaf-like.
Requirements: Well drained soil
Comments: A graceful small shrub with a pendulous habit. An attractive addition to the garden.
Localities: Kalorama, 58, 59
Distribution: Vic, NSW, SA

Pultenaea humilis

Dwarf Bush-pea

Size: 30 cm x 1 m — P
Habitat: Valley sclerophyll forest
Form: Hairy, erect to spreading low shrub
Foliage: Narrow, slightly concave, dull green leaves to 10 mm long, glabrous above and hairy below, crowded along stems. Stipules 2 mm long.
Flowers: Dense terminal heads of orange and yellow to red-brown flowers; October to December. Bracteoles hairy, long and narrow.
Requirements: Moist well drained soils. Tolerates dry shade once established but appreciates Summer watering
Comments: An attractive small shrub for a lightly shaded area. It will adapt to full sun if Summer watering is available. In heavy shade plants tend to grow taller and foliage is sparser. A grey-leafed form is available from nurseries.
Localities: 61
Distribution: Vic, NSW, Tas

Illustrated p. 172

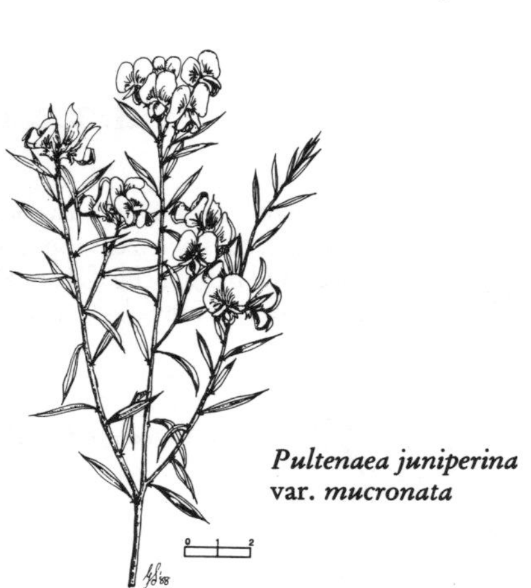

Pultenaea juniperina var. *mucronata*

Pultenaea juniperina var. mucronata

Prickly Bush-pea

Size: 1–3 m x 1–1.5 m — F P
Habitat: Valley and damp sclerophyll forests
Form: Erect to spreading shrub
Foliage: Stiff, sharply-pointed lanceolate leaves with incurved margins, to 30 mm long. Stipules erect, 2–3 mm long.
Flowers: Solitary fragrant yellow and red flowers in leaf axils; October to December. Short, hairy bracteoles at the base of calyx tube.
Requirements: Moist well drained soils tolerating some dryness once established
Comments: Similar in appearance to *P. muelleri*, the main difference being the axillary flowers. Seldom produces seed locally but suckers or resprouts after fire. Once common in the eastern part of the region, it is becoming locally rare.
Localities: Montrose, Lilydale, Kalorama, 34, 51–53, 55, 56
Distribution: Vic, NSW, Tas

Pultenaea muelleri var. *muelleri*

Pultenaea muelleri var. muelleri

Mueller's Bush-pea

Size: 1–3 m x 1–2 m — P
Habitat: Valley sclerophyll forest
Form: Tall, dense, hairy shrub
Foliage: Crowded, narrow lanceolate, concave leaves to 15 mm long, with pointed tip, stipules prominent
Flowers: Solitary yellow and red flowers at the ends of branchlets; November to January. Large oval bracteoles.
Requirements: Moist well drained soils
Comments: Similar in appearance to *P. juniperina* var. *mucronata*, but has solitary terminal flowers that are surrounded by persistent overlapping bracts, not flowers in axillary clusters. Easily grown in the garden adding colour to a shaded area. Restricted range within the Melbourne area where it is endangered and possibly extinct.
Localities: Dandenong Ranges#
Distribution: Endemic to Vic

Pultenaea paleacea var. sericea

Chaffy Bush-pea

Size: 0.1–0.6 m x 0.6 m **F P**
Habitat: Tea-tree heath
Form: Straggling to prostrate shrub
Foliage: Narrow grey-green leaves to 20 mm long, hairy below, with recurved margins, ending in a fine tip
Flowers: Dense terminal clusters of sessile gold and brown or red flowers surrounded by pale brown, papery bracts; late October to November. Brown, oblong bracteoles attached near middle of calyx tube.
Requirements: Moist, well drained soil
Comments: This variety is identified by its long, white-silky hairs on the bracts and stipules.
Localities: was Cheltenham, Brighton; Knox, 63, 67–69, 75
Distribution: Vic, Qld, NSW

Pultenaea pedunculata

Matted Bush-pea

Size: Prostrate x 1–3 m **F P**
Habitat: Dry sclerophyll forest, box ironbark woodland
Form: Layering, densely matted plant
Foliage: Tiny, flat, dark green elliptical leaves to 12 mm long, hairy below, margins sometimes recurved. Stipules prominent, 2–3 mm long.
Flowers: Masses of single yellow and red axillary flowers on long hairy stalks; October to November. Fine, long bracteoles.
Requirements: Well drained soils, tolerating dry periods once established
Comments: An excellent groundcover, useful for soil-binding, and cascading over rockeries and retaining walls. It provides an interesting base plant in a tub with other plants. The local form in Montmorency has yellow flowers and smaller leaves while a more vigorous plant occurs in the moister area of Warranwood. A pink-flowered form, while not local, is also available in nurseries.
Localities: 34–38, 58
Distribution: Vic, NSW, Tas, SA

Pultenaea scabra

Rough Bush-pea

Size: 1–2 m x 0.5–1.5 m **P**
Habitat: Damp and valley sclerophyll forests
Form: Hairy, erect or rounded shrub
Foliage: Small, rough, dark green, wedge-shaped leaves, notched at the end, to 15 mm long, paler below; stipules insignificant
Flowers: Masses of orange-yellow flowers in loose terminal clusters of 2–5; September to November. Lanceolate, hairy bracteoles attached at or below the centre of the calyx tube.
Requirements: Well drained soil which does not dry out
Localities: Kalorama, 49–51, 55–58, 71
Distribution: Vic, NSW, SA

Pultenaea stricta

Rigid Bush-pea

Size: to 1 m x 0.5–1 m **F P**
Habitat: Valley sclerophyll forest, tea-tree heath
Form: Slender upright shrub
Foliage: Ovate to oblong or elliptic leaves to 10 mm long, margins and short stiff point recurved, stipules insignificant (less than 1 mm long)
Flowers: Yellow and red flowers in loose terminal clusters; September to November. Bracteoles attached in the upper half of hairy calyx tube.
Requirements: Moist sandy soil
Comments: Now locally rare, it is still found on the Mornington Peninsula.
Localities: Was collected Oakleigh, Frankston 1894, Nth Croydon; 74, 75
Distribution: Vic, NSW, Tas, SA

Pultenaea subumbellata = Almaleea subumbellata

Pultenaea tenuifolia

Slender Bush-pea

Size: 10–50 cm x 10–30 cm **F P**
Habitat: Coastal banksia woodland, primary dune scrub
Form: Slender, open, trailing shrub
Foliage: Hairy, crowded, very narrow leaves to 8 mm long, the margins so recurved that the leaves appear terete, with a prominent channelled midrib
Flowers: Sessile, single or paired yellow and brown flowers at the ends of branchlets, surrounded by clusters of leaves with enlarged stipules; September to October. Long hairy bracteoles attached at the base of the calyx tube.
Requirements: Well drained soils
Localities: Brighton#, 67#
Distribution: Vic, Tas, SA, WA

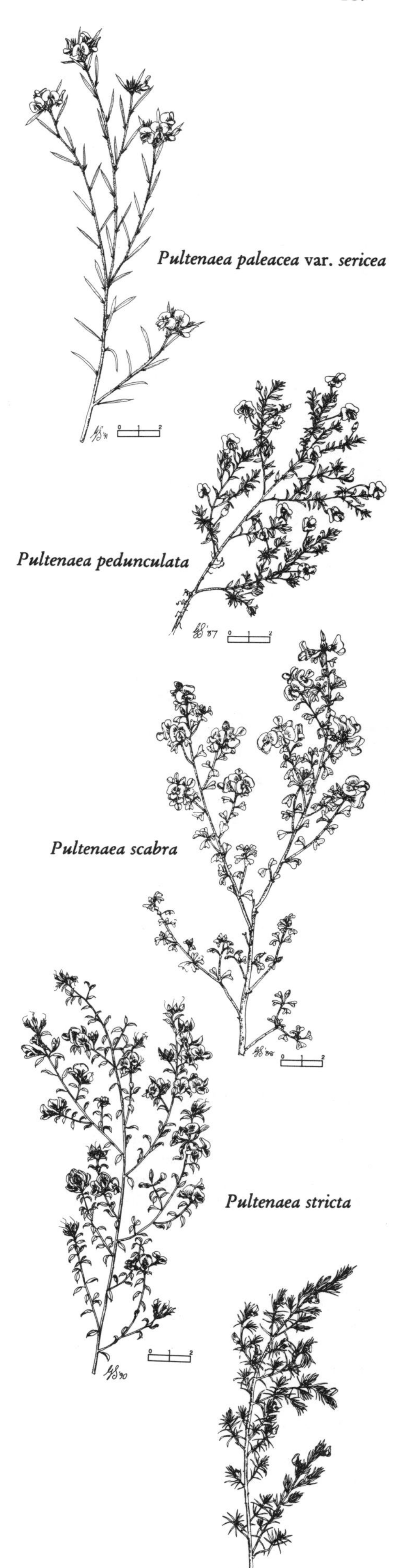

Pultenaea paleacea var. *sericea*

Pultenaea pedunculata

Pultenaea scabra

Pultenaea stricta

Pultenaea tenuifolia

SCALE: 0 1cm 2cm The scale representation on each plant equals 2cm.

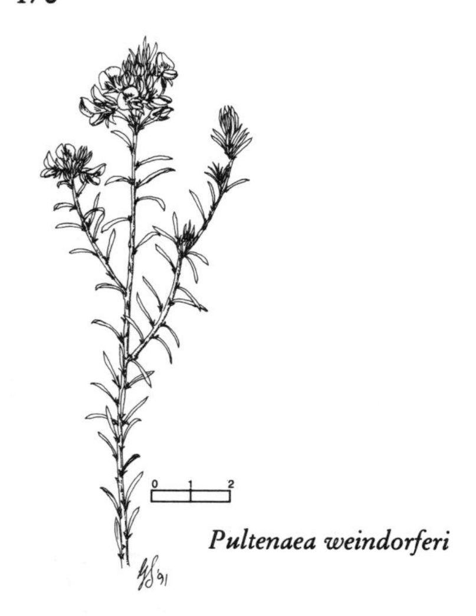

Pultenaea weindorferi

Pultenaea weindorferi

Swamp Bush-pea

P N

Size: 1.2 m x 0.8 m
Habitat: Wet depression in valley sclerophyll forest
Form: Glabrous upright shrub
Foliage: Erect, broad-linear to narrowly oblanceolate bright green leaves to 10 mm long
Flowers: Yellow flowers with orange-red centres in tight terminal leafy clusters; September to October
Requirements: Moist soil, drying out in Summer
Comments: A rare Victorian plant, recently discovered in a small pocket in Mt. Evelyn.
Localities: 56
Distribution: Endemic to Vic

Pycnosorus

Asteraceae

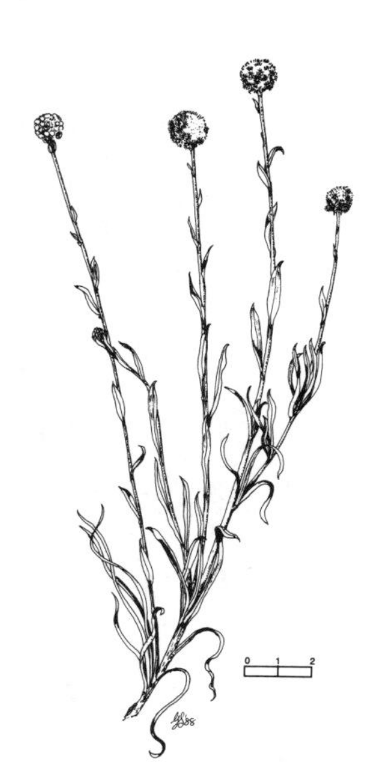

Pycnosorus chrysanthes

Pycnosorus chrysanthes

Golden Billy Buttons

F P

Size: 30 cm x 0.3–1 m
Habitat: Grassy wetlands on the basalt plains
Form: Tufted annual or perennial herb
Foliage: Narrow silvery leaves to 50 mm long
Flowers: Solitary bright yellow globular flowerheads to 15 mm across, held above the foliage; September to December and again in March to May.
Requirements: Heavy moist soils
Comments: An excellent garden or container plant. Tolerates waterlogging for extended periods. It remains in very few sites in Melbourne.
Propagation: Ripe seed, cuttings, division
Localities: St Albans, Sunbury, Sydenham, Sunshine, 7, 16, 26
Distribution: Vic, Qld, NSW, SA
Synonym: *Craspedia chrysantha*

Pycnosorus globosus

Drumsticks

F

Size: 10–20 cm high
Habitat: Moist depressions in plains grasslands
Form: Clumping perennial herb
Foliage: Erect, finely hairy, bluish-green fleshy leaves to 20 cm long
Flowers: Large, yellow globular flowerheads, on stems to 50 cm high; November to February
Requirements: Heavy moist soils
Comments: Found on few sites within the study area.
Propagation: Seed, division
Localities: Altona, Melton
Distribution: Vic, Qld, NSW, SA
Synonym: *Craspedia globosa*

Ranunculus

Ranunculaceae

Commonly known as buttercups because of their cupped, shiny yellow flowers, *Ranunculus* spp. are annual or perennial herbs of moist to wet areas. The leaves are either divided, frequently into 3 leaflets, or lobed. The fruit (achenes) are clustered together and have a short beak derived from the persistent style. They will grow in many positions in the garden if the soil is kept moist, and provide a bright splash of colour through Spring and Summer. Propagate from seeds or division.

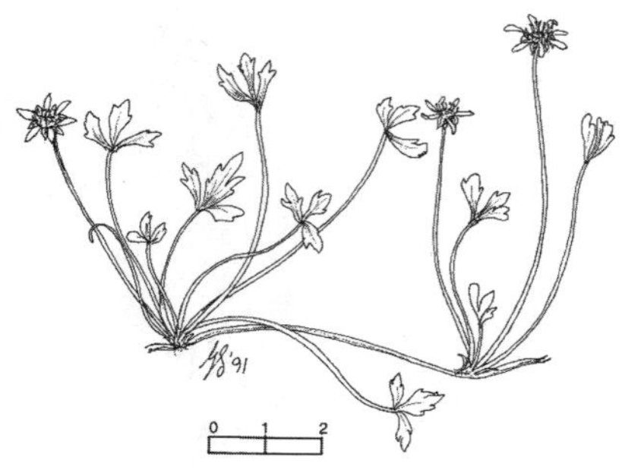

Ranunculus amphitrichus

Ranunculus amphitrichus

Small River Buttercup

F P

Size: 5 cm x 20 cm
Habitat: Red gum woodland, valley sclerophyll forest, wattle tea-tree scrub
Form: Very similar in habit to *R. inundatus*. Stoloniferous, forming a mat with leaves clustered at the nodes.
Foliage: Leaves glabrous and shiny. Submerged plants have deeply dissected narrow-linear segments, whilst those growing in damp soil have broad, wedge-shaped, 3-lobed segments.
Flowers: Small pale yellow flowers to 10 mm wide with 5–9 narrow petals. Achene has slender erect beak. Flowers most of the year.
Comments: An attractive small plant, useful in a shallow pond, or areas with permanently wet soil. Locally rare.
Localities: Dandenong, 34A, 35, 49, 67#, 71, 74, 75
Distribution: Vic, NSW, Tas, SA; NZ
Synonym: *R. rivularis*

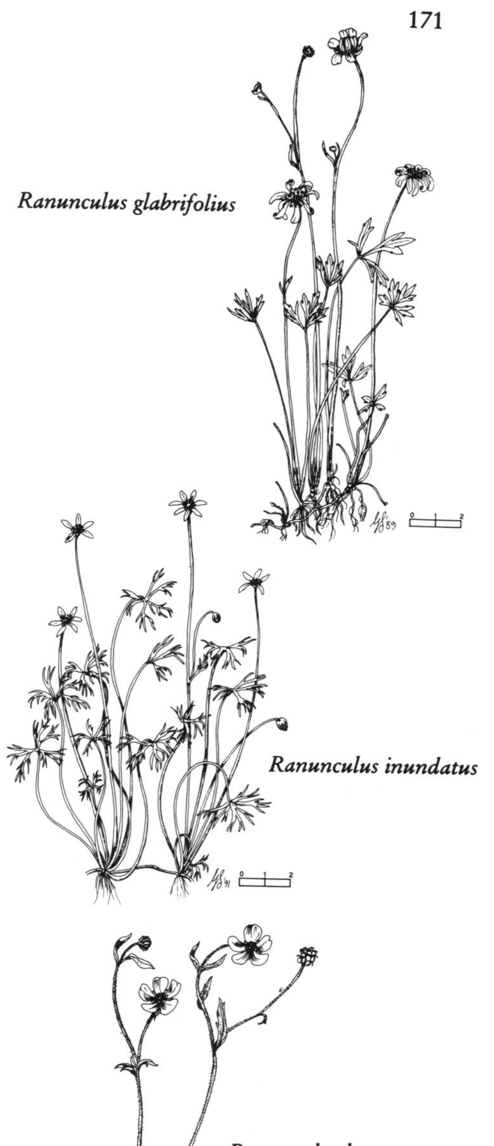
Ranunculus glabrifolius

Ranunculus inundatus

Ranunculus glabrifolius

Shining Buttercup

P

Size: Prostrate-10 cm high
Habitat: Swamp scrub, valley sclerophyll forest
Form: Slender, stoloniferous, perennial herb
Foliage: Leaves glossy and very variable, trifoliate with leaflets narrow and entire, or deeply dissected and toothed
Flowers: 5–10 narrow, yellow petals. Sepals hairy. Round, wavy and ridged achenes.
Requirements: Moist to wet soil
Comments: Grows in association with *R. amphitrichus* and *R. inundatus*. Locally rare.
Localities: Baxter, 41, 54, 61
Distribution: Vic, NSW, Tas; NZ

Ranunculus inundatus

River Buttercup

F P

Size: 5–30 cm high
Habitat: Red gum woodland, valley sclerophyll forest, in or near fresh water
Form: Vigorous stoloniferous perennial often forming large mats
Foliage: Basal leaves, to 30 mm long, deeply divided into very narrow segments; stem leaves smaller
Flowers: Long, erect flowering stalks with 1–3 yellow flowers to 15 mm wide; 5–7 elliptical petals; September to January. Sepals hairless. Rounded, warty achenes have down-turned beaks.
Localities: Knox, 35, 42, 51, 54, 59
Distribution: Vic, Qld, NSW, Tas, SA

Ranunculus lappaceus

Common or Australian Buttercup

F P

Size: 10–50 cm x 15 cm
Habitat: Widespread in grassy wetland, red gum woodland, wet, damp, valley and dry sclerophyll forests, wattle tea-tree scrub
Form: Soft, hairy, tufted perennial herb, long spreading hairs on lower stem
Foliage: Basal leaves divided into 3 deeply dissected or lobed leaflets to 80 mm long on stalks to 30 cm long; stem leaves fewer, narrower and less divided
Flowers: Single or pairs of 5-petalled golden flowers to 25 mm across, on long, erect, branched stalks; September to December. The hairy sepals are erect.
Requirements: Moist but not stagnant soils
Comments: The flattened achenes have slender coiled beaks. A bright, easy to grow herb for permanently moist areas.
Localities: St Albans, 12, 16, 26, 29, 34A, 35, 38, 39, 41–44, 47–49, 50A, 51, 53, 55–58, 62–64, 67#, 74, 76
Distribution: All states except WA; NZ

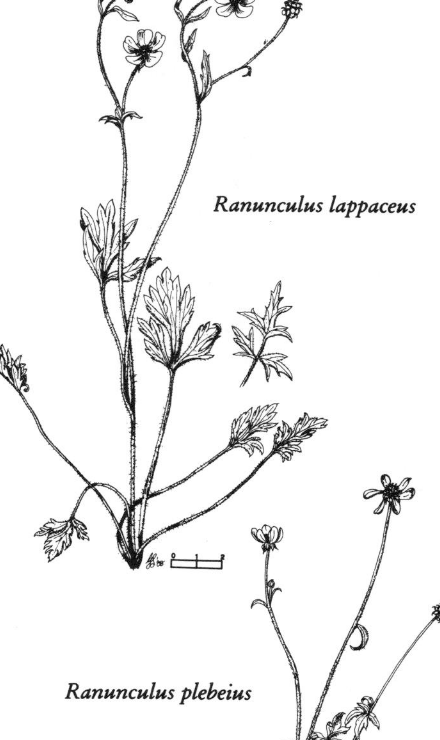
Ranunculus lappaceus

Ranunculus pachycarpus

Thick-fruited Buttercup

F P

Size: 6–40 cm high
Habitat: Valley sclerophyll forest
Comments: Very similar to *R. lappaceus* but the roots are tuberous rather than fibrous. The flowering stem is less branched and the achenes are plump and round with a stout beak; July to November.
Localities: ?42
Distribution: Vic, NSW, SA

Ranunculus papulentus

Large River Buttercup

F P

Size: 10–25 cm high
Habitat: Freshwater lagoons and along rivers in riparian scrub
Form: Similar to *R. inundatus*. Spreads by underground stolons.
Foliage: Leaves deeply dissected into several narrow segments
Flowers: Flowers to 20 mm wide have 9–15 petals; December to January
Localities: Plenty R, Yarra R
Distribution: Vic, Qld, NSW

Ranunculus plebeius

Ranunculus plebeius

Forest or Hairy Buttercup

P N

Size: 10–20 cm x 20–40 cm
Habitat: Riparian scrub, wet, damp and valley sclerophyll forests
Form: Tufted, hairy perennial herb
Foliage: Undivided or lobed leaves
Flowers: Small flowers with reflexed sepals to 15 mm wide, on long slender stalks high above the foliage; Spring to Summer. Achenes (2–3 mm long) have slender hooked beaks less than 1 mm long.
Localities: 29#, 42, 55–58
Distribution: Vic, Qld, NSW, Tas

SCALE: 0 1cm 2cm

The scale representation on each plant equals 2cm.

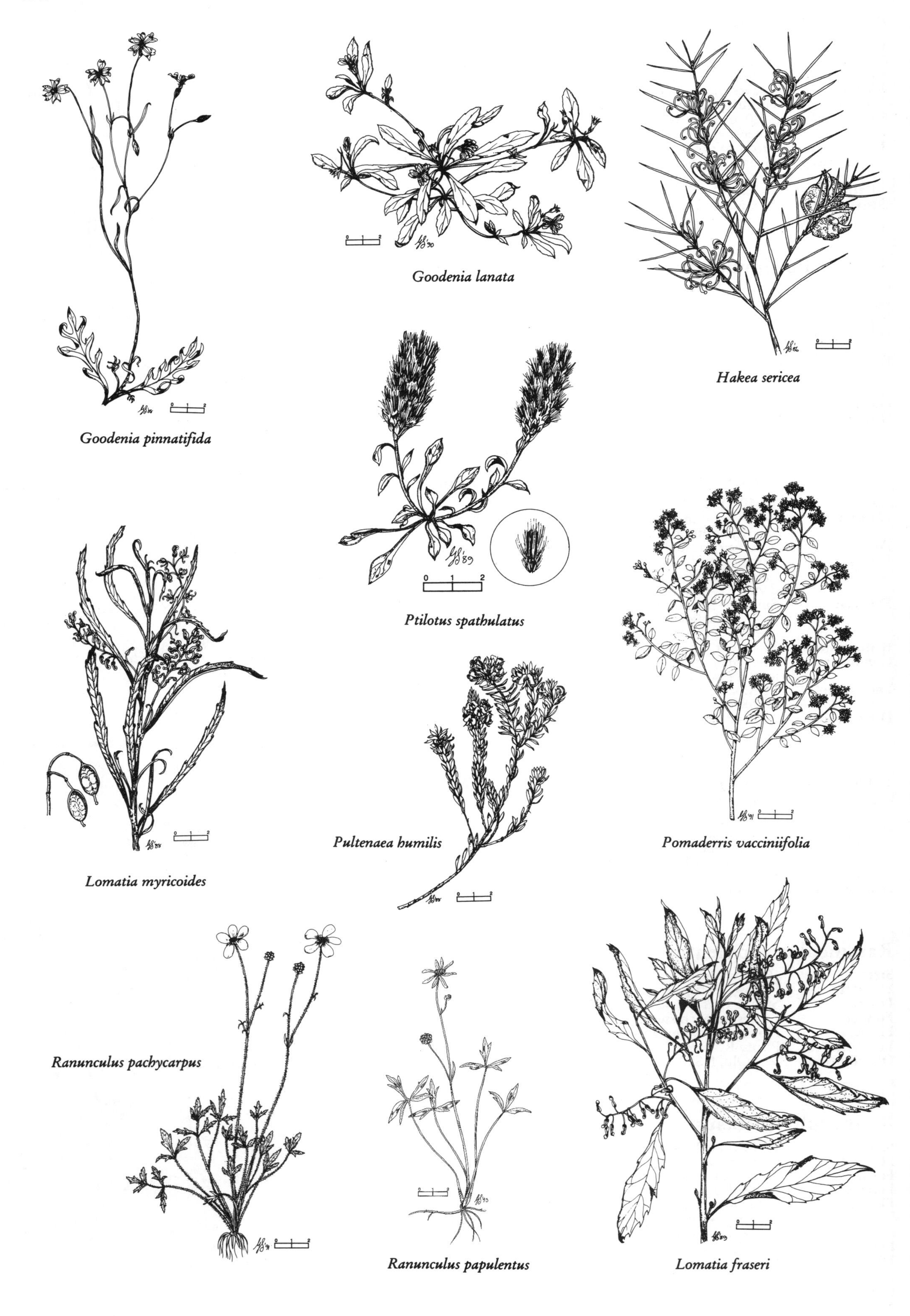

Goodenia pinnatifida

Goodenia lanata

Hakea sericea

Ptilotus spathulatus

Lomatia myricoides

Pultenaea humilis

Pomaderris vacciniifolia

Ranunculus pachycarpus

Ranunculus papulentus

Lomatia fraseri

Ranunculus pumilio var. pumilio
Ferny or Small-flowered Buttercup

Size: 1–35 cm high **F P**
Habitat: Floodplains and swamp margins in coastal banksia woodland, wattle tea-tree scrub and plains grassland
Form: Similar to *R. sessiliflorus* var. *sessiliflorus.* Densely hairy slender annual herb
Foliage: 3-lobed leaves up to 20 mm x 10 mm, lobes dissected on lower leaves. Longer leaf stalks to 70 mm long.
Flowers: Tiny stalked greenish flowers with 2–4 petals; August to November. Achenes round, short-beaked with numerous small protuberances bearing curved hairs.
Localities: Seaford, 5, 42, 74
Distribution: All states

Ranunculus rivularis = R. amphitrichus

Ranunculus robertsonii
Slender Buttercup

Size: 5–25 cm high **F P**
Habitat: Depressions in plains grassland
Form: Tufted, small hairy perennial herb with tuberous roots
Foliage: Leaves few, deeply dissected and pinnate, the 3–9 segments also deeply and narrowly lobed
Flowers: Bright yellow flowers with 5 petals; August to October. Recurved, strongly hooked beak on achene.
Localities: Melton, Sunbury
Distribution: Vic, SA

Ranunculus robertsonii

Ranunculus scapiger

Size: to 40 cm high **P N**
Habitat: Dry sclerophyll forest
Form: Upright perennial herb
Comments: Differs from *R. plebeius* in that the achenes are shorter (1–2 mm), and the beaks are more than 1 mm long, straight or arching with a recurved tip.
Localities: Sassafras
Distribution: Endemic to Vic

Ranunculus sessiliflorus var. sessiliflorus
Australian Small-flowered Buttercup

Size: 2–35 cm high **P**
Habitat: Riparian and wattle tea-tree scrub
Form: Small, hairy annual herb
Foliage: Leaves to 20 mm wide have 3 broad, toothed lobes. Leaf stalks to 50 mm long.
Flowers: Tiny flowers often stalkless with 0–2 petals; July to October. Achenes ovate, long-beaked with scattered conical protuberances bearing recurved hairs.
Localities: St. Kilda, 34A–36, 42, 67#
Distribution: All states

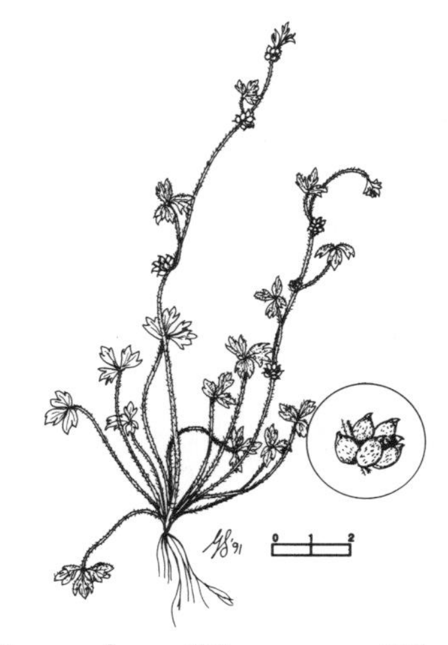

Ranunculus sessiliflorus var. *sessiliflorus*

Rapanea — Myrsinaceae

Rapanea howittiana
Muttonwood, Tulipwood

Size: 3–10 m x 2–4 m **P N**
Habitat: Damp sclerophyll forest, riparian scrub
Form: Pyramidal tall shrub or small tree
Foliage: Leathery, glossy dark green elliptical leaves to 90 mm long, paler green below, with wavy edges. Leaves bunched near the ends of branches. Juvenile leaves have toothed margins.
Flowers: Small greenish flowers clustered along older wood followed by small, round, violet to black drupes; late Winter to Summer
Requirements: Moist well drained soil
Comments: A useful screening plant for a shaded area provided it is watered during dry periods. An excellent replacement for *Pittosporum undulatum* which it superficially resembles.
Propagation: Fresh seed, cuttings
Localities: The Basin, Yarra R, 8, 16, 26, 33, 34A–36, 42, 57, 61
Distribution: Vic, NSW

Rapanea howittiana

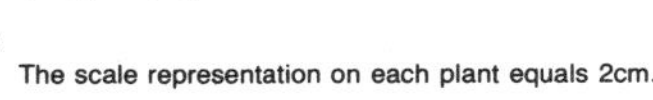

The scale representation on each plant equals 2cm.

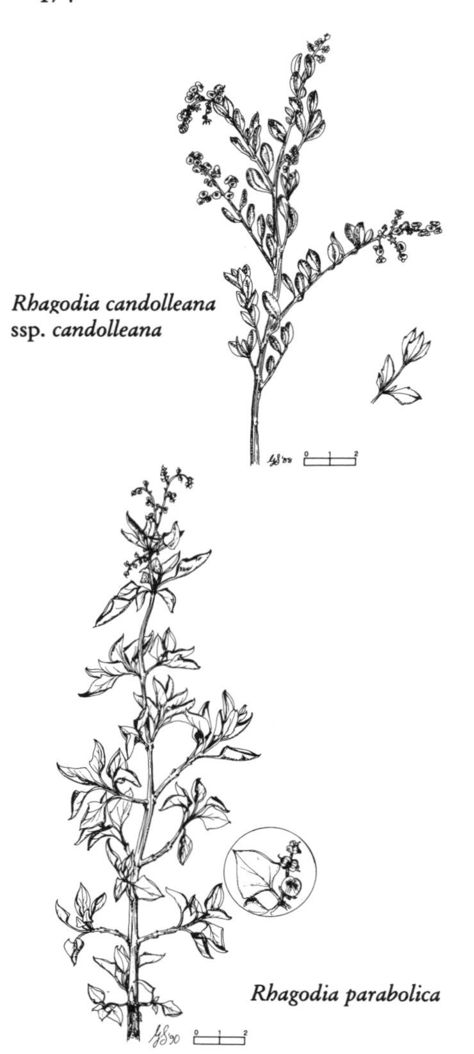
Rhagodia candolleana ssp. *candolleana*

Rhagodia parabolica

Rhagodia — Chenopodiaceae

Rhagodia candolleana ssp. candolleana — Seaberry Saltbush

Size: 2 m x 1–2.5 m — **F**
Habitat: Coastal banksia woodland, primary dune scrub, saltmarshes
Form: Dense sprawling or scrambling shrub
Foliage: Semi-succulent, dark green oblong-elliptic leaves, often broader near base, to 35 mm long, paler green and mealy below. Leaf margins often recurved.
Flowers: Generally dioecious; inconspicuous whitish flowers in mealy, pyramidal sprays; December to April. Small, shiny and flat dark red berries follow in Autumn.
Requirements: Well drained soils
Comments: The ribbed branchlets of this salt-tolerant shrub are mealy when young. When scrambling amongst other shrubs it may reach a height of 5 m. The Aborigines used the fruit, and possibly the leaves, for food.
Propagation: Cuttings
Localities: Altona, 4, 67–69A, 72, 74
Distribution: Vic, NSW, Tas, SA, WA
Synonym: Previously included with *R. baccata*

Rhagodia parabolica — Fragrant or Mealy Saltbush

Size: 0.8–2 m x 0.5–1.5 m — **F P**
Habitat: Sandstone cliffs of chenopod rocky open scrub, box woodlands
Form: Upright spindly to dense shrub
Foliage: Thin, broad, mealy grey-green leaves to 30 mm long, spade-like on long stalks, sometimes with broad basal lobes
Flowers: Dioecious; tiny, fragrant, mealy-white flowers in open sprays to 100 mm long; November to January followed by small red berries
Requirements: Well drained soils
Comments: A rare shrub of state significance in Victoria. Isolated occurrences remain in rocky gorges north-west of Melbourne.
Propagation: Cuttings
Localities: Sunbury, Melton, Werribee R, Sydenham, 26
Distribution: All mainland states

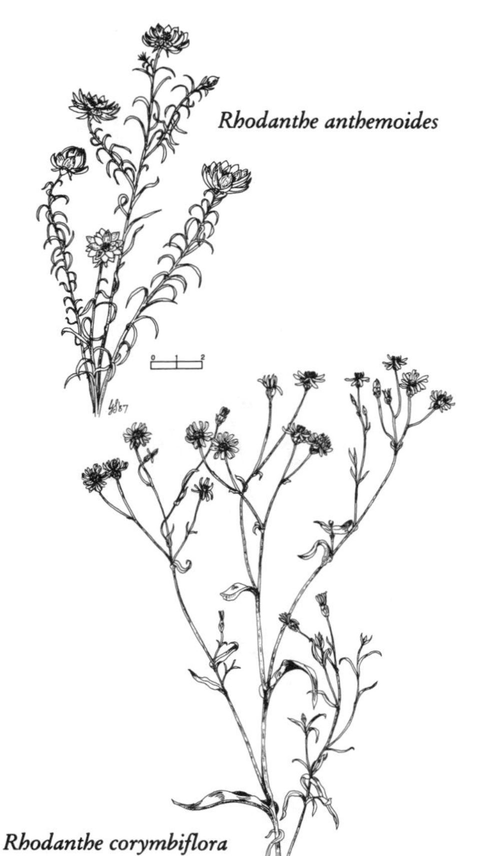
Rhodanthe anthemoides

Rhodanthe corymbiflora

Rhodanthe — Asteraceae

Rhodanthe anthemoides — Chamomile Sunray

Size: 20–40 cm x 20–60 cm — **F P**
Habitat: Plains grassland
Form: Compact perennial herb
Foliage: Blunt narrow bluish-green leaves to 20 mm long
Flowers: Terminal white papery daisies with yellow centres; October to May. Buds are deep pink to white.
Requirements: Moist well drained soils
Comments: A very attractive container or rockery plant requiring a hard prune after flowering. The variety readily available as "Paper Baby" is from NSW.
Propagation: Fresh seed
Localities: Sydenham#, 7, 16, 26
Distribution: Vic, Qld, NSW, Tas, SA
Synonym: *Helipterum anthemoides*

Rhodanthe corymbiflora — Paper or Grey Sunray

Size: 1–30 cm x 10–20 cm — **F**
Habitat: Plains grassland, coastal banksia woodland
Form: Slender annual, usually only a single stem
Foliage: Soft narrow cottony grey leaves to 15 mm long
Flowers: Loose terminal clusters of white daisies with yellow centres; June to October.
Requirements: Dry well drained conditions
Comments: Grows well in pots. May be locally extinct.
Localities: Sydenham#, 67#
Distribution: Vic, NSW, SA
Synonym: *Helipterum corymbiflorum*

Ricinocarpos **Euphorbiaceae**

Ricinocarpos pinifolius

Wedding Bush

Size: 1–3 m x 1–2 m **F P**
Habitat: Tea-tree heath
Form: Dense to open rounded shrub
Foliage: Mostly opposite, narrow, dull green leaves to 40 mm long, margins rolled under
Flowers: Masses of fragrant, open, white, petalled male flowers to 25 mm wide; September to November. Clusters of male flowers surround a cone-like female flower which swells to form a round fruit.
Requirements: Moist, well drained sandy soil
Comments: Spectacular in flower but difficult to propagate.
Propagation: Scarified seed, cuttings
Localities: Port Melbourne#, St Kilda#, Caulfield, Sth Yarra, Seaford, 63, 66–71, 73–75
Distribution: Vic, Qld, NSW, Tas

Ricinocarpos pinifolius

Rorippa **Brassicaceae**

Rorippa dictyosperma

Forest Bitter-cress

Size: 0.3–0.9 m high **P N**
Habitat: Wet and damp sclerophyll forests
Comments: Differs from *R. laciniata* in that the leaves are broader and basal leaves are pinnate. The white flowers are larger with petals to 10 mm long. Each flower has 6 stamens. Seeds are pitted.
Localities: 32, 49, 57, 58
Distribution: Vic, NSW, Tas, WA
Synonym: *Cardamine dictyosperma*

Rorippa laciniata

Jagged Bitter-cress, Perennial Marsh Cress

Size: 20–40 cm high **P**
Habitat: Shaded moist slopes and river flats
Form: Slender, erect perennial herb
Foliage: Basal rosette of narrow-lanceolate, leaves to 80 mm long. They are mostly basal and may be pinnatifid, toothed or entire. Stem leaves are few, small and narrow, entire or with a few teeth or lobes.
Flowers: Small white flowers with 4 narrow petals to 5 mm long, clustered together at the ends of long thin stalks; most of the year. Cylindrical fruit to 40 mm long, splits to release smooth seeds.
Requirements: Moist soils
Comments: The leaves of both species were an important food source for the Aborigines. Appears to be extinct within the Melbourne area.
Propagation: Seed
Localities: Collected from Darebin Ck 1896
Distribution: Vic, Qld, NSW, SA
Synonym: *Cardamine laciniata*

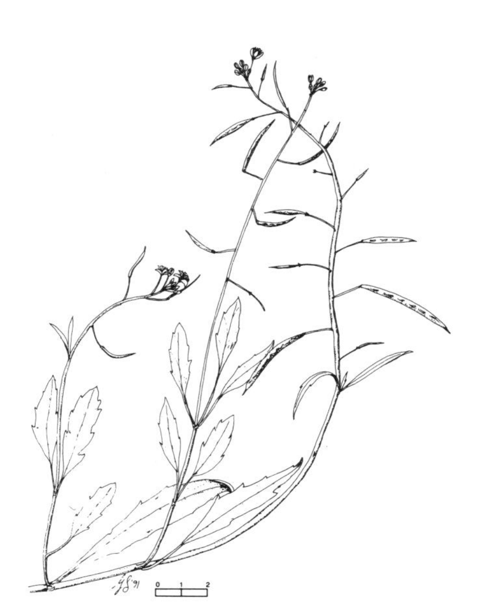

Rorippa dictyosperma

Rubus **Rosaceae**

Rubus parvifolius

Small-leaf Bramble, Native Raspberry

Size: 0.6–1 m x 0.5–2 m **P N**
Habitat: Wet, damp and valley sclerophyll forests, riparian scrub and woodland
Form: Rambling small shrub to trailing plant covered in hooked thorns
Foliage: Lobed to deeply-toothed pinnate leaves, the 3–5 leaflets ovate to 60 mm long, bright green above, silvery below. The terminal leaflet is largest.
Flowers: Small deep pink flowers to 15 mm wide; October to December, followed by small, edible red berries (10–12 mm wide); December to April
Requirements: Well drained soils
Comments: A hardy trailer which can be trained as a climber. Similar to the introduced raspberry.
Propagation: Fresh seed, cuttings, root suckers
Localities: Sunshine, St Albans, Kalorama, 1, 8, 16, 19, 26–33, 34A–37, 41–44, 49, 50A, 55–63, 67, 69A, 71, 74
Distribution: Vic, Qld, NSW, Tas, SA

Rubus parvifolius

The scale representation on each plant equals 2cm.

Rumex

Polygonaceae

Widespread in Australia, these water-loving herbaceous perennials have clusters of small flowers, arranged in simple or branched spike-like or panicle-like inflorescences. Flowers age to red. Fruit are 3-sided. The valves of the fruiting bodies provide identifying features for each species. The native spp. in the Melbourne area have fruiting valves with marginal teeth. Propagation is by seed or division. Rumex reproduce freely and may become invasive in ideal conditions. Some indigenous and introduced spp. are superficially similar.

Rumex bidens

Rumex bidens

Mud Dock

Size: 0.3–0.8 m high — F P
Habitat: Aquatic in Melbourne's rivers and creeks
Form: Perennial herb rooting in mud or shallow water, with hollow, swollen stems floating on or just under the water. Emergent upper stems erect.
Foliage: Narrow-lanceolate leaves with wavy margins to 30 cm on long stalks to 90 mm long, sheathed at base
Flowers: Clusters of tiny green flowers in whorls in the upper leaf axils of the upper stems, male flowers grouped above female flowers; all year, peaking Spring and Summer
Requirements: Shallow water or wet soil
Comments: The fruiting valves have 1–2 spreading basal teeth on each side. The submerged stem was an important food source for the Aborigines.
Localities: Maribyrnong R, 16, 26, 28, 32, 35, 42, 67#
Distribution: Vic, Qld, NSW, Tas, SA

Rumex brownii

Slender or Swamp Dock

Size: 0.3–1 m high — F P
Habitat: Riparian scrub and woodland, box and red gum woodland, valley sclerophyll forest, wattle tea-tree scrub
Form: Erect perennial herb
Foliage: Long-stalked, oblong to lanceolate leaves to 130 mm long, mostly at the base of the stems
Flowers: Flowers are in widely spaced whorls in clusters of 5–16 along the leafless stems; September to December. Fruiting valves have 3–5 hooked teeth on each side and a hooked tip.
Requirements: Moist soils
Comments: Widespread low-lying areas subject to inundation. The plant may die back to a perennial rootstock during Summer. Regrowth commences the following Spring.
Localities: Deer Park, 8, 9, 14–18, 23–33, 34A–36, 39, 41, 42, 44, 56, 58, 60, 62, 63, 71, 74
Distribution: All states *Illustrated p. 200*

Rumex dumosus

Rumex dumosus

Wiry Dock

Size: 0.4–0.9 m x 0.4–0.9 m — F P
Habitat: Saltmarshes, grassy wetlands, plains grassland, red gum woodland
Form: Tangled, wiry perennial herb becoming rounded in form
Foliage: Lower leaves are lanceolate to 22 cm long
Flowers: Tiny flowers in widely spaced clusters of 1–4, each with smaller, narrow floral leaves; August to January. Fruiting valves are veined and have 2 rigid teeth on each side.
Requirements: Moist soils
Comments: When dry, the plant can break off at the base and be blown along by the wind.
Localities: 2, 4, 6, 7, 12, 15, 17, 18, 23, 26, 28, 34A
Distribution: All states

Rumex tenax

Size: 10–50 cm high — F P
Habitat: Low-lying depressions in grasslands
Form: Erect, widely-branched perennial herb
Foliage: Basal and stem leaves are often linear, 90–160 mm long, with wavy margins. Leaves and stalks are of equal length.
Flowers: Widely spaced clusters of 12 or more small flowers in the axils of floral leaves, smaller than basal leaves; March to May and September to October. Fruiting valves are net-veined and have 2 spreading teeth on each side. They also have a callus.
Requirements: Moist soils
Localities: 7
Distribution: All mainland states

Rutidosis — Asteraceae

Rutidosis leptorrhynchoides — Button Wrinklewort

Size: 15–30 cm x 30 cm **F P**
Habitat: Plains grassland, grassy wetlands of basalt plains
Form: Slender, glabrous perennial herb, branching from the base
Foliage: Sessile, linear leaves to 20 mm long, with margins curled under
Flowers: Yellow button flowerheads to 20 mm wide with dull green bracts, on long stalks to 20 cm; November to May; followed by fluffy seed heads
Requirements: Well drained heavy soils
Comments: An endangered species of both national and state significance, this unusual button daisy would be interesting in a container or rockery. In Melbourne, it is now restricted to only a few sites.
Propagation: Seed, division
Localities: Early collections: Footscray, Altona, 15#; St.Albans, Laverton (10 plants remain), Werribee, Deer Park, 26
Distribution: Vic, NSW

Rutidosis leptorrhynchoides

Rutidosis multiflora — Small Wrinklewort

Size: 15–50 mm high **F P**
Habitat: Coastal banksia woodland, primary dune scrub, dry sclerophyll forest
Form: Open annual herb
Foliage: Succulent, sessile, linear leaves to 10 mm long with long hairs near the base, lower leaves often paired
Flowers: Tiny, sessile, whitish-cream flowerheads grouped together in clusters among floral leaves; August to October
Requirements: Well drained sandy soil, tolerating dry periods
Comments: A rare plant in the Melbourne area resembling a tiny cauliflower, suited to containers.
Propagation: Seed
Localities: 42, 49, 67#
Distribution: Vic, NSW, Tas, SA, WA

Rutidosis multiflora

Sambucus — Caprifoliaceae

Sambucus gaudichaudiana — Native Elderberry

Size: 0.6–2 m x 0.5–1.5 m **P**
Habitat: Riparian scrub and woodland, wet, damp and valley sclerophyll forests
Form: Upright herbaceous perennial herb
Foliage: Pairs of light green leaves divided into 5–9 coarsely-toothed, ovate-lanceolate leaflets each 80–150 mm long; lower leaflets on larger leaves divided again
Flowers: Terminal clusters of small, stalkless, waxy white fragrant flowers; November to December; followed by masses of sweet, white or yellowish fleshy berries
Requirements: Moist well drained soil
Comments: A bright shrub for a shady moist area. Aborigines ate the berries.
Propagation: Seed, cuttings
Localities: Kalorama, 8, 16, 26, 29, 35, 36, 55, 57, 58
Distribution: Vic, Qld, NSW, Tas, SA

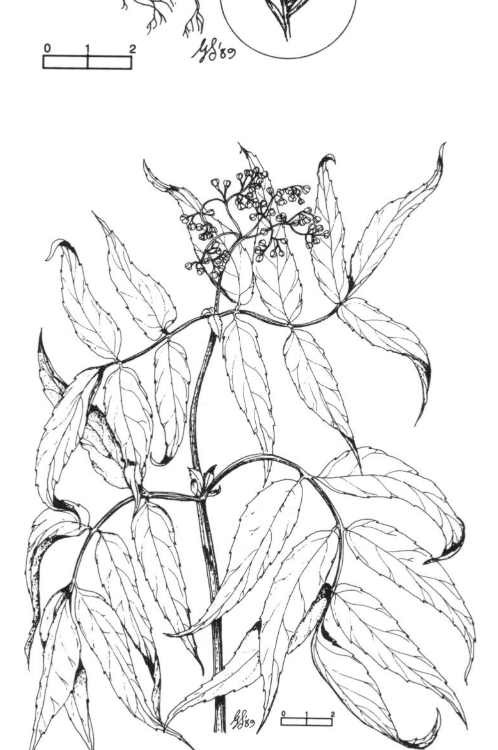

Sambucus gaudichaudiana

Samolus — Primulaceae

Samolus repens — Creeping Brookweed

Size: 30 cm high **F P**
Habitat: Saltmarshes, grassy wetlands, swamps in red gum woodland, primary dune scrub
Form: Tufted, perennial herb, with some stems decumbent and rooting at the nodes
Foliage: Dull green; basal leaves thick, obovate to 40 mm long; stem leaves narrower, oblong to spathulate to 15 mm long
Flowers: Short terminal cluster of tiny waxy pink or white flowers on erect stems; most of the year
Requirements: Moist sandy soil, salt tolerant
Comments: A spreading herb for moist coastal areas.
Propagation: Cuttings, division
Localities: 2–4, 6, 11, 16, 25, 26, 67, 70, 74
Distribution: All states except NT; NZ

Also illustrated p. 343

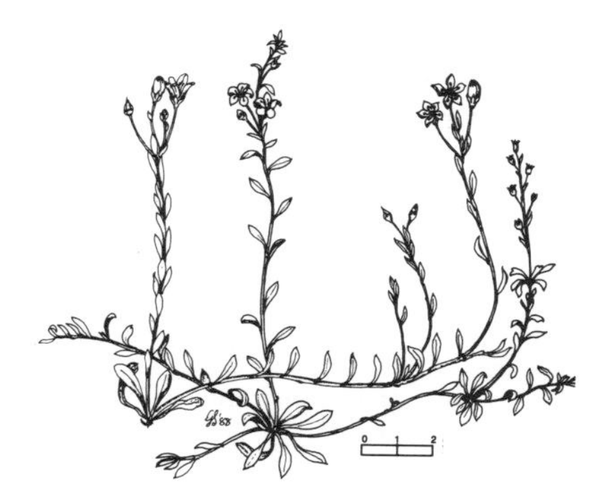

Samolus repens

SCALE: 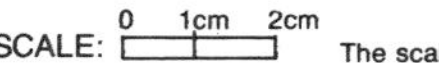

The scale representation on each plant equals 2cm.

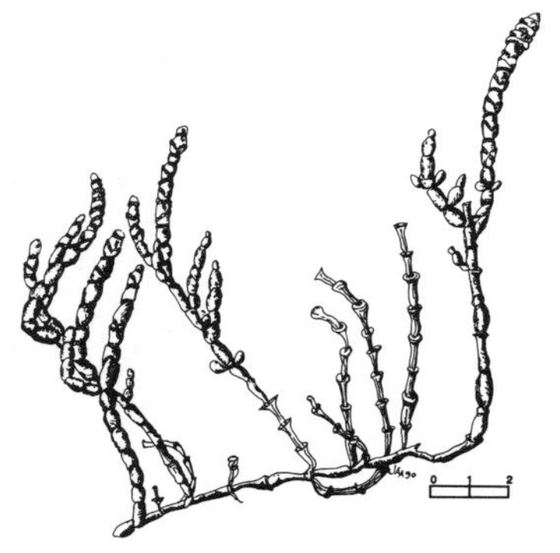
Sarcocornia blackiana

Sarcocornia — Chenopodiaceae

Sarcocornia blackiana

Thick-head Glasswort

Size: to 20 cm high — F
Habitat: Saltmarshes, estuaries, primary dune scrub
Form: Erect or spreading shrub, fleshy stems rooting at nodes
Foliage: Succulent, often reddish, cylindrical segments. Fruiting spikes to 50 mm long, 5–8 mm in diameter when in fruit.
Flowers: Rows of 5–13 green flowers embedded in the succulent axis, central flowers often in 2 rows; October to February
Requirements: Wet saline soil, tolerating dryness in Summer
Comments: Seeds are covered in small protuberances with short round hairs.
Propagation: Cuttings, division
Localities: Altona, 2, 67[#], 69A, 74
Distribution: Vic, Tas, SA, WA
Synonym: *Salicornia blackiana*

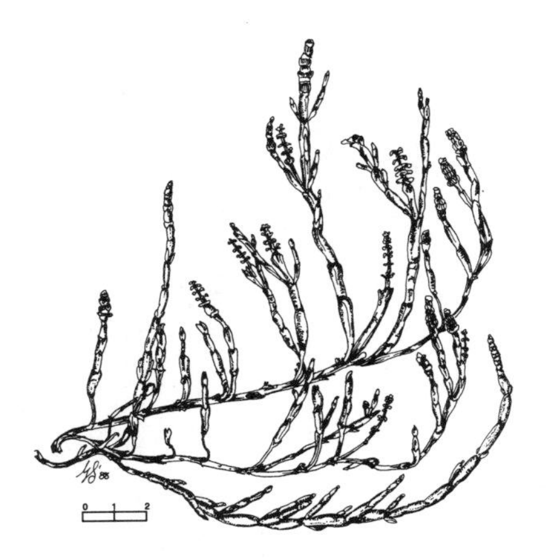
Sarcocornia quinqueflora ssp. *quinqueflora*

Sarcocornia quinqueflora ssp. quinqueflora

Beaded Glasswort or Samphire

Size: Prostrate x 0.5 m — F
Habitat: Estuaries, saltmarshes, grassy wetlands, primary dune scrub
Comments: Similar to *S. blackiana* but with more slender, longer segments. Fruiting spikes are narrower, to 5 mm in diameter. 5–9 flowers are in a single row; November to March. Seeds covered with curved bristles. Prefers less salty areas. *S. quinqueflora* ssp. *tasmanica* occurs just south of the Study area, in Mt. Martha.
Localities: Footscray, 2–4, 7, 67, 69A, 72, 74
Distribution: All states except NT; NZ
Synonym: *Salicornia quinqueflora*

Sclerolaena — Chenopodiaceae

Sclerolaena diacantha

Grey Copperburr, Two-spined Saltbush

Size: 10–30 cm x 20–50 cm — F P
Habitat: Plains grassland
Form: Rounded or prostrate perennial shrub, the branches and foliage covered in densely matted hairs
Foliage: Fleshy, narrow grey leaves to 20 mm long
Flowers: Single flowers in leaf axils; most of the year. Very hairy fruiting body has 2 tiny divergent spines.
Requirements: Dry soils, tolerant of salt and limestone
Comments: A short-lived coloniser of dry areas. It seeds readily and is valuable in stabilising soils prone to wind erosion. Very restricted range in the Melbourne area, possibly occurring just outside the study area.
Propagation: Seed
Localities: Melton
Distribution: All states except Tas
Synonym: *Bassia diacantha*

Sclerolaena muricata var. muricata

Black Roly-poly, Five-spined Saltbush

Size: 1 m x 1 m — F
Habitat: Saltmarshes, box woodland, riparian scrub, primary dune scrub
Form: Short-lived, rounded perennial shrub forming a tangled clump
Foliage: Dark blue-green or pale green, linear to narrowly oblong leaves to 15 mm long, hairless and slightly fleshy
Flowers: Single flowers in leaf axils; most of the year. Tiny, thick fruiting bodies are firmly attached to the branches. Each has 5 prominent spines, the 3 largest (to 10 mm long) being separate, the 2 smaller ones usually joined at the base.
Requirements: Moist soils, tolerating periodic inundation
Comments: A pioneer plant of disturbed or degraded areas. It has been declared a noxious weed in Victoria as the spiny fruit catch in sheep's wool making shearing and processing difficult. Dry plants break off at the base, and are blown along the ground by the wind.
Propagation: Seed
Localities: Toolern Vale, St. Albans, Sunshine, 4, 9, 12, 16, 23, 26, 67
Distribution: Vic, Qld, NSW, SA
Synonym: *Bassia quinquecuspis* var. *quinquecuspis*

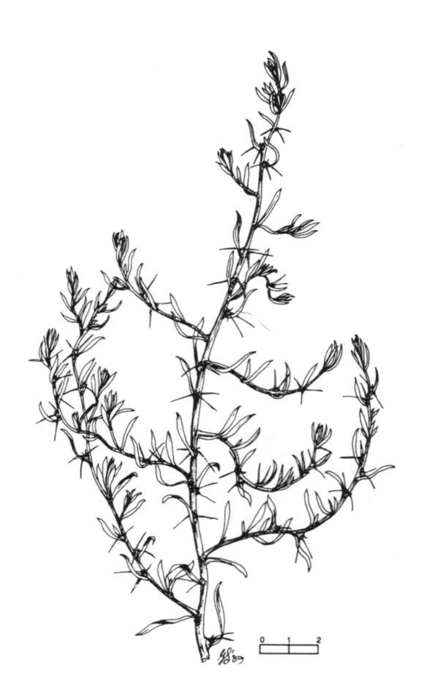
Sclerolaena muricata var. *muricata*

Sclerolaena muricata var. villosa

Grey Roly-poly

F P

Habitat: Riparian scrub on basalt plains
Comments: The branches have a covering of woolly hairs. The dark green obovate-lanceolate leaves to 10 mm long have a glabrous upper surface, sparsely downy below. Locally rare.
Localities: Melton, 16
Distribution: Vic, Qld, NSW, SA, NT
Synonym: *Bassia quinquecuspis* var. *villosa*

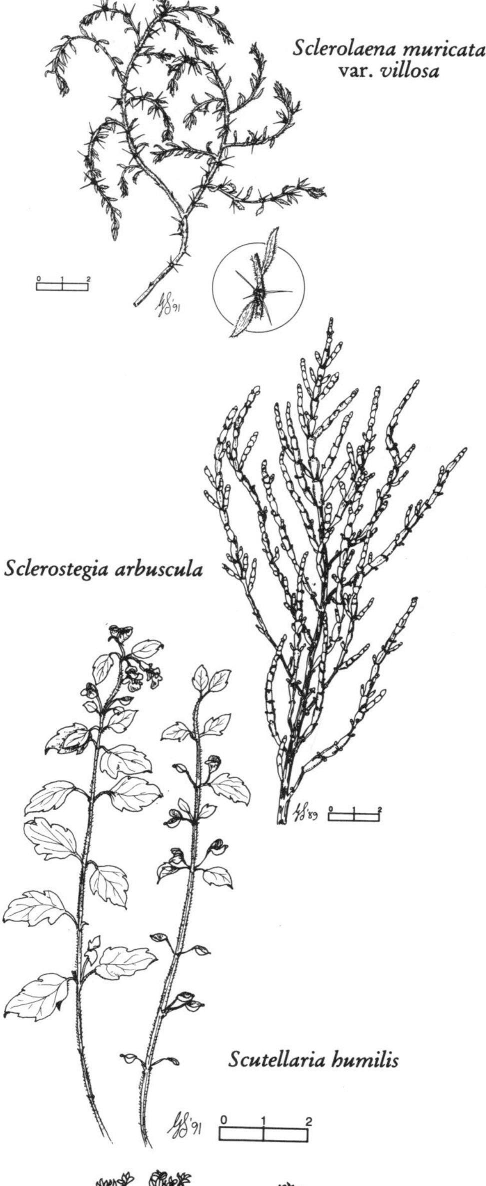
Sclerolaena muricata var. *villosa*
Sclerostegia arbuscula
Scutellaria humilis

Sclerostegia

Chenopodiaceae

Sclerostegia arbuscula

Shrubby Glasswort

F

Size: 1–2 m x 1–2 m
Habitat: Saltmarshes, shoreline
Form: Erect, much-branched shrub
Foliage: Succulent stems green or reddish, with segments to 5 mm long
Flowers: Flowers in spikes consisting of rows of 3 flowers; all year
Requirements: Moist to wet saline soils
Comments: Restricted distribution in the Melbourne area.
Propagation: Seed
Localities: 2–4, 67
Distribution: Vic, NSW, Tas, SA, WA
Synonym: *Arthrocnemum arbuscula*

Scutellaria

Lamiaceae

Scutellaria humilis

Dwarf Skull Cap

F P N

Size: 15 cm x 1 m
Habitat: Box woodland, tea-tree heath, along creeks and gullies
Form: Stoloniferous perennial herb with erect 4-sided stems
Foliage: Pairs of toothed, ovate leaves to 12 mm long
Flowers: Small mauve to pink flowers singly on slender stalks in leaf axils; October to February. The flowers appear to be paired as they often grow in the same direction.
Requirements: Moist, well drained soils, requiring Summer watering
Comments: Very rare small dainty plant which adds interest to a shady site. Spreads by layering.
Propagation: Cuttings, division
Localities: Mt Eliza, Sunbury#, 26, 29#, 74
Distribution: Vic, Qld, NSW, Tas, SA

Sebaea

Gentianaceae

Sebaea albidiflora

White Sebaea

P

Size: to 20 cm high
Habitat: Saltmarshes, valley sclerophyll forest, wattle tea-tree scrub
Form: Stiff, erect annual herb
Foliage: Pairs of erect, stem-clasping, ovate to lanceolate leaves to 10 mm long, smaller at the base and withering early
Flowers: Compact terminal cymes, composed of 1–5 repeatedly forked clusters with no more than 3 sessile, white to cream tubular flowers in each; September to November. Flowers divided to the base into 4 segments (4-partite). The calyx lobes are blunt, base clasped by leafy bracts.
Requirements: Moist to wet soil
Comments: Restricted distribution in Melbourne.
Propagation: Seed
Localities: 3, 4, ?42, 49, 67#
Distribution: Vic, Tas, SA

Sebaea ovata

Yellow Sebaea

P N

Size: 20 cm high
Habitat: Plains grassland, grassy wetlands, red gum woodland, damp and valley sclerophyll forest, tea-tree heath
Form: Similar to *S. albidiflora*. Stems are 4-sided with wider, ovate to almost round leaves to 12 mm long.
Flowers: Clusters seldom have more than 5 yellow flowers which are 5-partite and become stalked after flowering. The calyx lobes are pointed and bracts spreading. Locally rare.
Localities: Laverton Nth, Rockbank, 12, 17#, 18, 26, 34A, 35, 41, 42, 49, 58, 67#
Distribution: All states except NT; NZ

Sebaea albidiflora
Sebaea ovata

SCALE: 0 1cm 2cm — The scale representation on each plant equals 2cm.

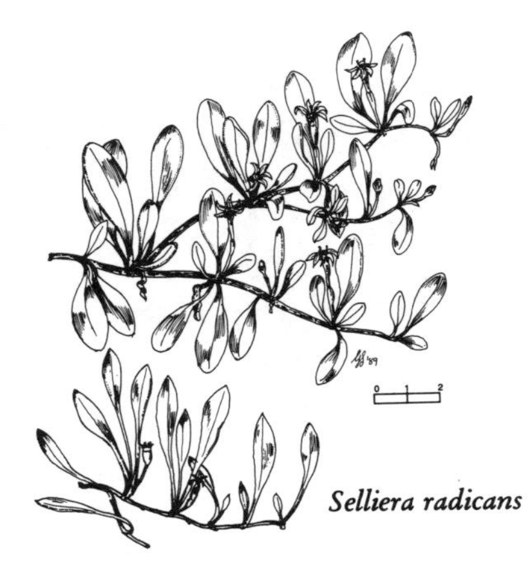

Selliera radicans

Selliera — Goodeniaceae

Selliera radicans

Swampweed

Size: Prostrate-40 mm x 1 m — **F P N**
Habitat: Saltmarshes, riparian scrub, coastal banksia woodland, grassy wetland
Form: Prostrate, creeping mat plant, rooting at the nodes
Foliage: Succulent, bright green spathulate leaves, 10–100 mm long
Flowers: Small white to mauve fan-shaped flowers; October to November
Requirements: Moist soil, salt tolerant
Comments: A fast-growing creeper, useful as a soil or sand binder. Tolerates both wet and dry periods.
Propagation: Cuttings, division
Localities: Keilor, 3, 4, 16, 26, 28, 60, 67, 69A, 71, 72, 74, 76
Distribution: Vic, NSW, Tas, SA; NZ, S Am

Senecio — Asteraceae

The Senecios are a very large genus of herbaceous plants represented by 16 species in the Melbourne area. Yellow flowerheads are in terminal clusters and are either radiate (having both tubular and ligulate florets) or, more frequently, discoid (having only tubular florets). The flowerhead is surrounded by a row of bracts. Fluffy seed heads follow flowering. The leaves often have ear-like growths at the base, called auricles. Senecios are pioneering plants, germinating quickly following bush-fires, and colonising disturbed areas. Generally understorey plants, some species may become invasive under ideal conditions. Propagation is by seed.

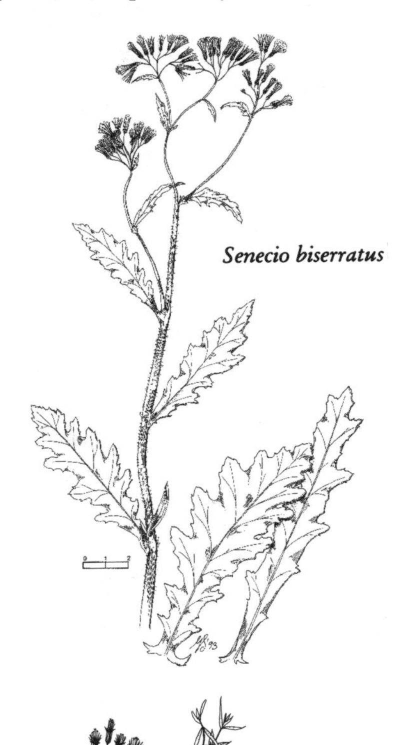

Senecio biserratus

Senecio biserratus

Jagged Fireweed

Size: 0.6–1 m high — **F P**
Habitat: Riparian scrub, grassy low open forest, primary dune scrub
Form: Erect annual herb, branching below the infloresence
Foliage: Glabrous, ovate to broad-lanceolate toothed leaves to 140 mm long. The leaves are prominently veined, shallowly lobed and irregularly toothed; the auricles are also toothed.
Flowers: Dense clusters of discoid flowerheads surrounded by few, narrow green bracts; October to March
Requirements: Moist soils tolerant of salty winds
Localities: Keysborough, Chelsea, 36, 42, 71, 74, 76
Distribution: Vic, NSW, Tas, SA; NZ

Senecio cunninghamii var. cunninghamii

Branching or Bushy Groundsel

Size: to 1 m x 1 m — **F P**
Habitat: Plains grassland
Form: Erect to spreading under-shrub
Foliage: Glabrous; sessile, usually entire, light green linear leaves 20–120 mm long, often with 2 grooves below and curled edges, auricles sometimes present. The branches are reddish.
Flowers: Dense flat clusters of discoid flowerheads, bracts broad and yellowish; August to April
Requirements: Moist soils tolerating inundation and saline conditions
Comments: May be useful as a coloniser of saline areas. The local form has smaller leaves to 20 mm long.
Localities: Sydenham, 15#, 16
Distribution: All states except Tas

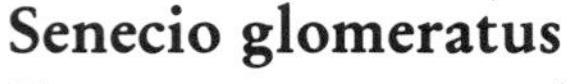

Senecio glomeratus

Annual Fireweed

Size: 0.5–1.2 m high — **F P**
Habitat: Widespread in red gum woodland, wet, damp, valley and dry sclerophyll forests, grassy low open forest, tea-tree heath
Form: Erect, softly hairy annual herb
Foliage: Lanceolate-ovate leaves to 120 mm long, coarsely toothed to lobed, lobes sometimes toothed, with large, toothed auricles
Flowers: Densely-bunched discoid flowerheads with a few narrow, woolly bracts; November to February
Requirements: Moist soils
Comments: Similar to *S. hispidulus* var. *hispidulus* but covered in soft, cobweb-like hairs.
Localities: Montrose, 16, 26, 28, 34A–36, 39–42, 44, 47, 48, 50–52 54–58, 60, 63, 64, 67–72, 74–76
Distribution: Vic, NSW, Tas, SA, WA; NZ — *Illustrated p. 18*

Senecio cunninghamii var. *cunninghamii*

Senecio hispidulus var. hispidulus

Rough Fireweed

Size: 0.2–1.3 m high **F P**
Habitat: Plains grassland, dry and valley sclerophyll forests, coastal banksia woodland, tea-tree heath
Form: Erect perennial, single stemmed or multi-branched from the base
Foliage: Sessile, lanceolate to obovate, toothed to sharply-lobed leaves to 60 mm long, erect bristly hairs below, rough on upper surface, auricles with 2 coarse teeth
Flowers: Branched clusters of inconspicuous spreading discoid flowerheads surrounded by green bracts; September to February
Requirements: Moist soils
Comments: Often occurs in clearings or by tracks.
Localities: Montrose, 28, 34A–36, 41–44, 47, 48, 50–56, 58–60, 63, 64, 67, 68, 69A–71, 74–76
Distribution: All states; NZ

Senecio hispidulus var. *hispidulus*

Senecio lautus

Senecio linearifolius

Senecio macrocarpus

Senecio hispidulus var. dissectus

Hill Fireweed

Size: to 0.8 m high **F P**
Habitat: Dry sclerophyll forest, amongst rocks
Comments: Leaves are deeply dissected to pinnate, and margins have more rounded teeth.
Localities: Bulla, Diamond Ck, 32
Distribution: All states

Senecio lautus

Variable Groundsel

Size: 0.1–1 m x 0.3–0.5 m **F P**
Habitat: Riparian scrub, valley and damp sclerophyll forests, coastal banksia woodland
Form: Very variable. An erect or sprawling perennial herb or under-shrub.
Foliage: Dark green leaves, variable from narrow to pinnate, entire to toothed or lobed, 10–70 mm long, may be stem-clasping
Flowers: Loose clusters of radiate flowerheads with 8–14 ray florets, many disk florets; September to March. 12–20 bracts with several minute bracts at base.
Requirements: Well drained soils, lime tolerant
Comments: Some forms are particularly attractive and long flowering. The coastal form is small and spreading, with fleshy leaves to 50 mm long and well displayed flowerheads. The foothills forms range from entire, stalked and elliptic to narrow-lanceolate, toothed and stem-clasping.
Localities: St. Kilda#; Olinda, 14, 30#, 49, 58, 67#, 74
Distribution: All states; NZ

Senecio linearifolius

Firewheel Groundsel

Size: 1–2 m x 1–1.5 m **P N**
Habitat: Wet, damp and valley sclerophyll forests
Form: Erect perennial herb
Foliage: Sessile, entire or sharply-toothed, linear-lanceolate, dark green leaves to 150 mm long. The undersurface is more or less glabrous.
Flowers: Large flat-topped clusters of numerous, small radiate flowerheads with 5 ray florets; November to February
Requirements: Moist soils
Comments: A brilliant display in flower. Alpine forms have broader leaves than the local form. Conspicuous after fire or clearing.
Localities: 47, 55–58, 62, 63
Distribution: Vic, NSW, Tas

Senecio macrocarpus

Size: 20–40 cm high **F**
Habitat: Plains grassland
Form: Straggly to erect perennial herb
Foliage: Downy grey narrow leaves to 60 mm long; lower leaves usually entire, stem leaves smaller, toothed, and with minute auricles
Flowers: Few large discoid flowerheads; September to October
Requirements: Well drained soils
Comments: Only recently rediscovered in the Melbourne area, on the basalt plains. Extinct through some of its range it is an endangered plant of both Melbourne and Victoria.
Localities: Laverton Nth, Sunbury, Diggers Rest, Melton
Distribution: Vic, Tas, SA

SCALE: 

The scale representation on each plant equals 2cm.

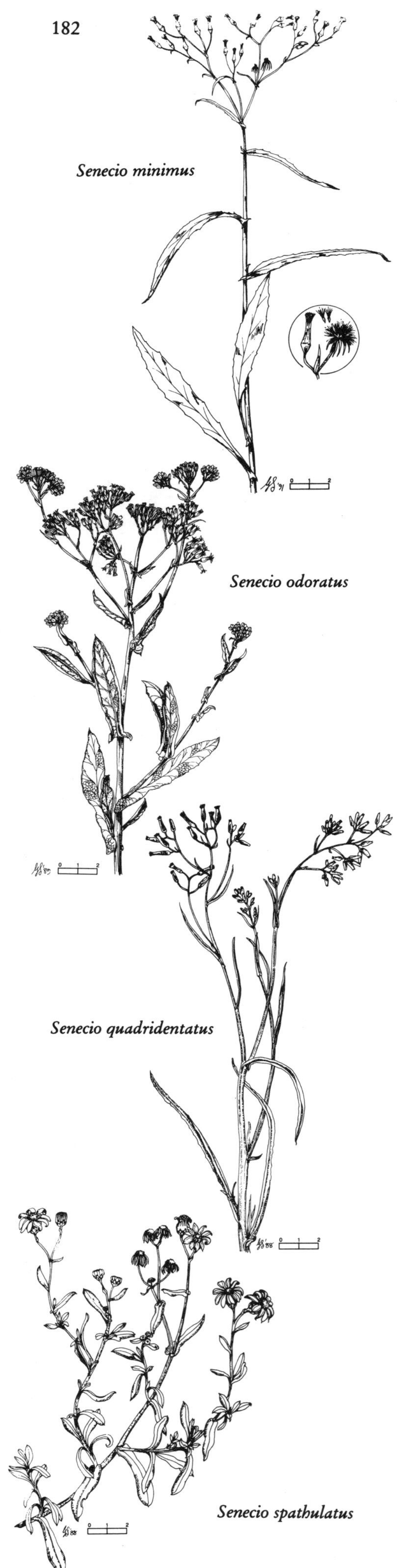
Senecio minimus

Senecio odoratus

Senecio quadridentatus

Senecio spathulatus

Senecio minimus

Shrubby Fireweed

P N

Size: 0.5–1 m high
Habitat: Red gum and riparian woodland, swamp scrub, damp and valley sclerophyll forests, tea-tree heath
Form: Erect annual herb often branched at the base or below flowerheads, parallel ridges along stems
Foliage: Lanceolate, evenly-toothed leaves to 90 mm long, sometimes larger, with toothed auricles
Flowers: Masses of discoid flowerheads, narrow green bracts; December to April
Requirements: Moist well drained soils
Localities: 35, 36, 42, 46, 47, 51, 54–58, 60, 71, 73–75
Distribution: All states except NT; NZ

Senecio odoratus

Scented Groundsel

F P

Size: 0.6–2 m x 0.6–1.5 m
Habitat: Grassy wetlands, valley sclerophyll forest, grassy low open forest
Form: Erect perennial undershrub
Foliage: Coarse, sessile, usually glaucous leaves, to 120 mm long, broadly lanceolate to ovate, toothed along recurved margins, and with auricles. The veins are conspicuous.
Flowers: Large flat-topped clusters of discoid flowerheads; October to January. 8 bracts.
Requirements: Well drained soils, tolerating salt spray
Comments: Coastal forms are lower and more bushy. Locally rare.
Localities: 5, 34A, 42, 74, 76
Distribution: Vic, Tas, SA

Senecio quadridentatus

Cotton Fireweed

F

Size: 0.4–1 m x 0.5–1 m
Habitat: Widespread in disturbed areas of plains grassland, red gum and riparian woodland, riparian scrub, dry and valley sclerophyll forests, tea-tree heath
Form: Erect, perennial herb, much-branched from the base. Both stems and leaves are covered with dense cottony hairs, giving the plant a greyish appearance.
Foliage: Narrow, pointed leaves to 100 mm long, becoming smaller up the stem, margins recurved. Leaves sometimes have a few teeth on the margins.
Flowers: Small greenish-yellow discoid flowerheads in loose clusters; October to March. 11–13 bracts.
Requirements: Very adaptable
Comments: The most common and widely distributed *Senecio* spp. Withstands very dry conditions, but may die back to a woody rootstock until rain occurs. Major features distinguishing it from *S. tenuiflorus* are the 3 prominent veins on the floral bracts and tapering achenes (or fruit) which have an elongated beak and prominent ribs.
Localities: 7, 8, 12, 16–18, 21, 26, 28, 31, 32, 34A–36, 39, 41–44, 46–49, 51–60, 62–68, 69A–71, 74, 76
Distribution: All states; NZ, Timor, N Caledonia

Senecio runcinifolius

Tall Groudsel

F

Size: 0.2–1 m high
Habitat: Saltmarshes
Form: Erect annual herb
Foliage: Lanceolate stem-clasping leaves, deeply lobed with more than 8 pairs of toothed lobes, lobes pointing towards the base of the leaf
Flowers: Broad loosely-branched clusters of discoid flowerheads; August to November. Fruiting heads are white and very fluffy.
Requirements: Moist soils, tolerating saline conditions
Comments: More common after good rains, it will grow larger if it is supported by other plants. Masses of silky seeds give the plant an interesting appearance. Locally rare.
Localities: Altona Nth
Distribution: Vic, NSW, SA

Illustrated p. 200

Senecio spathulatus

F

Size: to 0.5 m high
Habitat: Primary dune scrub
Comments: A weak herb often with fleshy obovate leaves to 55 mm long and few radiate flowerheads. A locally rare plant, often combined with *S. lautus.*
Localities: Seaford, Pt. Wilson
Distribution: Endemic to Vic
Synonym: *S. lautus* ssp. *maritimus*

Senecio squarrosus

Leafy Fireweed

Size: 0.3–0.5 m high **F P**
Habitat: Grassy low open forest, plains grassland
Form: Erect perennial herb, branching at the flowerheads
Foliage: Thick linear-lanceolate leaves to 100 mm long, rough above, sparse cottony hairs below, entire or sparsely toothed or lobed; upper leaves sessile, narrower with small coarsely-toothed auricles
Flowers: Terminal clusters of 4–16 discoid flowerheads; December to March
Requirements: Well drained soils
Comments: A rare plant in the Melbourne area. The form found on the basalt plains may be raised to species status after further research. It is in danger of extinction due to development occurring on the only known sites.
Localities: Braybrook 1889, Lysterfield 1903; Werribee, Deer Park, 50A, 74
Distribution: Vic, Tas, SA

Senecio tenuiflorus

Size: 0.3–0.6 m high **F P**
Habitat: Dry and valley sclerophyll forests, tea-tree heath, disturbed roadsides
Form: Erect annual or biennial herb branching at the base or below the flower clusters
Foliage: Crowded, obovate to oblanceolate lower leaves to 100 mm long, very hairy and usually purplish below, rough above. Mid-stem leaves shorter and lanceolate.
Flowers: Small discoid flowerheads; October to January
Requirements: Prefers moist soils
Comments: Similar to and often occurring with *S. quadridentatus* but has fewer flowerheads, one (sometimes 2) prominent veins on the bracts and a plump achene with flat ribs.
Localities: 34A, 36, 42, 44, 47, 48, 50–57, 70, 74
Distribution: All states except NT

Senecio vagus

Saw Groundsel

Size: to 1 m high **P N**
Habitat: Wet sclerophyll forest
Form: Erect or rounded hairless perennial herb
Foliage: Large, dark green lanceolate leaves to 15 cm long, on long stalks. Foliage is deeply divided, with irregular lobes or teeth.
Flowers: Many large radiate flowerheads in large, loose clusters; sporadic, peaking September to December
Requirements: Moist well drained soils
Comments: Very restricted range in Melbourne.
Localities: 55, 57
Distribution: Vic, NSW, Tas

Senecio velleioides

Forest Groundsel

Size: 0.5–1.5 m x 0.5–1 m **P N**
Habitat: Wet and damp sclerophyll forests
Form: Soft, many-branched perennial herb
Foliage: Stem-clasping, glaucous, heart-shaped leaves to 7–17 cm long, upper leaves almost entire while lower leaves are regularly toothed
Flowers: Clusters of large radiate flowerheads; November to February
Requirements: Moist well drained soils
Comments: Germinates after fire. This showy plant is becoming increasingly difficult to find locally.
Localities: 57, 58
Distribution: Vic, Qld, NSW, Tas

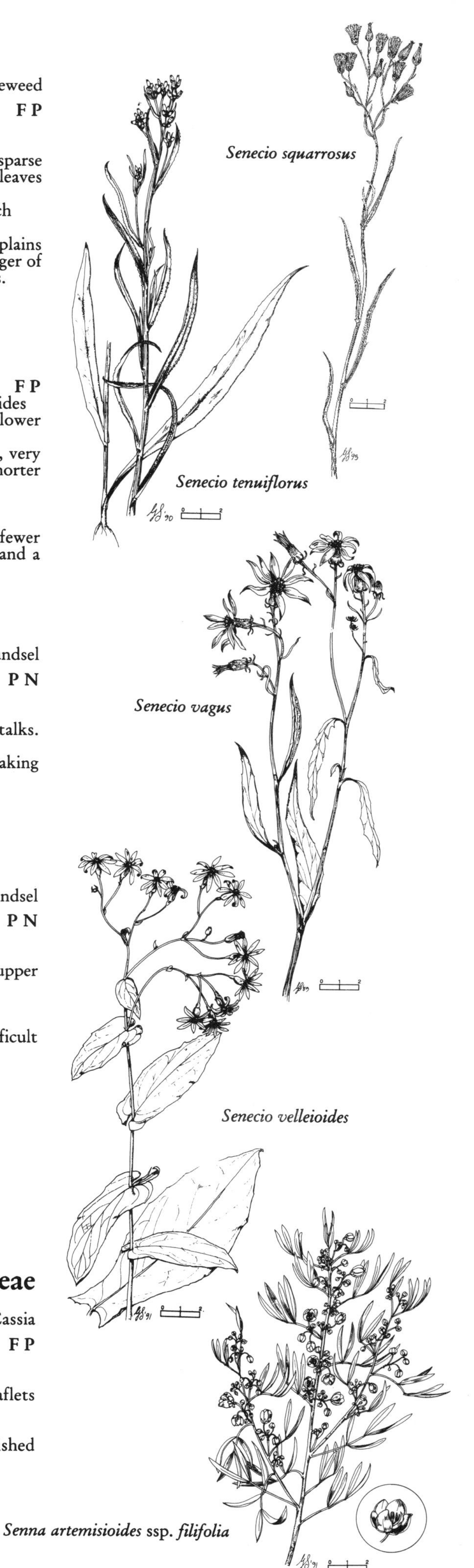

Senecio squarrosus

Senecio tenuiflorus

Senecio vagus

Senecio velleioides

Senna artemisioides ssp. *filifolia*

Senna — Caesalpiniaceae

Senna artemisioides ssp. filifolia

Desert Cassia

Size: 1–3 m x 1 m **F P**
Habitat: Box woodland
Form: Rounded or erect shrub
Foliage: Pinnate leaves to 50 mm long with 1–2 pairs of terete or narrow leaflets
Flowers: Abundant short racemes of golden flowers; June to November
Requirements: Well drained soils
Comments: An attractive and easily grown shrub which does well under established eucalypts. It also tolerates hot dry conditions.
Propagation: Scarified seed, cuttings
Localities: Essendon, Sunbury, Tullamarine, 16, 26
Distribution: Vic, SA, NT
Synonym: *Cassia nemophila* var. *nemophila*, *C. eremophila*

SCALE: 0 1cm 2cm The scale representation on each plant equals 2cm

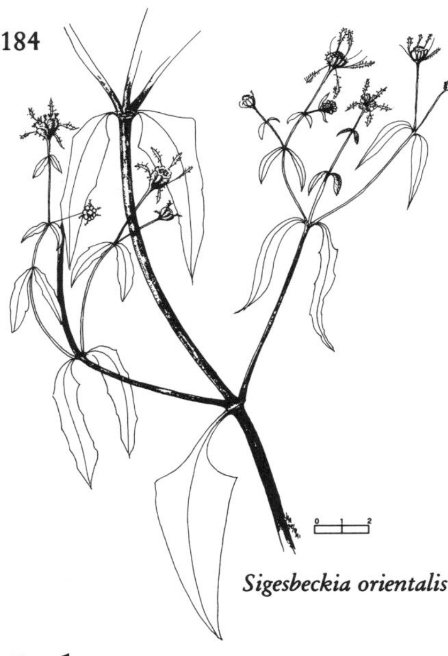
Sigesbeckia orientalis

Sigesbeckia — Asteraceae

Sigesbeckia orientalis — Indian Weed

Size: 0.1–0.8 m x 0.1–0.8 m — P
Habitat: Wet, damp and valley sclerophyll forests
Form: Stiff, erect, branched annual herb
Foliage: Widely-spaced pairs of soft, downy, lanceolate to arrow-shaped leaves to 120 mm long, with toothed margins
Flowers: Yellow daisy-like flowerheads on long stalks above the leaves; November to March. Ray florets which are tiny, number about 8, but as each is 3-lobed, it appears there are many. The 5 outer floral bracts are covered with sticky glandular hairs, somewhat like those of *Drosera* spp.
Requirements: Moist soils
Comments: Similar in appearance to *Senecio* spp., and may also be found in disturbed areas. It is not usually found in large numbers.
Propagation: Seed
Localities: Kalorama, 29, 55–58
Distribution: All states except Tas; NZ

Solanum — Solanaceae

Solanum spp. are often colonising plants of disturbed areas and tracks. They have an important role following fires, regenerating quickly from seed or underground stems. The five fused petals are pale mauve to purplish in the Melbourne spp. The fleshy berries were eaten by the Aborigines but only when very ripe, often being placed in sand heaps to ripen. Fast growing, some species make excellent screen plants in hot, dry conditions. Propagation is by seed or cuttings.

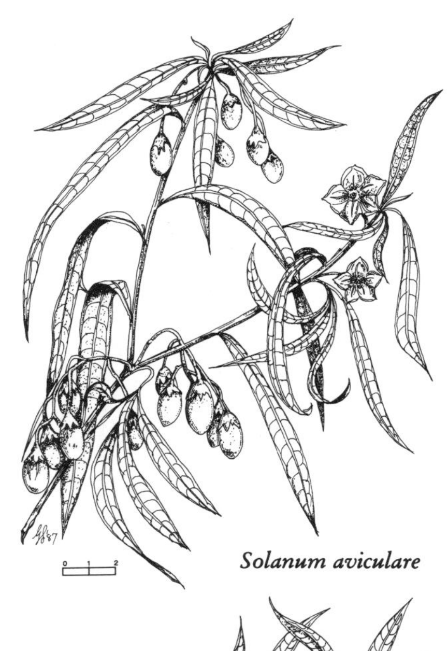
Solanum aviculare

Solanum aviculare — Kangaroo Apple

Size: 1–3 m x 1–4 m — F P N
Habitat: Red gum woodland, valley, damp and wet sclerophyll forests, grassy low open forest
Form: Erect, soft woody shrub, stems angular
Foliage: Dark green; leaves variably lobed, broadly elliptic to obovate to 30 cm long, with 3–11 deeply cut lobes; entire lanceolate leaves 5–20 cm long often borne on the upper parts of the plant
Flowers: Axillary cluster of up to 10 violet flowers, darker in centre, 25–40 mm across, deeply cut lobes are sharply pointed; January. Succulent egg-shaped fruit are orange-red to scarlet when ripe.
Requirements: Well drained soils
Comments: A decorative fast growing shrub becoming straggly with age but easily rejuvenated with heavy pruning.
Localities: 23, 33–34A, 42, 47, 49, 55, 57, 60–63, 74, 76
Distribution: Vic, Qld, NSW, Tas; NZ, PNG

Solanum laciniatum — Large Kangaroo Apple

Size: 1–3 m x 1–3 m — F P N
Habitat: Box and red gum woodlands, valley sclerophyll forest, riparian scrub
Foliage: Leaves either irregularly lobed and broadly ovate to 30 cm long with 1–7 lobes or entire and lanceolate to 100 mm long
Flowers: Bluish to purple flowers to 50 mm wide, September to March, have very shallow lobes. Fruit is yellow to orange-yellow when ripe.
Comments: Similar to *S. aviculare*. Edible when soft and orange but poisonous if eaten when green. Both species are being cultivated as a source of solasodine for making cortico-steroid drugs.
Localities: 1, 14, 16, 26, 29, 32, 33, 34A–36, 44, 47, 50A, 61, 64, 67–71, 74–76
Distribution: Vic, Tas, SA

Solanum laciniatum

Solanum prinophyllum — Toothed or Forest Nightshade

Size: 15–30 cm x 30–50 cm — P
Habitat: Wet and damp sclerophyll forests
Form: Sprawling annual or short-lived prickly perennial undershrub with minute downy hairs
Foliage: Lustrous dark green to purplish-green lanceolate-elliptic leaves to 80 mm long, with 7–10 rounded, toothed lobes
Flowers: Clusters of 1–4 lilac-blue flowers to 25 mm wide, with pointed lobes; Spring to Summer. Berry green with purplish tinge when ripe.
Requirements: Moist soils
Comments: Many scattered spines to 10 mm long cover the plant. Locally rare.
Localities: Mt Dandenong, 57, 58
Distribution: Vic, Qld, NSW

Illustrated p. 200

Solanum vescum

Gunyang

F P

Size: 1–2 m x 1–3 m
Habitat: Damp sclerophyll forest
Form: Erect or rounded shrub
Foliage: Variable, sessile; narrow entire leaves to 150 mm long, the leaf blades continuing down the stem as a ridge. Some leaves may have a few long lobes.
Flowers: Axillary cluster of pale mauve flowers to 40 mm wide, shallowly cut between broad lobes; Spring to Summer. Round, greenish-ivory berries have an unpleasant smell when ripe.
Requirements: Well drained soils, tolerating dryness once established
Comments: Restricted distribution in Melbourne.
Localities: 58
Distribution: Vic, NSW, Tas

Solenogyne — Asteraceae

Solenogyne dominii

F P

Size: Prostrate-20 cm x 10 cm
Habitat: Plains grassland, red gum woodland, dry sclerophyll forest, grassy low open forest
Form: Perennial herb
Foliage: Rosette of oblanceolate, dull green glabrous leaves to 60 mm long, paler below, 15–21 rounded marginal teeth per leaf
Flowers: Erect flowering stalks shorter than the leaves at flowering time, lengthening later, with a single, terminal greenish flowerhead; bracts and ray florets magenta-tinged. Most of the year.
Requirements: Well drained soils
Propagation: Seed
Localities: 2, 6, 12, 17#, 18, 25, 28, 34A, 35, 38, 42, 47, 48, 50A, 56, 74
Distribution: Vic, NSW, Tas, SA

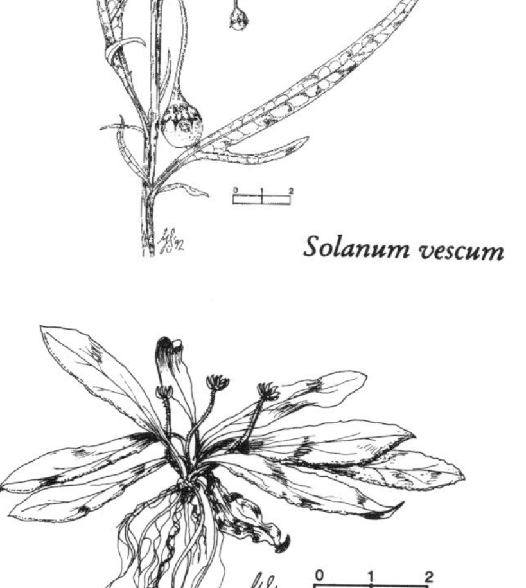

Solanum vescum

Solenogyne dominii

Solenogyne gunnii

P

Habitat: Plains grassland, red gum woodland, dry sclerophyll forest, grassy low open forest
Requirements: Prefers moist, shaded positions tolerating seasonal inundation
Comments: Similar to *S. dominii* but leaves distinctly hairy with 9–13 marginal teeth per leaf. Bracts and ray florets rarely tinged magenta. Both species may occur together in moister areas.
Localities: 7, 12, 13, 20, 23, 24, 26, 31, 42, 44, 46, 47, 63, 64, 74
Distribution: Vic, NSW, Tas, SA
Synonym: *S. bellioides* var. *gunnii*

Sphaerolobium — Fabaceae

Sphaerolobium vimineum

Leafless Globe-pea

F P

Size: 0.3–0.6 m x 0.3–0.6 m
Habitat: Valley sclerophyll forest, tea-tree heath
Form: Wiry upright shrub
Foliage: Leafless; occasionally a few tiny scale-like leaves are found on the unbranched rounded stems
Flowers: Terminal spikes of small yellow pea flowers, sometimes tinged with red; September to January; seed pods small and round
Requirements: Moist well drained soil
Comments: It is attractive in a rockery or planted with other small shrubs, remaining unnoticed until it flowers. Once widespread, it is rarely seen around Melbourne now.
Propagation: Scarified seed, cuttings
Localities: Montrose, ?42, 47, 49, 50A, 54, 56, 58, 67#, 74, 75
Distribution: All states except NT

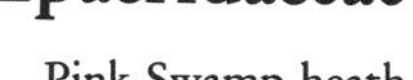

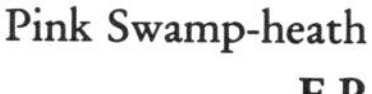

Sprengelia — Epacridaceae

Sprengelia incarnata

Pink Swamp-heath

F P

Size: 0.8–2 m x 0.2–0.7 m
Habitat: Swamps in tea-tree heath, swamp scrub
Form: Prickly, upright shrub
Foliage: Stiff, concave leaves to 12 mm long with sharp points, bases sheathing the stem
Flowers: Dense terminal spikes of small, pink, star-like flowers; August to November
Requirements: Wet sandy soils, tolerating periods of waterlogging
Comments: A most attractive plant for a wet position but requiring special care. It performs well in the garden if given good drainage and plenty of water.
Propagation: Cuttings, may be difficult to strike
Localities: Clayton, 66#, 67#, 73, 75
Distribution: Vic, NSW, Tas, SA

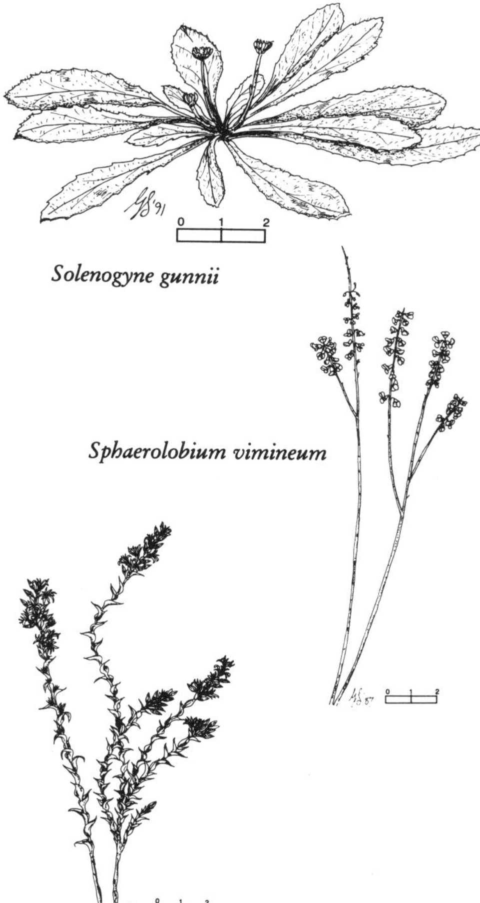

Solenogyne gunnii

Sphaerolobium vimineum

Sprengelia incarnata

SCALE: 0 1cm 2cm — The scale representation on each plant equals 2cm.

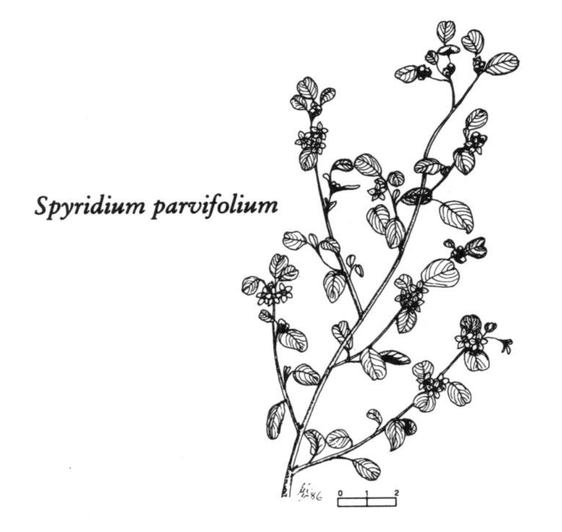

Spyridium parvifolium

Spyridium — Rhamnaceae

Spyridium parvifolium — Australian Dusty Miller

P N

Size: 1–3 m x 1–2 m
Habitat: Damp and valley sclerophyll forests
Form: Dense upright shrub
Foliage: Heavily-veined, dark green oval leaves to 25 mm long, with notched ends, pale green and hairy below
Flowers: Small white flowers in flat clusters surrounded by dusty-white floral leaves; July to November
Requirements: Well drained soils, tolerating dryness once established
Comments: An interesting shrub providing a light screen in dry, shady areas, where its most attractive feature, the floral leaves, are shown to advantage.
Propagation: Seed, cuttings
Localities: 30#, 34, 34A, 41, 42, 44, 46, 47, 49–51, 55–59, 62–64
Distribution: Vic, NSW, Tas, SA

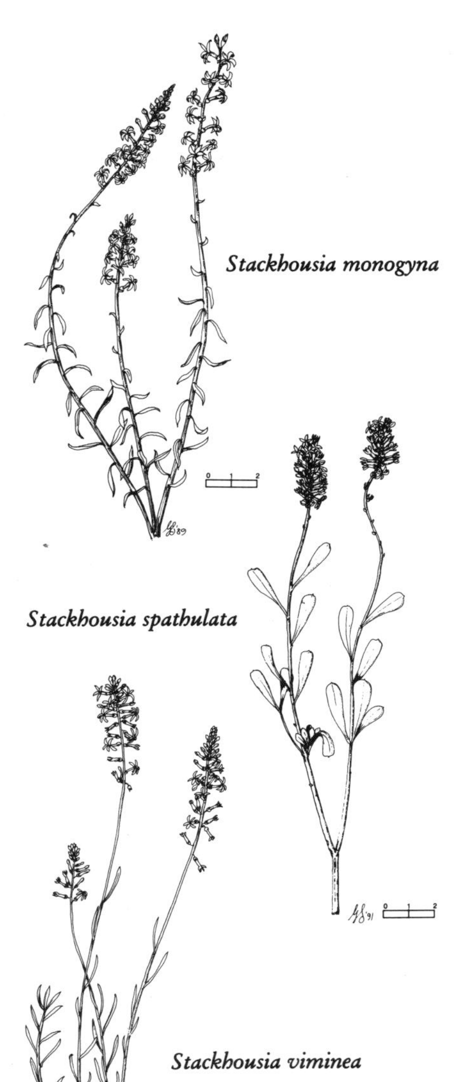

Stackhousia monogyna

Stackhousia spathulata

Stackhousia viminea

Stackhousia — Stackhousiaceae

Stackhousia monogyna — Candles, Creamy Stackhousiana

P N

Size: 10–30 cm x 10–30 cm
Habitat: Widespread in grassy wetlands, plains grassland, red gum woodland, wet, damp, valley and dry sclerophyll forests, grassy low open forest
Form: Erect herbaceous perennial
Foliage: Smooth narrow leaves to 40 mm long, often widely spaced on the stems
Flowers: Many tiny cream tubular flowers in a candle-like spike at the end of each stem; August to January. The perfume is especially noticeable at night.
Requirements: Moist well drained soil
Comments: Inconspicuous when not in flower, it usually grows in patches creating a massed display. An excellent rockery plant providing it is not allowed to dry out. New growth is often tinged with red.
Propagation: Cuttings from new leafy stems emerging from the rootstock.
Localities: Eltham, 4, 5, 7, 12, 16, 26, 29#, 30#, 34A–37, 41–44, 46–59, 61–64, 67#, 71, 74, 76
Distribution: Vic, Qld, NSW, Tas, SA

Stackhousia spathulata — Coast Stackhousia

F P

Size: 15–30 cm x 10–30 cm
Habitat: Primary dune scrub
Foliage: Similar in form to *S. monogyna*, its leaves are thicker, broader and blunt on the ends, to 30 mm long
Flowers: The cream flowers are densely crowded in spikes and have a broad subtending bract; July to January
Requirements: Well drained sandy soil, sometimes growing on the beach
Comments: Now locally very rare.
Localities: Werribee, 67#
Distribution: Vic, Qld, NSW, Tas, SA

Stackhousia viminea — Slender Stackhousia

F P

Size: 0.3–0.6 m x 0.3 m
Habitat: Tea-tree heath
Form: Similar to *S. monogyna*, spreading to form a clump
Foliage: Narrow, elliptic to wedge-shaped leaves to 30 mm long at the base of the stems. Leaves are sparse or non-existent on upper parts of stems.
Flowers: Small greenish-yellow flowers in clusters of 1–6 along the upper part of the stem, forming a dense or sparse spike. Plants with the denser spikes were known as *S. flava*.
Localities: Clayton, 66, 74, 75
Distribution: All states
Synonym: *S. flava*

Stellaria — Caryophyllaceae

Stellaria is a genus of mainly herbaceous perennials, with stems which are thickened where the pairs of leaves are attached. Plants are generally very soft in their growth and sprawl along the ground unless support is available from other plants, when they may climb weakly. The white star-like flowers superficially resemble those of daisies, having 5 petals deeply lobed to the base, so that there appears to be 10. Petals are absent in some species. Each flower is 15–25 mm across, and the plants are quite showy, brightening dark shady corners.

Stellaria flaccida

Forest Starwort

P N

Size: 10–50 cm x 0.5–1 m
Habitat: Wet, damp and valley sclerophyll forests
Form: Sprawling perennial herb
Foliage: Pairs of widely-spaced, bright green, ovate leaves to 25 mm long
Flowers: White starry flowers; September to November
Requirements: Moist to wet soils
Comments: A spreading ground cover for a poorly drained area. It may become invasive in ideal conditions.
Propagation: Cuttings, division
Localities: 55–58
Distribution: Vic, Qld, NSW, Tas

Stellaria flaccida

Stellaria palustris var. *palustris*

Stellaria multiflora

Rayless Starwort

F P

Size: 25–75 mm high
Habitat: Exposed cliff tops
Form: Sprawling annual herb
Foliage: Lanceolate leaves to 5 mm long
Flowers: Flowers have small sepals but lack petals; September to October
Requirements: Grows in well drained, disturbed soils
Comments: Now very rare or extinct within the Melbourne area.
Localities: St. Kilda#, 67#
Distribution: Vic, NSW, Tas, SA, WA

Stellaria palustris var. palustris

Swamp Starwort

P

Size: Sprawling to 1.2 m
Habitat: Grassy wetlands, tea-tree heath
Form: Perennial herb with weak, whitish stems
Foliage: Sessile, widely-spaced, narrow-lanceolate leaves to 40 mm long
Flowers: White axillary flowers on long stalks to 70 mm long; October to December
Requirements: Tolerates waterlogging. Locally rare.
Localities: Laverton Nth, Sunshine, 74
Distribution: Vic, NSW, Tas, SA

Stellaria pungens

Prickly Starwort

F P

Size: 10–30 cm x 0.5 m
Habitat: Riparian scrub, box and red gum woodland, damp and valley sclerophyll forests, primary dune scrub
Form: Perennial, suckering herb with hairy, tangled stems forming a loose mat
Foliage: Bright green, sessile, narrow-lanceolate leaves to 15 mm long, rigid and prickly and often in clusters
Flowers: Single white flowers to 20 mm wide; October to December
Requirements: Well drained moist soil
Comments: May dry out and look untidy in hot weather, but is readily rejuvenated by heavy pruning and watering.
Localities: 14, 16, 26, 29, 32, 34A–36, 39, 41, 42, 55, 56, 58, 60, 67#, 71
Distribution: Vic, Qld, NSW, Tas, SA

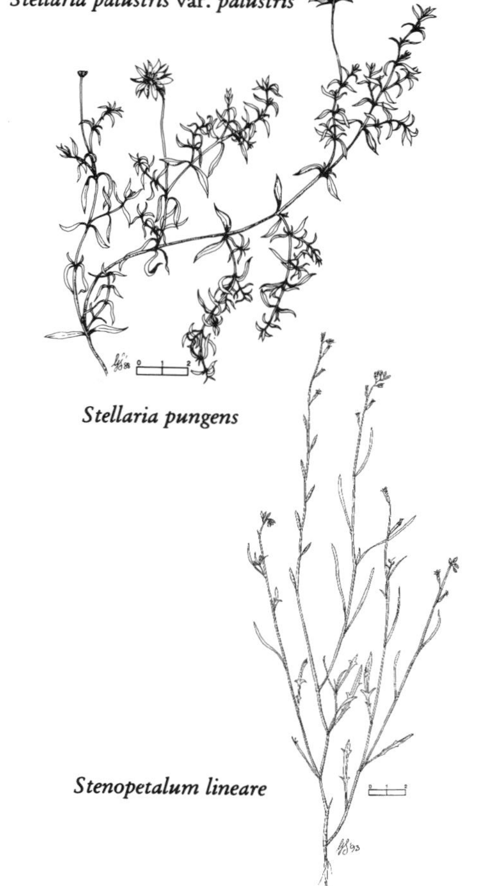

Stellaria pungens

Stenopetalum lineare

Stenopetalum — Brassicaceae

Stenopetalum lineare

Narrow Thread-petal

F

Size: 0.3–0.5 m high
Habitat: Plains grasslands, exposed coastal cliffs
Form: Slender, erect, branched annual herb
Foliage: Basal leaves to 50 mm long with 3 or more narrow, entire or toothed lobes; stem leaves to 70 mm long, lobed, entire or thread-like
Flowers: Brown to yellow flowers, the petals thread-like, hanging in loose clusters along the upper stem; September to November. Oblong pods held on erect stalks.
Requirements: Well drained soil, tolerating dryness
Comments: The upper branches are covered in stellate or irregularly-branched hairs. The plants and seeds, which have a taste of mustard, were eaten by the Aborigines. Not collected for some time, it may have become extinct within the Melbourne area.
Propagation: Seed
Localities: Werribee#, 67#
Distribution: All states

SCALE: 0 1cm 2cm — The scale representation on each plant equals 2cm.

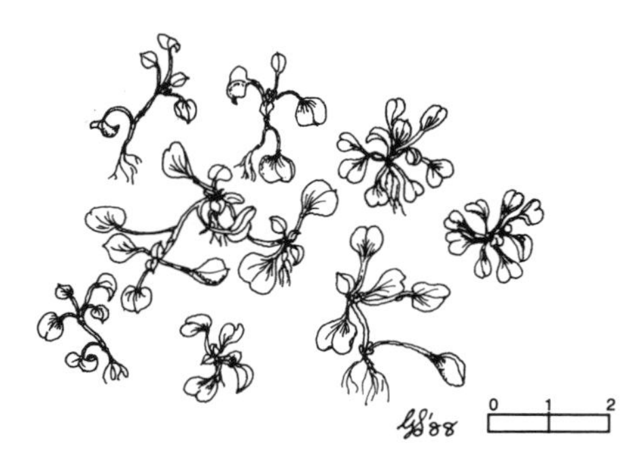
Stuartina muelleri

Stuartina — Asteraceae

Stuartina muelleri — Spoon Cudweed

Size: Prostrate-12 cm x 10–30 cm — F
Habitat: Coastal cliffs, chenopod rocky open scrub, primary dune scrub, tea-tree heath
Form: Erect or prostrate, spreading annual herb with woolly hairs
Foliage: Soft, greyish-green spathulate leaves to 18 mm long, whitish below
Flowers: Small terminal clusters of conical woolly, greenish-brown or whitish flowerheads, lacking ray florets; September to November
Requirements: Well drained soil, responding to extra moisture
Comments: Short-lived plants which germinate quickly following Autumn rains. Locally rare.
Propagation: Seed, cuttings
Localities: 34A, 67#, 74
Distribution: Vic, Qld, NSW, SA, WA; NZ

Stylidium — Stylidiaceae

Known as "trigger" plants because of their unique pollination method. The column is suddenly released when an insect lands on its base, hitting the insect and leaving pollen on its back. Flowering stems in the Melbourne spp. are held above tufts or rosettes of leaves. Each flower has 2 pairs of petals. Stylidiums make interesting container plants. Propagation is by seed, which does not set in great number.

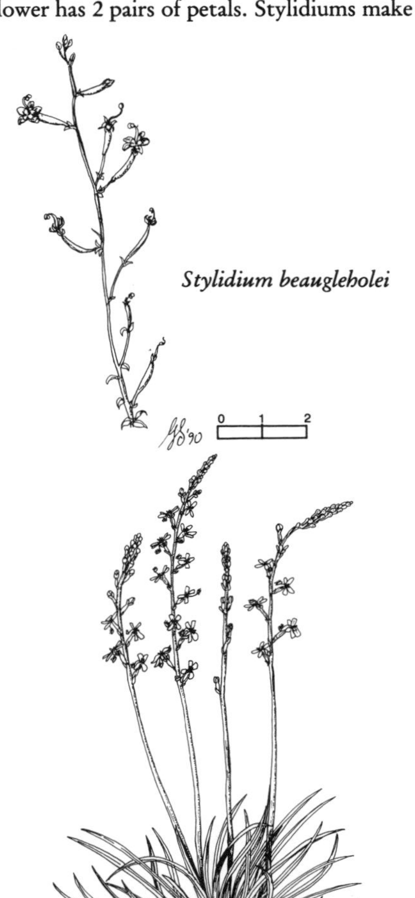
Stylidium beaugleholei

Stylidium graminifolium var. *graminifolium*

Stylidium beaugleholei — Beauglehole's Trigger-plant

Size: 25–100 mm high — P
Habitat: Shallow seasonal swamps of tea-tree heath
Form: Weak, short-lived annual with few basal leaves to 5 mm long
Flowers: Pale pink fan-shaped flowers have a linear calyx tube and a deeper pink stripe on outside edge; October to January.
Localities: 74
Distribution: Vic, SA, WA

Stylidium despectum — Dwarf Trigger-plant

Size: 15–80 mm high — F P
Habitat: Swamp flats of riparian scrub
Form: Short-lived erect herb
Foliage: Tiny, narrowly-ovate leaves to 4 mm long, alternate, not in a rosette
Flowers: Inconspicuous white or pale pink flowers on a long stalk, singly or in a raceme, petals paired vertically, calyx tube linear; October to December
Requirements: Wet soils
Comments: Differs from *S. inundatum* in petal orientation and lack of rosette.
Localities: It was collected in 1896 from along the Merri Ck; 74
Distribution: Vic, NSW, Tas, SA, WA

Stylidium graminifolium var. graminifolium — Grass Trigger-plant

Size: 0.2–0.6 m x 20–30 cm — F P
Habitat: Widespread in plains grassland, red gum woodland, dry and valley sclerophyll forests, grassy low open forest
Form: Basally tufted perennial
Foliage: Narrow, green to grey-green grass-like leaves 5–30 cm long, standing erect
Flowers: Flower stem ends in a spike of many small pale to bright pink flowers; September to December
Requirements: Moist well drained soils, tolerating both wet and dry periods once established
Comments: A very variable plant in size, leaf and flower colour. The alpine form has deep magenta flowers. An excellent rockery plant. Plants should be used in drifts for best effect.
Localities: 12, 26, 33–36, 38, 39, 41–44, 47–54, 59–64, 67, 69, 69A, 71, 74, 75
Distribution: Vic, Qld, NSW, Tas, SA

Stylidium graminifolium var. angustifolium

Habitat: Wet, damp, valley and dry sclerophyll forests
Comments: Leaves are very narrow-linear from 15–30 cm long but no more than 2 mm wide. Flowering stem is a little shorter than above.
Localities: 37, 55–58
Distribution: Endemic to Vic

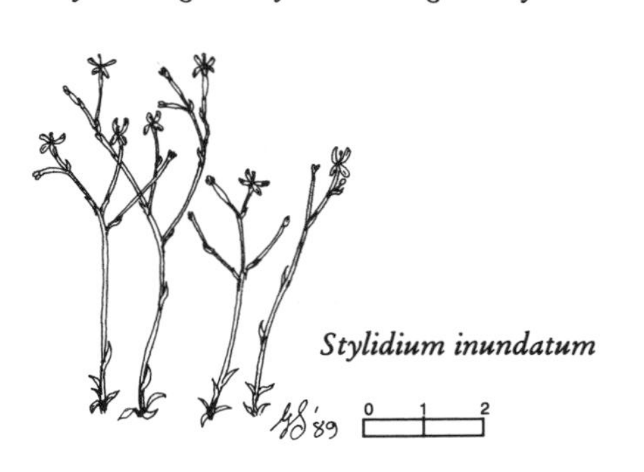
Stylidium inundatum

Stylidium inundatum — Hundreds and Thousands

Size: 15–50 mm high — F P
Habitat: Swamp scrub, tea-tree heath
Foliage: Similar to *S. despectum*. When present, basal rosette of narrow leaves to 6 mm long; stem leaves ovate to 4 mm long.
Flowers: Petals of inconspicuous flowers are paired laterally, calyx tube linear; September to November.
Localities: 62, 70, 75
Distribution: Vic, Tas, SA, WA

Stylidium perpusillum

Tiny or Slender Trigger-plant

Size: 15–40 mm high — F P
Habitat: Tea-tree heath
Form: Tiny slender annual herb
Foliage: Few narrow leaves to 3 mm long in a basal rosette
Flowers: Tiny white flowers, singly or 2–3, on a long stalk to 30 mm long, calyx tube globular; October to November.
Requirements: Moist sandy soil.
Localities: 67#, 74, 75
Distribution: Vic, NSW, Tas, SA, WA

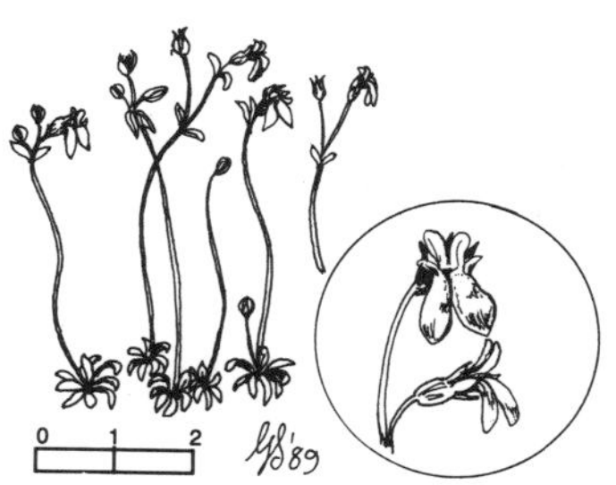

Stylidium perpusillum

Suaeda — Chenopodiaceae

Suaeda australis

Austral Seablite

Size: 0.15–0.8 m x 0.3–1 m — F
Habitat: Saltmarshes, coastal banksia woodland
Form: Rounded perennial shrub, branching from the base
Foliage: Succulent, narrow blue-green to red leaves to 30 mm long, becoming smaller up the stem
Flowers: Axillary clusters of minute greenish flowers followed by succulent, round fruit. Both are found all year, peaking January to June.
Requirements: Moist, saline soils
Propagation: Cuttings
Localities: Footscray, 2–4, 7, 67, 74
Distribution: All states except NT

Suaeda australis

Swainsona — Fabaceae

Swainsona lessertiifolia

Coast or Purple Swainson-pea, Poison Pea

Size: 10–30 cm x 0.4–1 m — F P
Habitat: Primary dune scrub
Form: Sprawling or scrambling perennial herb
Foliage: Dark green pinnate leaves to 90 mm long with 13–19 oblong leaflets, softly hairy below
Flowers: Spikes of bright purple pea flowers with a bright yellow mark at the base; June to October, at other times following rain
Requirements: Well drained sandy soil, tolerating dryness once established
Comments: Copes well with lime and salt spray but may be frost tender. It needs to be cut back each winter to encourage vigorous new growth. An endangered plant in the Melbourne area.
Propagation: Scarified seed
Localities: Port Phillip Bay area, Braybrook#, Seaford
Distribution: Vic, Tas, SA

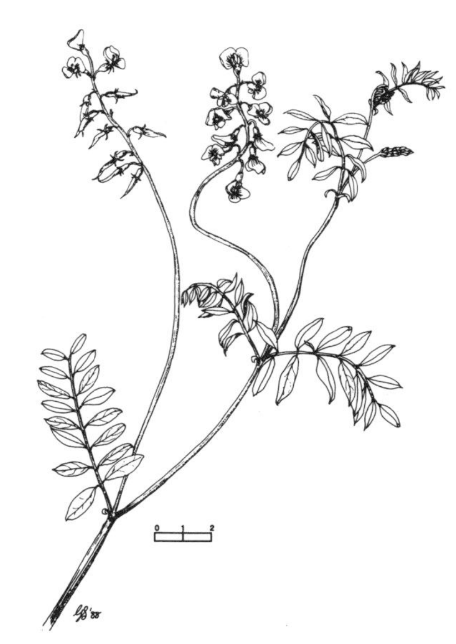

Swainsona lessertiifolia

Templetonia — Fabaceae

Templetonia stenophylla

Leafy Templetonia

Size: Prostrate-30 cm x 20–50 cm — F P
Habitat: Box woodland
Form: Trailing or arching shrub with ridged to quadrangular stems
Foliage: Sparse; narrow-oblong lower leaves, upper leaves linear, to 60 mm long
Flowers: Showy large yellow and reddish pea flowers solitary or in pairs in leaf axils or in small terminal clusters; August to November. Stalks have 2 bracteoles near the middle. Pods flat to 20 mm long.
Requirements: Well drained soils tolerating dryness once established
Comments: Known to occur in the Melbourne area at two sites south of Melton, it is becoming depleted throughout Victoria.
Propagation: Scarified seed
Localities: Melton South, 16#
Distribution: Vic, Qld, NSW, SA

Tetragonia — Aizoaceae

Tetragonia implexicoma

Bower Spinach

Size: Prostrate or straggling climber 0.3–3 m x 2 m — F P
Habitat: Coastal banksia woodland, primary dune scrub, saltmarshes
Form: Succulent, trailing or scrambling shrub
Foliage: Clusters of thick, bright green broadly-lanceolate to diamond-shaped leaves 20–80 mm long
Flowers: Single, scented small pale-yellow flowers on long stalks; August to February. Succulent reddish berry ripens to black.
Requirements: Well drained sandy soil
Comments: Useful for stabilising sand dunes, it is very common along beach foreshores. Plant at 1 m intervals for dense cover. The young shoots and leaves were cooked as a vegetable by the Aborigines.
Propagation: Fresh seed, cuttings
Localities: Melton Sth, Werribee R, 2–5, 67, 69, 69A, 74, 76
Distribution: Vic, Tas, SA, WA

Tetragonia implexicoma

SCALE: 0 1cm 2cm — The scale representation on each plant equals 2cm.

Tetragonia tetragonioides

New Zealand Spinach

Size: Prostrate x 1–2 m **F**
Habitat: Primary dune scrub
Form: Small spreading succulent herb similar to *T. implexicoma*. The fleshy stems become woody with age.
Flowers: Almost sessile small green flowers, singly or in pairs in leaf axils; November to February. Longer, ribbed fruit are green and succulent but become hard and pale brown.
Requirements: Moist, well drained soil
Comments: An important food source for the Aborigines and early settlers.
Localities: 67#, 69A
Distribution: All states except NT; Pacific Ocean Countries

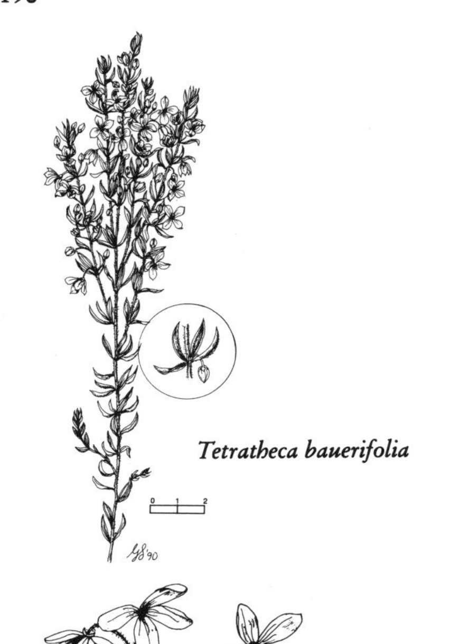
Tetratheca bauerifolia

Tetratheca — Tremandraceae

Tetratheca bauerifolia

Heath Pink-bells

Size: 20–40 cm x 20–30 cm **P**
Habitat: Valley sclerophyll forest
Form: Small, erect or rounded shrub
Foliage: Whorls of 4–6 linear to lanceolate leaves to 8 mm long, margins recurved, paler below
Flowers: Single, rosy to dark pink bell-like flowers on long, fine red stalks in upper whorls; August to December. The stalks are glabrous and distinctly hooked above the flower.
Requirements: Moist well drained soils
Comments: Prefers morning sun and is attractive in flower.
Propagation: Cuttings
Localities: ?42
Distribution: Vic, NSW, SA

Tetratheca ciliata

Tetratheca ciliata

Pink Bells, Black-eyed Susan

Size: 0.3–0.6 m x 0.3–0.6 m **P N**
Habitat: Damp, valley and dry sclerophyll forests, grassy low open forest
Form: An erect or, more often, spreading clumping shrub
Foliage: Oval leaves to 12 mm long in whorls of 3–4 distinctly fringed with hairs
Flowers: Fragrant mauve-pink, magenta or white flowers hang profusely from short glandular hairy stalks, petals spread as they age; July to December
Requirements: Well drained soil responding to extra moisture in Summer
Comments: Tolerates drier and heavier soils and lime. An attractive container specimen.
Localities: 34A, 35, 37, 38, 41–44, 47, 49–56, 58, 61, 63, 65#, 67#, 74–76
Distribution: Vic, NSW, Tas, SA

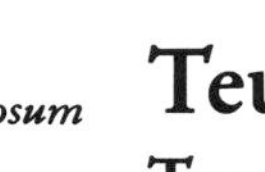
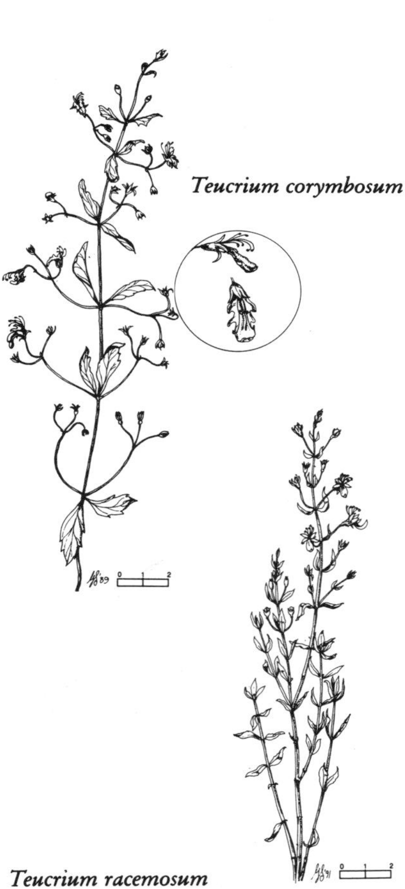
Teucrium corymbosum

Teucrium racemosum

Teucrium — Lamiaceae

Teucrium corymbosum

Forest Germander

Size: 0.3–1 m high **P N**
Habitat: Valley sclerophyll forest
Form: Erect perennial herb with rigid, scaly quadrangular stems
Foliage: Pairs of ovate leaves to 50 mm long, almost glabrous above, grey hairs below, with coarsely toothed margins
Flowers: Loose terminal spikes of white, 2-lipped flowers, the upper lip cut in two, lower lip 3-lobed, stamens are prominently exserted from the flower; December to February
Requirements: Moist, well drained soils
Comments: Regular pruning will maintain a tidy shape.
Propagation: Cuttings
Localities: Sth Morang, Bundoora, Diamond Creek, Kew, 36, 57
Distribution: Vic, Qld, NSW, Tas, SA

Teucrium racemosum

Grey Germander

Size: 0.4–0.6 m x 0.5–1 m **F**
Habitat: Grassy wetlands, red gum woodland
Form: Grey and woolly, erect perennial herb with quadrangular stems
Foliage: Pairs of shortly-stalked, silvery, lanceolate leaves to 25 mm long, with entire, often wavy margins
Flowers: Terminal racemes of white, 2-lipped flowers, lobed as *T. corymbosum*; November to February
Requirements: Moist well drained soils, tolerating occasional inundation
Comments: May sucker forming clumps. The grey foliage provides a good contrast in a damp area.
Propagation: Cuttings, division
Localities: Laverton, 10
Distribution: All mainland states

Thesium — Santalaceae

Thesium australe

Austral Toad-flax

F

Size: 30 cm high
Habitat: Plains grasslands
Form: Wiry, erect perennial herb
Foliage: Linear, yellow-green leaves to 30 mm long
Flowers: Minute, greenish-yellow tubular flowers singly on very short stalks in leaf axils; February to March
Requirements: Heavy soils
Comments: Extinct within the Melbourne area as a result of heavy grazing and grassland cultivation, it is known from only 3 sites in far East Gippsland. It is presumed extinct elsewhere in Australia.
Propagation: Seeds—difficult due to its semi-parasitic reliance on grassland herbs.
Localities: Once occurred on the basalt plains, Braybrook#
Distribution: Vic, Qld, NSW, Tas

Thesium australe

Threlkeldia — Chenopodiaceae

Threlkeldia diffusa

Wallaby Saltbush, Coast Bonefruit

F

Size: Prostrate–30 cm x 1 m
Habitat: Saltmarshes, primary dune scrub
Form: Spreading, succulent perennial herb, ribbed lower branches
Foliage: Narrow, nearly cylindrical grey-green leaves to 15 mm long
Flowers: Tiny tubular flowers singly in leaf axils; May to November. Fruit are succulent and often reddish; Summer.
Requirements: Moist saline soils
Comments: A matting plant for coastal conditions.
Propagation: Seed
Localities: Seaford, 5, 74
Distribution: Vic, NSW, Tas, SA, WA

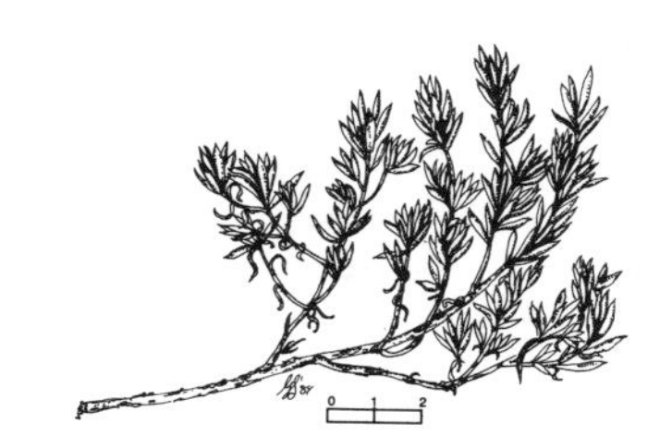

Threlkeldia diffusa

Trachymene — Apiaceae

Trachymene anisocarpa

Wild Parsnip, Parsnip Trachymene

F P

Size: stem 0.3–1.5 m high
Habitat: Tea-tree heath
Form: Stoutly erect, leafy annual or biennial herb, stem finely grooved
Foliage: Hairy leaves 20–100 mm long, mostly in a basal rosette, deeply divided into 3 wedge-shaped, lobed segments
Flowers: Umbels of up to 50 lacy white flowers on long stalks to 80 mm long; September to January. Leafy flower stem held erect, up to 1.5 m high.
Requirements: Sandy, well drained soil
Comments: Fast growing, it regenerates well after fire. Most attractive in flower.
Propagation: Seed
Localities: Port Melbourne#, St. Kilda#, 67, 71, 73–75
Distribution: Vic, NSW, Tas, SA, WA

Trachymene anisocarpa

Triptilodiscus — Asteraceae

Triptilodiscus pygmaeus

Common Sunray

F P

Size: 2–12 cm x 2–12 cm
Habitat: Red gum and box woodlands, dry sclerophyll forest
Form: Tiny erect annual herb
Foliage: Light green linear leaves to 30 mm long, covered in long scattered hairs. Leaf margins somewhat crinkled.
Flowers: Sessile, yellow, urn-shaped flowerheads lacking ray florets, with papery white and green bracts around the base; September to November. Flowerheads terminal or in leaf axils surrounded by leaves.
Requirements: Well drained soils tolerating some dryness, but responding to Summer watering, which lengthens its flowering season
Comments: Easily overlooked amongst herbs and grasses, it is more common in good seasons. Makes an interesting container plant.
Propagation: Seed, cuttings
Localities: Balwyn, 7, 29, 32, 35, 42, 67#
Distribution: Vic, Qld, NSW, SA, WA
Synonym: *Helipterum australe*

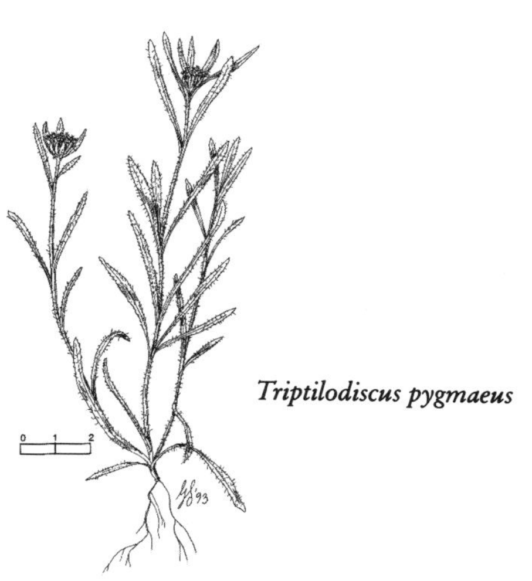

Triptilodiscus pygmaeus

SCALE: 0 1cm 2cm — The scale representation on each plant equals 2cm.

Urtica incisa

Urtica — Urticaceae

Urtica incisa — Scrub or Stinging Nettle

Size: 0.6–1 m high — **F P N**
Habitat: Riparian scrub and woodland, box woodland, damp sclerophyll forest
Form: Upright, scrambling perennial herb covered with brittle stinging hairs
Foliage: Pairs of coarsely-toothed, dark green leaves to 80 mm long, on long thin stalks
Flowers: Loose slender spikes of small green flowers, male and female flowers in separate clusters along the spike; Winter to early Summer. Fruit is a small nut.
Requirements: Adaptable to most sites but prefers moist, shaded conditions
Comments: Often a coloniser of disturbed sites, particularly if plenty of moisture is available. The coarse hairs produce a very painful sting. The Aborigines used the leaves to treat rheumatism and sprains. The leaves were also cooked when food was scarce.
Propagation: Seed
Localities: Tullamarine, 14, 16, 26, 34A, 35, 42, 57, 58
Distribution: Vic, Qld, NSW, Tas, SA

Utricularia — Lentibulariaceae

These tiny carnivorous herbs of wet places are known as Bladderworts due to the submerged globular bladder-like trap which sucks in minute aquatic animals. The lower petal of the flower forms an enlarged lip with a pouch-like spur extending from the base of the petal downward but shorter than the lip. *Utricularia* spp. make interesting and unusual pot specimens, requiring light soil, with the pot placed in a saucer of water. Propagation is by seed.

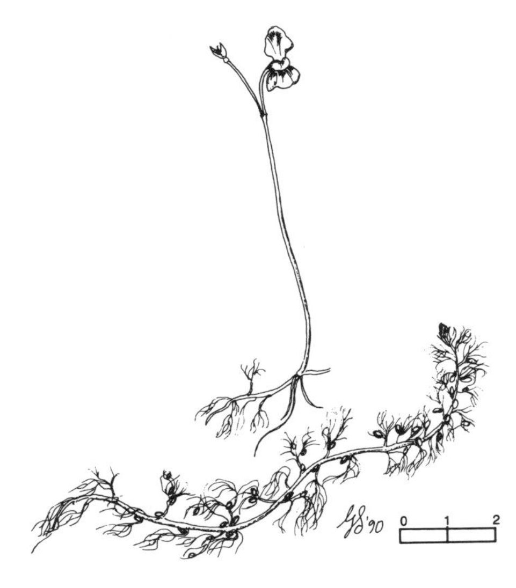

Utricularia australis

Utricularia australis — Yellow Bladderwort

Size: Stems 0.3–0.9 m long, depending on water depth — **P N**
Habitat: Aquatic in tea-tree heath, red gum woodland
Form: Submerged, floating rootless perennial herb with zig-zag stems
Foliage: Pinnate leaves divided into 2 branches at the base, 10–14 alternate leaflets divided into thread-like segments; bladders to 4 mm long at the base of the leaflets
Flowers: Spray of 2–8 yellow flowers on an erect, emergent stalk, lower lip to 18 mm wide; November
Requirements: Fresh, still water to 0.6 m deep
Comments: Locally rare.
Localities: Bundoora, 74
Distribution: All states except NT; NZ, PNG, Af, Asia, Eur

Utricularia dichotoma — Fairies Aprons

Size: 8–30 cm high — **P N**
Habitat: Swamp margins of riparian and swamp scrub, valley sclerophyll forest, tea-tree heath
Form: Rosette with creeping stems
Foliage: Linear to spathulate leaves 5–25 mm long. Tiny bladders to 1.5 mm long on some modified immersed leaves.
Flowers: Single or paired mauve to purple flowers with yellow throats on fine upright stalks; October to January. Lower lip to 20 mm wide.
Requirements: Shallow water or mud
Comments: Once widespread but becoming rarer in Melbourne through destruction of its habitat, it is now found in few sites. Well worth growing in a container. A yellow flowered form occurs in Frankston.
Localities: Sunshine#, Melton#, Kilsyth, 16, 26, 49#, 61–64, 67#, 74, 75
Distribution: All states except NT

Utricularia dichotoma

Utricularia sp. aff. dichotoma

Habitat: Grassy wetlands
Requirements: Shallow water or mud
Comments: An undescribed species with similarities to *U. dichotoma*. A distinguishing feature is found on the inflated section (or palate) at the base of the lower corolla lip. While this species has 4–10 slightly raised ridges on the palate, the palate of *U. dichotoma* has fewer, more strongly raised ridges. It has a disjunct distribution, mainly occurring in Western Victoria.
Propagation: Seed
Localities: Western suburbs
Distribution: Vic

Utricularia laterifolia — Small Fairies Aprons

Size: to 10 cm high — **P N**
Habitat: Swamp margins of tea-tree heath
Comments: Tiny annual herb, similar to *U. dichotoma*. The lower lip of the pale mauve flowers is 6 mm across and the flower stalks are shorter. An endangered plant in the Melbourne area.
Localities: Moorabbin#, Clayton#, 49#, 69#, 74, 75
Distribution: Vic, Qld, NSW, Tas, SA; NZ

Utricularia tenella

Pink Bladderwort, Pink Fans

Size: 20–75 mm high **P**
Habitat: Swamp margins of tea-tree heath
Form: Tiny herb with tufted stolons
Foliage: Narrow spathulate leaves to 6 mm long
Flowers: 1–2 pink flowers with a yellow or white throat on a fine erect stalk, the upper lip deeply divided into tapered lobes, the lower lip to 5 mm long with 3 blunt lobes. The spur is almost as long as the lower lip. This species has 4 sepals. The other species each have 2 sepals.
Localities: 49#, 67#, 74, 75
Distribution: Vic, Tas, SA, WA
Synonym: *Polypompholyx tenella*

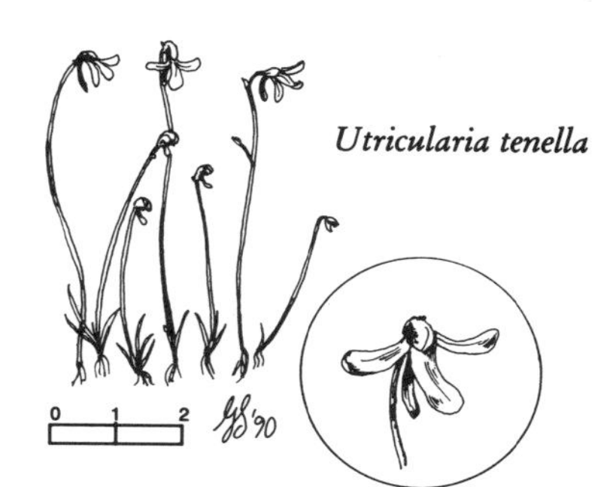

Utricularia tenella

Velleia

Goodeniaceae

Velleia paradoxa

Spur Velleia

Size: Prostrate-0.6 m x 0.3 m **F P N**
Habitat: Grassy wetlands, plains grassland, riparian scrub, red gum woodland
Form: Erect perennial herb with forked stems
Foliage: Basal rosette of bluntly-toothed, broadly oblanceolate light green leaves to 60 mm long; slightly hairy. Pairs of small toothed or lobed bracts at each fork.
Flowers: Widely branched, long stalks with open, 5–petalled yellow flowers to 20 mm wide; October to November, March to May. A conspicuous spur is at the base of the flower.
Requirements: Moist well drained soils, tolerating some wet periods
Comments: A showy ground cover for a moist place. Will germinate readily in cultivation. It is similar to *Goodenia pinnatifida* which has smaller bracts at the forks and more deeply lobed or toothed leaves.
Propagation: Seed
Localities: St. Albans, Brighton#, Hampton#, 7, 10, 12, 16, 17#, 18, 25, 26, 29, 34A, 42, 67
Distribution: All states except NT

Velleia paradoxa

Veronica

Scrophulariaceae

Perennial herbs of moist shady situations, *Veronica* spp. make useful groundcovers. The four blue to mauve petals join to form a tube at the base. Fruit is a flat capsule. Pruning after flowering encourages a denser habit. Propagate by division or cuttings.

Veronica calycina

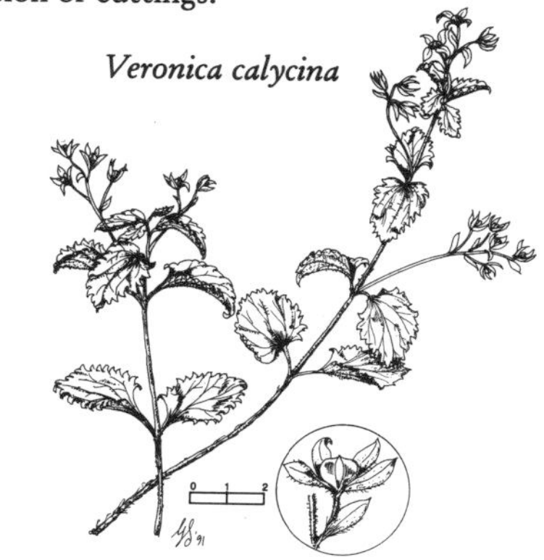

Veronica calycina

Cup or Hairy Speedwell

Size: Prostrate–20 cm x 0.5 m **P N**
Habitat: Widespread in wet, damp, valley and dry sclerophyll forests, riparian scrub, grassy low open forest
Form: Erect or trailing stoloniferous herb, covered with long fine hairs
Foliage: Pairs of dark green ovate leaves to 25 mm long with rounded teeth
Flowers: Small, loose clusters of pale blue flowers in upper leaf axils; October to December
Requirements: Moist soils, tolerating periods of poor drainage
Comments: May become invasive in ideal conditions.
Localities: 29, 34A–36, 38, 39, 41, 42, 51, 55–58, 71, 74, 76
Distribution: All states except NT

Veronica gracilis

Slender Speedwell

Size: 15–30 cm x 1 m **P N**
Habitat: Widespread in grassy wetlands, riparian scrub, red gum woodland, dry, valley and damp sclerophyll forests, tea-tree heath
Form: Slender, erect or trailing herb
Foliage: Pairs of bright green, narrow lanceolate leaves to 20 mm long
Flowers: Mauve to pale blue cup flowers with darker veins in small axillary clusters; September to December
Requirements: Moist, well drained soils
Comments: Roots freely from underground stems.
Localities: 2, 4, 5, 16, 17#, 18, 26, 28–30, 32, 34A–36, 38, 39, 41, 42, 44, 47, 49, 51, 54, 56, 58, 59, 61–64, 67, 74, 75
Distribution: Vic, NSW, Tas, SA

Veronica gracilis

SCALE: 0 1cm 2cm — The scale representation on each plant equals 2cm.

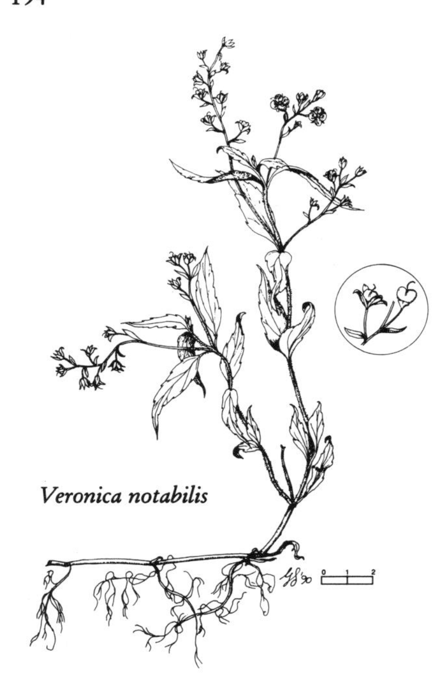

Veronica notabilis

Veronica notabilis

Forest Speedwell

Size: Prostrate-0.8 m x 0.3–1 m **P N**
Habitat: Damp and wet sclerophyll forests
Form: Spreading perennial herb with upright stems suckering lightly from underground stems
Foliage: Pairs of dull green broad-lanceolate leaves to 50 mm long have impressed veins
Flowers: Small white to pale blue flowers with purple veins in loose terminal sprays; September to January
Requirements: Cool moist soils
Comments: The whole plant is softly hairy, especially the stems. Locally rare.
Localities: Kalorama, 57
Distribution: Vic, Qld, NSW, Tas

Veronica plebeia

Creeping or Trailing Speedwell

Size: Prostrate x 2 m **F P N**
Habitat: Damp and valley sclerophyll forests, riparian woodland, grassy low open forest
Form: Creeping herb
Foliage: Dark green, ovate to heart-shaped coarsely-toothed leaves to 25 mm long but usually smaller
Flowers: Loose clusters of 2–10 violet flowers in upper leaf axils; September to January
Requirements: Moist well drained soils
Comments: Spreads readily in ideal conditions, and makes an attractive groundcover in shaded gardens.
Localities: Research, Kalorama, 34A, 36, 41, 42, 51, 60, 71, 74–76
Distribution: All states except NT *Illustrated p. 200*

Villarsia reniformis

Villarsia — Menyanthaceae

Villarsia exaltata

Erect or Yellow Marsh Flower

Size: 0.3 m x 1 m, flower stalks may grow to 1.5 m **F P**
Habitat: Aquatic in swampy tea-tree heath
Form: Tufted herb, the broad basal leaves floating if plant is growing in water
Foliage: Shiny oval to lanceolate leaves to 80 mm long on long stalks, length determined by water depth
Flowers: Yellow 5-petalled flowers on long branching flowering stems held above the leaves; November to January
Requirements: Wet soils or water to a depth of 1 m
Comments: An excellent water plant for a larger pond or dam.
Propagation: Seed, division
Localities: 49#, 73–75
Distribution: Vic, Qld, NSW, Tas *Illustrated p. 200*

Villarsia reniformis

Running Marsh Flower

Size: 0.4 m x 0.5–1 m **F P N**
Habitat: Swamps or shallow water to 0.6 m deep, in swamp scrub, red gum woodland, tea-tree heath
Form: Tufted, or stoloniferous if growing in water
Foliage: Tufts of shiny dark green kidney-shaped leaves to 100 mm long, on long stalks which float if aquatic
Flowers: Bright yellow flowers on stems to 1 m high; September to November
Comments: A most attractive plant for shallow water or damp soil beside a pond.
Localities: Black Rock, 35, 54, 60, 66, 67#, 69–70, 75
Distribution: Vic, NSW, Tas, SA

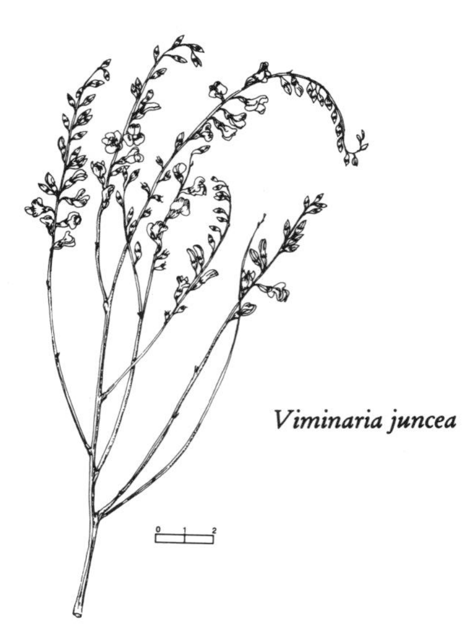

Viminaria juncea

Viminaria — Fabaceae

Viminaria juncea

Native Broom, Golden Spray

Size: 2.5–5 m x 2 m **F P**
Habitat: Widespread in red gum woodland, riparian and swamp scrub, valley sclerophyll forest, tea-tree heath, grassy low open forest
Form: Slender erect, usually leafless shrub with pendulous branches
Foliage: Long flexible needle-like branchlets to 30 cm long
Flowers: Long drooping sprays of yellow pea flowers; October to February
Requirements: Adaptable to poorly drained soils, tolerating salt and lime
Comments: A fast-growing shrub which is most attractive in flower, providing an excellent substitute for introduced broom species. Its open weeping habit is used to best advantage beside pools, where allowed to hang over the water.
Propagation: Scarified seed
Localities: 16, 26, 28, 34A, 42, 49, 54, 60–64, 66#–68, 70, 74–76
Distribution: All states except NT

Viola

Violaceae

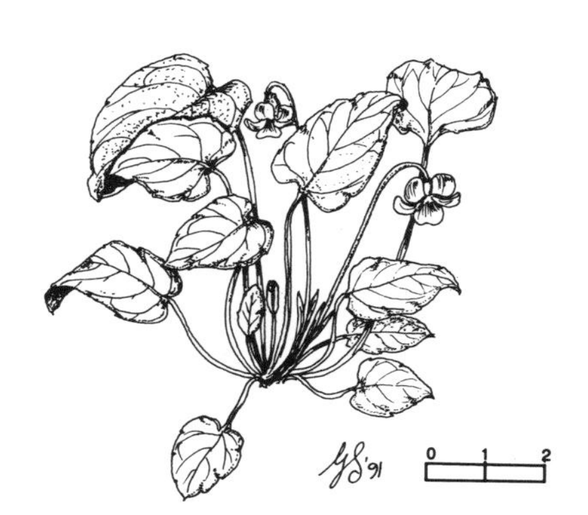

Viola betonicifolia

Viola betonicifolia

Showy or Mountain Violet

Size: 15 cm x 30 cm — P N
Habitat: Dry, valley and damp sclerophyll forests, grassy low open forest
Form: Erect tufted perennial herb
Foliage: Dark green triangular-ovate to lanceolate leaves to 80 mm long, on long stalks to 140 mm. Local form from the Ringwood area has much smaller, roundish to ovate leaves to 30 mm long
Flowers: Large purplish-blue to purple flowers to 20 mm across, borne singly on long stems to 100 mm; September to December
Requirements: Moist well drained soil
Comments: Seeds germinate freely in the garden. An attractive and adaptable plant which also thrives in protected coastal situations.
Propagation: Seed
Localities: Mordialloc 1892; 29#, 34A, 38, 42, 44, 46, 47, 49, 50A#, 58, 76
Distribution: Vic, Qld, NSW, Tas, SA

Viola hederacea

Viola cleistogamoides

P N

Habitat: Damp tea-tree heath, swamp scrub, valley sclerophyll forest
Form: Tiny stoloniferous perennial herb similar to *V. sieberiana*
Foliage: Coarsely toothed leaves ovate to narrowly cuneate
Flowers: Tiny cream flowers with a purplish tinge towards the centre on shorter stalks to 25 mm long; October to January
Requirements: Seasonally wet, sheltered conditions.
Localities: Early collections from Vermont to Lilydale, 67#, 74, 76
Distribution: Vic, NSW, Tas, SA
Synonym: *Viola hederacea* ssp. *cleistogamoides*

Viola hederacea

Native or Ivy-leaf Violet

Size: Prostrate–15 cm x 1–2 m — F P N
Habitat: Red gum woodland, wet, damp, valley and dry sclerophyll forests, grassy low open forest, wattle tea-tree scrub
Form: Fast-growing stoloniferous herb, forming a dense mat
Foliage: Light green kidney-shaped leaves to 30 mm long
Flowers: Small white flowers with purple centres held above the leaves, stalks to 100 mm long; flowers most of the year, especially June to March
Requirements: Moist to wet soils
Comments: A prolific grower once established. Larger leaves and flowers are produced when shelter and extra moisture is provided. It is an attractive hanging basket plant provided it is kept moist.
Propagation: Seed, division
Localities: 25, 26, 29#, 30, 33–36, 38, 40–45, 47–64, 67, 68, 70, 71, 73–76
Distribution: Vic, Qld, NSW, Tas, SA

Viola sieberiana

Viola sieberiana

Tiny Violet

Size: 30 mm x 0.5 m — P N
Habitat: Wet and damp sclerophyll forests, tea-tree heath
Foliage: Smaller than *V. hederacea* with denser, rhomboid to ovate, coarsely toothed leaves to 10 mm long in a tuft
Flowers: Tiny flowers hidden amongst the foliage on stalks to 50 mm long; October to December
Requirements: Moist soils
Localities: 58, 59, 67, 72, 74–76
Distribution: Vic, NSW, Tas
Synonym: *Viola hederacea* ssp. *sieberiana*

SCALE: 0 1cm 2cm The scale representation on each plant equals 2cm.

Vittadinia

Asteraceae

Small perennial sub-shrubs found in open woodlands and grasslands, and on disturbed soil, usually on the basalt plains. All species in Melbourne are similar and have tiny mauve to blue daisy flowerheads and cuneate-spathulate to oblanceolate leaves. The main distinguishing features between the species are the fruit (or achene) characteristics. Propagation is by seed, plants often regenerating readily in the garden once established.

Vittadinia cervicularis

Vittadinia cervicularis

Size: 15–25 cm high **F**
Habitat: Red gum and box woodlands
Form: Erect perennial sub-shrub
Foliage: Spathulate to obovate leaves to 20 mm long, entire or with 1 pair of teeth near the middle and a fine point on the end, becoming linear. Stems and leaves are covered in bristly hairs while the floral bracts are terminated by a tuft of hairs.
Flowers: White or mauve flowerheads most of the year. The fruit, to 10 mm long, is flattened and covered in glandular hairs. Ribs converge into a distinct neck.
Comments: Only known sites in Melbourne.
Localities: Yarra Bend, Sth of Melton
Distribution: Vic, NSW, SA, WA

Vittadinia cuneata var. *cuneata*

Vittadinia cuneata var. cuneata

Common or Woolly New Holland Daisy, Fuzzweed

Size: 10–30 cm x 30 cm **F P**
Habitat: Red gum woodland, plains grassland, grassy wetland, tea-tree heath
Form: Rounded to erect perennial sub-shrub, covered in rough spreading hairs
Foliage: Dark green oblanceolate to cuneate leaves, 5–30 mm long, entire or with 3 lobes at the tip
Flowers: Narrow heads of tiny yellow flowers, the ray florets mauve to purple in 2 or more rows. The flowers are held erect in loose clusters on leafy stalks most of the year. The fruit, to 7 mm long, is wedge- to top-shaped, and sparsely to densely hairy with numerous appressed hairs on the lower part.
Requirements: Well drained soils
Comments: An attractive small plant for drier areas. The fluffy seeds are a most conspicuous feature.
Propagation: Seed
Localities: Port Melbourne, 2, 7, 12, 21, 26, 29#, 67#
Distribution: Vic, NSW, Tas, SA, WA

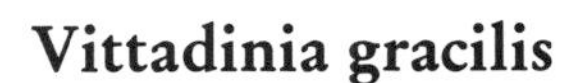

Vittadinia gracilis

Woolly New Holland Daisy

Size: 10–40 cm high **F P**
Habitat: Plains grassland, grassy wetland, red gum woodland
Form: Branched, erect woody perennial sub-shrub covered in fine white hairs, denser on stems
Foliage: Entire, linear to narrow lanceolate leaves to 40 mm long
Flowers: Purple flowers most of the year, bracts woolly. The fruit, to 6 mm long, has 5–7 ribs and is covered on the upper part in glandular and loose hairs.
Localities: Broadmeadows, Laverton, Melton, Parkville, 4, 17#, 18
Distribution: Vic, NSW, Tas, SA, WA

Vittadinia muelleri

Vittadinia muelleri

Narrow-leaf New Holland Daisy

Size: 10–30 cm x 30 cm **F P**
Habitat: Plains grassland, red gum woodland, dry sclerophyll forest
Form: Woody perennial subshrub, stems branching from the base
Foliage: Narrow to elliptical leaves to 45 mm long, entire or with a pair of pointed lobes. Minute and longer hairs are scattered along stems, but restricted to margins and lower midrib on the foliage.
Flowers: Dark blue flowerheads are held on stalks much longer than the foliage, most of the year. The fruit, to 5 mm long, is narrow-oblanceolate with a short tuft of appressed hairs at the base and spreading clubbed hairs on the upper part.
Localities: Sunbury, Eltham, Balwyn, 12, 17#, 18, 26, 38
Distribution: Vic, Qld, NSW, Tas

Wahlenbergia

Campanulaceae

Annual or perennial tufted herbs with well displayed blue or occasionally white, open, bell-shaped flowers at the ends of long slender erect stalks. The flower is 5-lobed. In most species the flowers nod in bud, becoming erect as they mature and open. Fruit is a capsule. Wahlenbergias are beautiful planted en masse throughout the garden and also make ideal container plants, flowering for a long period through Spring and Summer. Perennial species often die back in dry conditions and begin growing again during Winter. The petals are edible and are most attractive added to a salad. Propagation is by seed, which may germinate better if kept in the refrigerator at 1°C for 3 months once collected. (See stratification method.)

Wahlenbergia communis — Tufted Bluebell

Size: 15–50 cm x 15 cm — **F P N**
Habitat: Widespread on plains grassland, red gum and box woodland, riparian scrub
Form: Tufted or open perennial herb with sparsely branched erect flowering stems and a vigorous rhizomatous root system
Foliage: Small tufts or single hairy narrow leaves to 40 mm long, entire to slightly toothed
Flowers: Pale to bright blue flowers to 12 mm wide, singly on branching stalks to 45 cm high; November to May
Requirements: Moist well drained soils
Comments: In good seasons the foliage is denser. Often confused with *W. gracilis*, but may be easily distinguished by the flower size. In *W. gracilis*, flowers are only 6 mm wide.
Localities: St. Kilda, Broadmeadows, Clifton Hill, Ashburton, 2, 5, 12–14, 16–18, 20, 24–26, 28, 29, 32, 34A, 35, 63, 64, 74
Distribution: All mainland states

Wahlenbergia communis

Wahlenbergia gracilenta — Annual Bluebell

Size: 10–30 cm high — **F P**
Habitat: Plains grassland, red gum woodland, valley and damp sclerophyll forests, tea-tree heath
Form: Single to few-stemmed annual herb
Foliage: Entire, obovate hairy leaves 1–40 mm long with wavy margins, lower leaves opposite
Flowers: Minute pale blue flowers to about 6 mm wide on long branched stems; September to November.
Comments: Seeds readily in well drained soils. Withers early in Summer as the ground dries out.
Localities: 12, 25, 26, 35, 36, 42, 58, 67, 68, 74, 76
Distribution: Vic, NSW, Tas, SA, WA

Wahlenbergia gracilenta

Wahlenbergia gracilis — Australian or Sprawling Bluebell

Size: 10–50 cm high — **F P**
Habitat: Riparian scrub, valley, damp and wet sclerophyll forests, grassy low open forest
Form: Sprawling annual or perennial herb
Foliage: Alternate or opposite, entire narrow-lanceolate leaves to 30 mm long
Flowers: Soft blue flowers to about 6 mm wide; September to November. Similar to *W. communis* which has larger flowers, to 12 mm wide.
Localities: 18, 26, 28, 29, 32, 35, 36, 41, 42, 44, 47–49, 50A, 51, 53, 55–57, 59, 74, 76
Distribution: Vic, Qld, NSW, Tas, SA; NG, PNZ, N Cal
Synonym: *W. quadrifida*

Wahlenbergia gymnoclada — Naked Bluebell

Size: 10–50 cm high — **F P**
Habitat: Valley sclerophyll and grassy low open forest
Form: Small erect perennial herb with spreading rhizomes
Foliage: Whitish-green narrow-linear, almost glabrous leaves 5–50 mm long, at the base of long unbranched flower stalks, lower leaves opposite.
Flowers: Single large funnel-shaped flower with long lobes, to 16 mm wide; October to February
Requirements: Well drained light soil
Localities: 31, 47, 54–56, 61, 63, 64, 74, 75
Distribution: Vic, Tas, SA

Wahlenbergia luteola

Size: 6–40 cm high — **F**
Habitat: Red gum woodland, plains grassland
Form: Perennial tufted herb
Foliage: Linear leaves 4–60 mm long, lower leaves opposite
Flowers: Branched flowering stalk has flowers to 15 mm wide which are blue inside and yellowish-brown on the outside; most of the year.
Localities: Werribee 1899, 1926; Eltham, 21, 22, 25, 45
Distribution: Vic, NSW, SA
Synonym: *W. bicolor*

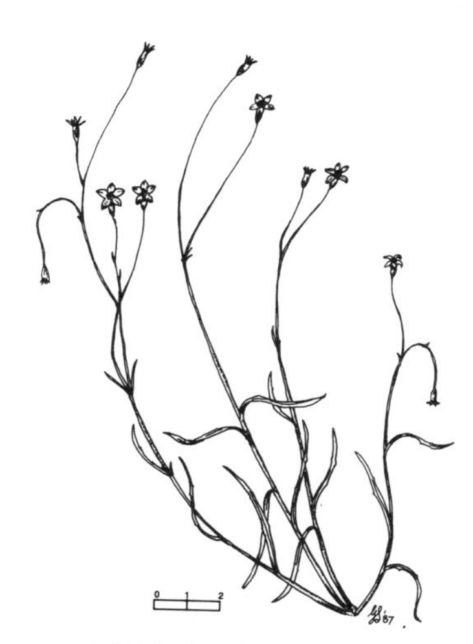

Wahlenbergia gracilis

SCALE: 0 1cm 2cm — The scale representation on each plant equals 2cm.

Wahlenbergia multicaulis

Wahlenbergia multicaulis — Tadgell's Bluebell

Size: 10–50 cm high **F P**
Habitat: Red gum woodland, dry sclerophyll and grassy low open forest
Form: Tufted perennial herb
Foliage: Narrow strap-like, often slightly toothed alternate leaves to 60 mm long with thickened edges, lowest leaves sometimes opposite. Lower leaves and stems sometimes sparsely hairy; upper leaves smaller and linear.
Flowers: Flowers pale blue, with a short tube; September to May. Flower stalk may be branched.
Requirements: Well drained soils
Localities: Eltham Lower, 25, 26, 42, 44, 47, 48, 74, 76
Distribution: Vic, NSW, Tas, SA, WA
Synonym: *W. tadgellii*

Wahlenbergia stricta — Tall Bluebell

Size: 0.4–0.9 m x 0.3–0.4 m **F P**
Habitat: Widespread in plains grassland, red gum woodland, wet, damp, valley and dry sclerophyll forests, grassy low open forest
Form: Erect clumping much-branched perennial herb
Foliage: Hairy, ovate, opposite lower leaves 10–70 mm long with wavy edges, set at right angles to the stem. Upper leaves smaller and linear.
Flowers: Light blue, occasionally all white, flowers with a white throat, to 25 mm wide, tube conspicuous; August to January
Requirements: Well drained soils, tolerating some dryness
Comments: The Aborigines picked and ate the flowers.
Localities: 1, 12, 16, 26, 28, 34A-36, 38, 41–44, 47, 48, 50A, 51, 53–59, 61, 63, 69A, 74–76
Distribution: All states except NT

Wahlenbergia stricta

Wilsonia — Convolvulaceae

Wilsonia backhousei — Narrow-leaf Wilsonia

Size: Prostrate-20 cm x 1–1.5 m **F**
Habitat: Primary dune scrub
Form: Perennial matting plant
Foliage: Succulent, glabrous dark green linear leaves to 15 mm long, sessile on woody stems
Flowers: Single, sessile white or cream tubular flowers to 15 mm long with greatly exserted purple-tipped stamens; October to December
Requirements: Moist to wet soils, tolerating salt
Comments: A good groundcover for coastal areas.
Propagation: Seed, cuttings
Localities: 67#, 74
Distribution: Vic, NSW, Tas, SA, WA

Wilsonia humilis — Silky Wilsonia

Size: Prostrate **F**
Habitat: Saltmarshes
Form: Very small matting plant
Foliage: Pairs of tiny, fleshy, silvery, ovate to oblong, concave leaves to 4 mm long, each opposite pair clasping the pair above
Flowers: Sessile, silky white tubular flowers longer than the leaves, to 6 mm long; September to December
Localities: Pt. Cook 1902, Port Melbourne#; 4
Distribution: Vic, NSW, Tas, SA, WA

Wilsonia backhousei

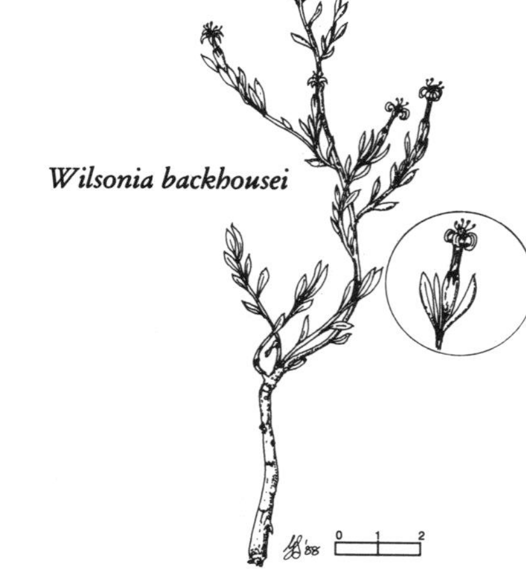

Wilsonia rotundifolia — Round-leaf Wilsonia

Size: Prostrate-20 cm x 0.3–0.6 m **F**
Habitat: Grassy wetlands, saltmarshes, mudflats, primary dune scrub
Form: Small matting plant
Foliage: Tiny round glossy green, somewhat succulent leaves to 4 mm long on short stalks. Loose hairs cover young leaves.
Flowers: Tubular cream flowers with reflexed petals, very shortly stalked; September to December
Reqirements: Moist soils, salt tolerant
Localities: Laverton, 2, 4, 67#, 74
Distribution: Vic, NSW, SA, WA

Illustrated p. 200

Xanthosia — Apiaceae

Xanthosia dissecta var. dissecta — Cut-leaf Xanthosia

Size: 10–30 cm x 30 cm — P
Habitat: Valley and damp sclerophyll forests, sclerophyll woodland, wattle tea-tree scrub
Form: Spreading perennial herb with a woody rootstock
Foliage: Finely divided dark green leaves to 30 mm long, on long stalks to 120 mm
Flowers: Axillary cluster of tiny green or reddish flowers; September to November
Requirements: Moist well drained soils
Propagation: Cuttings
Localities: 44, 47, 48, 50A, 51, 53–56, 58, 59, 63, 64, 66#, 67#, 70 74, 75
Distribution: Vic, NSW, Tas, SA

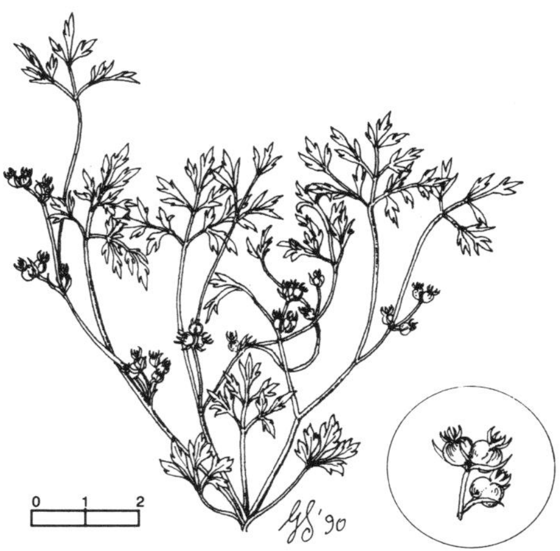

Xanthosia dissecta

Xanthosia pilosa — Woolly Xanthosia

Size: 20–50 cm x 20–30 cm — P
Habitat: Grassy low open forest
Form: Variable erect or trailing herb
Foliage: Soft grey or brown hairs cover the leaves and stems. Leaves, to 30 mm long, have 3–7 broad leaflets which may be toothed or deeply lobed.
Flowers: Small cream flowers in long-stalked axillary umbels, often containing only 1 or 2 flowers; October to March.
Requirements: Moist well drained soils, preferring some protection in coastal areas
Localities: 74, 76
Distribution: Vic, Qld, NSW, Tas

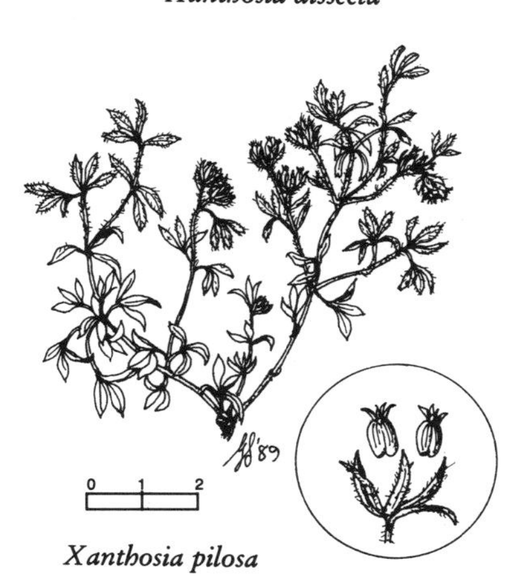

Xanthosia pilosa

Xanthosia pusilla — Common or Heath Xanthosia

Size: 5–20 cm x 20–40 cm — F P
Habitat: Tea-tree heath, grassy low open forest
Form: Hairy, spreading or erect perennial herb
Foliage: Leaves divided into 3 entire, narrowly elliptic segments to 15 mm long
Flowers: Clusters of 1–4 sessile green flowers; October to November
Requirements: Well drained sandy soils
Localities: 67–69, 74–76
Distribution: Vic, Tas, SA, WA

Ziera — Rutaceae

Ziera arborescens — Stinkwood

Size: 2–5 m x 3 m — P N
Habitat: Wet sclerophyll forest
Form: Tall erect or spreading shrub or small tree
Foliage: Pairs of dark green glabrous leaves on long stalks divided into 3 lanceolate leaflets to 100 mm long, paler green and downy below
Flowers: Axillary clusters of white flowers to 10 mm wide; August to December
Requirements: Moist well drained soils
Comments: The leaves and wood have a strongly aromatic smell when touched.
Propagation: Cuttings
Localities: 57
Distribution: Vic, Qld, NSW, Tas

Ziera arborescens

Zygophyllum — Zygophyllaceae

Zygophyllum billardieri — Coast Twin-leaf

Size: 0.3–0.6 m x 1 m — F
Habitat: Riparian scrub, primary dune scrub
Form: Scrambling perennial with a single central ridge on the stem
Foliage: Pairs of succulent 'Y'-shaped leaves, leaflets ovate to 15 mm long
Flowers: Masses of bright yellow, 4-petalled cup-shaped flowers to 15 mm wide, singly in leaf axils; most of the year. Fruit a drooping, acutely 4-angled capsule to 9 mm long, triangular in outline.
Requirements: Sandy well drained soils, tolerating dry periods
Comments: Suitable for exposed coastal conditions. Salt tolerant. Appears to be resistant to fires.
Propagation: Cuttings
Localities: Port Phillip, 29#
Distribution: All states except NT

Zygophyllum billardieri

SCALE: 

The scale representation on each plant equals 2cm.

Zygophyllum glaucum

Pale Twin-leaf

F

Size: Prostrate-75 mm x 0.8–2 m
Habitat: Riparian scrub
Form: Succulent, spreading annual herb with stout ridged stems
Foliage: Pairs of succulent glaucous or dull green 'Y'-shaped leaves on short stalks, leaflets obovate to 30 mm long
Flowers: Single bright yellow flowers on short stalks in leaf axils; July to November. Drooping oblong 4-angled capsule to 20 mm long
Requirements: Sandy loams
Comments: Forming extensive mats, it dies off after flowering.
Propagation: Seed
Localities: 16, 26
Distribution: All mainland states

Zygophyllum glaucum

Rumex brownii

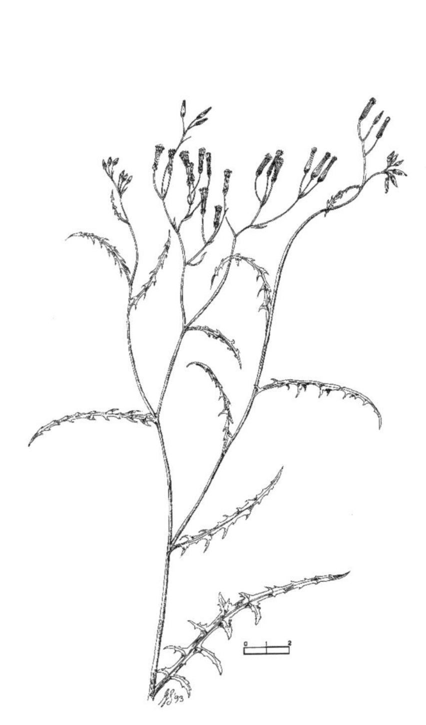

Senecio runcinifolius

Solanum prinophyllum

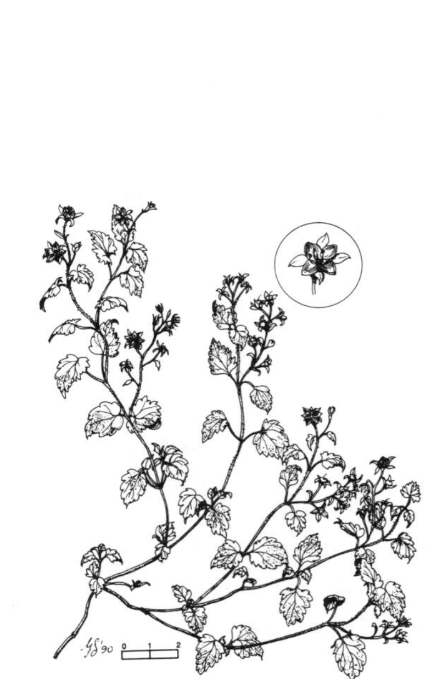

Veronica plebeia

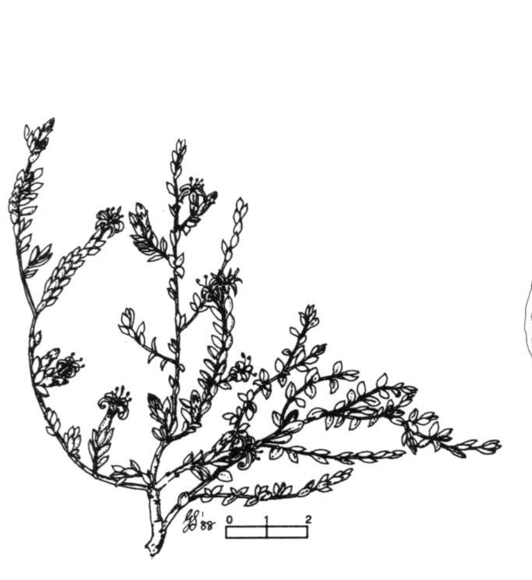

Wilsonia rotundifolia

Villarsia exaltata

Flowering Plants

Monocotyledons

Lilies and Irises

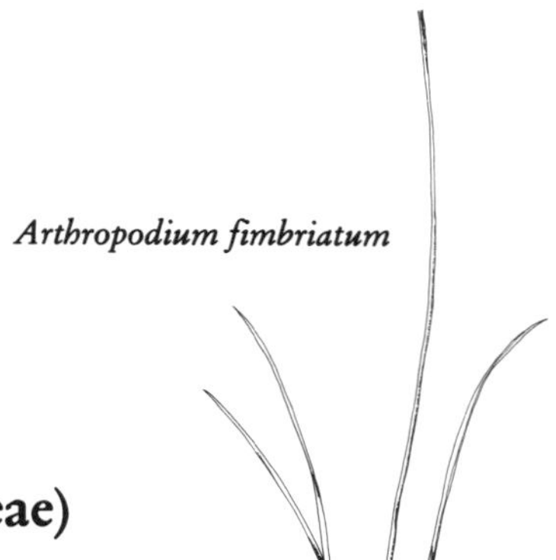

Arthropodium fimbriatum

Arthropodium — Liliaceae (Anthericaceae)

Arthropodium fimbriatum

Nodding Chocolate Lily

F

Size: 0.2–1 m x 0.2–0.8 m
Habitat: Box woodland, plains grassland
Form: Dwarf perennial herb
Foliage: Grass-like leaves to 40 cm long
Flowers: Each unbranched stem has several clusters of 1–4 blue to violet flowers held high above the foliage; September to December. Stalks nodding in fruit, and sometimes in flower.
Requirements: Warm, well drained soils
Comments: Flowers sweetly vanilla scented. Plants die back to a tuberous rootstock after flowering, and commence regrowth following Autumn rains. All species have edible tubers which were roasted by the Aborigines. Many botanists distinguish *Dichopogon* as a separate genus from *Arthropodium* because of the 2 beard-like appendages on each anther of those species.
Propagation: Seed, division
Localities: 12, 25, 26
Distribution: Vic, NSW, SA, WA
Synonym: *Dichopogon fimbriatus*

Arthropodium milleflorum

Pale Vanilla Lily

F P

Size: 0.3–1 m x 30 cm
Habitat: Riparian scrub, damp and valley sclerophyll forests, grassy low open forest
Form: Grass-like tufted perennial herb
Foliage: Slightly fleshy dark green leaves to 30 cm x 10–30 mm
Flowers: Pale pink, pale mauve or white flowers in clusters of 2 or 3 on branched, leafless slender stems to 1 m tall; September to March
Requirements: Moist clay soils
Comments: Leaves die down to a dormant fleshy tuberous rootstock during the dry season. Use to good effect in mass plantings or informal drifts. Suited to container growing. Another form occurs in Melton West.
Propagation: Seed or division of tuberous rootstock
Localities: 29, 37, 42, 44, 49, 50A, 51, 55, 56, 58, 60, 74, 76
Distribution: Vic, NSW, Tas, SA

Arthropodium milleflorum

Arthropodium minus

Small Vanilla Lily

F P

Size: 20–30 cm x 10–20 cm
Habitat: Plains grassland, red gum woodland
Form: Grass-like tufted perennial herb
Foliage: Linear leaves to 100 mm x 5 mm
Flowers: Purple sweetly scented small flowers singly on slender stems to 30 cm tall; September to December
Requirements: Well drained soil
Comments: Also dormant in dry weather, this plant is well suited to an open sunny rockery situation. It tolerates dry soil conditions where overhead protection is available. Distinguish from *A. milleflorum* by the solitary flowers.
Propagation: Seed or division
Localities: Laverton Nth, Sth of Melton, 7, 12, 25, 26
Distribution: Vic, NSW, Tas, SA

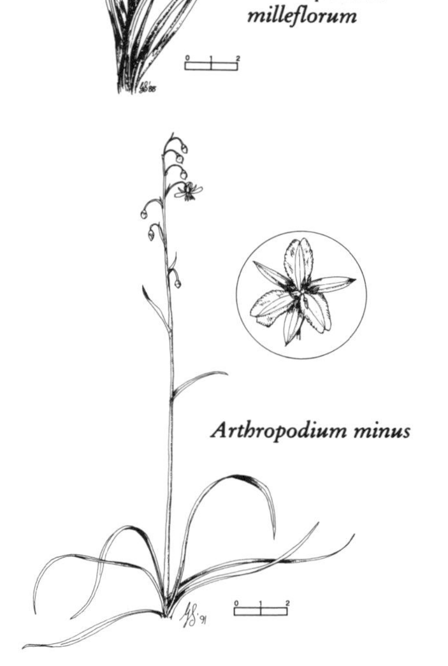

Arthropodium minus

SCALE: 0 1cm 2cm — The scale representation on each plant equals 2cm.

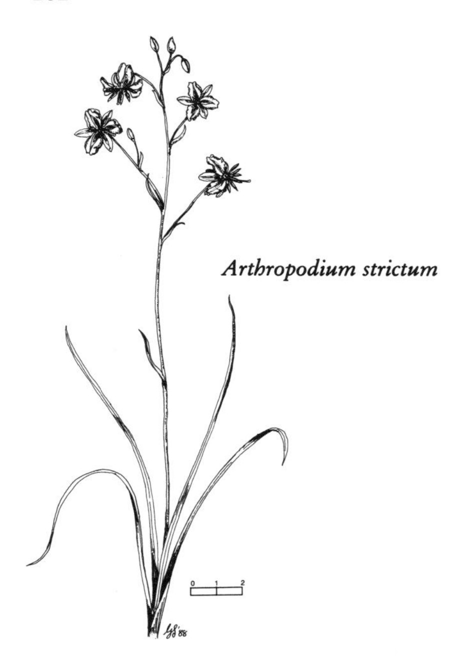

Arthropodium strictum

Arthropodium strictum — Chocolate Lily

Size: 0.2–1 m x 0.2–0.8 m — **F P**
Habitat: Plains grassland, red gum and sclerophyll woodland, dry, valley and damp sclerophyll forests, grassy low open forest
Form: Dwarf perennial herb
Foliage: Grass-like leaves to 40 cm long
Flowers: Violet, rarely white, flowers, singly on erect stalks, on branched flowering stems held high above the foliage; September to December
Requirements: Well drained soils
Comments: A most attractive and adaptable plant. Chocolate- or caramel-scented flowers brighten a rockery and add interest to natural bushland areas. Follows the same growth cycle as *A. fimbriatum* but differs in that the flowering stems are branched and flowers are solitary.
Propagation: Seed, division
Localities: St. Kilda#, 1, 2, 12, 13, 16, 21, 25, 26, 28–56, 58, 59, 61–64, 67–71, 74–76
Distribution: Vic, NSW, Tas, SA
Synonym: *Dichopogon strictus*

Arthropodium sp. aff. strictum

Comments: An unnamed species similar to *A. strictum* occurring in swampy areas of plains grassland. It differs in that there are more leaves in the rosette, several flowers occur at each node and the floral bracts are larger. The flowers have darker anthers, a different fragrance and flowering time is later.
Localities: Sunbury

Bulbine — Liliaceae (Asphodelaceae)

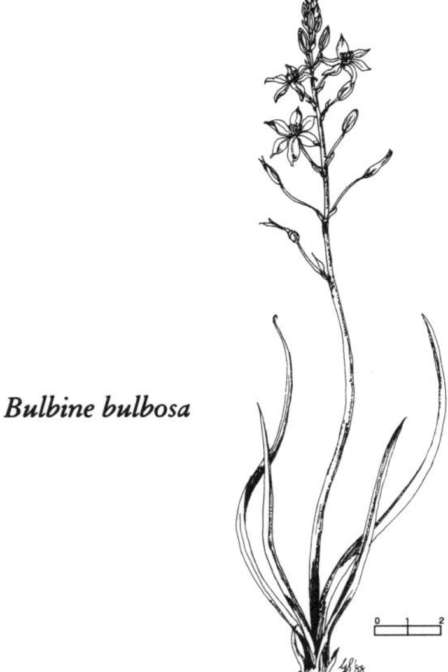

Bulbine bulbosa

Bulbine bulbosa — Bulbine Lily or Wild Onion

Size: 0.2–0.6 m x 30 cm — **F P**
Habitat: Widespread in plains grassland, red gum woodland, dry and valley sclerophyll forests
Form: Densely tufted perennial herb
Foliage: Erect green to grey-green succulent rush-like leaves to 40 cm long, hollow and channelled along their length
Flowers: Yellow star-like flowers to 20 mm wide clustered on leafless flowering stems to 60 cm high; September to January, also sporadic during the year
Requirements: Moist well-drained soils
Comments: Plants die back to a bulbous tuberous rootstock in dry weather, but may continue to produce new leaves and flower throughout the year with additional watering during Summer and Autumn. In ideal conditions they will regenerate readily, attractive informal drifts developing naturally. Differs from *B. semibarbata* in having a bulbous rootstock and all 6 staminal filaments bearded. The tubers of both species were steamed and eaten by the Aborigines.
Propagation: Seed or division
Localities: St Albans, 1, 12, 15, 16, 25, 26, 29, 33–39, 41, 42, 44, 45, 47, 49, 50A, 51, 58, 67#, 74
Distribution: Vic, Qld, NSW, Tas, SA

Bulbine semibarbata — Leek Lily

Comments: There is an unconfirmed report that *B. semibarbata* was once found in Warrandyte. This is considered unlikely however.

Burchardia — Liliaceae (Colchicaceae)

Burchardia umbellata

Burchardia umbellata — Milkmaids

Size: 20–50 cm high — **F P**
Habitat: Widespread in plains grassland, box, red gum and sclerophyll woodlands, dry and valley sclerophyll forests, grassy low open forest, tea-tree heath, coastal banksia woodland
Form: Small sparsely tufted perennial herb
Foliage: Grass-like, pale green leaves to 20 cm long and 1 or 2 narrow stem leaves
Flowers: Terminal umbels of 2–10 honey scented, white to light pink flowers to 30 mm wide on erect simple stems to 50 cm high; September to December. Pink triangular ovary in the centre of the flower remains after flowering as a dried capsule.
Requirements: Moist, well drained soils
Comments: This most attractive plant is best grown in informal drifts amongst other small plants, and is ideally suited to containers. Plants always die down during dry weather and regenerate from an edible, persistent fibrous rootstock.
Propagation: Seed
Localities: Somerton, 1, 12, 13, 18, 25, 26, 28–32, 34A, 35, 37–56, 58–71, 73–76
Distribution: All states except NT

Caesia — Liliaceae (Anthericaceae)

Caesia calliantha — Blue Grass Lily

Size: 10–50 cm x 10–50 cm — F P
Habitat: Plains grassland, red gum woodland, valley sclerophyll forest
Form: Tufted perennial herb
Foliage: Crowded grass-like basal leaves to 30 cm x 15 mm wide
Flowers: Lilac blue to deep blue star-like flowers in clusters of 2–3 along stout erect stems to 50 cm high; September to February. Petals tightly, spirally twisted after flowering.
Requirements: Moist soils which dry out in Summer
Comments: Useful rockery plant, which may grow larger and flower longer if Summer moisture is available. Best effect is gained when planted in drifts or groups. The root tubers of all species were an important part of the aboriginal diet.
Propagation: Seed or division
Localities: Doncaster, Laverton, Tottenham, Rockbank, Derrimut, DeerPark, 1, 10, 12, 15, 16, 20, 25, 26, 28, 33, 35, 39, ?42, 44, 49, 62, 63, 67#, 74, 76
Distribution: Vic, NSW, Tas, SA
Synonym: *C. vittata*

Caesia calliantha

Caesia parviflora var. parviflora — Pale Grass Lily

Size: 10–30 cm x 10–25 cm — F P
Habitat: Damp and valley sclerophyll forests, grassy low open forest, tea-tree heath
Form: Tufted perennial herb
Foliage: Grass-like basal leaves to 25 cm x 5 mm wide
Flowers: White to pale lavender flowers scattered singly along slender erect flowering stems to 30 cm high, branched several times; September to February.
Requirements: Moist to well drained soils
Comments: Similar to *C. calliantha* but generally smaller in all parts.
Propagation: Seed
Localities: Montrose, 42, 44, 46–51, 53, 54, 56, 58, 59, 61–64, 67–71, 74–76
Distribution: Vic, Qld, NSW, Tas

Caesia parviflora var. *parviflora*

Caesia parviflora var. minor

Size: 10–20 cm high
Comments: Smaller flowers and narrower leaves to 2 mm wide. Flowering stems 1-many-branched and spreading, becoming erect at the ends. Flowers are white, tinged with blue.
Localities: Early collections from Dandenong 1875, Oakleigh 1895
Distribution: Vic, Tas, SA

Chamaescilla — Liliaceae (Anthericaceae)

Chamaescilla corymbosa — Blue Stars

Size: 7–20 cm x 10–20 cm — F P
Habitat: Red gum woodland, damp and valley sclerophyll forests, grassy low open forest
Form: Tiny perennial herb
Foliage: Few basal, dull green, narrow grass-like leaves to 15 cm long, often smaller, lying flat on the ground
Flowers: Open terminal clusters of 1–10 bright blue flowers to 15 mm wide on slender branched stems to 20 cm high; August to November. Individual flowers only last one day.
Requirements: Moist soils
Comments: Plants die back to tuberous rootstock in dry weather, and are generally short lived.
Propagation: Seed
Localities: Research, Mooroolbark, 26, 29#, 34A, 35, 42, 44, 45, 47–56, 58, 59, 63, 64, 67–69A, 71, 74–76
Distribution: Vic, Tas, SA, WA

Chamaescilla corymbosa

Dianella — Liliaceae (Phormiaceae)

Dianellas are most attractive garden, rockery or container plants. Their many small blue to purple flowers are in panicles held above the foliage on long flowering stems and are followed by succulent glossy blue or purple berries. The tough strap-like leaves were used by the Aborigines for basket-making and plaiting into cords. Plants are long-lived, growing in tufts or spreading colonies. Propagation is by freshly sown seed or division of clumps. Current research indicates that there may be up to 14 spp. within the Melbourne area.

SCALE: 0 1cm 2cm — The scale representation on each plant equals 2cm.

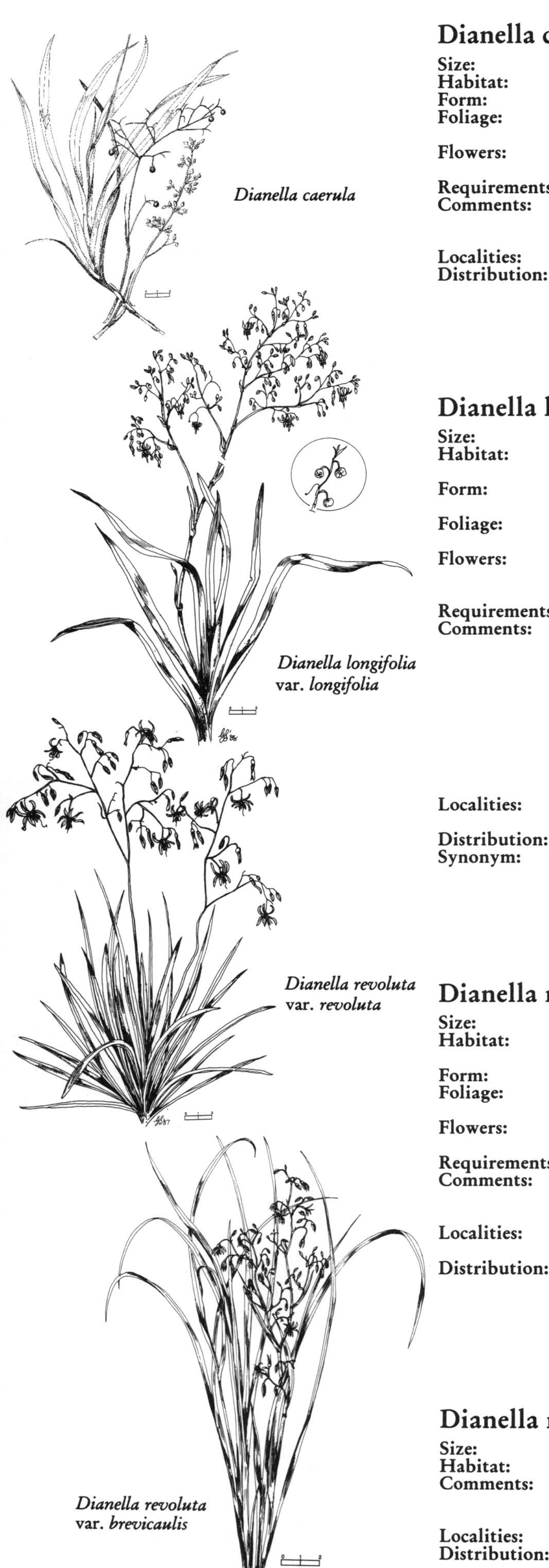

Dianella caerula

Dianella longifolia var. *longifolia*

Dianella revoluta var. *revoluta*

Dianella revoluta var. *brevicaulis*

Dianella caerula

Paroo Lily

Size: 20–35 cm x 0.3–1 m **F P**
Habitat: Valley sclerophyll forest
Form: Tufted perennial clump
Foliage: Dark green linear leaves 15–20 cm long, on branching stems, minutely saw-toothed on edges and midrib
Flowers: Loose panicle of pale to dark blue flowers on erect stems to 35 cm high; August to February, followed by round blue or purple berries
Requirements: Well drained soils
Comments: An attractive long-lived accent plant. Ideal for establishing under existing trees. Other varieties of this species are taller and may develop into large colonies.
Localities: Belgrave, Monbulk
Distribution: Vic, Qld, NSW, Tas

Dianella longifolia var. longifolia

Pale or Smooth Flax-lily

Size: 0.3–0.8 m x 0.5 m **F P**
Habitat: Plains grassland, box woodland, valley and dry sclerophyll forests, grassy low open forest
Form: Tufted perennial clump with thick short underground rhizome and tuberous roots
Foliage: Soft, linear glaucous, or sometimes light green, leaves to 80 cm x 12 mm wide, edges and midrib smooth
Flowers: Loose to dense panicles of pale blue flowers in groups of 2–12, on robust stems to 1 m high; August to January, followed by dark blue or purple berries
Requirements: Moist well drained soils
Comments: An attractive, easily maintained clumping plant, ideal for growing under trees. The leaves were favoured by the Aborigines for basket making. At least 3 varieties occur in the Melbourne area. The typical green form of the foothills from Hurstbridge to the Dandenong Ranges forms an evergreen tussock. The form from the basalt plains is blue with short very wide leaves that die off in Summer. It is rhizomatous and has only 2–3 'fans' if it clumps. Another form, found on the silurian sandstone around Greenvale and eastward, is also bluish, rhizomatous and summer-deciduous, but the foliage is very thin and has short tooth-like projections along the margins.
Localities: 2, 4, 12, 13, 16, 23, 25, 26, 28, 29, 32, 33–36, 39, 40–42, 44, 46–48, 50–56, 58, 60–64, 67, 69, 69A, 74, 76
Distribution: All states
Synonym: *D. laevis*

Dianella revoluta var. revoluta

Black Anther, or Spreading Flax-lily

Size: 0.3–1 m x 0.5–2.5 m **F P**
Habitat: Widespread in plains grassland, box and red gum woodland, dry, valley and damp sclerophyll forests, tea-tree heath
Form: Robust open tufted perennial, spreading by vigorous, branched rhizomes
Foliage: Dark green linear leaves to 70 cm long with recurved leaf margins which are finely serrated
Flowers: Loose to dense panicles of blue to whitish flowers on branched stems to 1 m high; August to May, followed by small, shiny dark blue berries
Requirements: Well drained soils
Comments: A very tolerant plant once established. Ideal for growing close to trees. More vigorous if moisture is available. The Aborigines ate the berries and also used them to obtain blue dye.
Localities: 1, 2, 5, 7, 10, 12, 13, 15–18, 24–26, 28, 29, 31–39, 41, 42, 44–56, 58–71, 74–76
Distribution: All states except NT

Dianella revoluta var. brevicaulis

Size: 30–50 cm x 30–50 cm **F P**
Habitat: Primary dune scrub and cliffs
Comments: Smaller tufts with slightly narrower yellow-green leaves. Flowering stems are amongst the foliage rather than above it, flowers on very short stalks. Prefers sandy soil.
Localities: 4, 69, 69A, 74, 76
Distribution: Vic, Tas, SA, WA

Dianella tasmanica

Tasman Flax-lily

Size: 0.6–1.5 m x 0.5–2 m **P N**
Habitat: Wet, damp and valley sclerophyll forests
Form: Very robust tufted perennial, usually a clump but may spread vigorously by strong rhizomes
Foliage: Broad linear leaves up to 1 m x 40 mm, distinctly serrated along the margins and underside of midrib
Flowers: Panicles of blue flowers with yellow anthers on strong many-branched stems to 1.5 m high; August to February, followed by large violet to blue berries
Requirements: Moist soils, preferably in a cool position
Comments: Plants are very tolerant once established and will adapt to most situations including snow cover. A most attractive addition to a fern garden. Seedlings often appear in gardens.
Localities: Floodplains west of Dandenong Rges, Kalorama, 42–44, 47, 49, 50A, 51, 54–60, 71, 74, 76
Distribution: Vic, NSW, Tas

Dianella tasmanica

Dichopogon fimbriatus = Arthropodium fimbriatum

Dichopogon strictus = Arthropodium strictum

Diplarrena — Iridaceae

Diplarrena moraea

Butterfly Flag

Size: 0.3–0.6 x 0.5–1 m **F P**
Habitat: Damp sclerophyll forest, sclerophyll woodland
Form: Tussock-forming perennial herb with rhizomatous rootstock
Foliage: Strap-like, bright green leaves to 60 cm x 1 cm wide, with 20–30 parallel veins
Flowers: Large flowers with 3 white outer petals enclosing 3 smaller white and yellow, and sometimes purple, petals; October to December. Flowers on robust stems as long or longer than the leaves.
Requirements: Well drained soils
Comments: Very attractive accent plant suitable for container cultivation. Each honey-scented flower lasts one day, but they are produced in profusion over a long period. Plants respond favourably to extra moisture in Summer. Restricted range in Melbourne.
Propagation: Seed, division
Localities: Belgrave, 67#
Distribution: Vic, NSW, Tas

Diplarrena moraea

Hypoxis — Liliaceae (Hypoxidaceae)

Hypoxis glabella var. glabella

Tiny Star

Size: 5–20 cm high **P**
Habitat: Plains grasslands, red gum woodland, dry and valley sclerophyll forests, grassy low open forest
Form: Sparse, glabrous perennial tufting herb
Foliage: Few narrow dark green grass-like leaves to 20 cm long, usually less, and 1 mm wide
Flowers: Single, or pairs of bright yellow star-like flowers to 20 mm wide, on stems as long as the leaves; July to March. Flowering stems have a pair of fine bracteoles 2–18 mm long near the middle.
Requirements: Moist, well drained soil
Comments: An attractive long flowering little herb which should be planted en masse for best effect. Plants regenerate from an edible bulbous tuber as soon as regular Autumn rains set in, then they flower quickly. The flowers close up in dull weather. Snails and slugs cause serious damage.
Propagation: Seed
Localities: 7, 12, 25, 26, 29, 34A, 35, 37, 38, 41, 42, 45–47, 49–51, 58, 59, 62, 63, 75
Distribution: Vic, NSW, Tas, SA, WA
Synonym: *H. hookeri*, *H. pusilla*

Hypoxis glabella var. *glabella*

Hypoxis hygrometrica var. hygrometrica

Golden Weather-glass

Size: 5–20 cm high **F P**
Habitat: Swamp scrub
Flowers: Usually a single yellow star-like flower. Differs from *H. hygrometrica* var. *villosisepala* in that the ovary and sepals are glabrous. The single bracteole is less than 4 mm long.
Comments: Rare within Melbourne, occurring in low-lying areas at the base of the foothills. More common just outside the study area.
Localities: 54
Distribution: Vic, NSW, Tas, SA

SCALE: 0 1cm 2cm — The scale representation on each plant equals 2cm.

Hypoxis hygrometrica var. *villosisepala*

Hypoxis hygrometrica var. villosisepala

Size: 5–30 cm high **F P**
Habitat: Plains grassland, valley sclerophyll forest
Form: Sparsely hairy perennial tuft
Foliage: Few, narrow, slightly fleshy grass-like leaves to 20 cm long
Flowers: Pairs of yellow star-like flowers to 30 mm wide with a few hairs on the ovary and ends of the sepals; August to December. The flowering stem has a single bracteole to 10 mm long below the flowers.
Requirements: Moist well drained soils
Comments: May be distinguished from *H. glabella* var. *glabella* by the presence of tiny hairs.
Propagation: Seed
Localities: Yarra, Montrose, 25, 26, 28, 42, 50A, 54, 55, 62, 63, 67, 68, 70, 74
Distribution: Vic, NSW, Tas

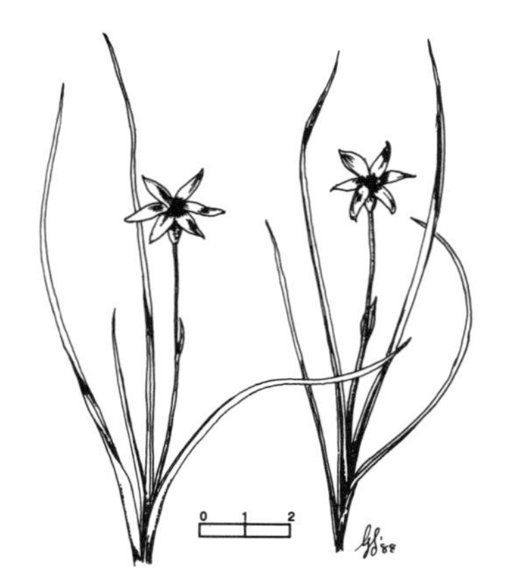

Hypoxis vaginata var. *vaginata*

Hypoxis vaginata var. vaginata

Yellow Star

Size: 5–35 cm high **F P**
Habitat: Valley sclerophyll forest, grassy low open forest
Comments: A variable species similar to and often confused with *H. glabella*. Leaves are longer, to 35 cm, and wider, to 3 mm, and flowers are larger, to 40 mm wide. It has a single sheathing bracteole to 70 mm long on the flowering stem.
Localities: Eltham, Doncaster, Boronia, 7, 26, 34A, 44, 55, 64, 66, 69, 74–76
Distribution: Vic, NSW, Tas, SA, WA
Synonym: Previously referred to as *H. glabella*

Hypoxis vaginata var. brevistigmata

Habitat: Tea-tree heath
Comments: Smaller herb to 10 cm high. Flowers occur singly on the flowering stem and are smaller in all aspects. The main distinguishing feature is the tiny size of the stigmatic lobes. Grows in damp situations.
Localities: An early collection in Melbourne; 69
Distribution: Vic, NSW, Tas

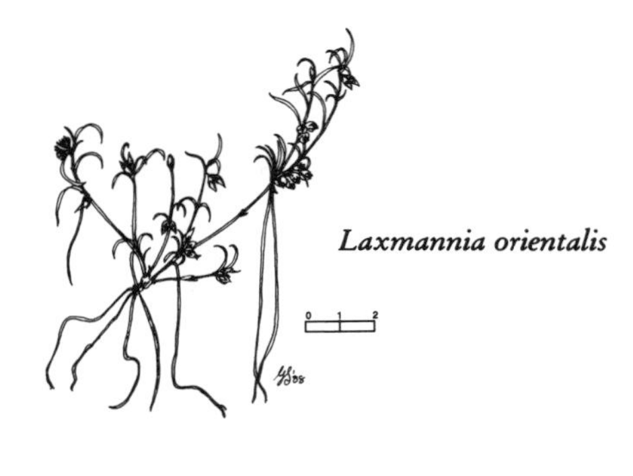

Laxmannia orientalis

Laxmannia — Liliaceae (Anthericaceae)

Laxmannia orientalis

Dwarf Wire Lily

Size: 2–5 cm x 5–15 cm **F P**
Habitat: Tea-tree heath
Form: Tiny wiry tufting plant, often with aerial roots descending from nodes on stems
Foliage: Narrow, stem-sheathing, needle-like leaves 5–25 mm long, with white, woolly hairs along sheath margins, borne at regular intervals
Flowers: Nodding clusters of 3–7 tiny stalkless white flowers with red-lined sepals in each tuft of leaves; September to November.
Requirements: Well drained soils in an open sunny position
Comments: Particularly suited to container cultivation. This slow growing plant is more of interest to collectors than regenerators. Locally rare.
Propagation: Division
Localities: Baxter, 67–69, 74
Distribution: Vic, Tas, SA
Synonym: Previously referred to as *L. sessiliflora*, which is now regarded as endemic to WA.

Libertia pulchella

Libertia — Iridaceae

Libertia pulchella

Pretty Grass-flag

Size: 7–30 cm x 30 cm **P N**
Habitat: Damp sclerophyll forest
Form: Sparsely tufting perennial herb
Foliage: Narrow, flat, overlapping leaves, 10–20 cm long, often in fan-shaped tufts
Flowers: Loose clusters of small white fragrant flowers on stems to 30 cm high; October to January, followed by interesting seed heads.
Requirements: Moist well drained soil, rich in humus, tolerating boggy periods
Comments: A dainty, long-lived plant but difficult to flower unless growing conditions suit. Ideal container plant, or used as a border in fern gardens. Requires Summer watering. Restricted range in Melbourne.
Propagation: Seed, division
Localities: Ferntree Gully
Distribution: Vic, NSW, Tas

Patersonia — Iridaceae

Patersonia fragilis — Short Purple-flag

Size: 10–20 cm x 40 cm **F P**
Habitat: Tea-tree heath, swamp scrub
Form: Tufting rhizomatous perennial herb
Foliage: Thick and fleshy, stiff, narrow dull green to blue-green leaves to 20 cm long
Flowers: Bright, deep purple iris-like flowers on stems shorter than the leaves; September to January. Flowers are in terminal clusters, enclosed by 2 large bracts, the floral tube extending beyond the bracts. They have 6 petals: 3 large, rounded and spreading outer petals and 3 tiny, erect inner ones.
Requirements: Moist open position tolerating inundation for short periods
Comments: An attractive plant even when not in flower especially planted in a rockery. Flowers are short lived, but are produced in great numbers on sunny days.
Propagation: Seed, division
Localities: Montrose, 54, 67, 69, 74, 75
Distribution: Vic, Qld, NSW, Tas, SA
Synonym: *P. glauca*

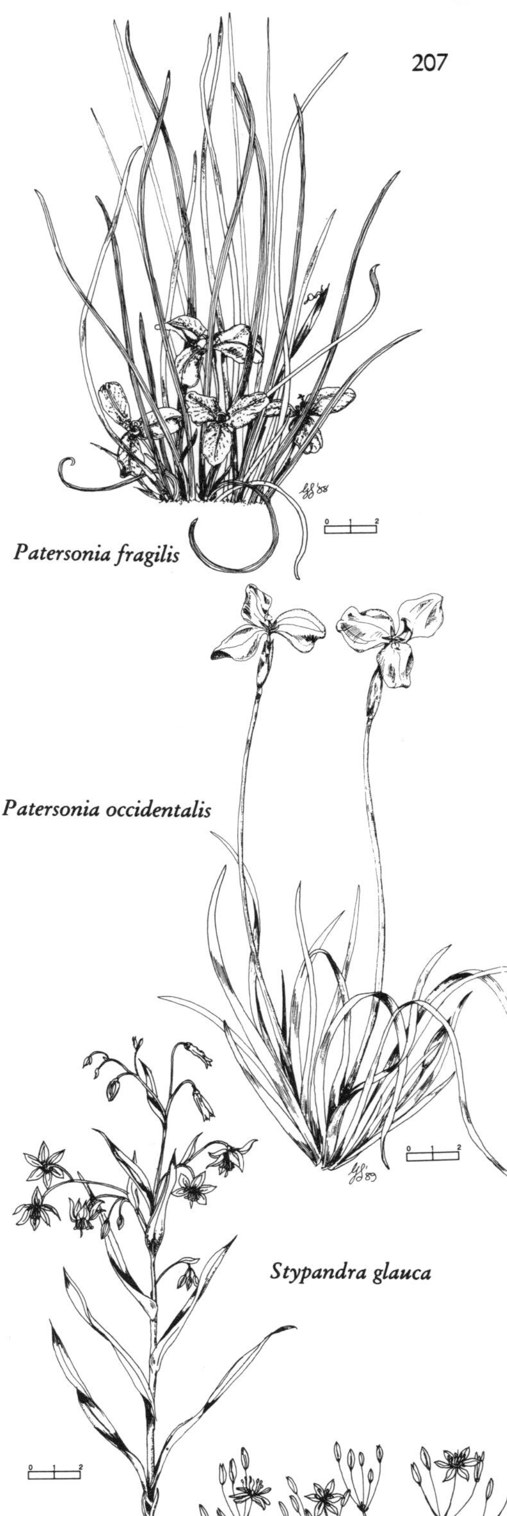

Patersonia fragilis

Patersonia occidentalis

Patersonia occidentalis — Long Purple-flag

Size: 20–40 cm x 0.3–0.6 m **F P**
Habitat: Valley sclerophyll forest, swamp and wattle tea-tree scrub
Form: Compact clumping perennial herb
Foliage: Long, flat leaves to 60 cm x 5 mm, convex on one surface
Flowers: The tube of the bluish-purple, or occasionally white, flowers is almost hidden by the bracts. Flowering stems are as long as, or longer than, the foliage, to 85 cm long; September to January.
Requirements: Tolerates inundation during Winter and drying out in Summer
Comments: Suitable for bog gardens or pond edges but also tolerant of much drier positions. Distinguished from *P. fragilis* by the wider leaves, longer flowering stems and hidden floral tube.
Propagation: Seed or division
Localities: Montmorency, Montrose, 49, 51, 54, 62, 63, 67–71, 73–76
Distribution: Vic, Tas, SA, WA
Synonym: *P. longiscapa*

Stypandra — Liliaceae (Phormiaceae)

Stypandra glauca — Nodding Blue Lily

Size: 0.5–1.5 m x 1.5 m **F P**
Habitat: Riparian and swamp scrub
Form: Soft, sprawling clump. Stems often twisted or bent, open-branched.
Foliage: Glaucous, lanceolate, sessile leaves to 20 cm long, but usually less, arranged alternately along the stems
Flowers: Bright blue nodding star-shaped flowers with bright yellow anthers, in open branching terminal clusters; July to November, also sporadic throughout the year
Requirements: Well drained, moist to dry soil
Comments: An attractive plant, especially in flower. Plants are at first herbaceous but become woody with age. Pruning encourages new growth from the centre of the clump and increases flower production. Regenerates vigorously after fire.
Propagation: Seed, division
Localities: 29, ?42, 61
Distribution: Vic, Qld, NSW, SA, WA

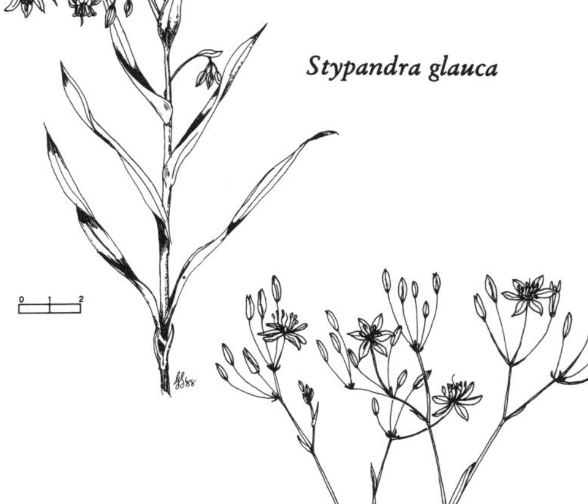

Stypandra glauca

Thelionema — Liliaceae (Phormiaceae)

Thelionema caespitosum — Blue Grass-lily

Size: 0.2–0.6 m x 0.3–0.6 m **F P**
Habitat: Valley sclerophyll forest, tea-tree heath, generally on damp peaty soil, swamp and wattle tea-tree scrub
Form: Tufted herbaceous perennial
Foliage: Blue-green to pale green linear leaves to 30 cm long, "V"-shaped in cross-section
Flowers: Blue, or sometimes white, star-shaped flowers on leafless wiry branched stems to 60 cm high; September to January
Requirements: Moist soils
Comments: An attractive, easily grown plant for a moist rockery. A white-flowered form occurs in the Frankston area.
Propagation: Division
Localities: Montrose, ?42, 44, 49, 54, 63, 64, 67, 70, 73–76
Distribution: Vic, Qld, NSW, Tas, SA
Synonym: *Stypandra caespitosa*

Thelionema caespitosum

SCALE: 0 1cm 2cm — The scale representation on each plant equals 2cm.

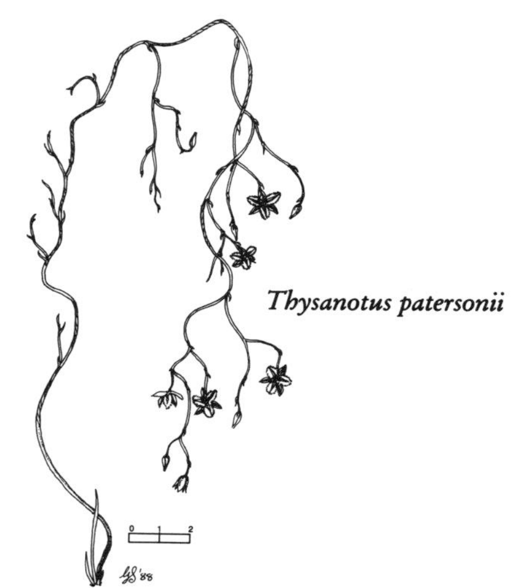

Thysanotus patersonii

Thysanotus — Liliaceae (Anthericaceae)

Thysanotus patersonii

Twining Fringe-lily

Size: Stems 0.1–1 m long **F P**
Habitat: Red gum woodland, plains grassland, riparian scrub, valley and dry sclerophyll forests, grassy low open forest, tea-tree heath
Form: Light perennial creeper or climber, twining weakly on other plants; usually a single stem, occasionally 2, terete and hairy at the base, glabrous and quadrangular towards the tips
Foliage: 1–2 annual short fine leaves, withering when the leafless flowering stem develops
Flowers: Numerous mauve to violet flowers 15 mm wide, consisting of three distinctly fringed petals, borne singly at the end of short branches on the flowering stem; August to November
Requirements: Well drained soils
Comments: A delightful little climber, not noticeable until in flower. Stem and leaves annual, emerging from the dormant tuber in Winter.
Propagation: Seed
Localities: 12, 16, 26, 29#, 34A–37, 39, 41–44, 47–51, 53–56, 58, 59, 61, 63, 64, 67–71, 74–76
Distribution: Vic, NSW, Tas, SA, WA

Thysanotus tuberosus ssp. *tuberosus*

Thysanotus tuberosus ssp. tuberosus

Common Fringe-lily

Size: 15–30 cm x 15–20 cm **F P**
Habitat: Riparian scrub, red gum woodland, valley and dry sclerophyll forests
Form: Slender, erect herbaceous perennial tuft
Foliage: Few narrow greyish leaves to 20 cm long, channelled for most of length
Flowers: Umbels of 1–8 fringed bright mauve flowers to 35 mm wide; November to January. Flowers held above the foliage on leafless many-branched wiry stems.
Requirements: Open well drained soils, tolerating dryness once established
Comments: An attractive herb which is usually not noticed unless it is flowering. The flowers only last 1 day, generally opening early in the morning and closing by midday in hot weather, but plants continue to produce flowers over some months. The leaves shoot annually from the tuberous rootstock and may persist until after flowering or wither as flowering commences. The Aborigines ate the tubers and cooked and ground the leaves and flowers. While widespread it is becoming less common locally.
Propagation: Seed
Localities: Cheltenham#, 29, 35, 42, 47–51, 53–56, 58, 59, 61, 67–69, 71, 74–76
Distribution: Vic, Qld, NSW, SA

Tricoryne elatior

Tricoryne — Liliaceae (Anthericaceae)

Tricoryne elatior

Yellow Rush-lily

Size: 30–50 cm x 30–50 cm **F P**
Habitat: Widespread in plains grassland, red gum and box woodland, dry and valley sclerophyll forests, grassy low open forest, tea-tree heath
Form: Wiry, many-branched, grass-like rhizomatous perennial herb
Foliage: Few, widely-spaced grass-like linear grey-green leaves to 90 mm long, often withering at flowering, reduced and scale-like on upper branches
Flowers: Many bright yellow star-shaped flowers in open clusters, held above the foliage; September to February
Requirements: Moist or dry soils
Comments: An attractive, long flowering little plant for the garden, which is not noticed until flowering commences. Used to good effect in mass plantings or informal drifts. Petals and sepals twist spirally after flowering.
Propagation: Seed, division
Localities: Laverton Nth, 5, 6, 12, 15–18, 21, 24–26, 28, 31, 32, 34A–42, 44, 45, 47–55, 58, 59, 61–68, 69A, 71, 74–76
Distribution: All states

Wurmbea

Liliaceae (Colchicaceae)

Wurmbea dioica

Early Nancy

Size: 5–30 cm x 10 cm **F P**
Habitat: Red gum and sclerophyll woodland, dry, valley and damp sclerophyll forests, grassy low open forest, tea-tree heath
Form: Small glabrous perennial herb
Foliage: 3 fleshy, narrow stem-sheathing leaves to 100 mm long
Flowers: 1–11 white starry 6-petalled flowers, usually with a purplish band (or nectary) toward the base of each sepal and petal. Most plants are either male or female. Males have red or purple anthers. Flowers July to October. Flowers spaced one above the other along the single zig-zagging flowering stem.
Requirements: Moist well-drained soils
Comments: The honey-scented flowers may be monoecious or dioecious. Dormant over Summer, it shoots again from its bulbous rootstock as soon as Autumn rains fall. It takes its common name from being the first lily to flower each year. Tubers were eaten by the Aborigines.
Propagation: Seed
Localities: 16, 25, 26, 29, 30, 32, 34A, 35, 37, 38, 41, 42, 44–51, 53–56, 58, 59, 61–64, 67, 68, 69A, 70, 74–76
Distribution: All states except NT
Synonym: *Anguillaria dioica*

Wurmbea dioica

SCALE: 0 1cm 2cm The scale representation on each plant equals 2cm.

Orchids *Orchidaceae*

Orchids occur in a number of diverse habitats, ranging from the coast to the mountains and may be found in heaths, scrub, open forests and woodlands. All orchids in Melbourne are terrestrial with the exception of *Sarcochilus australis*, the most southerly occurring epiphytic orchid in Australia.

The orchids which occur locally are perennial herbs and may be distinguished from other monocotyledons by their floral structure. All have 6 perianth segments (3 petals and 3 sepals). The labellum is the modified lowest petal and is usually different to the two side petals. The male and female parts are united in a structure known as the column. The labellum is modified in some genera to sexually attract the males of specific insects which then pollinate the flower. The fruit is a capsule which, in most species, dehisces (splits open at maturity) releasing a large number of minute seeds.

Most Australian terrestrial species grow from a tuberoid which is replaced annually. Some species also produce daughter tuberoids and may form extensive colonies. Other species including the saprophytic, *Dipodium roseum*, grow from rhizomes. *Cryptostylis* spp. and *Spiranthes sinensis* also grow by this means but, unlike other terrestrial orchids, these species do not undergo a Summer dormancy period.

The majority of Australian orchids are difficult to propagate as they rely on a symbiotic association (or mycorrhiza) between a soil-borne fungus and their seeds for at least some stages of their development. The fungus penetrates the seed and provides the necessary nutrients for the developing orchid.

Fire plays an important role in the regeneration of orchids and some species such as *Burnettia cuneata* may not be seen for many years, only reappearing after a major fire. Others will flower more prolifically, gradually having less blooms with each subsequent year after the bushfire.

The tuberoids of many indigenous orchid spp. provided a staple diet for the local aboriginal tribes. However continued development and human pressures in the Melbourne region have led to many species becoming rare and locally endangered. Some species are currently verging on extinction while others have already disappeared. Specific localities have not been given for the orchids as a means of protecting the remaining local populations.

Orchids must never be transplanted from the bush as, without specialist knowledge, they generally do not survive in cultivation. At the same time removal will lead to their ultimate extinction in their own habitat. Orchids may be obtained from time to time from specialist Australian plant nurseries or from the Australian Native Orchid Society during their sales and exhibitions. The more reliable species, plus advice, are available where orchids are offered for sale.

Currently the Australian Orchidaceae is undergoing revision. This has already led to many new species being described and many more changes are likely to occur in the future as the taxonomists continue their work.

ORCHIDS

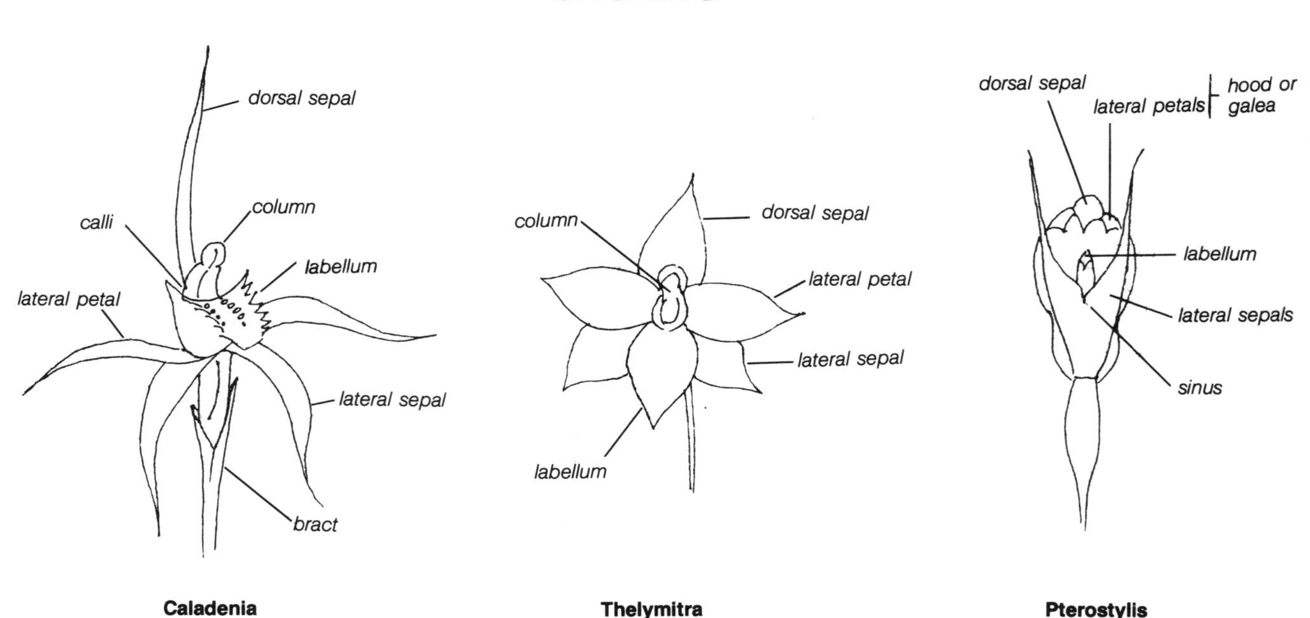

Acianthus

Acianthus caudatus

Mayfly Orchid

Size: Stem 5–25 cm high **P**
Habitat: Dry and valley sclerophyll forests, tea-tree heath, grassy low open forest
Form: Slender erect tuberous terrestrial herb
Foliage: Single heart-shaped dark green basal leaf to 30 mm long, purple below; held on stem, above ground level
Flowers: 1–9 crimson to dark purple-red flowers clustered at the end of the stem. Sepals long and thread-like, dorsal to 30 mm long, laterals to 15 mm long; petals to 5 mm long curve downwards.
Labellum is smooth, ovate and recurved, with 2 prominent glands at the base. May to October
Requirements: Well drained clay loam or sandy soils, remaining moist during the growing season
Comments: On warm days the flowers exude an unpleasant odour. While suited to a container this colony-producing species is difficult to keep growing. *Acianthus* spp. are pollinated by small flies.
Propagation: Seeds, increase in tuberoids
Localities: Eltham, Heathmont-Bayswater, Dandenong Rges, Belgrave, Langwarrin, Cranbourne, 34A, 42, 50A, 54, 74
Distribution: Vic, NSW, Tas, SA

Acianthus caudatus

Acianthus pusillus

Gnat or Mosquito Orchid

Size: stem 5–20 cm high **P**
Habitat: Widespread in dry, damp and valley sclerophyll forests, tea-tree heath
Form: Slender erect tuberous herb
Foliage: Single green heart-shaped leaf to 40 mm long, purplish below, margins entire, held up to 30 mm above the ground
Flowers: Terminal raceme of 3–20 greenish to pinkish flowers. Sepals small to 8 mm long, tapering and gland-tipped; petals smaller and bent backwards.
Labellum is narrow with 2 glands at the base. March to August
Requirements: Moist soils, drying out over Summer
Comments: Easily grown in a pot where it will flower well and form colonies if watered from late February. Mix must be well drained. Wild populations may form large colonies in ideal conditions. Distinguished from *A. exsertus* by its paler flower colour and smaller labellum.
Propagation: Seed, increase in tuberoids
Localities: Eltham, Heathmont-Boronia, Montrose, Hampton, Cheltenham, Seaford, Keysborough, Cranbourne, 34A, 42, 50A, 51, 56, 58, 63, 65#–67, 71, 74
Distribution: Vic, Qld, NSW, Tas, SA
Synonym: Previously included with *A. exsertus.*

Acianthus pusillus

Acianthus reniformis = Cyrtostylis reniformis

Arthrochilus

Arthrochilus huntianus

Elbow Orchid

Size: Stem to 15 cm high **P**
Habitat: Scattered in dry sclerophyll forest, often on ridges
Form: Leafless, erect tuberous herb with a reddish, wiry stem
Flowers: Terminal spike of 2–10 tiny, reddish-green insect-like flowers. Slender, reflexed sepals and petals to 5 mm long.
Labellum, to 6 mm long, is hinged at the base to the column. Its mid-section is fringed with long purplish-red hairs with 2 rough, hairy tails from the lower end. November to March
Requirements: Well drained soil
Comments: A saprophytic orchid feeding off dead and decaying organic matter. Locally rare and difficult to see but in good seasons it is more abundant.
Propagation: Impossible to cultivate
Localities: Dandenong Rges, Langwarrin, 42#
Distribution: Vic, NSW, Tas

Arthrochilus huntianus

SCALE: 0 1cm 2cm The scale representation on each plant equals 2cm.

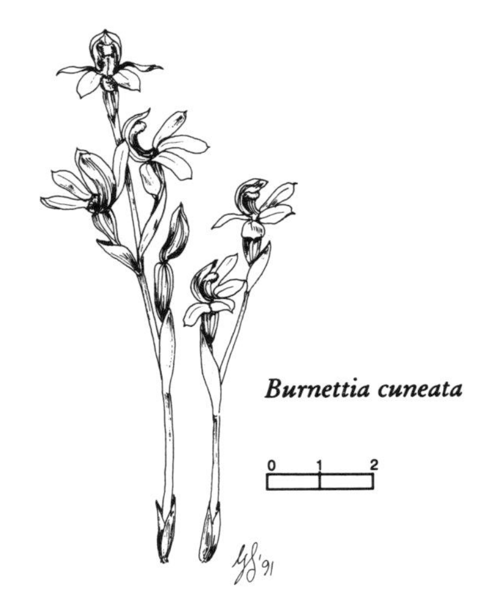

Burnettia cuneata

Burnettia

Burnettia cuneata

Lizard Orchid

Size: Stem 8–15 cm high — P
Habitat: Wet peaty heathland, tea tree swamp
Form: Terrestrial saprophytic herb with purplish-brown fleshy but brittle stem
Foliage: Reduced to brownish fleshy sheathing scales, sometimes with a well developed basal bract to 20 mm long
Flowers: Clusters of 1–7 flowers to 25 mm across, white inside, greenish-brown to purplish-brown with darker veins on the outside. Fleshy, widely-spreading sepals and petals to 13 mm long; dorsal sepal erect broad and deeply hooded. September to December
Requirements: Wet peaty soils
Comments: Rarely seen, remaining dormant for years and flowering for one season after a bushfire. Rare in Victoria, it may be extinct within the Melbourne area.
Propagation: Impossible to cultivate
Localities: Cheltenham#, 50A#, 67#, 74#
Distribution: Vic, NSW, Tas

Caladenia

Caladenias are dainty terrestrial orchids growing from a round tuberoid and are common in the grassy understorey of heathlands and open forests. Most species in Melbourne are now rare and in danger of extinction due to loss of habitat and weed invasion. They have a single basal leaf which is usually hairy. The hinged labellum is 3-lobed, usually fringed or toothed and bears rows of sessile or stalked calli. The column is erect, incurved and usually winged in the upper part.

Caladenia spp. may be divided into 2 groups. The first group has relatively small flowers and 4 of the perianth segments projecting forward like fingers. The Fairy or Finger Orchids usually occur in shades of pink, white or blue. The second group has larger flowers which are often suffused with red, and thread-like perianth segments. This group is commonly referred to as 'Spider Orchids'.

Species of *Caladenia* are difficult to grow and maintain in cultivation with most only reproducing by seed. Some will grow and reproduce through the production of daughter tuberoids, but these may be shy to flower. Bees pollinate the colourful species while the maroon and green flowered species sexually attract male thynnid wasps.

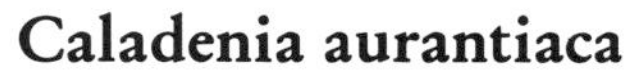

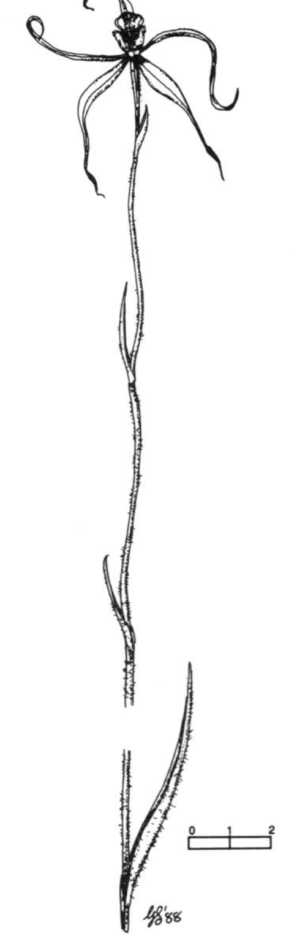

Caladenia australis

Caladenia aurantiaca

Orange-tip Caladenia

Size: stem to 15 cm high — P
Habitat: Beside swamps in tea-tree heaths
Form: Erect herb with thin wiry stem
Foliage: Narrow linear sparsely hairy leaf to 80 mm long
Flowers: 1–2 white flowers to 20 mm across. Perianth segments to 10 mm long. Labellum—3-lobed, lateral lobes erect, mid-lobe of labellum is orange with toothed margins. Stalked calli are clubbed and orange. September to November
Requirements: Moist peaty sands
Comments: Related to *C. carnea*, with which it is often confused. However, *C. aurantiaca* may be readily distinguished by the orange-tipped labellum. Impossible to cultivate. Known from one small colony in the Melbourne area.
Localities: Cranbourne
Distribution: Vic, NSW, Tas

Caladenia australis

Size: stem to 30 cm high — P
Habitat: Dry sclerophyll forest
Form: Erect herb with hairy, wiry stem
Foliage: Leaf hairy, to 120 mm long
Flowers: 1–2 creamy-yellow or reddish flowers to 60 mm across. Perianth segments to 50 mm long, with long dark clubbed tips.
Labellum is red, lateral lobes erect, mid-lobe recurved, margins shortly toothed. September to November
Requirements: Well drained soil
Comments: Differs from *C. reticulata* in that the labellum is red rather than cream with red stripes and margins.
Localities: Hurstbridge, Templestowe, Dandenong Rges, Frankston-Cranbourne, 42
Distribution: Vic, Tas, SA
Synonym: Previously confused with *C. reticulata* which does not occur further east than Stawell.

Caladenia caerula

Blue Fingers

Size: stem to 15 cm high **P**
Habitat: Dry sclerophyll forest, dry stony ground in box ironbark woodland, tea-tree heath
Form: Erect herb with hairy, wiry stems
Foliage: Oblong to linear-lanceolate, sparsely hairy leaf to 70 mm long
Flowers: Single blue flower to 25 mm across, paler on the outside. Perianth segments, to 20 mm long, have scattered tiny dark blue glands.
Labellum—3-lobed with dark blue transverse bands, lateral lobes are entire and erect. July to September
Requirements: Well drained soil
Comments: Difficult to maintain in cultivation.
Localities: Sth Morang, Diamond Ck, Eltham, Warrandyte, Heathmont, Belgrave, Black Rock#, 50A, 74
Distribution: Vic, Qld, NSW, Tas

Caladenia cardiochila

Fleshy-lipped Caladenia

Size: stem to 30 cm high **P**
Habitat: Coastal scrub and heathlands
Form: Erect herb
Foliage: Thick, hairy, linear-lanceolate leaf to 110 mm long
Flowers: Single yellowish flower to 30 mm across, each segment with a brown-red central stripe. Perianth segments spreading, to 20 mm long ending in glandular tips which are sometimes club-shaped; dorsal sepal hooded; lateral sepals wider than petals.
Labellum cordate to cordate-ovate, the tip thickened and slightly crenulate, very dark red stalked calli densely crowded in a narrow band from the base to about ½ its length. September to October
Requirements: Well drained sandy soils
Localities: Collected in Sandringham 1939; 76
Distribution: Vic, SA
Synonym: Previously included with *C. tessellata* from NSW, which also has isolated occurrences in East Gippsland.

Caladenia carnea var. carnea

Pink Fingers

Size: stem 8–25 cm high **F P**
Habitat: Widespread in dry sclerophyll forest, sclerophyll and red gum woodland, tea-tree heath
Form: Erect hairy herb with a wiry stem
Foliage: Narrow-linear leaf 8–20 cm long
Flowers: 1–3 pink flowers to 30 mm across, less commonly white to greenish-white. Labellum and column have dark red bars. Perianth segments to 15 mm long.
Labellum to 8 mm long, 3-lobed, lateral lobes erect, yellowish mid-lobe recurved, triangular, rarely with short marginal teeth. 2 rows of yellow calli. August to December
Requirements: Well drained soil
Comments: One of the easiest Caladenias to grow. White forms predominate in the Dandenongs.
Localities: Somerton, Bundoora, Hurstbridge-Eltham, Templestowe, Park Orchards, Box Hill, Heathmont, Dandenong Rges, Noble Park, Cranbourne, 33, 34A, 42, 44, 47, 49, 50A, 56, 58, 61, 65#, 67#, 74
Distribution: Vic, Qld, NSW, Tas, SA

Caladenia catenata

White Fingers, White Caladenia

Size: stem to 30 cm high **P**
Habitat: Dry and valley sclerophyll forests, red gum woodland, grassy low open forest
Form: Erect herb with hairy wiry stem
Foliage: Sparsely hairy linear leaf to 120 mm long
Flowers: 1–2 white flowers to 30 mm across. Perianth segments to 15 mm long, lateral sepals deflexed
Labellum—3-lobed, lateral lobes entire and erect, the longer mid-lobe recurved with marginal teeth, tip orange-yellow and calli club-like. April to October
Requirements: Well drained soils
Comments: Confused with *C. carnea* var. *carnea* but readily distinguished by the longer, toothed orange mid-lobe and lack of red bars on the labellum. The flowers are also more open. Seldom seen in Melbourne now, except after fire. Readily cultivated.
Localities: Bundoora, Eltham, Dandenong Rges, Belgrave, 42, 50A, 55, 63, 71, 74
Distribution: Vic, Qld, NSW
Synonym: *C. alba*

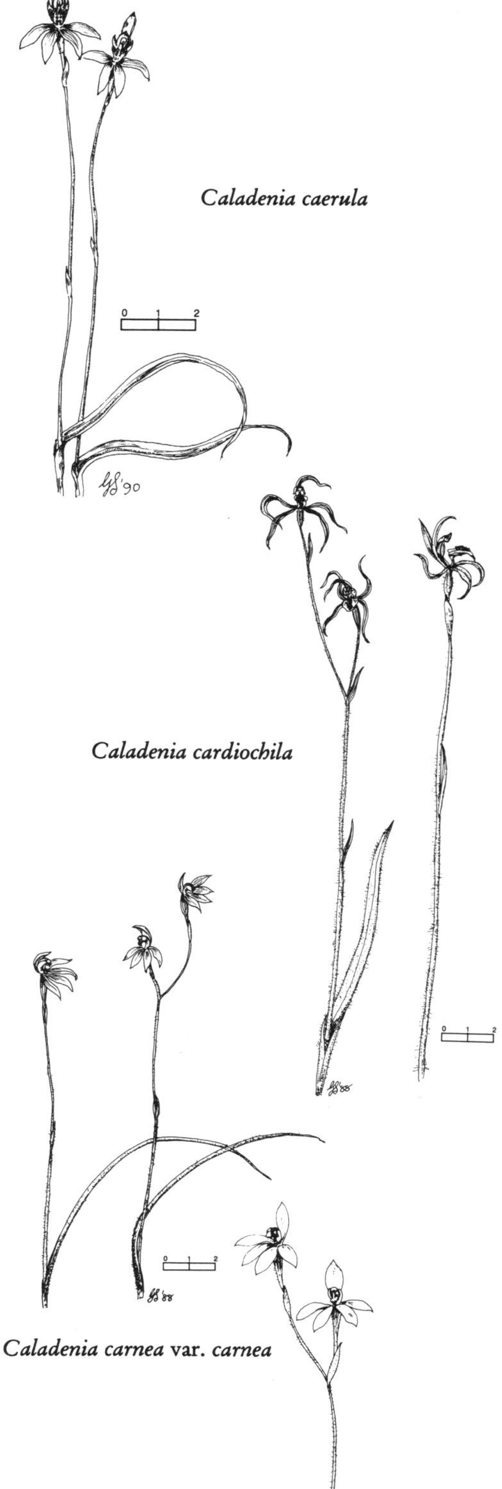

Caladenia caerula

Caladenia cardiochila

Caladenia carnea var. *carnea*

Caladenia catenata

SCALE: 0 1cm 2cm The scale representation on each plant equals 2cm.

Caladenia clavigera

Caladenia clavigera

Clubbed or Plain-lipped Spider Orchid

Size: stem 10–40 cm high **F P**
Habitat: Widespread but scattered occurrences in dry and valley sclerophyll forests
Form: Erect herb with hairy, wiry reddish stem
Foliage: Hairy lanceolate leaf to 15 cm long, red-spotted at the base
Flowers: 1–2 greenish-yellow flowers to 60 mm across. Perianth segments have a prominent red central stripe, sepals, to 50 mm long, taper to clubbed tips; petals are shorter and not clubbed.
Labellum to 12 mm long, cordate, greenish with dark red recurved mid-lobe and 4–6 rows of clubbed calli. September to December
Requirements: Moist well drained soils
Comments: Locally rare.
Localities: Heathmont-Boronia, Belgrave, 42, 44, 50A
Distribution: Vic, NSW, Tas, SA

Caladenia concinna

Size: stem to 20 cm high **P**
Habitat: Sparse scrub in dry sclerophyll forest
Form: Erect herb with a wiry, hairy stem
Foliage: Hairy oblong to elliptic leaf to 120 mm long, red-spotted at the base
Flowers: 1–2 pale yellowish-green flowers with red markings, to 50 mm across. Perianth segments bent backwards, with faint red stripe, to 35 mm long; dorsal sepal erect, sepals ending in a poorly developed, yellowish club.
Labellum—broadly flared, to 18 mm across, green with maroon in the upper half. Lateral lobes have few broad teeth, mid-lobe tip is recurved, dark red calli are club-like in 2 rows. September to October
Requirements: Well drained soils
Comments: Locally rare. Has been confused with *C. toxochila* in the past.
Localities: Wattle Glen, Greensborough, Belgrave
Distribution: Vic, NSW
Synonym: *C. dilatata* var. *concinna*

Caladenia deformis

Caladenia congesta

Black-tongue Caladenia

Size: stem to 0.6 m high **P**
Habitat: Valley sclerophyll forest, swamp margins of wattle tea-tree scrub
Form: Erect slightly hairy herb with slender stem
Foliage: Linear leaf to 18 cm long
Flowers: 1–3 bright pink or reddish flowers to 30 mm across, with a conspicuous black labellum. Perianth segments spreading and flat to 20 mm long; dorsal sepal erect, shorter and hooded.
Labellum—3-lobed, lateral lobes erect, mid-lobe longer and very narrow, completely covered with 2 rows of flat, sessile blackish calli. October to December
Requirements: Intolerant of high rainfall and high humidity
Comments: Very difficult to cultivate, requiring very well drained mixture.
Localities: Ringwood-Bayswater, Dandenong Rges, Belgrave, Lysterfield, Moorabbin#, 33, 34A, 67#
Distribution: Vic, NSW, Tas, SA

Caladenia deformis

Blue Fairies, Bluebeard Caladenia

Size: stem 10–20 cm high **F P**
Habitat: Widespread in dry sclerophyll forest, grassy low open forest, tea-tree heath
Form: Erect herb with wiry stem, growing in tufts
Foliage: Bright green linear leaf to 100 mm long
Flowers: Single dark blue faintly perfumed flower to 40 mm across, with scattered tiny purple glands. Perianth segments lanceolate to 25 mm long, spreading; dorsal sepal erect.
Labellum—3-lobed, lateral lobes erect, entire, mid-lobe triangular, recurved, deep purple and fringed. 4–8 dense rows of calli. June to October
Requirements: Well drained soils
Comments: Now locally rare. More commonly found in shrubby coastal heaths.
Localities: Campbellfield, Bayswater#, Belgrave, Cranbourne, 41, 42, 47, 49, 50A, 58, 67#, 74
Distribution: Vic, NSW, Tas, SA, WA

Caladenia dilatata

Green Comb Spider Orchid

Size: stem to 45 cm high **F P**
Habitat: Widespread in dry, valley and damp sclerophyll forests, red gum woodland, tea-tree heath
Form: Tall hairy herb with wiry stems
Foliage: Hairy oblong to elliptical leaf to 120 mm long
Flowers: 1–2 large green or yellowish-green flowers to 100 mm across. Perianth segments to 70 mm long, each having 3 red stripes; sepals tipped with yellowish hairy clubs, petals thread-like.
Labellum—green, 3-lobed, maroon towards the tip, lateral lobes have linear teeth on margins, mid-lobe is recurved with short, blunt teeth. Clubbed, reddish-purple linear calli crowded in 4 rows. Column has 2 yellow basal glands. August to January
Requirements: Well drained soils
Comments: One of the more common *Caladenia* species found in Melbourne. Variable in form, the species is currently undergoing revision.
Localities: Bundoora, Wattle Glen, Greensborough, Eltham, Belgrave, 34A, 42, 47, 49, 50A, 51, 55, 56, 58, 67#, 74, 76
Distribution: Vic, Qld, NSW, Tas, SA

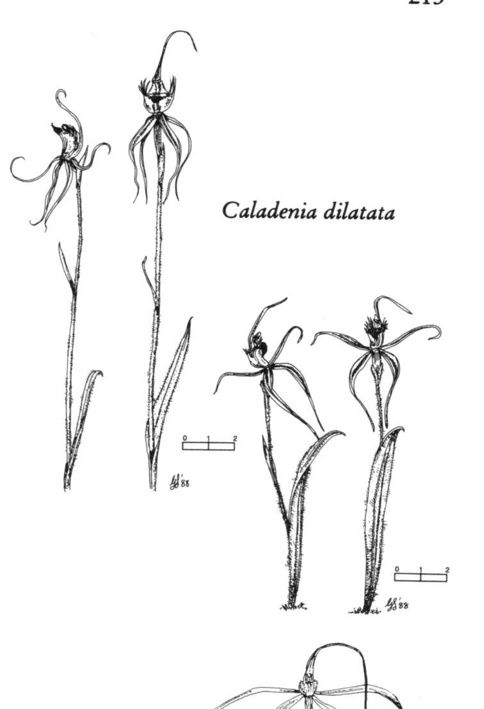

Caladenia dilatata

Caladenia filamentosa var. filamentosa

Daddy Long Legs

Size: stem 10–40 cm high **F P**
Habitat: Valley and damp sclerophyll forests
Form: Erect herb covered in soft long hairs with a thin wiry stem
Foliage: Narrow-linear leaf to 18 cm long
Flowers: 1–4 deep crimson, reddish, or occasionally greenish-white flowers, to 80 mm across. Perianth segments to 60 mm long, flat, becoming thread-like, droopy and entangled.
Labellum—narrow with darker veins, curved, with calli on margins, tip entire, 2 rows of calli on back half of tongue. September to October
Requirements: Moist, well drained soils
Comments: Usually grows in small colonies. Locally rare.
Localities: Yarrambat, Boronia, The Basin, 58
Distribution: Vic, NSW, Tas, SA

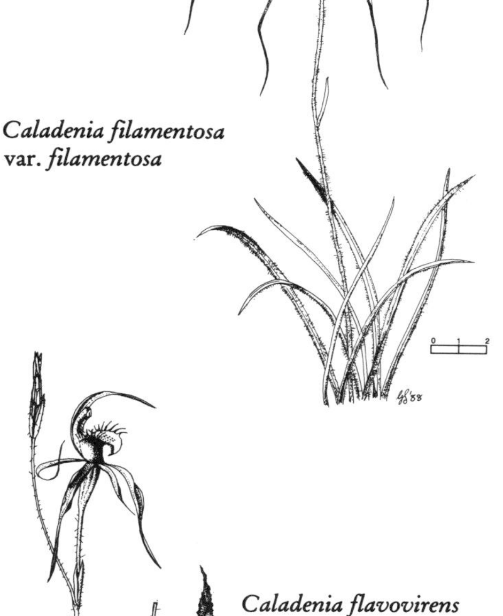

Caladenia filamentosa var. *filamentosa*

Caladenia flavovirens

Summer Spider Orchid

Size: stems to 40 cm high **P**
Habitat: Dry and valley sclerophyll forests with grassy understorey
Form: Robust, erect herb
Foliage: Coarsely-haired lanceolate leaf to 18 cm long
Flowers: 1–2 bright yellow-green flowers to 70 mm across. Perianth segments more than 50 mm long and drooping, sepals longer ending in club-like tips, dorsal sepal erect.
Labellum broadly ovate, undivided, sometimes with dark red tip. 4–6 rows of calli. November to January
Requirements: Well drained soil
Comments: Regenerates well after fire. Its habitat locally is being threatened by weed invasion and encroaching housing development.
Localities: Montrose, Boronia, The Basin, 42, 50A, 55, 58
Distribution: Vic, NSW, possibly Tas
Synonym: Formerly referred to as *C. pallida* which is endemic to Tasmania.

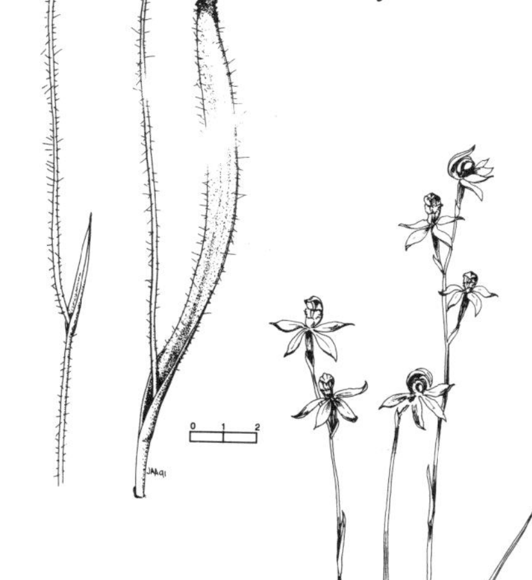

Caladenia flavovirens

Caladenia gracilis

Musky Caladenia

Size: stem 10–40 cm high **P**
Habitat: Dry and valley sclerophyll forests, grassy low open forest
Form: Sparsely hairy erect herb with thin, wiry stem
Foliage: Thick linear leaf to 30 cm long
Flowers: Raceme of 1–6 white musk-scented flowers to 30 mm across, outer surfaces purple or greenish-brown. Spreading perianth segments to 15 mm long; dorsal sepal erect, hooded.
Labellum fringed along the end with purple, red or yellow calli. 4 rows of stalked yellow or purple calli also along tongue. September to November
Requirements: Well drained soil
Comments: The hooded dorsal sepal may cause confusion with *C. cucullata* which grows north of Melbourne. *C. gracilis* may be distinguished by the strong musky scent exuded on warm days. Locally rare.
Localities: Park Orchards, Doncaster, Heathmont-Boronia, Belgrave, Montrose, 42, 51, 55, 56, 58, 74
Distribution: Vic, Qld, NSW, Tas, SA
Synonym: *C. angustata*

Caladenia gracilis

SCALE: 0 1cm 2cm The scale representation on each plant equals 2cm.

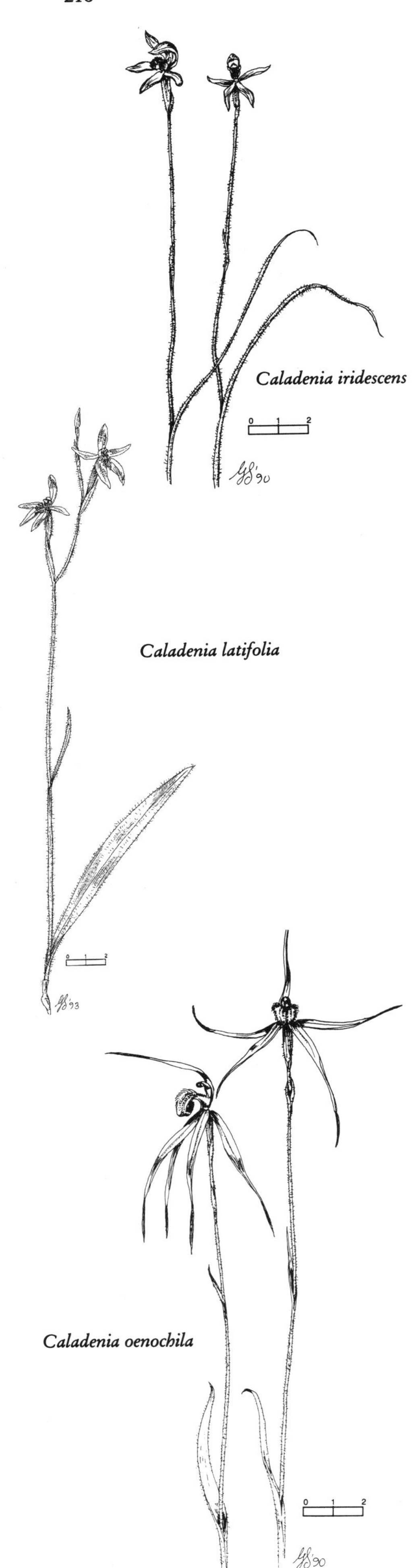

Caladenia iridescens

Bronze Caladenia

P

Size: stem 10–25 cm high
Habitat: Valley sclerophyll forest, grassy low open forest
Form: Erect herb with wiry purplish stems
Foliage: Narrow-linear leaf to 100 mm long
Flowers: 1–4 dusky red, purplish-crimson to greenish flowers to 20 mm across. Narrow, widely spaced perianth segments to 10 mm long.
Labellum 3-lobed, white with red or purple transverse bars, lateral lobes erect, purplish mid-lobe recurved with glandular-headed calli. September to November
Requirements: Well drained soils
Comments: Locally rare.
Localities: Heathmont-Boronia, Lysterfield, Montrose, Kilsyth, 50A, 51, ?55, 74
Distribution: Vic, NSW, Tas

Caladenia latifolia

Pink Fairies

F P

Size: stem to 40 cm high
Habitat: Tea-tree heath, coastal banksia woodland
Form: Hairy erect herb with wiry stems
Foliage: Bright green, very hairy oblong-lanceolate leaf to 20 cm long
Flowers: 1–4 bright pink, rarely white, flowers to 35 mm across. Perianth segments spreading; dorsal sepal erect, sepals to 18 mm long, petals shorter.
Labellum 3-lobed, narrow and pink-striped, lateral lobes erect, mid-lobe recurved with 3–4 pairs of long teeth on margin, calli in 2 converging rows. August to December
Requirements: Well drained sandy soil
Comments: Easily grown but rarely flowers in cultivation. Water regularly during growing season. Forms clumps which need to be separated to maintain vigour.
Localities: Hampton, Cheltenham, Beaumaris, Seaford, 67#, 74
Distribution: Vic, NSW, Tas, SA, WA

Caladenia menziesii

Hare or Rabbit Orchid

P

Size: stem 5–25 cm high
Habitat: Damp and valley sclerophyll forests, tea-tree heath, grassy low open forest
Form: Slender erect herb with glabrous, wiry stem
Foliage: Bright green glabrous ovate to ovate-lanceolate leaf to 90 mm long
Flowers: 1–3 pink and white flowers to 15 mm across. White lateral sepals spreading, to 10 mm long; dorsal sepal reddish, hooded; dark red petals held erect like ears, to 20 mm long.
Labellum white with transverse pink bars, sides erect, tip white and recurved, 2–4 rows of yellow calli. August to November
Requirements: Moist well drained soils
Comments: Flowers profusely after fires forming dense colonies. Easy to grow but shy to flower under cultivation, it reproduces by tuberoids, forming a clump. Banana skins placed beside the plants produce ethylene gas which may induce them to flower.
Localities: Belgrave, Cheltenham, Beaumaris, 34A, 42, 47, 49, 55–58, 67#, 74, 76
Distribution: Vic, NSW, Tas, SA, WA
Synonym: *Leptoceras menziesii*

Caladenia oenochila

P N

Size: stem to 40 cm high
Habitat: Damp and valley sclerophyll forests
Form: Hairy erect herb with wiry stem
Foliage: Linear-lanceolate leaf to 15 cm long
Flowers: 1–3 sweetly perfumed pale yellow-green flowers to 80 mm across, with very dark red hairs on the outer surface.
Labellum is undivided and usually deep red, paler towards the base and ovate-cordate. Marginal teeth and calli are deep red. August to November
Requirements: Moist well drained soil
Comments: Locally very rare. Will sometimes grow and flower in a pot for a few years but will not increase in number. Similar to *C. patersonii* from which it differs mostly in flower colour.
Localities: Nunawading-Boronia, The Basin, Lysterfield, 33, 34A, 42, 55, 56, 58, 63
Distribution: Endemic to Vic
Synonym: Previously known as *C. patersonii* which is endemic to Tas, and *C.* sp. aff. *patersonii* (foothills)

Caladenia praecox

Early Caladenia

Size:	stem to 15 cm high	**P**
Habitat:	Dry and valley sclerophyll forests	
Form:	Erect herb with thin wiry stem	
Foliage:	Sparsely hairy very narrow leaf to 15 cm long	
Flowers:	1–4 white, or rarely pink, flowers to 30 mm across, with pink or green markings. Perianth segments, to 15 mm long, are dark red on the outside. Labellum—white spotted with red, lateral lobes erect, mid-lobe crimson or purple, fringed white, yellow or purple. Stalked, clubbed calli white or yellow. August to October	
Requirements:	Well drained soil	
Comments:	Occurs in open forests where it is protected by grassy tussocks.	
Localities:	Diamond Ck, Eltham, Heathmont-Boronia, Mooroolbark, Montrose, The Basin, Belgrave, Lysterfield, 34A, 41, 49, 51, 56, 58	
Distribution:	Vic, NSW, Tas	

Caladenia pusilla

Tiny Caladenia

Size:	stem to 9 cm high	**P**
Habitat:	Valley sclerophyll forest, grassy low open forest	
Form:	Tiny erect herb	
Foliage:	Linear, sparsely hairy leaf to 60 mm long	
Flowers:	Tiny single cream to deep pink flower to 15 mm across, with a central stripe, reddish or dark brown on outside. Perianth segments to 7 mm long; lateral sepals differ from *C. carnea* var. *carnea* in that they are relatively broad and are joined together in the basal half. Labellum—3-lobed, white, transversely barred with red; lateral lobes oval, erect, mid-lobe narrow-triangular, fringed and yellow tipped. 2 rows of yellow calli. September to October	
Requirements:	Well drained soils	
Localities:	Croydon, Belgrave, 42#, 67#, 74, 76	
Distribution:	Vic, NSW, Tas, SA	
Synonym:	*C. carnea* var. *pygmaea*	

Caladenia robinsonii

Size:	stem to 35 cm high	**P**
Habitat:	Eucalyptus viminalis woodland with grassy understorey	
Form:	Small erect hairy herb	
Foliage:	Narrow-lanceolate leaf to 110 mm long	
Flowers:	1–2 cream or greenish flowers to 60 mm across. Perianth segments to 35 mm long, becoming thread-like. Labellum—small with short lateral teeth. September to November	
Requirements:	Well drained sandy soil	
Comments:	This species is possibly extinct as the only known recent occurrence has been destroyed for housing.	
Localities:	Frankston	
Distribution:	Endemic to Vic	
Synonym:	Previously known as C. sp. aff. *reticulata*	

Caladenia rosella

Size:	stem 10–17 cm high	**P**
Habitat:	Dry sclerophyll forest	
Form:	Small erect hairy herb with a greenish to reddish-purple stem	
Foliage:	Hairy, linear-lanceolate leaf to 100 mm long.	
Flowers:	Single brilliant pink flower to 60 mm across, with musky fragrance. Labellum has 6 widely-spaced rows of finger-like light rose pink or yellowy-pink calli. July to October	
Requirements:	Well drained soil	
Comments:	Similar to *C. patersonii* but has pink flowers and is smaller in all its parts. An endangered species with a very restricted occurrence.	
Localities:	Hurstbridge, Eltham	
Distribution:	Endemic to Vic	

0 1 2

GS '90

Caladenia rosella

SCALE: 0 1cm 2cm The scale representation on each plant equals 2cm.

Caladenia tentaculata

Spider Orchid

Size: stem to 40 cm high **P**
Habitat: Valley sclerophyll forest, grassy low open forest
Form: Erect hairy herb with a thin wiry stem
Foliage: Lanceolate leaf to 15 cm long, often red-spotted near the base
Flowers: 1–2 yellowish-green flowers to 100 mm across, with crimson stripes and markings. Perianth segments to 70 mm long, becoming thread-like, with 3 reddish stripes; sepals tipped with yellowish hairy clubs, lateral sepals projecting forward, dorsal sepal erect; petals thread-like, bent backwards.
Labellum—3-lobed, as broad as it is long, to 20 mm across, green with prominent white patch and maroon tip; lateral lobes have blunt marginal teeth to 10 mm long. Crowded reddish calli in 4 rows. August to October
Requirements: Moist, well drained soils
Comments: Similar to *C. dilatata*, but with a broader labellum.
Localities: 42, 74, 76
Distribution: Vic, SA

Caladenia thysanochila

Size: stem to 25 cm high **F P**
Habitat: Eucalyptus viminalis woodland
Form: Hairy erect herb
Foliage: Linear-lanceolate stem-clasping leaf to 20 cm long
Flowers: Small white flowers with reddish-purple tinges. Light purplish-brown club-like tips on petals and sepals.
Labellum densely fringed with reddish-purple teeth. Up to 4 rows reddish-purple calli.
Requirements: Well drained sandy soil
Comments: Known from 2 plants, it is on the verge of extinction.
Localities: Mt. Eliza
Distribution: Endemic to Vic

Caladenia tentaculata

Caladenia venusta

Size: stem to 45 cm high **P**
Habitat: Tea-tree heath
Comments: Similar to *C. patersonii* but distinguished by its larger flowers which are white except for the marginal teeth and calli. Teeth of the labellum are longer and its fragrance resembles mouldy oranges. A rare plant with one small colony within the Melbourne area. A new orchid found in Kilsyth in 1992 closely resembles this species.
Localities: Dingley#; Frankston
Distribution: Vic, Tas
Synonym: Previously known as *C.* sp. aff. *patersonii* (large white)

Caleana

Caleana major

Large Duck Orchid, Flying Ducks

Size: stem 15–40 cm high **F P**
Habitat: Dry sclerophyll forest, grassy low open forest
Form: Glabrous erect herb with thin, wiry, green or reddish-brown stem
Foliage: Single, narrow-lanceolate, reddish basal leaf to 120 mm long. Leaf often withers by flowering time.
Flowers: 1–5 shiny reddish-brown flowers, displayed upside down to resemble a duck flying. Perianth segments to 15 mm long, narrow to linear with pointed tips.
Labellum ovoid, to 8 mm long, hollow underneath. The labellum resembles a duck's head and is attached to the base of the winged column by a broad sensitive strap. September to February
Requirements: Well drained sandy soils
Comments: Often grows in association with *Eucalyptus macrorhyncha*. It is difficult to keep growing in cultivation. Pollinated by sexually attracted male sawflies.
Propagation: Seed
Localities: Moorabbin#, 42#, 50A, 63, 67#, 74
Distribution: Vic, Qld, NSW, Tas, SA

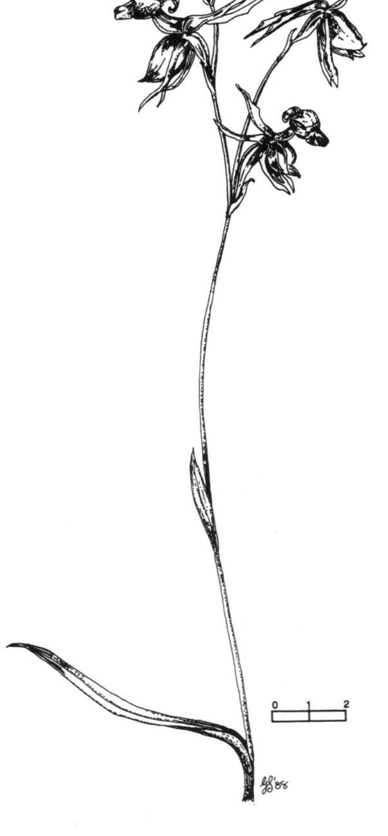

Caleana major

Calochilus

Calochilus campestris

Copper Beard-orchid

Size: stem 0.3–0.6 m high **P**
Habitat: Damp and valley sclerophyll forests, grassy low open forest
Form: Glabrous, erect herb with slender to stout, often greyish, stem
Foliage: Single rigid dark green linear-lanceolate leaf to 30 cm long, channelled with fleshy triangular cross-section
Flowers: 5–15 pale yellow-green flowers to 20 mm across, with reddish-brown markings and coppery beard. Erect dorsal sepal ovate and concave to 9 mm long, lateral sepals narrower and longer spreading below the labellum; petals erect, shorter and narrower than the dorsal sepal.
Labellum to 15 mm long, ovate, curved, basal part glabrous, with 2 metallic blue plates, central part covered with purple bristly hair-like calli resembling a beard. Labellum ends in a short glabrous tail. September to January
Comments: All *Calochilus* species are difficult in cultivation, dying out after a few years. They require moist, well drained soils. Most species can self-pollinate if not insect pollinated. This species remains in few Melbourne sites.
Localities: Dandenong Rges, Boronia, Belgrave, Lysterfield, Caulfield#, Cheltenham#, 57, 61, 67#, 74
Distribution: Vic, Qld, NSW, Tas, SA; NZ

Calochilus campestris

Calochilus paludosus

Red Beard-orchid

Size: stem to 35 cm high **P**
Habitat: Dry and valley sclerophyll forests
Form: Slender herb with wiry stem
Foliage: Thin, ribbed linear-lanceolate leaf to 18 mm long, triangular in cross-section, often reddish at base
Flowers: 1–9 reddish-bronze flowers to 25 mm across, with a coppery beard. Broadly elliptic hooded dorsal sepal to 15 mm long, lateral sepals smaller, narrow-lanceolate; petals to 8 mm long, triangular with pointed tip.
Labellum—to 30 mm long, basal part covered in calli, central section has a beard of coarse reddish hairs. Labellum ends in a glabrous strap-like tail to 15 mm long. September to January
Localities: Hurstbridge, Boronia, Bayswater, Belgrave, Kilsyth, Lysterfield, 41, 42, 50A, 51, 74
Distribution: Vic, Qld, NSW, Tas, SA; NZ

Calochilus robertsonii

Calochilus robertsonii

Common or Purplish Beard-orchid

Size: stem to 0.45 m high **P**
Habitat: Widespread in sclerophyll woodland, dry, valley and damp sclerophyll forests, grassy low open forest
Form: Glabrous erect herb with a slender stem
Foliage: Single fleshy, ribbed, dark green linear-lanceolate leaf to 40 cm long, triangular in cross-section and reddish at the base
Flowers: 1–9 green flowers to 30 mm across, with reddish or purple stripes and a bronze-purple beard. Erect dorsal sepal, ovate to 25 mm long, lateral sepals as long but narrower, petals to 10 mm long
Labellum—ovate to 35 mm long, basal part covered in purple callus-like glands, central part has a beard of purple to bronze-brown hair-like calli. Ends in a short glabrous tail, longer than *C. campestris*.
The base of each column wing bears a bead-like gland, the wings connected by a prominent purplish ridge. August to October
Comments: The most widespread and common beard orchid in Melbourne. Plants flower freely and are most prominent on warm sunny days when the flowers open widely to fully display their beards.
Localities: Hurstbridge, Bayswater, Dandenong Rges, 42, 44, 47, 49–51, 54–56, 58, 66#, 67#, 74, 76
Distribution: All states except NT; NZ

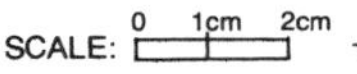

The scale representation on each plant equals 2cm.

Chiloglottis

Small terrestrial orchids with a single terminal flower and a pair of basal leaves. A floral bract surrounds the flower stalk. The dorsal sepal is erect and curved inwards. *Chiloglottis* spp. prefer sheltered areas and spread by increasing their tuberoid numbers vegetatively to form colonies. They are commonly called Bird Orchids, alluding to the resemblance of the flowers in some species to a baby bird with its beak open, waiting to be fed.

Some species may be grown, and flower well, in pots provided the mixture is well drained and includes well rotted organic material. They need watering from Autumn to Spring while in active growth and should dry out over Summer when they are dormant. Protection is needed from slugs and snails. Pollinated by sexually attracted male thynnid wasps. Propagate by division of tuberoids.

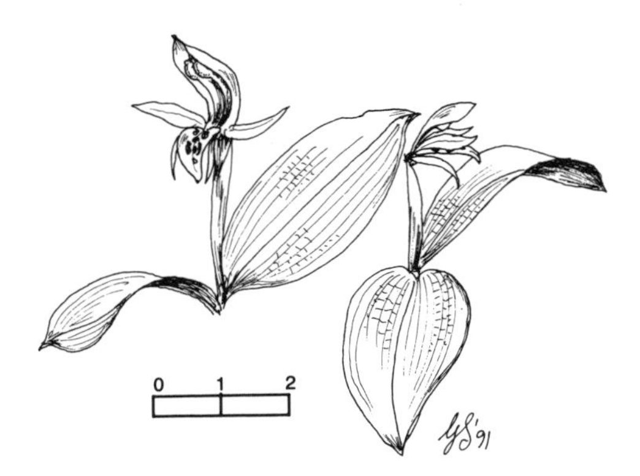

Chiloglottis cornuta

Chiloglottis cornuta

Green Bird-orchid

P N

Size: stem to 4 cm high
Habitat: Wet sclerophyll forest, along stream banks
Foliage: Bright green broadly-ovate leaves 30–100 mm long
Flowers: Pale green flower to 30 mm across, with reddish markings. Perianth segments to 20 mm long, lateral sepals curved downwards, petals erect. Labellum ovate, green to reddish with a few dark green to reddish sessile calli in the centre. October to January
Requirements: Moist soils in high rainfall areas
Localities: 57
Distribution: Vic, NSW, Tas, SA; NZ

Chiloglottis reflexa

Autumn Bird-orchid

P

Size: stem 8–18 cm high
Habitat: Dry sclerophyll forest, tea-tree heath, grassy low open forest
Foliage: Dark green elliptical stem-clasping leaves to 60 mm long with wavy margins
Flowers: Narrow greenish-bronze or purplish flower to 15 mm across, on a pinkish stem. Perianth segments to 20 mm long, petals bent backwards. Labellum brownish, obovate, to 12 mm long with reddish-black calli in the centre, ending in a prominent short point. March to August
Requirements: Well drained sandy soils
Comments: Flowering is sporadic, poor in some seasons, prolific in others, and may be stimulated by Summer fires. Grows well in a pot but is prone to rotting, so the mix must be perfectly drained.
Localities: Heathmont, Lysterfield, Cranbourne, 42, 67[#], 74
Distribution: Vic, NSW, Tas

Chiloglottis trapeziformis

Chiloglottis trapeziformis

Broad Lip or Dainty Bird-orchid

P

Size: stem to 8 cm high
Habitat: Dry sclerophyll forest, grassy low open forest
Foliage: Dark green ovate-lanceolate, shortly stalked leaves to 80 mm long, entire or with wavy margins
Flower: Brownish-green to reddish flower to 20 mm across. Perianth segments to 15 mm long.
Erect labellum broadly rhomboid (or trapeziform) to 12 mm long with a compact group of sessile black calli towards the base. September to November
Requirements: Well drained soils
Comments: In cultivation, the hardiest of the local *Chiloglottis* species. Closely related to the earlier-flowering *C. reflexa*, but is readily distinguished by the stalked leaves and more compact calli. Locally threatened and already extinct in most Melbourne sites.
Localities: Mt. Eliza, 34A, 51[#], 74[#], 76
Distribution: Vic, Qld, NSW, Tas

Chiloglottis valida

Chiloglottis valida

Common Bird-orchid

P

Size: stem to 40 mm high
Habitat: Widespread in damp and valley sclerophyll forests, grassy low open forest
Foliage: Dark green ovate leaves to 100 mm long
Flowers: Dark reddish-brown to purplish-green flower to 40 mm across. Perianth segments to 20 mm long.
Labellum purplish, broadly ovate to 16 mm long with dark red to black calli. September to January
Requirements: Moist well drained humus-rich soils
Comments: Widely distributed in cooler forests often forming very large colonies. Readily distinguished from *C. cornuta* by the calli, some of which are on short stalks.
Localities: Heathmont-Boronia, Kalorama, Belgrave, 34A, 42, 44, 47, 49, 50A, 51, 55–58, 63, 74, 76
Distribution: Vic, NSW, Tas; NZ
Synonym: Previously included with *C. gunnii*

Corybas

Dwarf terrestrial orchids of cool, sheltered areas reproducing by tuberoids to form colonies which are often hidden beneath shrubs and grassy tussocks. They have a single, flat, ground-hugging leaf and a single sessile or shortly stalked flower conspicuously hooded by the large erect dorsal sepal. Lateral sepals and petals are reduced and narrow, the large tubular labellum is erect at the base, expanding then curving downwards. Pollination is by small fungus gnats. Propagate by division.

Corybas aconitiflorus

Spurred Helmet-orchid

P N

Habitat: Damp sclerophyll forest
Foliage: Dark green cordate leaf to 35 mm long, purplish below
Flowers: Erect purplish flower to 30 mm long on a short slender stalk. Hooded dorsal sepal encloses most of the labellum; lateral sepals and petals are thread-like. Lower half of labellum is tubular, upper part widely flared. March to July
Requirements: Moist well drained soils
Comments: Forms large colonies under ideal conditions. Successful under cultivation.
Localities: Belgrave
Distribution: Vic, Qld, NSW, Tas

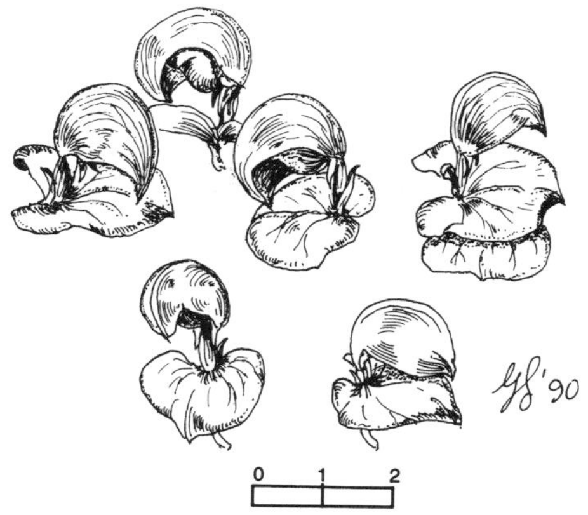
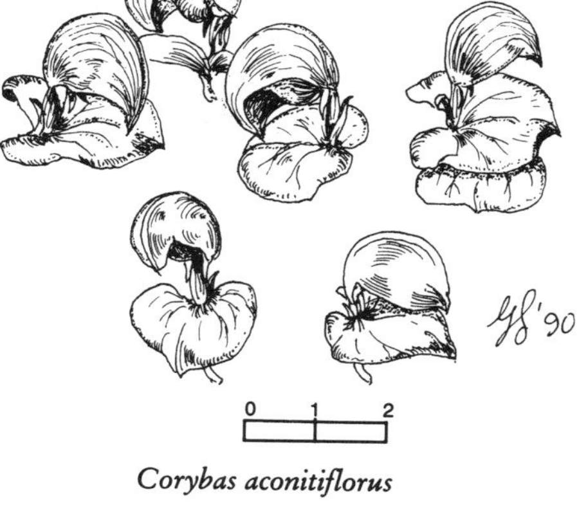

Corybas aconitiflorus

Corybas diemenicus

Veined Helmet-orchid

N

Habitat: Fern gullies in wet and valley sclerophyll forest, grassy low open forest
Foliage: Circular to cordate leaf to 25 mm diameter with a circular marginal vein
Flowers: Large dark reddish-purple flower to 25 mm long, erect or recurved on a short slender stalk. Lower part of labellum is erect, upper part is sharply recurved and widely flared, with prominent veins, a central white patch and short fringed marginal teeth pointed forward. June to September
Requirements: Moist soil with plenty of humus
Comments: Seldom flowers in cultivation. In fern gullies, often colonises treefern trunks.
Localities: Montrose, Dandenong Rges, Belgrave, 42, 57, 74
Distribution: Vic, NSW, Tas, SA, WA
Synonym: *C. dilatatus* has been included with *C. diemenicus*. The species previously known as *C. diemenicus* has now become *C. incurvus*.

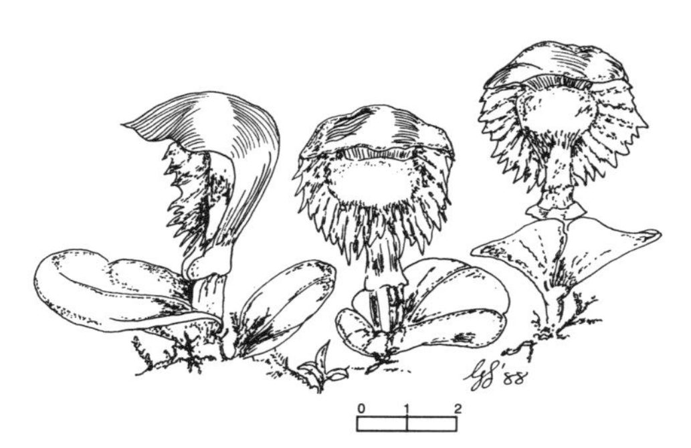

Corybas diemenicus

Corybas incurvus

Slaty or Toothed Helmet-orchid

P

Habitat: Moist sheltered slopes and gullies in valley sclerophyll forest, tea-tree heath, grassy low open forest
Foliage: Cordate to ovate leaf to 30 mm long
Flowers: Erect, sessile dark purple flower to 15 mm long. Crimson-veined labellum differs from *C. diemenicus* in that the white central spot is channelled and the fringed margins of the upper part are curved inwards. June to September
Requirements: Moist soils
Localities: Bundoora, Wattle Glen, Eltham, Bayswater, Heathmont, Montrose, Springvale, Cranbourne, Cheltenham, Hampton, Beaumaris, 42, 65–67, 74–76
Distribution: Vic, NSW, Tas, SA
Synonym: *C. diemenicus*

Corybas unguiculatus

Small Helmet-orchid, Pelicans

P N

Habitat: Protected sites in moist tea-tree heath, grassy low open forest
Foliage: Cordate grey-green, often 3-lobed, leaf to 30 mm long, reddish below
Flowers: Reddish-purple to purple-black flower to 15 mm long, held erect on a short stalk. Dorsal sepal narrow at base, expanded and hooded in upper half. Labellum is tubular with margins incurved and the tip flared. May to November
Requirements: Sandy or peaty soils, moist to wet in Winter
Comments: A solitary species which is difficult to grow. The flower profile resembles a duck's head.
Localities: Belgrave, Cranbourne, Beaumaris, Cheltenham, 74
Distribution: Vic, NSW, Tas, SA

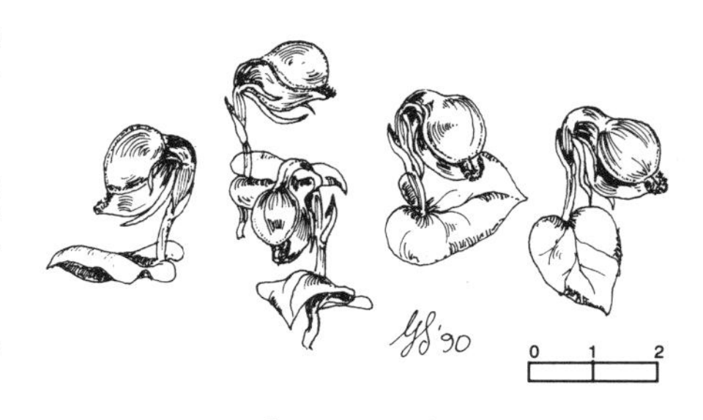

Corybas unguiculatus

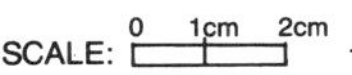

The scale representation on each plant equals 2cm.

Cryptostylis subulata

Cryptostylis

Cryptostylis leptochila

Small Tongue-orchid

Size: stem 20–40 cm high **P**
Habitat: Damp and valley sclerophyll forests, grassy low open forest
Form: Stiff, erect glabrous herb with tuberous rhizomes
Foliage: Stalked, leathery dark green ovate leaves to 120 mm long, held stiffly erect. Back of leaf brownish-purple.
Flowers: Terminal raceme of 9–12 brownish-purple flowers, each to 20 mm long. Thread-like green perianth segments to 20 mm long, stiffly spreading with margins rolled in.
Softly hairy labellum to 20 mm long with rounded, shiny black calli, projects forward before sharply curving up, margins rolled inwards. December to April
Requirements: Well drained soils
Comments: Forms small colonies and is slow to re-establish once disturbed. Pollinated by sexually attracted male ichneumonid wasps. Both *Cryptostylis* spp. grow actively over Spring and Summer, retaining leaves all year unless very dry.
Propagation: Division of rhizomes
Localities: Heathmont-Boronia, Dandenong Rges, Lysterfield, 42, 47, 49, 51, 56, 74
Distribution: Vic, Qld, NSW, Tas

Cryptostylis subulata

Large Tongue-orchid

Size: stem 0.3–0.8 m high **P**
Habitat: Moist depressions in valley and damp sclerophyll forests, wattle tea-tree scrub, grassy low open forest
Form: Same as *C. leptochila*
Foliage: 2 or 3 stalked leathery dark to yellow green lanceolate leaves to 15 cm long, held stiffly erect
Flowers: Terminal raceme of 3–20 yellow and reddish-brown flowers to 25 mm long. Green to yellow-green thread-like perianth segments to 30 mm long, margins inrolled.
Labellum oblong to 30 mm long, held rigidly forward, yellowish towards the base, margins rolled up to show the reddish underside; 2 dark purple ridges run along the labellum ending in a 2-lobed callus. August to April
Requirements: Moist soil
Comments: Easy to grow, it may be possible to establish in a bog garden or terrarium.
Propagation: Division of rhizomes
Localities: Heathmont-Boronia, Belgrave, Lysterfield, Noble Park, Springvale, Montrose, 42#, 47, 49, 50A, 51, 54, 56, 63–65#, 67#, 73, 74
Distribution: Vic, Qld, NSW, Tas, SA; NZ

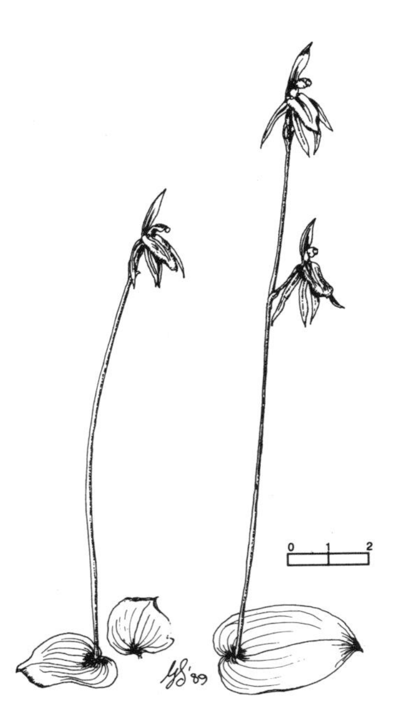
Cyrtostylis reniformis

Cyrtostylis

Cyrtostylis reniformis

Gnat Orchid

Size: stem to 10 cm high **P**
Habitat: Dry sclerophyll forest, tea-tree heath, coastal woodland
Form: Slender erect herb on wiry stem
Foliage: Single roundish ground-hugging grey-green leaf to 40 mm long with whitish veins, crystalline below
Flowers: 1–6 reddish-brown flowers to 10 mm long. Slender glabrous perianth segments to 8 mm long, dorsal sepal erect.
Labellum oblong with a conspicuous longitudinal vein along each edge. May to October
Requirements: Well drained soil
Comments: May form large dense colonies in moist shaded sites but is less prolific on drier forest slopes. Grows well in a pot and is often available through specialist nurseries. Dormant over Summer.
Propagation: Division of tuberoids
Localities: Dandenong Rges, Belgrave, Black Rock, Cheltenham, 32#, 33, 34A, 35, 42#, 49, 51, 67, 74, 76
Distribution: All states except NT; NZ
Synonym: *Acianthus reniformis*

Dipodium

Dipodium roseum

Hyacinth Orchid

Size:	stem 0.3–0.9 m high **P**
Habitat:	Widespread in dry and valley sclerophyll forests, coastal woodland, grassy low open forest
Form:	Erect, leafless saprophytic herb with thick, fleshy purplish-red stem
Flowers:	Long terminal raceme of 6–50 pale pink flowers to 40 mm across, with small pink spots. Reflexed oblong-lanceolate perianth segments to 17 mm long. Labellum erect to 13 mm long, 3-lobed, lateral lobes much shorter, tip of mid-lobe hairy. December to April
Requirements:	Well drained soils, growing in close association with *Eucalyptus* spp.
Comments:	Being saprophytic, it is impossible to cultivate. The fleshy roots were eaten by the Aborigines. Distinguished from *D. punctatum*, which does not occur in Melbourne, by the paler pink flowers, finer spots, and reflexed perianth segments.
Localities:	Montrose-Kilsyth, Belgrave, Heathmont-Boronia, Springvale, 35–37#, 42–44, 47–51, 55–58, 63, 67#, 71, 74, 76
Distribution:	Vic, NSW, Tas, SA
Synonym:	Previously included with *D. punctatum*

Dipodium roseum

Diuris

Glabrous terrestrial orchids growing in colonies. Diuris are readily recognised by their erect, ear-like petals, composed of a blade and a claw, giving them the common name of 'Donkey Orchid'. The lateral sepals are narrow-linear and pendent while the dorsal sepal is erect. The labellum is entire and 3-lobed, the mid-lobe being contracted at the base. The yellow or purple flowers are held in a terminal raceme of 2 or more and are often blotched or spotted with brown. The 2 or more grass-like leaves are in a basal clump. *Diuris* spp. hybridise readily. They increase in number by producing daughter tuberoids as well as by seeds and propagation can take advantage of both methods. Seeds should be sprinkled around the base of the parent plant. Pollination is by native bees. They grow well in pots using a well drained medium, in bush houses or cool glasshouses. Plants are dormant over Summer.

Diuris brevissima

Short-tailed Leopard Orchid

Size:	stem to 35 cm high **F P**
Habitat:	Dry sclerophyll forest, usually in hilly country
Foliage:	2 narrow channelled leaves to 20 cm long
Flowers:	6–9 yellow flowers to 30 mm across, with distinct red-brown blotches. Dorsal sepal ovate; lateral sepals parallel, to 10 mm; petals to 12 mm long, with a short dark brown claw. Labellum bent downwards, lateral lobes spreading. October to November
Requirements:	Well drained soil
Comments:	Similar to *D. pardina* with which it is often confused. However *D. brevissima* is later flowering, has broader lateral lobes on the labellum and broader lateral sepals. The claws of the petals tend to be shorter.
Localities:	42
Distribution:	Vic, NSW, SA

Diuris corymbosa

Wallflower or Donkey Orchid

Size:	stem 10–50 cm high **P**
Habitat:	Dry and valley sclerophyll forests, coastal woodland, grassy low open forest
Form:	Slender erect herb
Foliage:	2–3 deeply channelled linear leaves to 25 cm long
Flowers:	1–8 yellow, brownish-red and purple flowers to 40 mm across, the colours suffusing together. Dorsal sepal very broad and rounded to 10 mm long; narrow, green lateral sepals to 20 mm long, hang parallel; stalked petals to 20 mm long, blade oval. Labellum has broad, spreading or recurved lateral lobes as long as or longer than the mid-lobe, to 12 mm long; mid-lobe notched on the end with a single raised ridge down the centre. July to November
Requirements:	Well drained soils
Comments:	A widespread and variable species in Melbourne, with increased flowering after fire. Some forms have much larger flowers, to 70 mm across. Pure yellow forms are also found.
Localities:	Greensborough, Eltham, Doncaster, Blackburn-Boronia, The Basin, Belgrave, Baxter, 34A, 41, 42, 44, 51, 55, 56, 58, 63, 67, 71, 74–76
Distribution:	Vic, NSW, Tas, SA, WA
Synonym:	Previously confused with *D. longifolia*

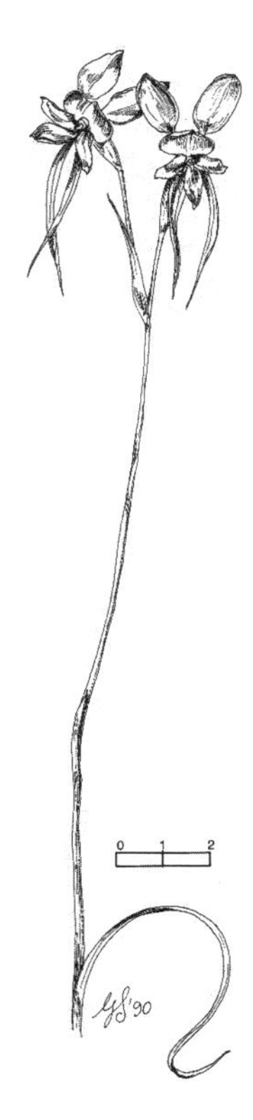

Diuris corymbosa

SCALE: 0 1cm 2cm The scale representation on each plant equals 2cm.

Diuris fragrantissima

Fragrant Doubletail

Size: stem to 0.2 m high **F**
Habitat: Plains grasslands
Comments: Similar to *D. punctata* but shorter and stouter. Leaves paired to 18 cm long. 2–7 highly perfumed white flowers to 50 mm across, with purple suffusions and streaks; October and November.
This orchid was once quite widespread on the Keilor Plains but is now endangered and has not been seen recently at some known sites. It has however been successfully propagated and has been reintroduced into sites where it would have previously occurred.
Localities: Tottenham[#], St. Albans, Sydenham[#], Williamstown[#], Sunshine, Laverton, Keilor[#]
Distribution: Endemic to Vic
Synonym: *D. punctata* var. *albo-violacea*

Diuris fragrantissima

Diuris lanceolata

Golden Moths, Snake-orchid

Size: stem 10–30 cm high **F P**
Habitat: Moist depressions in plains grasslands, red gum and sclerophyll woodland, dry and valley sclerophyll forests, tea-tree heath
Foliage: 3–6 linear leaves to 15 cm long
Flowers: 1–5 nodding, bright yellow flowers to 25 mm across. Broadly ovate dorsal sepal to 15 mm long; narrow channelled lateral sepals to 25 mm long, spreading below the labellum; petals shorter, spreading to the side. Mid-lobe of labellum broadly ovate to 20 mm long with 2 fleshy ridges, lateral lobes to 5 mm long, spreading, ends toothed. September to October
Requirements: Moist soils
Comments: Plants of dwarf populations on the plains west of Melbourne have deep orange labellums.
Localities: Sunbury, Essendon, Tottenham, St. Albans, Laverton, Camberwell-Mitcham, Scoresby, Belgrave-Rowville, Lyndhurst, Black Rock, 29, 33, 34A, 35, 38, 41, 42, 58, 63, 67, 74
Distribution: Vic, NSW, Tas, SA
Synonym: Was previously known as *D. pedunculata*, a species which only occurs in NSW.

Diuris x fastidiosa

Proud Doubletail

Size: stem to 20 cm high **F P**
Habitat: Moist grasslands
Foliage: Loose tussock of 7–8 grass-like, slightly twisted leaves to 100 mm long
Flowers: Similar to *D. lanceolata* but paler, smaller and not nodding, with darker striations on the outer edges and brown stripes at the base of the dorsal sepal. Dorsal sepals and petals are nerved; lateral sepals obliquely erect. Labellum has brown markings on outside. August to September
Comments: A naturally occurring hybrid between *D. palustris* and *D. lanceolata* with intermediate characteristics. The only known site in Melbourne has been destroyed. It also occurs in Stawell.
Localities: Tottenham[#]
Distribution: Endemic to Vic

Diuris lanceolata x pardina

Comments: A naturally occurring hybrid found in the dry sclerophyll forests of north east Melbourne. Intermediate between and found with both parents.
Localities: Heidelberg, Eltham, Templestowe, Warrandyte
Distribution: Endemic to Vic
Synonym: Previously confused with *D.* x *palachila* which does not occur in Melbourne.

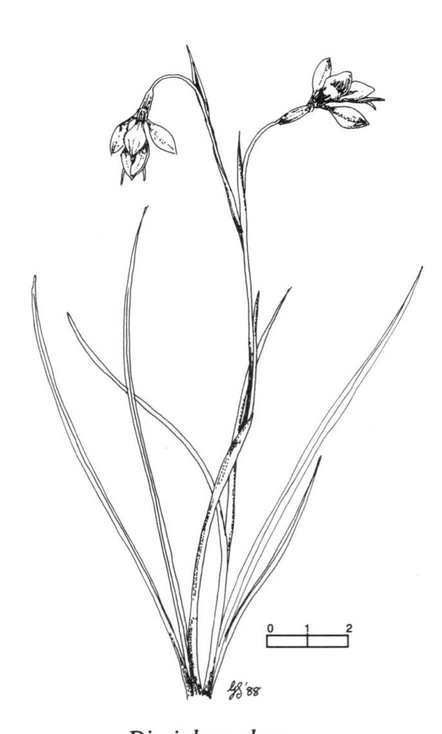

Diuris lanceolata

Diuris palustris

Swamp diuris

Size: stem 10–25 cm high **F P**
Habitat: Wet depressions in plains grassland, tea-tree heath
Foliage: Tuft of 8–10 channelled, narrow spirally-twisted leaves to 80 mm long
Flowers: 1–4 yellow flowers to 20 mm across, blotched with brown, especially on the outside. Dorsal sepal ovate to 8 mm long, recurved; lateral sepals green, parallel, to 16 mm long; petals to 10 mm long have a dark brown vertical stripe.
Labellum lobes similar in length with 2 thick, fleshy raised lines from the base to the middle of the mid-lobe, merging into one towards the tip. July to December
Requirements: Moist to wet soils
Comments: The flowers release a spicy perfume on warm days. This species is slow to establish in cultivation.
Localities: Laverton[#], Tottenham, Keilor Plains, St. Albans, 67[#]
Distribution: Vic, Tas, SA

Diuris pardina

Leopard Orchid

Size: stem 20–30 cm high **P**
Habitat: Dry and valley sclerophyll forests, tea-tree heath, grassy low open forest
Foliage: 2–3 narrow channelled leaves to 20 cm long
Flowers: 2–6 yellow flowers to 30 mm across, distinctly and heavily blotched with brown. Dorsal sepal ovate; green lateral sepals to 12 mm long, recurved and crossing each other; petals to 15 mm long, covered in dark brown blotches.
Lateral lobes of labellum as long as the mid-lobe. August to November
Requirements: Well drained soils
Comments: Confused with *D. maculata* which is not as heavily blotched and flowers earlier than *D. pardina*.
Localities: Greensborough-Eltham, Park Orchards, Blackburn-Boronia, Belgrave, Springvale, 34A, 35, 37, 41, 42, 44, 51, 58, 67#, 71, 74
Distribution: Vic, Tas, SA
Synonym: Previously confused with *D. maculata*, an orchid endemic to NSW.

Diuris punctata

Purple Diuris

Size: stem 20–60 cm high **F P**
Habitat: Moist areas in box, red gum and sclerophyll woodlands, grassy low open forest
Foliage: Pair of grass-like channelled leaves to 15 cm long
Flowers: 2–10 large purple flowers to 50 mm across. Broadly ovate dorsal sepal to 15 mm long; lateral sepals brownish or green, thread-like 40–80 mm long; petals elliptic to 30 mm long.
Mid-lobe of labellum fan-shaped to 20 mm long, with prominent yellow central blotch and 2 raised yellow ridges, lateral lobes much smaller and lobed to the base. October to November
Requirements: Moist soils
Comments: A very showy orchid which is now restricted to a few plants in the Melbourne area.
Localities: Werribee, Bundoora, Mentone, Hampton#, Mt. Eliza, Cranbourne, 26, 49, 50A#, 74
Distribution: Vic, Qld, NSW, SA

Diuris sulphurea

Tiger Orchid

Size: stem to 40 cm high **P**
Habitat: Red gum, box and coastal woodland, around swamp margins in valley and dry sclerophyll forests, tea-tree heath
Foliage: 1–3 channelled grass-like leaves to 35 cm long
Flowers: 2–7 yellow flowers to 30 mm across, with brown markings. Ovate dorsal sepal to 20 mm long has 2 dark brown to blackish spots near the base; lateral sepals to 22 mm long; petals, to 30 mm long, ovate on short stalks.
Lateral lobes of labellum short, to 5 mm long, wide and blunt, mid-lobe spade-shaped with a single raised ridge extending to the middle. October to December
Requirements: Moist well drained soils
Comments: Often growing in association with *Eucalyptus baxteri*. Rare hybrids with *D. corymbosa* have been found in the Dandenong Rges.
Localities: Tullamarine, Bundoora, Nunawading-Boronia, Lysterfield, Springvale, 26, 42, 44, 51, 55, 56, 58, 67, 74
Distribution: Vic, Qld, NSW, Tas, SA

Eriochilus

Eriochilus cucullatus

Parson's Bands

Size: stem 8–25 cm high **F P**
Habitat: Widespread in red gum and sclerophyll woodlands, dry and valley sclerophyll forests, grassy low open forest
Form: Glabrous erect herb with thin wiry stem
Foliage: Shiny dark green, ovate basal leaf to 35 mm long, becoming fully developed after flowering finishes
Flowers: 1–5 white, or sometimes pink, flowers to 20 mm across. Perianth segments to 15 mm long; greenish dorsal sepal erect to 8 mm long, hooded; lateral sepals spreading, elliptical-lanceolate, petals erect, narrower and shorter.
Labellum cream or yellowish with dark spots, upper half recurved and covered in stiff hairs. December to May
Requirements: Dry to moist well drained soils
Comments: Dormant over Summer. May be successful in a container provided it is left undisturbed.
Propagation: Seed, scattered around established plants.
Localities: Basalt plains, Bundoora, Heathmont-Boronia, Kalorama, Belgrave, Baxter, 42, 45#, 50A, 51, 56, 61, 67#, 71, 74–76
Distribution: Vic, Qld, NSW, Tas, SA

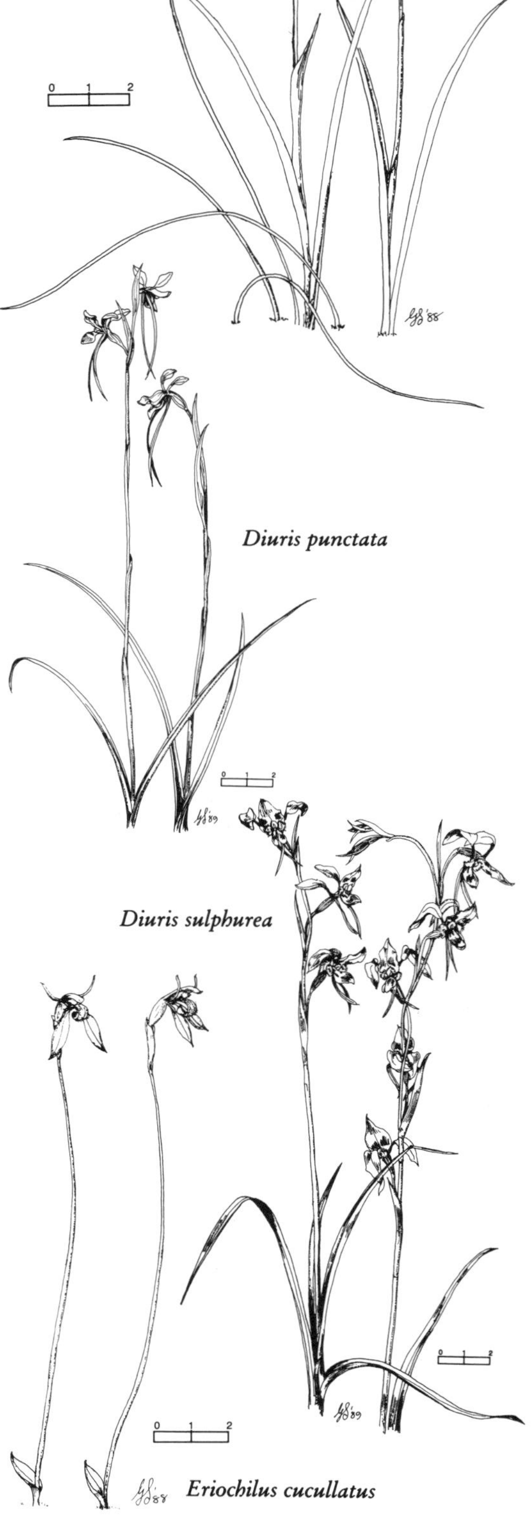

Diuris pardina

Diuris punctata

Diuris sulphurea

Eriochilus cucullatus

SCALE: 0 1cm 2cm
The scale representation on each plant equals 2cm.

Gastrodia

Gastrodia sesamoides

Gastrodia procera

Size: stem 0.7 m to over 1 m high **P N**
Habitat: Damp sclerophyll forest
Form: Tall leafless saprophytic herb with erect fleshy brown stem
Flowers: Terminal raceme of up to 75 tubular flowers to more than 20 mm long, cinnamon brown on outside, creamy inside.
Callus plate on upper part of labellum quite elevated, dividing into 2 widely spaced ridges from the middle. Fruits are larger and paler brown than *G. sesamoides*. November to January
Requirements: Moist soils with high organic content and high rainfall
Comments: Similar to *G. sesamoides*. Both species may occur together usually growing close by Eucalypt species. *G. procera* has a strong, sweet perfume, is more floriferous, with larger, darker flowers, and prefers moister habitats. Both are pollinated by native bees. Aborigines roasted and ate the tubers.
Propagation: Impossible
Localities: Dandenong Ranges, Olinda
Distribution: Vic, Qld, NSW, Tas
Synonym: Previously included with *G. sesamoides*

Gastrodia sesamoides

Potato Orchid, Cinnamon Bells

Size: stem 0.3–0.8 m high **P**
Habitat: Widespread in damp and valley sclerophyll forests, grassy low open forests
Form: Leafless erect saprophytic herb with a fleshy brown stem, nodding before flowering
Flowers: Terminal raceme of up to 25 drooping, tubular flowers to 20 mm long, rough and light grey-brown on outside, creamy inside.
Labellum yellowish-orange, calli plate less elevated than *G. procera* with dividing ridges closer together. October to December
Requirements: Moist humus-rich soils, in high rainfall areas
Comments: Flowers emit a sweet perfume on warm days.
Localities: Eltham, Heathmont-Kalorama, Belgrave, 42, 50A, 51, 55–58, 61, 63, 74
Distribution: Vic, Qld, NSW, Tas, SA; NZ

Genoplesium

Genoplesiums are terrestrial orchids with few to many very small dull-coloured flowers in short dense terminal spikes. Each flower is reversed with the labellum uppermost and hinged on a small claw. Flowering occurs during Summer and Autumn. Each orchid has a single, erect terete leaf which clasps the stem for most of its length. Pollination is by tiny flies. While propagation is by seed they are very difficult to grow in cultivation. *Genoplesium* spp. have been separated from *Prasophyllum* spp., which differ in details of the labellum and column.

Genoplesium despectans

Genoplesium archeri

Variable Midge-orchid

Size: stem 10–20 cm high **P**
Habitat: Valley sclerophyll forest, primary dune scrub, grassy low open forest
Foliage: Leaf 15 cm long, the top 25 mm free of the stem
Flowers: Squat spike of 2–15 pale yellowish-green or purplish flowers to 10 mm across, with reddish stripes and markings. Dorsal sepal hooded, ovate; lateral sepals and petals spreading, to 7 mm long.
Tiny dark purple labellum has hairy margins, 2 parallel ridges and upturned tip. December to June
Requirements: Well drained soils
Comments: Uncommon, it remains in few sites in Melbourne.
Localities: Bayswater, Dandenong Ranges, Belgrave, Lysterfield, 67#, 74
Distribution: Vic, Qld, NSW, Tas
Synonym: *Prasophyllum archeri*

Genoplesium despectans

Sharp Midge-orchid

Size: stem to 40 cm high **P**
Habitat: Dry and valley sclerophyll forests, grassy low open forest
Foliage: Leaf to 25 cm long, free for 15 mm
Flowers: Dense pyramidal spike of 1–45 tiny, glabrous, nodding, dark purplish-brown or green flowers with purple markings, to 3 mm across. Dorsal sepal is hooded; lateral sepals and petals very pointed.
Labellum also sharply pointed; January to June
Requirements: Well drained clay loam soils
Comments: Often found with *Eucalyptus baxteri*.
Localities: Eltham, Heathmont-Boronia, Belgrave, Lysterfield, 34A, 41, 42, 44, 51, 71, 74
Distribution: Vic, NSW, Tas, SA
Synonym: *Prasophyllum despectans*

Genoplesium morrisii

Bearded Midge-orchid

Size: stem to 30 cm high **P**
Habitat: Valley sclerophyll forest, grassy low open forest, on heavier soil
Foliage: Leaf to 30 cm long, free for 20 mm
Flowers: Dense spike of 3–25 dark purple or greenish flowers to 8 mm across with purple and reddish markings. Hooded dorsal sepal, petals and labellum fringed with long dark purple hairs. Lateral sepals glabrous, spreading, to 6 mm long. December to May
Requirements: Damp clay soils
Comments: Readily recognised by the fringed labellum.
Localities: Montrose, Belgrave, Eastern Bayside Suburbs#, 56, 74
Distribution: Vic, Tas
Synonym: *Prasophyllum morrisii*

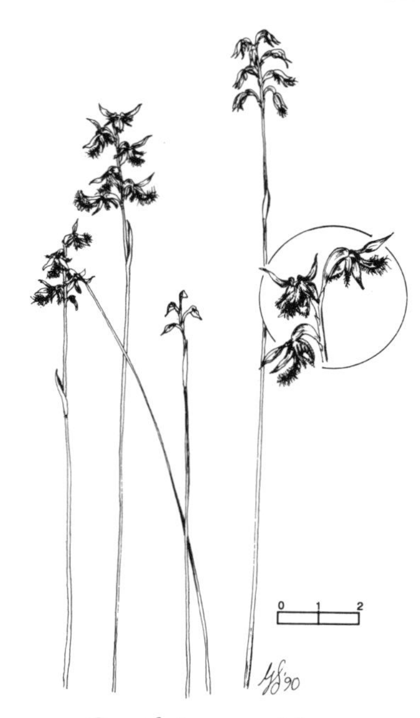
Genoplesium morrisii

Genoplesium rufum

Red Midge-orchid

Size: stem to 15 cm high **F P**
Habitat: Tea-tree heath, red gum woodland
Foliage: Leaf to 15 cm long, mostly sheathing
Flowers: Open spike of 3–20 tiny black to dark greenish flowers. Deeply hooded dorsal sepal; lateral sepals spreading, broad-lanceolate and often gland-tipped, petals toothed.
Labellum margins toothed, callus plate raised, very dark. Column is winged and lightly coloured. January to May
Requirements: Moist, well drained sandy soil
Localities: Noble Park, Sth Oakleigh, 67#
Distribution: Vic, Qld, NSW, Tas, SA
Synonym: *Prasophyllum rufum*

Glossodia

Glossodia major

Wax-lip Orchid

Size: stem to 30 cm high **F P**
Habitat: Widespread in box ironbark woodland, dry and valley sclerophyll forests, coastal woodland, tea-tree heath
Form: Erect, slender hairy herb
Foliage: Single, hairy, dark green oblong to oblanceolate leaf to 100 mm long
Flowers: 1–2 large purple to mauve flowers to 45 mm across, with a prominent white base on labellum. Perianth segments glabrous, broad, spreading, to 25 mm long.
Labellum cordate, hairy at the base. Notched, erect yellow basal calli. September to November
Requirements: Well drained soils
Comments: Plants usually occur singly or in scattered groups, but are much more abundant after fire. On warm days flowers exude a sweet perfume. They are difficult to cultivate, usually persisting only for a short while. All-white variants are found occasionally. Pollinated by native bees.
Localities: Eltham, Belgrave-Rowville, 34A, 36, 41, 42, 44, 47–51, 55, 56, 58, 61, 64, 67, 74, 76
Distribution: Vic, Qld, NSW, Tas, SA

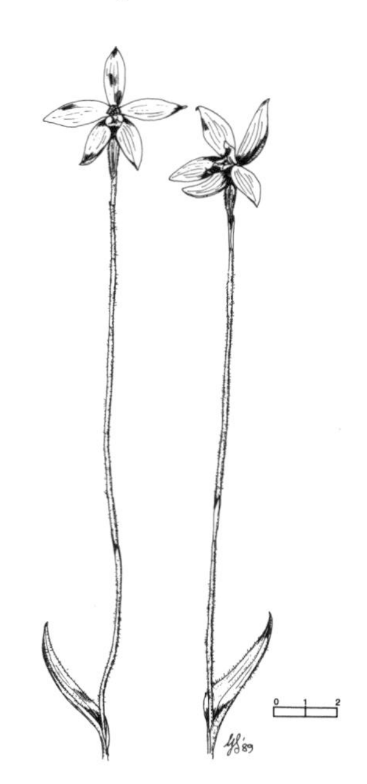
Glossodia major

Leporella

Leporella fimbriata

Fringed Hare-orchid

Size: stem to 25 cm high **F P**
Habitat: Tea-tree heath, grassy low open forest
Form: Slender erect glabrous herb
Foliage: 1, sometimes 2, bluish-green to yellowish-green, sessile, basal, broadly-lanceolate leaves to 30 mm long, developing 3–5 prominent parallel red veins after flowering.
Flowers: 1–3 reddish and yellow-brown flowers to 15 mm across. Perianth segments spreading; dorsal sepal wide, erect, to 10 mm long; lateral sepals very narrow, petals longer, erect, clubbed tips covered in black glandular hairs.
Labellum fan-shaped, greenish with hairy purple spots, recurved with deeply and coarsely fringed margins. March to August
Requirements: Well drained sandy soil
Comments: Once formed extensive colonies, especially prominent after fire. Pollinated by sexually attracted winged male ants. Difficult to maintain in cultivation. As it has not been collected recently it is presumed extinct within the Melbourne area.
Localities: Cheltenham#, Black Rock#, Beaumaris#, 67#, 74
Distribution: Vic, Tas, SA, WA
Synonym: *Leptoceras fimbriatum*

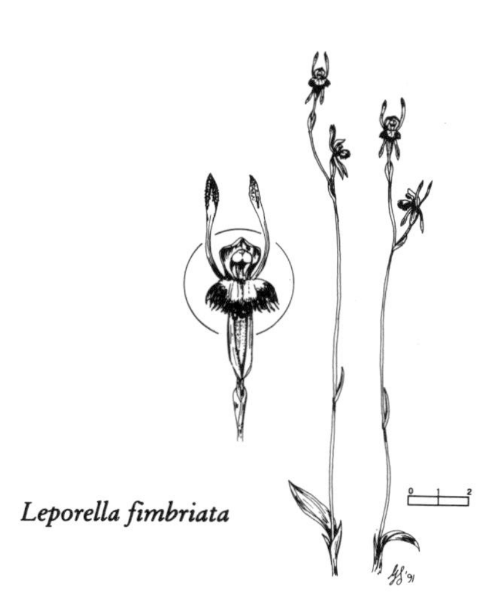
Leporella fimbriata

Leptoceras menziesii = Caladenia menziesii

SCALE: 0 1cm 2cm The scale representation on each plant equals 2cm.

Lyperanthus nigricans

Lyperanthus suaveolens

Lyperanthus

Lyperanthus nigricans

Red Beaks

Size: stem to 25 cm high **P**
Habitat: Coastal banksia woodland, tea-tree heath, grassy low open forest
Form: Erect fleshy herb with leaf-like stem bracts to 40 mm long
Foliage: Bright green cordate basal leaf, variable to 90 mm long, often with red or black markings, ground-hugging
Flowers: 2–8 large lightly perfumed flowers to 40 mm across, white with red stripes, each with a large floral bract. Perianth segments curved forward, to 35 mm long, spreading, red-tipped; dorsal sepal hooded, curved over column.
Labellum white with crimson lines, erect, deeply fringed. August to November
Requirements: Well drained soils
Comments: Flowers freely after fires but difficult to maintain in cultivation.
Propagation: Division of tuberoids
Localities: Springvale, Cheltenham#, Sandringham, Black Rock, Beaumaris, 74
Distribution: Vic, NSW, Tas, SA, WA

Lyperanthus suaveolens

Brown Beaks

Size: stem to 45 cm high **P**
Habitat: Dry and valley sclerophyll forests, tea-tree heath
Foliage: Stiff leathery dark green linear-lanceolate leaf to 20 cm long
Flowers: 2–8 yellowish-brown flowers to 30 mm across. Perianth segments narrow, stiff and leathery, to 30 mm long, spreading with margins curved downwards; petals erect.
Bright yellow labellum is curved and 3-lobed. August to November
Requirements: Well drained soils
Comments: Flowers are fragrant in warm weather. Plants display considerable variety in flower colour, from greenish, yellow-brown to dark brown or black. Grows and flowers well in a container. Locally very rare.
Propagation: Division of tuberoids
Localities: Nunawading-Bayswater, Kilsyth, Belgrave, 34A, 42, 44, 51, 58, 67#, 74
Distributin: Vic, Qld, NSW, Tas

Microtis

Slender glabrous terrestrial orchids which die back to their tuberoids over Summer and Autumn. A single, erect, terete, hollow leaf sheathes the stem. Tiny green flowers, in dense or open spikes, are on the end of larger ovaries. Each has a broad, erect, hooded dorsal sepal. Lateral sepals and petals are much narrower. Flowers are self-pollinated if not visited by insects. Propagation is by division of tuberoids. Easily overlooked in the bush due to their colour and size.

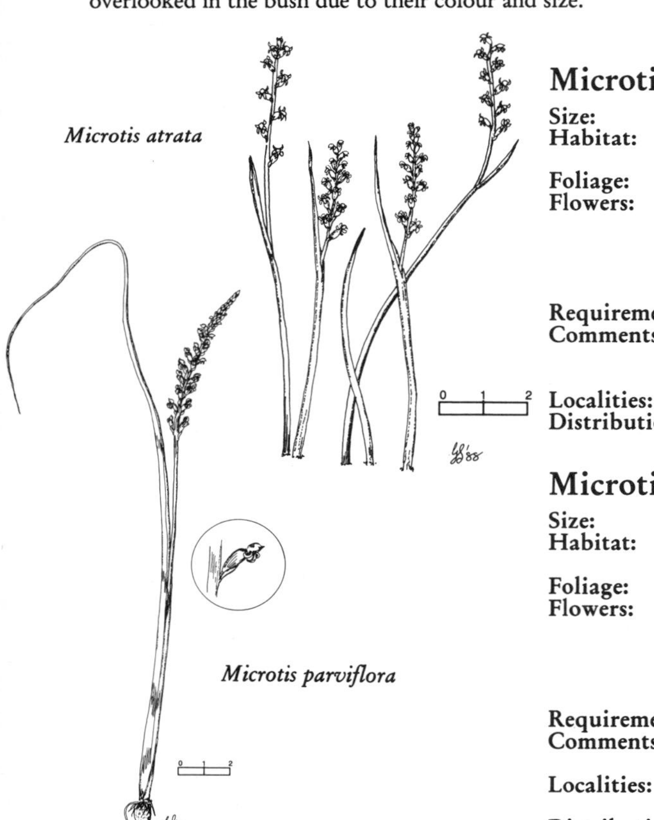
Microtis atrata

Microtis parviflora

Microtis atrata

Yellow or Tiny Onion-orchid

Size: stem 5–15 cm high **P N**
Habitat: Low-lying depressions and swamps of valley sclerophyll forest, tea-tree heath, grassy low open forest
Foliage: Leaf to 90 mm long, often yellow-green
Flowers: Dense spike of 2–40 minute semi-erect flowers less than 2 mm wide. Lateral sepals spreading, oblong and blunt-tipped, and not hidden by labellum.
Labellum—ovate and entire, bent sharply downwards, with no calli. September to December
Requirements: Boggy soils
Comments: The whole plant is yellowish-green drying to black with age. It forms dense colonies and is easy to cultivate tolerating inundation for some time. Locally rare.
Localities: Belgrave, 42, 47, 49, 50A, 67#, 74
Distribution: Vic, Tas, SA, WA

Microtis parviflora

Slender Onion-orchid

Size: stem to 0.5 m high **F P**
Habitat: Widespread in moist areas of dry and valley sclerophyll forests, grassy low open forest, tea-tree heath
Foliage: Leaf to 40 cm long
Flowers: Dense spike of 10–80 tiny erect flowers to 3 mm wide. Flowers similar to *M. rara*. Lateral sepals not as tightly curved back.
Labellum shorter, cordate, not pressed against the ovary, margins entire or wavy with a small recurved tip. 2 calli at the base. October to February
Requirements: Moist soils in Winter
Comments: A common orchid colonising lawns and disturbed areas, forming large colonies.
Localities: Bundoora-Warrandyte, Nunawading-Dandenong Rges, Belgrave, 63, 67, 74–76
Distribution: All states except NT; NZ, N Cal

Microtis rara

Scented Onion-orchid

Size: stem to 0.6 m high **F P N**
Habitat: Beside permanent swamps in areas of high rainfall and valley sclerophyll forest
Foliage: Leaf to 60 cm long
Flowers: Spike of 5–50 well-spaced fragrant flowers to 4 mm wide. Dorsal sepal only narrowly hooded; lateral sepals linear-oblong, spreading, curved backwards; petals erect.
Labellum oblong, pressed closely to and about the same length as the ovary, margin wavy and tip notched; 2 large dark green calli at the base and 1 at the tip. October to January
Requirements: Moist soils
Comments: Forms small clumps, flowering more freely after fires which may produce robust plants over 1 m high. Plants prefer sunny sites protected by grasses. A rare plant, first collected in Ringwood in 1920.
Localities: Mitcham-The Basin, Belgrave, 58, 74
Distribution: Vic, NSW, Tas, SA
Synonym: *M. oblonga*

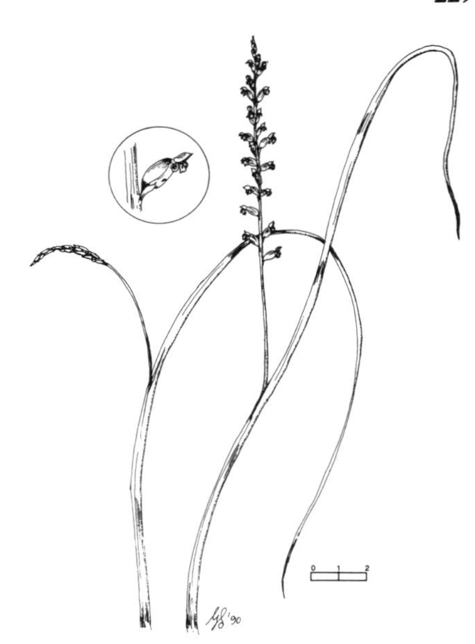

Microtis unifolia

Microtis unifolia

Common Onion-orchid

Size: stem 15–80 cm high **F P**
Habitat: Widespread, favouring swamps in heaths, dry and valley sclerophyll forests from coast to foothills, but also colonising drier soils throughout its range; grassy wetland, red gum woodland
Foliage: Leaf to 70 cm long
Flowers: Dense spike of 6–100 pale to golden-green erect flowers to 4 mm wide. Dorsal sepal is deeply hooded, partly hiding petals.
Labellum less than ½ as long as ovary with wrinkled margins, 2-lobed; 2 basal calli and a narrow central callus band. October to January
Requirements: Well drained to moist situations
Comments: May form extensive colonies.
Localities: Throughout the Greater Melbourne area
Distribution: All states except NT; countries of western Pacific

Orthoceras

Orthoceras strictum

Horned or Crow Orchid

Size: stem 25–60 cm high **F P**
Habitat: Swamp edges in valley sclerophyll forest, wattle tea-tree scrub, grassy low open forest
Form: Glabrous herb with a rigid stem
Foliage: Erect clump of 2–5 channelled, linear leaves to 30 cm long
Flowers: 2–9 green to dark brown flowers to 10 mm across. Dorsal sepal to 10 mm long, hooded and pointed at tip, hiding small petals; lateral sepals almost terete, erect and spreading on each side of hood, to 25 mm long.
Labellum 3-lobed, lateral lobes erect, mid-lobe elliptical with central yellow spot, curved downwards, large yellow callus at base. November to January
Requirements: Moist to wet soils
Comments: Plants are easily overlooked in grassy habitats, but are locally common.
Propagation: Not cultivated
Localities: Dandenong Rges, Belgrave, Lysterfield, Port Phillip, Cheltenham#, 47, 49, 67#, 74
Distribution: Vic, Qld, NSW, Tas, SA; NZ, N Cal

Orthoceras strictum

Prasophyllum

Terrestrial orchids with a single, erect, terete basal leaf which is stem-clasping only up to two thirds of its length. Prasophyllums have a spike of many small to medium, dull-coloured, reversed flowers in which the labellum is uppermost and usually a different colour to the perianth segments. The labellum is immovable and has a central callus which can occupy most of the surface. Margins are often crisped or wavy.

Prasophyllum spp. flower in Spring and Summer and are often strongly perfumed. They are pollinated by nectar-seeking wasps. Propagation is by seed, but all are difficult to grow. Autumn flowering species with movable labella and almost fully stem-clasping leaves are now called *Genoplesium* spp.

Prasophyllum affine = P. fuscum

Prasophyllum archeri = Genoplesium archeri

SCALE: 0 1cm 2cm The scale representation on each plant equals 2cm.

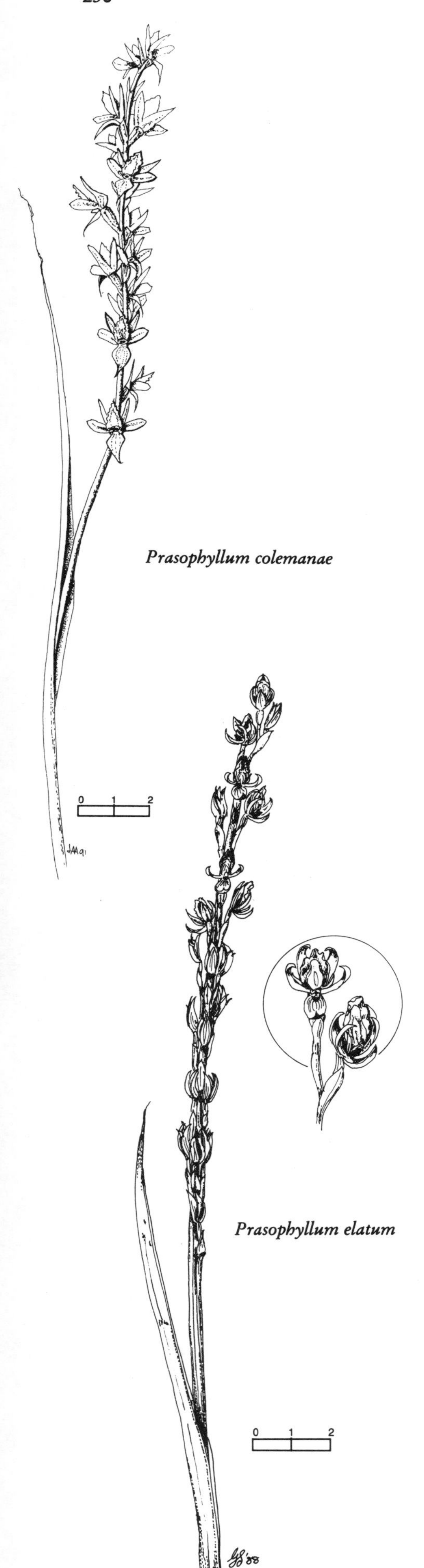

Prasophyllum colemanae

Prasophyllum elatum

Prasophyllum australe

Austral Leek-orchid

Size: stem to 0.75 m high **P**
Habitat: Damp and valley sclerophyll forests
Foliage: Slender to stout, erect leaf to 35 cm long, free for 30 cm of its length, reddish at base
Flowers: Dense spike of 15–60 sweetly perfumed flowers to 15 mm across, white with reddish-brown and greenish stripes on long slender ovaries, appressed against the stem. Perianth segments lanceolate, sharply pointed, to 8 mm long; lateral sepals usually united almost to the tip.
Labellum is white with curly margins and a swollen base, sharply recurved from the middle with a callus ridge ending at the bend with 2 raised lumps. September to January
Requirements: Moist to wet soils
Comments: Grows in colonies amongst grasses and sedges.
Localities: Bayswater, Scoresby, Lysterfield, 42, 58
Distribution: Vic, Qld, NSW, Tas, SA

Prasophyllum brevilabre

Short-lip Leek-orchid

Size: stem to 50 cm high **P**
Habitat: Damp and valley sclerophyll forests
Foliage: Slender, fleshy leaf to 35 cm long, often reddish at base
Flowers: Loose spike of 8–30 green flowers to 10 mm across with dark red to dark purplish-green markings. Perianth segments to 8 mm long, lateral sepals usually joined throughout.
White labellum curves sharply back on itself from the middle with green callus extending just beyond the bend, margins curly. August to January
Requirements: Moist soil
Comments: The ovaries in this and most other species stand out from the stem and are swollen, unlike *P. australe* and *P. elatum* which are pressed against the stem.
Localities: Nth Warrandyte, Bayswater, 55, 58
Distribution: Vic, Qld, NSW, Tas

Prasophyllum colemanae

Size: stem 0.25–0.9 m high **P**
Habitat: Valley sclerophyll forest
Comments: Very similar to *P. odoratum* but more robust with leaf often longer than the flowering stem. The lavender flowers are smaller, to 10 mm across, with up to 20 per spike. The dorsal sepal is greenish and petals have a narrow green central stripe. The labellum is flat and only slightly flexed. Last collected in 1922 in Bayswater.
Localities: Heathmont-Bayswater
Distribution: Endemic to Vic
Synonym: Previously included with *P. odoratum*

Prasophyllum despectans = Genoplesium despectans

Prasophyllum elatum

Tall Leek-orchid

Size: stem 0.6–1.2 m high **F P**
Habitat: Damp sclerophyll forest, wattle tea-tree scrub, moist tea-tree heath
Form: Robust herb varying from pale green to dark purple
Foliage: Thick fleshy leaf to 1 m long
Flowers: Dense spike of 15–60 relatively large, lightly perfumed yellow-green to brown or purple flowers to 15 mm across. Flowers and ovaries similar to *P. australe*. Perianth segments longer, to 10 mm long, and often curved, tips moderately pointed.
White labellum has a green callus ridge almost to the tip. It is slightly recurved and base is not swollen, margins are wavy. August to December
Requirements: Moist, well drained soils
Comments: A variable species which flowers well after fire. One of the tallest orchids in Melbourne.
Localities: Belgrave, Lysterfield, Beaumaris#, Cheltenham#, 67#, 74
Distribution: All states except NT

Prasophyllum flavum

Yellow Leek-orchid

Size: stem to 0.9 m high **P N**
Habitat: Wet sclerophyll forest
Foliage: Closely sheathing purplish leaf to 60 cm long, sometimes yellow at the base
Flowers: Crowded spike of 6–50 yellow to yellowish-green flowers to 10 mm across, sometimes with reddish-brown markings. Perianth segments to 10 mm long, lateral sepals usually fully united.
Labellum green with white or cream wavy margins, gently recurved; callus extending halfway. October to February
Requirements: Moist humus-rich soils
Comments: Saprophytic herb growing in dense undergrowth.
Localities: Sherbrooke, Olinda
Distribution: Vic, Qld, NSW, Tas

Prasophyllum frenchii

Maroon or Slaty Leek-orchid

Size: stem 30–60 cm high **F P**
Habitat: Valley sclerophyll forest, tea-tree heaths, wattle tea-tree scrub
Foliage: Slender to stout leaf to 50 cm long, free part withering at flowering time
Flowers: Dense spike of 30–60 flowers to 8 mm across, grey-brown or green with red markings. Perianth segments to 10 mm long, tips bent backwards; lateral sepals free.
Labellum broad and fleshy in basal section, tip erect and pointed, margins whitish and slightly wavy. Low broad callus with thickened margins, extends to bend. October to December
Requirements: Moist, well drained soils
Comments: Known from few Melbourne sites. Also rare throughout Victoria.
Localities: Bayswater#, Dandenong Rges, Mt. Eliza, 35, 51, 67#
Distribution: Vic, SA
Synonym: *P. hartii*

Prasophyllum fuscum

Tailed or Tawny Leek-orchid

Size: stem 25–45 cm high **F P**
Habitat: Moist grasslands of basalt plains, damp sclerophyll forest, wattle tea-tree scrub
Foliage: Slender to stout leaf as long as the flowering spike, free part often withering at flowering time
Flowers: Loose to dense spike of 10–30 perfumed green, greenish-brown or purplish flowers, to 7 mm across. Perianth segments to 8 mm long, lateral sepals joined in the basal half, becoming free with maturity, margins curved inwards.
Labellum erect from above the middle or near the tip, margins flat or wrinkled; callus narrow, raised, extending almost to the tip. September to November
Requirements: Moist soils
Comments: A widespread orchid, becoming increasingly restricted throughout Victoria. Flowers well after fire.
Localities: Keilor Plains, St. Albans, Belgrave, 67#
Distribution: Vic, NSW, Tas, SA
Synonym: Confused with *P. affine*

Prasophyllum lindleyanum

Green Leek-orchid

Size: stem to 35 cm high **P**
Habitat: Damp and valley sclerophyll forests, grassy low open forest
Foliage: Slender yellowish-green leaf to 35 cm long, free part usually withering at flowering time
Flowers: Loose slender spike of 12–50 yellowish-green flowers, to 7 mm across. Perianth segments to 8 mm long, curved back; lateral sepals spreading, free with margins inrolled.
White or pink s-shaped labellum with curly, hairy margins; narrow green callus ridge extending towards the tip. September to January
Requirements: Well drained soils
Comments: Vulnerable in Victoria. Flowers have a strong, sweet fragrance.
Localities: Mitcham-Bayswater, Dandenong Ranges, Belgrave, Black Rock, Cheltenham
Distribution: Vic, Tas
Synonym: *P. brainei*

Prasophyllum morrisii = Genoplesium morrisii

Prasophyllum odoratum

Scented or Sweet Leek-orchid

Size: stem to 0.9 m high **P**
Habitat: Damp and valley sclerophyll forests
Foliage: Slender or stout leaf to 70 cm long
Flowers: Spike of 10–40 perfumed green and white flowers to 15 mm across, sometimes with reddish stripes. Perianth segments to 12 mm long, pointed; lateral sepals free, widely spreading.
White labellum sharply curved back below the middle, tip passing through the lateral sepals, margins wavy; green callus extends just beyond the bend. August to February
Requirements: Moist, well drained soils
Comments: One of the most widespread *Prasophyllum* spp., prominent after fires.
Localities: Knox, Ringwood-Belgrave, Ferny Ck, 55, 56, 58
Distribution: Vic, Qld, NSW, Tas

Illustrated overleaf

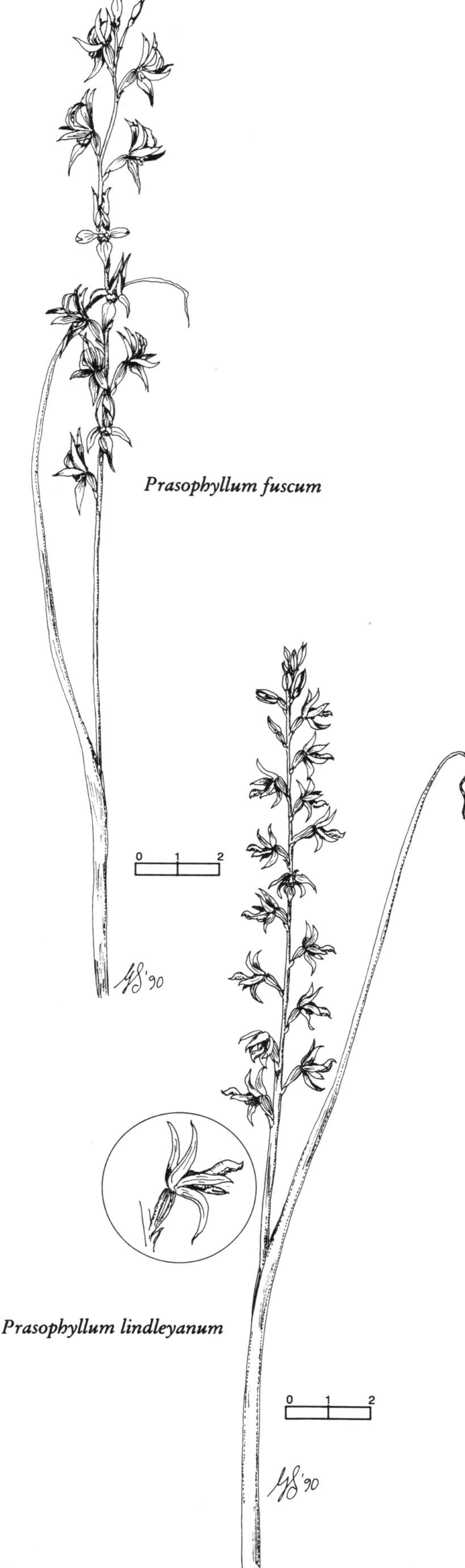

Prasophyllum fuscum

Prasophyllum lindleyanum

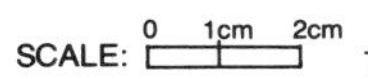

The scale representation on each plant equals 2cm.

Prasophyllum odoratum

Prasophyllum patens

Broad-lip Leek-orchid

Size:	stem 25–45 cm high **F P**
Habitat:	Primary dune scrub, tea-tree heath
Foliage:	Slender leaf to 30 cm long, free part often withering at flowering time
Flowers:	Loose or dense spike of 15–50 pinkish-green flowers, to 12 mm across. Perianth segments spreading, to 8 mm long, dorsal sepal ovate-lanceolate; lateral sepals lanceolate, free; petals narrower. White or pink labellum ovate-lanceolate with wavy margins, curved backwards; green callus ridge extends just beyond the bend, edges not thickened. September to December
Requirements:	Well drained sandy soil
Comments:	Rare in Victoria, it may already be extinct in Melbourne.
Localities:	Sandringham#
Distribution:	Vic, Qld, NSW, Tas, SA; NZ
Synonym:	Was confused with *P. truncatum* which is endemic to Tas.

Prasophyllum pyriforme

Graceful Leek-orchid

Size:	stem to 0.5 m high **P**
Habitat:	Valley sclerophyll forest
Foliage:	Slender leaf to 30 cm long, free part often wilting at flowering time
Flowers:	Dense spike of 15–40 fragrant yellowish-green, brownish or purplish flowers, to 12 mm across. Perianth segments to 15 mm long, lateral sepals free or joined in the basal third. White, pink or purplish labellum with wavy margins, upper half erect, fleshy green callus raised and extending almost to the tip. September to January
Requirements:	Well drained soil
Comments:	The original specimen was collected in Wonga Park. Plants favour lightly timbered sites, growing among grass tussocks.
Localities:	Doncaster, Wonga Park, Belgrave, 51, 58
Distribution:	Endemic to Vic
Synonym:	Previously known as *P.* sp. aff. *rostratum*. Wrongly named *P. gracile*.

Prasophyllum rufum = Genoplesium rufum

Prasophyllum spicatum

Size:	stem to 25 cm high **P**
Habitat:	Tea-tree heath
Comments:	Similar to *P. odoratum*. A very robust orchid with many green and white flowers in a dense spike to 15 cm long.
Localities:	Cranbourne, 74
Distribution:	Endemic to Vic
Synonym:	*P. odoratum* var. *album*

Pterostylis

A well represented genus of terrestrial orchids in Melbourne, common in cool moist forests, with a few species occurring on the basalt plains. Most *Pterostylis* spp. are glabrous and have a basal rosette of leaves which may either encircle the flower stem or appear to one side. The rosette may only be present in non-flowering plants. In those species where the rosette is absent from flowering plants, the leaves are scattered up the stem.

Pterostylis spp. are commonly known as Greenhoods because flowers are generally green, sometimes with brown or reddish tinges, and the dorsal sepal and petals are united into a hooded structure called the galea, which encloses the winged column. The galea is usually erect for about ¾ of its length before curving forward. The labellum is variable in shape and is attached by a movable claw to the foot of the column. The lateral sepals are united for part or most of their length to form a lower lip which may be erect, embracing the galea, or, in many species, bent downwards. The sinus, or recess, between the lateral sepals differs in shape and size and acts as a further distinguishing feature.

Many of the colony-forming species are amongst the easiest of the terrestrial orchids to grow. They are often available from specialist nurseries or at Native Orchid displays and shows and should not be removed from the bush. The main requirement is a well drained mix and the observance of a Summer dormancy period, when the pots are permitted to dry out. Solitary species can generally be grown but are sensitive to overwatering. Propagation is by division of tuberoids. Small flies or fungus gnats are the pollinators.

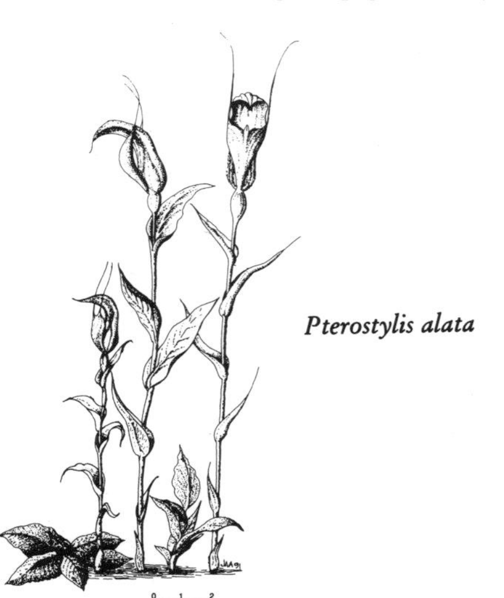
Pterostylis alata

Pterostylis alata

Striped Greenhood

Size:	stem 8–25 cm high **P**
Habitat:	Widespread in dry and valley sclerophyll forests, tea-tree heath
Form:	Erect slender herb on thin stem; non-flowering plants form leafy rosette
Foliage:	Rosette of 3–11 long-stalked, ovate dark green leaves with wavy margins, to 20 mm long; flowering plants have 3–4 sheathing sessile, lanceolate stem leaves to 40 mm
Flowers:	Single, occasinally 2, pale green or translucent white flowers, with dark green stripes, to 25 mm long. Galea ends in a fine point. Labellum green to brown, erect, narrowed in upper half. Lateral sepals erect, sinus broad and notched, free points to 25 mm long and thread-like. April to August
Requirements:	Moist, well drained soils
Comments:	Forms colonies but difficult to establish in cultivation. Similar to *P. robusta*, but taller and more slender with smaller leaves and flowers. Grows in higher rainfall areas. Becoming locally rare.
Localities:	Greensborough, Hurstbridge-Warrandyte, Eastern heathlands of Port Phillip Bay, 65#–67
Distribution:	Vic, NSW, Tas, SA

Pterostylis alpina

Mountain Greenhood

Size:	stem to 30 cm high	**P**
Habitat:	Damp and valley sclerophyll forests	
Form:	Stout herb with a rough fleshy stem, non-flowering plants form extended leafy rosette	
Foliage:	3–5 sessile, dark green, fleshy, ovate to elliptic leaves to 60 mm long scattered up the stem, margins entire or wavy	
Flowers:	Single translucent white flower to 30 mm long with dark green lines and tinges. Dark green labellum curved near end to protrude through the sinus. Lateral sepals erect, sinus broad with notch, free points to 15 mm long swept back behind galea. August to October	
Requirements:	Moist, well drained soil	
Comments:	An easily grown colonising *Pterostylis* which usually occurs on southern slopes growing amongst grassy tussocks. Often confused with *P. scabrida* which is endemic to Tasmania.	
Localities:	Montrose, Belgrave, 34A#, 41, 42, 47, 49, 51, 55–58	
Distribution:	Vic, NSW Tas	

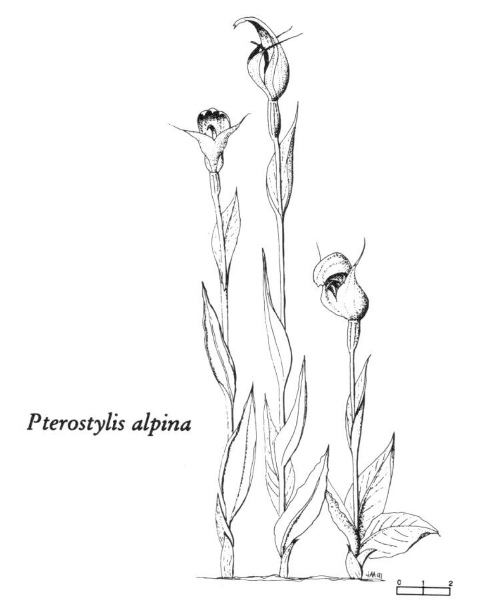

Pterostylis alpina

Pterostylis concinna

Trim Greenhood

Size:	stem 8–30 cm high	**F P**
Habitat:	Widespread in dry and valley sclerophyll forests, tea-tree heath, grassy low open forest, coastal woodland	
Form:	Wiry erect herb	
Foliage:	Rosette of 4–6 dark green ovate to oblong stalked leaves to 30 mm long, margins entire or wavy	
Flowers:	Single, sometimes 2, translucent pale green flowers to 15 mm long with dark green stripes and brown tinges near sepal points and sinus. Galea ends in a fine point. Brown labellum slightly curved, ending in 2 teeth. Lateral sepals erect, with a very wide sinus and fine erect points to 20 mm long held above the galea. Tips of the points appear clubbed. May to October	
Requirements:	Moist, well drained soils	
Comments:	May form dense colonies, usually in shaded areas, but will tolerate full sun in moist protected positions.	
Localities:	Eltham, Belgrave, Dingley, Cheltenham, Hampton, Beaumaris, 33, 34A, 42, 47, 49, 58, 65#–67, 69A, 74–76	
Distribution:	Vic, NSW, Tas, SA	

Pterostylis concinna

Pterostylis x toveyana

Mentone Greenhood

Size:	stem to 20 cm high	**P**
Habitat:	Dry sclerophyll forest, tea-tree heath, grassy low open forest	
Foliage:	Non-flowering plants have a rosette of 2–4 ovate leaves to 20 mm long similar to both parents. Flowering plants also have 2–3 lanceolate sheathing stem leaves to 30 mm long.	
Flowers:	The single flower, to 15 mm long, is translucent white with broad green stripes and brown tinges on the tips. Lateral sepals tightly embrace the galea. Free points erect to 20 mm long, tips expanded and clubbed. May to October	
Requirements:	Moist, well drained soil	
Comments:	A naturally occurring hybrid between *P. concinna* and *P. alata*. First collected in Mentone.	
Localities:	Greensborough, Mentone, Aspendale, Frankston	
Distribution:	Vic, SA, Tas	

Pterostylis x toveyana

Pterostylis cucullata

Leafy Greenhood

Size:	stem 8–15 cm high	**P**
Habitat:	Tea-tree heath	
Foliage:	Rosette of 5–7 sessile, oblong to elliptical dark green leaves to 100 mm long, with 2 or 3 leaf-like bracts scattered up the stem, the large, uppermost bract sheathing the base of the flower.	
Flowers:	Single, large softly hairy green flower to 30 mm long, petals and lower lip reddish-brown. Tip of galea curved down. Dark brown labellum, curved, blunt end not protruding. Lateral sepals erect with a very narrow sinus, points to 10 mm long, tapering, just exceeding the galea. August to October	
Requirements:	Sandy soil	
Comments:	Very restricted in Melbourne, it is also vulnerable throughout its range in Australia. Forms small colonies.	
Localities:	Hampton 1948; 29#, 67#, 74#	
Distribution:	Vic, NSW, Tas, SA	

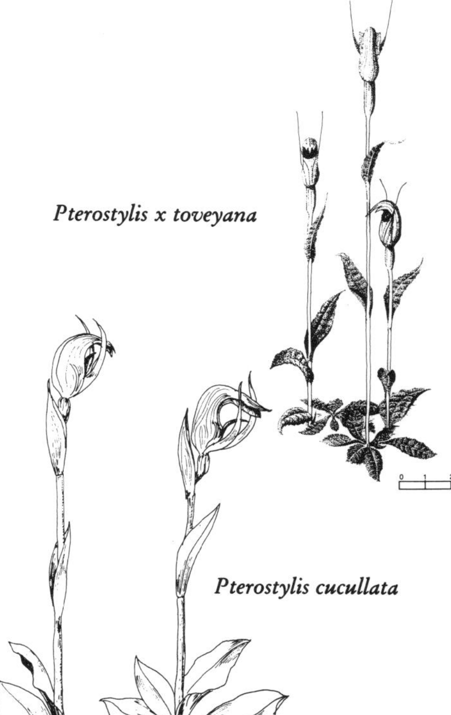

Pterostylis cucullata

SCALE: 0 1cm 2cm — The scale representation on each plant equals 2cm.

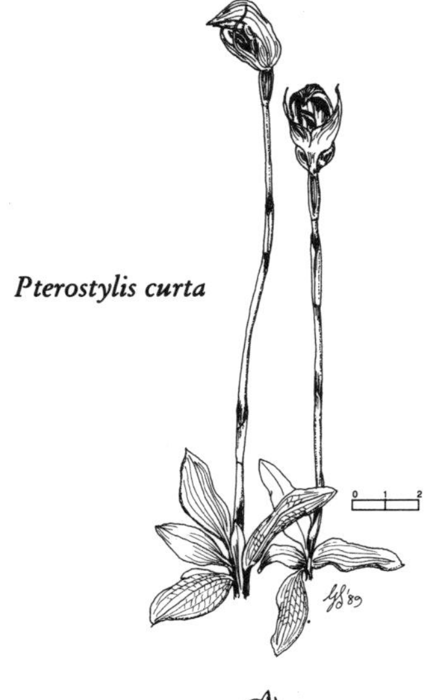

Pterostylis curta

Pterostylis curta

Blunt Greenhood

Size: stem 10–30 cm high **P N**
Habitat: Widespread in valley and damp sclerophyll forests, riparian scrub, tea-tree heath
Foliage: Rosette of 2–6 dark green ovate or oblong leaves to 100 mm long, on long stalks, margins wavy or flat
Flowers: Single green flower with darker stripes and brown tinges, to 35 mm long. Brown labellum has a raised central ridge and a distinctly twisted tip protruding through the sinus.
Lateral sepals erect, loosely embracing the galea, sinus very broad with free points to 12 mm long, not above the galea. July to October
Requirements: Moist, well drained soils
Comments: An easily grown free flowering plant.
Localities: Widespread from Heidelberg to Belgrave, 29#, 67, 69A, 74, 76
Distribution: Vic, Qld, NSW, Tas, SA

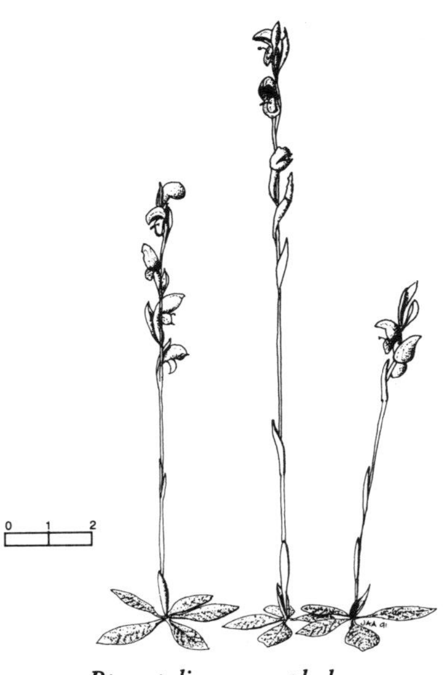

Pterostylis cycnocephala

Pterostylis cycnocephala

Swan Greenhood

Size: stem to 20 cm high **F P**
Habitat: Box woodland, dry sclerophyll forest
Foliage: Rosette of 6–12 sessile, ovate leaves to 25 mm long, with a pointed tip, crowded and overlapping. 2 or more closely sheathing stem bracts
Flowers: Spike of 2–24 tiny bright green and white flowers to 9 mm long. Galea curved throughout with a short, blunt, downward pointing tip. The labellum has a very dark shallowly notched tip, and the dark green basal appendage is curved towards the tip.
Lateral sepals, to 6 mm long, are bent downwards, concave, with free or united tips. August to January
Requirements: Well drained soils
Comments: Similar to the closely related *P. mutica*, but may be distinguished by the dark labellum tip, and the basal appendage curving towards the tip. Solitary plants often grow amongst rocks, sometimes occurring with *Allocasuarina* species. A drought tolerant plant.
Localities: Greensborough#, Keilor Plains
Distribution: Vic, Qld, NSW, Tas, SA

Pterostylis decurva

Pterostylis decurva

Summer Greenhood

Size: stem to 30 cm high **P N**
Habitat: Valley and damp sclerophyll forests
Foliage: Rosette of 2–5 long-stalked, dark green oblong leaves to 30 mm long, with a blunt or rounded tip; 4–5 sheathing stem leaves to 40 mm long on flowering plants
Flowers: Single yellowish-green and white flower to 25 mm long, with brown tinges especially on the petals. Galea bent abruptly downwards at the tip, ending in a thread-like point to 20 mm long. Blunt reddish-brown labellum is sharply curved down in the upper third, protruding through the sinus.
Lateral sepals tightly embrace the galea with wide sinus slightly protruding, free points to 40 mm long, extending well above the galea. October to March
Requirements: Moist soils
Comments: Plants are usually solitary, but may form small colonies amongst grassy tussocks. Easily grown in a container.
Localities: Knox, Boronia, Belgrave, 57, 58
Distribution: Vic, NSW, Tas

Pterostylis foliata

Slender Greenhood

Size: stem to 30 cm high **P N**
Habitat: Damp and valley sclerophyll forests
Foliage: 3–6 sessile, elliptical dark green leaves to 80 mm long, scattered along the stem, margins wavy; sometimes a few basal leaves form a loose rosette
Flowers: Single translucent white flower to 20 mm long with broad green stripes and brown tinges towards the tip. Galea at first erect, then curved forward. Brown labellum is curved in the upper third, protruding through the sinus.
Lateral sepals erect with a narrow sinus and free points to 20 mm long, exceeding the galea. August to January
Requirements: Moist soil
Comments: Locally rare in Melbourne.
Localities: Wattle Glen, Greensborough, Dandenong Rges
Distribution: Vic, NSW, Tas; NZ

Pterostylis furcata

Sickle Greenhood

Size: stem to 30 cm high **P N**
Habitat: Swamps and moist depressions in damp and valley sclerophyll forests
Foliage: Rosette of 4–5 bright green lanceolate leaves to 80 mm long
Flowers: Single large green and white flower to 60 mm long. Galea prominently curved and sickle-shaped. Curved, narrow dark green to brown labellum protruding through the sinus.
Lateral sepals erect, widely separated from the galea with very narrow free points to 30 mm long, curving forward above the galea. September to January
Requirements: Moist to wet soils
Comments: Needs to remain very wet during growth period.
Localities: Bayswater, Mooroolbark, Belgrave, The Basin, Wantirna South, Rowville, 33, 34A, 51
Distribution: Vic, Qld, NSW, Tas, SA
Synonym: *P. falcata*

Pterostylis grandiflora

Cobra or Superb Greenhood

Size: stem 10–40 cm high **P**
Habitat: Valley sclerophyll forest, grassy low open forest, tea-tree heath
Foliage: Flowering plants have 6–9 dark green, lanceolate sheathing stem leaves to 40 mm long. After flowering, plants develop a rosette of 3–5 shortly stalked, ovate leaves to 20 mm long, with wavy margins. A similar rosette is borne on non-flowering plants.
Flowers: Single translucent white flower to 35 mm long with green stripes and red-brown tinges. Galea is at first erect, then curves forward, then down with a fine tip to 10 mm long. Bronze-brown petals flared at right angles on the curved sepal. Erect red-brown labellum tapers sharply in the upper half and protrudes through the sinus.
Lateral sepals erect, sinus wide and protruding, free points very long, to 50 mm, extending high above the galea. May to August
Requirements: Moist soils
Comments: Very restricted now in Melbourne and rare throughout Victoria.
Localities: Sth Belgrave, Lysterfield, Eastern Port Phillip Bay, 67#
Distribution: Vic, Qld, NSW, Tas

Pterostylis longifolia

Tall Greenhood

Size: Variable, stem 0.15–0.9 m high **P**
Habitat: Widespread in dry and valley sclerophyll forests, tea-tree heath, grassy low open forest
Foliage: Basal rosette of 3–6 long-stalked, linear dark green leaves to 35 mm long on non-flowering plants only; 5–8 stem-clasping, dark green lanceolate stem leaves to 100 mm long, held erect
Flowers: Raceme of 1–15 green and white flowers with brown tips, to 15 mm long, widely spaced along the stem. Galea curved from the base, ending in a short point. Brown to dark green hairy labellum is narrowly 3-lobed with a notched tip turned upwards.
Lateral sepals bent downwards, joined for ½ their length then tapering to a short point. April to November
Requirements: Moist, well drained soils
Comments: Plants usually grow as solitary specimens, often close to Eucalypt trunks or through grass tussocks. Because of their height they are easily recognised. Although the most common species in Melbourne it can be difficult to maintain in cultivation.
Localities: Heidelberg to Dandenong Rges, 61, 63, 67#, 74–76
Distribution: Vic, Qld, NSW, Tas, SA

Pterostylis sp. aff. longifolia

Size: stem 0.4 m high
Habitat: Box ironbark woodland, dry sclerophyll forest
Comments: Similar to *P. longifolia* but more robust with larger flowers which are crowded towards the top of the stem rather than spaced along it. Labellum differs in that it is larger, with a slightly broader mid-lobe. Erect lateral lobes are tinged brown. Leaves are longer and curved rather than erect. An orchid known from 3 sites one of which has since disappeared for housing development. The other 2 sites are currently at great risk.
Localities: Eltham#, Greensborough, Diamond Creek
Distribution: Endemic to Vic

SCALE: 0 1cm 2cm The scale representation on each plant equals 2cm.

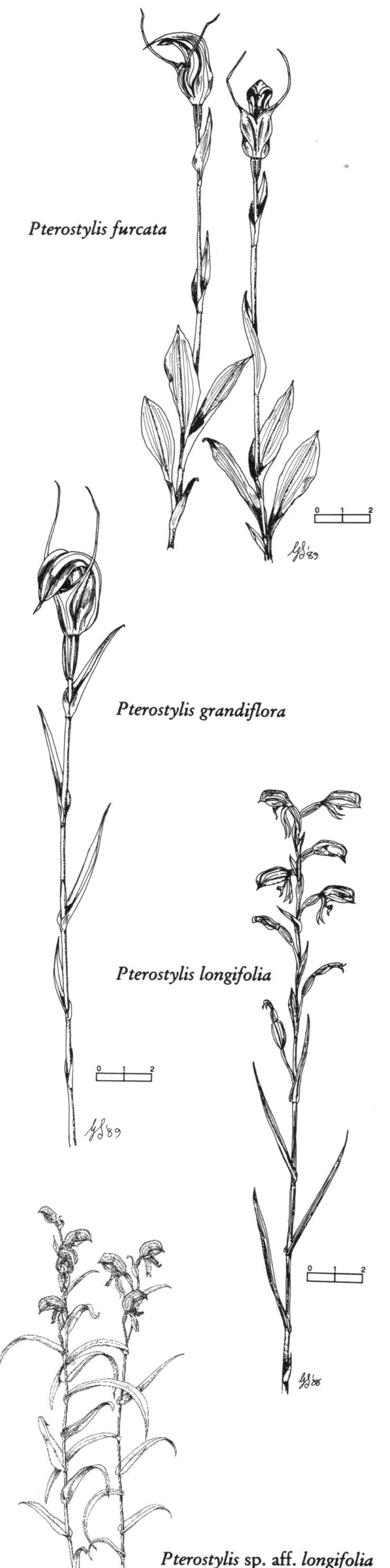

Pterostylis furcata

Pterostylis grandiflora

Pterostylis longifolia

Pterostylis sp. aff. *longifolia*

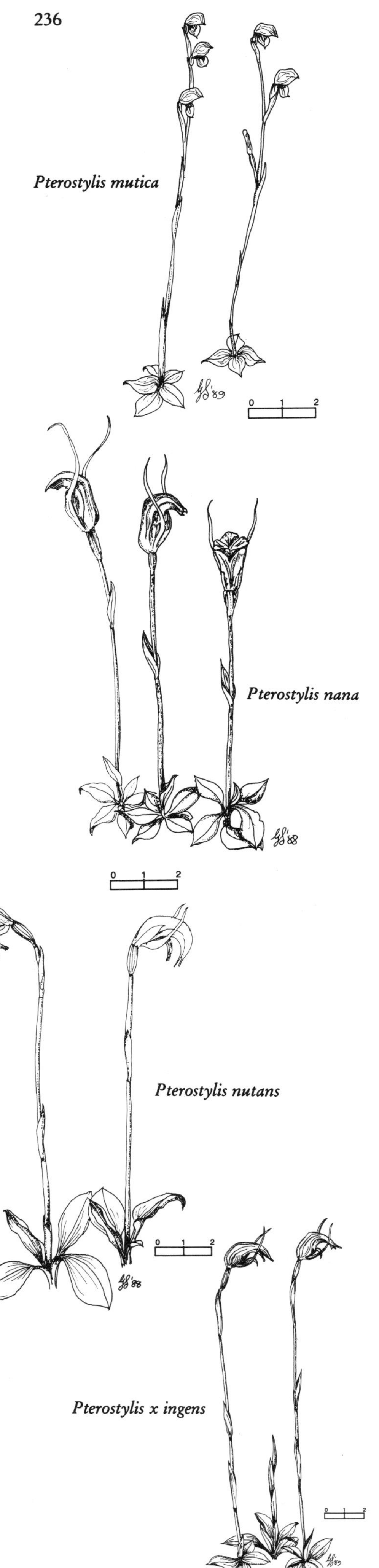

Pterostylis mutica

Midget Greenhood

Size: stem 8–25 cm high **F P**
Habitat: Woodlands of basalt plains, dry sclerophyll forest, tea-tree heath
Foliage: Rosette of 6–12 sessile, ovate dark green leaves to 25 mm long, with flat margins; 1–9 pointed sheathing stem bracts
Flowers: Dense spike of 2–10 tiny waxy green flowers to 8 mm long. Galea curved throughout, blunt-tipped. Nearly round pale green labellum has a notched tip and a fleshy appendage at the base curved like an 'S' away from the tip.
Lateral sepals bent downwards, concave and united almost to the tip. July to January
Requirements: Well drained soils
Comments: A solitary species propagated by seed. It usually grows in drier situations, often protected only by rocks or small grasses. When found on the basalt plains it commonly occurs with *Callitris glaucophylla*. May be extinct within the Melbourne area.
Localities: Melton#, Tottenham#, Werribee#, Greensborough#, 29#, 34A, 67#
Distribution: All states except NT; NZ

Pterostylis nana

Dwarf or Snail Greenhood

Size: stem 5–15 cm high **F P N**
Habitat: Dry sclerophyll forest, grassy low open forest, primary dune scrub
Foliage: Rosette of 4–8 dull green, shortly-stalked ovate leaves to 30 mm long, margins wavy; flowering plants also have 2–3 sheathing stem bracts
Flowers: Single bright green flower to 15 mm long with dark green stripes. Erect, thick greenish-brown labellum is hidden.
Lateral sepals erect with a central incurved tooth in the large sinus, free points to 25 mm long above the galea, tips often clubbed. July to October
Requirements: Well drained soils
Comments: A very adaptable orchid tolerating a wide range of soils and habitats. Plants exhibit a remarkable degree of variation, and may be solitary or grow in small colonies. In dry open situations the stem may be as small as 2 cm in length, but in moist protected sites, slender vigorous plants to 30 cm high have been observed. A white form is known from 1 site in Eltham.
Localities: Bundoora, Wattle Glen, Eltham, Belgrave, 34A, 42, 51, 58, 67#, 74–76
Distribution: Vic, NSW, Tas, SA, WA; NZ

Pterostylis nutans

Nodding Greenhood or Parrot's Beak Orchid

Size: stem 10–30 cm high **P N**
Habitat: Widespread in dry and valley sclerophyll forests, red gum woodland, tea-tree heath, grassy low open forest
Foliage: Rosette of 3–6 dark green shortly-stalked ovate to oblong leaves 25–80 mm long with wavy margins; 3 stem leaves on flowering plants
Flowers: Single nodding translucent flower to 25 mm long with green stripes, sometimes reddish towards the tip. Galea curved forward ending in a sharp point. Very hairy green labellum with reddish-brown central ridge, curved to protrude through the sinus.
Lateral sepals with narrow sinus, loosely embracing the galea, curved downwards at the base then curving forwards, free points extending just beyond the galea. March to October
Requirements: Moist soils
Comments: A locally common plant forming large colonies.
Localities: Bundoora, Greensborough-Dandenong Ranges, Hampton-Frankston, Cranbourne, 36, 63, 65#, 71, 74–76
Distribution: Vic, Qld, NSW, Tas, SA; NZ

Pterostylis x ingens

Large Pointed Greenhood

Size: stem to 30 cm high **P**
Habitat: Valley sclerophyll forest
Foliage: Rosette of 3–7 ovate leaves to 35 mm long, with wavy margins
Flowers: Displays similarities to both parents. Flower large to 35 mm long. Galea is humped near the base before bending forwards and then downwards from halfway. The greenish-brown labellum is hairy, with a raised central ridge and is prominent as in both parents.
Lateral sepals loosely embrace the galea with free points to 25 mm long, just beyond it. The sinus is narrow and does not protrude.
Comments: A naturally occurring hybrid between *P. nutans* and *P. furcata* with intermediate features. Hybrid populations are likely where the parents occur in close proximity in moister habitats of their range. Easily grown in cultivation, producing large colonies and flowering freely.
Localities: Bayswater, Wantirna South, Mooroolbark, Wonga Park, Blackburn, 61
Distribution: Vic, NSW, Tas

Pterostylis obtusa

Blunt-tongue Greenhood

Size: stem 10–25 cm high **P**
Habitat: Valley and damp sclerophyll forests, often growing with ferns or amongst grasses, tea-tree heath
Foliage: Rosette of 3–6 ovate to oblong, shortly-stalked leaves to 25 mm on non-flowering plants; flowering plants have 3–5 lanceolate stem leaves to 40 mm long
Flowers: Single translucent white flower to 30 mm long with bright green stripes and brown tinges. Galea is erect for most of its length, then curves forward, ending in a short fine tip. Dark brown oblong labellum slightly protruding through sinus.
Lateral sepals erect with very broad bulging sinus, free points to 25 mm long held high above the galea. February to June
Requirements: Moist soils
Comments: Plants may form extensive colonies when protected by dense understorey. Colonies are generally sparse in more open situations. Locally endangered.
Localities: Montrose, The Basin, 58, 67#, 74
Distribution: Vic, Qld, NSW, Tas, SA

Pterostylis obtusa

Pterostylis parviflora

Tiny Greenhood

Size: stem 15–30 cm high **P**
Habitat: Widespread in dry sclerophyll forest, tea-tree heath, grassy low open forest
Foliage: Rosette of 3–10 long-stalked, bright green to bluish-green ovate, pointed leaves to 15 mm long on non-flowering plants only; several small, closely sheathing stem bracts on flowering plants, with rosettes on side shoots off the flowering stem
Flowers: Spike of 1–13 green and maroon flowers to 10 mm long. Galea blunt ended. Blunt tip of labellum just visible.
Lateral sepals erect with broad sinus and very short free points. February to August
Requirements: Moist soils
Comments: Flowers are unusual in that they face towards the stem. A solitary species which is difficult to maintain in cultivation.
Localities: Eltham, Montrose, Nunawading-Bayswater, Belgrave, Springvale, Cheltenham, 42, 51, 56, 58, 67, 73, 74
Distribution: Vic, Qld, NSW, Tas, SA

Pterostylis parviflora

Pterostylis pedoglossa

Prawn Greenhood

Size: stem 10–15 cm high **P N**
Habitat: Peaty tea-tree heath, grassy low open forest
Foliage: Rosette of 3–6 dull greyish-green, ovate leaves to 25 mm long. The very thin flowering stem bears 2–4 sheathing bracts.
Flowers: Single translucent white flower to 15 mm long with green stripes at the base, brownish at the top. Galea ends in a fine point to 30 mm long. Labellum is tiny and hidden.
Lateral sepals erect, sinus narrow with free points to 30 mm long, held high above the galea. March to July
Requirements: Moist sandy soil
Comments: Plants are difficult to find, usually being well hidden in thick undergrowth or sedges and grasses, even when in large colonies. Readily identified by the long thread-like tips on all sepals. Difficult to cultivate. Vulnerable in Victoria and restricted to few sites in Melbourne.
Localities: Clayton#, Springvale#, Cheltenham#, 67#, 74
Distribution: Vic, NSW, Tas

Pterostylis pedunculata

Pterostylis pedunculata

Maroon Hood

Size: stem to 25 cm high **P N**
Habitat: Widespread in valley and dry sclerophyll forests, red gum woodland, tea-tree heath, grassy low open forest
Foliage: Rosette of 4–6 long-stalked, prominently veined, ovate to oblong dark green leaves to 40 mm long, margins sometimes wavy; 2–3 small pointed bracts closely sheathing the stem
Flowers: Single flower to 20 mm long, green and white at the base, the top tinged dark reddish-maroon. Tip of maroon labellum just visible.
Lateral sepals loosely erect, sinus narrow, free points to 30 mm long, held high above the galea. July to October
Requirements: Moist soil amongst leaf litter
Comments: Forms small dense colonies beneath low shrubs and grasses, or protected by tree trunks. In gullies, plants may grow on logs or fern trunks. Easily grown and flowers reliably.
Localities: Bundoora, Wattle Glen, Eltham, Park Orchards, Belgrave, Dingley, 34A, 36, 41, 42, 47, 51, 54, 57, 58, 61, 67, 69A, 74–76
Distribution: Vic, Qld, NSW, Tas, SA

The scale representation on each plant equals 2cm.

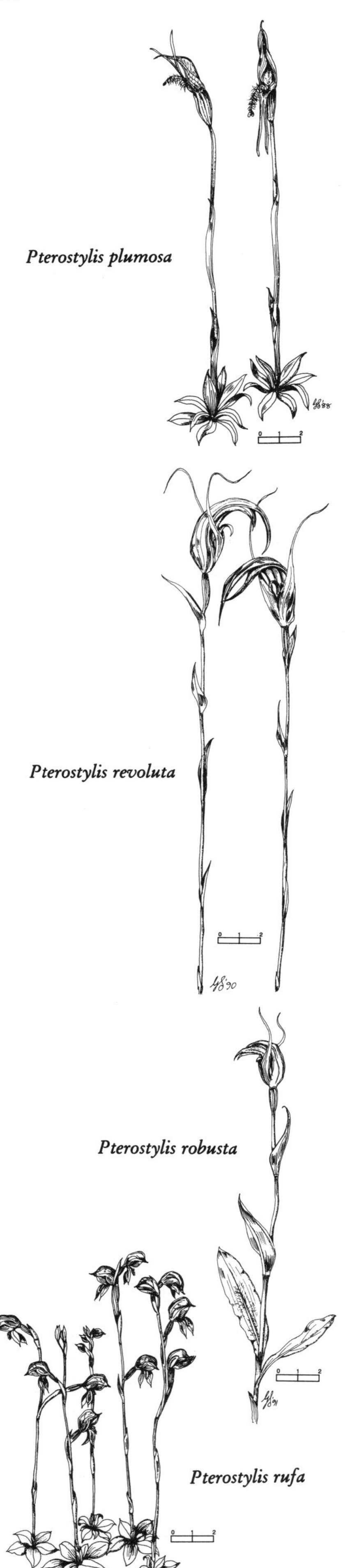

Pterostylis plumosa

Bearded Greenhood

Size: stem 20–30 cm high **P**
Habitat: Dry and valley sclerophyll forests, grassy low open forest
Foliage: Clump of 10–20 crowded, pale green or yellowish lanceolate leaves to 35 mm long, prominently veined, often extending for some distance up the stem
Flowers: Single, translucent, shiny green flower to 35 mm long, with dark veined markings. Galea is erect, ending in a short fine tip. Prominent thread-like labellum to 25 mm long, covered in long yellow hairs, ending in a dark knob.
Narrow lateral sepals bent downwards with inrolled margins, joined in lower third, free points nearly parallel. August to November
Requirements: Moist, well drained soils
Comments: Easily distinguished by its narrow, long yellow-haired tongue with an apical knob, and see-through galea. It usually occurs as solitary specimens but is sometimes found in small colonies. Difficult to cultivate.
Localities: Greensborough and Hurstbridge-Warrandyte, Heathmont, Bayswater, Belgrave, Moorabbin, 58, 67#, 74
Distribution: Vic, NSW, Tas, SA, WA; NZ

Pterostylis revoluta

Autumn Greenhood

Size: stem to 25 cm high **P**
Habitat: Dry sclerophyll forest, box ironbark woodland
Foliage: Rosette of 5–10 long-stalked, bluish-green ovate leaves to 20 mm long, only on non-flowering plants; 3–5 small pointed sheathing stem bracts on flowering plants
Flowers: Single translucent white flower with dark green stripes to 45 mm long, often with reddish-brown tinges. Galea leaning forward in a gentle curve, ending in a fine tip to 20 mm long. Curved pointed labellum protrudes through the sinus.
Lateral sepals loosely erect with narrow slightly protruding sinus, thread-like points to 35 mm long held high above galea. February to June
Requirements: Well drained soils
Comments: Plants generally occur in drier regions in the shelter of grass tussocks and small shrubs, and rely on good Summer/Autumn rains for flowering. Large free-flowering colonies are found in wetter years. Easy to cultivate. Locally rare.
Localities: Greensborough, Hurstbridge, Wonga Park, Park Orchards, 42, 49#, 50A#, 65#, 66
Distribution: Vic, Qld, NSW

Pterostylis robusta

Large Striped Greenhood

Size: stem 5–15 cm high **P**
Habitat: Dry and damp sclerophyll forests
Foliage: 6–7 ovate to elliptic basal leaves only present on non-flowering plants; flowering plants bear 4–5 broad lanceolate stem leaves to 50 mm long
Flowers: Large single flower to 40 mm long, bright green and white with deep green stripes. Labellum dark green.
Lateral sepals are held erect or curved, free points to 30 mm long, sinus deeply notched. June to September
Requirements: Well drained soil
Comments: Similar to *P. alata* but shorter on a more robust stem, sinus more deeply notched. Easy to cultivate but shy to flower.
Localities: Greensborough, Dandenong Rges, 42
Distribution: Vic, NSW, SA, WA

Pterostylis rufa

Rusty Hood

Size: stem to 30 cm high **P**
Habitat: Dry sclerophyll forest
Foliage: Rosette of 5–12 thick, dull green oblong to lanceolate leaves to 30 mm long, often withering by flowering time; 2–6 closely sheathing stem bracts
Flowers: Spike of 3–15 reddish flowers to 10 mm long. Galea leaning forward with a narrow opening and short tip, petal edges end before the base. Many tiny white hairs on margins of fleshy brown labellum.
Lateral sepals bent downwards, free points curved forwards from a narrow sinus. September to December
Requirements: Well drained gravelly soils
Comments: Widespread but not common, usually growing as solitary plants. They are not easy to cultivate as the tuberoids tend to rot.
Localities: Eltham, Park Orchards, 33#, 34A, 42, 50A, 51
Distribution: All states except NT

Pterostylis sanguinea
Banded Greenhood

Size: stem 10–40 cm high **F P**
Habitat: Coastal banksia woodland, grassy low open forest
Foliage: Rosette of 3–6 ovate grey-green leaves to 30 mm long on non-flowering plants; 5–8 sessile, sheathing lanceolate leaves to 80 mm long, becoming gradually smaller down the flowering stem
Flowers: Compact raceme of 1–10 nodding reddish-brown flowers with greenish-white stripes, to 15 mm long. Galea and lateral sepals very wide. Fleshy brown to purple labellum has hairy margins and ends in upturned notched tip.
Lateral sepals bent downwards, tapering, with a narrow sinus, ending in short pointed tips. April to September
Requirements: Well drained sandy soil
Comments: Solitary species which is never common. Grows in protection of shrubby plants, often in peaty soils, and is difficult to locate. Unreliable in cultivation.
Localities: Cheltenham[#], Baxter, 67[#], 74, 76
Distribution: Vic, Tas, SA, WA
Synonym: Previously known as *P. vittata* which is endemic to WA.

Pterostylis truncata
Little Dumpies, Brittle Greenhood

Size: stem to 15 cm high **P**
Habitat: Rocky or grassy sites on plains grassland, valley sclerophyll forest, sclerophyll woodland
Foliage: Rosette of 2–6 bright green ovate leaves to 30 mm long on non-flowering plants; 2–5 closely sheathing tapering stem leaves to 30 mm long, on flowering plants
Flowers: Single large greenish-white flower to 50 mm long with dark green or reddish stripes. Galea curved forward ending in a point, petals broadly dilated. Labellum tapered to a blunt point, protruding slightly through the sinus.
Lateral sepals erect, sinus narrow, free points to 30 mm long, held erect or recurved above the galea. February to July
Requirements: Moist, well drained soil
Comments: Grows in dense colonies. Easy to cultivate but rarely flowers well. Most of its habitat has been destroyed by housing development leaving it endangered throughout Victoria.
Localities: Tottenham[#], Sunshine[#], Sth Belgrave, Beaumaris[#], 5
Distribution: Vic, NSW

Sarcochilus

Sarcochilus australis
Butterfly Orchid, Gunn's Orchid

Size: 5–15 cm across, stems to 5 cm long **P N**
Habitat: Fern gullies in wet sclerophyll forest, cool temperate rainforest
Form: Semi-pendulous epiphytic orchid
Foliage: Thin, leathery, curved dark green linear-lanceolate leaves to 80 mm long
Flowers: Pendulous racemes of 2–14 fragrant green flowers to 15 mm across. Spreading perianth segments are narrow and fleshy, dorsal sepal incurved. Labellum is white with purple markings. October to December
Requirements: Moist humid conditions
Comments: The only epiphytic orchid in the Melbourne area, it lives on mossy branches and trunks of trees and shrubs such as *Coprosma quadrifida*, *Hedycarya* and *Bedfordia*, often occurring close to the ground. It is very restricted in its range in Melbourne.
Propagation: Impossible to cultivate
Localities: Dandenong Ranges
Distribution: Vic, Qld, NSW, Tas

Spiranthes

Spiranthes sinensis
Austral Ladies Tresses

Size: stem 25–50 cm high **F P**
Habitat: Swamps and bogs of wattle tea-tree scrub, valley sclerophyll forest, growing amongst rushes and sedges
Form: Erect tufted evergreen herb with a thin wiry stem
Foliage: Tuft of 3–5 erect, dark green narrow-lanceolate leaves to 15 cm long with 3–5 stem bracts
Flowers: Dense spirally-arranged spike of tiny pink and frosty white flowers. Perianth segments to 5 mm long, petals and dorsal sepal erect, lateral sepals spreading. Labellum is white with fringed margins. October to March
Requirements: Moist to wet soil
Comments: A very distinctive plant which is easily grown in a container. The flowers produce a sweet honey perfume, especially in the evenings. Very restricted in the Melbourne area and possibly already extinct.
Propagation: Seed, division
Localities: Bayswater[#], Sandringham[#], 74
Distribution: Vic, Qld, NSW, Tas, SA; NZ, Asia

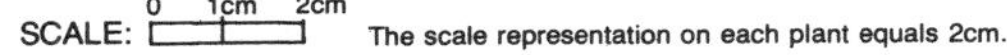

The scale representation on each plant equals 2cm.

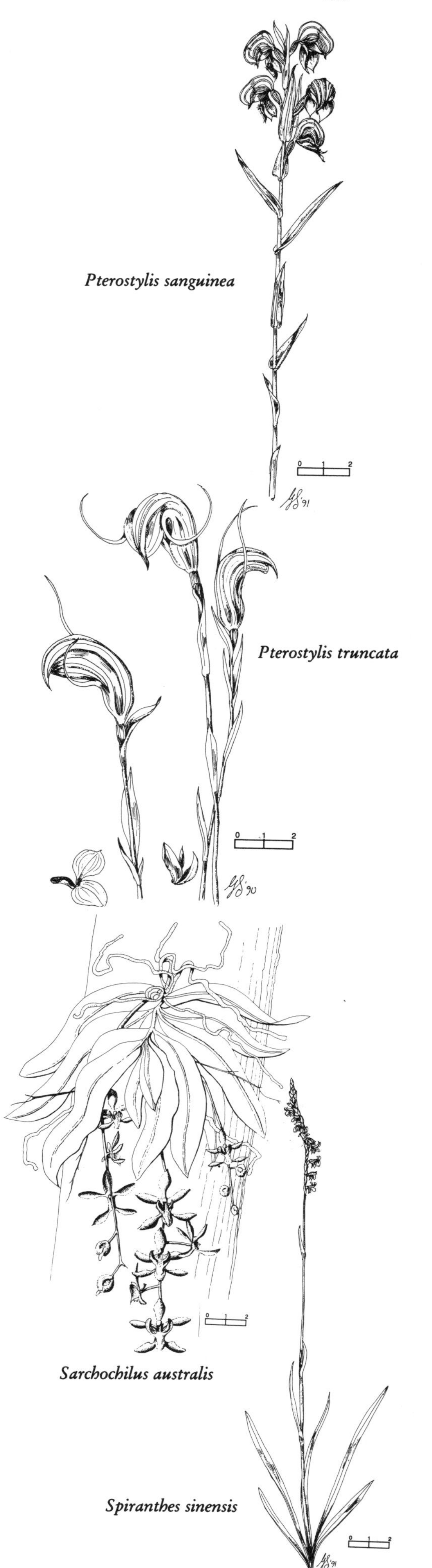
Pterostylis sanguinea

Pterostylis truncata

Sarchochilus australis

Spiranthes sinensis

Thelymitra

A colourful, glabrous group of terrestrial orchids. Flowers open wide on warm sunny days, giving them the common name of Sun Orchids. They have a solitary, erect, channelled leaf sheathing at the base of the stem and 1–2 leafy stem bracts. The flowers are simple, all perianth segments including the labellum similar in appearance. Identification is made through the column which varies considerably. Important features include the 2 column arms (or lateral lobes) found on either side of the anther, which have different forms, and may be covered in many hairy tufts; the post-anther (or mid) lobe—an erect projection between the column arms and behind the anther which sometimes forms a fleshy hood overhanging the anther; and the side lobule—a fleshy projection behind the column arm but distinct from the mid lobe, with jagged margins. Propagation is by seed. They are difficult to cultivate.

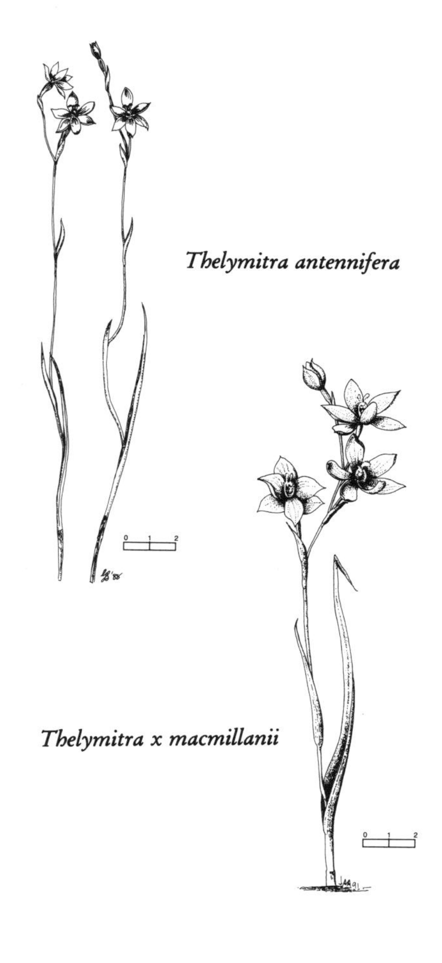

Thelymitra antennifera

Thelymitra x macmillanii

Thelymitra antennifera

Rabbit's Ears, Vanilla Orchid

Size: stem 10–20 cm high **F P**
Habitat: Sclerophyll woodland, damp and valley sclerophyll forest, tea-tree heath, grassy low open forest
Foliage: Long grass-like leaf to 120 mm long, often reddish at the base. The pinkish flexuose flower stem bears 2 leaf-like bracts
Flowers: Zig-zagging terminal raceme of 1–3 large fragrant yellow flowers to 40 mm across; September to November
Yellow column is erect with broad wings, not hoded; dark brown column arms are 2-lobed and ear-like, held high above the column.
Requirements: Moist, well drained soils
Comments: Widespread, fairly common orchid, growing in colonies and appearing in numbers after fire.
Localities: Bundoora, Montrose, Belgrave, Cheltenham, 42, 47, 49, 58, 67#, 74
Distribution: Vic, NSW, Tas, SA, WA

Thelymitra x macmillanii

Crimson Sun-orchid

Size: stem 15–20 cm high **F P**
Habitat: Grassy low open forest
Foliage: Thick, fleshy linear leaf, channelled inside.
Flowers: Slender wavy flower stem has 1–6 pink to crimson flowers to 40 mm across; September to October.
Column pink to crimson; post-anther lobe short, narrow and toothed; yellow to reddish column arms held high above anther, densely covered in small rounded teeth. Yellow anther is broad, thick, and hairy, curved horizontally forward.
Comments: A natural hybrid between *T. antennifera* and *T. nuda* occurring wherever the parents grow in close proximity. Because the parent plants are variable, the form of this hybrid also varies. In Melbourne it is only recorded for the eastern coastal fringe, but is more widespread in other areas. Flowers open freely on hot days, but in cooler weather the buds close and remain inflated as do those of *T. antennifera*.
Localities: Belgrave, 67#, Mt. Eliza
Distribution: Vic, Tas, SA, WA

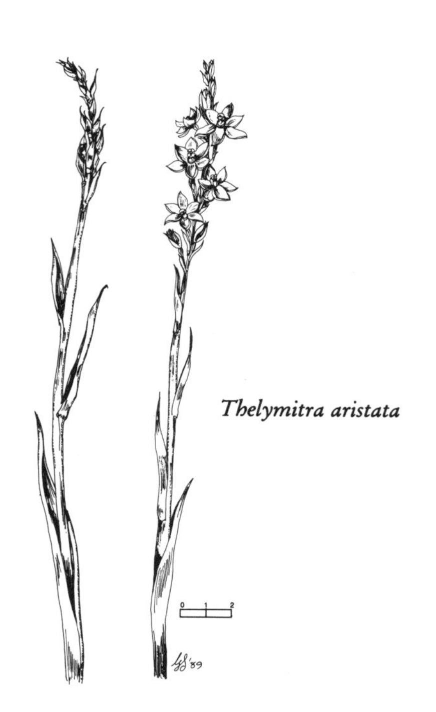

Thelymitra aristata

Thelymitra aristata

Scented Sun-orchid

Size: Robust stem to 0.8 m high **F P**
Habitat: Plains grassland, red gum woodland, dry sclerophyll forest
Foliage: Thick broad-lanceolate leaf to 35 cm long with 3–4 large leafy stem bracts
Flowers: Long terminal raceme of up to 30 blue to mauve flowers to 40 mm across; October to November.
White or bluish column erect, wings inflated; hood curved, 2-lobed and toothed; column arms erect, ending in a tuft of white hairs.
Requirements: Moist soils
Comments: An impressive orchid, very showy in flower. Plants appear in large numbers in moist to wet heathlands. They are generally more scattered in forested areas. Locally rare, flowering well after fire.
Localities: Werribee#, St. Albans, Sydenham, Eltham, 25, 33
Distribution: Vic, NSW, Tas, SA
Synonym: *T. grandiflora*

Thelymitra carnea

Pink Sun-orchid

Size: stem 20–35 cm high **F P**
Habitat: Valley sclerophyll forest, grassy low open forest
Foliage: Narrow, terete or channelled leaf to 15 cm long, 2–3 stem bracts
Flowers: Zig-zagging raceme of 1–4 pinkish, rarely cream flowers, to 15 mm across; September to November.
Column cream to reddish, post anther lobe yellow, short and narrow, not hooded, with notched end; yellow column arms erect, margins covered in blunt teeth.
Requirements: Soils wet in Winter, drying out in Summer
Comments: Flowers only open during hot humid weather and are self-pollinated. Distinguished from *T. rubra* by the smaller flowers, shorter column, narrower column arms and post anther lobe. Fairly common, growing in moist or wet soils among sedges and low shrubs of heathlands, less conspicuous in forests.
Localities: Blackburn, Bayswater, Belgrave, 34A, 47, 49, 67, 74
Distribution: All states except Qld; NZ

Illustrated p. 241

Thelymitra epipactoides

Metallic Sun-orchid

Size: stem 20–50 cm high **F P**
Habitat: Marshes in tea-tree heath
Foliage: Thick fleshy lanceolate leaf to 25 cm long. Stout flower stem bears 1 or 2 large sheathing leaf-like bracts.
Flowers: Raceme of 6–20 large blue-green or bronze flowers to 35 mm across, with a metallic shine; September to November.
Column widely winged, post-anther lobe incurved, end fringed with teeth; erect column arms end in dense white hair tufts.
Requirements: Moist to wet soils
Comments: Once widespread in Melbourne, mainly on near-coastal tracts, it is now presumed extinct due to destruction of its habitat. An endangered species throughout its Australian range.
Localities: Black Rock#, 67#
Distribution: Vic, SA

Thelymitra flexuosa

Twisted Sun-orchid

Size: stem 10–25 cm high **F P**
Habitat: Moist depressions and swamp margins in valley sclerophyll forest, wattle tea-tree scrub, grassy low open forest
Foliage: Linear terete leaf to 100 mm long. The reddish flowering stem is flexuose, bearing 2 stem bracts.
Flowers: Zig-zagging raceme of 1–3 pale yellow or cream flowers to 14 mm across; September to November.
Erect, white to cream widely winged column with 4 rows of short hairs down the back. Column arms reduced to small lumps, post-anther lobe not hooded, slightly notched and shorter than anther. Anther large, swollen and protruding, densely hairy.
Requirements: Winter wet soils
Comments: Flowers only open on hot days and are self-pollinated. Preferring wet sites, plants sometimes occur in shallow water. Similar to *T. antennifera*, the flowers are much smaller and lack the 'rabbit's ear' appendages or the column arms.
Localities: Blackburn, Belgrave, 33, 34A, 42, 67#, 74
Distribution: Vic, Tas, SA, WA

Thelymitra ixioides var. ixioides

Dotted Sun-orchid

Size: stem 20–60 cm high **F P**
Habitat: Wet grassy flats of valley and dry sclerophyll forests, grassy low open forest
Foliage: Dark green linear to lanceolate leaf to 20 cm long, often reddish at base
Flowers: Raceme of 3–9 mauve to blue flowers to 20 mm across, with darker spots on dorsal sepal and petals, but occasionally absent; October to November.
Column erect, white; erect column arms projected forward, ending in tufts of white, pink or mauve hairs; short post-anther lobe not hooded, end covered in rows of finger-like orange calli; side lobules fringed, often orange.
Requirements: Wet soils
Comments: Beautiful orchid which is quite variable. It may be robust and many-flowered, or slender with few flowers. Widespread throughout Melbourne favouring moist, open sites.
Localities: Blackburn-Boronia, Scoresby, Belgrave, Springvale, Moorabbin, 34A, 41, 42, 44, 51, 55, 56, 58, 67#, 74, 76
Distribution: Vic,Qld, NSW, Tas, SA; NZ, N Cal

Thelymitra ixioides var. subdifformis

Comments: Differs from *T. ixioides* var. *ixioides* in flower colour. Sepals are green, petals are pale blue to lavender.
Localities: Blackburn
Distribution: Endemic to Vic

Thelymitra luteocilium

Fringed or Pink Sun-orchid

Size: stem to 35 cm high **F P**
Habitat: Moist depressions in valley sclerophyll forest, wattle tea-tree scrub
Foliage: Fleshy, shallowly channelled dark green lanceolate leaf to 20 cm long. Slender, reddish-brown flower stem with 2–3 stem bracts.
Flowers: Raceme of 2–5 pale pink flowers to 20 mm across; September to December.
Column erect with narrow wings; post-anther lobe short, yellow, slightly hooded and densely fringed, behind the dense terminal tuft of yellow hairs of the short column arms.
Requirements: Moist, well drained soils
Comments: An inconspicuous orchid growing in the shelter of trees and shrubs, opening only on very hot humid days. Self-pollinating.
Localities: Ringwood, Bayswater, Langwarrin#, 34A
Distribution: Vic, NSW, Tas, SA

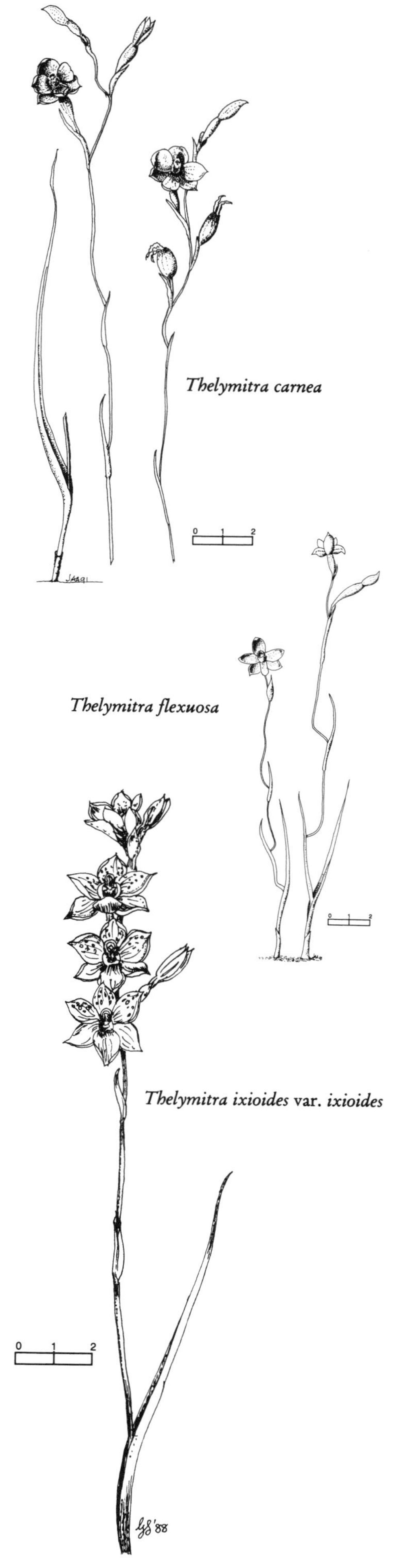

Thelymitra carnea

Thelymitra flexuosa

Thelymitra ixioides var. *ixioides*

SCALE: 0 1cm 2cm
The scale representation on each plant equals 2cm.

Thelymitra nuda

Thelymitra media var. media

Tall Sun-orchid

Size: stem to 0.9 m high **F P**
Habitat: Valley, damp and wet sclerophyll forests
Foliage: Thick lanceolate leaf to 30 cm long. Robust or slender stem, with bracts similar to *T. aristata*.
Flowers: Dense spike of 5–25 blue flowers to 30 mm across; October to January. Cream or bluish column with wide wings; post-anther lobe is not hooded and has a prominent band, fringed with short erect lemon calli; column arms extend forward ending in a tuft of white hairs.
Requirements: Moist soils
Comments: A beautiful orchid, of high rainfall areas. Flowers open freely on hot days, and are generally long-lasting. Similar to *T. aristata*, distinguished by the horizontal hair tufts on the column and a distinctive collar-like band of colour below the column lobes.
Localities: Boronia, Montrose, The Basin, Belgrave, Lysterfield, 55, 57, 58
Distribution: Vic, Qld, NSW, Tas *Illustrated p. 243*

Thelymitra megcalyptra

Scented Sun-orchid

Size: stem 20–40 cm high **F P**
Habitat: Plains grassland, coastal banksia woodland
Foliage: Very thick dark green lanceolate leaf 10–30 cm long, reddish at the base
Flowers: Raceme of 2–25 large fragrant mauve to deep blue flowers to 45 mm across; Octber to November.
White or bluish column; dark brown to blackish post-anther lobe with greatly expanded hood, deeply cleft; column arms projected forward ending in long dense white hairs.
Requirements: Well drained soil
Comments: Grows in large colonies. Flowers open readily in the sun producing an impressive display. Similar to *T. nuda* but more robust with larger flowers and a greatly swollen post-anther lobe.
Localities: Keilor, Sydenham, Toolern Vale, Diggers Rest, 67
Distribution: Vic, NSW, SA
Synonym: *T. aristata* var. *megcalyptra*

Thelymitra nuda

Scented or Plain Sun-orchid

Size: stem to 0.6 m high **F P**
Habitat: Dry sclerophyll forest, tea-tree heath
Foliage: Variable, thick, linear to lanceolate, dark green with a red base, or bluish-green, to 30 cm long. Flowering stem stout.
Flowers: Raceme of 2–20 large fragrant blue flowers to 40 mm across, mauve on outside, occasionally white, pink or mauve inside; August to November. Column erect, white or bluish; dark brown post-anther lobe with large, rounded hood, often yellow margins; column arms bent inward, with short dense white, rarely pink or lilac hairs in terminal tufts, held horizontally.
Requirements: Well drained soils
Comments: A beautiful orchid with flowers opening readily. Closely related to *T. pauciflora* which has smaller flowers that seldom open, and *T. aristata* which has a yellow, toothed post-anther lobe.
Localities: Montrose, 34A, 41, 74
Distribution: All states except NT

Thelymitra pauciflora

Thelymitra pauciflora

Slender Sun-orchid

Size: stem 20–50 cm high **F P**
Habitat: Plains grassland, dry and valley sclerophyll forests, red gum woodland, tea-tree heath, grassy low open forest
Flowers: Loose raceme of 3–15 blue flowers 10–20 mm across; August to January. Hood is smaller and narrower.
Column arms are erect with less dense white tufts of hair.
Requirements: Moist, well drained soils
Comments: Similar to *T. nuda* but smaller in all aspects. Flowers only open in very hot weather. Self-pollinating, it often matures without opening at all. This is the most common and widespread of Australia's *Thelymitra* species and is found in most temperate habitats. Populations often occur in large colonies, and show marked variations in flower size and colour. The plant is easily raised from seed and is reliable in cultivation.
Localities: Sunbury, Bundoora, Kew, Eltham, Montrose, Scoresby, Belgrave, Springvale, 25, 26, 33, 34A, 36, 42, 44, 47, 50A, 51, 54–56, 58, 63, 67, 69A, 74–76
Distribution: All states; NZ

Thelymitra rubra

Salmon or Pink Sun-orchid

Size: stem 15–40 cm high **P**

Habitat: Dry and valley sclerophyll forests, wet tea-tree heath, grassy low open forest

Foliage: Deeply channelled linear leaf to 20 cm long, reddish at base. 2–3 closely-sheathing bracts on the reddish, slightly flexuose stem

Flowers: Raceme of 1–4 pink flowers to 20 mm across; September to December. Column cream to pinkish; post-anther lobe above anther, rounded but not hooded, with a densely toothed yellow end; broad erect column arms yellow, covered in wrinkled, distinctive teeth.

Requirements: Moist soils

Comments: Opens readily in warm sun but is usually self-pollinated. Similar to *T. carnea* but flowers are larger and column arms are broader and warty.

Localities: Eltham, Nunawading-Bayswater, Montrose, Belgrave, Cranbourne, Cheltenham, 35, 42, 44, 51, 55, 56, 58, 67, 74–76

Distribution: All states

Synonym: *T. carnea* var. *rubra*

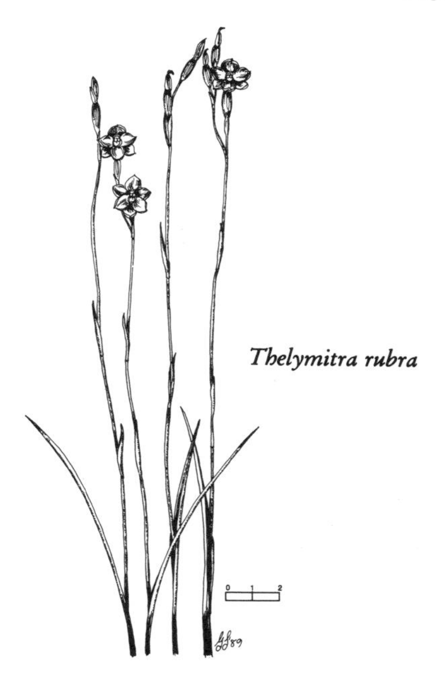

Thelymitra rubra

Thelymitra media var. *media*

SCALE: 0 1cm 2cm The scale representation on each plant equals 2cm.

Grasses, Rushes and Sedges, Aquatic and Semi-aquatic Herbs

Agropyron scabrum = Elymus scabrus

Agrostis — Poaceae

Annual or perennial grasses, generally tufted and with rhizomes, sometimes forming low spreading patches. A world-wide genus with 5 species indigenous to the Melbourne area, the majority of which are annuals. The inflorescence is an open or contracted, usually much branched, panicle of small single-flowered spikelets. The lemma (or lower bract) is toothed along the top and has an awn arising dorsally from near the middle or base. Propagation is generally by seed but division of the rhizome is also successful, however few of the Australian species have horticultural merit.

Agrostis aemula var. *aemula*

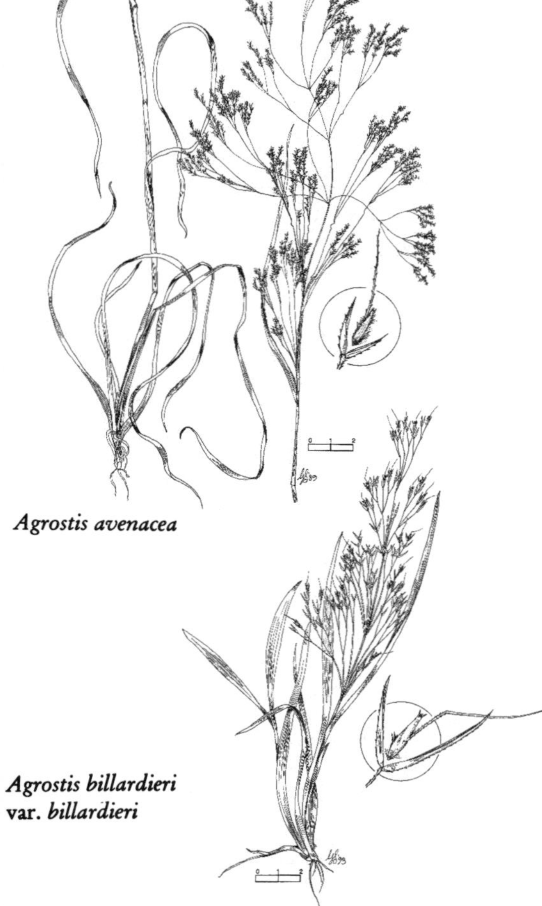

Agrostis avenacea

Agrostis billardieri var. *billardieri*

Agrostis adamsonii — Adamsons Bent

Comments: Similar to *A. billardieri* but spikelets are smaller, to 3.5 mm long, awns are straight and only shortly exserted. Previously known only from one collection, it has recently been rediscovered at another Victorian site. Extinct in the Melbourne area.
Localities: Studley Park#
Distribution: Endemic to Vic

Agrostis aemula var. aemula — Blown Grass

Size: to 10 cm high; stems 0.25–0.6 m high — **F P**
Habitat: Plains grassland, grassy wetland, valley sclerophyll forest
Form: Compact annual tuft
Foliage: Rough, linear, flat leaves to 7 mm wide
Flowers: Panicle is open and broadly spreading. Spikelets to 5 mm long, purplish at maturity. Lemma, to 3 mm long, is hairy on the back. September to January
Requirements: Heavy clay and basalt soils
Comments: A widespread grass.
Localities: Campbellfield, St. Albans, 4, 12, 26, 28, 34A, 41, 42, 44, 47, 48, 50A, 54, 55, 65# 70, 74
Distribution: All states except NT

Agrostis aemula var. setifolia — Blown Grass

Habitat: Grassy wetland
Requirements: Seasonally wet soils
Comments: Differs from *A. aemula* var. *aemula* in that the lemma is slightly longer, to 3.5 mm, and leaves are narrower, to 1 mm wide and inrolled.
Localities: Craigieburn
Distribution: Vic, Qld, NSW, Tas

Agrostis avenacea — Common Blown Grass

Size: stems to 0.6 m high — **F P**
Habitat: Plains grassland, grassy wetlands, box woodland, valley sclerophyll forest, grassy low open forest, primary dune scrub
Form: Annual, biennial or perennial tuft
Foliage: Linear leaves to 20 cm long, tapering to a fine point
Flowers: Grey-green to pale green spikelets to 4 mm long in spreading panicles to over 30 cm long, branches often drooping when young. Lemma hairy on back. October to February
Requirements: Moist clays or clay loams
Comments: Very similar to *A. aemula* and widespread throughout the region. Readily naturalises in areas of light disturbance. A useful volunteer in rough lawns.
Localities: Footscray, Research, 2, 4–9, 11, 12, 15–18, 24–29, 32, 34A–36, 42, 44, 47, 48, 50A, 51, 54–56, 58, 60, 61, 64, 67#, 69A–72, 74–76
Distribution: All states; NZ

Agrostis billardieri var. billardieri — Coast Blown Grass

Size: to 15 cm high; stems 0.15–0.6 m high — **F P**
Habitat: Primary dune scrub, riparian scrub
Form: Annual grassy tuft
Foliage: Flat linear leaves to 20 cm x 3–7 mm
Flowers: Very loose, spreading, straw-coloured panicles to 30 cm long, spikelets to 7 mm long. Lemma glabrous, 4-toothed, outer pair longer. October to February
Requirements: Moist soils
Comments: Usually confined to coastal tracts.
Localities: 5, 67#, 74
Distribution: Vic, NSW, Tas, SA; NZ

Agrostis billardieri var. robusta

Size: to 0.6 m high
Comments: Differs from *A. billardieri* var. *billardieri* in that the leaves are narrower and inrolled and the plant is usually taller. It does not occur in coastal areas.
Localities: Collected in Warrandyte, 1853
Distribution: Vic, Tas, SA

Agrostis aff. hiemalis

Winter Bent

P N

Size: to 30 cm high
Habitat: Damp sclerophyll forest
Requirements: Moist, well drained soils
Comments: Tufted perennial grass, sometimes with a short rhizome. The main distinguishing features are the small spikelets to 2 mm long and the awnless lemma.
Localities: 57
Distribution: Vic, Qld, NSW, Tas; Am, Asia

Agrostis aff. *hiemalis*

Alisma

Alismataceae

Alisma plantago-aquatica

Water Plantain

F P

Size: 0.5–1 m x 0.5 m
Habitat: Aquatic in riparian scrub, grassy wetlands
Form: Erect perennial semi-aquatic herb
Foliage: Erect long-stalked ovate to ovate-lanceolate leaves, blade to 30 cm long, with prominent network of veins
Flowers: Much-branched, whorled panicle, of many small, long-stalked, pale pink 3-petalled flowers, each lasting a single day, borne on rigid leafless stems to 1 m high or more; Summer
Requirements: Moist to wet soils, tolerating poorly drained sites
Comments: A most attractive, easily grown plant for bog gardens and shallow ponds. The closely related *A. lanceolatum*, from Europe and Asia, can often be distinguished by its lanceolate leaves. *Damasonium minus* is similar but may be distinguished by the lesser number of carpels (up to 10).
Propagation: Seed or division of bulbous rootstock
Localities: Laverton Nth, 4, 14, 16, 19, 26, 27, 32, 34A, 36, 42, 44, 51, 53, 54, 56, 62, 63, 65, 74, 76
Distribution: Vic, NSW; NZ

Alisma plantago-aquatica

Amphibromus

Poaceae

Slender tufted perennial grasses growing up to 1.5 m high, usually found growing in wet places beside pools and streams. Leaf blades are generally linear, either flat or inrolled. The inflorescence is a narrow, loose, elongated panicle with slender, erect or flexuose branches. Spikelets have 3 or more florets. The lemma of each floret ends in bristle-like teeth and has a dorsal awn arising from above the middle. A prominent hairy tuft surrounds the base of the lemma. Propagation is by seed or division.

Amphibromus archeri

Pointed Swamp Wallaby Grass

F P

Size: to 30 cm high; stems to 1.2 m high
Habitat: Riparian and swamp scrub
Form: Tufted perennial clump
Foliage: Greenish deeply ribbed leaves 30 cm x 2.5–4 mm
Flowers: Loose erect panicles to 35 cm long, spikelets to 18 mm long contain 2–4 florets. Glumes are very unequal. Lemma to 10 mm long, is 4-toothed (2 of which are much longer than the others), each ending in a bristle; awn to 15 mm long, is dark, bent, and arises well above the middle of the lemma, hair tuft large. October to January.
Requirements: Most soils with ample moisture
Comments: Useful grass for the bog garden but it is not tolerant of drying out. Very rare in Melbourne.
Localities: Oakleigh#, Kilsyth, 28, 69A, 71
Distribution: Vic, Tas, SA

Amphibromus archeri

Amphibromus fluitans

Graceful Swamp Wallaby Grass

P

Size: 0.15–0.7 m high
Habitat: Beside swamps in grassy low open forest, riparian scrub
Foliage: Leaf sheaths are rough
Flowers: Spikelets 7–10-flowered, glumes more or less equal, lemma 2-toothed, awn pale, straight, rising from the middle of the lemma; hair tuft tiny or absent.
Requirements: Moist soils, tolerating inundation
Comments: It was first collected along the Yarra R. flats. Probably extinct in the Melbourne area.
Localities: Camberwell#; Kew#, Balwyn#, 33#, 60#
Distribution: Vic, NSW; NZ
Synonym: *A. gracilis*

Illustrated p. 255

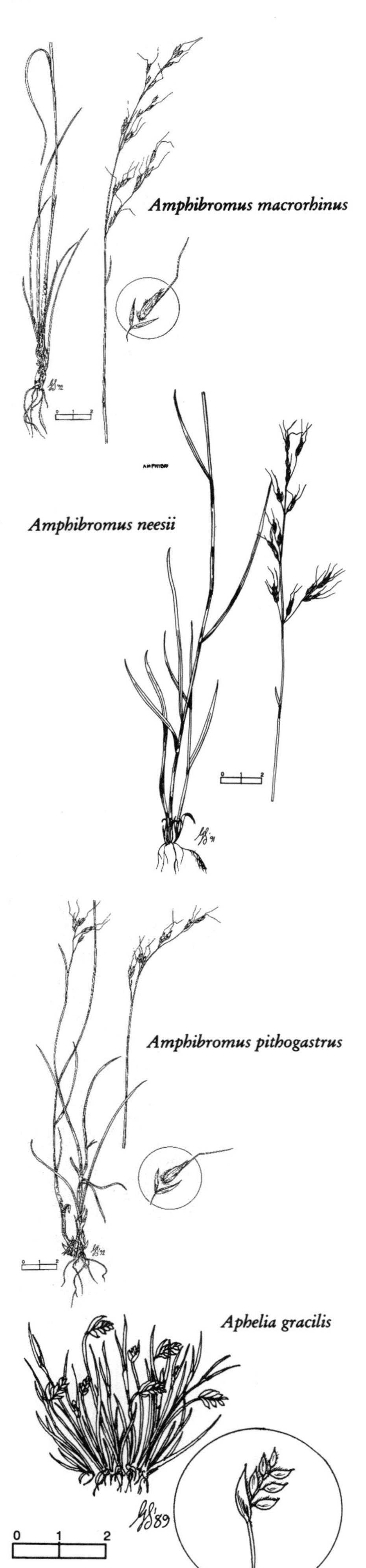
Amphibromus macrorhinus
Amphibromus neesii
Amphibromus pithogastrus
Aphelia gracilis

Amphibromus macrorhinus

Long-nosed Swamp Wallaby Grass

Size: to 25 cm high; stems to 1 m high **F**
Habitat: Grassy wetlands
Foliage: Flat or inrolled leaves to 25 cm long
Flowers: Green or purplish 4–5-flowered spikelets in erect, often spreading panicle to 40 cm long. Lemma has a drawn out, papery apex, very rough on lower back with awn rising from or just below middle. October to November
Requirements: Moist to wet soils. Plants do not tolerate drying out.
Comments: A rare plant in the Melbourne area.
Localities: Laverton
Distribution: Vic, NSW, Tas, SW, WA
Synonym: Previously included with *A. neesii*

Amphibromus neesii

Swamp Wallaby Grass

Size: to 25 cm high; stems 0.4–1 m high **F P**
Habitat: Grassy wetlands, swamps of plains grasslands, wattle tea-tree scrub
Form: Densely tufted perennial grass
Foliage: Flat narrow leaves to 25 cm long, with rough, glabrous surface
Flowers: Very loose panicle to 40 cm long on slender erect stems to 1 m high, with reddish, 4–7-flowered spikelets. Glumes (or bracts) at base of spikelet narrow. Lemma irregularly toothed, pale brownish awn slightly bent, rising just above the middle, small hair tuft. Spring to Autumn
Requirements: Moist to wet soils
Comments: A common grass of low-land wet areas with an attractive weeping habit. It is readily grown but does not tolerate drying out. Until recently this species has often been confused with *A. nervosus*.
Localities: 2, 7, 12, 18, 26, 34A, 35, 71, 75
Distribution: Vic, NSW, Tas, SA, WA

Amphibromus nervosus

Size: to 25 cm high; stems to 1.5 m high **F P**
Habitat: Grassy wetland
Foliage: Pale green linear leaves 5–25 cm x 1.5–6 mm, flat or loosely folded
Comments: Differs from *A. neesii* in that glumes are broad and lemma tapers away evenly.
Localities: Greenvale, Laverton, 4, 28, 34A, 47, 70
Distribution: Vic, NSW, SA, WA *Illustrated p. 255*

Amphibromus pithogastrus

Swollen or Plump Swamp Wallaby Grass

Size: to 20 cm high; stems to 1 m high **F P**
Habitat: Grassy wetlands
Form: Tufted perennial with swellings on lower internodes of stems
Foliage: Narrow, flat to inrolled leaves to 20 cm long
Flowers: Green 2–6-flowered spikelets in narrow, erect panicle to 25 cm long. Lemma is smooth or minutely warty and swollen towards the base with an awn rising shortly below the apex.
Requirements: Moist to wet soils
Comments: An endangered plant in Victoria, it has recently been found on a few scattered sites west and north of Melbourne.
Localities: Basalt plains
Distribution: Vic, NSW

Aphelia — Centrolepidaceae

Aphelia gracilis

Slender Aphelia

Size: 20–40 mm high **F P**
Habitat: Moist tea-tree heath, swamp scrub
Form: Tiny annual tuft
Foliage: Filiform leaves to 25 mm long
Flowers: Spike to 4 mm long, turned to one side, with 6–8 blunt bracts, the lowest one longest; September to November
Requirements: Moist open soil on temporarily wet ground
Comments: The flowerhead of Aphelia spp. is a spike with 6–16 paired bracts and unisexual flowers while the closely related Centrolepis spp. have flower-heads of bisexual flowers enclosed by a pair of bracts. Locally very rare.
Propagation: Seed
Localities: Dandenong, St. Kilda#, 49#, 61, 63, 67#, 74, 75
Distribution: Vic, NSW, Tas, SA, WA

Aphelia pumilio

Dwarf Aphelia

F P

Size: 10–30 mm high
Habitat: Moist tea-tree heath
Form: Tiny annual
Foliage: Linear leaves to 20 mm long
Flowers: Spike erect, to 6 mm long; 8–16 tapering bracts, the lowest 2 longer and leaf-like; October to November
Requirements: Seasonally wet ground
Propagation: Seed
Localities: Heathmont#, St. Kilda#, 67#, 74, 75
Distribution: Vic, NSW, Tas, SA

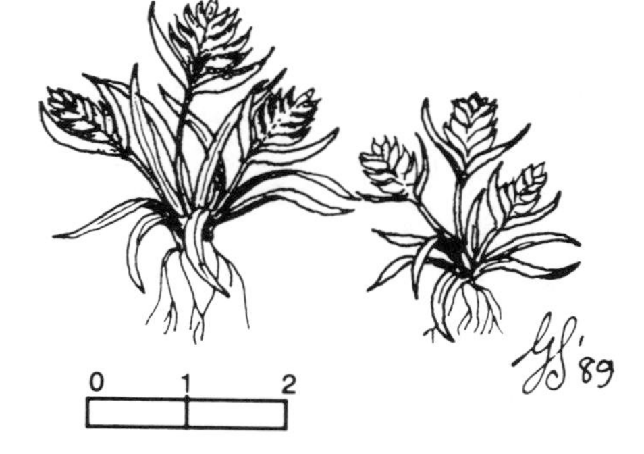

Aphelia pumilio

Aristida

Poaceae

Aristida ramosa

Purple or Cane Wiregrass

F

Size: 0.3–1 m high
Habitat: Plains grassland, box woodland, often in rocky areas
Form: Slender perennial grass tussock with stiff, wiry stems, branching at the upper nodes
Foliage: Leaves tightly inrolled
Flowers: Very narrow, loose panicle to 15 cm long with purplish 1-flowered spikelets. Distinguishing feature is the 3-branched awn on the lemma. August to October
Requirements: Well drained soils
Comments: An attractive summer-growing grass for a sunny position, tolerating poor soils. For best results and longer flowering, Summer moisture is desirable.
Propagation: Seed
Localities: 16, 26
Distribution: Vic, Qld, NSW, WA

Aristida ramosa

Austrofestuca

Poaceae

Austrofestuca hookeriana

Hooker's Fescue

F P

Size: 10–30 cm high; stems to 1.8 m high
Habitat: Swamp and wattle tea-tree scrub, valley sclerophyll forest
Form: Coarse, dense tussock-forming perennial grass
Foliage: Rough, bright green, flat linear leaves to 15 cm long, finely ridged, tips shaped like the bow of a boat
Flowers: Greenish 4–5-flowered spikelets to 20 mm long, ageing to straw coloured, in open conical panicles. Tiny awn to 3 mm long, lemma shortly hairy at base. November to January. Culms much taller than the leaves.
Requirements: Moist soils, tolerating Winter inundation and drying out in Summer
Comments: Being tolerant of heavy shade, this grass is ideal for use as a foliage contrast in fern gardens. Often confused with a serious introduced weed, *Festuca arundinacea*, which is distinguished by the panicles which tend to fall to one side, the glabrous lemmas and the different leaf tips.
Propagation: Seed, division
Localities: Bayswater, Montrose, 53, 54
Distribution: Vic, NSW, Tas
Synonym: *Festuca hookeriana*

Illustrated p. 255

Austrofestuca littoralis

Coastal Fescue

F

Size: 0.3–0.8 m high
Habitat: Primary dune scrub
Form: Tussock-forming perennial grass
Foliage: Rigid, sharp, narrow straw-coloured leaves to 45 cm long, often longer than the culms
Flowers: Dense yellowish spike-like panicle held rigidly erect, with overlapping 4–6-flowered spikelets. Lemma awnless and glabrous at base.
Requirements: Well drained sandy soils
Comments: Important plant for beach erosion control.
Propagation: Seed or division
Localities: Seaford, 2, 67#, 74
Distribution: Vic, NSW, Tas, SA, WA
Synonym: *Festuca littoralis*

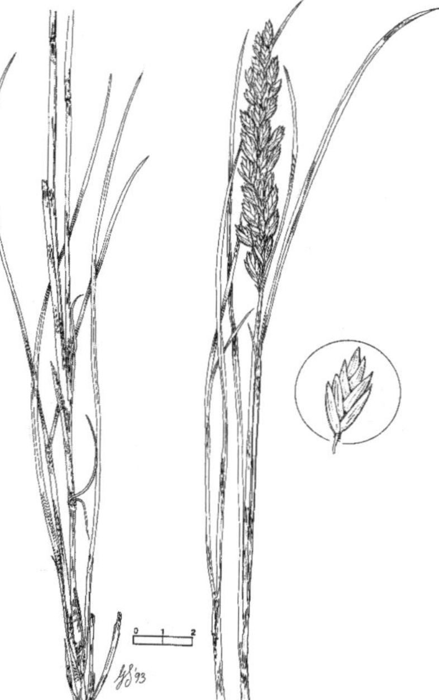

Austrofestuca littoralis

Baumea

Cyperaceae

Baumeas are slender, rush-like, rhizomatous perennial sedges. The flowerhead is a terminal panicle. Leaves and flowering stems (or culms) are similar in shape and usually in size. They are ideal as accent plants in a bog garden, occurring naturally along stream banks and in low-lying swampy areas. Propagation is by division of the rhizome or seed.
Synonym: Previously included with *Cladium*

SCALE: 0 1cm 2cm The scale representation on each plant equals 2cm.

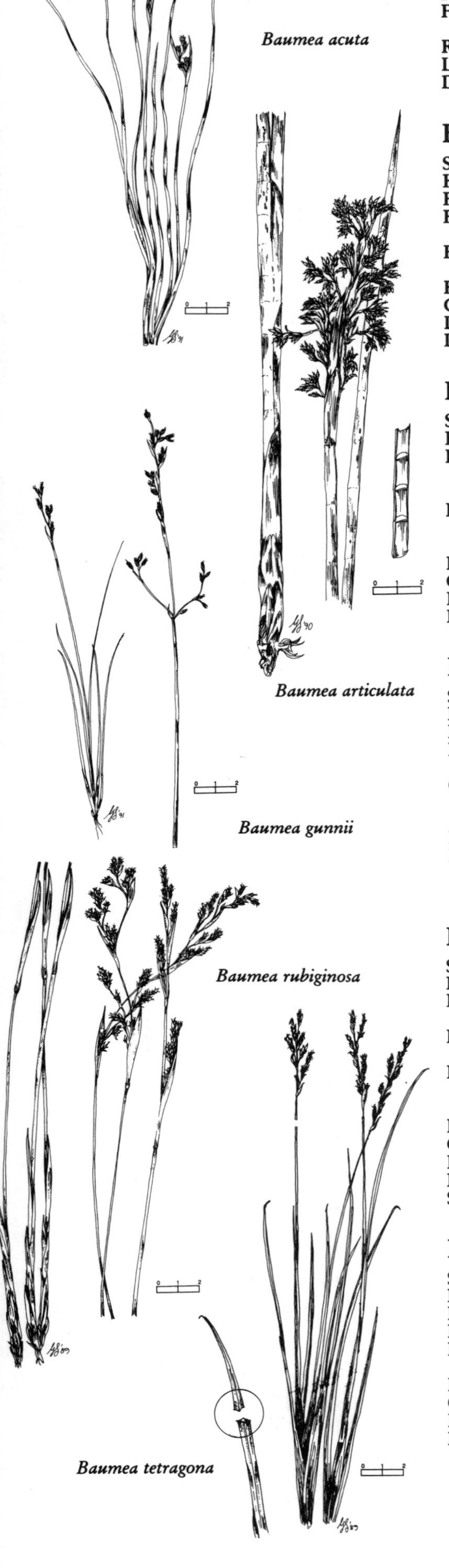

Baumea acuta

Pale Twig-rush

F

Size: 15–30 cm high
Habitat: Tea-tree heath
Foliage: Flattened leaves and flowering stems to 2 mm wide with blunt margins
Flowers: Reddish-brown 1-flowered spikelets to 5 mm long, densely congested in short panicles to 50 mm long; October to April
Requirements: Moist sandy soils
Localities: 50, 67#, 70, 71, 74, 75
Distribution: Vic, NSW, Tas, SA, WA

Baumea articulata

Jointed Twig-rush

F P

Size: 1–2 m high
Habitat: Riparian scrub
Form: Tall erect tussock
Foliage: Stout hollow cylindrical stems and leaves with pungent tips and prominent transverse partitions
Flowers: Numerous brown 3–5-flowered spikelets in large drooping panicles 20–40 cm x 3–6 cm; December to April. Nut light brown to whitish.
Requirements: Moist soils, tolerating inundation
Comments: Useful as a shelter plant for waterbirds. Very effective beside ponds.
Localities: 17#, 18, 35, 72, 75
Distribution: All states except NT; PNG, NZ, N Cal, Poly

Baumea gunnii

Slender Twig-rush

F P

Size: 0.3–1 m high
Habitat: Swamp and wattle tea-tree scrub
Foliage: Leaves reduced to basal sheaths, sometimes with 1 or 2, very short and pointed blades; stems slender with longitudinal furrow and several fine striations
Flowers: Loose elongated panicles to 20 cm long, branches erect, lower branches distant. Few brownish or greyish 1-flowered spikelets, distantly scattered. Flowers most of the year.
Requirements: Adaptable to any soils providing ample moisture is available.
Comments: Interesting bog garden plant.
Localities: 61, 74
Distribution: All states except NT; PNG, NZ

Baumea juncea

Bare Twig-rush

F P

Size: 0.3–1 m high
Habitat: Coastal banksia woodland, tea-tree heath
Form: Rush-like clump with creeping rhizomes
Foliage: Terete greyish stems with 2 or 3 nodes, leaves reduced to sharply pointed sheaths
Comments: Differs from *B. gunnii* in that the spike-like panicle is smaller, to 50 mm long, and the few reddish-brown spikelets are crowded together. September to April.
Localities: 28, 67, 68, 69A–71, 74
Distribution: All states except NT; NZ

Illustrated p. 255

Baumea rubiginosa

Soft Twig-rush

F

Size: 0.3–1 m high
Habitat: Swamp scrub
Form: Rhizomatous clump with round or slightly angled to flattened stems, usually with one node
Foliage: Basal leaves wider than stem; stem leaves with long sheaths and short channelled blades, both sharply pointed
Flowers: Narrow dense panicle to 12 cm long with reddish or brown, 3–5-flowered spikelets in erect clusters. Nut reddish-brown. Flowers most of the year.
Requirements: Ample moisture
Comments: Locally common along watercourses.
Localities: 51, 54, 63, 64, 69A, 70, 72, 74
Distribution: All states; NZ, Asia
Synonym: *B. glomerata*

Baumea tetragona

Square Twig-rush

F

Size: 0.3–1 m high
Habitat: Swamp and wattle tea-tree scrub, tea-tree heath
Form: Erect rush-like clump, stems and leaves strongly 4-angled
Foliage: Leaves basal with pointed tips, wider than stems
Flowers: Dense, erect reddish-brown panicles to 100 mm long. Spikelets 1-flowered, close together. Most of the year
Requirements: Ample moisture, but tolerates drying out in Summer
Comments: Attractive accent plant for bog gardens.
Localities: Knox, Clayton, 54, 67#, 69, 71, 73, 74, 75
Distribution: Vic, Qld, NSW, Tas, SA

Bolboschoenus — Cyperaceae

Bolboschoenus caldwellii — Sea Club-rush

Size: 0.3–0.9 m high — F P
Habitat: Saltmarshes, grassy wetland, wet depressions in red gum woodland
Form: Erect rhizomatous semi-aquatic perennial herb with leafy triangular stems
Foliage: Flat grass-like leaves of varying length, to 4 mm wide
Flowers: Flowerheads a terminal compound cluster of 1–3 many-flowered, golden or red-brown spikelets with 1–3 floral bracts. Glumes downy, keel ending in a point. Nut straw-coloured to golden-brown. October to April
Requirements: Fresh or brackish water on heavy clay or sandy soils
Comments: *Bolboschoenus* species are distinguished by the leaflike bracts which are much longer than and surround the flowerheads. The tubers of both species were roasted by the Aborigines, then pounded to make thin cakes.
Propagation: Seed, division
Localities: Rockbank, Sunshine, 2, 4, 25, 26, 72, 74
Distribution: Vic, NSW, Tas, SA, WA; NZ
Synonym: *Scirpus caldwellii, S. maritimus*

Bolboschoenus caldwellii

Bolboschoenus medianus — Marsh Club-rush

Size: 0.7–2 m high — F P
Habitat: Swamps in riparian scrub
Comments: Similar to but usually taller than *B. caldwellii*. The foliage is darker green, broader and more prominent to 50 cm x 6–11 mm. Clusters of 4–6 dull red-brown spikelets, surrounded by 2–6 floral bracts. Glume ends in a rough, recurved awn. Nut is red-brown to black. Also occurs in shallow brackish water.
Localities: 4, 28, 29, 34A, 35, ?42, 74, 75
Distribution: Vic, NSW, Tas, SA; NZ
Synonym: *Scirpus medianus, S. fluviatilis*

Illustrated p. 255

Bothriochloa — Poaceae

Bothriochloa macra — Redleg Grass

Size: 0.3–0.6 m high — F P
Habitat: Box and red gum woodland, plains grassland
Form: Tufted perennial grass with tough reddish-purple flowering stems
Foliage: Flat, linear, pointed leaves to 20 cm long
Flowers: Erect unbranched panicle of 2–5 racemes, to 60 mm long. Spikelets in very unequal pairs. Long white silky hairs on stalks of spikelets; whitish glume is 2-keeled, fertile lemmas are dimpled and have a brown awn to 20 mm long; anthers purple. December to April, August to September
Requirements: Well drained clay loam soils
Comments: An attractively flowered summer-growing grass, tolerant of extended dry conditions but responding well to extra moisture.
Propagation: Seed, division
Localities: Sunbury, Keilor, Laverton Nth, 2, 9, 16–18, 21, 25, 26, 32
Distribution: Qld, NSW, Tas, SA

Bothriochloa macra

Carex — Cyperaceae

Carex spp. are common in moist to wet sites, usually occurring along watercourses and in swamps. They are perennial, grass-like sedges forming tufts to 1 m high (often smaller), often with rhizomes. Flowers are unisexual, in plume-like terminal spikes with glumes spirally overlapping in several rows. Bracts at the base of the spike are either large and leaf-like, or small, inconspicuous and glume-like. The nut is enclosed in a loose covering. Some species are suited to bog gardens or moist sites in a garden as accent plants. Propagated by division or seed, the more attractive *Carex* spp. are becoming readily available through the specialist nurseries.

Carex appressa — Tall Sedge

Size: 0.5–1.2 m x 0.5–1 m — F
Habitat: Widespread in riparian scrub, dry and valley sclerophyll forests, red gum woodland, grassy low open forest, tea-tree heath
Form: Robust dense tuft, stems rough, sharply triangular and solid, the same length as leaves
Foliage: Slender, bright green, arching leaves to 6 mm wide, with rough edges; bracts inconspicuous
Flowers: Long narrow dense to loose panicle 5–25 cm long, with 20 or more spikes of brownish or dull yellow spikelets. Spikes bisexual (male florets above female florets), the few female florets inconspicuous. August to January
Requirements: Ample moisture, tolerating periods of inundation
Comments: Although slow growing, this tough sedge is suitable for stabilising eroded stream banks. It may be used as either an aquatic or bog garden plant. The Aborigines used the tough leaves in basket-making.
Localities: 7, 26, 27, 29, 31, 34A–36, 39, 42, 44, 46, 47, 49, 50A, 51, 54–57, 60, 62–66, 70, 71, 74–76
Distribution: All states except NT; NZ

Illustrated p. 255

The scale representation on each plant equals 2cm.

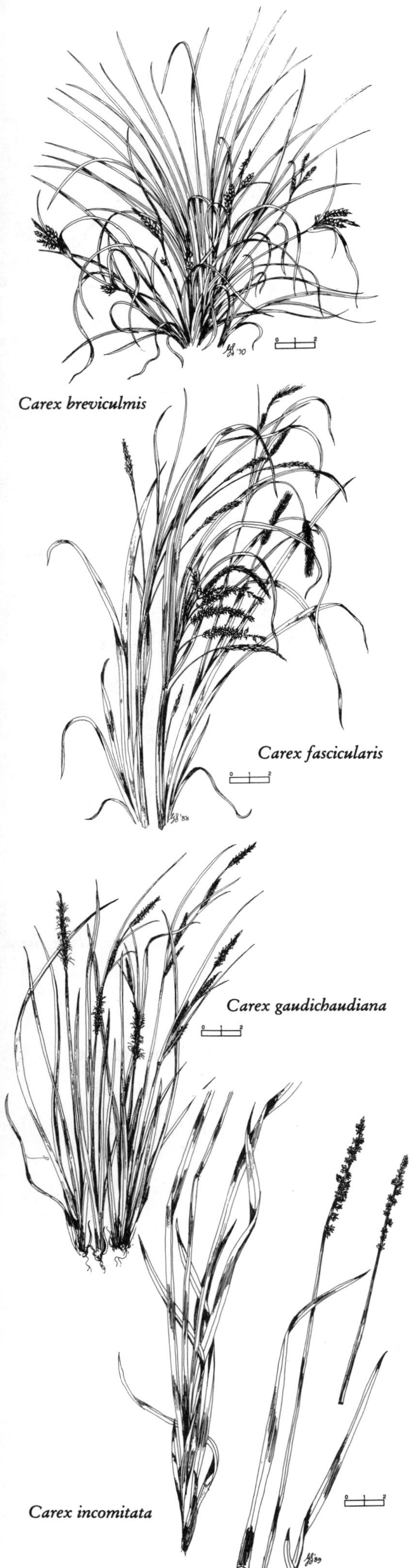

Carex breviculmis

Carex fascicularis

Carex gaudichaudiana

Carex incomitata

Carex bichenoviana — Sedge

F P

Size: stems 25–50 cm high
Habitat: Plains grassland, red gum woodland
Form: Tufted grass-like sedge, with long-creeping rhizome
Foliage: Narrow grass-like leaves and bracts shorter than the triangular stems
Flowers: Heads of 9–23 dense spikes with purple-brown to blackish glumes; terminal cluster of 6–20 sessile male spikes, few female spikes lower, sometimes stalked. October to February.
Requirements: Moist depressions on heavy clay
Comments: May form dense carpets in shady situations. Very rare in the Melbourne area.
Localities: St Albans, Deer Park
Distribution: Vic, Tas, SA

Carex breviculmis — Short-stem Sedge

F P

Size: to 15 cm high
Habitat: Widespread in saltmarshes, grassy wetland, plains grassland, red gum woodland, damp, valley and dry sclerophyll forests, grassy low open forest
Form: Small, densely tufted sedge with short woody rhizomes; stems triangular with rough margins, base covered with brown fibrous remains of old leaf sheaths
Foliage: Flat leaves, longer than flowering stems
Flowers: 2–5 cylindrical spikes, terminal spike male 4–25 mm long, others female to 20 mm long. Covering of nut often downy. Bracts long. August to December
Requirements: Very adaptable, from exposed slopes to moist depressions
Comments: Flower spikes hidden inside leaves. This plant is often overlooked because of its grass-like habit and stature.
Localities: 2, 4, 6, 8, 15, 17#, 18, 26, 28, 34A–36, 38, 39, 41, 42, 44, 45, 47, 48, 50–52, 54–56, 63, 64, 69A, 74–76
Distribution: Vic, Qld, NSW, Tas, SA; NZ

Carex fascicularis — Tassel Sedge

P

Size: 0.5–1 m high
Habitat: Valley sclerophyll forest
Form: Coarse tufted plant; triangular stems with rough margins
Foliage: Bright green partitioned leaves almost as long as stems, to 8 mm broad; leafy bracts much longer than the flowering spikes
Flowers: 3–7 long-stalked, cylindrical, drooping spikes 30–60 cm long, borne near the end of the stem. Terminal spike male. Glumes roughly awned. October to April.
Requirements: Moist soil, tolerating inundation
Comments: A common sedge found along watercourses and near swamps. This graceful tussock looks most attractive beside a pool. Avoid planting on heavy basalt soils.
Localities: Montrose, 35, 36, 56, 62, 63
Distribution: All states; NZ

Carex gaudichaudiana — Tufted Sedge

F P

Size: stems 0.1–0.6 m high
Habitat: Valley sclerophyll forest, swamp scrub
Form: Coarsely tufted plant sometimes covering large areas, with woody ascending rhizomes and triangular stems with rough margins
Foliage: Flat, erect, dark bluish-green leaves to 4 mm wide, often longer than the stems, lower bracts long
Flowers: 3–8 stalked, cylindrical spikes 1.5–6 cm long, at the top of stem, terminal spike male. Glumes almost black. Nut covering is distinctly 4–6-veined. September to February
Requirements: Grows in gravel or mud at the water's edge
Comments: The bluish foliage of this attractive low-growing sedge provides relief from the typical greens of other bog plants. It is easily grown and controlled. Although tolerant of drying out once established, it looks best in permanently moist soils.
Localities: 34A, 35, 42, 54, 56, 62, 63
Distribution: Vic, Qld, Nsw, Tas, SA

Carex incomitata

F

Size: stems 0.5–0.7 m high
Habitat: Plains grassland
Form: Differs from *C. appressa* in that it is a diffuse rather than dense tuft with a stout, short-creeping rhizome
Foliage: Leaves are paler green and wider, to 8 mm.
Flowers: Shorter spike-like panicle is always dense and narrow-oblong, to 80 mm long and mostly unbranched. The many female florets are widely reflexed, hiding the male section.
Comments: Unlike most other *Carex* spp. it prefers well drained soils and tolerates saline conditions.
Localities: Altona, Deer Park, 26, 36
Distribution: Vic, NSW
Synonym: Recently segregated from *C. appressa* as forma *minor*

Carex inversa

Knob Sedge

Size: stems 10–30 cm high
Habitat: Widespread in plains grassland, grassy wetlands, box and red gum woodland, valley sclerophyll forest, grassy low open forest, tea-tree heath
Form: Small tufted or spreading clump with shortly creeping rhizome, stems slender, flat and smooth, usually shorter than the leaves
Foliage: Bright green, grass-like leaves to 1–3 mm wide; 2 leaf-like bracts to 15 cm long
Flowers: Terminal cluster of 2–4 sessile, bisexual, ovoid spikes to 10 mm long, (sometimes one a little lower down). Florets mostly female, few male florets at the base. Glumes pale or greenish, midrib extending into an awn. September to April.
Requirements: Moist well drained soils
Comments: A variable species which sometimes becomes a weed in gardens.
Localities: Montrose, 6, 7, 17#, 18, 23–26, 29, 31, 32, 34A–36, 39, 41, 42, 44, 47, 49, 50A, 54–56, 62, 63, 69A–71, 74, 76
Distribution: All states except NT; NZ

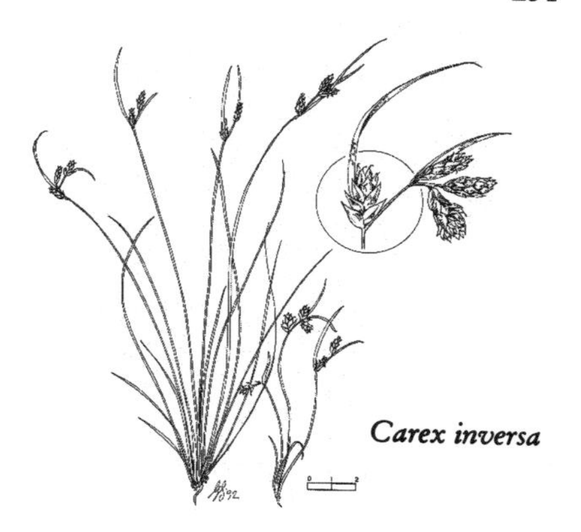

Carex inversa

Carex iynx

Size: to 40 cm high — P
Habitat: Valley sclerophyll forest
Form: Coarse tufted herb with short, ascending, woody rhizomes, forming large clumps; stems at base covered with fibrous remains of old leaf sheaths
Foliage: Bracts short, leaves similar in length to stems
Flowers: Densely-flowered spikes to 8 mm thick, in tufts of 1–5 at nodes, upper 1–4 spikes mostly male and shortly-stalked. Lowermost spikes drooping on long slender stalks. Yellow-chestnut glumes of female florets awned.
Requirements: Moist soils
Localities: Eltham, 34A, 41, 42
Distribution: Vic, NSW, Tas, SA

Illustrated p. 255

Carex pumila

Strand Sedge

Size: stems 10–30 cm high — F
Habitat: Coastal grassy wetlands, primary dune scrub
Form: Tufted herb with a creeping rootstock
Foliage: Flat leaves, keeled in the lower part, coiled at the tip; leaf bracts long, sometimes hiding flowerheads which are held on triangular stems shorter than the leaves
Flowers: 4–7 spikes, 1–4 terminal male spikes, close together, female spikes distant, reddish-brown, the lowest shortly-stalked. August to January. Nut covering is plump and yellowish.
Requirements: Moist sandy soil
Comments: Once locally frequent but remaining in few sites.
Localities: Port Melbourne#, Brighton#; Maribyrnong R, 67#, 69A
Distribution: All states except NT; NZ, S Am, Asia

Carex tasmanica

Size: stems to 0.4 m high — F P
Habitat: Grassy wetlands
Form: Tufted perennial sedge
Foliage: Leaves and stem bracts strongly veined with coiled tips, basal sheaths with papery margins
Flowers: Raceme, to 90 mm long of 2–4 short dense spikes, each to 25 mm long. Terminal spike of male flowers is narrower than spikes of female flowers.
Requirements: Heavy wet soils
Comments: The Melbourne occurrence is a major disjunction from its normal distribution in Southwest Victoria.
Propagation: Division, seed
Localities: Craigieburn
Distribution: Vic, Tas

Carex tereticaulis

Common Sedge

Size: 1 m x 1 m — F P
Habitat: Plains grassland, riparian scrub, valley sclerophyll forest
Form: Densely tufted clumps with terete, hollow, smooth stems which are finely striated
Foliage: Leaves rudimentary, to 4 mm wide, or reduced to sheaths
Flowers: Narrow, dense, spike-like panicle usually less than 10 cm long, with more than 20 spikes; August to April.
Requirements: Moist soils, tolerating occasional inundation
Comments: Similar in habit and appearance to *C. appressa*, but readily distinguished by the terete stems. The stems of *C. appressa* are distinctly triangular. The Aborigines split the stems while still green and used the fibre for string and baskets.
Localities: Rockbank, Altona, 4, 6, 16–18, 24–26, 33, 34A–36, 74
Distribution: Vic, NSW, Tas, SA, WA

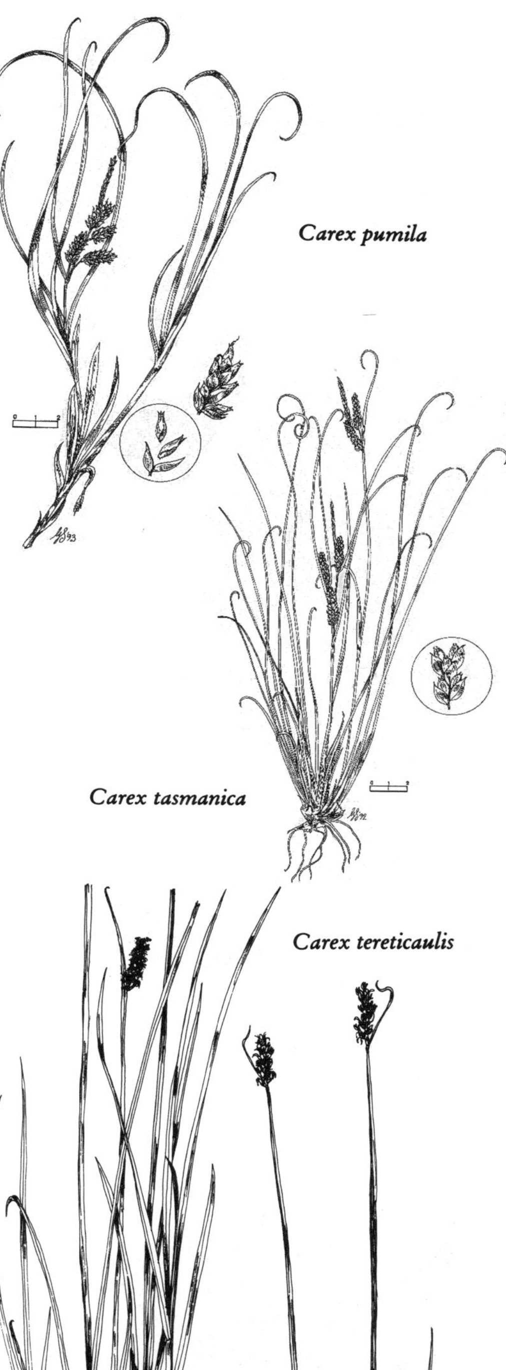

Carex pumila

Carex tasmanica

Carex tereticaulis

SCALE: 0 1cm 2cm — The scale representation on each plant equals 2cm.

Caustis

Cyperaceae

Caustis restiacea

Caustis restiacea

Slender Twist-rush

F P

Size: 0.3–0.6 m x 10–20 cm
Habitat: Swamp scrub
Form: Erect perennial herb with spreading rhizomes, leaves reduced to sheathing bracts, stems slender, terete and slightly twisted
Flowers: Flowers borne in unisexual spikelets to 4 mm long; August to January
Requirements: Moist open soil
Comments: Known from one site within the Melbourne area, also occurring around Gembrook. Distribution is highly restricted within Victoria.
Propagation: Seed, division
Localities: Kilsyth
Distribution: Vic, NSW

Centrolepis

Centrolepidaceae

Small or minute annual or perennial sedge-like or moss-like herbs with linear leaves forming a basal tuft. Flowers are sessile in a terminal head enclosed by 2 erect sheathing bracts which may continue upwards, resembling leaves. The flowering stem is erect and leafless. Found in a variety of habitats but usually in swampy ground or in moist depressions, and often quite common. Propagate by seed.

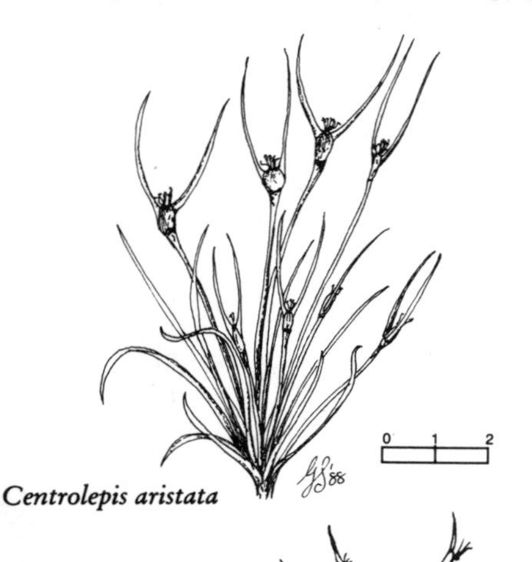

Centrolepis aristata

Centrolepis aristata

Pointed Centrolepis

P

Size: 2–10 cm high
Habitat: Red gum woodland, swamp scrub, valley sclerophyll forest, wattle tea-tree scrub
Form: Rigidly erect annual herb, bright green or becoming reddish after flowering, stems flattened
Foliage: Shiny leaves paired and folded with pointed tip, 10–60 mm long
Flowers: Flowering head flattened, to 3 mm wide with 10–40 flowers per head; September to December. Bracts with leaf-like awns, the lower awn to 40 mm long, upper one shorter.
Requirements: Moist infertile soils
Localities: 12, 26, 28, 35, 42, 44, 53–55, 60, 67#, 69A–71, 73–75
Distribution: Vic, NSW, Tas, SA, WA

Centrolepis fascicularis

Tufted Centrolepis

P

Size: 2.5–6 cm x 3–12 cm
Habitat: Swamp and wattle tea-tree scrub
Form: Bright green perennial herb forming dense cushions; stems terete and thread-like
Foliage: Many fine soft leaves to 45 mm long, lower half with sparse soft hairs
Flowers: Ovoid flowerhead to 3 mm long; November to February. Bracts hairy, just longer than flowerhead.
Requirements: Moist open soils
Localities: Dandenong Rges, 61, 74
Distribution: All states except NT; PNG

Illustrated p. 255

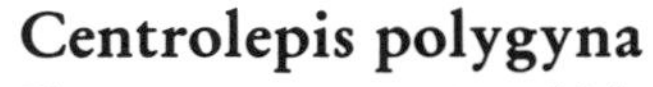

Centrolepis polygyna

Centrolepis polygyna

Wiry Centrolepis

F P

Size: 1.5–6 cm high
Habitat: Saltmarshes, tea-tree heath
Form: Dull green annual tufted herb, becoming red-brown after flowering, stems terete
Foliage: Narrow crowded glabrous leaves 4–12 mm long, rigidly recurved
Flowers: Cylindrical flowerhead 3–5 mm long, with a single flower; July to November. Lower bract has a leaf-like curved awn to 10 mm long, upper bract awnless.
Requirements: Moist sandy soil, tolerating saline conditions
Localities: 67#
Distribution: Vic, NSW, Tas, SA, WA

Centrolepis strigosa

Centrolepis strigosa

Hairy Centrolepis

F P

Size: 2–7 cm high
Habitat: Red gum woodland, valley sclerophyll forest, tea-tree heath, wattle tea-tree scrub
Form: Small hairy bright green annual herb forming a hemispherical tuft
Comments: Similar to *C. fascicularis*. Soft spreading leaves to 25 mm long are softly hairy all over. The flowerheads, to 4 mm long, are sheathed in hairy bracts which end in a short point no longer than the heads. September to November.
Propagation: Seed
Localities: St. Kilda, 35, 42, 44, 60, 63, 67#, 69–72, 74, 75
Distribution: All states except NT; NZ

Chionochloa **Poaceae**

Chionochloa pallida Silver Top Wallaby Grass, Red Anther Wallaby Grass

Size: to 0.3 m x 1 m; stems to 1.5 m high **F P**
Habitat: Sclerophyll woodland, dry and valley sclerophyll forests
Form: Spreading tufted perennial grass forming a tussock, or, when very large, a hummock with a sparse centre
Foliage: Fine green or bluish leaves to 70 cm long, with margins inrolled
Flowers: Spikelets ageing to straw-coloured, with prominent red anthers. Panicles to 35 cm long, held high above the leaves; October to January (mostly after fire)
Requirements: Well drained soils, tolerating periods of wetness
Comments: A most attractive grass, especially in flower, forming large clumps. Tolerates *Phytophthora cinnamomi* fungus, and poorer soils low in nutrient.
Propagation: Seed, division
Localities: Research, 25, 26, 33–36, 40–42, 44, 47, 48, 50–56, 58, 59, 62–64, 71, 74
Distribution: Vic, NSW, WA
Synonym: *Danthonia pallida*

Chloris **Poaceae**

Chloris truncata Windmill Grass, Umbrella Grass

Size: 15–45 cm high **F**
Habitat: Grassy wetland, plains grassland, red gum and box woodland
Form: Open or compact tufted grass forming a dense low crown, occasionally with short, branched stolons
Foliage: Bluish-green, narrow, rough leaves to 15 cm long x 2–5 mm
Flowers: Panicle of 6–9 purplish to black spikes, each to 13 cm long, radiating horizontally from a common point at maturity; November to January. Spikelets arranged in 2 rows along each radiating arm.
Requirements: Well drained conditions, preferring heavy soils
Comments: An attractive grass for a sunny rockery, with very decorative seed heads. Similar to the weed 'Couch' (*Cynodon dactylon*), but larger with the exception of the length of the stolons. The flowering season may be extended through Autumn with additional watering.
Propagation: Seed
Localities: Richmond, Basalt Plains, 2, 5, 7, 9, 12, 15–18, 21, 23–26, 29, 34A, 67#
Distribution: All states except Tas

Chorizandra **Cyperaceae**

Chorizandra cymbaria Heron Bristle Rush

Size: 0.3–1 m high **F P**
Habitat: Swamp scrub, valley sclerophyll forest, tea-tree heath
Form: Erect rush-like perennial herb with fleshy partitioned stems
Foliage: Fleshy basal leaves
Flowers: Solitary, dense, terminal flowerheads, globular dark brown with spikelets to 5 mm long, female floret terminal, surrounded by many male florets. Flowerhead sheathed by an erect bract which appears to extend the stem. September to November.
Requirements: Moist soils, tolerating drying out for short periods over Summer, but responds to Summer watering
Comments: An attractive rush-like plant for bog gardens. Flowerhead appears to burst out of the sides of the stems.
Propagation: Seed, division
Localities: 42, 54, 70, 73, 74
Distribution: All states except SA; N Cal

Cladium **Cyperaceae**

Cladium procerum Leafy or Tall Twig-rush

Size: 0.9–1.8 m high **F P**
Habitat: Riparian scrub, wattle tea-tree scrub
Form: Large grass-like tufting perennial herb with creeping rhizomes, stems hollow, erect, with several nodes
Foliage: Flat leaves with minutely toothed margins and keels
Flowers: Terminal panicle dense and leafy, to 30 cm x 80 mm; November to December
Requirements: Moist to wet soils
Comments: Usually found near watercourses, tolerating saline conditions.
Propagation: Seed, division
Localities: Mouth of Yarra#, 36, 67, 74
Distribution: All states except Tas; N Cal

Chionochloa pallida

Chloris truncata

Chorizandra cymbaria

SCALE: 0 1cm 2cm The scale representation on each plant equals 2cm.

Cymbopogon refractus

Cymbopogon — Poaceae

Cymbopogon refractus — Barb-wire or Turpentine Grass

F P

Size: stems to 1.2 m high
Habitat: Escarpments in plains grassland
Form: Tufted perennial grass
Foliage: Basal leaves to 50 cm long, narrow and rough, rolled in bud, stem leaves shorter. Nodes on stems purple.
Flowers: Narrow panicle comprising distant clusters of glabrous racemes with reddish sheathing bract at the base; racemes bending downwards and becoming darker at maturity. Lemmas either awnless or with twice bent awn to 15 mm long; October to January
Requirements: Well drained soil, usually growing on rocky ground
Comments: The reflexed heads on this grass provide an interesting effect. The leaves have a gingery aroma when crushed. Known from one site within the Melbourne area.
Propagation: Seed, division of rhizome
Localities: Sunbury
Distribution: Vic, Qld, NSW, NT; N Cal, Poly

Cyperus — Cyperaceae

Annual or perennial sedges with creeping rhizomes, found in moist, boggy sites. Leaves of the local species are long and grass-like, at the base of the triangular flowering stems. The terminal inflorescence is an umbel or ball of several-flowered flattened spikelets, with bracts spreading from the base and usually exceeding the infloresence. Glumes overlap in 2 opposite rows. Plants are propagated by division or seed but are rarely available through nurseries.

Cyperus brevifolius

Cyperus brevifolius — Globe Kyllinga

F

Size: 15–30 cm x spreading
Habitat: Known only from cultivated situations; usually on river flats
Form: Perennial herb with slender scattered or tufted stems
Foliage: Soft, limp leaves similar in length to the stems, to 3 mm wide; bracts 3–4, always longer than the flowerhead
Flowers: Tightly clustered, green or yellowish, single-flowered spikelets in a single rounded head. Flowers November to May.
Requirements: Permanently moist soils
Comments: Known only from lawn sites in Melbourne, it may be introduced.
Localities: Balwyn, Melbourne, ?69A
Distribution: Vic, Qld, NSW, SA; NZ, PNG, N Cal, N & S Am, Indon, Af, Philippines, S. Asia

Cyperus gunnii — Flecked Flat Sedge

P

Size: 0.6–1 m x spreading
Habitat: Riparian scrub
Form: Densely tufted perennial herb with rigid, sharply triangular stems as long as the leaves
Foliage: Leaves folded flat, with parallel ridges and finely toothed margins, to 1 m x 5 mm; 2 to 4 bracts similar to leaves, longest pair 0.3–1 m long
Flowers: Simple or compound umbel with 5–8 primary branches. Numerous spikelets in dense, flattened clusters; bright brown spikelets are 6–15-flowered and linear, to 10 mm long; October to April
Requirements: Moist to boggy soils
Localities: 56
Distribution: Vic, Qld, NSW, Tas, SA

Cyperus lhotskyanus — Flat Sedge

P

Size: 0.1–0.6 m high
Habitat: Moist depressions in box woodland on the basalt plains
Form: Tufted perennial herb with finely ridged stems as long as the leaves, and a short creeping rhizome
Foliage: Flat, rigid leaves to 60 cm long; several bracts like the leaves, the lower bract longer than the flowerhead
Flowers: Umbel of 3–7 spikes to 110 mm long; reddish-brown spikelets in dense, 8–12-flowered oblong-lanceolate heads; October to January.
Requirements: Wet soil
Localities: Toolern Vale, 14
Distribution: Vic, NSW, SA
Synonym: *C. rutilans*

Illustrated p. 255

Cyperus gunnii

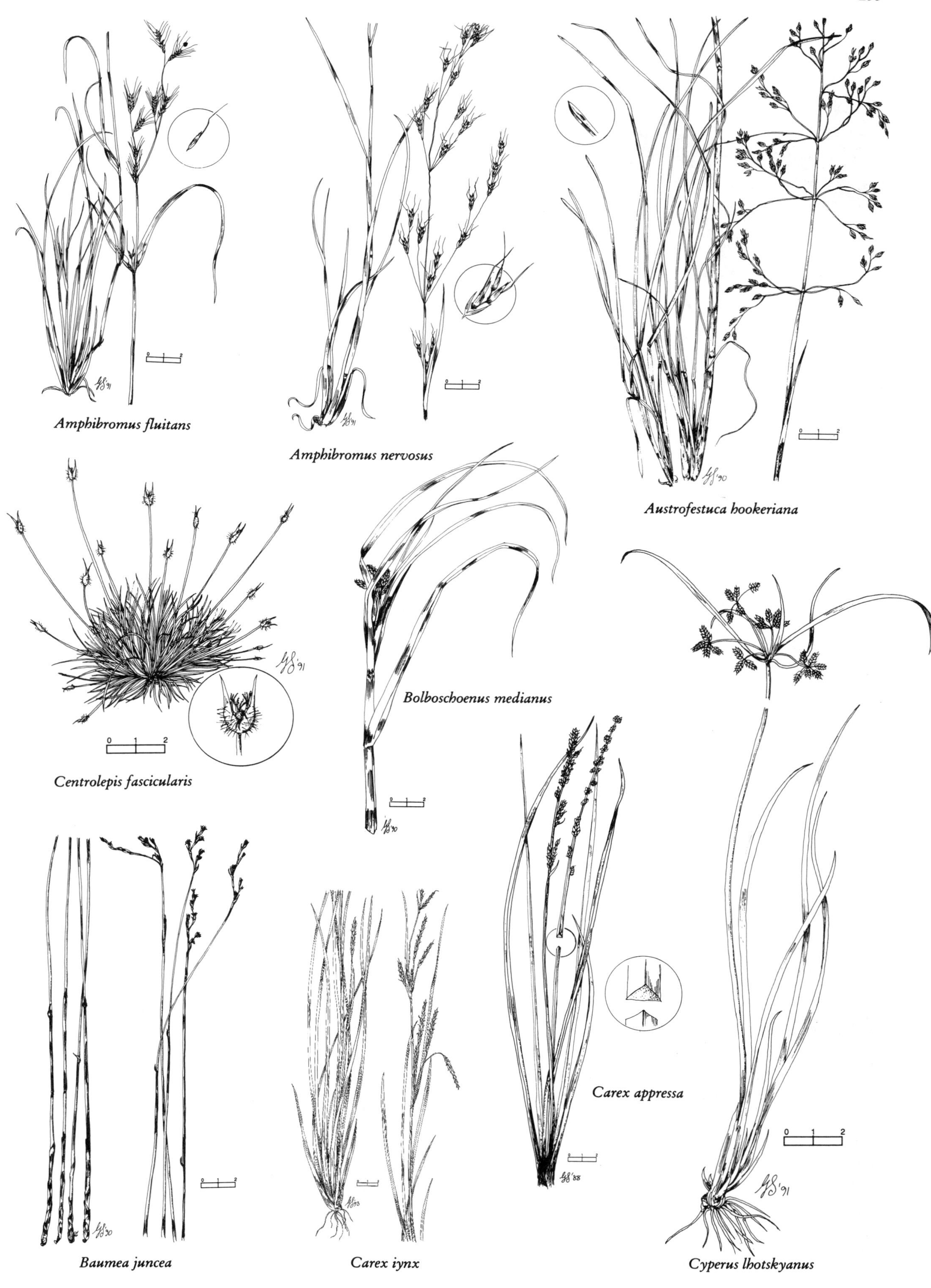

SCALE: 0 1cm 2cm The scale representation on each plant equals 2cm.

Cyperus lucidus

Cyperus lucidus

Leafy Flat Sedge

Size: 0.6–1.5 m high **P**
Habitat: Around swamps and water courses of dry, valley and damp sclerophyll forests
Form: Robust tufted perennial herb with sharply triangular stems
Foliage: Shiny dark green, flat or channelled leaves with rough margins and many shallow ridges, often longer than the stems, to 15 mm wide; 3–6 large bracts 5–15 cm long
Flowers: Compound umbel of up to 12 rigid branches to 20 cm long, divided again into secondary, dense cylindrical brown spikes to 5 cm long, loosely arranged spikelets 5–10-flowered; October to February.
Requirements: Wet soils or boggy conditions
Comments: Will grow as an aquatic plant.
Localities: 30, 34A, 35, 42, 46, 47, 55, 59, 61
Distribution: Vic, Qld, NSW, Tas, SA

Cyperus sanguinolentus

Dark Sedge

Size: 10–40 cm high **P**
Habitat: Riparian scrub
Form: Tufted annual herb
Foliage: Variable dark green leaves 10–40 cm x 3 mm, sometimes very short and thread-like; 3–4 bracts 8–10 cm long
Flowers: Umbel of few short spikes to 40 mm long, on slender stems as long as the leaves. Spikelets clustered, oblong and 8–20-flowered, to 14 mm long; glumes green with dark margins; November to April.
Requirements: Moist or wet soils with a sheltered aspect
Comments: May become a weedy in cultivation.
Localities: 29
Distribution: Vic, Qld, NSW, SA; PNG, Asia, Af

Damasonium minus

Damasonium

Alismataceae

Damasonium minus

Star Fruit

Size: to 0.5 m high **F P**
Habitat: Grassy wetlands, swamps and depressions in box woodland
Form: Emergent aquatic or semi-aquatic annual tufted herb
Foliage: Erect, long-stalked ovate-lanceolate to cordate leaves, blades to 100 mm long
Flowers: Stiff erect panicle with whorls of several 1-flowered branches held high above the foliage on leafless stems. Tiny pale pink 3-petalled flowers; October to July, followed by star-like fruit with 6–10 triangular sections.
Requirements: Shallow water in a sunny position
Comments: An interesting feature for a shallow pond. Plants may be perennial in permanent water, developing into dense, long-flowered colonies. May be confused with *Alisma* spp.
Propagation: Division
Localities: Melton, Yarra R., 6, 24, 26
Distribution: All states

Danthonia

Poaceae

Danthonias (or Wallaby Grasses) are common perennial grasses of open plains and lightly forested slopes, forming discrete clumps or tussocks varying in height from 0.1–1 m. Seventeen species occur within the Melbourne metropolitan area. They may be distinguished from other grasses by the characteristic arrangements of hairs, either covering the lemma, in tufts or in rows. The lemma is distinctly lobed along the top and has a central awn rising from the sinus between 2 pointed or awned lobes. These features also help to identify individual species of *Danthonia*.

Most species are excellent contrast plants in a native landscape requiring full sun or semishaded positions with well drained soil, often thriving on neglect.

Most *Danthonia* spp. show different characteristics in response to changes in their environment. They become much smaller if trampled or grazed regularly and the infloresence may become quite purple after fire. Older plants can be readily rejuvenated by either lifting and dividing or (in some species) by burning the tussock. In the wild, after fire, the first rains induce the plants to spring into life very quickly. Danthonias are an important component of natural pastures and several species have considerable agricultural potential. Other species make excellent lawns if infrequently mown.

Propagation is by seed or by division.

Danthonia auriculata

Lobed Wallaby Grass

Size: to 10 cm high; stems to 30 cm high **F P**
Habitat: Red gum woodland, plains grassland
Form: Slender tufted perennial grass
Foliage: Short, fine, densely hairy leaves to 10 cm long, margins inrolled
Flowers: Dense compact panicle to 40 mm long, spikelets usually 6-flowered. Immature spikelets pale green, often tinged purple, ageing to straw coloured. Outer edges of lobes on lemma end in triangular protuberances (auricles); lemma broad with 3 transverse rows of hair-tufts, hairs of upper ring to 6 mm long. Central awn to 15 mm long, strongly twisted 2 or more times near base. October to December
Requirements: Well drained clay or loam soils
Comments: A species which is well adapted to grazing and natural disturbance.
Localities: 2, 4, 7, 12, 16, 21, 25, 26, 35, 44, 45
Distribution: Vic, NSW, SA

Danthonia caespitosa

Common Wallaby Grass

Size: 20–40 cm x 40 cm; stems to 1.2 m high **F P**
Habitat: Grassy wetland, plains grassland, red gum woodland, valley sclerophyll forest, tea-tree heath
Form: Variable perennial grass often forming a dense tussock, but sometimes reduced to small tufts
Foliage: Leaves glabrous or hairy, flat or loosely rolled, and often blue-green on upper surface; vary substantially under dry conditions
Flowers: Panicles usually oblong to 15 cm, with 10–30 spikelets of 4–9 flowers. Lemma pale, to 6 mm long, with 3 transverse rows of hair-tufts, central awn usually dark, to 25 mm long, twisted 3–5 times near base. October to January, March
Requirements: Moist well drained soils
Comments: Widespread and common throughout the region and often a dominant component of the ground flora. Mature flowerheads appear bleached and fluffy. May persist under mowing or grazing. Large variability between forms may warrant future subdivision of this species.
Localities: Montrose, 2, 4–9, 12, 14–18, 21, 24–26, 28, 29, 32, 34A, 35, 50A, 54, 56, 58, 62, 63, 67, 68, 69A, 71, 74, 76
Distribution: Vic, NSW, Tas, SA, WA; NZ

Danthonia carphoides var. carphoides

Short Wallaby Grass

Size: to 10 cm high; stems to 30 cm high **F**
Habitat: Plains grassland, red gum woodland
Form: Small tufted perennial grass
Foliage: Short fine leaves 3–20 cm long, inrolled
Flowers: Dense ovoid raceme to 40 mm long with few 3–5-flowered greenish spikelets soon turning straw-coloured. Lemma to 6 mm long with hairs scattered over the back, lateral lobes tiny and awnless to 2 mm long, central awn short and thick. Glumes are broad and strongly boat-shaped. October to December
Requirements: Well drained soils, tolerating short wet periods in Winter
Comments: A rare and adaptable small tuft, often associated with *D. auriculata*. Ideal for filling small spaces between rocks. May persist under mowing or grazing.
Localities: Preston, 2, 4, 7, 21, 25, 26, 28
Distribution: Vic, NSW, Tas, SA

Danthonia duttoniana

Brown-back Wallaby Grass

Size: to 40 cm x 50 cm; stems to 1 m high **F P**
Habitat: Grassy wetland, low lying areas in plains grassland and red gum woodland
Form: Erect, densely tufted glabrous perennial grass
Foliage: Leaves typically 20 cm x 2–4 mm
Flowers: Numerous 5–7-flowered pale green spikelets, clustered towards ends of flowering branches in panicles to 120 mm long. Lower branches long, becoming reflexed. Lemma golden brown, lobes paler, with 2 rows of sparse hair-tufts. Central awn bent and twisted 2–3 times. October to January
Requirements: Moist, poorly drained soils, in basalt and peat
Comments: One of several *Danthonia* spp. which tolerate poorly drained conditions. The flowerheads are often distinctly reddish before maturity, making them most attractive.
Localities: 2, 4–7, 12, 16–18, 21, 24–26, 28, 35, 36
Distribution: Vic, NSW, SA

SCALE: 0 1cm 2cm — The scale representation on each plant equals 2cm.

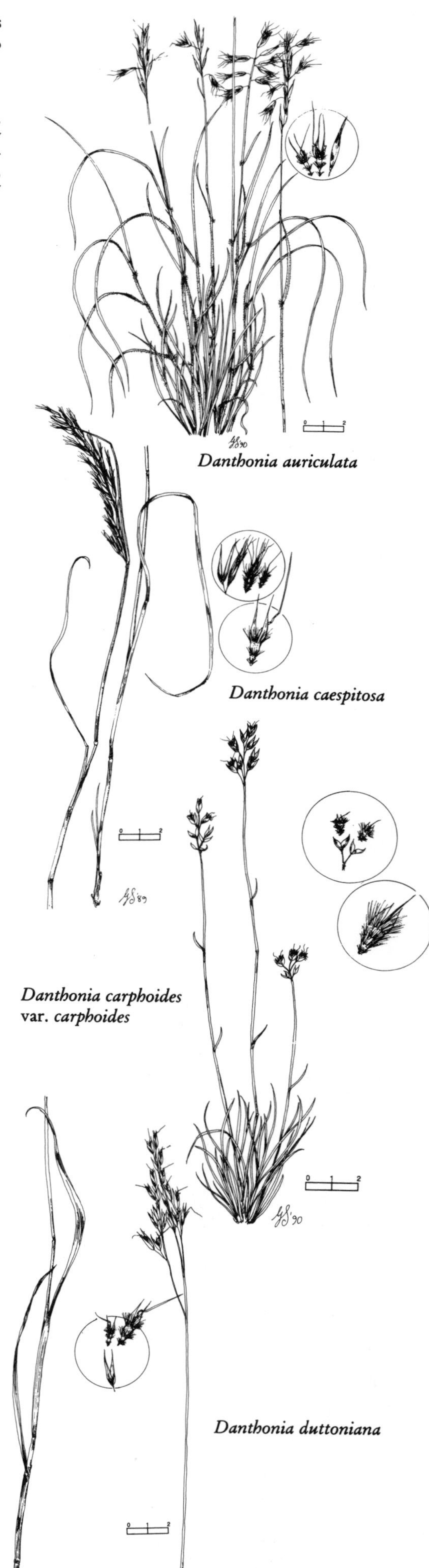

Danthonia auriculata

Danthonia caespitosa

Danthonia carphoides var. *carphoides*

Danthonia duttoniana

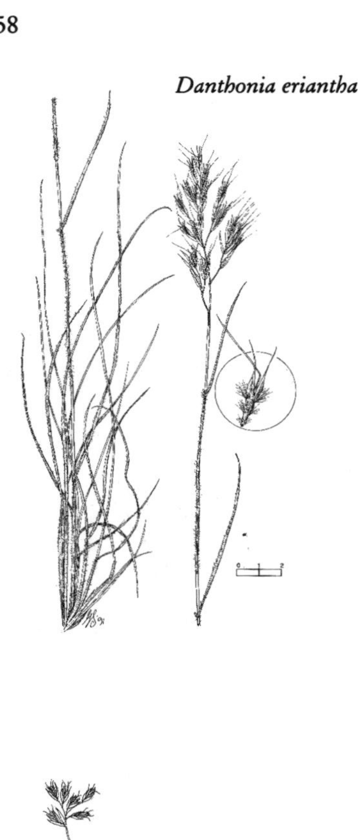
Danthonia eriantha

Danthonia eriantha

Hill Wallaby Grass

Size: to 20 cm x 30 cm; stems to 50 cm high **F P**
Habitat: Red gum woodland, plains grassland, dry sclerophyll forest
Form: Erect, densely tufted perennial grass
Foliage: Leaves fine, stiff, inrolled, to 25 cm long, hairy at least when young
Flowers: Short, dense, lanceolate to ovate panicle, 20–70 mm long, 4–15 greenish spikelets, on downy branches. 2 rows of hair tufts on lemma. Central awn of lemma to 15 mm long, twisted 3–4 times, long lateral lobes. Anthers yellow to pale orange-yellow. October to December
Requirements: Well drained soils on exposed sites
Comments: A widespread and common grass, often co-extensive with other *Danthonia* spp., particularly *D. caespitosa*. Persists in rough lawns.
Localities: Montmorency, 2, 4, 6, 12, 17#, 18, 24–26, 35, 41, 42, 47, 48, 74
Distribution: Vic, NSW, SA

Danthonia geniculata

Kneed Wallaby Grass

Size: to 15 cm x 20 cm; stems to 30 cm high **F P**
Habitat: Box and red gum woodland, dry sclerophyll forest, tea-tree heath
Form: Tufted perennial grass with slender stems, often bent near base
Foliage: Very fine hairy inrolled leaves to 15 cm long
Flowers: Dense panicle to 50 mm long, with pale, 4–6-flowered spikelets. Lemma hairs scattered, lateral lobes pointed, 2–4 times length of body, central awn bent at base, no longer than side lobes; October to December, March
Requirements: Tolerant, adapting to most soils
Comments: Useful in lawns but slow to establish.
Localities: Kilsyth#, Eltham, Prahran, 5, 6, 16–18, 21, 23–26, 32, 34A–36, 42, 44, 45, 49, 66–71, 74–76
Distribution: Vic, SA

Danthonia induta

Yellow Anther Wallaby Grass

Size: to 30 cm high; stems 0.6–1.2 m high **F P**
Habitat: Box woodland
Form: Robust erect tufted perennial grass
Foliage: Leaves to 30 cm long, flat to 4 mm wide or inrolled
Flowers: Loose, large, spreading panicle to 18 cm long bearing many green or straw-coloured spikelets with yellow-orange anthers. Lemma hairs scattered, increasing in size towards the apex, central awn strongly twisted at base.
Requirements: Heavy well drained soils
Comments: An attractive, vigorously growing grass which is never abundant. Responds to extra moisture during Summer, producing flowers over an extended period.
Localities: Keilor, 25, 26, 35, 42
Distribution: Vic, Qld, NSW *Illustrated p. 262*

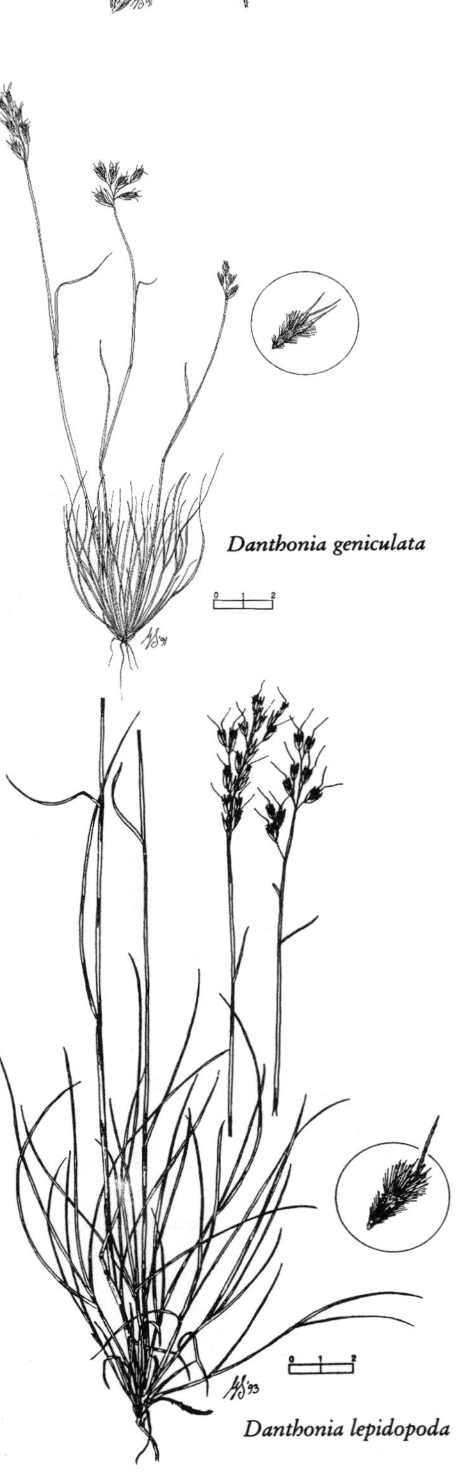
Danthonia geniculata

Danthonia lepidopoda

Danthonia laevis

Wallaby Grass

Size: to 40 cm x 40 cm; stems to 0.7 m high **F P**
Habitat: Plains grassland, red gum and box woodlands, dry and valley sclerophyll forests, tea-tree heath
Form: Erect densely tufted perennial
Foliage: Leaves to 30 cm long, inrolled in bud, becoming flat or loosely inrolled
Flowers: Panicle to 50 mm long with 4–7 greenish spikelets. Lemma has complete ring of long hair-tufts near the top and only small tufts (rather than a ring) below; lateral lobes broad, to 10 mm long ending in fine awns, central awn long to 30 mm, bent at 4 mm. Anthers yellow-orange to purple. October to January
Requirements: Moist soils
Comments: Extremely adaptable to different soils providing moisture is adequate. Often found bordering wet depressions with *D. duttoniana* on basalt or *D. semiannularis* elsewhere.
Localities: Silvan, Montmorency, 25, 26, 28, 34A, 35, 42, 44, 47, 48, 50A, 54–56, 63, 69A, 70, 73, 75
Distribution: Vic, NSW, Tas, SA *Illustrated p. 262*

Danthonia lepidopoda

Size: to 15 cm high; stems to 0.6 m high **P**
Habitat: Sclerophyll woodland
Form: Weakly tufted perennial grass, with long scaly rhizomes
Foliage: Flat or channelled leaves to 15 cm long, glabrous or sparsely hairy
Flowers: Narrow to narrowly ovate panicle to 80 mm long, with few, purplish, 3–4-flowered spikelets. Lemma covered in hairs which are weakly tufted, lobes ending in short bristly tips, central awn to 10 mm long, weakly twisted.
Requirements: Sandy soil
Comments: A newly named species known from 2 collections on the south-eastern slopes of the Dandenong Rges. More common in the Otways and Grampians. Differs from all other *Danthonia* spp. in that it develops a long creeping rhizome.
Localities: Belgrave Sth
Distribution: Endemic to Vic

Danthonia linkii var. linkii

Wallaby Grass

Size: to 40 cm x 40 cm; stems to 0.6 m high **F P**
Habitat: Red gum woodland, dry and valley sclerophyll forest
Form: Variable perennial grass, densely tufted and erect
Foliage: Leaves firm, 20–70 cm x 1–2.5 mm wide
Flowers: Loose, sometimes sparse, panicle to 120 mm long with pale green spikelets, crowded and 5–6-flowered. Lemma pale, fluffy, densely hairy at base, usually a row of fine long hairs around the top, back covered in hairs. Lateral lobes twice as long as lemma body, central awn twisted for 1.5 mm from base. Palea (or upper bract) lanceolate and pointed. Flowers mostly from November to March, but in a good season flowering may continue all year. Panicles ripen slowly from the top down, often showing the full range of stages of development.
Requirements: Heavy soils
Comments: High rates of foliage production may be useful for fodder or specimen plants, but very poor for lawns.
Localities: Heyington, Hurstbridge, 18, 21, 23, 25, 26, 34A–36, 39, 41, 42, 44, 51, 53, 56, 69A
Distribution: Vic, Qld, NSW

Danthonia linkii var. fulva

Wallaby Grass

Habitat: Box woodland, dry and valley sclerophyll forests
Comments: Generally more robust, with broader leaves (to 3 mm), than *D. linkii* var. *linkii*. The central awn is brown and more strongly twisted for 3–4 mm at the base. Both varieties commonly occur together.
Localities: Keilor basalt plains, Montmorency, Dandenong Rges, 62, 63
Distribution: Vic, NSW, SA

Danthonia linkii var. *fulva*

Danthonia pallida = Chionochloa pallida

Danthonia penicillata

Slender Wallaby Grass

Size: to 20 cm x 30 cm; stems to 0.6 m high **P**
Habitat: Dry, valley and wet sclerophyll forests, riparian woodland and scrub, grassy low open forest
Form: Fine, sparsely hairy, weeping perennial grass forming sparse open tussocks,
Foliage: Narrow flat or inrolled leaves to 15 cm long
Flowers: Slender, arching, furrowed stems to 60 cm high, bearing narrow weak racemose panicles to 15 cm long with scattered 4–6-flowered spikelets. Lateral lobes longer than lemma body; separate hair-tufts on sides and back of lemma; October to January.
Requirements: Moist well drained soil
Comments: A graceful distinctive little grass that is easily overlooked, and is ideal for establishing in shaded areas. Persists in unimproved pasture and rough lawn. Distinguished from *D. pilosa* by arching stems and short twisted part of awn.
Localities: 8, 16, 18, 25, 26, 29, 34A–36, 41, 42, 44, 47–50A, 54–57, 60, 63–67, 74, 76
Distribution: Vic, NSW, Tas; NZ

Danthonia penicillata

Danthonia pilosa var. pilosa

Velvet Wallaby Grass

Size: to 20 cm x 30 cm; stems to 0.5 m high **P**
Habitat: Sclerophyll woodland, valley sclerophyll forest, grassy low open forest, plains grassland
Form: Erect or flattened tufted perennial grass, depending on its environment
Foliage: Flat or inrolled, hairy linear leaves usually to 12 cm x 2 mm
Flowers: Short, ovate, stiff panicle to 70 mm long, contracting at maturity. 5–9-flowered pale spikelets crowded and overlapping. Top hair-tufts on lemma separated; dark central awn strongly twisted near base, coarse and long; November to February.
Requirements: Moist soils
Localities: 16, 23, 26, 28, 34A, 36, 40–42, 44, 47–50A, 54–56, 58, 60, 63, 64, 69A, 74–76
Distribution: All states except NT; NZ *Illustrated p. 262*

Danthonia procera

Tall Wallaby Grass

Size: to 0.5 m x 0.7 m; stems to 1.4 m high **F P**
Habitat: Red gum woodland, grassy low open forest
Form: Large, robust perennial tussock grass
Foliage: Fine, inrolled, glabrous leaves to 30 cm x 3 mm, bluntly pointed; similar to *Chionochloa pallida*
Flowers: Loose, open panicle to 15 cm long. Lemma pale with hair-tufts in rows, short awns on lateral lobes.
Requirements: Well drained soils, although very tolerant once established
Comments: Regionally rare and uncommon throughout its range.
Localities: 23, 28, 35, 74, 76,
Distribution: Vic, NSW, Tas

Danthonia procera

SCALE: 0 1cm 2cm — The scale representation on each plant equals 2cm.

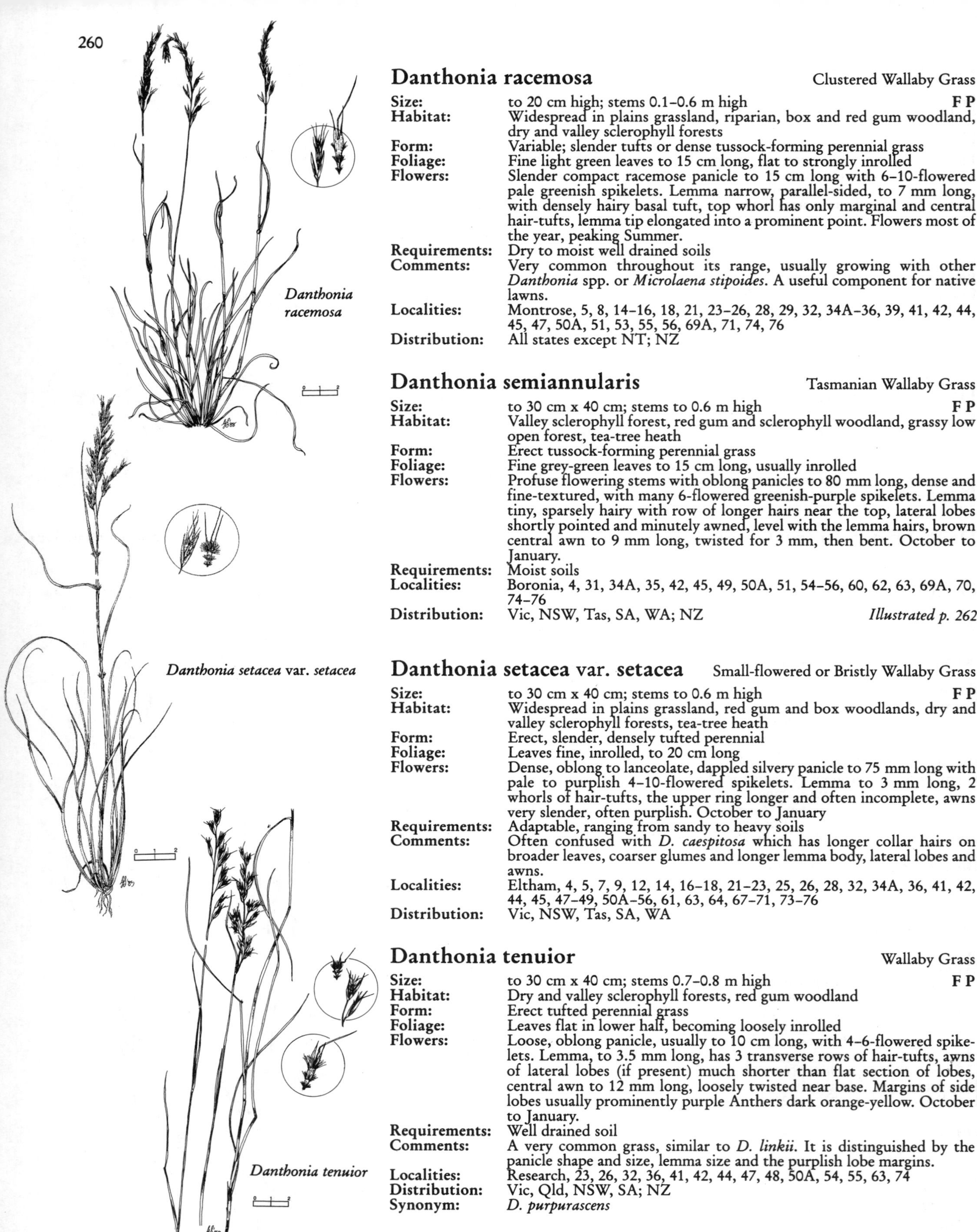

Danthonia racemosa

Clustered Wallaby Grass

Size: to 20 cm high; stems 0.1–0.6 m high **F P**
Habitat: Widespread in plains grassland, riparian, box and red gum woodland, dry and valley sclerophyll forests
Form: Variable; slender tufts or dense tussock-forming perennial grass
Foliage: Fine light green leaves to 15 cm long, flat to strongly inrolled
Flowers: Slender compact racemose panicle to 15 cm long with 6–10-flowered pale greenish spikelets. Lemma narrow, parallel-sided, to 7 mm long, with densely hairy basal tuft, top whorl has only marginal and central hair-tufts, lemma tip elongated into a prominent point. Flowers most of the year, peaking Summer.
Requirements: Dry to moist well drained soils
Comments: Very common throughout its range, usually growing with other *Danthonia* spp. or *Microlaena stipoides*. A useful component for native lawns.
Localities: Montrose, 5, 8, 14–16, 18, 21, 23–26, 28, 29, 32, 34A–36, 39, 41, 42, 44, 45, 47, 50A, 51, 53, 55, 56, 69A, 71, 74, 76
Distribution: All states except NT; NZ

Danthonia semiannularis

Tasmanian Wallaby Grass

Size: to 30 cm x 40 cm; stems to 0.6 m high **F P**
Habitat: Valley sclerophyll forest, red gum and sclerophyll woodland, grassy low open forest, tea-tree heath
Form: Erect tussock-forming perennial grass
Foliage: Fine grey-green leaves to 15 cm long, usually inrolled
Flowers: Profuse flowering stems with oblong panicles to 80 mm long, dense and fine-textured, with many 6-flowered greenish-purple spikelets. Lemma tiny, sparsely hairy with row of longer hairs near the top, lateral lobes shortly pointed and minutely awned, level with the lemma hairs, brown central awn to 9 mm long, twisted for 3 mm, then bent. October to January.
Requirements: Moist soils
Localities: Boronia, 4, 31, 34A, 35, 42, 45, 49, 50A, 51, 54–56, 60, 62, 63, 69A, 70, 74–76
Distribution: Vic, NSW, Tas, SA, WA; NZ *Illustrated p. 262*

Danthonia setacea var. setacea

Small-flowered or Bristly Wallaby Grass

Size: to 30 cm x 40 cm; stems to 0.6 m high **F P**
Habitat: Widespread in plains grassland, red gum and box woodlands, dry and valley sclerophyll forests, tea-tree heath
Form: Erect, slender, densely tufted perennial
Foliage: Leaves fine, inrolled, to 20 cm long
Flowers: Dense, oblong to lanceolate, dappled silvery panicle to 75 mm long with pale to purplish 4–10-flowered spikelets. Lemma to 3 mm long, 2 whorls of hair-tufts, the upper ring longer and often incomplete, awns very slender, often purplish. October to January
Requirements: Adaptable, ranging from sandy to heavy soils
Comments: Often confused with *D. caespitosa* which has longer collar hairs on broader leaves, coarser glumes and longer lemma body, lateral lobes and awns.
Localities: Eltham, 4, 5, 7, 9, 12, 14, 16–18, 21–23, 25, 26, 28, 32, 34A, 36, 41, 42, 44, 45, 47–49, 50A–56, 61, 63, 64, 67–71, 73–76
Distribution: Vic, NSW, Tas, SA, WA

Danthonia tenuior

Wallaby Grass

Size: to 30 cm x 40 cm; stems 0.7–0.8 m high **F P**
Habitat: Dry and valley sclerophyll forests, red gum woodland
Form: Erect tufted perennial grass
Foliage: Leaves flat in lower half, becoming loosely inrolled
Flowers: Loose, oblong panicle, usually to 10 cm long, with 4–6-flowered spikelets. Lemma, to 3.5 mm long, has 3 transverse rows of hair-tufts, awns of lateral lobes (if present) much shorter than flat section of lobes, central awn to 12 mm long, loosely twisted near base. Margins of side lobes usually prominently purple Anthers dark orange-yellow. October to January.
Requirements: Well drained soil
Comments: A very common grass, similar to *D. linkii*. It is distinguished by the panicle shape and size, lemma size and the purplish lobe margins.
Localities: Research, 23, 26, 32, 36, 41, 42, 44, 47, 48, 50A, 54, 55, 63, 74
Distribution: Vic, Qld, NSW, SA; NZ
Synonym: *D. purpurascens*

Deyeuxia

Poaceae

Deyeuxias (or Bent Grasses) are erect, sparsely-tufted perennials up to 1.5 m high, with mostly basal leaves, flat or convolute and tapering to a fine point. The inflorescence is an open or dense terminal panicle with numerous and often densely overlapping 1-flowered spikelets. An awn rises from the back of the lemma similar to *Agrostis* but the lemma is narrower and papery rather than transparent. None of the species are important as pasture grasses. Propagation is by seed or division of the tuft. Seed should be stored 6–12 months before sowing.

Deyeuxia contracta

Bent-grass

Habitat: Wet sclerophyll forest
Form: Leaves and flowering stems lax
Flowers: Panicle to 7–20 cm long, loose with spreading branches with green or purplish spikelets to 2.5 mm long. Lemma rough with minute awn attached to the upper third
Requirements: Moist rich soils
Localities: 57
Distribution: Vic, NSW, Tas

Illustrated p. 262

Deyeuxia densa

Bent-grass

Size: 0.5–1 m high **F P**
Habitat: Tea-tree heath, swamp scrub
Form: Stout or slender tufted perennial grass
Foliage: Leaves narrow, flat or folded
Flowers: Dense spike-like panicle to 120 mm long. Spikelet stalk ends in feathery bristle. Awn, to 5 mm long, rises from near the middle of the lemma. October to January
Requirements: Moist soil
Comments: Locally rare.
Localities: Clayton, Kilsyth, 74
Distribution: Vic, Tas, SA

Deyeuxia minor

Bent-grass

Size: to 0.4 m high **F P**
Habitat: Coastal banksia woodland, dry sclerophyll forest
Comments: A slender tufted perennial similar to *D. densa* but smaller with very fine leaves. Panicle is shorter to 40 mm and bristle is absent. A coastal grass which may be extinct within Melbourne.
Localities: Warrandyte#, 67#
Distribution: Vic, NSW, Tas, SA

Deyeuxia quadriseta

Reed Bent-grass

Size: to 15 cm x 40 cm; stems 1 m or more high **F P**
Habitat: Widespread in damp, valley and dry sclerophyll forests, sclerophyll woodland, grassy low open forest, plains grassland
Form: Open, sparsely tufted perennial tussock
Foliage: Flat to slightly inrolled leaf to 30 cm long
Flowers: Dense spike-like panicle to 15 cm long with pale green spikelets, awn almost basal; September to May
Requirements: Well drained soils
Comments: Although a coarse grass, large clumps are attractive in flower.
Localities: Research, 7, 26, 28, 34A–36, 41, 42, 44–48, 50–58, 61–64, 67, 68, 69A, 70, 74–76
Distribution: Vic, NSW, Tas, SA, WA

Illustrated p. 262

Deyeuxia rodwayi

Bent-grass

Size: to 10 cm high; stems 0.75 m high **P N**
Habitat: Wet, damp and valley sclerophyll forests
Form: Weakly ascending slender tussock
Flowers: Narrow but loose panicle to 15 cm long. Glumes widely gaping at maturity. Awn attached to the middle of the lemma, curved and longer than lemma.
Requirements: Moist soils
Localities: Belgrave, 55, 57
Distribution: Vic, Qld, NSW, Tas

Illustrated p. 262

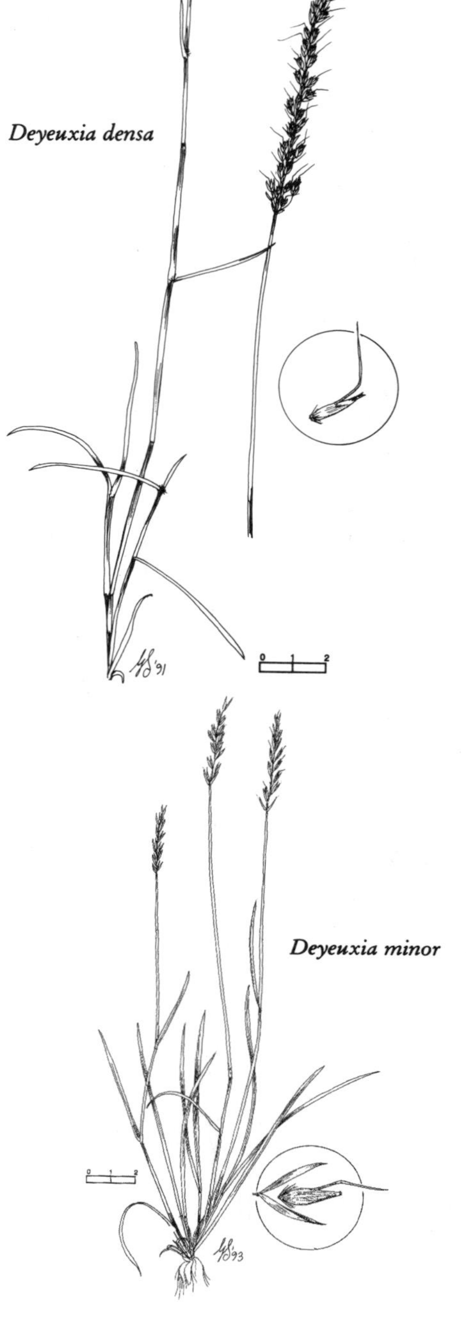

Deyeuxia densa

Deyeuxia minor

Dichanthium — Poaceae

Dichanthium sericeum

Queensland or Silky Blue-grass

Size: 30–50 cm high; stems to 0.8 m high **F**
Habitat: Plains grassland
Form: Upright grassy clump, nodes of flowering stems densely bearded with silky white hairs
Foliage: Flat, bluish leaves to 100 mm x 2–4 mm, often with purple tinges
Flowers: Groups of 2–6 sessile racemes to 50 mm long, densely covered in silky white hairs, radiating from the end of the flowering stem. Spikelets in very unequal pairs; awn of fertile lemma dark, twisted and bent, to 30 mm long. Flowering most of the year.
Requirements: Well drained heavy clay soils
Comments: Highly ornamental when growing vigorously because of its distinctive blue-grey appearance. Responds positively to extra water in Summer and also to hard cutting back.
Propagation: Seed or division
Localities: Sydenham, Sunshine, Footscray, Rockbank, Broadmeadows, 10, 15, 16, 25, 26, 29
Distribution: All mainland states; PNG, N Cal, Philippines

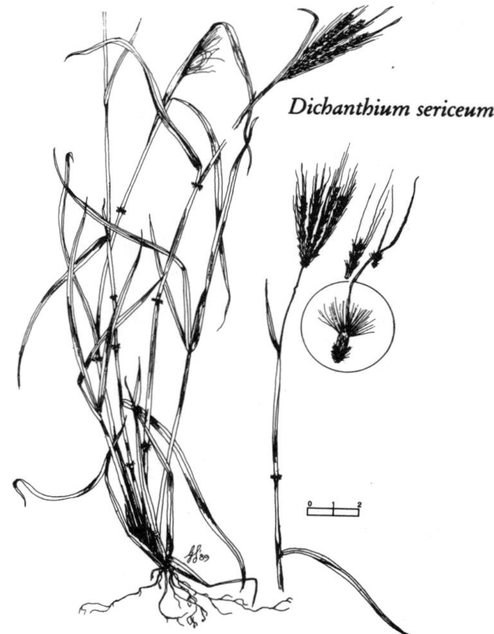

Dichanthium sericeum

SCALE: 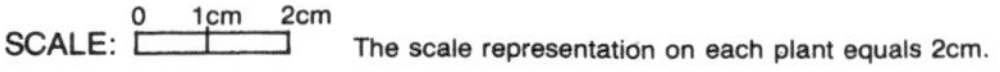

The scale representation on each plant equals 2cm.

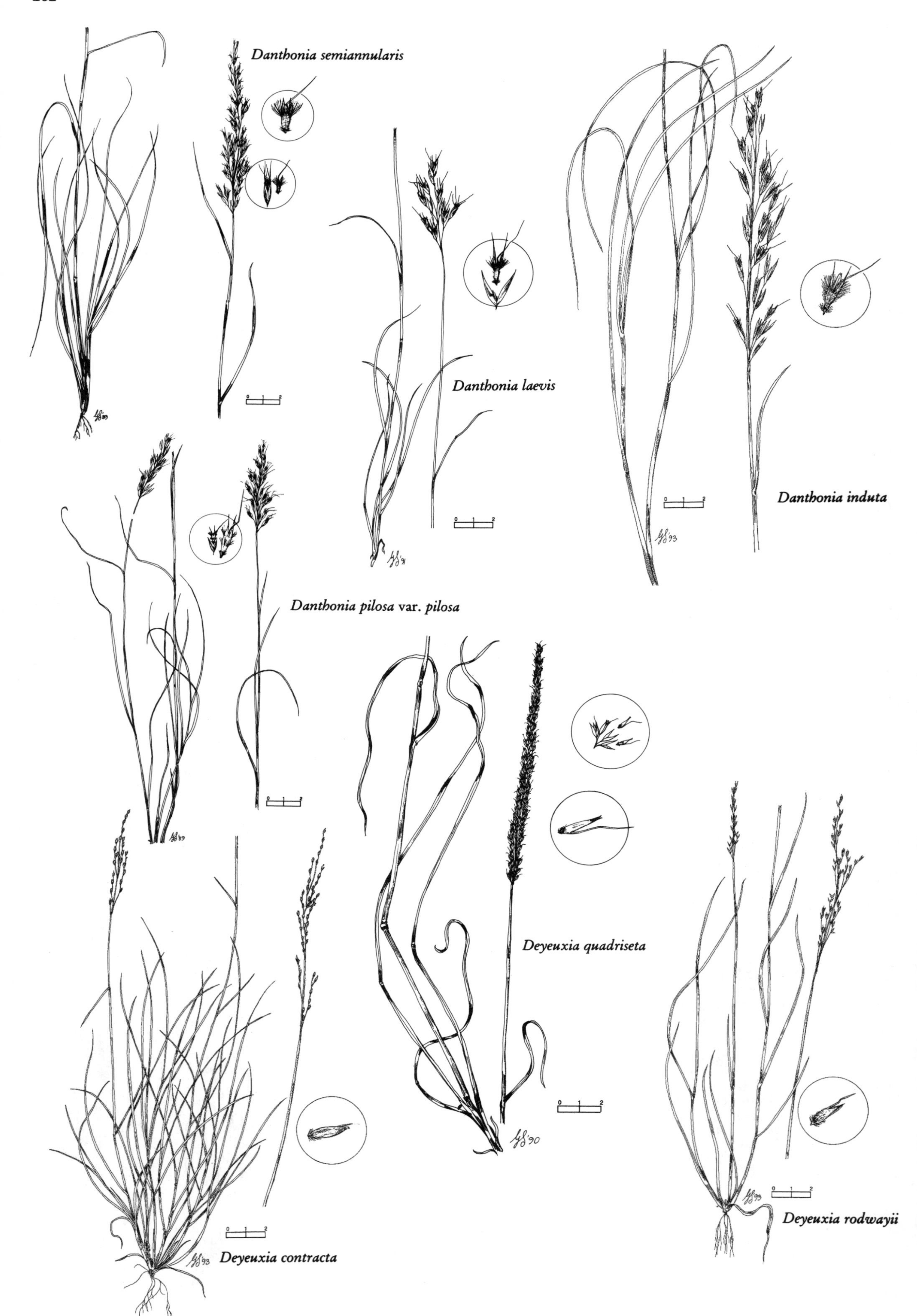
Danthonia semiannularis
Danthonia laevis
Danthonia induta
Danthonia pilosa var. *pilosa*
Deyeuxia quadriseta
Deyeuxia contracta
Deyeuxia rodwayii

Dichelachne

Poaceae

Sparsely tufted perennial grasses with fine, hairy flowerheads. Spikelets are single-flowered. Fine awns become curly at maturity. They are attached close to the top of the bilobed lemma and are more than twice the length of the lemma. Propagate by seed or division.

Dichelachne crinita

Long-hair Plume-grass

Size: to 10 cm high; stems 0.5–1 m high **F P**
Habitat: Widespread in plains grassland, red gum, box and riparian woodland, dry and valley sclerophyll forest, grassy low open forest, tea-tree heath
Form: Sparse open tuft
Foliage: Flat, green to bluish-green leaves to 20 cm long
Flowers: Dense spike-like panicle to 20 cm long, of more than 100 overlapping spikelets, awn to 55 mm long, thread-like and curly rather than bent; October to December
Requirements: Well drained soils
Comments: An ornamental grass which seeds readily. Seeds may irritate the skin. Distinguish from *D. micrantha* by the usually denser flowerheads and lack of a bend in the awn.
Localities: 2, 4, 7, 8, 12, 13, 15–18, 20, 21, 24–26, 28, 31, 32, 33–36, 41, 42, 44, 49, 61, 67–69, 74, 76
Distribution: All states except NT; NZ
Synonym: *D. longiseta*

Dichelachne crinita

Dichelachne micrantha

Short-hair Plume-grass

Size: to 10 cm high; stems 0.3–1.1 m high **F P**
Habitat: Dry sclerophyll forest, plains grassland
Foliage: Flat, dark green, mainly basal leaves to 20 cm long
Flowers: Dense panicle to 20 cm long, often looser at the base. Spikelets separated, from 30–100+. Awn to 20 mm long, slightly thickened and twisted in lower half, then often weakly bent. July to October
Requirements: Well drained soils
Comments: An ornamental grass
Localities: Research, 28, 36, 41, 42, 47, 48–49, 50A, 51, 53–58, 62, 74
Distribution: All states except NT; NZ
Synonym: Separated from *D. sciurea*

Dichelachne micrantha

Dichelachne sieberiana

Plume-grass

Size: to 10 cm high; stems to 1.3 m high **P**
Habitat: Dry sclerophyll forest
Form: Tufted perennial grass, nodes of flowering stems hairy
Foliage: Narrow, flat, rough leaves
Flowers: Sparse, loose open panicles to 25 cm long; awns up to 4 times length of lemma, very tightly twisted. Summer
Requirements: Well drained soils
Propagation: Seed or division
Localities: 36, 42, 44, 46–48, 56, 64
Distribution: Vic, NSW, Tas
Synonym: Segregated from *D. rara*

Illustrated p. 273

Distichlis

Poaceae

Distichlis distichophylla

Australian Salt-grass

Size: 5–20 cm x spreading **F**
Habitat: Saltmarshes, primary dune scrub
Form: Perennial grass with ascending branches and long-creeping rhizomes, forming a spreading lightly prickly clump
Foliage: Thin, rigid leaves 25–50 mm long, sometimes with short tips, alternate in 2 rows on opposite sides of the stem
Flowers: Dioecious; short terminal spike or raceme to 25 mm long, spikelets green to straw-coloured, flat, 2–4 on male plants; often more, crowded together on female plants and 6–14-flowered. Lemma keeled, awnless, stamens or styles often persisting. October to December
Requirements: Moist saline soils
Comments: Useful for soil stabilisation.
Propagation: Division of creeping stems
Localities: 2–5, 16, 21, 25, 26, 67, 69A, 71, 74
Distribution: Vic, NSW, Tas, SA

Distichlis distichophylla

SCALE: 0 1cm 2cm The scale representation on each plant equals 2cm.

Dryopoa — Poaceae

Dryopoa dives — Giant Mountain Grass

Size: stems to 1.5–4.5 m high — **P N**
Habitat: Cool temperate rainforest, wet sclerophyll forest
Form: Biennial, erect grass with cane-like flowering stems to 25 mm thick, forming large, loose tussocks
Foliage: Flat, arching, bright green leaves to 1.5 m x 25 mm, often with prominent white midrib
Flowers: Straw-coloured loose, spreading panicle to 50 cm x 20 cm, spikelets to 8 mm long. Lemma awnless, with 5 prominent dorsal ribs; October to March
Requirements: Moist, well drained, fertile soils
Comments: A graceful fast-growing grass which flowers in the second year. It has considerable ornamental appeal used amongst ferns and by watercourses.
Propagation: Fresh seed
Localities: 49, 57
Distribution: Vic, NSW, Tas
Synonym: *Festuca dives*

Dryopoa dives

Echinopogon — Poaceae

Echinopogon ovatus — Forest or Common Hedgehog Grass

Size: to 10 cm high; stems 15–40 cm high — **P**
Habitat: Riparian scrub, valley and damp sclerophyll forests, often in rocky areas
Form: Slender erect or ascending rhizomatous grass
Foliage: Very rough, flat bright green leaves, 2–16 cm x 8 mm, tapering to a point
Flowers: Bright green, bristly, ovoid spike-like panicle, spikelets to 5 mm long. Straight, stout awn to 15 mm long, rising from the top of the lemma, lemma bearded at the base. October to January
Requirements: Moist well drained soils
Propagation: Seed, division of rhizomes
Localities: Sunshine, Deer Park, Research, 26, 28, 29, 31, 32, 34A, 41, 42, 44, 50A, 55, 57, 58, 60, 62, 63
Distribution: All states except NT; NZ

Illustrated p. 273

Eleocharis — Cyperaceae

Annual or perennial leafless sedges growing in water or in heavy soils which receive periodic flooding, spreading by creeping rhizomes or stolons. Stems are hollow and tufted with 1 or more sheathing bracts at the base (instead of leaves) and a single erect flower spike at the tip. Glumes overlap in a spiral arrangement. They provide interest planted around dams and ponds and a safe habitat for waterbirds and fish. Propagation is by seed using the bog method, or division carried out in Spring and early Summer.

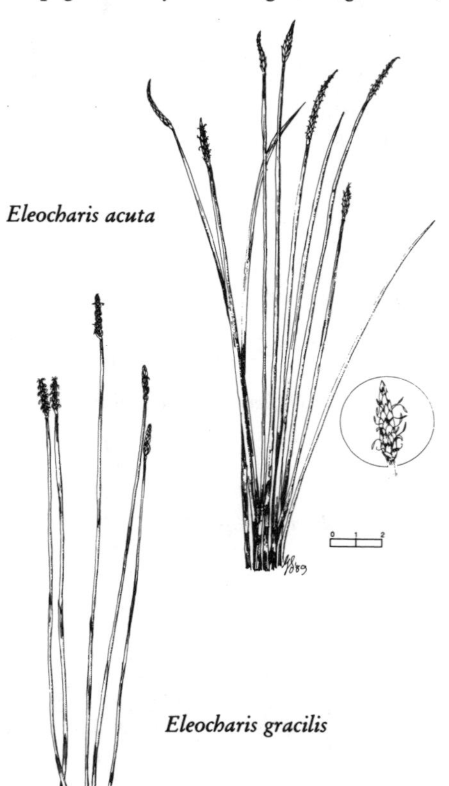

Eleocharis acuta

Eleocharis gracilis

Eleocharis acuta — Common Spike-rush

Size: 0.3–0.9 m high — **F**
Habitat: Widespread in swampy areas of grassy wetlands, red gum and box woodland, riparian scrub, tea-tree heath, grassy low open forest
Form: Perennial aquatic herb with tufts of foliage at intervals along slender rhizomes
Flowers: Small linear dark brown spikelet to 30 mm x 3–7 mm; glumes ovate-lanceolate to pointed; September to April
Comments: Easy to establish in a dam or heavy damp soils, but may spread rapidly in shallow water.
Localities: The Basin, 1, 2, 4, 6, 7, 9, 14–18, 24–26, 28, 29, 34A, 35, 60, 67#, 69A–72, 74, 76
Distribution: All states; Norfolk Is, NZ

Eleocharis atricha — Tuber Spike-rush

Size: 3–40 cm high — **P**
Habitat: Aquatic, grassy wetlands
Form: Tufted herb bearing small tubers along the stolons
Flowers: Lanceolate to linear chestnut brown spikelet to 20 mm x 3 mm; glumes oblong; January
Comments: The Aborigines may have eaten the tubers.
Localities: Laverton Nth, Keilor, 11, 60
Distribution: Vic, Qld, NSW, SA

Illustrated p. 273

Eleocharis gracilis — Slender Spike-rush

Size: 20–30 cm high — **P**
Habitat: Riparian scrub and moist depressions
Form: Slender, erect or curved tufted stems on creeping rhizomes
Flowers: Ovoid spikelet to 9 mm long, glumes ovate-oblong, rounded at the tip; October to March, June
Localities: 16, 62, 63, 69A
Distribution: All states except NT; Norfolk Is, NZ

Eleocharis minuta

Variable Spike-rush

Size: to 10 cm high **F**
Habitat: Grassy wetlands
Flowers: Spikelet 2–7 mm long, glumes less than 2 mm long
Comments: An endangered plant of Victoria which is now extinct within the Melbourne region.
Localities: Port Melbourne at the mouth of the Yarra R, 1892
Distribution: Vic, Qld, NSW; E Af and its major islands

Eleocharis pallens

Pale Spike-rush

Size: to 50 cm high **F P**
Habitat: Grassy wetlands
Form: Densely tufted herb with short rhizomes and prominently longitudinally ribbed, bluish culms
Flowers: Pale-coloured, linear cylindrical spikelet to 20 mm long; glumes shedding, ovate with triangular point; May, September
Requirements: Moist heavy soil, drying out in Summer
Comments: A vulnerable plant in Victoria, it was recently discovered in 2 sites in Melbourne, one of which was subsequently destroyed. Distinguish from *E. acuta* by the paler flowers, shorter rhizome and large pitted cells between the ribs on the stem.
Localities: Laverton Nth#, Rockbank
Distribution: All mainland states

Eleocharis pusilla

Small Spike-rush

Size: 2 mm to 25 cm high **F P**
Habitat: Aquatic in saltmarshes, grassy wetlands, box woodland
Form: Tiny perennial herb with thread-like stems and rhizomes
Flowers: Tiny few-flowered ovate to linear spikelet to 7 mm long; December to April
Comments: Readily grown and easily controlled around margins of a pond or as a bog plant.
Localities: Laverton Nth, Deer Park, Sunshine, 4, 6, 11, 17#, 18, 24, 26
Distribution: All states; NZ

Eleocharis sphacelata

Tall Spike-rush

Size: 0.5–2 m high **F P**
Habitat: Shallow freshwater swamps of red gum woodland, swamp scrub
Form: Robust perennial aquatic herb with stout, ribbed stems to 12 mm wide along a thick woody rhizome
Flowers: Large cylindrical spike to 60 mm long, flowers changing from light green to light brown, glumes stiff and flattish to 8 mm long; November to February. Differs from the other species in that the spike is narrower than the stem.
Comments: Provides protection for fish in shallow dams or ponds but may become invasive. The Aborigines used the stems whole for making mats and split for weaving bags.
Localities: Moorabbin#, 29, 34A, 35, 60–63, 67#, 69A, 71, 74, 75
Distribution: All states; NZ, PNG

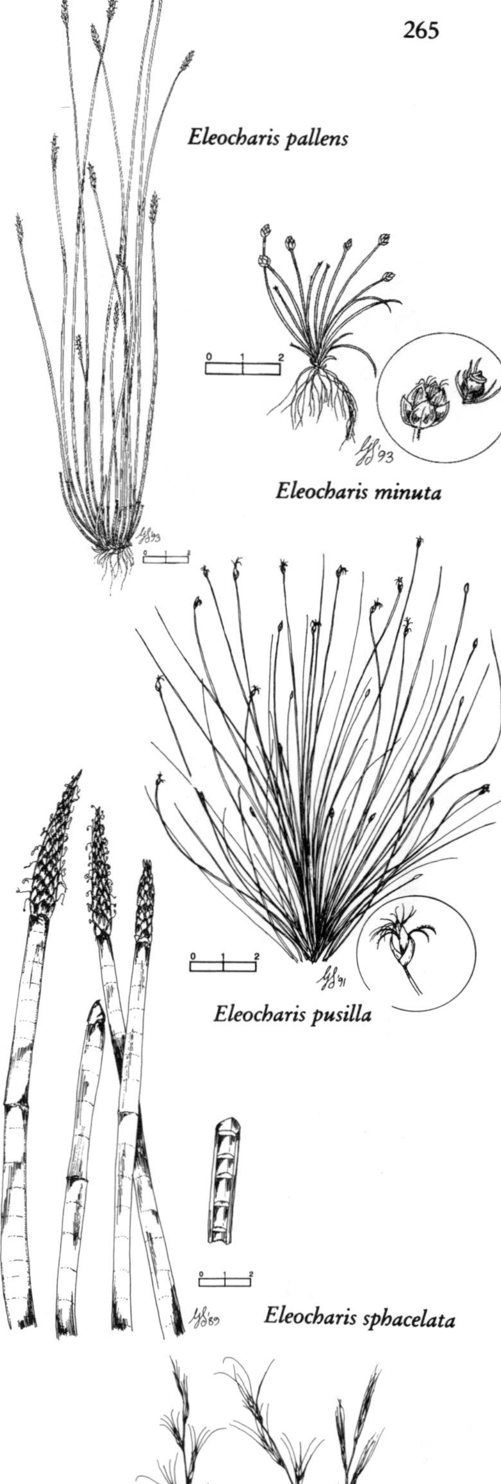

Eleocharis pallens

Eleocharis minuta

Eleocharis pusilla

Eleocharis sphacelata

Elymus

Poaceae

Elymus scabrus

Common Wheat-grass

Size: 20 cm x 40 cm; stems to 0.8 m high **F P**
Habitat: Widespread throughout plains grassland, red gum woodland, dry and valley sclerophyll forests
Form: Open-tufted perennial grass with slender erect or drooping stems, trailing to several metres in some grassland forms
Foliage: Flat green or bluish leaves to 80 cm x 2–4 mm, but usually less, tapering gradually to a fine point. Upper surface and margins are rough.
Flowers: Slender spike with 1–10 large, distant 6–12-flowered spikelets. Lemmas taper into awns to 50 mm long which curve outwards as the spikelet matures; October to January.
Requirements: Adaptable to all well drained soils, including gravelly soils and alluvial clays
Comments: There are probably several species within *E. scabrus*. Bluish-leafed forms make attractive garden plants. Sought after by butterflies as a food source.
Propagation: Seed
Localities: St Albans, Deer Park, 2, 4, 7, 12, 13, 15–18, 21, 23–26, 28, 32–36, 38, 39, 41, 42, 44, 49, 50A, 53–55, 57, 58, 67#, 69A
Distribution: All states except NT; NZ
Synonym: *Elymus scaber*, *Agropyron scabrum*

Elymus scabrus

SCALE: 0 1cm 2cm The scale representation on each plant equals 2cm.

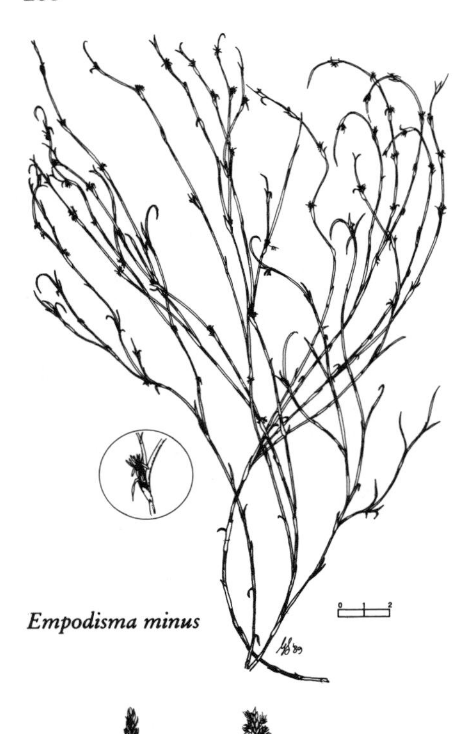

Empodisma minus

Empodisma — Restionaceae

Empodisma minus — Spreading Rope-rush

Size: stems 0.5 x 2 m long — F P
Habitat: Wet areas in sclerophyll woodland, swamp and wattle tea-tree scrub
Form: Dense, matted, perennial herb with bright green, wiry, curved branches, spreading from extensive rhizomes. May climb to 2 m when growing in dense undergrowth, developing into a tangled mass.
Foliage: Leafless; tiny pale green scales or sheathing bracts to 10 mm long along stems
Flowers: Dioecious; brown spikelets are sessile, axillary, solitary and distant, male spikelets 2–3-flowered to 4 mm long with 2 linear floral bracts and loose, narrow glumes; female spikelets single flowered with longer tight rigid glumes. September to March
Requirements: Ample moisture in poorly drained soils
Propagation: Seed, possibly division
Localities: Montrose, 50, 54, 56, 59, 60, 67#, 73–75
Distribution: Vic, Qld, NSW, Tas, SA; NZ
Synonym: *Calorophus lateriflorus*

Enneapogon nigricans

Enneapogon — Poaceae

Enneapogon nigricans — Niggerheads

Size: 20 cm x 30 cm; stems to 40 cm high — F
Habitat: Plains grassland, box woodland
Form: Tufted perennial grass, forming sparse tussocks
Foliage: Grey-green, downy, stiff narrow leaves to 15 cm x 2–3 mm, usually inrolled
Flowers: Dense terminal spike-like panicle 30–50 mm long, spikelets 3–4-flowered, becoming fluffy and dark purplish or black as seed matures and finally straw-coloured. Lemmas covered in silky hairs, with thin vertical ribs, each 9-awned, awns to 6 mm long. Mostly Summer, sporadically throughout the year.
Requirements: Dry, well drained soils, preferring exposed positions and no competition
Comments: Although plants are slow growing and short-lived, they are most attractive. Flowerheads are an ornamental feature.
Propagation: Seed, division
Localities: Sunbury, Essendon, Melton, Rockbank, Deer Park, 9, 16, 25, 26
Distribution: Vic, Qld, NSW, SA, WA

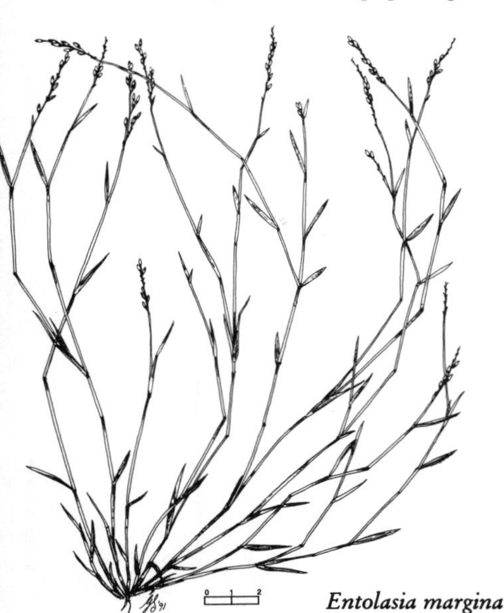

Entolasia marginata

Entolasia — Poaceae

Entolasia marginata — Bordered Panic

Size: to 0.3 m high — F P
Habitat: Grassy low open forest
Form: Wiry, erect to decumbent perennial grass with straggly stems which often branch
Foliage: Soft, flat lanceolate leaves 3–10 cm long, finely ribbed with numerous rough veins and pale, nerve-like margins
Flowers: Very narrow panicle to 75 mm long with few erect or slightly spreading branches, spikelets crowded. Upper glume prominently nerved, fertile lemma covered in silky hairs. October to December
Requirements: Tolerates infertile soils
Comments: Locally rare
Propagation: Seed, which may need to be stored first
Localities: 74
Distribution: Vic, Qld, NSW; PNG

Entolasia stricta

Size: to 0.6 m high — F P
Habitat: Grassy low open forest
Requirements: Sandy soils
Comments: Differs from *E. marginata* in that stems are mostly erect and leaves are narrow and inrolled. Panicles are narrower with shorter branches.
Propagation: Seed
Localities: 74
Distribution: Vic
Synonym: Recently separated from *E. marginata*

Eragrostis

Poaceae

Eragrostis brownii

Common or Brown's Love-grass

Size: to 15 cm x 30 cm; stems to 40 cm high **F P**
Habitat: Widespread and common in riparian scrub, red gum woodland, dry and valley sclerophyll forests, tea-tree heath
Form: Coarse, tufted perennial grass, leaves spreading rather than erect
Foliage: Slender, flat, bright green leaves to 80 mm long, margins smooth
Flowers: Very open pyramid-shaped panicle 2–20 cm long, branches often widely spaced. Spikelets dense, to 15-flowered, olive green to greyish, thin and flat or curved with a longitudinal furrow between the 2 rows of flowers. September to April
Requirements: Adaptable to most soils
Comments: A decorative grass for rockeries, especially when well watered. Suitable for use as a low maintenance lawn in areas not subject to heavy use.
Propagation: Seed
Localities: 16, 21, 25, 26, 28, 34A–36, 39, 41, 42, 44–47, 50A, 51, 54–56, 58, 60, 65–71, 74, 75
Distribution: All states

Eragrostis brownii

Eragrostis elongata

Close-headed Love-grass

Size: 10–20 cm high; stems 30–65 cm high **F P**
Habitat: Grassy wetlands
Form: Tufted perennial grass
Foliage: Leaves inrolled or flat, to 20 cm long, margins and upper surface rough
Flowers: Narrow, cylindrical spike-like panicle to 20 cm. Flat, white to purplish spikelets are sessile in dense clusters. December to March
Requirements: Moist heavy soils tolerating inundation
Comments: An isolated occurrence in Melbourne, more commonly found north of the Divide.
Propagation: Seed
Localities: Laverton Nth
Distribution: All mainland states; PNG

Eragrostis elongata

Eragrostis infecunda

Cane Grass

Size: to 0.7 m high **F**
Habitat: Grassy wetland
Form: Rhizomatous or stoloniferous wiry perennial grass
Foliage: Stiff, inrolled or folded leaves to 100 mm long, margins thickened and rough
Flowers: Panicle narrow, elliptical-lanceolate to 10 cm long, spikelets very loosely 5–11-flowered, the small stem visible between the florets. December to March
Requirements: Tolerates saline clays, heavy soils and temporary inundation
Propagation: Seed, division
Localities: Altona
Distribution: Vic, SA

Illustrated p. 273

Festuca hookeriana = Austrofestuca hookeriana

Festuca littoralis = Austrofestuca littoralis

Gahnia

Cyperaceae

Gahnia species are perennial sedges with woody rhizomes which may form very large tussocks. They are generally found in situations where the soil is moist or wet for much of the year, and often subject to periodic inundation. Leaves are strap-shaped and/or inrolled, sheathing around the stem and spirally arranged up the stem. Leaf margins, and sometimes longitudinal ridges, have very sharp bristles on some species. The terminal dark brown to black panicle is composed of many branched spikes each with a leaf-like bract. The last 2 glumes of each spikelet contain flowers, the others are empty. Flowers are cream and fruit are hard nuts.

The Aborigines ground the nuts to provide food. Gahnias are important, (sometimes exclusive) food plants for caterpillars of several butterflies and provide safe habitat for small birds. Both foliage and flower spikes provide attractive contrast in cut and dried floral arrangements. Plants are useful in stabilising soil and creek erosion but may be difficult to propagate. Seed is the most successful, division and transplanting having limited success with some species.

SCALE: 0 1cm 2cm The scale representation on each plant equals 2cm.

Gahnia filum

Gahnia clarkei

Brickmaker's Sedge, Tall Saw-sedge

Size: 1.5–4.5 m x 1–3 m **P N**
Habitat: Damp and valley sclerophyll forests
Form: Tall perennial palm-like tussock, stems woody to 30 mm wide
Foliage: Very long, narrow, inrolled leaves with sharp margins
Flowers: Panicle initially golden brown, turning dark brown, to 60 cm x 60 mm. Numerous spikelets have more than 12 tightly overlapping, blunt glumes, the lower ones without awn-like points. The upper glumes contain 2 flowers. Nuts shiny bright red. September to February
Requirements: Moist to wet soils, tolerating permanent inundation
Comments: Slow growing but can eventually form impenetrable thickets. Becoming very rare in Melbourne with only 1 plant remaining in one location.
Localities: 51, 58, 67#
Distribution: Vic, Qld, NSW, SA

Gahnia filum

Chaffy Saw-sedge

Size: 1–1.2 m high **F**
Habitat: Coastal saltmarshes and grassy wetlands
Form: Perennial leafy tussock
Foliage: Long, inrolled leaves tapering into slightly rough points; lower leaf-like bracts smooth, reddish-purple below, smaller floral bracts very broad and chaff-like
Flowers: Narrow pale brown panicle to 20–35 cm x 10–20 mm. Densely clustered, 1-flowered spikelets most of the year. Nuts pale brown.
Requirements: Moist sandy soil, tolerating saline situations
Comments: Attractive fruits
Localities: Seaholme, 3–5, 74
Distribution: Vic, NSW, Tas, SA, WA

Gahnia radula

Thatch Saw-sedge

Size: 1–2 m x 0.5–2 m **F P**
Habitat: Dry and valley sclerophyll forests, sclerophyll woodland, grassy low open forest, wattle tea-tree scrub
Form: Clumping perennial herb spreading by underground rhizomes
Foliage: Long, flat, raspy, deep green leaves with very sharp inrolled margins
Flowers: Ovate, loosely-arranged chestnut brown panicle to 60 cm x 70 mm, becoming black and pendulous; most of the year. Nuts dark brown to black.
Requirements: Moist soils, tolerating dryness once established
Comments: Plants are tolerant of *Phytophthora cinnamomi*. The vigorous rhizomes are useful in controlling soil erosion. The foliage has been used for roof thatching in the past.
Propagation: Difficult to propagate as it sets little seed and transplants do not adapt well. Young plants seem to suffer transplanting the least provided minimum root damage occurs.
Localities: 26, 34A, 37, 40–44, 46–49, 50A, 51, 53–56, 59–67, 70, 71, 73–76
Distribution: Vic, Qld, NSW, Tas, SA

Gahnia radula

Gahnia trifida

Gahnia sieberiana

Red-fruited Saw-sedge

Size: 1.5–3 m x 2–3 m **F P N**
Habitat: Valley and damp sclerophyll forest, wattle tea-tree scrub
Form: Clumping perennial sedge
Foliage: Long, channelled, rough spreading leaves, becoming pendulous
Flowers: Dense, yellowish-brown compound panicle becoming almost black, to 65 cm x 70 mm. Spikelets differ from *G. clarkei* in that there are up to 10 loosely overlapping pointed glumes, all with awns. Bright shining red nuts dot the panicle. October to January.
Requirements: Moist soils for most of the year, but tolerates drier soils once established
Propagaton: Easily grown from seed which has been stored for 12 months.
Localities: 50–51, 53–59, 70, 71, 73–75
Distribution: Vic, Qld, NSW, Tas, SA; PNG, N Cal *Illustrated p. 273*

Gahnia trifida

Coast Saw-sedge

Size: 0.6–1.5 m x 0.6–1 m **F P**
Habitat: Coastal, in moist tea-tree heath
Form: Upright perennial clumping herb
Foliage: Long narrow leaves with very rough inrolled margins and pendulous, thin tips
Flowers: Erect, narrow, interrupted dark brown panicle to 40 cm long with densely clustered 1-flowered spikelets; October to December. Nut shiny and black.
Requirements: Moist well drained sandy soils, tolerating extended dry periods once established and alkaline soils
Comments: Differs from *G. filum* in that lower leaf bracts are sharply toothed and the smaller floral bracts are narrow. Flower stems are cut commercially.
Propagation: Seed or division but difficult to establish
Localities: 74
Distribution: Vic, Tas, SA, WA

Glyceria

Poaceae

Glyceria australis

Australian Sweet-grass, Manna Grass

Size: 0.6–1 m x spreading **F P**
Habitat: Freshwater swamps and watercourses of riparian scrub, valley sclerophyll forest, grassy low open forest
Form: Perennial grass with individual stems arising from creeping rhizomes, lower part of the stems usually horizontal and rooting
Foliage: Flat leaves with rough edges and prominent veins
Flowers: Narrow panicle to 15 cm long with few pale green 6–20-flowered spikelets. Lemmas awnless with 7 distinct, parallel veins and tapered tips. October to February
Requirements: Moist or wet soils
Comments: May be used as a semi-aquatic grass in swampy ground. Easily confused with the introduced *G. declinata*, which has ragged-toothed tips of the lemmas.
Propagation: Seed, division
Localities: Yarra R, Plenty R, 35, 41, 42, 44, 51, 56, 74, 76
Distribution: Vic, Qld, NSW, Tas, SA

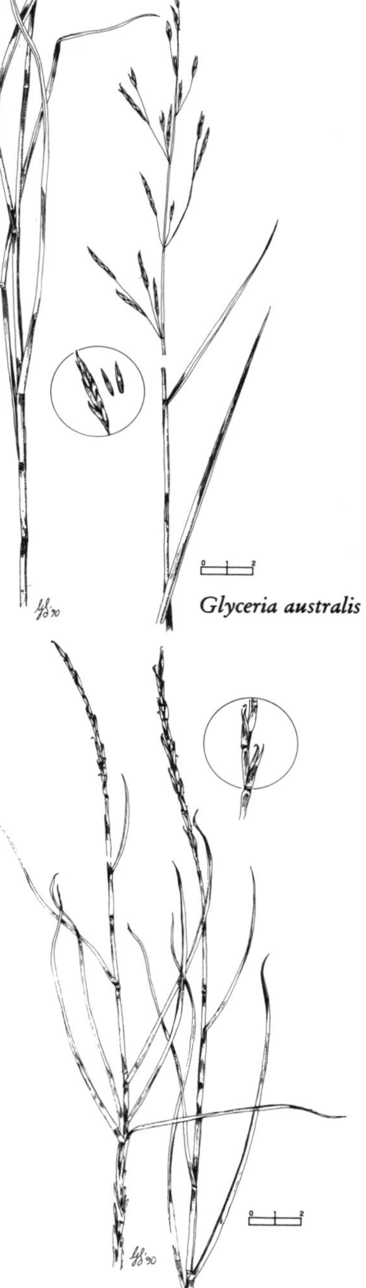

Glyceria australis

Hemarthria uncinata

Hemarthria

Poaceae

Hemarthria uncinata

Mat Grass

Size: to 40 cm x spreading **F P**
Habitat: Red gum woodland, swamp scrub, valley sclerophyll forest, tea-tree heath around swamps
Form: Perennial, rigid, matted grassy sward
Foliage: Flat, narrow-linear leaves to 20 cm long, keeled along the midrib
Flowers: Terminal, rigid, often curved spike to 130 mm long; 1-flowered spikelets paired, to 10 mm long, in 4 indistinct rows, appearing sessile, 1 of each pair in a hollow along the rhachis; December to February
Requirements: Moist often heavy clay soils
Comments: Vigorous plants may grow to 1 m high on sheltered sites, and spread may be up to 3 m. May be confused with the introduced *Hainardia* and *Parapholis* grasses, whose spikelets form 2 distinct rows on opposite sides of the stems.
Propagation: Seed, division
Localities: 25, 28, 34A–36, 51, 53, 54, 60, 69A–71, 74, 76
Distribution: All states except NT

Homopholis

Poaceae

Homopholis proluta

Rigid Panic

Size: 0.2–1 m high **F P**
Habitat: Red gum woodland, plains grassland, in low-lying areas
Form: Tufted, erect, leafy perennial grass
Foliage: Green or blue-green flat leaves (sometimes with margins inrolled), 2–15 cm x 2–7 mm
Flowers: Much branched, loose, very open panicle to 20 cm long, lower branches whorled. Short pointed spikelets to 4 mm long, greenish, tinged purple, on long thread-like stalks. September to April. The lower glume is as long as the spikelet, separating this genus from *Panicum* where the glume is never more than half as long.
Requirements: Heavy clay soils, plants forming extensive dense stands after wet winters. Drought resistant once established
Comments: Seeds are gathered by Aborigines and ground to make a kind of flour. Attractive used in dry arrangements.
Propagation: Seed
Localities: St. Albans, Laverton Nth, 4, 7, 11, 16–18, 21, 26
Distribution: Vic, Qld, NSW, SA, WA
Synonym: *Panicum prolutum*

Illustrated p. 273

Hypolaena

Restionaceae

Hypolaena fastigiata

Tassel Rope-rush

Size: 20–50 cm x 0.5–1.5 m **F P**
Habitat: Tea-tree heath
Form: Spreading grey-green rush-like rhizomatous perennial herb with slender, erect, much branched stems bearing up to 12 distinct longitudinal mealy-white ridges
Foliage: Leaves reduced to pointed dark sheathing bracts to 10 mm long
Flowers: Dioecious; many, stalked, pendulous reddish-brown male spikelets to 8 mm long, in a loose terminal panicle; few, solitary erect 1-flowered female spikelets to 10 mm long. Flowers and/or fruit most of the year.
Requirements: Moist sandy soils
Comments: Attactive foliage plant beside pools.
Propagation: Division of the creeping rhizome
Localities: 67–70, 73–75
Distribution: All states except NT

Hypolaena fastigata

SCALE: 0 1cm 2cm The scale representation on each plant equals 2cm.

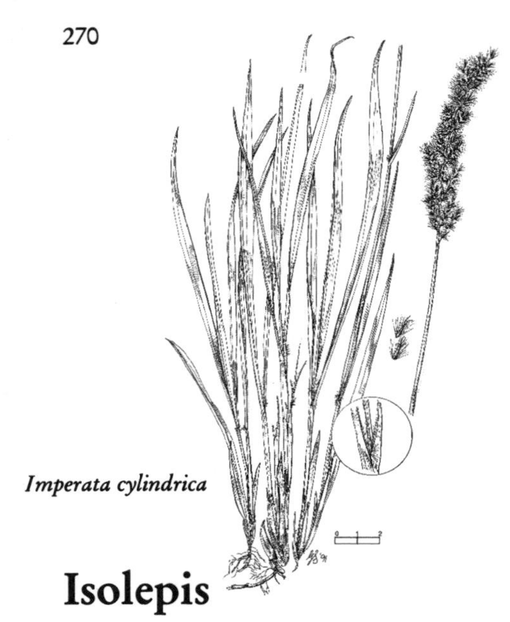

Imperata cylindrica

Imperata — Poaceae

Imperata cylindrica — Blady Grass

Size: 0.3–0.7 m high; stems to 1 m high — F P
Habitat: Grassy wetland, damp, valley and dry sclerophyll forests, tea-tree heath
Form: Erect coarse, vigorously spreading, rhizomatous perennial grass
Foliage: Pale mottled green linear leaves to 70 cm long, often with reddish parts, with a prominent midrib. The margins having tiny serrations.
Flowers: Dense, fluffy, cylindrical spike-like panicle to 20 cm long. Paired spikelets have stalks of different lengths, the whole spikelet covered with long, silvery silky hairs; November to March
Requirements: Moist, well drained soils
Comments: The seed heads are extremely ornamental but are mainly seen after fire or slashing. Regenerates rapidly after fires and may be unwelcome in cultivated areas; however it provides an important habitat for many small animals, and should be maintained in remnant vegetation.
Propagation: Seed, division
Localities: Altona, 5, 50–51, 54–56, 59, 60, 74, 75
Distribution: All states; NZ, PNG, N Cal, Asia

Isolepis — Cyperaceae

Annual or perennial sedges, *Isolepis* spp. may be rhizomatous, tufted, single-stemmed, creeping or floating. They are usually found in damp, swampy ground. Leaves are basal and are either small or reduced to sheaths on the nodeless stem. The brownish-yellow flowers are generally borne in dense terminal heads of 1 to many spikelets, a stiff erect terminal bract continuing the stem. Fruit are nuts. Some species are suited to garden culture, particularly in bog gardens. Propagation is by seed or division of the clumps.
Synonym: Previously included in the genus *Scirpus*

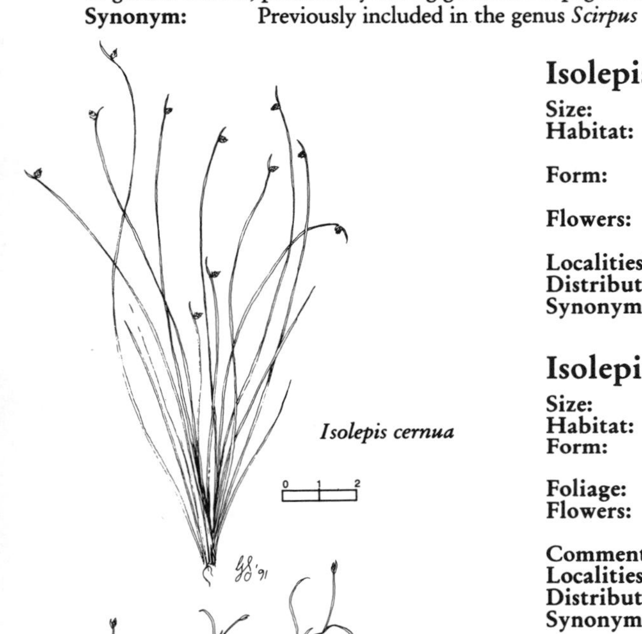

Isolepis cernua

Isolepis fluitans

Isolepis inundata

Isolepis cernua — Nodding, Low or Grassy Club-rush

Size: to 10 cm high — F P
Habitat: Grassy wetlands, saltmarshes, riparian scrub and woodland, frequently coastal
Form: Small erect tufted annual rush with leaves reduced to a small pointed sheath or non-existent; floral bract glume-like to 7 mm long
Flowers: Solitary broadly ovoid spikelet to 3 mm long; most of the year. Nuts are flattened and become dark brown or black on maturity.
Localities: 2, 4, 5, 8, 14, 16, 35, 36, 63, 67#, 69A, 70, 74
Distribution: All states except NT; most of the world
Synonym: *Scirpus cernuus*

Isolepis fluitans — Floating Club-rush

Size: to 15 cm high — P
Habitat: Swamps or aquatic in tea-tree heath, valley sclerophyll forest
Form: Weak, many-noded, fine-stemmed perennial rush, creeping or floating in water, or tussock-forming on drier ground
Foliage: Pale green thread-like leaves, shorter than stems
Flowers: Solitary ovoid spikelet to 5 mm long on a long stalk, glumes pale green to straw-coloured; October to February. Nut is ovoid.
Comments: An attractive feature in a water garden.
Localities: Research, 34A, 35, 46, 47, 54, 70, 72, 74–76
Distribution: All states except NT; Eur, Af, Asia
Synonym: *Scirpus fluitans*

Isolepis hookeriana

Size: to 15 cm high, often smaller — P
Habitat: Swamp scrub, depressions in grassy wetlands, valley sclerophyll forest
Form: Small tufted annual rush with fine, erect, bristly stems, leaves very fine to 3 mm long but usually absent
Flowers: Cluster of 1–2 slanted, oblong, several-flowered spikelets, to 3.5 mm long; September to February. Nut straw coloured to brown or black, longitudinally ridged and wrinkled.
Localities: Laverton Nth, Montrose, 5, 31, 44, 46, 50A, 54, 74, 75
Distribution: All states except NT
Synonym: *Scirpus hookeranus, S. calocarpus* *Illustrated p. 273*

Isolepis inundata — Swamp Club-rush

Size: 5–30 cm x 10–40 cm — P
Habitat: Wattle tea-tree and riparian scrub, valley and damp sclerophyll forests
Form: Tufted perennial rush, stems stiffly erect or arching, with offshoots proliferating from flowerheads; leaves reduced to a point, erect bract longer than spikelets
Flowers: Cluster of 3–12 oblong, angled spikelets to 6 mm long, often becoming dark purplish brown. Glumes have a green keel; October to April
Comments: A widespread and useful tufting plant for moist to wet soils, tolerating periodic inundation, but can be a problem in nurseries.
Localities: 8, 14, 16, 34A–36, 42, 44, 50–58, 60, 63, 64, 67#, 69A, 72, 74–76
Distribution: All states except NT; NZ, S Am, SE Asia
Synonym: *Scirpus inundatus*

Isolepis marginata

Tiny or Coarse Club-rush

Size: 25–100 mm high **F P**
Habitat: Wattle tea-tree and riparian scrub, tea-tree heath, saltmarshes, valley sclerophyll forest
Form: Tiny tufted leafy annual with bristly stems
Foliage: Well developed bristly leaves shorter than the stems; floral bract erect or spreading, longer than spikelets
Flowers: Single sessile cluster of 1–6 spikelets to 6 mm long. Rigid green glumes boat-shaped with a bright reddish or purplish-brown patch on sides; September to January
Comments: An adaptable species which tolerates drier conditions than most *Isolepis* spp. Often appears in gardens.
Localities: Montrose, The Basin, 2, 4, 12, 24, 26, 29, 32, 34A, 35, 44, 47, 48, 50A–52, 54–56, 69–71, 74, 75
Distribution:5 Vic, NSW, Tas, SA, WA; NZ, S Af
Synonym: *Scirpus marginatus*

Isolepis nodosa

Knobby Club-rush

Size: 0.5–1.5 m x 0.6–2 m **F P**
Habitat: Coastal banksia woodland, riparian, swamp and primary dune scrub, saltmarshes, tea-tree heath, grassy low open forest
Form: Tall, coarse, wiry densely tufted perennial rush with creeping rhizomes, leaves reduced to sheaths
Flowers: Dense globular cluster to 20 mm wide of sessile brown spikelets to 5 mm long; most of the year. Short erect floral bract behind flowerhead appears to continue the stem making the cluster lateral.
Requirements: Moist soils, tolerating dry periods once established
Comments: Widespread in Melbourne, its upright habit provides interest in the landscape as a contrast plant. It is of some benefit in binding soils in moist areas.
Localities: 2–4, 8, 14, 26, 28, 31, 32, 61–64, 67–69A, 71, 72, 74, 76
Distribution: All states except NT; NZ, S Af, S Am
Synonym: *Scirpus nodosus*

Isolepis platycarpa

Club-rush

Size: to 70 mm high **F P**
Habitat: Swamp and riparian scrub, damp sclerophyll forest
Form: Tiny tufted annual rush
Comments: Similar to *I. hookeriana* but leaves are short and well developed, to 30 mm long. Spikelets are often solitary, but sometimes paired, broader and less angled than *I. hookeriana*. Nut is shiny dark brown and wrinkled but not ridged. September to April.
Localities: The Basin, Montrose, 17#, 18, 28, 50A, 54, 58, 70, 72, 74
Distribution: Vic, NSW, Tas, SA, WA; NZ
Synonym: *Scirpus platycarpus*

Isolepis producta

P

Habitat: Aquatic, in riparian scrub
Comments: Similar to *I. fluitans* differing in that *I. producta* has purplish leaf sheaths and glumes, and stems are always floating. Flowers October to March
Localities: Yarra R., 36
Distribution: Vic, NSW, Tas, SA, WA
Synonym: *Scirpus productus*

Isolepis stellata

Star Club-rush

Size: 60–100 mm high **P**
Habitat: Valley sclerophyll forest
Form: Slender tufted annual rush with rigid stems
Foliage: Leaves bristly to 25 mm long
Flowers: Star-like clusters of 3–8 densely packed greenish spikelets to 4 mm long. Glumes spreading with broad keel and sharp point; October to February. Nut triangular and black
Localities: 62, 75
Distribution: Vic, NSW, Tas, SA, WA
Synonym: *Scirpus stellatus*

Isolepis subtilissima

Size: 5–12 cm high **P**
Habitat: Wet and valley sclerophyll forests
Form: Tufted bristly perennial rush with very slender stems and long-creeping rhizomes
Foliage: Very narrow channelled leaves sometimes longer than stems; floral bract erect and leaf-like to 30 mm long
Flowers: Single, or 2–3 ovoid, reddish spikelets to 3 mm long; March
Localities: 44, 57, 74, 76
Distribution: Vic, Qld, NSW, Tas, SA; NZ, PNG, Philippines
Synonym: *Scirpus subtilissimus*

Illustrated p. 273

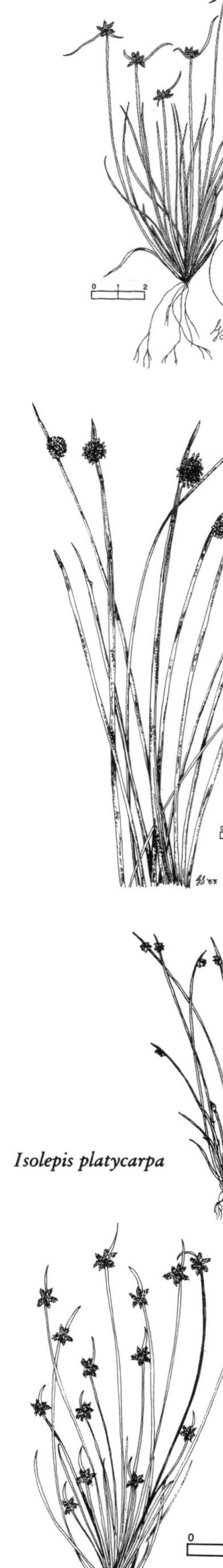

Isolepis marginata

Isolepis nodosa

Isolepis platycarpa

Isolepis stellata

SCALE:
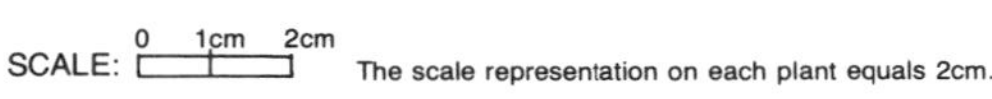

The scale representation on each plant equals 2cm.

Isolepis victoriensis

Size: 6–12 cm high — F
Habitat: Damp depressions in plains grassland, box woodland
Comments: Tufted annual rush. Heads of 3–4 spikelets to 5 mm long with strongly keeled glumes; August to November. Nut globular and pale grey.
Localities: Werribee#, Campbellfield#, Rockbank, 7, 17#, 18, 67#
Distribution: Endemic to Vic
Synonym: *Scirpus victoriensis*

Isolepis victoriensis

Juncus — Juncaceae

Juncus species are common plants of moist areas, and are often found in swamps and along watercourses. Several species are often found growing together. Many are adapted to growing in temporarily inundated areas, some being tolerant of saline conditions. They may be annual or perennial (perennials have a short-creeping rhizome), native or exotic, and mostly form robust tussocks of green stems. Flowers occur in terminal cymes or clusters varying in colour from greenish through browns to purple-black. The flowers usually appear to occur on one side of the stem, due to an erect bract which seems to continue the stem above the flowerhead. Fruit is a 3-celled capsule. Leaves are always glabrous and arranged in a basal rosette. They may be flat or terete, with or without spongy pith, or reduced to basal sheaths. *Juncus* spp. are useful in stabilising wet sloping soils, and for providing habitat for small birds and frogs as well as adding interest in a wet landscape area. Propagation is by fresh seed or division of rhizomes. Seed is produced prolifically and germinates readily. Some species may become invasive under certain conditions. Most species prefer a sunny to semi-shaded position.

Juncus species are difficult to tell apart. Features used here include the colour, stem length and diameter (measured midway between the rhizome and the base of the inflorescence); the appearance of the pith when cut longitudinally (solid, hollow or with air spaces); the length, colour and tightness of the basal sheaths; the arrangement of the inflorescence; the length of the capsule at maturity and the relative lengths of the capsule and the perianth (petals and sepals).

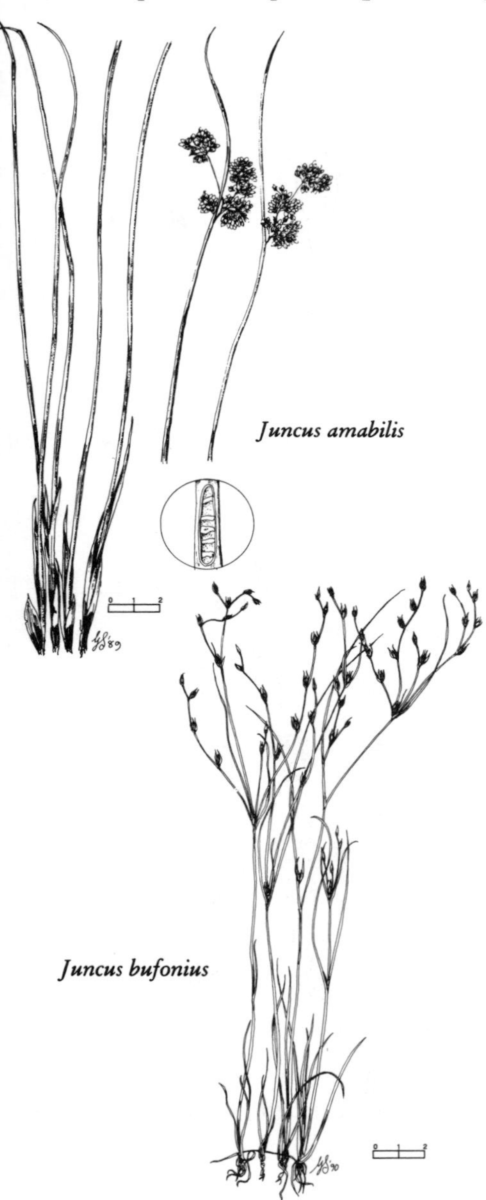

Juncus amabilis

Juncus bufonius

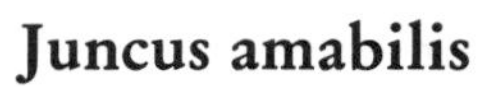

Juncus amabilis

Size: 0.2–1.2 m x 0.2–0.5 m — F P
Habitat: Grassy wetlands, plains grassland, valley sclerophyll forest, wattle tea-tree scrub
Form: Rhizomatous tufted perennial rush with blue-green stems 1–2.5 mm wide, pith very open with large air spaces
Foliage: Leaves reduced to dark brown basal sheaths
Flowers: Compact panicle with light brown flowers clustered along the branches; November to February. Capsule 2–2.5 mm long, somewhat longer than the perianth.
Comments: Tolerates both periods of inundation and dryness once established.
Localities: Montrose, 16, 25, 34A, 42, 44, 47, 48, 53, 54, 56, 63, 64, 70, 71, 74, 76
Distribution: Vic, NSW, Tas, SA, WA

Juncus australis — Austral Rush

Size: 0.6–1.2 m x 0.5–1 m — F P
Habitat: Riparian scrub, valley sclerophyll forest
Form: Tufted perennial rush with short-creeping rhizome; stems stout, shiny, blue-green 1–3 mm wide, pith open with large air spaces
Foliage: Leaves reduced to shiny dark brown basal sheaths, longest sheaths 5–15 cm long, standing away from the stem and broadly dilated at the tip
Flowers: Compound panicles with almost globular clusters to 30 mm wide, of pale brown flowers; most of the year. Capsule usually shorter than the perianth.
Requirements: Prefers moist to wet soils but will tolerate short, dry periods.
Localities: 15, 18, 28, 34A, 36, 47
Distribution: Vic, NSW, Tas, SA; NZ

Juncus bufonius — Toad Rush

Size: 2–30 cm x 30 cm — F P
Habitat: Widespread in grassy wetlands, plains grassland, red gum woodland, riparian and swamp scrub, wet, damp and valley sclerophyll forests, tea-tree heath
Form: Small slender annual herb
Foliage: 2–3 very narrow, solid, shiny flat channelled leaves on each stem
Flowers: Branched panicle to 120 mm long, of single pale green flowers scattered along the branches, bracts short and leafy; most of the year. Capsule shorter than perianth.
Comments: Considered by some botanists to be introduced to Australia. Often a weed, colonising anywhere sufficient soil moisture is available.
Localities: 2, 4, 5, 7, 12, 14–18, 24–26, 28, 31, 35, 41–44, 47, 49, 50A, 51, 53–58, 60, 61, 64, 67, 69A–72, 74, 75
Distribution: All mainland states; cosmopolitan

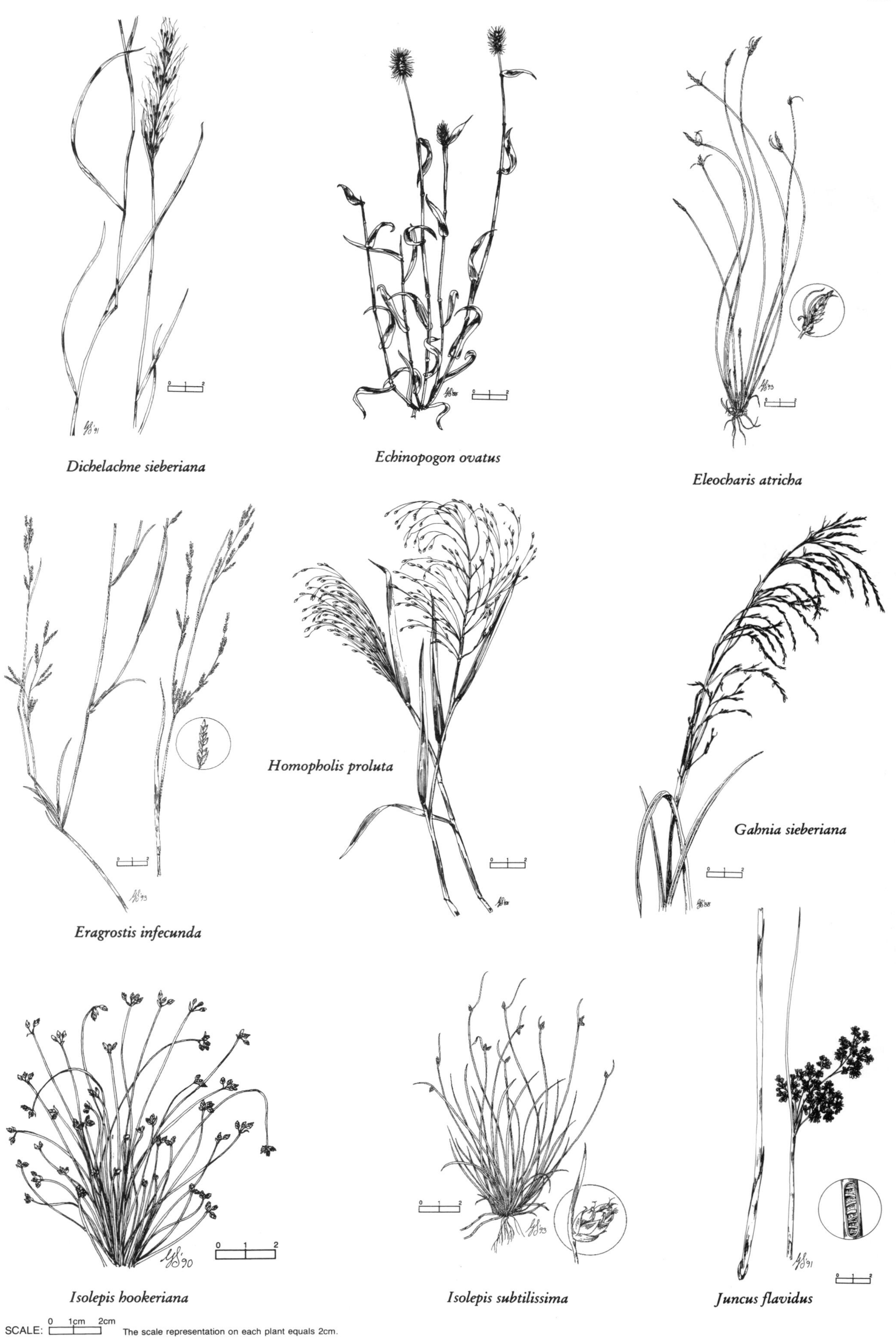

Dichelachne sieberiana

Echinopogon ovatus

Eleocharis atricha

Eragrostis infecunda

Homopholis proluta

Gahnia sieberiana

Isolepis hookeriana

Isolepis subtilissima

Juncus flavidus

SCALE: 0 1cm 2cm The scale representation on each plant equals 2cm.

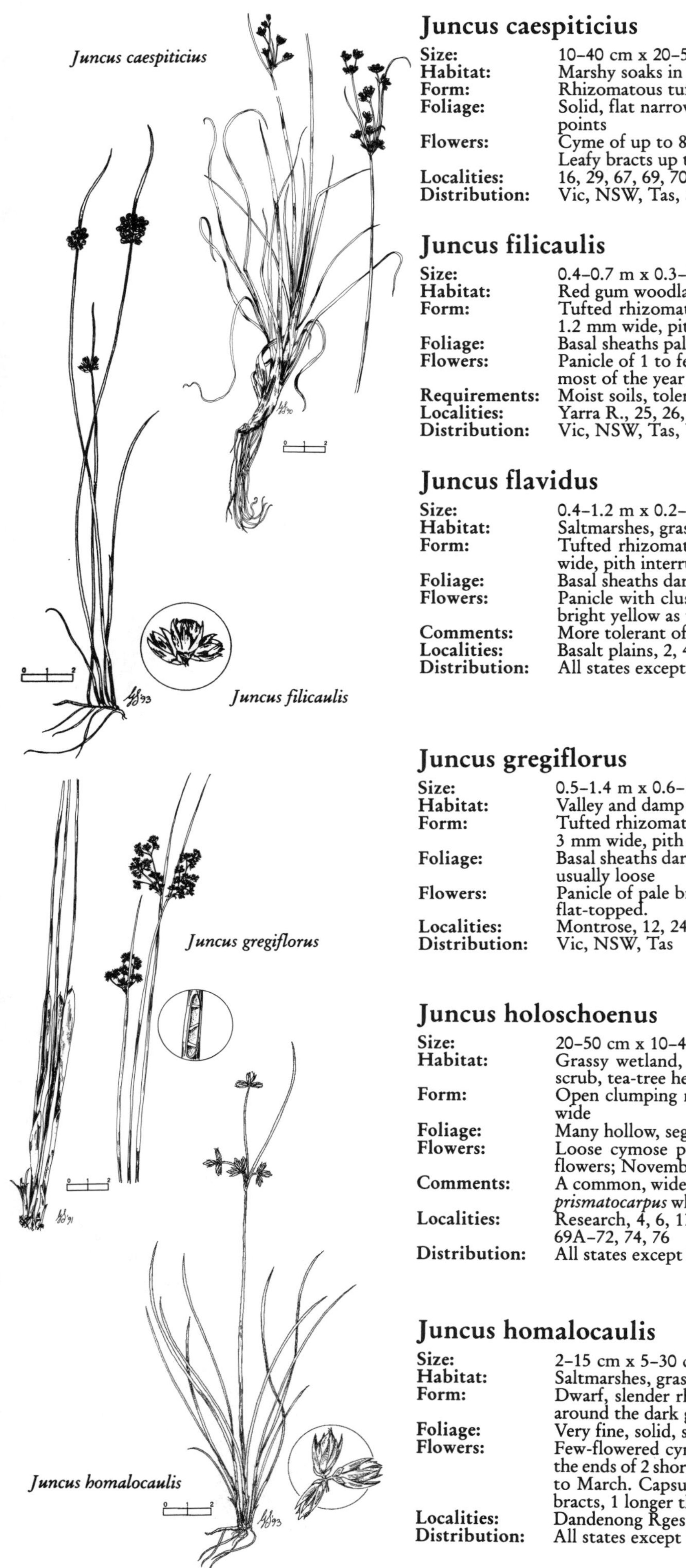

Juncus caespiticius

Grassy or Tufted Rush

Size: 10–40 cm x 20–50 cm **F P**
Habitat: Marshy soaks in riparian scrub, tea-tree heath
Form: Rhizomatous tufted perennial rush
Foliage: Solid, flat narrow incurved leaves to 20 cm x 2–4 mm, tapering to fine points
Flowers: Cyme of up to 8 globular heads of brownish flowers; most of the year. Leafy bracts up to the length of the inflorescence.
Localities: 16, 29, 67, 69, 70, 74
Distribution: Vic, NSW, Tas, SA, WA

Juncus filicaulis

Thread Rush

Size: 0.4–0.7 m x 0.3–0.5 m **F P**
Habitat: Red gum woodland
Form: Tufted rhizomatous perennial herb with slender blue-green stems to 1.2 mm wide, pith cobwebby with very small air spaces
Foliage: Basal sheaths pale brown to 50 mm long, closely pressed to the stem
Flowers: Panicle of 1 to few small, almost round straw-coloured flower clusters; most of the year
Requirements: Moist soils, tolerating dry periods once established
Localities: Yarra R., 25, 26, 69A
Distribution: Vic, NSW, Tas, WA

Juncus flavidus

Size: 0.4–1.2 m x 0.2–1 m **F P**
Habitat: Saltmarshes, grassy wetland, box and red gum woodlands
Form: Tufted rhizomatous perennial rush with yellow-green stems to 3 mm wide, pith interrupted by small air spaces
Foliage: Basal sheaths dark reddish-brown
Flowers: Panicle with clusters of pale yellow flowers along branches, becoming bright yellow as they mature; November to May
Comments: More tolerant of dry soils than other *Juncus* spp.
Localities: Basalt plains, 2, 4–6, 17#, 18, 25, 34A, 47, 48, 69A, 70
Distribution: All states except NT *Illustrated p. 273*

Juncus gregiflorus

Size: 0.5–1.4 m x 0.6–1.5 m **P**
Habitat: Valley and damp sclerophyll forest, riparian scrub
Form: Tufted rhizomatous perennial rush with bright green shining stems to 3 mm wide, pith interrupted
Foliage: Basal sheaths dark brown to dark reddish or purplish brown, top sheath usually loose
Flowers: Panicle of pale brown clustered flowers; November to March. Capsule flat-topped.
Localities: Montrose, 12, 24, 26, 34A, 36, 44, 50A, 53, 56, 63, 74
Distribution: Vic, NSW, Tas

Juncus holoschoenus

Joint-leaved Rush

Size: 20–50 cm x 10–40 cm **F**
Habitat: Grassy wetland, red gum woodland, valley sclerophyll forest, swamp scrub, tea-tree heath
Form: Open clumping rhizomatous perennial rush with leafy stems to 3 mm wide
Foliage: Many hollow, segmented, usually terete leaves as long as the stems
Flowers: Loose cymose panicle with 4–8 clusters each with 10–20 pale green flowers; November to March. Leafy bracts shorter than panicle.
Comments: A common, widespead plant often colonising garden areas. Similar to *J. prismatocarpus* which has multi-tubular partitions in the flattened leaves.
Localities: Research, 4, 6, 17#, 18, 25, 28, 34A, 35, 42, 44, 50A, 54–56, 58, 61–64, 69A–72, 74, 76
Distribution: All states except NT; NZ *Illustrated p. 286*

Juncus homalocaulis

Wiry Rush

Size: 2–15 cm x 5–30 cm **F**
Habitat: Saltmarshes, grassy wetland, box woodland
Form: Dwarf, slender rhizomatous perennial rush, old leaf sheaths remaining around the dark green stems
Foliage: Very fine, solid, slightly flattened leaves to 20 cm long
Flowers: Few-flowered cyme of 1 central cluster, often with another cluster on the ends of 2 short recurved branches; 2–6 flowers per cluster; November to March. Capsule light reddish-brown, shorter than perianth. 2 leafy bracts, 1 longer than the inflorescence.
Localities: Dandenong Rges, Laverton Nth, Deer Park, 2, 11, 17#, 18, 24–26, 60
Distribution: All states except NT

Juncus krausii

Sea Rush

Size: 0.6–2.3 m x 0.5–1.5 m **F**
Habitat: Marshes in coastal banksia woodland, primary dune scrub
Form: Rhizomatous perennial rush with terete stems, leaves and bracts, pith solid
Foliage: Few, dark green sharp-pointed leaves similar to and as long as the stems
Flowers: Loose or dense panicle with small clusters of dark brown flowers; November to March
Requirements: Brackish to saline areas
Comments: Plants are slow to re-establish after disturbance.
Localities: Footscray, 3, 4, 25, 67, 71, 72, 74
Distribution: All states except NT; NZ
Synonym: Previously included with *J. maritimus* which occurs in the Northern Hemisphere.

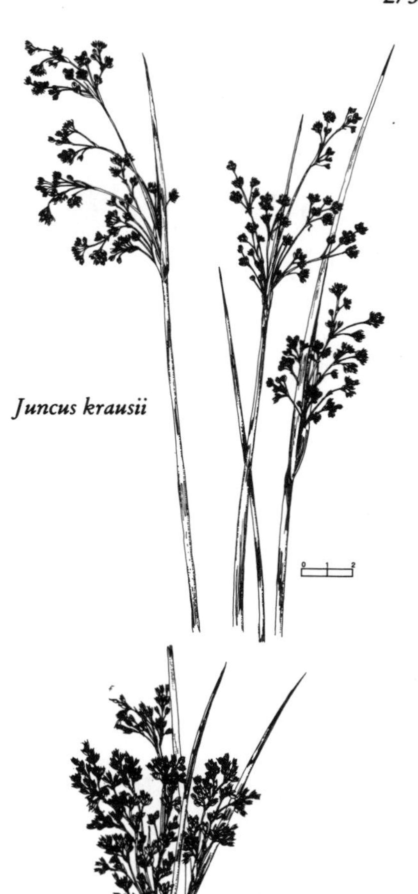

Juncus krausii

Juncus pallidus

Juncus pallidus

Pale Rush

Size: 0.5–2.3 m x 0.3–1 m **F P**
Habitat: Widespread in grassy low open forest, plains grassland, valley sclerophyll forest, tea-tree heath
Form: Tufted rhizomatous perennial rush, pith spongy and uninterrupted in pale green stems 3–8 mm wide
Foliage: Loose pale brown basal sheaths, darker brown below, to 15 cm long
Flowers: Erect, loose or dense panicles to 15 cm long with many pale yellow flowers; December to March. Capsule longer than perianth.
Comments: Vigorous grower adaptable to most situations, but requires periodic inundation for optimum growth.
Localities: Footscray, 16, 34A–36, 41, 42, 44, 46–48, 50–76
Distribution: Vic, NSW, Tas, SA, WA; NZ

Juncus pauciflorus

Loose-flower Rush

Size: 0.3–1 m x 0.2–0.6 m **P**
Habitat: Riparian and swamp scrub, valley sclerophyll forest, grassy low open forest
Form: Rhizomatous perennial rush forming a bright green, often arching tussock; pith spongy and continuous
Foliage: Tight, dark reddish brown basal sheaths
Flowers: Open, loose panicle to 80 mm long, with 20–60 reddish flowers (with 6 stamens) widely spaced along fine curved branches; December to March. Capsule longer than perianth.
Comments: An adaptable plant tolerating dryness once established.
Localities: 26, 27, 35, 36, 44, 47–49, 53–58, 60, 61, 63, 64, 67#, 74, 76
Distribution: Vic, NSW, Tas, SA, WA; NZ

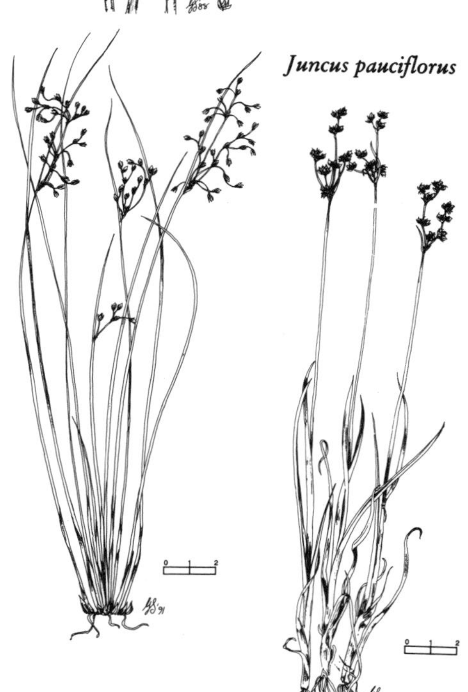

Juncus pauciflorus

Juncus planifolius

Juncus planifolius

Broad-leaf rush

Size: 10–50 cm x 10–30 cm **F P**
Habitat: Valley and damp sclerophyll forests, swamp and wattle tea-tree scrub
Form: Annual or perennial tufting rush with slender leafless stems, lacking a rhizome
Foliage: Broad flat solid leaves 20–30 cm x 3–8 mm, in basal grass-like tuft
Flowers: Umbel-like cymes of brown flowers in many small round heads to 7 mm wide; September to March. Bract shorter than infloresence.
Comments: Tolerates permanently moist soils. Differs from *J. caespiticius* in that leaves are wider, and lacks rhizome. Local forms frequently die around January.
Localities: 35, 43, 44, 54–56, 58–61, 63, 64, 67#, 69A, 71, 74, 75
Distribution: All states except NT; NZ, S Am

Juncus prismatocarpus

Branching Rush

Size: 0.2–0.6 m x 10–30 cm **P**
Habitat: Wet areas in damp sclerophyll forest, wattle tea-tree scrub
Form: Prolifically-flowered rush similar to *J. holoschoenus*
Foliage: Leaves are flattened, hollow with multi-tubular partitions, to 25 cm long
Flowers: Long-branched, cymose panicles with clusters of 10–40 flowers distantly spaced, with a single small bract; November to March
Comments: Distinguished from *J. holoschoenus* by flattened leaves.
Localities: 58, 63, 67#
Distribution: All states except NT; NZ, Asia

Illustrated p. 286

SCALE: 0 1cm 2cm — The scale representation on each plant equals 2cm.

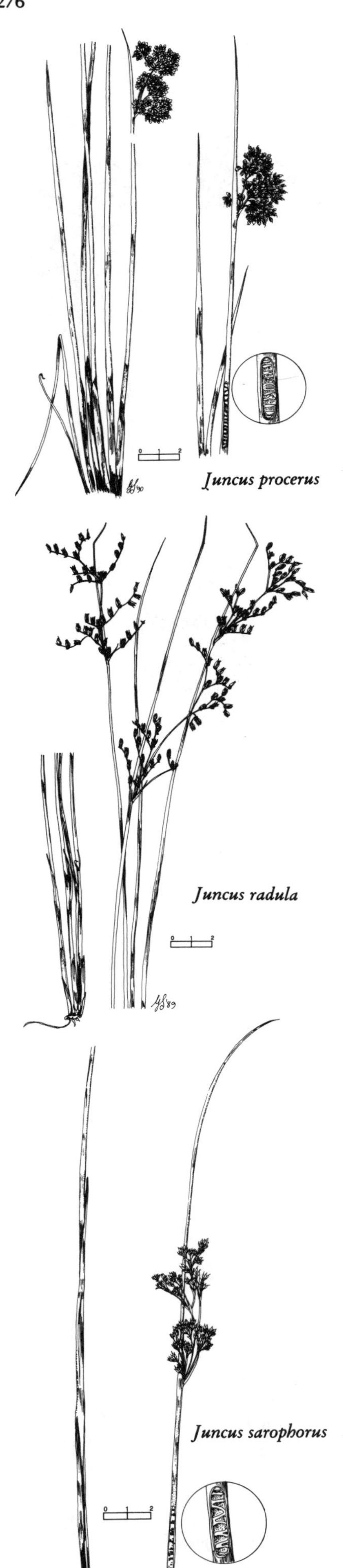
Juncus procerus
Juncus radula
Juncus sarophorus

Juncus procerus

Size: 1–2 m x 0.6–1.5 m — P
Habitat: Damp and valley sclerophyll forests
Form: Tufted rhizomatous perennial herb with soft, thick stems; large air spaces in pith (almost hollow), stems split lengthwise when compressed
Foliage: Large, broad, brown basal sheaths to 15 cm long, loosely surrounding the stem
Flowers: Compact panicle of single brown flowers; October to February. Capsule longer than perianth.
Requirements: Damp, well drained soils in sheltered situations
Localities: 34A, 35, 55, 56, 62, 63, 74, 76
Distribution: Vic, NSW, Tas, SA, WA; NZ

Juncus radula — Hoary Rush

Size: 0.3–0.7 m x 0.2–0.6 m — F P
Habitat: Plains grassland, red gum woodland, dry sclerophyll forest
Form: Tufted rhizomatous perennial rush with rough stems, branches of infloresences and flowers; greyish stems slender to 2.5 mm wide, pith solid
Foliage: Basal sheaths pale brown
Flowers: Loose panicle of single pale brown flowers spaced along the branches; October to March.
Comments: Often occurs in drier areas subject to periodic inundation.
Localities: Laverton Nth, Deer Park, 2, 5, 12, 17#, 18, 26, 35, 39
Distribution: Vic, NSW, SA, WA

Juncus revolutus — Creeping Rush

Size: 5–30 cm x 0.5–1.5 m — F
Habitat: Saltmarshes
Form: Perennial rush, with small tufts at intervals along creeping rhizome, stems sometimes with 1 stem-leaf
Foliage: Solid, thin, flattened leaves to 25 cm long, margins incurved
Flowers: Short one-sided racemes of pale brown flowers, singly or in groups of 2–3 along branches; November to March
Comments: A rare plant in the Melbourne region, it has applications for areas with saline soil.
Localities: Mouth of Yarra R, 2, 4
Distribution: Vic, NSW, Tas

Juncus sarophorus

Size: 0.6–2 m x 0.5–1 m — P
Habitat: Wattle tea-tree and riparian scrub, valley sclerophyll forest
Form: Tufted rhizomatous perennial rush with hard blue-green stems, pith interrupted by air spaces
Foliage: Basal sheaths dark brown to reddish-brown, longest to 30 cm
Flowers: Dense, fan-shaped panicle of pale brown to whitish flowers on erect branches; November to March
Comments: Capsules much longer than perianth
Localities: Montrose, 8, 14, 16, 25, 34A, 42, 44, 47, 48, 54, 56, 62, 63, 70, 74
Distribution: Vic, NSW, Tas, SA; NZ

Juncus sp. O.

Size: 1–1.6 m high — F P
Habitat: Grassy wetlands
Form: Tufted rhizomatous perennial rush, pith usually interrupted in top half of stem, continuous below, stems glaucous, becoming bluish-green with maturity
Foliage: Loose, tapering dark brown basal sheaths to 40 cm long, reddish-brown to black at base
Flowers: Large panicle with flowers usually clustered on branchlets, erect bract to 50 cm long above panicle
Requirements: Heavy soil
Comments: A rare species in Melbourne, more commonly found north of the Divide.
Localities: Laverton, 25
Distribution: Vic, NSW

Illustrated p. 286

Juncus subsecundus — Finger Rush

Size: 0.5–1 m x 0.5–1 m — F P
Habitat: Swampy depressions in plains grassland, riparian scrub, valley sclerophyll forest, grassy low open forest
Form: Tufted rhizomatous perennial rush with smooth, dull blue-green stems and air spaces in pith
Foliage: Basal sheaths pale to mid brown, longest to 120 mm long
Flowers: Loose or compact panicles of pale brown flowers, with a large cluster towards the base of the panicle and smaller terminal clusters; November to January, March to May.
Comments: May form large colonies in heavy, wet soils.
Localities: Research, 2, 4, 5, 16–18, 24–26, 28, 32, 34A, 36, 44, 47, 48, 58, 62, 63, 71, 74
Distribution: All states except NT

Juncus usitatus

Size: 0.3–1.2 m x 0.3–1.5 m **F P**
Habitat: Plains grassland, red gum woodland, valley sclerophyll forest, often growing in shallow water
Form: Tufted rhizomatous perennial rush with slender yellow-green stems, pith interrupted, with air spaces and pithy segments almost equal
Foliage: Basal sheaths dark brown to dark reddish-brown, shining
Flowers: Loose fan-shaped panicles of pale brown flowers; November to March
Comments: A vigorous grower, particularly in poorly drained soils.
Localities: 12, 26, 33, 34A, 36, 58, 62, 63, 65, 67#
Distribution: Vic, Qld, NSW

Juncus vaginatus

Clustered Rush

Size: 0.3–1 m x 0.5–1 m **F P**
Habitat: Wet depressions in red gum woodland
Form: Tufted rhizomatous perennial rush with robust stems to 8 mm wide, pith solid and spongy
Foliage: Basal sheaths loose, yellowish-green to light brown or greyish
Flowers: Large, much-branched and spreading panicle to 15 cm long, pale brown to deep orange-red flowers, with 6 stamens, in almost round clusters separated by bare primary branches; November to March
Comments: An attractive ornamental rush for wet gardens and poolside planting.
Localities: 25, 26
Distribution: Vic, Qld, NSW, Tas

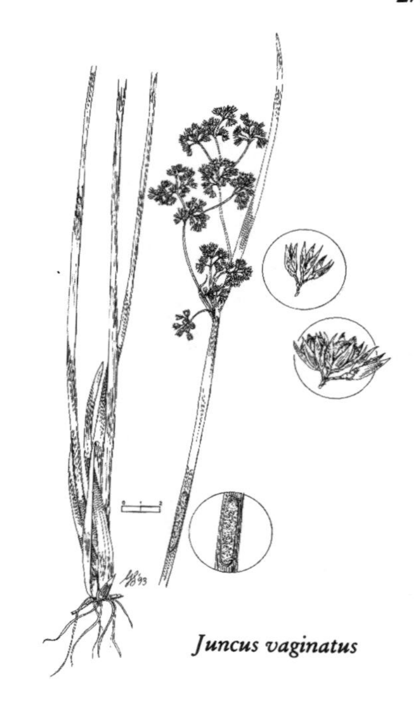

Juncus vaginatus

Lemna — Lemnaceae

Lemna disperma

Duckweed

Size: Individual plants 2–4 mm wide **F P N**
Habitat: Fresh, still water in grassy wetlands, riparian scrub, box woodland
Form: Floating mat plant, each plant consisting of a single leaf-like thallus and a single root 10–40 mm long, suspended in the water
Foliage: Bright green, flattened disk-like leaves
Flowers: Minute, almost insignificant white flowers on the margins of thallus; Spring
Comments: A rapid-growing and multiplying perennial aquatic plant providing good cover for fish and other aquatic animals. It is most prolific in Spring and Summer.
Propagation: Vegetative budding. Young thalli of *Lemna*, *Spirodela* and *Wolffia* spp. emerge from small pockets in the edges and eventually break away. Each species also occasionally produces minute seed.
Localities: 4, 6, 14, 16, 29, 34A–36, 42, 44, 49, 55, 60, 62, 63, 67#, 71, 75
Distribution: All states; NZ, cosmopolitan
Synonym: *L. minor*

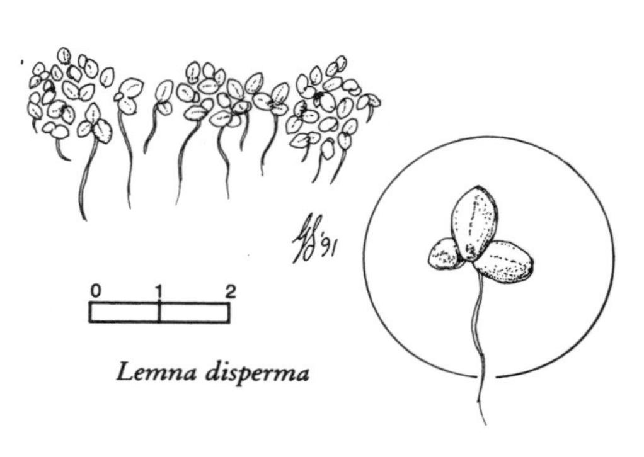

Lemna disperma

Lepidosperma — Cyperaceae

Lepidosperma species, commonly called sword-sedges and rapier-sedges because of the shapes of their leaves, are a relatively abundant group of perennial sedges occurring in heaths and moist sites such as stream sides and the edges of swamps. Plants are tufted, spreading by creeping rhizomes. The erect stems and leaves are very similar in appearance and length, with all leaves basal and sometimes flatter than the stems. Flowers are in terminal panicles or spikes with the lowest bract leaf-like, sheathing the base of the panicle. The fruit is a nut, surrounded by 6 thickened whitish scales (not to be confused with stamen filaments).

The erect foliage and graceful panicles of flowers make many *Lepidosperma* spp. attractive plants for accent planting, particularly near water. The flower heads are most decorative in bold dried flower arrangements. Plants can be propagated by seed, but are generally propagated by division of the clumps. They are not fussy as to soil type and often grow well in very heavy soils as long as there is plenty of moisture available, and full or partial sun.

Lepidosperma concavum

Lepidosperma concavum

Sand-hill or Hill Sword-sedge

Size: 0.6–1 m high **F P**
Habitat: Primary dune scrub, coastal banksia woodland, tea-tree heath
Foliage: Stems solid to 6 mm wide, flat on one side, convex the other side
Flowers: Short, widely pyramidal panicle 40–70 mm long with densely clustered blackish-brown spikelets; most of the year; bract broad. Nut dull brown, scales long and tapering.
Requirements: Moist well drained sandy soil
Localities: Clayton, 49, 67–71, 73–75
Distribution: Vic, Qld, NSW, Tas, SA

SCALE: 0 1cm 2cm — The scale representation on each plant equals 2cm.

Lepidosperma congestum

Clustered Sword-sedge

Size: 0.15–0.8 m high — **F P**
Habitat: Tea-tree heath
Foliage: Leaves sticky at sheath margins; stems flat, to 5 mm wide, margins sharp and slightly rough
Flowers: Narrow elongated blackish panicle to 80 mm long, with primary branches very short, spikelets in dense golden rounded clusters; most of the year. Bracts sharply pointed, upper ones with long awns. Nut shiny olive-green.
Requirements: Moist sandy soil
Localities: Black Rock, 69A, 75
Distribution: Vic, SA

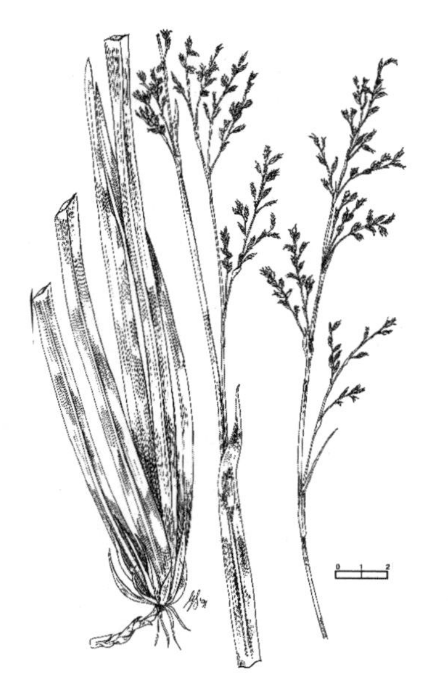

Lepidosperma elatius var. *elatius*

Lepidosperma elatius var. elatius

Tall Sword-sedge

Size: 1–2.5 m x 1–2 m — **P N**
Habitat: Wet, damp and valley sclerophyll forests, grassy low open forest in swamps and gullies
Foliage: Leaves to 10 mm wide, slightly shorter than stems which have sharp margins and a conspicuous mid-rib
Flowers: Loose panicle more than 100 mm long with numerous ovoid spikelets to 5 mm long; most of the year.
Comments: The Aborigines used the lower part of the leaf to obtain fibre for basket-making. A spectacular accent plant which should not be planted near walkways due to sharpness of leaves.
Localities: 34A, 46, 47, 50–52, 55–58, 60, 75
Distribution: Vic, NSW, Tas
Synonym: The var. *ensiforme* is now included within this variety.

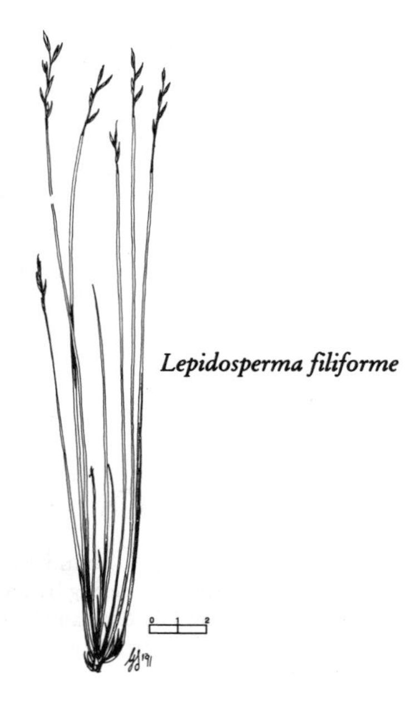

Lepidosperma filiforme

Lepidosperma filiforme

Common Rapier-sedge

Size: to 0.9 m high — **P**
Habitat: Swamp and wattle tea-tree scrub, sclerophyll woodland
Foliage: Leaves reduced to basal sheaths, stems terete and smooth to 1 mm wide
Flowers: Simple spike of brown or greyish flowers in up to 12 loosely arranged spikelets; Spring to Summer
Comments: Becoming rare in the Melbourne area.
Localities: Montrose, Clayton, 54, 67#, 74–76
Distribution: Vic, NSW, Tas; NZ

Lepidosperma forsythii

Large-flowered Rapier-sedge

Size: 0.6–1 m high — **F P**
Habitat: Tea-tree heath, in swamps
Foliage: Leafless, leaves reduced to bracts tapering to a point; stems terete to 1.5 mm wide, bracts large and broad, shorter than flowerhead
Flowers: Short flexuose panicle with 5 or more narrow, widely spreading spikelets
Requirements: Wet sandy soil
Localities: Beaumaris, 74
Distribution: Vic, NSW

Lepidosperma gladiatum

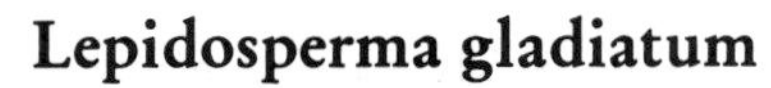

Lepidosperma gladiatum

Sword Rush, Coast Sword-sedge

Size: 1–1.5 m high — **F P**
Habitat: Primary dune scrub
Form: Similar to *L. concavum* but stems are convex on both faces, taller and broader, to 20 mm wide, with sharp edges and a prominent central rib (leaves flatter).
Flowers: The dense panicle is larger, to 15 cm long with pale brown spikelets. Nut is wrinkled and shiny brown, and scales beneath the nut are very broad.
Comments: Useful in dried floral arrangements. The tender leaf base was eaten by the Aborigines while the whole leaf was used for basket-making.
Localities: Seaford, 67#, 74
Distribution: All states except Qld, NT

Lepidosperma gunnii

Habitat: Tea-tree heath
Comments: Similar to *L. laterale* from which it has recently been separated. It has narrower leaves and stems to 2–3 mm wide and shorter panicles to 75 mm long.
Localities: 66, 67, 73, 74–76
Synonym: *L. laterale* var. *angustum*

Lepidosperma laterale var. laterale

Variable Sword-sedge

Size: 0.4–1 m high **P**
Habitat: Damp, valley and dry sclerophyll forests, sclerophyll woodland, swamp scrub, grassy low open forest
Foliage: Narrow, stiff shining dark green leaves and stems to 6 mm wide, hardly ribbed, flat to slightly concave on one side, margins sharp
Flowers: Narrow, loose panicle to 20 cm long with erect branches and narrow, brown spikelets to 8 mm long; September to March. Nut is wrinkled and shiny mid-brown.
Requirements: Very adaptable
Comments: As a species, *L. laterale* is the most common and widespread *Lepidosperma* in Victoria. It is very variable and several varieties have been described. Plants with narrow leaves occur at Diggers Rest, Warrandyte and Croydon. *L. lineare*, which does not occur within Melbourne, has been wrongly applied to some narrow leaf forms. A more robust variety is described below. *L. laterale* is currently undergoing revision.
Localities: Eltham, 26, 28, 32, 34A–36, 40–42, 44, 47, 48, 50–60, 62–66, 71, 74–76
Distribution: Vic, Qld, NSW, Tas, SA; NZ *Also illustrated p. 286*

Lepidosperma laterale var. *laterale*

Lepidosperma laterale var. majus

Variable Sword-sedge

Size: Very variable, up to 2 m high **P**
Habitat: Valley and wet sclerophyll forests, grassy low open forest
Comments: Differs from *L. laterale* var. *laterale* in that it is more robust, with broad, very flat stems. The flowers are borne on a longer panicle to 30 cm. Large plants resemble *L. elatius*, which has smaller nuts with shorter scales, not drawn out into long fine points or bristles. The red leaf base was used as a contrast colour in basket-making by the Aborigines.
Localities: 44, 45, 47, 48, 54, 57, 74, 76
Distribution: Vic, NSW

Lepidosperma laterale var. *majus*

Lepidosperma longitudinale

Pithy or Common Sword-sedge

Size: 0.6–1.7 m high **F P**
Habitat: Wattle tea-tree and swamp scrub, occurring in or near water
Foliage: Leaves and stems soft and pithy, sometimes hollowed, convex on both faces, to 8 mm wide, margins smooth
Flowers: Erect narrow panicle 10–30 cm long with densely crowded greyish-brown, 2–3-flowered spikelets to 7 mm long; most of the year. Nut shiny light brown to brown.
Requirements: Moist or wet soils
Localities: 60, 67, 69–71, 73–75
Distribution: All states except NT

Lepidosperma neesii

Stiff Rapier-sedge

Size: to 0.8 m high **P**
Habitat: Grassy low open forest, wattle tea-tree scrub
Foliage: Linear terete leaves, stems strongly angled
Flowers: Short, narrow blackish spike-like panicle to 25 mm long, with a rigid, very long bract beneath. Many spikelets to 8 mm long pressed flat against the branches.
Requirements: Swampy soils
Localities: 59, 74, 76
Distribution: Vic, NSW

Lepidosperma semiteres

Wire Rapier-sedge

Size: 0.3–1 m high **F P**
Habitat: Damp sclerophyll forest, tea-tree heath, grassy low open forest
Foliage: Leaves flat with thin margins; stems to 1 mm wide, strongly convex on both faces, sometimes with a deep groove
Flowers: Short, branched spike-like panicle to 60 mm long with 12 or more slender spikelets to 8 mm long, flowers brown or greyish; most of the year. Nut straw-coloured and wrinkled or smooth shiny olive-green.
Localities: 56, 67–70, 74, 76
Distribution: Vic, NSW, SA *Illustrated p. 286*

Lepidosperma tortuosum

Tortuous Rapier-sedge

Size: to 40 cm high **P**
Habitat: Damp sclerophyll forest
Foliage: Leaves are convex on both faces, to 25 cm long, stems biconvex to terete, channelled with a ridge on the other side
Comments: Similar to *L. forsythii* but smaller and more slender. The 2–5 spikelets to 8 mm long are close together on the short spike; January. Bracts are inconspicuous.
Localities: 56
Distribution: Vic, NSW, Tas, SA *Illustrated p. 286*

Lepidosperma longitudinale

Lepidosperma neesii

SCALE: 0 1cm 2cm The scale representation on each plant equals 2cm.

Lepilaena **Zannichelliaceae**

Aquatic annual or perennial rhizomatous grassy herbs, found in fresh or brackish water, some species tolerating salinities exceeding those of seawater. Rhizomes and stems are much-branched. Leaves are sheathed at the base with a well developed, cleft ligule (or growth between the sheath and leafblade). The unisexual flowers are inconspicuous and at first enclosed in a leaf sheath. The fruit and leaves are eaten by some seabirds.

Lepilaena cylindrocarpa

Lepilaena bilocularis

Small-fruited or Feather-style Water-mat

F P

Size: stems 5–15 cm long, occasionally to 1 m long
Habitat: Saltmarshes, lakes, in brackish water to 1 m deep
Form: Submerged slender perennial herb
Foliage: Fine, linear leaves to 20 mm long, tip truncate with 3 distinct points, borne at close intervals along thread-like stems
Flowers: Dioecious, flowers almost sessile; May to September
Requirements: Fresh to brackish water
Localities: Albert Park Lake, 4
Distribution: Vic, Qld, NSW, Tas, SA; NZ

Lepilaena cylindrocarpa

Long-fruit Water-mat

F

Size: stems to 35 cm long
Habitat: Saltmarshes, marine
Comments: Similar to *L. preissii*. Leaves end in a short point. Inconspicuous dioecious flowers are borne on stalks longer than the leaf sheaths. Petals are slightly notched. Stems are slender, branched and flexuose; stems on female plants shorter, to 25 cm high. Flowers August to November.
Localities: Western shores of Port Phillip, mouth of Yarra R, 2, 4
Distribution: Vic, Tas, SA, WA

Lepilaena preissii

Slender Water-mat

F

Size: stems 5–50 cm long
Habitat: Salt marshes, brackish lakes, marine
Form: Annual monoecious or dioecious herb
Foliage: Linear leaves to 80 mm long tapering to a sharp point
Flowers: Much-branched flowering stems with clusters of conspicuous white flowers (relative to other species) on short stalks no longer than the sheaths, petals deeply notched; September to February. Male and female flowers often together.
Localities: Western shores of Port Phillip, Albert Park, 4
Distribution: Vic, Tas, SA, WA

Leptocarpus brownii

Leptocarpus **Restionaceae**

Leptocarpus brownii

Coarse Twine-rush

F P

Size: 0.5–1 m high
Habitat: Swamp scrub, tea-tree heath
Form: Rush-like rhizomatous perennial herb with erect unbranched stems and scale-like leaves or sheathing bracts to 7 mm long
Flowers: Dioecious, in panicles; male flowers in few short reddish-brown spikelets to 10 mm long, on white-woolly stalks; female flowers in numerous 3–6-flowered golden-brown spikelets to 6 mm long, sessile, clustered together; most of the year
Requirements: Moist soils, tolerating dryness once established
Localities: 61, 67#, 70, 71 74
Distribution: Vic, NSW, Tas, SA

Leptocarpus tenax

Slender Twine-rush

F P

Size: 0.5–1 m high
Habitat: Swamp scrub, wattle tea-tree scrub
Foliage: Sheathing bracts 5–10 mm long
Flowers: Differs from *L. brownii* in that male spikelets are smaller, to 4 mm long, and more numerous in a loose, often drooping panicle with glabrous stalks. Female spikelets fewer, to 10 mm long, in rigidly erect panicles; mostly October to June.
Requirements: Moist soil
Comments: Endangered in the Melbourne area. Very attractive as an accent plant, and also when used in dried arrangements.
Localities: Collected in Sandringham 1905; 61
Distribution: All states except NT

Lepyrodia

Restionaceae

Lepyrodia muelleri

Common or Erect Scale-rush

P

Size: 0.4–0.6 m high
Habitat: Wattle tea-tree scrub
Form: Rush-like perennial herb with scaly rhizomes
Foliage: Leaves reduced to distant sheathing bracts to 25 mm long
Flowers: Dioecious on few stems, few of which are branched. Single, stalked pale brown flowers in a narrow panicle 30–120 mm long, glumes shorter than perianth segments; September to May. Floral bracts are very thin and fragile.
Requirements: Wet sandy soil
Localities: 59, 67, 68, 70, 73–75
Distribution: Vic, NSW, Tas, SA, WA

Lepyrodia muelleri

Lomandra

Xanthorrhoeaceae (Dasypogonaceae)

Lomandras are hardy perennial rhizomatous herbs forming rush-like tufts. Their basal leaves are often held stiffly erect, longer than and sometimes hiding the dense clusters or panicles of small yellow or yellow-brown flowers. All species are dioecious. The flowers are composed of 3 outer and 3 inner perianth segments. Lomandras are important butterfly food plants. The Aborigines made drinks from the nectar and used fibre from the leaves of some species to weave bags and baskets. Propagation is by seed or division of clumps. Previously included in the family *Liliaceae.*

Lomandra filiformis ssp. filiformis

Wattle Mat-rush

F P

Size: 15–50 cm x 15–20 cm
Habitat: Widespread in valley and dry sclerophyll forests, sclerophyll and red gum woodland, grassy low open forest
Form: Sparsely tufted grass-like perennial
Foliage: Narrow channelled bluish-green to green leaves to 5 mm wide, flexible, with margins inrolled, tip minutely 1-3-pointed
Flowers: Panicle to 20 cm long (occasionally to 30 cm). The numerous stalked, yellow female flowers are small and globular and borne on fine short branches, looking like tiny wattle buds. Female panicles are slightly shorter than the male. Outer segments of male flowers are purplish and stems whitish; September to December.
Requirements: Moist, well drained clays or sands tolerating dry shady situations once established
Comments: An attractive, long-lived rockery plant grown for form rather than flowers. A form from Montrose is rhizomatous and spreading.
Localities: 12, 13, 16, 18, 21, 23–26, 28, 29, 31, 32, 34A–49, 50A–56, 58–68, 69A–71, 74–76
Distribution: Vic, Qld, NSW

Lomandra filiformis ssp. *filiformis*

Lomandra filiformis ssp. coriacea

F P

Size: 15–30 cm high
Habitat: Riparian scrub, valley and dry sclerophyll forest
Foliage: Leaves are flat, leathery and lightly raspy on the edges, tip entire.
Flowers: Male panicle has a few whorled branches and is distinctly rough at the axes; stem yellowish. Female panicle is smaller, axes not as rough.
Comments: The two subspecies are often found growing together in the wild.
Localities: Montrose, Sth Yarra, Brighton, 13, 21, 32, 34A, 36, 46, 47, 50–51, 53–55, 65, 69, 73–76
Distribution: Vic, Qld, NSW

Lomandra longifolia

Spiny-headed Mat-rush

F P N

Size: 0.5–1 m x 0.5–1.2 m
Habitat: Widespread in red gum woodland, dry and valley sclerophyll forests, grassy low open forest, tea-tree heath, coastal banksia woodland
Form: Large tussock plant
Foliage: Smooth bright green strap-like leaves to 12 mm wide, tip with 2 or 3 teeth
Flowers: Numerous clusters of sessile, scented yellowish flowers with purplish bases, whorled panicles to 15 cm long; panicles many-branched on male plants; narrow on female plants; September to December. Shiny greenish brown or brownish-orange capsules remain on plant for most of year. Spiky bracts to 30 mm long extend beyond each flower cluster.
Requirements: Well drained soils tolerating dry shade
Comments: Grows well under established trees.
Localities: 1, 12, 16, 26, 28, 29, 31, 32, 34A–36, 38, 40–56, 58–71, 73–76
Distribution: Vic, Qld, NSW, Tas, SA

Lomandra longifolia

SCALE: 0 1cm 2cm — The scale representation on each plant equals 2cm.

Lomandra multiflora

Lomandra nana

Luzula meridionalis var. *densiflora*

Lomandra micrantha ssp. **micrantha** — Small-flowered Mat-rush

Size: 0.2–0.7 m x 0.5 m — P
Habitat: Plains grassland, box woodland
Foliage: Narrow, flexuose grass-like leaves to 2.5 mm wide, flat to terete, hiding flower stem
Flowers: Loose panicle with minutely-rough branches. Small, scattered flowers are stalked and greenish-yellow to dark red. Male flowers to 2 mm long, borne singly or in 2's, panicle branched; female flowers to 5 mm long, panicle may be unbranched; April to December. Shining pale yellow or greenish capsule.
Requirements: Suited to most soils
Localities: Sunshine, 17#, 18, 28, 38, 74
Distribution: Vic, NSW, SA, WA

Lomandra multiflora — Many-flowered Mat-rush

Size: 0.3–0.5 m x 0.3–0.5 m — P
Habitat: Box woodland, valley sclerophyll forest, tea-tree heath
Foliage: Rigid, narrow greyish leaves to 3 mm wide, surfaces slightly rough
Flowers: Male flowers are borne in showy, densely whorled clusters on branched stems to 30 cm high. Each flower is 2–3 mm long on a stalk to 10 mm long. Petals are yellow, sepals purplish. Female flowers are slightly larger, to 4 mm, and sessile. Panicles are unbranched, stems to 25 cm long; capsules become black and wrinkled. June to January
Requirements: Well drained soils, tolerating extended dry spells once established
Localities: Montrose, St Albans, 34A, 42, 44, 54, 56, 62, 63, 67–70
Distribution: Vic, NT, Qld, NSW

Lomandra nana — Pale Mat-rush

Size: 5–15 cm x 5–10 cm — F P
Habitat: Tea-tree heath, plains grassland
Form: Low densely tufted herb with flowers hidden at the base of the foliage
Foliage: Fine, rough, flat bluish-green leaves to 2 mm wide, erect or curved to one side
Flowers: Male panicle stout, unbranched, creamy-white flowers in sessile clusters. Female flowerhead almost stemless with flowers crowded into 1 to several sessile clusters. Flowers sessile; October to December.
Requirements: Well drained soils
Localities: Keilor, Melton, 63, 64, 68–69A, 74
Distribution: Vic, Tas, SA
Synonym: Segregated from *L. glauca*

Luzula — Juncaceae

Luzula meridionalis var. **meridionalis** — Field Woodrush

Size: to 10 cm x 15 cm; stem to 30 cm high — P
Habitat: Widespread in red gum woodland, dry, valley and wet sclerophyll forests, grassy low open forest
Form: Loosely tufted stoloniferous perennial herb
Foliage: Flat, linear grass-like basal leaves 2–5 mm wide, the edges fringed with long white hairs, denser towards the base, and blunt tips; 1–2 stem leaves
Flowers: Terminal umbel-like panicle to 10 mm wide, of 1–6 dense globular clusters of brown flowers subtended by 1–4 leaf-like bracts, held above the foliage; August to December. Flowers each have 6 tapering perianth parts and 6 stamens. Fruit brown to dark brown.
Requirements: Well drained soils, tolerant of both dry and wet periods, but not waterlogging
Comments: *Luzula* spp. often develop swollen onion-like bases.
Propagation: Seed, division
Localities: 35, 36, 39, 41, 42, 44, 46, 49, 50A, 51, 53, 55–57, 60, 62, 63, 64, 67, 74, 76
Distribution: Vic, NSW, Tas, SA, WA
Synonym: All varieties were originally combined under *L. campestris*.

Luzula meridionalis var. **densiflora** — Woodrush

Size: stem 25–40 cm high — F P
Habitat: Valley sclerophyll forest, wattle tea-tree scrub
Requirements: Moist well drained soils
Comments: Differs from the typical species in that leaves are narrower, to 3 mm wide and margins densely fringed. Panicle consists of 1 or more rigidly branched sessile clusters. Fruit is brown to dark red-brown. July to December
Localities: Eltham, 42, 44, 45, 56, 74, 75
Distribution: Vic, NSW, Tas, SA, WA
Synonym: *L. densiflora*

Luzula meridionalis var. flaccida

Woodrush

Size: 15–25 cm high **P N**
Habitat: Tea-tree heath, valley sclerophyll forest
Comments: Differs from the above varieties in that leaves are very narrow, 1–2 mm wide, lax and almost glabrous. The flowers are smaller and yellowish-brown on limp stems; August to November.
Localities: 32, 34A, 36, 44, 47, 48, 67, 69A, 74
Distribution: Vic, Qld, NSW, Tas, SA
Synonym: *L. flaccida*

Illustrated p. 286

Microlaena **Poaceae**

Microlaena stipoides

Weeping Grass

Size: Highly variable; to 30 cm x 0.6 m; stems to 1 m high **F P**
Habitat: Widespread in plains grassland, dry and valley sclerophyll forests, sclerophyll woodland, grassy low open forest, swamp, riparian and wattle tea-tree scrub
Form: Sparse, shortly rhizomatous perennial grass with gracefully arching, erect or semi-prostrate stems which may develop roots at the basal nodes
Foliage: Narrow flat leaves to 80 mm long
Flowers: Narrow nodding racemes or panicles to 20 cm long on slender stems. Spikelets (to 30 mm long) composed of minute glumes, 2 sterile lemmas with awns to 20 mm long and 1 fertile, awnless lemma; September to November
Requirements: Moist, well drained soils
Comments: One of the best lawn grasses for shady sites, where it is often found as a remnant of the original vegetation of Melbourne. Regularly mown or grazed plants form a fine sward with stems as short as a few cms. In rural areas, grazing by macropods (kangaroos etc) sometimes creates weeping grass lawns.
Propagation: Seed, division
Localities: Laverton Nth, Sunshine, Deer Park, 8, 10, 16, 18, 21, 23–26, 28, 29, 31–36, 38–42, 44, 45, 47–60, 62–64, 67–71, 74–76
Distribution: All states; NZ

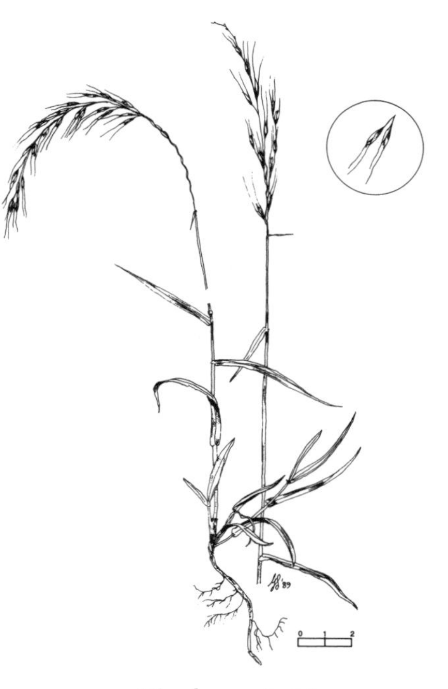

Microlaena stipoides

Ottelia **Hydrocharitaceae**

Ottelia ovalifolia

Swamp Lily

F P

Habitat: Freshwater pools and slow streams in water to 0.6 m deep
Form: Aquatic perennial herb with a tuft of floating leaves rising on long stalks from the base. Plants root in mud.
Foliage: Elliptic to ovate leaves, blades 50–150 mm long, with 7 prominent veins; juvenile leaves linear
Flowers: Large, showy single white flowers with dark reddish-purple base, to 75 mm wide, held just above water level; plants also bear unopened submerged flowers which are self-pollinating; November to March. Seeds ripen and are released under water.
Requirements: Fresh water, tolerating seasonal drying out of pool
Comments: An ornamental pond plant with attractive flowers and foliage. An alternative to water-lilies. Locally rare.
Propagation: Division
Localities: Melton West, Warrandyte, 9, 11, 35, 63, 67#
Distribution: All mainland states; N Cal

Ottelia ovalifolia

Panicum **Poaceae**

Panicum decompositum

Australian Millet or Umbrella Grass

Size: 0.3–0.5 m high, stems to 1.5 m high **F P**
Habitat: Moist depressions in grassy wetlands
Form: Coarse, densely tufted perennial grass
Foliage: Erect, flat glabrous blue-green leaves to 50 cm x 12 mm gradually tapering to a fine point; edges whitish
Flowers: Large, very open, much branched panicle to 30 cm long, held above foliage on stout, hollow stems. Lower branches clustered. Solitary spikelets along the rhachis of branches. First glume up to 30% length of spikelet. Flowers mostly in Summer.
Requirements: Heavy soils that do not dry out
Comments: Although perennial, plants may be short lived, suffering adversely during dry periods. Very attractive in dried arrangements. The flour from ground seeds was made into cakes by the Aborigines. A rare plant both in Melbourne and the rest of Victoria.
Propagation: Seed
Localities: Braybrook 1905; Laverton, Sunshine
Distribution: All mainland states

Panicum decompositum

SCALE: 0 1cm 2cm — The scale representation on each plant equals 2cm.

Panicum effusum var. *effusum*

Panicum effusum var. effusum

Hairy Panic

Size: 20–60 cm high — F P
Habitat: Grassy wetlands, plains grassland, box and red gum woodland
Form: Tufted perennial grass with thickened, hairy base
Foliage: Sparsely hairy, flat, dull greyish-green leaves 5–25 cm x 2–6 mm, nodes bearded with silky hairs
Flowers: Differs from *P. decompositum* in that panicle is smaller, to 20 cm long, with usually 2 purplish spikelets near the ends of thread-like rhachis. First glume pointed, about half the length of spikelet. October to May
Requirements: Heavy clay soils
Comments: The old flowerheads of *Panicum* spp. soon become brittle and break away. Blown along by the wind they are often seen in large numbers caught along fences.
Propagation: Seed
Localities: Sunshine, 6, 9, 15, 17#, 18, 21, 25, 26
Distribution: All mainland states

Panicum prolutum = Homopholis proluta

Paspalidium — Poaceae

Paspalidium constrictum

Knotty-butt or Box Grass

Size: 30–60 cm high — F P
Habitat: Rocky escarpments
Form: Tufted perennial herb
Foliage: Narrow, rough, flat or folded leaves to 15 cm long
Flowers: Narrow, slender spike-like panicle to 12 cm long, borne slightly above the leaves. Spikelets irregularly arranged on short panicle branches, lower glume downy; September to April
Requirements: Well drained rocky soils
Comments: A restricted species due to habitat destruction, it is now known from only 2 sites within the Melbourne area.
Propagation: Seed
Localities: Melton
Distribution: All mainland states

Paspalidium constrictum

Pentapogon — Poaceae

Pentapogon quadrifidus

Five-awned Spear-grass

Size: 8–18 cm high, stems 30–60 cm high — F P
Habitat: Plains grassland, red gum woodland, dry and valley sclerophyll forests
Form: Tufted erect annual or short-lived perennial grass
Foliage: Leaves 8–18 cm long, inrolled, glabrous or pubescent
Flowers: Open to moderately dense light brownish panicle to 15 cm long with narrow 1-flowered spikelets. Lemma 2-lobed, 2 small awns per lobe, longer central awn to 25 mm long, rigid and twisted in first 10 mm. November to February.
Requirements: Adaptable to all but very wet soil conditions
Propagation: Seed
Localities: Laverton Nth, 5, 12, 25, 26, 28, 36, 42, 44, 47, 48, 50A, 54, 55, 74
Distribution: Vic, NSW, Tas, SA — *Illustrated p. 286*

Philydrum lanuginosum

Philydrum — Philydraceae

Philydrum lanuginosum

Woolly Water Lily

Size: 0.5–1 m x 0.5 m — F P
Habitat: Freshwater pools and swamps
Form: Erect aquatic perennial herb
Foliage: Smooth, pointed, reddish-green strap-shaped leaves 15–45 cm x 5–10 mm, reducing in length up the flowering stem to become ovate floral bracts to 25 mm long
Flowers: Long spike of up to 20 sessile, velvety yellow, hooded flowers, on a stout woolly flowering stem to 0.9 m high. Each flower has just 1 perfect stamen and 2 staminodes and lasts for one day; Summer.
Requirements: Ample fresh water
Comments: Attractive flowering pond plant which appears to be extinct within the Melbourne area. Aboriginal women used the leaves for girdles.
Propagation: Division
Localities: Cheltenham#, 67#
Distribution: Vic, Qld, NSW, WA, NT; SE Asia

Phragmites **Poaceae**

Phragmites australis

Common Reed

Size: 1–3 m high **F P**
Habitat: Riparian and swamp scrub, coastal banksia woodland
Form: Semi-aquatic, fast growing bamboo-like perennial grass with strongly creeping rhizomes, flowering stems leafy and unbranched
Foliage: Glabrous grey-green leaves 20–60 cm x 1–3 cm, tapering to a fine point
Flowers: White to purplish panicles, fluffy and plume-like to 40 cm long. Spikelets 2–6-flowered, to 15 mm long, lemmas glabrous, ending in long points, surrounded by many silky hairs. January to April
Requirements: Wet and poorly drained soils, tolerating brackish sites
Comments: An attractive water-side plant for dams and large ponds but must be kept contained or else it can take over. Provides food and nesting for waterbirds. Important to the Aborigines who used the stems for spears and ornaments and leaves to weave baskets.
Propagation: Division, seed
Localities: 1, 3, 4, 8, 14, 16, 18, 21, 25–30, 32, 33, 34A–36, 42, 44, 46, 47, 49, 51, 53, 55, 56, 59–67, 69A–76
Distribution: All states; all continents

Phragmites australis

Poa **Poaceae**

Native *Poa* species found in Melbourne are perennial grasses with flowerheads arranged mostly in loose panicles. The lemmas are 5–9-veined while the glumes are 1–3-veined.

Some particularly attractive species are suited to ornamental horticulture. Their soft, graceful form makes them a very useful accent plant in a variety of landscape styles.

Propagation is from seed, or division (which is quicker and easier). The Aborigines used the leaves and stems of the larger species for string or basket-making.

Classification and identification of Poas into species is very difficult. Recognition must sometimes rely on a composite of rather variable features, and intermediates occur between what we presently call separate species.

Poa clelandii

Size: to 25 cm high; stems to 0.75 m high **F P**
Habitat: Plains grassland, tea-tree heath, valley sclerophyll forest
Form: Loose or dense tussocks with creeping rhizomes, new tufts forming at a distance from the parent
Foliage: Leaves flat, inrolled on drying, to 25 cm long, lower leaf sheaths purplish
Flowers: Narrow panicle to 20 cm long, with 3–5-flowered, purplish, greenish or straw-coloured spikelets on upper ends of branches. September to January
Localities: Beaumaris, 17#, 18, 51, 54, 74, 75
Distribution: Vic, SA

Poa ensiformis

Purple-sheath Tussock Grass

Size: 0.3–0.75 m x 1 m; stems to 1.5 m high **P N**
Habitat: Damp and valley sclerophyll forests
Form: Rhizomatous, forming loose to rather dense tussocks
Foliage: Long, narrow, flat dark green leaves to 75 cm x 6 mm, rough, especially on margins and back. Purple sheaths around lower leaves during most months. Old leaves inrolled and straw-coloured.
Flowers: Erect, spreading panicle to 30 cm long; October to March
Comments: Vigorous grass, ideally suited to moist, shaded sites. Useful for controlling erosion.
Localities: 34A, 36, 42, 44, 47, 48, 50A, 51, 53–57
Distribution: Vic, NSW
Synonym: Previously included with, and confused with *P. helmsii* which is found in the mountains of the Dividing Range. *Illustrated p. 286*

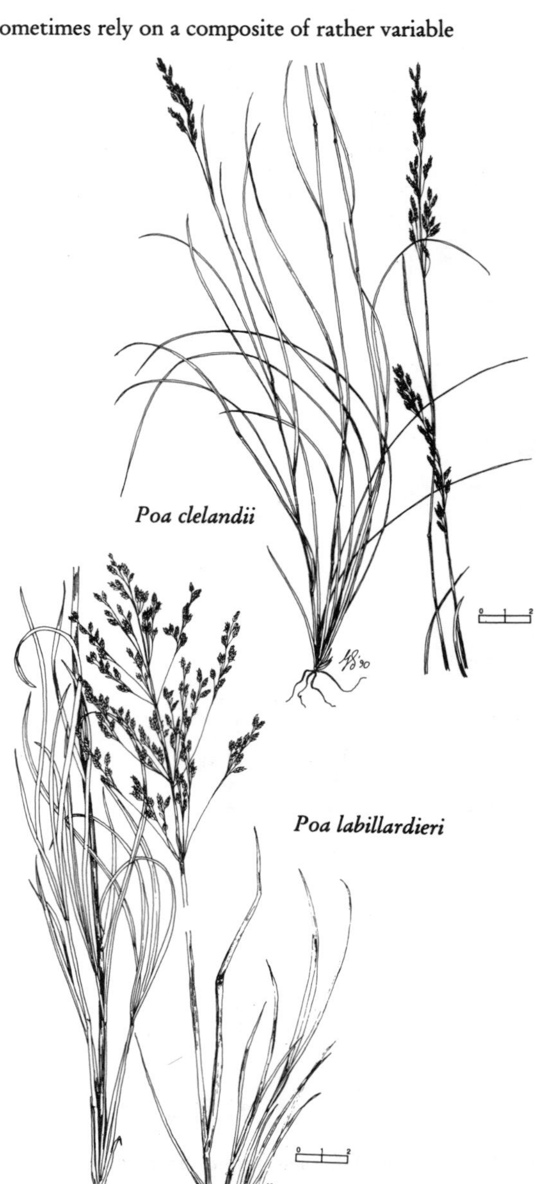

Poa clelandii

Poa labillardieri

Poa labillardieri

Common Tussock Grass

Size: 0.3–0.8 m high; stems to 1.2 m high F P
Habitat: Widespread in red gum woodland, riparian scrub, plains grassland, dry and valley sclerophyll forests
Form: Large, coarse densely tufted tussock
Foliage: Rough, green, greyish-green or blue-green leaves to 80 cm x 1–3.5 mm, flat to tightly inrolled, tips sometimes pungent-pointed.
Flowers: Open panicle to 25 cm long, branches spreading. Green or purplish 3–4-flowered flattened spikelets along the length of upper branches but only along upper half of lower branches. October to February
Requirements: Adapts to moist or slightly dry soils
Comments: A very vigorous grass with many forms. Colour may change with season or age.
Localities: 1, 2, 4–6, 8, 11, 14, 16–18, 25–28, 32, 34A–36, 39, 41, 42, 44, 50A, 51, 53–55, 58, 60, 62, 63, 67, 68, 69A–71, 74, 76
Distribution: Vic, Qld, NSW, Tas, SA

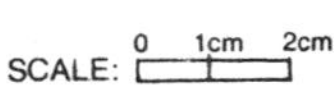

The scale representation on each plant equals 2cm.

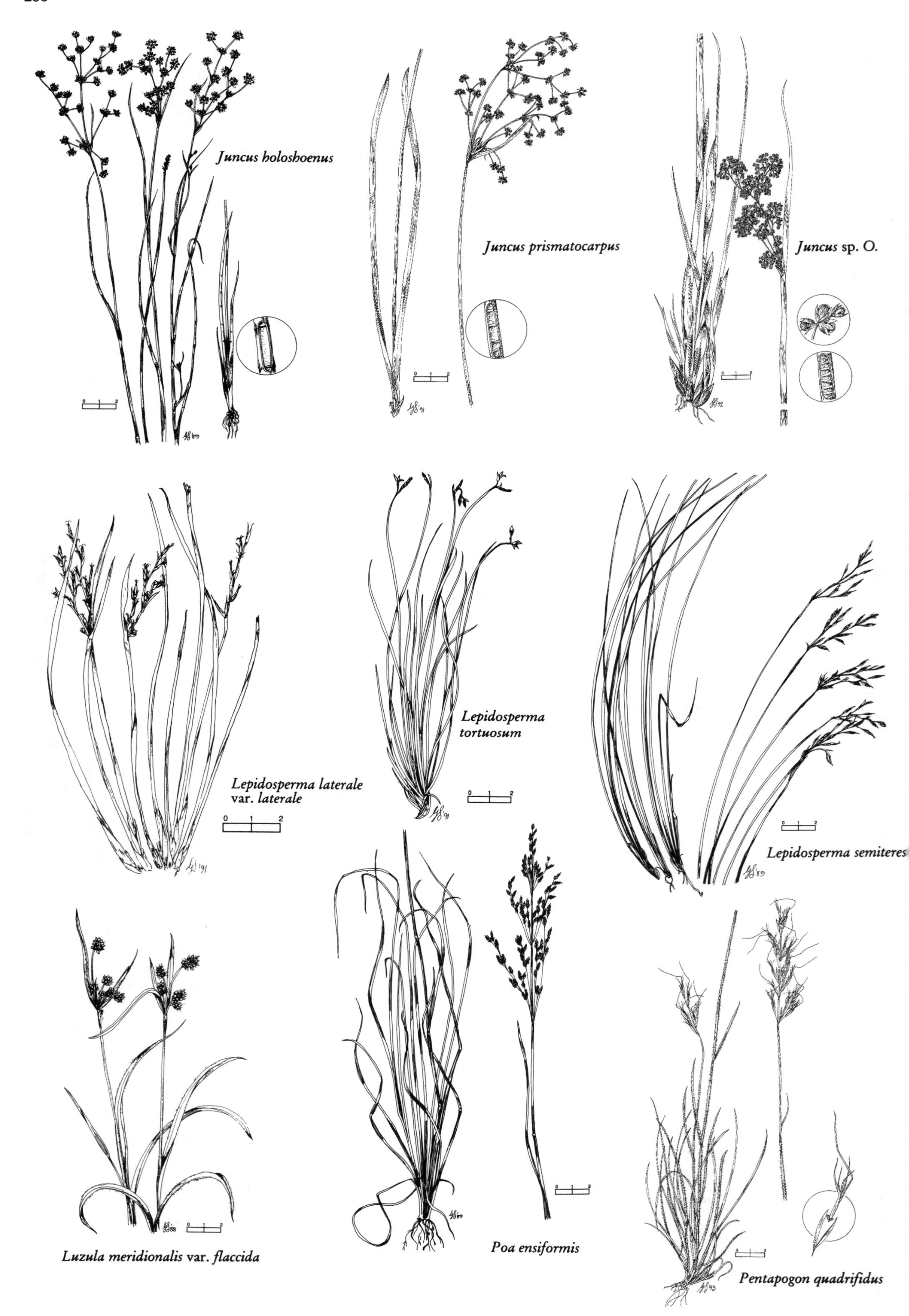
Juncus holoshoenus
Juncus prismatocarpus
Juncus sp. O.
Lepidosperma laterale var. *laterale*
Lepidosperma tortuosum
Lepidosperma semiteres
Luzula meridionalis var. *flaccida*
Poa ensiformis
Pentapogon quadrifidus

Poa morrisii

Velvet Tussock Grass

Size: to 30 cm high, stems 0.5–0.9 m high **F P**
Habitat: Dry and valley sclerophyll forests, sclerophyll woodland, grassy low open forest
Form: Soft dense greyish-green tussock-forming grass
Foliage: Loosely inrolled, soft, lightly to densely hairy leaves to 30 cm long, lower sheaths pale
Flowers: Open panicles to 25 cm long. Lemmas densely hairy on keel, soft downy hairs between veins. October to January
Requirements: Moist well drained soils
Comments: A most attractive grass, suited to a range of horticultural uses.
Localities: Eltham, 26, 28, 34A–36, 41, 42, 44, 47, 48, 50–51, 53–56, 59, 62–64, 70, 74, 76
Distribution: Vic, SA
Synonym: Previously included with *P. australis* sp. agg. a very variable group which has now been separated into several species.

Poa morrisii

Poa poiformis var. poiformis

Coast or Blue Tussock Grass

Size: 0.2–0.9 m x 1 m **F P**
Habitat: Primary dune scrub, coastal banksia woodland
Form: Densely tufting grass
Foliage: Rigidly erect, thickened terete or angular bluish leaves about as long as flowering stems
Flowers: Dense panicles to 30 cm long, at first narrow, becoming loose. Branches in whorls of 3–5. Large, pale green to straw-coloured spikelets almost to the base of the branches. Lemmas rough on upper keel and hairy on lower keel veins and margins. September to January
Requirements: Well drained sandy soil, tolerating saline soil and salt spray
Comments: Sometimes hard to distinguish from some coastal forms of *P. labillardieri*, whose distribution may overlap. Features which need to be considered are: proximity to sea, stem height relative to leaves, compactness of seed heads.
Localities: Seaford, 2, 4, 5, 62, 67, 69A, 71, 74
Distribution: Vic, NSW, Tas, SA, WA

Poa poiformis var. *poiformis*

Poa rodwayi

Size: 0.25–0.6 m high **F P**
Habitat: Grassy low open forest, valley sclerophyll forest, box woodland
Comments: Green to greyish-green tussock-forming perennial.
Localities: Tarneit, Sth of Melton, 62, 64, 74, 75
Distribution: Vic, NSW, Tas

Poa sieberiana var. sieberiana

Tussock Grass

Size: 15–30 cm x 40 cm; stems to 0.9 m high **F P**
Habitat: Widespread in grassy low open forest, wattle tea-tree scrub, plains grassland, red gum woodland, dry sclerophyll forest
Form: Dense green to greyish-green tuft
Foliage: Fne, almost glabrous terete leaves
Flowers: Panicle to 25 cm long, with green, purplish or straw-coloured spikelets; branches mostly in pairs. Lower part of lemma hairy between the veins.
Comments: Extremely variable species with different forms from coastal to alpine. Very adaptable in cultivation, this attractive grass establishes well under existing eucalypts. Grows larger in shaded forests.
Localities: Eltham, 2, 10, 12–18, 23, 25, 26, 28, 31, 32, 34A–36, 40–42, 44, 47, 50A, 51, 53, 56, 58, 60, 65, 67#, 69–71, 74–76
Distribution: Vic, Qld, NSW, Tas
Synonym: Previously included with *P. australis* sp. agg. a very variable group which has now been separated.

Poa sieberiana var. *sieberiana*

Poa sieberiana var. hirtella

Habitat: Valley sclerophyll forest
Comments: Distinguish from the typical form by the sparsely hairy leaves.
Localities: Montrose, 36
Distribution: Vic, Qld, NSW

Poa tenera

Slender Tussock Grass

Size: 5–20 cm high **P N**
Habitat: Damp and valley sclerophyll forests, swamp scrub, grassy low open forest
Form: Bright green, soft, trailing stoloniferous grass, sometimes forming open tussocks
Foliage: Soft, glabrous, inrolled linear leaves 5–20 cm long
Flowers: Delicate open panicle to 120 mm long with few pale green 2–4-flowered spikelets towards the end of the fine branches. Lower branches paired. October to January
Requirements: Moist well-drained soils
Comments: Very effective when trailing down embankments.
Localities: 34A, 41, 42, 44, 47, 48, 50A, 51, 53–58, 61, 74–76
Distribution: Vic, NSW, Tas, SA

Illustrated p. 294

The scale representation on each plant equals 2cm.

Potamogeton

Potamogetonaceae

Potamogeton species are perennial, rhizomatous aquatic herbs commonly known as pondweeds. They thrive in both still backwaters and lagoons and flowing streams, as long as the water is fresh. They may be totally submerged except for the flowers, or partly emerged with floating leaves. Flowers are brownish and generally inconspicuous, borne in spikes held above the water. After pollination spikes become submerged, where the fruit develops. Plants are attractive in ornamental ponds; however their growth can become quite vigorous and must be kept in check. Propagation is by division of rhizomes or setting the nut-like fruit into the muddy base of ponds.

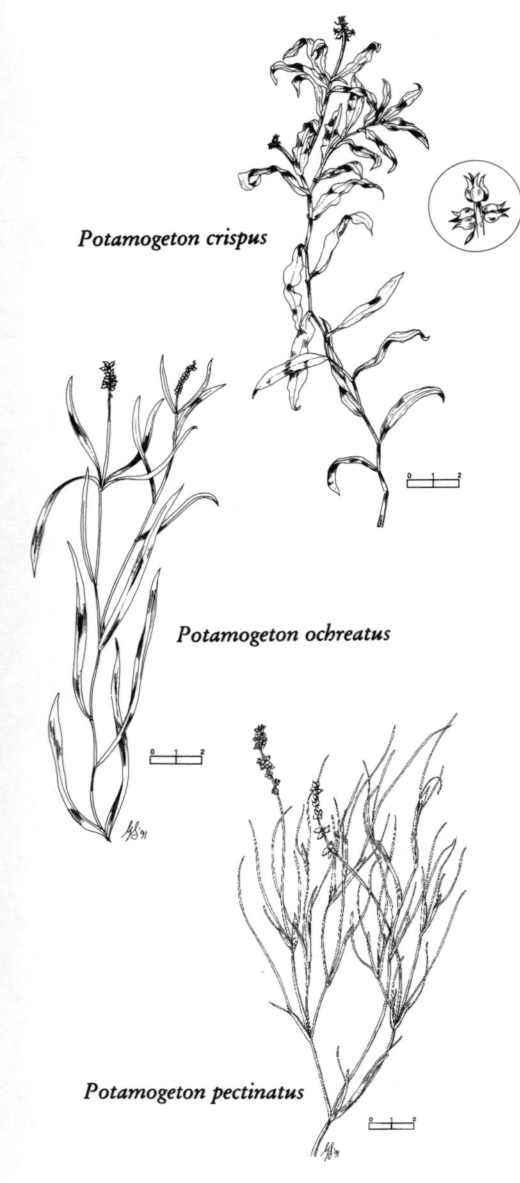

Potamogeton crispus

Potamogeton ochreatus

Potamogeton pectinatus

Potamogeton crispus

Curly Pondweed

Size: stems to 4 m long **F P**
Habitat: Still or flowing water to 4.5 m deep in riparian and red gum woodland
Form: Submerged aquatic
Foliage: Sessile, narrow-lanceolate to linear-oblong, green to reddish-brown translucent leaves to 70 mm long, margins distinctly wavy, with tiny teeth
Flowers: Short, emergent few-flowered spike, held on stems to 70 mm above the water. Fruit to 5 mm x 3 mm with a long pointed beak, in clusters 10–20 mm long at the end of the spike; November to May
Localities: 8, 35, 42, 67#
Distribution: All mainland states; NZ, Eur, Af, Asia

Potamogeton ochreatus

Blunt Pondweed

Size: stems to 4.5 m long **F P**
Habitat: Still or flowing water to 4.5 m deep
Comments: Differs from *P. crispus* in that leaves are entire, flat and linear, to 90 mm long, with stipule-like nerves on the leaf sheath. Flowering spike elongated, to 25 mm in fruit; August to March peaking late Spring
Localities: 4, 11, 29#, 34A, 42, 74, 76
Distribution: All states; NZ

Potamogeton pectinatus

Fennel Pondweed

Size: stems to 3 m long **F P**
Habitat: Fresh to saline, still or flowing water to 3 m deep
Foliage: Stipular sheath is joined to the stem and leaves at the base, free above; leaves entire, narrow-linear and grass-like to 15 cm long
Flowers: Spikes with several isolated clusters of 2–3 flowers, to 40 mm long in fruit
Localities: Altona, Footscray, 2, 4, 11, 67#
Distribution: All states except NT; NZ, world-wide

Potamogeton tricarinatus

Floating Pondweed

Size: stems to 2.7 m long **F P**
Habitat: Still and floating fresh water, mud beside receding water, grassy wetlands
Form: Aquatic or semi-aquatic, emergent leaves floating
Foliage: Long-stalked, thick and leathery, ovate to oblong emergent leaves 15–100 mm x 25 mm, with up to 16 parallel veins; submerged leaves thin, narrower, 5–23 cm long
Flowers: Flowering spike short and dense to 40 mm long at the end of stout, erect stalks. Fruit cluster to 45 mm long; September to April
Localities: Rockbank, Melton, 6, 7, 29, 35, 61, 67#, 71
Distribution: All states *Illustrated p. 294*

Puccinellia

Poaceae

Puccinellia stricta var. *perlaxa*

Puccinellia stricta var. stricta

Australian Saltmarsh-grass

Size: 15–60 cm high **F**
Habitat: Saltmarshes, grassy wetland
Form: Stiffly erect tufted annual grass
Foliage: Slender, bristle-like, erect leaves, sheaths loose, the uppermost leaf clasping the base of the panicle
Flowers: Very narrow erect panicle to 15 cm long with narrow 6–12-flowered spikelets to 10 mm long, pale green to greyish. September to January
Requirements: Poorly drained saline soils
Propagation: Seed
Localities: Laverton, Port Melbourne, 2–4, 26, 74
Distribution: Vic, NSW, Tas, SA, WA; NZ *Illustrated p. 294*

Puccinellia stricta var. perlaxa

Size: to 50 cm high **F**
Habitat: Saltmarsh
Comments: Annual or perennial grass with pale green to bluish-green folded to inrolled leaves to 30 cm long. Panicles are larger than the typical form, to 30 cm long, and widely spreading. Spikelets are smaller, to 8 mm long, often purplish and 4–5-flowered.
Localities: Altona, Werribee, Footscray, 4, 5
Distribution: Vic, Tas

Restio — Restionaceae

Restio tetraphyllus

Tassel Cord-rush

F P

Size: to 1.5 m high
Habitat: Swamps in wattle tea-tree scrub, tea-tree heath
Form: Tall bright green feathery perennial tussock, stems smooth and terete with brown sheathing bracts at regular intervals
Foliage: Fine soft much-divided leaves or branchlets from a node just below the inflorescence
Flowers: Dioecious; loose tassel-like panicles of many brown or reddish ovoid to round spikelets; glumes with awn-like points; October to February
Requirements: Permanently boggy sandy soils
Comments: An attractive gracefully arching but non-invasive sedge-like plant for planting in or around ponds. The foliage is useful in floral arrangements. Very rare in the Melbourne area.
Propagation: Seed, division
Localities: 73–75
Distribution: Vic, Qld, NSW, Tas, SA

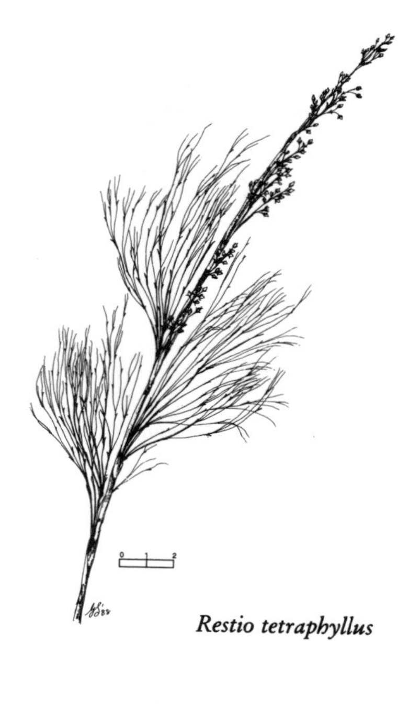

Restio tetraphyllus

Ruppia — Ruppiaceae/Potamogetonaceae

Ruppia maritima

Sea Tassel or Ditch Grass

F

Size: to 15 cm high
Habitat: Saltmarsh
Form: Rhizomatous, aquatic perennial with fine, erect branched stems to 50 mm long
Foliage: Clusters of thread-like leaves to 15 cm long, sheathed broadly at base
Flowers: 1 or 2 flowers on a straight stalk to 50 mm long, flowers pollinated below the surface; July to December
Requirements: Brackish water
Comments: Waterbirds eat the seeds, leaves and starchy leaf bases of all species.
Propagation: Division of rhizome, setting ripe fruit in mud
Localities: Port Phillip Bay, Kororoit Ck
Distribution: All states; NZ, cosmopolitan

Ruppia megacarpa

Widgeon Grass

F

Size: stems to 1.5 m high but usually 20–30 cm high
Habitat: Estuarine aquatic, in water to 0.3 m deep, salt pans
Comments: More robust perennial herb than the other 2 Melbourne species. Bright to olive green thread-like leaves 5–25 cm long with 2-lobed tip, sheath to 40 mm long. Flowers rise to the surface on stalk 0.3–1 m long, stalk becoming coiled after pollination drawing the flowers below the surface, where the fruit ripens. August to December.
Localities: Altona, 5
Distribution: Vic, NSW, SA, WA; NZ

Ruppia polycarpa

Widgeon Grass

F

Size: stems 20–40 cm high
Habitat: Saltmarshes and estuaries
Comments: Annual or delicate perennial similar to *R. maritima* but stems crowded. Dark green leaves to 15 cm long ending in a blunt tip. Flower stalks to 50 cm long each with 2 flowers, pollinated above the water surface but drawn underwater as fruit ripens. June to November
Localities: 2, 4
Distribution: Vic, NSW, Tas, SA, WA; NZ

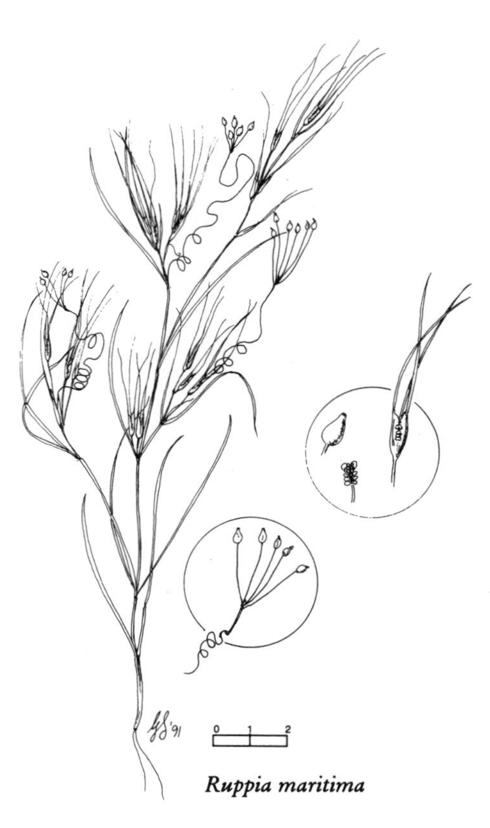

Ruppia maritima

Schoenoplectus — Cyperaceae

Schoenoplectus dissachanthus

Club-rush

F P

Size: stems to 30 cm high
Habitat: Grassy low open forest
Form: Slender annual rush-like herb with a creeping rhizome and tufted triangular stems; leaves reduced to sheaths
Flowers: Terminal cluster of 1–3 sessile, cylindrical yellow or greenish-yellow, many-flowered spikelets to 15 mm long with scales at the base of nut. Bract at base of cluster to 100 mm long, appears to extend stem. A single female flower is found in a sheath at the base of the flowering stem. March to April
Requirements: Moist to wet sandy soil
Comments: Extremely rare in the Melbourne area.
Localities: 74
Distribution: All mainland states
Synonym: *Scirpus dissachanthus*

SCALE: 0 1cm 2cm — The scale representation on each plant equals 2cm.

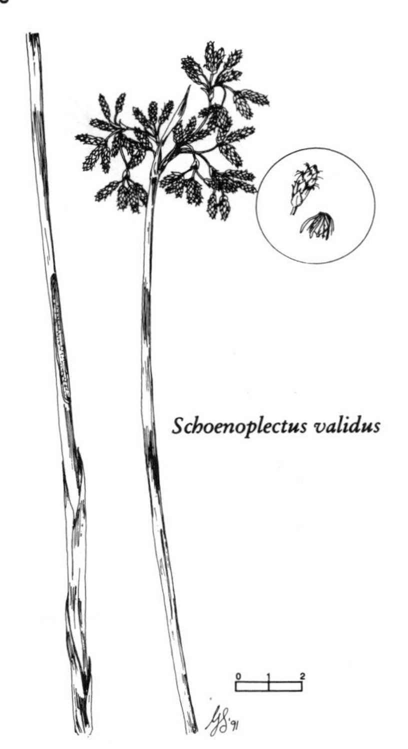
Schoenoplectus validus

Schoenoplectus pungens
American Club-rush, Sharp Leaf-rush

Size: stems 30–60 cm high F P
Habitat: Grassy wetlands
Form: Robust tufted rhizomatous herb, stems stout and sharply triangular
Foliage: Bluish grass-like basal leaves with long sheaths shorter than the stems
Flowers: Cluster of 1–6 usually sessile dark brown spikelets to 10 mm long. Bract at base of cluster to 60 mm long appears as a continuation of the stem. October to March
Requirements: Wet or swampy soils
Comments: Has become rare as a result of development in Melbourne.
Propagation: Seed
Localities: Rockbank, Broadmeadows
Distribution: Vic, SA, WA; NZ, Eur, N Am, S Am
Synonym: *Scirpus americanus* *Illustrated p. 294*

Schoenoplectus validus
River Club-rush

Size: stems to 2 m high F P
Habitat: Riparian and swamp scrub
Form: Robust tufted perennial rhizomatous herb, stems soft, terete and grooved
Flowers: Loose umbel-like panicle to 70 mm long, with numerus many-flowered ovoid spikelets to 10 mm long, glumes keeled and hairy along margins; bract shorter than flowerhead. November to April
Requirements: Wet soil
Comments: The stems have been used for weaving mats or baskets.
Localities: Sunshine, Deer Park, 11, 14, 16, 26, 28, 35, 36, 42, 72
Distribution: All states except NT

Schoenus — Cyperaceae

Schoenus, or bog sedges, are tufted annual or perennial plants with a short creeping rhizome, occurring in moist areas which are often subject to regular inundation. Leaves are usually basal, sometimes reduced to a sheath. Flowers are in a cluster of spikelets, the rhachilla (or spikelet stem) strongly zig-zagged and curved over each nut. Plants propagate readily by division or seed.

Schoenus apogon

Schoenus apogon
Common Bog-rush

Size: 5–30 cm high F P
Habitat: Sclerophyll and red gum woodland, plains grassland, valley sclerophyll forest, wattle tea-tree heath
Form: Slender perennial tufted herb, stems terete, longitudinally grooved with 1–3 nodes below the flowerhead
Foliage: Fine inrolled leaves as long as the stems, or shorter in tall plants
Flowers: 2–5 clusters of dense, blackish, 2–3-flowered spikelets to 7 mm long; 1 cluster terminal, the others at a node in the axil of a leafy bract. Bracts longer than clusters. October to January
Requirements: Moist or wet soils
Comments: A widespread and variable species giving a grass-like appearance to a moist area. Often found growing in gardens.
Localities: 2, 4, 6, 7, 12, 13, 16–18, 25, 26, 28, 29, 32, 34A–36, 41, 42, 44, 47–59, 62, 64, 67#, 69–71 73–76
Distribution: All states except WA; PNG, NZ

Schoenus breviculmis
Matted Bog-rush

Size: to 50 mm high F P
Habitat: Wattle tea-tree scrub
Form: Dwarf matting perennial herb with short erect stems hidden amongst the dense foliage, leaves flat
Flowers: Terminal cluster of 2 several-flowered spikelets to 10 mm long, surrounded by 2–3 floral bracts. Flowers most of the year.
Requirements: Moist peaty soil
Localities: 67, 68
Distribution: Vic, SA, WA

Schoenus brevifolius
Zig-zag or Short-leaf Bog-rush

Size: 0.3–0.6 m high F P
Habitat: Tea-tree heath, grassy low open forest
Form: Large leafless herb, leaves reduced to basal, glabrous brown sheaths to 10 mm long
Flowers: Long panicle with loose, branched clusters of 3–5-flowered spikelets to 10 mm long, rhachillas very flexuose; bracts much smaller than spikelets.
Requirements: Moist sandy soil
Localities: 68–70, 73–75
Distribution: Vic, Qld, NSW, Tas; NZ, N Cal *Illustrated p. 294*

Schoenus breviculmis

Schoenus latelaminatus

Medusa Bog-rush

Size: 10–25 cm high **P**
Habitat: Valley sclerophyll forest, red gum woodland
Form: Annual pale-green grass-like herb similar to *S. apogon* but stems are lax and do not have nodes
Flowers: Clusters of 1–3 tiny pale spikelets in the bract axils
Requirements: Temporarily wet sites
Comments: A very rare plant in the Melbourne area.
Localities: Epping, 42
Distribution: Vic, NSW, Tas, SA

Schoenus maschalinus

Schoenus maschalinus

Leafy Bog-rush

Size: stems to 25 cm long **P**
Habitat: Valley sclerophyll forest, wattle tea-tree scrub
Form: Weak slender herb with prostrate to ascending fine leafy stems, sometimes branched
Foliage: Very narrow weak flat leaves to 30 mm long
Flowers: Clusters of 1–3 tiny, 1–2-flowered spikelets to 3 mm long in the upper axils; October to February; bracts longer than spikelets
Requirements: Moist heavy soils
Comments: Forms a fine bright green mat along the water's edge of ponds.
Localities: Diamond Ck, 44, 51, 53, 55–57, 67#, 69, 69A, 74, 75
Distribution: All states; NZ, PNG, Philippines

Schoenus nitens

Shiny Bog-rush

Size: 3–15 cm high **F P**
Habitat: Saltmarsh
Form: Slender-stemmed perennial, few short basal leaves with glabrous shining sheaths
Flowers: Terminal cluster of 2–4 tiny ovate, blackish, 1–3-flowered spikelets; September to March
Requirements: Moist soils
Comments: A coastal plant tolerating brackish conditions.
Localities: 4, 5, 67#, 69A
Distribution: All states except NT; NZ, PNG *Illustrated p. 294*

Schoenus tenuissimus

Slender Bog-rush

Size: 10–25 cm high **F P**
Habitat: Wattle tea-tree and swamp scrub
Form: Slender wiry herb with leaves reduced to basal sheaths
Flowers: Single, 1-flowered, narrow blackish terminal spikelet to 10 mm long; most of the year.
Localities: Montrose, 50, 54, 67, 69, 70, 73–75
Distribution: Vic, NSW, Tas, SA *Illustrated p. 294*

Schoenus tesquorum

Schoenus tesquorum

Bog-rush

Size: 15–40 cm high **P**
Habitat: Swamp and riparian scrub, red gum woodland
Comments: Similar to and confused with *S. apogon*, but with coarser stems (to 40 cm long) and leaves (to 18 cm long). Stems have a single node below the flowerhead. A rare plant.
Localities: Craigieburn, Clayton, 54, 61, 74, 75
Distribution: Vic, SA

Sparganium

Sparganiaceae

Sparganium subglobosum

Floating Burr-reed

Size: 0.3–0.6 m x 0.3 m **F P**
Habitat: Aquatic in fresh, still or moving water to 0.5 m deep
Form: Rhizomatous grass-like plant
Foliage: Few, soft but stout, erect narrow leaves to 5 mm wide, floating or submerged, lowest leaves longest, to 60 cm, rising from the rhizome
Flowers: Unbranched stems to 30 cm high with a flexuose terminal spike of 2-9 sessile, globular flowerheads; male flowers at the top of the spike, female below. Burr-like clusters larger in fruit, to 15 mm wide, each nut beaked; Summer
Requirements: Permanent moisture
Localities: Yarra R. near Melbourne#, Cranbourne
Distribution: Vic, Qld, NSW; NZ
Synonym: S. antipodum

Sparganium subglobosum

SCALE: 0 1cm 2cm The scale representation on each plant equals 2cm.

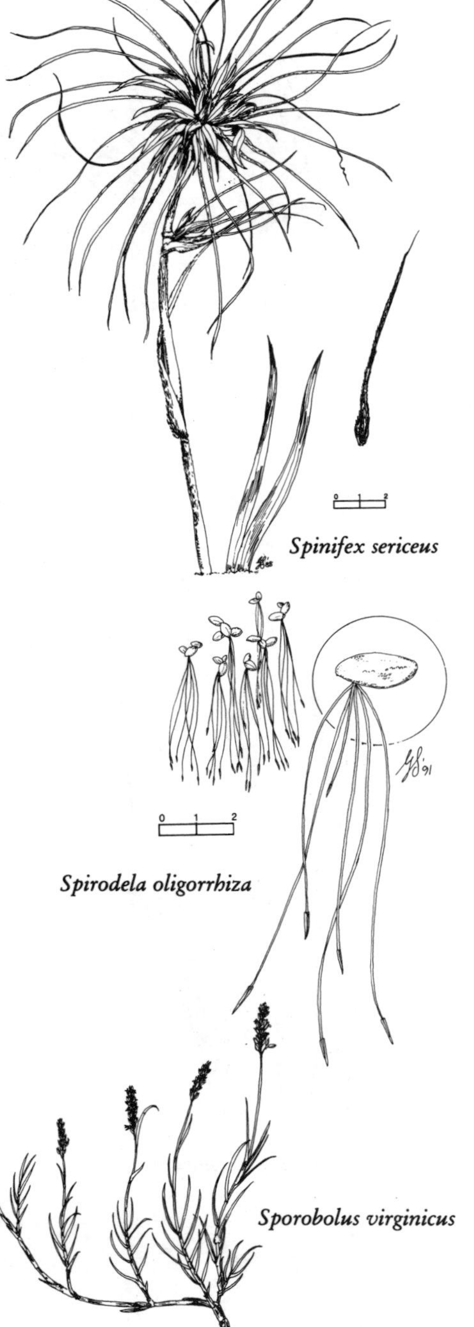

Spinifex sericeus

Spirodela oligorrhiza

Sporobolus virginicus

Spinifex **Poaceae**

Spinifex sericeus
Hairy Spinifex

F

Size: to 50 cm high
Habitat: Primary dune scrub, beaches
Form: Strong perennial grass with long-creeping stolons
Foliage: Limp, silvery, flat densely hairy leaves 10–40 cm long, inrolled in bud, tufts of leaves produced along the stolons at thickened nodes
Flowers: Dioecious; terminal clusters of spikes; stalked, orange-brown male spikelets to 12 mm long in erect racemes to 50 mm long; female plant has large silvery-green to straw-coloured head-like clusters to 22 cm wide of sessile 1–2-flowered spikelets, each at the base of a long bristle; September to January
Requirements: Excellent drainage in sandy soil, with deep moisture
Comments: A very useful plant for stabilising sand dunes. Seed heads on female plants snap off whole, like a "tumble weed".
Propagation: Seed
Localities: Altona, Seaford, 5, 67, 69A, 74
Distribution: Vic, Qld, NSW, Tas, SA
Synonym: Segregated from *S. hirsutus* which only occurs in WA

Spirodela **Lemnaceae**

Spirodela oligorrhiza
Thin Duckweed

F P

Size: thallus 3–6 mm long x 2–4 mm wide
Habitat: Fresh still water in riparian scrub, tea-tree heath
Form: Floating aquatic forming dense mats on the surface of still water. Individual plant consists of single thin ovate leaf-like thallus, often tinged purplish below, with 3–8 roots to 40 mm long.
Propagation: As for *Lemna disperma*
Localities: Yarra R., 36, 74, 76
Distribution: All mainland states; NZ, N Cal, Asia
Synonym: *Lemna oligorrhiza*

Sporobolus **Poaceae**

Sporobolus virginicus
Salt or Sand Couch

F

Size: 10–30 cm x spreading
Habitat: Estuaries, saltmarshes, primary dune scrub, coastal cliffs
Form: Rhizomatous perennial grass with leafy stems and thick, extensively creeping scaly rhizomes
Foliage: Pairs of rigid, wiry leaves with overlapping sheaths and short blades (to 50 mm long) and inrolled margins
Flowers: Dense, narrow spike-like panicle to 60 mm long with tiny, dark 1-flowered spikelets; all year.
Requirements: Moist sandy soils, tolerating saline conditions
Comments: A useful grass for salt-laden soils.
Propagation: Seed, division of rhizome
Localities: Port Melbourne, Altona, Seaford, around Port Phillip, 5, 74
Distribution: All states; NZ, PNG, Pacific, S Am, S Af

Stipa **Poaceae**

Stipa species are tufted perennial grasses, with 200 species occurring in the Melbourne region. Several species found on the grasslands of the basalt plains are now quite rare. They are commonly known as spear grasses as the mature seeds can penetrate the skin, mouths and eyes of stock. Leaves are overlapping and hairy, often terete. The inflorescence is a panicle of single, stalked 1-flowered spikelets which have a hard cylindrical lemma sharply-pointed at the base (or callus). The terminal awn twists and bends on drying and may be very long. The lower section is termed the column and twists, the section above the bend does not twist and is called the bristle. Glumes remain on the plant after the seeds have fallen.

As horticultural subjects they can add a graceful accent to a bushland garden or rockery and are generally at their best in Spring and Summer when the soft new growth and feathery flowering panicles are present. Hard pruning of tussocks after flowering is recommended to maintain vigour and to remove dead leaves and flower stems. Plants will grow in full sun to semi-shade.

Some species such as *S. elegantissima* are often available from specialist nurseries. Plants are usually readily grown from seed which is easily collected, but be wary of introduced *Nassella* spp. which appear very similar and are major weeds. Often a high proportion of florets do not produce viable seed. Division of clumps is also successful.

Stipa aristiglumis

Plump or Bristly Spear-grass

Size: to 40 cm high; stems 0.5–1 m high **F P**
Habitat: Plains grassland, red gum woodland
Form: Erect, densely tufted, stout or slender grass
Foliage: Narrow, glabrous, smooth leaves to 40 cm x 3–6 mm, inrolled from the base or only in the upper part
Flowers: Loose few-flowered panicle 10–40 cm long with long branches, lemmas swollen, awn twice bent, to 40 mm long, callus is hooked and very short in relation to lemma length, glumes prominently green-veined; October to February.
Requirements: Heavy soils
Comments: Becoming less common as habitat disappears.
Localities: Tottenham, St Albans, 5, 6, 7, 13, 26, 28
Distribution: Vic, Qld, NSW, SA

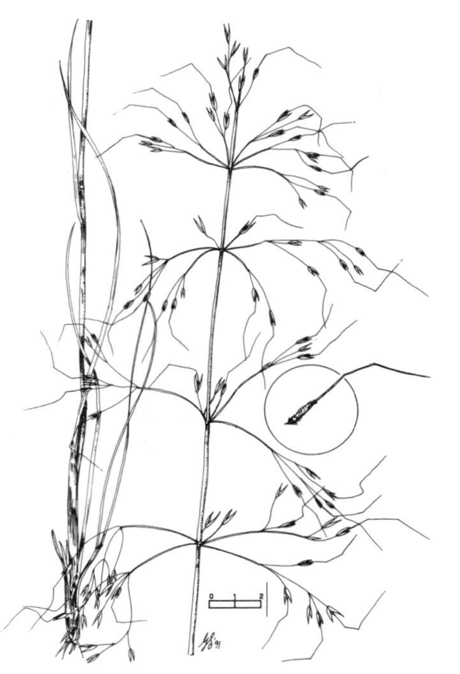

Stipa aristiglumis

Stipa bigeniculata

Tall Spear-grass, Plains Grass

Size: to 20 cm high; stems 0.3–1.2 m high **F P**
Habitat: Plains grassland, grassy wetland, red gum and box woodland
Form: Slender, erect tussock
Foliage: Narrow ridged leaves 8–20 cm long, lower leaves rough
Flowers: Very similar to *S. blackii*. Panicle 25–45 cm long; lemma to 10 mm long, hair tuft at the top to 2 mm long, awn to 60 mm long strongly twice bent, callus curved, longer in relation to lemma length; September to February.
Requirements: Heavy clay soils on flood plains
Localities: 4, 6, 12, 14, 15, 17#, 18, 21, 22, 23, 26
Distribution: Vic, NSW *Illustrated p. 294*

Stipa blackii

Crested Spear-grass

Size: to 20 cm high; stems 0.45–1 m high **F P**
Habitat: Red gum woodland, plains grassland, box woodland
Form: Densely tufted erect grass
Foliage: Rough, stiff, linear leaves to 20 cm x 2–5 mm, lower leaves hairy
Flowers: Similar to *S. aristiglumis* and *S. bigeniculata*. Panicle narrower, 10–25 cm long with purplish or straw-coloured spikelets. Lemma covered in white spreading hairs, becoming yellow to orange, with a conspicuous tuft of hairs to 5 mm long on apex; awn to 40 mm long and twice bent. September to November.
Requirements: Moist heavy soils
Comments: Disappearing from Melbourne areas as habitat is destroyed.
Localities: Toolern Vale, Melton Sth, Sunshine, Deer Pk, Sth Yarra, Mt Cottrell, 7, 12, 13, 15, 20, 26, 32
Distribution: Vic, NSW, SA, WA *Illustrated p. 294*

Stipa curticoma

Stipa curticoma

Spear-grass

Size: to 30 cm high; stems to 1.2 m high **F P**
Habitat: Grassy wetlands, plains grassland, red gum woodland
Form: Open tufted grass
Foliage: Leaves to 30 cm x 3–5 mm
Flowers: Sparse open panicle 15–30 cm long. Glumes broad. Lemma hairs white, with tiny hair-tufts at top of lemma, awn 45–65 mm long with dense, fine spreading hairs on twice-bent column. September to December.
Requirements: Moist heavy soils, intolerant of dry conditions
Comments: A rare grass in Victoria.
Localities: Diggers Rest, Laverton, Sunshine, Derrimut, Deer Park, St Albans, 2, 10, 17#
Distribution: Vic, SA

Stipa densiflora

Foxtail Spear-grass

Size: to 20 cm high; stems 0.5–1 m high **F P**
Habitat: Box and box ironbark woodland, dry sclerophyll forest
Foliage: Lax, hairy leaves to 130 mm long, flat or inrolled, tapering to a fine point
Flowers: Dense compact panicle, to 30 cm long. Glumes are downy, lemma to 15 mm long, awn to 45 mm long, column twice-bent, with feathery hairs. September to January.
Requirements: Well drained gravelly soils
Localities: Diamond Ck, 14, 26, 36, 42, 55
Distribution: Vic, Qld, NSW, SA

Stipa densiflora

SCALE: 0 1cm 2cm — The scale representation on each plant equals 2cm.

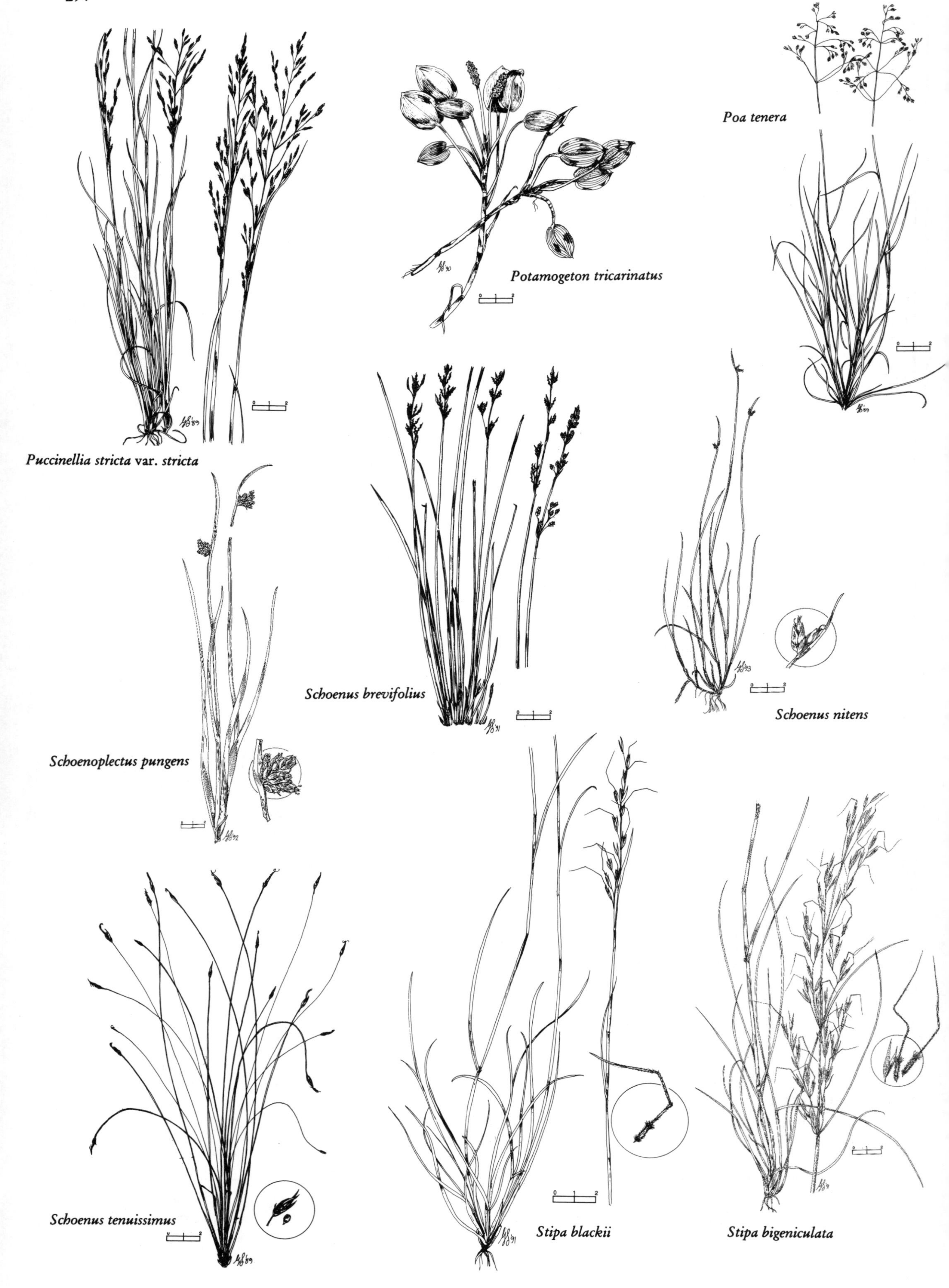
Puccinellia stricta var. stricta
Potamogeton tricarinatus
Poa tenera
Schoenus brevifolius
Schoenus nitens
Schoenoplectus pungens
Schoenus tenuissimus
Stipa blackii
Stipa bigeniculata

Stipa elegantissima

Feather Spear-grass, Spider Grass

Size: 0.5–0.8 m high; stems to 1 m high **F P**
Habitat: Box and red gum woodland
Form: Rhizomatous tussock, cane-like stems glabrous and often branched
Foliage: Rough, narrow, inrolled leaves 50–80 cm long,
Flowers: Large, very loose open panicle to 25 cm long, branches whorled, with long feathery, sometimes pinkish, hairs on branches and stalks. Glumes 3-ribbed, purplish with scattered hairs, lemma black at maturity. Awn to 50 mm long and strongly bent, column to 15 mm long, once-bent, with rough hairs. August to January
Requirements: Dry sandy or open soil
Comments: A particularly ornamental grass.
Localities: Altona, St Albans, Sth of Melton, Sunbury, 22, 23, 25, 26, 32, 74, 76
Distribution: Vic, NSW, SA, WA

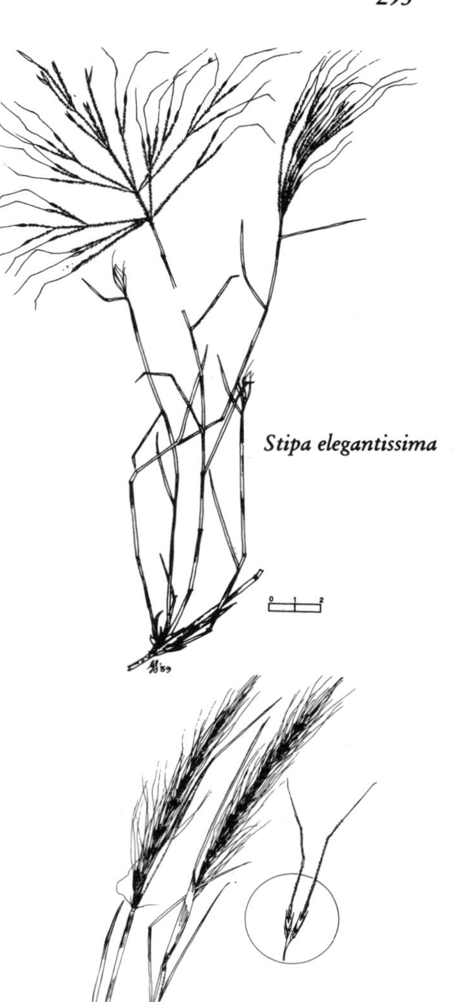

Stipa elegantissima

Stipa flavescens

Stipa exilis

Size: stems to 0.6 m high **F P**
Habitat: Woodland
Form: Small densely tufted perennial grass, stems erect, very fine with downy nodes
Foliage: Downy, flexuose, very narrow leaves to 20 cm long, tightly inrolled
Flowers: Narrow, few-flowered panicle to 20 cm long. Glumes purplish, narrow and tapering, unequal to 10 mm long; dark brown lemma lightly covered in whitish hairs with a short tuft of hairs at the apex, palea has band of silky hairs along centre back. Awn to 55 mm long, twice bent. August to November
Requirements: Well drained heavy soil
Comments: A rare grass in Victoria with a disjunct distribution in Melbourne.
Localities: Melton
Distribution: Vic, SA, WA

Illustrated p. 304

Stipa flavescens

Spear-grass

Size: 0.5–0.7 m high; stems to 1.2 m high **F P**
Habitat: Primary dune scrub, saltmarshes
Form: Open, shortly rhizomatous tufted grass, often branching after the season's first seeds begin to mature
Foliage: Narrow flexuose leaves to 70 cm x 7 mm
Flowers: Dense narrow many-flowered panicle to 40 cm long with erect branches. Glumes to 15 mm long, 3-ribbed, purplish with scattered hairs. Awn is slender to 70 mm long, column twice-bent, densely and softly hairy. September to February
Requirements: Moist well drained soils, tolerant of salt spray
Comments: Useful grass for front-line coastal planting and stabilisation of sand dunes.
Localities: Sandringham-Mt. Eliza, Altona, Mt Cottrell, 2–5, 49, 62, 63
Distribution: Vic, NSW, Tas, SA, WA
Synonym: *S. elatior*

Stipa gibbosa

Spear-grass

Size: to 30 cm high; stems to 1.5 m high **F P**
Habitat: Plains grassland, red gum woodland
Foliage: Few ridged leaves to 30 cm x 2.5 mm
Flowers: Narrow panicle on a rigid, erect stem. Differs from *S. bigeniculata* in that the lemma, to 6 mm long, is distinctly swollen, awn is shorter to 35 mm long; October to January.
Requirements: Moist soils which do not dry out
Comments: Becoming very rare in Melbourne as its habitat is destroyed for housing. Also rare throughout Victoria.
Localities: Laverton, Altona, Mt Cottrell, Rockbank, 4, 16–18
Distribution: Vic, NSW, SA

Illustrated p. 305

Stipa mollis

Stipa mollis

Soft Spear-grass

Size: to 30 cm high; stems to 1.5 m high **F P**
Habitat: Dry sclerophyll forest, red gum woodland, grassy low open forest
Form: Robust, erect tufted grass
Foliage: Limp, downy, tightly inrolled leaves to 30 cm x 1–3 mm
Flowers: Differs from *S. semibarbata* in that hairs on column are longer to 4 mm and spiral up the awn towards the end of the bristle, glume shorter, to 20 mm long; October to January
Requirements: Moist soils
Comments: A more robust species than *S. semibarbata.*
Localities: Alamein, Brighton, 26, 32, 34A, 36, 58, 59, 66–70, 74, 76
Distribution: Vic, NSW, Tas, SA, WA
Synonym: *S. semibarbata* var. *mollis;* segregated from *S. hemipogon*

SCALE: 0 1cm 2cm The scale representation on each plant equals 2cm.

Stipa muelleri

Stipa pubinodis

Stipa rudis ssp. rudis

Stipa muelleri

Wiry Spear-grass

F P

Size: to 1 m high x spreading
Habitat: Sclerophyll woodland
Form: Bright green wiry rhizomatous grass forming dense tangles, usually branching at the nodes, leaves scale-like
Flowers: Sparse unbranched panicle consisting of 1–3 large spikelets to 30 cm long, lemmas hairy with 2 erect lobes, awn rigid, 50–100 mm long; October to December.
Requirements: Well drained clay soil
Localities: Olinda, Montrose, 56, 59
Distribution: Vic, SA

Stipa nodosa

Spear-grass

F P

Size: to 30 cm high; stems 0.5–1 m high
Habitat: Red gum woodland, plains grassland
Form: Tufted grass without rhizomes, nodes on stems much wider than stem
Foliage: Coarse, flat or inrolled leaves to 30 cm long, many leaves also on stems
Flowers: Sparse, spreading panicle to 50 cm long, awns to 100 mm long with sickle-shaped bristles; August to September
Requirements: Moist well drained soils
Localities: Sth Yarra, 16, 20, 21, 31, 32, 34A, 35, 50A, 65
Distribution: Vic, Qld, NSW, SA
Synonym: Segregated from *S. variabilis* *Illustrated p. 305*

Stipa oligostachya

Spear-grass

F P

Size: to 20 cm high; stems to 1 m high
Habitat: Plains grassland, grassy wetlands, red gum woodland
Foliage: Erect, tightly inrolled leaves to 20 cm long
Flowers: Sparse, spreading panicle to 25 cm long, pale lemma warty, only hairy on veins, awn to 70 mm long, twice bent then slightly curved; November
Requirements: Moist heavy soils
Localities: Sunbury, Deer Park, St. Albans, 4, 6, 25
Distribution: Vic, SA *Illustrated p. 305*

Stipa pubinodis

Spear-grass

P

Size: to 35 cm high; stems 0.6–1.5 m high
Habitat: Valley and dry sclerophyll forests, grassy low open forest
Foliage: Rough, ridged tightly inrolled leaves to 35 cm x 1–2 mm
Flowers: Sparse panicle 15–25 cm long with more than 20 flowers. Lemma white hairy and granular, to 12 mm long, with a stout, rigid twice-bent awn to 100 mm long, column to 60 mm long; tip of glume appears cut off and soon tears; September to January.
Requirements: Moist soils
Comments: May be confused with *S. rudis* which has a smaller lemma and glume and much shorter, more slender awn column. It also prefers damper shadier positions although the two do overlap in habitat.
Localities: 16, 31, 32, 42, 44, 47, 48, 50A, 51, 54–56, 58, 61–64, 69A, 70, 74, 76
Distribution: Vic, Tas, SA
Synonym: Segregated from *S. pubescens* which does not occur in Victoria.

Stipa rudis ssp. rudis

Veined Spear-grass

P N

Size: to 40 cm high; stems to 1.2 m high
Habitat: Sclerophyll and red gum woodland, dry and valley sclerophyll forests, grassy low open forest
Foliage: Erect inrolled leaves to 40 cm long, woolly to slightly rough on one side; terete slightly ridged stems with 2–4 downy nodes, bent near the base
Flowers: Loose spreading many-flowered panicle to 40 cm x 15–40 mm. Lemma to 10 mm long, with fawn to golden hairs, awn twice bent, to 60 mm long with column to 25 mm long.
Requirements: Moist soils
Localities: Lilydale, Montmorency, 4, 12, 15, 26, 36, 42, 44, 47–49, 50A, 51, 53–56, 62–64, 69A, 71, 75
Distribution: Vic, Qld, NSW
Synonym: *S. nervosa* var. *neutralis*

Stipa rudis ssp. australis

Spear-grass

F P

Size: stems to 1 m high
Habitat: Dry sclerophyll forest, grassy low open forest
Comments: Leaves are densely woolly and flower parts are larger than in ssp. *rudis*. Lemma is straw-coloured or purple with an awn 60–90 mm long, column to 45 mm long.
Localities: Wantirna, 49, 73, 74
Distribution: Vic, Tas

Stipa rudis ssp. nervosa

Spear-grass

Size: stems 0.5–1.2 m high **F P**
Habitat: Valley sclerophyll forest
Comments: Very similar to ssp. *rudis*. The panicle is larger and narrower (to 50 cm x 30 mm). Awn and column are smaller (to 45 mm and to 20 mm respectively) and the lemma has white hairs.
Localities: Eltham, 45, 47, 50A, 55, 60, 61, 64
Distribution: Vic, Qld, NSW
Synonym: *S. nervosa* var. *nervosa*

Stipa rudis ssp. *nervosa*

Stipa scabra ssp. scabra

Rough Spear-grass

Size: to 25 cm high; stems 0.3–0.5 m high **F P**
Habitat: Plains grassland, box and red gum woodland
Form: Slender, tufted perennial grass with erect stems
Foliage: Fine, ridged inrolled or folded leaves to 25 cm long with short stiff hairs
Flowers: Dense narrow few-flowered panicle to 30 cm x 10–20 mm, with erect branches and spikelets; awn to 70 mm long, sickle-shaped with a short column to 15 mm long; glumes usually purplish; August to October
Requirements: Well drained soils
Localities: 9, 12, 14, 18, 21–23, 26, 29, 49
Distribution: All states
Synonym: Segregated from *S. variabilis*

Illustrated p. 305

Stipa scabra ssp. falcata

Slender Spear-grass

F P
Habitat: Plains grassland, box woodland
Flowers: Erect panicle to 25 cm long with spreading branches; August to December.
Comments: This subspecies has a more spreading panicle than the typical species. A form from Keilor is intermediate between the 2 subspecies.
Localities: 4, 10, 16, 17#, 24–26, 32
Distribution: Vic, NSW, SA
Synonym: *S. falcata*

Stipa scabra ssp. *falcata*

Stipa semibarbata

Fibrous Spear-grass

Size: to 30 cm high; stems 0.3–1 m high **F P**
Habitat: Plains grassland, red gum and box woodland, valley sclerophyll forest, grassy low open forest
Form: Erect, tufted grass
Foliage: Rough leaves 30 cm x 1–3 mm (occasionally to 7 mm), becoming torn and fibrous with age
Flowers: Large, dense stiffly erect panicle to 32 cm long with more than 30 spikelets. Awn to 90 mm long, twice bent, with short feathery hairs to 1 mm covering the stout column (but not present on the bristle) glumes to 25 mm long, tapering. August to November
Requirements: Well drained soil
Comments: This grass is suited to dry sandy soils. It is often confused with *S. mollis*.
Localities: Eltham, 2, 4, 12, 21, 24–26, 30, 32, 34A, 58, 65, 66, 71, 74–76
Distribution: Vic, NSW, Tas, SA

Illustrated p. 305

Stipa setacea

Corkscrew Grass

Size: to 30 cm high; stems 0.3–0.8 m high **F P**
Habitat: Red gum woodland, box woodland
Form: Slender tufted perennial grass
Foliage: Fine, rough or glabrous inrolled ridged leaves to 30 cm long
Flowers: Narrow but loose few-flowered panicle to 20 cm long, branches rough, the uppermost leaf sheath enveloping the base of the panicle. Lemma black with downy white hairs, awn to 40 mm long, twice bent; September to November.
Requirements: Heavy, well drained soil of basalt plains
Localities: Sunbury, Altona, Mt Cottrell, Rockbank, 16, 26, 49
Distribution: Vic, Qld, NSW, SA

Stipa setacea

Stipa stipoides

Coast or Prickly Spear-grass

Size: to 1 m high **F**
Habitat: Primary dune scrub, coastal cliffs, saltmarshes
Form: Hemispherical, densely-tufted rush-like tussock
Foliage: Long, prickly, glabrous, terete leaves to 70 cm long
Flowers: Tight narrow panicle to 25 cm long, mostly within the tussock. Glumes broad and erect to 20 mm long, lemmas covered in white to yellowish hairs, with 2 small hairy lobes, awn to 40 mm long, twice bent; October to March.
Requirements: Well drained sandy soil, tolerant of salt spray
Localities: 2, 3, 67, 69A, 74, 76
Distribution: Vic, NSW, Tas, SA
Synonym: *S. teretifolia*

Illustrated p. 305

The scale representation on each plant equals 2cm.

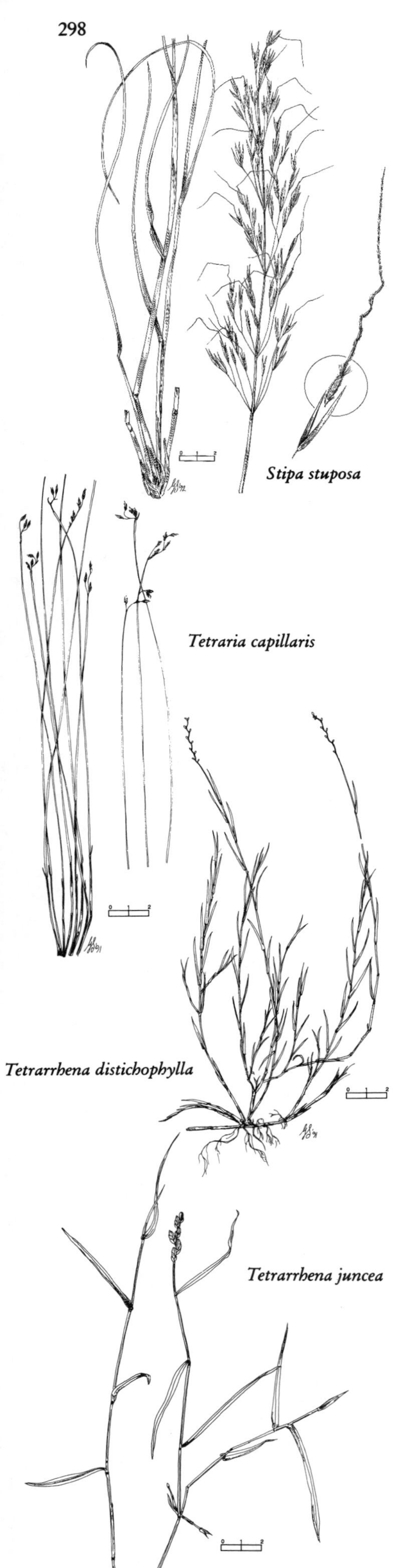
Stipa stuposa

Tetraria capillaris

Tetrarrhena distichophylla

Tetrarrhena juncea

Stipa stuposa

Tasmanian Spear-grass

Size: stems to 1.2 m high **F P**
Habitat: Plains grassland
Form: Robust tufted perennial grass, stem nodes downy
Foliage: Leaves to 40 cm long, glabrous or hairy
Flowers: Narrow, sparse to many-flowered panicle to 35 cm long. Glumes tapering, downy, to 25 mm long; lemma covered in white to yellow hairs, distinct tuft of hairs at the apex. Long awn to 70 mm, twice bent, column covered in soft hairs to 1.5 mm. November
Requirements: Well drained heavy soil
Localities: 29
Distribution: Vic, NSW, Tas, SA

Tetraria — Cyperaceae

Tetraria capillaris

Hair-sedge, Bristle Twig-rush

Size: 20–50 cm high **F P**
Habitat: Swamp scrub, damp and valley sclerophyll forest
Form: Slender rhizomatous perennial rush-like herb with many limp, thread-like, bright to yellow-green stems, terete with a groove along one side
Foliage: Leaves reduced to downy basal sheaths, sometimes with a bristly blade to 7 mm long
Flowers: Tiny loose panicle to 25 mm long of 1–8 narrow, reddish-brown 1–2-flowered spikelets to 6 mm long; March to June
Requirements: Moist soils
Propagation: Seed, division
Localities: Olinda, Montrose, 54, 56, 61
Distribution: All states except NT; NZ

Tetrarrhena — Poaceae

Tetrarrhena distichophylla

Hairy Rice-grass

Size: stems to 0.6 m long **F P**
Habitat: Grassy low open forest
Form: Decumbent rhizomatous perennial grass with hairy stems, sometimes forming mats
Foliage: Flat or inrolled rough leaves to 60 mm long in pairs along the stem, paler green above
Flowers: Short erect terminal spike-like raceme to 20 mm long, spikelets downy, sterile lemmas rough and pointed; September to March
Requirements: Moist sandy soil
Propagation: Seed, division
Localities: Baxter, 60, 73, 74
Distribution: Vic, SA, Tas

Tetrarrhena juncea

Forest Wire Grass

Size: stems scrambling 3–5 m long **P N**
Habitat: Wet, damp and valley sclerophyll forests, grassy low open forest
Form: Wiry, many-branched scrambling perennial grass with minutely hooked stems and extensive rhizomes
Foliage: Flat, rough leaves to 80 mm long, spread distantly and alternately up the stem
Flowers: Raceme with glabrous spikelets, glumes rounded and smooth
Requirements: Moist soils, tolerating drying out in Summer
Comments: This important component of forested areas is quick to re-establish after fire, preventing soil erosion until other plants regenerate. May cover large areas in moist environments, forming impenetrable barriers.
Propagation: Division
Localities: 43, 44, 49–52, 54–58, 62, 64, 75
Distribution: Vic, Qld, NSW, Tas

Themeda **Poaceae**

Themeda triandra

Kangaroo Grass

Size: to 40 cm x 0.75 m, stems 0.7–0.9 m high **F P**
Habitat: Widespread in plains grassland, sclerophyll, red gum and box woodlands, grassy wetland, grassy low open forest, dry and valley sclerophyll forests
Form: Soft, erect or sprawling perennial tussock
Foliage: Narrow-linear, limp, green, purple or sometimes quite blue, leaves to 30 cm x 3–4 mm, keeled below, sometimes rough above
Flowers: Leafy interrupted panicles 10–20 cm long on slightly arching stems; glossy-brown spikelets in groups of 6–8, central spikelet fertile and awned, each group surrounded by 4 sessile bract-like spikelets, each cluster sheathed in a leafy bract to 100 mm long; September to February.
Requirements: Adaptable to most soils which do not remain wet
Comments: A very common grass in many areas of remnant vegetation around Melbourne. The stems and leaves were used as string by the Aborigines to make nets.
Propagation: Seed, division
Localities: 2–7, 10, 12–18, 20, 21, 23–26, 28–32, 34A–36, 38–42, 44–48, 50–56, 58–71, 74–76
Distribution: All States; PNG, N Cal, SE Asia, Af
Synonym: *T. australis*

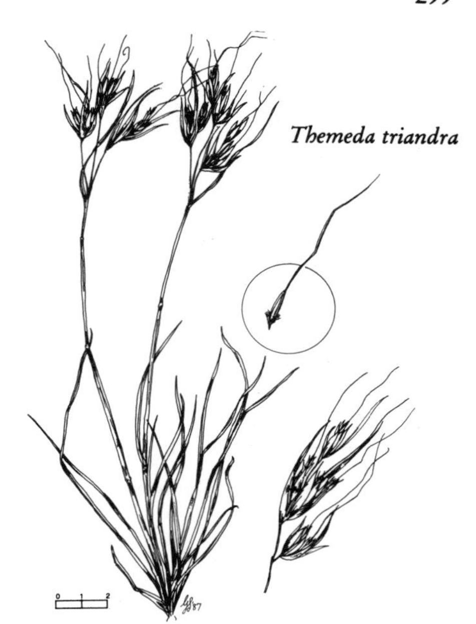

Themeda triandra

Thismia **Burmanniaceae (Thismiaceae)**

Thismia rodwayi

Fairy Lanterns

Size: stem 10–30 mm high **N**
Habitat: Cool temperate rainforest, wet sclerophyll forest
Form: Leafless saprophyte, often growing and flowering below the leaf litter, on a creeping mycorrhizal root system to 15 cm long; erect stem has 6 white scale-like bracts
Flowers: Single, terminal amber and red to rosy pink lantern-shaped flower to 20 mm long with 12 vertical coloured stripes, outer 3 petals recurved, inner 3 arching inwards.
Requirements: Damp humus
Comments: A very rare plant known from few sites in Victoria and 1 site in the Melbourne region.
Propagation: Impossible
Localities: 57
Distribution: Vic, Tas; NZ

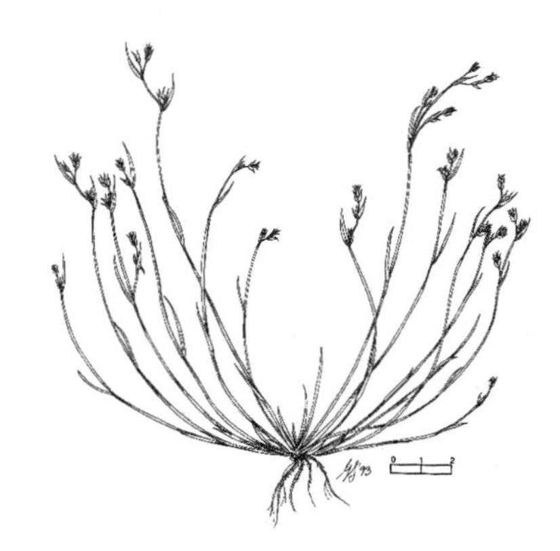

Tricostularia pauciflora

Tricostularia **Cyperaceae**

Tricostularia pauciflora

Needle Bog-rush

Size: 10–30 cm high **P**
Habitat: Tea-tree heath
Form: Tufted shortly rhizomatous perennial rush-like sedge, stems very fine, ridged and curved
Foliage: Few basal leaves, reduced to reddish sheaths, sometimes with a green tapering point to 15 mm long
Flowers: Short terminal spike to 25 mm long with 1–4 broad, brown 2-flowered spikelets to 6 mm long; December to February
Requirements: Damp sandy or peaty soil
Propagation: Seed, division
Localities: Mordialloc–Mentone, 67, 69
Distribution: Vic, NSW, Tas, SA

Triglochin **Juncaginaceae**

Triglochin centrocarpa

Dwarf Arrowgrass

Size: stem 5–15 cm high **F P**
Habitat: Tea-tree heath
Form: Slender annual herb
Foliage: Thread-like basal leaves to 50 mm long
Flowers: Terminal racemes to 60 mm long of 6–23 minute greenish flowers. Fruit narrow-pyramidal, 2–5 mm long with inconspicuous basal spurs; May to October.
Requirements: Damp sandy soil, intolerant of permanent water
Comments: Presumed extinct within the Melbourne area.
Propagation: Seed
Localities: 67#
Distribution: All States
Synonym: *T. centrocarpum*

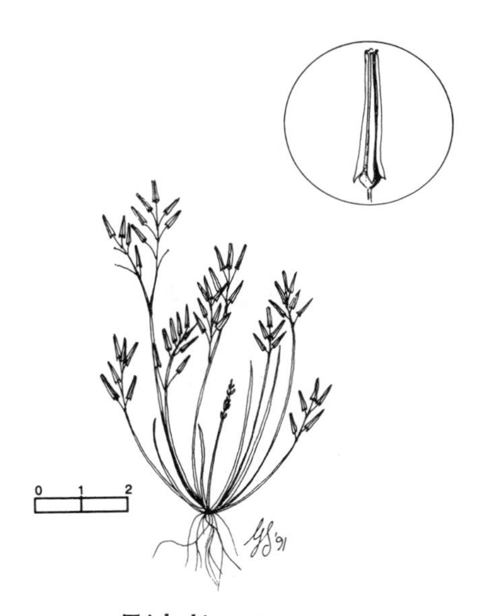

Triglochin centrocarpa

SCALE: 0 1cm 2cm The scale representation on each plant equals 2cm.

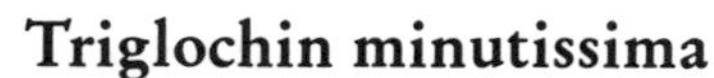

Triglochin minutissima

Tiny Arrowgrass

Size: stems 8–12 cm high **F P**
Habitat: Saltmarshes
Requirements: Moist saline soils
Comments: Similar to *T. centrocarpa* but smaller. Leaves 15–40 mm long, flowers are distant in the 4–11-flowered raceme and almost sessile. Fruit are minute to 1.5 mm long, basal spurs deflexed points; August to October. A rare Victorian plant which has almost disappeared in Melbourne.
Propagation: Seed
Localities: Altona, Port Melbourne#, Brighton#
Distribution: Vic, NSW, SA, WA
Synonym: *T. minutissimum*

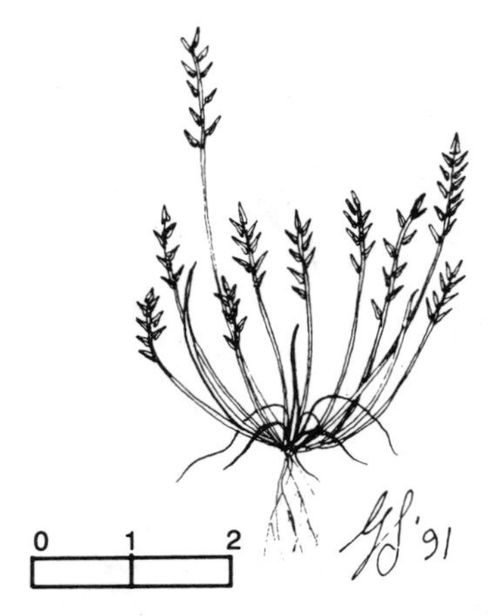

Triglochin minutissima

Triglochin mucronata

Prickly Arrowgrass

Size: stem 2–10 cm **F P**
Habitat: Saltmarshes
Requirements: Moist saline soil
Comments: Differs from *T. centrocarpa* in that the raceme is 1–7-flowered and up to 15 mm long and fruit, to 3 mm long, is broadly top-shaped with a 3-beaked tip; August to October. Very rare in the Melbourne area.
Propagation: Seed
Localities: Altona, Seaholme, Williamstown, Port Melbourne
Distribution: Vic, SA, WA
Synonym: T. mucronatum

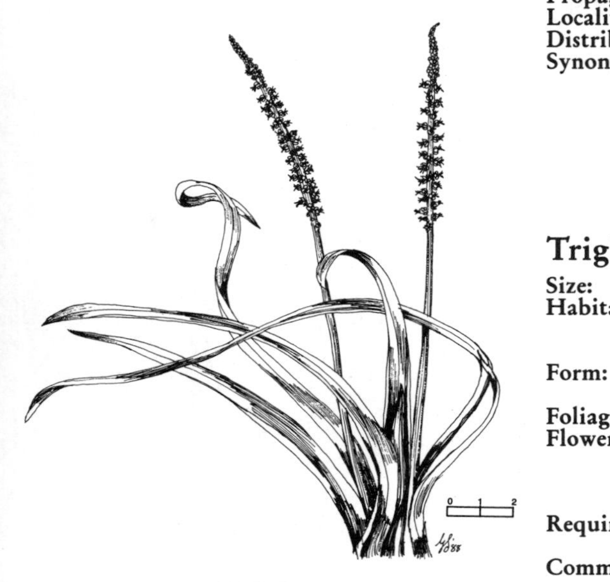

Triglochin procera

Triglochin procera

Water-ribbon

Size: stems 20–50 cm high **F P**
Habitat: Common in shallows of fresh water lakes and streams of riparian and swamp scrub, riparian woodland, damp and valley sclerophyll forests, grassy low open forest
Form: Variable and robust aquatic or amphibious perennial herb with a thick rhizome ending in numerous tubers
Foliage: Ribbon-like, erect or floating leaves 5–40 mm wide and 0.1–2 m long
Flowers: Dense terminal raceme to 30 mm long and 20 mm thick with 60–200 small greenish flowers held erect above the water. Spikes are shorter if not growing in permanent water. Fruit is broad elliptic 10–20 mm long; August to April.
Requirements: Submerged in freshwater to 1.5 m deep or areas subject to regular inundation
Comments: An attractive plant for water gardens, the long ribbon-like leaves flowing freely with the water currents. Leaves are erect in still water. Small forms also occur in areas of periodic inundation. The tubers were an important food source for the Aborigines and were either roasted or eaten raw.
Propagation: Division
Localities: Altona, Kororoit Ck, 1, 4, 8, 14, 16, 19, 26, 28, 29, 32, 33, 34A, 35, 42, 44, 47, 54, 56, 61–63, 65–67#, 69A, 71, 72, 74–76
Distribution: All States
Synonym: *T. procerum*

Triglochin striata

Triglochin striata

Streaked Arrowgrass

Size: stems 3–25 cm high **F P**
Habitat: Saltmarshes, swamp and riparian scrub, coastal banksia woodland
Form: Slender semi-aquatic perennial herb with small rhizomes
Foliage: Fine terete or flattened erect leaves 2–30 cm x 1–3 mm in tufts along the rhizome
Flowers: Slender, loose terminal racemes to 20 cm long with 2–100 tiny greenish-yellow flowers. Fruit globular to 3 mm; August to May.
Requirements: Moist, poorly drained soils
Propagation: Division
Localities: Altona, Montrose, 2–4, 11, 17#, 18, 25, 26, 29#, 32, 34A, 35, 42, 44, 47, 54, 56, 58–64, 67#, 69A–72, 74, 76
Distribution: All States; NZ, S Af, N Am
Synonym: *T. striatum*

Also illustrated p. 21

Tripogon — Poaceae

Tripogon loliiformis

Rye Beetle-grass, Five-minute Grass

Size: 5–25 cm high — **F P**
Habitat: Box woodland, plains grassland on very shallow soil above underlying rock
Form: Tufted annual or biennial grass
Foliage: Basal, narrow-linear or inrolled, glabrous or silky-hairy leaves to 50 mm long, with white sheaths
Flowers: Terminal open spike to 100 mm long. Narrow, erect 6–14-flowered spikelets, sessile in 2 rows along one side of the rhachis; lemma notched with a short awn and a short bearded callus; July to September.
Requirements: Dry soils on the basalt plains
Comments: A rare Victorian grass, found in few sites in Melbourne. Its common name refers to the speed with which it 'resurrects' after rain.
Propagation: Seed
Localities: Sunbury, Deer Park, St Albans, Melton, 7, 16–18, 26
Distribution: All mainland states

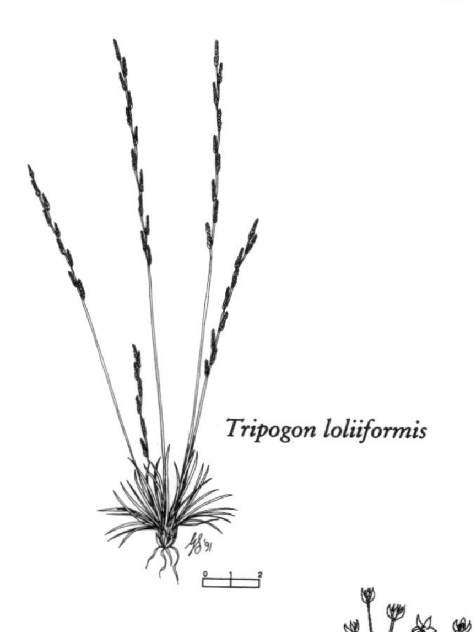

Tripogon loliiformis

Trithuria — Hydatellaceae

Trithuria submersa

Trithuria

Size: stems to 50 mm high — **F P**
Habitat: Grassy wetlands
Form: Tiny reddish annual herb
Foliage: Tuft of fine pointed leaves to 40 mm long
Flowers: Terminal head of reddish flowers lacking petals, each head surrounded by 4–6 spreading bracts on erect, unbranched, thread-like flowering stems; September to November
Requirements: Mud
Comments: Grows in Winter on the margins of seasonal pools on the Basalt Plains.
Propagation: Seed
Localities: Laverton
Distribution: Vic, NSW, Tas, SA, WA

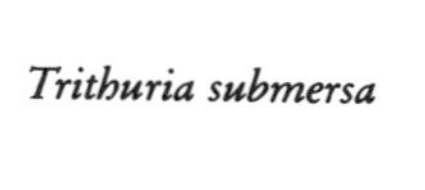

Trithuria submersa

Typha — Typhaceae

Typha domingensis

Bullrush or Cumbungi

Size: 1–3 m high x spreading — **F P**
Habitat: Fresh water lakes and pools in riparian scrub and woodland, box and red gum woodland, valley sclerophyll and grassy low open forest
Form: Vigorous, semi-aquatic perennial rush-like plant, spreading by rhizomes, stems erect and cane-like
Foliage: Stiff, flat narrow-linear leaves to 2 m x 4–10 mm, in pairs near the base of the stem
Flowers: Dense cylindrical spikes on tall stems above the foliage. Male flowers clustered 20–50 mm above the female spike which is usually 10–24 cm long and 5–15 mm wide. The stigmas are linear. Flowers all year.
Requirements: Grows in water along the shoreline and will not tolerate drying out
Comments: Often becomes invasive, particularly on farm dams and ornamental waterways. (See Chapter 5 on wetland regeneration for methods of containment.) Will not grow in water deeper than about a metre. The Aborigines roasted or steamed the rhizome, used stem and leaf fibres for string and wove baskets from the leaf.
Propagation: Seed, division
Localities: 1, 4, 16, 24, 26, 28, 33, 35, 36, 42, 44, 62–64, 67#, 71, 72, 74–76
Distribution: All States; N Af, SE Asia
Synonym: Both species were originally combined under *T. angustifolia*

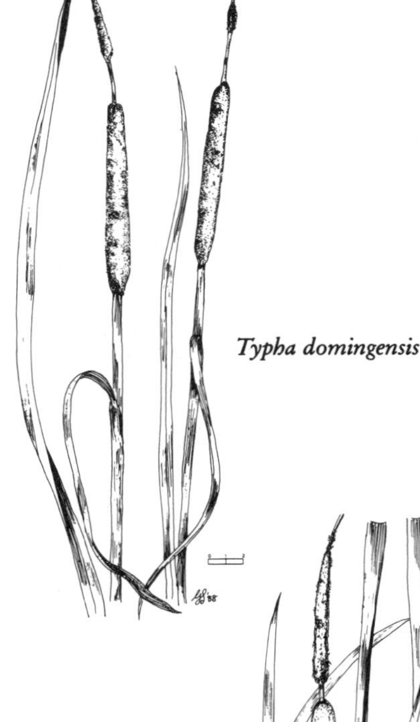

Typha domingensis

Typha orientalis

Size: 2–4.5 m high — **F P**
Habitat: Riparian and swamp scrub, saltmarshes
Comments: The main differences from *T. domingensis* are that the leaves are often broader, from 6–20 mm wide, the separation between the 2 spikes is less than 20 mm and the female spike is larger at 7–30 cm x 15–20 mm. The stigmas are narrow-ovate. Distinguishing *T. orientalis* from the introduced *T. latifolia* is less clear and requires microscopic examination for certainty. The flower spikes are often a darker brown in the latter. The introduced species dies down in Winter, while the native spp. remain green.
Localities: 4, 16, 26, 29, 35, 61
Distribution: All states except NT; NZ, SE Asia

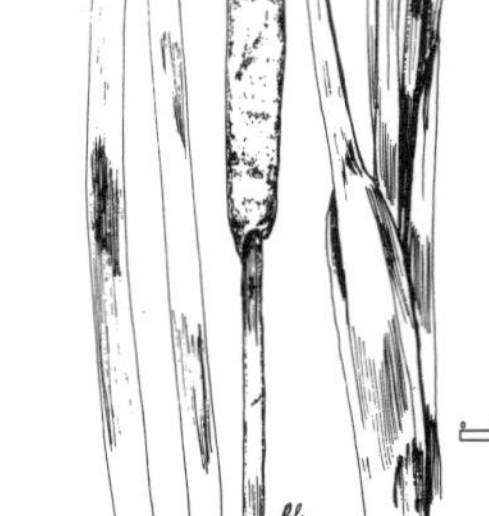

Typha orientalis

SCALE: 

The scale representation on each plant equals 2cm.

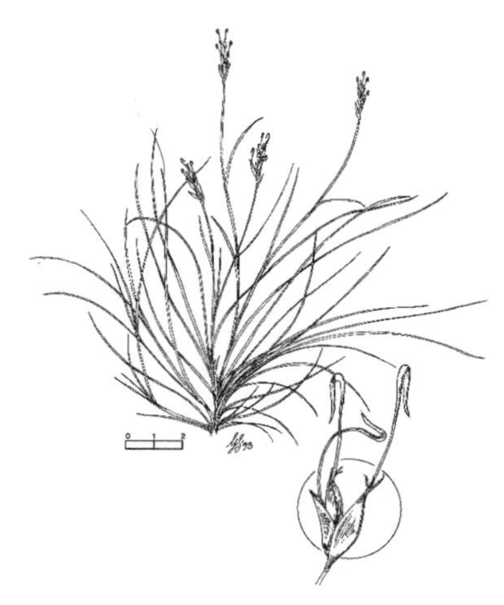
Uncinia tenella

Uncinia — Cyperaceae

Uncinia tenella — Delicate Hook-sedge

Size: stems to 15 cm high **P N**
Habitat: Cool temperate rainforest, wet sclerophyll forest
Form: Dwarf rush-like sedge
Foliage: Very fine grass-like leaves
Flowers: Dioecious; single terminal spikelet to 15 mm long, nut enclosed in a bag which ends in a long, projecting hooked awn
Requirements: Moist humus-rich soils where terrestrial
Comments: Frequently found growing on rotting logs and treefern trunks as well as beside watercourses. It has a very restricted range in the Melbourne area.
Propagation: Seed
Localities: 57
Distribution: Vic, NSW, Tas

Vallisneria spiralis

Vallisneria — Hydrocharitaceae

Vallisneria spiralis — Eel or Ribbon Weed, Eel Grass

Size: submerged x 30 cm **F P**
Habitat: Fresh water streams and lakes
Form: Submerged perennial stoloniferous herb
Foliage: Basal tufts of linear strap-like leaves 15–30 cm long with 5–9 longitudinal veins and tiny teeth along the margins towards the top of the leaf
Flowers: Dioecious; many minute male flowers in a head enclosed within a shortly-stalked bract to 20 mm long, flowerhead breaks off before pollen is released and floats on water surface; female flowers solitary to 25 mm wide enclosed in a bract on a very long and spirally-coiled stalk which lifts the flower to open on the surface of the water; November to May
Requirements: Fresh water
Comments: An excellent oxygenator for pools, providing habitat for water animals.
Propagation: Division
Localities: 35, 36, 60
Distribution: All states; NZ, cosmopolitan

Wolffia — Lemnaceae

Wolffia australiana — Duck Weed

Size: 1 mm long x 2 mm deep **F P**
Habitat: Fresh water aquatic of shallow ponds and streams to 30 cm deep
Form: Swollen rootless perennial herb, thallus elliptic above, convex below, most of plant submerged
Flowers: Single male and female flower erupt from a hollow on upper surface of thallus, rarely flowers
Requirements: Fresh or stagnant water
Comments: Many individual plants form a dense mat on the surface of the water. The smallest flowering plant in Australia.
Propagation: As for *Lemna disperma*. Budding is from a pit in the upper surface.
Localities: 4, 16, 60, 72
Distribution: Vic, NSW, SA; NZ

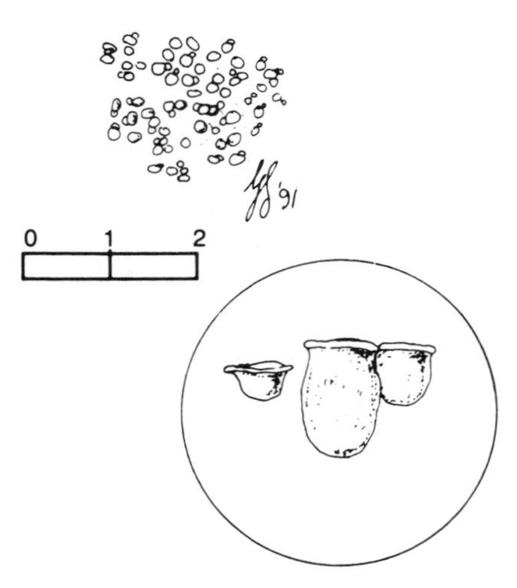

Wolffia australiana

Xanthorrhoea — Xanthorrhoeaceae

Xanthorrhoea australis — Austral Grass Tree

Size: to 3 m high (occasionally more) **F P**
Habitat: Grassy low open forest
Form: A slow-growing stout perennial plant with a thick woody trunk or butt surmounted by a grassy tuft of leaves and, if not burnt, skirted with old leaves
Foliage: Four-sided rigid bluish-green leaves to 1 m x 1–3 mm
Flowers: Dense clusters of creamy white, strongly scented flowers in a terminal spike 1–1.8 m x 50–80 mm, much longer than the stem (to 50 cm long); July to December
Requirements: Well drained soils tolerating dry conditions once established
Comments: One of the outstanding features of the Australian bush, particularly *en masse*. Prominent after bushfires which encourage bright green new leaves and prolific flowering. The *Xanthorrhoea* species were very useful to the Aborigines. The nectar provided drinks and the root was eaten. Adhesive was obtained from the resin while the flowering stem provided spears and firesticks. Very restricted distribution within the Melbourne area, although it occurs frequently just outside it to the north-east and south-east.
Propagation: Seed
Localities: 76
Distribution: Vic, NSW, Tas, SA

Illustrated p. vi and 304

Xanthorrhoea minor ssp. lutea

Small Grass Tree

Size: 0.6 m x 1 m **F P**
Habitat: Widespread in dry and valley sclerophyll forests, sclerophyll woodland, grassy low open forest, tea-tree heath
Form: Slow growing, stout perennial plant with a subterranean, often branched, woody trunk. Superficially looks like a dense grassy clump.
Foliage: Arching, triangular leaves to 1 m x 2–4 mm
Flowers: Dense clusters of yellowish, strongly-scented flowers in a terminal spike 5–20 cm long x 10–40 mm; slender stems (30–90 cm long), much longer than spike. Plants may bear several spikes; November to February.
Requirements: Well drained soils, tolerating dryness once established
Comments: An attractive grassy clump in the bush, particularly when the plant displays several flowering stems. Easily grown. The most obvious distinguishing feature of this subspecies is the very broad yellow flower. *X. minor* ssp. *minor* does not occur within the Melbourne area.
Propagation: Fresh seed
Localities: Research, 40, 42–44, 46–56, 58–64, 66–71, 73–76
Distribution: Vic, SA

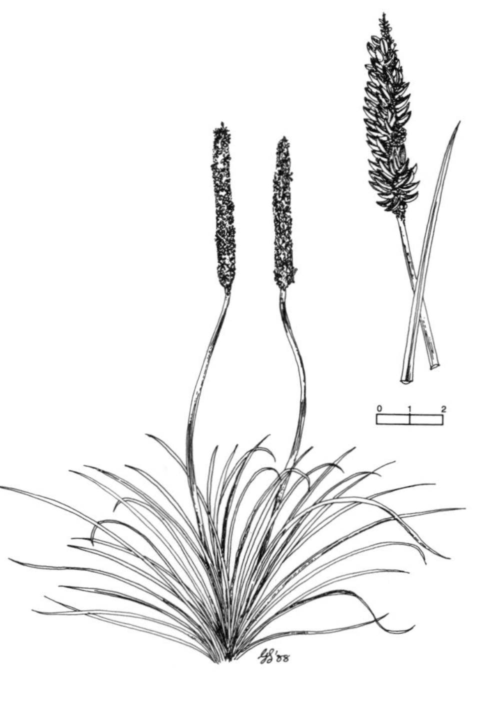

Xanthorrhoea minor ssp. *lutea*

Xyris

Xyridaceae

Xyris gracilis

Slender Yellow-eye

Size: 15–45 cm x 30 cm **F P**
Habitat: Tea-tree heath
Form: Erect perennial tufted herb with slender leafless stems
Foliage: Rush-like, basal pale green leaves to 30 cm x 1–2 mm
Flowers: Single terminal spike to 5 mm wide, composed of 6–12 conspicuous brown bracts with large pale centres, each holding a 3-petalled bright yellow flower, each flower lasting only 1 day; November to January.
Requirements: Damp peaty soils
Comments: An inconspicuous plant until in flower. Suitable for bog gardens. Almost extinct within the Melbourne area.
Propagation: Seed, division
Localities: Clayton, Moorabbin, 67#, 73–75
Distribution: Vic, NSW, Tas

Xyris operculata

Tall Yellow-eye

Size: to 0.6 m high, stems 0.5–1.5 m high **P**
Habitat: Tea-tree heath
Form: Large clumping perennial
Foliage: Terete leaves to 60 cm long, sheaths shiny
Flowers: Large globular head of many, often fringed, broad dark brown bracts in 5 rows, lower bracts empty. The yellow flowers open one at a time; November to January
Comments: Both species used to grow together but this species is now presumed extinct within Melbourne.
Localities: Eastern Port Phillip Bay, Macclesfield
Distribution: All states except WA

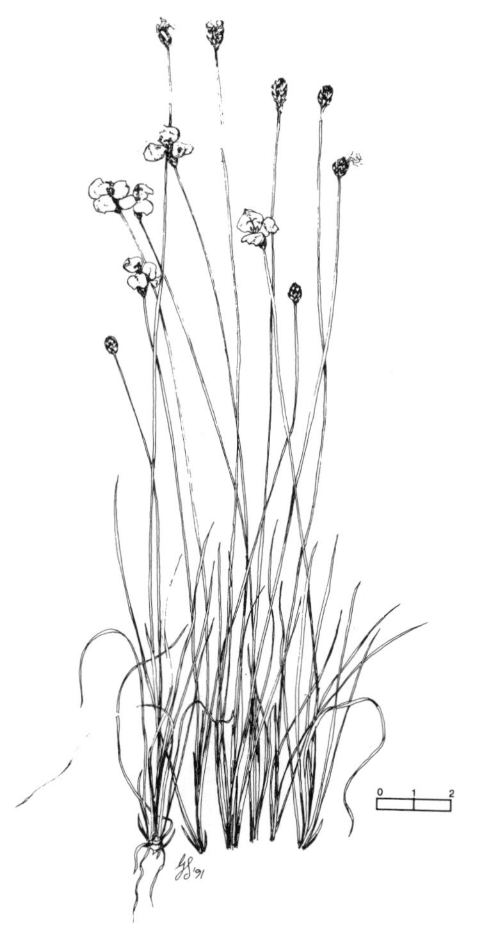

Xyris gracilis

Zostera

Zosteraceae

Zostera muelleri

Dwarf Grass-wrack

Habitat: Marine aquatic of mud flats and shallow coastal areas
Form: Perennial sea grass with creeping rhizomes forming extensive meadows at times, emergent at low tide
Foliage: Short vegetative shoots with 2–6 narrow-linear leaves to 100 mm long with notched end, deciduous, leaving old sheath
Flowers: Flowers enclosed in a shortly-stalked sheathing structure, 2–3 bracteoles on the rhachis; October to March.
Comments: Other sea-grasses occurring in Port Phillip Bay are:
Heterozostera tasmanica—similar to above but with rounded leaves and no bracteoles on rhachis, fertile shoots branched; found in coastal waters to 8 m deep.
Amphibolus antarctica (Zannichelliaceae)—submerged with wiry upright stems to 60 mm long, rigid, shiny leaves broad-linear to 50 mm long on the top half of the stem, flowers sessile, either dioecious or on separate shoots.
Propagation: Division
Localities: All occur along the coast of Port Phillip Bay within the study area.
Distribution: Vic, Tas, SA; NZ. Latter 2 also in NSW, WA (not NZ)

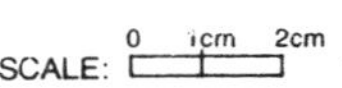

The scale representation on each plant equals 2cm.

Zoysia **Poaceae**

Zoysia macrantha

Prickly Couch

Size:	stem to 25 cm x spreading **F**
Habitat:	Saltmarshes, primary dune scrub
Form:	Low rhizomatous mat-forming perennial grass
Foliage:	Leaves small to 5 mm long, more than 2 mm wide with many smooth veins, ending in long pungent points
Flowers:	Terminal narrow spike-like raceme of small purplish 1-flowered spikelets to 5 mm long, single glume pointed
Requirements:	Moist to dry sandy soil, tolerating saline conditions
Propagation:	Seed, division
Localities:	Seaholme, Port Melbourne, 67
Distribution:	Vic, Qld, NSW, Tas

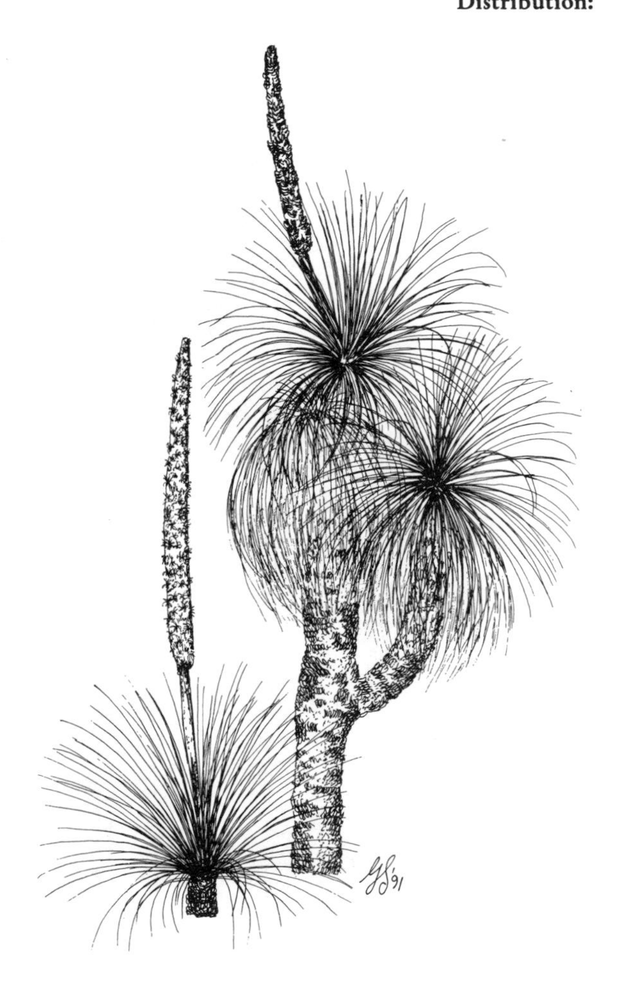

Xanthorrhoea australis

Stipa exilis

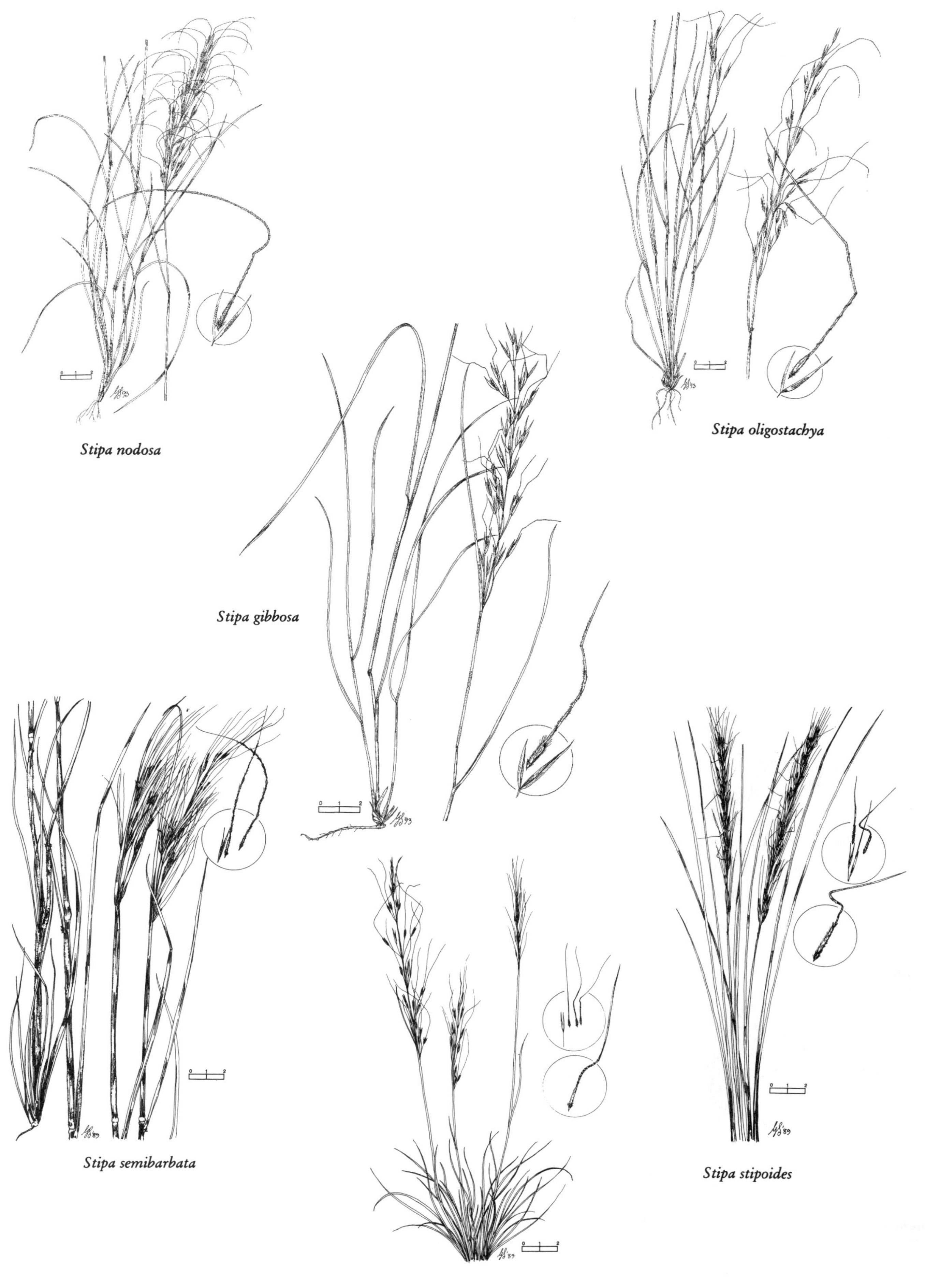

SCALE: 0 1cm 2cm The scale representation on each plant equals 2cm.

Ferns and Fern Allies

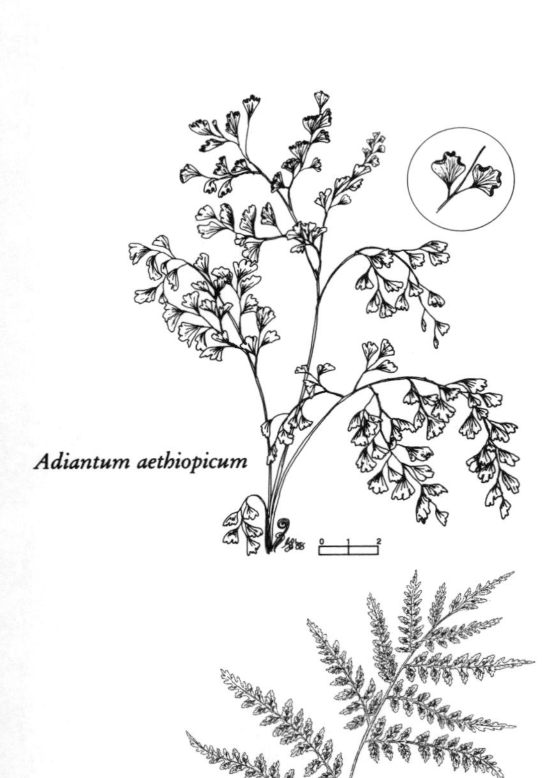

Adiantum aethiopicum

Adiantum — Adiantaceae

Adiantum aethiopicum — Common Maidenhair

Size: 10–45 cm high x spreading **P**
Habitat: Red gum woodland, wet, damp, valley and dry sclerophyll forests, grassy low open forest, riparian scrub in crevices of rocky outcrops
Form: Carpeting groundcover suckering by vigorous underground rhizomes
Foliage: Delicate bipinnate to tripinnate fronds, pinnules lobed and wedge-shaped, light yellow-green but darkening with age
Requirements: Moist, well drained soils. Becomes dormant during warm dry spells, but reshoots quickly from underground rhizomes once the soil moisture increases.
Comments: A well known and reliable fern which can cover large areas in ideal conditions. Suitable also as a container or basket plant if given ample moisture and protection from drying winds.
Propagation: Spore, division
Localities: Sunshine, St Albans, 1, 25, 26, 28–30, 34A–36, 38, 40–45#, 47, 49–51, 53, 55–65, 67, 74, 76
Distribution: All states; Lord Howe Is, NZ, Af

Allantodia australis

Allantodia — Athyriaceae

Allantodia australis — Austral Lady Fern

Size: 0.5–2 m tall **P N**
Habitat: Cool temperate rainforest, wet sclerophyll forest
Form: Erect tufted fern, with a small woody trunk in old plants
Foliage: Brittle, arching, bipinnate to tripinnate light green lacy fronds to 2 m long. Fronds are broadly triangular-shaped, pinnules to 25 mm long, prominently toothed.
Requirements: Cool, moist to wet well drained soils
Comments: An elegant fern for a moist outdoor area protected from wind. Old well grown plants resemble short-trunked tree ferns. Dormant during Winter. Suited to growing in a large tub indoors provided high humidity levels are maintained.
Propagation: Spores
Localities: 57
Distribution: Vic, Qld, NSW, Tas; NZ, N Cal
Synonym: *Diplazium australe, Athyrium australe*

Asplenium — Aspleniaceae

Asplenium bulbiferum ssp. gracillimum — Mother Spleenwort

Size: 0.5–1.2 m x 1 m **P**
Habitat: Cool temperate rainforest, wet and damp sclerophyll forests, epiphytic on logs, rocks and tree fern trunks
Form: Tufted perennial spreading clump with erect or semi-weeping fronds
Foliage: Thin, dark green shining fronds bipinnate to tripinnate, often with small plantlets borne near the tips of pinnae
Requirements: Moist, very well drained soils that do not dry out, preferably high in humus
Comments: A relatively common and easy to grow fern, hardy in a protected situation provided soil moisture can be maintained without becoming wet. The slowly growing plantlets on old fronds should be allowed to develop on the plant until the frond withers, when plantlets may be removed and potted individually until large enough to plant out.
Propagation: Plantlets produced on the fronds, spores
Localities: 57, 58
Distribution: Vic, Qld, NSW, Tas, SA; NZ

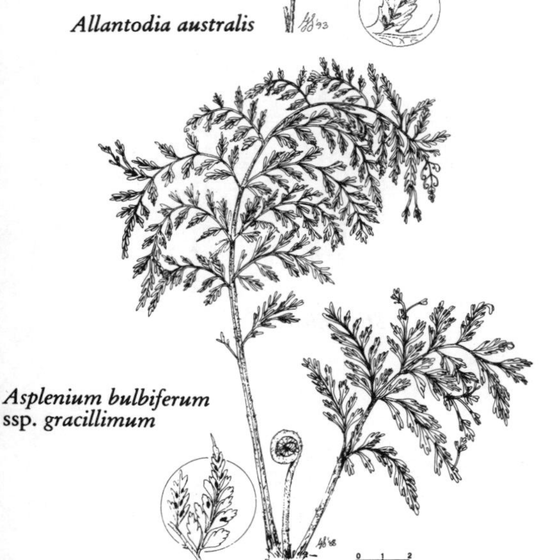

Asplenium bulbiferum ssp. *gracillimum*

Asplenium flabellifolium

Necklace fern

Size: 5–30 cm x spreading **P**
Habitat: Moist rocky outcrops of riparian scrub and woodland, red gum woodland, wet, damp and valley sclerophyll forests also epiphytic on tree fern trunks, logs and moist rocks
Form: Small procumbent or prostrate fern forming large spreading colonies by creeping rhizomes
Foliage: Delicate, pale green pinnate fronds to 30 cm long with plantlets borne on the tip of the frond. Pinnae are wedge- or fan-shaped.
Requirements: Rich light moist open soil
Comments: This dainty little fern is useful for terrariums and hanging baskets, but must have ample moisture and dappled shade. In nature, it can be epiphytic, and is often found in sunny situations, protected in crevices among boulders and grasses. Plantlets take root as the tip of the frond touches the ground, and a large colony is soon formed in humus rich soil.
Propagation: Spore, plantlets, division of the rhizomes
Localities: St Albans, Rockbank, 8, 16, 25, 26, 28–30#, 34A–36, 42, 54–58
Distribution: All States; NZ

Asplenium flabellifolium

Azolla

Azollaceae

Azolla filiculoides

Red Azolla or Pacific Azolla

Size: Prostrate-15 mm x 10–30 mm **F P**
Habitat: Billabongs and slow-moving watercourses in riparian scrub, grassy wetlands, box and red gum woodland, valley sclerophyll forest, grassy low open forest
Form: Free-floating fern forming carpets over still fresh water. Unbranched roots dangle below the water surface.
Foliage: Overlapping, irregularly divided sessile fronds with crinkled appearance, oblong-triangular in shape, to 50 mm long, green to deep red in colour
Requirements: Fresh still water
Comments: Can be very fast spreading but dies back in cold weather. Sometimes appears temporarily in lakes and slow flowing streams. Good cover for fish in ponds.
Propagation: Natural division as older plants break up
Localities: Maribyrnong Valley, Diamond Ck, 4, 6, 14, 24, 26, 27, 34A–36, ?42, 44, 48, 60, 67#, 71, 72
Distribution: All states; NZ, N Am, S Am

Azolla filiculoides

Azolla pinnata

Ferny Azolla

P

Habitat: Billabongs and ponds in damp and valley sclerophyll forests
Comments: Very similar in form to *A. filiculoides*. Branching is more regular (pinnate) and fronds are triangular in appearance. The lower surface of the fronds is rough while *A. filiculoides* is smooth all over. The main distinguishing feature is the feathery roots.
Localities: 34A, 42, 48, 59
Distribution: All States except Tas; PNG, Asia, Af

Azolla pinnata

Blechnum

Blechnaceae

Blechnum cartilagineum

Gristle Fern

Size: 0.5–1.5 m x 1 m **P**
Habitat: Damp and valley sclerophyll forests
Form: Upright tufting fern with short creeping stoloniferous rhizomes, forming spreading patches
Foliage: Very broad, slightly arching, leathery light green to yellow-green pinnate fronds to 1.5 m long, new growth often pinkish. Pinnae are longest at the base of fronds.
Requirements: Moist well drained soils, tolerating drier conditions once established
Comments: This attractive fern is readily available and quite easy to grow. It is the only Victorian *Blechnum* in which the fertile and barren fronds are similar in shape.
Propagation: Spore, division
Localities: Montrose, 42, 55–58, 60
Distribution: Vic, Qld, NSW, Tas; Philipines

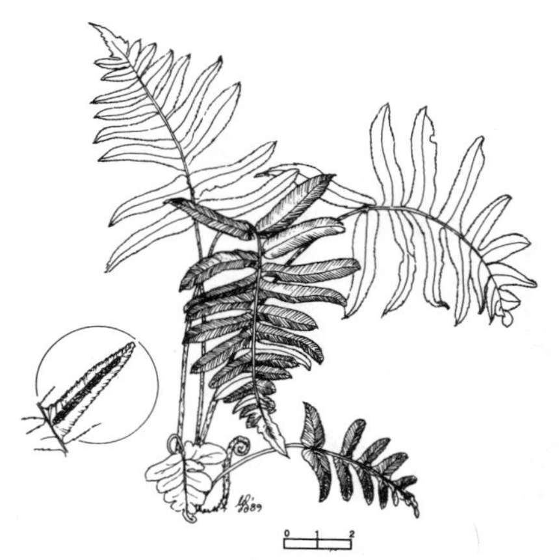

Blechnum cartilagineum

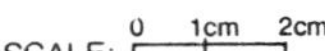

SCALE: 0 1cm 2cm The scale representation on each plant equals 2cm.

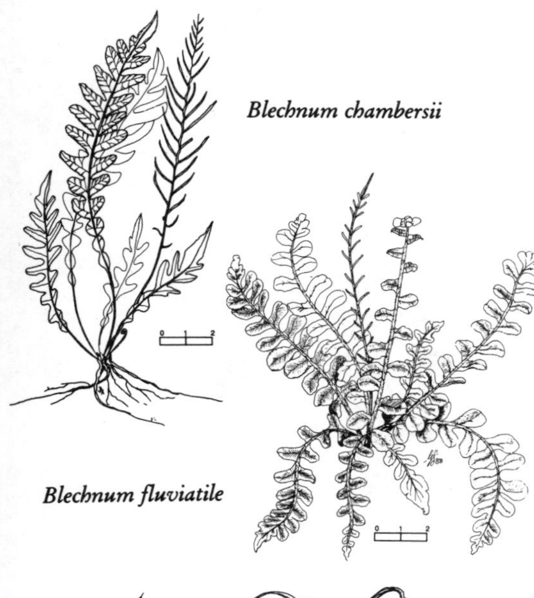

Blechnum chambersii

Blechnum fluviatile

Blechnum chambersii

Lance Water Fern

Size: 0.6 m x 0.6 m **P N**
Habitat: Wet and damp sclerophyll forests
Form: Semi-erect clump-forming fern
Foliage: Rough thin-textured dark green arching pinnate fronds to 60 cm long, but usually less. Pinnae small and broad at base of fronds, becoming longer towards the centre, then reducing again towards the tip. Fertile pinnae very narrow.
Requirements: Ample moisture in cool dark situations
Comments: Slow growing fern needing heavy shade and intolerant of dryness, or hot and cold winds. Locally rare.
Propagation: Spore, division
Localities: ?42, 57, 58, 60
Distribution: Vic, NSW, Tas, SA; NZ, Fiji, Norfolk Is

Blechnum fluviatile

Ray or Star Water Fern

Size: 20–40 cm x 0.5–1 m **P N**
Habitat: Wet and damp sclerophyll forests
Form: Prostrate to spreading rosetted fern, colonising small areas by underground stolons
Foliage: Thin light green pinnate fronds, spreading or prostrate, to 80 cm long. Pinnae sessile, the longest towards the centre of the frond, the lower ones rounded, the upper ones oblong. Fertile pinnae short, narrow and curved, on erect fronds.
Requirements: Well drained soil with ample moisture
Comments: Fast growing attractive small fern in ideal conditions but will not tolerate dryness.
Propagation: Spore, division
Localities: 47, 57, 58, 74
Distribution: Vic, NSW, Tas; NZ

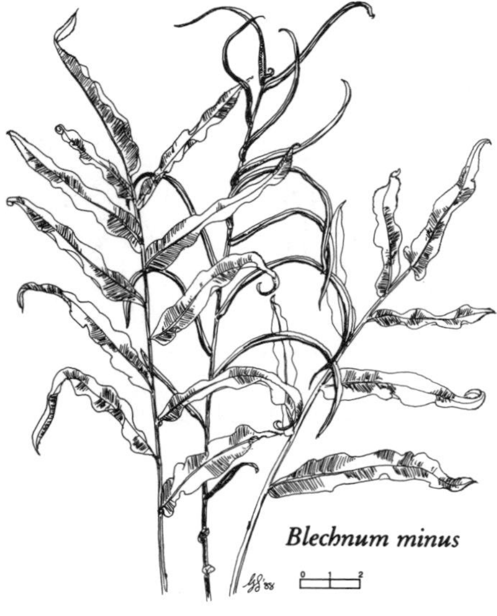

Blechnum minus

Blechnum minus

Soft Water Fern

Size: 0.5–1.2 m x 0.5–1 m **F P**
Habitat: Widespread in wet, damp and valley sclerophyll forests, grassy low open forest
Form: Dense erect clump, forming spreading patches from underground stolons
Foliage: Erect or arching, soft shiny green deeply pinnate fronds to 1.2 m long. Pinnae stalked, linear and well spaced along the rhachis, (or midrib), the lowest ones smallest. The new fronds are pinkish. Pinnae on fertile fronds very narrow.
Requirements: Likes humus rich soil but quite adaptable. Must have ample moisture, tolerating wet soils
Comments: Will tolerate exposure to the sun if the roots are well watered. Old plants produce short trunks.
Propagation: Spore, division
Localities: 41, 42, 55–57, 74–76
Distribution: Vic, Qld, NSW, Tas, SA; NZ

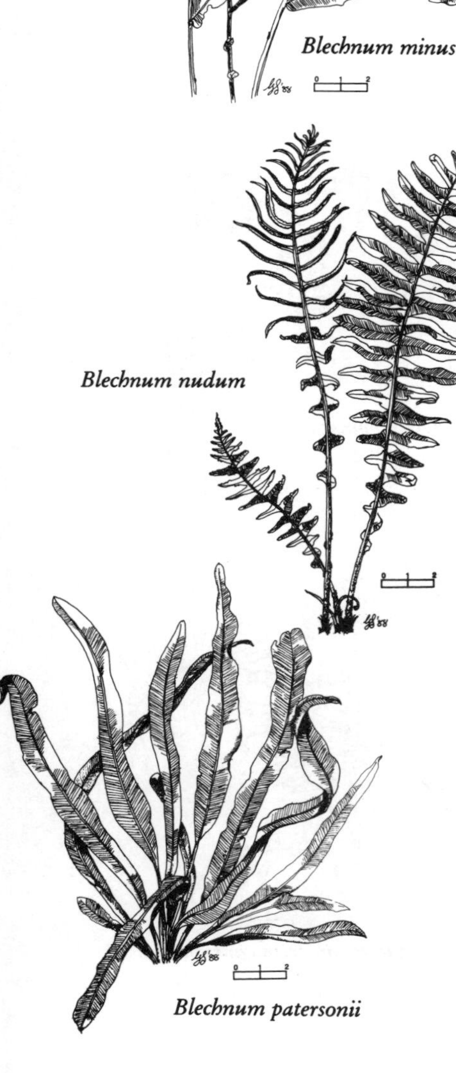

Blechnum nudum

Blechnum patersonii

Blechnum nudum

Fishbone Water Fern

Size: 0.5–1.2 m x 0.5–1 m **P N**
Habitat: Widespread in wet, damp and valley sclerophyll forests, grassy low open forest
Form: Individual plants form an erect rounded clump, with a small black fibrous trunk to 1 m in old plants. Plants spread by underground stolon to form large colonies.
Foliage: Erect or spreading dark green lanceolate pinnate fronds to 1.2 m long, young fronds yellow-green. Pinnae straight, held at right angles to the rhachis. Fertile fronds have much narrower pinnae.
Requirements: Very moist well-drained soil rich in humus. Adapts well to heavy soils.
Comments: Its attractive arching habit makes this fern an excellent long lived tub or garden plant but it must be protected from hot sun and drying winds.
Propagation: Spore, division
Localities: 42, 55, 56, 58, 75
Distribution: Vic, Qld, NSW, Tas, SA

Blechnum patersonii

Strap Water Fern

Size: 10–40 cm x 40 cm **P N**
Habitat: Cool temperate rainforest, wet sclerophyll forest
Form: Small erect fern forming open clumps
Foliage: Erect, leathery dark green fronds to 40 cm long, entire and strap-like or sometimes irregularly lobed. Young fronds reddish-pink. Fertile fronds narrower.
Requirements: Rich moist well drained soil
Comments: An attractive and hardy fern in a well protected moist position. The fertile fronds are simple when the plant has only simple fronds, but are divided and lobed when the plant is likewise.
Propagation: Spore
Localities: 57
Distribution: Vic, Qld, NSW, Tas

Blechnum wattsii

Hard Water Fern

Size:	to 1 m x spreading **P N**
Habitat:	Cool temperate rainforest, damp and wet sclerophyll forests
Form:	Vigorous rhizomatous creeping fern, generally forming extensive dense colonies, often excluding other ground species
Foliage:	Upright dark green coarsely pinnate fronds to 1 m long. Pinnae leathery and slightly serrated. Young fronds an attractive pink-bronze. Scales occur on all but the upper portion of the rhachis. Fertile fronds much narrower.
Requirements:	Moist, well drained soil, rich in humus
Comments:	Often the dominant ground cover in moist mountain forests, it is fairly hardy in cultivation, in a protected position .
Propagation:	Spore, division
Localities:	49, 57, 58
Distribution:	Vic, Qld, NSW, Tas, SA
Synonym:	Previously referred to as *B. procerum* which does not occur in Australia.

Blechnum wattsii

Botrychium — Ophioglossaceae

Botrychium australe

Austral Moonwort

Size:	10–40 cm x 10–30 cm
Habitat:	Moist depressions in plains grassland
Form:	Small open fern with thick fleshy roots and a non-creeping rhizome
Foliage:	Sterile fronds bipinnate to 4-pinnate, fleshy, bright green and lacy. The generally taller fertile fronds are borne as offshoots of the sterile fronds and bear grape-like clusters of spore cases at their tips.
Requirements:	Cool, acidic moist well drained soil, rich in humus
Comments:	A vulnerable plant throughout Victoria, presumed extinct in the Melbourne area. Plants grow in a mycorrhizal association with an invading fungus.
Propagation:	Division
Localities:	25#
Distribution:	All States except WA; NZ, S Am

Botrychium australe

Calochlaena — Dicksoniaceae

Calochlaena dubia

False Bracken, Rainbow Fern

Size:	0.5–2 m x spreading **P N**
Habitat:	Riparian scrub, damp and valley sclerophyll forests
Form:	Coarse open spreading fern, sometimes growing in dense clumps, with a stout, vigorous creeping rhizome
Foliage:	Large, broadly triangular, yellow-green 3–4 pinnate fronds on strong erect stalks (or stipes) to 2 m long (rarely to 4 m long)
Requirements:	Adaptable to most soils and exposed sites but thrives in moist clay soils
Comments:	This fern is often confused with common bracken (*Pteridium esculentum*). It is distinguished by its softer fronds, and a groove running along the main rib. Plants are quite vigorous once established and need room to spread. Growth may be controlled by pruning of creeping rhizomes.
Propagation:	Spore, division of rhizomes
Localities:	Montrose, 16, 18, 26, 42, 43, 50A, 51, 53, 55–60, 62, 63, 74
Distribution:	Vic, Qld, NSW, Tas
Synonym:	*Culcita dubia*

Calochlaena dubia

Cheilanthes — Adiantaceae

Cheilanthes austrotenuifolia

Rockfern

Size:	0.2–0.5 m x spreading **F P**
Habitat:	Widespread in red gum and box woodlands, damp, valley and dry sclerophyll forests, tea-tree heath
Form:	Dwarf fern forming open clumps, rhizomes short and branched
Foliage:	Fronds erect bipinnate to tripinnate, shiny, bright green and almost glabrous, to 30 cm long but often shorter. Fertile and sterile fronds similar.
Requirements:	Open position in well drained soil with root protection
Comments:	A surprisingly hardy fern in natural conditions, the fronds tolerant of direct sunshine and drying winds. They do eventually die down to the creeping rhizome in Summer but are renewed in Autumn. Plants resent disturbance and are difficult to establish, but have proved successful in sunny rockeries where the rhizomes are protected from extremes in temperature. In dry areas fronds may only reach 30–50 mm long.
Propagation:	Spore, division
Localities:	Tottenham, Sydenham, Tullamarine, 4, 7, 12, 15–18, 25, 26, 29, 30, 32, 34A–36, 42, 44, 46, 49, 50A, 51, 55, 56, 58–61, 67, 76
Distribution:	All States; NZ, PNG
Synonym:	Previously called *C. tenuifolia* var. *tenuifolia*

Cheilanthes austrotenuifolia

SCALE: 0 1cm 2cm The scale representation on each plant equals 2cm.

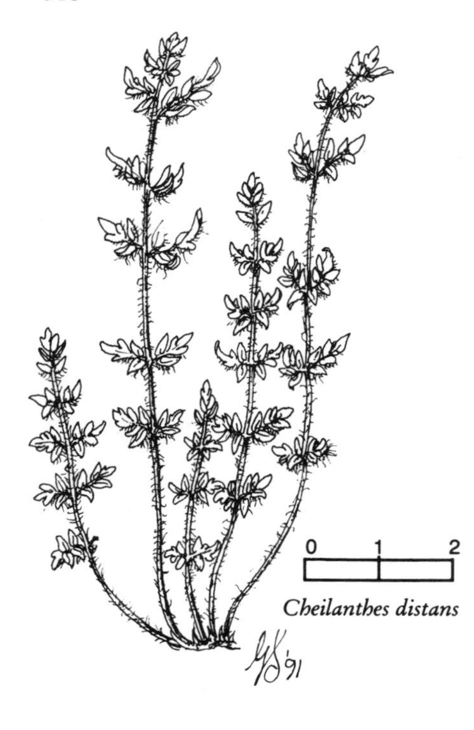

Cheilanthes distans

Cheilanthes distans
Bristly Cloak Fern

Size: to 30 cm high **F**
Habitat: Uncommon in riparian scrub, escarpments, crevices in rocky outcrops
Form: Tiny fern with short, much-branched rhizomes, spreading to form small, compact, separate clumps
Foliage: Small, slender upright pinnate to bipinnate fronds, to 30 cm long, but usually much less, covered with hair-like scales
Requirements: Warm open position, preferably in a well drained rockery situation. Resents disturbance
Comments: One of the easiest species to grow, this plant resents shade and overwatering. Often grows in similar habitats to *C. austrotenuifolia* but is easily distinguished by the dense covering of hair-like scales. Restricted range in the Melbourne area.
Propagation: Spore, division
Localities: Keilor, Diggers Rest, Rockbank, 16, 18, 26
Distribution: All States except Tas; Norfolk Is, NZ, N Cal

Cheilanthes sieberi ssp. sieberi
Mulga Fern

Size: to 0.4 m high **F**
Habitat: Box woodland, plains grassland, often amongst rocks
Form: Dwarf fern forming open spreading clumps
Foliage: Narrow erect, shiny bright green glabrous bipinnate to tripinnate fronds
Requirements: Warm well drained soils, resenting shade, but rhizomes need protection from temperature extremes.
Comments: Similar to *C. austrotenuifolia*, differing mainly in the narrower fronds and shorter rhizomes. Some water during the driest periods is beneficial.
Propagation: Spore, division
Localities: 14, 28, 34A
Distribution: All states except Tas; NZ, N Cal
Synonym: *C. tenuifolia* var. *sieberi*

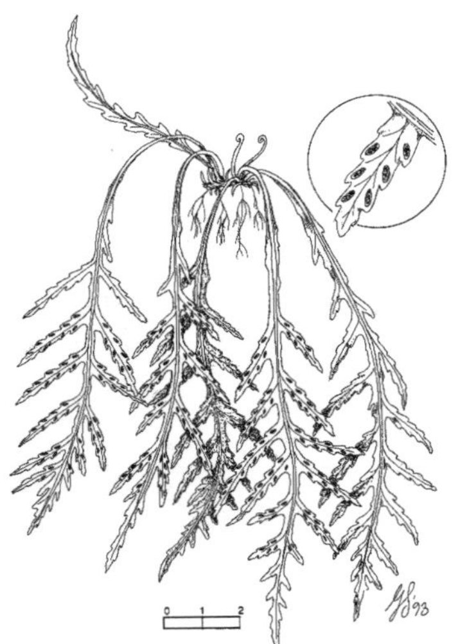
Ctenopteris heterophylla

Ctenopteris — Grammitidaceae

Ctenopteris heterophylla
Gipsy Fern

Size: 10–30 cm high **N**
Habitat: In mossy crevices or on rocks or mossy tree trunks in wet sclerophyll forest, cool temperate rainforest
Form: Pendant, tufted or shortly rhizomatous, epiphytic fern
Foliage: Variable, lobed or pinnate, rarely entire, lanceolate fronds to 30 cm long, leathery and dull green
Requirements: Extremely humus rich moist soil or preferably mossy rock, logs or tree trunks in a constantly humid situation
Comments: Very slow growing. May be suited to terrarium cultivation but has never been successfully grown.
Propagation: Spore, division
Localities: 57
Distribution: Vic, Tas; NZ

Culcita dubia = Calochlaena dubia

Cyathea australis

Cyathea — Cyatheaceae

Cyathea australis
Rough Tree Fern

Size: 5–15 m high **P N**
Habitat: Cool temperate rainforest, wet, damp and valley sclerophyll forests, banks of creeks and sheltered sites in drier areas
Form: Upright fibrous trunk with a head of long arching fronds. Base of trunk is often buttressed.
Foliage: Dark green tripinnate fronds, 2–5 m long x 1 m wide. Base of the stalks are covered with hard, pointed projections
Requirements: Moist soils tolerating dryness and some sun once established
Comments: Often confused with *Dicksonia antarctica*, the Soft Tree Fern—the chief vegetative difference being the rasp-like frond bases compared with the soft hairy frond bases of *D. antarctica*.
Propagation: Spore
Localities: 42, 51, 55–58, 60, 66#, 73–76
Distribution: Vic, Qld, NSW, Tas

Cyathea cunninghamii

Slender Tree Fern

Size: 10–20 m high **N**
Habitat: Wet sclerophyll forest
Form: Slender upright trunk with a small head of arching fronds
Foliage: Soft tripinnate fronds to 3 m long, dull, dark green above, paler below
Requirements: Ample moisture, particularly during Summer, with humus rich soil. Intolerant of wind and hot sun.
Comments: A most attractive treefern with a very slender, almost black trunk. Plants to 20 m in height are known with trunk diameters of only 15 cm. A rare plant in Victoria known from 1 site in the Melbourne region.
Propagation: Spore
Localities: Dandenong Ranges
Distribution: Vic, Qld, NSW, Tas; NZ

Dicksonia antarctica

Dicksonia

Dicksoniaceae

Dicksonia antarctica

Soft Tree Fern

Size: 2–15 m high **P N**
Habitat: Cool temperate rainforest, wet, damp and valley sclerophyll forests, often in pure stands
Form: Robust, often buttressed trunk with a head of arching fronds. Trunk covered in soft brown fibrous roots.
Foliage: Tripinnate fronds to 5 m long, dark green and glossy above, dull green below.
Requirements: Soils rich in humus and ample moisture. Will tolerate some sun once established.
Comments: This is the fern commonly sold as bare trunks in plant nurseries. All sale plants should carry a licence tag. Trunks are excellent hosts for small epiphytic ferns.
Propagation: Should be propagated by spore only, to protect plants in the wild.
Localities: 55–58, 60, 66#, 74, 76
Distribution: Vic, Qld, NSW, Tas, SA

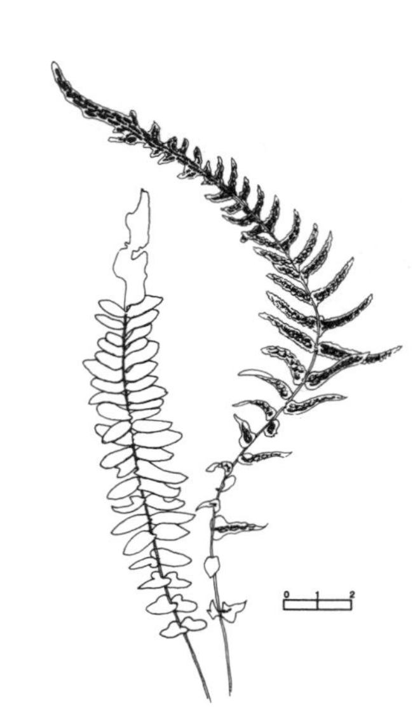

Doodia caudata

Doodia

Blechnaceae

Doodia caudata

Small Rasp Fern

Size: 10–30 cm x 30–50 cm **P N**
Habitat: Embankments and rock crevices in riparian scrub
Form: Small erect or weeping fern, producing separate tufted clumps on short creeping rhizomes
Foliage: Narrow, dark green, pinnate fronds, generally having terminal pinnae united into a tail. Fertile fronds more erect and about twice as long as sterile fronds.
Requirements: Acidic rich peaty soils that do not dry out. Will tolerate quite a sunny position with ample moisture.
Comments: An adaptable fern suited to garden, pot or hanging basket culture. This fern is both variable and widespread but is locally rare.
Propagation: Spore, division
Localities: Broadmeadows
Distribution: Vic, Qld, NSW, Tas, SA; NZ, N Cal

Doodia media var. *australis*

Doodia media ssp. australis

Common Rasp Fern

Size: 0.3–0.6 m x 0.3–0.5 m **P N**
Habitat: Valley sclerophyll forest, riparian scrub
Form: Small erect fern forming spreading tufted clumps along short creeping rhizomes
Foliage: Pinnate, dark green lanceolate fronds to 60 cm long, new growth often purplish-pink. Stipe is covered in tiny projections giving it a rough texture.
Requirements: Humus rich, moist well drained soils
Comments: A variable species which will tolerate sunshine in protected situations, provided it is kept moist.
Propagation: Spore or division
Localities: Somerton, Dandenong Ranges 1863, 42, 74
Distribution: Vic, Qld, NSW, Tas; NZ

SCALE: 0 1cm 2cm The scale representation on each plant equals 2cm.

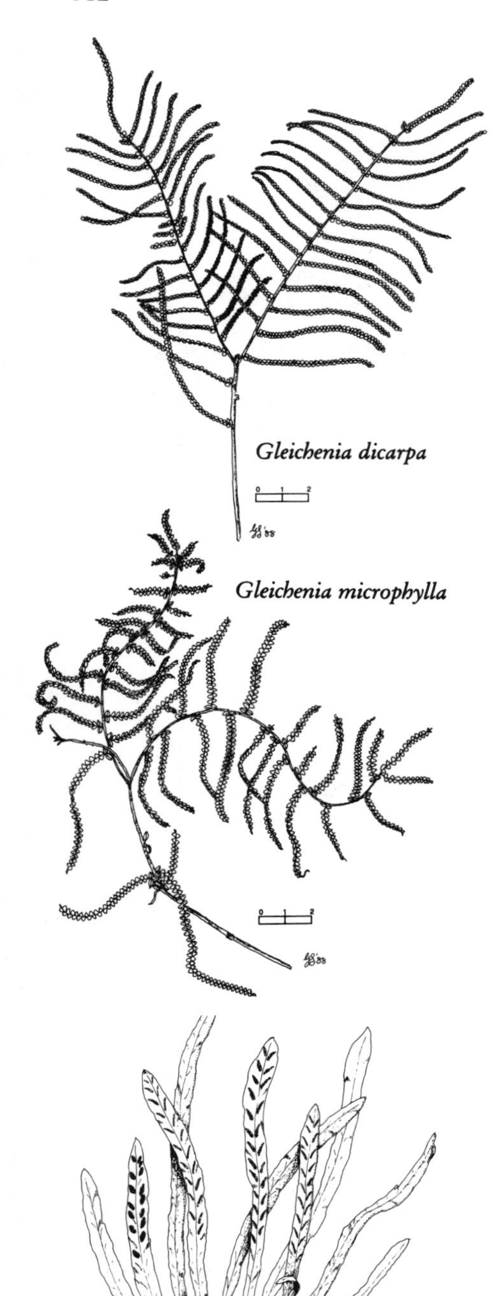

Gleichenia dicarpa

Gleichenia microphylla

Grammitis billardieri

Gleichenia — Gleicheniaceae

Gleichenia dicarpa

Pouched Coral Fern, Tangle Fern

Size: to 3 m in scrubby thickets but usually lower — **F P**
Habitat: Bogs and soaks in damp sclerophyll forest, wattle tea-tree scrub
Form: Scrambling or climbing fern forming extensive tangled colonies, with vigorous much-branched wiry rhizomes
Foliage: Erect, many branched and very wiry, light green fronds. Pinnae are up to 50 mm long and pinnatifid. Margins of rounded pinnules are strongly rolled under forming a pouch.
Requirements: Acidic, damp or wet soils. Prefers its foliage in the sun.
Comments: Sometimes forms impenetrable thickets. Roots resent disturbance and will not tolerate drying out.
Propagation: Spores, occasionally division of the creeping rhizomes
Localities: Bentleigh#, 58, 66#, 67#, 74, 75
Distribution: Vic, Qld, NSW, Tas; NZ, N Cal, Mal
Synonym: *G. circinnata*

Gleichenia microphylla

Scrambling Coral Fern, Umbrella Fern

Size: to 4 m high in scrubby thickets — **P N**
Habitat: Wet, damp and valley sclerophyll forests, wattle tea-tree scrub
Comments: Often confused with *G. dicarpa. G. microphylla* is a stronger-growing species, prefering cooler, shaded sites. Fronds are dark green to yellowish with almost triangular, flat pinnules, whereas the pinnules of *G. dicarpa* are distinctly pouched.
Propagation: Spores, occasionally division
Localities: Montrose, 56, 57, 67#, 73–76
Distribution: All states except NT; NZ, N Cal, Mal

Grammitis — Grammitidaceae

Grammitis billardieri

Common Finger Fern

Size: to 15 cm high — **N**
Habitat: Cool temperate rainforest, wet and damp sclerophyll forests
Form: Tiny erect epiphytic or lithophytic fern with a short creeping rootstock
Foliage: Few leathery, dark green linear fronds (rarely lobed near the tip) to 15 cm long, often smaller
Requirements: Moist, heavily shaded position with high humidity
Comments: This inconspicuous fern is common on mossy rocks, logs and tree fern trunks in cool, moist forests. It has proved difficult to maintain in cultivation.
Propagation: Spore
Localities: 57, 58
Distribution: Vic, NSW, Tas; NZ

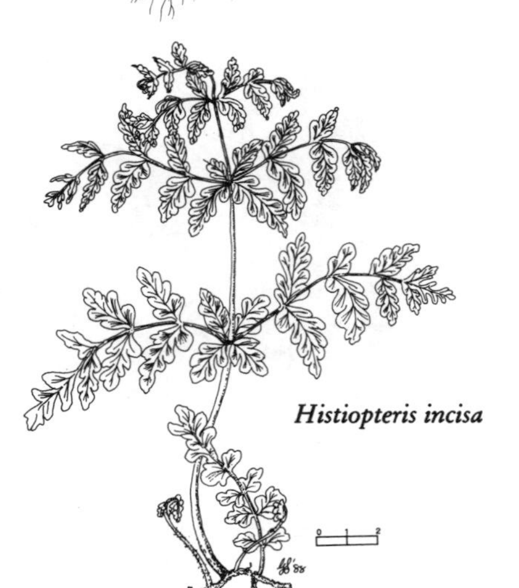

Histiopteris incisa

Histiopteris — Dennstaedtiaceae

Histiopteris incisa

Bat's Wing Fern

Size: 0.5–2 m high — **P N**
Habitat: Cool temperate rainforest, wet and damp sclerophyll forests
Form: Robust upright fern spreading by vigorous underground rhizomes
Foliage: Soft pale green or glaucous bipinnate to tripinnate fronds, triangular in outline, held erect on stout stalks, to 2 m high. Pinnae and pinnules in opposite pairs.
Requirements: Moist well drained soils, tolerating dryness once established
Comments: In the right conditions this plant can be extremely vigorous, forming spreading colonies. May also establish in more open areas such as escarpments where the young ferns are able to get sufficient moisture. It makes an interesting foliage contrast in a fernery, where its bluish fronds can be shown to advantage.
Propagation: Spore, division
Localities: 42, 56–58, 66#, 67#
Distribution: All States except WA; NZ, S Af, S Am, W Ind

Hymenophyllum

Hymenophyllaceae

Hymenophyllum australe

Austral Filmy Fern

N

Size: Fronds to 15 cm long
Habitat: Cool temperate rainforest
Form: Lithophytic or epiphytic filmy fern with wiry creeping rhizomes
Foliage: Erect, membranous dark green bipinnate fronds with secondary pinnae deeply divided into linear segments
Requirements: Constant high humidity and protection from sun and drying winds
Comments: Can form dense blankets on mossy rocks, logs and tree fern trunks. All species of *Hymenophyllum* have a restricted range in Melbourne.
Propagation: Spore, division
Localities: 57
Distribution: Vic, Qld, NSW, Tas

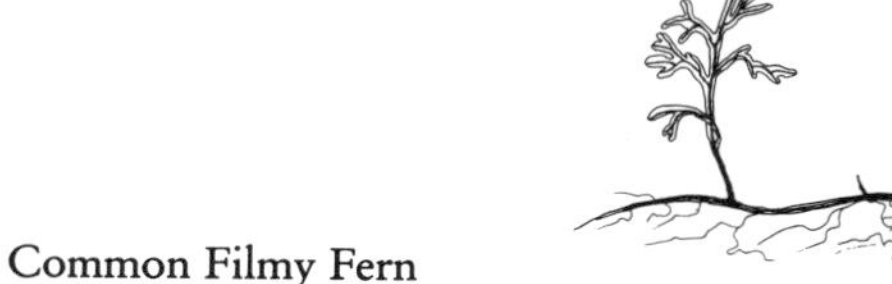

Hymenophyllum australe

Hymenophyllum cupressiforme

Common Filmy Fern

N

Size: Fronds to 10 cm long
Habitat: Cool temperate rainforest, wet and damp sclerophyll forests
Comments: Lithophytic or epiphytic filmy fern with threadlike creeping rootstock. The main distinguishing feature is the form of the fronds. They are small, weakly erect or arching, dark green and membranous, with toothed margins.
Localities: 42, 57, 58
Distribution: Vic, Qld, NSW, Tas; NZ

Hymenophyllum flabellatum

Shiny Filmy Fern

N

Size: Fronds to 25 cm long
Habitat: Cool temperate rainforest, wet and damp sclerophyll forests
Comments: Epiphytic fern with long creeping threadlike rootstock, often found growing on trunks of *Dicksonia antarctica*. Differs from *H. cupressiforme* in that the pale green pendent fronds are much longer, and from *H. australe* in that the fronds are usually pendent.
Localities: 57, 58
Distribution: Vic, Qld, NSW, Tas; NZ, Samoa, Tahiti

Hymenophyllum flabellatum

Hypolepis

Dennstaedtiaceae

Hypolepis glandulifera

Downy Ground Fern, Sticky Ground Fern

F P

Size: to 2.5 m high
Habitat: Wet sclerophyll forest
Form: A coarse vigorous spreading fern with a thick creeping much-branched rhizome, quickly developing into large colonies
Foliage: Large ovate to triangular, mostly 4-pinnate fronds, dull green and bracken-like on slender stalks, to 2 m long. Stalks, rhachises and young fronds covered densely with crooked sticky hairs
Requirements: Tolerant of most soils and positions but must have ample moisture in sunny positions
Comments: The fronds are less sticky if growing in sun. An easily grown fern which spreads quickly, but may be controlled by pruning the rhizome.
Propagation: Spore, division
Localities: 57
Distribution: Vic, Qld, NSW; S India, Sri Lanka to PNG and N Cal
Synonym: Previously referred to as *H. punctata.*

Hypolepis muelleri

Harsh Ground Fern

F P

Size: 0.5–1.5 m high
Habitat: Wet and damp sclerophyll forests
Form: Coarse, vigorous spreading fern with a slender creeping rhizome, often forming extensive colonies
Foliage: Large ovate tripinnate fronds, dark green and bracken-like on slender stems, to 1.5 m long
Requirements: Very moist, swampy soils
Comments: May become quite invasive under ideal conditions.
Propagation: Spore, division
Localities: 57, 58
Distribution: Vic, Qld, NSW, Tas

SCALE: 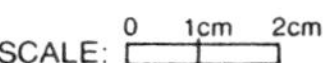

The scale representation on each plant equals 2cm.

Hypolepis rugosula

Ruddy Ground Fern

Size: 0.5–1.5 m high — **F P**
Habitat: Wet and damp sclerophyll forests, swamps in wattle tea-tree scrub
Form: A coarse vigorously spreading fern with strong branching rhizomes, forming large clumps
Foliage: Erect broadly-triangular tripinnate fronds, dull green and bracken-like with reddish-brown warty stems, to 1.5 m long
Requirements: Moist or wet soils
Comments: May become invasive. As with other *Hypolepis* species, suitable only for large gardens where its vigorous habit is not a problem. Looks best in shaded moist situations, but adaptable to full sun if ample moisture is available.
Propagation: Spore, division
Localities: 57, 58, 67#, 74, 75
Distribution: All States except NT

Hypolepis rugosula

Isoetes — Isoetaceae

Isoetes drummondii var. drummondii

Plain Quillwort

Size: 3–20 cm high — **F P**
Habitat: Red gum woodland
Form: Small, erect or spreading, tufted annual fern ally, corm-like rootstock usually 3-lobed
Foliage: Narrowly cylindrical fronds 3–20 cm long, bases abruptly wider and overlapping. Broadly elliptical spore-containing cases at base of fronds, liver brown becoming shiny when mature; membranous veil absent.
Requirements: Poorly drained soil or shallow water
Comments: A rare in plant in Melbourne.
Propagation: Unknown
Localities: Dandenong, Langwarrin
Distribution: Vic, Tas, SA, WA

Isoetes drummondii var. *drummondii*

Isoetes muelleri

Isoetes muelleri

Size: 5–30 cm high — **F P**
Habitat: Grassy wetlands
Form: Aquatic tufted fern ally with 2- or 3-lobed rootstock
Foliage: Erect or lax cylindrical fronds 50–150 mm long, becoming wider towards the base. Bases abruptly wider, flattened and loosely overlapping. Thin, rounded to elliptical, pale coloured spore-containing cases entirely or partly covered by pale membranous veil.
Requirements: Moist heavy soils subject to inundation
Comments: Known from one site in the Melbourne area.
Localities: Rockbank
Distribution: All states
Synonym: Previously confused with *I. humilior*

Lastreopsis — Dryopteridaceae

Lastreopsis acuminata

Shiny Shield Fern

Size: 0.5–0.8 m x 0.5–1 m — **P N**
Habitat: Wet, damp and valley sclerophyll forests
Form: Open, tufted or shortly rhizomatous fern
Foliage: Bipinnate (sometimes tripinnate) arching, glossy, dark green narrowly triangular fronds to 0.8 m long
Requirements: Moist, humus rich, well drained soils
Comments: An easily grown fern, its glossy fronds add interest to shaded gardens. Fronds become smaller in open or sunny situations, even with plenty of moisture. Locally rare.
Propagation: Spore, division
Localities: 57, 58, 62
Distribution: Vic, Qld, NSW, Tas, SA
Synonym: *L. shepherdii*

Lastreopsis hispida

Bristly Shield Fern

Size: 0.1–0.8 m x 0.3–0.6 m — **P N**
Habitat: Cool temperate rainforest, wet sclerophyll forest
Form: Open tufted or shortly rhizomatous fern
Foliage: Thin glossy broadly triangular dark green 3- to 4-pinnate fronds, erect or arching, to 0.8 m long. Bristly hairs on the stems and rhachis.
Requirements: Moist to wet, humus rich, well drained soils
Comments: Sometimes grows on rotting logs and mossy trunks. It is quite rare both in Victoria and in the region.
Propagation: Spore, division
Localities: Olinda
Distribution: Vic, NSW, Tas; NZ

Lastreopsis acuminata

Lindsaea — Lindsaeaceae

Lindsaea linearis — Screw Fern

Size: 5–30 cm x 20 cm — **F P**
Habitat: Widespread in damp and valley sclerophyll forests, tea-tree heath, grassy low open forest
Form: Small erect fern with a short wiry creeping rhizome
Foliage: Pinnate, pale green slender fronds to 30 cm long forming an arching rosette. Pinnae paired and fan-shaped to 10 mm long. Fertile fronds more slender and erect than sterile fronds.
Requirements: Moist soils, often in open sites when the rhizome is protected
Comments: The pinnae on the narrow fertile fronds are obliquely bent down, giving rise to the common name of screw fern. It is difficult to establish and maintain in cultivation.
Propagation: Spore
Localities: 41, 43, 44, 47–51, 53–56, 58, 59, 61–64, 67, 68, 70, 71, 73–76
Distribution: All States; Norfolk Is, NZ, N Cal

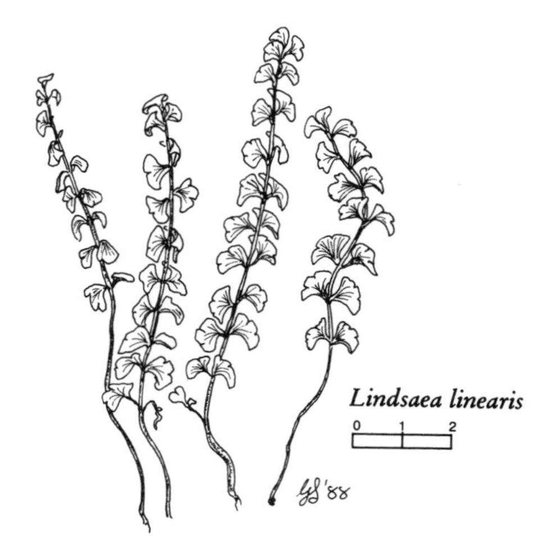

Lindsaea linearis

Lycopodiella — Lycopodiaceae

Lycopodiella laterale — Slender Clubmoss

Size: Branches 10–40 cm long — **P N**
Habitat: Peaty swamps amongst sedges in wattle tea-tree scrub
Form: Weakly erect or trailing single or few-stemmed non-woody plant, with thick branched underground rhizomes. Stems may be once or twice divided.
Foliage: Soft very narrow leaves to 6 mm long, sessile with incurved margins, crowded along the stems
Requirements: Moist to wet peaty, often sandy soils, protected by other scrubby plants
Comments: Small cone-like fruiting bodies (or stroboli) 10–15 mm long, are sessile and scattered along the stems. May be suited to terrarium culture. Possibly now extinct within the Melbourne area.
Propagation: Spore
Localities: Clayton#, 67#, 74
Distribution: All states except NT; NZ, N Cal
Synonym: *Lycopodium laterale*

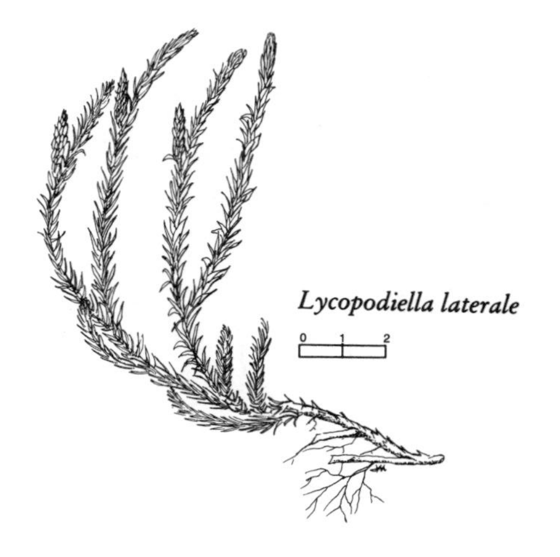

Lycopodiella laterale

Marsilea — Marsileaceae

Marsilea drummondii — Common Nardoo

Size: Stalks 2–30 cm high — **F P**
Habitat: Flood plains, bogs and swamps in box and red gum woodland, grassy wetlands, riparian scrub
Form: An aquatic with floating fronds and a creeping rhizome, glabrous on aquatic plants, covered in dense orange-brown hairs when terrestrial. Nodes on rhizome are close together.
Foliage: Silky, grey-green, "four-leaf clover" fronds on thin stalks to 30 cm long, held above the water surface. As the frond ages the stalk becomes more pliable and the rigid leaf floats. Glabrous wedge-shaped leaflets to 25 mm long (smaller and hairy on terrestrial plants).
Fruit: Light brown, rounded sporocarps to 10 mm wide singly on short stalks at the base of the frond. Fruiting generally occurs as water recedes, the sporocarps detaching from the plant as the soil dries out. They split following flooding to release the spores.
Requirements: Boggy soil, subject to inundation. Shallow water no deeper than 0.3 m.
Comments: Attractive in a pond or aquarium, plants may cover large areas in ideal situations, without being invasive. Tends to become dormant in cooler months. Spores form in hard structures the size of a pea, called sporocarps. They were an important food source for the Aborigines who either roasted them or ground them into flour.
Propagation: Spore or division
Localities: Sydenham, Brooklyn, Kew, 1, 6, 7, 9, 11, 25, 35, 36, ?42
Distribution: All mainland states

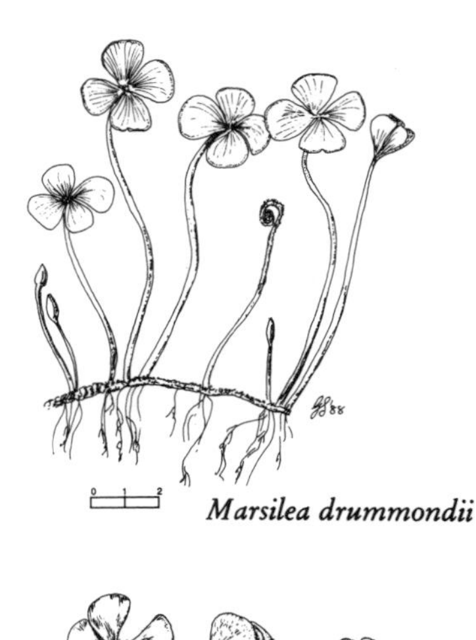

Marsilea drummondii

Marsilea hirsuta — Short-fruit Nardoo

Size: Stalks 2–17 cm high — **F P**
Habitat: Grassy wetlands on muddy sites beside swamps
Comments: Similar to *M. drummondii*, and although often with long silky hairs on top of the fronds, usually less hairy than that species. Stalks of fronds shorter, to 17 cm long. Narrow wedge-shaped leaflets to 15 mm long. Sporocarps to 5 mm, borne singly or in small groups, held horizontally on very short stalks. Nodes on rhizomes usually distant.
Localities: Laverton, 7
Distribution: All mainland states

Marsilea hirsuta

SCALE: 0 1cm 2cm — The scale representation on each plant equals 2cm.

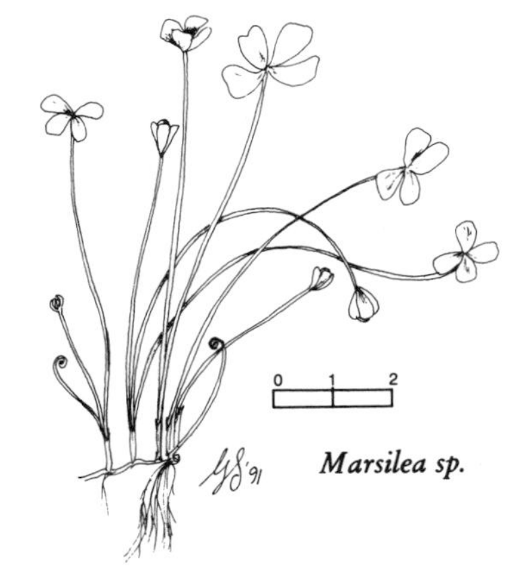

Marsilea sp.

Marsilea sp. — Narrow-leaf Nardoo

Size: Stalks to 10 cm high — **F P**
Habitat: Boggy areas subject to inundation in grassy wetlands, plains grassland
Foliage: Leaflets are narrowly obovate to 8 mm long, asymmetrically arranged, and sparsely hairy to glabrous
Fruit: Solitary ribbed sporocarps to 3 mm long on tiny stalks
Comments: Similar to *M. drummondii* and *M. hirsuta* but rhizomes are glabrous, stalks grow in clusters and plant is much more miniature in form. Plants form mats in boggy soils, or very shallow water. Much less common than previous species and locally rare.
Localities: Laverton, 17#, 18, 35
Distribution: All mainland states
Synonym: Previously confused with *M. angustifolia* which only occurs in tropical northern Australia.

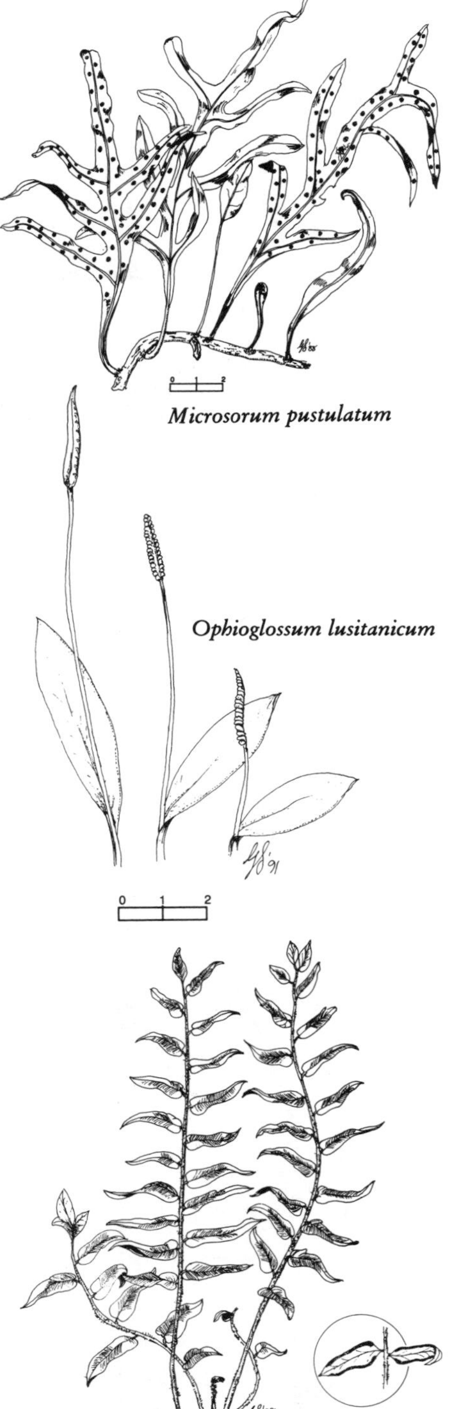

Microsorum pustulatum

Ophioglossum lusitanicum

Pellaea falcata var. *falcata*

Microsorum — Polypodiaceae

Microsorum pustulatum — Kangaroo Fern

Size: Scrambling or climbing fern — **P N**
Habitat: Cool temperate rainforest, wet sclerophyll forest
Form: Vigorous epiphytic or lithophytic fern with a creeping rhizome, favouring *Dicksonia antarctica* as a host
Foliage: Variable, linear, irregularly lobed or pinnate, leathery fronds to 60 cm long, but usually much less. Margins are wavy and lobes vary from 5–25 cm long.
Requirements: Shaded protected site with high humidity
Comments: An attractive creeping fern growing on mossy rocks, treefern trunks and logs in cool, moist forests. This fern is quite adaptable to cultivation in well watered, protected fern gardens.
Propagation: Spore, division
Localities: 55, 57, 58
Distribution: Vic, Qld, NSW, Tas; Norfolk Is, NZ, N Cal
Synonym: *M. diversifolium*

Ophioglossum — Ophioglossaceae

Ophioglossum lusitanicum — Adder's Tongue

Size: Fertile frond to 15 cm high — **F P**
Habitat: Valley sclerophyll forest, tea-tree heath, wattle tea-tree scrub, plains grassland
Form: Very small sparse fern with tuber-like rhizome
Foliage: Each plant consists of a solitary, erect broadly elliptic to lanceolate sterile frond to 35 mm long and a fertile spike to 15 mm long rising from the base of the sterile frond on a thread-like stalk to 70 mm long
Requirements: Protected situation with moist, well drained soil, tolerating some flooding
Comments: Difficult to maintain in cultivation but may occur in dense clumps in its natural habitat. Very rare within the Melbourne area.
Propagation: Spore
Localities: Laverton, Hurstbridge, 34A, 67#
Distribution: All States; almost cosmopolitan
Synonym: *O. coriaceum*

Pellaea — Adiantaceae

Pellaea falcata var. falcata — Sickle Fern

Size: 0.3–0.8 m x 0.3–0.6 m — **P N**
Habitat: Rocky outcrops in riparian scrub and woodland, wet and damp sclerophyll forests
Form: Rigid tufted fern with short creeping rhizomes
Foliage: Erect, linear-lanceolate, pinnate, shiny dark green leathery fronds to 50 cm long, rhachis dark brown. Pinnae 20–50 mm long, ovate to lanceolate, often curved upwards.
Requirements: Moist, well drained organic soils with root protection (such as rock crevices). Tolerates wet periods and some sun.
Comments: A reliable fern for pot or garden culture.
Propagation: Spore, division
Localities: Deer Park, 8, 16, 26, 29#, 42, 57, 58, 60
Distribution: Vic, Qld, NSW, Tas; NZ, Mal, India

Phylloglossum — Lycopodiaceae

Phylloglossum drummondi

Pigmy Club Moss

Size: 1–5 cm high — **P N**
Habitat: Swamp and wattle tea-tree scrub
Form: Tiny colony-forming fern with a basal tufted rosette and a central erect fleshy white stalk bearing a cone-like sporing structure
Foliage: Few, fleshy terete basal fronds to 20 mm long
Requirements: Wet peaty soils
Comments: The only species in the genus. Leaves die back as the ground dries, and resprout from a tiny white tuber during Winter and Spring. Locally rare.
Propagation: Spore
Localities: 49, 67#, 74
Distribution: Vic, NSW, Tas, SA, WA; NZ

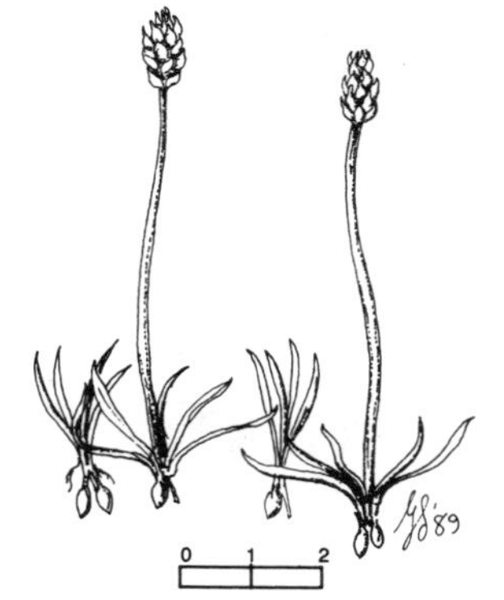

Phylloglossum drummondi

Pilularia — Marsileaceae

Pilularia novae-hollandiae

Austral Pillwort

Size: 2–7 cm high — **F P**
Habitat: Swamps and drying mud of temporary shallow water in box woodland
Form: Small perennial fern forming dense tufts along thread-like, glabrous green rhizomes
Foliage: Deep green grass-like sterile fronds to 70 mm long. Fertile fronds are buried in mud, and end in tiny globular sporocarps.
Requirements: Soft mud, tolerating temporary inundation
Comments: Growing amongst grasses and sedges it is easily overlooked. Recognised by the more or less flexuose fronds and the way they unfurl. A restricted occurrence.
Propagation: Spores, division
Localities: Keilor, Laverton Nth, Deer Park, Rockbank, 36
Distribution: Vic, NSW, Tas, SA, WA

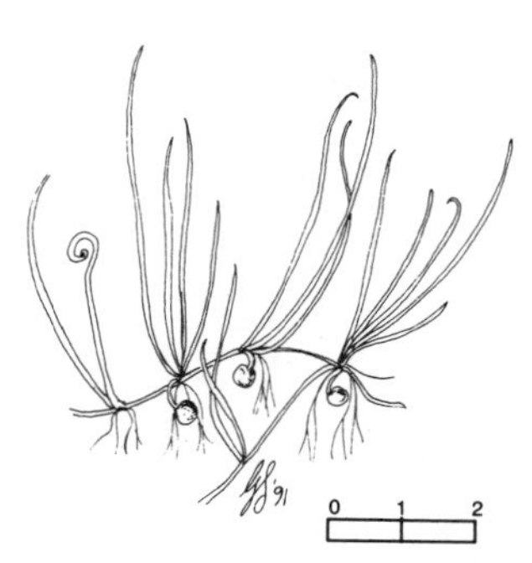

Pilularia novae-hollandiae

Pleurosorus — Aspleniaceae

Pleurosorus rutifolius

Blanket Fern

Size: to 17 cm high — **F**
Habitat: Rocky sites in riparian woodland and scrub, box woodland
Form: Small upright fern with a very short creeping rhizome covered in dark brown scales
Foliage: Erect, pinnate dark green fronds to 17 cm long, pinnae fan-shaped, notched or lobed, to 15 mm long
Requirements: Adaptable to most soils but resents overwatering and humidity. Like many Cheilanthes species, this fern prefers a sunny position with root protection such as afforded by rock crevices.
Comments: An attractive little fern which is quite drought resistant. It shrivels up at the height of Summer but resurrects with the onset of rain. Locally rare.
Propagation: Spore, division
Localities: Sunbury, Werribee, Altona, St Albans, 10, 11, 16, 26, 29, 36
Distribution: All States; NZ

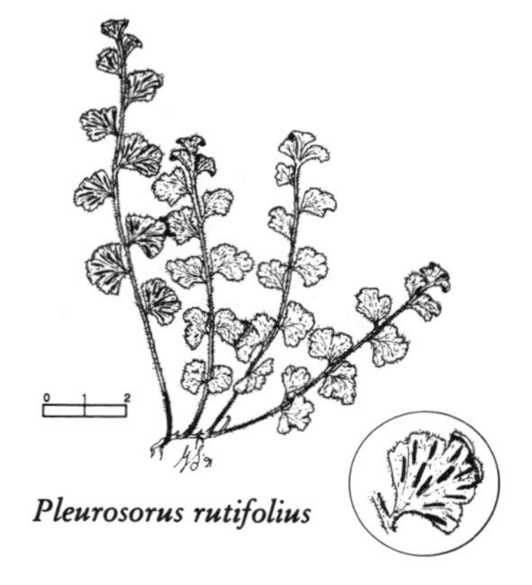

Pleurosorus rutifolius

Polyphlebium — Hymenophyllaceae

Polyphlebium venosum

Veined Bristle Fern

Size: Fronds to 15 cm long — **P N**
Habitat: Cool temperate rainforest, wet and damp sclerophyll forests
Form: A delicate rhizomatous epiphytic fern, the rhizome thread-like and much branched
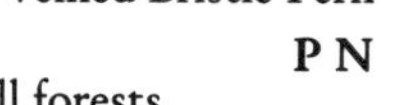
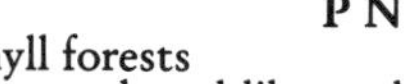
Foliage: Delicate translucent, pendulous, light green, lobed to irregularly pinnate fronds, with prominent, branched veins
Requirements: High humidity
Comments: This is the most common filmy fern in the outlying moist hills around Melbourne, preferring, and often completely covering the trunks of *Dicksonia antarctica.*
Propagation: Spore, division
Localities: 57, 58
Distribution: Vic, NSW, Tas; NZ

Polyphlebium venosum

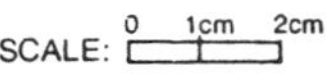

The scale representation on each plant equals 2cm.

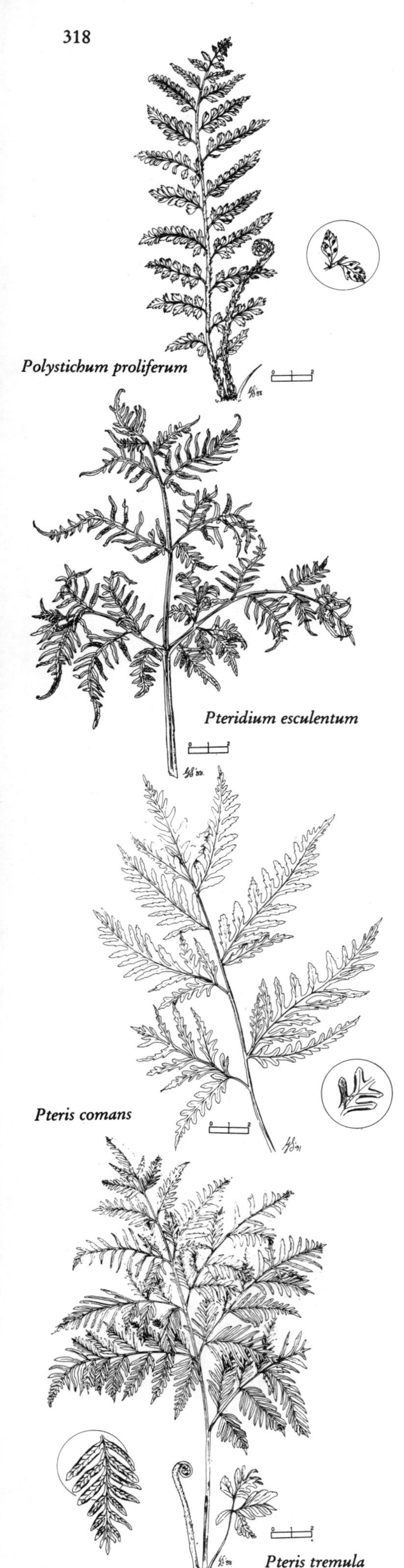
Polystichum proliferum

Pteridium esculentum

Pteris comans

Pteris tremula

Polystichum — Dryopteridaceae

Polystichum proliferum — Mother Shield Fern

Size: 1–1.5 m x 1–1.5 m — **P N**
Habitat: Cool temperate rainforest, wet and damp sclerophyll forests
Form: Tufted fern with long arching fronds, often occurring in large spreading colonies. Rhizomes are thick and become trunk-like in old plants.
Foliage: Young fronds bright light green, becoming dull dark green as they mature. At first erect, then arching, to 1 m long, bipinnate, often bearing bulbils near the tips. Stalks and rhachis densely covered with dark scales.
Requirements: Moist soils, tolerating dry periods once established
Comments: An excellent and reliable fern for garden culture that is readily propagated by layering the bulbils.
Propagation: Spore, bulbils
Localities: Deer Park, 42, 49, 55–58, 60, 74
Distribution: Vic, NSW, Tas

Pteridium — Dennstaedtiaceae

Pteridium esculentum — Austral Bracken

Size: to 1.5 m high — **F P**
Habitat: Widespread in wet, damp and valley sclerophyll forests, sclerophyll and red gum woodland, grassy low open forest, tea-tree heath, wattle tea-tree scrub, coastal banksia woodland
Form: Single erect frond, spreading vigorously from a strong creeping rhizome
Foliage: Dark green, broadly-triangular, leathery, 3- to 4-pinnate fronds, on rigid upright stalks, to 1.5 m long
Requirements: Moist or dry soils
Comments: An invasive fern that is poisonous to stock. Although this plant spreads readily by means of its branching underground rhizomes, it is difficult to propagate vegetatively. The sap from young fronds is a useful insect bite antidote. The rhizome was roasted in the hot ashes by the Aborigines, then beaten to a paste.
Propagation: Spore
Localities: 15, 16, 26, 29, 30, 32, 34A–36, 40–44, 46–76
Distribution: All States; NZ, South Pacific Is

Pteris — Pteridaceae

Pteris comans — Netted Brake

Size: to 1.5 m high — **N**
Habitat: Fern gullies of damp and wet sclerophyll forests
Form: Erect tufted fern
Foliage: Erect, dark green, 3- to 4-pinnate, broadly triangular lacy fronds to 1.5 m long. Pinnules are irregularly toothed and net veined. The grooved stalks are yellowish.
Requirements: Ample moisture and rich organic soils
Comments: This fern is rare in Victoria and endangered in the Melbourne region. It is difficult to maintain in cultivation as it resents disturbance.
Propagation: Spore
Localities: 57, 58
Distribution: Vic, Qld, NSW, Tas; NZ, South Pacific Is

Pteris tremula — Tender Brake

Size: 0.6–1.5 m high — **P N**
Habitat: Damp sclerophyll forest; isolated moist sites elsewhere
Form: Tufted fern sometimes with multiple crowns on old plants
Foliage: Erect, fine lacy, 2- to 4-pinnate, pale green, triangular fronds to 1.5 m long, on grooved, shiny brown stalks. Pinnules are oblong-linear, usually with fine teeth on margins. Veins are not netted.
Requirements: Moist to wet humus rich soils
Comments: A very attractive fern for a large container or protected fernery. In ideal conditions it freely colonises in gardens. Locally rare.
Propagation: Spore, division
Localities: 57, 58, 74
Distribution: Vic, Qld, NSW, Tas, SA; Norfolk Is, NZ, Poly

Pyrrosia — Polypodiaceae

Pyrrosia rupestris — Rock Felt Fern

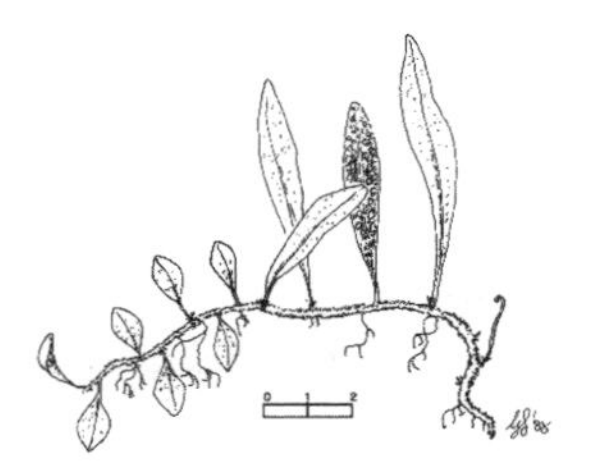
Pyrrosia rupestris

Size: Prostrate-10 cm x 20 cm — P N
Habitat: Wet sclerophyll forest
Form: An epiphytic or lithophytic mat-forming fern. The slender rhizome much branched and often exposed.
Foliage: Pale green, fleshy rounded to ovate button-like sterile fronds to 20 mm long, with lanceolate fertile fronds to 100 mm long. Covered in hairs when young, only on lower surface of frond when older.
Requirements: Ample moisture and humidity
Comments: This unusual fern is very rare in the Melbourne area, known only from two sites in the Dandenongs. It is more common in warm temperate and subtropical climates. Makes an interesting specimen in an open hanging basket on a mossy or fibrous host provided it has plenty of moisture and protection from winds. In times of drought fronds will shrivel, but swell again after rain.
Propagation: Spore, division
Localities: Wonga Park, 57
Distribution: Vic, Qld, NSW; PNG

Rumohra — Davalliaceae

Rumohra adiantiformis — Leathery Shield Fern

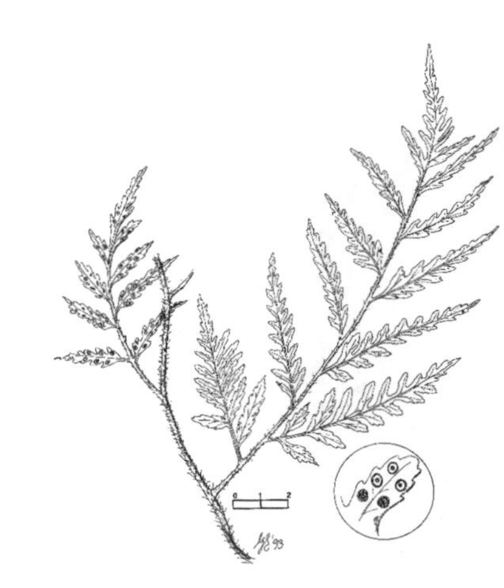
Rumohra adiantiformis

Size: Creeping or climbing epiphytic — P N
Habitat: Cool temperate rainforest
Form: Epiphytic on treefern trunks, mossy logs and boulders, or rarely terrestrial fern, sparsely foliaged with a robust hairy creeping rhizome
Foliage: Large broadly-triangular light green to shiny dark green, bipinnate to tripinnate erect or arching fronds to 50 cm long, on long grooved stalks
Requirements: Moist organic soils or a fibrous host, in humid conditions
Comments: Common on trunks of *Dicksonia antarctica*.
Propagation: Spore, division
Localities: 57,58
Distribution: Vic, Qld, NSW, Tas; NZ, Central & S Am, S Af

Schizaea — Schizaeaceae

Schizaea asperula — Rough Comb-fern

Schizaea asperula

Size: 10–40 cm high — P
Habitat: Wattle tea-tree scrub, tea-tree heath
Form: Upright tufted fern, with wiry stems and short creeping rhizome
Foliage: Distinctly rough, erect fan-shaped fronds forked several times. Sterile fronds 10–15 cm long, fertile fronds 15–30 cm long, with end segments consisting of pinnately arranged sori-bearing branches, resembling a comb.
Requirements: Dry to moist, well drained, peaty acidic soils
Comments: Does not tolerate root disturbance. It requires a symbiotic fungal relationship for successful growth. Once more widespread in Melbourne but now very restricted in its range. The three *Schizaea* species were often found growing together.
Propagation: Spores, division
Localities: Grew in Cheltenham to Sandringham area last century; 74
Distribution: Vic, NSW, Tas, SA

Schizaea bifida — Forked Comb-fern

Size: to 35 cm high — P
Habitat: Swamps in wattle tea-tree scrub, tea-tree heath
Form: Erect tufted fern with wiry stems and short rhizomes covered in glossy brown hairs
Foliage: Erect sterile fronds to 10 cm long, with simple flattened thread-like segments. Stems of fertile fronds wider, flattened and taller, to 35 cm long, similar to *S. asperula*.
Requirements: Moist to wet peaty soils
Comments: A slowly spreading fern now rare in the Melbourne area.
Propagation: Spores, division
Localities: 67#, 74
Distribution: Vic, Qld, NSW, Tas, SA; NZ

Schizaea fistulosa — Narrow Comb-fern

Size: 5–30 cm high — P
Habitat: Tea-tree heath, wattle tea-tree scrub beside swamps, often on mossy mounds
Comments: Similar to and often found with *S. bifida*. Rhizomes dark brown. Sterile fronds are simple, grass-like and few in number. Stems of fertile fronds simple and terete with a single terminal comb-shaped spore-bearing head, narrower than *S. bifida*.
Localities: Cranbourne, 67#
Distribution: All states except NT; NZ, N Cal, Mal, Madagascar, S Am

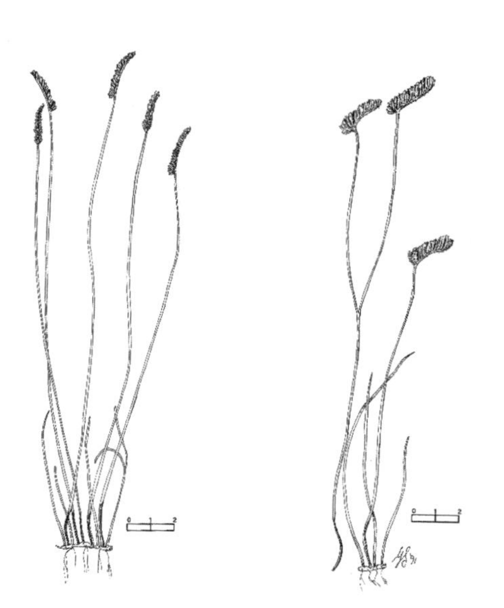
Schizaea fistulosa — *Schizaea bifida*

SCALE: 0 1cm 2cm — The scale representation on each plant equals 2cm.

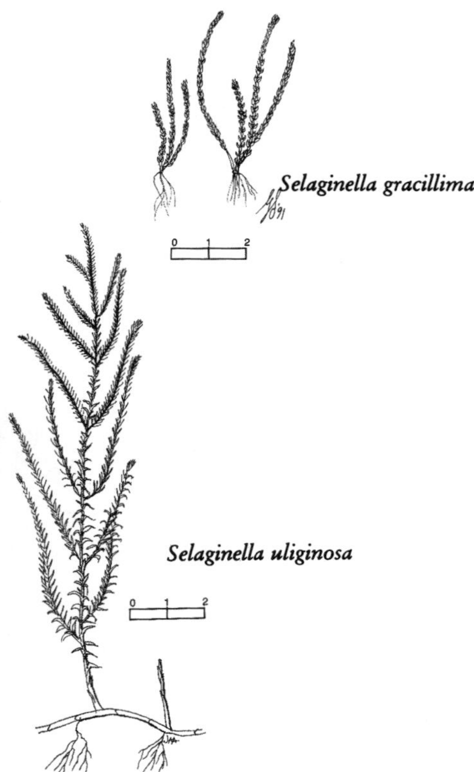

Selaginella gracillima

Selaginella uliginosa

Selaginella — Selaginellaceae

Selaginella gracillima — Tiny Selaginella or Clubmoss

Size: 2–6 cm high — P N
Habitat: Wet peaty depressions in wattle tea-tree scrub
Form: Almost moss-like wispy annual fern ally with erect stems, unbranched or branching once or twice
Foliage: Tiny pale green lanceolate leaves to 1 mm long scattered along the stem
Requirements: Ample moisture and humidity in water-holding peaty soils
Comments: Unknown in cultivation.
Propagation: Spore
Localities: Heatherton, 49, 67#, 74, 75
Distribution: All States except NT

Selaginella uliginosa — Swamp Selaginella or Clubmoss

Size: 5–25 cm x 5–30 cm — F P
Habitat: Moist depressions in swamp and wattle tea-tree scrub
Form: A soft erect rhizomatous fern-like plant, with slender pinnately branched stems
Foliage: Tiny scale-like, pale yellowish-green leaves turning red with stress. Spore cases bunched together in cone-like structures on the tips of some stems.
Requirements: Poorly drained, moist organic soils
Comments: An interesting plant, each branched stem somewhat resembling a tiny pine tree.
Propagation: Spore, division
Localities: Montrose, 49, 50A, 54, 67, 73–76
Distribution: All States except SA

Sticherus lobatus

Sticherus — Gleicheniaceae

Sticherus lobatus — Spreading Fan Fern

Size: to 1 m high — P N
Habitat: Cool temperate rainforest
Form: An erect fern with long creeping rhizomes and tough wiry stalks
Foliage: Dull green fronds, to 1 m long, are repeatedly branched, bipinnate and fan-shaped on slender stems. Pinnules, with entire margins, are arranged almost at right angles to the rhachis.
Requirements: Moist soils in a protected position
Comments: Plants generally resent disturbance and drying out. Restricted distribution in Melbourne. When growing along creeks, stems may reach 2 m high, supported by surrounding growth, and plants may cover large areas.
Propagation: Spore
Localities: Dandenong Ranges
Distribution: Vic, NT, Qld, NSW, Tas

Sticherus tener — Silky Fan Fern

Size: to 2 m high — P N
Habitat: Cool temperate rainforest, wet sclerophyll forest
Comments: Pinnules are entire, somewhat silky on the underside and arranged at an angle to the rhachis. The two local species of *Sticherus* are similar and easily confused. The angle of attachment of the pinnules to the rhachis is the major distinguishing feature. *S. tener* is much easier to cultivate, but will not tolerate drying out.
Propagation: Spore, division
Localities: 57
Distribution: Vic, NSW

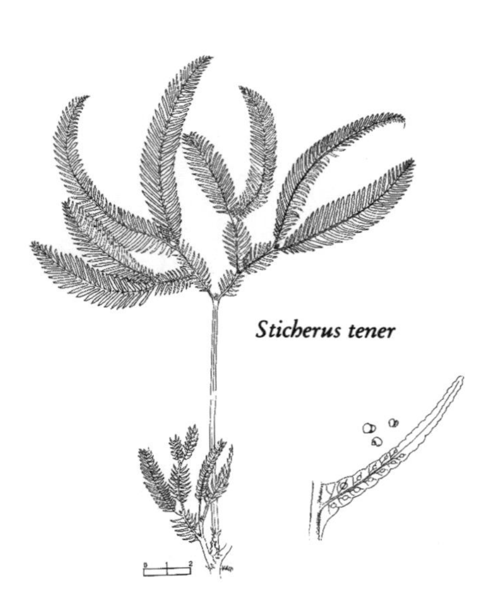

Sticherus tener

Tmesipteris — Psilotaceae

Tmesipteris billardieri — Long Fork Fern

Size: stems to 0.6 m long — N
Habitat: Cool temperate rainforest
Form: Fleshy rhizomatous epiphyte with pendulous leafy stems growing almost entirely on trunks of *Dicksonia antarctica*. The rhizomes are often deeply buried in the trunk.
Foliage: Weak flattened stems to 60 cm long are borne along the rhizome at regular intervals. The stems bear broad leaves to 25 mm long, with rounded tips and short point.
Requirements: Abundant water and high humidity
Comments: *Tmesipteris* spp. are not true ferns but a very primitive type of plant which lacks true roots. Well grown specimens can completely clothe the tops of large treeferns. This species is currently undergoing botanical revision.
Propagation: Spore
Localities: 55, 57
Distribution: Vic, NSW, Tas; Norfolk Is.

Illustrated p. 321

Tmesipteris parva

Small Fork Fern

N

Size: stems to 10 cm long
Habitat: Cool temperate rainforest
Form: Fleshy rhizomatous epiphyte with pendulous leafy stems, usually growing on trunks of *Cyathea australis*
Foliage: Fleshy tapering leaves to 15 mm long
Requirements: Abundant moisture and high humidity
Comments: Superficially similar to *T. billardieri*, but smaller in all parts. It may be distinguished by the leaves, which are narrow and curved and taper to an acute point.
Propagation: Spore
Localities: Silvan, 57
Distribution: Vic, NSW, King Is; Philippines

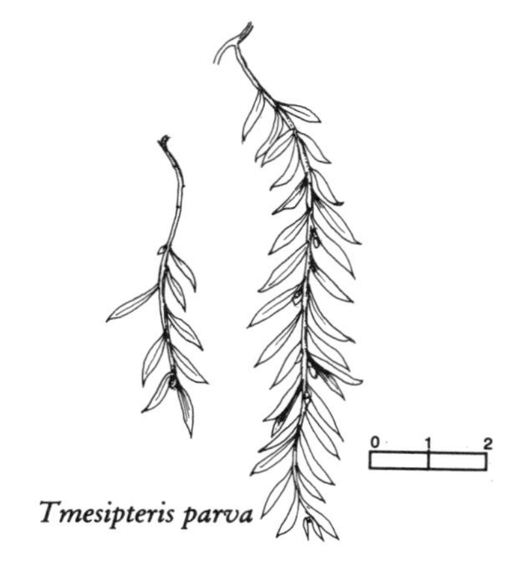

Tmesipteris parva

Todea — Osmundaceae

Todea barbara

King Fern

F P N

Size: 2–3 m x 4 m
Habitat: Wet and damp sclerophyll forests
Form: Spreading treefern-like plant with a dense crown of fronds, often with multiple crowns, from a stout, almost barrel-shaped trunk
Foliage: Upright to arching, dark green, glossy, leathery bipinnate fronds to 2.5 m long
Requirements: Moist, humus-rich soils
Comments: Very old plants can develop multi-crowned trunks rarely more than 1 m high but often up to 1.5 m wide. They are slow growing but extremely long lived. May be distinguished from other treeferns by the bipinnate rather than tripinnate fronds. Locally rare.
Propagation: Spore, transplant
Localities: 57, 58
Distribution: Vic, Qld, NSW, Tas, SA; NZ, S Af

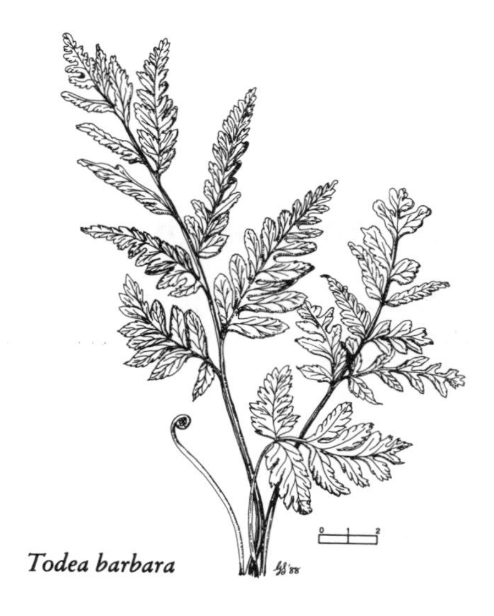

Todea barbara

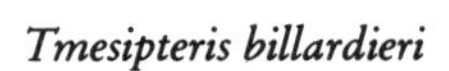

Tmesipteris billardieri

Conifer

Callitris — Cupressaceae

Callitris glaucophylla

White Cypress-pine

F

Size: 7–20 m x 5–10 m
Habitat: Plains grassland, isolated rocky scarps in box woodland
Form: Slender erect tree with a straight trunk
Foliage: Glaucous or green, leaves to 3 mm long are raised segments with rounded edges, forming branchlets
Cones: Tiny male cones borne in terminal clusters, female cones usually single or in pairs on stalks to 15 mm long, smooth, rounded to 25 mm wide, with 6 woody scales (or segments) splitting almost to the base as cone opens; Spring to early Summer. Cones usually fall once mature.
Requirements: Well drained soils, tolerating extended dry periods
Comments: An ornamental slow growing tree well known for its termite-resistant wood. Useful as a shade tree or windbreak, and for binding sand. It is depleted within Victoria mainly as a result of timber cutting and rabbit grazing. It has a very restricted range in the Melbourne area.
Propagation: Seed
Localities: Keilor, Sydenham, Sth of Melton, 15, 16, 27
Synonym: Previously included in *C. columellaris*, also confused with *C. hugelii*
Distribution: All mainland states

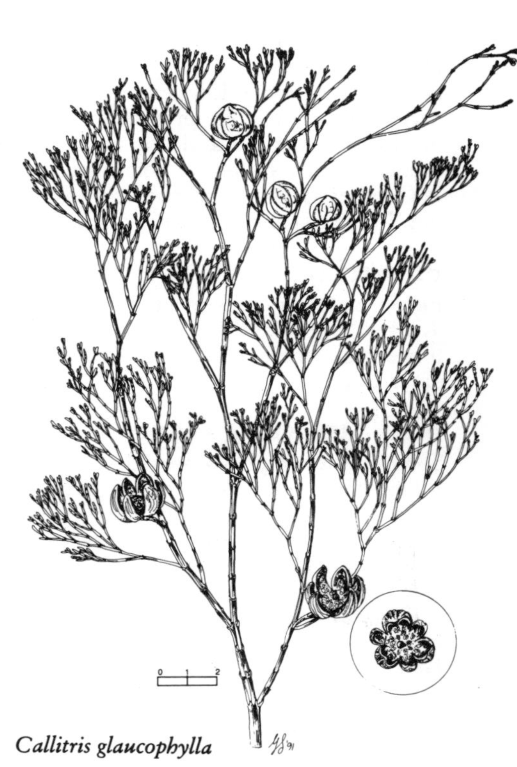

Callitris glaucophylla

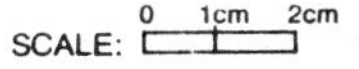

The scale representation on each plant equals 2cm.

Appendix 1. Cross Reference for Easy Plant Selection

The cross reference section should be used as an aid to find a plant or a group of plants quickly to fulfill a specific requirement. More information on each plant may then be obtained from the descriptions in the previous section.

Explanation of Key to the Cross Reference Section

Size and habit of plant

Sizes are an average and may vary according to the conditions in which a plant is grown.
The term 'tree' refers to a large woody plant with a distinct trunk.

TREE: Small—less than 8 metres high
Medium—8-15 metres high
Tall—more than 15 metres high

The term 'shrub' refers to a woody perennial plant which has several major branches growing from near the base of the plant.

SHRUB: Small—up to 1 metre high
Medium—1-2.5 metres high
Large—more than 2.5 metres high

A **Herb** does not develop a woody stem. It may be annual or perennial.
An **Annual** is a plant which flowers, seeds and dies in the one year.
A **Tuft** is a clumping plant where the leaves rise from the base of the plant. It is the common habit of grasses, lilies, irises and ferns.
A **Groundcover** is low and spreading, although it is not necessarily completely prostrate. It is always wider than its height and may be a shrub or herb, spreading from low branches or by stolons or rhizomes.
A **Climber** scrambles or twines up and/or over other plants.
An **Epiphyte** grows on other plants but is not a parasite.

Flowering Times

Flowering times are given in seasons: Summer, Autumn, Winter, Spring, Y—most of the year. The months of flowering, where known, are indicated in the individual descriptions.

Bird Attracting Plants

Some species of plants provide a rich source of nectar while others have sought-after seeds. Birds will seek insects from most plants and protection in prickly bushes. Waterbirds eat leaves, stems and/or roots of most water plants.

N—plants providing nectar
S—plants providing seeds
B—plants providing berries

Butterfly Attracting Plants

About 60 species of butterflies exist in the Melbourne area. The number of moth species is unknown but it would be in the thousands.

Indigenous vegetation is the key to the conservation of butterflies and moths. Their survival is under threat from heavy use of insecticides, clearing of native vegetation for agricultural and urban use and the invasion of native vegetation by weeds.

Butterflies require plants at 2 separate stages of their life cycle. As an adult they seek nectar-rich flowers as an energy source for flying and mating. As a caterpillar they require food for growth. This is usually, but not always, leaves.

This list is by no means complete and further information is welcome.

F—food plant for the caterpillar
N—a nectar plant for the butterfly or moth

Aspect

F—requires or tolerates full sun
P—prefers partial sun or dappled shade
N—prefers or tolerates full shade
A—will cope with all aspects

Screen or Windbreak Plants

S—may be used to screen unwanted vistas
W—will tolerate reasonable wind force and protect less sturdy plants

Soil and Drainage

D—dry, well drained soils—may be sandy, clayish or stony soils which do not accumulate water
M—moist, well drained soils—never dry out, holding water for short periods only
S—moist, swampy soils—poorly drained, includes areas subject to periodic inundation which may dry out in Summer
W—wet, boggy or waterlogged soils—remain wet all year. Includes semi-aquatic plants.
A—aquatic, in shallow or deep water

Coastal

1—plants which can withstand the full brunt of salt-laden winds
2—plants which require some protection from the strong, salty winds, either behind the front row, behind the sand dunes or a little further from the coast

Vegetation Communities

Covers the habitats found within the Melbourne region. While some plants are found in very specific locations, others may occur in a variety of habitats. (See Chapter 1 for further information.)

1 Aquatic
2 Cool temperate rainforest
3 Wet sclerophyll forest
4 Damp sclerophyll forest
5 Sclerophyll woodland
6 Swamp scrub
7 Grassy low open forest
8 Tea-tree heath
9 Wattle tea-tree scrub
10 Coastal banksia woodland
11 Primary dune scrub
12 Saltmarsh
13 Grassy wetland
14 Red gum woodland
15 Plains grassland
16 Riparian scrub
17 Chenopod rocky open scrub
18 Box ironbark woodland
19 Box woodland
20 Riparian woodland
21 Dry sclerophyll forest
22 Valley sclerophyll forest

Aboriginal Uses

* The Aborigines had a range of uses for plants. These include: food, medicine, weapons, containers, utensils, transportation.

Plant Selection List

Dicotyledons	Tree	Shrub	Other	Flowers	Bird	Butterfly	Sun Aspect	Screen Windbreak	Drainage	Coast	Vegetation Communities	Aboriginal Uses
Acacia acinacea		S-M		W-Sp	S		F P	S	D		14 17-19 21	
Acacia aculeatissima			G	W-S	S		P		D		21	
Acacia brownei		S		W-Sp	S		P		D	2	8 21	
Acacia dealbata	M-T			W-Sp	S	F	F P	W	M		3 4 7 14 16 22	*
Acacia genistifolia		M		A-Sp	S		F P		D M	2	21 22	
Acacia gunnii		S		W-Sp	S		F P		D		18 21	
Acacia implexa	S-M			S-A	S		F P	S	D M	2	14 19-22	
Acacia lanigera		S-M		A-Sp	S		F P		D		18 21	
Acacia leprosa	S-M	L		W-Sp	S		P N	S	M		4 22	
Acacia mearnsii	S-T			Sp-S	S	F	A	W	D M	1	7 14-16 20-22	*
Acacia melanoxylon	M-T			W-Sp	S	F	F P	S W	M	1	2 3 7 14-16 21 22	*
Acacia mucronata		M-L		Sp	S		F P	S	D M		4 22	
Acacia myrtifolia		M		W-Sp	S		A		D M		4 5 22	
Acacia oxycedrus		M		W-Sp	S		F P		M	2	8 21	
Acacia paradoxa		M-L		W-Sp	S		F P	S	D		7 14 15 21	
Acacia pycnantha	S-M	L		W-Sp	S		F P	S W	D	2	4 14 15 18 21 22	*
Acacia retinodes	S	L		Y	S		F P	S W	D M S	2	10 16 20	
Acacia sophorae		S-L		W-Sp	S		F	S W	D	1	7 10 11	*
Acacia stricta		M-L		W-Sp	S		A	W	D	1	7 8 10 22	
Acacia suaveolens		M		A-Sp	S		F P	W	D	2	8 9	
Acacia ulicifolia		M		A-Sp	S		P	S	M	2	7 8 22	
Acacia verniciflua		L		W-S	S		F P	S	D M S	2	4 7 22	*
Acacia verticillata	S	M-L		W-S	S		P		M S	2	3 4 9 16 22	*
Acaena agnipila			H	Sp			A		D M		13-15 21	
Acaena echinata			H	Sp			F P		D M		13-15 22	
Acaena novae-zelandiae			H G	Sp-S			A		M	1	3 6 14-16 20 22	
Acaena ovina			H	Sp			F P		D M	1	4 7 14 15 20 21	
Acrotriche prostrata			G	W	N		P N		M	2	4 5 7 22	*
Acrotriche serrulata			G	W-Sp	N		P N		D M	1	5 7 21 22	*
Actites megalocarpa			H	Sp-A			F		D	1	11	
Ajuga australis			H A	S			A		D	2	14 21 22	*
Allocasuarina littoralis	S		A	S			F P	W	D	2	7 14 21 22	*
Allocasuarina luehmannii	M		S	S			F		D		19	*
Allocasuarina paludosa		S		A-Sp	S		F		M	2	5 7 8 22	*
Allocasuarina paradoxa		S		W-Sp	S		P	S	D M	2	8	*
Allocasuarina verticillata	M			A-Sp	S		F	W	D	1	11 14 17-19	*
Almaleea subumbellata		S		Sp-S			P		M		6	
Alternanthera denticulata			H	Y			F P		M S	2	13-15 19 20 22	
Alyxia buxifolia		M		Sp-S	B		F		D	1	11	
Amperea xiphoclada		S		Sp-S			F		M	2	8 21	
Amyema linophyllum ssp. *orientale*				Sp-S	B	F	P N				19	*
Amyema miquelii				Y	B	F	P N				14 18 19	*
Amyema pendulum				S	B	F	P N			1	3 4 5 7 22	*
Amyema preissii				Sp-A	B	F	P N				11	*
Amyema quandang				Y	B	F	P N				22	*
Angianthus preissianus			H A	Sp			F		D M	1	11 12	
Aotus ericoides		M		Sp			F P		D M	2	8	
Apium annuum			H A	Sp			F		M	1	7 11 15	*
Apium prostratum ssp. *prostratum* var. *filiforme*			H	S-A			F		M W	1	10 16	*
Apium prostratum ssp. *prostratum* var. *prostratum*			H	S-A			F P		M W	1	10 16	*

	Tree	Shrub	Other	Flowers	Bird	Butterfly	Sun Aspect	Screen Windbreak	Drainage	Coast	Vegetation Communities	Aboriginal Uses
Asperula conferta			H G	Sp-S			P		D M	2	11 13-15 22	
Asperula euryphylla			H	Sp			P N		M		3 4	
Asperula scoparia			H G	Sp-S			P N		M	2	4 13 15 21	
Asterolasia asteriscophora		M		W-Sp			P		M		4 22	
Astroloma humifusum		S	G	W-Sp	N	B	F P		D	2	7 8 14 18 21	*
Atherosperma moschatum	T			A-W		F	P N		M		2 3	
Atriplex billardieri			H G				F		D	1	11	*
Atriplex cinerea		M		Sp-A			F P		D	1	11	*
Atriplex paludosa ssp. *paludosa*		S		Y			F		W	1	12 14	*
Atriplex semibaccata		S		S			F P		D	1	11 16 19	*
Atriplex suberecta			H A	Y			F		W	1	12	*
Australina pusilla ssp. *muelleri*			H G	S			P N		M		2-4	
Avicennia marina	S			S	B		F		A	1	1 12	*
Ballantinia antipoda			H A	Sp			F P		D M		13	
Banksia integrifolia	T			S-Sp	N	N	F	W	D	1	10 11	*
Banksia marginata	S	M-L		Sp-A	N	N	F P	S W	D M	1	5 7 8 16 22	*
Banksia spinulosa var. *cunninghamii*		M-L		A-W	N		F P	S W	M	2	5 22	*
Bauera rubioides		S-M	G	Y			P N		M S		3 4	
Bedfordia arborescens	S	L		Sp-S			P N		M		2 3 22	
Beyeria viscosa		L		W-S			P N	S	M		4	
Billardiera longiflora			C	W-S	N B		P		M		2 3 7 22	*
Billardiera scandens var. *brachyantha*			C	W-S	N B		P		D M		21	*
Billardiera scandens var. *scandens*			C	W-S	N B		A		D M	2	4 5 7 21 22	*
Boerhavia dominii			C G	Sp-S			F P		D	2	12	*
Boronia parviflora		S		Sp			P		M W	2	8	
Bossiaea cinerea		M		Sp			P		D M	2	8 10	
Bossiaea cordigera			G C	S	S		F P		M		5	
Bossiaea prostrata			G	Sp	S		A		D M	2	5 7 14 15 21 22	
Brachyloma ciliatum		S		Sp			F P		M	2	8	*
Brachyscome aculeata			H	Sp-A		N	F P		M		16	
Brachyscome basaltica var. *gracilis*			H	Sp		N	F		D M		13 15	
Brachyscome cardiocarpa			H T	W-Sp		N	F P		S	2	6 8 13	
Brachyscome ciliaris			H	W-S		N	F		D		15	
Brachyscome decipiens			H	Sp-S		N	F P		M S	2	14 15 21 22	
Brachyscome dentata			H	Sp		N	F		D M		13 15 16 19	
Brachyscome diversifolia var. *diversifolia*			H T	Sp-S		N	F P		D	1	10 11 21	
Brachyscome exilis			H	Sp-S		N	F P		S		13	
Brachyscome graminea			H	Y		N	F P		S	2	8 13 16	
Brachyscome leptocarpa			H A	Sp		N	F		D		15	
Brachyscome multifida var. *multifida*			H G	Y		N	F P		D M		19 21	
Brachyscome parvula var. *parvula*			H T	Sp-S		N	F		S	1	11	
Brachyscome perpusilla			H A	W-Sp		N	F		M		13	
Brachyscome scapigera			H T	Sp-S		N	F		D M		21	
Brachyscome spathulata			H	Sp-A		N	F P		D M		16	
Brachyscome trachycarpa			H	Y		N	F P		D M		15	
Brachyscome uliginosa			H	Sp-S		N	F		S		22	
Bracteantha bracteata			H A	Sp-A		N	F		D M	2	8 21	
Bracteantha viscosa			H	Sp-A		N	F P		D		14 19 21	
Brunonia australis			H	Sp-S		N	F P		D M	2	8 14 15 21 22	
Bursaria spinosa var. *macrophylla*	S	M-L		S		N F	F P	S	D M		15 16	
Bursaria spinosa var. *spinosa*	S	M-L		S		N F	F P	S	D M	1	7 11 14 16 20-22	
Calandrinia calyptrata			A	W-Sp			F		D	1	10 11 14 17 19	*
Calandrinia eremaea			A	W-Sp			F		D			
Callistemon sieberi	S	L		S-A	N S	N	F P	S	M S		16	
Callitriche brachycarpa			H	Sp-S			P		W		16 22	
Callitriche cyclocarpa			H	Sp-S			P		A		1	
Callitriche muelleri			H	Sp-S			P N		W A		1	
Callitriche palustris			H	Sp-S			P		A		1 16 22	
Callitriche umbonata			H	Sp-S			P		W A		1 13	
Calocephalus citreus			H	Sp-S		N	F P		D M		14 15	
Calocephalus lacteus		S		Sp-S		N	F P		D M		14 15 21	
Calotis anthemoides			H	Sp			F P		M S		15	
Calotis cymbacantha			A	A W-Sp			F P		D		15	
Calotis lappulacea			H	Y			F P		D		19	
Calotis scabiosifolia var. *scabiosifolia*			H	Sp			F P		M		14 15	
Calotis scabiosifolia var. *integrifolia*			H	Sp			P		M		21	
Calotis scapigera			H	Y			F P		M		13 14	
Calystegia marginata			C	Sp-S			P N		M S		4 22	
Calystegia sepium			C	Sp-S			P		M		13 16 22	

	Tree	Shrub	Other	Flowers	Bird	Butterfly	Sun Aspect	Screen Windbreak	Drainage	Coast	Vegetation Communities	Aboriginal Uses
Calytrix tetragona		M		Sp		N	F P		D		16	
Cardamine gunnii			H	Sp-S			P		M W		2 8	*
Cardamine paucijuga			H	W-Sp			P		D M		6 16	*
Cardamine tenuifolia			H	S			P		W S		15 22	*
Carpobrotus modestus			G	Sp-S			F		D		17	*
Carpobrotus rossii			G	Sp-S			F P		D	1	10 11	*
Cassinia aculeata		L		S			P		M	1	3-5 7 21 22	
Cassinia arcuata		M		S			F P		D	2	7 18 19 21 22	
Cassinia longifolia		L		S			P N		M	2	7 14 18 19 21 22	
Cassinia trinerva		L		S			P		M		3 4	
Cassytha glabella			C	Sp		F	F P			2	4 8 9 22	*
Cassytha melantha			C	W-Sp		F	F P		D	2	4 10 19 21 22	*
Cassytha pubescens			C	S-A		F	F P			2	4 8 14 21 22	*
Centella cordifolia			G	W-S			F P		S		4 6 7 16 21 22	
Centipeda cunninghamii			H	S-A			F P		M S	2	7 13 16	*
Centipeda minima			H	S-A			P		S		6 14 22	*
Ceratophyllum demersum			H	S					A		1	
Chenopodium desertorum ssp. *microphyllum*			H	W-Sp		F	F		S W		17	
Chenopodium glaucum			A	A-W		F	F P		M	1	11 12 15	
Chenopodium pumilio			A	S-W		F	F		S W		13 16	
Chrysocephalum apiculatum			H	Y		N	F		D M	2	8 14 19	
Chrysocephalum semipapposum			H	S-A		N	F P		D M		4 14 15 19 21	
Ciclospermum leptophyllum			A	S			P N		M		16	
Clematis aristata			C	W-S			A		D M		3 4 7 22	
Clematis microphylla			C	W-Sp			F P		D M	1	7 10 11 15 18-21	
Comesperma calymega		S		S			F P		D M	2	8	
Comesperma ericinum		M		S			P		D M	2	8 22	
Comesperma polygaloides		S		Sp-S			F		D		14 15	
Comesperma volubile			C	W-Sp			P		D M	2	7 8 21 22	
Convolvulus erubescens			C G	Sp-S			F		D	2	4 8 14 15 21	*
Convolvulus remotus			G	Sp-S			F		D		14 15	
Coprosma hirtella		M		Sp	B		P		M		3 4 22	
Coprosma quadrifida		M		Sp	B		P N		M		2-6	*
Correa alba		M		Y	N		F P	S	D	1	11	
Correa glabra		M		Y	N		A	S	D		16	
Correa reflexa		M		A-W	N		A		D M	2	4 5 7 8 21 22	
Correa reflexa x *glabra*		M		A-W	N		F P		D		21	
Cotula australis			H G	Sp-S			P N		M	1	5 10 14 16 21	
Cotula vulgaris var. *australasica*			A	Sp			F P		W	2	8 12	
Craspedia variabilis			T	Sp		N	F P		M S	2	5 7 8 13 14 16 21 22	
Crassula colorata var. *acuminata*			A	Sp			F		W		7 15 17	
Crassula decumbens var. *decumbens*			A	Sp			P		W	1	8 11 14 22	
Crassula helmsii			H	S-A			F		W A		1 7 16 20 22	
Crassula pedicellosa			A	Sp			F P		M		8 13	
Crassula peduncularis			A	S			P N		S	1	10 19	
Crassula sieberiana ssp. *sieberiana*			H	Sp-W			F P		S W	2	8 13-17 19	
Crassula sieberiana ssp. *tetramera*			A	Sp			P		W	2	8 22	
Cryptandra amara var. *amara*		S		W-Sp			F P		D		19	
Cuscuta tasmanica			C	S-A			F			1	12	
Cymbonotus lawsonianus			H	Sp			F		M		14 15 22	
Cymbonotus preissianus			H	Sp			P N		M	2	4 7 14 21	
Cynoglossum australe			H	Sp-S			F P		D		15	
Cynoglossum latifolium		S		Y			P		M S		3 4	
Cynoglossum suaveolens			H	Y			F P		D M	2	4 10 15 21	
Dampiera stricta			H G	A			F P		M		8 21	
Daucus glochidiatus			A	Sp			F P		D	1	10 15 21 22	
Daviesia latifolia		M		Sp			F P		D M	2	4 7 21 22	
Daviesia leptophylla		M		Sp-S			F P		D	2	5 10 21 22	
Daviesia ulicifolia		M		W-Sp			P		D M	2	8 16 21	
Derwentia derwentiana		S		S			P N		M		3 16 22	
Desmodium gunnii		S	G	Y			P		M		4 13 22	
Desmodium varians		S		W-Sp			F P		D		15 21	
Dichondra repens			H G	Sp			P N		M	2	7 10 15 16 20-22	
Dillwynia cinerascens		M		W-Sp			P		D	2	8 15 21 22	
Dillwynia glaberrima		M		Sp			F P		D M	2	7 8 22	
Dillwynia hispida		S		Sp			P		M	2	8	
Dillwynia juniperina		M		Sp			P		D		14	
Dillwynia phylicoides		M		Sp			P		D		21	
Dillwynia sericea		M		Sp			F P		D	2	5 8 21	

	Tree	Shrub	Other	Flowers	Bird	Butterfly	Sun Aspect	Screen Windbreak	Drainage	Coast	Vegetation Communities	Aboriginal Uses
Disphyma crassifolium ssp. *clavellatum*			G	Sp-S			F		D	1	10 12	*
Dodonaea viscosa ssp. *spatulata*		M		Sp			F P	S	D M		7 16 19 21	
Drosera binata			H	Sp-A			F P		W	2	8 22	
Drosera glanduligera			H	W-Sp			F P		S	2	8 14	
Drosera macrantha			H	W-Sp			F P		S	2	4-8 22	
Drosera peltata ssp. *auriculata*			H	Sp			F P		S	2	5 7-9 21 22	
Drosera peltata ssp. *peltata*			H	Sp			F P		S	2	8 14 15 21 22	
Drosera pygmaea			H	W-S			F		S	2	6 7	
Drosera spathulata			H	Y			P		S	2	6 8	
Drosera whittakeri			H	W-Sp			F P		S	2	7 8 14 15 21 22	
Eclipta platyglossa			H	Sp-S			F P		S		13	
Einadia hastata		S		S			F P		D	1	8 11 14 16-20	
Einadia nutans ssp. *nutans*			G	S-A			F P		D	1	11 14 16 17 19-21	
Einadia trigonos			G	S			P		M		14	
Elatine gratioloides			A G	Y			F		W A		1 13-15 19	
Enchylaena tomentosa		S	G	Sp-S			F P		D M	1	11 14-17 19	*
Epacris gunnii		S		A-Sp	N		P		M		6 22	
Epacris impressa		S		A-Sp	N		P		D M	1	4 5 7-9 21 22	
Epacris obtusifolia		M		W-Sp	N	N	P		M S	2	8	
Epilobium billardierianum ssp. *billardierianum*			H	S			F P		M S	2	6 9 14 16 21 22	
Epilobium billardierianum ssp. *cinereum*			H	S			F P		M S W	2	4 6 22	
Epilobium hirtigerum			H	S			F P		M S		5 7 14-16 22	
Eremophila deserti		L		A-Sp	B		F		D		19	
Erodium crinitum			H	W-Sp			F P		D	2	8 10 15	*
Eryngium ovinum			H	Sp-S			F		M		14 15	
Eryngium vesiculosum			H	Sp-S			F P		S		6 13 22	
Eucalyptus albens	M-T			A-W	N S F		F P	W	D		19	*
Eucalyptus baueriana	M-T			Sp-S	N S F		F	W S	M		16 19	*
Eucalyptus baxteri	M-T			S-A	N S F		F P	W	D M		4 22	*
Eucalyptus blakelyi	T			Sp-S	N S F		F P	W S	M		18	*
Eucalyptus camaldulensis	M-T			S	N S F		F		D M S	2	14-16 20	*
Eucalyptus camphora	M			A	N S F		F P	W	S		22	*
Eucalyptus cephalocarpa	M-T			A-Sp	N S F		F P	W	M S	2	4 5 7 9 22	*
Eucalyptus cypellocarpa	M-T			S-W	N S F		F P		M		3 4	*
Eucalyptus dives	M-T			Sp	N S F		F P	W S	D M		5 22	*
Eucalyptus globoidea	M-T			Y	N S F		F P		M S		22	*
Eucalyptus goniocalyx	M-T			A-W	N S F		F P	W	D		4 21 22	*
Eucalyptus ignorabilis	M-T			S-A	N S F		F	W	M		22	*
Eucalyptus leucoxylon ssp. *connata*	M-T			W-Sp	N S F		F P	W	D M		14 17-19 21	*
Eucalyptus macrorhyncha	M-T			S-A	N S F		F P		D		18 21 22	*
Eucalyptus melliodora	M-T			Sp-A	N S F	N	F P	W	D M	2	14 19 21 22	*
Eucalyptus microcarpa	M-T			S-W	N S F		F	W	D		17 19	*
Eucalyptus nortonii	M			Sp	N S F		F P	W	M		14	*
Eucalyptus obliqua	S-T			S-A	N S F		F P	W	M	2	3-5 7 21 22	*
Eucalyptus ovata	M-T			A-W	N S F		F P	W S	S	2	4 6 7 14-16 20 22	*
Eucalyptus pauciflora ssp. *pauciflora*	S-M			Sp-S	N S F		F P	W	D M	2	14 21	*
Eucalyptus polyanthemos ssp. *vestita*	S-T			Sp-S	N S F		F P	W S	D		21 22	*
Eucalyptus pryoriana	S-M			A-W	N S F		F	W S	D	1	7 8	*
Eucalyptus radiata	M-T			Sp-S	N S F		F P	W	D M		4 5 7 22	*
Eucalyptus regnans	T			S-W	N S F		F		M		2 3	
Eucalyptus rubida ssp. *rubida*	M-T			Sp-S	N S F		F P		D		21 22	
Eucalyptus tricarpa	M-T			W-S	N S F		F P	W	D		18 21	*
Eucalyptus viminalis	M-T			S-A	N S F		F P	W	M	2	3 6 7 20 22	*
Eucalyptus yarraensis	M			S	N S F		F P	W S	M S		22	*
Euchiton gymnocephalus			H	Y			F P		M	2	9 16 22	
Euchiton involucratus			H	Y			F P		M	1	10 16 19 21 22	
Euchiton sphaericus			A H	W-S			F P		M		15 19 22	
Euphorbia drummondii			A G	Sp			F		D		12 15 19	
Euphrasia collina ssp. *collina*			H	W-S			F P		M	2	5 8	
Euphrasia collina ssp. *muelleri*			H	W-Sp			F P		M		8	
Euphrasia collina ssp. *paludosa*			H	Sp-S			P		S		6 22	
Euphrasia collina ssp. *trichocalycina*			H	W-Sp			F		M		21	
Euphrasia scabra			H	Sp-A			F P		M		11 12	
Eutaxia diffusa		S		Sp			F		D	1	11 19	
Eutaxia microphylla var. *microphylla*		S	G	Sp			A		D M S		14 15	
Exocarpos cupressiformis	L			Y		F	F P	S	D M	1	4 7 8 14 18 19 21 22	*
Exocarpos stricta	M			W-Sp		F	F P		D	1	4 7 14 21 22	
Frankenia pauciflora		S	G	Y			F P		D	1	11 12	
Galium australe			H	S			P		M		7 16 22	
Galium binifolium			A	Sp			P		M		4	
Galium ciliare			H	Sp-S			P		D M		5	

	Tree	Shrub	Other	Flowers	Bird	Butterfly	Sun Aspect	Screen Windbreak	Drainage	Coast	Vegetation Communities	Aboriginal Uses
Galium compactum			H	Sp-S			F		D		21	
Galium gaudichaudii			H	Sp-S			P		M		3 4 7 16 22	
Galium migrans			H	Sp			P		M		16 20 22	
Galium propinquum			H	Sp-S			P N		M	2	7 10 19 20 22	
Geranium potentilloides			H	Sp-A			P N		M		4 5 22	*
Geranium retrorsum			H	W-S			P		M		14 15 19 20	
Geranium solanderi			H	Sp-S			P		M S		7 14 16 21 22	*
Glossostigma elatinoides			H G	S-A			F		W A		19	
Glycine clandestina			H C	Sp-S		F	P N		M	2	8 14 21 22	
Glycine latrobeana			G	Sp-S		F	F P		D		15 19 21	
Glycine microphylla			C	Sp-A		F	P N		M		4	
Glycine tabacina			C	S-A		F	F P		D		14-16 21	
Glycyrrhiza acanthocarpa			H	Sp-S			F P		M			
Gnaphalium indutum			H	Sp-S			F		D	2	7 10 13 14	
Gompholobium huegelii		S		Sp-S			P		D M	2	5 8 21	
Gonocarpus elatus			H	Sp-S			F P		D M		19	
Gonocarpus humilis		S		Sp-S			P		S		4 7 22	
Gonocarpus micranthus			G	S			P		S W	2	6 8 9	
Gonocarpus tetragynus			H	S			F P		D M	2	5 7-9 14 15 21 22	
Goodenia blackiana			H	Sp-S			F P		D M		21 22	
Goodenia elongata			H	Sp-S			P		M	2	6 8 22	
Goodenia geniculata			H	W-S			F P		M S	2	7 8	
Goodenia gracilis			H	Sp-S			F		S		13	
Goodenia heteromera			H	Sp-A			F P		S		13	
Goodenia humilis			H	Sp-S			F		M S	2	6 9	
Goodenia lanata			H	Sp-S			F P		D M		4 5 22	
Goodenia ovata		M		W-S			A		M S	1	3 4 7 14 19 22	
Goodenia pinnatifida			H	Sp-A			F		M	2	13-15	
Goodia lotifolia		M-L		Sp	S	F	F P		D M		4 21	
Gratiola peruviana			H G	Sp-A			P N		S	2	7 16 22	
Gratiola pubescens			H G	Sp-S			P		S		6	
Grevillea alpina		M		W-S	N		P		D M		21	
Grevillea infecunda		S	G	Sp S	N		F P		D	2	8	
Grevillea rosmarinifolia		M		W-Sp	N		F P		D M		15 21	
Gynatrix pulchella		M-L		W-Sp			P		M		4 15 16 22	*
Hakea nodosa		M-L		A-W	N		A	S	M S	2	5 6 22	
Hakea sericea		L		W-Sp	N	N	F P		D		5 19 22	
Hakea teretifolia ssp. *hirsuta*		L		Sp-S	N		F	S	M		5	
Hakea ulicina		M-L		W-Sp	N		F P		D M	2	5 8 21 22	
Haloragis aspera			H	Sp-A			F P		M		15 19	
Haloragis heterophylla			H	Sp-S			F P		S		15 16	
Halosarcia halocnemoides ssp. *halocnemoides*		S		S-A			F		W	1	12	
Halosarcia pergranulata ssp. *pergranulata*		S		S-A			F		W	1	12	
Hardenbergia violacea			C	W-Sp			F P		D	2	14 21 22	
Hedycarya angustifolia	S	L		Sp			N		M		2-4	*
Helichrysum leucopsideum			H	Sp-A		N	F P		D M		5 10	
Helichrysum rutidolepis			H	Sp		N	F P		M		13-15 21	
Helichrysum scorpioides			H G	Sp-S		N	F P		D M	2	5 8 21	
Hemichroa pentandra			H	Sp			F		W	1	12	
Hibbertia acicularis		S		Sp-S		F	F P		D M	2	5 8	
Hibbertia empetrifolia		S	G	Sp		F	F P		M		22	
Hibbertia obtusifolia		S		W-S		F	P		D		18 21	
Hibbertia prostrata		S		Sp		F	F P		M	2	8	
Hibbertia riparia		S		Sp-S		F	F P		M		5 7 8 22	
Hibbertia sericea var. *sericea*		S		Sp		F	F P		M	2	8	
Hibbertia stricta var. *stricta*		S		W-Sp		F	A		M	2	5 8 22	
Hibbertia virgata var. *virgata*		S		W-Sp		F	F P		M		8	
Hovea linearis		S		Sp			P N		D M	2	8 21 22	
Hydrocotyle callicarpa			A	Sp			A		M	1	7 11 22	
Hydrocotyle capillaris			A	Sp			F P		M		12 15 21	
Hydrocotyle foveolata			A	Sp			P		M S		8 22	
Hydrocotyle geraniifolia			H G	S			P N		M S		3 22	
Hydrocotyle hirta			H G	S			P		S		3 4 6 9 22	
Hydrocotyle laxiflora			H G	Sp			P N		S	2	20-22	
Hydrocotyle medicaginoides			A	Sp			P		S		9	
Hydrocotyle muscosa			H G	Sp-A			P		S W		7	
Hydrocotyle sibthorpioides			H G	Y			P		S		13 22	
Hydrocotyle tripartita			H	S-A			P		S W	2	7 19	
Hydrocotyle verticillata			H	S-A			P		S W	1	9 16 22	
Hymenanthera dentata		M-L		Sp			F P		M		14-16 19	
Hymenanthera sp. aff. *dentata*		S		Sp			F		D		15	

	Tree	Shrub	Other	Flowers	Bird	Butterfly	Sun Aspect	Screen Windbreak	Drainage	Coast	Vegetation Communities	Aboriginal Uses
Hypericum gramineum			H	Sp-S			F P		M S	2	5 7 9 14 15 21 22	
Hypericum japonicum			H	Sp-S			P		S	2	4 6 9	
Indigofera australis		M		Sp		F	A		D M		4 7 16 22	*
Isoetopsis graminifolia			A T	W-Sp			F		D		15	
Isopogon ceratophyllus		S		Sp			F P		M	2	8	
Isotoma fluviatilis ssp. *australis*			G	Sp			F P		S W		9 15 16	
Ixiolaena leptolepis			H	Sp		N	F		D		15	
Ixiolaena sp.		S		Sp-S			F		M		15	
Kennedia prostrata			G	A-S		F	F P		D	2	7 8 14-16 21 22	*
Kunzea ericoides		L		S		N	F P	S	D M		21 22	
Lagenifera gracilis			H	Sp-S			F P		M		7 9 21 22	
Lagenifera huegelii			H	Sp-A			F P		M		19 21	
Lagenifera stipitata			H	Sp-A			F P		M	2	3 4 7-9 22	
Lasiopetalum baueri		M		Sp-S			F		D	1	11	
Lavatera plebeia var. *plebeia*		S-M		W-Sp			F		D	1	12 16	
Lavatera plebeia var. *tomentosa*		S-M		Y			F		D	1	11	
Lawrencia spicata		S		Sp-S			F		S	1	8 12	
Lepidium aschersonii			H	Sp			F		S	2	12	*
Lepidium pseudohyssopifolium			H	W-Sp			F P		D M	1	15 16 19	*
Lepidium pseudotasmanicum			H	W-Sp			P		M		16	*
Leptinella reptans			H G	Y			F P		W	1	10 16	
Leptorhynchos elongatus			H A	Sp			F		D		21	
Leptorhynchos squamatus			H	Sp-S			F P		M		14 15 22	
Leptorhynchos tenuifolius			H	Sp-S			F P		D M	2	7 8 14 15 21 22	
Leptospermum continentale		M-L		Sp-A		N	F P		M S	2	5-9 22	*
Leptospermum grandifolium	S	M-L		Sp-S		N	F P	S	S W		4	*
Leptospermum laevigatum	S	L		Sp		N	F P	S W	D M	1	7 8 10 11	*
Leptospermum lanigerum	S	M-L		Sp-S		N	F P	S	S	2	8 16 20 22	*
Leptospermum myrsinoides		S-M		Sp		N	F P		M S	2	5 8 22	
Leptospermum obovatum		M-L		S		N	P	S	S		16	
Leptostigma reptans			H G	S			P N		S W		22	
Leucochrysum albicans ssp. *albicans* var. *albicans*			H	Sp-A		N	F P		D		21	
Leucophyta brownii		S	G	Sp-S			F P		D	1	11	
Leucopogon australis		S		Sp			P		M	1	8	*
Leucopogon ericoides		S		W-Sp			P		D		8 21	*
Leucopogon parviflorus		S-M		W-Sp			F P	S W	D	1	10 11	*
Leucopogon virgatus var. *virgatus*		S		W-S			F P		D	2	7 8 21	*
Levenhookia dubia			H	Sp			P		M	2	8 13 22	
Levenhookia sonderi			H	Sp			F P		M S	2	8 13 22	
Lilaeopsis polyantha			H	Sp-A			F P		W A	1	1 11 12	
Limonium australe			H				F		S W	1	12	
Limosella australis			G H	Sp			F		S W		6	
Linum marginale		S		Sp-A			F P		M	2	8 13 14 21	*
Lissanthe strigosa		S		Sp			P		D		21	*
Lobelia alata			H	Y			F P		M S	2	5 8 16 22	
Lobelia gibbosa			A	S			P		M	2	8	
Lobelia pratioides			H G	S			P		W		13 15 22	
Lobelia rhombifolia			A G	Sp			P		S W		4	
Lobelia simplicicaulis			H	S			F P		M	2	8 21 22	
Lomatia fraseri	S	L		S			P N		M		3 4	
Lomatia ilicifolia		S-M		S			F P		D		4 5 7 21	
Lomatia myricoides	S	M		S			P N		M		16	
Lotus australis			H	S-A		F	F		D M		15	
Lycopus australis			H	S-A			P N		S W		10 16 22	
Lysiana exocarpi				S-Sp	B	F	F P				19	*
Lythrum hyssopifolia			A	S-A			F P		M S	2	6 7 13 14 16 22	
Lythrum salicaria		S-M	H	S			F		S		16 22	
Maireana brevifolia		S		S-W			F		D		16 19	
Maireana decalvans		S		S-A			F P		S		15 19	
Maireana enchylaenoides			H	Sp-S			F		D		19	
Maireana pentagona			H	Sp			F P		M		15	
Mazus pumilio			H G	Sp-S			A		S W		8 21	
Melaleuca ericifolia	S	M-L		Sp	N	N	F P	S W	M S	2	6 9 10 14 22	*
Melaleuca lanceolata	S	L		Sp-S	N	N	F	S W	D M S	1	11 16 20	*
Melaleuca parvistaminea		M-L		Sp	N	N	F P	S W	S		6 16	*
Melaleuca squarrosa		M-L		Sp-S	N	N	F P		S W	2	4 6 9 22	*

	Tree	Shrub	Other	Flowers	Bird	Butterfly	Sun Aspect	Screen Windbreak	Drainage	Coast	Vegetation Communities	Aboriginal Uses
Mentha australis			H G	Sp-S			A		S W		16 22	*
Mentha diemenica var. *diemenica*			H	S			A		S		13 14	*
Mentha laxiflora			H G	Sp-S			P N		S		3 4 22	*
Mentha satureoides			H	S			P N		S		13 14	*
Microseris lanceolata			H T	W-Sp		N	P		D M	2	14 15 21	*
Millotia myosotidifolia			A	W			F P		D		14	
Millotia tenuifolia			A	Sp			F		D	1	11	
Mimulus repens			H G	Sp-A			F P		S W	2	12 13 16	
Minuria leptophylla			H	Y			F		D		15	
Mitrasacme distylis			A	Sp						1		
Mitrasacme paradoxa			A	Sp			P		D	1	11 21	
Monotoca scoparia		M		A			F P		M	2	8 21	*
Montia fontana			H T	Sp			P		S W		6	
Muehlenbeckia adpressa			C	Sp	B		F		D	1	10 11	*
Muehlenbeckia florulenta		M		Y			F		S	2	12 13 16	
Muellerina eucalyptoides			C	Sp-S	B	F	F P				3 4 7 14 19 22	
Myoporum insulare		M-L		Sp	B		F	S W	D	1	10 11	*
Myoporum parvifolium			G	S	B		A		D	2	12 13	*
Myoporum viscosum		S-M		Sp	B		F		D	1	11 16 17	*
Myosotis australis			A	Sp			F		D		7 21	
Myosotis exarrhena			H	Sp					D			
Myriocephalus rhizocephalus			A	Sp			P		M		13 14	
Myriophyllum amphibium			H	S			P		S W		9 14 21	
Myriophyllum caput-medusae			H	S			F P		A		1 16	
Myriophyllum crispatum			H	Sp-A			F P		W A		7 13 22	
Myriophyllum integrifolium			A	Sp			P		S W		13	
Myriophyllum muelleri			A	Sp			F P		A		1 13	
Myriophyllum salsugineum			H	Sp-S			F P		A		1	
Myriophyllum simulans			H	Sp			F P		A		1 9 13	
Myriophyllum variifolium			H	Sp-S			F P		A		1 8 13 22	
Myriophyllum verrucosum			H	Sp-A			F P		A		1 4 13	
Neopaxia australasica			H	G S			F P		S W A	1	1 6 8 13	
Nicotiana maritima			A	Y					D		14	
Nicotiana suaveolens			A	A-W			F		D		16 19	
Notelaea ligustrina	S	M-L		Sp	B		P N	S	M		2 3	
Olearia argophylla	S	M-L		Sp			P N		M		2-4 22	
Olearia asterotricha		S-M		S			P		M S		7 22	
Olearia axillaris		S-M		S-A			F		D	1	11	
Olearia ciliata		S		Sp			F P		D	2	8	
Olearia decurrens		S-M		S			F P		D		15 19	
Olearia erubescens		S		Sp			F P		D		4 21	
Olearia glandulosa		S-M		S-A			F P		S		6	
Olearia glutinosa		M		S			F		D	1	11	
Olearia lirata		M-L		Sp			P N		M		4 7 22	
Olearia myrsinoides		S-M		Sp-S			F P		D M		21 22	
Olearia phlogopappa var. *phlogopappa*		S-M		Sp-S			F P		D		22	
Olearia ramulosa var. *ramulosa*		S-M		Sp-A			F P		D	2	4 7 8 11 14	
Olearia rugosa		S-M		Sp			P		M		4	
Opercularia ovata			H	Sp			F P		M	2	7 14 21 22	
Opercularia varia			H	Sp			P N		M	2	7-9 21 22	
Oreomyrrhis eriopoda			H	Sp			F P		D		19 21	
Oxalis exilis			H	Y			F P		M S		4 7 16 19 22	
Oxalis perennans			H	Y			F P		M S		13-15 22	
Oxalis radicosa			H	A-Sp			F P		D		19	
Ozothamnus ferrugineus	S	M-L		Sp-S			F P		M	2	3 4 6 7 9 14 22	
Ozothamnus obcordatus		S-M		Sp-S			F P		D		18 19 21	
Ozothamnus rosmarinifolius		M-L		S			F P		M		6	
Ozothamnus turbinatus		S-M		A			F		D	1	11	
Pandorea pandorana			C	Sp			F P		M		3 4 7 21 22	
Parietaria debilis			A	Sp			A		M	1	10 16 22	
Parsonsia brownii			C	Sp			P N		M		2 3	
Pelargonium australe			H	Sp-S			F P		D	2	4 10 11 16 22	
Pelargonium inodorum			A	Sp-S			F P		D		7 21 22	
Pelargonium rodneyanum			H	S			F P		D		15	
Persicaria decipiens			A	Y	S		A		W A	2	4 8 14 16 20 22	
Persicaria hydropiper			A	S	S		F P		W A		16 19 22	*
Persicaria lapathifolia			A	Y	S		F P		S W		22	
Persicaria praetermissa			H	S-A	S		P		S W		22	
Persicaria prostrata			H	Sp-W	S		F P		S W		13 15 22	
Persicaria subsessilis			H/A		S		F P		S W		16	

	Tree	Shrub	Other	Flowers	Bird	Butterfly	Sun Aspect	Screen Windbreak	Drainage	Coast	Vegetation Communities	Aboriginal Uses
Persoonia juniperina		S-M		S	N		F P		D M	2	7 8 21 22	*
Pimelea axiflora ssp. *axiflora*		M		Sp		N	P N		M		3 4 22	*
Pimelea curviflora var. *sericea*		S		Sp-S		N	F P		D M		4 14 15 21 22	
Pimelea flava ssp. *flava*		S-M		Sp		N	P N		M		4 22	
Pimelea glauca		S		W-S		N	F P		D	2	11 15	
Pimelea humilis		S		Sp-S		N	F P		M	2	7 8 14 21 22	
Pimelea ligustrina ssp. *ligustrina*		S-M		Sp		N	P N		M		3 4	
Pimelea linifolia ssp. *linifolia*		S		W-S		N	F P		D		16 22	
Pimelea micrantha		S		Sp		N	F P		D		16	
Pimelea octophylla ssp. *octophylla*		S		Sp		N	F P		D	2	5 8	
Pimelea pauciflora		M		Sp		N	F P		M		22	*
Pimelea phylicoides		S		Sp-S		N	F		D	2	5 8	
Pimelea spinescens ssp. *spinescens*		S		A-Sp		N	F		D		15	
Pittosporum bicolor	S-M	L		Sp	S		P N		M		3 4	
Plantago debilis			H	Y		F	P		M		4 7 22	
Plantago gaudichaudii			H	Sp		F	F		M		14 15	
Plantago hispida			H	Sp		F	F		D		19	
Plantago varia			H	Y		F	F P		D	2	4 7 14 21 22	
Platylobium formosum		S-M		Sp			F P		M		4 8 22	
Platylobium obtusangulum		S		Sp			F P		D	2	5 7 8 14 21 22	
Platysace heterophylla			H	Sp-S			P		M	2	7 8	
Platysace lanceolata		S-M		S			P		D		21	
Podolepis jaceoides			T	Sp		N	F P		D		8 13-15 22	*
Podotheca angustifolia			A	Sp			F		D	2	10	
Polygonum plebeium			A	S	S		F P		W		13?	
Polyscias sambucifolius	S	M-L		Sp-S			P N		M		3 4 22	
Pomaderris aspera	M	L		Sp-S		F	P N		M		3 4 16 22	*
Pomaderris elachophylla		M-L		Sp			P		M		22	
Pomaderris elliptica		M-L		Sp			P		M		22	
Pomaderris ferruginea		M-L		Sp			F P		M		22	
Pomaderris lanigera		M		Sp			F P		M		21 22	
Pomaderris paniculosa ssp. *paralia*		S-M		Sp			F P		D	1	10	
Pomaderris prunifolia		M-L		Sp			A		M		22	
Pomaderris racemosa		M-L		Sp			A		D M		16	
Pomaderris vacciniifolia		M-L		Sp			F P		M		22	
Poranthera microphylla			A	Sp			F P		D M	2	7 14 19 21 22	
Portulaca oleracea			A G	Sp-S			F		D M	1	4 8 11 15	*
Pratia concolor			H G	S			P N		S W		13 15	
Pratia irrigua			H G	S			F P		S W		12 16	
Pratia pedunculata			H G	S			F P		S W		8 13-15 22	
Prostanthera lasianthos var. *lasianthos*	S-M	L		S			A	S	M		3 4 22	
Prostanthera melissifolia		M		Sp-S			P N	S	M		3	
Prunella vulgaris			H G	Sp-S			A		M S	2	3 4 6 8 14 16 22	
Pseudognaphalium luteo-album			A	Sp-A			A		D M	2	4 6 7 12 15 22	*
Psoralea adscendens			H G	Sp-S			P		M		15	
Psoralea parva			H	Sp			F		M		15	
Psoralea tenax			H	Sp-S			F P		M S		15	
Ptilotus macrocephalus			H	Sp			F		D M		14 15 19	
Ptilotus spathulatus			T	Sp A			F		D	1	11 15 19	*
Pultenaea daphnoides		M		Sp			A		M		7 21	
Pultenaea dentata		S		Sp			P		M		7 22	
Pultenaea gunnii		S-M		Sp			F P		D M		4 5 21 22	
Pultenaea hispidula		M		Sp			F P		D		4	
Pultenaea humilis		S	G	Sp			P		M		22	
Pultenaea juniperina var. *mucronata*		M		Sp			F P		M		4 22	
Pultenaea muelleri var. *muelleri*		M		Sp-S			P		M		22	
Pultenaea paleacea var. *sericea*		S		Sp			F P		M	2	8	
Pultenaea pedunculata		S	G	Sp			F P		D		21	
Pultenaea scabra		M		Sp			P		M		22	
Pultenaea stricta		S		Sp			F P		M	2	8 22	
Pultenaea tenuifolia		S		Sp			F P		D	1	10 11	
Pultenaea weindorferi		S		Sp			P N		M		22	
Pycnosorus chrysanthes			T	Sp A		N	F P		S		13	
Pycnosorus globosus			T	Sp-S		N	F		S		13	
Ranunculus amphitrichus			H	Y			F P		W	2	9 14 22	
Ranunculus glabrifolius			H	Sp			P		S W		6 22	
Ranunculus inundatus			H	Sp-S			F P		S W		14 22	
Ranunculus lappaceus			H	Sp			F P		M S	2	3 4 9 13 14 21 22	
Ranunculus pachycarpus			H	W-Sp			F P		M S		22	
Ranunculus papulentus			H	S			F P		W		16	
Ranunculus plebeius			H	Sp-S			P N		S W		3 4 16 22	
Ranunculus pumilio var. *pumilio*			A	Sp			F P		S W	2	9 10 15	
Ranunculus robertsonii			H	Sp			F P		S		15	

	Tree	Shrub	Other	Flowers	Bird	Butterfly	Sun Aspect	Screen Windbreak	Drainage	Coast	Vegetation Communities	Aboriginal Uses
Ranunculus scapiger			H	Sp-S			P N		M		21	
Ranunculus sessiliflorus var. *sessiliflorus*			A	W-Sp			P		S		9 16	
Rapanea howittiana	S	M-L		W-S			P N	S	M		16 22	
Rhagodia candolleana ssp. *candolleana*		M		S-A		F	F		D	1	10-12	*
Rhagodia parabolica		S-M		S		F	F P		D		17 19	
Rhodanthe anthemoides			H	Sp-A		N	F P		M		15	
Rhodanthe corymbiflora			H	W-Sp		N	F		D	2	10 15	
Ricinocarpos pinifolius		M		Sp			F P		M	2	8	
Rorippa dictyosperma			H	Y			P N		S		3 4	*
Rorippa laciniata			H	Y			P		S		16	*
Rubus parvifolius		S		Sp-S	B		P N		D M		3 4 16 20 22	*
Rumex bidens			H	Sp-S			F P		A		1	
Rumex brownii			H	Sp			F P		S		9 14 16 19 20 22	
Rumex dumosus			H	Sp-S			F P		S		12-15	
Rumex tenax			H	A Sp			F P		S		13	
Rutidosis leptorrhynchoides			H	Sp-A			F P		M		13 15	
Rutidosis multiflora			A	Sp			F P		D	2	10 11 21	
Sambucus gaudichaudiana		S	H	Sp	B		P		M		3 4 16 20 22	*
Samolus repens			H T	Y			F P		S	1	11-14	
Sarcocornia blackiana		S		Sp-S			F		S W	1	11 12	
Sarcocornia quinqueflora ssp. *quinqueflora*		S	G	S			F		S W	1	11-13	
Sclerolaena diacantha		S	G	Y			F P		D		15	
Sclerolaena muricata var. *muricata*		S		Y			F		S	2	11 12 16 19	
Sclerolaena muricata var. *villosa*		S		Y			F P		S		16	
Sclerostegia arbuscula		M		Y			F		S W	1	12	
Scutellaria humilis			H G	Sp-S			A		M	2	8 19	
Sebaea albidiflora			A	Sp			P		S W	2	9 12 22	
Sebaea ovata			A	Sp			P N		S W	2	4 8 13-15 22	
Selliera radicans			H G	Sp			A		M S	2	10 12 13 16	
Senecio biserratus			A	Sp-S		F	F P		S	1	7 11 16	
Senecio cunninghamii var. *cunninghamii*		S		Sp-A		F	F P		S W		15	
Senecio glomeratus			A	Sp-S		F	F P		S	2	3 4 7 8 14 21 22	
Senecio hispidulus var. *hispidulus*			H	Sp-S		F	F P		M S	2	8 10 15 21 22	
Senecio hispidulus var. *dissectus*			H	Sp-S		F	F P		D		21	
Senecio lautus		S	H	Sp-S		F	F P		D M	2	4 10 16 22	
Senecio linearifolius			H	Sp-S		F	P N		S		3 4 22	
Senecio macrocarpus			H	Sp		F	F		D		15	
Senecio minimus			A	S-A		F	P N		M		4 6 8 14 20 22	
Senecio odoratus			H	Sp-S		F	F P		D		7 13 22	
Senecio quadridentatus			H	Sp-S		F	F		M S	2	8 14-16 20-22	
Senecio runcinifolius			A	Sp		F	F		S		12	
Senecio spathulatus			H	Sp-S		F	F		M	1	11	
Senecio squarrosus			H	S		F	F P		D		7 15	
Senecio tenuiflorus			A	Sp-S		F	F P		S		8 21 22	
Senecio vagus			H	Sp		F	P N		M		3	
Senecio velleioides			H	Sp-S		F	P N		M		3 4	
Senna artemisioides ssp. *filifolia*		M		W-Sp			F P		D		19	
Sigesbeckia orientalis			A	Sp-S			P		M S		3 4 22	
Solanum aviculare		M		S	B		A		D M		3 4 7 14 22	*
Solanum laciniatum		M		Sp-S	B		A		D M		14 16 19 22	
Solanum prinophyllum		S	A	Sp-S			P		M		3 4	
Solanum vescum		M		Sp-S			F P		D M		4	
Solenogyne dominii			H	Y			F P		D		7 12 14 15	
Solenogyne gunnii			H	Y			P		M		7 14 15 21	
Sphaerolobium vimineum		S		Sp-S			F P		M		8 22	
Sprengelia incarnata		S-M		Sp	N		F P		S W	2	6 8	
Spyridium parvifolium		M		W-Sp			P N		D M		4 22	
Stackhousia monogyna			H	Sp-S		N	P N		M		3 4 7 13-15 21 22	
Stackhousia spathulata			H	W-S		N	F P		D	2	11	
Stackhousia viminea			H	Sp-S		N	F P		D	2	8	
Stellaria flaccida			H G	Sp			P N		M S		3 4 22	
Stellaria multiflora			A	Sp			F P		M	1	11	
Stellaria palustris var. *palustris*			H	Sp-S			P		S W		8 13	
Stellaria pungens			H G	Sp-S			F P		M	2	4 11 14 16 19 22	
Stenopetalum lineare			A	Sp			F		D	1	11 15	*
Stuartina muelleri			A G	Sp			F		D M	1	8 11 17	

	Tree	Shrub	Other	Flowers	Bird	Butterfly	Sun Aspect	Screen Windbreak	Drainage	Coast	Vegetation Communities	Aboriginal Uses
Stylidium beaugleholei			A	Sp-S			P		S	2	8	
Stylidium despectum			A	Sp			F P		W		16	
Stylidium graminifolium var. *angustifolium*			H T	Sp			P		M		3 4 21 22	
Stylidium graminifolium var. *graminifolium*			H T	Sp			F P		M	2	7 14 15 21 22	
Stylidium inundatum			A	Sp			F P		S		6 8	
Stylidium perpusillum			A	Sp			F P		S		8	
Suaeda australis		S		Y			F		S	1	10 12	
Swainsona lessertiifolia			H	W-Sp			F P		D	1	11	
Templetonia stenophylla		S		W-Sp			F P		D		19	
Tetragonia implexicoma			C	Sp-S			F P		D	1	10-12	*
Tetragonia tetragonioides			H G	Sp-S			F		M	1	11	*
Tetratheca bauerifolia		S		Sp-S			P		M		22	
Tetratheca ciliata		S		W-S			P N		D		4 7 21 22	
Teucrium corymbosum			H	S			P N		M		22	
Teucrium racemosum			H	Sp-S			F		M S		13 14	
Thesium australe			H	S			F		M S		15	
Threlkeldia diffusa			H G	W-Sp			F		S	1	11 12	
Trachymene anisocarpa			A	Sp-S			F P		D M	2	8	
Triptilodiscus pygmaeus			A	Sp			F P		D		14 19 21	
Urtica incisa			H	W-S		F	A		M S		4 16 19 20	*
Utricularia australis			H	Sp			P N		A		1 8 14	
Utricularia dichotoma			H	Sp-S			P N		W		6 8 16 22	
Utricularia laterifolia			A	Sp			P N		W		8	
Utricularia sp. aff. *dichotoma*			H	Sp			P N		S W		13	
Utricularia tenella			H	Sp			P		W		8	
Velleia paradoxa			H	Sp A			AA		M S		13-16	
Veronica calycina			H G	Sp			P N		M S		4 7 16 21 22	
Veronica gracilis			H	Sp-S			P N		M		4 8 13 14 16 21 22	
Veronica notabilis			H G	Sp-S			P N		S		3 4	
Veronica plebeia			H G	Sp-S			A		M		4 7 20 22	
Villarsia exaltata			H T	Sp			F P		W A		1 8	
Villarsia reniformis			H T	Sp			A		W A	2	1 6 8	
Viminaria juncea		M-L		Sp-S			F P		M S W	2	6-8 14 16 22	
Viola betonicifolia			H T	Sp-S			P N		M		4 7 21 22	
Viola cleistogamoides			H	Sp-S			P N		S		6 8	
Viola hederacea			H G	W-A			A		S W		3 4 7 9 21 22	
Viola sieberiana			H	Sp-S			P N		S		3 4 8	
Vittadinia cervicularis		S		Y			F		D		14 19	
Vittadinia cuneata var. *cuneata*		S		Y			F P		D M		8 13-15	
Vittadinia gracilis		S		Y			F P		D M		13-15	
Vittadinia muelleri		S		Y			F P		D		14 15 21	
Wahlenbergia communis			H	Sp-A			A		M		14-16 19	*
Wahlenbergia gracilenta			A	Sp			F P		M		4 8 14 15 22	*
Wahlenbergia gracilis			A/H	Sp			F P		M		3 4 7 16 22	*
Wahlenbergia gymnoclada			H	Sp-S			F P		D		7 22	*
Wahlenbergia luteola			H T	Y			F		M		14 15	
Wahlenbergia multicaulis			H T	Sp-A			F P		D		7 14 21	*
Wahlenbergia stricta			H	Sp-S			F P		D		3 4 7 14 15 21 22	*
Wilsonia backhousei		S	G	Sp			F		S W	1	11	
Wilsonia humilis		S	S	Sp			F		S W	1	12	
Wilsonia rotundifolia		S	G	Sp			F		S	1	11-13	
Xanthosia dissecta			H	Sp			P		M		4 5 9 22	
Xanthosia pilosa			H	Sp-S			P		M	2	7	
Xanthosia pusilla			H	Sp			F P		D	2	7 8	
Ziera arborescens	S	M-L		Sp			P N		M		3	
Zygophyllum billardieri			H	Y			F		D		11 16	
Zygophyllum glaucum			A	W-Sp			F		M		16	

Lilies and Irises

	Tree	Shrub	Other	Flowers	Bird	Butterfly	Sun Aspect	Screen Windbreak	Drainage	Coast	Vegetation Communities	Aboriginal Uses
Arthropodium fimbriatum			H T	Sp			F		D		15 19	*
Arthropodium milleflorum			H T	Sp-S			F P		S		4 7 16 22	*
Arthropodium minus			H T	Sp			F P		D M		14 15	*
Arthropodium strictum			H T	Sp			F P		D		4 5 7 14 15 21 22	*
Bulbine bulbosa			H T	Sp-S			F P		M		14 15 21 22	*
Burchardia umbellata			H T	Sp-S			F P		M		5 7 8 10 14 15 19	*
Caesia calliantha			H T	Sp-S			F P		M S	2	14 15 22	*
Caesia parviflora var. *minor*			H T	Sp-S			F P		M S	2	14	*
Caesia parviflora var. *parviflora*			H T	Sp-S			F P		M		4 7 8 22	*

	Tree	Shrub	Other	Flowers	Bird	Butterfly	Sun Aspect	Screen Windbreak	Drainage	Coast	Vegetation Communities	Aboriginal Uses
Chamaescilla corymbosa			H	Sp			F P		S	2	4 7 14 22	
Dianella caerula			T	Sp-S			F P		D M		22	*
Dianella longifolia var. *longifolia*			T	Sp-S			F P		M		7 15 19 21 22	*
Dianella revoluta var. *brevicaulis*			T	Sp-S			F P		D	1	11	*
Dianella revoluta var. *revoluta*			T	Sp-S			F P		D M	2	4 8 15 19 21 22	*
Dianella tasmanica			T	Sp-S			P N		S		3 4 22	*
Diplarrena moraea			T	Sp			F P		M		4 5	
Hypoxis glabella var. *glabella*			H T	W-S			P		M		7 14 15 21 22	*
Hypoxis hygrometrica var. *hygrometrica*			H T	Sp-S			P		M		6	
Hypoxis hygrometrica var. *villosisepala*			H T	Sp-S			F P		M	2	15 22	*
Hypoxis vaginata var. *brevistigmata*			H T	Sp-S			F P		M	2	8	*
Hypoxis vaginata var. *vaginata*			H T	W-S			F P		M		7 14 22	*
Laxmannia orientalis			H T	Sp			F P		M		8	
Libertia pulchella			H T	Sp-S			P N		M S		4	
Patersonia fragilis			H T	Sp-S			F P		S	2	6 8	
Patersonia occidentalis			H T	Sp-S			F P		S		6 9 22	
Stypandra glauca			H	W-Sp			F P		D M		6 16	
Thelionema caespitosum			H T	Sp-S			F P		S	2	6 8 9 22	
Thysanotus patersonii			C	Sp			F P		D M	2	7 8 14-16 21 22	
Thysanotus tuberosus ssp. *tuberosus*			H T	S			F P		D		14 16 21 22	*
Tricoryne elatior			H	Sp-S			F P		D M	2	7 8 14 15 19 21 22	
Wurmbea dioica			H	W-Sp			F P		M	2	4 5 7 8 14 21 22	*

Orchids

	Tree	Shrub	Other	Flowers	Bird	Butterfly	Sun Aspect	Screen Windbreak	Drainage	Coast	Vegetation Communities	Aboriginal Uses
Acianthus caudatus			H	W-Sp			P		M	2	7 8 21 22	*
Acianthus pusillus			H	A-W			P		M		4 8 21 22	*
Arthrochilus huntianus			H	Sp-S			P		D		21	
Burnettia cuneata			H	Sp-S			P		S W		8	*
Caladenia aurantiaca			H	Sp			P		D		8	*
Caladenia australis			H	Sp			P		D M		21	*
Caladenia caerula			H	Sp			P		D		8 18 21	*
Caladenia cardiochila			H	Sp			P		D	2	8 11	*
Caladenia carnea var. *carnea*			H	Sp-S			F P		D		5 8 14 21	*
Caladenia catenata			H	A-Sp			P		D		7 14 21 22	*
Caladenia clavigera			H	Sp			F P		M		21 22	*
Caladenia concinna			H	Sp			P		D		21	*
Caladenia congesta			H	Sp-S			P		D		9 22	*
Caladenia deformis			H	W-Sp			F P		D	2	7 8 21	*
Caladenia dilatata			H	Sp-S			F P		D		4 8 14 21 22	*
Caladenia filamentosa var. *filamentosa*			H	W-Sp			F P		M		4 22	*
Caladenia flavovirens			H	Sp-S			P		M		22	*
Caladenia gracilis			H	Sp			P		D		7 21 22	*
Caladenia iridescens			H	Sp			P		D		7 22	*
Caladenia latifolia			H	Sp			F P		D	2	8 10	*
Caladenia menziesii			H	Sp			P		S	2	4 7 9 22	*
Caladenia oenochila			H	Sp			P N		M		4 22	*
Caladenia praecox			H	Sp			P		D		21 22	*
Caladenia pusilla			H	Sp			P		D		7 22	*
Caladenia robinsonii			H	Sp			F P		M		7	*
Caladenia rosella			H	W-Sp			P		D		21	*
Caladenia tentaculata			H	Sp			P		D		7 22	*
Caladenia thysanochila			H	Sp			F P		D	2	7	*
Caladenia venusta			H	Sp			F		M	2	8	*
Caleana major			H	Sp-S			F P		D	2	7 21	
Calochilus campestris			H	Sp-S			P		M		4 7 22	*
Calochilus paludosus			H	Sp-S			P		M		21 22	*
Calochilus robertsonii			H	Sp			P		M		4 5 7 21 22	*
Chiloglottis cornuta			H	Sp-S			P N		S		3	*
Chiloglottis reflexa			H	S-A			P		M		7 8 21	*
Chiloglottis trapeziformis			H	Sp			P		D M	2	7 21	*
Chiloglottis valida			H	Sp-S			P		M		4 7 22	*
Corybas aconitiflorus			H	A-W			P N		M		4	*
Corybas diemenicus			H	W-Sp			N		S		3 7 22	*
Corybas incurvus			H	W			P		S		7 8 22	*
Corybas unguiculatus			H	A-Sp			P N		S W		7 8	*
Cryptostylis leptochila			H	S-A			P		D M		4 7 22	*
Cryptostylis subulata			H	Sp-A			P		S		4 7 9 22	*
Cyrtostylis reniformis			H	W-Sp			P		D M		8 14 22	*
Dipodium roseum			H	S-A			P		M		7 14 21 22	*
Diuris brevissima			H	Sp			F P		D M		21	
Diuris corymbosa			H	W-Sp			P		D M	2	7 14 21 22	*

	Tree	Shrub	Other	Flowers	Bird	Butterfly	Sun Aspect	Screen Windbreak	Drainage	Coast	Vegetation Communities	Aboriginal Uses
Diuris fragrantissima			H	Sp			F		M		15	*
Diuris lanceolata			H	Sp			F P		S		5 8 14 15 21 22	*
Diuris x *fastidiosa*			H	Sp			F P		S		15	*
Diuris palustris			H	W-Sp			F P		S W		8 15	*
Diuris pardina			H	Sp			P		D M		7 8 21 22	*
Diuris punctata			H	Sp			F P		S		5 7 14 19	*
Diuris sulphurea			H	Sp			P		M		8 14 19 21 22	*
Eriochilus cucullatus			H	S-A			F P		D M		5 7 14 21 22	
Gastrodia procera			H	S			F P		S		4	
Gastrodia sesamoides			H	Sp-S			P		S		4 7 22	
Genoplesium archeri			H	S-A			P		D M	2	7 11 22	*
Genoplesium despectans			H	S-A			P		D		7 21 22	*
Genoplesium morrisii			H	S-A			P		S		7 22	*
Genoplesium rufum			H	S-A			FP		M		8 14	*
Glossodia major			H	Sp			F P		D M		7 8 14 19 21 22	*
Leporella fimbriata			H	A-Sp			F P		M		7 8	*
Lyperanthus nigricans			H	Sp			P		D M	2	7 8 10	*
Lyperanthus suaveolens			H	Sp			P		D M		8 21 22	*
Microtis atrata			H	Sp			P N		S W		7 8 22	*
Microtis parviflora			H	Sp-S			F P		S		7 8 21 22	*
Microtis rara			H	Sp-S			A		S		22	*
Microtis unifolia			H	Sp-S			F P		M S		8 9 13 14 21 22	*
Orthoceras strictum			H	Sp-S			F P		S W		7 9 22	*
Prasophyllum australe			H	Sp-S			P		S W		4 22	*
Prasophyllum brevilabre			H	Sp-S			P		S		4 22	*
Prasophyllum colemanae			H	Sp			P		M S		22	*
Prasophyllum elatum			H	Sp			F P		M		4 8 9	*
Prasophyllum flavum			H	Sp-S			P N		S		3	*
Prasophyllum frenchii			H	Sp-S			F P		M		7 8 22	*
Prasophyllum fuscum			H	Sp			F P		S		4 9 15	*
Prasophyllum lindleyanum			H	Sp-S			P		D M		4 7 22	*
Prasophyllum odoratum			H	Sp-S			P		M		4 22	*
Prasophyllum patens			H	Sp-S			F P		M	2	8 11	*
Prasophyllum pyriforme			H	Sp-S			P		M		22	*
Prasophyllum spicatum			H	Sp-S			P		M		8	*
Pterostylis alata			H	A-W			P		M		8 21 22	*
Pterostylis alpina			H	Sp			P		M		4 22	*
Pterostylis cncinna			H	W-Sp			F P		M		7 8 14 21 22	*
Pterostylis x *toveyana*			H	W-Sp			P		M		7 8 21	*
Pterostylis cucullata			H	Sp			P		M		8	*
Pterostylis curta			H	W-Sp			P N		M		4 8 16 22	*
Pterostylis cycnocephala			H	Sp-S			F P		D M		19 21	*
Pterostylis decurva			H	Sp-S			P N		S		4 22	*
Pterostylis foliata			H	Sp-S			P N		S		4 22	*
Pterostylis furcata			H	Sp-S			P N		S W		4 22	*
Pterostylis grandiflora			H	W			P		S		7 8 22	*
Pterostylis longifolia			H	W-Sp			P		M		7 8 21 22	*
Pterostylis sp. aff. *longifolia*			H	W-Sp			P		M		18 21	*
Pterostylis mutica			H	W-S			F P		D M		8 19 21	*
Pterostylis nana			H	W-Sp			A		D M		7 11 21	*
Pterostylis nutans			H	A-Sp			P N		S		7 8 14 21 22	*
Pterostylis x *ingens*			H	Sp			P		S		22	*
Pterostylis obtusa			H	S-W			P		S		4 8 22	*
Pterostylis parviflora			H	S-W			P		S		7 8 21	*
Pterostylis pedoglossa			H	A-W			P N		S		7 8	*
Pterostylis pedunculata			H	W-Sp			P N		S		7 8 21 22	*
Pterostylis plumosa			H	Sp			P		M		7 21 22	*
Pterostylis revoluta			H	S-W			P		D M		18 21	*
Pterostylis robusta			H	W-Sp			P		D M		4 21	*
Pterostylis rufa			H	Sp-S			P		D		21	*
Pterostylis sanguinea			H	A-W			F P		D		7 10	*
Pterostylis truncata			H	S-W			P		M		5 15 22	*
Sarcochilus australis			E	Sp			P N				2 3	
Spiranthes sinensis			H	Sp-S			F P		S W		9 22	*
Thelymitra antennifera			H	Sp			F P		M		4 5 7 8 22	*
Thelymitra x *macmillanii*			H	Sp			F P		M		7	*
Thelymitra aristata			H	Sp			F P		S		14 15 21	*
Thelymitra carnea			H	Sp			F P		S		7 22	*
Thelymitra epipactoides			H	Sp			F P		S W		8	*
Thelymitra flexuosa			H	Sp			F P		S		7 9 22	*
Thelymitra ixioides var. *ixioides*			H	Sp			F P		W		7 21 22	*
Thelymitra ixioides var. *subdifformis*			H	Sp			F P		S		22	*
Thelymitra luteocilium			H	Sp			F P		M		9 22	*
Thelymitra media var. *media*			H	Sp-S			F P		S		3 4 22	*
Thelymitra megcalyptra			H	Sp			F P		D		10 15	*
Thelymitra nuda			H	Sp			F P		D M		8 21	*
Thelymitra pauciflora			H	Sp-S			F P		M		7 8 14 15 21 22	*
Thelymitra rubra			H	Sp			P		S		7 8 21 22	

Grasses, Rushes, Sedges and Aquatics

	Tree	Shrub	Other	Flowers	Bird	Butterfly	Sun Aspect	Screen Windbreak	Drainage	Coast	Vegetation Communities	Aboriginal Uses
Agrostis adamsonii			A T	Sp								
Agrostis aemula var. *aemula*			A T	Sp-S			F P		M S		13 15 22	
Agrostis aemula var. *setifolia*			A T	Sp-S			F P		S		13	
Agrostis avenacea			A T	Sp-S			F P		S		7 11 13 15 19 22	
Agrostis billardieri var. *billardieri*			A T	Sp-S			F P		S	1	11 16	
Agrostis billardieri var. *robusta*			A T	Sp-S			F P		M		21/22	
Agrostis aff. *hiemalis*			T	Sp-S			P N		S		4	
Alisma plantago-aquatica			H T	S			F P		W A		1 13 16	
Amphibromus archeri			T	Sp-S			F P		S W		6 16	
Amphibromus fluitans			T	Sp			P		S W		7 16	
Amphibromus macrorhinus			T	Sp			F		S W		13	
Amphibromus neesii			T	Sp-A			F P		S W		9 13 15	
Amphibromus nervosus			T	Sp-A			F P		S W		13	
Amphibromus pithogastrus			T	Sp			F P		S W		13	
Aphelia gracilis			A T	Sp			F P		S	2	6 8	
Aphelia pumilio			A	Sp			F P		S	2	8	
Aristida ramosa			H T	Sp			F		D		15 19	
Austrofestuca hookeriana			T	Sp-S			F P		S		6 9 22	
Austrofestuca littoralis			T	Sp			F		D	1	11	
Baumea acuta			T	Sp-A		F	F		S	2	8	
Baumea articulata			T	S-A		F	F P		S		16	
Baumea gunnii			T	Y		F	F P		S		6 9	
Baumea juncea			T	Sp-A		F	F P		S	2	8 10	
Baumea rubiginosa			T	Y		F	F		S W		6	
Baumea tetragona			T	Y		F	F		S	2	6 8 9	
Bolboschoenus caldwellii			T	Sp-A			F P		W A	1	12-14	*
Bolboschoenus medianus			T	Sp-A			F P		S W A	1	7 16	*
Bothriochloa macra			T	S-A Sp			F P		D M		11 14 15 19	
Carex appressa			T	Sp-S		F	F		S W		7 8 14 16 21 22	*
Carex bichenoviana			T	Sp-S			F P		S		14 15	
Carex breviculmis			T	Sp-S			F P		M-S		4 7 12-15 21 22	
Carex fascicularis			T	Sp-A			P		S W		22	
Carex gaudichaudiana			T	Sp-S		F	F P		S W		6 22	
Carex incomitata			T	Sp-S			F		D		15	
Carex inversa			T	Sp-A			F P		M		7 8 13-15 19 22	
Carex iynx			T	Sp			P		S		22	
Carex pumila			T	Sp-S			F		S	1	11 13	
Carex tasmanica			T	Sp			F P		S W		13	
Carex tereticaulis			T	Sp-A			F P		S W		15 16 22	*
Caustis restiacea			H T	Sp-S			F P		S		6	
Centrolepis aristata			A T	Sp			P		S		6 9 14 22	
Centrolepis fascicularis			H T	S			P		S		6 9	
Centrolepis polygyna			A T	W-Sp			F P		S	1	8 12	
Centrolepis strigosa			A T	Sp			F P		S		8 9 14 22	
Chionochloa pallida			T	Sp-S			F P		D M		5 21 22	
Chloris truncata			T	S			F		D		13-15 19	
Chorizandra cymbaria			T	Sp			F P		S		6 8 22	
Cladium procerum			T	Sp-S			F P		S W	1	9 16	
Cymbopogon refractus			T	Sp-S			F P		D		15	
Cyperus brevifolius			T	Sp-A		F	F		S		16	
Cyperus gunnii			T	Sp-A		F	P		S		16	
Cyperus lhotskyanus			T	Sp-S		F	P		W		19	
Cyperus lucidus			T	Sp-S		F	P		W A		4 21 22	
Cyperus sanguinolentus			T A	Sp-A		F	P		S W		16	
Damasonium minus			A T	Sp-W			F P		W A		1 13 19	
Danthonia auriculata			T	Sp-S			F P		D		14 15	
Danthonia caespitosa			T	Sp-S A			F P		M		8 13-15 22	
Danthonia carphoides var. *carphoides*			T	Sp-S			F		M S		14 15	
Danthonia duttoniana			T	Sp-S			F P		S W		13-15	
Danthonia eriantha			T	Sp-S			F P		D		14 15 21	
Danthonia geniculata			T	Sp-S			F P		D M S		8 14 19 21	
Danthonia induta			T	Sp-S			F P		M		19	
Danthonia laevis			T	Sp-S			F P		S		8 14 15 19 21 22	
Danthonia lepidopoda			T	Sp			P		M		5	
Danthonia linkii var. *fulva*			T	Sp-A			F P		M S		19 21 22	
Danthonia linkii var. *linkii*			T	Sp-A			F P		M S		14 21 22	
Danthonia penicillata			T	Sp-S			P		M		7 16 20-22	
Danthonia pilosa var. *pilosa*			T	Sp-S			P		S		5 7 15 22	
Danthonia procera			T	Sp-S			F P		D M		7 14	
Danthonia racemosa			T	Y			F P		D M		14 15 19-22	
Danthonia semiannularis			T	Sp-S			F P		S		5 7 8 14 22	
Danthonia setacea var. *setacea*			T	Sp-S		F	F P		D M		8 14 15 19 21 22	
Danthonia tenuior			T	Sp-S			F P		D		14 21 22	

	Tree	Shrub	Other	Flowers	Bird	Butterfly	Sun Aspect	Screen Windbreak	Drainage	Coast	Vegetation Communities	Aboriginal Uses
Deyeuxia contracta			T	Sp			P N		S		3	
Deyeuxia densa			T	Sp-S			F P		S		6 8	
Deyeuxia minor			T	Sp-S			F P		D	1	10 21	
Deyeuxia quadriseta			T	Sp-A			F P		D M		4 5 7 15 21 22	
Deyeuxia rodwayi			T				P N		S		3 4 22	
Dichanthium sericeum			T	Y			F		M		15	
Dichelachne crinita			T	Sp-S			F P		D		7 8 14 15 19-22	
Dichelachne micrantha			T	W-Sp			F P		D		15 21	
Dichelachne sieberiana			T	S			P		D		21	
Distichlis distichophylla			G	Sp-S			F		S	1	11 12	
Dryopoa dives			T	Sp-S			P N		M		2 3	
Echinopogon ovatus			T	Sp-S			P		M		4 16 22	
Eleocharis acuta			T	Sp-A			F		W A		1 7 8 13 15 16 19	
Eleocharis atricha			T	S			P		A		1 13	*
Eleocharis gracilis			T	Sp-S W			P		W		16	
Eleocharis minuta			T	S			F		W	1	13	
Eleocharis pallens			T	A S			F P		S W		13	
Eleocharis pusilla			T	S-A			F P		A		1 12-14	
Eleocharis sphacelata			T	S			F P		W A		1 6 14	*
Elymus scabrus			T	Sp-S		F	F P		D M		14 15 21 22	
Empodisma minus			G	Sp-A			F P		S W		5 6 9	
Enneapogon nigricans			T	S			F		D		15 19	
Entolasia marginata			T	Sp			F P		M		7	
Entolasia stricta			T	S			F P		D M		7	
Eragrostis brownii			T	Sp-A			F P		D M		8 14 16 21 22	
Eragrostis elongata			T	S-A			F P		S W		13	
Eragrostis infecunda			T	S			F		S W	1	13	
Gahnia clarkei			T	Sp-S		F	P N		S W		4 22	*
Gahnia filum			T	Y		F	F		S W	1	12 13	*
Gahnia radula			T	Y		F	F P		D M S		5 7 9 21 22	*
Gahnia sieberiana			T	Sp-S		F	A		S		4 9 22	*
Gahnia trifida			T	Sp-S		F	F P		M	2	10	*
Glyceria australis			G	Sp-S			F P		S W		7 16 22	
Hemarthria uncinata			T	S			F P		S		6 8 16 22	
Homopholis proluta			T	Sp-A			F P		S		14 15	*
Hypolaena fastigata			G	Y			F P		S	2	8	
Imperata cylindrica			T G	S		F	F P		M		4 8 13 21 22	
Isolepis cernua			A T	Y			F P		S W	1	12 13 16 20	
Isolepis fluitans			T	Sp-S			P		W A		1 6 8 22	
Isolepis hookeriana			A T	Sp-S			P		S		6 13 22	
Isolepis inundata			T	Sp-A			P		S W		4 9 16 22	
Isolepis marginata			A T	Sp-S			F P		M	1	8 12 16 22	
Isolepis nodosa			T	Y			F P		S	1	6-8 10 11 16	
Isolepis platycarpa			A T	Sp-A			F P		S		4 6 16	
Isolepis producta			H	Sp-A			P		A		1 16	
Isolepis stellata			A T	Sp-S			P		S		22	
Isolepis subtilissima			T	A			P		S		3 22	
Isolepis victoriensis			A T	Sp			F		S		15 19	
Juncus amabilis			T	S	S		F P		M S		9 13 15 22	
Juncus australis			T	Y	S		F P		S W		16 22	
Juncus bufonius			T	Y	S		F P		S W		3 4 6 8 13-16 22	
Juncus caespiticius			T	Y	S		F P		W		8 16	
Juncus filicaulis			T	Y	S		F P		S		14	
Juncus flavidus			T	S-A	S		F P		M		12-14 19	
Juncus gregiflorus			T	Sp-S	S		P		S		4 16 22	
Juncus holoshoenus			T	S	S		F		S		6 8 13 14 22	
Juncus homalocaulis			T	S	S		F		S		12 13 19	
Juncus krausii			T	S	S		F		S W	1	10 11	
Juncus pallidus			T	S	S		F P		S W		7 8 15 22	
Juncus pauciflorus			T	S	S		P		M S		6 7 16 22	
Juncus planifolius			A/T	Sp-S	S		F P		W		4 6 9 22	
Juncus prismatocarpus			T	S	S		P		W		4 9	
Juncus procerus			T	Sp-S	S		P		M		4 22	
Juncus radula			T	Sp-S	S		F P		S		14 15 21	
Juncus revolutus			T	Sp-S	S		F		S W	1	12	
Juncus sarophorus			T	Sp-S	S		P		S		9 16 22	
Juncus sp. O			T	S	S		F P		S		13	
Juncus subsecundus			T	S	S		F P		S W		7 15 16 22	
Juncus usitatus			T	S	S		F P		S W		14 15 22	
Juncus vaginatus			T	S	S		F P		S		14	
Lemna disperma				Sp			A		A		1 13 16 19	
Lepidosperma concavum			T	Y	S	F	F P		M	2	8 10 11	
Lepidosperma congestum			T	Y	S		F P		S		8	
Lepidosperma elatius var. *elatius*			T	Y	S		P N		S		3 4 7 22	*

	Tree	Shrub	Other	Flowers	Bird	Butterfly	Sun Aspect	Screen Windbreak	Drainage	Coast	Vegetation Communities	Aboriginal Uses
Lepidosperma filiforme			T	Sp-S	S		P		S		5 6 9	
Lepidosperma forsythii			T	Sp-S	S		F P		W	2	8	
Lepidosperma gladiatum			T	Sp-S	S		F P		D	1	11	*
Lepidosperma gunnii			T	Sp-S	S		F P		M		8	
Lepidosperma laterale var. *laterale*			T	Sp-S	S		P		M S		4-7 21 22	
Lepidosperma laterale var. *majus*			T	Sp-S	S		P		M S		3 7 22	*
Lepidosperma longitudinale			T	Y	S		F P		S W		6 9	
Lepidosperma neesii			T	Sp	S		P		S		7 9	
Lepidosperma semiteres			T	Y	S		F P		S		4 7 8	
Lepidosperma tortuosum			T	Sp-S	S		P		W		4	
Lepilaena bilocularis			H	W-Sp	B		F P		A	1	1 12	
Lepilaena cylindrocarpa			H	Sp	B		F		A	1	1 12	
Lepilaena preissii			A	Sp-S	B		F		A	1	1 12	
Leptocarpus brownii			T	Y			F P		S		6 8	
Leptocarpus tenax			T	Sp-W			F P		S		6 9	
Lepyrodia muelleri			T	Sp-A			P		W		9	
Lomandra filiformis ssp. *coriacea*			T	Sp	S	F	F P		M		16 21 22	*
Lomandra filiformis ssp. *filiformis*			T	Sp	S	F	F P		M		5 7 14 21 22	*
Lomandra longifolia			T	Y	S	F	A		D M	2	7 8 10 14 21 22	*
Lomandra micrantha ssp. *micrantha*			T	A-S	S	F	P		M		15 19	*
Lomandra multiflora			T	W-S	S	F	P		D M		8 19 22	*
Lomandra nana			T	Sp	S	F	F P		D M		8 15	*
Luzula meridionalis var. *densiflora*			T	W-S			F P		M		9 22	
Luzula meridionalis var. *flaccida*			T	Sp			P N		M	2	8 22	
Luzula meridionalis var. *meridionalis*			T	Sp			P		D M		3 7 14 21 22	
Microlaena stipoides			T	Sp		F	F P		M	2	5-7 9 15 16 21 22	
Ottelia ovalifolia			H T	S			F P		A		1	
Panicum decompositum			T	S			F P		M S		13	*
Panicum effusum			T	Sp-A			F P		M		13-15 19	*
Paspalidium constrictum			T	Sp-A			F P		D			
Pentapogon quadrifidus			A T	S			F P		M S		14 15 21 22	
Philydrum lanuginosum			H	S			F P		A		1	
Phragmites australis			T	S-A			F P		W A		6 10 16	*
Poa clelandii			T	Sp-S	S	F	F P		M		8 15 22	*
Poa ensiformis			T	Sp-A	S	F	P N		M		4 22	*
Poa labillardieri			T	Sp-S	S	F	F P		M	2	14 16 21 22	*
Poa morrisii			T	Sp-S	S	F	F P		M		5 7 21 22	
Poa poiformis var. *poiformis*			T	Sp-S	S	F	F P		D	1	10 11	*
Poa rodwayi			T	Sp	S		F P		M		7 19 22	
Poa sieberiana var. *hirtella*			T	Sp-S	S	F	P		M		22	
Poa sieberiana var. *sieberiana*			T	Sp-S	S	F	F P		M		7 9 14 15 21	*
Poa tenera			T	Sp-S	S	F	P N		M		4 6 7 22	
Potamogeton crispus			H	Sp-A			F P		A		1 14 16	
Potamogeton ochreatus			H	Sp-A			F P		A		1 13	
Potamogeton pectinatus			H	Sp-A			F P		A		1 13	
Potamogeton tricarinatus			H	Sp-A			F P		A		1 13	
Puccinellia stricta var. *perlaxa*			A T	Sp-S			F		W	1	12 13	
Puccinellia stricta var. *stricta*			A T	Sp			F		W	1	12	
Restio tetraphyllus			T	Sp-S			F P		W		8 9	
Ruppia maritima			H	W-S	S		F		A	1	1 12	
Ruppia megacarpa			H	Sp-S	S		F		A	1	1 12	
Ruppia polycarpa			A/H	W-Sp	S		F		A	1	1 12	
Schoenoplectus dissachanthus			A T	A			F P		S W		7	
Schoenoplectus pungens			Y	Sp-A			F P		S W		13	
Schoenoplectus validus			T	S-A			F P		W		6 16	*
Schoenus apogon			T	Sp-S			F P		S W	2	5 7 9 14 15 22	
Schoenus breviculmis			T	Y			F P		S		9	
Schoenus brevifolius			T	Sp-S			F P		S		7 8	
Schoenus latelaminatus			A	Sp			P		S		14 22	
Schoenus maschalinus			T	Sp-S			P		S		9 22	
Schoenus nitens			T	Sp-A			F P		S		12	
Schoenus tenuissimus			T	Y			F P		S W		6 9	
Schoenus tesquorum			T	Sp-S			P		S W		6 16	
Sparganium subglobosum			H	S			F P		A		1	
Spinifex sericeus			T G	Sp-S			F		D	1	11	
Spirodela oligorrhiza							F P		A		1 8 16 22	
Sporobolus virginicus			T G	Y			F		S	1	11 12	
Stipa aristiglumis			T	Sp-S	S		F P		S		14 15	
Stipa bigeniculata			T	Sp-S	S		F P		S		13-15 19	
Stipa blackii			T	Sp	S		F P		S		14 15 19	
Stipa curticoma			T	Sp	S		F P		S		13-15	
Stipa densiflora			T	Sp-S	S		F P		D		18 19 21	

	Tree	Shrub	Other	Flowers	Bird	Butterfly	Sun Aspect	Screen Windbreak	Drainage	Coast	Vegetation Communities	Aboriginal Uses
Stipa elegantissima			T	Sp-S	S		F P		D		14 19	
Stipa exilis			T	Sp	S		F P		M			
Stipa flavescens			T	Sp-S	S		F P		M	1	11 12	
Stipa gibbosa			T	Sp-S	S		F P		S		14 15	
Stipa mollis			T	Sp-S	S		F P		S		7 14 21	
Stipa muelleri			T	Sp	S		F P		D		5	
Stipa nodosa			T	Sp	S		F P		M		14 15	
Stipa oligostachya			T	Sp	S		F P		S		13-15	
Stipa pubinodis			T	Sp-S	S		P		S		7 21 22	
Stipa rudis ssp. *australis*			T	Sp-S	S		F P		S		7 21	
Stipa rudis ssp. *nervosa*			T	Sp-S	S		F P		S		22	
Stipa rudis ssp. *rudis*			T	Sp-S	S		P N		S		5 7 14 21 22	
Stipa scabra ssp. *falcata*			T	Sp	S		F P		D M		15 19	
Stipa scabra ssp. *scabra*			T	Sp	S		F P		D M		14 15 19	
Stipa semibarbata			T	Sp	S	F	F P		D M		7 14 15 19 22	
Stipa setacea			T	Sp	S		F P		M		14 19	
Stipa stipoides			T	Sp-A	S		F P		D	1	11 12	
Stipa stuposa			T	Sp	S		F P		M		15	
Tetraria capillaris			T	A-W			F P		S		4 6 22	
Tetrarrhena distichophylla			G	Sp-A			F P		S		7	
Tetrarrhena juncea			G	Sp-A			P N		M S		3 4 7 21 22	
Themeda triandra			T	Sp-S	S	F	F P		D M		5 7 13-15 19 21 22	*
Thismia rodwayi			H				N		S		2 3	
Tricostularia pauciflora			T	S			P		S		8	
Triglochin centrocarpa			A	Sp-A			F P		S		8	
Triglochin minutissima			A	Sp			F P		S	1	12	
Triglochin mucronata			A	Sp			F P		S	1	12	
Triglochin procera			H	Sp-A			F P		A		1 4 6 7 16 20 22	*
Triglochin striata			H	Sp-A			F P		W	1	6 10 12 16	
Tripogon loliiformis			A T	W			F P		D		15 19	
Trithuria submersa			A	Sp			F P		S W		13	
Typha domingensis			T	Y			F P		A		1 6 7 14 19 20 22	*
Typha orientalis			T	Y			F P		A		1 6 12 16	*
Uncinia tenella			T E				P N		S		2 3	
Vallisneria spiralis			H	S-A			F P		A		1 13	
Wolffia australiana			H				F P		A		1	
Xanthorrhoea australis	S		T	W-S	N	N	F P		D		7	*
Xanthorrhoea minor ssp. *lutea*			T	Sp-S	N	N	F P		D M		5 7 8 21 22	*
Xyris gracilis			T	S			F P		S		8	
Xyris operculata			T	S			P		S		8	
Zostera muelleri			H	Sp-A			F		A		1	
Zoysia macrantha			G				F		D M	1	11 12	

Ferns and Fern Allies

	Tree	Shrub	Other	Flowers	Bird	Butterfly	Sun Aspect	Screen Windbreak	Drainage	Coast	Vegetation Communities	Aboriginal Uses
Adiantum aethiopicum			G				P		M		3 4 7 14 16 21 22	
Allantodia australis			T				P N		M		2 3	
Asplenium bulbiferum			T				P		M		2-4	
Asplenium flabellifolium ssp. *gracillimum*			G E				P		M S		3 4 14 16 20 22	
Azolla filiculoides							F P		A		1 7 13 14 16 19 22	
Azolla pinnata							F P		A		1 4 22	
Blechnum cartilagineum			T G				P		M		4 22	
Blechnum chambersii			T				P N		S W		3 4	
Blechnum fluviatile			T G				P N		M		3 4	
Blechnum minus			T G				F P		S W		3 4 7 22	
Blechnum nudum			T G				P N		M S		3 4 7 22	
Blechnum patersonii			T G				P N		M		2 3	
Blechnum wattsii			G				P N		M		2-4	
Botrychium australe									M		15	
Calochlaena dubia			T G				P N		M S		4 16 22	
Cheilanthes austrotenuifolia			T G				F P		D		4 14 19 21 22	
Cheilanthes distans			T				F		D		16	
Cheilanthes sieberi ssp. *sieberi*			T G				F		D		15 19	
Ctenopteris heterophylla			E				N		S		2 3	
Cyathea australis	S-M						P N		M S		2-4 22	
Cyathea cunninghamii	M-T						N		S W		3	
Dicksonia antarctica	S-M						P N		S		2-4 22	
Doodia caudata			T				P N		W		16	
Doodia media ssp. *australis*			T G				P N		M		16 22	

	Tree	Shrub	Other	Flowers	Bird	Butterfly	Sun Aspect	Screen Windbreak	Drainage	Coast	Vegetation Communities	Aboriginal Uses
Gleichenia dicarpa			C				F P		S W		4 9	
Gleichenia microphylla			C				P N		S W		3 4 9 22	
Grammitis billardieri			E				N				2-4	
Histiopteris incisa			G				P N		M		2-4	
Hymenophyllum australe			E				N				2	
Hymenophyllum cupressiforme			E				N				2-4	
Hymenophyllum flabellatum			E				N				2-4	
Hypolepis glandulifera			G				F P		M S		3	
Hypolepis muelleri			G				F P		S W		3 4	
Hypolepis rugosula			G				F P		S W		3 4 9	
Isoetes drummondii var. *drummondii*			T				F P		S W		14	
Isoetes muelleri			T				F P		S W		13	
Lastreopsis acuminata			T				P N		M		3 4 22	
Lastreopsis hispida			T				P N		M S		2 3	
Lindsaea linearis			G				F P		M S		4 7 8 22	
Lycopodiella laterale							P N		S W		9	
Marsilea drummondii			G				F P		W A		13 14 16 19	*
Marsilea hirsuta			G				F P		W		13	
Marsilea sp.			G				F P		W A		13 15	
Microsorum pustulatum			E C				P N				2 3	
Ophioglossum lusitanicum			T				F P		M S		8 9 15 22	
Pellaea falcata var. *falcata*			T				P N		M S		3 4 16 20	
Phylloglossum drummondi			T				P N		S		6 9	
Pilularia novae hollandiae			T				F P		S W		19	
Pleurosorus rutifolius			T				F		D M		16 19 20	
Polyphlebium venosum			E				P N				2-4	
Polystichum proliferum			T G				P N		M S		2-4	
Pteridium esculentum							F P		D M	2	3-5 7-10 14 22	*
Pteris comans			T				N		S		3 4	
Pteris tremula			T				P N		S W		4	
Pyrrosia rupestris			E				P N				3	
Rumohra adiantiformis			E				P N				2	
Schizaea asperula			T				P		D M	2	8 9	
Schizaea bifida			T				P		S W	2	8 9	
Schizaea fistulosa			T				P		S W	2	8 9	
Selaginella gracillima			H				P N		S W		6 9	
Selaginella uliginosa			H				F P		S W		6 9	
Sticherus lobatus							P N		S		2	
Sticherus tener							P N		S		2 3	
Tmesipteris billardieri			E				N				2	
Tmesipteris parva			E				N				2	
Todea barbara	S						A		S		3 4	

Conifers

	Tree	Shrub	Other	Flowers	Bird	Butterfly	Sun Aspect	Screen Windbreak	Drainage	Coast	Vegetation Communities	Aboriginal Uses
Callitris glaucophylla	M-T				S		F	W	D		15	

Appendix 2. Reserves and Localities

These locations are representative of the plant communities that were once found across the greater Melbourne area and are referred to in the individual plant descriptions. Each is indicated on the map of the Melbourne Study on end papers.

Visits to these areas will provide an idea of the way plants relate to each other in a community. Unfortunately all are affected, to some degree, by invading weeds.

It must be stressed that removal of plant material should only occur with the permission of the land owner and that plants should never be transplanted from public land.

1. Weeroona Garden
   Set up by Brunswick Electricity Supply and Victorian Indigenous Nurseries Co-operative
   CERES, Lee St, East Brunswick
   Plants used by the local Wurundjeri tribe
2. Merrett Rifle Range, Williamstown
   Kororoit Creek Rd. Williamstown
   Communities: Primary Dune Scrub, Saltmarsh, Grassy Wetlands, Plains Grassland, Coastal and Marine vegetation
   Owner: Dept. Conservation & Environment
   Whilst the bay side of this area has been retained as a reserve (now known as Jawbone Conservation Reserve), the grasslands area was bulldozed for a housing estate in 1991.
3. Kororoit Creek mouth
   Altona Coastal Park
   Communities: Saltmarsh, Marine
   Owner: managed by Cities of Altona & Williamstown
4. Cherry Lake—Truganina Swamp
   Millers Rd. Altona
   Community: Saltmarsh
   Owner: Melbourne Water
5. Point Cook Metropolitan Park
   Point Cook—Homestead Rd, Werribee
   Communities: Primary Dune Scrub, Grassy Wetland, Saltmarsh, Plains Grassland
   Owner: Melbourne Water
6. Laverton RAAF Base Swamp
   Princes Highway, Laverton
   Community: Grassy Wetlands
   Owner: RAAF (prohibited access) & Public Transport Corporation (small area)
7. Altona Grasslands (including Laverton North Grassland Reserve)
   South and East of Princes Highway to Melbourne Water Drainage Basin, Altona
   Communities: Plains Grassland, Grassy Wetland, Saltmarsh
   Owner: Both private and public land.
   Latrobe University have reintroduced some rarer grassland species back into the Laverton North Grassland Reserve.
   A site of National significance, containing many rare and depleted species.
8. Cobbledicks Ford
   Cobbledicks Ford Rd, Werribee
   Community: Riparian Woodland
   Owner: Public land
9. Exford woodlands
   Melton South
   Community: Box Woodland (State significance)
   Owner: Private
10. North-western Rail Reserve
    Melton Reservoir through Melton
    Community: Plains Grassland
    Owner: Public Transport Corporation
11. Deans Marsh
    East of Rockbank, Sydenham West
    Community: Grassy wetland
    Owner: Mostly private
12. Evans St. Sunbury, Rail Reserve
    Community: Plains Grassland (State significance)
    Owner: Public Transport Corporation, Shire of Bulla
    Contains a wide range of grasses.
13. Melbourne–Bendigo Rail Reserve
    Sites between Sunbury and Diggers Rest railway stations
    Community: Plains Grassland (National significance)
    Owner: Public Transport Corporation
14. Jacksons Creek, Sunbury
    Communities: Box Woodland, Riparian Scrub, Chenopod Rocky Open Scrub
    Owner: Mostly private
15. Diggers Rest Rail Reserve Grasslands
    Between Calder Raceway and Diggers Rest
    Community: Plains Grassland (National significance)
    Owner: Public Transport Corporation
16. Organ Pipes National Park
    Calder Highway, Sydenham
    Communities: Riparian Scrub (mostly original flora); Box Woodland, Plains Grassland
    Owner: Managed by Dept. Conservation & Environment
    A revegetation project where many locally threatened species have been collected from nearby areas and reintroduced into the Park.
17. Taylors Lakes Grassland
    Between Keilor-Melton Rd and railway line, Taylors Lakes
    Community: Plains Grassland (National significance)
    Owner: Has now been cleared for housing, leaving tiny pockets of remnant vegetation which will ultimately disappear.
18. Taylors Creek
    St. Albans Rd to Calder Park Dve, Taylors Lakes
    Communities: Box Woodland, Riparian Scrub, Plains Grassland
    Owner: Mostly private; Surveys prepared by Melbourne Water

19. Steele Creek Grassland
West of confluence with Maribyrnong R., Avondale Heights
Communities: Riparian Scrub, Plains Grassland, escarpment vegetation
Owner: Melbourne Water
20. Braybrook Rail Reserve Grassland
West of Tottenham railway station, between Sunshine Rd and Duke St.
Community: Plains Grassland
Owner: Public Transport Corporation
21. Royal Park West
Manningham St, Parkville
Community: Red Gum Woodland
Owner: City of Melbourne
22. Union St. Brunswick, along Moonee Ponds Ck
Community: Riparian Scrub
Owner: Public
23. Napier Park, Essendon
Community: Red Gum Woodland
Owner: City of Essendon
24. Radar Hill, Tullamarine
Lancefield and Perimeter Rds, Melbourne International Airport
Community: Box Woodland
Owner: Commonwealth Government
25. Gellibrand Hill State Park
Oaklands and Somerton Rd, Oaklands Junction
Communities: Red Gum Woodland, Box Woodland
Owner: Managed by Dept. Conservation & Environment
26. Shire of Bulla
The vascular flora of the Shire of Bulla
Communities: Red Gum Woodland, Box Woodland, Plains Grassland, Riparian Scrub, Chenopod Rocky Open Scrub
27. Deep Creek environs
Konagaderra Rd, East of Sunbury
Community: Riparian Scrub
Owner: Private & public
28. Merri Creek, Cooper St, Somerton
Communities: Plains Grassland, Riparian Scrub
Owner: Public & Private; a small section along the Merri Ck has recently been acquired by the State Government to become part of the Merri Ck Metropolitan Park. At the time of writing the rest of this area is under threat of industrial development.
29. Merri Creek Valley
North Coburg to Campbellfield
Communities: Riparian Scrub, Plains Grassland
Owner: Public and private
Two lists were used: Rupp's species list of 1896 and Merri Ck Co-ordinating Committee study 1984
30. Yarra River to Studley Pk 1856
Community: Riparian Scrub and others
Early list by Hannaford of plants along the Yarra River.
31. Heyington Railway Reserve 1945
Communities: Escarpment, Red Gum Woodland
Owner: Public Transport Corporation
Early list of Yarra R. cliffs and the railway reserve at Heyington
32. Studley Park & Yarra Bend, Kew
Communities: Red Gum Woodland, Riparian Scrub, Dry Sclerophyll Forest
Owner: Some private, most managed by Melbourne Water
33. Heidelberg area
Communities: include Red Gum Woodland, Riparian Scrub
34. Templestowe area
Communities: Red Gum Woodland, Dry Sclerophyll Forest
34A. Yarra Valley Metropolitan Park
Communities: Riparian Scrub, Valley Sclerophyll Forest
Owner: Melbourne Water
35. Gresswell Forest
Bendoran Cres, Bundoora
Community: Red Gum Woodland
Owner: managed by Latrobe University Wildlife Reserve
36. Plenty Gorge
Plenty River from Wilton Vale Rd to Plenty River Ave
Communities: Valley and Dry Sclerophyll Forests, Box Ironbark Woodland
Owner: Mostly public, managed by Melbourne Water and Dept. Conservation & Environment
37. Yandell Reserve
St. Helena Rd, Greensborough
Community: Dry Sclerophyll Forest
Owner: Managed by Shire of Diamond Valley
38. Meruka Park
Karingal Dve, Eltham
Community: Dry Sclerophyll Forest
Owner: Managed by Shire of Eltham
39. Eltham Lower Park
Homestead Rd, Eltham
Community: Dry and Valley Sclerophyll Forests
Owner: Managed by Shire of Eltham
40. Bemboka Reserve
Bemboka Rd, Warranwood
Community: Dry Sclerophyll Forest grading to Valley Sclerophyll Forest
Owner: Managed by City of Croydon
41. Professors Hill
Research-Warrandyte Rd, Warrandyte Nth
Communities: Dry and Valley Sclerophyll Forests
Owner: Managed by Shire of Eltham
42. Warrandyte State Park
Several areas including 4th & 5th Hill, Jumping Ck Reserve
Communities: Dry and Valley Sclerophyll Forests, Riparian Scrub
Owner: Managed by Dept. Conservation & Environment
43. Koolunga Reserve
Forest Rd, Ferntree Gully
Community: Valley Sclerophyll Forest
Owner: Managed by City of Knox
44. Mullum Mullum/Koonung Valley
Doncaster to Ringwood
Communities: Dry and Valley Sclerophyll Forests, Riparian Scrub
Owner: Public and private land
45. Wattle Park 1917, 1958
Riversdale Rd, Wattle Park
Community: Left over remnant of Red Gum Woodland
Owner: Managed by Melbourne Water
46. Blackburn Lake
Central Rd, Blackburn
Community: Valley Sclerophyll Forest, some Riparian and Aquatic vegetation
Owner: Managed by City of Nunawading
47. City of Nunawading
Communities: Dry and Valley Sclerophyll Forests
48. Antonio Park
Maroondah Highway and Deep Creek Rd, Mitcham
Community: Dry Sclerophyll Forest
Owner: Managed by City of Nunawading
49. Mitcham area
General lists by J W Audas, 1937 and F Rogers 1970
Communities: Dry and Valley Sclerophyll Forests
50. 'Uambi'
Heathmont
Community: Valley Sclerophyll Forest
Owner: Private
50A. Ringwood
Lists of several reserves within the City of Ringwood personal knowledge by members of SGAP
Communities: Dry and Valley Sclerophyll Forests
51. Croydon
Lists of several reserves within the City of Croydon
Communities: Dry and Valley Sclerophyll Forests, Riparian scrub

52. Birts Hill
Alice St, Croydon
Community: Dry Sclerophyll Forest
Owner: Managed by Dept. Conservation & Environment
53. Hotchkins Ridge Flora Reserve
Exeter Rd, Croydon North
Community: Valley Sclerophyll Forest
Owner: City of Croydon & Dept. Conservation & Environment
54. Tereddan Dve Reserves
Kilsyth South
Communities: Valley Sclerophyll Forest, Swamp Scrub
Owner: Shire of Lillydale, Dept. Conservation & Environment & Melbourne Water
55. Mt. Dandenong National Park—west face
Mt. Dandenong Tourist Rd. to Glasgow Rd, Montrose
Communities: Dry and Valley Sclerophyll Forests, pockets of Damp Sclerophyll Forest
Owner: Managed by Dept. Conservation & Environment
56. Mt Evelyn area
Communities: Valley and Damp Sclerophyll Forests
57. Sherbrooke Forest
Dandenong Ranges
Communities: Cool Temperate Rainforest, Wet Sclerophyll Forest
Owner: Managed by Dept. Conservation & Environment
58. Ferntree Gully National Park
Burwood Highway & Mt Dandenong Tourist Rd, Ferntree Gully
Communities: Wet and Damp Sclerophyll Forests
Owner: Managed by Dept. Conservation & Environment
59. Baluk Willam Flora Reserve
Courtnays Rd, Belgrave South
Community: Sclerophyll Woodland
Owner: Managed by Dept. Conservation & Environment
60. Lysterfield Lake Park
Wellington Rd, Lysterfield
Communities: Grassy Low Open Forest, Wetland and Aquatic vegetation
Owner: Managed by Dept. Conservation & Environment
61. Churchill National Park
Churchill Park Dve, Rowville
Communities: Damp and Valley Sclerophyll Forests, Swamp Scrub
Owner: Dept. Conservation & Environment
62. Dandenong Valley Metropolitan Park
City of Waverley
Communities: Valley Sclerophyll Forest, Swamp Scrub, Aquatic
Owner: Melbourne Water
63. Waverley District
Communities: Valley Sclerophyll Forest, Swamp scrub
64. Valley Reserve, Mt. Waverley
Wills Ave, Mt. Waverley
Community: Valley Sclerophyll Forest
Owner: Managed by City of Waverley
65. Ashburton Wood 1931
High St. Rd, Gardiners Creek, Warrigal Rd
Community: Red Gum Woodland
Now totally developed.
66. Oakleigh area
General list of original species. Areas mostly developed
Community: Red Gum Woodland
67. City of Sandringham
Many plants noted as extinct within the area.
Communities: Tea-tree Heath, Wattle Tea-tree Scrub, Grassy Low Open Forest, Red Gum Woodland, Coastal Banksia Woodland, Primary Dune Scrub, Coastal Cliffs
68. Beaumaris High School
Balcombe & Reserve Rds, Beaumaris
Community: Tea-tree Heath
Owner: Ministry of Education & Training
69. Royal Melbourne Golf Course
Reserve & Cheltenham Rds, Black Rock
Communities: Primary Dune Scrub, Tea-tree Heath
Owner: Royal Melbourne Golf Club
69A. City of Mordialloc
Communities: Grassy Low Open Forest, Tea-tree Heath, Red Gum Woodland, Swamp Scrub, Primary Dune Scrub
70. The Grange Heathland Reserve
Osborne Ave, Clayton South
Community: Tea-tree Heath
Owner: City of Oakleigh
71. Braeside Metropolitan Park
Lower Dandenong Rd, Braeside
Communities: Tea-tree Heath, Grassy Low Open Forest, Red Gum Woodland, Swamp Scrub, Wattle Tea-tree Scrub
Owner: Melbourne Water
72. Edithvale-Seaford Wetlands
West of Wells Rd, Edithvale to Seaford
Community: Swamp Scrub, sub-saline wetlands
Owner: Dandenong Valley & Western Port Authority
73. Cranbourne Annexe
Ballarto Rd, Cranbourne; Annexe of Royal Botanic Gardens
Communities: Tea-tree Heath, Wattle Tea-tree scrub, Grassy Low Open Forest
Owner: Managed by Dept. Conservation & Environment
74. City of Frankston
General list including The Pines
Communities: Tea-tree Heath, Wattle Tea-tree Scrub, Grassy Low Open Forest, Primary Dune Scrub, Coastal Banksia Woodland
75. Langwarrin Flora and Fauna Reserve
Robinsons Rd, Langwarrin
Communities: Tea-tree Heath, Wattle Tea-tree Scrub, Grassy Low Open Forest
Owner: Managed by Dept. Conservation & Environment
76. Moorooduc Quarry Flora & Fauna Reserve & Moorooduc Plains
Between Moorooduc & Canadian Bay Rds, Moorooduc
Community: Grassy Low Open Forest
Owner: Managed by Dept. Conservation & Environment

Appendix 3. A. Associations & Contacts for Australian and Indigenous Plants

1. Society for Growing Australian Plants Maroondah Inc. (SGAP)
   PO Box 33 Ringwood 3134

   Caters for people from Kew to Montrose interested in growing and conserving Australian plants. Activities include monthly meetings, garden visits, field trips, camps and displays.

2. Society for Growing Australian Plants Victoria Inc.
   C/o 17 Craig Crt, Heathmont 3135

   The co-ordinating committee for the 24 district branches of SGAP, both city and country. All membership enquiries should be directed to them.

3. Indigenous Flora and Fauna Association Inc. (IFFA)
   C/o 69 Spenseley St., Clifton Hill 3068

   An organisation of professionals and amateurs from diverse backgrounds who are committed to the conservation of indigenous flora and fauna through preservation, restoration and management of habitat. Their objective is to both research and provide information.

4. Australasian Native Orchid Society, Victoria Inc. (ANOS)
   Secretary: PO Box 285, Cheltenham 3192

5. Conservation Council of Victoria, 247 Flinders Lane Melbourne 3000 Ph 654 4833

6. 'Friends' activities published in newsletters of IFFA (Indigenotes) and Victorian National Parks Association. (VNPA contact number (03) 650 8296)

   Local government departments can provide information on groups managing local bushland reserves or local environment groups.

7. Australian Trust for Conservation Volunteers

   Co-ordinate plantings throughout Australia during the week and on weekends, predominantly using indigenous plants.

   National Headquarters in Ballarat (053) 32 7490
   Melbourne (03) 532 8446

8. A project is underway to set up a database which will provide very detailed information on the indigenous plants of Melbourne and their management. A pilot program is currently being prepared. For further information contact Melbourne Water on (03) 615 4619.

9. Indigenous Nurseries Network (IFFA). Members represent more than 60 indigenous nurseries throughout Victoria. Contact: Sue Mills (03) 383 2937.

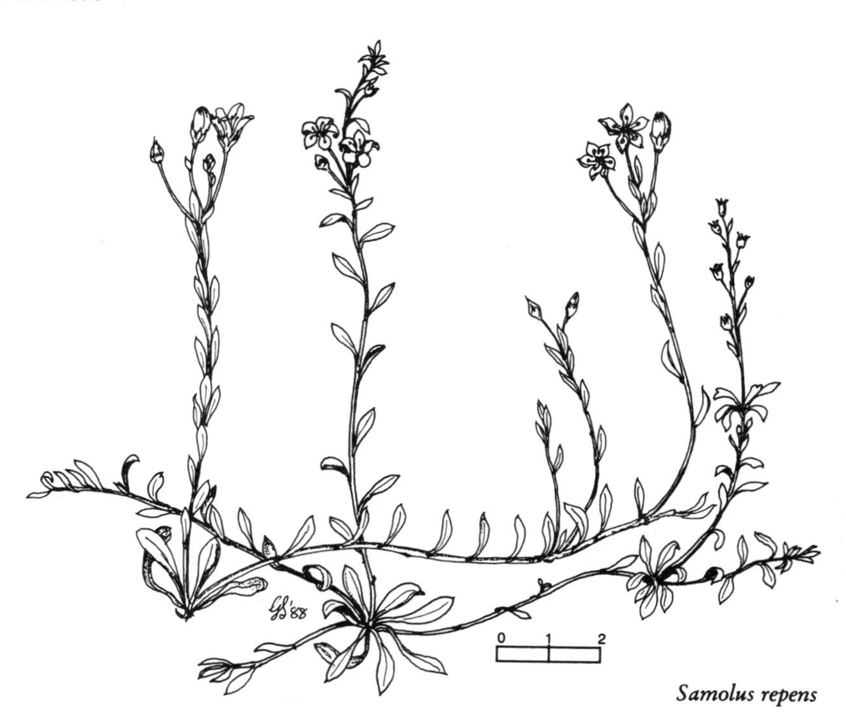

Samolus repens

Appendix 3. B. Nurseries Selling Indigenous plants of Melbourne

Locating plants from local provenances has been a difficulty experienced by many people involved in both large and small scale regeneration projects. Some large projects such as Nunawading Indigenous Plants Project (878 5998) and Friends of Warrandyte State Park grew their own to solve this problem. Fortunately, as the realisation of the benefits of growing indigenous plants increases, nurseries and individuals are beginning to cater for the demand.

The nurseries below are not an exhaustive list. Some nurseries also sell a general range of Australian plants. It is up to the buyer to check labelling on stock to ensure that the plants are indigenous to their area of need.

Many local councils are now setting up indigenous nurseries for their own areas. Some of these also have plants available to the public.

Austraflora Nursery, Belfast Rd, Montrose 3765
Ph (03) 728 1222 Proprietors: Bill Molyneux & Sue Forrester
Limited stock of indigenous plants.

Best Plant Brokers, 141 Stud Rd, Dandenong 3175
Ph (03) 791 8387 Proprietor: Darren Wallace
Tubestock to advanced sizes of species derived from provenance material within the Greater Knox region, also Lysterfield, Belgrave to Montrose.

Bimbadeen Nursery, 104 Webb St, Warrandyte 3113
Ph (03) 844 3906 Proprietor: Peter Hansen
Specialises in species from Warrandyte.

Bindelong Nursery (Yarra Valley Tubes), 55 Railway Ave, Wandin Nth 3139 Ph (059) 64 4974 Proprietor: Doug Pocock
Wholesale supplier of plants of the Yarra Valley.

Bush Garden Native Plants, 3 Burswood Close, Frankston 3199 (Melway 102 F10) Ph (059) 71 2585 Proprietor: Bev Courtney
Specialises in understorey species of the Mornington Peninsula, including Frankston, Langwarrin and Cranbourne. Species include grasses, orchids and wildflowers, also groundcovers, shrubs and small trees.

Bushland Flora, PO Box 312 Mt Evelyn 3796 Ph (03) 736 4364 Proprietors: Andrew Paget & Ian Shimmen
Contact re retail outlets throughout Melbourne.
Contract, retail and wholesale in tubestock. Species Melbourne-wide.

Bush Life Nursery, cnr Canterbury & Wantirna Rds, Ringwood 3134 Ph (03) 870 0016 Proprietor: Greg Jacobs
Specialises in plants from the Outer Eastern suburbs from Box Hill to Dandenong Ranges, also Warrandyte.

Chris Fletcher, 58 King St, Yarra Glen 3775 Ph (03) 730 1517 (by appointment only)
Species from Yarra Valley.

Dragonfly Aquatics, RMB AB 366, Colac 3250 Proprietor: Nick Romanowski
Specialises in water and moisture-loving plants, with the largest range in Australia. Send 2 stamps to the above address for a catalogue.

E.J. Fenton, Larapinta, Box 570 Hamilton 3300 Ph (055) 73 4555 Proprietor: Elizabeth Fenton
Seed and tubestock from the Hamilton district.

Geelong Indigenous Nursery, Ph (052) 298 087 Proprietor: Mark Trengove

Kareelah Bush Nursery, Lot 7 Luxton Dve, Balnarring 3926
Ph (059) 89 5801 Proprietor: Kathie Strickland
Tubestock from grasses to trees, from Mornington Peninsula. Retail and contract growing.

Kuranga Native Nursery, 393 Maroondah Highway Ringwood 3134 Ph (03) 879 4076 Proprietors: Evan Clucas & Leanne Weston
Specialises in tubestock, mostly from the Eastern suburbs, especially Ringwood. The source of all indigenous stock is marked on the label.

Local Native Flora, 4 Gull St, Rye 3941 Ph (059) 85 1122
Proprietor: Mark Adams
Southern Mornington Peninsula species and contract growing.

Otways Indigenous Nursery, 14 Tenth Ave, Anglesea 3230
Ph (052) 63 1630 (by appointment only) Proprietor: Geoff Clark
Specialises in coastal and heathland plant propagation from seeds and cuttings, from Point Addis to Apollo Bay to Colac and Winchelsea.

Put It Back Nursery, 1/51 Spenser St, St Kilda 3182 Ph (03) 534 3154 AH. Proprietor: Rob Scott
Contract seed collection and growing of plants throughout Melbourne.

Sandringham Community Nursery, cnr Reserve & Talinga Rds, Sandringham Ph (03) 598 8111 (Sandringham City Council) Open Saturdays.
Specialises in Sandringham provenances.

Victorian Indigenous Nurseries Co-op Ltd (VINC) CERES, Lee St., Brunswick East 3057 Ph (03) 387 4403
Collects seeds in and grows plants for the Northern, Western and Inner suburbs of Melbourne. Wholesale and retail nursery. Also contract growing and revegetation assistance.

Wildlife Reserve Nursery, Latrobe University, Bundoora 3083. Take Ring Rd at Latrobe University to the North East end of the campus, opposite Car Park 7
Specialises in plants from Heidelberg, Preston, Whittlesea, Diamond Valley and Eltham municipalities; also wetland plants of the Yarra Valley.

Wyeena Nursery, Smiths Gully Rd, Smiths Gully 3760.
Ph (03) 710 1340 Proprietors: Julie & Kahn Franke
Specialises in plants from Eltham Shire, Plenty Gorge, and Yarra Valley.

Appendix 4. Glossary

abaxial Away from the axis or stem.
achene A small dry one-seeded fruit which does not split on maturity (sometimes referred to as a cypsela).
annual A plant that completes its life cycle in one season.
anther The pollen bearing part of a stamen.
apex The free end or tip of a leaf.
appressed Pressed flat against something.
ascending Directed upwards.
auricle An ear-shaped lobe or appendage.
awn A bristle like appendage, e.g. on the seeds of many grasses.
axil The upper angle between two dissimilar parts e.g. that formed by a leaf in relation to the stem.
axillary Of buds or flowers arising in an axil.
basal rosette A cluster of leaves radiating from a common point at the base of the stem.
berry A fleshy fruit often containing many seeds.
bilobed Two lobed.
bipinnate Twice pinnately divided.
bract A leaflike structure which subtends a flower stem or inflorescence.
bracteole A small bract.
bulbil A specialized bud produced at the junction of main veins on the fronds of some ferns.
burr A prickly fruit.
callus (pl. calli) A thickening, eg the glandular, warty structure often found on the labellum in orchids; hardened, often hairy base of grass florets.
calyx Outer envelope of the flower, consisting of the sepals.
carpel Female reproductive organs.
column A fleshy growth in the flowers of orchids formed by the union of the stigmas and stamens.
compound Consisting of 2 or more parts.
concave Curves inward.
convex Curves or bulges outwards.
convolute Rolled around and overlapping, as in petals in a bud or lemmas in a spikelet.
coppice Wood of small trees grown for periodic cutting; growth arising from dormant buds in trunk, usually after lopping.
cordate Heart-shaped.
corolla The petals; whorl of floral segments inside the calyx.
crenulate Bordered by very small round teeth.
cuneate Wedge-shaped.
cyme An inflorescence where each branch is opposite and ends in a flower, the flowers opening sequentially downwards, and further development is by lateral branches.
decumbent Reclining on the ground with the tips of branches ascending.
decussate Of opposite leaves, each successive pair at right angles to the pair below.
dicotyledon The group of flowering plants which bear 2 seed leaves at the seedling stage.
dioecious Bearing male and female flowers on separate plants.
diffuse Widely spreading and much branched; of open growth.
discoid Flowerheads which only have central tubular disc florets (esp. Asteraceae).
drupe A fruit with a 'stone' or seed surrounded by a fleshy layer.

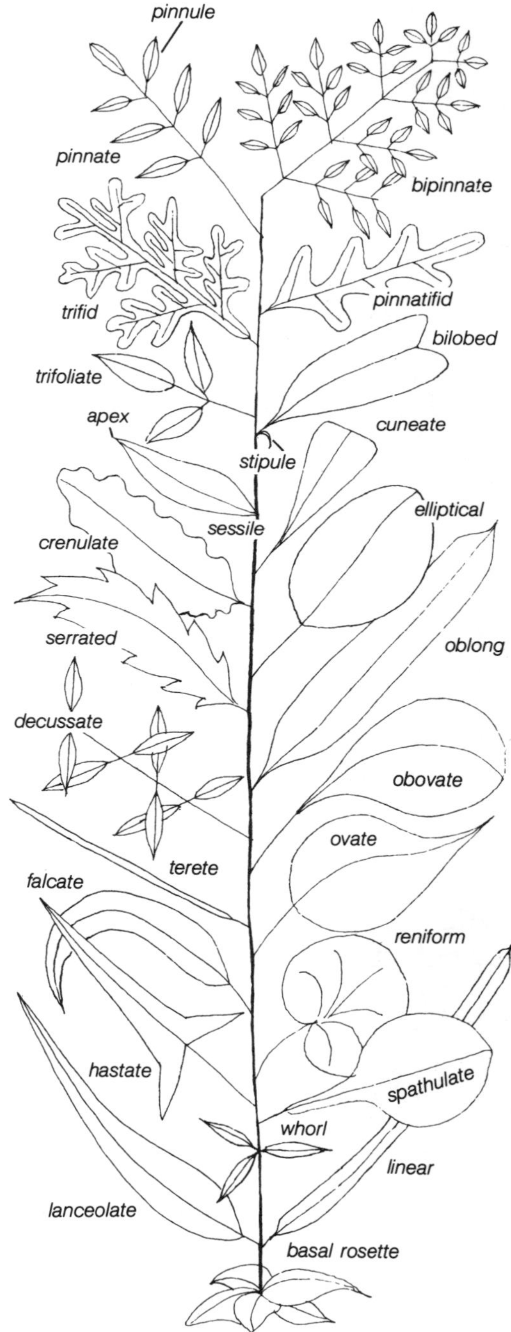

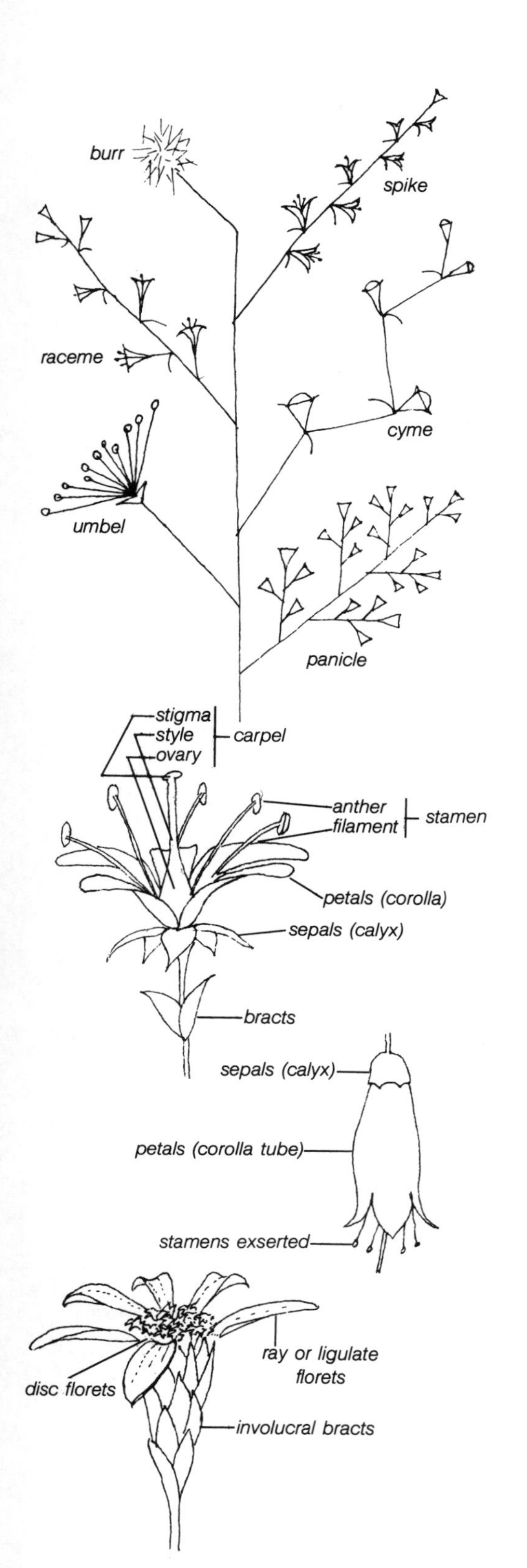

elliptical	Of a flat surface in the shape of an ellipse.
endemic	Found only in a specified location.
entire	Whole, not toothed or divided in anyway.
ephemeral	A plant completing its life cycle within a very short period e.g. 3–6 months.
epiphytic	A plant growing on another but not parasitic.
exserted	Protruding beyond adjacent parts.
falcate	Sickle-shaped.
filament	The stalk of a stamen supporting the anther..
filiform	Long and very slender; thread-like.
flexuose	Stem bent alternately in opposite directions.
floret	The smallest unit of a compound flower.
frond	Leaf of a fern.
frontline coastal	The closest to the water's edge, able to withstand salt-laden winds.
glabrous	Smooth, without hairs.
glaucous	Covered with a bloom, giving a bluish lustre.
globose	Like a globe; round.
glume	One of 2 bracts at the base of the spikelets of grasses and sedges.
hastate	Like an arrow head with spreading basal lobes.
herb	A plant that produces a fleshy rather than woody stem.
herbaceous	A perennial plant which dies down each year after flowering.
inflorescence	The flowering structure of a plant.
internode	Portion of stem between two adjacent nodes.
juvenile leaf	A seedling leaf that differs markedly from the adult leaf.
labellum	A lip; in orchids the petal in front of the column.
lanceolate	Lance-shaped; narrow and tapering at each end especially the apex.
lateral	Arising from the main axis; at the side of.
lemma	The lower of 2 bracts enclosing each grass flower.
lignotuber	A woody, usually underground, swelling at the base of a trunk, containing dormant buds.
ligulate	Of daisy flowers, a strap-like corolla lobe (ray floret).
linear	Long and narrow, with parallel sides.
linear-lanceolate	Long, narrow lance-shaped.
lithophyte	Of a plant growing on rock.
lobe	A rounded projecting part of a leaf, petal or sepal.
mallee	A shrub or tree with several trunks or stems rising from a lignotuber (esp. *Eucalyptus* spp.).
mealy	Covered with a flour-like powder.
monocotyledon	The group of flowering plants which bear a single seed leaf at the seedling stage.
monoecious	Bearing male and female flowers on the same plant.
mycorrhiza	A beneficial relationship between the roots or seeds of a plant and soil borne fungi resulting in a nutrient exchange system. Some plants (e.g. orchids) cannot grow without such a relationship.
node	The place on a stem marked by the attachment of a leaf or bracts.
oblanceolate	Lanceolate with the broadest part above the middle.
oblong	Greater in breadth than length.
obovate	Ovate with the broadest part above the middle.
obtuse	Blunt or rounded at the apex.
ovate	Egg-shaped and attached by the broad end.
palea	The upper of 2 bracts enclosing each grass flower.
pappus	A tuft of bristles, hairs or scales representing the calyx on the seeds of Asteraceae.
panicle	A much branched inflorescence.
parasitic	Of a plant living on another plant.
pendent	Hanging, swinging.
perennial	Living for more than two years.
perianth	Floral parts or segments (petals and sepals) of monocotyledons.
phyllode	A stem or stalk modified to act as a leaf.
pinna	A primary segment of a divided leaf.
pinnate	Once divided with the divisions extending to the midrib.
pinnatifid	Once divided with the divisions not extending to the midrib.
pinnule	The segment of a compound leaf divided more than once.
procumbent	Flat along the ground without rooting.
provenance	Source.
pungent	Very sharply pointed; also, smelling strongly.
quadrangular	Four-sided and angular.
raceme	A long unbranched inflorescence.

radiate A compound flowerhead (esp. in Asteraceae) comprising central tubular disc florets surrounded by ray florets.
ray floret One of the ligulate florets around the edge of inflorescence, as in daisies.
recurved Curved backwards.
reflexed Bent backwards and downwards.
reniform Kidney-shaped.
rhachilla The main axis of a grass spikelet.
rhachis The main axis of an inflorescence, compound leaf or frond.
rhizome An underground stem.
riparian Of or on a watercourse or drainage line.
saprophyte A plant which derives its food from dead or decaying matter.
scarified seed Seed that has had the surface scratched or lacerated (e.g. by sandpapering).
sclerophyll Referring to a forest dominated by eucalypts with an understorey of shrubs with small hard leaves.
scrub A plant community dominated by shrubs.
second line The second grouping of plants (usually used in reference to coastal plants), those behind the 'front line'.
sedge Waterside plant resembling grass.
sepal Free segment of the calyx or outer whorl of the perianth.
serrated Toothed with sharp, forward pointing teeth.
sessile Without a stalk.
simple Undivided, of one piece.
spathulate Spoon-shaped.
spike An inflorescence of sessile flowers on an unbranched axis.
spikelet Small spikes of the grass infloresence, bearing 2 glumes and one or more florets.
spore A simple asexual reproductive unit of ferns.
sporocarp A thick wall covering the spore cases.
stalk A support for a flower or leaf.
stamen The male part of a flower producing pollen, consisting of an anther and a filament.
stellate Star-shaped or of starlike form.
stigma Part of the style receptive to pollen.
stipule Small bract-like appendages borne in pairs at the base of the stalk.
stolon A basal stem growing above or just below the ground surface and rooting at intervals.
stoloniferous Bearing stolons; spreading by stolons.
style The elongated part of a carpel between the ovary and the stigma.
sward Expanse of short grass.
symbiotic Of a mutually beneficial partnership.
terete Cylindrical and slender.
terrestrial Growing in the ground.
terminal At the end or extremity.
trifid Divided almost to the middle into three parts.
tripinnate Divided three times.
trifoliate A leaf with three leaflets.
truncate With the apex appearing as if cut off.
tuberoid The swollen end of an underground root.
tuberous Resembling a tuber.
umbel An inflorescence in which all the stems arise at the same point and the flowers lie at the same level, more or less umbrella-shaped.
unisexual flowers Having only one sex.
valves A segment of the case of a woody fruit.
whorl An arrangement of three or more parts at the same level around an axis.

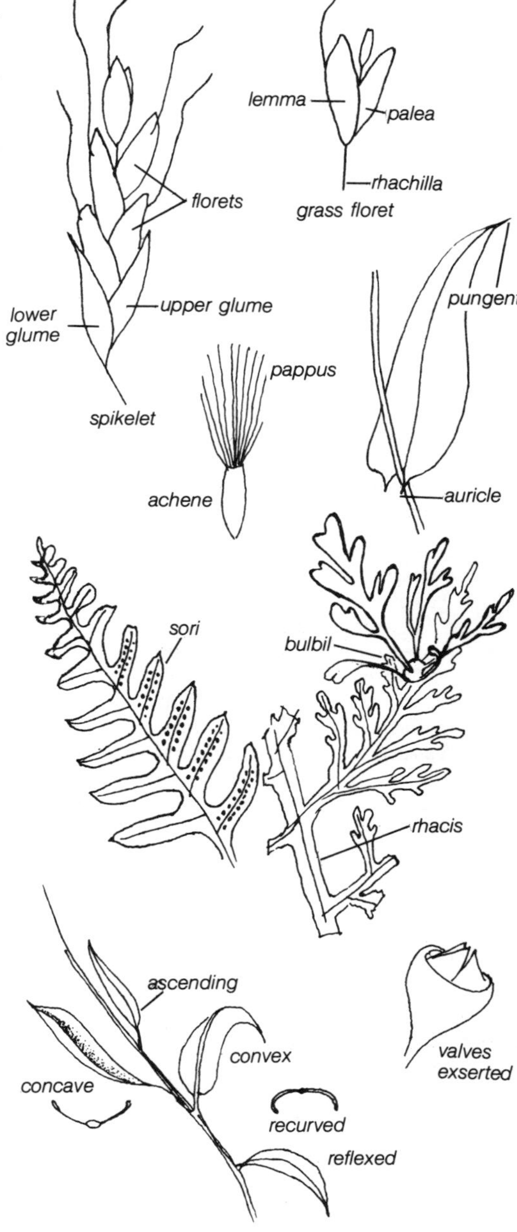

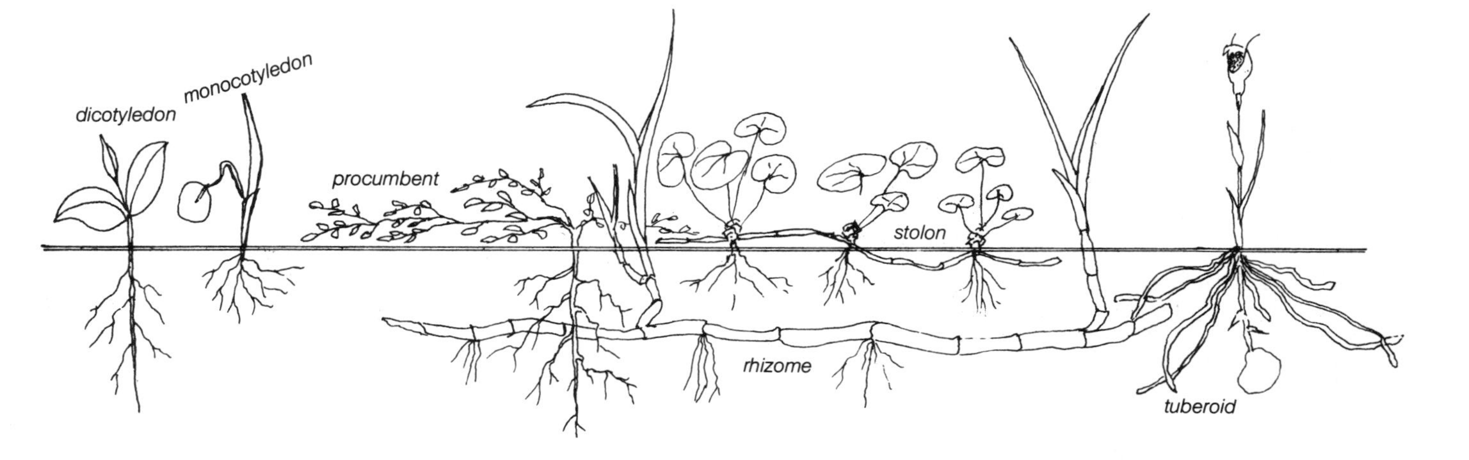

Appendix 5. Bibliography

Other references are listed under Further Reading after each chapter.

Albrecht, D. (unpubl) *A Review of Leafless Species of Juncus in Victoria.*

Aston, H.I. (1973) *Aquatic Plants of Australia*, Melbourne University Press.

Audas, J.W. (1937) *The Australian Bushland*, Robertson & Mullens Ltd, Melbourne.

Australian Daisy Study Group (1987) *Australian Daisies for Gardens and Floral Art*, Lothian Publishing Co., Melbourne.

Australian Plant Study Group (1987) *Grow What Small Plant*, Thomas Nelson (Australia) Ltd, Melbourne.

Australian Plant Study Group (1982) *Grow What Wet*, Thomas Nelson (Australia) Ltd, Melbourne.

Australian Plant Study Group (1980) *Grow What Where*, Thomas Nelson (Australia) Ltd, Melbourne.

Australian Systematic Botany Society (1981) *Flora of Central Australia*, (Ed. J. Jessop), A.H. & A.W. Reed, Sydney.

Australian Systematic Botany Society, (1982) Newsletter Nos. 32, 33 (Ed. G.P. Guymer), Queensland Herbarium, Indooroopilly, Qld

Austrobaileya Vol. 2 (1984), Periodical Journal of Queensland Herbarium, Dept. of Primary Industries, Brisbane, Government Printer, Qld.

Beadle, N.C.W. (1976) *Student's Flora of Northeastern New South Wales*, Pt. 3, University of New England, Armidale.

Beadle, N.C.W., Evans O.D., Carolin R.C. (1972) *Flora of the Sydney Region*, A.H. & A.W Reed, Sydney.

Beardsell, C. & D. (1983) *A Year of Orchids*, Richard Griffin, South Melbourne.

Beauglehole, A.C. (1983) *The Distribution and Conservation of Vascular Plants in the Melbourne area, Victoria*, Western Victorian Field Naturalists Clubs Association, Portland Vic.

Bentham, G. & Mueller, F. (1863–78) *Flora Australiensis* Pts 1–7, Lovell Reeve & Co., London.

Black, J.M. (1943–57) *Flora of South Australia*; 4th edition (1986) Pts 1–4 (Ed. J.P. Jessop & H.R. Toelken) Government Printer, Adelaide.

Blombery, A.M. (1967) *A Guide to Australian Native Plants*, Angus & Robertson, Sydney.

Bridgewater, P.B., Rosser, C. & de Corona, A. (1981) *The Saltmarsh Plants of Southern Australia*, Botany Dept., Monash University, Melbourne.

Brooker, M.I.H. & Kleinig, D.A. (1983) *Field Guide to Eucalypts* Vol. 1, Inkata Press Pty Ltd, Melbourne

Brunonia, (1979–87) Vols 2:1, 4:2, 5:1, 8:3, 9:2, Periodical Journal of the Herbarium Australiense, CSIRO, Melbourne.

Buckhorn, R. et al. (1989) *Urban Forestry Handbook*, Dept. Conservation, Forests & Lands, Melbourne.

Burbidge, N.T. (1984) *Australian Grasses*, revised by Jacobs, S.W.L., National Herbarium, Royal Botanic Gardens, Sydney, Angus & Robertson, Sydney.

Burbidge, N.T. & Gray, M. (1970) *Flora of the Australian Capital Territory*, Australian National University Press, Canberra.

Cady, L. & Rotherham, E.R. (1970) *Australian Native Orchids*, A.H. & A.W. Reed, Sydney.

Calder, W. (1975) *Langwarrin Military Reserve: Ecological Evaluation for the Shire of Cranbourne*, Report, Centre for Environmental Studies, University of Melbourne, Melbourne.

Carr, G.W. (1982) *Vegetation of Exeter Road Ridge, Croydon North, and its significance*, Report to Croydon Conservation Society, Croydon, Victoria.

Carr, G.W. (1983) *Report on the Vegetation and Management of the Proposed Eltham Lower Park Flora Reserve*, Society for Growing Australian Plants Yarra Yarra & Eltham Shire Council, Melbourne.

Carr, G.W. (1991) *New Taxa in Caladenia, Chiloglottis and Gastrodia (Orchidaceae) from South Eastern Australia*, Indigenous Flora & Fauna Association, Melbourne.

Carr, G.W. (1980) *Proposed development of the Vegetation of LaTrobe University Wildlife Reserve*, Wildlife Reserves Management Committee, LaTrobe University, Melbourne.

Carr, G.W., Reid, J. & Albrecht, D. (1987) *The Vegetation, Fauna and Management of Antonio Park*, City of Nunawading, Victoria.

Chandler, C. (1975) *Two Hundred Wattles for Gardens*, David G. Stead Memorial, Wildlife Research Foundation of Australia, Sydney.

Cheal, D.C. (1988) *Botanical Assessment of Grasslands, Merri Creek, Somerton, Cooper Street*, Dept. Conservation & Environment, Melbourne.

Cheal, D.C., et al. (unpubl.) *Vegetation Survey and Sites of Botanical Significance in the Melbourne Area*, Dept. Conservation & Environment, Melbourne.

City of Box Hill (undated) *Box Hill: An Introduction to the Natural Vegetation*, City of Box Hill, Victoria.

Clucas, R.D. (1980) *Peripheral Vegetation of Lysterfield Lake*, Ministry for Conservation, Victoria.

Cochrane, R.G., Fuhrer, B.A., Rotherham, E.R. & Willis, J.H. (1968) *Flowers and Plants of Victoria*, A.H. & A.W. Reed, Sydney.

Conabere, E. & Garnett, J.R. (1987) *Wildflowers of South-Eastern Australia*, Greenhouse Publications, Richmond.

Contributions from the New South Wales National Herbarium, (1962) No. 102, Dept. of Agriculture, NSW.

Costermans, L. (1981) *Native Trees and Shrubs of South-Eastern Australia*, Rigby, Adelaide.

Cribb, A.B. & Cribb, J.W. (1974) *Wild Food in Australia*, Collins, Sydney.

Croydon Conservation Society, (1988) *Trees and Wildflowers of Croydon*, Croydon Conservation Society, Croydon, Victoria.

Cunningham, G.M., Mulham, W.B., Milthorpe, P.C. & Leigh, J.H. (1981) *Plants of Western New South Wales*, Soil Conservation Service of New South Wales.

Curtis, W.M. (1956–67) *The Student's Flora of Tasmania* Pts 1–3, Government Printer, Tas.

Dandenong Valley & Western Port Authority (1991) *Edithvale-Seaford Wetlands*, Dandenong Valley & Western Port Authority, Melbourne.

Dashorst, G.R.M. & Jessop, J.P. (1990) *Plants of the Adelaide Plains and Hills*, State Herbarium of South Australia, Kangaroo Press, Kenthurst, Sydney.

Dockrill, A.W. (1969) *Australian Indigenous Orchids*, Vol 1 Society for Growing Australian Plants, Sydney.

Dunk, G. (1983) *Ferns for the Home and Garden*, Angus & Robertson, Sydney.

Ecological Horticulture Pty. Ltd. 'Appendix F' in Riedel, Byrne & Wilson Sayer Core (1987) *Merrett Rifle Range Environmental Effects Statement* Vol 2, Urban Land Authority, Melbourne.

Edwards, J., Reid, J. et al. (1988) *Mt. Evelyn's Original Garden: Plants of the Northern Dandenongs*, Mt. Evelyn Environment Protection & Progress Association, Melbourne.

Elliot, G. (1979) *Australian Plants for Small Gardens & Containers*, Hyland House, Melbourne.

Elliot, R. (1975) *An Introduction to the Grampians Flora*, Algona Guides, Melbourne.

Elliot, R. & Blake, T. (1984) *Common Native Plants of Sherbrooke Forest & Dandenong Ranges*, Pioneer Design Studio, Lilydale, Vic.

Elliot, R. & Jones, D.L. (1980-90) *Encyclopaedia of Australian Plants* Vol 1–5, Lothian, Melbourne.

Erickson, R. (1975) *Triggerplants*, Paterson Brokensha Pty. Ltd. Perth.

Fairley, A. & Moore, P. (1989) *Native Plants of the Sydney District*, Kangaroo Press, Kenthurst, Sydney.

Fisher, D. (1988) *Vegetation Survey and Sites of Botanical and Geological Significance: Taylors Creek*, Melbourne & Metropolitan Board of Works, Melbourne.

Fitzsimons, P.F. (1983) *Vegetation Management Strategy for Werribee Shire Coastline* (Unpubl. thesis), Monash University.

Flora of Australia (1981–91) (Ed. A.S. George), Vols 3, 4, 18, 45, 46, Australian Government Publishing Service, Canberra.

Friends of the Valley Reserve (undated) *The Valley Reserve, History, Plants, Birds*, Friends of the Valley Reserve & Waverley City Council, Melbourne.

Galbraith, J. (1977) *Collin's Field Guide to the Wildflowers of South-East Australia*, Collins, Sydney.

Geobotany, (1982) Acta Phytotax. Vol 33.

Gott, B. (unpubl.) 'Plant Species used by Koories, found in the Melbourne LCC Area', *Vicuse Database.*

Gullan, P.K. et al. (1989) *Rare or Threatened Plants in Victoria*, Dept. Conservation & Environment, Melbourne.

Gullan, P. & Walsh, N. (1986) *Ferns and Fern Allies of the Upper Yarra Valley & Dandenong Ranges*, National Herbarium of Victoria, Dept. Conservation & Environment, Melbourne.

Harrington, C.D. (1977) *How to Identify Grasses and Grass-like Plants*, Ohio University, Ohio.

Harris, T.Y. (1977) *Gardening with Australian Plants—Shrubs*, Thomas Nelson (Australia) Ltd., Melbourne.

Indigenotes (1990–91) Newsletter of Indigenous Flora & Fauna Association, Melbourne.

Jones, D.L. (1988) *Native Orchids of Australia*, Reed Books Pty. Ltd, Sydney.

Jones, D.L. & Clemesha, S.C. (1976) *Australian Ferns and Fern Allies*, A.H. & A.W. Reed, Sydney.

Jones, D.L. & Gray, B. (1988) *Climbing Plants in Australia*, Reed Books, Sydney.

Journal of the Adelaide Botanic Gardens (1979–81) Adelaide Botanic Gardens, S.A.

Kemp, B. (1987 unpubl.) *Organ Pipes National Park Flora.*

Lamp, C & Collet, F. (1976) *Weeds in Australia*, Inkata Press, Melbourne.

Lamp, C.A., Forbes, S.J. & Cape, V.W. (1990) *Grasses of Temperate Australia*, Inkata Press, Melbourne.

Land Conservation Council (1991) *Melbourne Area District 2 Review — Descriptive Report*, Land Conservation Council, Melbourne.

Launceston Field Naturalists Club (1981) *Guide to Flowers and Plants of Tasmania*, (Ed. M. Cameron), A.H. & A.W. Reed, Sydney.

Leigh, J., Boden, R. & Briggs, J. (1984) *Extinct and Endangered Plants of Australia*, Macmillan Co. Aust. Pty. Ltd., Melbourne.

McCubbin, C. (1971) *Australian Butterflies*, Thomas Nelson (Australia) Ltd., Melbourne.

McDougall, K. (1987) *Sites of Botanical Significance in the Western Region of Melbourne*, Dept. Conservation, Forests & Lands,Melbourne.

Marchant, N.G. et al. (1987) *Flora of the Perth Region*, Pts 1&2, Western Australian Herbarium, Dept. of Agriculture, Perth.

Morton, J. (1984 unpubl.) *The Design of Nature Parks on the Keilor Plains*, Final Project, Landscape Architecture, RMIT, Melbourne.

Miscellaneous species lists as part of published reports for various management committees, state and local government departments (see Appendix 2)

Miscellaneous unpublished species lists (refer to Appendix 2 for many of these).

Muelleria (1986–) Periodical Journal of the National Herbarium of Victoria, Government Printer, Vic.

Nicholls, W.H. (1964) *Orchids of Australia*, Complete Edition, (Ed. D.L. Jones & T.B. Muir), Thomas Nelson (Australia) Ltd, Melbourne.

Nuytsia (1984) Bulletin of the Western Australian Herbarium, Dept. Conservation & Land Management, Government Printer, W.A.

Pearson, L.G.C. (undated) *The Indigenous Plants of the Melbourne Region*, L.G.C. Pearson, Melbourne.

Port Phillip Authority (1982 unpubl.) *The Coastal Vegetation of Port Phillip Bay*, Port Phillip Authority, Melbourne.

Prescott, A. (1988) *It's Blue with Five Petals: Wildflowers of the Adelaide Region*, A Prescott, Prospect, S.A.

Raynor, C. (unpubl. photographic record) *Flora of the Keilor Plains*, Society for Growing Australian Plants, Keilor Plains.

Robinson, R.W. et al. (1986) *Vegetation Survey of the Melbourne Metropolitan Area* (preliminary Report), Dept. Conservation, Forests & Lands, Melbourne.

Rogers, F.J.C. (1978) *A Field Guide to Victorian Wattles*, Revised Edition, F.J.C. Rogers.

Ross, J.H. (1993) *A Census of the Vascular Plants of Victoria*, 4th Edition, National Herbarium of Victoria, Dept. Conservation & Environment, Melbourne.

Sandringham Environment Series (1979–89) Nos 3, 4, 7. Sandringham City Council, Sandringham, Victoria.

Sharpe, P.R. (1986) *Keys to Cyperaceae, Restionaceae and Juncaceae of Queensland*, Botany Branch, Dept. Primary Industries, Brisbane.

Simon, B.K. (1990) *A Key to Australian Grasses* Botany Branch, Dept. Primary Industries, Brisbane.

Society for Growing Australian Plants (1983–90) *Australian Plants*, Quarterly, Society for Growing Australian Plants, Sydney.

Society for Growing Australian Plants, Maroondah Inc. (Rev. 1991) *Attracting Birds to Native Gardens*, Society for Growing Australian Plants, Maroondah Inc. Ringwood.

Society for Growing Australian Plants, Maroondah Inc. (1978) *500 Australian Native Plants*, Society for Growing Australian Plants, Maroondah Inc., Ringwood.

Stanley, T.D. & Ross, E.M. (1983–86) *Flora of South-Eastern Queensland* Vol 2, Queensland Dept. of Primary Industries, Brisbane.

Sutton, C.S. (1916) 'A Sketch of the Keilor Plains Flora', *Victorian Naturalist*, Victorian Field Naturalists Club, Victoria.

Telopea (1981–89) Contributions from the National Herbarium of New South Wales, Government Printer, NSW.

Victorian Naturalist (1928–90) Newsletter of Victorian Field Naturalists Club, Victoria.

Waddell, W. (1976) *Wildflower Diary*, Native Plants Preservation Society.

Wheeler, D.J.B., Jacobs, S.W.L. & Norton, B.E. (1982) *Grasses of New South Wales* University of New England, Armidale, NSW.

Willis, J.H. (1962–72) *A Handbook to Plants in Victoria* Vols 1 & 2, Melbourne University Press, Melbourne.

Willis, J.H. (1964) *Vegetation of the Basalt Plains in Western Victoria*, Proceedings of the Royal Society of Victoria, Vol 77, Victoria.

Woolcock, C. and D. (1984) *Australian Terrestrial Orchids*, Thomas Nelson (Australia) Ltd, Melbourne.

Wrigley, J.W. & Fagg, M. (1979) *Australian Native Plants*, William Collins, Sydney.

Bibliography (third edition)

Backhouse, G.N. & Jeanes, J.A. (1995) *The Orchids of Victoria*, Melbourne University Press, Carlton.

Bishop, T. (1996) *Field Guide to the Orchids of NSW and Victoria*, UNSW, Sydney.

Department of Natural Resources & the Environment, (1997, 1998) *Victorian Flora Information System* Biological Database, Viridans, Brighton East.

Journal of the Adelaide Botanic Gardens (1998) Vol. 18. Adelaide Botanic Gardens, SA.

Muelleria (1995, 1998) Vol. 8, No. 3, Vol. 11. Periodical Journal of the National Herbarium of Victoria, Government Printer, Vic.

Ross, J.H. (2000) *A Census of the Vascular Plants of Victoria,* Sixth Edition, National Herbarium of Victoria, Melbourne.

Telopea (1992, 1998) Vol 5 (1), Vol 8 (1). Periodical Journal of the National Herbarium of New South Wales, Royal Botanic Gardens, Sydney.

Walsh, N.G. & Entwisle, T.J. (Eds.) (1994, 1996) *Flora of Victoria* Vols 2, 3, 4 (in press). Inkata Press, Melbourne.

Addendum 1. Name Changes and Alterations

Since the Revised Edition of the *Flora of Melbourne* was published in 1993 there have been many name changes as botanists throughout Australia continue to research our unique flora. Some changes result from the recognition of previous names which were applied to the species by early botanists, often in overseas herbaria where many original specimens were sent by collectors. The earliest name generally takes precedence. As more is learnt about a species it may become obvious to a botanist that subspecies, varieties or forms may in fact be sufficiently different to be given species status. This can also occur within a group of related species and a new generic name is applied. On the other hand, botanists may feel that differences between two (or more) species are insufficient to demand specific status and they are 'lumped' into the one species.

In several cases the species name has remained the same but the local form has been raised to subspecies or variety.

Undescribed plants which will ultimately be given specific status are referred to as **sp. aff.** while those whose affinities are still unclear are referred to as **aff.**

Where different botanists or herbaria recognise different nomenclature the alternatives have been listed for your assistance e.g. the **Liliaceae** family.

There have been a few omissions from the previous editions as plants have been recognised as a misidentification, are no longer believed to have occurred within our designated area or are now recognised as an introduced plant. One species has been relocated after many years and will be reinstated.

Updates in the Third Edition have been taken from *A Census of the Vascular Plants of Victoria* Sixth Edition January 2000 by J. H. Ross, published by the National Herbarium of Victoria. Further name changes occurring since then have been provided by the National Herbarium up until January 2001.

Changes as outlined below refer to spp. (ssp., varieties etc.) in the Melbourne area and may not be applicable throughout the range of the species.

≠ The new name is not a synonym for the former name but is a newly described species which has been separated from, or was confused with, the earlier description.

Dicotyledons

Acacia brownei = ***Acacia brownii***
Acacia lanigera = ***Acacia lanigera*** var. ***whanii***
Acacia mucronata (in part) = ***Acacia mucronata*** var. ***longifolia***
Acacia sophorae = ***Acacia longifolia*** var. ***sophorae***
Alternanthera denticulata Melton = ***Alternanthera*** sp. ***1***
Avicennia marina = ***Avicennia marina*** ssp. ***australasica***
Brachyscome angustifolia var. *angustifolia* = ***Brachyscome graminea***
Brachyscome leptocarpa = ***Brachyscome debilis***
Bursaria spinosa var. *macrophylla* included in ***Bursaria spinosa***
Cassytha glabella (Melb.) = ***Cassytha glabella*** forma ***dispar***
Crassula pedicellosa = ***Crassula closiana***
Cynoglossum latifolium = ***Austrocynoglossum latifolium***
Drosera whittakeri = ***Drosera whittakeri*** ssp. ***aberrans***
Eucalyptus ignorabilis ≠ ***Eucalyptus fulgens***
Eucalyptus camphora = ***Eucalyptus camphora*** ssp. ***humeana***
Eucalyptus ovata = ***Eucalyptus ovata*** var. ***ovata***
Eucalyptus pryoriana = ***Eucalyptus viminalis*** ssp. ***pryoriana***
Eucalyptus viminalis = ***Eucalyptus viminalis*** ssp. ***viminalis***
Euchiton gymnocephalus = ***Euchiton collinus***
Euphorbia drummondii = ***Chamaesyce drummondii***
Euphrasia scabra = ***Euphrasia caudata***
Eutaxia diffusa = ***Eutaxia microphylla*** var. ***diffusa***
Frankenia pauciflora = ***Frankenia pauciflora*** var. ***gunnii***
Goodia lotifolia = ***Goodia lotifolia*** var. ***lotifolia***
Hakea sericea ≠ ***Hakea decurrens*** ssp. ***physocarpa***
Hibbertia empetrifolia ≠ ***Hibbertia appressa***
Hibbertia prostrata = ***H. fasciculata*** var. ***prostrata***
Hibbertia stricta is currently included with ***Hibbertia riparia***
Lagenifera ssp. = ***Lagenophora*** spp.
Lavatera plebeia = ***Malva australiana***
Leptostigma reptans = ***Coprosma reptans***
Lissanthe strigosa = ***Lissanthe strigosa*** ssp. ***subulata***
Microseris lanceolata (in part) = ***Microseris*** sp. ***1*** (Basalt Plains)
Microseris lanceolata (in part) = ***Microseris*** sp. ***3*** (Foothills)
Mitrasacme distylis = ***Phyllangium distylis***
Mitrasacme paradoxa = ***Phyllangium sulcatum***

Montia fontana ssp. ***chondrosperma*** is referrable to the form found in Melbourne.
Myoporum viscosum = ***Myoporum*** sp. ***1***
Pimelea curviflora var. *sericea* has been absorbed into ***P. curviflora***
Podolepis jaceoides (Basalt Plains) = ***Podolepis*** sp. ***1***
Polyscias sambucifolia = ***Polyscias sambucifolia*** ssp. ***3***
Pratia spp. = ***Lobelia*** spp.
Psoralea adscendens = ***Cullen microcephalum***
Psoralea parva = ***Cullen parvum***
Psoralea tenax = ***Cullen tenax***
Pultenaea gunnii = ***Pultenaea gunnii*** ssp. ***gunnii***
Pultenaea juniperina var. *mucronata* = ***Pultenaea forsythiana***
Pultenaea paleacea var. *sericea* = ***Pultenaea sericea***
Rutidosis multiflora = ***Siloxerus multiflorus***
Senecio lautus = ***Senecio pinnatifolius***
Senecio spathulatus ≠ ***Senecio pinnatifolius*** var. ***2***
Stellaria palustris ≠ ***P. angustifolia***. Previously confused with *S. palustris* from Europe.
Stylidium graminifolium var. *angustifolium* = ***Stylidium graminifolium***
Stylidium graminifolium var. *graminifolium* = ***Stylidium*** sp. ***2***
Utricularia sp. aff. *dichotoma* = ***Utricularia beauglebolei***
Xanthosia pusilla = ***Xanthosia huegelii***

Monocotyledons

Lilies and Irises

Dianella revoluta var. *brevicaulis* = ***Dianella brevicaulis***
Wurmbea dioica = ***Wurmbea dioica*** ssp. ***dioica***

Orchids

Caladenia caerulea = ***Cyanicula caerulea***
Caladenia concinna (NSW endemic) ≠ ***Caladenia amoena***
Caladenia deformis = ***Cyanicula deformis***
Caladenia dilatata ≠ ***Caladenia phaeoclavia***
Caladenia menziesii = ***Leptoceras menziesii***
Caladenia oenochila ≠ *Caladenia lindleyana* (recent synonym, latter now Tas endemic)
Diuris brevissima (NSW endemic) ≠ ***Diuris pardina***
Diuris corymbosa (WA endemic) ≠ ***Diuris orientis***
Diuris lanceolata (Tas endemic) ≠ ***Diuris chryseopsis***
Genoplesium rufum (NSW endemic) ≠ ***Genoplesium*** sp. aff. ***rufum***
Lyperanthus nigricans = ***Pyrorchis nigricans***
Prasophyllum fuscum (Sydney endemic) ≠ ***Prasophyllum suaveolens***
Pterostylis furcata = ***Pterostylis falcata***
Pterostylis longifolia (Sydney endemic) ≠ ***Pterostylis melagramma***
Pterostylis obtusa (NSW endemic) ≠ ***Pterostylis atrans***
Pterostylis sp. aff. *longifolia* = ***Pterostylis smaragdyna***
Pterostylis rufa = ***Pterostylis squamata***
Spiranthes sinensis = ***Spiranthes australis***
Thelymitra ixioides var. *subdifformis* = ***Thelymitra hiemalis***
Thelymitra luteocilium ≠ ***Thelymitra*** x ***irregularis***

Grasses, Rushes, Sedges and Aquatics

Agrostis aemula var. *setifolia* = ***Agrostis punicea*** var. ***punicea***
Agrostis billardierei var. *robusta* = ***Agrostis robusta***
Caustis restiacea = ***Caustis flexuosa***
Chionochloa pallida = ***Joycea pallida***
Danthonia auriculata = ***Austrodanthonia auriculata***
Danthonia caespitosa = ***Austrodanthonia caespitosa***
Danthonia carphoides = ***Austrodanthonia carphoides***
Danthonia duttoniana = ***Austrodanthonia duttoniana***
Danthonia eriantha = ***Austrodanthonia eriantha***
Danthonia geniculata = ***Austrodanthonia geniculata***
Danthonia induta = ***Austrodanthonia induta***
Danthonia laevis = ***Austrodanthonia laevis***
Danthonia lepidopoda = ***Joycea lepidopoda***
Danthonia linkii var. *fulva* = ***Austrodanthonia fulva***
Danthonia linkii var. *linkii* = ***Austrodanthonia bipartita***
Danthonia penicillata = ***Austrodanthonia penicillata***
Danthonia pilosa = ***Austrodanthonia pilosa***
Danthonia procera = ***Austrodanthonia induta***
Danthonia racemosa = ***Austrodanthonia racemosa***
Danthonia semiannularis = ***Notodanthonia semiannularis***
Danthonia setacea = ***Austrodanthonia setacea***
Danthonia tenuior = ***Austrodanthonia tenuior***
Juncus krausii = ***Juncus krausii*** ssp. ***australiensis***
Juncus sp. O = ***Juncus semisolidus***
Leptocarpus brownii = ***Apodasmia brownii***
Paspalidium constrictum = ***Setaria constricta***
Restio tetraphyllus = ***Baloskion tetraphyllum***
Schoenus tenuissimus = ***Schoenus lepidosperma*** ssp. ***lepidosperma***
Spirodela oligorrhiza = ***Spirodela punctata***
Stipa spp. = ***Austrostipa*** spp.
Triglochin centrocarpum = ***Triglochin nanum***
Vallisneria spiralis = ***Vallisneria americana***

Ferns and Fern Allies

Allantodia australis = ***Diplazium australis***
Doodia media ssp. *australis* = ***Doodia australis***
Marsilea sp. = ***Marsilea costulifera***
Polyphlebium venosum = ***Crepidomanes venosum***
Schizaea asperula = ***Schizaea bifida***
Tmesipteris billardierei = ***Tmesipteris obliqua***

Carpobrotus modestus (p. 77)

Cladium procerum (p. 253)

Olearia rugosa (p. 151)

Luzula meridionales var. *meridionales* (p. 282)

Wilsonia humilis (p. 198)

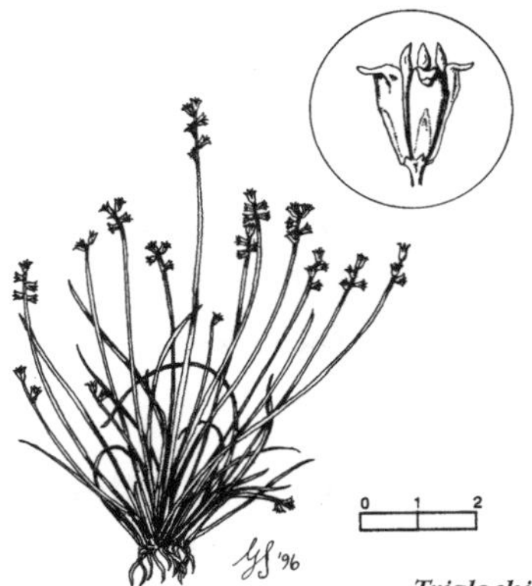

Triglochin mucronatum (p. 300)

SCALE: 0 1cm 2cm This scale representation on each plant equals 2 cm.

Addendum 2. New Species

Flowering Plants

Dicotyledons

Acacia obliquinervia

Mountain Hickory Wattle

Mimosaceae

Size: 3-9 m x 3-6 m **F P**
Habitat: Damp and valley sclerophyll forests
Form: Densely foliaged large shrub or small tree with a smooth grey trunk and ridged, red branchlets covered in a silvery bloom
Foliage: Greyish green, oblanceolate to elliptic phyllodes 5-17 cm x 1.5-5 cm, sickle-shaped with midrib closer to the top, single gland near base
Flowers: Racemes to 10 cm long of perfumed lemon-yellow or golden balls, stalk zig-zagging between flowers; August to November
Requirements: Well drained soils, tolerating dryness once established
Comments: A frost and light snow tolerant species which performs well under existing trees. Excellent as a higher altitude shelter tree or for erosion control. While widespread it has a restricted occurrence within the Melbourne area. See p. 52 for general comments on acacias.
Localities: Olinda, Monbulk
Distribution: Vic, NSW *Illustrated p. 359*

Acacia retinodes var. uncifolia

Habitat: Primary dune scrub, saltmarshes
Comments: Known from one surviving specimen in the Melbourne area this variety is more common on the Bellarine and Mornington Peninsulas. A suckering form, it differs in having shorter, narrower phyllodes 3-6.5 cm long, with a hooked tip and fewer flowers per head.
Localities: 5
Distribution: Vic, Tas, SA *Illustrated p. 359*

Acacia verticillata

Comments: A great deal of variation occurs within this species and 3 or 4 varieties have been noted. As intergrading occurs between these varieties they are not yet officially recognised. Distinguishing features are noted below.

A. verticillata var. verticillata

Comments: The most widespead variety with phyllodes to 25 mm long in whorls and flowers in cylindrical spikes generally more than 10 mm long. Localities are representative of this variety. A variant from Sydenham area has whorls of erect rather than spreading phyllodes.
Localities: Yarra R. 1852, Jacksons Ck 1900; Doncaster, Lilydale, Springvale-Clayton, 46, 50A, 58, 74

A. verticillata var. cephalantha

Comments: Long, narrow needle-like phyllodes 10-15 mm x 0.5 mm or less and round to ovoid spikes. Intergrades with both varieties making identification difficult.
Localities: Yarra R, St. Andrews, Greensborough, Box Hill-Doncaster, Boronia, 36, 44, 46, 47, 50A, 55, 57, 70

A. verticillata var. ovoidea

Comments: Phyllodes bunched or alternate, flowers in round to ovoid heads less than 10 mm long. A widespread variety.
Localities: Montrose, 55, 67, 73-75

Aphanes australiana

Australian Piert

Rosaceae

Size: 7-100 mm x 6-40 mm **F P**
Habitat: Dry sclerophyll forests
Form: Small, upright hairy annual herb
Foliage: Light green hairy fan-shaped leaves 4-12 mm x 3-7 mm with 6-9 deep lobes; stipules bowl-shaped with 7-9 lobes
Flowers: Clusters of 5-7 flowers without petals, appearing bell-shaped due to the enlarged, hairy floral bracts, 4 or 5 sepals 1/3 to 1/2 as long as floral bracts; August to November. Reddish-brown in fruit.
Requirements: Dry well drained soils
Comments: An uncommon species growing on very steep slopes which has been overlooked until recently.
Propagation: Seed
Localities: Around Port Phillip Bay 1853; 42
Distribution: Vic, NSW, Tas, SA

Atriplex australasica

Native Orache

Chenopodiaceae

Size: 0.4-1 m high **F**
Habitat: Saltmarshes or estuarine flats
Form: Erect annual shrublet
Foliage: Leaves variable, lower leaves entire or lobed, lanceolate to narrow-rhombic 5-10 cm x 1.5-4 cm, upper leaves narrower, smaller and entire
Flowers: Spike-like with small clusters of both male and female flowers along flowering stalk. Stalkless, thick, almost circular fruiting bracteoles (pair of small bracts which enlarge, covering the fruit when mature), back surface usually with 2 warty appendages. Fruit August to May
Requirements: Saline or brackish soils
Comments: Local forms have broader, usually toothed or lobed lower foliage.
Propagation: Seed
Localities: Yarra R. Melbourne, 2, 3
Distribution: Vic, NSW, Tas, SA
Synonym: Previously included with **A. patula*

Atriplex eardleyae

Size: 10-20 cm x 0.5-1 m **F P**
Habitat: Plains grassland
Form: Prostrate mealy-white annual herb
Foliage: Entire oblong leaves 6-15 mm x 4-9 mm
Flowers: Small globular clusters of male flowers near branch tips, female flowers in lower axils, sometimes both together. Fruiting bracteoles joined, trumpet-shaped, covered in bladder-like hairs, with a pair of wrinkled appendages near the base. Fruits October to April
Requirements: Heavy basaltic soil
Comments: An attractive silvery ground cover which is drought tolerant once established. May have been introduced years ago by agisted cattle from north western Victoria.
Propagation: Seed, cuttings
Localities: Craigieburn
Distribution: Vic, Qld, NSW, SA, WA
Synonym: *A. campanulata*

Atriplex leptocarpa

Slender-fruit Saltbush

Size: to 25 cm x 0.5-1.5 m **F**
Habitat: Depressions in plains grassland
Form: Spreading short-lived perennial shrub
Foliage: Oblong to oblanceolate scaly-grey leaves to 30 mm, margins sometimes toothed near tip
Flowers: Male and female flowers in leaf axils on the same plant, male flowers globular, clusters of female flowers in lower axils. Fruiting bracteoles narrow and joined to the tip which has 3 teeth. Most of the year
Requirements: Heavy soils, tolerating saline conditions
Comments: A drought resistant, layering groundcover suitable for embankments and roadsides to control erosion. Plants at this site may have been introduced by stock.
Propagation: Seed
Localities: Sydenham
Distribution: Vic, Qld, NSW, SA, WA

Baeckea ramosissima ssp. prostrata

Rosy Baeckea

Myrtaceae

Size: 8–20 cm x 0.3–1.5 m **F**
Habitat: Tea-tree heath
Form: Sparsely-branched spreading perennial shrub
Foliage: Narrow papery leaves 3–10 mm long with pointed tips
Flowers: Single, pendant small white to pale pink tea-tree-like flowers to 5 mm wide. June to February
Requirements: Sandy soils
Comments: An attractive small plant suited to coastal gardens. The more commonly available form is *B. ramosissima* ssp. *ramosissima*. Found in Monbulk, just outside the study area, its flowers are larger and are held erect. Some forms are a deep pink.
Propagation: Seed, cuttings
Localities: Frankston
Distribution: Vic, NSW, Tas

Brachyscome trachycarpa

Comments: As this species is only reliably known from a single specimen in north west Victoria, the Melbourne record is presumed to be a mis-identification.

Bracteantha palustris

Asteraceae

Size: 0.3–1 m high **F**
Habitat: Swamp scrub, winter wet grasslands, riparian scrub
Form: Erect rhizomatous perennial herb, rarely with one or two branches, short cobweb-like hairs on leaves and on stems to 5–15 cm below flowerhead
Foliage: Stalkless lanceolate-elliptic leaves spaced along the stem, from 3–10 cm x 3–8 mm, decreasing in size from the base
Flowers: Single golden yellow flowerhead to 5 cm; November to March
Requirements: Moist to wet clay soils
Comments: A rare species generally consisting of a few suckering plants in each population. Most sites are unprotected. *B. subundulata* differs in that it is shorter and occurs in alpine and subalpine areas.
Propagation: Root cutting, seed
Localities: Bayswater, Lyndhurst
Distribution: Vic, Tas *Illustrated p. 359*
Synonym: *B.* sp. aff. *subundulata*, *Helichrysum acuminatum* var. *angustifolium*

Calandrinia eremaea

Portulacaceae

Comments: (See p. 73) Previously believed to be extinct, this species has been rediscovered at Yarra Bend germinating from soil-stored seed after weed grasses had been removed.

Calandrinia granulifera

Pigmy Purslane

Size: 15–30 mm high
Habitat: Sand dunes and sandy depressions
Form: Tiny, erect ephemeral
Foliage: Almost rounded basal and stem leaves to 10 mm long
Flowers: Up to 10 tiny white to pale pink flowers in a terminal spray, 5–7 petals, sepals enlarging and falling before fruit ripens; September to November
Requirements: Moist sandy soil
Comments: Locally extinct, this tiny herb is still common in north west Victoria.
Propagation: Seed
Localities: St. Kilda 1852
Distribution: Vic, NSW, SA, WA

Callitriche sonderi

Matted Water Starwort

Callitrichaceae

Size: Prostrate x 10 cm **P**
Habitat: Riparian scrub, flood plains
Form: Mat-forming annual herb
Foliage: Narrow to narrow-obovate leaves 0.8–5 mm long
Flowers: Male and female flowers in pairs in leaf axils; September to December. Dark brown fruit is thicker at the base, with a very narrow wing.
Requirements: Damp soil
Comments: Tolerating inundation, this small plant would be a useful bog plant.
Propagation: Division
Localities: 42
Distribution: Vic, Qld, NSW, Tas, SA

Centaurium spicatum Spike Centaury

Gentianaceae

Size: 4-40 cm high **F P**
Habitat: Open forest and grassy areas following rain
Form: Erect, often greyish, annual herb with basal rosette which withers early
Foliage: Sessile, oblanceolate, obovate or elliptic leaves 10-25 mm x 3-6 mm, becoming smaller up the stem
Flowers: Simple or branched leafy spike-like flowerhead of pink to magenta flowers to 12 mm long x 6-8 mm across
Requirements: Moist heavy soils tolerating saline conditions
Comments: While sometimes considered to be introduced it is probable that some areas of distribution are indigenous occurrences while others may be introduced. It is uncertain which category the Melbourne population belongs to. This species also occurs in saltmarshes.
Propagation: Seed
Localities: 61
Distribution: All states; Sth Eur, Asia, N Cal

Chionogentias polysperes Early Forest Gentian

Gentianaceae

Size: 10-35 cm x 10-30 cm **F P**
Habitat: Open forests and woodlands in hilly areas
Form: Annual or biennial herb with several widely spreading, erect branches
Foliage: Deep green basal rosette of oblanceolate to spoon-shaped leaves 2-4 cm x 5-10 mm, stem leaves narrower and scattered
Flowers: Sparsely-flowering, terminal panicle of 5-7 erect, white to cream bell-shaped flowers with grey or violet vertical veins, to 20 mm long, stalks longer on upper flowers; January to April
Requirements: Moist well drained soils
Comments: Possibly extinct within the Melbourne area. An attractive species, it would make an ideal container plant but is short lived. Peaty soils are preferable for pots, maintaining a constantly moist medium. Frost and snow tolerant.
Propagation: Fresh seed which is stratified in the refrigerator
Localities: Mt. Dandenong 1869, Olinda Vale 1905, Ringwood 1922, Lilydale, Dandenong Rges gully
Distribution: Vic, NSW, Tas
Synonym: *Gentianella* aff. *diemensis* (Montane forests)

Chrysocephalum sp. **1**

Asteraceae

Size: Prostrate-40 cm x 1 m **F**
Habitat: Plains grassland, red gum woodland on basalt plains
Form: Erect to straggling perennial covered in dense cottony hairs
Foliage: Narrow, tapering silver-grey leaves 1-4 cm x 1-10 mm, hairier below
Flowers: Clusters of 3-many golden-yellow, sometimes brown-tinged, flowerheads 7-10 mm wide; spring to summer
Requirements: Well drained soils
Comments: Similar to *C. apiculatum* (see p. 82) but flowerheads are smaller and leaves narrower. An attractive groundcover with contrasting foliage which stands out well at night when lit.
Propagation: Seed cuttings
Localities: Keilor Plains
Distribution: Vic, ?Qld, NSW, SA, ?WA, ?NT
Synonym: *C.* aff. *apiculatum* (Inland Plain)

Ciclospermum leptophyllum

Comments: (See p. 82) This species is now considered to be introduced.

Correa reflexa var. **lobatus**

Rutaceae

Comments: The widespread and variable *C. reflexa* complex has recently been revised (1998) and several new varieties are now recognised. This variety differs from *C. reflexa* var. *reflexa* (throughout the rest of the Melbourne area) in that the calyx lobes are deeply triangular.
Localities: Dandenong Ranges, 73
Distribution: Endemic to Vic *Illustrated p. 359*

Correa reflexa × alba

Comments: This naturally occurring hybrid has been recorded in the Bay area. It can be distinguished from both parents by the short pale pink bell which is open and star-like at the end. Leaves are roundish.
Localities: Port Phillip Bay

Cotula coronopifolia

Water Buttons

Asteraceae

Size: 10–45 cm x 0.5–1 m **F P**
Habitat: Semi-aquatic, in both saline and fresh water
Form: Creeping perennial herb with succulent stems
Foliage: Toothed or lobed, oblong, sheathing leaves 2–5 cm long
Flowers: Flattish yellow flowerheads to 10 mm wide on long stalks; September to February
Requirements: Muddy to wet soils
Comments: A common species on edges of swamps, it is a good plant for bog gardens. There is considerable debate between botanists as to whether this species is indigenous or introduced or, in fact, cosmopolitan.
Propagation: Seed, cuttings, division
Localities: Collections 1892–1905 Preston, Moonee Ponds, Braybrook, Yarra banks, Vermont, Oakleigh, Caulfield, 69A; Altona, Coburg, Yarra Park, Cheltenham, Brighton, Mentone, 2, 4, 6, 7, 14, 16, 19, 21, 25, 26, 28–32, 35, 42, 44, 45–7, 49, 53, 58, 62, 64, 67, 70, 71, 74, 75
Distribution: All states; S Af, S Am *Illustrated p. 365*

Craspedia canens

Asteraceae

Size: 15–65 cm high **F P**
Habitat: Grassy low open forest, often near swamps
Form: Perennial herb covered in long fine white hairs
Foliage: Narrow-ovate, mainly basal, greyish leaves 6–25 cm x 5–15 mm, tapering at ends
Flowers: 1–5 globular to hemispherical yellow flowerhead to 25 mm each on separate woolly, green to purplish flower stalks; September to December
Requirements: Tolerates both dry and wet soils
Comments: More work on this variable species may result in further segregation.
Propagation: Seed
Localities: Clayton, Dandenong South, Lyndhurst, 73
Distribution: Vic, Qld, NSW

Craspedia paludicola

Swamp Billy-buttons

Size: to 75 cm high **F**
Habitat: Grassy wetlands, swampy areas
Form: Robust perennial herb
Foliage: Very large, narrow-obovate dark green leaves 15–30 cm x 8–20 mm tinged deep red at their broad bases. Leaves limp and often partly submerged.
Flowers: 1–3 bright yellow globular flowerheads to 30 mm held erect on separate long purplish stalks; October to January
Requirements: Moist to boggy soils
Localities: Croydon 1897; Laverton North, 34A
Distribution: Vic, NSW, Tas

Dysphania glomulifera ssp. glomulifera

Pigweed

Chenopodiaceae

Size: stems to 20 cm long **F**
Habitat: Grassy wetlands
Form: Prostrate to erect, fleshy annual or short-lived perennial herb
Foliage: Spoon-shaped leaves 2–12 mm long
Flowers: Tiny sessile hooded flowers in crowded axillary clusters, most flowers female; December to April
Requirements: Moist soils
Comments: Known from a single area within Melbourne this species is usually found further north in warmer areas. It is uncertain whether this species is indigenous to the area or whether it was brought in with agisted stock.
Propagation: Seed
Localities: Rockbank
Distribution: All mainland states
Synonym: *Atriplex glomulifera*, *D. myriocephala*

Eucalyptus camaldulensis

Myrtaceae

Comments: A form growing in the Hampton Park area differs from the red gums growing in other parts of Melbourne in that the tree is more upright, the juvenile leaves are broader and the buds are prominently horn shaped rather than beaked.
Localities: Lyndhurst, Hampton Park

Eucalyptus willisii ssp. willisii

Comments: Records of populations in the Melbourne area attributed to this name are likely to be referable to glossy leafed forms of *E. radiata*.

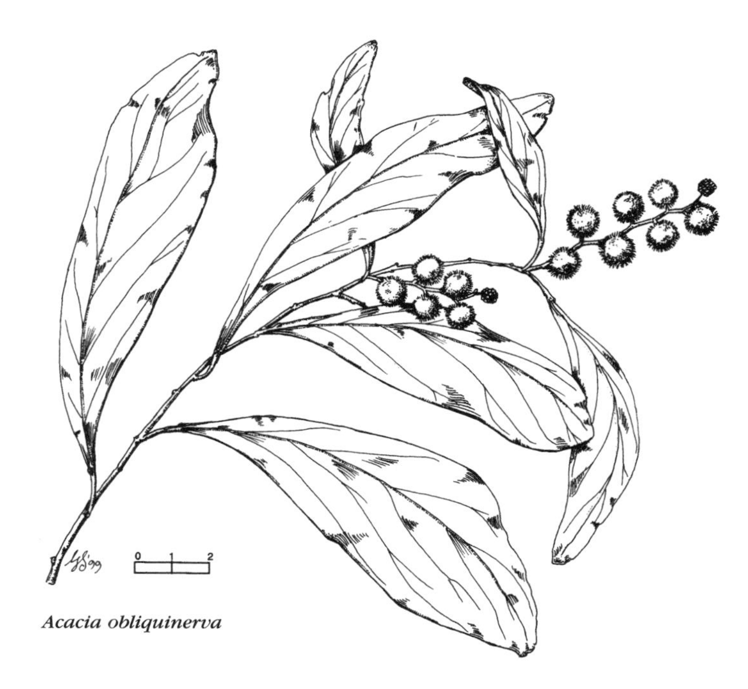

Acacia obliquinerva

Acacia retinodes var. *uncifolia*

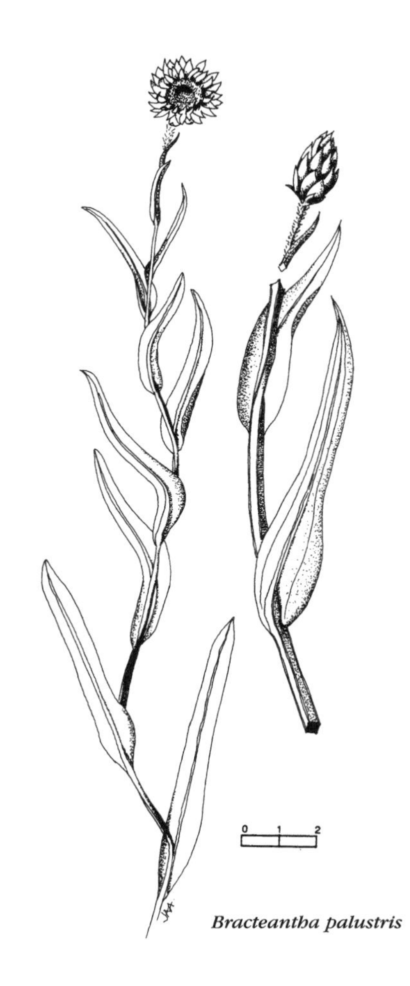

Bracteantha palustris

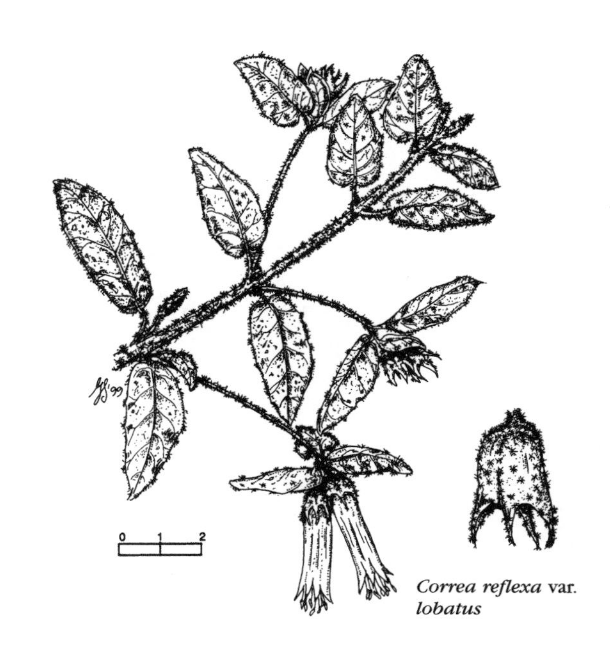

Correa reflexa var. *lobatus*

SCALE: 0 1cm 2cm This scale representation on each plant equals 2 cm.

Galium compactum

Comments: It is likely that the specimen collected from the Research area is attributable to another species.

Geranium — Geraniaceae

A recent revision of the genus Geranium has resulted in many new species and sub species. Most changes within the Melbourne area have resulted from the study of the *G. solanderi* complex. This group now includes a further 3-4 species as well as the original type. Most of these species are currently identified by number but manuscript (ms.) names have been attributed to them and these have been listed in the synonym field. The new descriptions below replace the description for *G. solanderi* on p. 111. Localities will remain confused as it may be difficult to attribute the original numbers to the new species.

Geranium homeanum — Rainforest Crane's-bill

Size: stems to 1 m long **F P N**
Habitat: Valley, damp and wet sclerophyll forests, margins of cool temperate rainforest
Form: Prostrate to scrambling perennial herb with a thickened, branched taproot and few recurved hairs on the stems
Foliage: Kidney-shaped to pentagonal leaves 1-4.5 cm long, deeply divided into 5 (-7) broad lobes, sometimes toothed, each divided with 3 final lobes ending in a small point; becoming glabrous or with few curved hairs above; stipules narrow-triangular with long taper
Flowers: Single or paired, small, bright pink flowers, becoming white towards the centre, 7-8 mm wide, anthers off white with fine purple lines; sepals usually obovate to 3.5 mm long, ending in a small point, edged with a broad translucent margin; peaking October to March. Beaked fruit 12-14 mm long.
Requirements: Moist soils
Comments: The small flowers, sepal shape, translucent margins and taproot help to distinguish this species. Not previously recorded from the greater Melbourne region.
Propagation: Seed, possibly cuttings
Localities: Kalorama, Montrose, Olinda Ck, Belgrave, 42, 55-58
Distribution: Vic, Qld, NSW; NZ *Illustrated p. 365*

Geranium solanderi var. solanderi — Austral Crane's Bill

Size: stems to 50 cm long **P**
Habitat: Damp to dry sclerophyll forests, grassy low open forest and woodlands, mostly along drainage lines
Form: Trailing to sub-erect perennial herb with rounded to turnip-shaped taproot and both long and short spreading to slightly recurved hairs on the stems
Foliage: Round to kidney-shaped leaves to 6 cm long, deeply divided into 5-7 lobes each forked 2 or 3 times, often more, ends rounded, stem leaves with narrow lobes; no or few scattered, curved hairs above, few long, spreading hairs below; stipules triangular to narrow-ovate and shortly tapered
Flowers: Paired or single bright pink flowers to 12 mm wide with slightly notched petals, on stalks to 25 mm long, anthers pink to lemon with dark purple lines; hairy ovate to narrowly oblong sepals 4-5.5 mm long with longer spreading hairs, ending in a tiny point, margins occasionally narrowly translucent; October to January. Beaked fruit to 15 mm long.
Requirements: Moist, sheltered positions
Comments: A vulnerable species in Melbourne.
Localities: Werribee, Diamond Creek, Blackburn, Dandenong, ?3, ?18, ?29, 42
Distribution: Vic, NSW, Tas, ?WA; NZ

Geranium sp. 1 — Large-flower Crane's-bill

Size: stems to 25 cm high
Habitat: ?Volcanic plains
Form: Trailing perennial herb with densely hairy stems
Foliage: Circular to kidney-shaped leaves 1.8-2.8 cm long deeply divided into 5-7 lobes, each again 3-lobed, rounded to pointed on tips; stipules tapering, lanceolate to arrow-shaped
Flowers: Large single or paired pink ?to white flowers 18-25 mm wide, often with darker veins, on stalks to 3.8 cm long; hairy ovate to oblong sepals to 8 mm long with rounded or indented tips and no points; margins broad and translucent; April. Beaked fruit 18-21 mm long.
Comments: Only 2 records of this species have been confirmed and, after fruitless searches, it is now assumed to be extinct.
Localities: Broadmeadows# 1903
Distribution: Endemic to Vic
Synonym: *G. carolinii* ms, removed from *G. solanderi* sens. strict

Geranium sp. 2

Variable Crane's-bill

Size: stems to 80 cm long **F P**
Habitat: Dry and valley sclerophyll forests
Form: Scrambling perennial herb with dense short and long recurved hairs on stems and turnip-shaped to egg-shaped taproot
Foliage: Large rounded to kidney-shaped leaves to 4 cm long, deeply divided into 5–7 lobes, each again 3-lobed, lobe tips square to rounded; hairless or long curved hairs above, few curved spreading hairs below; narrow-ovate to lanceolate, stipules tapering
Flowers: Single or paired pale pink to white flowers with translucent veins to 12 mm wide, on stalks to 35 mm long, petal tips cut squarely; lemon to yellow anthers lack purple lines; hairy sepals to 3.5 mm long with pale margins, pointed tip tiny; August to January. Beaked fruit to 14 mm long.
Requirements: Well drained soils tolerating dryness once established
Comments: A variable species. A form from Hurstbridge and Epping areas has larger, almost white flowers. This and other forms may need further revision.
Propagation: Seed, possibly cuttings
Localities: Hurstbridge, Montrose, ?32–41, 42, ?44–46, 50A–53 (Yan Yean)
Distribution: Vic, ?Qld, NSW, Tas, SA, ?WA *Illustrated p. 365*
Synonym: *G. ciliocarpum* ms, removed from *G. solanderi* sens. strict.

Geranium sp. 3

Pale Flower Crane's-bill

Size: stems to 30 cm long **F P**
Habitat: Grassy areas in dry sclerophyll forests
Form: Trailing perennial herb with broadly spreading hairs on young stems, hairs recurved and pressed against older stems; taproot turnip-shaped
Foliage: Hairy kidney-shaped to pentagonal leaves to 3.5 cm long, deeply divided by 3–5 narrow lobes which are deeply divided 2–3 times, tips pointed to rounded; tapering ovate to triangular stipules with hairy margins
Flowers: Single or paired pale pink flowers to 10–12 mm wide on stalks to 22 mm, tips rounded, pale lemon anthers with purple lines; hairy sepals have a small point and hairy, narrow translucent margins; September to January. Beaked fruit 15–17 mm long.
Requirements: Drier soils
Comments: A vulnerable species known from few locations it is similar to *G. retrorsum* but has paler flowers which have rounded rather than notched petals, purple lines on the anthers and hairier, less dissected leaves.
Propagation: Seed, possibly cuttings
Localities: Eltham, (Yan Yean)
Distribution: Vic, ?ACT, ?SA
Synonym: *G. pallidiflorum* ms; separated from *G. retrorsum*

Geranium sp. 4

Rough Crane's-bill

Size: stems to 2 m long **P**
Habitat: Valley, damp and wet sclerophyll forests
Form: Scrambling perennial herb with rough curved hairs and a thickened, tapering taproot
Foliage: Coarsely haired, kidney-shaped leaves to 4 cm long, triangular on upper stems, deeply dissected into 3–5 broad, sometimes toothed, lobes which are again divided 2–3 times; tips pointed or rounded with tiny point; stipules often lobed
Flowers: Single or paired bright pink flowers to 9 mm wide, becoming white towards the centre on stalks to 16 mm, anthers off-white with fine purple lines; narrow, pointed, hairy sepals with translucent hairy margins; October to April. Beaked fruits to 16 mm long.
Requirements: Moist soils in shelterd positions
Comments: Easily identified by the roughness of the stems.
Propagation: Seed, possibly cuttings
Localities: East Melbourne, Montrose, 50A, 51
Distribution: Vic, ?Qld, NSW, SA; NZ
Synonym: *G. trachycaule* ms, *G.* sp. *nova C.*, removed from *G. solanderi*

Geranium sp. 5

Naked Crane's-bill

Size: stems to 1 m long **F P**
Habitat: Moist to seasonally inundated sites
Form: Spreading, almost glabrous perennial herb with thickened, tapering to branched taproot
Foliage: Round to kidney-shaped leaves to 4 cm long with 5–7 deeply dissected lobes, forked 2–3 times and again dissected, often toothed, mostly narrow lobes, tips pointed to square; triangular tapering sepals
Flowers: Single or paired pink to bright pink flowers to 7 mm long, purple lines on mauve to lemon anthers; broad hairy sepals; October to March. Beaked fruit to 16 mm long
Requirements: Moist soils
Comments: Similar to *G. retrorsum* but plant is mostly glabrous, leaf lobes are broader, and taproot narrower and tapered. Further investigation is needed to ascertain whether this species may be introduced.
Propagation: Seed, stem cuttings, root division or cuttings
Localities: Sunshine, Epping, Bundoora, Fairfield, Kangaroo Ground, 3, 16, ?29, ?35, ?42, ?49, 50A, 51
Distribution: Vic, NSW, ?SA; NZ
Synonym: *G. inundatum* ms, previously misidentified as *G. retrorsum*

Hyalosperma demissum

Moss Sunray

Asteraceae

Size: 5-20 mm x 5-20 mm **P**
Habitat: Valley sclerophyll forest, open woodland
Form: Branched dwarf, rounded, annual herb, sparsely hairy to glabrous
Foliage: Narrow, tapering cylindrical leaves to 5 mm long
Flowers: Tiny cup-shaped stalkless flowerheads amongst foliage, florets 3-4 lobed, bracts pale green to straw-coloured; September to December
Requirements: Well drained soils
Comments: A short-lived herb appearing after rain.
Propagation: Seed
Localities: 42
Distribution: Vic, NSW, Tas, SA *Illustrated p. 365*
Synonym: *Helipterum demissum*

Hydrocotyle pterocarpa

Wing Pennywort

Apiaceae

Size: Prostrate **P**
Habitat: Riparian scrub
Form: Creeping perennial herb rooting at leaf nodes
Foliage: Kidney to heart-shaped leaves 1-5 cm across with 3-11 shallow broad lobes and wavy margins, on stalks 1-10 cm long
Flowers: Round clusters of 5-20 tiny off white flowers with purple blotches, on stalks 4-30 mm long; spring to early autumn. Prominently winged, flat fruit 4-5 mm wide is red spotted.
Requirements: Moist soil
Comments: General comments p. 123
Localities: Seaford, 42
Distribution: Vic, Tas, SA

Lavatera plebeia var. tomentosa

Comments: This variety is found growing in the guano deposits on Mud Is. outside the Melbourne area.

Lepidium hyssopifolium

Pepperweed, Perennial Peppercress, Dittander

Brassicaceae

Size: 30-70 cm x 20-50 cm **F P**
Habitat: Basalt plains
Form: Erect perennial herb covered in fine short spreading hairs
Foliage: Shortly hairy leaves with longer hairs on margins, basal leaves deeply divided or toothed; rough, narrow, toothed or entire stem leaves 1-4 cm long, base lobed
Flowers: Tiny flowers often lacking petals in branched, lengthening raceme, stalks hairy; fruit elliptical, sometimes hairy, to 5 mm long, with narrow wings forming a notch at the tip; summer to autumn
Requirements: Most free draining soils
Comments: A rare plant now only found in 2 locations in Melbourne. Differs from the 2 species separated from it by its covering of fine hairs.
Propagation: Seed
Localities: Yarra R. Port Melbourne 1850, West Melbourne 1850; Bulleen, Heidelberg
Distribution: Vic, NSW, Tas, SA

Ludwigia peploides var. montevidensis

Water Primrose, Clovestrip

Onagraceae

Size: 0.1-2 m long **F P**
Habitat: Aquatic
Form: Floating, downy perennial herb, rooting at nodes
Foliage: Glossy dark green elliptic leaves 1-10 cm x 4-30 mm on long stalks with 2 swollen dark green stipules
Flowers: Single bright yellow flowers to 30 mm across with 10 stamens, on slender stalks in upper leaf axils; November to May. Fruit is 10-ribbed cylindrical capsule.
Requirements: Dams or ponds
Comments: An ornamental species suitable for bog gardens and dams but needs to be watched for weediness. Very variable in hair covering and leaf shape and size.
Propagation: Seed, cuttings
Localities: Richmond#, 54
Distribution: All mainland states; NZ, N Am, S Am

Myriophyllum pedunculatum ssp. **longibracteolatum**

Mat Water-milfoil

Haloragaceae

Size: 0.25 cm x 1.5 m **F P**
Habitat: Swamps in tea-tree heath
Form: Perennial herb with weak erect stems, rooting at the nodes
Foliage: Thin, widely-spaced, thread-like leaves 15–22 mm long, forked or with 1 or 2 lobes near middle
Flowers: Small, single yellow to reddish flowers in leafy spikes, male flowers above, female below, sometimes on separate stems. Tiny reddish-purple to black cubic fruit.
Requirements: Permanently moist soil or ponds
Comments: A mat-forming aquatic or semiaquatic plant useful in bog gardens or pools. It is possible that ssp. *pedunculatum* also occurred in this area although it is more often found in higher altitudes. It can be distinguished by its stouter, prostrate stems with only the tips erect to 10 cm high and by its narrow, entire leaves which are fleshier, closer together and smaller. See p. 145 for general information.
Localities: Cranbourne
Distribution: Vic, NSW, Tas

Oxalis thompsoniae

Oxalidaceae

Size: stems to 45 cm long
Habitat: Disturbed sites
Form: Prostrate green to blue-green herb with poorly developed taproot
Foliage: Bilobed leaflets variable, hairy below and on margins, 3–16 mm x 5–20 mm; stalks 15–50 mm long; stipules obvious, with rounded tips
Flowers: 1–4 yellow flowers on stalks shorter than leaves, stalks bent over in fruit. Densely hairy, erect fruit capsule 5–16 mm long.
Comments: A poorly known species. While its status is uncertain it is believed by many botanists to be indigenous. Comments p. 152
Localities: Outer eastern suburbs, below Hurstbridge
Distribution: Vic, Qld, NSW, SA; NZ, PNG

Pelargonium littorale

Storksbill, Kopata

Geraniaceae

Size: 0.2–0.4 m x 0.3–1 m **F P**
Habitat: Primary dune scrub
Form: Erect perennial herb with lightly hairy stems and stalks and fleshy taproot
Foliage: Opposite, heart-shaped to rounded, entire to shallowly 5–7-lobed leaves to 6 cm x 6 cm on long stalks to 10 cm, margins wavy or bluntly toothed
Flowers: Long stalked clusters, to 8 cm long, of 2–7 deep pink flowers, or pale pink flowers with dark veins, 14 mm across; calyx hairs long and spreading; August to April
Requirements: Well drained soils
Comments: An attractive plant for small gardens and containers. Responds well to pruning. Usually frost hardy.
Propagation: Seed, stem cuttings
Localities: Williamstown
Distribution: Vic, Tas, SA, WA

Picris angustifolia ssp. **angustifolia**

Asteraceae

Size: 7–140 cm high **F P**
Habitat: Primary dune scrub, grassy low open forest, valley sclerophyll forest
Form: Sparsely branched annual or perennial herb covered in forked, hooked hairs, sap milky
Foliage: Narrow to oblancolate leaves to 40 cm x 3.5 cm, sometimes toothed; basal leaves with or without stalks, upper stem leaves sessile
Flowers: Clusters of slender, yellow radiate flowerheads 3–8 mm wide; outer floral bracts erect with 1–3 lines of branched hairs; September to December. Beaked fruit has both barbed and feathery bristles.
Requirements: Moist well drained soils
Comments: Once widespread this species is becoming increasingly rare. It has been confused with the more common introduced species.
Propagation: Seed
Localities: Deer Park, Yarrambat, Donvale, Vermont, Tremont, Montrose, Keysborough, 42, 44, 57, 60
Distribution: Vic, NSW, Tas, SA, WA
Synonym: Separated from *P. hieracioides*, an introduced species

Pimelea curviflora

Thymelaeaceae

Habitat: Valley sclerophyll forest
Comments: This form differs from *P. curviflora* var. *curviflora* in that the sepals are tiny (less than 1 mm long compared to 0.5-3mm). See p. 156. The National Herbarium of Victoria does not currently recognise any varieties within *P. curviflora*.
Localities: 44
Distribution: Endemic to Vic.
Synonym: *P. curviflora* aff. var. *subglabrata*

Podolepis sp. 1

Basalt Podolepis

Asteraceae

Size: 20-60 cm high **F**
Habitat: Plains grassland, grassy wetland
Form: Erect tufted perennial herb, mostly glabrous
Foliage: Narrow pointed leaves with fine hairs on margins and midrib below, basal to 17 cm long, stem leaves 1-8 cm long
Flowers: Single to a few bright yellow flowerheads 20-30 mm wide in loose cymes, ray florets lobed, floral bracts long and pointed; September to November
Requirements: Well drained soils
Comments: An attractive small plant for massed planting in rockeries or in containers. It appreciates summer watering. Similar to the more widespread *P. jaceoides* which has narrow lanceolate leaves and is more hairy.
Propagation: Seed
Localities: Basalt plains, Deer Park, Warrandyte, 6, 7
Distribution: Endemic to Vic
Synonym: *Podolepis* sp. aff. *jaceoides*

Pomaderris vaccinifolia

Comments: This species occurs in damp sclerophyll forest in the Kinglake and Healesville areas. The collection from Warrandyte is probably a small leaf form of *P. racemosa*.

Prunella vulgaris

Comments: This species is now considered to be introduced.

Ranunculus diminutus

Ranunculaceae

Size: 2-5 cm high **F**
Habitat: Grassy wetland
Form: Small tufted perennial herb, rooting at nodes
Foliage: Leaves to 20 mm long and wide divided into 3 oblong leaflets, central leaflet with 1-2 narrow lobes; stalks to 50 mm long
Flowers: Single tiny, glossy yellow flowers on erect stalks slightly shorter than leaves; 5-11 petals to 5 mm long; September to February
Requirements: Seasonally wet heavy soil
Comments: A rare plant in Victoria, only found near the edges of a few lakes. For comments see p. 170.
Localities: 4
Distribution: Vic, NSW
Synonym: *R.* sp. B

Rorippa gigantea

Forest Bitter-cress

Brassicaceae

Size: to 1.2 m high **P**
Habitat: Damp and wet sclerophyll forests
Form: Scrambling to erect annual herb
Foliage: Sessile, oblong to lanceolate leaves to 12 cm long, lobed at the base, margins entire or with widely spaced teeth
Flowers: Tiny white flowers with 6 stamens on horizontal stalks less than 8 mm long; spring to summer. Narrow fruit to 35 cm long.
Requirements: Moist soils
Propagation: Seed
Localities: Dandenong Rges 1853; 57
Distribution: Vic, Qld, NSW, Tas

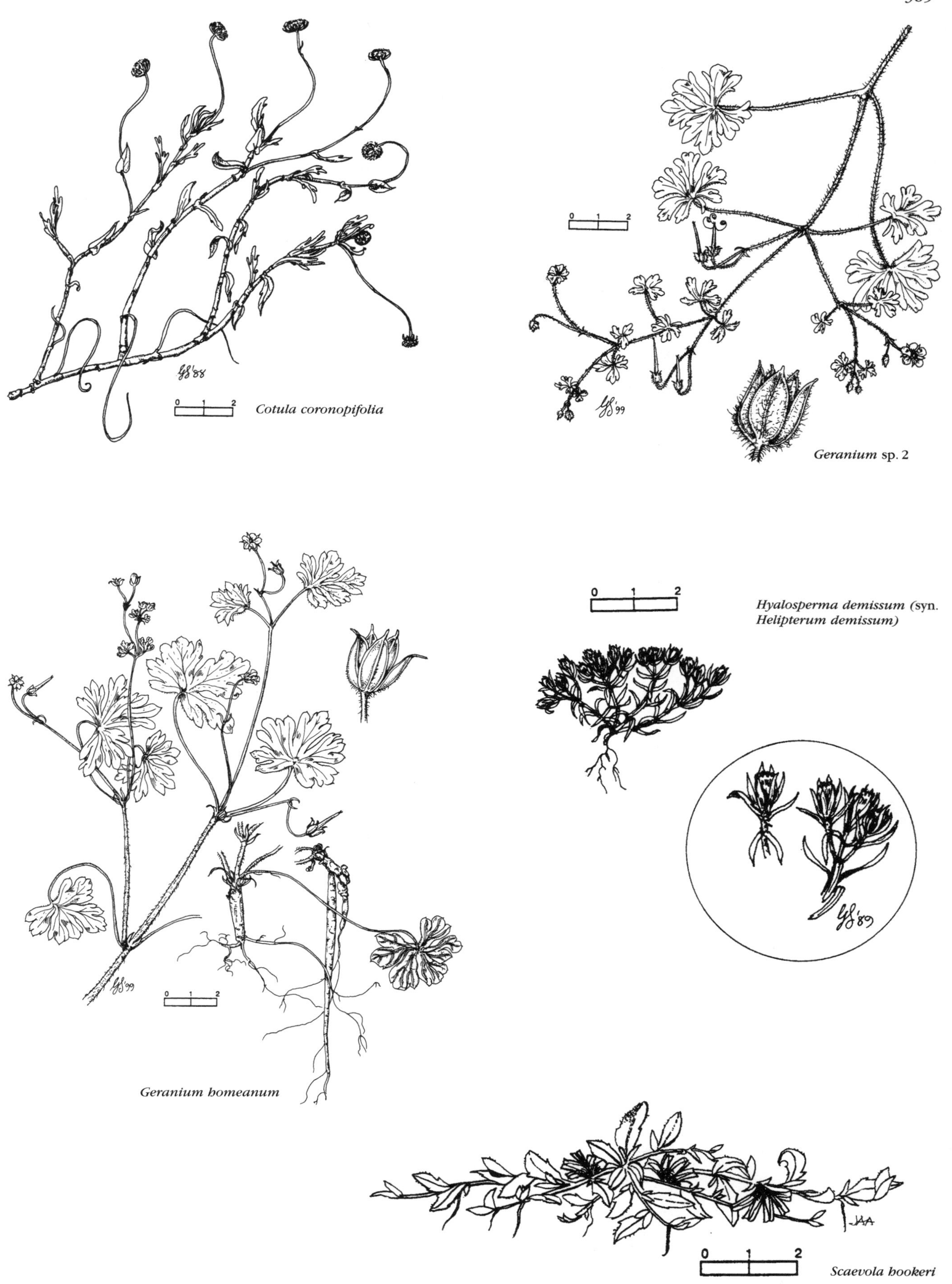

Cotula coronopifolia

Geranium sp. 2

Geranium homeanum

Hyalosperma demissum (syn. *Helipterum demissum*)

Scaevola hookeri

SCALE: 0 1cm 2cm This scale representation on each plant equals 2 cm.

Rumex stenoglottis

Polygonaceae

Size: 30-50 cm x 30-50 cm **F**
Habitat: Grassy wetlands
Form: Tangled, wiry perennial herb
Foliage: Narrow-oblong leaves to 16 cm long with curled margins, quickly withering; few stem leaves
Flowers: Branched flowering stems with well-spaced whorls of 3-5 tiny flowers, floral leaf below each whorl; September to January. Fruiting valves similar to *R. dumosus* but narrower, tapering to a pointed, recurved tip, 1- (rarely 2) toothed near base.
Requirements: Moist soils
Comments: Very similar to *R. dumosus* (see p. 176). Known from 4 sites in Victoria and 1 site in Melbourne.
Localities: St. Albans
Distribution: Vic, Qld, NSW

Scaevola hookeri

Creeping Fan-flower

Goodeniaceae

Size: Prostrate x 1 m **P N**
Habitat: Wet tea-tree heath
Form: Hairy, stoloniferous matting perennial herb
Foliage: Light green ovate to oblong leaves to 25 mm x 12 mm with toothed or entire margins
Flowers: Single white or blue flowers with yellow throats to 8 mm long in leaf axils on stalks 1-8 mm long; November to March
Requirements: Moist to wet soils
Comments: More commonly found in alpine areas, it makes a useful bog plant. Frost tolerant.
Propagation: Stem and root cuttings
Localities: 73
Distribution: Vic, NSW, Tas *Illustrated p. 365*

Senecio glossanthus

Asteraceae

Size: 5-40 cm high **P**
Habitat: Saltmarsh
Form: Erect ephemeral or annual herb with few branches and sparse downy hairs
Foliage: Narrow sessile leaves 0.5-4 cm long
Flowers: Few flowered clusters of bell-shaped flowerheads to 3.5 mm wide, ray florets pale yellow, disc florets yellow; September to December
Requirements: Moist soil
Comments: Plants appear on drying soils following inundation. Was common in Werribee but possibly disappeared due to grazing.
Propagation: Seed
Localities: Werribee, 4
Distribution: All mainland states

Senecio pinnatifolius var. pinnatifolius

Variable Groundsel

Size: to 50 cm x 30-50 cm **F P**
Habitat: Red gum woodland, ?plains grassland
Form: Annual or short-lived perennial herb or sub-shrub
Foliage: Pinnate or bipinnate leaves, ovate in outline, 5-8 cm x 2-5 cm; 5-13 divisions, segments narrow and entire, toothed or lobed. Largest stem leaves lobed.
Flowers: Loose clusters of radiate flowerheads with 8-14 yellow ray florets; September to January
Requirements: Dry well drained soils
Comments: *S. lautus* is now regarded as a NZ species. Australian plants formerly referred to that name have been separated into several varieties. The type variety is probably extinct in the Melbourne area. (Original description p. 181.)
Localities: Werribee 1901, Oakleigh 1902
Distribution: All states
Synonym: *S. lautus* ssp. *dissectifolius*

Senecio pinnatifolius var. 2

Size: to 30 cm high **F**
Habitat: Primary dune scrub
Form: Rhizomatous perennial herb
Foliage: Fleshy, entire or pinnate obovate leaves 3-60 mm x 3-12 mm
Comments: See p. 182 for description. Flowers August to November.
Localities: Seaford, Pt. Wilson
Distribution: All states except NT
Synonym: *S. lautus* ssp. *maritimus.* Confused with *S. spathulatus*

Senecio pinnatifolius var. 3

Size: 0.5–1 m x 0.3–0.5 m **P N**
Habitat: Valley, damp and wet sclerophyll forests, tea-tree scrub
Form: Robust, non-rhizomatous perennial herb or sub-shrub
Foliage: Narrow elliptic to lanceolate, coarsely-toothed leaves 4–15 cm x 4–20 mm
Requirements: Moist soils
Comments: The most commonly found variety in the Melbourne area. Flowers September to April.
Localities: Lilydale 1901; Olinda, Sassafras, Belgrave, 36, 51, 57, 58, 60, 73
Distribution: Vic, Qld, NSW
Synonym: *S. lautus* ssp. *lanceolatus*

Spergularia marina Lesser Sea-spurrey

Caryophyllaceae

Size: 5–35 cm x 12–18 cm **F**
Habitat: Saltmarshes, mud flats
Form: Spreading annual herb with slender stems and taproot
Foliage: Narrow fleshy leaves 5–50 mm long with rounded end and small tip, small stipules
Flowers: Branched flower heads, flowers 4–8 mm wide, petals pink with white base, hairy sepals longer, green or purplish with dark red basal dots, stamens 2–5 but usually 4; most of the year. Capsule just longer than sepals, seeds orange- to deep red-brown.
Requirements: Moist saline soils
Comments: A widespread plant of salty areas it was originally believed to be introduced but is now accepted as an indigenous species.
Propagation: Seed
Localities: St. Kilda, Footscray, 7, 67
Distribution: All states; NZ

Spergularia sp. 1

Size: 10–40 cm x 0.4–0.7 cm **F**
Habitat: Saltmarshes, saline wetlands
Form: Erect annual or perennial herb with thick woody root
Foliage: Narrow, flattened fleshy leaves 10–60 mm long with small tip or awn, small stipules
Flowers: Loosely branched flower head with pink flowers 7–10 mm wide, petals shorter than densely hairy sepals, stamens 5–10; October to December. Capsules longer than sepals, seeds black and winged.
Requirements: Moist saline soils
Comments: Presumed to be extinct within the Melbourne area.
Propagation: Seed
Localities: Early collections in Brighton 1852, 1885, Williamstown 1885
Distribution: Vic, NSW, Tas, SA, WA; NZ
Synonym: *S.* sp. *B* (NSW)

Spergularia sp. 3

Size: 6–20 cm x 10–12 cm **F**
Habitat: Saltmarshes, drier sites
Form: Prostrate to straggling annual or short-lived perennial herb with slender stems and slender woody taproot
Foliage: Bundles of fine, glandular-hairy leaves with prominent tip or awn, silvery stipules tapering
Flowers: Loose, few- to many-flowered cluster of rose-pink to lilac flowers, petals smaller or equal to densely hairy, green or purplish sepals, stamens 6–8; September to November. Capsule about equal to sepal length, seeds iridescent grey-brown to black.
Requirements: Moist to drier soils
Propagation: Seed
Localities: Werribee, Melton, Port Phillip Coast
Distribution: All states except NT

Sphaerolobium minus Globe-pea

Fabaceae

Size: 0.2–0.5 m high **F P**
Habitat: Damp and valley sclerophyll forests, grassy low open forest, tea-tree heath
Form: Upright, rush-like shrub
Foliage: Occasional scattered narrow leaves to 5 mm long in seedling stage
Flowers: Clusters of 2–3 yellow flowers with reddish markings forming long terminal spikes, wings and keel equal length, calyx lead-grey, style wing more than 1/2 length of style; September to December
Requirements: Moist well drained soils
Comments: *S. vimineum* differs from *S. minus* in that the wings are longer than the keel, the calyx is green with dark spots and the wing on the style is less than 1/2 its length. The two species can be found growing together.
Propagation: Seed
Localities: Croydon 1897, Bayswater 1900, Ringwood Nth 1901, Cheltenham 1902; Olinda Ck, 59, 60
Distribution: Vic, Qld, NSW, Tas, SA
Synonym: Separated from *S. vimineum*

Stellaria caespitosa

Starwort

Caryophyllaceae

P

Size: Prostrate, stems 5-15 cm long
Habitat: Riparian scrub
Form: Weak, straggling annual herb, rooting at nodes to form large mats
Foliage: Narrow sessile leaves 3-6 mm long
Flowers: Single white flowers held on long stalks to 10 mm in upper axils, 5 petals longer than sepals; November to February
Requirements: Moist soil tolerating inundation
Propagation: Seed, Division
Localities: Wonga Park, 42
Distribution: Vic, NSW, Tas, SA
Synonym: *S. palustris* var. *tenella*

Utricularia uniflora

Lentibulariaceae

P N

Size: 10-20 cm high
Habitat: Swamp margins of tea-tree heath
Form: Stoloniferous terrestrial perennial herb, traps on stolons
Foliage: Tiny obovate leaves to 8 mm long
Flowers: Single erect flowering stem 10-20 cm long with 1 or 2 mauve to lilac flowers to 15 mm long, central pair of ridges on lower lip yellow, not longer than white ridges on sides; August to March
Requirements: Wet soils
Comments: Known from a single old record in the Melbourne area it is now possibly extinct. General comments p 192.
Localities: 73
Distribution: Vic, Qld, NSW, Tas
Synonym: *U. dichotoma* var. *uniflora*

Wahlenbergia victoriensis

Campanulaceae

F P

Size: stems 10-40 cm high
Habitat: Plains grassland, woodland
Form: Erect simple or few-branched annual herb with slender taproot
Foliage: Opposite, obovate to elliptic, hairy leaves on hairy lower stems, ovate to lanceolate, alternating, glabrous leaves on glabrous upper stems, 2-35 mm long, margins flat to wavy
Flowers: Branched flowering stems at least 1/2 size of the plant with many blue bell-shaped flowers to 15 mm long on stalks 2-12 cm long, sepals narrowly triangular; August to January
Requirements: Well drained soils
Comments: A seldom collected species which is usually found further north in Victoria. Similar to *W. gracilenta* which has much smaller flowers and oblong sepal lobes. General comments p. 197.
Localities: Sunbury, ?70
Distribution: Vic, NSW
Synonym: *W.* sp. aff. *gracilenta*

Xanthosia tridentata

Hill Xanthosia

Apiaceae

F P

Size: to 30 cm high
Habitat: Grassy heath, heathy woodland
Form: Erect to spreading dwarf shrub, hairy or glabrous
Foliage: Wedge-shaped to elliptic leaves 6-15 mm x 2-8 mm on short stalks, 3-notched end, margins recurved; downy white below
Flowers: 1-3-flowered clusters of tiny pale green or cream flowers, sometimes edged pink, on long stalks opposite leaves or at ends of branches; winter
Requirements: Well drained soils
Comments: More commonly found just outside the Melbourne area.
Propagation: Cuttings
Localities: Narre Warren, ?74
Distribution: Vic, NSW, Tas, WA

Flowering Plants — Monocotyledons

Lilies and Irises

Bulbine glauca — Rock Lily

Liliaceae (Asphodelaceae)

F

Size: to 50 cm high
Habitat: Rock escarpment
Form: Tufted perennial herb with thick, fleshy roots
Foliage: Erect, fleshy, blue-green onion-like leaves to 30 cm long
Flowers: Few to many yellow star-like flowers to 35 mm wide with yellow anthers, clustered on leafless flowering stems to 50 cm high; September to January. All 6 stamens are bearded.
Requirements: Well drained soil
Comments: Differs from *B. bulbosa* (p. 202) in that stamens are loosely grouped or spreading rather than bunched, roots are not tuberous and foliage is bluish.
Propagation: Seed or division
Localities: 16
Distribution: Vic, ?Qld, NSW, Tas

Bulbine semibarbata — Leek Lily

F P

Size: 20–40 cm x 10–30 cm
Habitat: Dry sclerophyll forest
Form: Tufted annual herb with fibrous roots
Foliage: Erect to spreading, flattish, slightly fleshy, rush-like leaves to 20 cm long
Flowers: Yellow star-like flowers to 14 mm wide, on stems to 40 cm high, anthers orange; September to December, also sporadic. Only 3 of the staminal filaments in each flower are bearded.
Requirements: Usually occurs on sandy soil.
Comments: This entry is reinstated after its rediscovery in Warrandyte.
Propagation: Seed
Localities: 34A,42
Distribution: All states except NT *Illustrated p. 370*

Dianella amoena — Matted Flax-lily

Liliaceae (Phormiaceae)

F P

Size: to 45 cm x up to 5 m
Habitat: Plains grassland, grassy wetland, red gum woodland
Form: Tufted mat-forming perennial with long, slightly fleshy and much-branched rhizomes
Foliage: Narrow, tapering grey-green leaves to 45 cm, often dull crimson at base, edges and midrib with small, irregularly-spaced teeth. Leaves deciduous in summer if water-stressed.
Flowers: Small, loose panicles of large, sweetly scented pale to deep violet flowers, anthers pale yellow with orange base, on slender stems 20-90 cm high; Summer followed by small, round off white to dark blue berries
Requirements: Well drained to seasonally wet soils
Comments: An endangered species with few plants in each population.
Propagation: Division. Plants are not regenerating from seed in situ.
Localities: Broadmeadows, Mernda, Bundoora, Coburg, Eltham, 29, 34A
Distribution: Vic, Tas *Illustrated p. 370*
Synonym: *D.* sp. *nov.*

Dianella callicarpa — Swamp Flax-lily

P N

Size: 0.3–1.6 m x 1.5 m
Habitat: ?Wet sclerophyll forest
Form: Densely tufted or shortly rhizomic perennial with fibrous roots
Foliage: Thin, tapering, mid to dark green glossy leaves to 1.6 m x 8–20 mm, minutely toothed along the edges and underside of midrib especially towards the tip; arching or bent downwards
Flowers: Attractive lightly scented, nodding bluish-violet flowers with maroon on the back in widely spreading panicles to 50 cm long on tall stems to 1.9 m high. Anthers pale yellow with an orange base, petals strongly recurved; Summer, followed by large, lumpy, glossy purple berries
Requirements: Moist to wet soils
Comments: Known presently from few scattered populations but may be more widespread. Occurs in one site in Melbourne. The more open panicle and the lumpy berries help to distinguish it from *D. tasmanica*.
Localities: Dandenong Ranges
Distribution: Endemic to Vic *Illustrated p. 370*
Synonym: Previously included with *D. tasmanica*

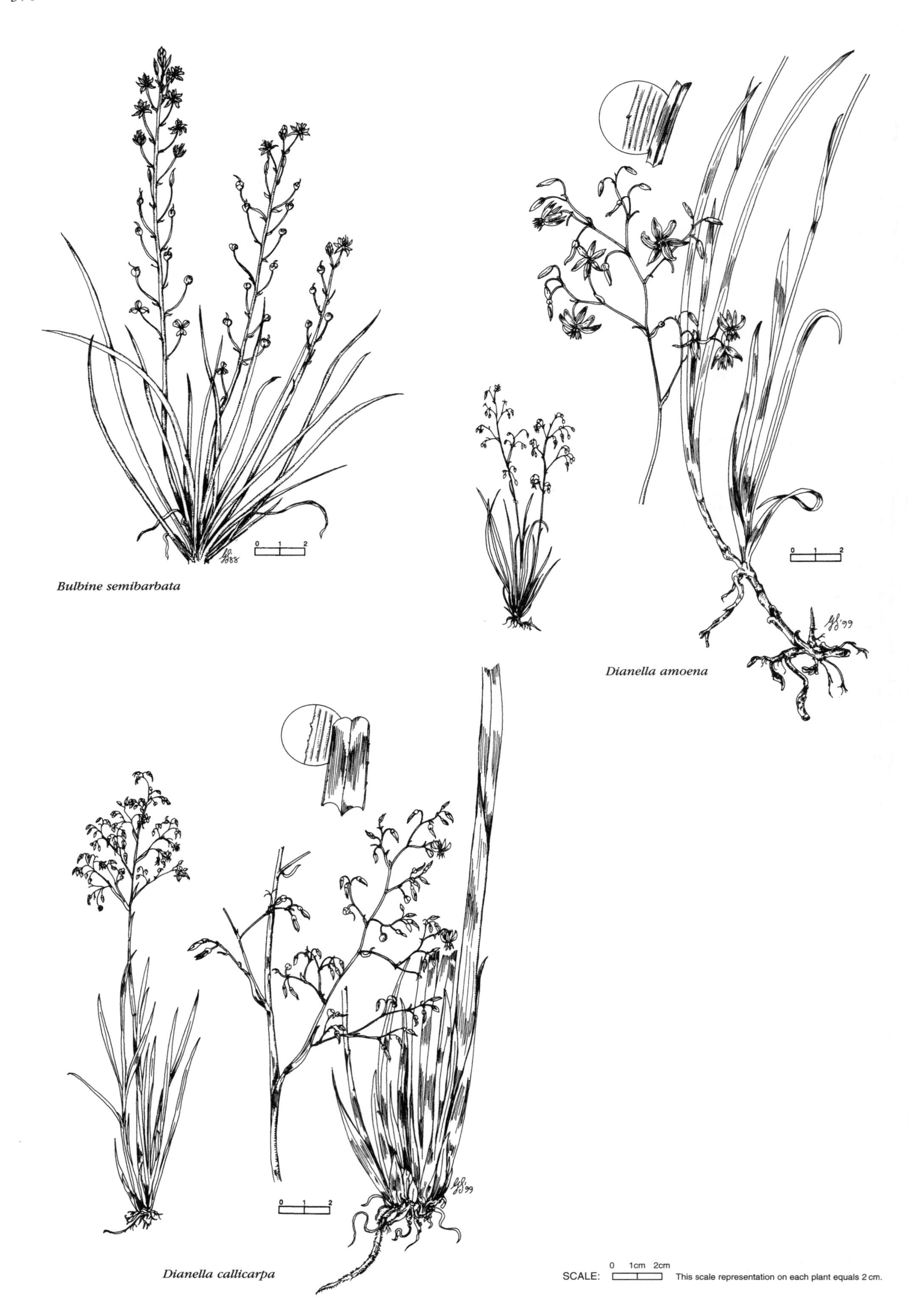

Bulbine semibarbata

Dianella amoena

Dianella callicarpa

Dianella longifolia var. grandis

Size: to 1.3 m x 0.4 m
Habitat: Plains grassland, grassy woodland
Foliage: Leaves with red or white bases, 8–25 mm wide
Flowers: Panicles of greenish-white to pale blue flowers; November to December
Requirements: Well drained soil
Comments: Once widespread over the volcanic plains it is now extinct in most localities in the Melbourne region.
Localities: Volcanic plains[#], 25
Distribution: Vic, Qld, NSW, SA

Thelionema umbellatum

Liliaceae (Phormiaceae)

Size: to 35 cm high **P**
Habitat: Tea-tree heath
Form: Tufted herbaceous perennial
Foliage: Narrow linear leaves to 35 cm x 2–3 mm with ridged midrib
Flowers: 3–10 small white to cream flowers with yellow anthers in an umbel, stems to 0.4 m; October to December
Requirements: Wet sandy soil
Comments: Differs from the more widespread *T. caespitosum* (p. 207) in the narrower leaves which lack a keel, the umbel-like flowering stem and the white flowers.
Propagation: Division
Localities: 73
Distribution: Vic, NSW, Tas
Synonym: *Stypandra umbellata, S. caespitosa* var. *umbellata*

Orchids

Orchidaceae

Caladenia amoena

Charming Spider Orchid

Size: stem to 10 cm high **P**
Habitat: Dry sclerophyll forest on ridge tops
Form: Erect herb with slender, green to reddish hairy stem
Foliage: Densely hairy lanceolate leaf to 80 mm with red spots near the base
Flowers: Single yellowish-green flower with a crimson stripe, to 20 mm wide. Perianth segments to 25 mm long, hanging, recurved and tapering abruptly at ends; erect dorsal sepal curves over column.
Labellum V-shaped, green with maroon tip. Clubbed maroon calli in 4 crowded rows. Lateral lobes are erect with a few short teeth. August to October
Requirements: Poorer quality dry soils
Comments: Similar to *C. toxochila* from the Wimmera but flowers smaller and lighter in colour with less congested, dark red rather than black calli. An endangered species found only on private property to the north east of Melbourne. (See p. 212 for general description of caladenias.)
Localities: Wattle Glen, Greensborough, 36
Distribution: Endemic to Vic
Synonym: Recently described. Previously included with *C. concinna*, a NSW endemic, and *C. toxochila*.

Caladenia aff. carnea

Size: stem to 20 cm high **F P**
Habitat: Dry and valley sclerophyll forests
Foliage: Narrow, thin, dark green leaf to 12 cm long, shiny above, duller and hairy below, purplish near base
Flowers: 1–2 dull greenish-white flowers 15–20 mm wide, with greenish-brown stripe; narrow, erect finger-like perianth segments to 20 mm long, almost closed obscuring labellum and column; dorsal sepal erect, slightly incurved
Labellum pale pinkish-white or pure white, 3-lobed with red transverse stripes, lateral lobes broad and erect, mid-lobe small with yellow tip and 2 rows of stalked, yellow, clubbed calli. October to November
Requirements: Dry stony soil
Comments: The local form differs from *C. carnea* in that the perianth segments are almost closed around the labellum and column, possibly resulting in the plants being self-pollinating. It differs from *C. prolata* in that the dorsal sepal is erect rather than hooded, the ovary is smaller and hardly swollen and the leaf is thinner. This species is extremely rare being known from 2 plants at one site and 1 plant at the other.
Localities: Warrandyte, Dandenong Ranges
Distribution: Endemic to Vic.
Synonym: *C.* sp. aff. *prolata* (Brisbane Ranges); separated from *C. carnea*

Caladenia fuscata

Dusky Caladenia

Size: stem 6–15 cm high **F P**
Habitat: Dry sclerophyll forest, tea-tree heath
Form: Erect, sparsely hairy herb with wiry green to reddish stem
Foliage: Narrow leaf to 12 cm long
Flowers: Single white to pink flower to 15 mm with dark brown hairs and red median stripe on the back of lower segments, greenish-brown towards tips, red bars on the labellum and column. Obovate perianth segments to 12 mm long, lateral sepals and petals spreading.
Labellum 3-lobed, lateral lobes surrounding column, with triangular extensions pointing forward. Yellow calli along small deflexed mid-lobe and on margins. September to October
Requirements: Well drained soils
Comments: The tightly column-embracing lateral lobes and their triangular extensions help to distinguish this species from *C. carnea*.
Localities: Wattle Glen 1930; 34A, 42, 73
Distribution: Vic, Qld, NSW
Synonym: *C. carnea* var. *fuscata*

Caladenia leptochila

Narrow-lip Spider Orchid

Size: stem 15–24 cm high
Flowers: 1 or 2 yellowish-green flowers with a red central stripe. Perianth segments to 30 mm, upturned, sepals finely tapering, ending in a club with a blackish gland.
Narrow dark red labellum 12 mm x 4 mm lacks lateral lobes. 2 rows of short, black calli. September to November
Comments: Has not been seen in Victoria recently. There is now some doubt as to the origin of the Victorian specimens as this species is quite common in its only known habitat in the Adelaide Hills.
Localities: Collected in Cheltenham 1925
Distribution: ?Vic, SA

Caladenia parva

Small Spider Orchid

Size: stem to 15 cm high **P**
Habitat: Coastal grassy low open forest
Form: Slender hairy herb
Foliage: Lanceolate leaf 10 cm x 10 mm with red spots near the base
Flowers: Single green flower to 30 mm across with crimson stripe and fine yellowish glandular tips on sepals. Dorsal sepal incurved
Labellum similar to that of *C. phaeoclavia* but smaller. September to October
Requirements: Moist soils
Comments: Differs from *C. phaeoclavia* in that flower is smaller in all aspects, sepal tips yellower and flowers earlier. More study is required on this species.
Localities: ?Brighton#, ?Frankston#, Cranbourne, Sth Belgrave
Distribution: Vic, ?SA
Synonym: Separated from *C. dilatata*

Caladenia patersonii

Paterson's or Common Spider Orchid

Size: stem 15–35 cm high **F**
Habitat: Tea-tree heath
Form: Slender hairy herb with green-brown stem
Foliage: Sparsely hairy lanceolate leaf to 15 cm with reddish spots at base
Flowers: One or two fragrant cream to pale yellow flowers to 80 mm across with red streaks at base of segments. Perianth segments to 80 mm long, broad at base tapering to drooping thread-like tips covered in reddish-brown glandular hairs.
Labellum yellow, curved forward with tip curved under, long fine tooth-like calli along reddish margins, mid lobe with 4–6 rows of stalked calli. September to October
Requirements: Well drained sandy soil
Comments: Probably extinct within the Melbourne area. There is some doubt as to the status of these early specimens. It is probable that they belong to either *C. venusta* or *C. fragrantissima*, both occurring on the Mornington Peninsula.
Localities: Oakleigh 1890, Clayton 1892; 67#
Distribution: Vic, Tas

Caladenia phaeoclavia

Brown-clubbed Spider Orchid

Size: stem 10–25 cm high **F P**
Habitat: Dry and valley sclerophyll forests, tea-tree heath
Form: Small hairy herb with green or reddish stems
Foliage: Narrow lanceolate leaf to 13 cm with red spots near the base
Flowers: Single flower to 40 mm across; slender perianth segments to 40 mm long, green with a crimson stripe and fine, brown glandular tips on sepals.
Labellum 3-lobed, lateral lobes green, erect, with teeth to 3.5 mm long; mid-lobe whitish with short, blunt teeth on recurved maroon tip and 4 rows of crowded, clubbed maroon calli. October to November
Requirements: Well drained soils
Comments: More widespread in Melbourne than *C. dilatata* which is larger in all respects and later flowering. Dark brown glandular clubs on sepals are longer and column is strongly recurved before becoming erect. *C. phaeoclavia* is also confused with *C. parva* which is a smaller, earlier-flowering coastal form.

	New evidence suggests that both species may ultimately be combined under *C. parva*.
Localities:	Between Warrandyte, Park Orchards & Ringwood, Hurstbridge, Wattle Glen, Research, South Belgrave, 34A, 42, 50A, 67, 74
Distribution:	Vic, NSW
Synonym:	Separated from *C. dilatata* which possibly occurred in Frankston and Brighton.

Caladenia sp. aff. **venusta**

Habitat:	Grassy open forest
Comments:	Similar to *C. venusta* (p. 218). Its flowers are smaller and cream in colour and lack the distinctive mouldy orange fragrance.
Localities:	Kilsyth South

Calochilus gracillimus

Slender or Late Beard-orchid

Size:	stem to 50 cm high
Habitat:	Grassy low open forest
Form:	Slender erect herb
Foliage:	Narrow fleshy channelled leaf to 30 cm long, V-shaped in cross-section
Flowers:	2–9 widely spaced green flowers to 30 mm across with purplish stripes on perianth segments, purple to reddish-brown beard. Hooded ovate dorsal sepal to 25 mm long, ending in a pointed tip; lateral sepals triangular, broadest at base; petals incurved, to 10 mm long. Narrow ovate labellum to 35 mm long with short purplish glands at base, long wiry hairs in central part, ending in a short, glabrous tail. December to February
Requirements:	Well drained soils
Comments:	A rare orchid for Melbourne, also occurring just outside the study area in Christmas Hills. This species is poorly known due to its similarities with *C. robertsonii* which flowers earlier, is shorter and less slender, has a more crowded flowering stem and a denser beard.
Localities:	Langwarrin
Distribution:	Vic, Qld, NSW

Calochilus imberbis

Naked Beard Orchid

Size:	stem 20–45 cm high **P**
Habitat:	Dry sclerophyll forest
Form:	Slender erect herb
Foliage:	Single, narrow, fleshy dark green leaf to 40 cm, ribbed and broadly V-shaped
Flowers:	1–5 green flowers to 35 mm across with red stripes on perianth segments. Broadly ovate, hooded dorsal sepal to 15 mm long, lateral sepals to 15 mm narrowing to a point, incurved ovate petals to 10 mm. Labellum ovate to 15 mm long, lacking beard or calli. Purple gland at base of each wing on column is connected by a ridge. October to November
Requirements:	Well drained gravelly sands and clay soils
Comments:	Very similar to *C. robertsonii*, and often occurring together but less common. Lacks the beard and calli on the labellum.
Localities:	Ringwood# (still occurs in Emerald)
Distribution:	Vic, NSW, Tas, SA

Chiloglottis jeanesii

Mountain Bird Orchid

Size:	stem to 5 cm high **P**
Habitat:	Wet sclerophyll forest, cool temperate rainforest
Foliage:	Fleshy dark green basal leaves 25–70 mm x 10–25 mm, paler below
Flowers:	Single green to purplish-brown flower to 30 mm across. Perianth segments to 20 mm long, lateral sepals narrow, petals lanceolate and spreading. Labellum heart-shaped with up to 5 pairs of green, reddish or purple stalked and sessile calli, central gland long and stalked. October to January
Requirements:	Moist rich soil
Comments:	Grows with *C. cornuta* and *C. valida* at the base of trees but is not a hybrid between these species. It can be distinguished from the former by the shape of the labellum and from the latter in its smaller flowers and widely spreading petals. (General information p. 220.)
Localities:	57
Distribution:	Endemic to Vic
Synonym:	*C.* sp. aff. *valida, C.* sp. A.

Chiloglottis x **pescottiana**

Bronze Bird Orchid

Size:	stem 4–14 cm high
Habitat:	Grassy low open forest
Foliage:	Oblong to ovate dark green leaves to 60 mm long
Flowers:	Single greenish-bronze to purplish flower to 30 mm across. Perianth segments to 15 mm, dorsal sepal spoon-shaped, lateral sepals narrow and pointed downwards, petals spreading, sickle-shaped. Labellum elliptic to ovate to 14 mm long, stalked and sessile black calli. September to November
Requirements:	Well drained soils
Comments:	A naturally occurring hybrid between *C. trapeziformis* and *C. valida*. A rare plant found in one site in the Melbourne area.
Localities:	Mt. Eliza
Distribution:	Vic, NSW

Corybas fimbriatus — Fringed Helmet-orchid

Size: flower to 30 mm; stemless **P N**
Habitat: Valley sclerophyll forest, wattle tea-tree scrub, in leaf and bark litter
Foliage: Cordate to round leaf 13–45 mm long
Flowers: Almost sessile purplish-red to crimson flower to 30 mm long. Ovate dorsal sepal hooded over labellum, transparent with reddish spots. Lower part of labellum erect, upper section circular, widely flared with incurved or spreading, deeply fringed margins. May to June
Requirements: Moist soils
Comments: A disjunct distribution with a small colony in Melbourne, otherwise found in South and East Gippsland. (see p. 221)
Localities: Frankston 1920; Greensborough, Plenty R.
Distribution: Vic, Qld, NSW, Tas

Cyrtostylis robusta — Large Gnat Orchid

Size: stem 4–25 cm high **P**
Habitat: Wattle tea-tree scrub
Form: Slender erect herb
Foliage: Single round ground-hugging bright green leaf with pale veins, almost transparent below, 15–50 mm across
Flowers: 2–7 pinkish-red to green flowers to 14 mm long. Perianth segments narrow and tapering, to 13 mm long, dorsal sepal curved forward.
Labellum oblong, projecting forward, to 15 mm long, tip scalloped with short tapered point. July to August
Requirements: Sheltered position in humus-rich, well drained sand
Comments: A colony-forming orchid which may now be extinct within the Melbourne area. Similar to *C. reniformis* (p. 222) but larger with distinctly green leaves and often an earlier flowering period.
Localities: Brighton, Mentone, Seaford, 67, 69A,
Distribution: Vic, SA, WA
Synonym: Separated from *C. reniformis*

Dipodium punctatum — Purple Hyacinth Orchid

Size: stem to 1m high **P**
Habitat: Open forests
Form: Erect leafless saprophytic herb with a stout, fleshy dark brown stem
Flowers: 15–60 pale to bright pink flowers to 25 mm across with dark red spots, in an open to crowded spike. Perianth segments similar, linear-elliptic with rounded tips, to 20 mm long.
Labellum tri-lobed, pointed forward, band of hairs towards tip sparser than in *D. roseum* (p.223). January to February
Requirements: Well drained soils
Comments: An extremely rare species with 10 plants recently discovered in Melbourne. Only 1 specimen occurs in each of 2 sites.
Localities: Greensborough, Yarrambat, Abbotsford, 18
Distribution: Vic, NSW

Diuris behrii — Golden Cowslips

Size: stem to 50 cm high **F P**
Habitat: Grassy low open forest, swamp scrub
Form: Herb forming an erect grass-like tussock
Foliage: 3–6 grass-like leaves to 20 cm long
Flowers: 1–4 drooping bright lemon-yellow flowers with brown stripes on the dorsal sepal and labellum, to 40 mm across. Ovate dorsal sepal to 20 mm, pointed forward, narrow lateral sepals parallel, greenish to 25 mm, stalked elliptical petals are spreading or drooping to 23 mm long.
Labellum tri-lobed, lateral lobes long and narrow, mid-lobe broadly wedge-shaped, margins irregularly toothed; 2 raised ridges becoming single ridge on mid-lobe, continuing almost to the tip. October to November
Requirements: Moist soils, tolerating winter wet conditions
Comments: A recently located species in the outer east of Melbourne, this orchid is possibly extinct elsewhere in the study area.
Localities: South eastern suburbs#, Croydon South
Distribution: Vic, SA

Diuris sp. aff. *lanceolata* (Basalt Plains) — Small Golden Moths

Size: stem to 18 cm high **F**
Habitat: Plains grasslands
Foliage: Loose tussock of 3–9 erect grass-like leaves to 10 cm long
Flowers: 1–3 partially opened yellowish-orange flowers to 20 mm across. Ovate dorsal sepal projects forward with margins slightly curved in; narrow, pale yellow lateral sepals to 15 mm long; stalked elliptical petals to 18 mm long, curved inwards.
Ovate mid-lobe of labellum 12 mm long, callus deeper golden. September to October
Requirements: Moist basalt soil
Comments: An endangered species consisting of less than 200 plants on private property. Similar to but smaller and darker than *D. orientis* (syn. *D. lanceolata*) (p. 224).
Localities: Laverton, Altona
Distribution: Endemic to Vic.
Synonym: *D. lanceolata*

Genoplesium ciliatum

Fringed Midge Orchid

Size: stem 10–15 cm high **P**
Habitat: Tea-tree heath
Foliage: Leaf to 12 cm long, free for 20 mm, reddish at base
Flowers: Crowded spike of 1–10 semi-erect yellowish-green flowers with red markings, to 7 mm across. Ovate, hooded dorsal sepal; lateral sepals and petals narrow and spreading.
Maroon, oblong labellum to 5 mm long, sparsely hairy on margins, tip upturned,callus thick and channelled. February to April
Requirements: Tolerates seasonally moist soils
Comments: A rare plant in the Melbourne area which may have already become extinct. *G. archeri* is similar but is larger with more flowers which are nodding and have a hairier labellum. (notes p. 226)
Localities: Sandringham
Distribution: Vic, SA
Synonym: Separated from *G. sagittiferum*; previously included with *G. archeri*

Microtis arenaria

Notched Onion Orchid

Size: stem 10–60 cm high **F P**
Habitat: Widespread in dry and valley sclerophyll forests, grassy low open forest, tea-tree heath, adjoining saltmarshes
Foliage: Single leaf to 40 cm long
Flowers: Crowded spike of 8–100 fragrant, pale green to yellowish flowers to 4 mm across. Hooded dorsal sepal has an upturned tip; lateral sepals strongly coiled back.
Labellum hanging rather than pressed against the ovary as *M. unifolia*, with wavy margins and bi-lobed tip. September to November
Requirements: Tolerates both moist, heavy soils and well drained soils
Comments: An invader of disturbed sites it can occur in large numbers after fires.
Localities: 69A 1897, Mentone 1902, Brighton, Frankston to Skye 1907; Port Melb., Park Orchards, 34A, 42, 55, 57, 58
Distribution: Vic, NSW, Tas, SA
Synonym: *M. biloba*

Prasophyllum suaveolens

Fragrant Leek Orchid

Size: stem to 25 cm high **F**
Habitat: Plains grassland
Foliage: Slender erect leaf to 25 cm long, reddish at base, tip often withering at flowering
Flowers: Short, open spike of 10–30 fragrant greenish-brown flowers with reddish stripes, to 7 mm across. Dorsal sepal ovate to 7 mm long with pointed tip; erect lateral sepals joined for half their length, margins curved inwards, petals spreading.
Labellum erect and curved backwards at right angles near the middle; smooth, raised green callus almost to tip. September to October
Requirements: Rich basaltic soils
Comments: An endangered species which is now extinct on the basalt plains of Melbourne due to destruction of its habitat. (notes p. 229)
Localities: Keilor Plains#, St. Albans#
Distribution: Endemic to Vic.
Synonym: Previously included in *P. fuscum*, now recognised as a NSW endemic. *P. affine* is not synonymous, occurring in NSW and East Gippsland. There is disagreement amongst botanists as to the specific name of the latter specimens.

Prasophyllum sylvestre

Forest Leek Orchid

Size: stem 20–50 cm high **P**
Habitat: Grassy low open forest
Foliage: Sub-erect, non-sheathing leaf to 40 cm long
Flowers: Open spike of 10–30 fragrant yellowish-green flowers with brown stripes, to 10 mm across, labellum pink to white. Ovate dorsal sepal with long pointed tip, obliquely curved back; lateral sepals erect to 12 mm, joined about half way, tips keeled, narrow petals spreading.
Oblong labellum curved at right angles near middle, margins slightly wavy, yellow or pinkish callus raised and glistening. November to December
Requirements: Well drained sandy loams
Comments: A poorly known species due to confusion with other species but probably extinct within the Melbourne area. Believed to flower only after disturbance such as fire.
Localities: Dandenong area 1859#
Distribution: Vic, NSW
Synonym: A recently described species which was previously included with *P. frenchii* and *P. gracile*.

Pterostylis aciculiformis

Slender Ruddyhood

Size: stem to 25 cm high **F P**
Habitat: Dry sclerophyll forest
Foliage: Basal rosette of 4–12 often overlapping, ovate to elliptic dull green leaves 10–30 mm long, usually withering at flowering; 2–6 small sheathing bracts on flower stem

Flowers:	2–10 semi-erect greenish flowers to 12 mm long with tan tones, especially on pendant lateral sepals and labellum. Galea ends in fine upturned point. Fleshy oblong labellum to 5 mm with few white hairs on margins, basal lobe with numerous white hairs. Lateral sepals bent downwards, joined and ovate at the base, shallowly concave, free points curved forward, to 7 mm long. October to November
Requirements:	Well drained soil
Comments:	A poorly known species which appears to be extinct in the Melbourne area. (See p. 232 for general information.)
Localities:	Hurstbridge 1933
Distribution:	Vic, NSW, SA
Synonym:	*P. rufa* ssp. *aciculiformis*

Pterostylis sp. aff. **parviflora** (Eastern Melbourne)

Corranwarrabul Greenhood

Size:	stem to 20 cm high **P**
Habitat:	Valley sclerophyll forests, sclerophyll woodland, swamp scrub
Foliage:	4–10 leaves in ground-hugging radical rosettes. Leaves ovate, grey-green to 20 mm x 10 mm, pointed with wavy margins, on side shoots off the flowering plants; 3–5 small sheathing stem leaves. Rosettes on both fertile and sterile plants.
Flowers:	2–8 small white flowers with green stripes to 12 mm long, facing the stem; petals brown, lateral sepals brown with white stripes. Galea with blunt brown tip. Labellum elliptic, rufous and white, tip visible but not protruding through broad sinus. Lateral sepals erect, free points very short and tapering, to top of galea. March to May
Requirements:	Well drained loams, tolerating extra moisture during the growing season
Comments:	Colony forming, often growing at the base of trees. It is readily distinguised from *P. parviflora* by its brown tips and from other related forms by its less curved petals, its smaller size and the shape of the labellum. Known from few sites its status is vulnerable.
Localities:	Heathmont[#], Belgrave, Kilsyth South, 42
Distribution:	Vic, SA
Synonym:	Separated from *P. parviflora* (p. 237)

Pterostylis planulata

Flat Rustyhood

Size:	stem to 35 cm high **P**
Habitat:	Box-ironbark woodland
Foliage:	Overlapping basal rosette of 5–12 ovate dull green leaves to 30 mm long, often withered at flowering; 2–6 stem-sheathing leaves
Flowers:	2–7 translucent flowers to 30 mm long with greenish stripes. Galea with fine upturned point to 30 mm long. Thin dark green oblong-ovate labellum to 7 mm long with short hairs along the margin and a pair of longer hairs at the base. Lateral sepals broadly ovate and shallowly concave with hairy upcurved margins, free points thread-like to 30 mm long
Requirements:	Well drained soil
Comments:	A recently described species which may now be extinct in Melbourne.
Localities:	Diamond Creek
Distribution:	Vic, NSW, SA
Synonym:	Was included in *P. biseta* a SA endemic

Pterostylis tasmanica

Southern Bearded Greenhood

Size:	stem to 15 cm high **F P**
Habitat:	Sclerophyll woodland
Foliage:	8–14 fleshy, dark green lanceolate leaves to 25 mm long with white veins, in a crowded rosette, often extending up the flower stem; 2–3 stem-sheathing leaves
Flowers:	Single translucent shiny white and green flower to 25 mm long with darker veins. Galea bulbous at base, constricted in the middle, with a blunt end. Thread-like labellum to 15 mm long densely covered in long yellow hairs, ending in a dark brown knob. Narrow, parallel lateral sepals bend downwards with incurved free points to 10 mm long. October
Requirements:	Well drained soils
Comments:	Differs from *P. plumosa* in its more slender habit and smaller flower. The galea lacks a fine point, the labellum hairs are much denser and the terminal knob is more prominent.
Localities:	Belgrave
Distribution:	Vic, Tas; NZ
Synonym:	Separated from *P. plumosa*

Thelymitra circumsepta

Naked Sun-orchid

Size:	stem 15–60 cm high **P**
Habitat:	Heathy swamps
Foliage:	Thick, channelled, dark green lanceolate leaf 9–40 cm long
Flowers:	Raceme of 2–17 lilac to pale blue flowers to 25 mm across; December to January Column white or pink, tipped with yellow; central part of post anther lobe short and irregularly toothed with longer side lobes deeply fringed; column arms ending in dense tuft of yellow hairs.

Requirements: Moist rich soils
Comments: A vulnerable species recently located near Melbourne.
Localities: Cranbourne
Distribution: Vic, NSW, Tas, SA

Thelymitra holmesii
Slender Blue Swamp Sun-orchid, Blue Star Sun-orchid

Size: stem 18–50 cm high **F P**
Habitat: Valley sclerophyll forests and heathlands in swampy areas and winter-wet depressions
Foliage: Narrow channelled fleshy leaf 8–33 cm long
Flowers: Raceme of 1–10 deep blue or violet flowers to 20 mm across, opening on warm days. November to December
Blue column has blackish band; yellow post anther lobe hooded and deeply notched; white column arms with tangled white hair tufts.
Requirements: Moist or seasonally inundated soils
Comments: A poorly known species that may still occur in a few sites in Melbourne.
Localities: Kilsyth South
Distribution: Vic, Tas, SA, WA
Synonym: *T. pauciflora* var. *holmesii*

Thelymitra luteocilium
Crested Sun-orchid

Comments: This species is known to occur in western Victoria. Thelymitras hybridise readily when 2 or more species occur together. It is more likely that pinkish sun orchids previously attributable to *T. luteocilium* are in fact natural hybrids between unspotted forms of *T. ixioides* and *T. rubra*, or *T. ixiodes* and *T. carnea* (sometimes referred to as *T.* x *irregularis*).

Thelymitra sp. aff. pauciflora (Laverton)

Habitat: Plains grassland
Comments: A recently discovered species. The smooth column and pale blue flower colour is similar to *T. nuda* but the smaller flower size is closer to *T. pauciflora*. It has a raceme of 9–10 flowers.
Localities: Laverton
Distribution: Endemic to Vic

Thelymitra × truncata

Size: stem 15–55 cm high **F P**
Habitat: Open forests, heathlands
Foliage: Fine dark green channelled leaf to 20 cm long
Flowers: 1–10 pale to deep blue flowers with few scattered spots on dorsal sepal and petals. October to November
Column bluish; short, erect, yellow post anther lobe, scalloped on top; column arms end in dense tuft of white hairs.
Requirements: Tolerates both well drained soils and heavier moist loams
Comments: Natural hybrid between *T. ixioides* and *T. pauciflora-nuda* group.
Localities: Warrandyte, Sth Belgrave
Distribution: Vic, NSW, Tas, SA
Synonym: *T. ixioides* var. *truncata*

Grasses, Rushes and Sedges, Aquatic and Semi-aquatic Herbs

Austrodanthonia monticola
Wallaby Grass

Poaceae

Size: to 15 cm high; stems to 45 cm high **F P**
Habitat: Dry sclerophyll forest
Form: Densely tufted perennial grass
Foliage: Fine inrolled leaves to 15 cm long with short, coarse hairs
Flowers: Small, narrow-ovate panicle 10–40 mm long with 5–15 few-flowered, purplish spikelets on hairy branches. Lemma broad to 2.5 mm long with 2 rows of hairs, the lower hairs reaching the base of the upper layer; lateral lobes erect to 6 mm long, tapering to awns 1–2 mm long; central awn 2–4.5 mm long, twisted near base. November
Requirements: Well drained soil
Comments: This is a grass with scattered populations in Victoria, known from one site in Melbourne. See general comments p. 256.
Localities: Plenty R. near Greensborough
Distribution: Vic, NSW
Synonym: *Danthonia monticola*. All Australian species formerly included in *Danthonia* are now regarded as belonging to the genera *Austrodanthonia, Rytidosperma, Joycea* and *Notodanthonia*.

Austrostipa hemipogon

Spear Grass

Poaceae

Size: to 20 cm long; stems to 1 m high **F P**
Habitat: Plains grassland, low grassy open forest
Foliage: Rough inrolled leaves to 20 cm long
Flowers: Narrow, loose panicle to 25 cm long. Glumes purplish or green, tapered; finely granular brown lemma to 7.5 mm long with white to gold hairs pressed against it; awn 30–60 mm long, column twice-bent, covered in dense feathery hairs and a spiral of short hairs. October to December
Requirements: Dry sandy soils
Comments: A rare Victorian grass. For general comments see p. 292.
Localities: Toolern Vale, 71
Distribution: Vic, SA, WA
Synonym: *Stipa hemipogon*

Baumea arthrophylla

Cyperaceae

Size: stems 0.3–1.3 m high **F P**
Habitat: Freshwater swamps, seasonal creek lines
Form: Aquatic perennial sedge with long rhizomes
Foliage: Basal leaves terete, similar or wider but shorter than stems, indistinctly transversely partitioned; stem leaves small; sheath reddish or straw-coloured
Flowers: Narrow, erect reddish-brown panicle to 55 cm long with many 2–4-flowered spikelets. Pale to whitish 3-angled nut. Spring to Summer
Requirements: Ample moisture, sometimes growing in water to 1 m deep
Comments: Often confused with *B. rubiginosa* which has somewhat flattened leaves and bracts and densely clustered spikelets. See p. 247 for general notes.
Localities: Mordialloc 1934; Craigeburn, Lilydale,
Distribution: All states; NZ

Bolboschoenus fluviatilis

Cyperaceae

Size: stems 1–2 m high **P**
Habitat: Swamps in valley sclerophyll forest
Form: Semi-aquatic rhizomatous perennial rush
Foliage: Recurved grass-like leaves along stems
Flowers: Panicle of 6–9 branches 2–10 cm long with clusters of 1–6 yellow brown spikelets. Dull pale yellow to grey or blackish and shiny 3-angled nut, 2 angles blunt, dorsal angle sharp. Spring to summer
Requirements: Moist to wet situations
Comments: A very rare plant in Melbourne known from few specimens. Useful as a pond plant.
Propagation: Seed, division
Localities: Wonga Park, 42
Distribution: Vic, Qld, NSW; NZ, Asia, N Am
Synonym: *Scirpus maritimus* var. *fluviatalis*

Carex brownii

Cyperaceae

Size: stems 0.2–1 m high **F P**
Habitat: Swamp scrub, drainage lines
Form: Loose tuft; triangular stems noded and rough above
Foliage: Leaves shorter and wider than stems
Flowers: Bright green, erect panicle 2–20 cm long with 3–4 erect, mostly sessile spikes to 25 mm long, lowest spike at a distance from the rest; lower spikes female, upper spike male or with some female flowers in the middle. Glumes whitish with green midrib, tip as long or longer than body. Lowest floral bracts longer than flowerhead. Spring to summer. Nut envelope has central bulge and many prominent veins.
Requirements: Moist soils
Comments: A rare sedge in the Melbourne area. See p. 249 for general comments.
Localities: Warrandyte, 61
Distribution: Vic, Qld, NSW

Carex chlorantha

Size: stems to 35 cm high **F P**
Habitat: Swamps
Form: Small erect loosely-tufted sedge with long creeping rhizomes; 3-angled stems slender, glabrous and smooth
Foliage: Soft leaves usually shorter than the stems
Flowers: Short, narrow terminal panicle to 25 mm long with 4–12 green to pale brown spikes to 7 mm long, male flowers above female flowerson top spike, lower all female or as above. Lowest floral bract smaller than flowerhead and awned. Spring to summer. Nut envelope green to red-brown with no veins or very faintly veined.

Requirements:	Moist to wet fertile soil
Comments:	Plants are generally scattered and never common. Rare in Melbourne.
Localities:	Warrandyte
Distribution:	Vic, NSW, Tas, SA

Carex polyantha

Size:	0.2–0.8 m high	**F P**
Habitat:	Riparian scrub	
Form:	Densely tufted sedge; stems triangular	
Foliage:	Bright green leaves as long as stems, 4–9 mm wide	
Flowers:	Erect panicle 10–55 cm long of 5–8 distantly spaced cylindrical spikes, 2–17 cm long; top 1–5 spikes male, sometimes with female flowers below, lower spikes female, sometimes with male flowers above. Narrow, pointed red-brown glumes. Spring to summer. Nut envelope pale brown covered with red dots, veins faint or absent.	
Requirements:	Moist soils	
Comments:	A rare species in Melbourne.	
Localities:	34A, 42	
Distribution:	Vic, Qld, NSW	

Chorizandra australis

Cyperaceae

Size:	stems 0.9–2.2 m high	**P**
Habitat:	Tea-tree heath	
Form:	Erect rush-like perennial with smooth, yellow-green ridged stems 4–9 mm wide	
Foliage:	Leaves shorter and more slender than stems; loose pale brown to purplish sheaths to 38 cm long	
Flowers:	Single, terminal globular to hemispherical flowerhead 10–18 mm wide with 14–16 dark red-brown glumes. Erect floral bract to 20 cm long.	
Requirements:	Moist soil	
Comments:	Known from a single plant on the margin of a Melaleuca swamp. Differs from *C. cymbaria* in that the floral bract does not sheath the flowerhead.	
Localities:	Frankston	
Distribution:	Vic, Tas, SA	
Synonym:	Previously confused with *C. cymbaria*	

Cyperus brevifolius

Comments:	Now considered to be introduced

Dichelachne rara

Plume-grass

Poaceae

Size:	stems to 0.7 m, rarely up to 1m high	**F P**
Habitat:	Dry and valley sclerophyll forests, grassy low open forest	
Foliage:	Flat, rough glabrous or shortly hairy leaves to 15 cm long	
Flowers:	Erect, dense panicle 5–15 cm long, spikelets to the base of short branchlets. Lemma and awn glabrous and slightly rough, awn inserted 1 mm below lemma tip, once bent, 10–25 mm long, column tightly twisted at maturity. October to February	
Requirements:	Moist to dry soils	
Comments:	A very widespread species. Most specimens previously noted as *D. micrantha* are *D. rara*. See notes for this genus on p. 263.	
Localities:	Research, Kalorama, Montrose, Vermont Sth, Boronia, Wantirna, 41, 42, 50A, 53–58	
Distribution:	Vic, Qld, NSW, Tas, SA	

Eleocharis macbarronii

Cyperaceae

Size:	25–75 cm high	**F**
Habitat:	Grassy wetlands	
Form:	Tufted perennial with fine bluish green stems, long rhizomes and small tubers	
Flowers:	Pale straw-coloured cylindrical spikelets 5–18 mm long; glumes pointed or blunt to 3.5 mm long. Yellow-brown nut tinged dark brown has 8–15 prominent longitudinal ridges. Spring to summer	
Requirements:	Heavy soils which are inundated in winter but dry out in summer	
Comments:	A rare species that has only recently been described, it does not usually produce viable seed but spreads by rhizomes.	
Localities:	Sunshine, 7, 17	
Distribution:	Vic, Qld, NSW	

Eleocharis minuta

Comments: Now considered to be introduced.

Festuca asperula

Graceful Fescue

Poaceae

F P

Size: stems to 1.2 m high
Habitat: Valley sclerophyll forests
Form: Tufted, glaucous perennial grass
Foliage: Rough, inrolled or folded leaves to 30 cm x 1 mm, brown to purplish leaf sheath open to base
Flowers: Narrow, erect, loose panicle to 25 cm long, branches sometimes drooping or spreading; 3-7-flowered pale green to purplish spikelets to 15 mm long; narrow lemma 6-9 mm long is pointed with a short awn and rounded on the back, keeled towards the top. Callus hairless. November to February
Requirements: Well drained soils
Comments: *Austrofestuca* has been separated from *Festuca*. Its lemmas are keeled throughout and the callus is downy.
Propagation: Seed
Localities: Yarrambat, Warrandyte, Mt. Dandenong
Distribution: Vic, NSW, Tas

Isachne globosa

Swamp Millet

Poaceae

F

Size: stems to 60 cm high
Habitat: Swamps
Form: Semi-aquatic perennial grass
Foliage: Linear-lanceolate, flat stem leaves 3-10 cm x 3-8 mm, slightly rough on margins and below
Flowers: Open pyramidal panicle to 10 cm x 8 cm, branches fine and wavy with roundish single spikelets towards ends, 2 florets-upper female or bisexual, lower male. September to June
Requirements: Moist to boggy soils
Comments: A rare plant for the Melbourne area. It may be an interesting plant for a bog garden.
Propagation: Seed
Localities: Plenty Lagoon, Yarrambat
Distribution: Vic, Qld, NSW, SA; PNG, NZ, SE Asia

Isolepis congrua

Cyperaceae

F

Size: to 20 cm high
Habitat: Damp depressions in plains grassland
Form: Tufted annual herb with fine stems
Foliage: Leaves to 9 cm long
Flowers: Flowerhead of 1-5 spikelets to 5 mm long, each with longer, erect to spreading floral bract to 15 mm. Glumes broad, pointed, strongly keeled with tip often curved back; spring. 3-sided nut glistening dark red-brown to dark grey with tiny whitish spots.
Requirements: Moist soil
Comments: A small bog plant which is rare in Victoria and seldom collected in Melbourne.
Propagation: Seed
Localities: Derrimut, Deer Park
Distribution: Vic, NSW, SA, WA, NT
Synonym: *Scirpus congruus*

Juncus ingens

Giant Rush

Juncaceae

F

Size: 1-5 m high
Habitat: Shallow lagoons
Form: Rhizomatous tufted perennial rush forming dense stands; erect dull green stems 4-10 mm wide, pith interrupted, sometimes dense at base
Foliage: Reduced to basal sheaths to 40 cm long, dark brown and straw-coloured
Flowers: Plants dioecious; large, loose, many-flowered panicles, flowers scattered along branches. Long erect bract to 50 cm. Straw coloured capsules equal to or longer than perianth. October to January
Requirements: Heavy soil, tolerating inundation
Comments: Known from one large stand where it grows to about 1 m high. Comments on *Juncus* on p. 272
Localities: Bulleen
Distribution: Vic, NSW

Juncus remotiflorus

Size: 0.3–0.9 m high **F P**
Habitat: Along drainage lines in valley sclerophyll forests, tea-tree heath
Form: Loosely tufted perennial rush; erect dull-green to blue-green stems to 3 mm wide, sometimes with a waxy bloom or tinged reddish-purple, pith interrupted with very large air spaces
Foliage: Pale to medium brown leaf sheaths to 13 cm long, tight or loose to stem
Flowers: Open erect panicle with flowers scattered along branchlets; erect bract to 30 cm long. Capsule similar size to perianth, to 4 mm long. November to January
Requirements: Tolerates dry soils for most of the year with temporary inundation
Comments: An unusual species which occurs in areas that are dry for much of the year. Bears similarities to *J. subsecundus* and *J. radula*.
Localities: Armidale (early collection), Ringwood 1951, Warrandyte, Oakleigh, 70
Distribution: Vic, Qld, NSW
Synonym: *J.* sp. *A*

Lomandra longifolia var. exilis

Xanthorrhoeaceae

Habitat: Valley sclerophyll forest
Requirements: Tolerates drier conditons than *L. longifolia* var. *longifolia*
Comments: Differs from the more common variety in that the leaves are narrower, from 2–4 mm wide; the male flowerhead is either unbranched or with short branches pressed to the stem and narrower, to 3 cm wide; the bracts usually not much longer than flower clusters. Flowering stem is often purplish.
Localities: City of Maroondah, 56
Distribution: Vic, NSW

Ruppia tuberosa

Potamogetonaceae

Size: Flowering axis 5–80 cm long **F**
Habitat: Brackish swamps and channels
Form: Annual or short-lived perennial herb with reduced branches to 5 mm long
Foliage: Thread-like leaves 8–10 cm long
Flowers: Surface-flowering with axis coiling after pollination; 9-11 flowers per cluster, fruiting carpels stalkless or almost so, stalk not lengthening. September to November
Localities: Fishermans Bend, 5
Distribution: Vic, SA, WA

Schoenoplectus dissachanthus

Comments: This record is most likely to be a misidentification as it has only been collected from Kaniva and Quambatook in NE Victoria.

Tetrarrhena turfosa

Smooth Rice-grass

Poaceae

Size: stems 0.2–1.3 m high
Habitat: Valley sclerophyll forest
Form: Densely tufted or scrambling perennial grass, stems smooth and glabrous
Foliage: Erect, smooth, tightly inrolled leaves 20–70 mm long and very narrow with blunt or swollen tip
Flowers: Short, erect spike-like raceme 10–30 mm long with 3–10 often purplish spikelets; sterile lemmas blunt with 5–7 prominent veins; November to March
Requirements: Moist soil
Comments: A single specimen is known in the Melbourne area.
Propagation: Seed, division
Localities: Heathmont
Distribution: Vic, NSW
Synonym: *T.* sp.

Triglochin alcockiae

Size: to 90 cm long **F P**
Habitat: Usually still fresh water, ephemeral swamps
Form: Slender, tufted aquatic perennial herb with small, plump vertical tubers
Foliage: Slender flat leaves 25–90 cm x 2–10 mm, submerged or floating on water surface
Flowers: Loose, erect terminal racemes to 13.5 cm long with few to many flowers on slender stalks. Fruit distinctively globular or depressed to 10 mm wide, opening to 41% of their length in the local populations; October to December.
Requirements: Freshwater to 50 cm deep
Comments: Similar to *T. procerum* floating form but less robust and more slender.
Propagation: Division
Localities: Bayswater, Dandenong, Dingley, Seaford, 54, 56
Distribution: Vic, SA

Ferns and Fern Allies

Anogramma leptophylla

Annual Fern

Adiantaceae

Size: fronds 2–8 cm long **P N**

Habitat: Sheltered positions such as log hollows in open forest

Form: Delicate tufted annual fern with a poorly developed rhizome

Foliage: Pale green, deeply lobed to bipinnate fertile fronds, scattered pinnae stalked and fan-shaped; pinnules deeply lobed, spore cases clustered along veins on underside; if present sterile fronds smaller and fan-shaped

Requirements: Moist sheltered position

Comments: A rare occurrence in the Melbourne area although may be overlooked. Ferns die down in dry summers to a tuber formed on the perennial gametophyte (the first stage of a fern after spore germination).

Propagation: Spore

Localities: 42

Distribution: Vic, NSW, Tas, SA, WA; NZ, S Am, Af, Eur, India

Asplenium flaccidum

Weeping Spleenwort

Aspleniaceae

Size: fronds 0.2–0.9 m long **P N**

Habitat: Along creeks in wet sclerophyll forest

Form: Weeping epiphytic fern, fronds tufted with a short, thick rhizome

Foliage: Thick, leathery, bright green bipinnate fronds, narrow in shape; mid-rib (rhachis) grooved. Both pinnae and pinnules scattered and linear, pinnae to 20 cm long, pinnules to 15 mm long.

Requirements: Humid position on tree ferns or tree trunks

Comments: A very rare occurrence in the Melbourne area. Plants may be grown in hanging baskets or on tree fern slabs in sheltered positions.

Propagation: Spores, division

Localities: Olinda

Distribution: Vic, Qld, NSW, Tas; NZ, Pacific Islands

Sticherus urceolatus

Gleicheniaceae

Size: to 0.9 m high **P N**

Habitat: Wet sclerophyll forest

Form: Densely scrambling erect fern with long creeping rhizomes

Foliage: Branched up to 4 times. Differs from *S. tener* (p. 320) in that final branch segments arise obliquely to the axis or rachis, at an angle of 40–75°, rather than almost at right angles. Final branch is more lance-shaped than linear.

Requirements: Permanently moist clay soils

Localities: Kalorama

Distribution: Vic, NSW, Tas

Synonym: Segregated from *S. tener*

Index of Photographs

Index of Botanical and Common Names

Current botanical names are written in bold type. Synonyms, common names and weed species are in medium type. Common names based directly on generic names have not been listed. Page numbers in bold type refer to the plant description while numbers preceded by Col refer to Colour Plates. Name changes in the 3rd edition are listed with the original entry. *represents species introduced to Melbourne.

Reserves and Localities

1 Weeroona Garden, East Brunswick
2 Merrett Rifle Range, Williamstown
3 Kororoit Creek mouth, Altona
4 Cherry Lake, Truganina Swamp, Altona
5 Point Cook Metropolitan Park
6 Laverton RAAF Base Swamp
7 Altona Grasslands (& Laverton North Grassland Reserve)
8 Cobbledicks Ford, Werribee
9 Exford woodlands, Melton South
10 North-western Rail Reserve, Melton
11 Deans Marsh, Sydenham West
12 Evans St, Sunbury
13 Melbourne-Bendigo Rail Reserve, Sunbury-Diggers Rest
14 Jacksons Creek, Sunbury
15 Diggers Rest Rail Reserve Grasslands
16 Organ Pipes National Park, Sydenham
17 Taylors Lakes Grassland
18 Taylors Creek, Taylors Lakes
19 Steele Creek Grassland, Avondale Heights
20 Braybrook Rail Reserve Grassland
21 Royal Park West, Parkville
22 Union St, Brunswick
23 Napier Park, Essendon
24 Radar Hill, Tullamarine
25 Gellibrand Hill State Park, Oaklands Junction
26 Bulla area
27 Deep Creek, East of Sunbury
28 Merri Creek, Cooper St, Somerton
29 Merri Creek Valley, North Coburg to Campbellfield
30 Yarra River - Studley Park 1856
31 Heyington Railway Reserve 1945
32 Studley Park & Yarra Bend, Kew
33 Heidelberg area
34 Templestowe area
34A Yarra Valley Metropolitan Park
35 Gresswell Forest, Bundoora
36 Plenty Gorge, Greensborough-Sth Morang
37 Yandell Reserve, Greensborough
38 Meruka Park, Eltham
39 Eltham Lower park
40 Bemboka Reserve, Warranwood
41 Professors Hill, Warrandyte Nth
42 Warrandyte State Park
43 Koolunga Reserve, Ferntree Gully
44 Mullum Mullum/Koonung Valley, Doncaster to Ringwood
45 Wattle Park 1958
46 Blackburn Lake
47 City of Nunawading
48 Antonio Park, Mitcham
49 Mitcham area
50 `Uambi', Heathmont
50A Ringwood area
51 Croydon area
52 Birt's Hill, Croydon
53 Hotchins Ridge, Croydon Nth
54 Terraden Dve, Kilsyth
55 Mt Dandenong - west face
56 Mt Evelyn area
57 Sherbrooke Forest
58 Ferntree Gully National Park
59 Courtney Rd, Belgrave Sth
60 Lysterfield Lake
61 Churchill National Park
62 Dandenong Valley Metropolitan Park
63 Waverley area
64 Valley Reserve, Mt Waverley
65 Ashburton Wood 1931
66 Oakleigh area
67 Sandringham area
68 Beaumaris High School
69 Royal Melbourne Golf Course, Black Rock
69A City of Mordialloc
70 The Grange, Clayton Sth
71 Braeside Metropolitan Park
72 Edithvale-Seaford Wetlands
73 Cranbourne Annexe
74 Frankston area
75 Langwarrin Flora and Fauna Reserve
76 Moorooduc Quarry Reserve & Moorooduc area

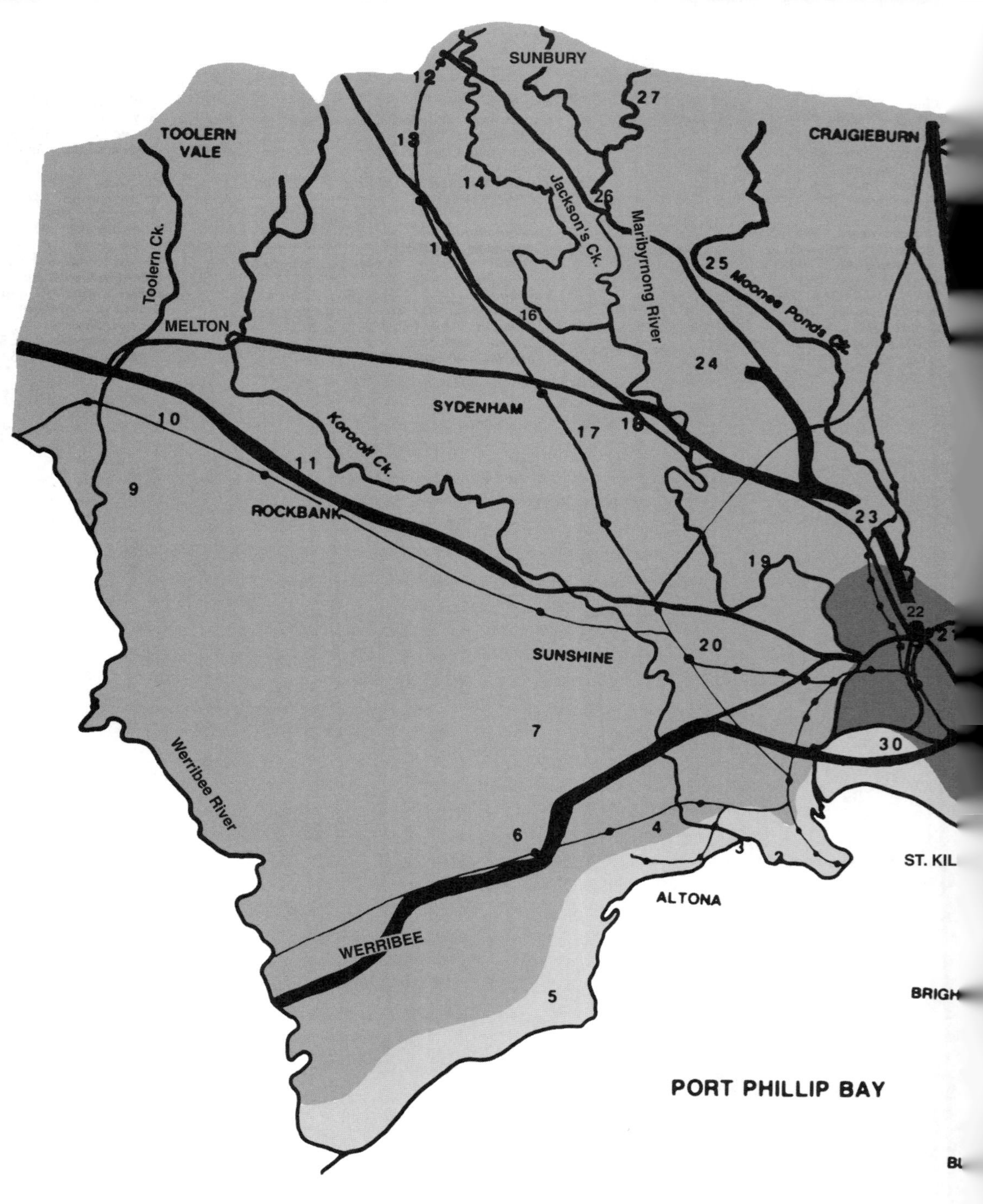

LEGEND

BASALT PLAINS

TERTIARY SANDS

COASTAL AREAS

SILURIAN DERIVED SEDIMENTARY HILLS

MAIN ROADS

RAILWAYS

WATERWAYS

RESERVES, PARKS OR AREAS REFERRED TO IN TEXT

REFERENCE MAP

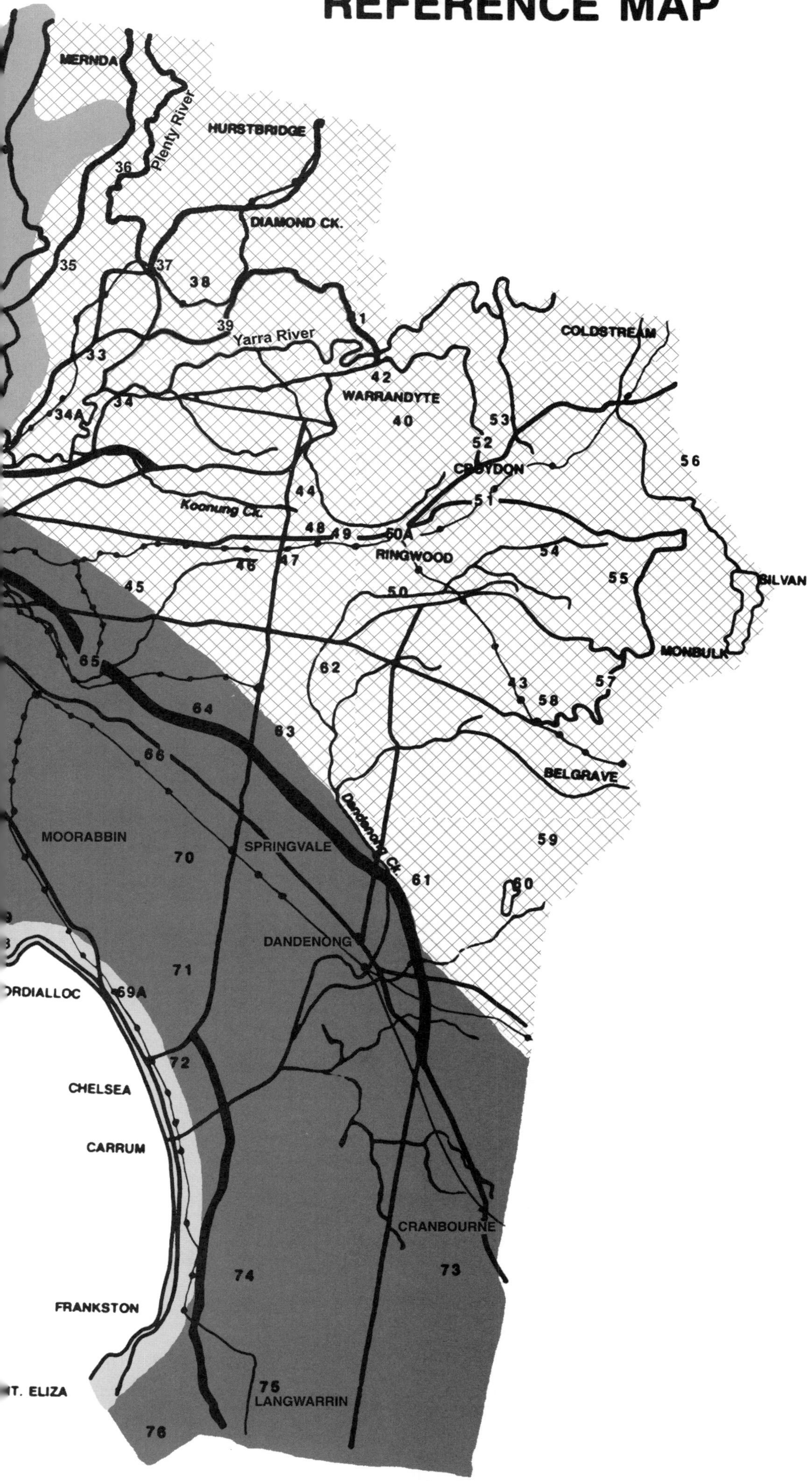

Key To Easy Plant Selection

This replaces the bookmark of the previous edition. It is an abbreviated version of the Cross Reference for Easy Plant Selection given in Appendix 1, page 322.

Size and Habit

TREE: **S** Small (to 8m high)
M Medium (8-15m)
T Tall (over 15m)

SHRUB: **S** Small (to 1m high)
M Medium (1-2.5m)
L Large (over 2.5m)

H: Herb
A: Annual
T: Tuft
G: Groundcover
C: Climber
E: Epiphyte

Flowering Times
S: Summer
A: Autumn
W: Winter
Sp: Spring
Y: Most of the Year

Bird Attracting
N: Nectar
S: Seeds
B: Berries

Butterfly Attracting
F: Food plant
N: Nectar plant

Aspect
F: Full sun
P: Partial or dappled sun
N: Full shade
A: All aspects

Screen or Windbreak Plants
S: Screen
W: Windbreak

Soil and Drainage
D: Dry, well drained
M: Moist, well drained
S: Moist, poorly drained
W: Wet all year, semi-aquatics
A: Aquatic

Coastal
1: Front-line
2: Second-line

Vegetation Communities
1: Aquatic
2: Cool temperate rainforest
3: Wet sclerophyll forest
4: Damp sclerophyll forest
5: Sclerophyll woodland
6: Swamp scrub
7: Grassy low open forest
8: Tea-tree heath
9: Wattle tea-tree scrub
10: Coastal banksia woodland
11: Primary dune scrub
12: Saltmarsh
13: Grassy wetland
14: Red gum woodland
15: Plains grassland
16: Riparian scrub
17: Chenopod rocky open scrub
18: Box ironbark woodland
19: Box woodland
20: Riparian woodland
21: Dry sclerophyll forest
22: Valley sclerophyll forest

Aboriginal Uses *